Spain

John Noble
Damien Simonis
Mark Armstrong
Susan Forsyth
Corinne Simcock

Spain

1st edition

Published by
Lonely Planet Publications
Head Office: PO Box 617, Hawthorn, Vic 3122, Australia
Branches: 155 Filbert St, Suite 251, Oakland, CA 94607, USA
              10 Barley Mow Passage, Chiswick, London W4 4PH, UK
              71 bis rue du Cardinal Lemoine, 75005 Paris, France

Printed by
Colorcraft Ltd, Hong Kong

Photographs by

Mark Armstrong	Bethune Carmichael	John Noble
Damien Simonis	Nick Tapp	David Waterman

Front cover: Near the entrance to Parc Güell, Barcelona (Bethune Carmichael)

First Published
May 1997

National Library of Australia Cataloguing in Publication Data

Spain.

   1st ed.
   Includes index.
   ISBN 0 86442 474 4.

   1. Spain – Guidebooks. I. Noble, John, 1951 Oct. 11- .
   (Series: Lonely Planet travel survival kit).

914.60483

text & maps © Lonely Planet 1997
photos © photographers as indicated 1997
Alicante and Santiago de Compostela climate charts compiled from information supplied by Patrick J Tyson,
©Patrick J Tyson, 1997

John Noble

John comes from the Ribble valley in northern England. Increasing interruptions to a mainstream journalism career, for travel to various bits of the globe, saw him eventually abandon Fleet Street for a Lonely Planet trail which has taken him to four continents and more than a dozen LP books, from *Sri Lanka* and *Mexico* to *Central Asia* and *Russia, Ukraine & Belarus*. For over two years he has enjoyed being based in southern Spain, together with his wife and co-author Susan Forsyth and their children Jack and Isabella.

Damien Simonis

Damien is a London-based freelance journalist. With a degree in languages and several years newspaper experience on, among others, the *Australian* and the *Age*, he left Australia in 1989. He has worked and travelled widely in Europe, the Middle East and North Africa. In addition to this book he has worked on Lonely Planet guides to *Jordan & Syria*, *Egypt & the Sudan*, *Morocco*, *North Africa* and *Italy*, as well as contributing to several shoestring guides and other publications in the UK, Australia and North America.

Mark Armstrong

Mark was born in Melbourne. When he was nine he moved with his family to Barcelona, where they lived for a couple of years. Back home he studied at Melbourne Uni and has worked in computer sales and marketing, as a restorer of old houses and as a fencing contractor. His travels have taken him through South-East Asia, North America and Europe, including regular trips back to Spain. Being robbed there three times has in no way diminished his passion for Spain or its people (or, unfortunately, honed his instincts), but as a precaution he now travels with the words 'I already gave' stencilled on his money belt. Mark has written LP's *Melbourne*, *Victoria* and *Queensland* guides and worked on updates of *Islands of Australia's Great Barrier Reef*, *Australia* and the Spain chapter of *Mediterranean Europe*.

Susan Forsyth

Susan hails from Melbourne and survived a decade teaching in the Victorian state education system before activating long-postponed travel plans and heading off for a year as a volunteer lecturer in Sri Lanka, where she met her future husband John Noble. Susan has since helped update LP's *Australia*, *Indonesia*, *Sri Lanka* and *Mexico* guides and *Travel with Children*, travelled lengthily in the ex-USSR, given birth to and nurtured two little *rubios* (blondies), and weathered five years in England's cold, wet but beautiful Ribble valley. For this book, the family relocated to southern Spain, where they enjoy the semitropical climate and improving their Spanish.

Corinne Simcock

Corinne, based in London, spent the first 10 years of her career as a sound engineer in the music industry. In 1988, sick of spending 18 hours a day in a basement listening to people who could not play make mistakes, she chucked it all in to become a journalist, writing for national newspapers and magazines about everything from travel and crime to business and personal finance. She has travelled through more than 30 countries and her passion in life is deserts.

From the Authors

From John & Susan We would like to thank all the many people who helped in so many ways with their parts of this book, notably: Albert Padrol and Josep Maria Romero for their generous hospitality and insights into Cataluña and Andorra; the host of residents and visitors to Cómpeta, Andalucía, who shared their knowledge and experience of Spain – among them the Smarts, Wrightsons, Brannagans, Hillekamps and Boyletts, Dorothy Sim and friends, Rachel Allsop, Patricia Luce, Keith & Lynette Smith, Mike Smith, Sandra Costello, Scott and Jacquetta, David Waterman, Aden Penn and Matthew Taylor; also Rupert in Sevilla; Charlotte Hindle (our Port Aventura correspondent);

the many Spanish tourist office staff who were generous with their time, including those in Algeciras, Almería, Andorra, Córdoba, Gibraltar, Granada, London and Málaga, and Isabel and colleagues in Jerez de la Frontera; the Instituto Cervantes in London; and Ski Andorra. Not least, thank you Damien, Mark and Corinne for doing a great job; ditto to Adrienne, Nick and everyone else in Melbourne (and for your patience!); and to the LP London office for continued help with communications.

From Damien Staff at many tourist offices throughout Spain were patient and obliging. An especial vote of thanks goes to those in Zaragoza, Cuenca, Teruel, Segovia, Valladolid, Estella, Bilbao and San Sebastián. In Madrid, I owe a host of people thanks for ideas willingly given on the project, help with things that had nothing to do with it at all and for a load of good times. They include, in no particular order: Bárbara Azcona; Ángeles Sánchez Caballero; Luis Soldevila; Chris La Riche; Susan Kempster; David Ing, Isabel, Pachi 'El Conejo' and the gang, Radek Divis, Debby Luhrman and others. *A todos muchísimas gracias*. J Luis López García in Astorga was kind enough to take time to explain some local history. Paul Gowan of the RAC in London helped out with information on motoring in Spain. Lucrezia and Ariana shared many travelling adventures in Castilla-La Mancha, Galicia and Asturias and still managed to smile through a frantic schedule. Elisabeth Mead not only came along for the ride in the País Vasco, but was brave enough to wade through some of my chapters in search of howlers. Special thanks to Mum, who, in spite of many difficulties, proved an ideal companion on the road in northern Spain. A long overdue vote of thanks goes to all the guys at LP London, who have not only gone beyond the call of duty in helping me keep bits of life ticking over, but have always kept the welcome mat out. In Melbourne, Nick Tapp and the team did a great editing job, and I am indebted to John Noble for casting a careful eye over my text and to John and Susan for rolling out the welcome mat. My share of this book is for Ariana, *que creció un poquito aquí, compartió algunos de mis descubrimientos y con quien aprendí aún más*.

From Mark Special thanks to Alicia Navarro Verdeguer for her friendship and invaluable assistance, and to Ashley Chan for his (famed) hospitality in New York. Thanks also to the staff in all the tourist offices, especially Manel Pons (Menorca) and Eva Mollá Palomares (Alicante). Thanks also to the following people for their good company, advice and/or suggestions: Susannah Kornherr, Britta Wilhelmi, Massimo Bonannini, Steffi Hahnzog and Matthias, Maria Alonso Borso, Paula, Natalia, Raquel, Federico, Pedro, Helen, Olivia, Marcus and the Man in the Bar with the Blue Couches. And thanks to Tor Jorgensen (the Vegemite kid) for the photos.

From Corinne Thanks to Emilia Gonzales Marin from the tourist office in Badajoz and to all my friends in Spain, particularly Gerry & Issy Coleman, Dr Peter & Ulli Hawthorne, Colin & Linda Martin and Carmel Rogers. A special thanks to Mick for saving my sanity and for generally being the best man on the planet.

From the Publisher
This 1st edition of *Spain* was edited in Lonely Planet's Melbourne office by Nick Tapp with assistance from Brigitte Barta, Craig MacKenzie, Cathy Oliver, Miriam Cannell, Kirsten John and Anne Mulvaney. Janet Austin, Adrienne Costanzo, Paul Harding and Anne Mulvaney helped with proofing. Marcel Gaston designed and laid out the book, and coordinated a mapping and illustrating team consisting of Rachel Black, Trudi Canavan, Tony Fankhauser, Mark Griffiths, Jane Hart, Matt King, Ann Jeffree, Jenny Jones, Chris Lee Ack, Dorothy Natsikas (*Adios*, Dot), Anthony Phelan, Jacqui Saunders, Michael Signal, Lyndell Taylor and Andrew Tudor. Paul Clifton prepared the colour map. David Kemp designed the cover and Michael Signal drew the back-cover map. Nick did the index and cooked the *paella*. Thanks to Lou Callan for help with languages, to Leonie Mugavin for help in hunting down stray facts, to Sarah Mathers for additional map-checking, and to Adrienne and Jane, who oversaw the project from start to finish.

This Book
Coordinating author John Noble wrote parts of Facts about the Country and Facts for the Visitor, the entire Barcelona, Cataluña and Andorra chapters and parts of the Andalucía and Extremadura chapters; Damien Simonis wrote Getting There & Away and Getting Around, the chapters on Madrid, Comunidad

de Madrid, Castilla y León, Castilla-La Mancha, Aragón, País Vasco, Navarra & La Rioja, Cantabria & Asturias and Galicia, and parts of Facts about the Country and Facts for the Visitor; Susan Forsyth wrote parts of Facts about the Country, Facts for the Visitor and the Andalucía chapter; Mark Armstrong wrote the Balearic Islands and Valencia chapters; and Corinne Simcock wrote the Murcia chapter and parts of Andalucía and Extremadura.

Warning & Request

Things change: prices go up, schedules change, good places go bad and bad places go bankrupt – nothing stays the same. So, if you find things better or worse, places recently opened or long since closed, please tell us and help us to make the next edition of *Spain* even more accurate and useful.

We value all the feedback we receive from travellers. Julie Young coordinates a small team who read and acknowledge every letter, postcard and e-mail, and ensure that every morsel of information finds its way to the appropriate authors, editors and publishers.

Everyone who writes to us will find their name in the next edition of the appropriate guide and will also receive a free subscription to our quarterly newsletter, *Planet Talk*. The very best contributions will be rewarded with a free Lonely Planet guide.

Excerpts from your correspondence may appear in updates (which we add to the end pages of reprints); in new editions of this guide; in our newsletter, *Planet Talk*; or in the Postcards section of our Web site – so please let us know if you don't want your letter published or your name acknowledged.

Contents

Boxed Asides

Map Legend

BOUNDARIES

International Boundary
Regional Boundary

ROUTES

Freeway
Highway
Major Road
Minor Road
Unsealed Road or Track
City Road
City Street
Railway
Underground Railway
Tram
Walking Track
Ferry Route
Cable Car or Chairlift

AREA FEATURES

Parks
Built-Up Area
Pedestrian Mall, Plaza
Market
Cemetery
Reef
Beach or Desert
Rocks

HYDROGRAPHIC FEATURES

Coastline
River, Creek
Intermittent River or Creek
Rapids, Waterfalls
Lake, Intermittent Lake
Canal
Swamp

SYMBOLS

CAPITAL .... National Capital
Capital .... Regional Capital
CITY .... Major City
City .... City
Town .... Town, Village

Place to Stay, Place to Eat
Cafe, Pub or Bar
Post Office, Telephone
Tourist Information, Bank
Transport, Parking
Museum, Youth Hostel
Caravan Park, Camping Ground
Church, Cathedral
Mosque, Synagogue
Buddhist Temple, Hindu Temple
Hospital, Police Station

Embassy, Petrol Station
Airport, Airfield
Swimming Pool, Gardens
Shopping Centre, Zoo
Winery or Vineyard, Picnic Site
One Way Street, Route Number
Stately Home, Monument
Castle, Tomb
Cave, Hut or Chalet
Mountain or Hill, Lookout
Lighthouse, Shipwreck
Pass, Spring
Beach, Surf Beach
Archaeological Site or Ruins
Ancient or City Wall
Cliff or Escarpment, Tunnel
Railway Station

Note: not all symbols displayed above appear in this book

Introduction

It has been said that Europe ends at the Pyrenees. While that has always been an exaggeration, any journey south of those mountains proves that, as an old tourism promotion campaign once had it, Spain *is* different. With its plethora of colourful fiestas and unbelievably vibrant and late nightlife, its complete spectrum of scenery and environments and its unique and well-preserved architectural and artistic heritage, Spain provides a variety of fun and fascination that few countries can match.

Travel is easy, accommodation plentiful, the climate generally benign, the people relaxed and fun-loving, the beaches long and sandy, and food and drink easy to come by and full of regional variation. More than 40 million foreigners a year take holidays in Spain to enjoy these things. Yet you can also travel for days and hear no other tongue but Spanish. Once away from the holiday *costas*, you could only be in Spain. In the cities, narrow, twisting old streets suddenly open out to views of daring modern architecture, while spit-and-sawdust bars serving wine from the barrel rub shoulders with blaring, glaring discos. Travel out into the back country and you'll find, an hour or two from some of Europe's most stylish and sophisticated cities, villages where time has done its best to stand still since the Middle Ages.

Geographically, Spain's diversity is immense. In Andalucía, for example, you could ski in the Sierra Nevada and later the same day recline on a Mediterranean beach or traverse the deserts of Almería. There are

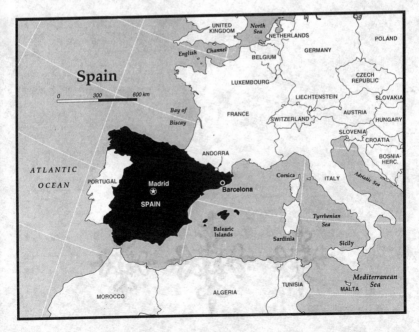

endless tracts of wild, crumpled and crinkled *sierra* to explore, and some spectacularly rugged stretches of coast between the beaches – many of which are far less crowded and developed than you might imagine. Culturally, the entire country is littered with superb old buildings, from Roman aqueducts and Islamic palaces to Gothic cathedrals. Almost every second village has a medieval castle. Spain has been the home of some of the world's great artists – El Greco, Goya, Picasso and more – and has museums and galleries to match. The country vibrates with music of every kind.

The more you travel in Spain, the bigger it seems to get. It's surprising just how many Spains there are. Cool, damp, green Galicia is a world away from hot, dry Andalucía, the home of flamenco and bullfighting. Fertile Cataluña in the north-east, with its separate language and independent spirit, seems a different nation from the Castilian heartland on the austere *meseta* at the centre of the Iberian Peninsula. Once you leave the beaten track, it can take as long to wind your way through a couple of remote valleys and over the sierra between them as it would to travel the highway or railway from Madrid to Barcelona. All you need to do is get out there and enjoy it!

Facts about the Country

HISTORY

The ancestors of today's Spaniards included prehistoric hunters from Africa, Phoenicians, Jews and Arabs from the Middle East, Berber tribes from Morocco and the Sahara, Visigoths from the Balkans and numerous other European peoples. The ancestors of a good half of the people of the Americas today – and others dotted across the rest of the globe – were Spaniards. The key to this great ebb and flow of peoples, cultures and empires is Spain's location – on both the Mediterranean Sea and the Atlantic Ocean, in Europe yet half cut off by the Pyrenees, a stone's throw from Africa, and as near to America as anywhere in the Old World. Such a pivotal position has entangled Spain in the affairs of half the world, and half the world in Spain's.

In the Beginning

Caves throughout the country tell us plenty about Spain's earliest inhabitants. The most impressive are at Altamira near Santander, and date from around 12,000 BC. Altamira's sophisticated, colourful paintings of bison, stag, wild boar and horses show confident brush strokes and realistic perspective – not primitive efforts!

The beginnings of Spanish art – a detail from the 14,000 year old paintings at Altamira

Altamira was part of the Magdelanian hunting culture of southern France and northern Spain, the high point of Palaeolithic (Old Stone Age) life in the Iberian Peninsula. Magdelanian culture lasted from around 20,000 BC to the end of the Ice Age in about 8000 BC. One of the many theories about the origins of the Basque people of northern Spain and south-western France is that they are descended from the Magdelanians.

But the story goes much further back. In recent years archaeologists in Spain have discovered two lots of human bone fragments reckoned to be older than any others found in Europe. Those found in 1994 in the Sierra de Atapuerca near Burgos are widely accepted to be about 780,000 to 800,000 years old, and may come from a hitherto unknown species of hominid, a remote ancestor of the later Neanderthals. These bones' similarities to others from Africa have disturbed the previously accepted view that early humans first reached Europe from Asia (about 800,000 years ago). The second set of bones, from Orce near Granada and Cueva Victoria in Murcia, are reckoned to be the remains of meals eaten by giant hyenas 1.2 to 1.6 million years ago. Some experts have still to be convinced that there were people in Spain so long ago, but the Spanish finds taken together are certainly causing serious rethinking about the origins of European humanity.

From the later Neanderthal era comes 'Gibraltar Woman', a skull dating from about 50,000 BC, which was found in 1848. The Cueva de Nerja in Andalucía is one of many sites of the Cro-Magnons (the first real modern humans), who may also ultimately have been of African origin and who displaced the Neanderthals from about 40,000 BC, during the last Ice Age. These cave dwellers hunted mammoth, bison and reindeer.

After the Ice Age, new peoples known today as Iberians or proto-Berbers arrived, probably from North Africa. Their rock-shelter paintings of hunting and dancing survive on the east coast. Meanwhile, in about 5000 BC, the Neolithic (New Stone Age) revolution had begun in Egypt and Mesopotamia. Its many innovations included the plough, crops, livestock raising, pottery and fabrics, boats and permanent fortified villages. Spain's first Neolithic society appeared in the south-east, near Almería, in about 2500 BC. Out of this developed a first stepping stone to the Bronze Age, the Los Millares culture, based on Almería's rich copper resources.

The third and second millennia BC also saw the building of megalithic tombs (dolmens) by unknown peoples in many parts of the peninsula's perimeter, Brittany and the British Isles. Spain's best examples are near Antequera in Andalucía.

By 2000 BC bronze, an alloy of copper and tin, was replacing stone, bone and wood for tools, weapons and adornments. El Argar, again near Almería, was the early centre of this activity but the new ways quickly spread over two-thirds of the peninsula. By 1500 BC there was a flourishing culture in the Guadalquivir valley in Andalucía. This was probably the lost civilisation of Tartessos mentioned in classical sources and the Old Testament – but traces of its capital, thought to have been near Huelva, have so far eluded discovery.

Celts

From around 1000 to 500 BC, Celts (originally from central Europe) and other tribes from beyond the Pyrenees started to settle north of the Ebro. By contrast to the dark-featured Iberians, who consumed wine and olive oil, the Celts were fair, drank beer and ate lard. Celts and Iberians who merged on the central *meseta* became the Celtiberians. The Celts introduced iron technology to the north at about the same time as the Phoenicians brought it to the south.

Phoenicians

As early as 1200 BC the Phoenicians, a Semitic people from present-day Lebanon, were trading with Iberians on Spain's Mediterranean coast, attracted by its mineral wealth and bountiful marine life. They founded Gadir (Cádiz) in 1100 BC and other outposts including Malaca (Málaga), Onuba (Huelva) and Sexi (Almuñecar). The Phoenicians exposed Spain to a more advanced Mediterranean society and brought an alphabet which the Iberians adopted. They called the Iberian Peninsula 'i-schephan-im', from which, it's reckoned, the name 'España' is ultimately derived.

Greeks

With Phoenicia's decline, Greeks began trading and setting up colonies on Spain's coasts around 600 BC. They were after metals and the esparto grass used for making rope. They introduced the potter's wheel, money and some musical instruments.

The people the Greeks encountered were a mixture of tribes who spoke a uniform language and lived in sizable hill fort towns. Their well-developed art – with an emphasis on ceramic paintings and large stone sculptures – fused with Greek influences, as is seen in the famous sculpture of a woman, the *Dama de Elche*, found near Alicante in the 19th century.

Greek dominance in the Mediterranean was ended by the Carthaginians in a naval battle off Corsica in 535 BC. But the main Greek colony in Spain, Emporion (Empúries) in Cataluña, survived till Roman times.

Carthaginians

Carthage was founded by the Phoenicians near present-day Tunis in 814 BC, 50 years before Rome. After defeating the Greeks, the expansionist Carthaginians supported the Phoenician colony at Gadir against the troublesome Tartessians – whose capital somehow vanished in the process. Gadir became the Carthaginians' main Iberian city, but there was a flourishing colony on Ibiza too.

The Carthaginians took on the Romans unsuccessfully in the First Punic War (264 to 241 BC). In 237, seeking a base from which to launch another attack on Rome, they

Madrid Metro
Hours: 6 am to 1:30 am

◀ **Metro** ▶

- 🔕 Cercanías Station
- ⮂ RENFE Station
- 🅿 Parking

9 Herrera Oría

Barrio del Pilar

Ventilla

Valdeacederas

Tetuán

Estrecho

Alvarado

Guzmán el Bueno

Metropolitano

Ciudad Universitaria

2 Cuatro Caminos

3 Moncloa

4 Argüelles

Ventura Rodríguez

Plaza de España

🔕 🅁 Príncipe Pío

Lago

Batán

Alto de Extremadura

Lucero

Campamento

Empalme

Laguna 🔕

Carpetana

10 **5** 🅿 Aluche

🔕 🅿

Carabanchel

Vista Alegre

Opañel

Plaza Elíptica

Usera

6 Legazpi **3**

Delicias

Méndez Álvaro 🔕

Urgel

Oporto

Marqués de Vadillo

Pirámides

Acacias — Embajadores

Lavapiés

Puerta de Toledo

La Latina

Puerta del Ángel

Santo Domingo

🅁 Opera

Callao

Sol

Tirso de Molina

Antón Martín

Atocha

Atocha Renfe 🔕 ⮂

Menéndez Pelayo

Conde de Casal

Pacífico

Puente de Vallecas

Nueva Numancia

Portazgo

Buenos Aires

Alto del Arenal

Miguel Hernández **1** 🅿

Pavones **9**

Artilleros

Vinateros

Estrella

Sáinz de Baranda

Ibiza

O'Donnell

Retiro

Banco de España

Sevilla

Gran Vía

A. Martínez

Chueca

Tribunal

Bilbao

10

Noviciado

San Bernardo

Quevedo

Iglesia

Colón

Serrano

Velázquez

Príncipe de Vergara

Goya

Núñez de Balboa

Rubén Darío

Avda. de América **7** **8**

Diego de León

Lista

Manuel Becerra

Ventas **2**

El Carmen

Quintana

Pueblo Nuevo

García Noblejas

Simancas

San Blas

Ascao

Ciudad Lineal

Suanzes

Torre Arias

Las Musas **7**

🅿 **5** Canillejas

Barrio de la Concepción

Parque de las Avenidas

Cartagena

Prosperidad

Alfonso XIII

Avda. de la Paz

Arturo Soria

Cruz del Rayo

Concha Espina

República Argentina

Esperanza **4**

Colombia

Pío XII

Duque de Pastrana

Chamartín 🔕 ⮂

Begoña

Fuencarral **8**

Plaza de Castilla **1**

Cuzco

Lima

Nuevos Ministerios 🔕

Ríos Rosas

6

DAMIEN SIMONIS

Modernisme in Madrid – the Sociedad General de Autores y Editores building on Calle de Pelayo

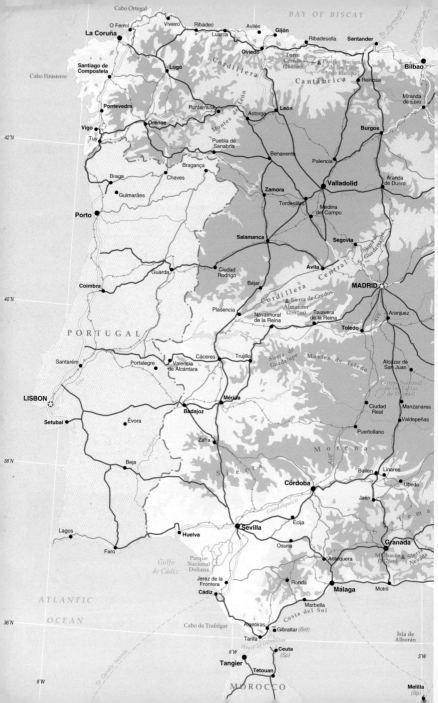

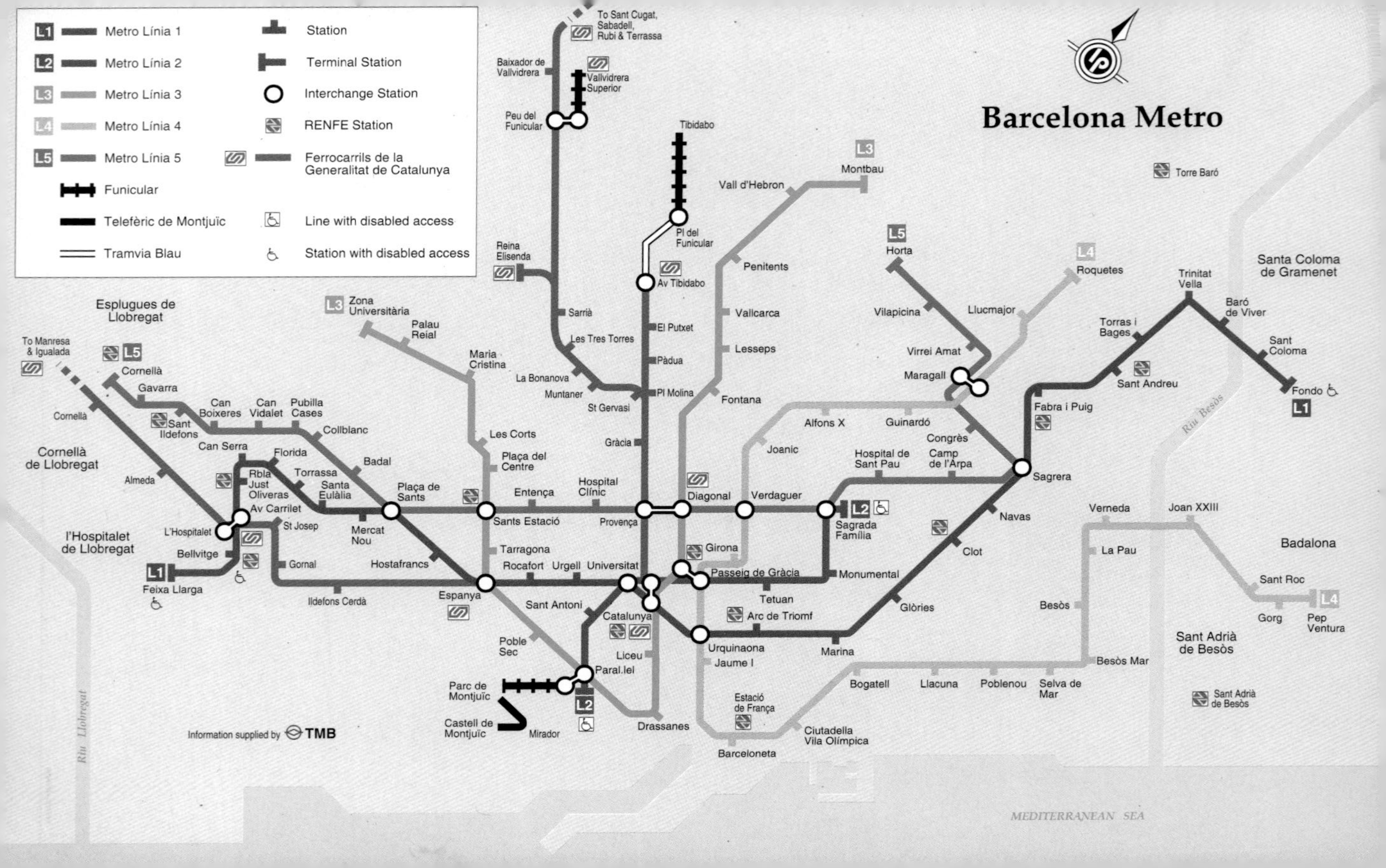

Barcelona Metro
L1 Metro Línia 1
L2 Metro Línia 2
L3 Metro Línia 3
L4 Metro Línia 4
L5 Metro Línia 5
Funicular
Telefèric de Montjuïc
Tramvia Blau
Station
Terminal Station
Interchange Station
RENFE Station
Ferrocarrils de la Generalitat de Catalunya
Line with disabled access
Station with disabled access
To Sant Cugat, Sabadell, Rubí & Terrassa
Baixador de Vallvidrera
Vallvidrera Superior
Peu del Funicular
Reina Elisenda
Sarrià
Les Tres Torres
La Bonanova
Muntaner
St Gervasi
Tibidabo
Pl del Funicular
Av Tibidabo
El Putxet
Pàdua
Pl Molina
Gràcia
Montbau
Vall d'Hebron
Penitents
Vallcarca
Lesseps
Fontana
Horta
Vilapicina
Virrei Amat
Maragall
Llucmajor
Roquetes
Torre Baró
Santa Coloma de Gramenet
Trinitat Vella
Baró de Viver
Sant Coloma
Fondo
Torras i Bages
Sant Andreu
Fabra i Puig
Sagrera
Navas
Clot
Glòries
Marina
Alfons X
Guinardó
Congrès
Camp de l'Arpa
Hospital de Sant Pau
Joanic
Verdaguer
Sagrada Família
Monumental
Diagonal
Provença
Hospital Clínic
Girona
Passeig de Gràcia
Tetuan
Arc de Triomf
Urquinaona
Jaume I
Catalunya
Liceu
Drassanes
Universitat
Urgell
Rocafort
Tarragona
Entença
Sants Estació
Plaça del Centre
Les Corts
Maria Cristina
Palau Reial
Zona Universitària
Esplugues de Llobregat
To Manresa & Igualada
Cornellà
Gavarra
Sant Ildefons
Can Boixeres
Can Vidalet
Pubilla Cases
Collblanc
Badal
Plaça de Sants
Can Serra
Florida
Torrassa
Santa Eulàlia
Rbla Just Oliveras
Av Carrilet
L'Hospitalet
Bellvitge
Feixa Llarga
St Josep
Gornal
Ildefons Cerdà
Mercat Nou
Hostafrancs
Espanya
Sant Antoni
Poble Sec
Paral.lel
Parc de Montjuïc
Castell de Montjuïc
Mirador
Estació de França
Barceloneta
Ciutadella Vila Olímpica
Bogatell
Llacuna
Poblenou
Selva de Mar
Besòs Mar
Besòs
La Pau
Verneda
Joan XXIII
Sant Roc
Gorg
Pep Ventura
Badalona
Sant Adrià de Besòs
Cornellà de Llobregat
l'Hospitalet de Llobregat
Almeda
Riu Besòs
Riu Llobregat
MEDITERRANEAN SEA
Information supplied by TMB

began an all-out campaign to conquer the Iberian Peninsula; they founded Barcelona and Carthago Nova (Cartagena) but were fiercely resisted by the inland Celtiberians.

In 226 Carthage and Rome agreed to divide the peninsula between them, with the Río Ebro as the border. But the young leader Hannibal was determined to master Rome and began the Second Punic War by sacking Saguntum, a town on the east coast allied to Rome, before marching on and over the Alps to give the Romans a hiding at Cannae in northern Italy in 216. Hannibal failed to follow up this success, however, was forced to retreat, and was eventually routed by the Roman general Scipio in North Africa in 202.

Romans

Though the Romans held sway on the peninsula for 600 years, it took them 200 years to subdue the fiercest of the Celtiberian, Celtic and Iberian tribes; and the Basques in the north, though defeated, were never Romanised like the rest of Hispania, as the Romans called it. Legendary stands against the Romans included the eight year revolt led by the shepherd turned guerrilla Virathius in the west and centre from around 150 BC, and the siege of Numancia near Soria in 133 BC. Rome had to bring in the most illustrious of its generals to deal with these and other insubordinations. Pompey and Julius Caesar even fought it out among themselves here, transplanting their Roman power struggles to Iberian soil.

By 50 AD most of the peninsula, particularly the south, had adopted the Roman way of life. This was the time of the Pax Romana, a long and prosperous period of stability. Hispania became urbanised and highly organised. The early Roman provinces were called Hispania Citerior and Hispania Ulterior, with their capitals at Carthago Nova (Cartagena) and Corduba (Córdoba), but in the 1st century BC they were reorganised into Baetica (roughly present-day Andalucía and southern Extremadura), with its capital at Corduba; Lusitania (Portugal and northern Extremadura), with its capital at Augusta Emerita (Mérida), the greatest Roman city on the peninsula; and Tarraconensis (the rest), with its capital at Tarraco (Tarragona).

Rome gave the peninsula a road system, aqueducts, theatres, temples, amphitheatres, circuses, baths, the basis of its legal system and languages, and eventually Christianity. The Roman era also brought many Jews, who spread throughout the Mediterranean part of the empire. Hispania gave Rome incredible wealth – gold from the north, silver from the south, grain and wine – soldiers, emperors (Trajan, Hadrian and Theodosius), and even some of the greatest Latin literature – that of Seneca, Martial, Quintilian and Lucan. One other notable export was *garum*, a spicy sauce derived from fish and used as a seasoning. The finest of Spain's Roman ruins today are at Empúries, Itálica, Mérida, Tarragona and Segovia.

The Pax Romana started to crack when two Germanic tribes, the Franks and the Alemanni, swept across the Pyrenees in the late 3rd century AD, causing devastation. Massive defensive walls were built around Hispania's towns and cities to stave off these threats. The end came when the Huns arrived in eastern Europe from Asia a century later. Germanic peoples displaced by the Huns moved west – among them the Suevi and the Vandals, who overran the Iberian Peninsula around 410.

Visigoths

Another Germanic people, the Visigoths, took Rome itself under their leader Alaric in 410. Having spared the Roman emperor, the Visigoths made a pact with him to rid Hispania of other invaders in return for lands in southern Gaul (France). But in the 6th century the Franks pushed the Visigoths out of Gaul. The Visigoths then settled in the upper reaches of Spain's Tajo and Ebro rivers, and Toledo became their capital.

The rule of the roughly 200,000 long-haired Visigoths, who had a taste for gaudy jewellery, over the several million more-sophisticated Hispano-Romans was precarious, and was undermined by strife among their own nobility. The Hispano-Roman nobles still ran the fiscal system and their Catholic bishops were the senior figures in urban centres. Town life declined in quality under Visigothic rule.

Ties between the Visigoth monarchy and the influential Hispano-Roman church were greatly strengthened in 587 when King Reccared converted to Roman Catholicism from the Visigoths' Aryan version of Christianity (which denied that Christ was God). But the Visigoth kings still had to contend with regular revolts by nobles, bishops and others.

The Visigoths had no long-standing culture of their own and tended to ape Roman ways. A few Visigothic churches can be seen today in northern Spain. One, at Baños de Cerrato near Palencia, dating from 661, is probably the oldest church in the country.

The Muslim Conquest

The Visigoths achieved their success because of their military superiority but they fell out of practice. By 700, with famine and disease in Toledo and chaos throughout the peninsula, their kingdom was falling apart. This set the scene for the successful Muslim invasion of 711, which set Spain's destiny quite apart from the rest of Europe.

Following the death of Mohammed in 632, Arabs had spread through the Middle East and North Africa, taking Islam with them. If you believe the myth, they were finally ushered onto the Iberian Peninsula by the sexual exploits of the last Visigoth king, Roderick. Ballads and chronicles written long after the event relate how Roderick seduced (to put it mildly) young Florinda, the daughter of Count Julian, the Visigothic governor of Ceuta in North Africa; and how Julian sought revenge by approaching the Muslims with a plan to invade Spain. In dull fact Julian probably just wanted outside help in a struggle for the Visigothic throne.

In 711, on orders from Musa, the Arab governor of North Africa, a general named Tariq landed at Gibraltar with around 10,000 men, mostly Berbers (indigenous North Africans). He also had some of Roderick's Visigoth rivals as allies. In the same or the following year, probably near the Río Guadalete in Andalucía, Roderick's army was decimated and he drowned while fleeing the scene. Visigothic survivors fled north.

Within a few months Tariq had taken Toledo and, with Arab reinforcements, the Muslims quickly took over the rest of the peninsula except for small areas in the Cantabrian mountains. They even went on over the Pyrenees, but were decisively repulsed by the Franks at Poitiers in 732 and retreated south of the Río Duero. In the Iberian Peninsula they were welcomed by Jews and slaves, who had been badly treated under Visigoth rule.

Muslim Spain

The Muslims (often referred to as Moors) were to remain the dominant force on the peninsula for nearly four centuries, a potent force for 170 years after that, and a lesser one for a further 250 years. Between wars and rebellions, Al-Andalus, the name given to this Muslim territory, developed the most highly cultured society of medieval Europe.

Al-Andalus never had any long-term unified government, and it suffered its share of internal conflicts. Political power and cultural developments centred initially on Córdoba (756-1010), then Sevilla (c 1040-1248) and lastly Granada (1248-1492). In these cities the Muslims built beautiful palaces, mosques, monuments and gardens. They were great imitators rather than innovators but they imbued their art, architecture and environment with their own style and sensuous nature. Their lands were made as productive as possible through irrigation, the introduction of exotic fruits and crops (oranges, lemons, peaches, sugar cane, rice) and advanced farming techniques.

The Muslims mostly ruled tolerantly, allowing freedom of worship. Christians under their rule (mozárabes or Mozarabs) had to pay a special tax so there were many conversions to Islam. Before long, as the Muslims had not brought women with them, Muslim and local blood merged. This applied as much to the rulers as the ruled, for as well as the acquisition of women for royal harems, there was frequent intermarriage with the Christian royalty and aristocracy of the north – for tribute, appeasement or even alliance.

The Córdoban Emirate & Caliphate From 711 to 756, Muslim Spain was a province of the Emirate of Ifriqiya (North Africa), part of the Caliphate of Damascus which ruled the Muslim world. In 756, following the shift of the caliphate to Baghdad under a rival dynasty, Muslim Spain became an independent emirate under Abd ar-Rahman I, who began the construction of the Córdoba Mezquita (mosque), one of the world's greatest Muslim monuments. Most of Al-Andalus was unified under Córdoban rule for some fairly long periods. A complete break with Muslim central authority was made in 929 when Abd ar-Rahman III established the independent Caliphate of Córdoba, under which Al-Andalus reached its political and cultural peak.

At this time Córdoba, with by some estimates as many as 500,000 people, was the biggest and most dazzling city in western Europe, thriving on a productive agriculture and the work of its skilled artisans. Abd ar-Rahman III's court was frequented by Jewish, Arab and Christian scholars.

Later in the 10th century the fearsome Córdoban general Al-Mansour struck terror into Christian northern Spain with 50-odd forays into Christian territory in 20 years. He destroyed the cathedral at Santiago de Compostela in 997 and forced Christian slaves to carry its doors and bells to Córdoba, where they were incorporated into the great mosque. Al-Mansour even conquered Morocco. But after his death in 1002 rebels looted Córdoba, and in 1031 the caliphate broke up into 20 or so *taifas* (small kingdoms), of which Sevilla, Granada, Toledo and Zaragoza were among the most powerful.

Almoravids & Almohads Political unity was restored to Al-Andalus by the Almora-vid invasion (at the invitation of the Sevilla taifa) of 1086. The Almoravids were a fanatical Muslim sect of Saharan nomads who had conquered North Africa. Sixty years later another fanatical Berber sect, the Almohads from the Atlas Mountains, invaded the Iberian Peninsula after stamping out the Almoravids in Morocco. Both these sects soundly defeated the Christian armies that they encountered.

Under both the Almoravids and the Almohads, religious intolerance sent refugees fleeing north to Christian territory. But in time both mellowed in their adopted territory and Almohad rule saw a revival of the cultural achievements that the Almoravids had interrupted in Sevilla. In Córdoba the philosopher Averroës translated Aristotle into Arabic, and a Latin version of his commentary introduced Greek thought to medieval Europe, causing uproar among Christian theologians.

The Reconquista
The Christian Reconquista (Reconquest) of the peninsula began in about 722 at Covadonga and ended with the fall of Granada in 1492. It was a stuttering affair, conducted by a tangled sequence of emerging, merging and demerging Christian states that were as often at war with each other as with the Muslims. There were also Christian-Muslim alliances. The concept of 'Spain' – a single unified country covering most of the peninsula – did not arise till later. But the Muslims were gradually pushed south as the northern kingdoms of Asturias, León, Navarra, Castilla and Aragón developed and ultimately forged a sufficiently united front to oust Muslim rule from the peninsula.

Santiago Matamoros An essential ingredient in the successes of the Reconquista was the cult of St James (Santiago), one of the 12 Apostles. In 813, strange celestial happenings were reported at the saint's supposed tomb in Galicia. Pilgrims began arriving and the town of Santiago de Compostela grew around the church that was built on the spot, eventually to become the third most popular medieval Christian pilgrimage goal after Rome and Jerusalem. Visions of St James appeared to various Christian leaders before forays against the Muslims, inspiring their soldiers to acts of great bravery. Here was the answer to the war cry of Islam. St James became the special protector of soldiers in the Reconquista, earning the sobriquet 'Matamoros' (Muslim-Slayer), and is today the patron saint of Spain.

The First 500 Years – the Rise of Castilla

Covadonga lies in the Picos de Europa in Asturias, where Visigothic nobles took refuge after the Muslim conquest. Christian versions of what happened there tell of a small band of fighters under their leader Pelayo crushing a truly ginormous force of Muslims; Muslim accounts make it a rather less important skirmish. Whatever the facts of the matter, the Muslims gave up taking on the Asturian mountaineers thereafter. By 757 Christians occupied nearly a quarter of the peninsula. Progress was a lot slower, however, from then on.

The Asturian kingdom eventually moved its capital to León, which spearheaded the Reconquista until the Christians were set on the defensive by Al-Mansour in the 10th century. Then Sancho III (the Great) of Navarra in the western Pyrenees took over in the early 11th century.

A new Christian setback came with the Almoravids, against whom Alfonso I of Aragón, the kingdom east of Navarra, led the counterattack, taking Zaragoza in 1118. After his death Aragón was united through royal marriage with Cataluña, to its east, creating a formidable new Christian power block. Portugal, too, emerged as an independent Christian kingdom in the 12th century. But it was Castilla, originally a small principality in eastern León, that developed as the dominant Reconquista force. Taking its name from the castles built by its Christian conquerors, Castilla grew from the 11th century as hardy adventurers set up towns in the vulnerable no-man's-land of the Duero basin, spurred on by huge land grants in

conquered territory and other rights and privileges (fueros).

The Castilians suffered a terrible defeat at the hands of the Almohads at Alarcos, south of Toledo, in 1195, and this had the effect of unifying Christians against the Muslims. The pope called an international crusade, its spirit embracing the cult of St James. In June 1212 a united army of Spanish and European soldiers annihilated a huge Almohad force at Las Navas de Tolosa in the Sierra Morena. This was the beginning of the end for Al-Andalus.

The Castilian king Fernando III El Santo (the Saint) took Córdoba in 1236 and Sevilla (with help from the rival Muslim kingdom of Granada) in 1248. Fernando triumphantly returned the bells of Santiago de Compostela's cathedral, which had been taken by Al-Mansour to Córdoba in 997. Jaume I of Aragón took the Balearic Islands and Valencia in the 1230s, and Portugal expelled the Muslims in 1249. The sole surviving Muslim state on the peninsula was the Emirate of Granada, which comprised roughly half of present-day Andalucía.

There were no great reprisals against the defeated Muslims. Until the Black Death a century later, Castilla and Aragón were cosmopolitan communities.

The Lull (1250-1479)

Fernando III's son, Alfonso X El Sabio (the Learned, 1252-84) proclaimed Castilian the official language of his realm, and gathered around him at Toledo scholars regardless of their religion, particularly Jews who knew Arabic and Latin and could translate ancient texts, thus contributing to a cultural revival. But politically Alfonso was plagued by constant uprisings and plots, even from within his own family. This unrest continued in Castilla until the 15th century, with the nobility, increasingly rich from wool production on their huge estates, repeatedly challenging the crown.

The late 13th and the 14th centuries were a time of cultural malaise in Castilla, architecture and music being the exceptions. Architecture was the great art of the late Middle Ages, reaching its heights in great cathedrals such as those at Toledo and León. This was also an era of growing intolerance towards the Jews and foreigners – especially Genoese – who were taking over Castilian commerce and finance while the Castilians were preoccupied with their low effort/high profit wool production. Jews were blamed for economic crises and even for the Black Death in the mid-14th century. Events culminated in pogroms around the peninsula in the 1390s.

Aragón, meanwhile, looked outwards to the Mediterranean, and relations between its crown and subjects were kept fairly free of strife by a form of parliament. Aragón took Sardinia and Sicily, from where Catalan soldiers went off to fight the Ottoman Turks. The cathedral and other buildings in the kingdom's main city, Barcelona, attest its wealth at that time, but Aragón's star started to wane with the Black Death.

Both Castilla and Aragón suffered series of ineffectual monarchs from the late 14th century until the time of Isabel and Fernando, whose marriage in Segovia Castle in 1469 would merge the two kingdoms. Isabel succeeded to the Castilian throne in 1474, and Fernando to Aragón's in 1479, both coming through civil wars to hang on to their inheritances. The joint rule of the Reyes Católicos (Catholic Monarchs), as they are known, dates from 1479. (Castilla and Aragón, however, remained legally separate states until the 18th century, and have a tradition of conflict and tension right up to the present day.)

The Fall of Granada The Nasrid dynasty ruled the Muslim Emirate of Granada from the lush Alhambra palace for over 250 years from 1237. Their city saw Spain's final Muslim cultural flowering and their state prospered with the influx of refugees from the Reconquista. It reached its peak in the 14th century under Yousouf I, then Mohammed V, both of whom contributed to the splendours of the Alhambra.

Granada survived by playing off Castilla, Aragón and Muslim Morocco against each other. It was also helped by Castilla's internal conflicts. Castilian armies eventually started nibbling at the Emirate of Granada in the 15th century. After Emir Abu al-Hasan refused in 1476 to pay any more tribute to Castilla, Isabel and Fernando launched the final crusade of the Reconquista in 1482, with an army largely funded by Jewish loans and the Catholic church.

By now Granada's rulers had retreated to a pleasure-loving existence in the Alhambra and were riven by harem jealousies and other feuds. Matters degenerated into a confused civil war, and the Castilians took full advantage. Fernando and Isabel mopped up the rest of the emirate, then entered Granada, after a long siege, on 2 January 1492 – an appropriate start for the most momentous year in Spanish history.

The surrender terms were fairly generous to Boabdil, who got the Alpujarras valleys south of Granada and 30,000 gold coins. His subjects were to be allowed political and religious freedom, though this was reversed within a few years.

From Granada, the crusading spirit of the Reconquista briefly moved on to North Africa, where Spain took a few fortresses before being distracted by European affairs after 1510.

The Catholic Monarchs
From 1479 to 1516 the pious Isabel and the Machiavellian Fernando were an unbeatable team. The war against Granada was just one of several steps they took to cement their subjects' loyalty. They checked the power of the Castilian nobility, granting Andalucían land to their supporters and excluding aristocrats from the royal administration. They also reformed a corrupt, immoral clergy.

Jews & the Inquisition Despite Fernando's part-Jewish background and Jewish loans for the Granada war, Jews were considered Muslim allies on top of their other problems. Capitalising on anti-Jewish feeling, the Catholic Monarchs revived the almost extinct Inquisition – founded earlier to deal with heretics in France – to root out false Christians. The Inquisition focused most of all on *conversos*, Jews who had converted to Christianity, and accused many of continuing to practise Judaism in secret. It was responsible for perhaps 12,000 deaths over 300 years, 2000 of them in the 1480s.

Under the influence of the Grand Inquisitor Tomás de Torquemada, in April 1492 Isabel and Fernando ordered the expulsion from their territories of all Jews who refused baptism. Around 50,000 to 100,000 Jews converted to avoid expulsion, but some 200,000 – the first Sephardic Jews (Jews of Spanish origin) – left for other Mediterranean destinations. In September the bankrupt monarchy seized all unsold Jewish property. A talented urban middle class was decimated.

Christopher Columbus

Persecution of the Muslims A few years later, Cardinal Cisneros, Isabel's confessor and overseer of the Inquisition, took the spirit of the Reconquista to its logical conclusion by trying to eradicate Muslim culture altogether. He forced mass conversions, had Islamic books burnt and banned the Arabic language. Muslims in Andalucía revolted but were quickly suppressed. In 1502 Muslims under Castilian rule were ordered to convert to Christianity or leave. Most Muslims – an estimated 300,000 – underwent baptism and stayed, to be known as Moriscos (converted Muslims), but their conversion was barely skin-deep and they were never assimilated. The Moriscos were finally expelled from Spain between 1609 and 1614.

Christopher Columbus In April 1492 the Catholic Monarchs finally granted Christopher Columbus (Cristóbal Colón to Spaniards) funds for his long-desired journey across the Atlantic in search of a new trade route to the Orient. The Genoese Columbus had presented his ideas to other European monarchs without success. Isabel and Fernando were motivated by the urgent need to fill their empty coffers and the possibility of more Christian conversions.

Columbus set off from Palos de la Frontera, near Huelva, on 3 August with three small ships and 120 men. They stopped at the Canary Islands, then sailed west for 31 days sighting no land. The rebellious crew gave Columbus two more days. He sighted the island of San Salvador, Bahamas, and returned to his benefactors eight months after his departure, with Indians and riches. He made three more voyages, founding Santo Domingo on Hispaniola and reaching the coasts of Honduras and Venezuela, but proved an incompetent administrator and was eventually shipped home as a prisoner, though released on his return. He died poor, and apparently still believing he had reached Asia, in Valladolid in 1506.

After Isabel Fernando entangled Spain in European affairs, and Europe in Spain's, by marrying his and Isabel's four children into the royal families of Portugal, Burgundy and England and the powerful Habsburg family of central Europe. (The English connection failed when the youngest, Catalina, or Catherine of Aragón, was cast aside by Henry VIII.) The early death of two of the children left the third, Princess Juana, heir to the Castilian throne when Isabel died in 1504. Juana's husband was Felipe El Hermoso (the Handsome), who was heir to the Low Countries and to the Habsburg lands in central Europe. But Juana, dubbed Juana la Loca (the Mad), was unfit to rule, and when Felipe died soon after, Fernando took over as regent of Castilla until his own death in 1516. During this time he conducted a war with France over interests in Italy and Navarra: by taking Navarra he united Spain under a single rule for the first time since Visigothic days.

The Habsburgs

Carlos I In 1517 Fernando's 17 year old grandson Carlos – son of Juana la Loca and Felipe El Hermoso and already ruler of the Low Countries – came with his supporters from Flanders to take up his Spanish inheritance. Juana la Loca was kept under house arrest, though she remained nominally queen till she died in 1555.

In 1519 Carlos succeeded his other grandfather Maximilian to the Habsburg lands in Austria, and managed to win the election to follow Maximilian as Holy Roman Emperor (becoming Charles V in that role). Carlos now ruled more of Europe than anyone since the 9th century – all of Spain, the Low Countries, Austria, several Italian states and parts of France and Germany – plus the Spanish colonies in the Caribbean and Panama. To these he would add more of central Europe and big slices of the American continent.

Carlos spent only 16 years of his 40 year reign in Spain. At first the Spanish did not care for a king who spoke no Castilian, nor for his luxurious lifestyle and Flemish entourage, nor for his appropriating their wealth. Castilian cities revolted in 1520-21 (the Guerra de las Comunidades or War of the Communities) but were crushed by Carlos' foreign troops. Eventually the Spanish came round to him, at least for his strong stance against emerging Protestantism and his learning of Castilian. Under Carlos, Spain could have developed into an early industrial power, but he blew it by being drawn into an endless series of European conflicts, even with the pope. These consumed the bulk of the monarchy's new wealth from the Americas. War-weary, Carlos abdicated shortly before his death in 1556, dividing his territories between his brother Fernando and his son Felipe, who got the lion's share, including Spain, the Low Countries and the American possessions.

The American Empire Carlos I's reign saw Spain take over vast tracts of the American mainland, beginning with the ruthless but brilliant conquest of the Aztec empire by Hernán Cortés and his small band of adventurers in 1519-21, followed by Francisco Pizarro's similar subjugation of the Inca empire in 1531-33. These conquistadors, with their odd mix of brutality, bravery, gold lust and piety, were the natural successors to the warriors of the Reconquista.

By 1600 Spain controlled Florida, all the biggest Caribbean islands, nearly all of present-day Mexico and Central America, and a strip of South America from present-day Venezuela to Argentina. The new colonies sent hugely valuable cargoes of silver, gold and other riches back to Spain, where the crown was entitled to one-fifth of the bullion (the *quinto real* or royal fifth). Sevilla enjoyed a monopoly on this trade and grew into one of Europe's biggest and richest cities by 1600.

Whether the Spanish empire was any more or less greedy and inhumane than comparable enterprises – such as the later British conquest of North America – is a topic of much rather pointless debate. One of the few certainties is that to try to judge it by 20th century liberal standards is silly. The conquistadors sprang from one war culture and confronted others – which also indulged in practices such as slavery and mass human sacrifice. Many Spaniards considered the conquest to have as much a moral as an economic and political mission – that of winning new Christian souls. Though the welfare of the bodies the souls inhabited wasn't always paramount, the clergy managed to spare the natives some of the worst excesses of the colonists. At the instigation of the friar Bartolomé de Las Casas, Spain enacted laws which gave a measure of protection to the natives – something no other European colonial power of the time did. The native population of the colonies may indeed have been decimated, but this was at least as much a result of new diseases as of colonial oppression.

Felipe II Carlos I's son, Felipe II (1556-98), presided over the zenith of Spanish power. Not surprisingly, his reign is a study in contradictions. Felipe enlarged the overseas empire but lost wealthy capitalist Holland to a long, drawn-out rebellion; thrashed the Ottoman Turks, Spain's great Mediterranean rivals, at the sea battle of Lepanto (Greece) in 1571, but saw his Spanish Armada in 1588 routed by England; received greater flows of silver than ever from the Americas, but went bankrupt; was a fanatical Catholic who spurred the Inquisition to persecution of anyone suspected of Protestant views or of Jewish or Muslim blood, yet readily allied with Protestant England against Catholic France when it suited Spain's interests; and spent his life conscientiously drowning under state papers but increasingly unable to take big decisions.

When Felipe claimed Portugal on its king's death in 1580, he not only united the Iberian Peninsula but also Europe's two great overseas empires: Portugal's was dotted across the globe from sugar-growing Brazil to spice-rich Asia. But there was no plan to absorb the new wealth. The Castilian gentry's disdain for commerce and industry allowed Genoese and German merchants to dominate trade, even in Sevilla, produced a trade deficit because wool was the only serious export, and left the countryside dominated by sheep and cattle ranches, with grain having to be imported. Such money as didn't find its way into foreign pockets or wasn't owed for costly European wars went on churches, palaces and monasteries. Spain, it was said, had discovered the magic formula for turning silver into stone.

One of Felipe's most lasting decisions, made in 1561, was to turn the minor country town of Madrid into a new, permanent capital from which to mould his kingdom. Over past centuries Toledo, Segovia, Valladolid and other cities had all served as Castilla's capital.

The 17th Century Under a trio of ineffectual kings, Spain saw its chickens come home to roost. Felipe III (1598-1621) preferred hunting to ruling and left government to the self-seeking Duke of Lerma. Felipe IV (1621-65) concentrated on a long line of mistresses and handed over affairs of state to Count-Duke Olivares, who tried bravely to reverse Spain's slide but retired a broken man in 1643. Spain fought unsuccessful wars with France and Holland, lost Portugal and faced revolts in Sicily, Naples and Cataluña. Silver shipments from the Americas shrank disastrously. The physically and mentally feeble Carlos II (1665-1700), who liked picking strawberries and was unable to produce children, bequeathed only the War of the Spanish Succession.

The Cultural Golden Age Mid-16th to late 17th century Spain was like a gigantic artisans' workshop, in which architecture, sculpture, painting and metalwork consumed around 5% of the nation's income. Education spread, increasing literacy, though this hardly touched the masses. The age was immortalised on canvas by artists such as Velázquez, El Greco, Zurbarán, Murillo and Ribera; and in words by Miguel de Cervantes, the mystics Santa Teresa of Ávila and San Juan de la Cruz (St John of the Cross) and the unbelievably prolific playwright Lope de Vega.

The 18th Century

Under the new Bourbon dynasty – still in place today – the 18th century was one of limited recovery from the nadir of the 17th.

Felipe V Carlos II had bequeathed his throne to his young relative Philippe, Duke of Anjou, who happened to be grandson of Louis XIV of France – and second in line to the French throne. In 1700, aged 16, Philippe reluctantly left Versailles for Madrid, where he became Felipe V (1701-46). But France's big rival, the Austrian emperor Leopold, wanted to see his son Charles, a nephew of Carlos II, on the Spanish throne. The resulting War of the Spanish Succession (1702-13) was a contest for the balance of power in Europe, involving England, Holland and even a rebellious Cataluña. In the end Felipe V held on to Spain but renounced his right to the French throne. Spain lost several Italian states and Flanders, its last possession in the Low Countries, to Austria, and Gibraltar and Menorca to the British. The suppression of the Catalan rebellion in 1714 finally put an end to Aragón's theoretical independence of Castilla.

Felipe, with many French and Italian advisers, instituted reforms in economy and government and strengthened the navy. But land reform proved impossible – two-thirds of the land was in the hands of the nobility and church and underproductive, and large numbers of males from nobles to vagrants were unwilling to work.

This was the age of the Enlightenment, but traditional Spanish values, fostered by the powerful church and Inquisition, were at odds with the rationalism which trickled in from France. Bullfighting, Spanish folkloric dress and religious festivals became firmly entrenched.

Fernando VI & Carlos III The next two Bourbon kings made efforts to modernise Spain. Fernando VI (1746-59) replaced all foreign advisers with Spanish, reorganised finance, further strengthened the navy, and ended the Inquisition's dreaded *autos de fe* (elaborate execution ceremonies). The economy was on an upturn largely due to a revitalised Cataluña, with growing industries such as weaving, and the Basque shipbuilding industry. But agricultural Castilla was left behind, unable to increase yields due to lack of land reforms.

Carlos III (1759-88) was an enlightened despot in the new European mould. He expelled the backward-looking Jesuits, transformed the face of Madrid, sent a new road system spoking out to the provinces, and tried to improve agriculture. But food shortages fuelled unrest among the masses, provoking fear among the upper echelons that the growing democratic fever in France would spread to Spain.

French Revolution & Spanish War of Independence (Peninsular War)

Carlos IV (1788-1808), a son of Carlos III, was dominated by his Italian wife, Maria Luisa of Parma; she hooked up with a handsome royal guard called Godoy, who became chief minister. This unholy trinity was less than ideally suited to coping with the crisis presented by the French Revolution of 1789.

When Louis XVI of France (Carlos' cousin) was guillotined in 1793, Spain declared war on France. Two years later, with France's Reign of Terror spent, Godoy made peace, pledging military support for France against Britain in return for the withdrawal of French forces from northern Spain. In 1805 a combined Spanish-French navy was beaten by the British fleet under Nelson off Cape Trafalgar (between Cádiz and Gibraltar). This put an end to Spanish sea power and sealed Spain's colonial decline.

Two years later, Napoleon and Godoy agreed to divide Britain's ally Portugal between them. French forces poured into Spain, supposedly on the way to northern Portugal. By 1808 this had become a French occupation of Spain. The king, queen and Godoy fled to their Aranjuez palace outside Madrid, which angry mobs soon surrounded. Carlos abdicated to his son Fernando VII. Godoy only escaped the mob's wrath by rolling himself up in a carpet.

Napoleon summoned the royal family and Godoy to Bayonne and forced Fernando to abdicate to Carlos, and Carlos in turn to abdicate to Napoleon's brother Joseph Bonaparte (José I). Back in Madrid crowds revolted, and country-wide the Spanish populace took up arms. Napoleon scored a number of victories but the Spanish guerrillas plugged on.

The Spanish were reinforced by British and Portuguese forces led by the Duke of Wellington. By 1812, Napoleon's attention was diverted to his Russian campaign and French forces withdrew in large numbers. They were finally expelled following their defeat at Vitoria in the País Vasco in 1813. Fernando VII took the throne, to the acclaim of the masses, in 1814. As it turned out,

Fernando was a very poor advertisement for monarchy.

The 19th Century

Liberals vs Conservatives During the war, a national Cortes (parliament), meeting at Cádiz in 1812, had drawn up a new liberal constitution which incorporated many of the principles of the American and French prototypes. But the assembly was not really representative, and the constitution was bound to upset the church and monarchy – setting the pattern for a confused contest, which would occupy most of the century, between conservatives, who had a vested interest in the status quo, and liberals, who wanted vaguely democratic reforms.

Fernando VII (1814-33) revoked the 1812 constitution, exiled, imprisoned or executed liberal opponents, re-established the Inquisition and invited the Jesuits back. In 1820 Colonel Rafael de Riego made the first of the 19th century's many *pronunciamientos* (pronouncements of military rebellion) in the name of liberalism. But French troops put Fernando back on the throne in 1823. Severe reprisals and corrupt government drastically cut the king's popularity before he died in 1833.

Meanwhile the restless American colonies had taken advantage of Spain's internal problems to strike out on their own. By 1824 only Cuba and Puerto Rico remained part of Spanish America.

First Carlist War Fernando's dithering indecision over the succession to the throne resulted in the First Carlist War (1833-39), between supporters of his brother Don Carlos and his infant daughter Isabel. Don Carlos was supported by the church, other ultraconservatives, and regional rebels in the País Vasco, Navarra, Cataluña and Aragón – all together known as the Carlists. The Isabel faction had the support of liberals and the army.

During the war violent anticlericalism emerged. Religious orders were closed and church property and lands seized and sold. As usual, only the wealthy benefited. At the war's end the defeated Don Carlos went to France. The army emerged victorious and confident, with General Baldomero Espartero ruling as regent for Isabel from 1840 to 1843.

Isabel II In 1843 Isabel, now all of 13, declared herself Queen Isabel II (1843-68). Her inept reign saw a series of constitutional crises and revolving governments of gently liberal persuasion, overshadowed by a power struggle between senior generals. One achievement of sorts was the creation of a rural police force, the Guardia Civil, mainly to protect the wealthy in the bandit-ridden countryside. There was an upturn in the economy with progress in business, banking, mining and railways, plus some reforms in education, but the benefits accrued to few.

Under the influence of French, German and English philosophy and political events, plus a growing hatred for the dissolute Isabel and her feeble governments, liberal sentiments advanced even within the army. Eventually radical liberals, and discontented soldiers led by General Juan Prim, overthrew Isabel in the Septembrina Revolution of 1868. Isabel fled to France.

Second Carlist War & First Republic Prim and General Francisco Serrano formed a liberal government, but Spaniards still wanted a monarch. Eventually Amadeo of Savoy, a son of the Italian king and known for his liberal sentiments, accepted the job in 1870. The day Amadeo arrived in Madrid, Prim, his main supporter, was assassinated. Then things got worse. Amadeo's supporters squabbled among themselves, and the church and aristocracy opposed him outright. The aristocracy split into two camps, one favouring Isabel II's teenage son Alfonso, the other backing Don Carlos' grandson Carlos. Thus began the three-way Second Carlist War (1872-76).

With the Carlists holding most of the north, Barcelona a law unto itself and anarchism making strides in Andalucía, Amadeo gave up and left Spain in 1873. The liberal-dominated Cortes proclaimed Spain a federal republic of 17 states the same month.

But this First Republic, riven by internal divisions and unable to keep a grip on the regions, lasted only 11 months. In the end the army, no longer liberal, put Alfonso on the throne as Alfonso XII (1874-85), in a kind of coalition with the church and landowners. Yet another constitution, recognising both monarchy and parliament, was declared in 1876. All it really produced was a sequence of orderly changes of government *(turnos)* between supposed conservatives and liberals – though little actually separated their political persuasions. Electoral rigging was part of the process.

Social Unrest

The 1890s brought overall stability, economic growth and improved schooling, but there were growing rumblings among the industrial working class. And in the humiliating Spanish-American War of 1898, Spain lost the last of its once vast overseas possessions – Cuba, Puerto Rico, the Philippines and Guam.

Alfonso XIII (1902-1930), who came to the throne at 17 after a long regency by his mother, was initially sensitive to the liberal mood of the time but soon became fed up with constitutional government and started interfering. There were 33 different governments during his reign. His friends were among the military, church and wealthy landowners.

At the other end of the social scale, a powder keg was forming. Industry had brought large-scale migration to Barcelona, Madrid and Basque cities. On the surface, these cities looked prosperous, but their workers lived in squalid slums. In the countryside, where most of the population still lived, the old problems of underproduction, and land ownership by the few, persisted. Many Spaniards left for Latin America. The remaining working class increasingly gravitated towards Marxism and anarchism. The wealthy, powerful church had already failed them.

Anarchism

This offshoot of Marxism arrived in Spain in 1868 and gained support

rapidly. It favoured one outburst of revolutionary violence to bring down the system and replace it with an egalitarian society. In the 1890s and 1900s anarchists were responsible for the bombing of Barcelona's Liceu opera house, assassinations of two prime ministers, and a bomb at Alfonso XIII's wedding in 1906, which killed 24 people.

Anarchism appealed both to the rural communities of Andalucía, Aragón, Cataluña and the north-west, and to industrial workers who lived and worked in appalling conditions in Barcelona and other cities. In 1910, the anarchist unions were organised by the syndicalists (anarchist trade unionists) into the powerful CNT (Confederación Nacional del Trabajo, National Confederation of Work). The syndicalists saw organisation of labour as the way to an anarchist society, their main weapon being the general strike.

Socialism This grew more slowly than anarchism because of its idea of steady change through parliamentary processes. Spanish socialists rejected Soviet-style communism. The UGT (Unión General de Trabajadores, General Union of Workers), established in 1888, was moderate and disciplined. Its appeal was greatest in Madrid and Bilbao, both fearful of Catalan separatism. Its sharpest growth was between 1906 and 1910.

Regionalism Parallel with the growth of the left was the growth of Basque and Catalan separatism. In Cataluña, which had always liked to steer its own ship, separatism was taken over by big business interests which had been hard hit by the loss of the Cuban market and wanted to pursue policies independent of Madrid. Basque nationalism emerged in the 1890s largely due to the perceived threat to Basque identity posed by the large numbers of Castilians who had flocked to work in Basque industries.

The Tragic Week & General Strikes When in 1909 Berbers wiped out a contingent of Spaniards in Morocco – part of which had become a Spanish protectorate when the

European powers carved up North Africa – the government called up Catalan reserves to go to Morocco. The result was the so-called Tragic Week (Semana Trágica) in Barcelona, which began with a general strike and turned into a frenzy of violence. In a furious government response, many workers were executed.

Spain stayed neutral during WWI (1914-18) and enjoyed an economic boom. In 1917 parliamentary reforms were demanded by industrialists, liberals, unionists and the general public. The king and the right refused, leading to a general strike which was crushed by the army. But anarchist and socialist numbers grew, inspired by the Russian Revolution, and political violence and general mayhem continued, especially in lawless Barcelona.

Primo de Rivera's Dictatorship

In 1921 the Spanish army suffered a catastrophe at Anual in Morocco, with 10,000 men killed by a small force of Berbers. The finger of blame was pointed at King Alfonso, who had intervened to select the Spanish commander for the campaign. But just as a report on the event was to be submitted to parliament in 1923, General Miguel Primo de Rivera led an army rising in support of the king, then launched his own mild six year dictatorship.

Primo was an eccentric, unpredictable aristocrat and a centralist. He censored the press and upset intellectuals but kept a lid on worker discontent by gaining the cooperation of the socialist UGT. Anarchists went underground. Primo's successes included increased industrialisation, better roads, punctual trains, new dams and power plants. Eventually he was unseated by an economic downturn following the Wall Street crash and by discontent in the army, with Alfonso taking the chance to return to public life and dismiss him.

The Second Republic

Alfonso had brought the monarchy into too much disrepute to last long himself. When a new republican movement scored sweeping victories in municipal elections in April 1931, the king departed for a life of exile in Italy. The Second Republic (1931-36) that now ensued was an idealistic, tumultuous and increasingly violent period that polarised Spanish politics and ended in civil war.

The Left in Charge (1931-33) La Niña Bonita (the Pretty Child), as the Second Republic was called by its supporters, was welcomed by leftists and the poor masses, but conservatives were alarmed and the middle class undecided. Strife began within a month of the king's departure. A new Carlist pretender, Don Jaime, with Navarran peasant support, called on antirepublicans. There were church burnings and lootings, mostly initiated by anarchists but also by those in the pay of the right.

Elections in 1931 brought in a government composed of socialists led by Francisco Largo Caballero, the so-called Radicals (actually more like centrists) led by Alejandro Lerroux, and the Republican Action Party led by Manuel Azaña. The Cortes contained few workers – and no-one from the anarchist CNT, which saw any sort of government as reprehensible and continued to use violence to bring on the revolution. Azaña, the Minister of War, immediately trimmed back the military, even closing the Zaragoza Military Academy, the director of which was a short, shrill-voiced Galician general called Francisco Franco. (Franco, aged 38, was enjoying a meteoric career built on brave, disciplined leadership in Morocco.)

A new constitution, passed in December 1931, alienated many. It outraged Catholics by ending Catholicism's status as the official religion, disbanding the Jesuits, ending government payment of clerics' salaries, legalising divorce and banning clerical orders from teaching. The constitution gave autonomy-minded Cataluña its own parliament and president in return for ultimate support for the republic, but socialists and the right saw this as a threat to national unity. The constitution promised land redistribution, which pleased the Andalucían landless, but failed to deliver much. Even new universal suffrage rebounded on the republic because newly enfranchised women led a swing to the right in the next elections in 1933.

The Right in Charge (1933-36) Continuing anarchist disruption, an economic slump and increasing alienation of big business, and disunity on the left, all helped the right win the 1933 election. The new Catholic party CEDA (Confederación Española de Derechas Autónomas, Spanish Confederation of Autonomous Rights), led by José María Gil Robles, won more seats than any other party. Other new forces on the right included José Calvo Sotelo's monarchist Renovación Española party, and the fascist Falange led by José Antonio Primo de Rivera, son of the 1920s dictator. Falange practised blatant street violence. The left, including the emerging communists (who, unlike the socialists, supported the Russian Revolution), now called increasingly for revolution.

By 1934 the situation was reaching crisis point as violence soared out of control. The socialist UGT called for a general strike, Cataluña's president declared Cataluña independent (albeit within a federal Spanish republic), and workers' committees took over the northern mining region of Asturias after attacking police and army posts. All these moves were quashed, but in Asturias it took a campaign of violent repression by the Spanish Foreign Legion (set up to fight Moroccan tribes in the 1920s), led by generals Millan Astray and Franco.

The events in Asturias firmly divided the whole country into left and right. The many now in jail included Largo Caballero and Azaña. The government suspended Catalan autonomy and repealed agrarian reform.

Popular Front Government & Army Uprising The February 1936 elections were a straight fight between the Popular Front left-wing coalition (with the communists now to the fore) and the right-wing National Front. The Popular Front won and Azaña headed its government. Now the left feared an army coup, the right a revolution. Catalan autonomy was restored. Suspect generals were moved out of the way (Franco to the Canary Islands).

Violence continued on both sides. Extremist groups grew bigger (the anarchist CNT now had over a million members), and peasants were on the verge of revolution. The army was divided. Then right-wing leader Calvo Sotelo was murdered by a group of off-duty policemen and the government was blamed.

On 17 July the Spanish garrison in Melilla in North Africa revolted, followed the next day by some garrisons on the mainland. The leaders of the plot were five generals, among them Franco, who on 19 July flew to Morocco to take command of his legionnaires. The civil war had begun.

The Civil War
This was not to be the usual quick, decisive military revolt. The Spanish Civil War split communities, families and friends. Both sides committed atrocious massacres and reprisals, and employed death squads to eliminate members of opposition organisations, in the early weeks especially. This was partly out of simple hatred, partly to eliminate dangerous opponents, and, on the rebels' side at least, partly to terrorise the populace into submission. The rebels, who called themselves Nationalists because they thought they were fighting for Spain, shot or hanged tens of thousands of supporters of the Republic. Republicans, known as Loyalists, did likewise to Franco sympathisers, including some 7000 priests, monks and nuns, even though the church was not involved in the initial uprising. Political affiliation often provided a convenient cover for settling old scores. In the whole war perhaps 350,000 Spaniards died.

Much of the military and the Guardia Civil went over to the Nationalists, whose campaign quickly took on overtones of a holy crusade against the enemies of God. In Republican areas, anarchists, communists or socialists were often the only groups organised enough to resist the rebellion and ended up running many towns and cities. Social revolution followed.

Foreign Intervention From autumn 1936 the International Brigades (armed foreign idealists and adventurers organised by the communists) arrived to aid the Republicans, but they never numbered more than 20,000, suffered high casualties, and couldn't turn the tide against the better armed and organised Nationalist forces.

What really tipped the scales in the Nationalists' favour was support from Nazi Germany and Fascist Italy – weapons, planes and men (75,000 from Italy, 17,000 from Germany). These turned the war into a rehearsal for WWII. The Republicans had some Soviet support – planes, tanks, artillery and advisers – but the rest of the international community refused to get involved, though 25,000 or so French fought on the Republican side. The war came to be seen internationally as a struggle between fascism and communism, but it was a more complex conflict than that – and an essentially Spanish one, which evolved out of centuries-old tensions.

Nationalist Advance The basic battle lines were already drawn up within a week of the rebellion in Morocco. Whether a city fell into Nationalist hands depended both on whether its military leadership and garrison backed the rebels (most did), and on whether it was strong enough to overcome whatever Republican opposition there was. North of Madrid, all of Spain except Cataluña, the eastern half of Aragón, the Basque coast, Cantabria and Asturias was in Nationalist hands, as were western Andalucía and Granada in the south. Franco's force of legionnaires and Moroccan mercenaries was airlifted from Morocco to southern Spain by German warplanes in August. Essential to the success of the revolt, they moved through Andalucía and Extremadura towards Madrid, wiping out fierce resistance in some cities. At Salamanca, the Nationalists' nerve centre, in October, Franco pulled all the Nationalists into line behind him, styling himself Generalísimo (Supreme General). Before long he was to declare himself head of state and adopt the title *caudillo*, roughly equivalent to the German *Führer*.

By the time Franco reached Madrid in November the capital was being reinforced by the first International Brigades battalions and managed to repulse the Nationalist assault. It then endured, under communist inspiration, over two years siege.

Republican Quarrels The Republican government, with Largo Caballero now prime minister, moved to Valencia to continue trying to preside over the diversity of political persuasions on the Republican side – from anarchists and communists to moderate democrats and regional secessionists. Barcelona was even more revolutionary than Madrid, with anarchists and the POUM (Partido Obrero de Unificación Marxista) Trotskyite militia running it for nearly a year. The Basques, by contrast, were not leftists. They supported the Republicans because the Republicans promised them autonomy.

Italian troops took Málaga in February 1937. In April the Basque town of Gernika (Guernica) was bombed by German planes, with terrible casualties; this became the subject of Picasso's famous pacifist painting. All the north coast fell in the summer, which gave the Nationalists control of Basque industry. Republican counterattacks near Madrid and in Aragón failed.

Meanwhile tensions among the Republicans erupted into fierce street fighting in Barcelona in May 1937, with the communists – who under growing Soviet influence were trying to unify the Republican war effort – crushing the anarchists and the POUM. Largo Caballero was replaced as prime minister by Juan Negrín. The Republican government moved to Barcelona in autumn 1937.

Nationalist Victory In early 1938 Franco repulsed a Republican offensive at Teruel in Aragón, then swept eastward with 100,000 troops, 1000 planes and 150 tanks, cutting the Republican zone in two and isolating

Barcelona from Valencia. Italian bombers from Mallorca started battering Barcelona, and Franco turned south towards Valencia. In July the Republicans launched a daring last offensive on the Nationalists as they moved through the Ebro valley. The bloody encounter resulted in 50,000 casualties, including 20,000 dead, and the Nationalists won.

The USSR withdrew from the war in September 1938. The Nationalists received more German aid for their offensive against Barcelona, which they launched in December. In January 1939 they took the city unopposed. The Republican government and hundreds of thousands of supporters sought refuge in France. In February Britain and France recognised Franco's government.

But Republicans still held Valencia and Madrid and had 500,000 men under arms. Negrín returned to Spain to try to negotiate surrender terms. Other Republicans wanted to fight to the death. In Madrid Republicans even fought each other over how to end the war while the Nationalists waited outside the city. In the end the Republican army simply evaporated. The Nationalists entered Madrid on 28 March 1939 and Franco declared the war over on 1 April.

Franco's Spain (1939-75)

War's Aftermath The victors were merciless. Instead of reconciliation, more bloodletting ensued. Informing, private vendettas and executions were rife. Altogether an estimated 100,000 people were killed, or died in prison, after the war, including thousands of teachers as the education system was purged. The hundreds of thousands imprisoned included many artists and intellectuals; others fled abroad, depriving Spain of a whole generation of scientists, artists, writers, educationalists and more. Others simply abandoned liberal principles for the sake of survival.

Dictatorship Franco ruled absolutely, dismissing, imprisoning, exiling or executing opponents, and sacking ministers as he pleased. He was commander of the army and leader of both the government and the sole political party, the Movimiento Nacional (National Movement). The Cortes was merely a rubber stamp for such decrees as Franco chose to submit to it. Aspirations towards regional autonomy were simply not tolerated.

Franco hung on to power by never allowing any single powerful group – the church, the Movimiento, the army, monarchists or bankers – to become dominant. The army provided many ministers and enjoyed a generous budget, with plenty of jobs and sinecures for its now sedentary soldiers. Catholic orthodoxy was fully restored, with most secondary schools being entrusted to the Jesuits, divorce made illegal and church weddings compulsory. The Movimiento Nacional was a development of the old fascist Falange, which Franco had hijacked during the civil war as a unified organisation for all Nationalists, with him as its leader. After the war the Movimiento was given control of press, propaganda and unions, with labour organised into vertical unions

General Francisco Franco, Spain's absolute ruler from 1939 to his death in 1975

covering entire sectors of the economy. Franco won some working-class support with carrots such as paid holidays, job security, bonuses and social security, but there was no right to strike. As for the monarchy, in theory Franco was merely the regent, but he had no intention of installing Don Juan, son of Alfonso XIII (who died in 1941), as king.

WWII & After WWII began a few months after the civil war ended. Franco kept Hitler at bay by promising an alliance but never committing himself to a date. Spanish 'volunteers' did fight for Germany against the USSR, but Franco refused German troops entry to Spain for a planned attack on Gibraltar. Spanish communists and Republicans who had been active in the French Resistance crossed the Pyrenees to attack Franco's Spain but failed in September 1944; they continued their struggle in small guerrilla units in the north, Extremadura and Andalucía right up to 1951.

Franco's ambiguous stance during WWII won him no friends abroad. At the war's end in 1945, most countries withdrew recognition of his government. Spain was excluded from the United Nations and NATO and suffered a UN-sponsored trade boycott which turned the late 1940s into the *años de hambre* (years of hunger). With the onset of the Cold War, Franco's anticommunist stance helped him gain international legitimacy. In 1953 he agreed to the USA's request for four bases in Spain in return for large sums in aid. In 1955 Spain was admitted to the UN.

Economic Miracle Spain was on the brink of insolvency by the late 1950s but the Stabilisation Plan of 1959, with its devaluation of the peseta and other deflationary measures, brought an economic upswing. The plan was engineered by a new breed of technocrats linked to Opus Dei, a powerful lay Catholic group which aimed to combine Catholicism with a work ethic (see the boxed aside under Religion later in this chapter).

Under development plans resulting from the visit of a World Bank team in 1962,

Spanish industry boomed. Thousands of young Spaniards went abroad to study economics, education, sociology and science, and returned with a new attitude of teamwork. Spain's late industrialisation enabled it to learn from the experience of other countries. Modern machinery, techniques and marketing were introduced, transport was modernised, and even agriculture moved forward with new dams providing irrigation (as well as hydro power), and conservation and reforestation schemes reclaiming land from civil war blight and sheep grazing.

The recovery was funded in part by US aid and remittances from more than a million Spaniards working abroad, but above all by tourism. From 1960 to 1965, the number of tourists arriving in Spain annually jumped from four to 14 million. (Today the number is about 45 million.) Construction – much of it in concrete, and ugly – boomed in the cities and on the coast. Though the tourism boom created lots of jobs, many were seasonal and the chief beneficiaries were building and property companies and tour operators.

Social Change Such a boom could not occur without social repercussions. A massive population shift took place from impoverished rural regions to the cities and tourist resorts. Many Andalucíans went to Barcelona, with Sevilla, Valencia, Madrid and Bilbao also growing considerably; elegant suburbs developed as well as shantytowns and, later, high-rise housing for the workers. Education and wealth started to replace heredity or profession as the keys to success. The trappings of material wealth – cars, fashions, hairdos, TVs, pop music – were eagerly adopted. Young people began to challenge traditional attitudes to authority, women and marriage – though family and religious values remained intact till well after Franco's death. Labour disputes increased, too.

The Final Decade In 1964 Franco celebrated 25 years of peace, order and material progress. But the jails were still full of political prisoners and large garrisons were maintained outside every major city. Franco controlled parliament and the press. Crime was low but there was political apathy.

Over the next decade, as the European economic boom faltered, labour strife grew and there were political rumblings in the universities and even the army and church – where some radical young priests now supported workers and students. The old political order was proving incompatible with economic and social change.

Regional problems resurfaced. The Basque terrorist group ETA (Euskadi Ta Askatasuna, or Basques and Freedom), founded in 1959, gave cause for the declaration of six states of emergency between 1962 and 1975, and heavy-handed police tactics won it support from moderates who eschewed violence.

Looming over everything was the question of what would happen after Franco. The dictator, who always made out that he was a monarchist at heart, chose as his successor the Spanish-educated Prince Juan Carlos, son of the still-living Don Juan (with whom Franco had never got on). When officially named successor in 1969, Juan Carlos swore loyalty to Franco and the Movimiento Nacional.

In 1973 Franco relinquished the prime ministership (though keeping his other titles) to his right-hand man Luis Carrero Blanco, who was then blown up by ETA. His successor Carlos Arias Navarro, heeding the winds of change, initiated a few cautious reforms. These produced violent reactions from right-wing extremists. By 1975 Spain seemed to be descending into chaos as Franco's health visibly declined. Franco gave a final faltering speech, warning of a 'Judaeo-Masonic-Marxist conspiracy', at the Plaza de Oriente in Madrid in October. On 20 November he died.

Transition to Democracy
Juan Carlos I & Adolfo Suárez Juan Carlos I, aged 37, took the throne two days after Franco's death. The new king's links with Franco and the army inspired little confidence in a Spain now clamouring for democracy. But Juan Carlos had kept his

cards very close to his chest and takes a large measure of the credit for the successful transition to democracy that followed. As it became clear that Prime Minister Arias Navarro was not going to produce serious reforms, the king sacked him in July 1976. As replacement the king chose Adolfo Suárez, a little-known 43 year old Franco apparatchik with film-star looks. The choice was a shock but a success. First Suárez railroaded through the Francoist-filled Cortes a proposal for a new, two chamber parliamentary system, then in early 1977 political parties, trade unions and strikes were all legalised and the Movimiento Nacional abolished.

New Constitution Suárez's centrist UCD (Unión del Centro Democrático) won nearly half the seats in elections to the new Cortes in 1977. The left-of-centre PSOE (Partido Socialista Obrero Español, Spanish Socialist Worker Party), led by a charismatic young lawyer from Sevilla, Felipe González, came in second. In 1978 the Cortes passed a new constitution, which made Spain a parliamentary monarchy with no official religion. In response to the regional autonomy fever which gripped Spain after the stiflingly centralist Franco era, the constitution also provided for a large measure of devolution. By 1983 this resulted in the country being divided into 17 'autonomous communities' with their own regional governments controlling a range of policy areas. The most autonomy-minded regions – Cataluña, the País Vasco (Basque Country), and to a lesser extent Andalucía and Galicia – have greater local powers than others. (Autonomy in the País Vasco initially did nothing to curb ETA terrorism, which peaked in 1980. ETA has now killed more than 700 people.)

New general elections in 1979 produced a result similar to 1977.

Social Liberation Personal and social life too enjoyed a sudden liberation after Franco. UCD governments decriminalised contraceptives, homosexuality, adultery and divorce, and it was during this era that the *movida* – the late-night bar and disco scene that enables people almost anywhere in Spain to party till dawn or after – emerged. But Prime Minister Suárez faced mounting resistance, from his own party's right wing, to further reforms in areas such as the police, army, administration, education, the legal system and broadcasting. Finally, in January 1981, Suárez resigned.

Attempted Coup During the investiture of Suárez's UCD successor as prime minister, Leopoldo Calvo Sotelo, in February 1981, Lieutenant-Colonel Antonio Tejero Molina of the Guardia Civil marched with an armed detachment into the Cortes and held it captive for almost 24 hours. This attempted military putsch, provoked by the regional autonomy policy and a supposed threat of political and economic turmoil, was snuffed out by the king, who made clear to any wavering generals that the action did not have his support, and ordered them to obey him. The ridiculous but nightmarish images of the wing-helmeted Tejero waving his pistol at cowering deputies proved to be the last spasm of Francoism's corpse.

The PSOE Years
In 1982 Spain made a final break with the past by voting the PSOE into power with a sizable overall majority. González was to be prime minister for over 13 years.

Economic Squeeze & Boom The PSOE's young, highly educated leadership came from the generation that had opened the cracks in the Franco regime in the late 1960s and early 70s. It legalised narcotics use in 1983 and abortion in 1985. But it quickly showed that social equality and redistribution of wealth came second to an overall improvement in the economy. The party persuaded the unions to accept wage restraint and job losses in order to streamline industry. Unemployment rose from 16% to 22% by 1986.

In 1986 the PSOE won a second term and Spain joined the EC (now the EU), bringing on its second great post-civil war economic

boom, which lasted till 1991 and cut unemployment back to 16%. Spaniards as a whole now had more money than ever before and flung it about lavishly. The middle class was growing ever bigger. Spain's traditionally stay-at-home women poured into higher education and jobs.

Legislation for a proper national health system was passed in 1986 (it achieved its aims by the early 1990s).

Rumblings of Discontent It was around halfway through the boom that the good life began to go a bit sour. People observed that many of the glamorous new rich were making their money by unpopular methods such as property or share speculation, or plain corruption. Meanwhile the government had failed to improve welfare provision for those who were left out of the fun. Further, the PSOE, always secretive and ready to use its powers of patronage, began to figure in a series of scandals. Most of these were matters of petty abuse of privilege, but the ultimately far more serious GAL affair (see below) also first came to light in mid-1988.

All this contributed to a widely observed one day general strike in 1988, which did result in some welfare improvements. The same year a school teachers' strike finally raised teachers' pay to respectable levels (other changes in education in the PSOE years saw schoolchildren achieve better results, class sizes reduced, church influence cut back, and a jump in the university population to well over a million).

In the 1989 elections, the PSOE won just half the seats in the Cortes but managed to continue governing alone. By now some of the social side effects of the post-Franco liberalisation were becoming clear. Alcoholism and drug addiction were real problems and out-of-control drunkenness, once a rarity, was a growing phenomenon, especially among the young. Public narcotics use became illegal in 1992.

The same year – exactly five centuries on from the pivotal year of its history – Spain celebrated its return to the modern world in style with the Barcelona Olympics and the Expo 92 world fair in Sevilla.

Slump & Scandal The economic boom had now turned into a slump and the PSOE was increasingly mired in corruption scandals. Questions were being asked about where, and how, it got hold of its substantial party funds. González's long-standing No 2, Alfonso Guerra, resigned as deputy prime minister in 1991 over an affair involving his influential wheeler-dealer brother's use of a government office.

By 1993 unemployment was back up to 22.5%. It was a testament both to González's personal popularity and to voters' lingering post-Franco fears of the right that the PSOE government survived that year's election. It lost its overall majority, however, and had to rely on support from the moderate Catalan nationalist party Convergència i Unió (CiU).

The slump bottomed out in 1993, but the scandals multiplied. Among the most bizarre was the case of Luis Roldán, the González-appointed head of the Guardia Civil from 1986 to 1993, who suddenly vanished in 1994 after being charged with embezzlement and bribery. He was arrested the following year in Bangkok and jailed in Spain. In another scandal Mariano Rubio, a former head of the Spanish central bank and another González appointee, was arrested on suspicion of fraud and illegal share deals. There were several forced resignations by government ministers – including two in 1995 over illegal tapping of phones, including the king's.

Most damaging of all was the GAL affair, named after the Grupos Antiterroristas de Liberación, death squads that had murdered over 20 suspected ETA terrorists (some of whom turned out to be innocent) in southwest France in the mid-1980s. The big question was: who was ultimately responsible for GAL? By 1996 a dozen senior police and PSOE men had been charged in connection with GAL, including José Luis Barrionuevo, who had been González's interior minister in the mid-1980s. The GAL affair seemed to be mixed up with other scandals too. The interior ministry, it

appeared, had operated a huge slush fund in its fight against ETA and organised crime, and some people suspected that this was the source of Luis Roldán's huge personal fortune. The government's reluctance to face questions on the matter only heightened suspicions, though few people believed that González himself had ordered the killings.

The PP Takes Over
In the face of all this CiU withdrew parliamentary support for the PSOE, forcing an election in March 1996. The winner was the PP (Partido Popular, People's Party), a descendant of an old post-Franco right-wing party which had recast itself as a respectable centre-right party under the leadership of the uncharismatic José María Aznar, an Elton John fan and former tax inspector. But despite the mess the PSOE was in, the PP failed to get an overall majority. After two months of talks Aznar stitched together a coalition with CiU and moderate Basque and Canary Islands nationalists. The main challenges ahead of the PP were economic. Unemployment was still 23%, easily the highest in the EU – and an alarming 42% among 16 to 25 year olds.

GEOGRAPHY
Spain is probably Europe's most geographically diverse country, ranging from the near-deserts of eastern Andalucía to the green countryside and deep coastal inlets of Galicia, and from the sunbaked uplands of Castilla-La Mancha to the rugged, snow-capped Pyrenees. It covers 84% of the Iberian Peninsula and spreads over nearly 505,000 sq km, making it the biggest country in Western Europe after France.

Uplands
Spain is a mountainous country, and with an average altitude of 650 metres it's the highest European country after Switzerland. In the past this rugged topography not only separated Spain's destiny from that of the rest of Europe, but encouraged the rise of separate statelets in both the Christian and Islamic parts of medieval Spain. These leave their

imprint today in the divergent characters of the regions of modern Spain.

Meseta & Cordillera Central At the heart of Spain, occupying some 40% of the country, is the meseta – a tableland of boundless horizons, 400 to 1000 metres high. It covers most of the regions of Castilla y León, Castilla-La Mancha and Extremadura. Apart from a handful of major cities (including Madrid), the meseta is sparsely populated and much given over to grain-growing, though there are vineyards and long lines of olive trees in the south and extensive pastures in Extremadura. Contrary to what Henry Higgins taught Eliza Dolittle, the meseta is not where most of Spain's rain falls, nor is it really a plain! Much of Castilla y León is rolling, and the meseta is split in two by the Cordillera Central mountain chain, running from north-east of Madrid to the Portuguese border. The two main ranges in the Cordillera Central are the Sierra de Guadarrama north of Madrid and the Sierra de Gredos to the west, both of which reach above 2400 metres. South of the cordillera are the lower Montes de Toledo and Sierra de Guadalupe.

Mountains around the Meseta On all sides except the west (where it slopes gradually down across Portugal), the meseta is bounded by mountain chains.

Across the north, close to the Bay of Biscay (Mar Cantábrico), is the damp Cordillera Cantábrica, straddling Castilla y León's borders with Cantabria and Asturias and rising above 2500 metres in the spectacular Picos de Europa. In the north-west the Montes de León and associated ranges cut off Galicia from the meseta.

The Sistema Ibérico runs down from wine-growing La Rioja to the olive orchards of southern Aragón, peaks at 2316 metres in the Sierra de Moncayo, and varies from plateaus and high moorland to deep gorges and strangely eroded rock formations as in the Serranía de Cuenca.

The southern boundary of the meseta is the fairly low, wooded Sierra Morena running across northern Andalucía.

Outlying Mountains Spain's highest mountains, however, lie on or towards its edges. The Pyrenees stride 400 km along the French border, virtually from the Mediterranean Sea in the east to the Bay of Biscay in the west, and reach down into Cataluña, Aragón and Navarra, with the foothills extending west into the País Vasco. There are numerous 3000 metre peaks in Cataluña and Aragón, the highest being Aragón's Pico de Aneto (3404 metres).

Across southern and eastern Andalucía stretches the Sistema Penibético, a rumpled mass of ranges which includes mainland Spain's highest peak, Mulhacén (3478 metres) in the Sierra Nevada south-east of Granada. This system continues east into Murcia and southern Valencia, dips under the Mediterranean, then re-emerges as the Balearic Islands of Ibiza and Mallorca. On Mallorca it rises to over 1400 metres in the Serra de Tramuntana. The other main Balearic Island, Menorca, is a tip of the same underwater massif as Sardinia and Corsica.

Lowlands

Around and between all the mountains are five main lower-lying areas.

Fertile Cataluña, in the north-east, is composed mainly of ranges of lower hills.

The Ebro basin, between the Sistema Ibérico to its south and the Cordillera Cantábrica and Pyrenees to its north, supports wine production in La Rioja, grain-growing in Navarra, and horticulture in eastern Aragón, though other parts of Aragón are near-desert.

Galicia in the north-west is hilly and green with mixed farming, and reminiscent of other Celtic lands like Ireland or Brittany.

Coastal areas of Valencia and Murcia are dry plains transformed by irrigation into green *huertas* (market gardens and orchards). Similar areas further south, in the Almería area of eastern Andalucía, are virtually desert.

The Guadalquivir basin, stretching across Andalucía between the Sierra Morena and

Sistema Penibético, is a highly fertile zone growing a wide range of produce, from grain to olives and citrus fruit.

Rivers

The major rivers are the Ebro, Duero, Tajo (Tagus), Guadiana and Guadalquivir, each draining a different basin between the mountains. All of these, and many of their tributaries, are dammed here and there into long, snaking reservoirs to provide much of Spain's water and electricity.

The Ebro is the largest in volume, rising in the Cordillera Cantábrica and draining the southern side of the Pyrenees and the northern side of the Sistema Ibérico. It flows across north-eastern Castilla y León, La Rioja, Navarra and Aragón to enter the Mediterranean Sea in southern Cataluña.

All the other major rivers empty into the Atlantic Ocean. The Duero flows west from the northern Sistema Ibérico and drains the northern half of the meseta, then continues across Portugal as the Douro.

The Tajo and the Guadiana both rise in the southern Sistema Ibérico and flow across the southern half of the meseta, the Tajo draining the part north of the Montes de Toledo and the sluggish Guadiana the southern part. The Tajo continues west across Portugal to Lisbon as the Tejo, while the Guadiana turns south: its last stretch into the Golfo de Cádiz forms the Portuguese border.

The Guadalquivir flows from east to west across the middle of Andalucía.

Coasts

Spain's coasts are as varied as its interior.

Mediterranean Coast The long Mediterranean coast begins in the north with Cataluña's Costa Brava (Rugged Coast), pockmarked with rocky coves and inlets that have to some extent restricted the growth of concrete tourist resorts. The Costa Daurada, south of Barcelona, and the Costa del Azahar north of Valencia are flatter, with some long sandy beaches and fairly mundane resorts (lively Sitges excepted). Between the two is the fertile, rice-growing Ebro delta, an area of

freshwater marshes made up of rich sediments brought down by the river. Sea temperatures on all these *costas* average 19°C or 20°C in June and October, and a comfortable 22°C to 24°C from July to September.

South of Valencia, there are some attractive coves around Denia and Jávea, before the coast rounds Cabo La Nao to the infamous Costa Blanca, whose good sandy beaches are disfigured by concrete package resorts like Benidorm and Torrevieja. Alicante, in the same way as Málaga on the Costa del Sol, is a refreshingly Spanish city in the midst of all this. Murcia's Mar Menor lagoon has warm waters, more good beaches and more high-rise development, but the hard-to-reach beaches on the Golfo de Mazarrón west of Cartagena are almost undeveloped. Sea temperatures on the Costa Blanca and the Murcian coast are mainland Spain's warmest – a degree or two higher than further north.

Entering Andalucía, there's more resort development at Mojácar before you reach the rugged, beautiful 50 km coast around Cabo de Gata, where near-desert and mountains come right down to beaches lapped by warm, turquoise waters. Development is starting here, but slowly, and several beaches can only be reached by foot or boat. Immediately west of Almería is a narrow coastal plain covered by hideous plastic greenhouses, before you reach the string of middle-sized resorts that includes Almuñecar and Nerja. These last are sometimes considered an eastern extension of the Costa del Sol but are a haven of tranquillity compared to the Costa del Sol proper between Málaga and Gibraltar. Here the package tourism pressure cookers of Torremolinos, Fuengirola and Marbella form an almost continuous built-up strip 70 km long, backed by barren mountains. Perhaps surprisingly, Andalucían coastal waters are generally a couple of degrees cooler than Cataluña's further north.

Atlantic Coasts The Atlantic coasts generally have a wilder climate and colder seas than the Mediterranean.

Stretching north-west from Tarifa, west of Gibraltar, to the Portuguese border is the Costa de la Luz, much less developed than the Costa del Sol. It has some fine, wide, dune-backed beaches, especially south of Cádiz and west of the Guadalquivir delta, which is an important water-bird and wildlife habitat.

Galicia's coast is Spain's most rugged, deeply indented with majestic estuaries called *rías*, reminiscent of Norway's fjords, dotted with appealing coves, beaches and fishing villages, and almost ignored by foreign package tourism. Best known are the Rías Bajas on the west-facing coast, but the Rías Altas on the north-facing coast are just as impressive in decent weather and include Spain's most awesome cliffs, at Cabo Ortegal and Serra de la Capelada.

All along the Bay of Biscay, the Cordillera Cantábrica comes almost down to the coast, providing a fine backdrop for resorts big and small (the biggest are Santander and San Sebastián), many of which have good beaches, and surfing centres like Zarautz and Mundaka. Tourism here is mainly Spanish and French. The coast and valleys support a varied agriculture including dairy farms and cider apple orchards.

Balearic Islands The waters here are warmer than on the mainland, averaging 21°C in June and October and 25°C in August. The north coast of Mallorca is lined with high, wild cliffs and the hard-to-reach beaches on its coves are much quieter than those around Palma de Mallorca, on Mallorca's lower-lying east coast or on Menorca. Ibiza is dotted with dozens of remote little beaches.

CLIMATE

The meseta and the Ebro basin have a continental climate: very hot in summer, cold in winter, and dry. Madrid regularly freezes in December, January and February, and temperatures climb above 30°C in July and August. Valladolid on the northern meseta and Zaragoza in the Ebro basin are even

drier, with only around 300 mm of rain a year (little more than Alice Springs in Australia). The Guadalquivir basin, in Andalucía, is only a little wetter, and positively broils in high summer, with temperatures of 35°C-plus in Sevilla which kill people every year. It doesn't get so cold as the meseta in winter, though.

The Pyrenees and the Cordillera Cantábrica backing the Bay of Biscay coast bear the brunt of cold north and north-west air-streams, which bring moderate temperatures and heavy rainfall (three or four times as much as Madrid's) to the north and north-west coasts. In winter the rains here hardly seem to stop, except when they turn to snow. Temperatures are cooler than Madrid from April to September, but less cold (though not very much so in Galicia) from November to March.

The Mediterranean coast as a whole, and the Balearic Islands, get little more rain than Madrid, and the south can be even hotter in summer, though the whole coast is markedly warmer in winter. The south-east, from the Costa Blanca to Cabo de Gata, is the driest part of Spain, and the conditions produce near-desert in parts of eastern Andalucía. The Mediterranean also provides Spain's warmest waters – reaching 27°C or so in August – and you *can* swim as early as April or even late March in the south-east.

In general you can rely on pleasant or hot temperatures just about everywhere from April to early November (plus March in the south, but minus a month at either end on the north and north-west coasts). In Andalucía there are plenty of warm, sunny days right through winter. In July and August, temperatures can get unpleasant, even unbearable, anywhere inland (unless you're high enough in the mountains). Spaniards themselves abandon their cities in droves for the coastal resorts at this time.

Rain in most areas is heaviest from around October to April, though in the north – especially in the Pyrenees and Galicia – there are quite a lot of wet days year round, even in summer, which tends to be humid. Rainfall from year to year, however, is inconsistent to

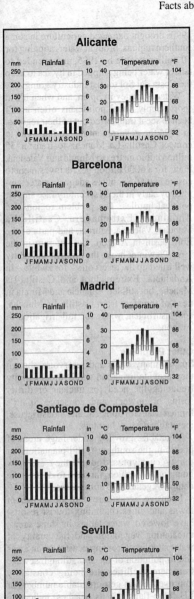

Alicante

Barcelona

Madrid

Santiago de Compostela

Sevilla

say the least (see Drought in the following section).

Snowfalls in the mountains start as early as October and some snow cover lasts all year on the highest mountains. Weather in the high mountains generally is unreliable.

ECOLOGY & ENVIRONMENT
The Past

Spain's environment has been radically altered by human hands over two millennia. It was the Romans who began to cut, for timber, fuel and weapons, the country's very extensive woodlands and forests – which until then even covered half the meseta. Over the next 2000 years further deforestation, along with overtilling and overgrazing (especially by huge sheep herds), brought substantial topsoil erosion – most of the 300 sq km delta of the Río Ebro has been formed by eroded deposits in the last 600 years. Many animal species were drastically depleted by hunting. Urban and industrial growth, joined in the 20th century by construction of numerous dams for hydroelectricity and irrigation, inevitably caused further change.

Any assessment of the health of Spain's environment must surely take the historical human impact as a starting point, and consider how well the resulting situation can sustain human as well as animal and plant life. On the whole, things don't seem too bad. Despite uncertain rainfall and, in many areas, impoverished soils, Spain supports a varied, often low-tech, and mostly healthy agriculture, though the irrigation and chemicals on which some of this now depends have brought other problems. Most Spaniards live in towns and cities, which reduces their impact on the countryside. There's still lots of wilderness. Serious urban pollution is limited, since Spain is relatively lightly industrialised and urban authorities have taken appropriate action in many places. Protection given to many animal and bird species has brought big increases in numbers for some, though it's probably too late for others.

Conservation

Environmental awareness was not quick to emerge in the 1960s and 70s under Franco, but took a quantum leap forward in the 1980s with the advent of the PSOE government, which made environmental pollution a crime and spurred a range of actions by regional governments, which now have responsibility for most environmental matters. If you take the number and size of environmentally protected areas as a yardstick, things have improved by leaps and bounds. In 1981 Spain had just 35 such areas, covering 2200 sq km. Today there are over 400, covering more than 25,000 sq km. The attention paid to the environment in education and the media is now strong, too – though there's resistance to conservation measures among politicians, bureaucrats and local people where such measures are seen as economically damaging.

Another problem is that different regions give conservation very different priorities: Andalucía has over 80 protected areas, while neighbouring Extremadura has just three. Nor are protected areas always very well protected. Bird life in the important wetlands of Doñana in Andalucía, the Ebro delta in Cataluña and the Albufera in Valencia has been severely damaged by agricultural pesticide pollution. Some protected areas suffer because their ecosystems extend to unprotected areas elsewhere; Doñana and the Tablas de Daimiel wetlands in Castilla-La Mancha have lost water to industry, irrigation or drainage outside their boundaries.

Drought

Probably Spain's worst environmental problem is drought, which struck in the 1950s and 60s, and again in the early 1990s. This is despite huge investment in reservoirs (which cover a higher proportion of the land in Spain than in any other country in the world), and projects like the Tajo-Segura water diversion system, which can transfer 600 million cubic metres of water a year from the Tajo basin in central Spain to the heavily irrigated Valencia and Murcia regions on the Mediterranean coast. The

1990s drought damaged agriculture in some southern regions, brought water rationing for 10 million people by 1995, and even led to talk of water being shipped in by sea to keep the Costa del Sol tourist industry going.

Water is money in Spain, and when it's in short supply, local politicians often aren't keen to see it transferred out of their regions. In 1994 the government had to intervene to compel Castilla-La Mancha to transfer 55 million cubic metres to Murcia and Valencia. Plans for a 6000 billion peseta investment to ensure that all Spain has adequate water supplies by early in the 21st century face similar political hurdles. The problem regions are Andalucía, Extremadura, Castilla-La Mancha, Valencia, Murcia, and parts of the Ebro basin in Aragón. Lots of rain in the 1995-96 winter broke the drought and pretty well filled up the reservoirs – for awhile – in Andalucía, Extremadura and Castilla-La Mancha, but still left Valencia and Murcia in need of transfers from Castilla-La Mancha, and insufficient water for full irrigation in Aragón.

Other Problems

Spain's many dams and reservoirs, though they provide irrigation and hydroelectricity (reducing the need for nuclear or dirtier forms of power), and conserve Spain's limited water for domestic and industrial use, inevitably destroy habitats.

Vegetables growing under huge areas of plastic in the south-east, and plantations of thirsty eucalyptus, though they are now going out of fashion, threaten to destroy the natural vegetation of some areas.

Intensive agriculture and the spread of towns and cities (including tourist resorts) have lowered water tables in some areas, threatening vegetation and the quality of water supplies. Growing coastal urban areas add to pollution of the seas, though sewage treatment facilities are being constantly improved. Spain gets creditable numbers of EU 'blue flags' for its beaches, indicating that they meet certain minimal standards of cleanliness and safety, but EU standards are not very stringent. The tests are carried out by local public authorities, not by outside researchers.

Hunting, though subject to restrictions, is a deeply ingrained side of Spanish life. Over 15,000 sq km are set aside as national hunting reserves and over 1.25 million shooting licences are issued annually. Many species are now protected from hunting, but a lot of illegal shooting and trapping of animals and birds still goes on. Nevertheless, species like the wild boar and red deer have recovered in some areas to the point where they are now legally culled. The Spanish ibex, a species of mountain goat, wàs almost extinct by 1900 but protection since then has raised its numbers to around 10,000.

Industrial pollution is probably at its worst around Bilbao, in the País Vasco, and the small chemical-producing town of Avilés in Asturias.

FLORA & FAUNA
Flora
The variety of Spain's flora is astonishing, as anyone who witnesses the spectacular wild-flower displays on roadsides and pastures in spring and early summer will testify. Spain has around 8000 plant species, many of them unique to the Iberian Peninsula, and it's a paradise for orchid hunters. This special abundance is largely due to the fact that the last Ice Age did not cover the entire peninsula, enabling plants which were killed off further north to survive in Spain. The natural barrier of the Pyrenees then prevented many from recolonising northwards.

High-Altitude Plants Spain's many mountain areas – principally the Pyrenees, Cordillera Cantábrica, Sierras de Guadarrama and Gredos, Sistema Ibérico, Sierra Nevada, and Serra de Tramuntana on Mallorca – claim a lot of the variety. The Pyrenees have about 150 unique species, and even the Sierra Nevada in the south, covering a much smaller area, has 40. When the snows melt, the alpine and subalpine zones – above the tree line in these ranges – become spectacularly abloom with small rock-clinging plants and high pastures full of gentians,

orchids, crocuses, narcissi and sundews. Particularly good orchid areas include the alpine meadows of the Picos de Europa (with 40 species) and the Serranía de Cuenca in the Sistema Ibérico.

Mountain Forests Higher mountain forests tend to be coniferous, and are often commercial. The silver fir is common in the Pyrenees and Sistema Ibérico, while the Spanish fir is confined to the Ronda area in Andalucía. The Scots pine, with its flaking red bark, is common on the cooler northern mountains; the umbrella pine, with its large spreading top and edible kernel, is commoner near coasts. Many pine forests are threatened by the yellow pine processionary moth, whose hairy caterpillars devour pine needles. The caterpillars' large silvery nests are easy to spot in the trees and best steered clear of, as touching the caterpillars can provoke a nasty allergic reaction (see Stings & Bites under Health in the Facts for the Visitor chapter). Deciduous forests – predominantly beech but also Pyrenean oak and other trees – are found mainly on the lower slopes of the damp northern mountains. Many orchids grow on the forest floors.

Lowland Forests Mixed forests are dotted here and there over the lowlands and meseta, and occasionally elsewhere, as around Ronda in Andalucía. Many contain two useful evergreen oaks – the cork oak (*alcornoque*), whose thick outer bark is stripped every eight or 10 years for cork (*corcho*), and the holm or ilex oak, whose acorns are gobbled up by pigs destined to become *jamón ibérico* (see Food in Facts for the Visitor). Where the tree cover is scattered, the resulting combined woodland-pastures are known as *dehesas*. These mostly occur in the south-western meseta and bloom with flowers in early summer. Mixed forests may also contain conifers for timber or eucalyptus grown for wood pulp.

Scrub & Steppe Where there's no woodland and no agriculture, the land is likely to be either maquis scrub or steppe. Maquis occurs where forests were felled and the land then abandoned. Herbs like lavender, rosemary and thyme are typical maquis plants, as are shrubs of the cistus family in the south and gorse, juniper, heather and the strawberry tree in the north. If the soil is acid, there may also be genista. Orchids, gladioli and irises may flower beneath these shrubs, which themselves can be quite colourful in spring. Steppe is produced by overgrazing or occurs naturally in areas of hot, very dry climate. Much of the Ebro valley and Castilla-La Mancha are steppe, as is the almost desert-like Cabo de Gata in Andalucía. Plant life is scrubby and can be sparse, but bursts into colour after rain.

Fauna

Spain's wildlife is certainly among the most varied in Europe thanks to its wild terrain, which has allowed the survival of several species that have died out in many other countries – though some are now in perilously small numbers. Many of Spain's animals are, however, nocturnal and you need to be both dedicated and lucky to track them down.

Mammals There are about 50 brown bears (*oso pardo* in Spanish) in the Picos de Europa and further west in the Cordillera Cantábrica, and a few in the Pyrenees (most of those on the French side). Though hunting or killing these bears has been banned since 1973 – and is punishable by heavy fines or up to a year in jail – numbers have continued to decline. The Pyrenean population is effectively extinct, and the Cantabrian one may be going that way too. Introduction of mates from Eastern Europe is being considered to keep bears in the Pyrenees. In 1900 Spain had about 1000 brown bears: hunting and poisoning (accidental and deliberate) have been the main reasons for their decline.

Up to 1000 wolves (*lobo*) survive in the mountains of the north-west, the south-western meseta and the Sierra Morena. Though the few in Andalucía are fully protected, they're still regarded as an enemy by many local people elsewhere.

Things look better for the ibex (*cabra montés*), a stocky high-mountain goat whose males have distinctive, long horns. It spends summer hopping agilely around precipices high in the mountains and descends to pasture land in winter. Almost hunted to extinction by 1900, the ibex was protected by royal decree a few years later, and recent estimates are of as many as 70,000, the main populations being in the Sierra de Gredos and Andalucía's Sierra de Cazorla. The Pyrenean subspecies, however, was down to two females in 1996.

The rare Pyrenean ibex *(cabra montés)*

The pardel lynx *(lince ibérico)*, a uniquely Spanish species smaller than the lynx of northern Europe, has been reduced to possibly a few hundred by hunting and by a decline in the numbers of rabbits, its staple diet. Now stringently protected, it lives in wild woodlands of the south and west, including Doñana National Park and Monfragüe Natural Park.

Less uncommon beasts – though you still need to go looking for them – include the mainly nocturnal wild boar (*jabalí*), which likes thick woods, marshes and farmers' root crops; the chamois (rebeco, sarrio, isard or gamuza), not unlike a smaller, shorter-horned ibex but actually a member of the antelope family, which lives above and just within the tree line in the Pyrenees and the Cordillera Cantábrica, descending to pasture land in winter; the red, roe and fallow deer (ciervo, corzo, gamo) in forests and woodlands of all types; the nocturnal genet (gineta), rather like a short-legged cat with a white coat spotted with black and a long, striped tail, in woodland and scrub in the south and north; the red squirrel (ardilla) in mountain forests; the nocturnal badger (tejón), mainly in woods with thick undergrowth; the mainly nocturnal Egyptian mongoose (meloncillo) in woods, scrub and marshes in the southern half of the country; the fox (zorro), common in scattered areas; the otter (nutria); the beech marten (garduña) in scattered deciduous forests and on rocky outcrops and cliffs; and the pine marten (marta) in some Pyrenees pine forests.

Birds of Prey Spain has lots of birds of prey – around 25 breeding species, some of them summer visitors from Africa. In the mountains or on the meseta you'll often see them circling or hovering. Monfragüe Natural Park and the Serranía de Cuenca are two places particularly noted for birds of prey. (Identifying them is a different matter! See Books in Facts for the Visitor for some useful field guides.)

The threatened lammergeier, with its majestic two-metre-plus wingspan, is recovering slowly in the high Pyrenees (to 55 pairs in 1996) but has disappeared from its other Spanish habitat, the Sierra de Cazorla. Poisoned food and furtive hunting by those who consider it a pest have been its main threats. Its Spanish name, quebrantahuesos (bone-breaker), reflects its habit of smashing bones by dropping them on to rocks so that it can get at the marrow.

Even bigger (it's Europe's biggest bird of prey) is the black vulture (buitre negro), also slowly increasing in numbers. The few

hundred pairs in Spain are probably the world's biggest population. Its strongholds are all in the central west – the Sierra Morena, Monfragüe Natural Park in Extremadura, the Montes de Toledo in Castilla-La Mancha, and the Sierra de la Peña de Francia in Castilla y León.

Another emblematic bird is the Spanish imperial eagle (águila imperial), which was almost killed off by hunting and the decline in the rabbit population. Its white shoulders distinguish it from other imperial eagles. Around 100 pairs remain, about 20 of them in Doñana National Park, others in Monfragüe Natural Park, the Pyrenees and Cantabria.

Other notable large birds of prey include the golden eagle (águila real) and the griffon vulture (buitre leonado) and Egyptian vulture (acantilados alimoche), all found in high mountain regions. Among smaller birds of prey, many of them found around deciduous or lowland woods and forests, are the kestrel (cernícalo) and buzzard (ratonero), which are both common, the sparrowhawk (gavilán), various harriers (aguiluchos), and the acrobatic red kite (milano real) and black kite (milano negro). Black kites may be seen over open ground near marshes, rivers and rubbish dumps.

Around 100 pairs of Spanish imperial eagles survive in the wild.

Water Birds Spain is a haven for numerous water birds, thanks to some large wetland areas. The many reservoirs, however, support little bird life because of their lack of shoreline vegetation. Most famous and important of the wetlands is the Guadalquivir delta in Andalucía, large sections of which are included in the Doñana National Park and its surrounding buffer zones. Hundreds of thousands of birds winter here and many more call in during spring and autumn migrations. Other important coastal wetlands are the Albufera de Valencia, and the Ebro delta and Aiguamolls de l'Empordà in Cataluña.

Inland, thousands of ducks (pato) winter on the Tablas de Daimiel wetlands in Castilla-La Mancha and, with cranes (grulla) too, at Laguna de Gallocanta, Spain's biggest natural lake (though it can virtually dry up in summer), 50 km south of Calatayud in Aragón. Laguna de Fuente de Piedra near Antequera in Andalucía is Europe's main breeding site for the greater flamingo (flamenco), with as many as 13,000 pairs rearing chicks in spring and summer. This beautiful pink bird can be seen in many other saline wetlands along the Mediterranean and southern Atlantic coasts, including the Ebro delta, Cabo de Gata and Doñana National Park.

Other Birds Two rare large birds famous for their elaborate male courtship displays are the great bustard (avutarda), which inhabits the plains of the meseta, and the capercaillie (urogallo), a kind of giant black grouse, in the northern mountain woodlands. Spain has perhaps 8000 great bustards, more than the rest of Europe combined, though it's under pressure from modernisation of agriculture. Weighing up to 14 kg, the male in flight has been compared to a goose with eagle's wings.

More easily seen is the large, ungainly white stork (cigüeña blanca), actually black and white, which nests from spring to autumn on chimneys and towers right in the middle of towns like Cáceres and Trujillo in Extremadura, as well as on trees in lowland mixed forest. The much rarer black stork (cigüeña negra), all black, has been reduced to probably less than 200 pairs in Spain by destruction of its woodland habitat and by industrial poisoning of its watering and feeding places, but the population at least seems stable. Its stronghold is the western part of the southern meseta, especially Monfragüe Natural Park. Both types of stork winter in Africa.

Among the most colourful of Spain's many other birds are the golden oriole (oropéndola) in orchards and deciduous woodlands in summer (the male has an unmistakable, bright yellow body); the orange, black and white hoopoe (abubilla), with its distinctive crest, common in open woodlands, on farmland and golf courses; and the gold, brown and turquoise bee-eater (abejaruco), which nests in sandy banks in summer. All three are more common in the south. Various woodpeckers (pitos or picos) and owls (búhos) inhabit mountain woodlands.

Other Fauna From spring to autumn, Spain is paradise for butterfly and moth enthusiasts. Most of Europe's butterflies are here, including some that are unique to the Iberian Peninsula. There are 20-odd bat species, four types of salamander, midwife toads, chameleons in the far south, numerous lizards, and snakes. See the Health section in Facts for the Visitor for info on Spain's few dangerous beasts.

Reserves & National Parks

Much of Spain's most spectacular and ecologically important country is under some kind of official protection. Nearly all of these areas are at least partly open to visitors, but degrees of conservation and visitor access vary widely. Parques naturales, for instance, the largest category of protected area, may include villages with hotels, hostales and camp sites, or may limit access to a few walking trails with the nearest accommodation 10 km away. A few reserves require special permits, and others include sections with no public access. Fortunately the most interesting usually have visitor centres with ample suggestions about how to spend your time, and information on where you can and can't go. You'll find information on access, accommodation etc under specific destinations in the regional chapters of this book.

National Parks Mainland Spain and the Balearic Islands have five national parks *(parques nacionales)* administered by the central government: Picos de Europa, covering the beautiful Picos de Europa mountains, a refuge for endangered species straddling Asturias, Cantabria and Castilla y León; Ordesa y Monte Perdido, a spectacular section of the Pyrenees in Aragón, with over 30 mammal species and bird life that includes the lammergeier; Tablas de Daimiel, which protects important wetlands for birds in Castilla-La Mancha; Doñana in Andalucía's Guadalquivir delta, a vital haven for birds and mammals, containing a range of ecosystems from beach and marshes to woodland and dunes; and Archipiélago de Cabrera, a group of rocky islets in the Balearics. A sixth 'national park', Aigüestortes i Estany de Sant Maurici in the Catalan Pyrenees, contains small hydroelectric installations which put it outside international criteria for national parks, and is administered locally.

Other Protected Areas These are administered by Spain's 17 regional governments. There are literally hundreds of them, falling into at least 16 classifications and ranging in size from 100-sq-metre rocks off the Balearics, classified as Áreas Naturales de Especial Interés, to the mountainous 2140 sq km Parque Natural de Cazorla, Segura y Las Villas in Andalucía, a beautiful refuge of unique plants, ibex, pine martens and birds of prey.

A few of the other most important and interesting reserves are: Parque Natural de Monfragüe in Extremadura, with spectacular birds of prey; the Parc Natural Delta de l'Ebre in Cataluña's Ebro delta, a wetland vital for birds; mountainous Parque Natural Sierra de Grazalema in Andalucía, one of Spain's wettest areas, with luxuriant vegeta-

tion including the rare Spanish fir, and a rich bird life; the Parque Natural Sierra Nevada, covering Spain's highest mountain range, south-east of Granada, with 40 unique plants; the Áreas Naturales de la Serra de Tramuntana, covering most of this spectacular mountain range on Mallorca; and Menorca's S'Albufera des Grao wetlands, which were central to the whole of Menorca being declared a UNESCO Biosphere Reserve in 1993.

The most widespread classification is *parque natural*. The complicated classification system results from three factors: successive bouts of legislation that established new categories without requiring existing areas to be reclassified; the adoption of categories specific to some of the country's 17 administrative regions, which now have responsibility for most nature conservation; and the inclusion of some Spanish reserves in international conservation programmes.

Reservas Nacionales de Caza Many fine wilderness areas are Reservas Nacionales de Caza (national hunting reserves), which cover over 15,000 sq km around the country. These are usually well conserved for the sake of the wildlife that is to be hunted – which has to be exploited in a 'rational' manner. Public access is usually pretty open – some hunting reserves include villages and even towns – and you may well hike or drive across one without even knowing it. If you hear shots, though, caution is advisable!

GOVERNMENT & POLITICS

Since 1978, three years after the death of Franco, Spain has been a constitutional monarchy. The king is commander of the armed forces, a role that proved decisive in the February 1981 coup attempt, when Juan Carlos I came down unequivocally against any move to impose a military government.

The Cortes Generales, or parliament, is bicameral and comprises the Congreso de los Diputados (lower house) and Senado (upper house). Both houses are elected by free, universal suffrage. From December 1982 until

March 1996, the PSOE ruled modern Spain's destinies, guided by the seemingly invincible Felipe González Márquez. His fall in 1996 in an atmosphere of scandal and disillusion ushered in a new period of uncertainty as the centre-right PP embarked on a government supported by pacts with Catalan, Basque and Canary Islands nationalists.

What concerns many about the PP is its ambiguous attitude to one of the most fundamental changes in recent Spanish history, the devolution of power from the central state to the 17 regions, now known as Comunidades Autónomas, (autonomous communities or regions), under the 1978 constitution. What began as a response to long-standing desires for greater self-rule by the obviously distinct communities of Cataluña and the País Vasco has become a generalised decentralisation from Madrid to all the regions. It could hardly be claimed that, for instance, Castilla-La Mancha has a historical or cultural identity and heritage terribly distinct from that of, say, Castilla y León. And yet both regions now have their own autonomous governments. The city-enclaves of Melilla

and Ceuta in North Africa were granted a degree of autonomy in 1995.

The physiognomy of the regions in fact changed after the demise of the Francoist state. Castilla y León is made up of what had been the separate regions of León (you can see graffiti in León even today calling for separation from Castilla) and Castilla la Vieja. The latter lost the coastal province of Cantabria, which became a separate region, and the province of Logroño, which in turn became the region of La Rioja. Castilla la Nueva absorbed Albacete province to its

Autonomous Communities & Provinces

ANDORRA

Cataluña

Girona

Barcelona

0   100   200 km

Palma de Mallorca

Baleares

Galicia	Autonomous Community Name
	Autonomous Community Boundary
	Province Boundary
⊙ Mérida	Autonomous Community Capital
⊙ Valladolid	Autonomous Community/ Province Name & Capital
● La Coruña	Province Name & Capital
● Bilbao	Province Capital

south-east from the region of Murcia and was renamed Castilla-La Mancha.

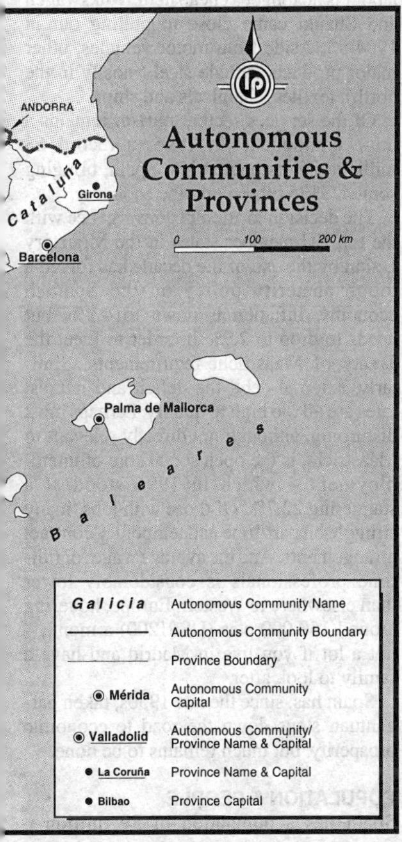

One result of the autonomous regions policy has been a massive duplication of bureaucracy, with each *comunidad* having its own parliament, while the central state also has separate representation in each comunidad.

Article 148 of the constitution lists areas of power eligible for transfer to the comunidades, including transport, agriculture, tourism, health policy and environment. Negotiations on the transfer of powers continue even now, with Cataluña and the País Vasco particularly eager to attain as much elbowroom as possible. The pacts signed in April 1996 between the PP and nationalists opened the way for yet more concessions, and not a few observers are asking when the process will finally be deemed complete.

The 17 autonomous regions are divided into provinces, most of which are named after their capital city – Segovia, for instance, is the capital of Segovia province. The provinces are further subdivided into town and district administrative units, called *municipios*.

ECONOMY

By the time the civil war ended in 1939, Spain's already weak economy had been devastated. Throughout WWII and into the early 1950s, the country laboured under a self-sufficiency programme that appealed to the nationalist sensibilities of the country's more comfortably placed political elite, but did little to alleviate the extreme poverty in which many Spanish people languished. US economic aid from the early 1950s and a 1959 stabilisation plan helped the wheels turn a little faster, and from the early 1960s an unprecedented boom set in that was soon touted as a Francoist-inspired economic 'miracle'. Up until the world oil crisis in 1973-74, the miracle was in fact fuelled largely by growing foreign investment (Spain was the land of cheap labour *par excellence*), tourism and remittances from emigrant Spaniards; almost two million left the country to work abroad between 1959 and 1973.

Tourism has since the early 1960s played a key role in boosting the economy. In fact, throughout the 1960s and into the 1970s it was the single most important pillar in Spain's spectacular growth.

The oil crisis hit Spain hard, and by 1982 inflation and unemployment had reached crippling levels. The arrival in power of the Socialists ushered in a period of renewed, if more modest, growth with inflation coming down to single figures but unemployment remaining high. A new period of stagnation which began in 1989 has since 1994 shown some signs of reversal, but the country has serious problems to deal with.

Entry into the EC, as it was then, in 1986 has proven a mixed blessing. While opening up markets for Spanish exports and freeing up the local economy, it has brought competition from the outside, which has also caused pain. Farmers and fishermen in particular have had trouble coping with quotas imposed from Brussels and the need to modernise in order to remain competitive. One notable advantage has been the flow of funds into infrastructure projects across the country. Everything from roads and the high-speed Tren de Alta Velocidad Español (AVE) rail link between Madrid and Sevilla to ports and airports has benefited from subsidies.

Agriculture accounts for some 4.5% of Spain's GDP, well above the EU average. The most profitable farming is carried out along the Mediterranean coast and the Río Ebro. Intense plasticulture farming on the south coast, particularly around Almería and Huelva, contributes year-round high yields of everything from tomatoes to strawberries and cucumbers. Inland, farmers have to contend with extreme conditions in winter and summer and persistent rainfall shortages and drought. The main products are wine, olives, citrus fruit, almonds, wheat and rice.

Fishing is another traditionally important sector. Spain's fleet, the largest in the EU, has to cast its nets far and wide to maintain its activities – a contentious issue that led to an acrimonious war of words in 1995 between Canada and the EU over halibut fishing off Newfoundland. The biggest fleets operate out of Galicia and Andalucía.

Some 35% of Spain's GDP comes from industry, but although Spain is among the top 10 industrialised nations in the world, the sector is problematic. Much of its activity has traditionally been fuelled by foreign investment. Nowhere is this more evident than in the motor industry, where giants such as General Motors, Volkswagen, Ford, Renault and Nissan are heavily involved. The danger with this state of affairs is that the foreign companies may not necessarily choose to hang around, especially as Spanish labour is no longer a cheap item. Volkswagen and Suzuki came close to pulling out in 1994-95. Aside from motor vehicles, other major products include steel (mostly in the north), textiles, chemicals and ships.

Of the services sector, tourism remains a huge component. In 1995, a record 63 million visitors poured into Spain, bringing some US$25 billion into the economy.

The decision to attempt convergence with the top EU member states in the Monetary Union by the end of the decade has forced a tough austerity policy on the Spanish economy. Inflation is down to 4.3%, but needs to drop to 2.9% in order to meet the Treaty of Maastricht requirements. Similarly, external debt, the deficit and interest rates are all too high to qualify. Perhaps most disturbing, although not directly relevant to Maastricht, is the open social sore of unemployment – which in 1996 stood at a staggering 22.7%. Of those with jobs, many struggle on part-time and temporary contract arrangements. And the average wage for full-time professionals is considerably lower than elsewhere in Western Europe, hovering around 150,000 ptas (US$1200) a month – not a lot if you live in Madrid and have a family to look after.

Spain has, since the late 1950s, taken gargantuan steps down the road to economic prosperity, but much remains to be done.

POPULATION & PEOPLE

Spain has a population of 39 million –

roughly two-thirds of a Spaniard for each of the 60 million or so visitors (of whom around three-quarters can be classed tourists) who flood into the country each year!

Spain never received any significant immigration from its empire, and its main ancestral peoples – Iberians, Basques, Celts, Romans, Jews, Visigoths, Franks, Arabs and Berbers – had all arrived by 1000 years ago. Though large numbers of Jews and Muslims were expelled in the 15th, 16th and 17th centuries, these peoples had already inter-mingled with the rest of the population.

Distribution

Spain is one of Europe's least densely popu-lated countries, with about 77 people per sq km. Spaniards like to live together, in cities, towns or *pueblos* (villages) – a habit which probably goes back to past needs for defence and must have a lot to do with their gregari-ous nature. Only in the Basque lands are you likely to see much countryside dotted with single farmsteads and small fields. Else-where, farmers travel out from their pueblos to their fields in the morning and back at night. As a result much of the countryside looks oddly empty to those of us who come from places where settlement is more spread out.

Since the civil war there has been a big shift of people from the country to the cities – and more specifically, from poor agricul-tural regions like Andalucía, the meseta and Galicia to industrialised areas in Cataluña, the País Vasco and elsewhere. More than half of all Spaniards live in cities now, and most of the rest live in towns of 10,000 or more people. Most major cities, past and present, grew up as ports (Barcelona, Tarragona, Valencia, Cartagena, Málaga, La Coruña, Cádiz, even Sevilla, which is linked to the Atlantic by the Río Guadalquivir), or at stra-tegic sites on major rivers (Zaragoza, Valladolid, Mérida, Badajoz, Córdoba). The major exception is Madrid, chosen in the 16th century – mainly for its central location – as the country's new capital.

The biggest cities today are Madrid (popu-lation: three million), Barcelona (1.7 million), Valencia (750,000), Sevilla (715,000), Zaragoza (594,000) and Málaga (556,000). Greater Madrid and greater Bar-celona each number about four million people, and there are sizable conurbations around Bilbao, Valencia, Zaragoza and Sevilla. At the other end of the scale are Aragón, with only around 20 people per sq km outside its capital Zaragoza, and the three meseta regions of Castilla-La Mancha (21 people per sq km even including cities), Extremadura (25) and Castilla y León (27).

Regional Differences

Most of the more obvious cultural and politi-cal differences you'll notice between regions today probably owe more to developments in the last three or four centuries, including nationalist movements around the turn of the century and since the 1970s, than to older roots. Though Andalucía, for instance, has some very distinct cultural features, few of them seem directly traceable to the medieval Muslim culture which dug its deepest roots there. Even the two most enduringly inde-pendent-minded regional peoples – the Basques, who may have been defending their current territory since the Stone Age, and the Catalans, whose sense of difference can be traced back to 9th century Frankish roots – owe a lot of their sense of identity to 19th century cultural and political reawakenings, provoked in part by the arrival of people from other Spanish regions looking for jobs in early Catalan and Basque industries.

These and the other regions with the strongest local identities are on the fringes of the country. Some Basques and Catalans, and a handful of Galicians, feel so strongly about their identity that they don't consider themselves Spaniards. All three of these peoples have their own languages, and minority independence movements – the Basque terrorist organisation ETA being the most infamous of these.

Politics aside, distinctive features of Basque culture include farmsteads scattered over the countryside (instead of the rural population being concentrated in villages), an excellent cuisine, tolerance of drunkenness, a fondness for gambling, some unique musical instruments, and unusual sports such as *pelota*.

Catalans are renowned for being hardworking and sober, pragmatic and prosperous, yet also avant-garde and cosmopolitan. They don't like bullfighting to the death and think of flamenco as a foreign art form.

Galicians are known for their poetry and music (their instruments include bagpipes), smuggling, emigrating and a tendency to melancholy – these last two probably both induced by their region's poverty and gloomy climate.

Andalucía is the home of several things sometimes considered typically Spanish, including flamenco, bullfighting, gazpacho, hot weather and lots of colourful, noisy fiestas. There are noticeably fewer people of fair features here than in the north of the country. Andalucíans like to enjoy life to the full, but their reputation for being lazy seems entirely unjustified.

Ethnic Minorities

Some consider Spain's Gypsies to be its only true ethnic minority, interbreeding having made the rest of the population fairly homogeneous (though some Basques might dispute that). Generally reckoned to be the originators – as well as the best performers – of flamenco, Gypsies are thought to have originated in India and reached Spain in the 15th century. As elsewhere, they have suffered discrimination. There are about 500,000 Gypsies in Spain, more than half of them in Andalucía. Though some still lead a wandering existence, most are settled. Granada, Madrid, Barcelona, Murcia and Sevilla are among cities with sizable Gypsy communities.

Spain has about 200,000 permanent residents, and perhaps 250,000 semipermanent ones, from other EU countries, mostly from Britain, Germany, Holland, Belgium and Scandinavia. They are concentrated mainly on the Costa del Sol and Costa Blanca, and a good proportion of them are retired. In the last decade or two there has been a trickle of immigrants from North Africa and the Caribbean, though on a much smaller scale than in other European countries such as France or Britain.

ARTS
Painting
The Beginnings Humans have been creating images in Spain for as long as 14,000 years, as the cave paintings in Altamira (Cantabria) attest. More strictly speaking, the origins of Spanish painting lie in the early Middle Ages. From this period some magnificent frescos have been conserved. Although much-faded examples of such religious art remain visible in some of the pre-Romanesque churches of Asturias, among the oldest and most invaluable frescos to have survived are those in the 11th century Mozarabic Ermita de San Baudelio, near Berlanga de Duero in south-eastern Castilla y León. In the same unique building is a rich serving of Romanesque frescos from the following century. The 12th century indeed produced some magnificent work. Those in the Panteón Real of the Real Basílica de San Isidoro in León are possibly the most outstanding, although the ones executed in the apse of Sant Climent in Taüll (now on display in the Museu Nacional d'Art de Catalunya in Barcelona) are equally masterpieces.

Catalan & Valencian Schools A great deal of the painting to emerge from medieval Spain, most of a religious nature, has remained anonymous, but a few leading lights managed to get some credit. Ferrer Bassá (c1290-c1348) can with good reason be considered one of the country's first masters. Influenced above all by the Siennese school, his only surviving works are murals with a slight caricatural touch in Barcelona's Pedralbes convent. The style of which he is commonly considered the originator in Spain is also known as Italo-Gothic. He was succeeded by the brothers Jaume and Pere Serra, Luis Borrassa and Ramón de Mur.

The style soon displayed a more international flavour, best embodied in the work of Bernat Martorell, a master of chiaroscuro who worked in the mid-15th century. As the Flemish school gained influence, so painters like Jaume Huguet adopted the sombre realism lightened with Hispanic splashes of gold, as can be seen from his *San Jorge* in the Museu Nacional d'Art de Catalunya.

Closely linked to Cataluña was the school of painters that emerged in neighbouring Valencia, producing a style more directly influenced by Italian fashions. Its major exponents included Lorenzo Zaragoza (1365-1402), Pere Nicolau (died 1410) and Andrés Marzal de Sax (died 1410), but Bartolomé Bermejo (died 1495) was the most interesting of the lot, incorporating Flemish influences and exploring the use of oil. Nothing better illustrates the Córdoba-born artist's gifts than the *Pietà* in Barcelona's cathedral museum.

Castilla Local artists tended to be passed over in favour of foreigners in 15th century Castilla. Their 'surnames' often give this away: Nicolás Florentino (from Florence: born Dello Delli, he did the retablo in the Catedral Vieja in Salamanca), Nicolás Francés (from France) and Juan de Flandes (Flemish).

One local exception was Fernando Gallego (1466-1507), heavily influenced by Flanders' Rogier van der Weyden. Zamora's cathedral houses altarpieces by him, and others can be seen in the Prado.

Also initially imbued with Hispano-Flemish thinking, Pedro Berruguete (1438-1504) is traditionally said to have done a stint in Urbino, Italy. Although there is no direct proof of this, his later work as court painter to Fernando and Isabel tends to support the claim. His son, Alonso (1488-1561), definitely enjoyed an extended stay in Urbino and, although a fine painter, is remembered for his sculpture – the most superior in 16th century Spain. His alabaster Resurrection in Valencia's cathedral is a master work, and he also carved the choir stalls in Toledo's cathedral.

16th Century One of the most remarkable artists at work in all Spain in the latter half of the 16th century was an 'adopted' Spaniard. Domenikos Theotokopoulos (1541-1614) – usually known simply as El Greco (the Greek) – was schooled in Crete and Italy, but spent his productive working life in Toledo. His slender, exalted figures and, in the latter part of his career, a striking simplicity of colour and fluidity of movement are hallmarks that many tried to imitate but none emulated. One of his earlier works is also one of his greatest – *El Entierro del Conde de Orgaz* (The Burial of the Count of Orgaz), in Toledo's Iglesia de Santo Tomé. His son Jorge was more an architect than a painter. Luís Tristán (1586-1624), who continued the work of El Greco's studio, never achieved the mastery of his mentor.

El Greco and Spanish artists in general had a hard time raising interest in their material at the court of Felipe II, who above all preferred Titian and a series of lesser Italian Mannerists. Holding up the Spanish side to a certain extent was 'El Mudo' (the Mute), Juan Navarrete (1526-79), who tried to distract the emperor's attention away from the Italians and became one of the first of Spain's practitioners of 'tenebrism', a fashion that largely aped Caravaggio's chiaroscuro style and became particularly popular in 17th century Sevilla.

The Golden Age As the 16th century gave way to the 17th, a remarkably fecund era in the history of Spanish painting dawned.

One of Navarrete's protégés was Francisco Ribalta (1565-1628). He ended up in Valencia, where he turned out mostly religious portraiture in which he deployed to great effect the tenebrist methods he had learned.

Across the Mediterranean in Italy, José (Jusepe) de Ribera (1591-1652) also came under the influence of Caravaggio. Many of his works found their way back to Spain and are now scattered about various galleries, but he himself remained in Naples until the end of his days. It is odd that a Spaniard who spent most of his life in Italy should be known today as a Spanish artist, while El Greco is *not* known as Cretan! Ribera's mastery of light was bettered perhaps only by his contemporary Velázquez, and his success lay largely in revealing a profoundly human sympathy with his characters. He is considered a seminal protagonist of European baroque.

In Sevilla, meanwhile, another school began to gather momentum under the guiding hand of Francisco Pacheco (1564-1654). A true Renaissance man, he was too interested in both painting and literature to achieve greatness in either. He did however have an alumnus whom he set in the right direction. Not only did Diego Rodríguez de Silva Velázquez (1599-1660) marry Pacheco's daughter, he soon rose to prominence after leaving his native Sevilla for Madrid. Within a year he was admitted to the magic circle of court painters. He knew on which side his bread was buttered and stayed with the court for the rest of his life. This did not stop him making several trips to Italy.

Velázquez stands in a class of his own. He composed scenes that owe their life not only to his photographic eye for light and contrast but to a compulsive interest, not unlike Ribera's, in the humanity of his subjects. With him any trace of the idealised stiffness that characterised a by-now spiritless Mannerism falls by the wayside. Realism becomes a key, and the majesty of his royal subjects springs from his capacity to capture the essence of the person – king or infanta – and the detail of their finery. His job was one thing, but between commissions he'd take just as sympathetic a view of the less fortunate inhabitants of the royal menagerie – court jesters and dwarfs.

His masterpieces include *Las Meninas*, *La Rendición de Breda*, both on view in the Prado, and a portrait of Pope Innocent X he carried out while in Rome in 1650.

A less exalted contemporary and close friend of Velázquez, Francisco de Zurbarán moved *to* Sevilla as an official painter. Probably of Basque origin but born in Extremadura, he is best remembered for the startling clarity and light in his portraits of monks. He travelled a great deal and in Guadalupe a series of eight portraits can still be seen hanging where Zurbarán left them in the Hieronymite monastery. Other good series are on view in the Museo de Cádiz and the Real Academia de Bellas Artes de San Fernando in Madrid. Himself an ascetic, Zurbarán fell on hard times in the 1640s and was compelled by plague to flee Sevilla. He tried to reverse his sagging fortunes in Madrid, but died in poverty.

Zurbarán has come to be seen as one of the masters of the Spanish canvas, but in his own lifetime it was a younger and less inspired colleague who took all the prizes. Bartolomé Esteban Murillo (1618-82) took the safe road and turned out stock religious pieces and images of beggar boys and the like with technical polish but little verve. He was good without being a genius, and it is not surprising that he ended up as president of the Sevilla Academy he founded.

Yet another solid artist of the same period and a student of Pacheco was Alonso Cano (1601-67), who spent his working life in Granada. Also a gifted sculptor and architect, he is sometimes referred to as the Michelangelo of Spain. Not a great deal of his work remains, and his stormy life didn't help matters. He might well have joined the Velázquez gravy train in Madrid had he not been accused of his second wife's murder there and obliged to leave.

A parade of late-baroque artists working over the course of the century have been loosely lumped together as the 'Madrid school'. Among their number, a few names worth mentioning include Antonio de Pereda, the monk Fray Juan Rizi, Juan Carreño de Miranda and Francisco Rizi (the monk's younger brother). The last of them, and the most gifted, was Claudio Coello (1642-93). He specialised in the big picture – literally. Some of his enormous decorative canvases decorate El Escorial, among them his magnum opus, *La Sagrada Forma*.

18th Century The Bourbon kings had little interest in sponsoring Spanish talent, being obsessed rather with all things French and, to a lesser extent, Italian. Carlos III had Anton Raphael Mengs (1728-79) brought across from Bohemia as court painter and he became the man who could make or break rising artists. Aided by Francisco Bayeu (1734-95), he was a gifted if unexciting portraitist. One of the few halfway respectable painters of the same period was Luís Paret y Alcázar (1746-99), whose pleasant rococo creations display talent without knocking you over.

Goya Mengs could spot talent. He encouraged Francisco José de Goya y Lucientes (1746-1828), a provincial hick from Fuendetodos in Aragón, as a cartoonist in the Fábrica Real de Tapices in Madrid, where the long and varied career of Spain's only truly great artist of the 18th (and, indeed, even the 19th) century began.

In this early stage of his rise, Goya's portrayals of everyday scenes appear to owe something to the candour of Hogarth, and in some cases also to the influence of Tiepolo, whom Carlos III had attracted to Spain to work on the Palacio Real.

Prior to his arrival in Madrid, married to Francisco Bayeu's sister, he had somehow managed to finance a trip to study art in Italy and carried out some commissions in Zaragoza, notably frescos depicting the lives of Christ and the Virgin Mary in the Cartuja de Auli, a monastery just outside the city. They have been restored and can be seen today.

In 1776 he began designing for the tapestry factory and by 1799 he had been appointed Carlos IV's court painter. Illness in 1792 left him deaf, and this perhaps had an influence on his style, which was increasingly unshackled by convention and often mercilessly objective.

Several distinct series and individual paintings mark the progress of his life and work. In the last years of the century he painted such enigmatic masterpieces as *La Maja Vestida* and *La Maja Desnuda*, identical portraits but for the lack of clothes in the latter. At about the same time he did the remarkable frescos in Madrid's Ermita de San Antonio de la Florida and *Los*

Caprichos, a biting series of 80 etchings lambasting the follies of court life and ignorant clergy.

The arrival of the French and war in 1808 profoundly affected his work. An unforgiving portrayal of the brutality of war is conveyed by *El Dos de Mayo* and, more dramatically, *El Tres de Mayo*. The latter depicts the execution of Madrid rebels by French troops. The war ground on for five years and provided Goya the gruesome raw material for his most disturbing etchings, *Los Desastres de la Guerra*, a sometimes sickening review of human barbarity.

With the return of Fernando VII at the end of the war, Goya's position became more tenuous. But he kept working, churning out portraits and another series of etchings, *La Tauromaquia*, one of the few artistic approaches to that most Spanish of activities, the bullfight. After he retired to the Quinta del Sordo (deaf man's house), as he called his modest lodgings west of the Manzanares in Madrid, age and perhaps an angry bitterness prompted the creation of his most extraordinary paintings, the nightmare images of the *Pinturas Negras* (Black Paintings). Done on the walls of the house, they were later removed and now hang in the Prado. *Saturno Devorando a Su Hijo* is emblematic of the hallucinatory horror of these works. The last years of his life he spent in voluntary exile in France, where he continued to paint until his death.

It is difficult fully to do justice to Goya's role in the evolution not so much of Spanish, but of European painting. An obvious precursor to many subsequent strands of modern painting, he was an island of grandeur in a sea of mediocrity in Spain.

Late 19th Century Although no-one of the stature of Goya can be cited, new trends were noticeable in the latter decades of the century. For the first time in centuries, the focus shifted briefly back to Valencia. A trio from this region merit a mention: Ignacio Pinazo (1849-1916), Francisco Domingo (1842-1920) and Emilio Sala (1850-1910). Sala, who was clearly influenced by Dégas, and Domingo lived and worked in Paris, but neither achieved great success. More successful in the long run was the Basque Ignacio Zuloaga (1870-1945).

Joaquín Sorolla (1863-1923), if anything, flew in the face of the French impressionists, preferring the blinding sunlight of the Valencian coast to the muted tones favoured in Paris. He is best known for his cheerful, large-format images of beach life. His work can be studied at the Museo de Sorolla in Madrid.

About the only true Spanish impressionists were Aureliano de Beruete (1845-1912) and Darío de Regoyos (1857-1932), neither of them of any great stature.

20th Century In a sense, the history of Spanish art turned full circle at the close of the 19th century, returning to Cataluña. Barcelona, a hothouse of social agitation and the home of Spanish modernism (see also Architecture below), was about the only environment in an otherwise depressed and sluggish Spain in which creative artists could hope to flourish. It was the perfect place for someone like Pablo Ruiz Picasso (1881-1973), born in Málaga, to come and flex his brushes.

Picasso is one of the monumental characters of Western European art. Having shown prodigious aptitude at an early age, he started visiting Paris in 1900. He had already absorbed lessons from his greatest forerunners – Goya, Velázquez and El Greco – and in Paris opened himself to the riches of Gauguin, Toulouse-Lautrec and Van Gogh.

Picasso was a turbulent character and an artist gifted not only on canvas, but as a sculptor, graphic designer and ceramicist, and his work knew many abruptly changing periods. His Blue Period, until 1904, is characterised by rather sombre renditions of the lives of the down and out. The common denominator was the predominance of blues in his palette. After his definitive move to Paris in 1904, he began the so-called Pink Period; the subjects became merrier and the colouring leaned towards light pinks and greys.

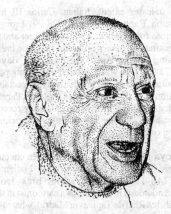

Pablo Ruiz Picasso, who changed the face of Western European art

Picasso remained ever in search of new forms. *Les Demoiselles d'Avignon* (1907) broke with all forms of traditional representation, introducing a deformed perspective that would spill into cubism, of which he and Georges Braque were the pioneers. From then until the early 1920s, cubism went through several stages, since given labels such as 'analytical' and 'synthetic'. Picasso experimented continually with different methods, and by the mid-1920s was dabbling with surrealism. His best-known work is *Guernica*, a complex canvas portraying the horror of war and inspired by the German aerial bombing of the Basque town, Gernika, in 1937.

Picasso's output during and after WWII remained prolific, and indeed he was cranking out paintings, sculptures, ceramics and etchings until the day he died.

While Picasso went his own way, his friend and countryman Juan Gris (1887-1927) remained faithful to cubist orthodoxy, and among other strong works produced an intriguing portrait of Picasso. Another painter of the time worthy of mention is José Gutiérrez Solana (1885-1945), whose subject matter tends to walk a little on the bleak side.

Separated from Picasso by barely a generation, two other names reinforced the Catalan contingent in the vanguard of first class Spanish contributions to this century's art: Dalí and Miró. Although he started off dabbling in cubism, Salvador Dalí (1904-89) became more readily identified with the surrealists. This complex character's 'hand-painted dream photographs', as he called them, are virtuoso executions brimming with fine detail and nightmare images dragged up from a feverish and Freud-fed imagination. Preoccupied with Picasso's success and fame, Dalí built himself a reputation as an outrageous showman and self-promoter. The single best display of his works can be seen at the 'theatre-museum' he created in Figueres, Cataluña.

Slower to find his feet, Joan Miró (1893-1983) developed a joyous and almost childlike style that earned him the epithet 'the most surrealist of us all' from André Breton. His later period is his best known, characterised by simple use of bright colours and forms.

Today Picasso, Dalí and Miró make a pretty hard act to follow, and contemporary painters lack the greatness of this extraordinary trio.

In the wake of the civil war, Fernando Zóbel collected his own works and those of his contemporaries in the 1950s 'Generación Abstracta' under one roof in a private museum in Cuenca. Gustavo Torner and Eusebio Sempere figure among those on display. Other names worth looking for include Antonio Saura, Manuel Millares and Antoni Tàpies.

Among working artists today, Eduardo Arroyo is steeped in the radical spirit that led him to co-found Paris' Salon de la Jeune Peinture in 1963 and put his art to the service of solidarity actions with the Cuban revolution and in Vietnam. A more traditional but highly talented counterpoint lies in the work of Antonio López García.

Architecture

Spain's place on the 'edge' of Europe and centuries of Muslim rule left an indelible imprint on the country's architectural heritage, setting it quite apart from the rest of the Continent. The ancient civilisations of Greece, Phoenicia and Rome all left their mark, overshadowed later by the genius of the Arabs, who not only left behind them extraordinary monuments, but an artistic legacy that would continue to find expression in Spanish building long after the last Muslim kingdom in Granada had fallen to the Reconquista.

Usually later than elsewhere in Europe, and often altered to suit Spanish tastes and needs, all the great European architectural movements did eventually seep into Spain, from Romanesque to Gothic, from the baroque to neoclassicism. But no other European country can boast quite the diversity of Spain. While the towering Gothic cathedrals of Burgos, León and Toledo were being raised to the greater glory of God in the first half of the 13th century, Granada became home to the Alhambra, one of the most remarkable monuments the Muslim world has ever produced.

Across the country, countless magnificent churches and monasteries vie for your attention with castles and palaces of all shapes and sizes. The range, from startling feats of Roman engineering to the fantastical caprice of Gaudí and the *modernistas*, can seem a little overwhelming, but is never tiresome.

Celtiberians & Greeks The various tribes that inhabited the Iberian Peninsula prior to the arrival of the Romans, collectively known as Celtiberians, have left behind a wealth of evidence of their existence. The most common living arrangement, the *castro*, was basically a hamlet surrounded by stone walls and made up of small, circular stone houses. Several have been partly preserved in locations as disparate as La Guardia, on Galicia's southern coast, and Vinaceite, deep in Zaragoza province in Aragón. One of the best is just near Coaña, in Asturias.

The Greeks and Carthaginians rarely made it far into the Spanish interior, being interested primarily in sea trade. Apart from some Carthaginian necropolises in Ibiza, a couple of spots in Andalucía and some Greek remains at Empúries (Cataluña), little is left to remind you of their presence.

Romans With some spectacular exceptions, the Roman legacy in Spain is not as great as in some other of the empire's former vassals. The exceptions include the remarkable aqueduct in Segovia (Castilla y León), the bridge at Alcántara (Extremadura) and the stout walls of Lugo (Galicia).

The vestiges of various Roman towns can still be seen across the country, although many of the lesser sites are hardly ever visited. Among the more important sites are: the ancient town of Augusta Emerita, in Mérida (Extremadura); the remains of the ancient town of Tarraco at Tarragona (Cataluña); the amphitheatre and other ruins at Itálica (near Sevilla, Andalucía); and Sagunto (Valencia). Modest remains have been imaginatively converted into underground museums in Barcelona and Zaragoza.

The site of ancient Numancia, north of Soria (Castilla y León) is largely Roman, although it was preceded by a Celtiberian city that for a long time resisted Roman rule.

Visigoths Filling the vacuum left by the departing Romans, the Visigoths employed a much humbler but remarkably attractive architectural style, which survives in a handful of small churches. The 7th century Ermita de Santa María de Lara, at Quintanilla de las Viñas in Burgos province (Castilla y León) is one of the best examples, with fine sculpted bas-reliefs in a band around the outside. Fragments of this unique style of decoration can be seen in several cities across Spain, including Toledo, a major Visigothic centre prior to the arrival of the Muslims.

Reputedly the oldest church in Spain is that of 7th century San Juan, in Baños de Cerrato, while the cathedral in nearby Palencia (Castilla y León) conserves Visigothic origins in the crypt. The horseshoe arch, later perfected by the Arabs and North Africans, is a characteristic element of the Visigothic aesthetic.

Pre-Romanesque When Spain was swamped by the Muslim invasion of 711, only the unruly northern strip of the country in what is today Asturias remained in the locals' hands. During the 9th century, a unique building style emerged in this green corner of Spain cut off completely from the rest of Christian Europe. Of the 30 or so remaining examples of pre-Romanesque scattered about the Asturian countryside, the little Iglesia de Santa María del Naranco and Iglesia de San Miguel de Lillo, both just outside Oviedo, are about the best (see the boxed aside under Oviedo in the Cantabria & Asturias chapter). The complete vaulting of the nave, the semicircular arches in the windows and porches, and the angular simplicity of these churches are all a foretaste of the Romanesque style that would sweep across all Europe a couple of centuries later.

Muslim Architecture Meanwhile, the Muslims were settling in for a long occupation: they would remain for almost 800 years in their southernmost enclave, Granada.

While Muslim Spain remained at least nominally unified, Córdoba was its capital. The Omayyad dynasty that set up shop here had come from Syria, and brought with it architects already imbued with ideas and experience won in Damascus. This was soon put to use in the construction of the Mezquita (mosque) in Córdoba, and its style was echoed across Muslim Spain. Horseshoe-shaped and lobed arches; the use of exquisite tiles in the decoration – mostly calligraphy (usually verses from the Qur'an) and floral motifs; peaceful inner courtyards; complex stucco work and stalactite ceiling adornments are all features easily recognisable and comparable with buildings raised in Damascus. Just outside Córdoba, the ruined city of Medina Azahara was built in similar style.

Remnants of this rich Muslim legacy abound across Spain, although many grand examples have been lost. The oft-converted mosque of Cristo de la Luz is a modest reminder of the genre in Toledo, but the city's great central mosque was completely destroyed after the Reconquista rolled in. The most striking piece of Islamic architecture in northern Spain is the palace of the Aljafería in Zaragoza, a proud residence subsequently much altered when the Christians retook the city.

In the 12th century, the armies of Morocco's Almohad dynasty stormed across the by now hopelessly divided lands of Muslim Spain. To them we owe some of the marvels of Sevilla, in particular the square-based minaret known as the Giralda – more beautiful perhaps even than the minaret of the Koutoubia mosque, raised by the Almohads in Marrakesh.

Muslim art reached new heights of elegance with the construction of the Alhambra palace in Granada. Built from the 13th to the 15th centuries by Granada's Nasrid rulers, it is symptomatic of the direction taken by much Islamic art at the time. Eschewing radical innovation, the Alhambra expresses a desire to perfect and refine already well-tried forms. In this it is an unqualified success, and surely one of the Muslim world's most beautiful creations – preserved despite the bullish destructive tendencies of Carlos I.

Mudéjar & Mozarabic The single greatest element that sets much of Christian Spain's great monumental architecture apart from its counterparts elsewhere in Europe is the deep-seated influence exercised over it by Islamic styles.

Already in the 10th century, Christians practising in Muslim territory – known as *mozárabes* (Mozarabs) – began to adopt elements of classic Islamic construction and export them to Christian-held territory. Although Mozarabic artisans contributed to quite a number of buildings, 'purely' Mozarabic structures are few and far between. Among the outstanding examples

DAVID WATERMAN

An example of the intricate stucco work and elegant arches of the Alhambra palace, Granada, the high point of Muslim architecture in Spain

are: the Iglesia de San Miguel de Escalada (east of León), the Ermita de San Baudelio (in Soria province) and the Iglesia de Nuestra Señora de Lebeña, on the eastern side of the Picos de Europa.

More important was the *mudéjar* influence, that of Muslims who remained behind in the lands of the Reconquista and employed their art in construction all over Spain. Their skills were found to be priceless (though cheap), and throughout Spain their influence in building many of the country's greater and lesser monuments is evident.

One unmistakable mudéjar feature was the use of brick: castles, churches and private mansions all over the country were built of this material. This alone sets much of the country's architecture apart from contemporary work elsewhere in Europe.

Another telltale feature is in the ceilings. Extravagantly decorated timber creations, often ornately carved, are a mark of the mudéjar hand. Several different types get constant mention, and the terminology seems a little fluid, depending on who is using it. In a general sense, the term *armadura* refers to any of these wooden ceilings, especially when they have the appearance of being an inverted boat. *Artesonado* ceilings are characterised by interlaced beams leaving regular spaces (triangular, square or polygonal) for the insertion of decorative *artesas.* The truly mudéjar ones generally bear floral or simple geometric patterns, but Renaissance variations also abound, with less Oriental patterns.

The term *techumbre* (which can simply mean 'roof') applies more specifically to the most common of armaduras, where the skeleton of the ceiling (looked at from the end rather than from below) looks like a series of As. This structure was sometimes left open; in other examples, boards filled the spaces between the crossbeams to form a flat ceiling surface.

About the closest view you are likely to get of this kind of ceiling is in the Convento de Santa Clara in Salamanca, where ramps have been installed allowing close inspection of the original ceiling, which had been hidden for centuries by subsequent baroque overlays.

Romanesque As the Muslim tide was turned back and the Reconquista gathered momentum, the first great medieval European movement in design began to take hold in Spain, spreading from Italy and France. From about the 11th century, churches, monasteries, bridges, pilgrims' hospices and other buildings in the Romanesque style mushroomed, mostly in the north of the country. No doubt the growing importance of the pilgrimage routes to Santiago de Compostela at just this time helped speed the process.

The first wave came in Cataluña, where Lombard artisans soon covered the countryside with comparatively simple churches

JOHN NOBLE

The simple lines and semicircular arches of the church of Sant Climent in Taüll, Cataluña, are characteristic of the Romanesque style.

JOHN NOBLE

The Gothic cathedral of Sevilla viewed from La Giralda, which was once the minaret of a great Almohad mosque that stood on this site

that were cheap to build – emblematic of which is the church of Sant Climent in Taüll. But soon more home-grown styles began to emerge across the rest of northern Spain.

The Romanesque is easily identified by a few basic characteristics. The exterior of most edifices bears little decoration, and they tend to be simple, angular structures. In the case of churches in particular, the concession to curves comes with the semicylindrical apse – or, in many cases, triple apse. The single most striking element of decoration is the semicircular arch or arches that grace doorways, windows, cloisters and naves. The humble church of the Monasterio de Sigena, east of Zaragoza, has a doorway boasting no less than 14 such arches, one encased in the other.

Other Romanesque stars in Aragón, often overlooked by visitors, are Huesca's Iglesia de San Pedro El Viejo, the proud Castillo de Loarre, the cathedral in the pre-Pyrenean town of Aínsa, and the monastery of San Juan de la Peña, west of Jaca.

Romanesque bridges abound in northern Spain, but the most impressive is the Puente de los Peregrinos at Puente de la Reina, a key point along the Camino de Santiago in Navarra.

North of the Camino, some outstanding examples include the collegiate church in Santillana del Mar and the Monasterio de San Pedro in Cervatos, near Reinosa.

With all the baroque baubles, you could be excused for overlooking that the cathedral in Santiago de Compostela is itself a seminal work of Romanesque design – much imitated, for instance in Orense and Tuy.

The Camino de Santiago is studded with Romanesque beauties. These include, to name a few (from east to west), the Monasterio de Santo Domingo de Silos, the smaller cloister (Las Claustrillas) in the Monasterio de las Huelgas in Burgos (which otherwise is more of a Transitional structure – see below), the restored Iglesia de San Martín in Frómista and the Romanesque frescos in León's Real Basílica de San Isidoro.

South of this line, the Romanesque mantle thins out – for the simple reason that no-one was building Romanesque churches in Muslim territory. Segovia is an island of a peculiar style, with arcaded porches added to the sides of its churches, and in Ávila the Basílica de San Vicente is a largely Romanesque structure. What really stands out in Ávila, however, is the Romanesque walls that still surround the city.

The Transition In the course of the 12th century, modifications in the Romanesque recipe became apparent, particularly with the rapid spread of monasteries built for the Cistercian order. The pointed arch and ribbed vault of various kinds are clear precursors of the Gothic revolution to come.

The Monasterio de Santa María de la Oliva in Navarra was among the first to incorporate such features, and others followed. Cathedrals such as those in Ávila (part fortress), Sigüenza (Castilla-La Mancha), Tarragona (Cataluña) and Tudela (Navarra) all display at least some Transitional elements.

A peculiar side development affected only south-western Castilla. The cathedrals in Salamanca, Zamora and Toro all boast Byzantine lines, particularly in the cupola.

Gothic In northern Europe, everyone marvelled at the towering new cathedrals made possible by the use of flying buttresses and other technical innovations.

The idea caught on a little later in Spain, but three of the most important Gothic cathedrals in the country went up in the 13th century, those of Burgos, León and Toledo. Although the former two in particular owe much to French models, the Spaniards soon introduced other elements. The choir *(coro)* located in the centre of the nave and huge decorative *retablos* towering over the high altar were just two such innovations that became pretty much generalised in Spanish church-building. On the subject of churches, chapel-building was a favourite pastime of the well-lined. Construction of a cathedral tended to take a long time, and it was not uncommon for more and more chapels to be added to the basic structure for decades. Dedicated to a particular saint, they are generally fronted by a *reja* or wrought-iron grille.

The main structural novelty in Spanish Gothic was star-vaulting, while a clearly Hispanic touch is the cloister, inherited directly from Romanesque monasteries but a logical continuation of a long tradition not only in religious building (whether church or mosque) but also in palaces and right down to private mansions.

A problem with identifying what style any one monument belongs to is that often they belong to several. Many great buildings

DAMIEN SIMONIS

Work on the huge Gothic cathedral in Burgos spanned three centuries. Begun in 1221, it was completed in the 15th century.

started at the height of Romanesque glory were only completed long after Gothic had gained the upper hand. And although, for instance, the cathedral in Burgos was one of the first to go up, its magnificent spires were a result of German-inspired Late Gothic imagination. In many cases, these Gothic or Romanesque-Gothic buildings received a plateresque or baroque overlay at a later date.

It is important not to forget that mudéjar influences were alive and well, still most easily recognised in the giveaway penchant for working in brick rather than stone. Toledo is covered in Gothic-mudéjar combinations, while Aragón was blessed with a singular version of the theme. Zaragoza, Teruel, Tarazona and Calatayud all contain marvellous works. The tower of Teruel's Iglesia de San Salvador, for example, is an outstanding example of a mudéjar fantasy in brick and ceramics.

Finally, the so-called Isabelline style was a late addition to the cocktail. Taking some decorative cues from the more curvaceous traits of Islamic design, it was in some ways an indirect precursor to plateresque. Perhaps the ultimate expression of this style is Toledo's San Juan de los Reyes, originally destined to be the final resting place of the Catholic Monarchs (they changed their minds after capturing Granada, which they preferred). Designed by the French-born Juan Güas (1453-96), it is a medley of earlier Gothic and mudéjar elements, with a final decorative Isabelline flourish.

The 16th century saw a revival of pure Gothic, perhaps best exemplified in the new cathedral in Salamanca, although the Segovia cathedral was about the last, and possibly most pure, Gothic house of worship to be constructed in Spain.

Not only religious buildings flourished. The majority of the seemingly innumerable castles scattered across the country went up in Gothic times. Many never saw action and were not intended to. A couple of the more extraordinary samples of mudéjar castle-building from this era are the Castillo de la Mota (Medina del Campo, Castilla y León) and the sumptuous castle at Coca, not far

away. Others intended more for warfare were built of sturdier materials, such as the one at Peñafiel on the Río Duero, long the front line between Muslim and Christian Spain. A long way further south, near Almagro (Castilla-La Mancha), the warrior knights of Calatrava built a castle in a stunning position controlling a valley into what was by then left of Muslim territory – the kingdom of Granada. It's in a ruinous state but impressive for all that.

A surprising number of more humble establishments survive in hundreds of small towns and villages that have managed to retain something of their medieval – and hence largely Gothic-era – past. Noble mansions can be picked by the sculpted coats of arms that adorn them. More imposing are the likes of Guadalajara's Palacio del Infantado.

Renaissance The Renaissance in Spain can be roughly divided into three distinct styles. Firstly, the Italian-influenced special flavour that was plateresque. To visit Salamanca is to receive a concentrated dose of the most splendid work in the genre, which refers more to decoration rather than to structural style. The university façade especially is a virtuoso piece of intricate sculpture, featuring busts, medallions and swathes of complex floral design. It is busy but controlled, and the Italian influence is clearly evident. Not far behind in intensity comes the façade of the Convento de San Esteban. Little of the work can be convincingly traced to any one hand, and it appears that the principal exponent of plateresque, Alonso de Covarrubias (1488-1570), was busier in places such as his home city of Toledo (the Alcázar and the Capilla de los Nuevos Reyes in the cathedral).

Next is the more purist Renaissance style that prevailed in Andalucía and has its maximum expression in the Palacio de Carlos I in Granada's Alhambra. Diego de Siloé (1495-1563) and followers in his school are regarded as masters. Siloé made his mark with Granada's cathedral, and was followed by others with such masterpieces as the cathedral of Jaén and the Iglesia del San Salvador in Úbeda.

Juan de Herrera (1530-97) is the last and perhaps greatest figure of the Spanish Renaissance, but his work bears almost no resemblance to anything else of the period. His masterpiece, austere to the point of being devoid of ornament, was the grand palace-monastery complex of San Lorenzo de El Escorial. Even after his death, Herrera's style lived on. Madrid's Plaza Mayor and *ayunta-miento* (town hall) were built pretty much in imitation of his work, even as a new architectural fad was washing over the country.

Baroque The heady frills and spills of baroque can be seen all over Spain, but usually in the form of additions rather than complete buildings. Cádiz's baroque cathedral is an exception. Three loose phases can be identified, starting with a sober baroque still heavily influenced by Herrera (see above), followed by a period of greater architectural exuberance (some would say, a sickening amount), and finally running into a mixture of baroque with the beginnings of neoclassicism.

The leading exponents of this often over-blown approach to building and decoration were the Churriguera brothers. Alberto (1676-1750) designed Salamanca's Plaza Mayor, but he and José (1665-1735) are best known for their extraordinary retablos, huge carved wooden backdrops for altars, with twisting gilded columns and burdened with all manner of angels and saints.

Baroque reached heights of opulence with the Sagrario in Granada's La Cartuja monastery and the Transparente in Toledo's cathedral. The Transparente is a device loaded with trompe-l'oeil painting by which an opening was made in the vault of the church to allow in more light; it looks positively weird in among the Gothic clutter.

Among some of the outstanding baroque achievements are the façade superimposed over the Romanesque original in the cathedral of Santiago de Compostela, several of

DAMIEN SIMONIS

Alberto Churriguera, the designer of Salamanca's Plaza Mayor (pictured), and his brother José lent their name to the churrigueresque style of baroque architecture.

Galicia's monasteries, the cathedral in Murcia and the façade on Madrid's Museo Municipal.

More reserved were the many royal palaces that began to go up in and around Madrid in the 16th century. The Palacio Real and those in Aranjuez and La Granja de San Ildefonso all owe something to baroque.

Neoclassicism In Spain as elsewhere, the pendulum swung away from the gaudy extremes of baroque as the 18th century closed. Tastes became more sober and the cleaner, restrained lines of neoclassicism came into fashion. In Spain, minor churches, bullrings and public buildings were built in this style, but nothing of greatness was achieved, making the 19th century a bleak patch in the history of Spanish architecture.

Modernisme The end of the 19th century ushered in arguably one of the most imaginative periods in Spanish building. Cataluña was home to the *modernistas*, whose master was Antoni Gaudí (1852-1926). Although he exercised his fantasy outside Cataluña (in Astorga, León and Comillas), it was in Barcelona that he and his peers left their most singular mark. Work continues even now on his most exciting project, the immense La Sagrada Família church.

An utterly weird, swirling piece of *modernisme* in Madrid is the Sociedad General de Autores y Editores building.

Modern The main central boulevards of Madrid are filled with the portentous façades that were the property of banks and ministries around the turn of the century. Together

JOHN NOBLE

The south-western spires of Antoni Gaudí's unfinished masterpiece, the Temple Expiatori de la Sagrada Familia, Barcelona

DAMIEN SIMONIS

Detail from the Sociedad General de Autores y Editores building, a rare example in Madrid of the *modernista* style

they make an agreeable impression, without being of any notable architectural worth. It has largely been a disappointing century.

Music

Spain pulsates with music. As if awakened from a long torpor, all the elements that make up the patchwork quilt of the country's musical geography seem to be gathering force. Flamenco, revived earlier this century but subsequently much ignored by most Spaniards, is undergoing a startling transformation. No longer the preserve of the initiated or dished up sloppily for tourists, it has become increasingly fashionable among locals as it has demonstrated greater innovation. The country's rock and pop scene, while not wildly successful beyond Spanish shores, is nonetheless busy and vibrant – a good deal more so than in other European countries. Folk music peculiar to the many different regions of Spain is also blossoming, and even on the classical front there are stirrings.

Classical Of the great or once great European nations, Spain has been noticeable in the realm of classical music by its absence. Rather, it has generally fallen to outsiders to pick up the country's vibrant rhythms and translate them into lasting homages. Who has not at least heard of *Carmen*, an opera whose leading lady epitomises all the fire, guile and flashing beauty of Andalucía and its women? Its composer, Frenchman Georges Bizet, had been mesmerised by Moorish-influenced melodies of southern Spain in much the same way as Claude Debussy, whose penchant for the Iberian found expression in *Images*. Another Frenchman, Emmanuel Chabrier, immortalised his love for the country's sounds in *España*, while Maurice Ravel whipped off his *Bolero* almost as an aside in 1927. Russians too, have been swept away by the Hispanic. Mikhail Glinka went to Granada in 1845 and the compositions that resulted inspired a new movement in Russian folk music. Rimsky-Korsakov popped into Spain on shore leave while in the Russian navy. At heart more composer than captain, he penned his delightful *Capriccio Espagnol*.

Spain itself was bereft of composers until the likes of Manuel de Falla and Enrique Granados came onto the scene early this century. Granados and Isaac Albéniz became great pianists and interpreters of their own compositions, such as the latter's *Iberia* cycle. Joaquín Rodrigo is another composer of note.

Best known of Spain's operatic performers is Plácido Domingo, followed closely by José Carreras. With Italy's tenor Luciano Pavarotti, they form the big three of contemporary male opera singers. All three have recently taken to giving big open-air concerts – which have proved surprisingly successful. At present artistic director of the Washington Opera, Domingo has even toyed with the idea of going into politics. One of the world's most outstanding sopranos is Cataluña's Montserrat Caballé.

Flamenco This generic term covers a broad range of music and dance. It is rooted in the *cante hondo* (deep song) of the Gypsies of Andalucía and probably influenced by North African rhythms. The poet García Lorca and the composer Manuel de Falla helped keep the genre alive with their grand competition in 1922, but by then it already had a well-established history. The Gypsies had settled in Andalucía early in the 15th century, and by the end of the 18th century several centres of cante hondo (also known as *cante jondo*) had emerged – among them Cádiz, Jerez de la Frontera and the Triana area of Sevilla.

The melancholy cante hondo is performed by a singer, who may be male (in which case he is a *cantaor*) or female *(cantaora)*, to the accompaniment of a blood-rush of guitar from the *tocaor*. Although in its pure, traditional form this is sometimes a little hard for the uninitiated to deal with, it is difficult not to be moved by what is a very physical experience. The accompanying dance is performed by one or more *bailaores*. A dance style that closely resembles, but should not be confused with, what the bailaores do is the *sevillana* – more an Andalucían form of folk

Top: The ubiquitous olive
Bottom: Fun at the Feria de Málaga, Andalucía

DAMIEN SIMONIS

DAMIEN SIMONIS

DAMIEN SIMONIS

BETHUNE CARMICHAEL

Top Left: The oldest *cruceiro* in Galicia, in Melide, on the Camino de Santiago
Top Right: Façade of the Palacio de los Duques del Infantado, in Guadalajara, Castilla-La Mancha
Bottom Left: Detail from the façade of the Convento de San Esteban, in Salamanca, Castilla y León
Bottom Right: Renaissance fountain in the Alhambra, Granada, Andalucía

dancing. Girls all over the country try to learn sevillanas at some time during their school careers.

It is impossible in this limited space to delve into the intricacies of the various orthodox schools of flamenco that have emerged over the past century (schools of Cádiz, Sevilla, Jerez, Córdoba and so on), or of the different kinds of song and music (*bulerías*, boleros, *soleares*, *fandangos*, *alegrías*, *farrucas* and so on). Suffice to say that there is more to it than immediately meets the eye.

Although flamenco's home turf is in the south, many artists establish themselves in other major cities, especially Madrid, with its Gypsy *barrios* or districts and longtime flamenco bars.

Some of the greatest figures around the turn of the century, to some the Edad de Oro (golden age) of flamenco, include the guitarist Ramón Montoya and the singer Silverio Franconetti. Manolo Caracol joined the great singer Lola Flores (died 1995) to introduce theatrical elements and even orchestral accompaniment – which purists considered an unwelcome development, but which injected new life into the genre.

Flamenco's real golden age may well be opening up before us right now. Never has it been so popular both in Spain and abroad, and never has there been such a degree of imaginative innovation. Strangely, the most successful proponents of modern flamenco (or flamenco-style) music are the Gipsy Kings – who happen to be from southern France, not Spain.

Of the many great Spanish guitarists, Paco de Lucía stands out the most. Born in 1947 and internationally renowned, he has a virtuosity few would dare to claim they can match. He is for many the personification of *duende*, that indefinable capacity to transmit the power of flamenco. There is a wealth of albums to choose from; *La Fabulosa Guitarra de Paco de Lucía* is a nice introduction. Paco de Lucía spends more time abroad than in Spain now, but plenty of other good musicians fill the gap at home. The list of fine flamenco guitarists is long, among them the Habichuela family, especially Juan and Pepe. Other artists to watch for include Tomatito, Manolo Sanlúcar and Moraíto Chico. A relatively new star is Vicente Amigo: get hold of his *Vivencias Imaginadas*.

Paco de Lucía's friend El Camarón de la Isla, who died in 1992, personified the new heights of cante hondo, and plenty of flamenco singers today pretty much try to emulate him. Another who has reached the level of cult figure is Enrique Morente, referred to by one Madrid paper as 'the last Bohemian'. Among other leading vocalists figure such greats as Carmen Linares, from the province of Jaén, and the Sevillan José Menese. El Camarón's successors include Antonio Vargas, known as El Potito, Juan Cortés Duquende, Miguel Poveda and José Parra. Rising female vocalists include Aurora and the Cádiz-born Niña Pastori.

A couple who have added their own particular sound to the flamenco repertoire are Lole y Manuel. Lole's strong, melancholy voice is accompanied by her partner's equally emotive guitar. In the past few years, though, they have displayed a marked inability to come up with anything new.

Of Spain's flamenco dancers and choreographers, the greatest name this century is with little doubt Antonio Ruiz Soler, who died in early 1996. Leading figures today include Joaquín Cortés and Manuela Vargas. Traditionalists dislike fashionable attempts to mix flamenco dance with ballet and other forms. One of the great traditional bailaores, Farruco, spends most of his time touring outside Spain now, and argues that dancers such as Cortés don't really dance flamenco. The only *'puro masculino'* bailaor these days, says Farruco, is his teenage grandson Farruquito.

If you want to give yourself a general introduction to the best of flamenco today, try to see Carlos Saura's 1994 flick, *Flamenco*. A double-CD set of the music is also available.

Tourist-oriented flamenco shows, often called *tablaos*, usually lack the genuine emotion of real flamenco, though a few are worth seeing if you have no alternative. To catch the real thing, watch out for concerts by some of the names mentioned earlier, and for the fairly numerous flamenco festivals that take place – usually in the summer and mostly in Andalucía. A few venues that stage regular flamenco are mentioned in city sections of this guide.

Fusion Possibly the most exciting developments in flamenco have taken it to other musical shores. Two of the best-known groups that have experimented with flamenco-rock fusion since the 1980s are Ketama (some of whose members come from the Habichuela family) and Pata Negra, whose music is labelled by some as Gypsy rock. One of Ketama's best albums is *Canciones Hondas*, while Pata Negra's seventh, *Como Una Vara Verde*, is a good choice. A former member of Pata Negra, Raimundo Amador, has gone his own way and in 1996 made a CD with the American blues master BB King.

In the early 1990s, Radio Tarifa emerged with a mesmerising mix of flamenco, North African and medieval sounds. The first CD, *Rumba Argelina*, was a great hit. The main problem with these guys is that they have not produced any new material since. A more traditional flamenco performer, Juan Peña Lebrijano, has done some equally appealing combinations with classical Moroccan music. His CD *Encuentros*, recorded with the Andalusian Orchestra of Tangier, is a good sample.

Pop & Rock In purely monetary terms, Julio Iglesias must be the country's most successful performer ever. Long resident in the USA, he has for many years had millions swooning with his crooning in Spanish and various other languages. Apart from Iglesias, the success of Spanish popular music abroad has been limited. In the mid-1990s, however, the Sevilla duo Los del Río's song *Macarena* has proven a hit – in several versions – on radios and in discos around the world.

Kiko Veneno is one of the durables of Spanish rock. His flamenco roots still show through, but this in no way detracts from his crisp rock sound. Although he's been around

for quite awhile, he has cut relatively few albums – all of them good. Danza Invisible is another longtime mainstream band from Málaga. One of the country's more popular groups at home and abroad is Mecano, two male musicians fronted by a powerful woman singer.

A couple of male vocalists with a big following are Miguel Bosé and Antonio Vega. Vega's mood leans to the melancholy, while Bosé is perhaps a little more whimsically cerebral. For awhile in the early 1990s you heard little else on the radio. From those days, Bosé's *Bajo el Signo de Caín* and Vega's *Océano del Sol* were their best albums. Another popular singer with a little more oomph is Manolo Tena. Easily the most popular female vocalist is Luz, a fairly middle-of-the-road performer.

Moving up the rock scale a little, El Último de la Fila is a fine Barcelona duo – one of the best musical products of the city. Another duo worth catching is Amistades Peligrosas – Cristina del Valle and Alberto Comesaña do some great harmonies. *La Última Tentación* is one of their better albums.

For something a little racier, Celtas Cortos has a sound reminiscent of the Pogues (some would say too much so, and with less inspired lyrics). If it appeals, *Cuéntame un Cuento* is a good choice of CD. Another good band that split up at the beginning of the 1990s is Radio Futura.

One of the few rock bands to have survived from the days of the post-Franco *movida* in Madrid is La Unión, which now dabbles with a mix of white soul and techno.

A recent success story is the Gijón trio Australian Blonde, an indie band that is rising fast in the popularity stakes, along with another group of the same ilk, Los Planetas.

A heavy rock scene still animates many a Spanish bar, and one gutsy, fun band to revel in that scene is Seguridad Social. You have to like your music loud and thumping, and the lyrics are not without a strong dose of irony. Madrid was long a hothouse for good old-fashioned rock. Two young bands emerging on the local scene and defying the trendy taste for Latin American influences and fusion experiments are Sobrinus and Buenas Noches Rose. They crank out unabashed rock and are acquiring quite a local following.

Plenty more hard stuff animates the adolescent rock scene, and the bands' names alone clue you in a little: popular rap-rockers Def Con Dos, Pleasure Fuckers and Soziedad Alkohólika, just to name a few.

A whole subterranean world of loud and, for many, unbearable dance noise is most commonly known as *bakalao*. For this ear-splitting Spanish contribution to the wonderful world of techno, Valencia seems to be something of a headquarters. A subcategory (for those capable of discerning a difference) is *mákina*.

Folk Although the odd group playing traditional folk music can be found across several regions, the best and most prolific source is Galicia. Its rich heritage is closely related to that of its Celtic cousins in Brittany and Ireland, and has nothing at all in common with what might be considered quintessential 'Spanish' music, such as flamenco. Emblematic of the music is the *gaita*, Galicia's version of the bagpipes. The most successful purveyor of Galicia's Celtic tradition is the highly polished group Milladoiro. They indulge in a little adventure occasionally and in 1995 brought out a CD with the English Chamber Orchestra.

Another group worth seeking out is Palla Mallada, from Santiago de Compostela, which does a mix of instrumental pieces, dances and traditional songs. Others include Na Lua, Citania and Alecrín. Uxía is an enchanting female vocalist, a gutsy version of Enya, who also seeks her inspiration in traditional *gallego* folk music.

A highly versatile gallego performer of gaita and a variety of wind instruments is Carlos Núñez. He presents a slick show with his group A Irmandade da Estrela, which is made up of violins, percussion, guitar and lute. He often invites a wide range of guest artists to play at his concerts, providing for a highly entertaining and eclectic mix of styles.

The Celtic tradition is also alive in Asturias and even Cantabria, but not to nearly the same extent as in Galicia.

From the País Vasco, Oskorri is a fine electrical and acoustic band and one of the best folk-inspired groups to emerge from the region.

Cantautores Some of the great singer-songwriters of the *movida* are still in circulation. People like Pedro Guerra and Javier Krahe, who might loosely be compared with France's Georges Brassens or Germany's Wolf Biermann, still cover the late-night circuit in Madrid with their biting, witty ballads of protest and mordant social commentary, and are even experiencing something of a revival. For non-Spaniards they are the most challenging, for it is their lyrics that matter, not the music. Luís Pastor is a younger member of this crowd.

Festivals For information on when and where to catch some of the more important music festivals, see Public Holidays & Special Events in the Facts for the Visitor chapter.

Literature
Medieval Works It is difficult to talk of a 'Spanish' literature much before the 13th century, if by this is meant literature in Castilian. Before this, troubadours working in Vulgar Latin, Arabic and other tongues were doing the rounds of southern Europe, and the great writers and thinkers in a Spain largely dominated by Muslims produced their treatises more often than not in Arabic or Hebrew. Alfonso X, king of Castilla and León (1252-84) and known as El Sabio (the Learned), did much to encourage the use of Castilian as a language of learning and literature, himself writing on diverse subjects.

Of all the works produced in Spanish in the Middle Ages, the *Poema de Mio Cid*, which has survived in a version penned in 1307 (although first written in 1140), is surely the best known. The epic tale of El Cid

Campeador, or Rodrigo Díaz, whose exploits culminated in mastery over Valencia, bears little resemblance to the facts. Rather, it is concerned with telling a good story in which a towering figure overcomes all odds by his prowess and so attains glory.

This was an age of didactic writing, of poetry and injunctions working at once on a literal, moral and allegorical level. Gonzalo de Berceo, who died in the late 1200s, composed some of the most elegant writing in this genre, culminating in his *Milagros de Nuestra Señora* (Miracles of Our Lady). Juan Ruiz, who wrote in the first half of the 14th century, was one of the period's finest poets and something of a humorist who often descended into the downright bawdy. His *Buen Amor* (1330) leads the reader along paths of Good and Evil, with a less constrained view of earthly peccadillos than usually propounded in the edifying literature of the day.

El Siglo de Oro The end of the Reconquista in 1492 and the glory days of the Catholic Monarchs imbue with optimism the writing of the first half of the 16th century. Garcilaso de la Vega (1501-36), steeped in Italian literary sensibilities and *au fait* with the likes of Ariosto and Bembo, left behind sonnets and eclogues of unparalleled beauty. His successor and perhaps the greatest of all Spanish poets was Luís de Góngora (1561-1627). Unconcerned by theories, morals or highminded sentiments, Góngora manipulated words with a majesty that has largely defied attempts at critical 'explanation'; his verses are above all intended as a source of sensuous pleasure. With Góngora we are in the greatest period of Spanish letters, El Siglo de Oro (the Golden Century), which stretched roughly from the middle of the 16th century to the middle of the 17th.

This was equally the age of some of the country's greatest mystics. For St John of the Cross (San Juan de la Cruz), poetry, especially of a lightly erotic flavour, serves as the best of imperfect tools to render the ecstasy of union between God and the soul. His works, such as *Noche Oscura* and *Llama de Amor Viva*, didn't appear until well after his death in 1591. His contemporary, Santa Teresa de Ávila (1515-82), was heading down another road, capturing in evocative if not always strictly correct prose accounts of her explorations of her own spiritual life, among them *Camino de Perfección* and *Las Moradas o el Castillo Interior*.

Histories were gaining in popularity, and among the most meticulous of their compilers was the Jesuit Juan de Mariana (1535-1624).

The advent of the *comedia* in the early 17th century in Madrid produced some of the country's greatest ever playwrights. Lope de Vega (1562-1635), also an outstanding lyric poet, was perhaps the most prolific: more than 300 of the 800 plays and poems attributed to him remain. Disabused, he explored the falseness of court life and roamed political subjects with his imaginary historical plays. Less playful and perhaps of greater substance is the work of Tirso de Molina (1581-1648), in whose *El Burlador de Sevilla* we are presented with the immortal character of Don Juan, a likeable seducer who meets an unhappy end.

Yet another great name of the period is Pedro Calderón de la Barca (1600-81). The beauty of the works of this grand master of the stage lies in his agile language and inventive techniques as a dramatist. The themes and story lines of his work were, however, comparatively run-of-the-mill. Among his more powerful pieces are *La Vida es Sueño* and *El Alcalde de Zalamea*, in both of which Calderón upholds an idea of righteousness and justice irrespective of class and caste.

Also noteworthy is Francisco de Quevedo (1580-1645), an accomplished poet working in almost diametric opposition to Góngora. His verse is heavily burdened with the weight of his philosophising and musing on the depth and nature of passion. He is perhaps better known today for his prose – a sparkling virtuoso game of metaphor and wordplay, but often laden with a heavy dose of bitter and unforgiving social commentary. His *La Historia de la Vida del Buscón*

Llamado Don Pablos, tracing the none too elevating life of an antihero, El Buscón, is laced with what appears to be a special venom reserved for the lower classes.

Cervantes & the Novel His life something of a jumbled obstacle course of trials, tribulations and peregrinations, Miguel de Cervantes Saavedra (1547-1616) had little immediate success with his forays into theatre and verse. But today he is commonly thought of as the man who gave modern literature a new genre: the novel.

El Ingenioso Hidalgo Don Quijote de la Mancha started life as a short story, designed above all to make a quick peseta, but Cervantes found himself turning it into an epic tale by the time it appeared in 1605. The ruined *ancien régime* knight and his equally impoverished companion Sancho Panza embark on a trail through the foibles of his era – a journey whose timelessness and universality marked the work out for greatness. The successor to the picaresque novellas that emerged alongside the new theatre of the

Miguel de Cervantes Saavedra, the foremost figure in Spanish literature, who died on the same day as William Shakespeare – 23 April 1616

comedia at the beginning of the 17th century, *Don Quijote* would a century later be a fundamental source of inspiration for the further development of the modern novel, particularly in France and Britain.

18th & 19th Centuries The 18th century was not exactly a halcyon period for Spanish literary creation. The century's greatest figure was with little doubt Juan Meléndez Valdés (1754-1817). His *Poesías* bring together his finest work, ranging from the humanistic and even a hint of the coming romanticism through to a more personal, sometimes erotic verse. Another outstanding figure of the times was the Benedictine monk Benito Jerónimo Feijóo (1676-1764), an enlightened essayist whose defence of rational thought and the diffusion of culture is summed up in the eight volume collection of his finest essays, the *Teatro Crítico Universal*. Leandro de Moratín (1760-1828) was perhaps the best of a mediocre crowd of playwrights through the 18th century.

The age of the romantics touched Spain less than much of the rest of Europe. Its greatest poetic exponent, José de Espronceda (1788-1842), reached the pinnacle of his often anguished work with *El Diablo Mundo*, an unfinished history of man that incites to feverish life in the face of the enigma of existence and death. Less tortured but with a fine sense of nuance was Gustavo Adolfo Becquer (1836-70). Galicia's Rosalía de Castro (1837-85) was another bright light of the age.

One novelist towers above the rest through to the end of the 19th century. Benito Pérez Galdós (1843-1920) is the closest Spain produced to a Dickens or a Balzac. His novels and short stories ranged from social critique to the simple depiction of society through the lives of its many players. His more mature works, such as *Fortunata y Jacinta*, display a bent towards naturalism and, in the early 20th century, even symbolism. Another harsh realist and early feminist was Doña Emilia, Condesa de Pardo-Bazán. Her *Los Pazos de Ulloa* is a masterpiece.

From 1900 to Franco Miguel de Unamuno (1864-1936) was among the leading figures of the so-called Generation of 98, a group of writers and artists working around and after 1898 (this was a bad year for Spain with the loss of its last Caribbean colonies and an economic crisis at home). Unamuno's work is difficult, but among his most enjoyable prose is the *Tres Novelas Ejemplares*, imbued, as most of his novels and theatre are, with what could be termed a disquieting existentialism. The leading poet of the era was with little doubt Antonio Machado. Steeped in symbolism, his poetry moves towards the metaphysical in his mature years, particularly in *Proverbios y Cantares*. *Nuevas Canciones* were written from 1917 to 1930.

The leading light in early 20th century modernist poetry was the Nicaraguan Rubén Darío (1867-1916). Another experimental writer of note was Ramón María del Valle Inclán (1869-1936).

A little later came the brief flourishing of Andalucía's Federico García Lorca (1898-1936), whose verse and theatre leaned towards surrealism, leavened by a unique musicality and visual sensibility. Among his many offerings are *Canciones*, *Poema del Cante Jondo* and plays such as the powerful *Bodas de Sangre* (Blood Wedding). His career was cut short by Nationalist executioners in the early stages of the civil war.

The Franco Years The censors of Fascist Spain kept a lid, albeit far from watertight, on literary development in Spain. One of the few writers of quality who managed to work throughout the years of the dictatorship, and who continues to thrive, is the Galician Nobel Prize-winning novelist Camilo José Cela (born in 1916). His most important novel, *La Familia de Pascual Duarte*, appeared in 1942 and marked a rebirth of the Spanish realistic novel.

Much of worth was also produced by writers in exile, among them Francisco Ayala, Max Aub, Juan Larrea and Mercé Rodoreda.

Contemporary Writing The death of Franco in 1975 signalled the end of the constraints placed on Spanish writers. Many of those now able to work in complete freedom were already active in exile during the Franco years, and some choose to remain outside Spain. Juan Goytisolo (born 1931) started off in the neorealist camp but his more recent works, such as *Señas de Identidad* and *Juan sin Tierra*, are decidedly more experimental and tend to contain ferocious attacks on Spanish sacred cows.

Jorge Semprun (born 1923) ended up in a Nazi concentration camp for his activities with the French Resistance in WWII. He writes in Spanish and French. His first novel, *Le Grand Voyage*, is one of his best.

Of course, younger authors are emerging all the time. One to note is Antonio Muñoz Molina (born 1956), whose *El Invierno en Lisboa* is a touching novel that won him considerable acclaim when it appeared in 1987.

Notable female writers to emerge in the past 30 years include Adelaida García Morales, Rosa Montero, Ana María Matute and Montserrat Roig.

Dance

Mention dance and Spain together, and what traditionally springs to mind is flamenco and its associated forms – for which, see Music. However, contemporary dance and ballet are alive and well here too. Though contemporary dance pops up all round the country, Barcelona is probably its capital, with several shows to choose from almost any week of the year. The Ballet Nacional de España, founded in 1978, has two companies, one devoted to *ballet español*, a kind of fusion of flamenco, classical ballet and contemporary dance, the other to classical ballet. The current star of ballet español is Antonio Márquez, who also has his own company. The outstanding classical ballet company in recent years has been the Ballet Víctor Ullate, directed by the leading Spanish dancer of that name and based at Madrid's Teatro de Madrid, though it tours elsewhere too. One interesting company if you can catch it on its travels is the Compañía Andaluza de Danza (Andalucían Dance Company), which has been pushing flamenco dance well beyond its traditional frontiers by, among other things, 'flamencoising' other dance forms and using music by Peter Gabriel, Tom Waits and others.

Here and there you'll find the occasional regional folk dance, such as Cataluña's *sardana*.

Cinema

While a handful of directors and actors keep the modern Spanish cinema industry ticking over, occasionally with some success beyond their own shores, the history of film in Spain has been a largely barren expanse with the occasional burst of brilliance.

Way back in 1897 a short film was made showing people at Zaragoza's basilica, and later studios were set up in Barcelona.

Luís Buñuel The man now universally regarded as the greatest Spanish film maker ever, emerged with the surrealist movement in the 1920s. Luís Buñuel, born in Teruel in 1900, only developed an interest in film after moving to Paris in 1926. By then he had already established himself in Spanish literary and art circles, and for a long time was a close friend of Salvador Dalí.

Buñuel's first full attempt at film production, made when he was already under the sway of the surrealists, was *Un Chien Andalou* (1929), followed a year later by *L'Age d'Or*. Both were made with Dalí. They have lived on as classics, as has his next effort, a hard-hitting account of the desperation of rural life for which he returned to Spain. *Las Hurdes – Terre Sans Pain*, filmed in the hilly Las Hurdes region of Extremadura and the surrounding area, was banned in Spain and hence originally appeared in its French version. Buñuel remained in Spain dubbing for Warner Brothers. He did not really move back into film making until winding up in Mexico in the mid-1940s, an exile from Francoist Spain. Mexico City then

became his base, although he also continued to work in France. Among his successes was *Belle de Jour*, done in 1966.

The Civil War & the Franco Years Meanwhile, in Spain itself, censorship tended to stifle most creative impulses. During the civil war, the Republican side had beaten the Nationalists in the use of film as a propaganda tool, but this didn't prevent them losing the war. Once Franco installed himself in power in 1939, a tight if not always consistent clamp was applied to the industry.

There were exceptions to the rule. Luis García Berlanga's *Bienvenido Mr Marshall* (Welcome Mr Marshall), made in 1952, was a breath of Italian-style neorealism that managed to get through the net. It observes the belated agreement on US aid to Spain under the Marshall Plan (in which the USA ignored its own disapproval of Franco in return for military bases) from a small Spanish village; about the only tangible result for the villagers is a rain of dust as Marshall's cavalcade of VIP cars charges through the town.

Juan Antonio Bardem followed in 1955 with *Muerte de un Ciclista* (Death of a Cyclist), and Berlanga chimed in again with *El Verdugo* (The Executioner) in 1964. Buñuel was himself asked back to Spain at this time to produce a film. *Viridiana* was a biting performance deemed worthy of a Palme d'Or at Cannes and subsequently banned by Franco after the Vatican objected to certain irreverent scenes.

The next star to emerge was Carlos Saura, whose first film, *Los Golfos* (The Scoundrels) came out in 1959. He developed a more subversive style in the early 1970s, peaking with *Ana y los Lobos* (1973), in which the power of the church and army in Francoist Spanish society comes in for thinly camouflaged attack. In the same year, Victor Erice's *El Espíritu de la Colmena* (The Spirit of the Beehive) hit the screen; it is a quiet and beautifully crafted picture in which one of the cinema's outcast figures, Frankenstein's monster, becomes real for a beekeeper's little daughter in postwar Spain.

Cinema after Franco The late 1970s and the 1980s breathed new life into Spanish cinema, with a few directors doing work appreciated not only in Spain, but abroad as well. Pedro Almodóvar is with little doubt Spain's best-known cinema export, having won many fans with such quirkily comic looks at modern Spain as *Átame* (Tie Me Up, Tie Me Down) and *Mujeres al Borde de un Ataque de Nervios* (Women on the Edge of a Nervous Breakdown). Darker sentiments are explored in productions like *Matador*, where the blood lust of the *corrida* (bullfight) and the lust of the bed are closely tied together.

Ten years after his success with *El Espíritu de la Colmena*, Erice brought another classic to the screen with *El Sur*. Saura had another popular success in 1990 with *¡Ay Carmela!*. Set in the civil war, it is a clever balance of tragedy and comedy that follows a roving theatre duo around the country as they unwittingly stumble from Republican to Nationalist zones. A completely different turn came in 1994 with *Flamenco*, not so much a film as an exciting review of the best in this vein of Spanish dance and song.

Vicente Aranda has been less prolific than Almodóvar, but found acclaim with *Amantes* (1991), set in the Madrid of the 1950s and based on the real story of a love triangle that ends particularly badly. The following year, Fernando Trueba brought out *Belle Epoque*, which examines the melancholy underside to bliss through the story of four sisters' hounding of a young chap in their house. It won an Oscar.

Almodóvar in particular has moved away from the deadening burden of Franco and the civil war years, and other directors are following suit, picking up new themes. This does not imply the disappearance of such a sombre heritage as a source of material, and in 1995 British director Ken Loach tried his hand. The UK-Spanish co-production that resulted is probably one of the most even-handed and successful treatments of the Spanish Civil War on film to date – *Tierra y Libertad* (Land and Freedom).

The arrival of the PSOE in power in 1982 also meant a revived programme of subsidies and state help for the industry. This may all be about to change. The conservative PP, since taking over from the Socialists in early 1996, has been threatening to reduce, if not simply remove, state aid for film making. This, worried directors have warned, could be the death of home-grown material. Many fear that, faced with the overwhelming flood from Hollywood, as indeed is the rest of European cinema, Spanish cinema may struggle to survive.

The big names sometimes vote with their feet. While screen stars like Carmen Maura and Victoria Abril have continued to work mainly in Spain, Antonio Banderas has opted for Hollywood – where he probably makes a lot more money and also met the love of his life, Melanie Griffiths, with whom he starred in a comparatively silly number called *Two Much* in 1995.

Theatre

Thanks mainly to a big theatre development programme by the PSOE governments of the 1980s and 90s, most cities of any significance – and some of no significance at all – have a theatre. There's usually something on at them, too, ranging from old Lope de Vega through Lorca and other Spanish classics to modern comedy or avant-garde fare, with a fair swag of foreign drama in translation too. Madrid and Barcelona are the epicentres of the scene, with Barcelona having an edge when it comes to avant-garde productions. Straight theatre is unlikely to appeal, however, if your understanding of Spanish – or, in Barcelona, Catalan – is less than fluent. Just the occasional visiting foreign company does a show in English, French or some other tongue. A possible alternative is music hall or cabaret, both alive and well in the two big cities.

SOCIETY & CONDUCT

Spaniards can be economical with etiquette and thank-yous but this does not signify unfriendliness. One small way in which you may notice people expressing their fellow-

❉ ❉

What's in an Apellido?

You may soon notice that there's something not quite straightforward about Spaniards' names. María García and Pedro Blanco present no problem, but what to make of Almudena López López, Francisco Sánchez G, or Isabel de Colón Villalobos?

Basically, a Spaniard has three names: a given name *(nombre)*, and two surnames *(apellidos)*. The first of the surnames is the person's father's first surname. The second surname is the mother's first surname. So Isabel, the daughter of Antonio Romero Cervantes and Alicia Ruiz Álvarez, is Isabel Romero Ruiz.

In practice many people don't bother with their second surname, or occasionally just shorten it to an initial – so our Isabel is simply Isabel Romero, or maybe Isabel Romero R. But if the first surname is a particularly common one (García, Fernández, López, González and Rodríguez are the commonest), a person is more likely to keep the second one in use too – and may even, when a short version of her/his name is wanted, use only the second surname. A famous case of this is the writer Federico García Lorca, who is known as either García Lorca or just Lorca, but never as García.

Women don't change their names when they marry, but may tack their husband's surnames (preceded by *de*) on to the end of their own. So if Isabel Romero Ruiz were to marry Pedro Colón Villalobos, she could call herself Isabel Romero Ruiz de Colón Villalobos – and, for short, she might end up being called anything from Isabel Romero to Isabel de Colón! ∎

❉ ❉

feeling is the general *'Buenos días'* they often utter to all present when they enter a small shop or bar, and the *'Adiós'* when they leave. The Spanish are generally tolerant and easy-going, and often welcoming, towards the 60 million foreigners who invade their country each year, and now have several decades experience in making life easy for them. They don't expect foreigners to speak much Spanish – though you need some words to get by outside tourist centres, and of course it helps a lot if you *can* communicate in Spanish. Nor do they imagine outsiders will know much about their internal disputes: even calling an ardent Catalan nationalist a Spaniard will probably bring nothing more than a patient explanation to the contrary.

Equally, most Spaniards don't really expect, or show much interest in, communicating more than superficially with transient visitors. Invitations to Spanish homes are rare enough to be a mark of true friendship.

Spaniards are famous for being very gregarious, and the family is of paramount importance, with children adored and always a good talking point. At the same time they're an individualistic, proud people. But short of blatantly insulting someone, it's not easy to give offence. Disrespectful behavi-our – including excessively casual dress – in churches won't go down well, though.

Everywhere in Spain, people like to look their best and take every opportunity to dress up well – though not often to the extent of a formal suit and tie. They know that foreigners don't go to quite the same lengths, but you may feel a little uncomfortable in an unfresh T-shirt, jeans and trainers in some restaurants or discos – and some of the latter wouldn't let you in, in any case.

Day, Night & Time

The Spanish attitude to time *is* more relaxed than in most Western cultures. But things that need a fixed time – trains, buses, cinemas, football matches – get one, and it's generally stuck to. Things that need to get done, get done. Waiters may not always be in a hurry, but they come before too long.

What's different is the daily timetable. The Spanish *tarde* (afternoon) doesn't really start till 4 pm or so and goes on till 9 pm or later. Shops and offices close from around 2 to 5 pm, then mostly open again till around 8 pm. In hot summer months people stay outside till very late at night, enjoying the coolness. At fiestas don't be surprised if you should see a merry-go-round packed with tiny children at 3 am. And of course Friday and Saturday nights, all year round, barely begin till midnight for those doing the rounds of bars and discos.

Siesta Contrary to popular belief, most Spaniards do not sleep in the afternoon. The siesta is generally devoted to a long, leisurely lunch and lingering conversation. Then again, if you've stayed out until 6 am...

RELIGION
Roman Catholicism

It's impossible not to notice the importance of the Roman Catholic church in Spain. So many of the country's great occasions are religious fiestas; so many of its most magnificent buildings are cathedrals or churches, lavishly adorned and lovingly tended by the faithful. The great majority of Spaniards have church baptisms, weddings and funerals. According to surveys, around 85% of them say they are Catholics. Spain has around 20,000 Catholic priests, over 15,000 monks and 50,000 nuns.

All this is hardly surprising in a country whose very existence is the result of a series of medieval anti-Muslim crusades, and which gave the world the Jesuits to fight the Protestant Counter-Reformation in the 16th century. Under Franco the church and state were so closely tied that the Vatican allowed the government to appoint Spanish bishops, while the government paid priests' salaries and granted the church numerous other privileges, including lots of money. The government still subsidises the church heavily, and one-sixth of schools are still run by religious orders and groups, even though Spain has had no official religion since 1978.

Yet the church's hold is slipping in the face of modern distractions and opposition. Only some 40% of Spaniards now go to church once a month or more, and those who do go are increasingly old, poor and rural. The numbers of priests, monks and nuns are all falling.

Spain has a long-standing anticlerical tradition too, originating in the 19th century when the church became identified with conservative opposition to any form of liberal or revolutionary political change. Liberal and left-wing movements were often accompanied by church-burnings and killings of priests, monks and nuns. This reached a bloody crescendo in the civil war, when some 7000 were killed.

Nevertheless, so deeply is Catholicism

Opus Dei

Though the lay Catholic organisation Opus Dei (Work of God) hasn't had quite the influence on post-Franco Spain that it did during the dictatorship, it remains powerful in areas like the media, education and business. Founded in 1928 by an Aragonese, Josemaría Escrivá (1902-75), Opus Dei now has members in 80 countries around the world. Its basic philosophy is salvation through work. Escrivá noticed that economic progress tended to turn people away from Catholicism, and attempted to reverse this by inspiring Catholics with a new ethic of work and self-reliance, concentrating Opus Dei's efforts in influential areas like higher education, in a successful effort to gain support among the country's elite.

Though the organisation sees itself as nonpolitical, it is religiously conservative – with a strong emphasis on confession, for instance – and its philosophy lends itself to conservative capitalist economic policies. Opus Dei members and supporters were at the forefront of Spain's 1960s economic takeoff under Franco. Partly because of its rather clandestine nature, the fellowship is the subject of all sorts of conspiracy theories among people at the other end of the political spectrum.

Senior members of Opus Dei live in communities, take vows of poverty, chastity and obedience and practise self-mortification, yet they do normal (often senior) jobs in the outside world and don't wear any kind of special clothing. They hand over most of their often large earnings to their communities. Only a few are priests.

Opus Dei runs its own university – the Estudio General de Navarra near Pamplona – and a business school in Barcelona. For more on Opus Dei, see the Torreciudad section in the Aragón chapter. ■

ingrained in the Spanish way of life that men who hardly ever go to church vie for membership of the brotherhoods that carry holy images round the streets in Easter processions, while thousands of less than pious folk take part in giant pilgrimages to holy sites and other religion-based fiestas. The early 20th century philosopher Miguel Unamuno's quip, 'Here in Spain we are all Catholics, even the atheists', is still largely true.

Other Faiths

Protestantism was eradicated by the Inquisition in the 16th century before it could even get a toehold. Today there are only around 60,000 active Protestants in Spain, many of those in Cataluña. The Jehovah's Witnesses are one of the leading Protestant churches.

Muslims and Jews played enormous roles in medieval Spain but were stamped on at the end of that period (see History). Today Spain has around 150,000 to 200,000 Muslims, half of whom are in the North African enclaves, Ceuta and Melilla. Most of the others are Muslim immigrants, though there are perhaps 1000 native-born converts, many of them living in Granada's old Muslim quarter, the Albaicín.

The Jewish community numbers about 15,000, many of whom have come from Morocco. Franco, despite his anti-Jewish stance, did permit Jewish refugees to enter Spain in WWII, and in 1982 Sephardic Jews (Jews of Spanish origin) were officially invited to return to Spain, 490 years after their expulsion by the Catholic Monarchs.

LANGUAGE

Spanish, or Castilian (*castellano*), as it is often and more precisely called, is spoken throughout Spain, but there are also three widely spoken regional languages: Catalan (*català*; another Romance language, with close ties to French) is spoken in Cataluña, the Balearic Islands and Valencia; Galician (*galego*; similar enough to Portuguese to be regarded by some as a dialect) is spoken in Galicia; and Basque (*euskara*; of obscure,

non-Latin origin) is spoken in the País Vasco and Navarra.

English isn't as widely spoken as many travellers seem to expect. It's much easier to find people who speak at least some English in the main cities and tourist areas, but generally you'll be better received if you at least try to communicate in Spanish.

Spanish

Pronunciation Pronunciation of Spanish is not difficult, given that many Spanish sounds are similar to their English counterparts, and there is a clear and consistent relationship between pronunciation and spelling. If you stick to the following rules you should have very few problems in being understood.

Vowels Unlike English, each of the vowels in Spanish has a uniform pronunciation which does not vary. For example, the Spanish letter 'a' has one pronunciation rather than the numerous pronunciations we find in English, such as the 'a' in 'cake', 'cat', 'cart' and 'call'. Many Spanish words have a written accent. This acute accent (as in *días*) indicates a stressed syllable; it doesn't change the sound of the vowel. Vowels are pronounced clearly even if they are in unstressed positions or at the end of a word.

a   somewhere between the 'a' in 'cat' and the 'a' in 'cart'
e   like the 'e' in 'met'
i   somewhere between the 'i' sound in 'marine' and the 'i' in 'flip'
o   similar to the 'o' in 'hot'
u   like the 'u' in 'put'

Consonants Some Spanish consonants are the same as their English counterparts. The pronunciation of other consonants varies according to which vowel follows and also according to which part of Spain you happen to be in. The Spanish alphabet also contains the letter 'ñ', which is not found within the English alphabet. Until recently, the clusters 'ch' and 'll' were also officially separate consonants, and you're likely to encounter many situations – eg in lists and dictionaries – in which they are still treated that way.

b   soft; also (less commonly) like the 'b' in 'book' when initial or preceded by a nasal such as **m** or **n**

c   a hard 'c' as in 'cat' when followed by **a**, **o**, **u** or a consonant; like the 'th' in 'thin' before **e** or **i**

ch   like the 'ch' in choose

d   like the 'd' in 'dog' when initial or preceded by **l** or **n**; elsewhere as the 'th' in 'then'

g   like the 'g' in 'gate' when initial or before **a**, **o** or **u**; elsewhere much softer. Before **e** or **i** it's a harsh, breathy sound, similar to the 'ch' in Scottish 'loch'

h   always silent

j   a harsh, guttural sound similar to the 'ch' in Scottish 'loch'

ll   usually, rather like the 'y' in 'yellow'

ñ   a nasal sound like the 'ni' in 'onion'

q   'q' is always followed by a silent **u** and one of the vowels **e** (as in *que*) and **i** (as in *aquí*); the combined sound of 'qu' is like the 'k' in 'kick'

r   a rolled 'r' sound; longer and stronger when initial or doubled

s   like the 's' in 'send'

v   same as **b**

x   like the 'x' in 'taxi' when between two vowels; like the 's' in 'say' when preceding a consonant

z   like the 'th' in 'thin'

Semiconsonant Spanish also has the semiconsonant 'y'. This is pronounced as the Spanish 'i' when it's at the end of a word or when it stands alone as a conjunction. As a consonant, its sound is somewhere between the 'y' in 'yonder' and the 'g' in 'beige', depending on the region.

Greetings & Civilities

Hello.	*¡Hola!*
Goodbye.	*¡Adiós!*
Yes.	*Sí.*
No.	*No.*
Please.	*Por favor.*
Thank you.	*Gracias.*
That's fine/ You're welcome.	*De nada.*
Excuse me.	*Perdón/Perdone.*
Sorry/Excuse me.	*Lo siento/ Discúlpeme.*

Useful Phrases

Do you speak English?
  ¿Habla inglés?
Does anyone speak English?
  ¿Hay alguien que hable inglés?
I (don't) understand.
  (No) Entiendo.
Just a minute.
  Un momento.
Please write that down.
  ¿Puede escribirlo, por favor?
How much is it?
  ¿Cuánto cuesta?/¿Cuánto vale?

Getting Around

What time does the ... leave/arrive?
  ¿A qué hora sale/llega el ... ?

next	*próximo*
first	*primer*

Signs

BUS STATION	*ESTACIÓN DE AUTOBUSES*
CAMPING GROUND	*CAMPING/ZONA DE ACAMPADA*
ENTRANCE	*ENTRADA*
EXIT	*SALIDA*
FULL	*OCUPADO/ COMPLETO*
GUESTHOUSE	*PENSIÓN/CASA DE HUÉSPEDES*
HOTEL	*HOTEL*
INFORMATION	*INFORMACIÓN*
OPEN/CLOSED	*ABIERTO/CERRADO*
POLICE	*POLICÍA*
PROHIBITED	*PROHIBIDO*
ROOMS AVAILABLE	*HABITACIONES LIBRES*
TOILETS	*SERVICIOS/ASEOS*
TRAIN STATION	*ESTACIÓN (DE FERROCARRIL)*
YOUTH HOSTEL	*ALBERGUE JUVENIL*

last	*último*
the boat	*el barco*
the bus (city)	*el autobús/el bus*
the bus (intercity)	*el autocar*
the train	*el tren*
the metro/underground	*el metro*

I would like ...	*Quisiera ...*
a one-way ticket	*un billete sencillo*
a return ticket	*un billete de ida y vuelta*

1st class	*primera clase*
2nd class	*segunda clase*

Where is the bus stop?
¿Dónde está la parada de autobús?
I want to go to ...
Quiero ir a ...
Can you show me (on the map)?
¿Me puede indicar (en el mapa)?
far/near
lejos/cerca
Go straight ahead.
Siga/Vaya todo derecho.
Turn left.
Gire a la izquierda.
Turn right.
Gire a la derecha.

Around Town

I'm looking for ...	*Estoy buscando ...*
a bank	*un banco*
the city centre	*el centro de la ciudad*
the ... embassy	*la embajada ...*
my hotel	*mi hotel*
the market	*el mercado*
the police	*la policía*
the post office	*los correos*
public toilets	*los servicios/ aseos públicos*
the telephone centre	*la central telefónica*
the tourist office	*la oficina de turismo*

the beach	*la playa*
the bridge	*el puente*

the castle	*el castillo*
the cathedral	*la catedral*
the church	*la iglesia*
the hospital	*el hospital*
the lake	*el lago*
the main square	*la plaza mayor*
the mosque	*la mezquita*
the old city	*la ciudad antigua/ el casco antiguo*
the palace	*el palacio*
the ruins	*las ruinas*
the sea	*el mar*
the square	*la plaza*
the tower	*el torre*

Accommodation

Where is a cheap hotel?
¿Dónde hay un hotel barato?
What is the address?
¿Cuál es la dirección?
Could you write the address, please?
¿Puede escribir la dirección, por favor?
Do you have any rooms available?
¿Tiene habitaciones libres?

I would like ...	*Quisiera ...*
a single room	*una habitación individual*
a double room	*una habitación doble*
a room with bathroom	*una habitación con baño*
to share a dorm	*compartir un dormitorio*
a bed	*una cama*

How much is it per night/per person?
¿Cuánto cuesta por noche/por persona?
Can I see it?
¿Puedo verla?
Where is the bathroom?
¿Dónde está el baño?

Food

breakfast	*desayuno*
lunch	*almuerzo/comida*
dinner	*cena*

I would like the set lunch.
Quisiera el menú del día.

Is service included in the bill?
¿El servicio está incluido en la cuenta?
I am a vegetarian.
Soy vegetariano/vegetariana (m/f).

Time & Dates

What time is it?	*¿Qué hora es?*
today	*hoy*
tomorrow	*mañana*
in the morning	*de la mañana*
in the afternoon	*de la tarde*
in the evening	*de la noche*
Monday	*lunes*
Tuesday	*martes*
Wednesday	*miércoles*
Thursday	*jueves*
Friday	*viernes*
Saturday	*sábado*
Sunday	*domingo*
January	*enero*
February	*febrero*
March	*marzo*
April	*abril*
May	*mayo*
June	*junio*
July	*julio*
August	*agosto*
September	*setiembre/septiembre*
October	*octubre*
November	*noviembre*
December	*diciembre*

Health

I'm...	*Soy...*
diabetic	*diabético/a*
epileptic	*epiléptico/a*
asthmatic	*asmático/a*

I'm allergic to antibiotics/penicillin.
Soy alérgico/a a los antibióticos/la penicilina.

antiseptic	*antiséptico*
aspirin	*aspirina*
condoms	*preservativos/ condones*
contraceptive	*anticonceptivo*
diarrhoea	*diarrea*
medicine	*medicamento*
nausea	*náusea*
sunblock cream	*crema protectora contra el sol*
tampons	*tampones*

Emergencies

Help!	*¡Socorro! ¡Auxilio!*
Call a doctor!	*¡Llame a un doctor!*
Call the police!	*¡Llame a la policía!*
Go away!	*¡Vete!*

Numbers

0	*cero*
1	*uno, una*
2	*dos*
3	*tres*
4	*cuatro*
5	*cinco*
6	*seis*
7	*siete*
8	*ocho*
9	*nueve*
10	*diez*
11	*once*
12	*doce*
13	*trece*
14	*catorce*
15	*quince*
16	*dieciséis*
17	*diecisiete*
18	*dieciocho*
19	*diecinueve*
20	*veinte*
21	*veintiuno*
30	*treinta*
31	*treinta y uno*
40	*cuarenta*
41	*cuarenta y uno*
50	*cincuenta*
60	*sesenta*
70	*setenta*
80	*ochenta*
90	*noventa*
100	*cien/ciento*
1000	*mil*
one million	*un millón*

Basque

The Basque language is one of the oldest in the world, and a key to primitive Europe. It's the oldest surviving pre-Indo-European language in Europe; Hungarian and Finnish arrived considerably later. In a territory straddling France and Spain, and divided by the Pyrenees, Basque is spoken by 800,000 of the 2.4 million people who live in the territory known in Basque as Euskadi.

Pronunciation An English-speaker shouldn't have many difficulties with Basque pronunciation. There are no written accents, and stress is flexible. Vowels are pronounced as in Castilian. There are two distinct 'r' sounds to be aware of: one, much as the English 'r' when at the beginning or middle of a word; and the other, like a cross between the Scottish 'r' and the growl of a two-stroke motorbike: 'r-r-r-r-r-r'. Consonants are pronounced as in English with the exception of the following:

g	always hard, as in 'goat'
h	silent in the País Vasco; as in English in French Basque Country
rr	the growly 'r'
tx/ts	like the 'ch' in 'chew'
tz	like the 'tz' in 'tzetze'
x	like the 'sh' in 'ship'
z	like the 's' in 'sun'

Basics

Hi!	*Kaixo!*
Good morning.	*Egunon.*
Good night.	*Gabon.*
Goodbye.	*Agur.*
See you later.	*Gero arte.*
Please.	*Mesedez.*
Thank you.	*Eskerrik asko.*
Excuse me.	*Parkatu.*

How do you say that in Basque?
  Nola esaten da hori euskaraz?

Finding Your Way

Where's the toilet, please?
  Non dago komuna, mesedez?

At the end.	*Azkenean.*
Straight ahead.	*Zuzen-zuzenian.*
On the left.	*Ezkerretara.*
On the right.	*Eskuinetara.*

Small Talk

How are you?	*Zer moduz?*
Very well, thanks.	*Oso ongi, eskerrik asko.*
What's your name?	*Nola duzu izena?*
I'm called John.	*Nire izena Jon da.*
Where are you from?	*Nongoa zara?*
I'm from …	*Ni … naiz.*

Food

Waiter!	*Aizan!* (f)
	Aizak! (m)
I'd like …	*… nahi nuke.*
A little bread, please.	*Ogi piska bat, mesedez.*
A bottle of wine.	*Botila bat ardo.*
A beer.	*Garagardo bat.*
Beefsteak with chips.	*Xerra patata frijituekin.*
water	*ura*
mineral water	*metalura*
fish	*arraina*
vegetables	*barazkiak*

Catalan

Catalan is one of the Romance, or neo-Latin, languages, like French, Italian, Portuguese, Romanian and Spanish. It is not a dialect of any other language and its nearest relative is Occitan, spoken colloquially in southern France. It is the mother tongue of up to seven million people, most of whom also speak at least one other language. It is spoken, with various local dialect variations, in Cataluña, most of Valencia, the Balearic Islands, the strip of Aragón that borders Cataluña, Andorra, Roussillon (in France), and in and around L'Alguer (Alghero) in Sardinia.

Letters are pronounced approximately as in English with the following exceptions.

a	when stressed, as the 'a' in 'father'; when unstressed, as in 'about'
b	pronounced 'p' at the end of a word

c	hard before **a**, **o** and **u**; soft before **e** and **i**
ç	like 'ss'
d	pronounced 't' at the end of a word
g	hard before **a**, **o** and **u**; before **e** and **i**, like the 's' in 'measure'
h	always silent
i	like the 'i' in 'machine'
j	like the 's' in 'pleasure'
o	when stressed, as in 'pot'; when unstressed, like the 'oo' in 'zoo'
r	as in English in the middle of a word; silent at the end of a word
rr	growly and rolled, like a Scottish 'r'
s	like the 's' in 'sun' at the beginning of a word; in the middle of a word, like the 'z' in 'zoo'
v	at the start of a word, like the 'b' in 'big'; elsewhere, as in English
x	mostly as in English but sometimes like the 'sh' in 'shoe'

There are a few odd letter combinations:

ll	like the 'y' in 'you'
l.l	like the 'll-l' in 'doll-like'
tx	like 'ch' in 'cheese'
gu	a hard 'g', as in 'goat'
qu	before **e** or **i**, like 'k'; otherwise, as in English
ig	at the end of a word, pronounced like the 'tch' in 'itch'

Basics

Hi!	*Hola!*
Good morning/ Goodbye.	*Bon dia.*
Good afternoon.	*Bona tarda.*
Good night.	*Bona nit.*
Goodbye.	*Adéu.*
See you later.	*A reveure.*
Please.	*Sisplau/Si us plau.*
Thank you.	*Gràcies.*
Thank you very much.	*Moltes gràcies.*
You're welcome.	*De res, company.*
Excuse me.	*Perdoni.*
today	*avui*
tomorrow	*demà*
How much is it?	*Quant val?*

How do you say that in Catalan?
Com es diu això en català?

Finding Your Way

Where's the toilet, please?
On és el lavabo, si us plau?

At the end.	*Al fons.*
On the left.	*A mà esquerra.*
On the right.	*A la dreta.*

Small Talk

I'd like you to meet ...	*Li presento ...*
Pleased to meet you.	*Molt de gust.*
Delighted!	*Encantat* (m)/ *Encantada* (f).
What's new?	*Què hi ha?*
How are you?	*Com esteu?*
Very well, thanks.	*Molt bé, gràcies.*
Take care.	*Passi-ho bé.*
What's your name?	*Com es diu?*
My name's ...	*Em dic ...*
I like ...	*M'agrada ...*
OK.	*Val/D'acord.*
Where are you from?	*D'on ets?*

I'm from the UK/the USA/New Zealand/
Australia.
Sóc de Anglaterra/América/Nova Zelanda/Austràlia.

Food

Catalan food is among the best in Spain. For names and descriptions of typical dishes, see the boxed aside in the Barcelona chapter.

Waiter!	*Cambrer!*
I'd like ...	*Voldira ...*
A little bread, please.	*Una mica de pa, si us plau.*
A drop of wine. (No byo here!)	*Un glop de vi.*
A bottle.	*Una ampolla.*
A beer.	*Una cervesa.*
I'm vegetarian.	*Soc vegetarià.*

Galician

The language of the natives of Galicia tends not to be promoted as vigorously as Basque or Catalan. Although signs in Galician (*galego* to the locals) have popped up all over the region, you will generally hear Castilian spoken, not Galician. As you get further off the beaten track, your chances of encountering people who prefer not to speak Castilian will grow. A close cousin of Portuguese, Galician is nevertheless distinct from its neighbour.

Basics

Please.	*Por favor.*
Thank you.	*Gracias/Graciñas.*
Excuse me/I'm sorry.	*Perdoa.*
open	*aberto*
closed	*pechado*

Useful Phrases

Do you speak English?
  ¿Falas inglés?

I don't understand.
  Non entendo.
Please write that down
  ¿Por favor, pódemo escribir?
What time does the bus/train arrive/leave?
  ¿A qué hora chega/sae o autobús/tren?
Where is a cheap hotel?
  ¿Onda hay un hotel/unha fonda?
I'm looking for ...
  Estou buscando ...
What is the address?
  ¿Cal é o enderezo?
What time is it?
  ¿Qué hora é?

Emergencies

Help!	*¡Socorro!*
Call a doctor!	*¡Chame un doctor/médico!*
Call the police!	*¡Chame a policia!*
Go away!	*¡Vaite!*

Facts for the Visitor

PLANNING

When to Go

Spain can be enjoyable any time of year. The *ideal* months to visit are May, June and September (plus April and October in the south). At these times you can rely on good to excellent weather, yet avoid the sometimes extreme heat – and the main crush of Spanish and foreign tourists – of July and August, when temperatures may climb to 45°C in inland Andalucía, and Madrid is unbearable and almost deserted.

But there's decent weather in some part of Spain virtually year-round. Winter along the southern and south-eastern Mediterranean coasts is mild, while in the height of summer you can retreat to the north-west, or to beaches or high mountains anywhere, if you need to get away from excessive heat elsewhere.

The best festivals are mostly concentrated between Semana Santa (the week leading up to Easter Sunday) and September/October. See this chapter's Public Holidays & Special Events section for info on some festivals you might like to plan your visit around.

If you plan to pursue some specific activity, you may need to choose your time carefully – see the Activities section of this chapter and destination sections in the regional chapters.

Maps

Small-Scale Maps Some of the best maps for travellers are published by Michelin, which produces a 1:1 million *Spain Portugal* map and six 1:400,000 regional maps covering the whole country. These are all pretty accurate, even down to the state of minor country roads, frequently updated, and detailed yet easy to read. The country map doesn't show railways, but the regional maps do. They're widely available in Spain if you don't manage to pick them up before you go. Also good are the GeoCenter maps published by Germany's RV Verlag. Like Michelin, RV Verlag produces a 1:1 million *España Portugal* map, and also divides the country into 10 regional sheets at a scale of 1:300,000.

Probably the best physical map of Spain is *Península Ibérica, Baleares y Canarias* published by the Instituto Geográfico Nacional (IGN). Ask for it in good bookshops or map shops.

Road Atlases See under Car & Motorcycle in the Getting Around chapter.

City Maps For finding your way around cities, the free maps handed out by tourist offices are often adequate. If you want something more comprehensive, most cities are covered by one or another of the Spanish series such as Telstar, Alpina and Everest, with street indexes – available in bookshops. But check their publication dates as some are rather out of date.

Large-Scale Maps Two organisations publish detailed close-up maps of small parts of Spain. The IGN covers the country in over 4000 1:25,000 (1 cm to 250 metres) sheets, most of which are fairly up to date. The IGN and the Servicio Cartográfico del Ejército (SCE, Army Cartographic Service) both publish a 1:50,000 series (over 1000 maps for the whole country); the SCE's tend to be more up to date but the IGN's are more oriented towards travellers and hikers.

Also useful for hiking and exploring small areas are the *Guía Cartográfica* and *Guía Excursionista y Turística* series published by Editorial Alpina. Covering most of the mountainous parts of the country (except the south), these series combine information booklets in Spanish (or sometimes Catalan) with detailed maps at scales ranging from 1:25,000 to 1:50,000. They're well worth their price (around 500 ptas), though the maps have their inaccuracies. The Institut Cartogràfic de Catalunya does good

1:50,000 maps for each of the 41 *comarcas* (districts) of Cataluña, but there's no equivalent of these for other parts of Spain.

Editorial Alpina publications and IGN and SCE maps are often available in town bookshops near hiking and trekking areas, but to be sure of obtaining them you're safest visiting a specialist map or travel bookshop such as La Tienda Verde in Madrid, or Altaïr or Quera in Barcelona. Some map specialists in other countries, such as Edward Stanford, 12-14 Long Acre, London WC2E 9LP, also have good ranges of Spain maps. The IGN (☎ 91-554 14 50), Calle General Ibáñez de Íbero 3, 28003 Madrid, can supply you with a free catalogue of its maps.

What to Bring
Bring as little as possible. Everything you bring, you have to carry. You can buy just about anything you need in Spain, in any case.

Luggage If you'll be doing any walking with your luggage, even just from stations to hotels and back, a backpack is the only sensible answer. A backpack whose straps and openings can be zipped inside a flap is more secure and less at risk of getting trapped in escalators, caught on door handles etc. If you'll be using taxis, or your own car, you might as well take whatever luggage is easiest to open and shut, unpack and pack. Either way, a small day pack is a useful addition.

Inscribing your name and address on the inside of your luggage, as well as labelling it on the outside, increases your chances of getting it back if it's lost or stolen. Packing things in plastic bags inside your backpack/suitcase is a good way of keeping them organised and – if it rains – dry.

Clothes & Shoes In high summer you may not need more than one layer of clothing even at 4 am. At cooler times, layers of thin clothing, which trap warm air and can be peeled off if necessary, are better than a single thick layer. See Climate in the Facts about the Country chapter for the kind of temperatures and rainfall you can expect on your trip. It's a good idea to pack a set of good clothes (something other than jeans and T-shirts) for some discos and smart restaurants – they don't have to be too formal, though.

You need a pair of strong shoes – even strong trainers – no matter what type of trip you're making. You'll probably also appreciate having a lighter pair sometimes. And if you plan on going to smart discos or restaurants, you'll need something other than trainers. If you can combine these requirements into two pairs or even one, you'll save space in your luggage!

Useful Items Apart from any special personal needs, or things you might require for particular kinds of trips (camping gear, hiking boots, surfboard etc), consider the following:

- an under-the-clothes money belt or shoulder wallet, useful for protecting your money and documents in cities
- a towel and soap, often lacking in cheap accommodation
- sunscreen lotion, which can be more expensive in Spain than elsewhere
- a small Spanish dictionary and/or phrasebook
- books, which can be expensive, and hard to find outside main cities and tourist resorts
- photocopies of your important documents, kept separate from the originals
- a Swiss army knife
- minimal unbreakable cooking, eating and drinking gear if you plan to prepare your own food and drinks
- a medical kit (see Health)
- a padlock or two to secure your luggage to racks and to lock hostel lockers
- a sleeping sheet to save on sheet rental costs if you're using youth hostels (a sleeping bag is unlikely to be particularly useful unless you're camping)
- an adapter plug for electrical appliances
- a torch (flashlight)
- an alarm clock
- sunglasses
- binoculars if you plan to do any wildlife spotting

SUGGESTED ITINERARIES
Where you should go depends entirely on what you like doing. Every part of Spain has

its own compelling claims to be visited. Nor does it matter much in which order you take your chosen destinations – Spain is easy enough to travel around for you to make up your itinerary as you go.

The basic choice is between a wide-ranging tour that takes you to as many varied parts of the country as you can manage, or a narrower focus on a smaller number of places to explore in greater depth. Following are a few highlights to help you start planning. Also check the Flora & Fauna section in the Facts about the Country chapter, and the Public Holidays & Special Events and Activities sections of this chapter, for further ideas on places and events you might like to work into your timetable.

Cities & Towns

Madrid and Barcelona are obviously the most vibrant cities, with the most to see and do. They're a strong contrast and as close to essential as anywhere for giving you a feel for the country.

Sevilla, with its exciting southern atmosphere, isn't far behind the 'big two' for excitement and introduces you to the distinctive region of Andalucía. Other cities and towns with a particularly strong pull include Santiago de Compostela and Pontevedra in Galicia; San Sebastián in the País Vasco; Segovia, Ávila, Salamanca, León, Toledo and Cuenca in the old Castilian heartland; Trujillo in Extremadura; Valencia on the Mediterranean coast; and Granada and Ronda in Andalucía.

Coasts

The Costa Brava in Cataluña is rugged enough not to have been completely overwhelmed by tourist development and still secretes many pretty coves, villages and beaches. The Balearic Islands have many fine, isolated little beaches, especially on Ibiza and Formentera, while Mallorca's cliff-strewn north coast is one of the most spectacular in the country. Cabo de Gata in eastern Andalucía is strung with excellent, isolated, and by Spanish standards under-populated beaches, backed by some fine,

rugged coastal scenery. The Costa de la Luz on Andalucía's Atlantic coast has more good beaches and is relatively underdeveloped; Tarifa at its southern end is one of Europe's top windsurfing centres.

In Galicia, the Rías Bajas and Rías Altas are two series of majestic estuaries not unlike the Norwegian fjords, dotted with good beaches, fishing villages and low-key resorts. Spain's most awesome coastal scenery is to be found here too. On the Bay of Biscay coast are the country's best surf beaches and, at San Sebastián, probably its most beautiful city beach.

Countryside & Wilderness

The Pyrenees, especially in Cataluña and Aragón, are strung with imposing peaks and lovely valleys. Two of the best areas to head for are the national parks: Aigüestortes i Estany de Sant Maurici in Cataluña, and Ordesa y Monte Perdido in Aragón.

In the north-west, the Picos de Europa range, which straddles Cantabria, Asturias and Castilla y León, is justly famous for its wild and beautiful mountain scenery. Galicia is Spain's greenest area – rolling countryside abutting a dramatic coast.

In the central west, the Sierra de Gredos and its western offshoots such as the Sierra de Peña de Francia contain further impressive ranges and charming, rather remote valleys such as those of La Vera and the Jerte and Ambroz rivers in northern Extremadura. There's yet more impressive mountainous terrain in the Serranía de Cuenca area on the borders of Castilla-La Mancha and Aragón, and in Mallorca's Serra de Tramuntana.

In Andalucía, the mountains around Ronda, the Alpujarras valleys south of the Sierra Nevada, and the sierras of Cazorla and Segura east of Baeza stand out for their beauty, while the semidesert scenery east of Almería is weird enough to have been used as the setting for dozens of Western movies.

THE BEST & THE WORST

It's tough trying to pick just 10 of the best things about Spain. In fact, as the list below shows, we haven't quite managed it. These are our personal favourites, the places and activities the authors of this book would most like to dedicate a lot more of their time to:

1 Sevilla (except in July and August)
2 The Rías of Galicia
3 Valencia's mid-March Las Fallas festival
4 The Picos de Europa
5 Parc Nacional Aigüestortes i Estany de Sant Maurici, Cataluña
6 Beaches, bars and discos of the Balearic Islands
7 Cabo de Gata
8 Madrid nightlife
9 Granada
10 Toledo and
    White Andalucían villages at night (equal)

Thinking of things we don't like about Spain is a lot harder, but we'd be quite content never to experience any of the following again:

1 Albacete
2 The Costa del Sol
3 Benidorm
4 Spanish bureaucracy (don't tangle with it!)
5 Reinosa, Cantabria
6 Spanish motorbike noise
7 Callos (tripe – a popular food item)
8 Beach wear on the Costa Blanca
9 The 'Costa Plástica' – vast areas around Almería covered in plastic sheeting for forced vegetable cultivation
10 Heavy industry around Bilbao

TOURIST OFFICES

All the big cities and many smaller towns have what is generally called an *oficina de turismo* or *oficina de información turística*. In provincial capitals you'll sometimes find more than one office – one specialising in information on the city alone, the other carrying mostly provincial or regional information. There seems, however, to be no set rule on this division of labour.

Opening hours vary widely, as does the quality of the information. There are times when you could swear these people are paid not to tell you anything, but happily this is more of an exception than the rule. If you can see stacks of brochures and pamphlets on shelves behind the counter and have some

idea of what you're after, it is always worth while pointing these out and being insistent. Sometimes it's all irrelevant stuff on distant regions, but occasionally it's the useful local stuff they couldn't be bothered reaching back to retrieve for you.

Tourist Offices Abroad

Information is available from the following branches of the Oficina Nacional Española de Turismo abroad:

Argentina
    Avenida Florida 744, 1°, 1005 Buenos Aires (☎ 01-322 7264)
Austria
    Rotenturmstrasse 27, 1010 Vienna-I (☎ 0222-535 3191)
Belgium
    Rue de la Montagne 18, 1000 Brussels (☎ 02-512 5735)
Brazil
    Rua Zequinha de Abreu 78, Cep 01250 São Paulo (☎ 011-655999)
Canada
    102 Bloor St West, 14th Floor, Toronto, Ontario M5S 1M8 (☎ 416-961 3131)
Denmark
    Store Kongensgade 1-3, 1264 Copenhagen (☎ 33 15 11 65)
Finland
    Mecgelininkatu 12-14, 00100 Helsinki (☎ 90-441 992)
France
    43ter Ave Pierre 1er de Serbie, 75381 Paris, Cedex 08 (☎ 01 47 23 37 75)
Italy
    Piazza di Spagna 55, Rome 00187 (☎ 06-679 8272)
    Piazza del Carmine 4, 20121 Milan (☎ 02-72 00 46 12)
Germany
    Kurfürstendamm 180, W1000 Berlin 15 (☎ 030-8 82 60 36)
    Graf Adolfstrasse 81, Düsseldorf 1 (☎ 0211-3 70 47 67)
    Myliusstrasse 14, 6000 Frankfurt/Main 1 (☎ 069-72 50 33)
    Schubertstrasse 10, 8000 Munich 15 (☎ 089-5 38 90 75)
Japan
    Daini Toranomon Denki Bldg 4F, 3-1-10 Toranomon, Minato Ku, Tokyo 105 (☎ 03-34 32 61 44)
Netherlands
    Laan Van Meerdervoort 8-8a, 2517 Gravenhague, The Hague (☎ 070-346 59 00)

Norway
    Ruselökkveien 26, 0251 Oslo-2 (☎ 22 83 40 92)
Portugal
    Avenida Fontes Pereira de Melo 51-4° andar,
    D1000 Lisbon (☎ 01-354 1992)
Sweden
    Grev Turegatan 7-1TR, 114-46 Stockholm
    (☎ 08-611 41 36)
Switzerland
    40 Blvd Helvétique, 67 Rue du Rhône, Geneva
    1207 (☎ 022-735 9594)
    Seefeldstrasse 19, CH 8008 Zürich
    (☎ 01-252 7930/1)
UK
    57-58 St James's St, London SW1A 1LD
    (☎ 0171-499 1169)
USA
    665 Fifth Ave, New York, NY 10022
    (☎ 212-759 8822)
    8383 Wilshire Blvd, Suite 960, Beverly Hills,
    Los Angeles, CA 90211 (☎ 213-658 7188)
    Water Tower Place, Suite 915, East 845 North
    Michigan Ave, Chicago, IL 60611
    (☎ 312-642 1992)
    1221 Brickell Ave, Miami, FL 33131
    (☎ 305-358 1992)

VISAS & DOCUMENTS
Passport
Citizens of the 15 European Union member
states can travel to Spain with their national
identity cards alone. People from EU countries that do not issue ID cards, such as the
UK, must have a valid passport. UK Visitor
passports are not acceptable in Spain. All
non-EU nationals must have a full valid
passport.

If you've had the passport for awhile,
check that the expiry date is at least some
months off, otherwise you may not be
granted a visa (should you need one). If you
travel a lot, keep an eye on the number of
pages you have left in the passport. US consulates will generally insert extra pages into
your passport if you need them, but others
tend to require you to apply for a new passport. If your passport is nearly full when you
are preparing to leave home and you are
likely to have this trouble, do yourself a
favour and get a new one before you leave.

Bear in mind that by law you are supposed
to have your ID card (or passport) with you
at all times in Spain. It doesn't happen often,
but it could be embarrassing if you are asked

by the police to produce a document and you
don't have it with you. You will always need
one of these documents for police registration when you take a hotel room.

Visas
For visits to Spain of up to 90 days, the
nationals of many countries require no visa
at all. Those who do need a visa can find the
process a little irritating. With the imple-
mentation of the Schengen Agreement in
April 1995, the situation has, if anything,
become more confusing.

Spain, along with Portugal, France,
Germany, the Netherlands, Belgium and
Luxembourg, forms part of the new border-
free travel zone known as the Schengen
Area. Italy and Greece are expected to join
at a later date. Travel *between* these countries
normally entails no passport control on land
frontiers, at ports or in airports, although spot
checks are always possible. A common
police data bank has been established, and to
compensate for the dropping of internal controls, vigilance at all non-Schengen frontiers
and for flights and vessels arriving from
non-Schengen countries (including other EU
countries) has been tightened, as have the
visa requirements. Extraordinarily, the seven
member countries have *not* standardised
their lists of countries whose nationals
require visas to enter. The resulting situation
is farcical.

Among those who need no visa for any
Schengen country are citizens of the non-
Schengen EU countries, the USA, New
Zealand, Japan, Israel, Switzerland and
Norway. Among those who require one for
Spain, but not necessarily the other
Schengen countries, are Australians and
South Africans (including those resident in
another EU country *not* party to the
Schengen Agreement). Residents of one
Schengen country do *not* require a visa for
another Schengen country.

Possession of a visa for any Schengen
state allows travel to *all* other Schengen
countries.

Now comes the ridiculous part. The Australian traveller who, for argument's sake,

wants to tour around several European countries, including Spain (or France, where Australians also require a visa), often has only a vague notion of where and when he or she wants to go. That traveller does not need a visa to enter the other Schengen countries. So what is to stop said traveller going first to, say, the Netherlands, and then proceeding without a visa to Spain and/or France (by air or land)? The short answer is: nothing. The obvious idiocy of this aspect of a system that has taken years to 'perfect' is breathtaking. Although the official line is that a traveller requiring a visa for one of the Schengen countries should not be naughty and use this 'loophole', the temptation is great.

That said, it should be noted that at the time of writing France had reimposed some border controls in a fairly feeble effort to keep potential Algerian terrorists out. And all countries reserve the right to make random spot checks.

Many Australians report being able to cross into France from non-Schengen neighbours Italy and Switzerland without having their passports checked. This is often the case, but you can't count on it. If you have no luck at one crossing point, you could always try another. Again, once inside France you might technically be able to cross into Spain undetected, should you wish to take the risk.

Deportation Travellers who need a visa and are discovered entering Spain without one can be deported. You'd be unlucky to be caught on crossing Spain's land borders, although checks on trains, including the Lisbon-Madrid run, *do* occur. Your chances of slipping past unnoticed at airports are zero. Take this seriously, as travellers have been bundled onto planes and sent back to the country they flew from.

Coming from Morocco Spain's main non-Schengen frontier is with Morocco. It is unlikely you will get into Spain's North African enclaves of Ceuta or Melilla without a Spanish visa (if you are supposed to have one); even the Moroccan border guards will ask if you have a visa to enter Spain. Even should you manage to slip into Ceuta or Melilla without one, you are still not home and hosed, as passports are generally checked again when you head on to the Iberian Peninsula.

You may well be able to get onto a boat from Tangier (Morocco) to Algeciras, and certainly to Gibraltar. Again, if you ordinarily require a visa for Spain, you are taking a risk. Passports are generally quite closely checked by the Spaniards on arrival at Algeciras, and you could find yourself being sent back to Morocco. If you go via Gibraltar, you may just sneak across La Línea without having your passport checked – but don't bank on it.

Types of Schengen Visa There are several types of Schengen visa. Various transit visas allow you to cross the Schengen Area in order to reach a non-Schengen country. One version of this covers air transit.

Of interest to travellers are the 30-day and 90-day visas. At the Spanish embassy in London they cost £14.40 and £28.80, respectively. The longer visa usually entitles you to three entries, and you are allowed to apply for only one 90 day visa in any six month period. Check and compare prices and validity periods with those of the French version if you are going to France too. Each country sets its own prices depending on length of validity, so compare to get the best value.

You need to fill in an application form and provide four passport-sized photos. If you are resident in the country where you apply and do so in person, the process should take 24 to 48 hours (it's never completed the same day). Postal applications should include a self-addressed envelope stamped for registered mail.

If you apply for the visa in a country where you are *not* resident, the process can be lengthy. Your request may be forwarded to Madrid, and a reply could take weeks. In addition you may be asked to present tickets for onward or return flights, evidence of hotel accommodation and solvency, or even an invitation from someone in Spain. Finally, it is unlikely you will be given the option of the 90 day, three entry visa.

Visa Extensions & Residence Nationals of EU countries, as well as Norway and Iceland, can virtually (if not technically) enter and leave Spain at will. Those wanting to reside and work in Spain for longer than 90 days can apply for a *permiso de residencia* during the first month of their stay. The bureaucracy involved in getting the residence permit can be trying, although not nearly as much as in pre-EU days. You will need a work contract in Spain or proof of adequate funds to support yourself. With the former, the process is long but the outcome assured. Your *tarjeta de residencia* (resident's card) entitles you to five years residence. Arm yourself with lots of photocopies of work contracts, passport pages, bank statements and passport-sized photos. You will have to go the *comisaría*, or police HQ, of the town you intend to stay in; count on making several visits.

Other nationals in Spain with work contracts or on one year study programmes and the like can expect to go through similar hoops, but in most cases the initial application has to be made at the Spanish consulate in your present country of residence. It is wise to enquire at a Spanish consulate about what you may require prior to arriving in Spain.

Non-EU spouses of EU citizens resident in Spain can apply for residence too. The process is lengthy, and those needing to travel in and out of the country in the meantime could ask for an *exención de visado* – a visa exemption. In most cases, the spouse is obliged to make the formal application in his/her country of residence. A real pain.

Photocopies
It is a wise precaution to keep photocopies of all the data pages of your passport and any other identity cards, and even your birth certificate if you can manage it. This will help speed up replacement if the originals are lost or stolen. If your passport is stolen or lost, notify the police and obtain a statement,

and then contact your embassy or consulate as soon as possible.

Other worthwhile things to photocopy include airline tickets, travel insurance documents with emergency international medical aid numbers, credit cards (and international phone numbers in case of card loss), driving licence, vehicle documentation and any employment or educational qualifications you may need if you are considering work or study. Keep all of this, and a list of the serial numbers of your travellers' cheques, somewhere separate from the originals. Leave extra copies of all this stuff with someone reliable at home.

Some spare cash tucked away into a money belt, stuffed into a pair of socks or otherwise concealed could come in very handy if you lose your wallet, purse and/or money pouch.

Travel Insurance
Don't, as they say, leave home without it. You may never need it, but you'll be glad you've got it if you get into trouble. These papers, and the international medical aid numbers that generally accompany them, are valuable documents, so treat them like air tickets and passports. Keep the details (photocopies or handwritten) in a separate part of your luggage. See the Health section of this chapter for more on travel insurance.

Driving Licence & Vehicle Papers
EU licences (pink or pink and green) are fully recognised in all member states of the Union, including Spain, as of July 1996. Other foreign licences are supposed to be accompanied by an International Driving Permit (although in practice, for renting cars or dealing with traffic police, your national licence will suffice). The International Driving Permit is available from automobile clubs in your country and is valid for 12 months. If you are driving your own vehicle, you will require its registration papers and an International Insurance Certificate (or Green Card). Your third party insurance company will issue this. For further details, see the Car

& Motorcycle section in the Getting There & Away chapter.

Hostelling Card
A valid HI hostelling card is required in pretty much all the HI youth hostels in Spain. You can get this in your home country or at offices in Spain. Some hostels can issue one on the spot. Otherwise, the TIVE youth travel organisation, which has offices in many of Spain's regional and some provincial capitals (see Useful Organisations for details of its Madrid head office), can issue one to foreigners for 1800 ptas.

Student, Teacher & Youth Cards
An ISIC (International Student Identity Card) or similar card will get you discounted entry prices into some museums and other sights, and is of course an asset in the search for cheap flights out of Spain. It can also come in handy for such things as cinema and theatre and other travel discounts.

The fake student card business is alive and well, and some travel agents will even issue cards with certain discounted air tickets without asking to see any proof of student status.

More legitimately, the cards are available from many student and budget travel offices, including the following:

Australia
    Student Services Australia, 1st Floor, 20 Faraday St, Carlton, Vic 3053 (☎ 03-9348 1777)
Canada
    Travel Cuts, 187 College St, Toronto (☎ 416-977 3703)
    Voyages Campus, Université McGill, 3480 Rue McTavish, Montreal (☎ 514-398 0647)
UK
    Cards are best obtained from STA Travel and Campus Travel offices (see under Air in the Getting There & Away chapter)
USA
    CIEE, 205 East 42nd St, New York, NY 10017 (☎ 212-822 2600)
    CIEE, 10904 Lindbrook Dve, Los Angeles, CA 90024 (☎ 310-208 3551)
    CIEE, 530 Bush St, San Francisco, 94108 (☎ 415-421 3473)

There are also similar cards for teachers

(ITIC). They are good for various discounts and also carry a travel insurance component.

If you're aged under 26 but not a student you can apply for a GO25 card issued by the Federation of International Youth Travel Organisations (FIYTO) or a Euro26 card (in the UK known as the Under 26 Card), both of which give much the same discounts as an ISIC. They don't automatically entitle you to discounts everywhere, but you won't find out until you flash the card. The head office of FIYTO is in Denmark, at Islands Brygge 81, DK-2300 Copenhagen S, where you can write to request a brochure. Otherwise, the organisations listed above for the USA and Canada will issue GO25 and Euro26 cards. Both types of card are also issued by student unions, hostelling organisations and some youth travel agencies (such as Campus Travel in the UK). TIVE in Madrid (☎ 91-347 77 00; see Useful Organisations for the address) issues GO25 and Euro26 cards for 700 ptas.

You can also obtain a Carnet Joven Europeo, or European Youth Card, in Madrid. This is also for under-26s, costs 1000 ptas and can be used for discounts in museums, theatres, cinemas and sports centres, as well as for reductions on air and rail tickets, throughout Spain and in some other European countries. You do not need to be a Spanish citizen to obtain it, and you can do so in Madrid at the Consejería de Educación y Cultura (☎ 91-580 41 96), Calle de Alcalá 31.

The ISIC/ITIC seems to be the best card to have (if you can get one), followed by Euro26, GO25 and Carnet Joven Europeo.

EMBASSIES
Spanish Embassies Abroad
Here follows a list of Spanish embassies in a selection of countries throughout the world:

Algeria
    46 Rue Mohammed Chabane, El Biar, Algiers (☎ 02-922713, 922752, 922789)
Argentina
    Mariscal Ramón Castilla 2720, 1425 Buenos Aires (☎ 01-802 6031/6032)

Australia
15 Arkana St, Yarralumla, Canberra, ACT 2600
(☎ 06-273 3555)
Austria
Argentinierstrasse 34, A, 1040 Vienna
(☎ 01-505 5780/5788)
Belgium
19 Rue de la Science, 1040 Brussels
(☎ 02-230 0340)
Brazil
SES, Avenida das Nações, 44, 70429-900
Brasília, DF (☎ 061-244 2776/2023)
Canada
350 Sparks St, Suite 802, Ottawa (Ontario) K1R
7S8 (☎ 613-237 2193/2194)
Denmark
Upsalagade 26, 2100 Copenhagen
(☎ 31 42 22 66)
France
22 Avenue Marceau, 75381 Paris Cedex 08
(☎ 01-44 43 18 00/53)
Germany
Schlossstrasse 4, 53115 Bonn
(☎ 0228-21 70 94/95)
Ireland
17A Merlyn Park, Balls Bridge, Dublin 4
(☎ 01-269 1640/2597)
Israel
'The Tower', Rehov Daniel Frish 3, 64731 Tel
Aviv (☎ 03-696 5210/5218)
Japan
1-3-29, Roppongi, Minato-Ku, Tokyo 106
(☎ 03-35 83 85 31/32)
Morocco
105 Ave Allal ben Abdellah, 3 Zankat Madnine,
Rabat (☎ 07-707600, 707980)
New Zealand
Spain has no diplomatic representation in New
Zealand
Norway
Oscarsgate 35, 0258 Oslo (☎ 22 55 20 15/16)
Netherlands
Lange Voorhout 50, 2514 EG The Hague
(☎ 070-364 38 14/15/16)
Portugal
Rua do Salitre 1, 1200 Lisbon
(☎ 01-347 2381/2382/2383)
Sweden
Djurgardsväen 21, 115 21 Stockholm
(☎ 08-667 9430)
Switzerland
Kalcheggweg 24, Berne (☎ 031-352 04 12/13)
Tunisia
24 Avenue Dr Ernest Conseil, Cité Jardin, 1002
Tunis (☎ 01-782217, 787796)
UK
Embassy: 39 Chesham Place, London SW1X
8SB (☎ 0171-235 5555)
Consulates: 20 Draycott Place, London SW3

2RZ (☎ 0171-589 8989)
Suite 1A, Brook House, 70 Spring Gardens,
Manchester M2 2BQ (☎ 0161-236 1233)
63 North Castle St, Edinburgh EH23LJ
(☎ 0131-220 1843)
USA
2375 Pennsylvania Ave NW, Washington, DC
20037 (☎ 202-452 0100)

Foreign Embassies in Spain

Most countries have diplomatic representation in Spain, and all the main embassies are
located in Madrid. Some countries also
maintain consulates in major cities around
the country. Embassies and consulates in
Madrid (telephone area code ☎ 91) include
the following:

Algeria
Calle de General Oráa (☎ 562 97 05)
Argentina
Paseo de la Castellana 53 (☎ 442 45 00)
Consulate: Calle de José Ortega y Gasset 62
(☎ 402 51 15)
Australia
Paseo de la Castellana 143 (☎ 579 04 28)
Austria
Paseo de la Castellana 91 (☎ 556 53 15)
Belgium
Paseo de la Castellana 18 (☎ 577 63 00)
Canada
Calle de Núñez de Balboa 35 (☎ 431 43 00)
Denmark
Calle de Claudio Coello 91 (☎ 431 84 45)
France
Calle de Salustiano Olozaga 9 (☎ 435 55 60)
Consulate: Paseo de la Castellana 79
(☎ 597 32 67)
Germany
Calle de Fortuny 8 (☎ 319 91 00)
Ireland
Calle de Claudio Coello 73 (☎ 576 35 00)
Italy
Calle de Lagasca 98 (☎ 577 65 29)
Consulate: Calle de Agustín Bethencourt 1
(☎ 534 69 09)
Israel
Calle de Velázquez 150 (☎ 562 68 78)
Japan
Calle de Serrano 109 (☎ 590 76 00)
Morocco
Calle de Serrano 179 (☎ 562 42 84)
Consulate: Calle de Leizaran 31 (☎ 561 89 12)
Netherlands
Avenida del Comandante Franco 38
(☎ 359 09 14)

New Zealand
Plaza de la Lealtad 2 (☎ 523 02 26)
Norway
Paseo de la Castellana 31 (☎ 310 31 16)
Portugal
Calle del Pinar 1 (☎ 561 78 00)
Consulate: Paseo de General Martínez Campos 11 (☎ 445 46 00)
Sweden
Calle de Caracas 25 (☎ 308 15 35)
Switzerland
Calle de Núñez de Balboa 35 (☎ 431 35 17)
Tunisia
Plaza Alonso Martínez 3 (☎ 447 35 08)
UK
Calle de Fernando el Santo 16 (☎ 319 02 00)
Consulate: Calle del Marqués Ensenada 16 (☎ 310 29 44)
USA
Calle de Serrano 75 (☎ 577 40 00)

CUSTOMS

People entering Spain from outside the EU are allowed to bring in duty-free a maximum of one litre of spirits, 50 ml of perfume and 200 cigarettes. If you are travelling from one EU country to another, you can bring two litres of wine *and* a litre of spirits, but the same limits apply on the rest. For *duty-paid* items bought at normal shops and supermarkets in one EU country and taken into another, the allowances are more than generous: 800 cigarettes, 90 litres of wine, 10 litres of spirits and unlimited quantities of perfume.

There are duty-free shops at all main airports. Remember that tax-free shopping is also possible in Spain's North African enclaves of Ceuta and Melilla.

MONEY

A combination of travellers' cheques and credit cards is the best way to take your money.

Costs

Spain is one of Western Europe's more affordable countries. If you are particularly frugal, it's just about possible to scrape by on 2500 to 3000 ptas a day; this would involve staying in the cheapest possible accommodation, avoiding eating in restaurants or going to museums or bars, and not moving around too much. Places like Madrid, Barcelona, Sevilla and San Sebastián will place a greater strain on your money belt.

A more comfortable budget would be 5000 ptas a day. This could allow you 1500 to 2000 ptas for accommodation; 300 ptas for breakfast (coffee and a pastry); 800 to 1000 ptas for a set lunch; 250 ptas for public transport (two metro or bus rides); 500 ptas for a major museum; and 600 ptas for a light dinner, with a bit over for a drink or two and intercity travel.

If you've got 20,000 ptas a day you can stay in excellent accommodation, rent a car and eat some of the best food Spain has to offer.

Ways to Save Two people can travel more cheaply (per person) than one by sharing rooms. You'll also save money by avoiding the peak tourist seasons, when room prices go up: these vary from place to place, depending on local festivals and climate, but run from about July to mid-September in most places (sometimes plus a month or two either side). A student or youth card, or a document such as a passport proving you're over 65 (63 for some things), brings worthwhile savings on some travel costs and entry to some museums and sights (see Visas & Documents earlier in this chapter). Occasional museums and sights have free days now and then, and a few are cheaper for EU passport holders.

More info on accommodation, food and travel costs can be found in the Accommodation and Food sections of this chapter and in the Getting Around chapter.

Carrying Money

Spain has a high rate of theft from tourists. According to the British organisation Card Protection Plan, no fewer than 200,000 British credit cards and cash cards went missing in Spain in just four months (June to September) in 1995. Barcelona was ranked Europe's worst city for card theft, and Madrid the third worst.

So obviously it pays to look after your money – whatever form it's in – with a deal of care. Keep only a limited amount as cash, and the bulk in more easily replaceable forms such as travellers' cheques or plastic. If your accommodation has a safe for your use, use it. If you have to leave money in your room, divide it into several stashes and hide them in different places.

For carrying money on the street – it's in cities and tourist resorts that you have to take particular care – the safest thing is a shoulder wallet or under-the-clothes money belt. Since these are not always the most convenient, some people prefer an external money belt, which is only really safe if it can't be sliced off by a quick knife cut. If you prefer to keep your funds in your pockets, don't use your back pockets, and watch out for people who touch you or seem to be getting unwarrantedly close, in any situation.

Cash

Even if you're using a credit card you'll make most of your purchases with cash, so you need to carry some of this stuff all the time. But it's best to have the bulk of your funds in some other form – not only for security reasons but because cash generally attracts a worse exchange rate than travellers' cheques or credit cards. Buying a few pesetas before you come to Spain might save you a bit of time on arrival in the country, but isn't really necessary as you can change money at virtually every entry point.

Obviously you don't want to carry too much cash at any one time, but bear in mind that many exchange outlets give you better rates for larger amounts, and you can also reduce commission costs by changing relatively large sums at one go.

Try not to be left with any Spanish cash – especially coins, which most exchange outlets refuse to change – when you leave the country.

Travellers' Cheques

These protect your money because they can be replaced if they are lost or stolen. In Spain they can be cashed at the many banks and exchange offices, and usually attract a slightly higher exchange rate than cash.

American Express and Thomas Cook are widely accepted brands with efficient replacement policies. It doesn't really matter whether your cheques are denominated in pesetas or in the currency of the country you buy them in: most Spanish exchange outlets will change most non-obscure currencies. What you should avoid is cheques in a third currency (such as US dollars if you're not coming from the USA) because then you'll have to pay two lots of exchange charges. Get most of your cheques in fairly large denominations (the equivalent of 10,000 ptas or more) to save on any per-cheque commission charges. American Express exchange offices charge no commission to change travellers' cheques (even other brands).

Read up on the replacement procedures and conditions when you buy the cheques: it's vital to keep your initial receipt, and a record of your cheque numbers and the ones you have used, separate from the cheques themselves. For American Express travellers' cheque refunds you can call ☎ 900-99 44 26 from anywhere in Spain.

Take along your passport when you go to cash travellers' cheques.

Plastic Money

You can use plastic to pay for many purchases (including meals and rooms at many establishments, especially from the middle price range up, and long-distance trains), and you can use it to withdraw cash pesetas from banks and automatic teller machines (ATMs). Among the most widely usable cards are Visa, MasterCard, Eurocard, Eurocheque, American Express, Cirrus, Plus, Diners Club and JCB.

Card purchases and cash advances are normally charged to your account via an exchange rate which may be slightly worse than you'd be quoted for exchanging cash or travellers' cheques in Spain. Once you consider the commission on the exchange transaction, however, you'll find that you usually win by using plastic, even taking into account the handling charge, usually of about 1.5%, that's levied for cash advances (though not for direct purchases by credit card).

A very high proportion of Spanish banks, even in small towns and some villages, have an ATM *(cajero automático)* which will conveniently dispense cash pesetas at any time, any day or night of the week, if you have the right piece of plastic to slot into it – *and* will save you having to queue at a bank counter. The only problems with ATMs occur when a machine is out of order, doesn't service your particular brand of card, or eats your card (none of which happens any more often in Spain than in other countries). You can avoid the risk of your card getting eaten by getting your cash advances over the counter when the bank is open, though this is usually a lot more time-consuming than using an ATM.

Check with your card's issuer before you come to Spain on how widely usable your card will be, on how to report a lost card, on daily or weekly withdrawal/spending limits, and on whether your personal identification number (PIN) will be acceptable (some European ATMs don't accept PINs of more than four digits). If you think you may go over your credit limit while away, you can deposit cash in your account before you leave to give you access to extra.

American Express card-holders can get cash or at least travellers' cheques – up to various maximums depending on the type of card – from American Express offices around Spain by writing a personal cheque drawn on their home bank account.

All in all, it's best to take more than one card if you have them, and try to keep them all separately in case one gets lost or stolen. American Express tend to be the easiest cards to replace – you can call ☎ 91-572 03 03 or ☎ 91-572 03 20 (in Madrid) at any time. Other cards may not be replaceable till you get home, but of course you must report their loss straight away. You can report Visa, MasterCard or Access loss on ☎ 91-435 30 40 or ☎ 91-519 21 00 (Madrid) or ☎ 93-315 25 12 (Barcelona). For Diners Club card losses call ☎ 91-547 40 00 (Madrid) or ☎ 93-320 14 28 (Barcelona).

International Transfers

To have money transferred from another country, you need to organise someone to send it to you (through a bank there or a money-transfer service such as Western Union or MoneyGram) and a bank (or Western Union or MoneyGram office) in Spain at which to collect it. If there's money in your bank account back at home, you may be able to instruct the bank yourself.

For information on Western Union services, you can call Western Union free on ☎ 900-63 36 33 from anywhere in Spain. MoneyGram (☎ 900-20 10 10) has offices in Madrid, Barcelona, Sevilla and Málaga, and in other cities throughout the world. To send sums up to US$400 the sender is charged US$20. The money can supposedly be handed over to the recipient within 10 minutes of being sent.

To set up a transfer through a bank, either get advice from the bank at home on a suitable pick-up bank in Spain, or check with a Spanish bank about how to organise it. You'll need to let the sender have full, exact details of the Spanish bank branch – its name, full address, city and any contact or code numbers required. It's probably easiest and quickest to have the money sent in pesetas.

A bank-to-bank telegraphic transfer typically costs the equivalent of about 3000 or 4000 ptas and should take about a week. Western Union is likely to be quicker but a bit more expensive.

It's also possible to have money sent by American Express.

Currency

Spain's currency is the peseta (pta). The legal denominations are coins of one, five, 10, 25, 50, 100, 200 and 500 ptas, and notes of 1000, 2000, 5000 and 10,000 ptas. Until 1996 there were no fewer than 52 different types of coin spread over the eight denominations, but all except one type for each denomination were due to be phased out by 1 January 1997. The following list specifies the only coins that are legal tender after that date:

Denomination	Colour	Diameter (mm)	Comments
1 pta	silver	14	tiny
5 ptas	gold	17.5	
10 ptas	silver	18.5	
25 ptas	gold	19.5	hole in the middle
50 ptas	silver	20.5	dented edge
100 ptas	gold	24.5	
200 ptas	silver	25.5	
500 ptas	gold	28	don't confuse with 100 ptas coin!

A five ptas coin is widely known as a *duro*, and it's fairly common for small sums to be quoted in duros: *dos duros* for 10 ptas, *cinco duros* for 25 ptas, even *veinte duros* for 100 ptas.

Sometimes it's hard to get change for a 5000 or 10,000 ptas note. If you're getting cash from a bank or ATM, asking for a sum that's not a multiple of 5000 ptas will prevent you being stuck with 5000 or 10,000 ptas notes only.

Currency Exchange

Currencies of the developed world can be changed without problems – except queues! – in any bank or exchange office. If you're coming from Morocco, get rid of any dirham before you leave Morocco. You can change them for pesetas in Ceuta and Melilla but rates are worse than in Morocco.

Exchange rates fluctuate, of course, but the peseta has been fairly stable since its last devaluation in 1993.

Australia	A$1	=	104 ptas
Canada	C$1	=	96 ptas
France	1FF	=	25 ptas
Germany	DM1	=	84 ptas
Japan	¥100	=	114 ptas
New Zealand	NZ$1	=	93 ptas
Portugal	100$00	=	84 ptas
UK	UK£1	=	223 ptas
USA	US$1	=	131 ptas

Changing Money

You can change cash or travellers' cheques at virtually any bank or exchange office.

International airports and major train and bus stations usually have both, and road border crossings will have one or the other close by. Banks tend to offer the best rates, with minor differences between them. They're very common in cities and even small villages often have one. They're mostly open Monday to Friday from 8.30 am to 2 pm, and Saturday from 9 am to 1 pm – though some don't bother with Saturday opening in summer. A great many banks have ATMs.

Exchange offices – usually indicated by the word *cambio* (exchange) – exist mainly in tourist resorts and other places that attract high numbers of foreigners. Generally they offer longer opening hours and quicker service than banks, but significantly worse exchange rates (though American Express exchange offices are an honourable exception here).

Travellers' cheques usually bring a slightly better exchange rate than cash, and in many places, the more money you change, the better the exchange rate you'll get.

Wherever you change, it's well worth asking about commissions first, and confirming that exchange rates are as posted (in other words that they haven't changed since the sign was last updated). Every bank seems to have a different commission structure: commissions may be different for travellers' cheques and cash, and may depend on how many cheques, or how much in total, you're cashing. A typical commission is 3%, with a minimum of 300 to 500 ptas, but there are places with a minimum of 1000 and sometimes 2000 ptas. Places that advertise 'no commission' usually offer poor exchange rates to start with (American Express exchange offices are again an honourable exception.)

Tipping & Bargaining

In restaurants, the law requires menu prices to include service charge, and tipping is a matter of personal choice – most people leave some small change if they're satisfied, and 5% is usually plenty. It's common to leave small change at bar and café tables.

The only places in Spain where you are

likely to bargain are markets – though even there most things have fixed prices – and, occasionally, cheap hotels, particularly if you're staying for a few days.

Taxes & Refunds

In Spain, value-added tax (VAT) is known as *impuesto sobre el valor añadido* (IVA, pronounced as one word, 'EE-ba'). On accommodation and restaurant prices, there's a flat rate of 7% IVA which is usually – but not always – included in quoted prices. To check, ask '*¿Está incluido el IVA?*' ('Is IVA included?').

On retail goods, IVA is 16%. Visitors are entitled to a refund of IVA on any item costing more than 15,000 ptas that they are taking out of the EU. Ask the shop for a Europe Tax-Free Shopping Cheque when you buy, then present the goods and cheque to customs when you leave within three months. Customs stamps the cheque and you then cash it at a booth with the 'Tax-Free' logo and 'Cash Refund' sign. There are booths at all main Spanish airports, the border crossings at Algeciras, Gibraltar and Andorra, and similar refund points throughout the EU.

POST & COMMUNICATIONS
Stamps & Post Offices

Stamps are sold at most *estancos* (tobacconist shops with 'Tabacos' in yellow letters on a maroon background), as well as at all post offices *(oficinas de correos)*. Cities have quite a lot of post offices and most villages have one too. Main post offices in cities and towns are usually open Monday to Friday from about 8.30 am to 8.30 pm, Saturday from about 9 am to 1.30 pm. Smaller offices

Postal Rates *Destination*	*Up to 15g*	*15 – 20g*	*20 – 30g*	*30 – 35g*	*35 – 45g*	*45 – 50g*
Same city	19*	19*	30	30	30	30
Elsewhere in Spain, Andorra, Gibraltar, Philippines	30*	30*	42	42	42	42
Rest of Europe	60*	60*	140	140	140	140
Morocco, Tunisia, Algeria	60*	60*	77	77	174	174
Other African countries, the Americas, Hong Kong	87*	114*	194	221	221	248
Australia, New Zealand, China, Malaysia, Japan, Singapore	108*	156*	236	284	284	332

* Letters and cards weighing 20 grams or less are subject to an extra charge of 12 ptas if going to Spanish destinations, and 80 ptas to other countries, if they don't fit the arcane concept of *normalizado*. Normalizado essentially refers to certain maximum and minimum dimensions: for a letter the minimum is 14 by 9 cm and the maximum 23.5 by 12 cm; for a postcard the minimum is 14 by 9 cm, the maximum 14.8 by 10.5 cm; in both cases the length must be at least 1.4 times the width. Don't worry – most envelopes and cards meet these specifications!

may be open shorter hours. Estancos are usually open during normal shop hours.

Postal Rates

The table shows some standard postal rates in pesetas for letters and postcards within and from Spain. International rates are for air mail. Two A4 sheets in an air-mail envelope weigh less than 15 grams.

Certificado (registered mail) costs an extra 150 ptas for international mail and an extra 130 ptas for domestic mail. *Urgente* service, which means your letter may arrive two or three days quicker, costs an extra 200 ptas for international mail and from an extra 140 ptas for domestic mail. You can send mail both urgente and certificado if you wish.

Perhaps a day or two quicker than urgente service – but a lot more expensive – is Postal Exprés service, sometimes called Express Mail Service (EMS). This is available at most post offices and uses courier companies for international deliveries. Packages weighing up to one kg cost 3300 ptas to most of Western Europe, 5500 ptas to North America, and 7000 ptas to Australia or New Zealand.

Sending Mail

It's quite safe and reliable to post your mail in the yellow street postboxes *(buzones)* as well as at post offices.

Mail to other Western European countries normally takes up to a week; to North America up to 10 days; to Australia or New Zealand up to two weeks. Sometimes service is quicker; occasionally there are long delays or disappearances. See the previous Postal Rates section for the faster urgente and Postal Exprés services.

Receiving Mail

Delivery times are similar to those for outbound mail. All Spanish addresses have five-digit postcodes, use of which may help your mail arrive a bit quicker.

Poste restante mail can be addressed to you at poste restante (or better, *lista de correos*, the Spanish name for it), anywhere

in Spain that has a post office. It will be delivered to the place's main post office unless another one is specified in the address. Take your passport when you go to pick up mail. It's a fairly reliable system, although you must be prepared for mail to arrive late. It helps if people writing to you capitalise or underline your surname, and include the postcode in the address. Postcodes for poste restante/lista de correos at some main post offices are given in this book's destination sections. A typical lista de correos address looks like this:

> Jane SMITH
> Lista de Correos
> 08080 Barcelona
> Spain

For some quirks of Spanish address abbreviations, see the Getting Addressed box.

American Express card or travellers' cheque holders can use the free client mail-holding service at American Express offices in Spain. You can obtain a list of these from American Express offices inside or outside Spain. Take your passport when you go to pick up mail.

Telephone

Spain is very well provided with street pay phones, which are blue, common and easy to use for both international and domestic calls. They accept coins and/or phonecards *(tarjetas telefónicas)* and, in some cases, credit cards. Phonecards come in 1000 and 2000 ptas denominations and, like postage stamps, are sold at post offices and estancos.

An alternative in some places, though being phased out in favour of pay phones, is the telephone centre. Usually called a *locutorio*, a telephone centre has a number of booths, where you do your own dialling, then pay someone sitting at a desk afterwards. These places can be useful if you don't have enough coins or a card, or if pay phones are in short supply. They also usually have a good stock of telephone directories.

Public phones inside bars and cafés, and phones in hotel rooms, are always a good

Top: Street parade during the Fiesta de San Vicente Ferrer in Valencia
Bottom Left & Middle: Corpus Christi celebrations in Granada, Andalucía
Bottom Right: *Nazarenos* of the Hermandad (brotherhood) de las Cigarreras cross the Puente de
  Isabel II during Semana Santa in Sevilla, Andalucía

Top: Twirling flamenco dancers at the Feria de Málaga, Andalucía
Bottom Left: Mule trappings in Arenas, Andalucía, home of the Feria de la Mula
Bottom Right: Dressed for the *feria*, Málaga

Getting Addressed

You might think that if you have the address of a hotel, office or café, you should have little trouble locating it. But if the Pensión España should turn out to be at C/ Madrid 2°D Int, not far from Gta Atocha and just round the corner from P° del Prado, you could be forgiven for being a little confused. Here's a key to common abbreviations used in addresses:

Almd	Alameda
Av or Avda	Avenida
C/	Calle
Cllj	Callejón
Cno	Camino
Cril	Carril
Ctra or Ca	Carretera
Gta	Glorieta (major roundabout)
Pje	Pasaje
Pllo	Pasillo
P° or Po	Paseo
Pl or Pza or Pª	Plaza
Pte	Puente
Rda	Ronda
s/n	*sin número* (without number)
Urb	Urbanización

The following are used where there are several flats, *hostales*, offices etc in a building. They're often used in conjunction, eg 2°C, or 3°I Int:

2°	2nd floor
3°	3rd floor
4°	4th floor
C	*centro* (middle)
D or dcha	*derecha* (right-hand side)
I or izq	*izquierda* (left-hand side)
Int	*interior* (a flat or office too far inside a building to look on to any street – the opposite is Ext, *exterior*)

If someone's address is Apartado de Correos 206 (which might be shortened to Apdo Correos 206 or even just Apdo 206), don't bother going looking for it at all. An *apartado de correos* is a post office box.

Note also that the word *de* is often omitted: Calle de Madrid (literally 'Street of Madrid') may be truncated to C/ Madrid. In fact it's not uncommon for streets to be referred to by their names alone: Calle de Alfonso Rodríguez will just as likely be referred to as Alfonso Rodríguez. ■

deal more expensive than street pay phones. Managements set their own rates for these; always ask the cost before using one.

Costs These are not straightforward. Different operators at Telefónica, the state phone company, often have different answers to the same question. Then when you actually make the call you'll probably find that you pay more than any of them said. Pay phones often seem to run through your coins or phonecard credit faster than they have any right to, and private phone bills, even though calls are itemised, often seem to be higher than you could have anticipated even with the most careful calculations. Bearing all this in mind, you can expect a three minute pay phone or private-line call to cost around 30 ptas within your local area, 80 ptas to other places in the same province, 190 ptas to other provinces, 350 ptas to other EU countries, 600 ptas to North America and 1100 ptas to Australia. Calls are around 15% cheaper between 10 pm and 8 am, after 2 pm on Saturday, and all day Sunday and holidays.

Domestic Calls Spanish telephone codes all begin with 9 and consist of either two or three digits. Codes are given in this book's regional chapters. With a few minor exceptions, each code covers one of Spain's 50 provinces. Two-digit codes are followed by seven-digit numbers; three-digit codes, by six-digit numbers.

To make a call within an area covered by one code, just dial the six or seven digit number. To speak to a domestic operator, including for domestic reverse-charge (collect) calls, dial ☎ 009. A reverse-charge call is *una llamada por cobro revertido*. For directory enquiries dial ☎ 003; calls cost about 50 ptas.

International Calls To make an international call dial ☎ 07, wait for a new dialling tone, then dial the country code, area code and number. International collect calls are simple: dial ☎ 900 99 00 followed by a code for the country you're calling: ☎ 61 for Australia; ☎ 44 for the UK; ☎ 64 for New Zealand; ☎ 15 for Canada; and for the USA, ☎ 11 (AT&T) or ☎ 14 (MCI); codes to use for other countries are usually posted up in pay phones. You'll get straight through to an operator in the country you're calling. If for some reason this doesn't work, in most places you can get an English-speaking Spanish international operator on ☎ 008 (for calls within Europe) or ☎ 005 (rest of the world).

For international directory enquiries dial ☎ 025 and be ready to pay about 150 ptas.

Calling Spain from Other Countries
Spain's country code is ☎ 34. Always omit the initial 9 of the area code.

Fax & E-Mail
Most main post offices have fax service: sending one page costs about 350 ptas within Spain, 950 ptas to elsewhere in Europe, and 1700 to 2000 ptas to other countries. However you'll often find cheaper rates at shops or offices with 'Fax Público' signs.

For people travelling in Spain with their own computers, ease of access to e-mail and the Internet is a matter of being able to plug your computer into a phone line – which generally means staying in accommodation which might has a phone. If you're discreet, you might plug a laptop into the phone jack in a telephone centre. Check what connection procedures and pay rates you can expect through your server before leaving home. CompuServe as yet only has nodes in Madrid and Barcelona. Spain also has a growing number of *cafés internet* – cafés with Internet connections which you can use for a few hundred ptas an hour. Many of these also offer e-mail receiving services. There were about 40 such cafés at the time of writing; you'll find some mentioned in city sections of this guide. In addition, there are some 'Internet bureaus', often telephone locutorios with computer terminals, typically charging 600 ptas for 30 minutes Internet access.

BOOKS
Spain has inspired a deep fascination among foreign writers for two centuries. There's a huge wealth of literature in English on the country. It's best to stock up before you go on any reading matter you particularly want:

availability of foreign-language books is patchy in Spain. Main cities and resorts usually have a few sources, but the choice may be limited. Books on Spain (☎ & fax 0181-898 7789), PO Box 207, Twickenham TW2 5BQ, England, can send you a catalogue of hundreds of old and new titles available by mail order.

Lonely Planet
If trekking or hiking is on your agenda, you'll find a wealth of route descriptions for all the main areas, and lots of practical and informative background, in Lonely Planet's *Trekking in Spain* by Marc Dubin. For people travelling on from Spain, other Lonely Planet travel guides include *France*, *Portugal*, *Morocco* and *North Africa*.

Guidebooks
Blue Guide Spain isn't a bad companion if you want lots of detail about the country's architecture and art in historical context. The separate *Blue Guide Barcelona* is full of intriguing detail about the city's bars and nightspots as well as its churches and museums. For walking guides, see the Activities section later in this chapter.

Of the many guides in Spanish to different parts of Spain, those published by El País/Aguilar stand out for their concise, intelligent, honest coverage and handy format. There are around 60 guides in various series, covering provinces, cities, routes such as the Camino de Santiago, tapas bars in various cities, and one-offs such as the excellent *Pequeños Hoteles con Encanto* (Small Hotels with Charm), *Alojamientos en Monasterios* (Lodgings in Monasteries) and *Pequeños Pueblos con Encanto* (Small Villages with Charm).

Travel
19th Century Classics Washington Irving was an American who took up residence in Granada's Alhambra palace when it was in an abandoned state in the early 19th century. His *Tales of the Alhambra* (1832) weaves a series of still-enchanting stories around the folk with whom he shared his life there, and

was largely responsible for the romantic image of Al-Andalus – and by extension of Spain in general – which persists to this day.

A Handbook for Travellers in Spain by Richard Ford (1845) set standards that few guidebook writers have matched since. It remains a classic not only for telling us how things were then in places we see now, but also for its irascible English author, who is by turns witty, prejudiced, highly informative and downright rude. Unfortunately the most easily available edition (Centaur Press) comes in three volumes and costs around £75.

The Bible in Spain by George Borrow is an English clergyman's view of the 19th century Spain around which he tried to spread the Protestant word. It's an amusing read both for the man himself and for his experiences.

20th Century In the 1920s Englishman Gerald Brenan settled in a remote village south of Granada aiming to educate himself unimpeded by British mores and traditions. *South from Granada* (1957) is his absorbing account of local life and visits from members of the Bloomsbury set with whom he was associated. In 1949 Brenan returned to explore Franco's Spain, an experience recounted in *The Face of Spain* (1950).

Laurie Lee, meanwhile, walked off from his Gloucestershire home, aged 19, in 1934. He arrived by boat at Vigo, then walked the length of Spain, playing his fiddle for a living. *As I Walked Out One Midsummer Morning* (1969) is a delightful, poetic account of his adventures which also records the sights, smells and contrasting moods of turbulent pre-civil war Spain. *A Moment of War* (1991) describes Lee's bizarre experiences in the International Brigades during the civil war, encapsulating the confusion among the Republicans towards the end of the war. In the third of his Spanish 'trilogy', *A Rose for Winter*, Lee tells of his return to Andalucía 15 years later.

If you can trace Rose Macauley's out-of-print *Fabled Shore*, which recounts a trip along the coast from Cataluña to the Algarve in 1949, it will leave you wondering whether this really could have been the same seaboard as spawned the Costa Blanca and Costa del Sol.

Of recent travel writings, David Gilmour's *Cities of Spain* and Adam Hopkins' *Spanish Journeys*, both culture and history-focused, and Michael Jacobs' amusing *Between Hopes and Memories: A Spanish Journey*, stand out. Travels along the Camino de Santiago are recounted by Robin Hanbury-Tenison in *Spanish Pilgrimage – A Canter to St James* and Bettina Selby in *Pilgrim's Road*. He had a penchant for white horses; she did it by bike.

History

For a colourful but thorough and not over-long survey of Spanish history, *The Story of Spain* by Mark Williams is hard to beat. Also concise and worthwhile is Juan Lalaguna's *A Traveller's History of Spain*.

John A Crow's *Spain: The Root and the Flower* is an American Hispanophile's insightful, scholarly, but rarely dry, ramble through history and culture from early times to the 1980s.

Moorish Spain by Richard Fletcher is one of the best histories of Spain's fascinating Islamic era. *Imperial Spain, 1469-1716* by JH Elliot is probably the best single book covering the country's golden age and its immediate aftermath.

Gerald Brenan's *The Spanish Labyrinth* (1943) is an in-depth but readable unravelling of the tangle of political and social movements in the half-century or so before the civil war.

Civil War & Franco Era The Spanish Civil War of 1936-39 is said to be the second most written-about conflict in history (after WWII), and has spawned some wonderful books. *The Spanish Civil War* by Hugh Thomas is probably the classic account of the conflict in any language, long and dense with detail, yet readable, even-handed and humane. Raymond Carr's more succinct *The Spanish Tragedy* is another well-written and respected account.

Homage to Catalonia is George Orwell's participant's version of the civil war in Cataluña, moving from the euphoria of the early days in Barcelona to disillusionment with the disastrous infighting on the Republican side.

The murky story of one of the war's more infamous atrocities, the killing near Granada of the great poet and playwright Lorca, is chillingly and fascinatingly pieced together in *The Assassination of Federico García Lorca* by the noted Irish Lorca scholar (and now Spanish citizen) Ian Gibson, who also gives background on Lorca and the war. Ronald Fraser's *Blood of Spain* is a fascinating and voluminous collection of eye-witness accounts of the war.

Paul Preston's *Franco* is the big biography of one of history's little dictators.

Regions

Andalucía and Cataluña, two strongly contrasting regions at opposite ends of the country, seem to have inspired foreigners more than any other part of Spain.

The Sierras of the South by Alastair Boyd is a vivid, evocative story of life around Ronda in the Andalucían hill country in the 1950s and 60s, when foreigners were still a rarity. (The same author has also penned *The Essence of Catalonia*.) Nicholas Luard does a similar job for the valleys behind Tarifa in *Andalucia: A Portrait of Southern Spain* (1984). *Inside Andalusia* by David Baird (1993) is an always-interesting collection of portraits of people and places in this region.

Homage to Barcelona by Colm Tóibín (1990) is an excellent personal introduction to the city's modern life and artistic and political history, by an Irish journalist who has lived there. *Barcelona* by Robert Hughes (1992) goes into more depth, especially about the past.

Two books that give a revealing insight into Spanish attitudes to the changes of the past decades (notably tourism, which in many ways was welcomed because of the money it brought in) are Ronald Fraser's *The Pueblo*, about the village of Mijas on the Costa del Sol, and Norman Lewis' semi-

fictional *Voices of the Old Sea*, set on the Costa Brava.

A Winter in Mallorca is George Sand's account of an 1830s sojourn in an abandoned monastery on the island with her lover, the composer Chopin, and her two children; the locals didn't approve of the couple's relationship and made it hard for them to obtain food, but Chopin still composed some of his best work there.

Hemingway

Ernest Hemingway's *For Whom the Bell Tolls* (1941) is probably the most-read of all English-language books set in Spain – and justly so. This characteristically terse tale of the civil war, which Hemingway experienced as a journalist, is full of Spanish atmosphere and all the emotions unleashed in the war. Its plot keeps you hanging on until the last sentence. Hemingway's earlier novel *Fiesta* made the Sanfermines bull-running festival at Pamplona world-famous. *Death in the Afternoon* is his book on bullfighting.

Society, Culture & Arts

The two best overall introductions to modern Spain are *The New Spaniards* by John Hooper, a former *Guardian* Madrid correspondent, who ranges comprehensively from the arts through politics and bullfighting to sex, and the more controversial and personal *Fire in the Blood* by Ian Gibson, based on a British TV series.

It's a surprise to find that James Michener's *Iberia* (1968) is not an epic novel in his usual mode, but rather an absorbing treatise reflecting a lifetime love affair with the country, covering just about every topic that the word Spain readily conjures up.

Titus Burckhardt's *Moorish Culture in Spain* is a classic book on the unique architecture and culture of Islamic Spain. In the handy Thames & Hudson series on artistic movements, *Romanesque Art* by Meyer Schapiro covers this pre-Gothic architectural and artistic era, while *The Arts of Spain* by José Guidol ranges from cave paintings to the 20th century.

Flora & Fauna

Wildlife Travelling Companion Spain by John Measures is a good traveller's guide, focusing on 150 of the best sites for viewing flora and fauna, with details of how to reach them and what you can hope to see. It also contains a basic field guide to more common animals and plants.

Spain's Wildlife by Eric Robins covers the country's most interesting animals and birds – and their prospects for survival – in an informative way, spiced with plenty of personal experience and some good photos.

For more detailed flora and fauna spotting, Collins produces some good field guides, including *Collins Photoguide to the Wild Flowers of the Mediterranean* by Ingrid & Peter Schönfelder; *Collins Field Guide to the Birds of Britain and Europe* by Roger Peterson, Guy Mountfort & PAD Hollom; *Collins Pocket Guide Birds of Britain and Europe* by H Heinzel, RSR Fitter & J Parslow; *The Alpine Flowers of Britain and Europe* by Christopher Grey-Wilson & Marjorie Blamey; and *A Field Guide to the Butterflies of Britain and Europe* by LG Higgins & ND Riley.

From other publishers, there's *Flowers of South-West Europe, A Field Guide* by Oleg Polunin & BE Smythies; *Flowers of the Mediterranean* by Oleg Polunin & Anthony Huxley; *Wild Flowers of Southern Spain* by Betty Molesworth Allen; *Field Guide to the Orchids of Britain and Europe* by KP Buttler; *The Hamlyn Guide to the Trees of Britain and Europe* by CJ Humphries, JR Press & DA Sutton; *Field Guide to the Butterflies and Moths of Britain and Europe* by H Reichholf-Reihm; *Field Guide to the Mammals of Britain and Europe* by John Burton; and *Birds of Britain and Europe* by Bertel Bruna.

Food & Wine

There are dozens of books on Spanish cookery. Four of the best are *The Foods and Wines of Spain* by Penelope Casas, *Cooking in Spain* by Janet Mendel, and the slimmer *Spain on a Plate* by María-José Sevilla and *The Best of Spanish Cooking* by Janet

Mendel. All have good background on the country's widely varied regional cuisines as well as recipes. Mendel has an encyclopedic knowledge of the subject and her bigger book includes a good section on food market shopping.

CD ROM

There are some interesting CD ROMs available on Spain, but most of them have text and any voice-over in Spanish only and could be hard to come by outside Spain. Nearly all need Windows 3.1 or 95, a 16-bit sound card and at least a 386 computer with two to four MB of memory. You'll do better with at least a 486SX and eight MB: installing key files which enhance performance takes up eight to 10 MB of hard disk.

España Guía Turística CD-ROM (Círculo Multimedia, 4200 ptas) is really a souped-up tourist database, grouped by provinces or large settlements from which you click into categories like hotels, restaurants, golf courses and sailing facilities. Check the edition date. *Catalunya Interactiva* (BSI Multimedia/Enciclopèdia Catalana, 14,500 ptas) has encyclopedic info on Cataluña and is available in an English/Spanish/Catalan multilingual version.

Parques Nacionales de España (Indesmedia, 8500 ptas) has lots of info, photos, video and a useful plant and animal index. It's available for PC and Mac. *Visual Map Pirineo* (Visual Gis Engineering, Madrid, 4900 ptas) focuses on the Aragonese Pyrenees but also covers large slices of Zaragoza and Lleida provinces, with lots of stuff on facilities, features and routes. It's on three 3.5-inch diskettes and needs True Type fonts. *El Camino de Santiago* (Micronet SA, 8500 ptas) traces all Spanish variations of the pilgrim route, with 1000 colour pictures and info on 900 hotels and camp sites.

Art lovers could delve into *La Obra de Velázquez en el Museo del Prado*, the digital equivalent of a coffee-table book, available in Mac format too (Dynamic Multimedia, 4950 ptas); *El Palacio Real de Madrid*, which takes you into more rooms than a real visit to the palace (Micronet SA, 8900 ptas);

or *La Colección*, which explains hundreds of works in Madrid's Centro de Arte Reina Sofía (Micronet SA, 8500 ptas).

ONLINE SERVICES

A search of the World Wide Web under 'Spain, Travel' will reveal dozens of sites including the national tourist office's useful, though not too frequently updated one, *Discover Spain* (http://www.spaintour.com). It includes worldwide Spanish tourist office addresses; guides to 30-odd cities, coasts, regions and routes; temperature info; festival and holiday listings; national parks and quite a lot more. For Cataluña, the *Publintur Catalonia Tourist Guide* (http://www.Publintur.es/) is worth a look.

Spain Online (http://www.spainonline.com) offers travel information, Spanish news and events listings, *Lookout* magazine and other material, plus links to other useful Spanish Web sites.

Lonely Planet's enormously popular site (http://www.lonelyplanet.com/) has a 'Destination Spain' page, which includes recent travellers' tips and links to a number of other sources of information on Spain.

CompuServe's Spanish Forum has a data library with copious info on various aspects of Spanish travel, and you can post messages asking for specific tips.

For a couple of hints on access to the Internet in Spain, see the Fax & E-Mail section earlier in this chapter.

NEWSPAPERS & MAGAZINES
Spanish Press

Spain has a thriving and free press which is the subject of some of the country's more revealing statistics. According to a mid-1980s government survey, more than half of all Spaniards had never read a newspaper even once in their lives. Daily newspapers sell around four or five million copies between them, one for every eight to 10 people (a similar figure to Italy), compared to one for every 2½ people in Britain. Sales figures reflect not only still-widespread illiteracy among older generations and a degree of apathy about nonimmediate con-

cerns, but also the Spanish habit of sharing newspapers; it's actually reckoned that about one-third of Spaniards read papers regularly.

For some reason Spaniards have never taken to the idea of what's generously called a 'popular' press. There's no equivalent of the *Sun* or the *New York Daily News* here. However, one of the best-selling dailies is *Marca*, which is devoted exclusively to sport.

The major daily newspapers are the liberal *El País*, the conservative *ABC*, and *El Mundo*, which specialises in breaking political scandals. For solid reporting of national and international events, *El País* is hard to beat. It also has good regional sections, which include what's-on guides. There's also a welter of regional dailies, some of the best being Barcelona's *La Vanguardia* and *El Periódico*, both in Spanish, and *Avui* in Catalan, and Andalucía's *Sur* and *El Correo*. The País Vasco has two papers produced partly in the Basque language, *Deia* and ETA's mouthpiece *Egin*.

For a laugh, have a look at *¡Hola!*, a weekly picture magazine devoted to the lives and loves of the rich and famous.

Foreign-Language Press

Coastal areas with large expatriate populations have a few mainly English-language publications. Some of them are best for wrapping your fish and chips in, but in Andalucía the free weekly *Sur in English* reviews local news quite thoroughly and has good small ads, while *Lookout* is a glossy monthly magazine with some interesting features on aspects of Spain.

International press such as the *International Herald Tribune*, *Time* and *Newsweek*, and newspapers from Western European countries, reach major cities and tourist areas on the day of publication; elsewhere they're a bit harder to find and a day or two late.

RADIO & TV
Radio

There are several hundred radio stations around the country, mainly on FM, and they run the gamut from a lot of loud babble interspersed with silly noises, to nonstop good music. Many are independent but a few hundred are run by town councils. The state network Radio Nacional de España (RNE) has four stations. RNE 1, with general interest and current affairs programmes, and RNE 5, with sport and entertainment, are on AM (medium wave); RNE 2, with classical music, and RNE 3 (or 'Radio d'Espop'), with admirably varied pop and rock music, are on FM (VHF). Most listened-to of all is the commercial pop and rock station 40 Principales, on FM. Frequencies vary from place to place: El País publishes local wavelength guides in its 'Cartelera' (what's-on) section.

Some of the expat-populated costas have the odd foreign-language station, such as the English-language Onda Cero International (101.6 MHz FM) on the Costa del Sol. These stations' programming is mostly very middle-of-the-road, though they often carry BBC World Service news (on the hour), with better reception than the BBC itself.

The BBC World Service broadcasts to Spain on 3.955, 6.195, 7.150, 9.410, 12.095 and 15.070 MHz (short wave). There's transmission on one or other of these frequencies from 4.30 am to 11.15 pm GMT/UTC. In parts of the southern mainland you may get better reception on the BBC's Madeira/Canary Islands frequency, 15.400 MHz. Voice of America can be found on various short-wave frequencies, including 9.700, 15.205 and 15.255 MHz, depending on the time of day.

TV

Spaniards are Europe's greatest TV watchers after the British, but do some of their watching in bars and cafés, which makes it more of a social activity.

Most TVs receive between five and seven channels – two from the state-run Televisión Española (TVE1 and La 2), three independent (Antena 3, Tele 5 and Canal Plus), and in some areas one or two run by regional governments, such as Madrid's Telemadrid, Cataluña's TV-3 and Canal 33, Galicia's TVG, the País Vasco's ETB-1 and ETB-2,

Valencia's Canal 9 and Andalucía's Canal Sur. Most of the national channels broadcast round the clock. Apart from news (of which there's a respectable amount), TV programming consists largely of game and talk shows, sport, telenovelas (soap operas) and English-language films dubbed into Spanish.

On-screen logos tell you which channel you're watching: they're fairly obviously identifiable except for Antena 3's, which is a kind of blue, yellow and red upside-down teardrop. Canal Plus is a pay channel: non-subscribers can get usually some kind of reception, but it's very fuzzy on the most popular programmes such as sport and films.

Satellite TV is popular too – mainly in private homes, though some bars, cafés and top-end hotels have it too. Foreign channels you may come across include BBC World (mainly news and travel), BBC Prime (other BBC programmes), CNN, Eurosport, Sky News, Sky Sports, Sky Sports 2, Sky Movies, and the German SAT 1. Among Spanish satellite channels are Documenta and Canal Clásico, which have some good documentaries and arts programmes.

VIDEO SYSTEMS

If you want to record or buy video tapes to play back home, you won't get a picture if the image registration systems are different. Spanish TVs, and nearly all prerecorded videos on sale in Spain, use the PAL (phase alternation line) system common to most of Western Europe and Australia. France uses the incompatible SECAM system, and North America and Japan use the incompatible NTSC system. PAL videos can't be played back on a machine that lacks PAL capability.

PHOTOGRAPHY

Most main brands of film are widely available, and processing is fast and generally efficient. A roll of print film (36 exposures, ISO 100) costs around 650 ptas and can be processed for around 1700 ptas – though there are often better deals if you have two or three rolls developed together. The equivalent in slide *(diapositiva)* film is around 850 ptas plus 850 ptas for processing. Kodachrome slide film exists but isn't as common as some other brands.

Your camera and film will be routinely passed through airport x-ray machines. These shouldn't damage film but you can ask for inspection by hand if you're worried. Lead pouches for film are another solution.

Some museums and galleries ban photography, or at least flash, and soldiers can be touchy about it. It's common courtesy to ask – at least by gesture – when you want to photograph people, unless perhaps when they're in some kind of public event like a procession.

Bright middle-of-the-day sun tends to bleach out your shots. You get more colour and contrast earlier and later in the day.

TIME

Spain is on GMT/UTC plus one hour during winter, and GMT/UTC plus two hours during the daylight-saving period from the last Sunday in March to the last Sunday in October. Most other Western European countries have the same time as Spain year round, the major exceptions being Britain, Ireland and Portugal. Add one hour to these three countries' times to get Spanish time.

Morocco is on GMT/UTC year round. From the last Sunday in March to the last Sunday in October, subtract two hours from Spanish time to get Moroccan time; the rest of the year, subtract one hour.

Spanish time is normally USA Eastern Time plus six hours, and USA Pacific Time plus nine hours. But the USA tends to start daylight saving a week or two later than Spain (meaning you must add one hour to the time differences in the intervening period).

In the Australian winter (Spanish summer), subtract eight hours from Sydney time to get Spanish time; in the Australian summer subtract 10 hours. The difference is nine hours for a few weeks in March.

For comments on attitudes to time in Spain, see the Society & Conduct section of the Facts about the Country chapter.

ELECTRICITY

Electric current in Spain is 220V, 50 Hz, as in the rest of Continental Europe, but a few places are still on 125V or 110V (sockets are often labelled where this is the case). Voltage may even vary in the same building. Don't plug 220V (or British 240V) appliances into 125V or 110V sockets unless they have a transformer. Several countries outside Europe (such as the USA and Canada) have 60 Hz, which means that appliances from those countries with electric motors (such as some CD and tape players) may perform poorly.

Plugs have two round pins, again like the rest of Continental Europe.

WEIGHTS & MEASURES

The metric system is used. Like other Continental Europeans, the Spanish indicate decimals with commas and thousands with points.

LAUNDRY

Self-service laundrettes are rare. Small laundries *(lavanderías)* are fairly common but not particularly cheap. They will usually wash, dry and fold a load for 1000 to 1200 ptas, and can usually do it the same day or by the next day. Some youth hostels and budget hostales have washing machines for guests' use.

TOILETS

Public toilets are not particularly common in Spain, but it's OK to wander into most bars and cafés to use their toilet even if you're not a customer. It's worth carrying some loo paper with you when out and about as many toilets lack it. If there's a bin beside the loo, put paper etc in it – it's there because the local sewerage system couldn't cope otherwise. Here and there you'll still find a hole-in-the-ground squat toilet.

HEALTH

Spain is a pretty healthy country. Your main risks are likely to be sunburn, dehydration, foot blisters, insect bites, or mild gut problems at first if you're not used to a lot of olive oil.

Travel Health Guides

Two books worth considering are:

Travellers' Health by Dr Richard Dawood – comprehensive, easy to read and authoritative, though rather large to lug around

Travel with Children by Maureen Wheeler – a Lonely Planet book, which includes basic advice on travel health for younger children

Predeparture Planning

Health Insurance Travel insurance to cover theft, loss and medical problems is a wise idea.

EU citizens are entitled to free medical care under the Spanish national health system on provision of an E111 form, which is available in your home country before you come. Even with an E111, you will still have to pay for any medicines bought from pharmacies, even if a doctor has prescribed them, and perhaps for a few tests and procedures. Your own national health system may reimburse these costs.

An E111 is no good, however, for private medical consultations or treatment in Spain, which includes virtually all dentists and some of the better clinics and surgeries. If you want to avoid paying for these, you'll need medical as well as theft and loss insurance on your travel policy.

In Britain, E111s are issued free by post offices; all you need to supply is your name, address, date of birth and National Insurance number. In other EU countries ask your doctor or health service how to get the form.

Most, but not all, US health insurance policies stay in effect, at least for a limited period, if you travel abroad. On the other hand, most non-European national health plans (including Australia's Medicare) don't, so you must take out special medical as well as theft and loss insurance.

A wide variety of travel insurance policies is available and your travel agent will be able to make recommendations. The international student travel policies handled by STA Travel or other student travel organisations are usually good value. Check the small print:

- Some policies exclude 'dangerous activities', which can include scuba diving, motorcycling, even trekking. If such activities are on your agenda, you don't want that sort of policy.
- Some policies may impose a surcharge for expensive photo equipment and the like.
- Policies often require you to pay up front for medical expenses, then to claim from the insurance company afterwards, showing receipts, but you might prefer to find a policy on which the insurance company pays the doctor or hospital direct.
- Check whether the policy covers ambulances or an emergency flight home. If you have to stretch out, you will need two seats and somebody has to pay for them!

For more hints on travel insurance turn to the start of the Getting There & Away chapter.

Medical Kit Medicines are easily available in Spain, but a small, straightforward medical kit is a wise thing to carry. It could include:

- Aspirin or Panadol – for pain or fever
- Antihistamine (such as Benadryl) – useful as a decongestant for colds and allergies, to ease the itch from insect bites or stings, and to help prevent motion sickness
- Kaolin preparation (Pepto-Bismol), Imodium or Lomotil – for stomach upsets
- Antiseptic such as Betadine, which comes as impregnated swabs or ointment, and an antibiotic powder or similar 'dry' spray – for cuts and grazes
- Calamine lotion – to ease irritation from bites or stings
- Bandages and Band-aids – for minor injuries
- Scissors, tweezers and a thermometer (note that mercury thermometers are prohibited by airlines)
- Insect repellent, sunscreen and water purification tablets

Health Preparations If you wear glasses, take a spare pair and a copy of your prescription. You can usually get new ones made up quickly, fairly cheaply and competently.

If you require a particular medication take an adequate supply, as it may not be readily available in remote areas. If you're likely to need to buy supplies in Spain, it's best to take a letter from your doctor translated into Spanish explaining the condition and the medicines needed, and to carry part of the packaging showing the generic rather than the brand name (which may not be locally available).

Immunisations No jabs are normally needed to visit Spain, but the odd one might be required if you're coming from an infected area – yellow fever is the most likely one. You can check with your travel agent or Spanish embassy.

There are, however, a few routine vaccinations that are recommended whether you're travelling or not. They include polio, tetanus and diphtheria, and sometimes measles, mumps and rubella (German measles). All these are usually administered in childhood, but some require later booster shots. For details, check with your doctor or nearest health agency.

All vaccinations should be recorded on an International Health Certificate, which is available from your physician or government health department.

Basic Rules

Water Domestic, hotel and restaurant tap water is safe to drink virtually everywhere in Spain, though it varies a lot in taste quality. In places with water shortages you might want to check: lowering of water tables might introduce some undesirable ingredients into the supply. Ask '¿Es potable el agua?' if you're in any doubt.

Water from public spouts and fountains is not reliable unless it has a sign saying 'Agua Potable'. Often there are signs saying 'Agua No Potable': don't drink here.

Natural water, unless it's straight from a definitely unpolluted spring, or running off snow or ice with no interference from people or animals, is likewise not safe to drink unpurified.

Safe bottled water is available everywhere, generally for 40 to 75 ptas for a 1.5 litre bottle in shops and supermarkets.

The simplest way of purifying any water you're dubious about is to boil it vigorously for five minutes. However, at high altitude water boils at a lower temperature, so germs are less likely to be killed. If you can't boil water it should be treated chemically. Chlorine tablets (Puritabs, Steritabs or other brand names) will kill many pathogens. Iodine is also very effective in purifying water and is available in tablet form (such as Potable Aqua).

Nutrition If you're travelling hard and fast and missing meals, or if you simply lose your appetite, you can soon start to lose weight and place your health at risk. Make sure your diet is well balanced. Eggs, meat, pulses and dairy products are all safe ways to get protein. Fruit and vegetables are good sources of vitamins. Try to eat plenty of grains (including rice) and bread.

In hot weather make sure you drink enough; don't rely on feeling thirsty to indicate when you should drink. Not needing to urinate, or very dark yellow urine, is a danger sign. Carry a water bottle on long trips. Excessive sweating can lead to loss of salt and therefore muscle cramping.

Everyday Health Normal body temperature is 98.6°F or 37°C; more than 2°C higher indicates a high fever. The normal adult pulse rate is 60 to 80 per minute (children 80 to 100, babies 100 to 140). As a general rule the pulse increases about 20 beats per minute for each °C rise in fever.

Respiration (breathing) rate is also an indicator of illness. Count the number of breaths per minute: between 12 and 20 is normal for adults and older children (up to 30 for younger children, 40 for babies). People with a high fever or serious respiratory illness (like pneumonia) breathe more quickly than normal. More than 40 shallow breaths a minute usually means pneumonia.

You can help yourself by a few simple precautions like washing your hands before eating, limiting your exposure to hot sun, and dressing warmly when it's cold.

Medical Treatment

For serious medical problems and emergencies, the Spanish public health service provides care to rival that anywhere in the world. If you need to see a doctor about something more mundane, obscure appointment systems, queues and grumpy personnel can make it less than enchanting, though you should still get decent attention in the end. If you want to see a doctor quickly, or need emergency dental treatment, one way is to go along to the *urgencias* (emergency) section of the nearest hospital. Otherwise, the expense of going to a private clinic or surgery is often worth the saving in time and frustration. A consultation at a private clinic or surgery typically costs somewhere between 3000 and 6000 ptas (not counting medicines). If you have travel insurance you will probably be covered for this expense. All dental practices are private in any case.

Take along as much documentation as you can muster when you deal with medical services – passport, E111, insurance papers, ideally with photocopies too. Tourist offices, the police, and usually your accommodation, can all tell you where to find doctors, dentists and hospitals, or how to call an ambulance. You could also contact your country's nearest consulate in Spain for advice. Many major hospitals and emergency medical services are mentioned and/or shown on maps in this book's city sections.

Pharmacies *(farmacias)* can help with many ailments. A system of duty pharmacies *(farmacias de guardia)* operates so that each town or district of a city has one open all the time. When a pharmacy is closed, it posts the name of the nearest open one on the door. Lists of farmacias de guardia are often given in local papers, too.

Climatic & Geographical Considerations
Sunburn You can get sunburnt quickly in Spain, even through cloud. Use a sunscreen and take care to cover areas which don't normally see sun – eg your feet. A hat provides added protection. Calamine lotion is good for mild sunburn.

Prickly Heat This itchy rash, caused by excessive perspiration trapped under the skin, usually strikes people who have just arrived in a hot climate and whose pores have not yet opened enough to cope with greater sweating. Keeping cool but bathing often, using a mild talcum powder, or even resorting to air-conditioning, may help until you acclimatise.

Heat Exhaustion Dehydration or salt deficiency can cause heat exhaustion. Take time to acclimatise to high temperatures and make sure you get enough liquids. Wear loose clothing and a broad-brimmed hat. Don't do anything too physically demanding. Salt deficiency is characterised by fatigue, lethargy, headaches, giddiness and muscle cramps and in this case salt tablets may help. Vomiting or diarrhoea can deplete your liquid and salt levels.

Heat Stroke Long, continuous periods of exposure to high temperatures can leave you vulnerable to the serious, sometimes fatal, condition of heat stroke. It can occur if the body's heat-regulating mechanism breaks down and the body temperature rises to dangerous levels. You should avoid excessive alcohol or strenuous activity when you first arrive in a hot climate.

The symptoms are feeling unwell, not sweating very much or at all, and a high body temperature (39°C to 41°C). Severe, throbbing headaches and lack of coordination will also occur, and the sufferer may be confused or aggressive. Eventually the victim will become delirious or convulse. Hospitalisation is essential, but meanwhile get victims out of the sun, remove their clothing, cover them with a wet sheet or towel and then fan continually.

Fungal Infections Fungal infections happen more often in hot weather, and are most likely to occur on the scalp, between the toes or fingers (athlete's foot), in the groin (jock itch or crotch rot) or on the body (ringworm). You get ringworm (which is not a worm) from infected animals or by walking on damp areas, like shower floors.

To prevent fungal infections wear loose,

comfortable clothes, avoid artificial fibres, wash frequently and dry carefully. If you do get an infection, wash the infected area daily with a disinfectant or medicated soap and water. Apply an antifungal powder like the widely available Tinaderm. Try to expose the infected area to air or sunlight as much as possible and wash all towels and underwear in hot water.

Cold Too much cold is just as dangerous as too much heat, particularly if it leads to hypothermia. If you are out at high altitudes in cold or cool, wet weather, be prepared.

Hypothermia occurs when the body loses heat faster than it can produce it. It's surprisingly easy to progress from very cold to dangerously cold due to a combination of wind, wet clothes, fatigue and hunger, even if the air temperature is above freezing. It is best to dress in layers; silk, wool and some of the new artificial fibres are all good insulating materials. A hat is important, as a lot of heat is lost through the head. A strong, waterproof outer layer is essential. Carry basic supplies, including food containing simple sugars to generate heat quickly and lots of fluid to drink. A space blanket is something all travellers in cold environments should carry.

Symptoms of hypothermia are exhaustion, numb skin (particularly toes and fingers), shivering, slurred speech, irrational or violent behaviour, lethargy, stumbling, dizzy spells, muscle cramps and violent bursts of energy.

To treat mild hypothermia, first get the person out of the wind and/or rain, and replace their wet clothes with dry, warm ones. Give them hot liquids – not alcohol – and some high-kilojoule, easily digestible food. Do not rub victims; instead, allow them to slowly warm themselves. Early treatment of mild hypothermia is the only way to prevent severe hypothermia, which is a critical condition.

Altitude Sickness Acute Mountain Sickness, or AMS, occurs at high altitude and can be fatal. There's no firm rule about how high

is too high, but 3500 to 4000 metres is the usual range, so it's unlikely to be a major concern in Spain.

Breathlessness, a dry, irritative cough, severe headache, loss of appetite, nausea and sometimes vomiting are all danger signs. Increasing tiredness, confusion and lack of coordination and balance are real danger signs. Mild altitude sickness generally abates after a day or so but if symptoms persist the only treatment is to descend – even 500 metres can help.

Motion Sickness Eating lightly before and during a trip will reduce the chances of motion sickness. If you are prone to it, try to find a place that minimises disturbance – near the wing on aircraft, close to midships on boats, near the centre on buses. Fresh air usually helps; reading and cigarette smoke don't. Commercial motion-sickness preparations, which can cause drowsiness, have to be taken before the trip commences. Ginger is a natural preventative and is available in capsule form.

Infectious Diseases

Diarrhoea A change of water, food or climate can all cause the runs; diarrhoea caused by contaminated food or water is more serious. A few rushed toilet trips with no other symptoms are not indicative of a serious problem. Moderate diarrhoea, involving half-a-dozen loose movements in a day, is more of a nuisance.

Dehydration is the main danger with diarrhoea, particularly for children, and fluid replacement is the mainstay of management. Weak black tea with a little sugar, soda water, or soft drinks allowed to go flat and diluted 50% with water are all good. With severe diarrhoea a rehydrating solution is necessary to replace minerals and salts. Commercially available oral rehydration salts are very useful. You should stick to a bland diet as you recover.

Lomotil or Imodium brings relief from the symptoms but does not actually cure the problem. Only use these drugs if absolutely necessary – eg if you *must* travel – and don't use them if the victim has a high fever or is severely dehydrated, or the diarrhoea is watery, with blood and mucus. In cases of watery diarrhoea with blood and mucus, watery diarrhoea with fever and lethargy, or persistent diarrhoea for more than five days, see a doctor. Antibiotics may be needed.

Hepatitis Hepatitis is inflammation of the liver. The discovery of new strains has led to a virtual alphabet soup, with hepatitis A, B, C, D, E and a rumoured G. But hepatitis C, D, E and G are fairly rare worldwide, and Hepatitis A, which is spread by contaminated food and water, is only common in countries with worse sanitation than Spain.

Hepatitis B, however, has almost 300 million chronic carriers in the world, and Spanish children are now routinely vaccinated against it. It's spread through contact with infected blood, blood products or bodily fluids, for example through sexual contact, unsterilised needles and blood transfusions. Other risk situations include having a tattoo or having your ears pierced. The symptoms are much the same as for hepatitis A – fever, chills, headache, fatigue, weakness, aches and pains, followed by loss of appetite, nausea, vomiting, abdominal pain, dark urine, light coloured faeces, jaundiced skin – but they are more severe and may lead to irreparable liver damage or even liver cancer.

Although there is no treatment for hepatitis B, an effective vaccine is available, but it requires two injections at least a month apart followed by a third dose five months after the second. People who should especially consider having it include those who intend to stay in the country a long time and who anticipate contact with blood or other bodily secretions, for example through sexual contact.

Rabies Rabies has been very rare in mainland Spain and the Balearic Islands for some time, but there are occasional scares about it crossing the Strait of Gibraltar from Morocco or Spain's North African enclaves of Melilla and Ceuta. It's caused by a bite or scratch by an infected animal. Dogs are noted carriers, as are monkeys and cats. Any bite, scratch or even lick from a warm-blooded, furry animal should be scrubbed with soap and running water, then cleaned with an alcohol solution. If there is any possibility that the animal is infected, medical help should be sought immediately. Even if the animal is not rabid, bites can become infected or result in tetanus.

Sexually Transmitted Diseases Sexual contact with an infected sexual partner spreads these diseases. Abstinence is the only 100% preventative, but condoms *(condones, preservativos)*, available in many pharmacies, are also effective. Gonorrhoea and syphilis are the most common of these diseases; sores, blisters or rashes around the genitals, discharges or pain when urinating are common symptoms. Symptoms may be less marked or not observed at all in women. Syphilis symptoms eventually disappear completely but the disease continues and can cause severe problems in later years. Treatment of gonorrhoea and syphilis is by antibiotics. There's also effective treatment for numerous other sexually transmitted diseases, but there is no cure for herpes and currently none for AIDS.

HIV/AIDS HIV, the human immunodeficiency virus, may develop into AIDS, acquired immune deficiency syndrome. Any exposure to blood, blood products or bodily fluids may put a person at risk of HIV. It can be transmitted through heterosexual or male homosexual activity, or via contaminated needles shared by intravenous drug users. This last is the major reason for Spain having one of the highest rates of AIDS in Europe (over 600 new cases a month in 1996, and a total of over 40,000 cases, 80% of them males, since 1981). Apart from abstinence, the most effective preventative is always to practise safe sex using condoms.

HIV/AIDS can also be spread through infected blood transfusions and by dirty needles; vaccinations, acupuncture, tattooing and body piercing are potentially as dangerous as intravenous drug use if the equipment is not clean.

HIV and AIDS are VIH and *sida*, respectively, in Spanish. Several cities have a Comité (or Asociación) Ciudadano Anti-Sida, which is an AIDS information service. Madrid's comité is on ☎ 91-531 10 19, Monday to Friday from 10 am to 2 pm and 4 to 8 pm. Many gay organisations, including Barcelona's Coordinadora Gai-Lesbiana (☎ 93-237 08 69), can provide AIDS information and advice or put you in touch with an organisation that can.

Cuts, Bites & Stings

Cuts & Scratches Skin punctures can easily become infected in hot climates and may be difficult to heal. Treat any cut with an antiseptic such as Betadine. Where possible avoid bandages and Band-aids, which can keep wounds wet.

Stings & Bites For bee and wasp stings, calamine lotion will give relief and ice packs will reduce the pain and swelling. Scorpion stings are notoriously painful but Spanish scorpions are not considered fatal. Scorpions often shelter in shoes or clothing, so shake these out before you put them on when camping. Some Spanish centipedes *(escolopendras)* also have a very nasty, but not fatal, sting. The ones to steer clear of are those composed of hard, clearly defined segments, which may be patterned with, for instance, alternate black and yellow stripes.

Also beware of the hairy, reddish-brown caterpillars *(procesionarias)* of the pine processionary moth, which live in easily discernible silvery nests in pine trees in many parts of Spain, and have a habit of walking around in long lines (hence the name). The caterpillars' hairs contain a chemical which sets off a severely irritating allergic skin reaction. It's even more harmful to animals, which get gangrene of the tongue if not treated straight away.

Mosquito and other insect bites can be a nuisance – in the Pyrenees, for instance – but Spanish mosquitoes are not carriers of malaria. You can avoid bites by covering your skin and using an insect repellent.

Local advice is the best way of avoiding stinging and biting sea creatures. Jellyfish *(medusas)*, with their stinging tentacles, generally occur in large numbers or hardly at all, so it's fairly easy to know when not to go into the sea. Dousing in vinegar will deactivate any jellyfish stingers which have not 'fired'. Calamine lotion, antihistamines and analgesics may reduce the reaction and relieve the pain.

Snakes The only venomous snake that is even relatively common in Spain is the hognosed viper (*víbora hocicuda* in Spanish). This is a smallish, triangular-headed creature, rarely more than 50 cm long, and grey with a zigzag pattern along its back. It lives in dry, rocky areas, away from humans. Its bite can be fatal and needs to be treated as soon as possible with a serum which state clinics in major towns keep in stock. Also to be avoided are the Montpellier snake *(culebra bastarda)*, which is blue with a white underside and prominent ridges over the eyes, and Lataste's viper. These two live mainly in scrub and sandy areas – including parts of Doñana National Park – but they keep a low profile and are very unlikely to be a threat unless trodden on. To minimise your chances of being bitten by a snake, wear boots, socks and long trousers when walking where they may be present. Don't put your hands into holes and crevices, and be careful when collecting firewood.

Snake bites do not cause instantaneous death and antivenenes are usually available. Keep the victim calm and still, wrap the limb tightly, and attach a splint to immobilise it. Then seek medical help, if possible with the dead snake for identification. But don't try to catch the snake if there is even a remote possibility of being bitten again.

Women's Health

Gynaecological Problems Poor diet, lowered resistance due to the use of antibiotics for stomach upsets, and even contraceptive pills can lead to vaginal infections in hot weather. Maintaining good personal hygiene, and wearing skirts or loose-fitting trousers and cotton underwear, will help to prevent infections.

Yeast infections, characterised by a rash, itch and discharge, can be treated with a vinegar or lemon-juice douche, or with yoghurt. Nystatin suppositories are the usual medical prescription. Trichomoniasis is a more serious infection; symptoms are a discharge and a burning sensation when urinating. Male sexual partners must also be treated, and if a vinegar-water douche is not effective medical attention should be sought.

Pregnancy Most miscarriages occur during the first three months of pregnancy. They can occasionally lead to severe bleeding. The last three months of pregnancy should also be spent within reasonable distance of good medical care. A baby born as early as 24 weeks stands a chance of survival, but only in a good modern hospital. Pregnant women should avoid all unnecessary medication and take additional care to prevent illness, paying particular attention to nutrition. Alcohol and nicotine, for example, should be avoided.

Women travellers often find that their periods become irregular or even cease while they're on the road. A missed period in these circumstances doesn't necessarily indicate pregnancy.

WOMEN TRAVELLERS

The best way for women travellers to approach Spain is simply to be ready to ignore stares, catcalls and unnecessary comments. Spain actually has one of the lowest incidences of reported rape in the developed world, and harassment is much less frequent than you might expect, but you still need to use common sense about where you go on your own. Think twice about going alone to isolated stretches of beach or lonely country areas, or down dark city streets at night. Where there are crowds – as there often are very late into the night in towns and cities –

you're safer. It's highly inadvisable for a woman to hitchhike alone – and not a great idea even for two women together.

Topless bathing and skimpy clothes are in fashion in many coastal resorts, but people tend to dress more modestly elsewhere. Many Spanish women feel it only natural to emphasise their femininity by clothes and hairstyle, to both of which they devote considerable care – yet feel no obligation to respond to any male interest this arouses.

You may notice a shift in behaviour patterns as you move around the country. One northern European woman with many years experience of living and travelling in Spain observed to us that sexual stereotyping becomes more pronounced, and local men become more predatory, as you move south – and that men under about 30, who have grown up in relatively permissive post-Franco Spain, are less obsessed with foreign women than their older counterparts.

In Spain women's liberation, after the amazingly constricting Franco era (when wives could not legally take a job, open a bank account or even go on a long journey without their husband's permission), took the form less of radical feminism than of sexual permissiveness and of women flooding into the workforce and higher education, for the first time ever in Spanish history. Some of the causes of the 1970s women's movement were taken up, and some of its leaders absorbed, by the PSOE governments of the 1980s, and the movement rather fizzled out as a major independent force. Today it's stronger in the north than the south. Gender roles in the home haven't changed all that much, and many working women still run the household and take full responsibility for the children as well as going out to work. One consequence is that they're having fewer children now.

The Asociación de Asistencia a Mujeres Violadas (☎ 91-574 01 10), Calle O'Donnell 74, Madrid, offers advice and help to rape victims, and can tell of similar centres in other cities, though only limited English is spoken. The phone line is open Monday to Friday from 10 am to 2 pm and 4 to 7 pm;

there's a recorded message in Spanish at other times.

Recommended reading is the *Handbook for Women Travellers* by M & G Moss.

There are women's bookshops in Madrid, Barcelona and a few other cities (see city sections) which are also useful sources of information on women's organisations, activities and topics.

GAY & LESBIAN TRAVELLERS

Gay and lesbian sex are both legal in Spain, and the age of consent is 16 years, the same as for heterosexuals. The gay male scene is more developed than the lesbian one, though the latter certainly exists. Lesbians and gay men generally take a fairly low profile, but can be more open in the cities. Madrid, Barcelona, Sitges and Ibiza have particularly lively scenes. Sitges, in particular, is a major gay tourist destination, and is on the international gay party circuit; gays take a leading role in the wild *carnaval* there in February/March. As well, there are gay parades, marches and events in several cities on and around the last Saturday in June, when Madrid's Gay & Lesbian Pride march takes place.

You'll find gay and lesbian bars, discos, bookshops and information or social centres listed in some city sections of this book.

Guía Gay Visado is a guide to gay and lesbian bars, discos, contacts etc in Spain. You can find it, along with one or two similar publications, at some of the newsstands on La Rambla in Barcelona and in lesbian/gay bookshops. *Entiendes*, a gay magazine, is on sale at some newsstands for 500 ptas. International gay and lesbian guides worth tracking down are the *Spartacus Guide for Gay Men* (the Spartacus list also includes the comprehensive *Spartacus National Edition España*, in English and German), published by Bruno Gmünder Verlag, Mail Order, PO Box 11 07 29, D-1000 Berlin 11; *Places for Women*, published by Ferrari Publications, Phoenix, AZ, USA; and *Women Going Places*, published in London by Women Going Places.

There are a few Spanish queer sites on the World Wide Web, one of the best of which is *Gay Spain* (http://www.gayspain.com). It has city and regional listings of bars, clubs, accommodation, organisations etc – in Spanish.

DISABLED TRAVELLERS

Some Spanish tourist offices in other countries (including the one in London) can provide a basic information sheet with some useful addresses for disabled travellers, and give info on accessible accommodation in specific places.

You'll find some accessible accommodation in main centres but it may not be in the budget category – though 25 Spanish youth hostels are classed as suitable for wheelchair users. All new public buildings are now required to have wheelchair access, but of course most public buildings went up long before this law took effect.

The British-based Royal Association for Disability & Rehabilitation (RADAR) publishes a useful guide, *Holidays & Travel Abroad: A Guide for Disabled People*, with a section on Spain covering contact addresses, transport, services and accommodation. Contact RADAR (☎ 0171-250 3222) at 12 City Forum, 250 City Rd, London EC1 8AF. Mobility International (☎ 02-410 6274, fax 02-410 6297), Rue de Manchester 25, Brussels B1070, Belgium, has researched facilities for disabled tourists in Spain.

Organisations

Cruz Roja Española, the Spanish Red Cross (☎ 91-533 45 31, fax 91-253 35 79), Calle Doctor Santero 18, 28010 Madrid, may be able to give some assistance in travel arrangements and has available an access guide to Madrid. A Barcelona access guide is available from ECOM (☎ & fax 93-451 69 04), Spain's federation of private organisations for the disabled, at Gran via de les Corts Catalanes 562 principal 2ª, 08011 Barcelona.

INSERSO (☎ 91-347 88 88), Calle Ginzo de Limea 58, 28029 Madrid, is the Spanish government department for the disabled, with branches in all the country's 50 provinces. ONCE (☎ 91-597 47 27), Planta 28, Paseo de la Castellana 95, Madrid, is the Spanish association for the blind.

SENIOR TRAVELLERS

There are reduced prices for people over 60, 63 or 65 (depending on the place) at some museums and attractions, and occasionally on transport. Some of the luxurious *paradores* (see Accommodation later in this chapter) have recently been offering discounts for people over 60.

TRAVEL WITH CHILDREN

Spanish people as a rule are very friendly to children. Any child whose hair is less than jet black will get called *rubia* (blonde) if she's a girl, or *rubio* if he's a boy. Accompanied children are welcome at all kinds of accommodation, and in virtually every café, bar and restaurant. The large number of places with outside tables allows kids a bit of space and freedom while their grown-ups sit and eat or drink. Spanish children stay up late and at fiestas it's commonplace to see even tiny ones toddling the streets at 2 or 3 am. Visiting kids like this idea too – but can't cope with it quite so readily.

Of course you need to tailor your trip partly to what the kids like and can cope with. Most of them don't like travelling or moving around too much but are happier if they can settle into places and make new friends. It's easier on the parents too if you don't have to pack up all their gear and move on every day or two. Children are also likely to be more affected by unaccustomed heat, and need time to acclimatise and extra care to avoid sunburn. There are few special child health risks specific to Spain, but be prepared for minor effects brought on by change of diet or water, disrupted sleeping patterns, or even just being in a strange place.

Spanish street life and bustle, and the novelty of being in new places, provide some distraction for most kids but they'll get bored unless at least some of the time is devoted to their own favoured activities. Apart from the obvious attractions of beaches, playgrounds

are fairly plentiful and in many places you can find some excellent special attractions such as funfairs (among which Cataluña's Port Aventura reigns supreme), aquaparks, boat and train rides, child-friendly museums, zoos, aquariums – and let's not forget Mini-Hollywood and other Western movie sets in the Almería desert. Do bring some of the children's own toys, books etc with you and let them have adequate time to get on with some of the same activities they are used to back at home.

An extraordinary fascination is exercised over most children by the ubiquitous street-corner *kioscos* selling sweets or *gusanitos* (corn puffs) for a duro (5 ptas) or two. The magnetism of these places often overcomes children's inhibitions enough for them to carry out their own first Spanish transactions there.

Nappies, creams, lotions, baby foods and so on are all as easily available in Spain as in any other Western country, but if there's some particular brand you swear by it's best to bring it with you. Calpol, for instance, isn't easily found.

Children benefit from reduced or nonexistent entry fees at many sights and museums. Those under four travel free on Spanish trains and those aged four to 11 normally pay 60% of the adult fare.

Lonely Planet's *Travel with Children*, by Maureen Wheeler, has lots of practical advice on the subject, and first-hand stories from many Lonely Planet authors, and others, who have done it.

USEFUL ORGANISATIONS

The Instituto Cervantes, with branches in over 30 cities around the world, exists to promote the Spanish language and the cultures of Spain and other Spanish-speaking countries. It's mainly involved in Spanish teaching and library and information services. The library at the London branch, for instance – 22 Manchester Square, London W1M 5AP (☎ 0171-935 1518, fax 935 6167) – has a wide range of reference books, literature, books on history and the arts, periodicals, over 1000 videos including feature films, language-teaching material, electronic databases and music CDs.

TIVE, the Spanish youth and student travel organisation, is good for reduced-price youth and student travel tickets. It also issues various useful documents such as HI youth hostel cards, and FIYTO and ITIC cards (see Visas & Documents earlier in this chapter). TIVE has branches in many cities and its head office is at Calle José Ortega y Gasset 71, 28006 Madrid (☎ 91-347 77 00).

DANGERS & ANNOYANCES

Spain is generally a pretty safe country. The main thing you have to be wary of is petty theft (which may of course not seem so petty

to you if your passport, cash, travellers' cheques, credit card and camera all go missing). But with a few simple precautions you can minimise the risk and any worries about it.

For some specific hints about looking after your luggage and money, and on safety for women, see the What to Bring, Money and Women Travellers sections earlier in this chapter.

Before you leave home, inscribe your name, address and telephone number *inside* your luggage, and take photocopies of the important pages of your passport, travel tickets and other important documents. Keep the copies separate from the originals and

---

La Policía

Spanish police are on the whole more of a help than a threat to the average law-abiding traveller. Most of them are certainly friendly enough to be approachable for directions on the street. Highway police can be hard on locals but tend to steer clear of foreign vehicles unless they stop to give help (but see the Getting Around chapter for the list of documents and equipment that you should carry in your vehicle). Unpleasant events such as random drug searches do occur, but not with great frequency.

There are three main types of *policía*: the Policía Nacional, the Policía Local (sometimes called Policía Municipal) and the Guardia Civil (we use the words policía and guardia here to refer to the forces, but they also stand for each individual member).

Guardia Civil Most numerous are the green-uniformed members of the Guardia Civil, 70,000 strong, whose main responsibilities are roads, the countryside, villages, prisons, international borders and some environmental protection. These are the guys who used to wear those alarming winged helmets, which were phased out in the 1980s but still resurface on some ceremonial occasions.

The Guardia Civil was set up in the 19th century to quell banditry but soon came to be regarded as a politically repressive force clamping down on any challenge to established privilege. Though its image has softened since Franco and responsibility for it has been switched from the Defence Ministry to the Interior Ministry, it's still a military body in some ways: most officers have attended military academy and members qualify for military decorations.

Policía Nacional This force, 50,000 strong, covers cities and bigger towns and is the main crime-fighting body because most crime happens on its patch. Those of its number who wear uniforms are in blue. There is also a large contingent in plain clothes, some of whom form special squads dealing with drugs, terrorism and the like, but most of whom are to be found in large bunker-like police stations called *comisarías*, shuffling masses of paper dealing with things like the issuing of passports, DNIs (*documentos nacionales de identidad*, national identity cards) and residence cards for foreigners who like Spain enough to opt for long-term entanglement with its bureaucracy.

Policía Local The 35,000 members of the Policía Local are controlled by city and town councils and deal mainly with minor matters such as parking, traffic and bylaws. They wear blue-and-white uniforms. In Cataluña the equivalent force is called the Guàrdia Urbana. Spain has no real equivalent of 'bobby on the beat' street-patrol police.

Regional Police Finally, four of Spain's 17 autonomous communities have their own police forces in addition to the above three: Cataluña (where it's called the Mossos d'Esquadra), the País Vasco (the Ertzaintza), Valencia and Galicia.

Contacting the Police If you need to go to the police, any of them will do, but you may find the Policía Local are the most helpful.

Anywhere in Spain you can call ☎ 091 for the Policía Nacional or ☎ 092 for the Policía Local. Guardia Civil numbers vary from place to place. Some further police numbers, and locations of main stations, are given in the city and town sections of this book. ■

ideally leave one set of copies at home. These steps will make things easier if you do suffer a loss or theft.

Travel insurance against theft and loss is another very good idea; see the Health section in this chapter.

Theft & Loss

Theft is most a risk in tourist resorts, big cities, and when you first arrive in the country or a new city and may be off your guard, disoriented or unaware of danger signs. Barcelona, Madrid and Sevilla have the worst reputations for theft.

The main things to guard against are pickpockets and bag snatchers, and theft from cars. Carry valuables under your clothes if possible – certainly not in a back pocket or in a day pack or anything which could be snatched away easily – and keep your eyes open for people who get unnecessarily close to you at airports, at stations, in trains, buses or on the metro, or on the street. Don't leave baggage unattended, and avoid crushes. Also be cautious with people who come up to offer or ask you something, or start talking to you for no obviously good reason. These could be attempts to distract you or to get you to stop walking and make you an easier victim.

Car contents – including fitted radios and cassette players – are sitting ducks for thieves. Unfortunately it's safest to remove any radio or cassette player from your car before you go to Spain. When you leave the car, don't leave visible anything that looks even remotely useful – and preferably don't leave anything at all, visible or invisible. Even if thieves who get into your car end up taking nothing, they will probably have broken a window first.

Take care with your belongings on the beach; anything lying on the sand could disappear in a flash when your back is turned. Also avoid dingy, empty city alleys and backstreets, or anywhere that just doesn't feel 100% safe, at night.

You can also help yourself by not leaving anything valuable lying around your room, above all in any hostel-type place. Use a safe if there's one available.

If anything valuable does get stolen or lost, you'll need to report it to the police, and get a copy of the report, if you want to make an insurance claim. Occasionally, this might even help you get it back. If your passport has gone, contact your embassy or consulate for help in issuing a replacement. Many countries have consulates in a few cities around Spain (such as Barcelona, Valencia, Alicante, Málaga and Sevilla) and your embassy can tell you where the nearest one is. Embassies and consulates can also give help of various kinds in other emergencies, but as a rule cannot advance you money to get home.

Other Emergencies

Medical emergency numbers and locations of many hospitals and clinics are given in this book's city and town sections. In many – but not all – places, ☎ 061 is the number for an ambulance, while ☎ 22 22 22 (☎ 222 22 22 if local numbers have seven digits) is the Cruz Roja (Red Cross) number in many cities. See the Health section earlier in this chapter for more on Spanish medical facilities and health problems. If you're seriously ill or injured, someone should let your embassy or consulate know.

In many places the fire brigade (bomberos) is on ☎ 080 or ☎ 085, but in other places it's on some completely different number.

Terrorism

In the summers of 1995 and 1996 the Basque terrorist organisation ETA exploded a number of small bombs in tourist spots such as Granada, Málaga and Cataluña's Costa Daurada. One of the 1996 bombs, at the Costa Daurada's Reus airport, went off earlier than planned and injured over 30 people, mostly foreign tourists. But otherwise ETA violence has not generally been aimed at foreigners, and the total number of ETA-related deaths – averaging 17 a year since 1992 – has actually been lower in the mid-1990s than at any time for 20 years.

Annoyances

Spain is really a pretty mellow place and there ain't much to get annoyed about. That said, you should expect a few attempts to short-change you – and you've got to be prepared for more noise than you're probably used to! While a certain amount of noise and crowds can make anybody feel more alive, it can be hard to understand why young Spanish males deliberately tinker with their motorbike exhausts to make the blessed things even noisier than they need to be. There's some sort of legislation about silencers but no-one dreams of enforcing it.

The Libro de Reclamaciones

Most public establishments of any kind – places to stay, places to eat, post offices, businesses – have a sign up saying that they have a complaints book *(libro de reclamaciones)* available for anyone who would like to use it. If you have a serious gripe or are in dispute about a bill, asking for the libro de reclamaciones might just bring a swift change of attitude from whoever you're at odds with. If you actually go as far as making an entry in the book, there'll be a copy for you and a copy for the establishment concerned. On the back of your copy will be instructions on what to do if you want to take the matter further. The books are supposedly checked from time to time by government consumer agencies.

LEGAL MATTERS

If you're arrested you will be allotted the free services of a duty solicitor *(abogado de oficio)*, who may speak only Spanish. You're also entitled to make a phone call. If you use this to contact your embassy or consulate, it will probably be able to do no more than refer you to a lawyer who speaks your language. If you end up in court, the authorities are obliged to provide a translator.

Drugs

Spain's liberal drug laws were severely tightened in 1992. The only legal drug is cannabis, and only in amounts for personal use – which means very small amounts.

There is, however, inconsistency in enforcement. For example, a Madrid acquaintance of one of the authors of this book was found in possession of a small amount of cannabis by a policeman, who took the dope and told our friend to be on his way. Our friend, however, before departing, asked for his dope back, whereupon he was arrested and spent a night in the clink.

Public consumption of any drug is apparently illegal, yet there are still some bars where people smoke joints openly. Other bars will ask you to step outside if you light up. The only sure moral of these stories is to be very discreet if you do use cannabis. There is a reasonable degree of tolerance when it comes to people having a smoke in their own home, but it would be unwise in hotel rooms or guesthouses, and could be risky in even the coolest of public places.

Travellers entering Spain from Morocco should be ready for intensive drug searches, especially if they have a vehicle.

BUSINESS HOURS

Generally, people work Monday to Friday from about 9 am to 2 pm and then again from 4.30 or 5 pm for another three hours. Shops and travel agencies are usually open these hours on Saturday too, though some may skip the evening session. Big supermarkets, and department stores such as the nationwide El Corte Inglés chain, often stay open all day Monday to Saturday, from about 9 am to 9 pm. A few shops in tourist resorts open on Sunday in the summer. A lot of government offices don't bother with afternoon opening any day of the year.

Museums all have their own unique opening hours: major ones tend to open for something like normal Spanish business hours (with or without the afternoon break), but often have their weekly closing day on Monday, not Sunday.

See earlier sections of this chapter for bank and post office hours.

PUBLIC HOLIDAYS & SPECIAL EVENTS
Public Holidays

Everywhere in Spain there are at least 14

official holidays a year – some observed nationwide, some very local. When a holiday falls close to a weekend, Spaniards like to make a *puente* (bridge) – meaning they take the intervening day off too.

The eight national holidays are:

1 January
  Año Nuevo (New Year's Day)
March/April
  Viernes Santo (Good Friday)
1 May
  Fiesta del Trabajo (Labour Day)
15 August
  La Asunción (Feast of the Assumption)
12 October
  Día de la Hispanidad (National Day)
1 November
  Todos Santos (All Saints' Day)
6 December
  Día de la Constitución (Constitution Day)
25 December
  Navidad (Christmas)

In addition, regional governments everywhere set four holidays and local councils a further two. Common dates include:

6 January
  Epifanía (Epiphany) or *Día de los Reyes Magos* (Three Kings' Day), when children receive presents; observed everywhere
March/April
  Jueves Santo (Maundy Thursday, the day before Good Friday); everywhere except Cataluña and Valencia
June
  Corpus Christi (the Thursday after the eighth Sunday after Easter Sunday); widespread
24 June
  Día de San Juan Bautista (Feast of St John the Baptist), King Juan Carlos' saint's day; widespread
25 July
  Día de Santiago Apóstol (Feast of St James the Apostle), Spain's patron saint; widespread
8 December
  La Inmaculada Concepción (Feast of the Immaculate Conception); most places except Barcelona

Vacation Periods

The two main periods when Spaniards go on holiday are Semana Santa (the week leading up to Easter Sunday) and the month of August. At these times accommodation in resorts can be scarce and transport heavily booked, but other cities are often half-empty.

Festivals

Spaniards indulge their love of colour, noise, crowds, dressing up and partying at innumerable local fiestas and *ferias* (fairs): even small villages will have at least one, probably several, in the year, all with their own unique twists. Many fiestas are religion-based but still highly festive and party-spirited. Main local festivals are noted in city and town sections of this book and tourist offices can supply more detailed info. A few of the most outstanding include:

20 January
  Festividad de San Sebastián in San Sebastián – the whole town dresses up and goes berserk
February/March
  Carnaval (Carnival) – several days of fancy-dress parades and merrymaking in many places, usually ending on the Tuesday 47 days before Easter Sunday (wildest in Cádiz and Sitges, also good in Ciudad Rodrigo)
15-19 March
  Las Fallas in Valencia – several days of all-night dancing and drinking, first class fireworks and processions; also celebrated in Gandía and Benidorm
March/April
  Semana Santa (Holy Week, the week leading up to Easter Sunday) – parades of holy images and huge crowds, notably in Sevilla, but also big in Málaga, Córdoba, Toledo, Ávila, Valladolid, Zamora and other places
22-24 April
  Moros y Cristianos in Alcoy, near Alicante – colourful parades and 'battles' between Christian and Muslim 'armies', one of the best of several similar events in Valencia and Alicante provinces through the year
Late April
  Feria de Abril in Sevilla – a week-long party counterbalancing the religious fervour of Semana Santa
Last Sunday in April
  Romería de Andújar – hundreds of thousands of people in a mass pilgrimage to a shrine of the Virgin at Andújar, Andalucía
Early/mid-May
  Concurso de Patios Cordobeses – scores of beautiful private courtyards open to the public for two weeks in Córdoba

Third week of May

>Fiestas de San Isidro in Madrid – the capital's major fiesta, with bullfights, parades, concerts and more

May/June

>Romería del Rocío – festive pilgrimage of up to one million people to the shrine of the Virgin at the Andalucían village of El Rocío, focused on Pentecost weekend, the seventh after Easter

May/June

>Corpus Christi – religious processions and celebrations in Toledo and other cities, on or shortly before the ninth Sunday after Easter Sunday

Around 24 June

>Hogueras de San Juan – midsummer bonfires and fireworks, notably along the south-east and south coasts

6-14 July

>Sanfermines in Pamplona, with the famous Running of the Bulls (an activity also pursued in dozens of other cities and towns through the summer)

16 July

>Día de la Virgen del Carmen – on or near this day of the patron of fisherfolk, her image is carried into the sea, or paraded on it amid a flotilla of small boats, at most coastal towns

25 July

>Día de Santiago (Feast of St James) – the national saint's day, spectacularly celebrated in Santiago de Compostela, site of his tomb

August

>Semana Grande or Aste Nagusia – a week of general celebration, heavy drinking and hangovers on the north coast (dates vary from place to place)

Last Wednesday of August

>La Tomatina in Buñol, Valencia – wild tomato-throwing festival

Around 24 September

>Festes de la Mercè – a week-long party in Barcelona

Arts Festivals Spain's calendar also abounds in arts festivals (any excuse for a party!). Mérida's Festival de Teatro of drama and dance from late June to August, Barcelona's concurrent Grec festival of music, dance and theatre, Córdoba's two week Festival Internacional de la Guitarra starting in late June, San Sebastián's International Jazz Festival in July, Santander's mainly musical Festival Internacional in July and August, Sevilla's Bienal de Flamenco in September of even-numbered years, the November Festival Internacional de Jazz de Barcelona, which also includes blues – all these and many others will enliven visits to their cities at the right times.

Rock, Pop & Dance Festivals These are growing in number and popularity among a younger crowd, and the summer positively overflows with them in some parts of the country. In July 1996 David Bowie, Lou Reed, Blur and Patti Smith topped the bill at the first Doctor Music Festival near Esterri d'Aneu in the Catalan Pyrenees – the first staging of what's planned to be an annual event. Cáceres in Extremadura staged Spain's Womad world music festival every May from 1992 to 1996, but unfortunately there's doubt over whether it will continue to do so. Madrid's big one is Festimad, an early-May orgy of varied music in bars, halls and open-air stages. The Benicàssim festival north of Valencia is a long-weekend indie get-together in early August. Badalona near Barcelona has its Pop Festival, with international and Spanish names, in early September. There are many other smaller-scale festivals in summer, some just one night long. You'll see plenty of posters telling you about them. Outside the summer season Granada holds the one day Espárrago Rock festival in March, highlighting Spanish and foreign alternative rock.

The biggest numbers get together for modern dance gatherings with DJs (*pinchadiscos*) and bands pumping out techno, house, eurobeat, euroenergy and their relatives for a night or two. An estimated 200,000 people converged on the port at Málaga for the one-off World Dance Málaga in May 1996. Barcelona's Festival Sonar is the main annual event of this kind.

ACTIVITIES

Spanish tourist offices can provide quite detailed information on possibilities for many activities from hiking, skiing, mountaineering or windsurfing to horse riding, bird-watching, golf or wine tours. If you fancy going in a guided group, see the Organised Tours section of the Getting There & Away chapter for a few pointers. Spanish tourist offices can also usually tell you about tour companies running a vast range of activity holidays.

Trekking & Hiking

With its large tracts of wilderness, Spain offers limitless opportunities for short and long walks. Some wonderful areas are easily accessible and can be enjoyed on day or half-day walks, as well as by committed trekkers.

Trekking Trekking is popular among Spaniards as well as foreigners: outstanding mountain areas are the Pyrenees in Aragón and Cataluña, the Picos de Europa straddling Cantabria, Asturias and León provinces, the Sierra de Gredos west of Madrid, the Sierra Nevada and Alpujarras valleys in Andalucía, and the Serra de Tramuntana on Mallorca.

GRs, PRs & Other Paths Spain, particularly the north, has an extensive network of long-distance footpaths, the *senderos de Gran Recorrido* (GRs). Wherever possible these cross-country routes, some several hundred km long, avoid roads and tracks used by vehicles. Not all, however, are marked or maintained for their full length – or even for much of their length in some cases.

Among the longest of the GRs are the well-marked, well-established and spectacular GR-11 or Senda Pirenáica, which runs the length of the Spanish Pyrenees from Cap de Creus on the coast of Cataluña to Hondarribia (Fuenterrabía) on the Bay of Biscay in the País Vasco; the GR-10 from Puçol on the coast of Valencia to La Alberca, just 70 km from the Portuguese border (though the stretch across Ávila province doesn't yet exist); and the GR-7 from Andorra all the way south to Murcia province.

But Spain's most famous long walk is the Camino de Santiago (part of which forms the GR-65). This ancient pilgrim route, in use since the 11th century, can be started at various places in France. It then crosses the Pyrenees at Roncesvalles and runs across Navarra, La Rioja, Castilla y León and

Galicia to the cathedral in Santiago de Compostela, shrine of Spain's patron saint St James (Santiago). Variations run along the Bay of Biscay coast and through Aragón, and there are also routes from Portugal, Cataluña and elsewhere. Lots of people still walk or cycle the route (or parts of it), for religious purposes or otherwise. There are numerous guidebooks to the Camino, in various languages, and you'll find special sections devoted to it in this book's chapters on Galicia, Castilla y León, and the País Vasco, Navarra & La Rioja.

Of course most people don't walk the full length of these long-distance paths. Most are quite easily accessible by road (and often public transport) at many points, and it's perfectly feasible to join them for just a few hours amble if you're not committed to more serious walking.

Spain also has many *senderos de Pequeño Recorrido* (PRs), shorter footpaths suitable for day or weekend hikes. Like GRs, these vary widely in quality of trails and markings. In addition there are lots of good paths which haven't become either GRs or PRs.

National parks, natural parks and other protected areas (see Flora & Fauna in the Facts about the Country chapter) may restrict visitors to limited zones and routes, but often have well-marked walks through some of their most interesting areas, with interpretive information available.

Simply walking country roads and paths between villages and towns, instead of taking the bus, can be highly enjoyable, and a great way to meet the locals.

Not all Spain's coasts are covered with concrete hotels and there are some good coastal walks to be had in places such as Galicia, the Costa Brava and Andalucía's Cabo de Gata.

Seasons The best seasons for hiking and trekking vary from region to region. In the Pyrenees, late June to early September is best; in Andalucía, mid-April to mid-June, and September through to mid-October, are generally the most pleasant months, but the high Sierra Nevada is only really accessible from mid-July to September; the best months for trekking in the Picos de Europa are May, June and September. The weather in high mountains is never predictable at any time, however.

Sources of Information Tourist offices can often help. There are a number of Spanish mountain walking and climbing clubs which can give information on routes, refuges and equipment shops, including the Federación Española de Montañismo (☎ 91-445 13 82) in Madrid. Others are mentioned in regional chapters. A number of hiking guides to parts of Spain are available in English, French and other languages, as well as in Spanish. Lonely Planet's *Trekking in Spain*, by Marc Dubin, covers routes in all the main trekking areas, and has plenty of advice on equipment, preparation, seasons, accommodation and so on. A good companion on the Camino de Santiago is *The Way of St James – The Pilgrimage Route to Santiago de Compostela* by Dr Elias Valiña Sampedra, a book of detailed colour maps with a 20-odd page introduction to the route. Mountain guides worth tracking down include *Walks & Climbs in the Pyrenees* by Kev Reynolds, and *Walks & Climbs – Picos de Europa* by Robin Walker. In Spanish, the Colección El Búho Viajero series of hiking and walking books published by Libros Penthalon covers many regions of Spain in detail. *Gran Recorrido, Guía de Senderos del Estado Español* published by Prames (Zaragoza, 1994), gives basic details of the routes and condition of many of the GRs, and details of relevant maps, local guidebooks and information sources. Detailed Spanish walking guides are generally called *topoguías*. You may well find some available in local areas, but it's best to obtain them before you head off, from specialist bookshops in your own country or bookshops like Altaïr or Quera in Barcelona or La Tienda Verde in Madrid.

For information on maps for hikers, see the Planning section at the start of this chapter. References to some appropriate maps for specific areas are made in regional chapters of this guide.

Skiing

Spain is not exactly the first country that leaps to mind when talk turns to Europe's ski centres, but its profile was significantly lifted by the staging of the world skiing championships in the Sierra Nevada near Granada in 1996. Andorra is much better known, and has several good, well-established resorts.

In fact skiing facilities and conditions in Spain are surprisingly good, and costs are low, though in general the snow is not quite up to the standards of the Alps or even the French side of the Pyrenees. The season normally runs from December to April, with the best snow in February. But snow cover can be unpredictable, even in the higher altitude resorts: some years you may be able to ski from November to May, yet the Sierra Nevada's world championships actually happened 12 months late because there wasn't enough snow in the originally scheduled year, 1995.

Spain's main ski resorts are in the Pyrenees (plus the one in the Sierra Nevada), but there are others in the Sierra de Guadarrama north of Madrid, the Cordillera Cantábrica, and even La Rioja and southern Aragón. A recent survey by the premier national newspaper *El País* selected nine of the best resorts overall, judged by their length of piste, lift capacity, prices, landscape, services and popularity among users. The table on pages 122-3 shows the vital statistics of those nine, and of Andorra's resorts.

Ski package holidays from other countries are rather a novelty to Spain (though not to Andorra). But travel agencies in Spanish cities offer affordable packages for one day or longer. If you prefer to organise it yourself on the spot, a day's ski pass *(forfait)* at the better resorts in Spain and Andorra costs from around 2500 to 3900 ptas a day (depending on resort and season), or about 13,000 to 20,000 ptas a week, and equipment rental is usually around 1500 to 2000 ptas a day. Ski school costs around 1800 ptas for two hours or 9000 ptas for 15 hours. You can find a range of accommodation, from mid-priced hostales up, in or near most resorts.

The high season – when the slopes are

most crowded and prices for lift passes, ski school and accommodation are at their highest – generally means the Christmas-New Year holiday period, February, Semana Santa, and Saturday and Sunday almost all season long. At these times, the slopes are emptiest from 9 to 11 am and 1 to 3 pm while the Spanish skiers take breakfast and lunch.

Spanish and Andorran pistes are all graded green *(verde)* for beginners, blue *(azul)* for easy, red *(rojo)* for intermediate and black *(negro)* for difficult, though there's some variation in criteria between resorts.

Good resorts for cross-country skiing include Baqueira-Beret (Cataluña), Candanchú (Aragón), and several in Andorra. Snowboarding is growing fast in popularity at many ski resorts.

Spanish tourist offices in other countries, and tourist offices in Spanish and Andorran cities/towns near the ski resorts, usually have fairly detailed information on skiing.

Cycling

Mountain biking is popular among both Spaniards and foreigners. There are km upon km of good and bad tracks and roads for this in many areas, including Andalucía and Cataluña. Tourist offices often have info on routes. A good general source for mountain bikers who can read Spanish is *100 Rutas en Bicicleta de Montaña* by Juanjo Pedales (Espasa Calpe, 1995). Some tourist offices in Andalucía sell an English-language booklet, *120 Itineraries around Andalusia on a Mountain bike*, for 400 ptas. The Spanish for mountain bike is *bici todo terreno* (BTT).

See the Getting Around chapter for info on cycle touring in Spain.

Finding bikes of any kind to rent is a hit-or-miss affair with regard to both availability and price, which can vary enormously. Cataluña is fairly well provided with rental outlets for both mountain bikes and touring bikes, but elsewhere you should bring your own if you're dead set on the idea.

Surfing

The País Vasco has some good waves, at San Sebastián, Zarautz, which stages a round of the world championship each September, and Mundaka, with its legendary left, among others. Santander in Cantabria also attracts surfers in force, and there are other good spots in Cantabria and Asturias. You'll find boards (and wet suits) available in most surf spots if you're not carrying your own.

Windsurfing

Tarifa, Spain's southernmost point, is windsurfer's heaven, with strong breezes all year, a big windsurfing scene, and long, uncrowded beaches. In Galicia, Praia de Lariño on the Ría de Muros and La Lanzada beach on the Ría de Pontevedra can be good.

Snorkelling & Scuba Diving

Some of the rockier parts of the Mediterranean coast – notably the Illes Medes off L'Estartit, Cataluña, but also San Sebastián, Cadaqués, Isla de Tabarca, Cabo de Gata and Almuñecar and elsewhere – are good for these. Snorkelling and diving trips, and diving gear rental, are available at all these places.

Rafting, Canoeing & Hydrospeed

The turbulent Noguera Pallaresa in northwest Cataluña is Spain's top white-water river, with a string of grade 3 and 4 drops. Rafting, canoeing and hydrospeed (watertobogganing) are at their best here in May and June, and numerous local companies offer outings. The Río Sella in Asturias also has some good white water, and more than 1000 canoeists from around the world take part in the 22 km Descenso del Sella race, from Arriondas in the Picos de Europa to Ribadesella on the coast, on the first weekend in August.

Work You Pay to Do

SEO/Birdlife, the Spanish ornithological society, offers the chance to take part in bird surveys and ringing at places like Doñana National Park and the Strait of Gibraltar, a key migration route. You pay around 35,000 to 40,000 ptas for a week including accommodation and meals. Contact Centro de Migración de Aves, SEO/Birdlife, Carretera de Humera 63-1, 28224 Pozuelo, Madrid (☎ 91-351 10 45, fax 91-351 13 86).

Another organisation that sends paying volunteers to Spain is Earthwatch, Belsyre Court, 57 Woodstock Rd, Oxford OX2 6HU, UK (☎ 01865-311600, fax 01865-311383).

Projects include archaeological digs in Mallorca and Aragón and wildlife study on Mallorca. Earthwatch's representative in Spain is Pamela Cooper, Apartado de Correos 35078, 28080 Madrid (☎ 91-320 00 91, fax 91-742 36 52).

Spanish & Andorran Ski Resorts

Resort	Location	Telephone (Information)	Altitude (max/min, metres)	No of Lifts	Capacity (skiers/hour)
Spain					
Alto Campóo	Valle de Campóo, Cantabria (Cordillera Cantábrica)	942-77 92 22	2175/1650	9	7000
Baqueira-Beret	Vall d'Aran, Catalan Pyrenees	973-64 44 55	2510/1500	24	28,700
Candanchú	North of Jaca, Aragonese Pyrenees	974-37 31 94	2400/1560	24	19,650
Cerler	Near Benasque, Aragonese Pyrenees	974-55 10 12	2630/1500	13	9822
La Molina	Near Puigcerdà, Catalan Pyrenees	972-89 20 31	2537/1600	15	16,330
La Pinilla	Near Riaza, Sierra de Guadarrama, 110 km north of Madrid	921-55 03 04	2273/1500	12	12,500
San Isidro	Sierra de Murias (Cordillera Cantábrica), on León-Asturias Provincial Boundary	987-73 11 16	2155/1500	12	10,400
Sierra Nevada	33 km south-east of Granada	958-24 91 00	3300/2100	19	31,965
Valdezcaray	Sierra La Demanda, 60 km west of Logroño, La Rioja	941-42 70 40	2262/1530	11	7680
Andorra					
Arinsal		864389	2650/1550	14	12,200
Ordino-Arcalís		864389	2600/1940	12	13,500
Pal		864389	2358/1780	14	11,400
Pas de la Casa-Grau Roig		864389	2600/2050	27	27,415
Soldeu-El Tarter		864389	2560/1710	21	19,500

COURSES

A spot of study in Spain is a great way not only to learn something but also to meet people – Spaniards as well as other travellers – and get more of an inside angle on local life than the average visitor.

Language

Branches of the Instituto Cervantes (see Useful Organisations in this chapter) can send you long lists of places offering Spanish-language courses in Spain. Some Spanish embassies and consulates also have

Total No of Pistes	No of Red or Black Pistes	Length of Pistes (km)	No of Cannons	No of Instructors	Approx Cost of Day Pass (ptas)	Comments
10	7	12	80	36	1700-2200	Small resort with views of Picos de Europa
46	27	73.5	243	200	3900	Varied range of well-kept slopes, modern lifts, beautiful scenery, select clientele including the Spanish royal family
46	29	40	109	85	3200	Good range of runs, fine scenery, lift passes valid for nearby Astún too
26	16	34	79	50	2400-2800	Good for families and beginners, fine scenery
27	14	38	218	160	2600-3250	Long, easy runs
18	9	18	169	27	2200-3350	Popular with *madrileños*, poor snow record in recent years, little accommodation at resort
25	18	21.6	–	43	1600-2300	Small and relaxed
39	23	61	200	300	2725-3150	Quick access from Granada; liveliest ambience of Spanish resorts; long, easy runs; ugly resort development
14	7	14	20	25	1150-2600	Family atmosphere, antiquated lifts
21	12	28	68	60	2600-3000	Good for beginners and intermediates
22	10	24	12	40	2650-3300	Good scenery; can be windy
20	13	30	186	80	2600-3000	Good for beginners, intermediates and families
47	25	75	242	150	3300-3800	Andorra's highest, and its most reliable snow conditions; notoriously hideous resort development
29	14	60	241	125	3100-3600	Good for beginners and intermediates

information on courses. In Spain you can contact the Servicio Central de Cursos de Español (☎ 91-593 19 49, fax 91-445 69 60), Calle Trafalgar 32, 1° D, 28010 Madrid.

Universities, which exist in most sizeable cities, offer some of the best-value language courses: those at Salamanca, Santiago de Compostela and Santander are among those with the best reputations. Sevilla, Granada, Madrid and Barcelona are also very popular places to study Spanish. Private language schools as well as universities cater for a wide range of levels (from beginners up), course lengths, times of year, intensiveness and special requirements. Many courses have a cultural component as well as language pure and simple. University courses often last a term, though some are as short as two weeks or as long as a year. Private colleges can be more flexible about when you can start and how long you stay. One with a good reputation is ¿Don Quijote?, which has branches in Salamanca, Barcelona and Granada. There's further information on some courses in city sections of this book.

Costs vary widely. A typical four week course at a university, with 20 one-hour classes a week, will be around 40,000 or 50,000 ptas. Many places offer accommodation with families, in student lodgings or in flats if you want it. It's up to you whether you prefer the extra language practice a family can give you, or more of the company of your fellow students – or whether you value a bit of privacy more highly than either. Accommodation offers generally range from around 30,000 ptas a month with no meals to about 60,000 ptas for full board.

Other things to think about when you're weighing up your choice of course include its intensiveness (*intensivo* means different things at different schools), class sizes, who the other students are likely to be, and whether you want organised extracurricular social activities. It's also worth asking whether your course will lead to any formal certificate of competence. The Diploma de Español como Lengua Extranjera (DELE) is a qualification recognised by Spain's Ministry of Education and Science.

It's also easy to arrange private classes in many places; check notice boards in universities, language schools and foreign cultural institutes, or small ads in the local press. Expect to pay around 2000 ptas per hour for individual private lessons.

Other Courses

You can take courses in lots of other things too. Some places offering language courses also offer courses in other aspects of Spanish culture. The Instituto Cervantes and Spanish tourist offices are good places to start asking about possibilities. A number of foreigners living in Spain have set up residential centres where you can combine your learning experience with comfortable surroundings, company and, often, extras like excursions. These include:

Can Xanet School of Painting, Pollensa, Mallorca – workshops and courses in country home, some led by guest tutors; Contact Sheila Peczenik, 8 Pitt St, Kensington, London W8 4NX, UK (☎ 0171-937 0727)

Castillo San Rafael (☎ & fax 958-64 02 47), 18697 La Herradura, Granada – two-week painting or ceramics courses near the coast; around 160,000 ptas

Cortijo Romero (☎ 958-78 42 52) – personal development and alternative living centre in the Alpujarras area south of Granada, with vegetarian food and week-long programmes ranging from dance to yoga, walking to clowning; typical price around 60,000 ptas; contact Janice Gray, Little Grove, Grove Lane, Chesham, Bucks HP5 3QQ, UK (☎ 01494-782720)

Learning for Pleasure (☎ 956-64 01 02, fax 956-64 09 34), Apartado 25, 11330 Jimena de la Frontera, Cádiz – courses in painting, wildlife, Spanish cooking (led by well-known cooks), herbal medicine and other things, at a restored farmhouse

Los Pinos Photo Workshops (☎ 95-211 53 55), Apartado de Correos 102, 29754 Cómpeta, Málaga – one-week workshops led by well-known British photographers in Andalucían hill country, emphasising landscape, nature and darkroom work; around 80,000 ptas

The Spirit of Andalucía (☎ & fax 95-215 13 03, 95-215 12 22), Apartado 20, 29480 Gaucín, Málaga – cooking courses with 'name' cooks, painting and interior decorating courses

Trasierra (☎ 95-488 43 24, fax 95-488 33 05), 41370
Cazalla de la Sierra, Sevilla – week-long art
courses in converted Sierra Morena olive mill;
around 160,000 ptas.

WORK

With easily the EU's highest unemployment
rate, Spain doesn't exactly have a labour
shortage. Unlike in France, there's no casual
work for foreigners in fruit picking or har-
vests. But there are a few ways of earning
your keep (or almost) while you're here. If
you have any contacts – perhaps among the
many foreigners living in Spain – sound
them out, as word of mouth counts for a lot.

Bureaucracy

Nationals of EU countries, Norway and
Iceland are allowed to work in Spain without
a visa, but if they plan to stay more than three
months, they are supposed to apply within
the first month for a *tarjeta de residencia*
(residence card); for information on this
laborious process, see Visas & Documents
earlier in this chapter. Virtually everyone
else is supposed to obtain, from a Spanish
consulate in their country of residence, a
work permit and, if they plan to stay more
than 90 days, a residence visa. These procedures are well-nigh impossible unless you
have a job contract lined up before you begin
them; in any case you should start the processes a long time before you aim to go to
Spain. That said, quite a few people do work,
discreetly, without bothering to tangle with
the bureaucracy.

Opportunities

Language Teaching This is an obvious
option, for which language-teaching qualifications are a big help. There are lots of
language schools in all the big cities, and
often one or two even in smaller towns.
They're listed under 'Academias de Idiomas' in the yellow pages. Getting a job in one
of them is harder if you're not an EU citizen.
Some schools do employ people without
work papers, though often at lower than
normal rates. Giving private lessons is

another worthwhile avenue, though unlikely
to bring you a living wage straight away.

Sources of information on possible teaching work – school or private – include
foreign cultural centres (the British Council,
Alliance Française etc), foreign-language
bookshops, universities and language
schools. Many of these have notice boards
where you may find work opportunities, or
can advertise your own services. The local
press is also worth scanning for small ads and
may be worth placing your own ad in.

Tourist Resorts Summer work on the Mediterranean *costas* is another possibility,
especially if you get in there early-ish in the
season and are prepared to stay awhile. Many
bars, restaurants and other businesses are run
by foreigners. Check any local press in
foreign languages, such as the Costa del
Sol's *Sur In English*, which carries some ads
for waiters, nannies, chefs, baby-sitters and
cleaners – as well as 'closers', 'liners' and
others wanted to hawk time-share properties
to foreign holiday-makers.

Busking A few travellers earn a crust (not
much more) busking in the main tourist
cities.

ACCOMMODATION
Seasons & Reservations

Prices at any type of accommodation may
vary with the season. Many places have separate price structures for the high season
(*temporada alta*), mid-season (*temporada
media*) or the low season (*temporada baja*),
all usually displayed on a notice in reception
or close by. (Though these notices look official and the prices on them have indeed been
registered with the tourism authorities, hotel-
iers are not actually bound by them. They are
free to charge less, which they quite often do,
or more, which happens fairly rarely.)

What the high season is depends on where
you are, but in most places it's summer –
which can mean a period as short as mid-July
to the end of August or as long as Easter to
October. The Christmas-New Year period
and Semana Santa are also high, or at least

mid, season in some places. Local festivals which attract lots of visitors often count as high season too.

Differences between low-season and high-season prices vary widely around the country. They tend to be biggest – typically 30% or 50% – in coastal resorts and other places which attract a lot of tourism in summer. But even in these places you may still find some accommodation that keeps virtually the same prices year round. Occasionally there are bigger differences. Some hotels and hostales in Sevilla, for instance, charge three times as much during the city's Semana Santa and the Feria de Abril festivities as they do in the preceding winter months.

Major seasonal price variations are noted in Places to Stay sections through this book.

In the low season there's generally no need to book ahead, but when things get busier it's advisable, and at peak periods it can be essential if you want to avoid a wearisome search for a room. At most places a phone call is all that's needed, giving your approximate time of arrival.

Camping

Spain has something like 1000 officially graded camp sites *(campings)*. Some are well located in woodland or near beaches or rivers, but others are stuck away on the unattractive edges of towns and cities. Very few are near city centres, and camping isn't generally a very convenient way to go if you're relying on public transport.

Sites are officially rated as 1st class (1^a C), 2nd class (2^a C) or 3rd class (3^a C). There are also a few nonofficially graded sites, usually equivalent to 3rd class. Facilities generally range from reasonable to very good, though any site can be crowded and noisy at busy times. Even a 3rd class site is likely to have hot showers, electrical hook-ups and a cafeteria. The best sites have heated swimming pools, supermarkets, restaurants, travel agencies, laundry service, children's playgrounds, tennis courts and more. Sizes range from a capacity of under 100 people to over 5000.

Camp sites usually charge per person, per tent and per vehicle – anywhere between 250 and 800 ptas for each, though 450 or 500 ptas is typical. Children usually pay a bit less than adults. Many sites are open all year, though quite a few close from around October to Easter. Some are very crowded in July and August.

The annual *Guía Oficial de Campings*, available in bookshops for about 800 ptas, lists most of the country's sites and their facilities and prices. Tourist offices can always direct you to the nearest camp site.

Here and there you come across a *zona de acampada*, a country site often used by local campers but with no facilities, no supervision and no charge.

With certain exceptions – such as many beaches and environmentally protected areas, and a few municipalities which ban it – it is legal to camp outside camp sites (though not within one km of official ones!). Signs usually indicate where wild camping is not allowed. If in doubt you can always check with tourist offices. You'll need permission to camp on private land.

Note that Camping Gaz is the only common brand of camping gas: screw-on canisters are near-impossible to find.

Youth Hostels

Spain's approximately 180 youth hostels *(albergues juveniles*, not be confused with *hostales* – see the next section) are often the cheapest places to stay for lone travellers, but two people can usually get a double room elsewhere for a similar price. Many hostels are only moderate value, with night-time curfews, daytime closing hours, and no cooking facilities (though if there is nowhere to cook, they usually have a cafeteria). They can, too, be rather spartan and lacking in privacy, and are often heavily booked by school groups. Others, however, are conveniently located, relaxed about curfews, composed mainly of double rooms or small dorms, or even sited in fine historic buildings. Hostels can be good places for meeting people, too.

Most youth hostels are members of the

Red Española de Albergues Juveniles (REAJ, Spanish Youth Hostel Network), the Spanish affiliate of Hostelling International (HI), which used to be called the International Youth Hostel Federation. REAJ's head office (☎ 91-347 77 00, fax 91-401 81 60) is at Calle José Ortega y Gasset 71, 28006 Madrid.

Most hostels, however, are actually managed by the government of whichever of Spain's 17 autonomous regions they are in. Each region usually sets its own price structure. Some have central booking services where you can make reservations for most hostels in the region. These include Andalucía (☎ 95-455 82 93, fax 95-455 82 92), Cataluña (☎ 93-483 83 63, fax 93-483 83 50) and Valencia (☎ 96-386 92 52, fax 96-386 99 51).

HI's annual Europe hostels directory contains details of all REAJ hostels, and REAJ also publishes its own annual list. Some of the autonomous regions publish their own hostel guides, too.

Just a few hostels are run by other organisations or as private concerns, in which case they probably won't appear in regional guides – though they may still be REAJ members and appear in REAJ and HI directories!

Prices often depend on the season or whether or not you're under 26: typically you pay 900 to 1500 ptas a night. In some hostels the price includes breakfast. If there's an age distinction, 26 and overs will usually pay 300 or 400 ptas more. Many hostels require you to rent sheets – for around 300 ptas for your stay – if you don't have your own or a sleeping bag.

Some hostels require an HI card or membership card from your home country's youth hostel association; others don't (even though they may be HI hostels) but may charge more if you don't have one. You can buy HI cards for 1800 ptas at many hostels, at REAJ or regional youth hostel offices, or at branches of the youth travel agency TIVE (see Useful Organisations in this chapter). If you like, you can pay your 1800 ptas in 300 ptas nightly instalments. All you need to show is your passport. HI cards are valid for one year from purchase.

Hostales, Hospedajes, Pensiones, Hotels, Paradores etc

Officially, all these establishments are either *hoteles* (from one to five stars), *hostales* (one to three stars) or *pensiones* (one or two stars). These are the categories used by the annual *Guía Oficial de Hoteles*, sold in bookshops for about 1000 ptas, which lists a high proportion of all such places in Spain, with approximate prices. (Frustratingly for shoestringers, the *Guía Oficial* omits one star pensiones, though this fault is often remedied by more comprehensive local listings from tourist offices).

In practice, places to stay use all sorts of overlapping categories to describe themselves, especially at the budget end of the market. In broad terms, the cheapest are usually places just advertising *camas* (beds), *fondas* (traditionally a basic eatery and inn combined, though one or other function is now often missing), and *casas de huéspedes* or *hospedajes* (guesthouses). A pensión (basically a small private hotel) is usually a small step up from these, but in any of them bathrooms are likely to be shared, with single/double rooms costing 1000/2000 to 1500/3000 ptas. They'll be bare and basic, and your room may be small and even lack a window and towel, but most of them are kept pretty clean. Most discomfort is likely to come from lumpy beds, failure of hot water supplies, or insufficient bedding to keep you warm in winter (ask for more).

Next up the scale are hostales, essentially little different from pensiones, except that some are considerably more comfortable and more rooms tend to have their own bathrooms. Hostales may have more lounge space too. Hostal prices range from pensión levels up to 6000 ptas or so for a double in the best ones. Some hostales are bright, modern and pleasant places to stay; others are less so. A *hostal-residencia* is a hostal without any kind of restaurant – but since this is the case at a lot of 'hostales' too, the extra label seems a bit pointless.

Establishments calling themselves hotels range from simple places, where a double room could cost 4000 ptas or less, up to wildly luxurious, five star places where you could pay 60,000 ptas. Even in the cheapest ones rooms are likely to have an attached bathroom and there'll probably be a restaurant.

In a special category are the *paradores*, officially *paradores de turismo*, a state-run chain of 80-odd high-class hotels around the country, many of them in converted castles, palaces, mansions, monasteries or convents. These can be wonderful places to stay if you have 14,000 ptas or more (sometimes a lot more) for a double room. Occasional special offers, such as discounts of 35% to 50% for people aged 60 or more, may make paradores more affordable. You can book a room at any parador through their Central de Reservas (Central Booking Service; ☎ 91-559 00 69, fax 91-559 32 33), Calle Requena 3, 28013 Madrid.

Many places of all these types have a range of rooms at different prices. At the bottom end prices will vary according to whether the room has a washbasin (*lavabo*), shower (*ducha*) or full bathroom (*baño completo*). At the top end you may pay more for a room on the outside (*exterior*) of the building or with a balcony (*balcón*), and will often have the option of a suite.

Casas Rurales

Spaniards' burgeoning interest in their own countryside and environment has brought a boom in recent years in tourism to rural areas and the opening of many small new places to stay there. These *casas rurales* are usually comfortably renovated country houses or farmhouses, with just a handful of rooms. Some have meals available; some are self-catering. A double room typically costs from 3000 to 8000 ptas or so. Tourist offices can usually provide leaflets listing casas rurales and other country accommodation in their areas.

Refugios

Refugios are mountain shelters for hikers and climbers, and they're quite liberally scattered around most of the popular mountain areas. They're mostly run by mountaineering and hiking organisations. Accommodation – normally bunks tightly squeezed

into a dormitory – is usually apportioned on a first come, first served basis. In busy seasons (July and August in most areas) they can fill up quickly, and you should try to book or arrive by mid-afternoon to be sure of a place. Prices per person range from nothing to 1100 ptas or so a night. Most have a bar and meals available, and in many you can cook for yourself. Blankets are usually provided but you'll have to bring any further bedding yourself.

Apartments

In many places there are self-catering apartments, and even larger places such as houses and villas, to rent. A simple one bedroom apartment for two or three people might cost as little as 1500 ptas a night, or a two bedroom place for up to six people as little as 3000 ptas – though more often you're looking at twice that much, and prices can jump further in peak seasons. Apartments are most worth considering if you plan to stay several days or more, in which case there will usually be discounts from the daily rate. Tourist offices can supply lists of apartments, villas and houses for rent.

Tax

Virtually all accommodation prices are subject to IVA, the Spanish version of value-added tax, at a rate of 7%. This is often included in the quoted price at cheaper places, but less often at more expensive ones. To check, ask: '*¿Está incluido el IVA?*' ('Is IVA included?').

Room prices given in this book include IVA unless stated otherwise.

FOOD

Spanish cooking is typically Mediterranean in its liberal use of olive oil, garlic, onions, tomatoes and peppers. Traditionally it is simple fare based on fresh ingredients with a hint of herbs and spices. It reflects Roman, Arabic, Jewish, New World and (in the north) French influences, but the Arabic contribution is what sets it apart in Europe. Spices such as saffron and cumin, the use of fruits and almonds with savoury dishes

Top Left: Urbel del Castillo, in northern Burgos province, Castilla y León
Top Right: The 15th century Castillo de los Mendoza, in Manzanares El Real, Comunidad de Madrid
Bottom: The Gothic-mudéjar brick castle in Coca, Castilla y León

Top & Middle: Scenes from the Plaza de Toros, Valencia
Bottom: The famous *torero* El Cordobés making a comeback in the Plaza de Toros, Valencia

Paella

Despite its striking appearance, Spain's most famous dish – served throughout the country in various guises – is a simple one. It takes its name from the wide, shallow, two-handled metal pan in which it is cooked and served. Outside restaurants, it appears mainly on festive occasions, but in Spain that can include any Sunday or holiday; it's best cooked on a wood fire out of doors, and what better way to feed a crowd!

Paella as we know it is a fairly recent invention, but it has evolved from rice dishes that emerged in medieval times in the Valencia area. Rice came to Spain in a big way in the 8th century with the Muslims. The Arabic word for rice is *aroz*, thus the Spanish *arroz*. Rice cultivation in Spain declined in the 17th century with the expulsion of the Muslims and then was banned because the wetlands necessary to its growth were associated with malaria. In the late 19th century, the prohibition was lifted and land on the Ebro delta in Cataluña and in the marshlands of the Guadalquivir in Andalucía was given over to rice cultivation.

Traditional ingredients that went into the paella pan were seasonal vegetables, wetland wildlife (frogs, ducks, snails, eels, partridge), seafood and saffron, if available. Tourism increased the popularity of this attractive food with its bright yellow colour, titbits of chicken (instead of wild duck) and seafood, and its flavour produced by the simmering rice absorbing the juices of the other ingredients.

In Valencia, paella contains green beans, white butter beans, snails, chicken and pork bites, but no seafood. In Sevilla and Cádiz, big prawns and sometimes lobster are added while some other ingredients are omitted. On the Costa del Sol, green peas, clams, mussels and prawns garnished with red peppers and slices of lemon are a popular combination. Saffron is expensive so today food colouring or paprika *(pimentón)* is more commonly used.

Spaniards usually eat paella at lunchtime because it's considered 'heavy'. Sometimes it's served as a tapa or a starter. A lot of restaurants will only serve paella to a minimum of two people because it's not worth the effort to prepare a single portion. Some require you to order it in advance, as the ingredients need to be super fresh.

This recipe was provided by Lorraine Smart, Bar Villa Chile, Cómpeta, Málaga. It serves three or four people and requires a pan about 30 cm in diameter. The meat, fish, seafood and vegetable content can vary. The essential ingredients are olive oil, rice, stock, and saffron or its substitute.

Ingredients

Olive oil
1 onion, chopped
3 cloves garlic, chopped
1 red pepper, chopped
1 large tomato, chopped
Approx 500g rabbit or chicken,
  cut roughly

125g cubed pork
1 chorizo sausage (or salami),
  sliced
100g peas
150g peeled prawns
250g mussels
250g clams

650 ml chicken or seafood stock
250g short grain white rice
¼ teaspoon saffron threads (or
  paprika or food colouring)
Salt and pepper to taste

For the garnish: lemon wedges dipped in chopped parsley, three or four unshelled medium-sized prawns (or one king prawn) per person.

Method

Several hours before cooking, put the unshelled prawns, mussels and clams in cold water with a handful of porridge oats. This flushes out the shellfish.

Fry the onions, garlic and red pepper in olive oil until soft. Add the tomatoes and simmer for five minutes. Take the mixture out of the pan and put it to one side. Now, in more olive oil, fry the rabbit/chicken and the pork until they're half-cooked. Add the onion/tomato mix, chorizo slices, stock, rice and saffron. The paella now needs to cook slowly with the lid on for a total of 20 minutes. Stir as little as possible. (Meanwhile, the shellfish need to be cooked quickly in boiling water. Take them out as soon as they open and discard any that do not open. Keep the mussel shells for garnish.) After 10 minutes, add the peeled prawns and peas to the paella. Five minutes later, add the cooked shellfish. Five minutes more and the 20 minutes are up. Your paella is ready to garnish and serve! To garnish, you can arrange the mussel shells around the edge of the pan and the unshelled prawns overlapping in the centre. Place the lemon wedges as desired. ■

NICK TAPP

honeyed sweets and pastries are all legacies of the Muslim era.

But traditional food habits are fast changing, in part because of greater availability of imported foodstuffs and convenience foods, increased exposure to other cuisines and the hectic pace of modern life. Over the past 30 years, gas cookers have replaced open fires in all but the most rustic kitchens. Electric blenders are seeing off the mortar and pestle, and fridges and freezers have much altered the scene.

There are many dishes and foods that are considered typically Spanish and eaten country-wide, though often prepared differently in different regions. These include *paella* and other rice dishes (see the boxed aside), *gazpacho* (a cold, blended soup of tomatoes, capsicums, onion, garlic, breadcrumbs, lemon and oil), *sopa de ajo* (garlic soup), *jamón* (ham), *tortilla española* (potato omelette), *allioli* (garlic sauce made with oil and egg yolks), *garbanzos* (chickpeas), *habas* (broad beans), *pinchitos*, aka *pinchos morunos* (Moroccan-style kebabs usually made with pork), *chuletas* (chops or cutlets of pork, beef or lamb), all manner of *mariscos* (shellfish) and *pescado* (fish), *charcutería* (pork products including many forms of *embutido* (sausage), some eaten cold, some to be cooked), and *flan* (a caramel custard dessert). In the past the *cocido* or stew, a one pot feast of meat, sausage, beans and vegetables, was the mainstay of the Spanish diet. It's less common today as it's time-consuming to prepare, but you could find yourself at a bar when a cocido appears from the kitchen to be served as a tapa or a full meal. Cocido can be divided into parts to make up a three course meal, with the broth eaten first followed by the vegetables and lastly the meat.

Seafood, as well as meat, is eaten almost everywhere. Once Madrid was established as Spain's capital in the 17th century, carriers relayed fresh seafood to Madrid daily. The seafood is fantastic on all coasts, particularly the Atlantic, where every variety imaginable seems to be available. Unfortunately, it doesn't usually come cheap, but if you can afford seafood, eating in Spain will be a pleasure. Spaniards have a thousand and one ways of cooking seafood. Freshwater fish, crays, eels and even the occasional lizard are also eaten. Of course, in times of hardship meat and fish have not been readily available to all. Andalucíans, for example, still recall the days of the civil war and the ensuing lean years when soup made only of water and various grasses including fennel *(inojo)* provided sustenance. Also for economy, many varieties of soaked dried beans have traditionally made up the bulk of cocidos, and meat has only been added for flavouring if available.

The heavy emphasis on meat and fish in the Spanish diet is not good news for vegetarians, although there is a growing awareness of the benefits of vegetarianism, particularly among the young. Most big cities have some vegetarian restaurants.

Regional Specialities

Many of Spain's regions, especially Cataluña and the País Vasco, are extremely proud of their culinary heritages, and a vastly varied array of regional food flourishes away from the tourist enclaves. Basque and Catalan food preparation is generally more elaborate than elsewhere and results in arguably the best food in Spain.

The North Catalan cuisine has strong French and Italian influences, and sauces are typically served with meat and fish. Pasta is also common. The Basques are really serious

---

For Those with a Sweet Tooth

Spain has a strong tradition of elaborate sweets, cakes and pastries, much influenced by its Islamic past. The Spanish eat these delectables at any time of the day, especially on holidays or feast days, often with coffee, brandy or sweet wine. Some of the best sweets are sold at convents; others are available in *patiserías*. Try *turrón* (almond nougat), *yemas* (candied egg yolks), marzipan, sugared almonds or pine nuts, candied fruits or some of the fancy-looking tortes, cakes and pastries displayed in bars and patiserías. ■

✤ ✤

Vegetarian Food

Outside the big cities and university towns, Spain can be difficult if you're a vegetarian, and a real headache if you're a vegan. Even in places where there are vegetarian restaurants, they may only be open for lunch, or they may be tucked away in a far corner of town; vegetarian restaurants also tend to come and go depending on demand. Some restaurants in tourist or student areas cater for vegetarians in the *menú del día*, but you certainly can't count on it.

Now for the good news: Spanish fruits and vegetables are wonderfully fresh year round, so salads in any restaurant are a good bet. To be on the safe side, when you order add something like *'Soy vegetariano/a, no me gusta carne* (meat)*/jamón* (ham)*/pollo* (chicken)*/atún* (tuna)*/huevos* (eggs)*'* or whatever it is you don't want in your salad. Or simply say *'Sin ...'* ('Without ...').

More generally, you need to ask *'¿Qué hay sin carne, jamón, pollo, marisco o pescado?'* ('What is there without meat, ham, chicken, seafood or fish?'). *Alcachofa* (artichoke) and *espárragos* (asparagus) often appear on menus; they may be lightly cooked and served with mayonnaise, or tossed in oil and garlic. Red pepper salads such as *pipirrana* are also common. You may come across *escalivada*, a Catalan cold dish of aubergines, peppers and onions in an oil-and-garlic sauce. Vegetables are traditionally eaten on their own or with a touch of meat as a separate course after soup. Check the 'Vegetales/Verduras' (vegetables) section of the menu but remember that even dishes listed here won't necessarily come without meat unless you specify.

A good vegetarian dish is *pisto manchego*, similar to ratatouille, a fry-up of zucchinis (courgettes), green peppers, onions and potatoes. *Berenjenas* (aubergines) are common and excellent; they're often sliced thinly, dipped in batter and quickly fried – good as a side dish or a tapa. A full serve is usually plenty for two people. *Menestra* is another vegetarian dish – of artichokes, chard, peas and green beans – but you might have to ask for no *chorizo* (sausage), ham or egg to be included. *Garbanzos con espinacas* (chickpeas with spinach) is a filling and tasty stew. You'll often see *setas* (wild mushrooms) on menus; usually they're cooked in olive oil and garlic, but they are better in a sauce *(salsa)*. *Pimientos rellenos* (stuffed peppers) are available in some restaurants, but the filling is likely to have meat or prawns. Tofu and *seitán*, a miso-like vegetable protein, usually only crop up in vegetarian restaurants.

If you eat eggs, *tortillas* and *huevos revueltos* are good stand-bys; you can order them with asparagus, artichokes or other vegetables. Sad to say, a *cocido*, though it may include plenty of beans, will more often than not include bits of meat or contain meat stock. The same goes for soups although gazpacho is a safe bet. Occasionally a meat and fish-free *empanada* (pie) will turn up. And a *bocadillo vegetal* (salad sandwich) is filling.

If you get fed up, the only alternative, other than going on a diet, is to cater for yourself. ∎

✤ ✤

about food; there are whole cooking societies (for men only) devoted to fine food. Basque cuisine, like Catalan, incorporates ingredients from the mountains and the sea and gives importance to sauces. In Cantabria and Asturias, the food reflects the cool, wet climate with stews, apples, chestnuts, freshwater fish, seafood and cured meats predominating. Galicia is famous for its octopus, oysters, scallops, fish soups and stews and *empanadas* (pies). Lamb, game birds and freshwater fish are common fare in Navarra and Aragón. Islamic-influenced sweets such as *mazapán* (marzipan) are also typical of Aragón, while the small La Rioja region is renowned for its use of hot chillies and its wines. High and bleak, Castilla y León is the *zona de los asados*, the region of roasts – pork, lamb and game.

The Centre Castilla-La Mancha has similar fare to Castilla y León; game and wheat dishes are common. In the west, Extremadura is short on resources and has two contrasting cuisines: that of simple peasant foods, and that of rich cooking harking back to its medieval monasteries. In Valencia and Murcia, rice dishes, seafood and freshwater eels, and an abundance of high-quality fruit and vegetables make for a tasty cuisine. Murcia is known for its sweet pepper salads, whole baked fish and snails.

Andalucía This large region's various cuisines reflect its geographical diversity. In the high sierras, hams are cured (see the Jamón box) and game dishes abound. On the coasts, the abundant seafood ends up in soups, fried or, in the case of sardines, grilled on spits over driftwood fires. Pinchitos and gazpacho are true Andalucían foods. Everywhere the fruit and vegetables are delicious and fresh, for the growing season here lasts all year round.

The Balearic Islands Mallorca has strong links with Cataluña and thus French and Italian influences appear in its cuisine.

Added to this is the influence of numerous other invaders: Greeks, Romans, Arabs, Barbary pirates and modern-day tourists. Pork and seafood take first place. Menorca has a different culinary influence – that of Britain, which ruled it for 80 years. English gin, puddings, jams, stuffed turkey and even macaroni cheese have become a part of the local fare. Ibiza has just about lost its traditional cuisine.

Jamón, Jamón

Appetising is not usually the word that springs to mind when a foreigner first sets eyes on a dozen or so pigs' back legs dangling from the ceiling of a Spanish bar. But to most Spaniards, there's no more mouthwatering prospect than a few thin, succulent slices of this cured *jamón* (ham). The country consumes some 27 million of these hams every year. If you try it out you'll probably see why. You can eat two or three slices as a *tapa*, or have it in a *bocadillo*, or get a *ración*.

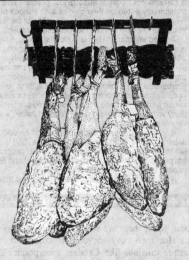

Most of these hams are *jamón serrano* (mountain ham), which is good enough. Even better (and more expensive), is *jamón ibérico*, from the black Iberian breed of pig, and the best jamón ibérico is *jamón ibérico de bellota*, from Iberian pigs fed on acorns *(bellotas)*. A glass of *fino* sherry is the traditional accompaniment to jamón ibérico.

Murcia, Galicia, Teruel in Aragón and Piornal in Extremadura all produce noted jamón serrano, while Salamanca has a fair ibérico. But the best jamones of all are considered to be those from Montánchez in Extremadura, Trevélez in the Alpujarras south of Granada, and above all the jamón ibérico of Jabugo in northwest Andalucía, from pigs free-ranging in the Sierra Morena oak forests. The best Jabugo hams are graded from one to five *jotas* (Js), and *cinco jotas* (JJJJJ) hams are said to come from pigs that have never eaten anything but acorns.

The curing process basically involves leaving the leg of the slaughtered pig in sea salt for a few days, then removing the salt (this process may be done twice) before hanging it up to mature – for periods ranging from a few months to over two years, depending on the ham. Great attention has to be paid to the temperature (gradually increasing) and humidity (not too dry) during the drying process. The curing process 'seals' the hams, which is why they're not covered with swarms of flies when you see them hanging in bars.

Traditionally hams were cured in cellars at home by the pig-owning family, but the business is becoming more and more industrialised. The Navidul factory at Torrijos, 87 km from Madrid, processes two million hams a year. But some families still hold traditional *matanza* (slaughtering) gatherings around 11 November, which marks the beginning of the slaughter season after the pigs have indulged on the autumn acorn harvest.

A *bocadillo de jamón serrano* in a bar or café is likely to cost 300 or 400 ptas, while a ración might be 600 to 1000 ptas; one kg in a shop is likely to be about 2000 ptas. Ibérico can be up to double those prices.

Ordinary uncured cold ham, by the way, is called *jamón York*. It's dull as ditchwater after you've tasted serrano or ibérico. ■

Meal Times & Typical Meals

Spaniards have their own timetable for eating so it's a good idea to reset your stomach clock, unless you want to eat alone or only with other tourists.

Breakfast Most Spaniards start the day with a light breakfast *(desayuno)*, perhaps coffee with a *tostada* (toasted roll) or *pastel* (pastry). *Churros con chocolate* – long, deep-fried doughnuts to dip in thick hot chocolate – are a delicious start to the day and unique to Spain. They are also popular at town fairs (you'll always see stands set up) and after drinking expeditions; Madrid, for instance, has several late-night *chocolaterías*. A *tortilla* (omelette) is a good option for a more substantial breakfast, though Spaniards eat eggs at other times of the day. *Huevos fritos* are fried eggs and *huevos revueltos* scrambled eggs; *huevos pasados por agua* will get you lightly boiled eggs; ask for *huevos cocidos* if you want hard-boiled eggs.

Lunch This is usually a Spaniard's main meal of the day; it is eaten between about 1.30 and 4 pm and is known as *almuerzo* or *comida*. It can consist of several courses including a soup or salad, meat or fish with vegetables or a rice dish or bean stew, followed by fruit, ice cream or flan.

Dinner A Spaniard's evening meal, or *cena*, tends to be lighter, perhaps an egg dish with bread, and may be eaten as late as 10 or 11 pm. But lots of people also go out to a bigger dinner in restaurants – though before about 9 pm you're unlikely to see anyone but foreigners doing this.

In-Between Times It's common (and a great idea!) to go to a bar or café for a snack, or *merienda*, around 11 am and again around 7 or 8 pm. One great Spanish snack is a *bocadillo*, a long white-bread roll filled with cheese or ham or salad or tortilla – the list goes on. You probably won't leave Spain without sampling a *bocadillo de tortilla española* or *de jamón serrano*, a roll filled, respectively, with potato omelette or cured ham. Then there are *tapas*... (see the boxed aside).

Tapas

These saucer-sized mini-snacks are part of the Spanish way of life and come in infinite varieties. You can make a meal of tapas, or go on to a meal afterwards, or hop on to another bar to sample more tapas, a great Spanish pastime. Tapas are generally consumed standing at the bar and accompanied by wine from the barrel or a beer.

Tapa translates as lid. Today's snacks supposedly originated in the sherry area of Andalucía last century when bar owners placed a piece of bread on top of a drink to keep away flies; this developed into the custom of putting a titbit, such as olives or a piece of sausage or ham, on a lid to cover the drink – something salty to encourage drinking. Today, tapas have almost become a cuisine of their own and each region and city has its specialities. Typical tapas include olives, slices of cured meat or cheese, potato salad, diced salad, bite-sized portions of fried fish, *albóndigas* (meat or fish balls), chickpeas with spinach, rabbit stew, *callos* (tripe), *gambas* (prawns) in garlic, or *boquerones* (anchovies) marinated in vinegar or *rebozados* (fried in batter).

Bars often display a range of tapas on the counter, or chalk a list on a board. If you're very lucky, there may even be a tapas menu. Otherwise, it seems, you're expected to know what's available and the situation *can* be rather confusing. A place that appears not to have tapas may actually specialise in them! Failing all else, you just have to ask what tapas there are, then try to recognise a few words in the long stream of verbiage that you're likely to be answered with. A *ración* is a meal-sized serving of these snacks, a *media ración* is half a ración.

Tapas are sometimes free though this custom is fast disappearing. A typical tapa costs between 100 and 200 ptas but check before you order as some are a lot dearer. Prices may also vary widely from bar to bar. Make it clear if it's a tapa you're after, not a media ración or ración, or you'll end up paying three or five times what you planned.

In the País Vasco and Asturias, tapas are often called *pinchos*. ■

Types of Eatery

Cafés & Bars If you're looking to get into Spanish ways, you'll be spending plenty of time in cafés and bars. The latter come in various guises, including *bodegas* (old-style wine bars), *cervecerías* (beer bars), *tascas* (bars that specialise in tapas), *tabernas* (taverns) and even *pubs*. In almost any of them you'll find tapas available. Some may serve more substantial fare too. You will often save 10% to 20% off the bill by standing (or sitting) at the bar rather than sitting at a table, particularly if the tables are outside on a picturesque terrace or in a smart attached dining room.

Restaurants Throughout Spain you'll find plenty of *restaurantes* serving good simple food at affordable prices, and often featuring regional specialities. There are also some unexceptional to woeful places, particularly in tourist resorts. If the *menú del día* (set menu) is chalked on blackboards out the front in several languages, the food will be nothing to rave about, though it may be cheap.

A *mesón* is a simple eatery with home-style cooking, attached to a bar, while a *comedor* is usually a dining room attached to a bar or hostal; in a comedor, the food is likely to be functional and cheap. A *venta* is a family-run establishment, probably once an inn, off the beaten track; the food here can be delectable and cheap, but ventas are gradually disappearing. A *marisquería* is a seafood restaurant. A *chiringuito* is basically an open-air bar serving drinks and snacks (you'll find them at ferias and fiestas, and some spring up in city plazas over summer), but the word can also refer to a permanent beachside eatery serving more substantial food.

Most restaurants offer a menú del día – the budget traveller's best friend – and post it outside. For anywhere between 600 and 2000 ptas – but usually 800 to 1200 ptas – you typically get a starter, a main course, *postre* (dessert), bread and wine. Often there's a choice of two or three dishes for each course. Before you go in and sit down, it's worth checking exactly what you're getting for your money. If the written description of the menú makes no mention of drinks, dessert, bread, coffee or 'IVA incluido', your meal may cost a lot more than the stated price.

The *plato combinado* is a near relative of the menú. It literally translates as 'combined plate' and may consist of a steak and egg with chips and salad, or fried squid with potato salad. Insipid pictures on the wall of what's available can be off-putting, but more often than not a plato combinado is fine.

Spanish law requires restaurant menu prices to include a service charge, and any tip beyond that is a matter of personal choice.

À la Carte You'll pay more for your meals if you order à la carte but the food will be better. The Spanish menu (*carta* – not *menú*, which means the menú del día) begins with starters such as *ensaladas* (salads), *sopas* (soups) and *entremeses*, the Spanish equivalent of hors d'oeuvres or an antipasto plate. Entremeses may consist of a mound of potato salad with peppers, olives, asparagus, anchovies and a selection of cold meats or, at their simplest, cold meats, slices of cheese and olives. Entremeses can be almost a meal in themselves.

Later courses on the menu will probably be listed under headings like *pollo* (chicken), *carne* (meat) – which may be subdivided into *cerdo* (pork), *ternera* (beef or veal) and *cordero* (lamb) – *mariscos* (seafood), *pez* or *pescado* (fish), *arroz* (rice), *huevos* (eggs) and *vegetales*, *verduras* or *legumbres* (all meaning vegetables).

Desserts have a low profile: *helados* (ice cream), fruit and flan are often the only choices. If you're lucky you may encounter *arroz con leche* (creamy rice pudding) or *tocino del cielo* (heavenly bacon), which is actually a type of caramel custard of bacon-like appearance.

Ethnic Restaurants Spain has lots of Chinese restaurants. They're generally mundane though quite often cheap. Large cities also have other types of ethnic restaurants but there has been no great flourishing of these as in some other European countries. Italian restaurants are pretty common and vary in quality: pizzas are mostly tasty enough and filling. There are some good Arabic restaurants in Málaga and Granada and a largely tourist-based revival of the cuisine of Al-Andalus in a few restaurants in Córdoba. Of course, if you're after ethnic US food, you'll find McDonald's and the like in big cities and tourist areas.

Self-Catering

Spain's *mercados* (food markets) are fun places to visit. Buy a selection of fruits, vegetables, cold meat or sausage, olives, nuts and cheese, pick up some bread from one of the many excellent *panaderías* (bakeries), stop in at a supermarket for a bottle of wine and head for the nearest picturesque spot. This can make a pleasant change from sitting in restaurants and, if you shop carefully, can be the most economical way of eating: you could put together a filling meal for as little as 400 ptas.

Only some youth hostels and just a few pensiones and hostales have facilities for cooking.

Cheese

Except in the north, Spain's climate and landscape are unsuitable for dairy cattle. Oil and lard are used in cooking rather than butter, and the common Western custom of spreading butter on bread is almost alien in Spain. That said, Spain does produce at least 36 varieties of *queso* (cheese). Most are fairly strong and some of the best are made from goat's or ewe's milk. One wonderful goat's-milk cheese is found in and around Ronda in Andalucía.

Spanish supermarkets stock a selection of local cheeses, many cheeses from other parts of Europe, and also Spanish copies of non-Spanish cheeses such as Brie and Camembert. Spanish cheese is generally pricey, around 1500 ptas a kg, while you can buy Edam or Gouda for as little as 900 ptas a kg. Spanish cheeses you might like to sample include:

Burgos – made from ewe's milk, this cheese comes in a rindless round and is particularly delicious eaten with honey, nuts and fruit.

Cabrales – strong Asturian cow's, goat's and sheep's-milk cheese matured in caves; it's encased in leaves, and the inside is creamy.

Manchego – the most famous of Spanish cheeses, traditionally made from ewe's milk, now often other milk, and cured in oil. It can be soft, fresh and mild or hard, crumbly and strong. The rind is brown/black, the inside pale yellow.

Pasiego – made from cow's milk near Santander; the inside is firm, white and creamy.

Roncal – made in the Roncal valley in Navarra from ewe's milk, sometimes combined with cow's milk. This is a hard, sharp cheese with tiny holes inside; the rind is brown.

Table Talk

Here are a few basic words that can come in handy whatever kind of meal you're eating:

bill (check)	*cuenta*
bread	*pan*
bread roll	*panecillo, bollo*
breakfast	*desayuno*
butter	*mantequilla*
change	*cambio*
cold	*frío/a*
cup	*taza*
dining-room	*comedor*
dinner	*cena*
food, meal	*comida*
fork	*tenedor*
glass	*vaso* or *copa*
hot (temperature)	*caliente*
ice	*hielo*
jam	*mermelada*
knife	*cuchillo*
lunch	*almuerzo* or *comida*
menu	*carta*
milk	*leche*
olive oil	*aceite de oliva*
plate	*plato*
pepper	*pimienta*
salt	*sal*
sauce	*salsa*
spoon	*cuchara*
sugar	*azúcar*
table	*mesa*
vinegar	*vinagre*
waiter/waitress	*camerero/a*

Food Glossary

Spain has such huge variety in food, and food terminology, from place to place, that you could travel the country for years and still find unfamiliar items on almost every menu you looked at. You should be able to decipher about half of most worthwhile menus with the help of the following list:

a la vasca	with parsley, garlic and peas; a Basque green sauce
aceite	oil
aceituna	olive
acelga	chard
adobo	battered
agua	water
aguacate	avocado
ahumado/a	smoked
ajo	garlic
albóndiga	meatball, fishball
alcachofa	artichoke
allioli	garlic sauce
almejas	clams
almendra	almond
alubia	bean
anchoa	anchovy
anguila	eel
apio	celery
arroz	rice
asado	roasted
atún	tuna
bacalao	salted cod
berenjena	aubergine, eggplant
bistek	beef steak
bocadillo	bread roll with filling
boquerones	anchovies
brasa	char-grill
butifarra	thick sausage (to be cooked)
cabra	goat
cacahuete	peanut
calabacín	zucchini, courgette
calabaza	pumpkin
caldereta	stew

caldo	broth, stock, consommé
callos	tripe
calamares	squid
camarón	small prawn, shrimp
canelones	cannelloni
cangrejo	crab
cangrejo de río	crayfish
carabinero	large prawn
caracol	snail
carne	meat
caza	hunt, game
cazuela	casserole
cebolla	onion
cerdo	pig, pork
cereza	cherry
champiñones	mushrooms
chanquetes	whitebait (illegal, but still served up on coasts)
charcutería	cured pork meats, or a shop selling them
chipirón	small squid
chivo	kid, baby goat
choco	cuttlefish
chorizo	red sausage
chuleta	chop, cutlet
churrasco	slabs of grilled meat or ribs in a tangy sauce; a Galician meat dish
churro	long, deep-fried doughnut
cocido	cooked; also hotpot/stew
cocina	kitchen
cochinillo	suckling pig
conejo	rabbit
cordero	lamb
crudo	raw
dorada	sea bass
dulce	sweet
empanada	pie
ensaimada	sweet bread (of lard)
ensalada	salad

entremeses	hors-d'oeuvres	*infusión*	herbal tea
escabeche	pickled or marinated fish	*jabalí*	wild boar
espagueti	spaghetti	*jamón*	ham
espárragos	asparagus	*jengibre*	ginger
espinacas	spinach	*judías blancas*	butter beans
estofado	stew	*judías verdes*	green beans
faba	type of dried bean	*langosta*	spiny lobster
faisán	pheasant	*langostino*	large prawn
fideo	vermicelli noodle	*lechuga*	lettuce
filete	fillet	*legumbre*	pulse
frambuesa	raspberry	*lengua*	tongue
fresa	strawberry	*lenguado*	sole
frijol	dried bean	*lentejas*	lentils
frito	fried	*lima*	lime
fruta	fruit	*limón*	lemon
fuerte	strong	*lomo*	pork loin
		longaniza	dark pork sausage
gachos	type of porridge		
galleta	biscuit, cookie	*macarrones*	macaroni
gamba	prawn, shrimp	*maíz*	sweet corn
garbanzo	chickpea	*mandarina*	tangerine
gazpacho	cold, blended soup of tomatoes, peppers, cucumber, onions, garlic, lemon and breadcrumbs	*manzana*	apple
		manzanilla	camomile; also a type of sherry and a type of olive
gazpachos	game dish with garlic and herbs	*marinado*	marinated
		marisco	shellfish
girasol	sunflower	*mayonesa*	mayonnaise
granada	pomegranate	*mejillones*	mussels
gratinada	au gratin	*melocotón*	peach
guindilla	hot chilli pepper	*menta*	mint
guisante	pea	*merluza*	hake
		migas	fried breadcrumb dish
haba	broad bean	*miel*	honey
hamburguesa	hamburger	*mojama*	cured tuna
harina	flour	*morcilla*	blood sausage, ie black pudding
helado	ice cream		
hierba buena	mint		
hígado	liver	*naranja*	orange
higo	fig	*nata*	cream
hongo	wild mushroom	*nuez*	nut, walnut; plural *nueces*
horno	oven		
horneado	baked		
hortalizas	vegetables	*olla*	pot
huevo	egg	*orejón*	dried apricot
huevos revueltos	scrambled eggs	*ostra*	oyster

paella	rice, seafood and meat dish	rosada	ocean catfish, wolf-fish
paloma	pigeon		
pajarito	small bird	salado	salted, salty
parrilla	grilled	salchicha	fresh pork sausage
pasa	raisin	salchichón	cured sausage
pastel	pastry, cake	sandía	watermelon
patisería	cake shop	sardina	sardine
patata	potato	seco	dry, dried
patatas bravas	spicy, fried potatoes	sepia	cuttlefish
patatas fritas	chips, French fries	serrano	mountain-cured ham
pato	duck		
pavía	battered	sesos	brains
pavo	turkey	seta	wild mushroom
pechuga	breast, of poultry	sobrasada	soft pork sausage
perdiz	partridge	soja	soy
peregrina	scallop	solomillo	sirloin
pescado	fish	sopa	soup
pescadilla	whiting	sopa de ajo	garlic soup
pez espada	swordfish		
picadillo	minced meat		
picante	hot, spicy, piquant	tapa	snack on a saucer
pil pil	garlic sauce sometimes spiked with chilli	tarta	cake
		ternera	beef, veal
		tocino	bacon
pimiento	pepper, capsicum	tomate	tomato
pinchitos	Moroccan-style kebabs	torta	round flat bun, cake
		tortilla	omelette
pincho	a tapa-sized portion of food	tortilla española	potato omelette
		tostada	toast
piña	pineapple	trigo	wheat
piñón	pine nut	trucha	trout
plancha	grill, grilled, on the hot plate	trufa	truffle
		turrón	almond nougat
plátano	banana		
platija	flounder	uva	grape
potaje	stew		
pollo	chicken		
postre	dessert	vaca, carne de	beef
puerro	leek	vegetal	vegetable
pulpo	octopus	vegetariano/a	vegetarian
		venera	scallop
queso	cheese	verdura	green vegetable
		vieira	scallop
rabo	tail		
rape	monkfish	yema	candied egg yolk
rebozado/a	battered and fried		
riñón	kidney	zanahoria	carrot
relleno	stuffed	zarzuela	fish stew

DRINKS
Nonalcoholic Drinks

Coffee Coffee in Spain is strong and slightly bitter. Addicts should specify how they want their fix. A *café con leche* is about 50% coffee, 50% hot milk; ask for *grande* or *doble* if you want a large cup, *en vaso* if you want a smaller shot in a glass, or *sombra* if you want lots of milk. A *café solo* is a short black; *café cortado* is a short black with a little milk. For iced coffee, ask for *café con hielo*: you'll get a glass of ice and a hot cup of coffee, to be poured over the ice – which, surprisingly, doesn't all melt straight away!

If you're having trouble sleeping, check your coffee consumption!

Tea Spaniards prefer coffee, but tea is served in most cafés and bars. The brew (a tea bag) is invariably weak and locals drink it black. Ask for milk to be separate; otherwise, you'll end up with a cup of milky water with a tea bag thrown in. Most places also have camomile tea (*té de manzanilla*), not to be confused with manzanilla sherry of the same name and colour. *Teterías* (Islamic-style tea-rooms) have become fashionable in some cities – here are served all manner of teas, including herbal concoctions (*infusiones*). The bill inevitably ends up hefty, you pay for the ambience – soft cushions, floaty music – so check the cost before you order.

Chocolate Spaniards brought chocolate back from the New World and adopted it enthusiastically. At one time it was even a form of currency. The Spanish serve it thick; sometimes it even appears on the *postres* (desserts) section of menus. Generally it's a breakfast drink consumed with churros; see the Food section.

Soft Drinks Orange juice (*zumo de naranja*) is the main freshly squeezed juice available but, though delicious, it's expensive at around 200 ptas a glass. Boxed juices come in all varieties in shops and are good and cheap.

Refrescos (cool drinks) include the usual international brands of soft drinks, local brands such as Kas, and expensive *granizado* (iced fruit crush).

Clear, cold water from a public fountain or tap is a Spanish favourite – but check that it's *potable*. For tap water in restaurants, ask for *agua de grifo*. Bottled water (*agua mineral*) comes in innumerable brands, either fizzy (*con gas*) or still (*sin gas*). A 1.5 litre bottle of agua mineral *sin gas* costs between 40 and 75 ptas in a supermarket, but out and about you may be charged as much as 175 ptas for the same.

A *batido* is a flavoured milk drink or milk shake; the bottled variety is sickly. *Horchata* (*orxata* in Catalan) is a Valencian drink of Islamic origin. Made from the juice of *chufa* (tiger nuts), sugar and water, it is sweet and tastes like soya milk with a hint of cinnamon. You'll come across it both fresh and bottled: Chufi is a delicious brand.

Alcoholic Drinks

Wine Spain is a wine-drinking country and so wine (*vino*) accompanies almost every meal. Spanish wine is strong because of the sunny climate. It comes white (*blanco*), red (*tinto*) or rosé (*rosado*). In general wine remains cheap though there is no shortage of expensive wines. A 500 ptas bottle of wine bought from a supermarket or wine merchant will be better than average. The same money in a restaurant will get you a mediocre drop. Cheap *vino de mesa* (table wine) sells for less than 200 ptas a litre, but wines at that price can be pretty rank.

You can order wine by the glass (*copa*) in bars and restaurants. In a restaurant they may bring you the bottle anyway but you only pay for what you drink. Or the restaurant's *vino de la casa* (house wine) will come from a barrel or jug at 125 ptas, sometimes less, a glass. In some more rustic eateries wine may arrive in a *porrón* – a jug with a long, thin spout through which you're supposed to pour it into your mouth. If you don't fancy wine dribbling down your chin and clothes, just pour it into a glass first.

Spain, like other European countries, regulates its wine fairly carefully so that you can judge what kind of quality you're getting from the wording on the label. Two important indicators of decent wine are the terms DOC and DO. DOC stands for *denominación de origen calificada* and refers to wine areas that have maintained consistent high quality over a very long period. Rioja is the only DOC at present, though Jerez may join it. DO, *denominación de origen*, is one step down from DOC. There are 40-odd DO areas spread around most of the country. Each DOC and DO covers a wide range of wines, of varying quality (usually indicated by the price), but a DOC or DO label does tell you that the wine has been produced to certain supervised standards by serious wine growers. On the other hand, there are also some good wines from places that haven't bothered about gaining DO status.

Regional Wine Specialities

Wine is made everywhere in Spain, with La Rioja, Castilla-La Mancha, Catalonia and the Jerez de la Frontera area in Andalucía producing the country's best (Jerez wine is, of course, sherry). However, the scene is dynamic; with wine production thriving and experimentation rife, competition is fierce and new wines are constantly entering the scene.

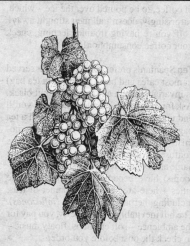

For ordinary drinking, some of the cheaper reds from La Rioja or even Valdepeñas (Castilla-La Mancha) are generally OK, as are Cataluña's *cavas* (sparkling wines like champagne) and still whites, such as Penedès. Rosé is cheap; those from Navarra, Rueda (Castilla y León) and Utiel-Requena (Valencia) are good.

Galicia's best wines include white Albariños from the Rías Baixas and red or white Ribeiros. In the País Vasco, a sharp, white wine known as *txacolí* is popular. In Aragón the Somontano area near Huesca is into high-tech wine production and is coming up with some good whites. Cataluña's best wines come from Penedès (cava and fruity whites) and Priorato (red).

The Rioja DOC region includes areas of Navarra and the País Vasco bordering its heartland in La Rioja. The region is best known for its reds – the current trend is towards production of mature wines rather than those for the cheaper end of the market. Navarra is an upcoming wine producer with lots of experimentation happening.

In Castilla y León, the Ribera del Duero region produces excellent reds that rival those of Rioja while the Rueda area was famous for its whites until challenged by developments in Galicia. Now rosé is fast overtaking whites in Rueda. Toro, near Salamanca, is a rising star on the scene, producing some notoriously powerful reds.

Extensive Castilla-La Mancha produces 50% of all the wine made in Spain. It has a reputation for cheap and (if you're lucky) cheerful wine, but this is fast changing with new wines hitting the scene. Its La Mancha and Valdepeñas DOs offer the best ranges of budget-priced wines in the country.

Valencia and Murcia have traditionally produced bulk wine and, more recently, concentrated grape juice, for export. However, there are some good-value wines being produced in the Utiel-Requena area of Valencia (whites and rosés), and in Murcia's Jumilla (reds) and Yecla (reds, whites and rosés) areas. Extremadura mainly produces wine for local consumption, grape juice or distilled liquor.

Andalucía is where wine production began in Spain when the Phoenicians founded Cádiz in around 1100 BC and introduced vine cultivation. The region is famous for sherry, a fortified wine produced by a special ageing process, mostly in the Jerez de la Frontera area. For more on sherry, see the boxed aside in the Andalucía chapter. Málaga dessert wines made from the muscatel grape were fashionable at the turn of the century and, though their popularity has declined, they are served today from the barrel in some of the city's bars. ∎

Other categories of wine, in descending order, are: *denominación de origen provisional* (DOp), *vino de la tierra* (from wine areas on the way up; there are about 30 of these), *vino comarcal* (about 30 of these too), and *vino de mesa*.

Yet more terms help interpret wine labels. *Vino joven* is wine made for immediate drinking, while *vino de crianza* has to have been stored for certain minimum periods: if red, it must have been stored for two full calendar years with a minimum of six months in oak; if white or rosé, it must have been stored for a minimum of one calendar year. *Reserva* requires longer storage – three years for reds and two years for whites and rosés. *Gran reserva* is a title permitted for particularly good vintages. These wines must have spent at least two calendar years in storage and three in the bottle. They're mostly reds.

Beer The most common way to order a beer *(cerveza)* is to ask for a *caña*, which is a small draught beer. *Corto* and, in the País Vasco, *zurrito*, are other names for this. A larger beer (about 300 ml) is usually called a *tubo* (which comes in a straight glass) or in Cataluña a *jarra*, which has a handle. All these words apply to draught beer *(cerveza de barril* or *cerveza de presión)*; if you just ask for a cerveza you're likely to get bottled beer, which is more expensive. A small bottle of beer is called a *botellín* or a *quinto*; a bigger one is a *tercio* or a *mediana*. Estrella de Galicia is the best beer we have found in Spain. San Miguel, Cruzcampo and Victoria are other popular brands.

A *clara* is a shandy, a beer with a dash of lemonade.

Other Drinks *Sangría* is a wine and fruit punch sometimes laced with brandy. It's refreshing going down but can leave you with a sore head. You'll see jugs of it on tables in restaurants but it also comes ready-mixed in bottles at around 300 ptas for 1.5 litres. *Tinto de verano* is a mix of wine and Casera, a brand of lemonade or sweet,

---

❀ ❀ ❀ ❀ ❀ ❀ ❀ ❀ ❀ ❀ ❀ ❀ ❀

Sangría

There are many recipes for *sangría*. Some include spices and many more varieties of fruit than just lemons, and are left to steep for a day or more. A fairly basic sangría mix with which to begin contains the following:

1 bottle dry red wine
60 ml brandy (optional)
juice of a lemon
1 lemon, sliced
sugar to taste
soda or mineral water to taste

Sangría should be served very cold or over ice. ∎

❀ ❀ ❀ ❀ ❀ ❀ ❀ ❀ ❀ ❀ ❀ ❀ ❀

---

bubbly water. Cider *(sidra)* is produced and largely consumed in Asturias and the País Vasco.

Spanish brandy *(coñac)* is popular and cheap. In bars, you'll notice locals starting the day with a coffee and a brandy, or a glass of *anís* (aniseed liqueur). Popular brandies include Centenario, Magno, 103 and Soberano. If you want other spirits, the Spanish-produced versions are generally much cheaper than imports. Larios gin made in Málaga is an example.

Spain produces a huge range of liqueurs *(licores)*. *Aguardiente* is a grape-based liqueur. *Pacharán* is a red liqueur made with aniseed and sloes, the fruit of the blackthorn.

ENTERTAINMENT
Listings

Local papers often carry fairly thorough entertainment listings, and Madrid and Barcelona both have their own good what's-on magazines. In Andalucía, try to pick up *El Giraldillo*, a what's-on publication for the whole region, from tourist offices. Some national papers such as *El País* have regional sections giving pretty good local listings for the part of the country you're in. The Friday 'Tentaciones' section in El País lists highlight events around the country for the coming week. Tourist offices can always tell you about major events, too.

Those Other Bulls

As you roam the highways of Spain, every now and then you'll observe the silhouette of a truly gigantic black bull on the horizon up ahead, looking your way. When you get closer to the creature, you realise it's only two-dimensional, made of metal and held up by bits of scaffolding. But what's it for?

Well, it's not a silent homage to bullfighting erected by the local folk. Nor is it a sign that you're entering a notable bull-breeding area. It's a sherry and brandy advert, for the Osborne company of Andalucía. And in recent years the *toros de Osborne* have been raising almost as much passion as bullfighting itself.

At the last count there were 93 of them, looming beside roads all over the country. Why doesn't the Osborne company put its name on the bulls if it wants to advertise, you might ask? From 1957, when the first bull was erected on the Madrid-Burgos road, until 1988 it did, in big letters. The bulls, which each weigh 50 tonnes, and at one time numbered 500, grew into a much-loved national symbol. Then in 1988 a new law banned advertising hoardings beside main roads, to prevent drivers being distracted. Osborne removed its name but left the bulls standing, which seemed to pacify the authorities – until 1994, when word got about that the law was going to be enforced strictly, meaning no more bulls. This provoked an enormous outcry, with intellectuals writing to the newspapers about the national heritage, the government of Andalucía talking about declaring the bulls protected monuments, and Osborne's home town of El Puerto de Santa María threatening to take the matter to the supreme court.

In 1996 the bulls were still standing. ∎

DAMIEN SIMONIS

Bars & Discos

Spain has some of the best nightlife in Europe; wild and *very* late nights, especially on Friday and Saturday, are an integral part of the Spain experience. Even some surprisingly small cities have very lively scenes. Many young Spaniards don't think about going out till midnight or so. Bars, which come in all shapes, sizes and themes, are the main attractions until around 2 or 3 am. Some play great music, which will get you hopping before you move on to a disco, if you can afford it, till 5 or 6 am – or later! Discos can be expensive, and some won't let you in wearing jeans or trainers, but they aren't to be missed if you can manage to splurge. Techno in various guises is the go in most discos. Spain's contributions to dance music in recent years have been *bakalao* and *mákina*, kinds of frenzied (150 to 180 bpm) techno, but eurobeat – where Eurovision meets techno – was the *sonido de moda* as this edition was being prepared.

Live Rock, Pop & Jazz

The home-grown Spanish rock and pop scene is large and lively but doesn't tend to be very original (see Music in the Facts about the Country chapter for some of the better bands). However, the bigger cities usually offer a reasonable and varied choice of bands, including foreign visitors, several nights of the week. Elsewhere gigs are mainly on weekends. The summer spawns hosts of festivals (see the Public Holidays & Special Events section earlier in this chapter).

Jazz has its following, with venues in most big cities.

Flamenco

Some of the best flamenco music and dance happens almost unadvertised in small bars, and so is hard to catch. Tourist offices will direct you towards *tablaos*, regular shows for a tourist audience with high-ish prices. Though not exactly spontaneous, some of these are still good. Otherwise, a few bars have regular performances of variable quality, and there are occasional one-off shows by name artists in concert halls. Your best bet, though, is to catch one of the summer flamenco festivals. Flamenco is biggest in its home, Andalucía, but is also strong in Cataluña (which has a large Andalucían population), Madrid and parts of Extremadura.

Classical Music, Dance & Theatre

For the culturally inclined, there's lots of all these going on all around the country. They often come in the form of festivals. Theatre is nearly all in Spanish, of course. For some background, see Arts in the Facts about the Country chapter.

Cinemas

Cinemas abound and are good value, though foreign films are usually dubbed into Spanish. In the biggest cities a few cinemas show films in their original languages with Spanish subtitles – look for the letters 'v.o.' *(versión original)* in listings.

SPECTATOR SPORT
Football

Never mind bullfighting, Spain's national sport is *fútbol* (soccer). Around 300,000 spectators attend the games in the Primera División (First Division) every weekend from September to May, with millions more following on TV. Acres of press space and hours of men's bar talk are dedicated to transfer rumours and speculation about team selection. Spain suffers very little football hooliganism but Spaniards still take their favoured teams' fortunes very seriously. It's wise to keep your emotions in check if a bar TV is showing your country taking on Spain in an international!

Almost any game in the Primera División will be worth attending for the Spanish crowd experience even if you're not a huge fan of the game itself. But those involving the big two clubs, Real Madrid and Barcelona, have an extra passion to them.

This pair have large followings throughout the country and something approaching a monopoly on the silverware: between them they have carried off the league champion-

ship in all but 13 seasons since 1950. Their players, coaches and directors are national celebrities. Both have huge stadiums. Other leading clubs are Atlético Madrid (which won one of its occasional league titles in 1996), Athletic Bilbao, Valencia, Deportivo La Coruña, Real Zaragoza, Espanyol (of Barcelona), Racing Santander, Sevilla and Real Betis (both of Sevilla) and Real Sociedad of San Sebastián. A promotion and relegation system from the Segunda División allows a few makeweight teams their hour of glory among the big boys. The 1996-97 season witnessed the odd spectacle of the Extremadura club, whose ground holds only 11,000 people, entertaining teams whose stadiums hold three times the population of Extremadura's home town, Almendralejo. Below the Segunda División is Segunda B, divided into four regional sections.

League games are played on Saturday and Sunday and you can pay at the gate (from about 1500 ptas) for all but the biggest matches. Games in the Copa del Rey (Spain's equivalent of the FA Cup), and matches in European competitions, are held midweek at night. Watch the press (including the sports paper *Marca*) for details of upcoming fixtures.

Other Sports

Champions such as Miguel Induráin (cycling), Severiano Ballesteros and José-María Olazábal (golf), and Arantxa Sánchez Vicario and Conchita Martínez (tennis) have all inspired booming popularity in their sports. All appear a few times a year in competitions in their home country, though Spain regularly stages none of the really big international events in any of their sports. Golf's Ryder Cup competition between Europe and the USA, however, takes place at Valderrama, near Gibraltar, in 1997 – the first time it has been held in Europe outside Britain.

The Spanish Formula 1 motor racing Grand Prix takes place at the Montmeló circuit near Barcelona early in the summer. Spain's version of the Tour de France cycle

The Bullfight

The low-lying sun floods the arena with heavy, sweaty summer light from the west. There is a buzz as places fill. Families jostle for space with older, beret-bearing aficionados, their faces creased with years of farm toil, and bright young things sporting sky-blue sunglasses. Some clutch plastic cups of beer, others swig red wine from animal-hide *botas*. All but those who have paid for the comfort of real seats in the shade *(sombra)* have brought some kind of cushion: bare concrete or wooden slats can pall after a while on unprotected behinds. Many have chosen to huddle on the cheap benches facing the unforgiving midsummer sun *(sol)*. At one end of the ring, high up in the top rows, a brass band strikes up a stirring *pasodoble*, while on the opposite side the president of the fight and his adjutants await the arrival of the *toros* (bulls).

The *corrida* (bullfight) is a spectacle with a long history and many rules. It is not, as many would suggest, simply a ghoulish alternative to the slaughterhouse (itself no pretty sight). Aficionados will say that the bull is better off dying at the hands of a *matador* (killer) than in the *matadero* (abattoir). The corrida is about many things – death, bravery, performance. No doubt, the fight is bloody and cruel, and about that hackles will always rise. To witness the fight is not necessarily to understand it, but it might clue you in to some of the thought and tradition behind it. Although many Spaniards themselves consider it a cruel and 'uncivilised' activity (no-one would call it a sport), there is no doubting its popularity. If on a bar-room TV there is football on one channel and a corrida on another, the chances are high that football fever will cede to the fascination of the fiesta.

Contests of strength, skill and bravery between man and beast are no recent phenomenon. The ancient Etruscans liked a good bullfight, and the Romans caught on. Julius Caesar, who came up with the idea of pitting gladiators and other unfortunates against lions, also had a weakness for the bulls. Of course things got a little kinky under the Romans, and half the time there was no fight at all, merely the merciless butchery of slaves and other human fodder to satisfy the morbid passions of the crowd.

La lidia, as the art of bullfighting is also known, really took off in an organised fashion in Spain in the mid-18th century. In the 1830s, Pedro Romero, the greatest *torero* (bullfighter) of the time, was at the age of 77 appointed by King Carlos IV director of the Escuela de Tauromaquia de Sevilla, the country's first bullfighters' college. It was around this time too that breeders succeeded in creating the first reliable breeds of *toro bravo* or fighting bull.

El Matador & La Cuadrilla Traditionally, young men have aspired to the ring in the hope of winning fame and fortune, in much the same way as boxers have often done. Most attain neither one nor the other. Only champion matadors make good money, and some actually make a loss. For the matador must rent or buy his outfit and equipment, pay for the right to fight a bull and pay his *cuadrilla* (team).

If you see a major fight, you will notice this team is made up of quite a few people. Firstly there are several *peones*, junior bullfighters under the orders of the main torero, who is the matador. The peones come out to distract the bull with great capes, manoeuvre him into the desired position and so on. Then come the *banderilleros*. At a given moment during the fight, one or two banderilleros will race towards the bull and attempt to plunge a pair of colourfully decorated *banderillas* (short prods with harpoon-style ends) high into the withers of the bull. This has the effect of spurring the animal into action. The horseback-mounted *picadores* play a different role. Charged by the bull, which tries to upend or eviscerate the horse, the picador shoves his lance into the same area of the bull in an attempt to weaken it. Animal-lovers will take some small consolation from the fact that for a long time the horses at least have been protected by heavy padding that bulls rarely manage to penetrate.

Then there is the matador himself. His dress could be that of a flamenco dancer. At its simplest, in country fiestas, it is generally a straightforward combination of black trousers or tights, white shirt and black vest. At its most extravagant, the *traje de luces* (suit of lights) can be an extraordinary display of bright, spangly colour – the name is apt. All the toreros (matadors, banderilleros etc) wear the black *montera* (the hat that looks a little like a set of Mickey Mouse ears). The torero's standard weapons are the *estoque* or *espada* (sword) and the heavy silk and percale *capa* (cape). You will notice, however, that the matador, and the matador alone, employs a different cape with the sword – a smaller piece of cloth held with a bar of wood called the *muleta* and used for a number of different passes.

La Corrida To summarise all that takes place on the day of a corrida is no easy task. In many cases, corridas are held over several days or even weeks, and the whole fiesta is known as the *feria*. The bulls are transported from their farms to a location near the ring, and in some cases directly to the ring, often days in advance. In Madrid, the bulls are kept at an Andalucían-style ranch in the Casa de Campo known as Batán until their big day arrives.

In some towns, the bulls are not transported directly to the ring, but rather to another point in town from where they are let loose on the morning of the corrida to charge to the ring. The *encierro*, as it is known, was made most famous in Pamplona by Ernest Hemingway, but scores of towns across the

country celebrate it. Barriers are set up along a set route to the ring, and some people feel inclined to run with the bulls (see also the section on Pamplona). It's a dangerous business and people always get hurt, sometimes mortally.

When the bulls arrive, the cuadrillas, president and breeders get together to look over the animals and draw lots to see who is going to fight which one. It depends a little on how many breeders are represented, how many matadors and teams there are and so on. The selected bulls are later huddled into individual, darkened corrals, where they await their moment. When this comes, the corrals are opened, light gushes in and the bulls charge out, sensing a chance to escape; one wonders if they feel disappointment as they barrel out into the ring.

The bullfight generally begins at about 6 pm, hence the title of Hemingway's manual on the subject, *Death in the Afternoon*. As a rule, six toros are on the day's card, although small country fiestas may feature only four. If any are considered not up to scratch, they are booed off (at this point the president will display a green handkerchief) and replacements brought on. Each fight takes about 10 to 15 minutes, so six bulls are quite enough entertainment for one day.

In very general terms, the bull is led about and calmed down a little by the peones, darting about and flashing their rose-and-yellow coloured capes at the heaving beast. The matador then appears and executes his *faenas* (moves) with the bull. To go into the complexities of what constitute well and badly executed *faenas* would require a book. The specialised vocabulary alone is such that a competent reader of Spanish can wade through a newspaper article about a fight and be lucky to understand the meaning of half the words, let alone the sense of the article.

Suffice to say that the more closely and calmly the torero works with the bull, pivoting and virtually dancing before the bull's horns, the greater will be the crowd's approbation. After a little of this, the matador strides off and leaves the stage first to the banderilleros, then to the picadores, before returning for another session. At various moments during the fight, the brass band will hit some stirring notes, adding to the air of grand spectacle. The various moves must be carried out in certain parts of the ring, which is divided into three parts: the *medios* (centre); *tercios* (an intermediate, chalked-off ring); and *tablas*, the outer ring.

When the bull seems tired out and unlikely to give a lot more, the matador chooses his moment for the kill. Placing himself head-on, he aims to sink the sword cleanly into the animal's neck *(estocada)* for an instant kill. It's an awful lot easier said than done.

A good performance followed by a clean kill will have the crowd on its feet waving handkerchiefs in the air in clear appeal to the president to award the matador an *oreja* (ear) of the animal. The president usually waits to see how great is the crowd's enthusiasm before finally flopping a white handkerchief onto his balcony. If the fight was exceptional, the matador might *cortar dos orejas* – cut two ears off. What he does with them when he gets home is anyone's guess.

The sad carcass is meanwhile dragged out by a team of dray-horses and the sand raked about in preparation for the next toro. The meat ends up in the butcher's.

When & Where Although bullfights are mainly a spring and summer activity, it is occasionally possible to see them at other times of the year. The season begins more or less officially in the first week of February with the fiestas of Valdemorillo and Ajalvir, near Madrid. In this case the encierros and corridas are part of the celebrations to mark the feast day of San Blas. Virtually all encierros and corridas are in fact organised as part of one town's fiesta or other. Given that there are so many fiestas, there is no shortage of bullfighting for a good part of the year.

In the Comunidad de Madrid, for instance, there are any number of local fiestas, and the encierros can be a wild and unpredictable affair. In many towns the Plaza Mayor also serves as a makeshift bullring. Often the smaller-town fights are amateurish affairs known as *capeas*. Rarely are the bulls involved fully mature, but rather young *novillos*.

The biggest and most prestigious feria in the world is that held in Madrid over four weeks from mid-May as part of the Fiesta de San Isidro, the feast of the city's patron saint.

Local tourist offices should be able to tell you if there are any bullfights going on in nearby towns, but a tip is to keep an eye out for town fiestas. Where there's a fiesta there's often a corrida and maybe an encierro.

The Matadors If you are spoiling for a fight, it is worth looking out for the big names among the matadors. A big name is no guarantee you'll see a high-quality corrida, as that depends in no small measure on the animals themselves, but it is a good sign. The last true star of the fiesta, Luís Miguel Dominguín, a hero of the 1940s and 50s, died in 1996. His present-day successors count among their number some fine performers, but perhaps none of his stature.

Names to look for include: Jesulín de Ubrique, a true macho whose attitudes to women don't go down well with everyone; Enrique Ponce, a serious class act; Joselito; and El Cordobés, one of the biggest names, although for some tastes his style borders on mocking the animal and is thus considered unnecessarily cruel.

Ethics of the Fight Anyone in any doubt about the danger to the human participants in this contest of bravery should remember that people *do* die in the ring. That it no longer happens often is perhaps to be welcomed, although there are those who cry foul. Time and again corrida reviewers lament the poor quality of the bulls and of the matadors, whose main concern appears to some to be to stay in one piece and fight (and earn) again another day. The most fraudulent practice, however, is the *afeitado* – the filing down of the bull's horns. This is a little like cutting your fingernails to the quick and makes the bull, however frightened or angry, just that little bit less anxious to make a full effort to charge and attack its tormentors.

Is the bullfight 'right'? Passions are frequently inflamed on the subject of the doubtless cruelty of the bullfight. Many people feel ill at the sight of the kill, although this is really a merciful relief to the bull and surely no worse than being lined up for the production-line kill in an abattoir. The preceding 10 or so minutes torture is cruel. The animal is frightened and in pain. Let there be no doubt about that. Aficionados will say, however, that these bulls have been bred for conflict and that their lives prior to this fateful day are better by far than those of any other farm animals. Toros bravos are treated like kings. To other Western cultures – and to many Spaniards too – the bullfight is cruel and 'uncivilised'. Yet there is something about this direct confrontation with death that invites a little more thought on the matter. Meat-eaters at any rate should reflect carefully before passing too ready a judgment. As an integral part of Spanish culture, it deserves to be experienced; there is nothing to say anyone should also *like* it.

Beyond Spain La lidia is not merely a Spanish preoccupation. It is a regular if lower-profile part of the calendar of events in southern France and Portugal. The Portuguese specialise in horseback toreros.

Beyond Europe, the bullfight has a big following in Latin America, particularly in Mexico, although Spaniards consider the general quality of the fight there to be inferior. ■

Women's Touch

The rising star in the ring today is not another brash don from the south, but a young blonde torera from outside Madrid – Cristina Sánchez. A successful fighter, she carries a double burden: not only must she face the danger of the bulls, but also the potential wave of derision and criticism that could crash upon her at any moment for simply being a woman in a man's world. She represents not only herself, but the claim of women to be taken seriously in this man's arena. And that fight is far from over. Most of her male counterparts accept Sánchez but at least one, Jesulín de Ubrique, still refuses to fight in the same corrida with her (not that he doesn't like women, you understand – he even stages corridas for women *spectators* only). For women, the fight has always been as intense outside the ring as in.

Nicolasa Escamilla, 'La Pajuelera', was the first woman to take on the bulls seriously, back in the late 18th century. Goya was so impressed that he left behind him a sketch of her in combat in Zaragoza. Martina García, born in 1814, was fighting until the age of 66, and as often as she killed her toros, she found herself being flipped by them. Towards the end of the century, Sevilla's Dolores Sánchez, 'La Fragosa', became one of the first toreras to don the traje de luces and abandon the skirt. Machismo and the fight go hand in hand, and the former caught up with the handful of active toreras in 1908, when a law was promulgated forbidding women to fight bulls, considering it 'improper practice and contrary to civilised manners and all delicate sentiment'.

The law was modified in 1934 but reimposed under Franco. Only in 1974 did Ángela Hernández succeed in having the law repealed, but this did nothing to change attitudes within bullfighting circles. Maribel Atiénzar began her career in 1977 and found she could only appear if she renounced the right to take on mature bulls as a fully recognised matador. In the language of the bullring, she was unable to *tomar la alternativa*. In this ritual the senior matador acknowledges a junior's capacity as a full matador in the ring and hands him or her the sword and cape. With this a torero's right to fight as a full matador (and hence be paid considerably more) is recognised everywhere in Spain but Madrid – the mecca of the corrida, which has its own qualifying hurdle. Maribel 'took the alternative' in Mexico, an achievement not recognised at all in Spain.

Cristina Sánchez, born in 1972, has achieved the unimaginable, taking the alternative in Madrid's Las Ventas – the ultimate achievement for any bullfighter – in mid-1996. But in any profession you're only as good as your last performance, and this is nowhere more true than in the potentially hostile world of the bullring. ■

race is the Vuelta de España, a three week round-the-country jaunt traditionally staged in spring, but moved to September in 1995 and 1996.

THINGS TO BUY

You can find some very attractive and reasonably priced handicrafts in Spain if you look in the right places. In some crafts there's wide regional variation between products and styles, and many products tend not to be found very far afield from where they are made. Apart from craft shops – which abound in the producing areas – you may pick up crafts at weekly or daily markets in villages or towns, and even in department stores. There are some excellent flea markets and car boot sales (rastros) around the country where you can at times find incredible bargains.

Pottery

This comes in many attractive regional varieties and is cheap. Crockery, jugs, plant pots, window boxes and tiles are likely to cost a fraction of the price of similar products at home. Islamic influence on design and colour is evident in much of the country. In Granada, the dominant colours are white splashed with green and blue, often with a pomegranate as the centrepiece of the pattern. In Córdoba the product is finer, with black, green and blue borders on white. Brighter colours are used in other parts of the country. Some excellent, more individual pieces are made in Níjar in eastern Andalucía. Many of the towns and villages around Valencia city are famous for their ceramics and pottery. There are plenty of speciality shops in the city – which is also a good place to buy your own paella dish!

Textiles & Clothes

Inexpensive, colourful rugs and blankets are made all over the country; try places like the Alpujarras and Níjar in Andalucía. Other textiles include lacework (from Galicia and elsewhere) and embroidery. (The finest embroidery – not for sale, though! – is seen on religious garments such as priests' vestments and the ornate outfits adorning the various images of the Virgin in churches and processions. The Virgins have whole wardrobes of richly embroidered dresses and cloaks. Bullfighters' costumes are also elaborately embroidered; some exquisite old examples are on display in the bullfighting museums of Ronda and Córdoba.)

Ibiza city is something of a drawing card for fashion victims and a surprisingly good place to buy clothes, with everything ranging from the latest and most extreme grunge statements to hippy gear straight out of Carnaby Street. Barcelona and the Costa Brava resort of Cadaqués have interesting boutiques too.

Leather

Spanish leather goods used to be quite a bargain and, though prices have gone up, you can still get good deals on leather jackets, bags, belts, shoes and boots in many places, especially Andalucía. Exquisite riding boots can be purchased in 'horsy' places like Jerez de la Frontera and El Rocío. Embossed, polychrome leather products such as poufs make a good not-too-bulky present: you can simply roll up the leather and insert the filling back at home.

Other Crafts

Gold and silver jewellery abound; some of the best is the filigree made in Córdoba. Damascene weapons (made of steel inlaid with gold, silver and copper) are still produced in Toledo. (Spain's very finest gold and silverware, much of it reflecting the influx of wealth from the New World, remains in the country's splendid churches and museums.)

There's some pleasing woodwork available, such as Granada's marquetry boxes, chess sets and more.

Basketwork is produced throughout Spain but is most evident on the coasts. Esparto grass products are durable and inexpensive.

Getting There & Away

Spain is one of Europe's top holiday destinations and is well linked to other European countries by air, rail and road. Regular ferries (most of which carry vehicles) also link it with Morocco to the south.

If you're coming to Spain from elsewhere in Europe, flying is the simplest option. Never assume that the cheapest way is by land (or sea). More often than not it is more attractive to fly – you lose nothing in price and save a lot of time and hassle – unless of course you want to enjoy the journey to Spain as much as your trip inside the country.

Some good direct flight deals are also available from North America. Those coming from Australasia have fewer choices and should watch out for deals including free internal European flights (see the Australia section under Air).

Insurance
However you're travelling, it's worth taking out travel insurance. Work out what you need. You may not want to insure that grotty old army surplus backpack, but everyone should be covered for the worst possible case: an accident, for example, that will require hospital treatment and a flight home. It's a good idea to make a photocopy of your policy, in case the original is lost. If you are planning to travel for a long time, the insurance may seem expensive, but if you can't afford it, you certainly won't be able to afford to deal with a medical emergency overseas.

Standard insurance should at least cover theft and loss of luggage, and cancellation of, and delays in, your travel arrangements. Cover depends on your insurance and type of ticket, so ask both your insurer and ticket-issuing agency where you stand. Ticket loss is also covered by travel insurance, but make sure you have a separate record of your ticket details. Buy travel insurance as early as possible. If you buy it in the week before you fly or hop on the bus, you may find, for example,

that you are not covered for delays to your trip caused by industrial action.

Paying for your ticket with a credit card often provides limited travel accident insurance, and you may be able to reclaim payment if the operator doesn't deliver. Ask your credit card company what it will cover.

See the Health section in the Facts for the Visitor chapter for more on aspects of travel insurance.

AIR
Always reconfirm your onward flight or return bookings by the specified time – at least 72 hours before departure on international flights. Otherwise you risk turning up at the airport only to find you've missed your flight because it was rescheduled, or that you've been classified as a 'no-show'.

Airports & Airlines
Spain is well connected with other European centres and for much of the year it is possible to dig up good deals, especially with charter companies. The main gateway is Madrid's Barajas airport, but there is no shortage of direct flights to other strategically located centres, particularly Barcelona in the north, Málaga in the south and Palma de Mallorca in the Balearic Islands. Occasional flights, mostly charters, also fly direct to a range of other Spanish cities from main European centres such as Paris and London.

Iberia, the Spanish national carrier that has been on the verge of bankruptcy for several years, is generally one of the most expensive ways to fly. Iberia flies to 11 Spanish cities from around the world.

The high season for travel to Spain is July and August, as well as the Easter and Christmas periods.

Buying Tickets
The plane ticket will probably be the single most expensive item in your budget, and buying it can be intimidating. It is worth

putting aside a few hours to research the market and check around the many travel agents hoping to separate you from your money. Start early: some of the cheapest tickets have to be bought months in advance, and some popular flights sell out early. Talk to other recent travellers; they may be able to stop you making some of the same old mistakes. Look at the ads in newspapers and magazines (including any Spanish press in your home country), consult reference books and watch for special offers. Then phone round travel agents for bargains. (Airlines can supply information on routes and time-tables; however, except at times of inter-airline war they do not supply the cheapest tickets.) Find out the fare, the route, the duration of the journey and any restrictions on the ticket (see the Air Travel Glossary). Then sit back and decide which is best for you.

You may discover that those impossibly cheap flights are 'fully booked, but we have another one that costs a bit more ...' Or that the flight is on an airline notorious for its poor safety standards and leaves you in the world's least favourite airport for 14 hours in mid-journey. Or they claim only to have the last two seats available for where you want to go for the whole of July, which they will hold for you for a maximum of two hours. Don't panic: keep ringing around.

If you are travelling from the UK or the USA, you will probably find that the cheapest flights are being advertised by obscure bucket shops whose names haven't yet reached the telephone directory. They sell airline tickets at up to a 50% discount where places have not been filled, and although airlines may protest to the contrary, many of them release tickets to selected bucket shops – it's better to sell tickets at a huge discount than not at all. Many such firms are honest and solvent, but there are a few rogues who will take your money and disappear, to reopen elsewhere a month or two later under a new name. If you feel suspicious about a firm, don't give them all the money at once. Leave a deposit of 20% or so and pay the balance when you get the ticket. If they insist on cash in advance, go somewhere else. And once you have the ticket, ring the airline to confirm that you are actually booked on the flight.

You may decide to pay more than the rock-bottom fare by opting for the safety of a better known travel agent. Firms such as STA Travel, which has offices worldwide, Council Travel in the USA and UK or Travel CUTS in Canada are not going to disappear overnight and leave you clutching a receipt for a nonexistent ticket, but they do offer good prices to most destinations.

Once you have your ticket, write its number down, together with the flight number and other details, and keep the information somewhere separate from the ticket. If the ticket is lost or stolen, this will help you get a replacement.

Use the fares quoted in this book as a guide only. They are approximate and based on the rates advertised by travel agents at the time of going to press. Quoted airfares do not necessarily constitute a recommendation for the carrier.

Travellers with Special Needs

If you have special needs of any sort – you've broken a leg, you're vegetarian, travelling in a wheelchair, taking the baby, terrified of flying – you should let the airline know as soon as possible so that they can make arrangements accordingly. You should remind them when you reconfirm your booking, and again when you check in at the airport. It may also be worth ringing round the airlines before you make your booking to find out how they can handle your particular needs.

Airports and airlines can be surprisingly helpful, but they do need advance warning. Most international airports will provide escorts from check-in desk to plane where needed, and there should be ramps, lifts, accessible toilets and reachable phones. Aircraft toilets, on the other hand, are likely to present a problem; travellers should discuss this with the airline at an early stage and, if necessary, with their doctor.

Guide dogs for the blind will often have

Air Travel Glossary

Apex Apex, or 'advance purchase excursion', is a discounted ticket which must be paid for in advance. There are penalties if you wish to change it.

Baggage Allowance This will be written on your ticket: usually one 20 kg item to go in the hold, plus one item of hand luggage.

Bucket Shop An unbonded travel agency specialising in discounted airline tickets.

Budget Fare These can be booked at least three weeks in advance, but the actual travel date is not confirmed until seven days prior to travel.

Bumped Just because you have a confirmed seat doesn't mean you're going to get on the plane; see Overbooking.

Cancellation Penalties If you have to cancel or change an Apex ticket there are often heavy penalties involved. Insurance can sometimes be taken out against these penalties. Some airlines impose penalties on regular tickets as well, particularly against 'no-show' passengers.

Check-In Airlines ask you to check in a certain time ahead of the flight departure (usually one to two hours on international flights). If you fail to check in on time and the flight is overbooked, the airline can cancel your booking and give your seat to somebody else.

Confirmation Having a ticket written out with the flight and date you want doesn't mean you have a seat until the agent has checked with the airline that your status is 'OK' or confirmed. Meanwhile you could just be 'on request'.

Discounted Tickets There are two types of discounted fares: officially discounted (see Promotional Fares) and unofficially discounted. The lowest prices often impose drawbacks like flying with unpopular airlines, inconvenient schedules, or unpleasant routes and connections. A discounted ticket can save you other things than money: you may be able to pay Apex prices without the associated Apex advance booking and other requirements. Discounted tickets only exist where there is fierce competition.

Full Fares Airlines traditionally offer 1st class (coded F), business class (coded J) and economy class (coded Y) tickets. These days there are so many promotional and discounted fares available from the regular economy class that few passengers pay full economy fare.

Lost Tickets If you lose your airline ticket an airline will usually treat it like a travellers' cheque and, after enquiries, issue you with another one. Legally, however, an airline is entitled to treat it like cash: if you lose it, then it's gone forever. Take good care of your tickets.

No-Shows No-shows are passengers who fail to show up for their flight, sometimes due to unexpected delays or disasters, sometimes due to simply forgetting, sometimes because they made more than one booking and didn't bother to cancel the one they didn't want. Full-fare passengers who fail to turn up are sometimes entitled to travel on a later flight. The rest of us are penalised (see Cancellation Penalties).

On Request An unconfirmed booking for a flight; see Confirmation.

---

to travel in a specially pressurised baggage compartment with other animals, away from their owner; smaller guide dogs may be admitted to the cabin. All guide dogs will be subject to the same quarantine laws (six months in isolation etc) as any other animal when entering or returning to countries currently free of rabies, such as Britain or Australia.

Deaf travellers can ask for airport and in-flight announcements to be written down for them.

Children under two travel for 10% of the standard fare (or free, on some airlines), as long as they don't occupy a seat. They don't get a baggage allowance either. 'Skycots'

should be provided by the airline if requested in advance; these will take a child weighing up to about 10 kg. Children between two and 12 can usually occupy a seat for half to two-thirds of the full fare, and do get a baggage allowance. Push chairs can often be taken as hand luggage.

The UK & Ireland

London is one of the best centres in the world for discounted air tickets. The price of RTW tickets, especially, is about the best available anywhere and tickets can be had for well under UK£1000; unfortunately, Spain rarely figures in such a ticket.

Open Jaws A return ticket where you fly out to one place but return from another. If available, this can save you backtracking to your arrival point.

Overbooking Airlines hate to fly with empty seats, and since every flight has some passengers who fail to show up (see No-Shows), airlines often book more passengers than they have seats. Usually the excess passengers balance those who fail to show up, but occasionally somebody gets bumped. If this happens, guess who it is most likely to be? The passengers who check in late.

Promotional Fares Officially discounted fares like Apex fares, available from travel agents or direct from the airline.

Reconfirmation At least 72 hours prior to departure time of an onward or return flight, you must contact the airline and 'reconfirm' that you intend to be on the flight. If you don't do this the airline can delete your name from the passenger list and you could lose your seat. You don't have to reconfirm the first flight on your itinerary or if your stopover is less than 72 hours. It doesn't hurt to reconfirm more than once.

Restrictions Discounted tickets often have various restrictions on them; advance purchase is the most usual one (see Apex). Others are restrictions on the minimum and maximum period you must be away, such as a minimum of 14 days or a maximum of one year. See Cancellation Penalties.

Stand-By A discounted ticket which lets you fly only if there is a seat free at the last moment. Stand-by fares are usually only available on domestic routes.

Tickets Out An entry requirement for many countries is that you have an onward or return ticket – in other words, a ticket out of the country. If you're not sure what you intend to do next, the easiest solution is to buy the cheapest onward ticket to a neighbouring country or a ticket from a reliable airline which can later be refunded if you do not use it.

Transferred Tickets Airline tickets cannot be transferred from one person to another. Travellers sometimes try to sell the return half of their ticket, but officials can ask you to prove that you are the person named on the ticket. This is unlikely to happen on domestic flights, but on an international flight tickets may be compared with passports.

Travel Agencies Travel agencies vary widely and you should ensure you use one that suits your needs. Some simply handle tours; full-service agencies handle everything from tours and tickets to car rental and hotel bookings. A good one will do all these things and can save you a lot of money, but if all you want is a ticket at the lowest possible price, then you really need an agency specialising in discounted tickets. A discount ticket agency, however, may not be useful for other things, such as hotel bookings.

Travel Periods Some officially discounted fares – Apex fares in particular – vary with the time of year. There is often a low (off-peak) season and a high (peak) season. Sometimes there's an intermediate or shoulder season as well. At peak times, when everyone wants to fly, not only will the officially discounted fares be higher but so will unofficially discounted fares – or there may simply be no discounted tickets available. Usually the fare depends on your outward flight: if you depart in the high season and return in the low season, you pay the high-season fare. ■

Some of the best sources of information about cheap fares around the world are the weekend editions of the national newspapers. In London try also the *Evening Standard*, the listings magazine *Time Out*, and *TNT*, a free weekly magazine ostensibly for antipodeans but full of relevant travel information for anyone. *TNT* comes out every Monday and is found in dispenser bins outside underground stations. Those with access to Teletext on television will find a host of travel agents advertising as in the publications already listed. As in North America, the Internet is another possible source of information.

Most British travel agents are registered with ABTA (Association of British Travel Agents). If you have paid for your flight with an ABTA-registered agent who then goes bust, ABTA will guarantee a refund or an alternative. Unregistered bucket shops are riskier but sometimes cheaper.

The Globetrotters Club (BCM Roving, London WC1N 3XX) publishes a newsletter called *Globe* that covers various obscure destinations and can help in finding travelling companions.

One of the more reliable, but not necessarily cheapest, agencies is STA (☎ 0171-361 6161 for European flights). STA has several offices in London, as well as branches on many university campuses and in cities such as Bristol, Cambridge, Leeds, Manchester and Oxford. The main London branches are:

86 Old Brompton Rd, London SW7 3LH
117 Euston Rd, London NW1 2SX
38 Store St, London WC1E 7BZ
Priory House, 6 Wrights Lane, London W8 6TA
11 Goodge St, London W1

A similar place is Trailfinders (☎ 0171-937 5400 for European flights), 42-50 Earls Court Rd, London W8 6EJ, with an office around the corner (☎ 0171-938 3232) at 194 Kensington High St, London W8 7RG. The latter offers an inoculation service and a research library for customers. Trailfinders also has agencies in Bristol, Birmingham, Glasgow and Manchester.

Campus Travel is in much the same league and has the following branches in London:

52 Grosvenor Gardens, London SW1W 0AG (European flights on ☎ 0171-730 3402)
University College of London, 25 Gordon St, London WC1H 0AH (☎ 0171-383 5377)
YHA Adventure Shop, 174 Kensington High St, London W8 7RG (☎ 0171-938 2188)
YHA Adventure Shop, 14 Southampton St, London (☎ 0171-836 3343)
South Bank University, Keyworth St, London SE1 (☎ 0171-401 8666)

The two flag airlines linking the UK and Spain are British Airways (☎ 0171-434 4700; 24 hour line (local rate) ☎ 0345-222111), 156 Regent St, London W1R, and Iberia (☎ 0171-830 0011), 11 Haymarket, London SW1Y 4BP. Of the two, BA is more likely to have special deals lower than the standard scheduled fares.

BA's standard open return ticket to Madrid costs £414; one way is £359. You would have to be very unlucky, however, or be feeling generous, to pay that kind of money.

Before going further into fares, think about where in Spain you want to end up. Although often there is not a huge difference in price between destinations, this is no hard-and-fast rule. If you're not tied to a particular region, you may find there are more com-petitive fares to places like Málaga or Alicante than to Madrid or Barcelona.

If you are over 26 and have no student card, you will be looking at about £230 with BA return to Madrid for a month (fixed dates). Don't despair, the bucket shops can often get you across for much less, more often than not on charter flights.

Still with the main airlines and scheduled flights, at the time of writing STA had discounted high-season return flights with BA from Gatwick airport to Madrid for £168 and to Málaga for £204. Heathrow to Madrid was £192. These were all open return fares valid for a year. Note that the difference between high and low season can be considerable. The above-mentioned Málaga flight could drop to as low as £120 in winter – although with restrictions (one month validity and fixed dates).

Council Travel (☎ 0171-437 7767), 28a Poland St, London W1V 3DB, which specialises in student and under-26 fares, plus the occasional charter, had shoulder-season six-month returns for students (ISIC sufficient) with Viva Air (connected with Iberia) for £125 to Madrid. Similar tickets with BA, valid for a year, cost £149.

You might like to ask about smaller airlines such as UK Air, which flies daily from Stansted airport (£10, 45 minutes train ride from Liverpool St Station) to Madrid. At the time of writing they had student return flights for £149. The Spanish private airline, Air Europa, had low-season return fares between Madrid and London Gatwick of 19,900 ptas, or £90 (maximum stay one month).

Spanish Travel Services (☎ 0171-387 5337), 138 Eversholt St, London NW1 1BL, often has a good range of charter flight options. If STS doesn't offer anything outstanding, look around other bucket shops. STS has charter flights from as low as £89 return to Madrid or Málaga in the low season. Check the arrival and departure times on these flights, as they can often be inconvenient. And remember that if you miss a charter flight, you have lost your money. There is little rhyme or reason to the kinds of deal that can come up out of nowhere; the explanation is usually a last-minute attempt to fill empty seats with rock-bottom fares.

Several times a year, usually around Easter and again in autumn (anytime from September to November), various charter companies put on four and five day long-weekend fares to Madrid, Málaga and other destinations for silly prices: £49 return is not unheard-of. Keep your eyes open for ads around these times, because it is often worth your while to buy the ticket and ditch the return leg. Otherwise, charter flights are always worth investigating. The most fruitful destination/exit point is Málaga. If you are flying out of here during winter, return flights can come in at less than 20,000 ptas.

In southern Spain, keep your eyes on the local English-language rags for cheap flights. Otherwise, check around the budget travel agents for student fares, charters and other last-minute deals.

Non-European passport-holders should note a curious version of racism in operation between Spain and the UK. Some charter flights running between these countries will accept only EU passport-holders as passengers. Even non-European residents in the EU are refused tickets. The 'reasoning' is that priority for cheap flights should be given to European holiday-makers, the implication being that non-EU citizens (including residents) are in some way *not* holiday-makers or are engaged in activities more nefarious than lying around on the *costas*! Try to work out this absurd and distasteful piece of bureaucracy.

Open-jaw tickets are a possibility. At the time of writing STS had one going into Barcelona and out of Madrid, or the other way around, for £159 return in June and £195 in July.

You needn't necessarily fly from London, as many good deals are as easily available from other major centres in the UK.

Flying as a courier (see also the USA section later in this chapter) might be a possibility. You'll have to go through the Yellow Pages to find companies that do this. DHL,

for instance, no longer sends people from outside the company.

If you're coming from Ireland, it might be worth comparing what is available direct and from London; getting across to London first may save you a few quid.

Fly-Drive Packages including flights and prebooked hire cars can be an attractive option, especially in the high season when local car hire prices will always exceed (often double) those of prebooked cars. Numerous travel agents and tour operators can make arrangements.

Continental Europe
Air travel between Spain and other places in Continental Europe is worth considering if you are pushed for time. Very short hops can be expensive, but for longer journeys you can often find airfares that beat overland alternatives on cost.

Germany In Munich, a great source of travel information and equipment is the Därr Travel Shop (☎ 089-28 20 32) at Theresien-strasse 66. Aside from producing a comprehensive travel equipment catalogue, this place also runs an 'Expedition Service' with current flight information available.

In Berlin, ARTU Reisen (☎ 030-31 04 66), at Hardenbergstrasse 9, near Berlin Zoo (with five branches around the city) is a good travel agent. In Frankfurt/Main, you might try SRID Reisen (☎ 069-43 01 91), Berger-strasse 118.

Netherlands Amsterdam is a popular departure point. Some of the best fares are offered by the student travel agency NBBS Reiswinkels (☎ 020-620 5071), which has seven branches throughout the city. Their fares are comparable to those of London bucket shops. NBBS Reiswinkels has branches in Brussels, Belgium, as well.

Italy The best place to look for cheap flights to Spain is the CTS (Centro Turístico

Studentesco), which has branches all over the country. The one in Rome (☎ 06-46791) is at Via Genova 16.

France In Paris, Voyages et Découvertes (☎ 01 42 61 00 01), 21 Rue Cambon, is a good place to start hunting down the best airfares, although given the proximity you should compare the advantages of travelling overland. At the time of writing, about the best deal from Madrid to Paris was with Aerolíneas Argentinas for 13,700 ptas one way or 24,700 ptas return. A company called Regional Air operates direct flights between Barcelona and Nice.

Portugal Only those in a tearing hurry will want to consider flying between Madrid and Lisbon. Iberia and TAP do it for around 38,000 ptas return; the one-way fare is almost the same! You will get a better deal if you are a student under 26.

North Africa

There is precious little in the way of cheap flights between Spain and North Africa. Among the cheaper tickets available from Madrid at the time of writing was one for about 30,000 ptas return to Tangier with a maximum stay of six months. To Marrakesh was 45,000 ptas. Such prices are themselves not always easy to find, and flights can easily cost 20,000 ptas more. The options *from* Morocco are more limited still. One way to Madrid from Casablanca, regardless of the airline, comes to about Dr 2800 (around 40,000 ptas). Iberia has four flights weekly between Madrid and Casablanca and two between Madrid and Tangier.

While the UN air embargo against Libya remains in place, there are no flights whatsoever between that country and Spain, and Algeria is virtually a no-go area too.

Canary Islands

Although part of Spain, Las Islas Canarias are so far away that many peninsular Spaniards can't resist jokes in poor taste about the islanders being Africans. Few visitors to mainland Spain end up combining their trip with another to the Canary Islands. There is certainly no particular financial incentive to do so, as charter flights to the Canaries from major European capitals often cost less than flights from mainland Spain. From Madrid, Iberia, Air Europa, Spanair and charters all fly to Tenerife. A return charter fare can be as low as 18,900 ptas. Aviaco links five Canary Islands airports with the mainland.

Tourist class return flights with Air Europa between Tenerife and mainland destinations range from 26,900 ptas (from Málaga) through 28,900 ptas (to Madrid) to 33,900 ptas (to Barcelona or Santiago de Compostela).

The USA

The North Atlantic is the world's busiest long-haul air corridor and the range of flight options is bewildering. Several airlines fly direct to Spain, landing in Madrid, Barcelona and other Spanish destinations. These include Iberia, British Airways and KLM. Many flights involve a stop elsewhere in Europe before reaching their final destination. If your European trip is not going to be confined to Spain, consult your travel agent on whether cheaper flights are available to other European cities.

The *New York Times*, the *LA Times*, the *Chicago Tribune* and the *San Francisco Examiner* produce weekly travel sections in which you'll find any number of travel agents' ads. Council Travel and STA Travel have offices in major cities nationwide. The magazine *Travel Unlimited* (PO Box 1058, Allston, Mass 02134) publishes details of cheap airfares.

Standard fares on commercial airlines are expensive and probably best avoided. However, travelling on a normal, scheduled flight can be more secure and reliable, particularly for older travellers and families, who might prefer to avoid the potential inconveniences of the budget alternatives.

Discount and rock-bottom options from the USA include charter flights, stand-by and courier flights. Stand-by fares are often sold at 60% of the normal price for one-way tickets. Airhitch (☎ 212-864 2000; e-mail airhitch@netcom.com), 2641 Broadway, New York, NY 10025, specialises in this sort of thing. You will need to give a general idea of where and when you need to go, and a few days before your departure you will be presented with a choice of two or three flights. Airhitch has several other offices in the USA, including Los Angeles (☎ 310-726 5000), as well as others in London, Paris, Amsterdam, Prague, Rome and Bonn. You can contact their Madrid representative on ☎ 91-541 30 83.

On courier flights you accompany freight or a parcel to its destination. A New York-Madrid return on a courier flight can cost under US$200 in the low season (more expensive from the west coast). Generally courier flights require that you return within a specified period (sometimes within one or two weeks, but often up to one month). You will need to travel light, as luggage is usually restricted to what you can carry onto the plane (the parcel or freight you accompany comes out of your luggage allowance), and you may have to be a US resident and apply for an interview before they take you on. Most flights depart from New York.

A good source of information on courier flights is Now Voyager (☎ 212-431 1616), Suite 307, 74 Varrick St, New York, NY 10013. This company specialises in courier flights, but you must pay an annual membership fee (around US$50), which entitles you to take as many courier flights as you like. Phone after 6 pm to listen to a recorded message detailing all available flights and prices. The Denver-based Air Courier Association (☎ 303-278 8810) also does this kind of thing. You join the association, which is used by international air freight companies to provide the escorts.

Prices drop as the departure date approaches. It is also possible to organise courier flights directly through the courier companies. Look in your Yellow Pages under 'courier services'.

Charter flights tend to be significantly cheaper than scheduled flights. Reliable travel agents specialising in charter flights, as well as budget travel for students, include STA and Council Travel, both of which have offices in major cities:

STA
    48 East 11th St, New York, NY 10003
    (☎ 212-477 7166)
    914 Westwood Blvd, Los Angeles, CA 90024
    (☎ 213-824 1574)
    166 Geary St, Suite 702, San Francisco, CA 94108 (☎ 415-391 8407)
Council Travel
    148 West 4th St, New York, NY 10011
    (☎ 212-254 2525)
    205 East 42nd St, New York, NY 10017
    (☎ 212-661 1450)
    1093 Broxton Ave, Los Angeles, CA 90024
    (☎ 213-208 3551)
    Suite 407, 312 Sutter St, San Francisco, CA 94108 (☎ 415-423473)

Other travel agents specialising in budget airfares include Discount Travel International in New York (☎ 212-362 3636).

For the truly high-tech traveller, another potential source of info and flights is the variety of travel forums open to users of the Internet and assorted computer information and communication services. They are a step further down the travellers' superhighway from TV Teletext services – another source of flights and fares.

Iberia flies direct between Madrid and New York, but it is rarely the most competitive deal. If you don't mind changing flights en route, some of the other major European airlines fly from New York and other US cities to most Spanish destinations. British Airways, for instance, has a shoulder-season US$475 return fare via London to Madrid, Barcelona or Málaga. KLM offers a similar deal to Madrid via Amsterdam. With Iberia or Delta you are looking at more like US$620 to US$680 return from New York, Miami, Atlanta or Chicago. Fares from the west coast hover around US$750. In the high season (mid-June to mid-September) expect high prices and low availability.

At the time of writing, one of the best deals out of Madrid to New York was with Air Europa. Low-season return fares on regular scheduled flights (twice a week) cost as little as 48,000 ptas. In the high season flights run Sunday to Friday and cost as much as 74,900 ptas return. Similar deals are available from the USA for between about US$360 and US$560. You can also make connections from New York to Barcelona for the same fares. The airline offers discounts for students under 26 and senior citizens (over 60), as well as a *tarifa genial*, which gives you the same discount if you make the return flight within three months.

If you can't find a particularly cheap flight, it is always worth considering getting a cheap transatlantic hop to London and prowling around the bucket shops there. See the UK & Ireland section below and make some calculations.

Canada

Iberia has direct flights to Madrid from Toronto and Montreal. In much the same way as from the USA, other major European airlines offer competitive fares to most Spanish destinations via other European capitals. Travel CUTS, which specialises in discount fares for students, has offices in all major cities. Otherwise scan the budget travel agents' ads in the *Toronto Globe & Mail*, the *Toronto Star* and the *Vancouver Sun*. The magazine *Great Expeditions* (PO Box 8000-411, Abbotsford BC V2S 6H1) is sometimes useful.

See the USA section above for information on courier flights. For courier flights originating in Canada, contact FB on Board Courier Services (☎ 514-633 0740 in Toronto or Montreal, or ☎ 604-338 1366 in Vancouver). Airhitch (see the USA section) has stand-by fares to/from Toronto, Montreal and Vancouver.

Australia

STA Travel and Flight Centres International are major dealers in cheap airfares, although heavily discounted fares can often be found at the travel agent in your local shopping centre. The Saturday travel sections of the Melbourne *Age* and the *Sydney Morning Herald* have many advertisements offering cheap fares to Europe, but don't be surprised if they happen to be 'sold out' when you contact the agents: they are usually low-season fares on obscure airlines with conditions attached.

Discounted return airfares on mainstream airlines through reputable agents can be surprisingly cheap, with low-season fares around A$1600 to A$1800 return and high-season fares up to A$2500.

As a rule there are no direct flights from Australia to Spain. Often you will have to change flights, if not airlines, and fly to Europe via Asia or South America. Aerolíneas Argentinas is one airline that connects Australia indirectly with Spain this way.

On some flights between Australia and main European destinations such as London, Paris and Frankfurt, a return ticket between that destination and another European capital is thrown in. Madrid and Barcelona are generally both possible choices for such a deal.

The following are some addresses for agencies offering good-value fares:

STA Travel
224 Faraday St, Carlton, Vic 3053
(☎ 03-9347 6911)
Shop 3, 702-730 Harris St, Ultimo, NSW 2007
(☎ 02-9281 1530)
1st Floor, New Guild Building, University of Western Australia, Crawley, WA 6009
(☎ 09-380 2302)
Flight Centres International
Bourke Street Flight Centre, 19 Bourke St, Melbourne, Vic 3000 (☎ 03-9650 2899)
Martin Place Flight Centre, Shop 5, State Bank Centre, 52 Martin Place, Sydney, NSW 2000
(☎ 02-9235 0166)
City Flight Centre, Shop 25, Cinema City Arcade, Perth, WA 6000 (☎ 09-325 9222)

New Zealand

As with Australia, STA Travel and Flight Centres International are popular travel agents in New Zealand. The cheapest fares to Europe are generally routed through the USA, although in the case of Spain you may get a deal via Latin America. A round-the-world (RTW) ticket may be cheaper than a normal return. Otherwise, you can fly from Auckland to pick up a connecting flight in Melbourne or Sydney.

Useful addresses include:

Flight Centres International
Auckland Flight Centre, Shop 3A, National Bank Towers, 205-225 Queen St, Auckland (☎ 09-309 6171)
STA Travel & International Travellers Centre
10 High St, Auckland (☎ 09-309 0458)
Campus Travel
Gate 1, Knighton Rd, Waikato University, Hamilton (☎ 07-856 9139)

LAND

If you are travelling by bus, train or car to Spain it will be necessary to check whether you require visas to the countries you intend to pass through.

The UK

Bus If you plan to head straight into Spain from the UK, bus is probably the cheapest option. Eurolines (☎ 0171-730 8235), 52 Grosvenor Gardens, Victoria, London SW1 (the terminal is a couple of blocks away), runs buses to Barcelona on Monday, Wednesday and Saturday, leaving at 11 am and arriving 24 hours later. The one-way and return fares are, respectively, £77 and £119 (£71 and £109 for those under 26 and senior citizens). A bus goes to Madrid on Monday and Friday, leaving at 10 pm and arriving as much as 34 hours later (there's a seven hour layover in Paris). One-way and return fares are £77 and £138 (£69 and £125 for under-26s and seniors). The single biggest disadvantage of the bus is that you can't get off along the way. Fares rise in the peak summer season.

You can also take a National Express bus from the same terminal to connect with the Brittany Ferries service to Santander. The standard adult return fare is £125, or £161 in the high season. If you do want to take this route from London, you may as well take the combined ticket, as it saves you a couple of pounds. The bus only runs on Sunday. In summer there is another bus to Santander via

France for £115 return, or £127 in the peak season (mid-July to mid-September).

Under-26s pay around 10% less on most bus services, as do seniors over 60 (over 50 in the case of some National Express channel crossing services). Children up to the age of 12 generally pay half-price on all services.

Train Effectively your choices from London are limited by the options in Paris, as any train journey to Spain from the UK involves changing trains in Paris. From there you usually have the choice of two daily services to Madrid and two others to Barcelona.

If you optimise your choice of departure from London to keep waiting times for connections to a minimum, the trip by train to either Barcelona or Madrid is comparable with the bus for journey times. Obviously there are plenty of possibilities for the Paris leg via ferry and hovercraft on the Dover-Calais run. If you leave at 7 am, you can be in Madrid at 9.50 am the following day.

Trains run from Charing Cross or Victoria station to Paris (via ferry or hovercraft from Dover to Calais or Folkestone to Boulogne). You arrive at the Gare du Nord, and must get to the Gare d'Austerlitz (take the RER B to St Michel and change there for the RER C to Austerlitz). From Paris there are two services each per day to Madrid and Barcelona; for more details see France later in this chapter.

The return fares to Barcelona and Madrid are £172 and £193 (marginally less if you are under 26), and tickets are valid for two months. Under-26s can get Wasteels or BIJ (Billet International de Jeunesse) tickets. They amount to the same thing, and from London at any rate represent a surprisingly small saving on normal tickets.

There are discounts for children, and seniors over 60 can get a special international rail travel card (valid only for trips that cross at least one border). UK citizens pay £5 for the card, and they must already have a British Rail card (£16). The pass entitles you to roughly 30% off standard fares.

Channel Tunnel An alternative rail option from London involves taking the new

Eurostar Chunnel train for the Paris leg. It only takes three hours, but given the timetables from Paris probably won't take much off your travel time. Fares will also be dearer.

Car & Motorcycle Refer to the Sea section later in this chapter for details of getting your car direct by ferry to Spain from the UK, or to France. A new option for those taking their cars to France is the Channel Tunnel car train connecting Folkestone with Calais, known as Le Shuttle. It runs around the clock, with up to four crossings (35 minutes) an hour in the high season. You pay for the vehicle only and fares vary according to time of day and season. The cheapest fare is £109 one way for a car and £45 for a motorcycle (ranging up to £159 and £55, respectively, for peak daytime crossings on Friday or Saturday in July or August). You can book in advance (☎ 0990-35 35 35), but the service is designed to let you just roll up and get on the next train.

Paperwork & Preparations Proof of ownership of a private vehicle should always be carried (Vehicle Registration Document for UK-registered cars) when driving through Europe. As of July 1996, all EU member states' driving licences are fully recognised throughout the Union, regardless of your length of stay. Note that the old-style UK green licence is not accepted. It is wise to get an International Driving Permit if yours is a non-EU licence (see Visas & Documents in the Facts for the Visitor chapter).

Third party motor insurance is a minimum requirement in Spain and throughout Europe, and it is compulsory to have a Green Card, an internationally recognised proof of insurance, which can be obtained from your insurer. Also ask your insurer for a European Accident Statement form, which can simplify matters in the event of an accident. Never sign statements you can't read or understand: insist on a translation, and sign that only if it's acceptable.

A European breakdown assistance policy such as the AA Five Star Service or the RAC Eurocover Motoring Assistance is a good investment. In Spain, assistance can be obtained through the RACE. See the Getting Around chapter for details.

Every vehicle travelling across an international border should display a nationality plate of its country of registration. A warning triangle (to be used in the event of a breakdown) is compulsory in Spain and throughout Europe. Recommended accessories are a first-aid kit, a spare bulb kit and a fire extinguisher. If the car is from the UK or Ireland, remember to have the headlights adjusted for driving in Continental Europe.

In the UK, further information can be obtained from the RAC (☎ 0181-686 0088) or the AA (☎ 01256-20123).

Rental Rather than take their own car all the way to Spain, many people opt to get there by other means, then rent a car once they arrive. Planning ahead and prebooking a rental car through a multinational agency – such as Hertz, Avis, Budget Car or Europe's largest rental agency, Europcar – before leaving home will enable you to find the best deals. Multinational agencies will provide a reliable service and good standard of vehicle. Prebooked and prepaid rates are always cheaper, and it may be worth your while looking into fly-drive combinations and other programmes. You will simply pick up the vehicle on arrival and return it to a nominated point at the end of the rental period. Ask your travel agent for information, or contact one of the major rental agencies.

Another possibility if you don't know when you want to rent is to call back home from Spain (more or less practical to the UK and the USA) and reserve through an agent there. This way you get the benefits of booking from home. One US reader suggested taking out American Automobile Association membership before leaving home: companies such as Hertz often have discounts for AAA members booking a car through a US office.

No matter where you rent, make sure you understand what is included in the price (unlimited km, tax, insurance, collision damage waiver etc) and what your liabilities are. The minimum rental age in Spain is 21 years. A credit card is usually required.

For more details of rental rates and options within Spain, see Car & Motorcycle in the Getting Around chapter.

Purchase Only residents may legally purchase vehicles in Spain; for more information consult the Car & Motorcycle section of the Getting Around chapter.

Otherwise, the UK is probably the best place to buy a vehicle for travelling in Europe, as second-hand prices are good and, whether buying privately or from a dealer, the absence of language difficulties for English-speakers will help you to establish exactly what you are getting for your money. Bear in mind that you will be getting a left-hand drive car (ie steering wheel on the right) if you buy in the UK. If you want a right-hand drive car and can afford to buy new, prices are relatively low in Belgium, the Netherlands and Luxembourg.

Camper Van A popular way to tour Europe is for three or four people to band together and buy a camper van. London is the usual embarkation point. Look at the ads in London's free *TNT* magazine if you want to form a group or buy a van. Private vendors gather daily at the Van Market in Market Rd, London N7 (near Caledonian Rd tube station). Some second-hand dealers offer a 'buy-back' scheme for when you return from Europe but, if you have the time, buying and re-selling privately is more advantageous. A good reason for travelling in a camper van is the flexibility, but they can be a pain to manoeuvre around towns. Some people take a cheap motor scooter or bicycles on board for urban commuting and keep the van in camping grounds outside the cities.

Motorcycle Spain, like the rest of Europe, is ideal for motorcycle touring, with every possible kind of terrain from mountain back roads to coastal highways. Wearing crash helmets is obligatory in Spain, as in the rest of Europe – although you wouldn't think so to judge by the way some locals behave. It is

easier to squeeze around city traffic and park, and you will never need to book ahead to get a bike onto a ferry.

Anyone considering joining a motorcycle tour from the UK might want to join the International Motorcyclists Tour Club (£19 per annum plus £3 joining fee). The club counts 400 members, and in addition to holidays on the Continent, also runs social weekends. The present secretary, James Clegg, can be contacted on ☎ 01484-66 48 68.

France

Bus Enatcar and ALSA, among the bus companies representing Eurolines in Spain, have buses between various Spanish cities (including Madrid, Barcelona, Santiago de Compostela, Oviedo and Málaga) and Paris, with other destinations en route.

Eurolines has offices in several French cities. There is one in Paris at 28 Ave du Générale de Gaulle (☎ 01 49 72 51 51).

Local bus services cross the Franco-Spanish frontier at several locations. Details appear in the appropriate regional and city chapters.

Train Trains leave Paris for Madrid at 6.05 pm and 10.24 pm, crossing the Franco-Spanish border via Hendaye (France) and Irún (País Vasco). One of these services is a sleeper-only job and requires no change of train at the border. Of the two runs to Barcelona, the 9.15 pm train to Barcelona's França station similarly requires no change of train and has sleepers only. The cheaper and slower 9.45 pm train from Paris to Barcelona (Sants) requires a change at Portbou.

The direct sleeper trains are equipped with mechanisms which allow them to change from the international line to Spain's narrow-gauge track. The cheapest option on this train is in a sleeper cabin of four, and the ticket from Madrid to Paris costs 17,500 ptas per person. In the case of the Barcelona version, the lowest fare is 16,500 ptas.

There are also direct trains from Barcelona and Valencia to Montpellier, and vice versa. Additional direct cross-border services are between Barcelona and Cerbère (the French coastal border town north of Barcelona) and Latour-de-Carol (in the Pyrenees), and between Hendaye and Irún and San Sebastián in the País Vasco.

In all other cases you will be obliged to change trains. Travelling from Madrid by anything but the direct train described will involve such a change but also give you the option of sitting – which can mean a saving of around 3000 ptas. The best bet in this case is the 3.30 pm departure for Paris from Chamartín station. In the case of Barcelona the saving can be more than 4000 ptas. Take the 5.20 pm departure for Paris from Sants station; see also the Barcelona chapter for more details.

Car & Motorcycle See the UK section above for general information on taking your own vehicle across Europe. The main crossings from France into Spain are the main highways to Barcelona and San Sebastián at either end of the Pyrenees. But there are plenty of more attractive back roads through the mountains into Spain. Many of them are discussed in the course of the book.

Portugal

Bus From Madrid there are three Eurolines buses a week to Lisbon (nine hours; around 4125 ptas one way) via Salamanca, departing from the Estación Sur de Autobuses at 10 pm and arriving at Avenida Casal Ribeiro at 6 am. AutoRes also has a daily bus (5675 ptas) from its station on Calle de Fernández Shaw in Madrid. A weekly service connects Lisbon with Barcelona. Other services to the Portuguese capital run from Málaga (via Sevilla and Badajoz), Benidorm (via Alicante and Toledo) and La Coruña (via Santiago de Compostela and Tuy). There are also services to the Algarve from Madrid, and local services from towns like Huelva (Andalucía), Badajoz (Extremadura) and Verín (Galicia).

Train A daily train makes its way from San Sebastián to Lisbon via Madrid, Salamanca and Oporto. From Madrid it takes 11 hours and a 2nd class one-way ticket costs 6700

ptas. The train leaves Chamartín station at 10.30 pm. You can also pick up local trains from Tuy (turn to the Galicia chapter for more information).

Car & Motorcycle Main roads run into central Portugal from Salamanca, Badajoz and Cáceres, while the highway from Sevilla via Huelva takes you to the Algarve region. In the north there are plenty of minor approach roads from Galicia, but the main highway runs via Tuy across the Río Miño and down the Portuguese coast. See the UK section above for general information on taking your own vehicle across Europe.

Andorra

Bus Regular buses connect Andorra with Barcelona and other destinations in Spain, including Madrid, and France. Turn to the Andorra chapter for more details. Travellers technically requiring visas for Spain but not having them might try this route, as passport checks are not always made – but don't bank on this.

Rest of Europe

Bus Eurolines and other companies operate buses from Madrid, Barcelona and other major cities across France and into Germany (Frankfurt, Hamburg, Munich and Düsseldorf), the Benelux countries, Italy, Switzerland and occasionally on to Eastern Europe.

Train Direct trains link Barcelona with Geneva, Zürich, Turin and Milan at least three times a week. Reaching other destinations in Europe beyond these will require a change in these cities or in Paris.

Morocco

An ambitious plan to unite Spain and Morocco (or, as the hyperbole merchants like to say, Europe and Africa) by tunnel looks as though it may well become reality in the early years of the 21st century. In the meantime, you'll have to adopt a more conventional approach. Buses from several Spanish cities converge on Algeciras to

BETHUNE CARMICHAEL

BETHUNE CARMICHAEL DAMIEN SIMONIS BETHUNE CARMICHAEL

Top: Detail from the *modernista* Mercado Central, Valencia
Bottom Left: Tiles and mosaics in Antoni Gaudí's unfinished garden-city, Parc Güell, Barcelona
Bottom Middle: Detail from the Alhambra, in Granada, Andalucía
Bottom Right: Colourful tiles, Parc Güell, Barcelona

DAMIEN SIMONIS

The charming village of Orbaneja del Castillo, in northern Burgos province, Castilla y León

make the ferry crossing to Tangier and head into Morocco. The trip to Tangier from Madrid can cost as little as 7000 ptas. Consult the Sea section of this chapter for more details on Spain-Morocco ferries.

Bus Passes

Eurolines (see the earlier UK section) offers the option of a Eurolines Pass. A pass valid for 30/60 days costs £229/279 (£199/249 for under-26s and senior citizens) and allows unlimited travel between 18 European cities. Unfortunately, the only Spanish city is Barcelona, so the pass is useless inside Spain. The pass is available at Eurolines offices across Europe.

Another option for students and young people is to climb aboard the Eurobus. This works something like Eurail. You buy a pass (from US$139 for two weeks up to US$325 for three months) and get on and off buses running a set route across much of Europe (including Madrid, Barcelona and Valencia) as you choose. Ask about this at youth travel agencies such as Campus Travel in London.

Train Passes

InterRail If you are resident in the UK (or indeed any other European country in the InterRail network) and plan to travel far and wide, it is worth thinking about an InterRail pass. The InterRail map of Europe is divided into zones, one of which is composed of Spain, Portugal and Morocco. The ticket is designed for people under 26 (there is a ticket for older people, but Spain does not recognise it). Fifteen days unlimited 2nd class travel in one zone costs £179. Better value is the one month ticket for two zones for £209 (which would get you across France too). If you think you can stand careering around virtually all of Europe, you could go for the one month all-in £249 ticket. Bear in mind that InterRailers must pay part of the fare on certain high-speed trains like Spain's Talgos, and full fare on the AVE.

Card-holders get discounts on travel in the country of residence where they purchase the ticket, as well as on a variety of other services such as ferry travel. In Britain you can buy InterRail cards at the International Rail Centre (☎ 0171-834 2345) at London's Victoria station, or several other main-line stations.

Eurail These passes are for non-European residents, which means you are not entitled to one if your passport shows you have been in Europe continuously for six months or more. For some odd reason, people over 26 pay for a 1st class pass and those under 26 for a 2nd class pass. If you are only going to be travelling in Spain, you are unlikely to cover the cost of the pass. For it to be worth considering, you need to be planning a *lot* of long-distance travel in Europe: even Eurail says you need to do at least 2400 km before you start to get value for money.

The standard Consecutive passes are expensive. You can get one valid for 15 days or one, two or three months. The 15 day pass costs £313, or £392 for over-26s.

Eurail also offers Flexipasses, with which the traveller is entitled to five, 10 or 15 days rail travel over a two month period. These cost, respectively, £201/274, £313/440 and £425/582 for under/over-26s. There is a growing range of permutations on the Eurail pass, largely because the original idea is so costly. Enquire about Eurail Youthpass, Europass Youth, Euraildrive Pass and Europass Drive (for combined rail travel and car rental), and Eurail Saverpass.

People generally purchase Eurail passes in their country of origin, but you *may* be able to get them at the International Rail Centre. If not, the French Railways (0171-493 9731) office in London does sell them. It's at 179 Piccadilly, W1V 0BA.

Explorer Pass Yet another possibility is a Spanish Explorer pass, offered by a youth rail travel group known as Eurotrain. This costs £215 for a two month ticket along a return route from London to Paris, Toulouse, San Sebastián, Madrid, Barcelona, Lyon, Paris and back to London. Passes are available at Campus Travel (☎ 0171-730 3402), 52 Grosvenor Gardens, London SW1W 0AG.

Other Passes You can also get Freedom passes (known as Euro-Domino outside the UK) for any one of 25 European countries, valid for three, five or 10 days travel over a month. For Spain, a 1st class, 10 day pass costs £289. Second class is £239 and a youth version (under 26) costs £189. This is a more attractive option than Eurail if you intend to spend a decent amount of time exploring Spain rather than rocketing all over the Continent. But again, you would need to be on trains a good amount of the time to get full value out of the pass. On balance, you are better off with an InterRail card if you can get one.

A comparatively new rail pass for non-Europeans is the Europass, which gives between five and 15 days unlimited travel within a two month period. Youth (aged under 26) and adult passes are available and can be purchased at the same outlets as Eurail passes. You choose from a list of combinations of adjacent countries. The available combinations range from three to five countries. A youth pass for one of the five-country combinations for 15 days costs £375. Adults can save a little on the standard pass prices by purchasing a pass for two people.

For information on passes inside Spain, turn to the Getting Around chapter.

SEA
The UK
Portsmouth-Bilbao P&O European Ferries (in Britain ☎ 0990-980980) operates a ferry from Portsmouth to Bilbao throughout the year. As a rule there are two sailings a week and voyage time is about 35 hours from England and 30 hours the other way. There are only two boats in January. For more details, turn to the Bilbao Getting There & Away entry in the País Vasco, Navarra & La Rioja chapter.

Plymouth/Portsmouth-Santander Brittany Ferries (in Britain ☎ 0990-360360), at Milbay Docks in Plymouth, operates a twice-weekly car ferry to Santander (24 hours travel time) from mid-March to mid-November. In the remaining months, the service drops to once a week and departs from Portsmouth (30 to 33 hours). For more details, see the Santander Getting There & Away entry in the Cantabria & Asturias chapter.

Via France You can transport your car by ferry to France (return fare of £116 to £139 per car, including passengers, depending on the service you take) and drive to Spain from there. You end up in Calais, Dunkirk – or Ostende (Belgium). For the Le Shuttle car train service through the Channel Tunnel, see the UK in the Land section earlier in this chapter. With your foot flat on the floor through France, you may save a little time over the direct Spain ferries. Whether or not it is cheaper depends on the French tollways you take, how much juice your vehicle burns and mechanical problems en route. It's a bit of a toss-up.

Morocco
Trasmediterránea, Isleña de Navegación SA and a couple of Moroccan companies operate frequent daily roll-on, roll-off car ferries and hydrofoils between Algeciras and Tangier in Morocco. The ferry takes about 2½ hours and the hydrofoil an hour. There is another daily ferry from Tarifa to Tangier too.

There are also at least six car ferry and six hydrofoil crossings from Algeciras to the Spanish enclave of Ceuta, from where you can easily travel overland into Morocco. Travel times are 1½ hours and 30 minutes, respectively.

On most days a Trasmediterránea car ferry also departs from Almería for Melilla, Spain's enclave in eastern Morocco. The trip takes up to eight hours. A similar service runs to Melilla from Málaga.

You could also go to Morocco via Gibraltar. A couple of ferries leave for Tangier each week.

For more details see the Getting There & Away entries for Algeciras, Almería, Málaga, Gibraltar and Tarifa.

Algeria

Romeu y Compañía runs summer (June to September) car and passenger ferries from Alicante to Oran and Algiers in Algeria.

Canary Islands

Most people choose to fly to the Canaries, but a car ferry leaves from Cádiz for Santa Cruz de Tenerife and Las Palmas (Gran Canaria) every Saturday at 6 pm. It's a long and often bumpy ride, arriving in Tenerife on Monday at 9 am and later the same day in Las Palmas. A one-way ticket for one person (without a vehicle) costs from 26,750 ptas. Unless you especially like ocean voyages or have to transport a car, you are better off flying.

LEAVING SPAIN

There are departure taxes when leaving Spain by air (fluctuating around 1000 ptas for European flights and rising to as much as 5000 ptas beyond Europe), but these are included in the price of the ticket at purchase. For European flights they are generally only charged if you are taking a *return* flight.

Passport formalities are minimal (on land borders with France, Andorra and Portugal, generally nonexistent). Those who are supposed to have a visa will usually have passports checked at airports, so if you have entered illegally, think twice about leaving by air if you don't want any unpleasant scenes.

ORGANISED TOURS

A lot of companies offer tours to Spain, generally concentrating on a couple of regions for a week or two. Spanish tourist offices can sometimes provide a list of tour operators that could be useful to you. What follows is a guide only to the kinds of options available in the UK, and should not be read as an endorsement of any of the mentioned companies. In other countries, try the organisations mentioned earlier in this chapter as sources of airfares. It is always worth shopping around for value, but such tours rarely come cheap.

Short Breaks

Brittany Ferries (see the earlier Sea section) is one of several companies that offer brief trips, lasting from two to seven days, in northern Spain. Such holidays can cost from £200 to £400, which includes the ferry crossing and usually decent accommodation.

Kirker Travel Ltd (☎ 0171-231 33 33), 3 New Concordia Wharf, Mill St, London SE1 2BB, offers pricier short breaks from London in more exclusive hotels in the main cities of Spain. As a rule, these trips will set you back from £250 per person (two to a room) for three nights, breakfast only included.

Walking Holidays

Several companies offer organised walking tours in selected areas of Spain. Explore Worldwide (☎ 01252-34 41 61), 1 Frederick St, Aldershot, Hants GU11 1LQ, UK, can take you trekking in the Picos de Europa in northern Spain or the Sierra Nevada near Granada, or trekking and sightseeing combined in Andalucía.

Alto Aragón (☎ 0181-398 13 21), 31 Heathside, Esher, Surrey KT10 9TD, UK, specialises in guided walking holidays in the Aragonese Pyrenees, which include some of the most spectacular mountain terrain in the country.

Cycling Holidays

Bolero International Holidays does cycling holidays to the Costa Brava from £169 to £258, depending on the time of year. The holidays are designed to allow experienced cyclists to travel with less enthusiastic pedallers – combining riding with relaxing. They can be contacted through European Bike Express (☎ 01642-25 14 40), 31 Baker St, Middlesbrough, Cleveland TS1 2LF, UK.

Under-35s

Young people interested in a party atmosphere as much as anything else could opt for one of the many tours that head from London to Pamplona (Navarra) in July for the running of the bulls. Hemingway would probably be left aghast, but these trips, usually for a week and taking in a few other towns along the way, are popular. Top Deck Travel (☎ 0171-370 4555), 131-135 Earls Court Rd, London SW5 9RH, does such tours. They range in cost from £149 to £219 depending on the length of stay and whether you opt to camp or stay in a hotel.

Top Deck also takes a decker home (a double-decker bus converted to a hotel on wheels) on a gruelling 36 day jaunt through Spain, Portugal and Morocco.

Contiki Travel Ltd (☎ 0171-637 0802), c/o Royal National Hotel, Bedford Way, London WC1H 0DG, also does a range of tours through Europe that take in Spain.

Coach Tours

Plenty of tour operators cater for a less boisterous clientele. Mundi Color Travel (☎ 0171-828 6021), 276 Vauxhall Bridge Rd, London SW1V 1BE, is one of several operators offering tours in Spain, especially in the south. Mundi Color has two one-week coach tours, one of Andalucía and the other taking in Madrid and parts of Castilla as well. The all-in price hovers around the £800 mark, including flights, tour, accommodation and half-board, but rises in the heart of the high season (July to August). Magic of Spain (see below) also does organised coach tours of Andalucía.

Saga Holidays (☎ 0800-30 05 00), The Saga Building, Middleburg Square, Folkestone, Kent CT20 1AZ, UK, offers three different coach tours with half-board (several departures from May to September) at £800 and up per person for 10 to 12 nights sharing a twin room. Saga can also do car hire for as little as £99 a week for guests who choose to stay in certain of the company's resorts rather than take a coach tour.

Magic of Spain (☎ 0181-748 7575), 227 Shepherds Bush Rd, London W6 7AS, does a tour of Andalucía, but specialises more in setting you up in a resort or one of the country's posher hotels.

Fly-Drive

Some companies will put together a full package getting you to Spain and including accommodation and car hire. You could do worse than start your enquiries with Spanish Affair (☎ 0171-385 8127), George House, 5-7 Humbolt Rd, London W6 8QH.

Cruises

If all you really want to do is touch the country while cruising by for a couple of weeks, a couple of companies run trips of about two weeks duration that make several stops in Spain as part of a Mediterranean cruise or a trip to the Canary Islands. Fares per person start at about £1000. One company is Fred Olsen Cruise Lines (☎ 01473-29 22 22), Fred Olsen House, White House Rd, Ipswich, Suffolk IP1 5LL, UK. More expensive still are the cruises run by the Holland America Line (☎ 0171-729 1929), 77-79 Great Eastern St, London EC2A 3HU.

WARNING

The information in this chapter is particularly vulnerable to change: prices for international travel are volatile, routes are introduced and cancelled, schedules change, special deals come and go, and rules and visa requirements are amended. Airlines and governments seem to take a perverse pleasure in making price structures and regulations as complicated as possible. You should check directly with the airline or a travel agent to make sure you understand how a fare (and ticket you may buy) works. In addition, the travel industry is highly competitive and there are many lurks and perks.

The upshot of this is that you should get opinions, quotes and advice from as many airlines and travel agents as possible before you part with your hard-earned cash. The details given in this chapter should be regarded as pointers and are not a substitute for your own careful, up-to-date research.

Getting Around

AIR

Several airlines link the major cities of Spain with a network of internal flights, but as a rule air travel within Spain is an expensive luxury. The most frequent connections are between Madrid and Barcelona, primarily aimed at business travellers. Generally you are better off with buses and trains. Possibly more useful, but expensive nonetheless, are flights to further-flung corners like the Balearic Islands.

Principal airports include Madrid, Barcelona, Málaga, Santiago de Compostela and Palma de Mallorca (Balearic Islands).

Iberia takes care of some domestic flights, but its principal subsidiary, Aviaco, is the main workhorse, connecting 24 cities on the mainland and Balearics. For info on Canary Islands flights, see the Getting There & Away chapter.

Fares with Iberia and Aviaco vary depending on what time of day you choose to go, the season and the type of ticket. Be sure to ask about discounts and special rates. You get 25% off on flights departing after 11 pm (though, admittedly, there are few of these). People under 22 or over 63 get 25% off *return* flights, another 20% off night flights and 15% off special deal minifares. These last can shave as much as 50% off weekend return tickets.

A standard one-way fare from Madrid to Barcelona in July is 12,300 ptas. Even with the discounts, Iberia and Aviaco tend to be more expensive than Spanair and Air Europa, their two main private competitors on the more important routes. The latter is emerging as one of the bigger carriers, with regular flights connecting Madrid, Barcelona and the Canary Islands, plus occasional flights to major internal destinations (such as Madrid, Barcelona, Palma de Mallorca and Málaga) and several minor airports. These include Alicante, Asturias, Bilbao, Salamanca, Sevilla, Valladolid, Vitoria and Zaragoza, but flights from these are largely limited to the Canary Islands and the odd charter to other European destinations.

Up to eight Air Europa flights connect Madrid with Barcelona daily. The one-way fare is 9900 ptas. The same airline also flies from the capital to Palma de Mallorca, Santiago de Compostela and Málaga. The return fare to all is 18,900 ptas (less if you take a special weekend fare).

Another small airline, Air Nostrum, flies from Sevilla to Ibiza, Madrid, Valencia and Zaragoza.

As a rule, one-way fares are somewhat more than half the tourist-class return fare. Tickets can easily be booked with nationwide travel agents such as Halcón Viajes. For youth fares, you could enquire at offices of TIVE (see Useful Organisations in the Facts for the Visitor chapter) in major cities around Spain.

BUS

A plethora of companies provide bus links within Spain, from local routes between small villages to fast and generally reliable major intercity connections. It is often cheaper to travel by bus than by train, particularly on long-haul runs, such as those from Madrid to the south. Check first though, as this is not a cast-iron rule.

One way or another, the local services can get you to just about any location throughout the country. However, most buses connecting small villages and provincial towns are not geared to tourist needs. This means that even frequent weekday services can drop off to a trickle on weekends. Often just one bus daily runs between smaller places during the week, and none on Sunday. Increased private car ownership over the past 10 years has led to a drastic drop in bus services too. It is not uncommon on runs between small *pueblos* for the driver to be the only person on the bus.

It is usually unnecessary to make reservations; just arrive early enough to claim a seat (on some routes the companies sometimes provide an additional bus if needed).

For longer trips (such as Madrid-Sevilla, or to the *costas*), and certainly during the peak season, buy your ticket in advance to ensure a seat. The main bus stations, like the Estación Sur de Autobuses in Madrid, can be a stifling sea of queues during major holidays: don't wander in at the last minute at these times.

In most larger towns and cities, buses leave from a single main bus station *(estación de autobuses)*, where the various companies have ticket windows, sometimes with timetables posted. If the windows are closed, no buses to your destination are leaving in the immediate future. In some cases, however, tickets are simply sold on the bus.

Bear in mind that on many regular runs (say, from Madrid to Toledo) the ticket you buy is for the next bus due to leave and *cannot* be used on a later bus. Advance purchase in such cases is generally not possible, mainly because there are sufficiently frequent departures.

In smaller places buses tend to operate from a set street or plaza, often in no way discernibly marked. If you find yourself in a small village searching for a bus, you'll have to ask around; in such cases everyone generally knows where to go. Usually a specific bar sells tickets and can give you timetable information.

People under 26 should always enquire about special discounts on long-distance trips. Companies that offer reduced fares for inter-regional travel include Enatcar, Auto-Res, Bacoma, Ecavisa and Aratesa.

Occasionally a return ticket is cheaper than two singles. Always enquire.

Fares between Madrid and major cities are often cheaper than shorter trips between two other places – compare the Madrid-Sevilla and Sevilla-Granada fares among the samples below:

Departure Point	Destination	Fare
Madrid	Alicante	2895 ptas
Madrid	Barcelona	2880 ptas
Madrid	Córdoba	1540 ptas
Madrid	Granada	1875 ptas
Madrid	Salamanca	2210 ptas
Madrid	San Sebastián	3685 ptas
Madrid	Santiago de Compostela	5440 ptas
Madrid	Sevilla	2680 ptas
Barcelona	San Sebastián	2450 ptas
Barcelona	Zaragoza	1640 ptas
Sevilla	Granada	2710 ptas

TRAIN

Travelling by train in Spain can be a mixed experience. Generally, the main-line trains with the national rail network, RENFE (Red Nacional de los Ferrocarriles Españoles), are reliable, if not always super fast, but on some of the minor lines they can be a test of your patience. To be fair though, the situation has improved out of sight over the past 20 years; anyone returning for the first time to Spain after a long absence will hardly recognise it.

It's always worth checking the relative merits of the bus as opposed to the train. Trains tend to be more agreeable for long trips, but in many cases are more expensive. Express buses between major cities are often faster, with more frequent departures, than the train. For information (in Spanish), call the local RENFE office (there's also a 24 hour information line in Madrid on ☎ 91-563 02 02).

Types of Train

A host of different train types coasts the narrow-gauge lines of the Spanish network. For the traveller, the difference is usually in the speed of the journey, the number of stops made and often, as a consequence, the price. A saving of a couple of hours on a faster train can mean a big hike in the fare, so if time is no object and money short, go for the slower options.

For short hops, many of the bigger cities have a local network known as *cercanías*. From Madrid, for instance, cercanías trains cover the entire Comunidad de Madrid region around the city, and such cities beyond as Toledo and Segovia.

Most long-distance *(largo recorrido)*

trains have 1st and 2nd class. The cheapest and slowest of these are the *regionales*, generally all-stops jobs that run between provinces within one region.

Rápidos and *estrellas* are the standard long-distance inter-regional trains. The latter is the night-time version of the former (a few old *expresos* fall into the same category as the estrellas, but are being phased out). Higher-quality rápidos are known as Inter-City trains.

Faster, more comfortable and expensive are the Talgos (Tren Articulado Ligero Goicoechea Oriol). They make only major stops and have such extras as TVs in the carriages for showing movies.

A classier derivative is the Talgo 200, basically a normal Talgo using the high-speed, standard-gauge Tren de Alta Velocidad Español (AVE) line between Madrid and Sevilla on part of the journey to such southern destinations as Málaga and Cádiz. The trip from Madrid to Cádiz takes five hours, and that to Málaga a little less. The most expensive way to go is to take the high-speed AVE train itself along the Madrid-Sevilla line (another line between Madrid and Barcelona, which would link up with the French TGV, is planned). Even in the cheapest class, AVE passengers have access to everything from videos and telephones to children's games and facilities for the disabled.

A new AVE service on the narrow-gauge lines from Madrid to Barcelona and Valencia, perhaps to be known as Euromed, was due to begin operation from late 1996.

Autoexpreso and Motoexpreso wagons are sometimes attached to long-distance services for the transport, respectively, of cars and motorbikes.

Passes

Apart from the many international passes described in the Getting There & Away chapter, three types of pass are available in Spain. The Carnet Joven Europeo is a youth pass for people under 26, obtainable in Madrid and at TIVE offices (see Visas & Documents and Useful Organisations in the Facts for the Visitor chapter).

The Tarjeta Dorada is a senior citizens' pass issued by RENFE for 500 ptas. The kind of rail discounts available are outlined above. You must be over 60 and resident in Spain.

RENFE also issues a Tarjeta Turística, a rail pass valid for four to 10 days travel in a two month period: in 2nd class, four days cost 22,646 ptas; 10 days cost 48,374 ptas.

Couchettes & Sleepers

Couchettes are known as *literas* in Spain and are fold-out bunk beds (generally in compartments of six berths). The standard price in addition to your ticket is 1300 ptas. The discounts noted above are also applied to literas.

If you want a sleeper, you have half a dozen choices, ranging from shared cabins through to luxury singles. Prices vary according to your choice and the distance you travel. At the top end of this kind of service is the so-called *tren hotel*, a sleek and comfortable train with 1st class sleepers.

Timetables & Reservations

Train timetables are generally posted at all stations. *Llegadas* (arrivals) tend to be listed on white posters and *salidas* (departures) on yellow ones. Often separate information on specific lines is also posted, or you can ask at the *taquillas* (ticket windows). Timetables for specific lines are generally available free of charge at stations, but RENFE does not sell a comprehensive rail guide. In fact, no-one seems to.

On most trains you'll never need to book ahead. If you want to be sure of a place, it may nevertheless be wise to do so. Bookings can be made at stations and RENFE offices and through many travel agents. There is usually no booking fee unless you have the ticket(s) mailed to you. Also, people with Eurail or InterRail cards will be charged 500 ptas to reserve a seat.

Costs & Discounts

The variety of possible fares is even more astounding than the number of train types.

All fares quoted in this guide should be considered a rough sample of basic 2nd class fares.

Starting at the simpler end, cercanías generally have one fare (unless you get a season pass for a particular line). On regionales and some of the faster long-distance trains (rápidos and InterCitys) you generally have the easy choice of 2nd or 1st class seats. The evening trains (estrellas and expresos) offer 1st and 2nd class seats, couchettes and in some cases *camas* (sleeping compartments) – see Couchettes & Sleepers below. The ordinary Talgos are basically a faster and more comfortable version of the other long-distance services.

A further distinction is made between peak traffic *días blancos* (white days) and off-peak *días azules* (blue days), with marginally lower fares in both 1st and 2nd class on the latter. Most days are in fact blue, and to avoid paying the extra you should get hold of one of the free pocket calendars with white days marked. Travelling on Friday and Sunday usually involves a small increase in fare too – on average, around 10% of the standard basic fare.

In some cases, the fare also depends on the time of day you travel. This mainly applies to major lines, such as Madrid-Barcelona, and the Talgo 200 and AVE lines. The cheapest train from Madrid to Barcelona leaves at the predictably uncomfortable hour of 7 am.

On blue days (ie most days), you are entitled to a 10% discount if you buy a return ticket (20% for same-day return). Children under four travel free and those from four to 11 get 40% off on blue days. Reductions are also possible for holders of certain discount passes, such as the Carnet Joven (20% off) and Tarjeta Dorada (35% off); see Passes below for details of these.

On some major lines like Madrid-Zaragoza and Madrid-Valencia you can purchase multiple-trip Bonocity passes. These are four-journey passes (ie two each way) valid for six months and *transferable*, offering a slight reduction over normal single fares. There are several other types of commuter pass along these lines.

Some typical one-way 2nd class fares on rápido/estrella class trains include:

Departure Point	Destination	Fare
Madrid	Alicante	3700 ptas
Madrid	Barcelona	4700 ptas
Madrid	Granada	3300 ptas
Madrid	León	2550 ptas
Madrid	Salamanca	1560 ptas
Madrid	Santander	3550 ptas
Madrid	San Sebastián	4600 ptas
Madrid	Zaragoza	2450 ptas
Barcelona	Zaragoza	2500 ptas
León	Santiago de Compostela	2550 ptas
San Sebastián	Vitoria	940 ptas

With the Talgo 200 the story becomes more complex. Firstly there are two classes – turista and the more luxurious *preferente*. Then there are three fare types for each class: from lowest to highest, *valle*, *llano* and *punta*. Which one of these three you pay depends on what time you want to take the train: the peak-time service corresponds to the punta fare. The cheapest one-way fare from Madrid to Málaga is 6800 ptas. Finally, you need to see if any discounts apply to your requirements. The return ticket discounts noted above rise to 20% and 25% respectively. Holders of Carnet Joven and Tarjeta Dorada passes get 25%, although this can vary depending on which of the three fares you are paying.

The various recognised international rail passes, such as Eurail, Europass, Eurodomino and so on (see the Getting There & Away chapter for more information on international rail passes) may be used for heavily discounted, but not free, travel on Talgo 200 trains – 85% off in turista and 65% off in preferente.

The AVE is complicated still more by the existence of a third, ultra-luxury class – *club* – to which the three fare bands also apply. The Madrid-Sevilla trip can be done in as little as 2¼ hours with no stops. Similar discounts apply to the AVE as to the Talgo 200, though holders of InterRail passes pay full fare. You can also buy an open return ticket valid for six months.

You have the right to request a full refund on your AVE ticket if you arrive more than five minutes late. The cheapest one-way fare to Sevilla from Madrid is 7600 ptas.

Fines

If you board a train without a ticket, the inspector will sell you a one-way ticket on the train – for double the price. If your destination is further than 100 km away, you pay double on the first 100 km.

Private Railways

Several private railway lines operate in northern Spain. The Ferrocarriles de Vía Estrecha (FEVE) company runs trains along the north coast from O Ferrol in Galicia to Gijón and Oviedo in Asturias, and from there to Bilbao in the País Vasco via Santander in Cantabria.

The Eusko Trenbideak (ET/FV) line in the País Vasco complements RENFE services with lines serving northern towns and linking Bilbao, San Sebastián, Irún and Hendaye (France).

The international rail passes normally valid on RENFE trains cannot be used for free travel or discounts on these lines.

CAR & MOTORCYCLE

If bringing your own car, remember to have your insurance and other papers in order (see the Getting There & Away chapter).

Road Rules

If fitted, rear seat belts must be worn; fines for failure to comply range from 50,000 to 100,000 ptas. The minimum driving age is 18.

Motorcyclists should note that headlights must be used at all times. Crash helmets are obligatory on bikes of 125 cc or more. The minimum age for riding bikes and scooters under 75 cc is 16 (no licence is required).

Spanish truck drivers often have the courtesy to turn on their right indicator to show that the way ahead of them is clear for overtaking (and the left one if it is not and you

are attempting this manoeuvre). This does not absolve you from the need to exercise the usual caution, but can be a great help.

In built-up areas the speed limit is 50 km/h, rising to 100 km/h on major roads and 120 km/h on *autopistas* and *autovías*. Cars towing caravans are restricted to a maximum speed of 80 km/h.

The blood-alcohol limit is 0.08% and breath-testing is carried out on occasion. Fines ranging up to 100,000 ptas are imposed if you are caught driving under the influence. Fines for many traffic offences range from 50,000 to 100,000 ptas.

Nonresident foreigners can be fined on the spot – the minor compensation being that they get 20% off normal fines for immediate settlement.

Road Atlases

Several road atlases are available, including the *Mapa Oficial de Carreteras*, put out by the Ministry of Public Works, Transport & Environment for around 1900 ptas. This even comes in a CD-ROM version! One of the best atlases on the market, and available both in and outside Spain, is the *Michelin Motoring Atlas – Spain & Portugal*. In Spain it's called *Michelin Atlas de Carreteras España Portugal* and costs about 2600 ptas. Although sometimes deficient on minor roads, it is for the most part faithfully accurate, in spite of the multitude of road works being carried out across the country.

Both these atlases include maps of all the main towns and cities. You can find them at most decent bookshops and some petrol stations in Spain.

Road Assistance

The Real Automóvil Club de España's head office (☎ 91-447 32 00) is at Calle de José Abascal 10 in Madrid. For RACE's 24 hour, country-wide emergency breakdown assistance, call ☎ 91-593 33 33. This service is available to members of foreign motoring organisations such as the RAC and AA.

City Driving & Parking

While not quite as hair-raising as in some

Italian cities, driving in the bigger Spanish centres can be a little nerve-racking at the start. Road rules and traffic lights are generally respected, but the pace and jostling take a little getting used to.

Parking can be difficult. Where possible, avoid leaving luggage and valuables in unattended vehicles. Sevilla has a particularly bad reputation for robbery from cars. If you must leave luggage in vehicles, you should probably take the safe option and use paid car parks (around 200 ptas per hour). Most of the bigger cities operate some kind of restricted parking system. Most people ignore the fines, but if you double park or leave your vehicle in a designated no-parking zone, you risk being towed – and recovering the vehicle can cost 10,000 ptas.

Tollways & Road Works

Spain, fortunately, is not yet 'blessed' with too many tollways *(autopistas)*, and pretty much all of them are located in the north. Keep in mind if you are driving into Spain from France that the A-7 from the French border to Barcelona via Girona (Gerona), which continues south to Murcia, and the A-8 from Irún to Bilbao are both tollways – and quite expensive.

Some stretches along the autopistas are toll-free, although in general toll-free dual-carriage highways are known as *autovías*.

You can pay tolls with cash or with many credit/debit cards, which you simply swipe in machines at the tollgate. The tolls are fairly hefty. For example, Irún to Burgos costs 4140 ptas; Bilbao to Barcelona, 7505 ptas; and La Jonquera to Alicante, 7815 ptas.

Others tollways include: the A-1 from Burgos to Miranda de Ebro (975 ptas); the A-2, which connects the A-7 with Zaragoza (1890 ptas); the A-4 from Sevilla to Cádiz (1395 ptas); the A-6, a stretch of motorway along the Madrid route to La Coruña that starts at Villalba and cuts out in Adanero (870 ptas); the A-9 that links La Coruña to Vigo (830 ptas); the A-15 from Pamplona to Tudela (1245 ptas); the A-16 from Barcelona to Sitges (645 ptas); the A-19 from Barcelona to Blanes (460 ptas); the A-66 from

Oviedo to León (1105 ptas); and the A-68 from Bilbao to Zaragoza (3180 ptas).

In some cases, the tollways can easily be avoided in favour of virtually parallel and sometimes more scenic highways. If you are intent on slipping them, keep an eye open for the magic word, *peaje* (toll). The downside is that these alternative roads are sometimes clogged with traffic.

Those on the road will sooner or later come up against road works. Detours are sometimes a little rough, but you are left in no doubt that the more mediocre of Spain's roadways are being improved.

Petrol

Gasolina is as expensive in Spain as just about anywhere else in Europe. Most of the petrol stations you'll see are home-grown companies such as Campsa, Cepsa and Repsol, but you'll see some foreign ones too.

Prices vary slightly between service stations and fluctuate with oil tariffs and tax policy, so what follows serves as a guide only. Super costs 119 ptas/litre and the increasingly popular diesel (or *gasóleo*) 88 ptas/litre. Lead-free *(sin plomo;* 95 octane), also sometimes known as Eurosuper, and a 98 octane variant (also lead free) that goes by various names, are also widely available and cost from 110 to 117 ptas a litre. You can pay with major credit cards at many service stations.

Petrol is about 30% cheaper in Gibraltar than in Spain, and 15% cheaper in Andorra. It's also cheap in Spain's tax-free enclaves of Ceuta and Melilla in North Africa (although technically it is illegal to carry spare fuel on sea crossings).

Rental

All the major international car rental companies are well represented throughout Spain, and there are some local operators too. Car hire is generally expensive, and it is worth organising prebooked car rental before arriving in Spain, for example in a fly-drive deal (see the UK section under Land in the Getting There & Away chapter).

If you do decide to hire after arriving, shop

around. You need to be at least 21 years old and have held a driving licence for a minimum of two years. It is easier, and with some companies obligatory, to pay with a credit card.

Standard rates with the bigger firms hover around 3000 to 4000 ptas per day for a week for a small car. Hertz, for instance, will give you a Peugeot 106 for 3200 ptas per day with unlimited km. On top of this you need to calculate 1800 ptas a day in collision damage waiver, as well as 910 ptas a day in theft and third party insurance. Add 16% IVA to all of this and you have the total daily cost.

In the touristy areas on the costas, local firms undercut the big boys considerably, and it's possible to get a small car for 20,000 ptas a week – but be sure to examine the rental agreement carefully (admittedly difficult if it is in Spanish only).

The bulk of companies offer better rates on weekends, as their fleets are used primarily by business people paying premium rates during the week.

At the time of writing, Avis had a flexible weekend deal allowing up to five days rental that had to include a Saturday or a Sunday (or both). Two days cost 5830 ptas for a Renault Clio, Fiat Punto or Opel Corsa with unlimited km. The full five days was 12,550 ptas. Insurance is extra.

Renting motorcycles and mopeds can be an expensive business. A sample weekday rate is 4000 ptas plus 16% IVA a day (8 am to 8 pm) for a 49 cc Vespino. You have to leave a refundable deposit of 40,000 ptas. Something like a Yamaha 250 cc can cost you 10,000 ptas a day plus tax, and the deposit is 75,000 ptas. Unlike in the Greek islands or some resort areas on the Italian coast, rental outlets for bikes and scooters, even on the holiday costas, are few and far between.

Purchase

Only people legally resident in Spain may buy vehicles there. One way around this is to have a friend who is a resident put the ownership papers in their name. Anyone can buy vehicle insurance; it is unlikely that proof of residence will be required. One company

that seems disinclined to insure foreigners – resident or otherwise – is the national insurance group Mapfre.

Car-hunters obviously need a reasonable knowledge of Spanish to get through all the paperwork and understand dealers' patter. Trawling around showrooms or looking through classifieds can turn up second-hand Seats and Renaults (4 or 5) in good condition from around 300,000 ptas. The annual cost of third party insurance, with theft and fire cover and national breakdown assistance, comes in at between 40,000 and 50,000 ptas.

Vehicles of five years and older must be submitted for roadworthiness checks, known as Inspección Técnica de Vehículos (ITV). The first one (you get a sticker for the car) is valid for two years. As a rule the car must be checked annually thereafter. Check that this has been done when buying: the test costs about 4500 ptas.

You can get your hands on second-hand 50 cc *motos* for anything from 40,000 to 100,000 ptas.

BICYCLE

Bicycle rental is not terribly common in Spain, although it is more so in the case of mountain bikes. If you plan to bring your own bike, check with the airline about any hidden costs. It will have to be disassembled and packed for the journey.

You should travel light on a cycle tour, but bring tools and some spare parts, including a puncture repair kit and a spare inner tube. Panniers are essential to balance your possessions on either side of the bike frame. A bike helmet is a good idea, as are a solid bike lock and chain to prevent theft.

One organisation that can help you plan your bike tour is the Cyclists' Touring Club (☎ 01483-417217), Cotterell House, 69 Meadrow, Godalming, Surrey GU7 3HS, UK. It can supply information to members on cycling conditions, itineraries and cheap insurance. Membership costs £25 per annum or £12.50 for people aged under 18.

If you get tired of pedalling and want to put your feet up on a train, it is possible to take your bike on the train, but the conditions are restrictive. You have to be travelling overnight in a sleeper or litera (couchette) in order to have the (dismantled) bike accepted as normal luggage. Otherwise, it can only be sent separately as a parcel.

The European Bike Express is a bus service that enables cyclists to travel with their machines. It runs in summer from north-east England to Spain, with pick-up/drop-off points en route. The one-way/return fare is £99/149 (£139 return for CTC members). Phone ☎ 01642-251440 in England for details. See Activities in the Facts for the Visitor chapter for one or two hints on mountain biking in Spain.

Books

If you read Spanish, you may find some of the locally produced cycling guides of use. There are many to choose from. Libros Penthalon publishes a series of cycling and hiking books on many areas called the Colección El Búho Viajero. They generally come with maps and route planning tips that shouldn't require too deep a knowledge of the language.

HITCHING

Hitching is never entirely safe and we don't recommend it. Travellers who decide to hitch should understand that they are taking a small but potentially serious risk. You'll also need plenty of patience and common sense. Women should avoid hitching alone, and even men should consider the safer alternative of hitching in pairs.

Hitching is illegal on autopistas and autovías and difficult on major highways. You can try to pick up lifts before the toll-booths on tollways. Otherwise you need to choose a spot where cars can safely stop prior to highway slipways, or use minor roads. The going can be slow on the latter, as traffic is often light. On the plus side, vehicles can stop easily and their drivers may be more inclined to do so than those screaming up and down the fast lanes. Overall, Spain is *not* a hitchhiker's paradise. Veterans of the road seem to have particular trouble in the south, where drivers seem most suspicious.

There is little point in trying to hitch from city centres. Take local transport to town exits and carry a sign with your destination in Spanish. There are one or two organisations that organise car pooling – a kind of organised hitching service for which you pay a contribution to petrol and often a small fee. This can work out well for long-distance trips.

Dedicated hitchhikers might like to get a hold of Simon Calder's *Europe – a Manual for Hitch-hikers*.

BOAT

Ferries and hydrofoils link the mainland ('La Peninsula' to Spaniards) with the Balearic and Canary islands and with Spain's North African enclaves of Ceuta and Melilla. Turn to the Sea section of the Getting There & Away chapter and the appropriate Getting There & Away entries throughout this guide for details.

LOCAL TRANSPORT

In most Spanish cities you will not need to use the local public transport much, as accommodation, attractions and main-line bus and train stations are generally within fairly comfortable walking distance. Where this is not the case, local buses connect bus and train stations with city centres.

Bus

The bus networks in larger cities can be complicated and, with some exceptions, are probably best avoided. In Madrid and Barcelona the underground rail systems are an easier option, and in most other cities you can cover most of the ground on foot.

Metro

Known as *el metro*, Madrid's and Barcelona's extensive underground rail networks make getting around easy if your feet are protesting. For more details, see the appropriate city Getting Around entries.

Taxi

By European standards, taxis are fairly cheap in Spain and decent value if split between three or four. Flag fall and fares vary between cities, and you pay extra for luggage and airport pick-up. For more details, see the appropriate city Getting Around entries.

ORGANISED TOURS

If you want to travel around Spain in an organised tour, this is best arranged through travel agents in your own country (see the Getting There & Away chapter for suggestions).

Guided coach tours can be organised in Spain if you wish. Pullmantur, which operates through local travel agents, offers a series of tours ranging from two days in Toledo from Madrid to 12-day trips through Andalucía and Morocco or 14-day journeys through Andalucía, Portugal and Galicia.

Guided tours of the major cities are an option if you prefer not to go independently. In Madrid, for instance, many travel agents can book you on one day tours not only of Madrid, but to outlying places like Toledo, Segovia, Ávila and El Escorial. Information about the availability of such tours can be obtained from tourist offices, but as a rule it is much cheaper and not a great deal more trouble to do it under your own steam.

Madrid

There is little point in portraying Madrid as something it is not. It is not one of Europe's awe-inspiringly beautiful cities. It is not even particularly old, and much of what may have constituted its historical legacy has over the centuries been all too quickly sacrificed to make way for the new. Madrid is a largely modern city, a product of this and the 19th centuries, and the expanses of its outer dormitory suburbs and peripheral high-rise apartment jungles are an oppressive introduction for anyone driving into the city for the first time.

Seen from the air, this city of three million (the surrounding region, known as the Comunidad de Madrid, counts a further two million) appears to rise out of nothing upon an unforgivingly dry plateau some 700 metres above sea level.

Madrid may lack the historical richness and sophistication of Rome or Paris and, moving closer to home, the physical beauty of Barcelona, but it oozes a life and character that, given the opportunity to work its magic (it doesn't take long), cannot leave you indifferent.

Leaving aside the great art museums, the splendour of the Plaza Mayor and Palacio Real, and the elegance of the Parque del Buen Retiro, the essence of Madrid is in the life pulsing through its streets. In no other European capital will you find the city centre so thronged so late into the night as here, especially on weekends. Everyone seems to stay out late, as though some unwritten law forbade sleeping before dawn. In this sense it is a city more to be lived than seen. This can work out fine, as Madrid also happens to make an ideal base for plenty of diverse sightseeing and day trips in the vicinity. Toledo, Segovia, El Escorial, Ávila, Aranjuez and the Sierra de Guadarrama – just to name some – are all within comparatively easy striking distance of Madrid.

History

Few historians place much credence in

HIGHLIGHTS

- *Churros y chocolate* at Chocolatería San Ginés after a night (and early morning) out in the bars of Santa Ana & Huertas
- Bargain-hunting in El Rastro flea market
- A Sunday morning stroll in the Parque del Buen Retiro
- Summertime *cañas* and magnificent views to the Sierra de Guadarrama at Las Vistillas
- The big three art galleries: the Prado, the Reina Sofía and the Thyssen-Bornemisza
- A chicken-and-cider lunch at Casa Mingo
- Coffee and a paper on Plaza Mayor

claims that a Roman settlement called Mantua (not to be confused with the Italian version) once stood on the banks of the Río Manzanares, and the first concrete references to Madrid emerge around the 10th century. Then it was the Muslim centre of Magerit, ceded to Alfonso VI in 1083. Surrounded by cities of far greater importance, such as Toledo, Segovia and Valladolid, Madrid was little more than a fortified village when Felipe II decided in 1561 to make it the permanent capital of the Spanish empire. The monarch conceived the city, then dominated by a stout *alcázar*, or Muslim-era fortress, as the future administrative centre of the country, the hub from which the spokes of power would reach out to the furthest corners of the empire. He was driven by another consideration. Toledo to the south was a more obvious choice for the capital, but its role as seat of the Church in Spain was incentive enough for Spain's temporal ruler to seek less claustrophobic lodgings.

Valladolid briefly assumed the role of capital in 1601, but the aberration lasted only five years. Madrid attracted not only civil servants: writers such as Cervantes, Lope de Vega and Calderón all lived and worked here through the 17th century.

The arrival of Carlos III in the 18th century was good news for the people's noses. He not only cleaned the city up (it had a reputation for being among the filthiest capitals in Europe), but completed the new Palacio Real, inaugurated the botanical gardens and carried out numerous other public works. Known as 'Madrid's best mayor', he was an enlightened ruler who did much to foster the intellectual life of the city. For a time he ran into trouble with his unpopular Italian minister, Squillace, declared long capes illegal in an attempt to reduce crime. Squillace argued that, now that the sewerage system and street cleaning had been improved, the capes were no longer necessary for keeping muck off other garments. The *madrileños* would have none of it, and after long riots the measure was repealed.

Calamity befell Madrid and the rest of the country with invasion by Napoleon. On 2 May 1808, a motley band of madrileños rose up in vain against the occupation, which lasted with some interruptions until May 1813.

As Joseph Bonaparte marched out, Fernando VII waltzed in, marking the restoration of the Bourbon family to the throne. But the country's problems were far from at an end. The turbulence of the Carlist wars followed and political uncertainty remained the rule well into the 20th century. In 1931 the Second Republic was proclaimed in Madrid. Franco's troops first attempted, and failed, to take Madrid in 1936, and the subsequent siege and slow, grinding advance of the Francoists lasted until the civil war ended in 1939.

Orientation

One of the most striking aspects of Madrid's layout is the absence of water. The pathetic dribble that constitutes the Río Manzanares doesn't flow through the city centre like the Thames, Seine or Tiber – indeed, it barely

✦ ✦

Pablo Iglesias & the Birth of Spanish Socialism

Madrid, for hundreds of years the political nerve centre of Spain and its one-time empire, has produced surprisingly few of its leading political figures. Kings and queens were almost always from somewhere else, and in more recent times Franco came from Galicia, while the long-running Socialist prime minister until 1996, Felipe González, is from Andalucía.

The founder of González' party, however, was a local boy. Well, almost. Born in Franco's home town of O Ferrol in 1850, Pablo Iglesias was brought to Madrid in his infancy and there he remained. A printer by trade, he began trade-union activities at the age of 20. One year later he got a workers' paper, La Emancipación, off the ground. With the rise of Marxist ideas across Europe, in 1879 Iglesias was elected president of a new association that constituted Spain's first clandestine workers' party. Two years later, the Partido Socialista Obrero Español (Spanish Socialist Workers' Party) went public. Its advances were rapid. Within seven years it had branches across the country and Iglesias was running its mouthpiece, El Socialista. The Unión General de Trabajadores (General Workers' Union) was organised thereafter, with strong PSOE influence. By the turn of the century Socialist MPs were winning seats in local government, and Iglesias himself was elected several times to the Cortes, or national parliament, from 1910 to 1916. By then ailing and increasingly shy of the limelight, Iglesias had become a working-class myth. Even in the wake of the general strike called in 1917 by the UGT, which was suppressed without any ceremony, Iglesias was left in peace. He remained president of the PSOE and UGT, albeit in a largely honorary fashion, until his death in 1925. ■

✦ ✦

MADRID

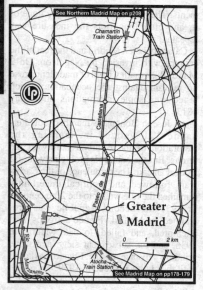

See Northern Madrid Map on p208

Chamartín
Train Station

Castellana

Paseo de la

Greater
Madrid

0   1   2 km

Río Manzanares

Atocha
Train Station

See Madrid Map on pp178-179

flows at all – and most visitors to Madrid leave the city blissfully unaware that there is a 'river' here.

Madrid, particularly the area likely to interest visitors, is also surprisingly compact in comparison with its great European counterparts. The main north-south artery, Paseo de la Castellana (which becomes Paseo de los Recoletos and Paseo del Prado at its southern end), lies in a shallow natural depression, along which a stream once flowed, and connects the city's two main train stations, Chamartín and Atocha.

It is the area around the southern portion of this promenade that captures the interest of out-of-towners. The core of the city's oldest quarters is squeezed in between Paseo del Prado in the east and the Palacio Real to the west. Roughly halfway between them is the Puerta del Sol, once a city gate but long since the official centre from which distances are measured to all corners of the country.

The majestic Plaza Mayor lies a short stroll west of the Puerta del Sol, surrounded by a warren of the more interesting back streets of Madrid. East of Sol, the old *barrios* are a happening, dynamic mix of seemingly endless restaurants, bars and cafés. The tangle of lanes spills southward into the equally fascinating working-class barrio of Lavapiés. This latter is perhaps one of the last barrios with a real feeling of local community, where the people, a mix of *gatos* (true madrileños), *gitanos* (Gypsies) and migrants (many from North Africa and the Middle East), live cheek by jowl. In the heat of the long summer nights, families jostle with revellers for space in the streets in a voluble but good-natured competition to fill the air with an energy rarely wasted on sleep – except in the hot, languid afternoons of the siesta. Moving westward to the area around Calle de Toledo you enter a slightly more polished version of Lavapiés, La Latina. On the way to the Palacio Real it in turn feeds into one of the oldest quarters of the city, once known as the *morería* – the Moorish quarter.

Madrid's great art galleries – the must-sees on everyone's list – are clustered about the Paseo del Prado, and a short walk behind the gallery of the same name spreads out one of the city's green lungs, the elegant Parque del Buen Retiro (referred to by most people as 'El Retiro'). Once the preserve of royals and dandies, it now throws open its gates to all those in search of respite from the city's hectic atmosphere.

The densest concentration of accommodation can be found in a couple of zones. The area around the Puerta del Sol and Plaza de Santa Ana is saturated with little *pensiones* and *hostales* of most conceivable classes. Similarly blessed is the labyrinth of narrow lanes that make up the barrios of Malasaña and Chueca, immediately north of Gran Vía. The same area is also seething with nightlife.

Buses arrive at numerous points throughout the city, depending on their origin. Pretty much everything south of Madrid (and much that is not) is served by buses from the Estación Sur de Autobuses near Atocha train station. From both the bus and train stations here you have a fairly short walk into the centre. Airport buses terminate at Plaza de

Finding Your Way in Madrid
Where necessary in this chapter, the information about places and sights includes a reference to the map on which you will find them (in addition, sometimes, to a reference to the nearest metro station), eg Centro de Arte Reina Sofía, Calle de Santa Isabel 52 (metro: Atocha; map: Central). The references use the following abbreviations, and the maps appear on the pages listed.

Abbreviation	Map	Page(s)
Madrid	Madrid	178-9
Central	Central Madrid	184-6
Ana & Hue	Plaza de Santa Ana & Huertas	204-5
España	Plaza de España & Around	197
Mal & Ch	Malasaña & Chueca	200-1
Sal	Salamanca	206
North	Northern Madrid	208

Colón and from there you are best off taking the metro to your final destination. Chamartín train station is a long way north, and from there you'll definitely need either a *cercanías* train or the metro to approach the city centre.

Maps The free maps at tourist offices are sufficient for most people's needs, but plenty of others are on sale. The central Madrid map in the Copiloto series published by Anaya Touring Club is clear and comes with a street directory. A far more comprehensive option is the *Plano-Guía Madrid* published by Neguri Editorial. It covers all Madrid and outlying suburbs and comes in a handy pocket-book format – much better than unfolding huge maps while sitting in the metro. Only long-termers, however, are likely to want to shell out 2700 ptas for it.

Information

Tourist Offices The main tourist office (☎ 541 23 25) is on the ground floor of the Torre de Madrid, Calle de la Princesa 1 (the entrance is around the corner on Plaza de España). You'll find another office (☎ 429 49 51) at Calle del Duque de Medinaceli 2 (map: Central). Both open Monday to Friday

from 9 am to 7 pm, and on Saturday from 9 am to 1 pm. The office at Barajas airport (☎ 305 86 56) is open Monday to Friday from 8 am to 8 pm and Saturday from 9 am to 1 pm. The one at Chamartín train station (☎ 315 99 76) keeps the same hours.

There is another tourist office (☎ 366 54 77) at Plaza Mayor 3 which specialises in the city. It opens Monday to Friday from 10 am to 8 pm and Saturday from 10 am to 2 pm.

Foreign Consulates For a list of foreign embassies and consulates in Madrid, see the Embassies section in the Facts for the Visitor chapter.

Money There is no shortage of banks across central Madrid, most with ATMs that accept a wide range of plastic, including Visa and MasterCard. When changing cash or cheques, always ask about commission. This can vary from bank to bank, but not greatly.

Exchange booths abound all over the centre of town. Don't be fooled by all the 'No Commission' signs: the exchange rates are often inferior to official bank rates. A rare exception is Cambios Uno, Calle de Alcalá 20, which generally offers sporting rates. It's open daily from 9.30 am to 8 pm.

Some of these places act as agents for Western Union and MoneyGram, in case you need to have money sent to you urgently. See Money in the Facts for the Visitor chapter for more on how these work. MoneyGram has a booth on Plaza de España, as well as at Atocha and Chamartín train stations.

American Express (☎ 322 54 24) has an office at Plaza de las Cortes 2. It's open Monday to Friday from 9 am to 5.30 pm and on Saturday from 9 am to noon.

Post The main post office is in the ornate and unmistakable Palacio de Comunicaciones on Plaza de la Cibeles. The postcode for poste restante *(lista de correos)* at the main post office is 28080. For stamps (which you can also buy at tobacconists), the post office is open Monday to Friday from 8 am to 10 pm and Saturday from 8.30 am to 8 pm. To send big parcels, head for Puerta N on the south

MADRID

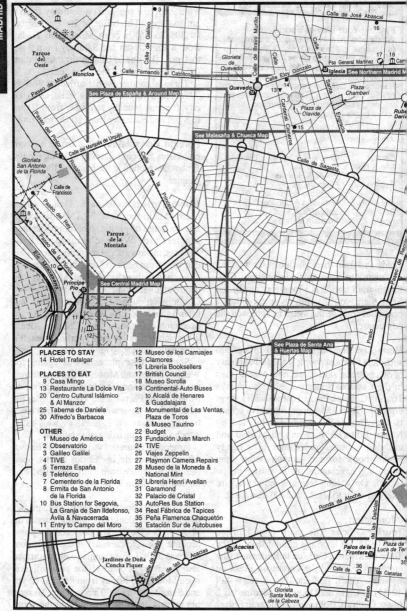

PLACES TO STAY
14 Hotel Trafalgar

PLACES TO EAT
9 Casa Mingo
13 Restaurante La Dolce Vita
20 Centro Cultural Islámico
   & Al Manzor
25 Taberna de Daniela
30 Alfredo's Barbacoa

OTHER
1 Museo de América
2 Observatorio
3 Galileo Galilei
4 TIVE
5 Terraza España
6 Teleférico
7 Cementerio de la Florida
8 Ermita de San Antonio
   de la Florida
10 Bus Station for Segovia,
   La Granja de San Ildefonso,
   Ávila & Navacerrada
11 Entry to Campo del Moro

12 Museo de los Carruajes
15 Clamores
16 Librería Booksellers
17 British Council
18 Museo Sorolla
19 Continental-Auto Buses
   to Alcalá de Henares
   & Guadalajara
21 Monumental de Las Ventas,
   Plaza de Toros
   & Museo Taurino
22 Budget
23 Fundación Juan March
24 TIVE
26 Viajes Zeppelin
27 Playmon Camera Repairs
28 Museo de la Moneda &
   National Mint
29 Librería Henri Avellan
31 Garamond
32 Palacio de Cristal
33 AutoRes Bus Station
34 Real Fábrica de Tapices
35 Peña Flamenca Chaquetón
36 Estación Sur de Autobuses

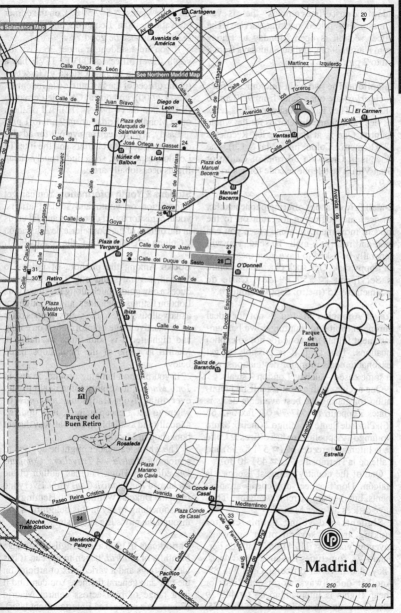

See Salamanca Map

Cartagena

19

Av de América

Avenida de América

Calle Diego de León

See Northern Madrid Map

Martínez Izquierdo

Calle de

Juan Bravo

Diego de León

los Toreros

21

El Carmen

Castelló

Calle de Francisco Silvela

Avenida de

Alcalá

Plaza del Marqués de Salamanca

23

22

Ventas

José Ortega y Gasset

24

Calle de

Núñez de Balboa

Lista

Calle de

Calle de Velázquez

Plaza de Manuel Becerra

Calle de Alcántara

Calle de

Manuel Becerra

Avenida de la Paz

25

Alcalá

Goya

26

Calle de

Goya

Plaza de Vergara

Calle de Jorge Juan

27

29

Calle del Duque de Sesto

28

O'Donnell

31

Calle de

30

Retiro

Calle de

O'Donnell

Avenida

Plaza Maestro Villa

Ibiza

Calle de Ibiza

Calle del Doctor Esquerdo

Parque de Roma

Menéndez Pelayo

Sainz de Baranda

32

Parque del Buen Retiro

Avenida de la Paz

La Rosaleda

Estrella

Plaza Mariano de Cavia

Paseo Reina Cristina

Conde de Casal

Avenida del

Mediterráneo

Atocha Train Station

34

Plaza Conde de Casal

33

Calle de Fernández Shaw

Menéndez Pelayo

Avenida

de la Ciudad

Calle Doctor

Avenida de la Paz

Madrid

Pacífico

de Barcelona

0   250   500 m

side of the post office complex – there is even a reasonably priced packing service. The parcel section is open Monday to Friday from 8 am to 9 pm, and on Saturdays from 8 am to 2 pm.

Telephone The two main Telefónica offices *(locutorios)* are open daily from 9.30 am to 11.30 pm. They have telephone cabins, telex services and phone directories for the whole country. One is at Paseo de los Recoletos 37-41 (metro: Colón; map: Mal & Ch). The other is at Gran Vía 30 (metro: Callao or Gran Vía). The telephone code for Madrid is ☎ 91.

E-Mail Private shops offering phone and fax services are beginning to catch on to the modem movement. In some cases you can send and receive e-mail. To send, you will generally be asked to have your message(s) on floppy disk. One such place in the centre is Serviprint (☎ 559 99 58), Calle de Jacometrezo 15 (metro: Santo Domingo).

Travel Agencies Madrid is not the ideal European capital for hunting down bargain-basement flights to exotic (or not so exotic) locations. That said, it is possible to get reasonable deals to major destinations, and in some cases – such as London – steals.

One agency with a well-established reputation for getting the best available deals is Viajes Zeppelin (☎ 547 79 03; fax 542 65 46), Plaza de Santo Domingo 2 (metro: Santo Domingo). Zeppelin also has offices at Calle de la Infanta Mercedes 62 (☎ 571 82 58) and Calle de la Hermosilla 92 (☎ 431 40 36).

One of the country's biggest agencies is Halcón. Don't expect dirt cheap arrangements, but they are extremely reliable. They have offices all over Madrid.

Students and young people can try looking around several other agencies. Juventus Viajes (☎ 319 41 35), Calle de Fernando VI, sometimes has some good deals. They also have an office at Gran Vía 88. Another one always worth checking for cheap flights is Intercambio 66 (☎ 449 79 99), Calle de Fernández de los Ríos 95.

Cadimar Viajes (☎ 542 59 05), on the corner of Calle de San Leonardo and Plaza de España, can also be good.

If you are a student or under 26, visit the youth travel offices of TIVE. TIVE has a branch at Calle de José Ortega y Gasset 71 (in the offices of the Instituto de la Juventud; ☎ 347 77 00), and one at Calle de Fernando El Católico 88 (☎ 543 74 12). All of them open Monday to Friday from 9 am to 1 pm.

Lastly, always keep an eye out for ads for outrageous deals on charters and the like. To London, especially, some ludicrously cheap flights occasionally arise.

Student & Youth Information You can get information on youth and student affairs, youth cards for travel discounts and HI cards in the offices of the Consejería de Educación y Cultura (☎ 580 41 96), Calle de Alcalá 31.

Books Among the plethora of guides to Madrid, several stand out. *Time Out* produces a city guide much along the lines of its London listings magazines, and although not a marvellous guide to the sights, it does offer an exhaustive range of information on eating and nightlife. It is sometimes available in Madrid in some of the bookshops listed below.

If you plan on hanging around, invest in *Todo Madrid*, a weighty tome dealing with everything from traditional *tabernas* to where to get a cheap haircut. It is updated annually and available in any halfway decent bookshop in Madrid.

The whimsical reader might be advised to search out *Madrid – A Travellers' Companion*, edited by Hugh Thomas (author of the acclaimed *The Spanish Civil War*). Everyone from the Duke of Wellington to Hemingway has something to say in this delightful stroll through the city's life and history.

Periodicals In 1996 a free English-language monthly, *In Madrid*, began to appear. It has local listings and a varied mix of articles on the city and general themes. You can find it in a range of bars across central Madrid (Finnegan's is one; see Entertainment later).

Bookshops La Casa del Libro, Gran Vía 29-31 (map: Central), has a broad selection of books on all subjects, and a respectable section with books in English, French and other languages.

For English-language books, you could also try either the Librería Turner, Calle de Genova 3 (map: Mal & Ch), or Booksellers, Calle de José Abascal 48 (map: Madrid). The former also stocks books in French and German.

There are a couple of specialist French bookshops: Librería Henri Avellan, Calle del Duque de Sesto 5 (map: Madrid), and El Bosque, Calle de Añastro 19. For German stuff, there's Lesen, Calle de Serrano 222 and Librería Alemana, Calle del Príncipe de Vergara 205 (map: North). Those in need of Italian books can head for the Librería Italiana, Calle de Modesto Lafuente 47 (map: North).

Librería de Mujeres, Calle de San Cristóbal 17 (map: Central), is a women's bookshop and well-known feminist meeting place.

Along Cuesta de Claudio Moyano, which runs along the southern edge of the botanic gardens, there is a row of 30-odd bookstalls selling an amazing selection of second-hand books, mostly in Spanish. For a more conventional selection, Librería Carmelo Blázquez, at Calle de Alfonso XII 66, 1st floor, is Madrid's largest second-hand bookshop.

About the best shop in Madrid for hiking and walking literature and maps is La Tienda Verde, Calle de Maudes 38 (map: North). They have another shop across the road at No 23 dedicated more to general travel books and ecology issues.

On Plaza de Chueca is a gay bookshop, Berkano (map: Mal & Ch). It's also not a bad place for info on the gay scene in Madrid and for looking for accommodation on the notice board.

Libraries One of the most venerable old libraries you'll find in Madrid is in the Ateneo de Madrid, Calle del Prado 21 (map: Ana & Hue). It is worth poking your head in here just to admire the study rooms of another age and the hall lined with portraits of important personages – also of another age.

Otherwise there are plenty of public libraries; look under Bibliotecas Públicas in the Páginas Amarillas (Yellow Pages). You could also try the various cultural centres or subject libraries at the Universidad Complutense.

Film & Photography You can have film developed all over the city. Photo Express at Gran Vía 84, right on Plaza de España, is reliable.

A reputable place for camera repairs is Playmon (☎ 504 21 95; map: Madrid), Calle de Jorge Juan 133.

For second-hand camera equipment of all sorts, head for Fotocasión (☎ 467 64 91), Calle de Carlos Arniches 22, near El Rastro.

Cultural Centres If you're yearning for a little culture from home, a first port of call should be the foreign cultural centres. They generally all have libraries and organise film nights and other activities.

France
    Institut Français, Calle del Marqués de la Ensenada 10 (☎ 319 92 99; map: Mal & Ch)
Germany
    Goethe Institut, Calle de Zurbarán 21 (☎ 319 32 35; map: Mal & Ch)
Italy
    Istituto Italiano di Cultura, Calle Mayor 86 (☎ 547 52 04; map: Central)
UK
    British Council, Paseo del General Martínez Campos 31 (☎ 337 35 00; map: Madrid)
USA
    Washington Irving Center, Paseo de la Castellana 52 (☎ 564 55 13; map: Sal)

Laundry There are a few strategically placed coin-op style laundrettes in central Madrid, a rarity in Spain. They include: Lavandería Alba, Calle del Barco 26; Lavomatique, Calle de Cervantes; Lavandería España, Calle del Infante; and in the northern end of town, Lavandería Automática, Calle de la Infanta Mercedes 88.

Hairdressers If you need a haircut, Peluquería Chiqui, Calle de Salitre 46 (metro:

Lavapiés) is one of the cheapest in the centre of town.

Medical Services If you have medical problems you can try popping into the nearest Insalud clinic – often marked 'Centro de Salud'. Make sure you have all your insurance details with you (including your E-111 if an EU citizen). A handy one in the centre is at Calle de las Navas de Tolosa 1 – which is also the city's main public AIDS information centre. You can also get help at the Anglo-American Medical Unit, or Unidad Médica (☎ 435 18 23), Calle del Conde de Aranda 1 (metro: Retiro; map: Mal & Ch). Staff speak Spanish and English.

At least one pharmacy opens 24 hours a day in each district of Madrid. They operate on a rota basis and details appear daily in *El País* and other papers. Alternatively, dial ☎ 098 to find out where the nearest one is. At the time of writing, there was talk of loosening laws on pharmacy trading hours, so you may find many open long hours.

Emergency In police emergency you can call the Policía Nacional on ☎ 091 or the Guardia Civil on ☎ 062. The Dirección General de Policía – Extranjeros (☎ 900-15 00 00), Calle de los Madrazo 8, sometimes has an interpreter service in summer, but otherwise is of limited use to the traveller in distress. Try instead the nearest *comisaría* (police station).

There are six first-aid stations (Urgencias) scattered about Madrid in case of medical emergency. They remain open 24 hours a day. Among them are Centro (☎ 521 00 25), Calle de las Navas de Tolosa (see Medical Services above); Retiro (☎ 420 03 56), Calle del Gobernador 39; and Tetuán (☎ 579 12 23), Calle de Bravo Murillo 357.

For an ambulance call the Cruz Roja on ☎ 522 22 22 or Insalud on ☎ 409 55 30. In a general medical emergency, you can always dial ☎ 061.

Gay & Lesbian Information The Colectivo de Gais y Lesbianas de Madrid operates an information phone service daily from 5 to 9 pm (24 hour answering machine service) on ☎ 523 00 70. The collective also has an AIDS support group called Nexus (☎ 522 45 17), where they answer the phones during the same hours. Otherwise, drop in at the Berkano bookshop in Chueca.

Help Line There is an English-language help line for those with the blues, or who simply have a request for information. Dial ☎ 559 13 93 from 7 to 11 pm.

Lost Property The main train stations and the Estación Sur de Autobuses all have lost-property offices. If you lose something in a taxi, head for the Negociado de Objetos Perdidos (☎ 588 43 44), Plaza de Legazpi 7 (metro: Legazpi). It opens from 9 am to 2 pm.

Dangers & Annoyances Pickpockets are rife in the more touristy parts of Madrid and on some metro lines, and of course foreigners are the prime targets. There is no need to be paranoid, but a few simple precautions are advisable. Keep to a minimum the valuables you carry around with you, and never put a wallet in your back pocket.

Madrid is not a terribly unsafe place to walk around but common sense should rule. Hanging around deserted areas, especially parks, at night is not a wise policy.

Parts of the Parque del Oeste are given over to prostitution by night and not ideal for a late-evening stroll. Paseo de Camoens y Valero and Paseo de Ruperto Chapi are where most of the tricks are done. The Casa de Campo is also swarming with ladies of the night, pimps and junkies right through the night.

The area around Calle de la Luna, near Gran Vía, can also be a little unsavoury, with a combination of prostitutes, pimps and dealers. Most of the time you will have no problems, but it is as well to be aware of what you are walking into.

The area behind the Templo de Debod is a popular summertime cruising patch. In El Retiro the same activity is carried on in the south-western corner around La Chopera. This may not appeal to all tastes.

Walking Tour

What follows aims to suggest a general route through 'essential Madrid'. If you intend to spend time in any of the monuments and museums, or prefer simply meandering at will and stopping in at the many enticing bars, cafés and restaurants, you will need at least several days to begin to do justice to such a circuit. Pick and choose using the more detailed sight descriptions that you'll find after this Walking Tour, and make judicious use of the metro system to get around.

Unless you want to hit the big art galleries first, the most fitting place to begin exploration of Madrid is the **Puerta del Sol**, or Sol as it is known to locals, the official centre of Madrid (map: Central).

Walk up Calle de Preciados and take the second street on the left, which will bring you out to Plaza de las Descalzas. Note the **baroque doorway** to the Caja de Ahorros in the Caja de Madrid building – it was built for King Felipe V in 1733 and faces the **Monasterio de las Descalzas Reales**.

Moving along, head south down Calle de San Martín until you come to the **Iglesia de San Ginés**, one of Madrid's oldest churches. Behind the church is the wonderful **Chocolatería de San Ginés**, generally open from 7 to 10 pm and 1 to 7 am.

Continue down to and cross Calle Mayor, and then into Madrid's most famous square, **Plaza Mayor**. After a coffee on the plaza, head west along Calle Mayor until you come to the historic **Plaza de la Villa**, with Madrid's 17th century *ayuntamiento* (town hall). On the same square stand the 16th century **Casa de Cisneros** and the Gothic-mudéjar **Torre de los Lujanes**, one of the city's oldest buildings, dating from the Middle Ages.

Take the street down the left side of the Casa de Cisneros, cross the road at the end, go down the stairs and follow the cobbled Calle del Cordón out onto Calle de Segovia. Almost directly in front of you is the *mudéjar* tower of the **Iglesia de San Pedro**. Proceed south down Costanilla de San Pedro until you reach **Iglesia de San Andrés**.

From here you cross Plaza de la Puerta de Moros and head south-west to the **Basílica de San Francisco El Grande**, or east past the market along Plaza de la Cebada – once a popular spot for public executions – to head into the Sunday flea market of **El Rastro**.

Otherwise, head west into the tangle of lanes that forms what was once the Islamic quarter, or **morería**, and emerge on Calle de Bailén and the wonderful *terrazas* of Las Vistillas – great for drinking in the views.

Follow the viaduct north to Madrid's cathedral, the **Catedral de Nuestra Señora de la Almudena**, the **Palacio Real** (royal palace) and Plaza de Oriente, with its statues, fountains and hedge mazes. On the far east side of the plaza is the **Teatro Real**.

At its northern end, Calle de Bailén runs into **Plaza de España**. Nearby, you could visit the **Museo de Cerralbo**, the **Templo de Debod** and, close to the Río Manzanares, the **Ermita de San Antonio de Florida**, which contains a masterpiece by Goya. If you were to continue north past the square you would pass through the Barrio de Argüelles, with some pleasant summer terrazas, and on towards the main centre of Madrid's Universidad Complutense.

The eastern flank of Plaza de España marks the beginning of **Gran Vía**. This Haussmannesque boulevard was slammed through the tumbledown and disreputable barrios and slums north of Sol in insensitive fashion in 1911.

At the east end of Gran Vía, the length of which you can walk in 15 minutes if you are in a hurry, note the superb dome of the **Metropolis Building**. Continue east along Calle de Alcalá until you reach **Plaza de la Cibeles**, Madrid's favourite roundabout.

Head north (left) up the tree-lined promenade of Paseo de los Recoletos. On the left you'll pass some of the city's best known cafés, including Gran Café de Gijón, El Espejo and El Gran Pabellón del Espejo, which, in spite of its 19th century appearance, was only built in 1990. On your right is the enormous **Biblioteca Nacional** (National Library), and a little further on a statue of Columbus in Plaza de Colón.

From here walk around the back of the

See Plaza de España & Around Map

See Malasaña & Chueca Map

Central Madrid

0   100   200 m

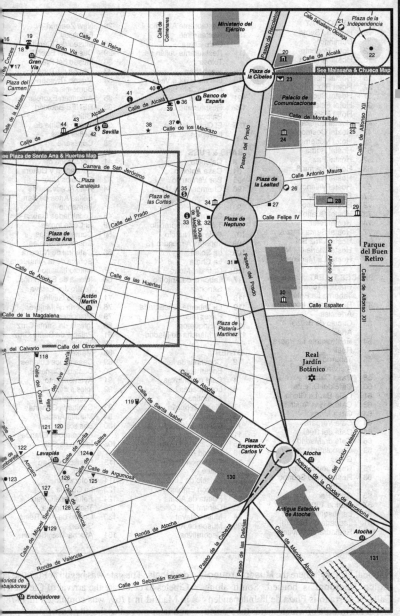

MADRID

PLACES TO STAY
5	Hotel de Santo Domingo
12	Hotel Regente
13	Hostal Andorra
14	Hotel California
16	Hostal Flores
27	Hotel Ritz
31	Hostal Sudamericano
32	Hotel Palace
43	Hotel Regina
45	Hostal Eureka
47	Hostal Cosmopólitan
48	Hotel Moderno
51	Hostal Roma
52	Hostal Paz
53	Hostal Jeyma & Hostal Ivor
59	Hostal Valencia
67	Pensión Luz
72	Hostal Riesco
73	Hostal Ruano
74	Hostal Rifer
77	Hostal Santa Cruz & Hostal Cruz Sol
78	Hostal María del Mar
86	Hostal La Macarena

PLACES TO EAT
1	Prada a Tope
3	Taberna La Bola
17	Restaurante Integral Artemisa
39	Círculo de Bellas Artes
54	Restaurante La Paella Real
55	Taberna del Alabardero
58	Casa Ciriaco
60	Café del Oriente
61	Café-Bar La Gloria
62	Café de los Austrias
63	Casa Marta
64	Café Vergara
65	Café del Real
66	Café de Madrid
69	Chocolatería de San Ginés
75	Restaurante Pontejos
83	Restaurante Sobrino de Botín
85	Casa Paco
87	Madrid 1600
97	La Tasquita
101	Taquería de Birrä (II)
102	Restaurante Rayuela

103	Restaurante Alamillo
104	Restaurante Gure-Etxea
111	Restaurante Julián de Tolosa
115	Manhattan
116	Cervecería La Vega
120	Nuevo Café Barbieri
121	Babilonia
122	Restaurante La Pampa
125	El Granadero de Lavapiés

BARS & PUBS
9	Calentito
84	Casa Antonio
95	Bar Ventorrillo
96	Champañería María Pandora
98	Travesía
99	Bar Irreal
106	Taberna Tempranillo
107	Café del Nuncio
108	Taberna Almendro 13
109	La Soleá
110	La Chata
112	Café del Mono
117	Taberna de Antonio Sánchez
118	Candela
119	La Taberna Encantada
127	PakesTeis
128	El Boquerón
129	La Mancha de Madrid

OTHER
2	Convento de la Encarnación
4	Café de Chinitas
6	Localidades La Alicantina
7	Viajes Zeppelin
8	Serviprint
10	Centro de Salud
11	FNAC
15	La Casa del Libro
18	Madrid Rock
19	Telefónica Phone Office
20	Palacio de Linares
21	French Embassy
22	Puerta de Alcalá
23	Central Post Office
24	Museo Naval
25	Museo de Artes Decorativos

26	New Zealand Embassy
28	Museo del Ejército
29	Casón del Buen Retiro
30	Museo del Prado
33	Oficina de Turismo
34	Museo Thyssen-Bornemisza
35	American Express
36	RENFE Booking Office
37	Teatro & Cine de Bellas Artes
38	Comisaría
40	Metropolis Building
41	Consejería de Educación y Cultura
42	Cambios Uno
44	Real Academia de Bellas Artes de San Fernando
46	Localidades Galicia
49	El Corte Inglés
50	Convento de las Descalzas Reales
56	Catedral de Nuestra Señora de la Almudena
57	Istituto Italiano
68	Iglesia de San Ginés
70	Teatro Joy Eslava
71	Palacio Gaviria
76	Librería de Mujeres
79	Multicines Ideal
80	Iglesia de Santa Cruz
81	Palacio de Santa Cruz
82	Tourist Office
88	Market
89	Casa de los Lujanes
90	Casa de Cisneros
91	Ayuntamiento
92	Iglesia del Sacramento
93	Capitanía General
94	Muralla Árabe
100	Basílica de San Francisco el Grande
105	Iglesia de San Andrés
113	Basílica de San Isidro
114	Fotocasión
123	La Corrala
124	Peluquería Chiqui
126	Teatro Olimpia
130	Centro de Arte Reina Sofía
131	Atocha Train Station

National Library, where the **Museo Arqueológico Nacional** is housed. South along Calle de Serrano is Plaza de la Independencia, in the middle of which stands the **Puerta de Alcalá**. The gate was begun at Plaza de la Cibeles to celebrate the arrival of Carlos III in Madrid in 1769, was completed in 1778, and later moved as the city grew.

Turn right and then left at Plaza de la Cibeles to head south down Paseo del Prado, an extension of the city's main tree-lined boulevard, and you'll soon reach the art gallery with which it shares its name. On the other side of the boulevard, the **Museo Thyssen-Bornemisza** is, along with the **Prado**, a must on the Madrid art gallery route.

The area around and north of the Prado is laced with museums, while stretching out behind it to the east are the wonderful gardens of the **Parque del Buen Retiro**. Immediately south of the Prado is the **Real Jardín Botánico**. Looking onto the mania of the multilane roundabout that is Plaza del Emperador Carlos V are the city's main railway station, **Atocha**, and the third in Madrid's big league of art galleries, the **Centro de Arte Reina Sofía**.

Head a few blocks north along Paseo del Prado again and turn west up Calle de las Huertas (through the tiny Plaza de Platería Martínez). The **Convento de las Trinitarias** (closed to the public), which backs onto this street, is where Cervantes lies buried. Turn right up Costanilla de las Trinitarias and continue along Calle de San Agustín until you come to Calle de Cervantes, and turn left. On your right you will pass the **Casa de Lope de Vega** at No 11. If the 'abierto' ('open') sign is up, just knock and enter.

A left turn at the end of Calle de Cervantes into Calle de León will bring you back onto Calle de las Huertas, which you may have already noticed is one of Madrid's happening streets loaded with bars and cafés. Anywhere along here or up on Plaza de Santa Ana will make a great place to take a load off at the end of this gruelling tour! For specific tips, consult the Entertainment section.

Museo del Prado

Built towards the end of the 18th century in what was then the Prado (meadow) de los Jerónimos, the Palacio de Villanueva was originally conceived as a majestic house of science, incorporating a natural history museum and laboratories. Events overtook the noble enterprise, and during the Napoleonic occupation the building was converted ignominiously into cavalry barracks.

Perhaps inspired by the ideas of the French Revolution and Napoleon's short-lived administration, King Fernando VII resolved in 1814 to create a museum to put on public display a representative chunk of the country's artistic wealth. Five years later it opened with 311 Spanish paintings. Today there are 6999 catalogued works in the Prado collection (including those in the Casón del Buen Retiro), but fewer than half are on view at any given time.

Since 1819, the museum (metro: Banco de España or Atocha; map: Central) has undergone numerous changes, but has rarely received the financial attention it deserves – far less, say, than the Louvre in Paris. That said, plans are afoot for a major overhaul. Work to restore something of the building's original look, especially that of the roof, will keep some rooms closed until well into 1997.

✺ ✺ ✺ ✺ ✺ ✺ ✺ ✺ ✺ ✺ ✺ ✺

Museum & Gallery Admission in Madrid

You can take advantage of several options to reduce the cost of entry to Madrid's museums and galleries. Standard entry to the three big art galleries – the Prado, Centro de Arte Reina Sofía and Museo Thyssen-Bornemisza – costs 400 ptas each. But admission to the first two is free on Saturday afternoon and Sunday. You can get a Paseo del Arte ticket for 1050 ptas for all three, valid all year round. Obviously this is only worth it if you can only visit when you'd normally pay the full price.

A year's ticket for unlimited visits to either the Prado or the Reina Sofía costs 4000 ptas. A yearly ticket to both and a series of nine other museums throughout the country is 6000 ptas.

Many other galleries, museums and other sights have free entry at least one day a week. In a few cases this is restricted to citizens of the EU, but others may be able to sneak through too. Saturday afternoon, Sunday and Wednesday are the most common free times.

Most, but not all, museums and monuments shut on Monday. Just about everything is closed on Sunday afternoon. In July and August some close parts of their displays for want of staff, most of whom take annual leave around this time. A few minor museums even close entirely through August. ■

✺ ✺ ✺ ✺ ✺ ✺ ✺ ✺ ✺ ✺ ✺ ✺

Suggestions for extending the museum include incorporating the nearby Museo del Ejército building and linking it, the main building and the Casón del Buen Retiro by a series of tunnels.

One of the beauties of the collection is the generous coverage given to certain masters. Whole strings of rooms are devoted to the works of a trio of Spain's greatest – Velázquez, Goya and El Greco. These three elements of the Prado's offerings are the cream, but there is plenty of good stuff by a range of Flemish, Italian and other painters too. The Prado demands more than one visit to fully savour its riches. One way of approaching it is to concentrate on themes, perhaps starting artist by artist. Bear in mind that parts of the collection are moved about as improvements and maintenance of the museum are carried out.

Velázquez Of this 17th century old master's works, it is *Las Meninas* that most people come to see, and rightly so. Executed in 1656, the work is more properly known as *La Familia de Felipe IV*. It depicts Velázquez himself on the left and, in the centre, the Infanta Margarita. There is more to it than that, though: the artist in fact depicts himself depicting the king and queen, whose images appear, according to some experts, in mirrors behind Velázquez. His mastery of light and colour are never more apparent than here. It takes pride of place in room 12, the focal point of the Velázquez collection on the 1st floor.

The bulk of Velázquez' works are hung together in rooms 11 to 15, as well as a few in room 27. Among some of his outstanding portraits are *La Infanta Doña Margarita de Austria* (who stars in *Las Meninas*) and *Baltasar Carlos a Caballo*. *Cristo Crucificado* manages to convey the agony of the Crucifixion, a subject that often descends into bathos, with great dignity. *La Rendición de Breda* (The Surrender of Breda) is another classic.

El Greco Domenikos Theotokopoulos, 58 years Velázquez' senior, is also represented on the 1st floor, in rooms 9B and 10B. The long, slender figures characteristic of this singular Cretan artist, who lived and worked in Toledo, are hard to mistake. Particularly striking are *La Crucifixión* and his *San Andrés y San Francisco*, finished towards the end of the 16th century.

Goya Francisco José de Goya y Lucientes is the most extensively represented of the Spanish masters in the Prado. Late to reach the heights of his grandeur, Goya, more than anyone, captured the extremes of hope and misery his country experienced before, during and after the Napoleonic invasion. In room 36 hang probably his best known and most intriguing oils, *La Maja Vestida* and *La Maja Desnuda*, portraits of an unknown woman, identical save for the lack of clothing in the latter. Other portraits are located in rooms 34 to 38.

The horrors of war had a profound effect on Goya's view of the world. *El Dos de Mayo* and, still more dramatically, *El Tres de Mayo*, bring to life the 1808 anti-French revolt and subsequent execution of insurgents in Madrid. They're in room 39.

The Goya exhibit continues on the ground floor in rooms 66 and 67, which house his *Pinturas Negras* (Black Paintings), so-called because of the dark browns and black that dominate. Painted in the last years of his life, these paintings and their sombre colouring reflect his probable mood in the wake of serious illness. Among the most disturbing of these works is *Saturno Devorando a Su Hijo* (Saturn Devouring One of His Children). It's probably better that we don't really know what was going through his mind when he did this.

Other Spanish Artists After these greats, the remaining members of the Spanish contingent come in looking a little insipid. There are nonetheless some fine works by other outstanding figures of the 17th century, such as Bartolomé Esteban Murillo, Francisco de Zurbarán, Alonso Cano and José de Ribera.

Flemish Artists Indeed, the 17th century is very much the backbone of the museum's collection, and while for most visitors the Spanish contribution is paramount, there is a wealth of Flemish art.

The pick of the work of Hieronymus Bosch (c1450-1516) lives in room 57A on the ground floor. While *The Garden of Earthly Delights* is no doubt the star attraction of this wildly fantastical painter's collection, all reward close inspection. The closer you look, the harder it is to escape the feeling that he must have been doing some pretty extraordinary drugs.

Peter Paul Rubens (1577-1640) also gets a big run here. His works, on themes ranging from religion to myth, interspersed with portraits, are distributed across several rooms from No 60 to 63A. He is joined by Anton van Dyck, Jacob Jordaens, David Teniers and others of the same epoch.

Italian Artists The Italians haven't been left out either. They fully occupy rooms 2 to 10A, and count among their number Sandro Botticelli (1445-1510), Andrea Mantegna (1431-1506), Raphael (1483-1520), Tintoretto (1518-94) and, especially, Titian (Tiziano Vecelli; 1487-1576).

Elsewhere (in rooms 18A and 41, respectively) there are some works by Tiepolo (1692-1770) and Caravaggio (1571-1610).

Dutch & German Artists Apart from a Rembrandt (Protestant Holland) and a few samples of Dürer and Carlos III's court painter, Anton Rafael Mengs (1728-79), there is not much to speak of from Germany or independent Holland. Mengs' stuff is mostly portraits, particularly of his boss, Carlos III (with the nose; room 17A).

French Artists Nicolas Poussin (1594-1665), an important French painter of the 17th century, dominates room 15A. There is precious little else from France, but in room 16A you can see a few contributions from Louis Michel Van Loo (1707-71) and Jean-Antoine Watteau (1684-1721).

Casón del Buen Retiro A short walk east of the Prado, the one-time ballroom of the now nonexistent Palacio del Buen Retiro houses a selection of lesser-known 19th century works. Artists represented include Joaquín Sorolla, Aureliano de Beruete and Vicente López. The latter's portrait of Goya hangs here.

Entry The Prado and the Casón are open Tuesday to Saturday from 9 am to 7 pm. On Sunday and holidays they close at 2 pm. They close all day Monday. You can enter the Prado by either the northern Puerta de Goya or the southern Puerta de Murillo. The latter leads you into the ground floor, while you can access the ground and 1st floors from the Puerta de Goya.

One ticket covers the Prado and Casón and costs 400 ptas (half for students). Entry is free on Sunday and Saturday afternoon (2.30 to 7 pm), as well as on selected national holidays. See the boxed aside 'Museum & Gallery Admission' earlier in this chapter for other possible tickets. You'll be required to leave your day pack in the *consigna*.

Guides & Information Unfortunately, there is little in the line of free printed information. The handout map guides you to the main schools and major artists. In rooms 9B, 12, 32 and 61 you'll find decent brochures on, respectively, El Greco, Velázquez, Goya and the Flemish artists. They cost 100 ptas each. The downside is that you'll usually only find the Spanish version. The only remaining option is one of the various guidebooks on sale in the museum bookshop on the ground floor.

Museo Thyssen-Bornemisza
Accumulated over two generations by the Thyssen-Bornemiszas, a family of German-Hungarian magnates, this collection is one of the most wide-ranging private assemblies of mostly European art in the world. Spain managed to acquire the prestigious collection when it offered to completely overhaul the neoclassical Palacio de Villahermosa specifically to house the main body of the

collection. Some 800 works have hung here since 1993, with a further 80 at the Monestir de Pedralbes (Barcelona). The museum is at Paseo del Prado 8 (metro: Banco de España; map: Central).

The exhibition is spread out over three floors, so you could do worse than follow the museum pamphlet's advice and start on the 2nd floor (there is a lift) and work your way down chronologically from 13th and 14th century religious art through to the avant-garde and pop art on the ground floor. The eclectic nature of the collection is such that many artists of a great number of epochs and schools are represented – if only by one or two pieces. What follows is a brief guide to where you can find some of our favourites.

Second Floor The first four rooms are dedicated to a range of medieval art, with a series of remarkable Italian triptychs and paintings to get the ball rolling. They include some by Duccio Buoninsegna, who led the nascent Sienese school into a gentle break from Byzantine forms in the late 13th and early 14th centuries.

Room 5 contains, among others, some works by Italy's Piero della Francesca (1410-92) and a *Henry VIII* by Holbein the Younger (1497-1543). Some of the jewellery Henry VIII commissioned Holbein to design is on display in room 6 (the long Galería Villahermosa). In room 7 are some exemplary works by the brothers Gentile (1429-1507) and Giovanni Bellini (1430-1516), who together with their father, Jacopo (1400-70), launched the Venetian Renaissance in painting. Titian also pops up here, although you'll see more later in room 11. Rooms Nos 8, 9 and 10 are given over to German and Dutch 16th century masters. Among them are a few works by Cranach (1472-1553).

Room 11 is dedicated above all to Titian and Tintoretto, although El Greco too contributes a few pieces, including an *Asunción*. Although Caravaggio dominates the next room, Spain gets a look in with some works by the early baroque painter José de Ribera (El Españoleto), himself influenced by Cara-

vaggio. Look out also for the fine views of Venice by Canaletto (1697-1768), accompanied by some of the best works of Francesco Guardi (1712-93), in room 17. Rubens leads the way in the last rooms on this floor, which are devoted to 17th century Dutch and Flemish old masters.

First Floor The Dutch theme continues on the next floor, with interiors and landscapes. They are followed by a room (No 27) devoted to a still-life series, and in room 28 you'll find a Gainsborough (1727-88) – one of the few British works in the entire collection. Next up comes a good representative look at North American art of the last century, including some pieces by John Singer Sargent (1856-1925) and James Whistler (1834-1903).

All the great impressionist and post-impressionist names seem to get a mention in rooms 32 and 33, with works by Pissarro, Renoir, Sisley, Monet and Manet. They are followed by Toulouse-Lautrec, Cézanne, Dégas, Gauguin and Van Gogh. The rest of the floor is dedicated to various movements in expressionist painting. In room 35 you'll find some of the earlier greats, including canvases by Egon Schiele, Henri Matisse, Edvard Munch and Oskar Kokoschka.

Ground Floor Here you move into the 20th century, from cubism through to pop art. In room 44 you'll see a nice mix of Picasso, Juan Gris and Georges Braque. More Picasso beyond cubism follows in the next room, accompanied by works of Marc Chagall, Max Ernst, Kandinsky and Joan Miró. In room 46 the leap is made back across the Atlantic, and Jackson Pollock and Willem de Kooning (actually a Dutchman who moved to the USA in 1926) are the stars. Lucien Freud (Sigmund's grandson and Berlin-born) and Francis Bacon are among the UK's few contributions to the collection, figuring in room 47.

Entry The gallery is open from Tuesday to Saturday from 10 am to 7 pm, and on Sunday from 9 am to 2 pm. Entry is 600 ptas (350 ptas for students), but is free on Sunday, from 2.30 pm on Saturday and on selected national holidays. Separate temporary exhibitions are regularly put on, and generally cost more.

Centro de Arte Reina Sofía

Adapted from the crumbling remains of an 18th century hospital, the Centro de Arte Reina Sofía, Calle de Santa Isabel 52 (metro: Atocha; map: Central), is the home of the best Madrid has to offer in modern art, principally spanning the beginning of this century into the 1960s.

The permanent collection is on the 1st floor (the 2nd floor to the Spanish), while the two floors above are used for temporary exhibits. There are a café and an excellent art bookshop on the ground floor.

The star attraction for most visitors is Picasso's *Guernica*. Don't just rush straight for it, though, as there is plenty of other good material to see.

In room 2, José Gutiérrez Solana is represented by sombre works, and a downright menacing one in the case of *La Procesión de la Muerte* (1930).

Room 4 is dedicated to cubism, with a couple of Picassos, including a still life, *Naturaleza Muerte – Los Pájaros Muertos*, done in 1912. Dalí also has a *naturaleza muerte* here, but the best work is a series of 10 pieces by Juan Gris, executed between 1913 and the 1920s. In room 6 you can see work of Joan Miró in his surrealist phase of the 1920s – enormously different from what he was doing in the 1970s (on display in room 13).

The star of the show, *Guernica*, fully dominates room 7, surrounded by a plethora of preparatory sketches. Already associated with the Republicans when the Spanish Civil War broke out in 1936, Picasso was commissioned by the Madrid government to do the painting for the Paris Exposition Universelle in 1937. Picasso incorporated features of others of his works into this, an eloquent condemnation of the horrors of war – more precisely, of the German bombing of Gernika (Guernica), in the País Vasco, in April of the same year. It has from the begin-

ning been surrounded by controversy, and was at the time viewed by many as a work more of propaganda than of art. In any case, the 3.5 by 7.8 metre painting subsequently migrated to the USA and only returned to Spain in 1981, to languish in the Casón del Buen Retiro until its transfer to the Reina Sofía. Calls to have it moved to the País Vasco are now growing louder.

There are some nice Dalís in room 8, including a portrait of the film maker Luis Buñuel (1924). Dalí continues in the next room, with such surrealist extravaganzas as *El Gran Masturbador* (1929). Room 17 has a few Picassos and a Francis Bacon.

Since mid-1996, Buñuel himself has had room 12 devoted to a permanent exhibition on his work. It may turn out to be pretty short-lived, because Buñuel's relatives don't consider the museum the right place to store his material.

Entry The gallery is open Monday to Saturday from 10 am to 9 pm (except Tuesday, when it is closed), and Sunday from 10 am to 2.30 pm. Entry is 400 ptas (half that for students).

Habsburg Madrid

Spain under Carlos I and Felipe II reached the apogee of its imperial greatness, its possessions spreading from Vienna to the Low Countries, from Sevilla to the Americas. Felipe's immediate Habsburg successors were largely responsible for expressing that glory in the centre of Madrid.

Puerta del Sol Once the site of a city gate, the Puerta del Sol is Madrid's most central point. On the south side a small plaque marks Km 0, from where distances along the country's highways are measured.

The semicircular junction actually owes much of its present appearance to the Bourbon king Carlos III, whose statue (the nose is unmistakable) stands proudly in the middle. Just to the north of Carlos, the statue of a bear nuzzling a *madroño* (strawberry tree, so-called because its fruit looks something like a strawberry on the outside) is not

MADRID

Madrileños often meet at this statue in Puerta del Sol, the popular centre of Madrid

only the city's symbol but a favourite meeting place for locals, as is indeed the clock tower on the south side. The square was the central stage for the popular rising against Napoleon's troops on 2 May 1808, quickly put down and immortalised in some of Goya's most moving works (to be seen in the Prado). On New Year's Eve, people thronging the square wait impatiently for the clock to strike 12, and at each gong swallow a grape. You may choke in the process, but the attempt must be made!

Plaza Mayor A short stroll west of Puerta del Sol, the heart of imperial Madrid beats in the 17th century Plaza Mayor. Designed in 1619 and built in typical Herrerian style, of which the slate spires are the most obvious expression, it was long a popular stage for royal festivities and *autos de fe*.

On a sunny day the plaza's cafés do a roaring trade, with some 500 busy tables groaning under the weight of the rather expensive drinks. In the middle stands an equestrian statue of Felipe III, who ordered construction of the square. The colourful frescos on the **Real Casa de la Panadería**, so-called for the bakery housed here in the 16th century, were painted in 1992. Just off

El Dos de Mayo

In early 1808, the French army marched into Madrid amid much confusion in the wake of the voluntary and cowardly abdication of Carlos IV and Fernando VII. General Tomás de Morla, who had armed the citizenry to help defend the city, soon found he could not control his unruly forces, and they were quickly overwhelmed by Napoleon's troopers. Morla's decision to surrender probably saved the city from the wholesale destruction promised by the French emperor in the event of continued resistance.

But the madrileños were not to be so easily pacified. In the last days of April, men began to converge on Madrid from the neighbouring countryside. Pamphlets exhorting the populace to revolt were circulated and tension grew. On the morning of 2 May, the blood-letting began, with isolated troops coming under attack from armed townspeople, starting around the Palacio Real. The French commander Murat soon had units camped outside the city move in. The 'mob', as he saw them, was concentrated at various points throughout the city, but those in the centre, at the Puerta del Sol, have gone down in history as a symbol of Spanish patriotism. Murat sent in Polish infantry and Mameluke cavalry – a fearsome unit brought to Europe from Egypt for precisely this kind of situation.

The motley band of madrileños gathered in the Puerta del Sol fought with whatever came to hand – rifles, knives, bricks. As the Mamelukes charged into the crowds, sabres cutting into the rebels, local women joined in the fight, stabbing at the Mamelukes' horses and bombarding them with household items from the houses above. As the imperial forces gained the upper hand, the rebels were pushed into Calle Mayor, where some commandeered houses to subject the troops to a bloody crossfire.

All was in vain. By the end of the day the streets, here and elsewhere in the city, had been cleared. Some of the rebels were rounded up to be shot the next day, and road blocks around the city cut off all chance of escape.

Goya immortalised the events of this day and the shootings of the following day in his grim paintings, *El Dos de Mayo* and *El Tres de Mayo*, which now hang in the Prado. And *el dos de mayo* (2 May) went into the annals of Spanish history as the quintessence of the country's patriotic fervour. It also marked the beginning of the Guerra de la Independencia (War of Independence), which to the British, who ultimately tipped the balance and forced Napoleon out of Spain five years later, came to be known simply as the Peninsular War. ■

the south-east corner of the square is the baroque edifice housing the Ministerio de Asuntos Exteriores, formerly the court prison.

South of the square, Calle de Toledo is no longer the main road to Madrid's one-time competitor for title of national capital. It's an interesting boulevard though, and you might want to have a quick look at the **Basílica de San Isidro**, long the city's principal church until Nuestra Señora de la Almudena was completed. The Instituto de San Isidro next door once went by the name of Colegio Imperial, and in it from the 16th century many of the country's leading figures were schooled.

At this point the road forks. Calle de Toledo leads down to the triumphal arch at the Puerta de Toledo and beyond to the 18th century bridge of the same name across the Río Manzanares. The left fork, Calle de los Estudios, leads into the heart of El Rastro, the crowded Sunday flea market (see Things to Buy later in this chapter).

Iglesia de San Ginés Situated between Calle Mayor and Calle del Arenal, directly north of Plaza Mayor, this is one of Madrid's oldest churches; it has been here in one form or another since the 14th century. It houses some fine paintings, including El Greco's *Cleansing of the Temple* depicting Christ's expulsion of the moneychangers, but it is only open for services.

Plaza de la Villa Back on Calle Mayor and heading west, you pass the central market in Plaza de San Miguel before entering Plaza de la Villa.

The 17th century **ayuntamiento**, on the west side of the square, is a typical Habsburg edifice with Herrerian slate-tile spires. Leaning more to the Gothic on the opposite side of the square is the **Casa de los Lujanes**, its brickwork tower said to have been 'home' to the imprisoned French monarch François I after his capture in the Battle of Pavia. The **Casa de Cisneros**, built in 1537 by the cardinal's nephew, is plateresque in inspiration. A block south looms the 18th century baroque remake of the **Iglesia del Sacramento**.

Monasterio de las Descalzas Reales Halfway between Calle del Arenal and Plaza de Callao, the grim walls of this one-time palace serve as a mighty buttress to protect the otherworldly interior from the 20th century chaos outside.

Doña Juana, daughter of Carlos I and mother of Portugal's ill-fated Dom Sebastian, commandeered the palace for conversion into a convent in the 16th century. She was followed by the Descalzas Reales (the Barefooted Royals), a group of illustrious women who became Franciscan nuns. A maximum of 33 nuns can live here, perhaps because Christ is said to have been 33 when he died. At present 26 nuns are in residence, still living according to the rules of the closed order.

The compulsory guided tour (in Spanish) takes you up a gaudily frescoed grand stairway to the upper level of the cloister. The vault was painted by Claudio Coello, and at the top of the stairs is a portrait of Felipe II and family members at the royal balcony.

You then pass several of the convent's 33 chapels. The first contains a remarkable carved figure of a dead Christ recumbent. This is paraded around in a moving Good Friday procession every year. At the end of the passage you are led into the ante-choir and then the choir stalls themselves, where Doña Juana is buried and a remarkable *Virgen la Dolorosa* by Pedro de la Mena is seated in one of the 33 oaken stalls.

The former sleeping quarters of the nuns now house a museum with some of the most remarkable tapestries you are likely to see. Woven in the 17th century in Brussels, they include four based on drawings by Rubens. Four or five artisans could take as long as a year to weave a square metre of premium-quality tapestry, so imagine how many years must have gone into these! While on the subject of impressive numbers, Spain and the Vatican were the biggest patrons of the tapestry business, and Spain alone is said to have collected four million of them.

The convent is open Tuesday to Saturday from 10.30 am to 12.30 pm and again (except Friday) from 4 to 5.30 pm. On Sunday and holidays it opens from 11 am to 1.30 pm. It is closed all day Monday. Admission costs 650 ptas (250 ptas for students), but is free on Wednesday for EU citizens.

Monasterio de la Encarnación While in the area, you could also drop into this less well known monastery. Founded by Empress Margarita de Austria, it is still inhabited by nuns of the Augustine order (Agustinas Recoletas). Inside you'll find a copious collection of works of art, mostly from the 17th century, and a host of gold and silver reliquaries. The most famous of these contains the blood of San Pantaleón, which purportedly liquefies every year on 28 June.

Located in Plaza de la Encarnación just north of the Teatro Real (metro: Ópera), it is open to visitors on Wednesday, Saturday (10.30 am to 12.30 pm and 4 to 5.30 pm) and Sunday (11 am to 1.30 pm). Admission costs 425 ptas, but is free on Wednesday to EU citizens.

Palacio Real, La Latina & Lavapiés

Palacio Real When the Alcázar, the oft-altered forerunner of the Palacio Real, burned down in 1734, few mourned its demise. Felipe V took the opportunity to indulge in a little architectural magnificence, planning to build a palace that would dwarf all its European counterparts. The result, which Felipe did not live to see completed, is the Palacio Real as it stands today, a colossus with some 2800 rooms – of which you are allowed to visit around 50. Carlos III was the first monarch to move in, but the present king is only rarely in residence. It is occasionally closed for state ceremonies of pomp and circumstance.

The **Farmacia Real** is the first set of rooms you strike after buying your tickets at the south end of the grand patio known as the Plaza de Armas (Plaza de la Armería). The pharmacy is a seemingly endless parade of medicine jars and stills for mixing royal concoctions. West across the Plaza is the **Armería Real** (Royal Armoury), a shiny collection of weapons and armour, mostly dating to the 16th and 17th centuries. The full

suits of armour, such as that of Felipe III, are among the most striking items on show.

Access to the main apartments lies at the northern end of the Plaza de Armas. The main stairway is a grand statement of imperial power leading first to the Halberdiers' rooms and on eventually to the Salón del Trono (throne room). The latter is sumptuous to the point of making you giddy, its crimson velvet wall coverings complemented by a Tiepolo ceiling. Shortly thereafter you'll encounter the Salón de Gasparini, with its exquisite stucco ceiling and embroidered silks covering the walls. The Sala de Porcelana is an extraordinary flourish, with myriad pieces from the one-time Retiro porcelain factory screwed into the walls. The themes change as you progress, with the grand Comedor de Gala (gala dining room) marking a distinct break. Shortly after this you encounter a couple of rooms given over to the display of musical instruments, including no less than five made by the Stradivari family.

The **Biblioteca Real** (Royal Library) has not been open since the late 1980s. Only students with appropriate permission may enter.

The palace is open Monday to Saturday from 9 am to 6 pm, and Sunday and holidays 9 am to 3 pm. Entry costs 850 ptas (350 ptas for students), but is free on Wednesday. There are optional guided tours to the Salones Oficiales, but you may have to wait awhile for your language to come up. The tour takes about 50 minutes. If you're really lucky, you may catch the fanciful changing of the guard in full 18th century parade dress. This is supposed to occur on the first Wednesday of every month between the palace and the Catedral de Nuestra Señora de la Almudena. However, it appears that more often than not the day is changed or the ceremony doesn't take place at all.

Jardines de Sabatini Several entrances allow access to this somewhat neglected, French-inspired garden on the north flank of the Palacio.

Campo del Moro Much more inspired are the wonderful gardens of the Campo del Moro, so-called because a Muslim army drew up here beneath the walls of Madrid in 1090 in the hope of retaking the town. The only entrance to the gardens is on the west side, from Paseo de la Virgen del Puerto. The gate closes at 8 pm.

Acquired by Felipe II, the partly English-style gardens as they are now were not laid out until 1844, with reforms in 1890. The fountain known as Fuente de las Conchas, between the visitors' entrance and the Palacio, was designed by Ventura Rodríguez. Inside the grounds is the Museo de los Carruajes (map: Madrid), in which royal carriages could be seen until it was closed for restoration.

Plaza de Oriente East across Calle de Bailén from the palace is the majestic Plaza de Oriente, which was once partly occupied by dependencies of the Alcázar and was given its present form under French occupation in the early 1800s. The square is dominated by an equestrian statue of Felipe IV and littered with 44 statues of monarchs, many of which had been destined to adorn the Palacio Real until it was found they were too heavy and would have caused bits of the building to collapse. Backing on to the eastern side of the square is what was once the city's premier opera house, the Teatro Real. It may well hit a high note again if restoration and improvements being carried out ever finish.

In mid-1996 a storm broke over a decision to demolish an area between the plaza and the Palacio Real to make way for an underground bus parking zone. Archaeologists had discovered two façades of the 16th century Casa del Tesoro, a royal mint and the seat of royal court offices connected to the then Alcázar. All that remains of these now are the archaeologists' photos taken before the demolition.

Catedral de Nuestra Señora de la Almudena This stark and cavernous church, Madrid's cathedral, was only completed in mid-1992 after more than 110 years under construction.

Muralla Árabe Behind the cathedral apse and down Cuesta de la Vega is a short stretch of the so-called Arab Wall, the city wall built by Madrid's early medieval Muslim rulers. Open-air theatre performances are generally held here in summer.

Viaduct & Calle de Segovia The leafy area around and beneath the southern end of the viaduct that crosses over Calle de Segovia is an ideal spot to take a break from the hubbub (see in particular the entry on Terrazas under Bars & Pubs in the Entertainment section). It has also long been a popular spot for suicides. Head down to the busy Calle de Segovia, once a dribbling tributary of the Manzanares, and cross to the south side. Just east of the viaduct on a characterless apartment block (No 21) is conserved one of the oldest coats-of-arms of the city. The site once belonged to Madrid's ayuntamiento. Calle de Segovia itself runs west between parks to a nine arched bridge of the same name, built in 1584.

Climb up the other side and you reach Calle de la Morería. The area running from here south to the Basílica de San Francisco el Grande and south-east to the Iglesia de San Andrés was the heart of the **morería**, or Islamic quarter. Strain the imagination a little and the maze of winding and hilly lanes even now retains a whiff of the North African medina. Across Calle de Bailén, the *terrazas* of Las Vistillas offer one of the best vantage points in Madrid for a drink, with views to the Sierra de Guadarrama. During the civil war Las Vistillas was heavily bombarded by Nationalist troops from the Casa de Campo, who in turn were shelled from a Republican bunker here.

Basílica de San Francisco el Grande Completed under the guidance of the 18th century Sicilian architect Francesco Sabatini, the basilica has a number of outstanding features, including frescoed cupolas and chapel ceilings by Francisco Bayeu.

Iglesia de San Andrés The decoration inside the dome of this church is rather unusual and worth a look if it is open. It was otherwise pretty much gutted during the civil war. As much for this reason as any it, like a good many of Madrid's churches, looks its best when lit up at night as a backdrop for the local café life.

Barrio de Lavapiés With the exception of **La Corrala**, an intriguing traditional tenement block built around a central courtyard, which functions even now as a makeshift stage for (mainly summertime) theatre, there are no specific sights in this lively quarter. La Corrala is at Calle de Mesón de Paredes 65, opposite the ruins of a church. The real attraction of Lavapiés is the sweaty feel of one of Madrid's last true barrios, a busy working-class district.

Plaza de España & Around

A curiously unprepossessing square given its grand title, Plaza de España is flanked to the east by the Edificio de España, reminiscent of some of the bigger efforts of Soviet monumentalism, and to the north by the rather ugly Torre de Madrid (which houses a tourist office). Taking centre stage in the square itself is a monumental statue of Cervantes. At the writer's feet is a bronze of his most famous creations, Don Quixote and Sancho Panza.

Museo de Cerralbo You could walk past this noble mansion and barely notice it among the bustle and traffic jams in the tight, narrow streets just west of Plaza de España. Inside is a haven of 19th century opulence. The 17th Marqués de Cerralbo – politician, poet and archaeologist – was also an inveterate collector. You can see the results of his efforts in what were once his Madrid lodgings, at Calle de Ventura Rodríguez 17. The upper floor boasts a gala dining hall with billiard room attached, and a grand ballroom. The mansion is jammed throughout with the fruits of the collector's eclectic meanderings – from Oriental pieces to suits of armour and from clocks to religious paintings. Occasion-

ally there's a gem, like El Greco's *Éxtasis de San Francisco*. The museum is open Tuesday to Saturday from 9.30 am to 2.30 pm, and Sunday from 10 am to 2 pm. Entry costs 400 ptas.

Templo de Debod Looking rather out of place in the Jardines del Paseo del Pintor Rosales, this 4th century BC Egyptian temple was saved from the rising waters of Lake Nasser, formed by the Aswan High Dam, and sent block by block to Spain in 1970.

The temple opens Tuesday to Friday from 10 am to 1 pm and 4 to 7 pm, and on the weekend from 10 am to 1 pm. Admission is 300 ptas, but is free on Wednesday and Sunday.

Ermita de San Antonio de la Florida Among the finest works produced by Goya are some of those in this small hermitage, also known as the Panteón de Goya, about a 10 minute walk north of the Campo del Moro (metro: Príncipe Pío; map: Madrid). You'll find two small chapels here. In the southern one the ceiling and dome are covered in frescos by the master (restored in 1993). Those on the dome depict the miracle of St Anthony, who is calling on a young man to rise from the grave and absolve his father, unjustly accused of his death. Around them swarms a typical Madrid crowd. Usually in this kind of scene the angels and cherubs appear in the cupola, above all terrestrial activity. Goya goes his own route and places the human above the divine.

The painter is buried directly in front of the altar. His remains were transferred here in 1919 from Burdeos, where he died.

The chapel is open Tuesday to Friday from 10 am to 2 pm and 4 to 8 pm, and on the weekend from 10 am to 2 pm. Entry is 300 ptas (free on Wednesday and Sunday).

Just across the road is one of Madrid's great little eating institutions, the chicken and cider house, Casa Mingo (see Places to Eat later in this chapter).

Across the railway tracks on Calle de Francisco is the **Cementerio de la Florida**,

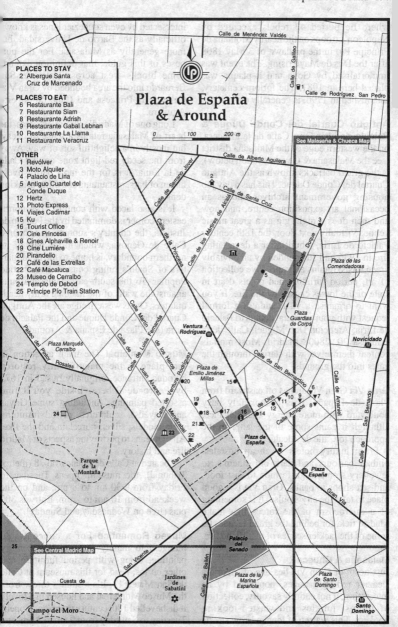

Plaza de España
& Around

0   100   200 m

PLACES TO STAY
2 Albergue Santa
   Cruz de Marcenado

PLACES TO EAT
6 Restaurante Bali
7 Restaurante Siam
8 Restaurante Adrish
9 Restaurante Gabal Lebnan
10 Restaurante La Llama
11 Restaurante Veracruz

OTHER
1 Revólver
3 Moto Alquiler
4 Palacio de Liria
5 Antiguo Cuartel del
   Conde Duque
12 Hertz
13 Photo Express
14 Viajes Cadimar
15 Ku
16 Tourist Office
17 Cine Princesa
18 Cines Alphaville & Renoir
19 Cine Lumiére
20 Pirandello
21 Café de las Extrellas
22 Café Macaluca
23 Museo de Cerralbo
24 Templo de Debod
25 Príncipe Pío Train Station

Calle de Menéndez Valdés
Calle de Gallieo
Calle de Rodríguez San Pedro
See Malasaña & Chueca Map
Calle de Alberto Aguilera
Calle de Serrano Jover
Calle de Santa Cruz
Calle de los Mártires de Alcalá
Calle de la Princesa
Calle del Conde Duque
Plaza de las Comendadoras
Novidicado
Plaza Guardias de Corps
Calle de San Bernardino
Calle de Amaniel
Calle de San Bernardo
Calle Martin de los Heros
Calle de Luisa Fernanda
Calle de Juan Álvarez Mendizábal
Calle de Ventura Rodríguez
Ventura Rodríguez
Plaza de Emilio Jiménez Millas
Plaza Marqués Cerralbo
Paseo del Pintor Rosales
de Dios
Calle Amigos
Calle de
Plaza de España
Plaza España
Gran Vía
Parque de la Montaña
San Leonardo
Calle de Mendizábal
See Central Madrid Map
San Vicente
Cuesta de
Campo del Moro
Jardines de Sabatini
Calle de Bailén
Palacio del Senado
Plaza de la Marina Española
Plaza de Santo Domingo
Santo Domingo

where lie buried 43 rebels executed by Napoleon's troops on the nearby Montaña de Príncipe Pío in the predawn of 3 May 1808 after the Dos de Mayo rising. The event was immortalised by Goya and a plaque was placed here in 1981. The forlorn cemetery, established in 1796, is generally closed.

Antiguo Cuartel del Conde Duque & Palacio de Liria Over Calle de la Princesa, on the western edge of the Malasaña district (see the Malasaña & Chueca section below), is the grand barracks known as the Antiguo Cuartel del Conde Duque. This has a day job housing government archives and as an occasional art exposition centre, and now and then does a night gig as a great music venue. Virtually next door, the 18th century Palacio de Liria, rebuilt after a devastating fire in 1936 and surrounded by an enviably green oasis, retains an impressive collection of art, period furniture and objets d'art in spite of the losses caused by the fire. If you want to organise a visit, address a formal request with your personal details to Palacio de Liria, Atención Don Miguel, Calle de la Princesa 20, 28008 Madrid. Most mortals content themselves with staring through the gates into the grounds.

Gran Vía Gran Vía arches off eastward from Plaza de España. It is a chokingly busy boulevard with more energy than elegance, although it gains some of the latter in the approach to Calle de Alcalá.

From luxury hotels to cheap hostales, pinball parlours and dark old cinemas to jewellery stores, high fashion to fast food, and sex shops to banks, Gran Vía is a good place to take the city's pulse. It is something of a microcosm of the forces that make Madrid tick, for behind the grand façades lie some of the tackier scenes of madrileño life.

Malasaña & Chueca
Just north of Gran Vía lies one of Madrid's sleazier red-light zones, populated by an interesting, if not entirely savoury, collection of pimps, junkies and wasted-looking hookers. This warren of long, narrow streets intersected by even squeezier lanes is known officially as the Barrio de Universidad, but more generally as Malasaña. For the purposes of this guide, that definition extends some blocks west across Calle de San Bernardo into the area bounded by Gran Vía, Calle de la Princesa and Calle de Alberto Aguilera.

Long one of Madrid's slummiest areas, the heart of Malasaña retains a sense of decay, but mostly in a delightful sort of way. Away from the seedy red-light zone around Calle de la Luna, it is for the most part a lively haven of bars, restaurants and other drinking dens.

It is also laced with contrast. The north-eastern corner is dominated by the Palacio de Justicia, the country's supreme law courts. Calle de Génova, which forms part of its northern boundary, is home to the headquarters of Spain's ruling conservative Partido Popular. To the south-east, Malasaña butts against the walls of the national army headquarters. On its western edge are the Antiguo Cuartel del Conde Duque and the Palacio de Liria (see Plaza de España & Around).

Museo Municipal The main attraction in this place is the magnificently restored baroque entrance, originally raised in 1673 by Pedro de Ribera. Inside you'll find assorted paintings (including some Goyas and Bayeus), sculptures, period furniture, scale models, silver, porcelain and the like. All of it leans to portraying aspects of Madrid life and history.

Located at Calle de Fuencarral 78 (metro: Tribunal), the museum opens Tuesday to Friday from 9.30 am to 8 pm, and on the weekend from 10 am to 2 pm. Entry is 300 ptas (free on Wednesday and Sunday).

Museo Romántico For a concentrated plunge into mainly Spanish 19th century painting, along with period furniture and other curios, head for this museum at Calle de San Mateo 13. It's a stone's throw from the Museo Municipal and housed in a lovely if dishevelled 18th century mansion. It opens Tuesday to Saturday from 9 am to 3 pm, and

Sunday and holidays from 10 am to 1.45 pm.
Entry costs 400 ptas.

Sociedad General de Autores y Editores
Only a couple of blocks east of the Museo
Romántico on Calle de Pelayo, this joyously
self-indulgent ode to *modernisme* looks
somewhat akin to a huge ice-cream cake half
melted by the scorching summer sun. It is
one of a kind in Madrid.

Plaza de Colón to the Prado
The modern Plaza de Colón (metro: Colón;
cercanías: Recoletos; map: Mal & Ch), with
the almost surreal Torres de Colón on its west
side, is at first glance a rather bare and uninspired affair. Its physical aspect, although

St Valentine's Bones
Nobody much thinks about poor old St Valentine on what in Spain is called 'Lovers' Day' (El
Día de los Enamorados), 14 February. This 3rd
century bishop and academic was born in
Terni, Italy, and according to the legend had
quite a thing about young people. Apparently
he was so enchanted by the blossoming of
young love that he'd help write love letters,
hand out flowers to young newlyweds and even
send a little money to struggling lovers in strait-
ened financial circumstances. Whether for this
or some other reason, Bishop Valentine was
not popular with the Roman administration –
and Christianity had yet to become Rome's
official faith. So the authorities had Valentine
arrested and executed on 14 February 269 AD.
Make of all that what you will.

Valentine seems then to have disappeared
from sight and mind, until in the 18th century
his bones, along with those said to belong to
hundreds of other saints, were dug up during
excavations in Rome. Since the Eternal City
had insufficient churches to each host one of
these venerable skeletons, the Church
decided to send some of them on a trip to other
good Catholic countries. And so it was that St
Valentine's bits landed in the crypt of the Iglesia
de San Antón (more properly known as San
Antonio Abad) in central Madrid. In 1986 it was
decided to put this skull-and-crossbones
arrangement on public view in the church
proper, at Calle de Hortaleza 65, just north of
Chueca metro station. The church is open for
services and an hour before for confession. ∎

softened by the fountains of the Centro Cultural de la Villa, is certainly nothing to write
home about. The statue of Colón (Columbus) seems somehow neglected, and the
Monumento al Descubrimiento (Monument to the Discovery – of America, that is),
for all its cleverness, does not leave a lasting
impression. It was cobbled together in the
1970s.

Still, the area is a cultural nerve centre.
The Centro Cultural plays host to any
number of theatrical and musical events, and
just south of the square looms the Biblioteca
Nacional and two museums. These could be
looked upon as the beginning of museum
row – since the walk from Colón to the Prado
(already dealt with in the Walking Tour
section earlier in this chapter) is laced with
them.

Biblioteca Nacional & Museo del Libro
Perhaps one of the most outstanding of the
many grand edifices erected in the 19th
century on the great avenues of Madrid, the
Biblioteca Nacional was ordered built by
Isabel II in 1865 and completed in 1892.

Some of the remarkable collections held
by the library have been imaginatively
arranged among displays recounting the
history of writing and the storage of knowledge. The Museo del Libro is a worthwhile
stop for any bibliophile yearning to see a
variety of illuminated manuscripts, Arabic
texts, centuries-old books of the Torah and
still more. If your Spanish is up to it, the
displays come to life with interactive video
commentaries of everything from the invention of writing through to the modern press.

The museum is open Tuesday to Saturday
from 10 am to 9 pm and Sunday from 10 am
to 2 pm. Admission is free.

Museo Arqueológico Nacional Out the
back of the same building, at Calle de
Serrano 13, the portentous entrance to this
museum of archaeology may seem just a
little too heavy for your liking. Inside you
will find a delightfully varied collection
spanning everything from prehistory
through the Iberian tribes, imperial Rome,

MADRID

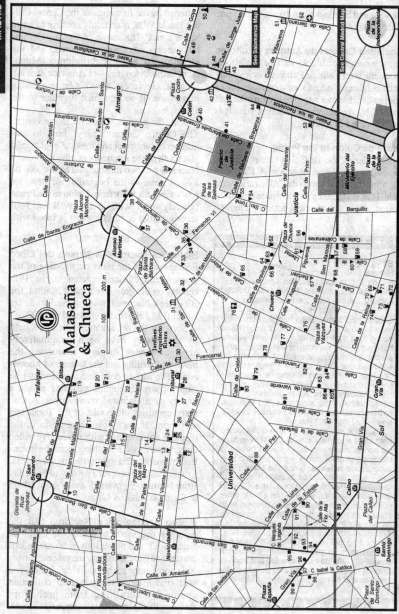

Malasaña
& Chueca

Visigothic Spain, the Muslim conquest and specimens of Romanesque, Gothic and mudéjar handiwork. There is a lot in here, and those passing through Madrid more than once while touring Spain could well benefit from repeated visits. In this way you will deepen your understanding of the extraordinary architectural wealth and history of the country.

The basement contains displays on prehistoric man, the Neolithic age and so on through to the Iron Age. Modest collections from ancient Egypt, Etruscan civilisation in

Italy, classical Greece, and southern Italy under imperial Rome can also be seen, as well as some Spanish specialities: ancient civilisation in the Balearic and Canary islands and a section on rock art in the Western Sahara, an African territory abandoned by Spain in 1975 and subsequently occupied by Morocco.

The ground floor is the most interesting. Sculpted figures such as the *Dama de Ibiza* and *Dama de Elche* reveal a flourishing artistic tradition implanted among the Iberian tribes – and no doubt influenced by contact with Greek, Phoenician and Carthaginian civilisation. The arrival of imperial Rome brought predictable changes. Some of the mosaics here are splendid, particularly the incomplete *Triumph of Bacchus* in room 22. The display on Visigothic Spain, and especially material from Toledo, marks a clear break, but only previous experience with Muslim Spain (eg the great cities of Andalucía) or other Muslim countries can prepare you for the wonders of Muslim art. The arches taken from Zaragoza's Aljafería are a centrepiece.

The influences of pure Islamic precepts persist in the later mudéjar style of re-Christianised Spain, which stands in remarkable contrast with Romanesque and later Gothic developments – all of which can be easily appreciated by soaking up the best of this eclectic collection.

Outside, stairs lead down to a partial copy of the cave paintings of Altamira (Cantabria), which will be as close to the paintings as many people get.

The museum is open Tuesday to Saturday from 9.30 am to 8.30 pm, and Sunday from 9 am to 2 pm. Entry costs 400 ptas (students pay half), but is free on Sunday and from 2 pm on Saturday.

Museo de Cera This is a rather pathetic version of a wax museum. Still, 450 characters have been captured in the sticky stuff – though you'll need a good dose of imagination to recognise some of them.

Located next to Colón metro station, it opens daily from 10 am to 2 pm and 4 to 8.30 pm. Entry is a whopping 900 ptas.

Palacio de Linares Walk south down Paseo de los Recoletos and you reach this 19th century pleasure dome (metro: Banco de España; map: Central), built in 1873 and a worthy member of the line-up of grand façades on Plaza de la Cibeles. The innards of this noble palace are notable particularly for the copious decoration in Carrara marble.

It opens on Tuesday, Thursday and Friday from 9.30 to 11.30 am, and on weekends and holidays from 10 am to 1.30 pm. Entry is 300 ptas.

Plaza de la Cibeles The fountain of the Cybele is one of Madrid's most beautiful. Since it was erected in 1780, the assessment of it has remained much the same. Carlos III thought it so nice he wanted to have it removed to the gardens of the Granja de San Ildefonso, on the road to Segovia, but the madrileños were so incensed that he was persuaded by leading figures of the day to let it be. The goddess Cybele has Atalanta and Hippomenes, recently paired off thanks to the intervention of Aphrodite, converted into lions and shackled to her chariot for having profaned her temple. They had been put up to this by Aphrodite, irritated by the apparent ingratitude of the newlyweds for her good work.

The building you are least likely to miss on the square is the sickly-sweet Palacio de Comunicaciones – or, more humbly, the central post office. Newcomers to town always seem to take a while in being convinced that this truly is only the post office.

It is more or less in keeping with the delayed baroque flavour of the great banks and other landmarks that, in particular, line Calle de Alcalá as it inclines westward from Cibeles and then forks at Gran Vía. Most of them went up around the turn of this century.

Museo Naval A block south, maritime history freaks may find some interest among the charts, instruments and other seafaring paraphernalia in this museum. Juan de la Cosa's 'sea-going map of the Indies' was supposedly the first to depict the New World. The entrance is at Calle de Montalbán 2, on the corner of the Paseo del Prado (map: Central). It opens Tuesday to Sunday from 10.30 am to 1.30 pm, and entry is free.

Museo de Artes Decorativos At Calle de Montalbán 12, this museum is full of sumptuous period furniture, ceramics, carpets, tapestries and the like spanning the 15th to the 19th centuries. It is open Tuesday to Friday from 9.30 am to 3 pm, and on the weekend and holidays from 10 am to 2 pm. Entry costs 400 ptas (half for students).

Museo del Ejército Filled with weapons, flags, uniforms and other remnants of Spanish military glory, the army museum is housed in what was the Salón de Reinos del Buen Retiro, part of the former Palacio del Retiro, at Calle de Méndez Núñez 1 (metro: Retiro). An interesting room with portraits of Franco is devoted to the glorious Nationalist campaign in the civil war, while the Sala Árabe (decorated Alhambra style) contains various curios including the sword of Boabdil, the last Muslim ruler of Granada, who signed the surrender in 1492 that marked the end of the Reconquista. Lovers of famous swords can also admire Tizona, one of the two mighty blades wielded by El Cid: it is displayed in the Sala de Armas. The museum opens Tuesday to Sunday from 10 am to 2 pm. Admission is 100 ptas (free on the weekend).

Plaza de Neptuno Officially known as Plaza de Cánovas del Castillo, the next roundabout south from Cibeles is commanded by an 18th century sculpture of the sea god, done by Juan Pascual de Mena. It is a haughty focal point, flanked not only by the Prado and the Thyssen-Bornemisza gallery, but by the city's famous competitors in the hotel business, the Ritz and the Palace. A block east on Calle de Felipe IV is the custodian of the Spanish language, the Academia Española de la Lengua.

Parque del Buen Retiro After a heavy day at the art galleries and other museums, a stroll in Madrid's loveliest public gardens might be the best way to end the day. They're at their busiest on the weekend, when street performers of all categories crawl out of the woodwork.

Once the preserve of kings, queens and their intimate friends, the park is now open for all to enjoy. You can hire boats to paddle about on the artificial lake (*estanque*), watched over by the statue of Alfonso XII. Weekend buskers and tarot readers ply their

trade around the same lake, while art and photo exhibitions take place at one of a couple of places, especially the Palacio de Exposiciones. Puppet shows for the kids are a summertime feature (look for Tiritilandia, or Puppet Land). At the southern end of the park near the rose gardens (La Rosaleda), a statue of El Ángel Caído (the fallen angel, ie Lucifer) brings a slightly sinister note to the place. The south-western end of the park is a popular cruising haunt for gay young bloods.

The park is a bit of a honey pot for pickpockets and bag-snatchers, so be careful.

Real Jardín Botánico Ask most madrileños about the city's botanic gardens and they won't know what you are talking about. All the worse for them, as the Real Jardín Botánico is a refuge still more beautiful than El Retiro, although not nearly as extensive. Created in 1755 under Fernando VI at El Huerto de Migas Calientes, the gardens were transferred to their present location under Carlos III. The eight hectares of these fine gardens are open daily from 10 am to 7 pm and entrance costs 200 ptas (half that for students).

Antigua Estación de Atocha The old train station at Atocha has become something of a botanical sight in itself. From here the high-speed AVE departs for Sevilla, and the interior of the old terminal has been converted into a tropical garden – certainly a pleasant departure or arrival point. Virtually across the road is the Centro de Arte Reina Sofía (see the section earlier in this chapter).

Real Fábrica de Tapices Founded in the 18th century to provide the royal family and other bigwigs with tapestries befitting their grandeur, this workshop still produces them today. You can see the work being done or just admire the products, which also include carpets. For years, unfortunately, it has been on the edge of bankruptcy, and a dark cloud hangs over its future. Have a look while you can; it's at Calle de Fuenterrabía 2 (metro: Menéndez Pelayo; map: Madrid) and opens Monday to Friday from 9 am to 12.30 pm.

The Prado to Sol

The main reason for heading into the area known to locals as Huertas, roughly contained in the triangle west of Paseo del Prado and between Calle de Atocha and Carrera de San Jerónimo, is to eat and drink. It is a smaller, brighter and perhaps more touristy version of Malasaña.

Mention has already been made, in the Walking Tour section, of Cervantes' burial place and the **Casa de Lope de Vega**. The latter, at Calle de Cervantes 11 (metro: Antón Martín), should be open Tuesday to Friday from 9.30 am to 2 pm and Saturday from 10 am to 1.30 pm. Entry costs 200 ptas. The playwright lived here for 25 years until his death in 1635, and the place is filled with memorabilia related to his life and times and those of the city around him.

A block to the north along Calle de León is the **Ateneo de Madrid** (see Libraries in the Information section earlier in this chapter) and on Calle de San Jerónimo are **Las Cortes**, the 19th century lower house of the national parliament, and its modern extension.

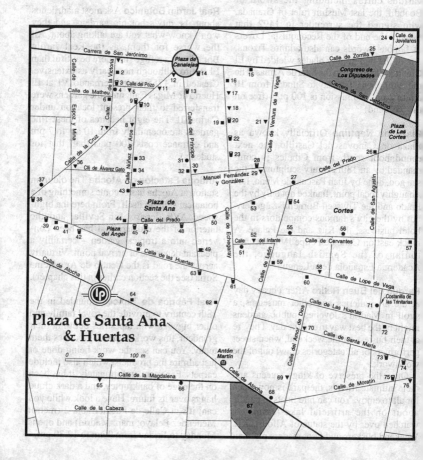

Plaza de Santa Ana & Huertas

If you need another art injection, try the **Real Academia de Bellas Artes de San Fernando**. This is a rather fusty old institution on Calle de Alcalá 13 (map: Central), founded in the 18th century by Fernando VI as a centre to train promising artists. Little seems to have changed since then. The 1st floor is mainly devoted to a mix of 16th to 19th century paintings. Among the stodgy portraits are some items of interest, including a couple of self-portraits by Goya and a series of full-length portraits by Zurbarán of white-cloaked friars. Non-Spaniards with a work or two scattered about include Tiepolo, Tintoretto, Rubens and Van Dyck. The 2nd floor is an odd combination of further portraits, porcelain and silverware, and a series of drawings by Picasso. It is open Tuesday to Friday from 9 am to 7 pm, and the rest of the week from 9 am to 2.30 pm. Entry costs 200 ptas.

Salamanca & Around
About Madrid's most chichi quarter, the Salamanca area to the north-east of the city centre is lined with elegant apartments and smart department stores. The snappy dressers wandering the grid-pattern boulevards around here seem to be on a different planet from the people of the gritty inner-city districts like Lavapiés. Apart from shopping, you can take in a little culture while up this way.

Museo Sorolla If you liked Sorolla's paintings in the Casón del Buen Retiro, don't miss this museum. It's in the artist's former residence and contains the most comprehensive collection of his work in Spain, mostly the sunny Valencian beach scenes for which he is best known. The residence-museum, set amid cool gardens, is at Paseo del General Martínez Campos 37 (metro: Rubén Darío;

PLACES TO STAY		PLACES TO EAT		23	Los Gabrieles
2	Hostal Esmeralda	1	Museo de Jamón	28	Carbones
6	Hostal Tineo & Hostal Gibert	5	Antigua Pastelería del Pozo	38	Bar Matador
15	Hostal Aguilar, Hostal León & Hostal Mondragón	7	La Casa del Abuelo	39	España Cañí
		8	La Trucha	42	Café Central
		12	Bar	45	Bar Hawaiano
16	Hotel Santander	17	Mesón La Caserola	47	La Moderna
19	Hotel Inglés	18	Restaurante Donzoko	48	Cervecería Alemana
26	Hotel Villa Real			54	Casa Pueblo
32	Hostal Carreras & Hostal Villar	21	Restaurante Integral Artemisa	61	Café Populart
33	Pensión Poza	25	Restaurante Al Natural	63	Casa Alberto
34	Hostal Lucense & Hostal Prado	29	Taberna Toscana	73	El Ratón
		30	La Trucha II	74	La Taberna Celta
35	Hostal Santa Ana	36	Las Bravas	75	El Parnaso
40	Hostal Plaza D'ort	49	Café Principal		
41	Hostal Persal	52	Gula Gula	**OTHER**	
43	Hostal la Rosa & Villa Rosa	58	Restaurante Pasadero	4	Bullfight Ticket Offices
44	Gran Hotel Reina Victoria	65	Asociación Hispano-Árabe	9	La Cartuja
				24	Teatro de la Zarzuela
46	Hostal Vetusta	69	Restaurante La Sanabresa	27	Ateneo de Madrid
53	Hostal Lamar, Hostal Mocelo	70	Restaurante La Biotika	31	Teatro de la Comedia
		76	Champagnería Gala	37	Torero
57	Hostales Gonzalo, Corberó & Cervantes			50	El Cenador del Prado
		BARS & PUBS		51	Lavandería España
59	Hostal Castro & Hostal San Antonio	3	La Fontana de Oro	55	Lavomatique
60	Hostal Casanova	10	Suristán	56	Casa de Lope de Vega
62	Hostal Matute	11	El Trébol	66	Sacromonte
64	Hostal Castilla I & Hostal Martín	13	Cuevas de Sésamo	67	Filmoteca Nacional
		14	Bar Cuatro Calles	68	Teatro Monumental
72	Hostal López	20	La Venencia	71	Convento de las Trinitarias
		22	Cardamomo		

MADRID

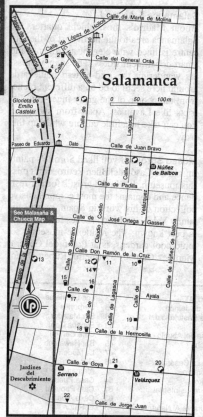

Salamanca

0   50   100m

PLACES TO STAY
3   Hotel Emperatriz
19   Hostal Don Diego

PLACES TO EAT
11   Casa Julián
14   Restaurante Oter
22   Thai Gardens

OTHER
1   Museo Lázaro Galdiano
2   St Andrew's Pub
4   Washington Irving Center
5   US Embassy
6   Boulevard 37
7   Museo de la Escultura Abstracta
8   Bolero
9   Italian Embassy
10   Mallorca
12   Irish Embassy
13   Belgian Embassy
15   Terraza de Serrano
16   Max 63
17   Marks & Spencer
18   Teatriz
20   Canadian Embassy
21   Iberia

map: Madrid). It is open Tuesday to Saturday from 10 am to 3 pm, and on Sunday and holidays from 10 am to 2 pm. Entry costs 400 ptas (200 ptas for students). Entry is free on Sunday.

Museo Lázaro Galdiano A surprisingly rich former private collection awaits you in this museum at Calle de Serrano 122 (metro: República Argentina). Aside from some fine works by artists such as Van Eyck, Bosch, Zurbarán, Ribera, Goya, Gainsborough, Constable and others, there is a rather oddball assembly of all sorts of collectables, including jewellery, silver, arms, furniture, ceramics and so on. The ceilings were all painted according to the function of the room. The one exception is room 14, where the artist created a collage from some of Goya's more famous works, including *La Maja* and the frescos of the Ermita de San Antonio de la Florida, in honour of the genius. It's open Tuesday to Sunday from 10 am to 2 pm. Admission is free.

Museo de la Escultura Abstracta This interesting open-air collection of 17 abstracts includes works by some of Spain's better known modern sculptors, such as Chillida, Miró, Sempere and Toledo's Alberto Sánchez. The sculptures can be found under the overpass where Paseo de Eduardo Dato crosses Paseo de la Castellana (metro: Rubén Darío). All but one are on the east side of Paseo de la Castellana.

Outside the Centre
Museums As you may already have noticed, Madrid seems to have more museums and art galleries than the Costa del Sol has high-rise

apartments. The following are a sample of those not covered earlier. Look for others in the *Guía del Ocio* entertainment guide.

Museo de América For centuries Spanish vessels plied the Atlantic between the mother country and the newly won colonies in Latin America. Although most of them were carrying gold one way and adventurers the other, the odd curio from the indigenous cultures also filtered across. Back in the 1940s, someone decided they should be put together in a museum. The two levels show off a representative display of ceramics, statuary, jewellery and the instruments of hunting, fishing and war, along with some of the paraphernalia of the colonisers. Items come from across South and Central America (with a few anomalous pieces from the Philippines and Polynesia thrown in). The Colombian gold collection, dating as far back as the 2nd century AD, and a couple of shrunken heads are rather eye-catching.

Located at Avenida de los Reyes Católicos 6 (metro: Moncloa; map: Madrid), this museum is open Tuesday to Saturday from 10 am to 3 pm, and closes half an hour earlier on Sunday and holidays. Admission is 400 ptas (half for students), or free from 2 pm on Saturday and all day Sunday.

The odd tower just in front of the Museo de América is designed not to control air traffic, but to transport visitors up for panoramic views of Madrid. The **Observatorio** opens Tuesday to Sunday from 11 am to 1.45 pm and 5.30 to 8.45 pm, and the ride in the lift costs 200 ptas. There is no café or anything of the sort once up there, and this is arguably not the ideal place for such views.

Museo de la Ciudad Described perfectly by one traveller as 'a must for the infrastructure buff', this rather dry technical museum traces the growth and spread of Madrid. Opened in 1992, it's at Calle del Príncipe de Vergara 140 (metro: Cruz del Rayo; map: North), and opens Tuesday to Friday from 10 am to 2 pm and 4 to 6 pm, and on the weekend from 10 am to 2 pm. Entry is free.

Museo de la Moneda If you like coins, this is the place for you: it's the national mint. Collections in the slightly dingy museum range from ancient Greek to the present day. The museum is at Calle del Doctor Esquerdo 36 (metro: O'Donnell; map: Madrid), and opens Tuesday to Friday from 10 am to 2.30 pm and 5 to 7.30 pm, and on weekends and holidays from 10 am to 2 pm. Entry is free.

Art Galleries The city is sprinkled with small private galleries and a couple of important foundations where you can check out the latest trends in contemporary work. There are many exhibition spaces, so the best advice is to keep an eye on newspapers and gig guides such as the *Guía del Ocio*.

Among the most important and established is the **Fundación Juan March**, Calle de Castelló 77 (metro: Núñez de Balboa). The foundation has its own collection and is responsible for organising some of the better temporary exhibits each year. The **Fundación La Caixa**, patronised by the Catalan bank of the same name, is another busy bee, putting on regular contemporary art exhibits. It's at Calle de Serrano 60.

Parque del Oeste Spread out between the university and Moncloa metro station, this is a tranquil and, in parts, quite beautiful park for a wander or shady laze in the heat of the day.

By night it undergoes something of a transformation, as the city's transsexual prostitute population and their clients come out to play. Part of the beat is reserved for female streetwalkers too. Most of the activity takes place in cars, which become remarkably numerous as the night wears on. Although you are unlikely to be bothered – police keep an eye out for anything more untoward than the routinely untoward – the area is not the ideal choice for a late-evening family stroll.

Casa de Campo This huge and rather unkempt semiwilderness stretching west of the Río Manzanares undergoes similar metamorphoses. It was in regal hands until 1931,

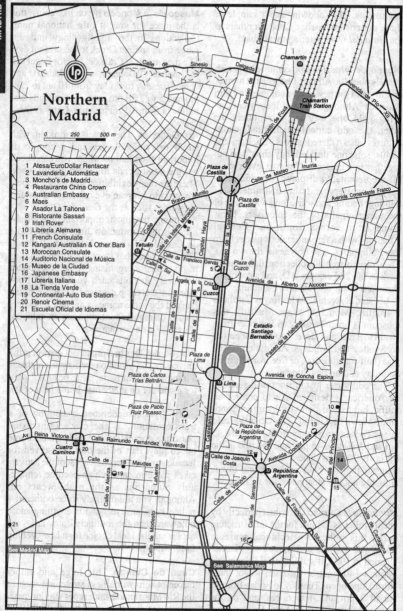

Northern Madrid

0   250   500 m

1 Atesa/EuroDollar Rentacar
2 Lavandería Automática
3 Moncho's de Madrid
4 Restaurante China Crown
5 Australian Embassy
6 Maes
7 Asador La Tahona
8 Ristorante Sassari
9 Irish Rover
10 Librería Alemana
11 French Consulate
12 Kangarú Australian & Other Bars
13 Moroccan Consulate
14 Auditorio Nacional de Música
15 Museo de la Ciudad
16 Japanese Embassy
17 Librería Italiana
18 La Tienda Verde
19 Continental-Auto Bus Station
20 Renoir Cinema
21 Escuela Oficial de Idiomas

See Madrid Map

See Salamanca Map

when its 1200 hectares were thrown open to the people.

By day cyclists and walkers eager for something resembling nature, but with no time or desire to leave Madrid, clog the byways and low roads that crisscross the park. There are also tennis courts and Madrid's most central swimming pool (see Swimming below) as well as an amusement park for the kids (see Entertainment).

Madrid's **zoo**, also in the park, contains some 3000 animals and a respectable aquarium (metro: Batán). It opens daily from 10 am to dusk. On a different animal note, the Andalucían-style ranch known as Batán is used to house the bulls destined to do bloody battle in the Fiesta de San Isidro (see Special Events). Finally, the none-too-exciting **teleférico** (cable car) from Paseo del Pintor Rosales (on the corner of Calle del Marqués de Urquijo; map: Madrid) ends up at a high point in the middle of the park. It starts operating at 11 am and continues until 10 pm. Tickets cost 345 ptas one way and 490 ptas return and it operates from 1 April to 30 September, as well as weekends and holidays through the rest of the year.

Many people just come to sip a drink by the small artificial lake (metro: Lago).

As night sets in, the scene takes on other hues. The occasional junkie, whore or pimp you may have espied in the area around the lake during the day turns into something of an avalanche. As the girls (and on occasion the boys who want to be girls) jockey for position to attract customers with wheels, not a few punters keep their places around the lakeside *chiringuitos* (makeshift bars) as though nothing out of the ordinary were happening around them. The traffic in the middle of the night here is akin to rush hour in the city centre!

Swimming

There are outdoor municipal pools in several locations around the city, open from June to September. During the rest of the year several municipal indoor pools open their doors. There are also various private pools.

About the handiest location is the Instituto

The Battle of Madrid

When Franco's Nationalists rose in revolt in July 1936, the army planned a lightning assault on the capital. General Mola quickly moved several thousand troops south from Pamplona and east from Valladolid, with the object of crossing the Somosierra and other passes and descending rapidly on Madrid before the Republicans could get organised. They never made it over the passes, which were held tenaciously by Republican militia who knew their loss would mean the loss of Madrid.

With Mola stopped in his tracks, the element of surprise was lost, but soon the capital faced a new threat as Franco's columns advanced rapidly from Seville through Extremadura and halted in the Casa de Campo, at the western gates of the city. In November the government fled to Valencia, but Madrid was not abandoned. A medley of Spanish Republican forces of all political persuasions were joined by Soviet advisers and the International Brigades. The latter would bear the brunt of Franco's assaults directed at the university part of town. Although these attacks met with some success – at the cost of a great many lives – the Nationalists never made it much beyond the barrio of Argüelles. As fortunes seesawed and then declined for the Republicans, Madrid remained out of Nationalist hands. Fighting continued on the Madrid front, but even when communist forces clashed with other Republicans in early 1939, the Nationalists failed to move. Of course, by that time they did not really need to. The writing was on the wall and the Republicans' days were numbered. As their forces in the centre crumbled and Franco's columns advancing from Toledo and on to Guadalajara linked up, the few commanders who had not already fled surrendered Madrid on 27 March. Four days later the war was over. ■

Municipal de Deportes in the Casa de Campo (metro: Lago). In summer (June to September) it opens daily from 10 am to 8 pm. During the rest of the year, the indoor pool opens Monday to Friday from 10 am to 6 pm. Entry costs 450 ptas, or you can buy a *bono*, good for 20 visits, for 7100 ptas.

Language Courses

There are several options for those wanting to study Spanish in Madrid. The Universidad Complutense offers a range of language and culture courses throughout the year, ranging from beginners to advanced level. For further information, contact the Secretaría de los Cursos para Extranjeros (☎ 394 53 25; fax 394 52 98), Facultad de Filosofía y Letras (Edificio A), Universidad Complutense, Ciudad Universitaria, 28040 Madrid.

You could also sign up directly at the rather overworked and chaotic Escuela Oficial de Idiomas (☎ 533 58 05, 554 98 94, 554 99 77), Calle de Jesús Maestro s/n. It offers courses in Spanish for foreigners (Español para Extranjeros) at most levels from beginners up. You will have to do an entry test to establish your level.

Many of the language schools aimed at teaching locals English and other foreign tongues also run courses in Spanish for foreign visitors.

Work

About the most common source of work for foreigners in Madrid is teaching their native language. You can start your job search at the cultural centre of your country, but there is a sea of language schools around Madrid. Non-EU citizens will have a harder time getting a job, but it is quite possible to find schools to employ you without work papers; expect to be paid below normal rates.

For English-speakers, the top choices are the British Council (see Cultural Centres under Information earlier in this chapter) and International House (☎ 310 13 14), Calle de Zurbano 8.

Organised Tours

Central Circuit You can pick up a special Madrid Vision bus around the centre of Madrid up to five times a day (except Monday, when it doesn't run at all). There are only three on Sunday and holidays. A full return trip costs 1500 ptas and you can board the bus at any of 13 clearly marked stops. Taped commentaries in four languages, including English, are available, and the bus stops at several major monuments, including the Prado and near Plaza Mayor. If you buy the 2200 ptas ticket, you can use the buses all day for two days to get around; frankly, you're better off investing in 10-trip metro tickets.

Descubre Madrid The Patronato Municipal de Turismo has chosen 80 itineraries around the capital. Tours are conducted in Spanish, and you can pick up calendars detailing when and where the walks are held at any branch of the Caja de Madrid bank, which co-sponsors the programme.

Other Tours Several companies organise city tours. These range from half-day jaunts around Madrid that can cost 5000 ptas through to an evening of somewhat artificial flamenco flouncing with a meal for up to 12,000 ptas. Most central Madrid travel agents can fill you in on the details. They will also organise day trips to towns surrounding Madrid, such as Toledo, Aranjuez, Segovia, Ávila, San Lorenzo de El Escorial and so forth.

Special Events

Fiestas de San Isidro Labrador Madrid's single greatest *fiesta* is without doubt the one which celebrates the city's patron saint, San Isidro, in the third week of May. It kicks off with the *pregón*, a speech delivered by the mayor, on the Friday or Saturday in the middle of the month and goes on for a week. There are free music performances around the city, and the country's most prestigious *feria*, or bullfight season, at the huge Plaza de Toros Monumental de las Ventas – the feria lasts for a month. Compulsive aficionados of bullfighting may want to take a peek at the Museo Taurino out the back of the bullring; it's usually open on weekdays from 9.30 am to 2.30 pm.

Other Fiestas The Malasaña district, busy enough at any time, has its biggest party on 2 May, which follows straight on from a national holiday on 1 May (Labour Day). For obvious reasons, the celebrations are centred on Plaza de Dos de Mayo.

The Fiesta de San Juan is held in the Parque del Buen Retiro over the seven days leading up to 24 June.

The few locals who haven't left town in the second week of August will be celebrating the consecutive festivals of San Caye-

Dyed in the Wool

Especially around the Fiesta de San Isidro, the *chulapos* and *manolas* of Madrid come out of the woodwork. The gents dress in their traditional short jackets and berets and the women in *mantones de Manila*, and put their best feet forward in a lively *chotis*. What is all this? The mantón de Manila is an embroidered silk shawl, which few people now wear except during fiestas. The chotis is a traditional working-class dance not unlike a polka. One of the most common versions involves a quick three-step to the left, the same to the right, and is topped off with a brisk twirl. Only a small portion of the truly *castizo* (true-blue) madrileños bother with this any more, but those who do so do it with a certain pride. The chulapo – or dyed-in-the-wool, born-and-bred madrileño, is now more commonly known as a *chulo*. Now this is a word to beware of. It generally implies a degree of bravado and even arrogance of character, although in the eyes of madrileños this is no bad thing. But to many people the word bears quite negative qualities – brash, showy. The word can also mean 'pimp', so you'd want to be sure of your company and context before bandying it around too much. The fast-talking, hard-living, Madrid version of James Dean is also typecast as a *macarra*, which at its worst also means a spiv.

These breezy types, especially the kind you'd come across in the inner working-class barrios like Lavapiés, were also once generally referred to as *manolos* (Manolo is a common first name). So it stands to reason that their girls should be known as manolas! To complete the picture, full-blood madrileños are also known to the rest of Spain as *gatos*, or cats – a nice image to reflect their city savvy. ∎

tano (Lavapiés), San Lorenzo (La Latina) and La Paloma (around Calle de Calatrava in La Latina). In the last week of September the Fiesta de Otoño (autumn festival) is held in Chamartín; this is about the only time you'd be tempted to hang around here and *not* get a train out.

September is a big month for local fiestas in several barrios of Madrid and assorted towns around the capital.

About halfway through September, the Partido Comunista de España (Spanish Communist Party) holds its yearly fundraiser in the Casa de Campo. The Fiesta del PCE lasts a whole weekend and is a mixed bag of regional food pavilions, rock concerts and political soap boxing.

Places to Stay

Madrid is positively crawling with pensiones, hostales and hotels, so there should rarely be trouble finding a place to stay. If you arrive by air and catch the airport bus to Plaza de Colón, you'll find an accommodation service and, often, touts offering rooms in cheaper pensiones.

The Spanish classification system is at its most expansive here, with *casas de huéspedes* (CH), pensiones, hostales, *hostal-residencias* and more, all sub-classified by a

star system. CHs, pensiones and one star hostales generally hover around the cheapest end of the scale. Prices quoted should be seen as indicative only. Proprietors often modify them at whim and have their own scale according to the size of individual rooms, length of intended stay and so on.

Places to Stay – bottom end

Camping & Youth Hostels There are two camping grounds within striking distance of central Madrid. *Camping Osuna* (☎ 741 05 10), on Avenida de Logroño near the airport, is the better of the two. Take metro No 5 to Canillejas (the end of the line), from where it's about 500 metres. *Camping Madrid* is at Km 11 along the N-I to Burgos. Take the Alcobendas bus from Plaza de Castilla (metro: Plaza de Castilla) to Los Dominicos, from where you have a 15 minute walk. Both charge 525 ptas per person, tent and car.

There are two HI youth hostels in Madrid. The *Albergue Richard Schirrman* (☎ 463 56 99) is in the Casa de Campo, Madrid's biggest park (metro: El Lago; bus No 33 from Plaza Ópera). B&B in a room of four costs 900 ptas (under 26) or 1200 ptas. Full board in a double room is 2550/3450 ptas per person (under/over 26).

The *Albergue Santa Cruz de Marcenado*

(☎ 547 45 32), Calle de Santa Cruz de Mar-cenado 28 (metro: Argüelles; bus Nos 1, 61 & Circular; map: España), has rooms for four, six and eight people. In terms of meals it offers breakfast only – but it does have a bar. B&B costs the same as in the other hostel.

An HI membership card is necessary for both hostels. You can obtain one at the hostels or in central Madrid at the offices of the Consejería de Educación y Cultura (☎ 580 41 96), Calle de Alcalá 31. The youth hostel section is on the left towards the end of the ground floor. The offices are open Monday to Friday from 9 am to 2 pm. Alter-natively, try the TIVE offices (see Travel Agencies under Information earlier in this chapter). The card costs 1800 ptas.

Other Accommodation – Atocha to Plaza de Santa Ana Atocha train station is close to the centre, so although there are quite a few places to stay around the station, it is worth making the effort to walk up Calle de Atocha towards Plaza de Santa Ana if you arrive here.

Roughly halfway between the station and Santa Ana, *Hostal López* (☎ 429 43 49), Calle de las Huertas 54, is a good choice. Singles/doubles start at 2400/3800 ptas without own bath, or 3600/4800 ptas with. It's on a fairly quiet part of an otherwise lively street.

There are a few places along the noisy Calle de Atocha itself and, if you can't be bothered tramping around and looking, you could do worse than *Hostal Castilla I* (☎ 429 00 95), at No 43. Small, spotless rooms with private bath and TV come in at 4000/5000 ptas.

The *Hostal Casanova* (☎ 429 56 91), Calle de Lope de Vega 8, has simple rooms at 1800/2600 ptas. Up around the corner, *Hostal Castro* (☎ 429 51 47), Calle de León 13, is an attractive place with good, clean rooms at 2000/3500 ptas with own bath. *Hostal San Antonio* (☎ 429 51 37), one floor up, also has some nice rooms at similar prices.

Hostal Gonzalo (☎ 429 27 14), Calle de Cervantes 34, is in sparkling nick and comes recommended by several travellers. It's on the 3rd floor and the owners are a little cagey about prices. Singles/doubles with private shower should not be more than about 3000/4500 ptas. If it doesn't satisfy, *Hostal Cervantes* (☎ 429 27 45), on the 2nd floor, is OK but more expensive, with doubles ranging up to 6000 ptas. On the 1st floor, *Hostal Corberó* (☎ 429 41 71) is not as good as the Gonzalo but charges similar rates.

Hostal Plaza D'Ort (☎ 429 90 41), Plaza del Ángel 13, looks rather grand from the outside, but some of the rooms are really very pokey. Singles/doubles with shower start at 2500/3500 ptas, but there are defi-nitely better deals around. *Hostal Persal* (☎ 369 46 43), next door at No 12, is a better bet but more expensive, with singles/doubles starting at around 3000/5500 ptas.

At Calle del Príncipe 18, *Hostal Carreras* (☎ 522 00 36) is a decent if unexciting choice with rooms at 2000/3500 ptas without own bath and 1000 ptas more with. In the same building, *Hostal Villar* (☎ 531 66 09) is in much the same category.

Hostal Matute (☎ 429 55 85), Plaza de Matute 11, has spacious singles/doubles for 2500/4300 ptas without own bath and 3500/5500 ptas with. *Hostal Vetusta* (☎ 429 64 04), Calle de las Huertas 3, has admittedly small, but cute, rooms with own shower for 2000/3500 ptas; try for one looking onto the street.

Hostal Santa Ana (☎ 521 30 58), at No 1 right on the square, has average rooms for 2000/3500 ptas. Try for a room with a view. *Hostal La Rosa* (☎ 532 58 05), Plaza de Santa Ana 15, has quite roomy singles/doubles for 1800/3000 ptas.

Hostal Lucense (☎ 522 48 88), Calle de Núñez de Arce 15, and *Pensión Poza* (☎ 232 20 65), at No 9, are owned by the same people (who used to live in Australia). Small and in some cases windowless rooms start at 1000/2000 ptas, but you can get better ones for 1500/2200 ptas. A hot shower costs 200 ptas extra. In the same building as the Lucense, *Hostal Prado* (☎ 521 30 73) on the 2nd floor offers rooms of a similar quality from 1500/2800 ptas.

North of Plaza de Santa Ana, *Hostal Mondragón* (☎ 429 68 16), Carrera de San Jerónimo 32, is pretty good value at 1800/2700 ptas for a biggish single/double without own bathroom. There are at least four other places in the same building. Of these, the *Hostal León* (☎ 429 67 78) is not bad and has heating in winter. It charges 2000/3500 ptas. Another acceptable option in the same building is *Hostal Aguilar* (☎ 429 36 61), which charges from 2700/4000 ptas.

Other Accommodation – around Puerta del Sol *Hostal Tineo* (☎ 521 49 43), Calle de la Victoria 6, is perfectly adequate and charges a standard 2000/3500 ptas. In the same building, *Hostal Gibert* (☎ 522 42 14) has rooms without bath for the same price, or doubles with private bath for 4000 ptas.

If you don't mind the traffic, *Hostal Cosmopolitan* (☎ 522 66 51), Puerta del Sol 9 (3rd floor), has singles/doubles from 1800/3000 ptas. *Hostal Eureka* (☎ 531 94 60), Calle de la Montera 7, also has reasonable singles/doubles for 2000/3000 ptas.

A much better deal is *Hostal Riesco* (☎ 522 26 92), Calle del Correo 2, which has comfortable rooms looking right onto Puerta del Sol. Singles/doubles with shower cost 3200/4300 ptas, or 3600/5000 ptas with full bathroom.

Hostal Rifer (☎ 532 31 97), Calle Mayor 5, is not quite as good but still reasonable at 4000/5000 ptas. A cheaper possibility is *Hostal Ruano* (☎ 532 15 63), at No 1, with no-frills doubles for 2900 ptas.

Another pretty decent place at this price level is the *Hostal Esmeralda* (☎ 521 00 77), Calle de la Victoria 1. Bright, clean rooms with private bath, TV and phone cost 3700/4900 ptas.

South-west of Puerta del Sol towards Plaza Mayor, the *Hostal Santa Cruz* (☎ 522 24 41), Plaza de Santa Cruz 6, is in a prime location. Rooms here start from about 2000/3600 ptas. A cheaper option in the same building is *Hostal Cruz Sol* (☎ 532 71 97). Rooms there start from 2000/2500 ptas without private bath. Doubles with bath cost 4000 ptas.

Hostal María del Mar (☎ 531 90 64), Calle del Marqués Viudo de Pontejos, has similarly basic rooms starting at 1800/2500 ptas.

Other Accommodation – Plaza Mayor *Hostal La Macarena* (☎ 365 92 21), Cava de San Miguel 8, has good rooms with private bath, but at 3900/6200 ptas for its cheapest rooms, you pay mainly for the position.

Other Accommodation – around Ópera *Pensión Luz* (☎ 542 07 59), Calle de las Fuentes 10, is a friendly place with decent little rooms at 2000/3500 ptas.

Calle del Arenal is a good hunting ground for places, although it's a noisy thoroughfare. *Hostal Jeyma* (☎ 541 63 29), at No 24, is a cheap option with small rooms starting at 1300 ptas a head. If it's too basic for your tastes, *Hostal Ivor* (☎ 547 10 54), in the same building, might be better. Its doubles with private bath go up to 5400 ptas.

Just by the Monasterio de las Descalzas Reales is *Hostal Roma* (☎ 531 19 06), Travesía de Trujillos 1, a reliable place with singles/doubles starting at 3500/4600 ptas with own shower, or 4600/5500 ptas with full bathroom.

Hostal Paz (☎ 547 30 47), Calle de la Flora 4, looks horrible outside, but the cheap rooms inside are reasonable value at 2200/3200 ptas without private bath, or a few hundred ptas more with bath.

An attractive option is the *Hostal Valencia* (☎ 559 84 50), Plaza de Oriente 2, with rooms starting at 3500/5000 ptas.

Other Accommodation – Paseo del Prado If you want to be a stone's throw from El Prado, you have a couple of choices on this grand boulevard. *Hostal Sudamericano* (☎ 429 25 64), at No 12, is not a bad one with singles/doubles starting at 2300/4200 ptas.

Other Accommodation – around Gran Vía & Malasaña Gran Vía is laden with accommodation, but it's a noisy avenue. At the cheaper end of the scale you could try *Hostal Alcázar Regis* (☎ 547 93 17), at No 61.

Singles/doubles cost 2500/ 4100 ptas. Across the road and up the hill a little, *Hostal Lamalonga* (☎ 547 26 31), at No 56, is reliable. Rooms with private bath start at 3800/5000 ptas. *Hostal Margarita* (☎ 547 35 49), a little further along at No 50, charges 3000/4300 ptas for rooms, also all with private bath.

The stylish *Hostal Besaya* (☎ 541 32 07), Calle de San Bernardo 13, has good rooms, some with private bath, starting at 4300/ 5600 ptas.

Hostal Gago (☎ 521 22 75), Calle de la Estrella 5, is a friendly, family-run place that seems a little at odds with the seedy streetwalker scene around nearby Calle de la Luna. Modest but clean rooms with shower cost 2000/3000 ptas. There are some singles without private shower for 1600 ptas. In the same building, *Hostal Romero* (☎ 522 19 36) charges about the same for simple, small rooms.

Hostal Flores (☎ 522 81 52), Calle de Gonzalo Jiménez de Quesada 2 (just off Gran Vía), has reasonable rooms for 2800/4000 ptas. *Hostal El Pinar* (☎ 547 32 82), Calle de Isabel la Católica 19, has similar rooms for the same price.

Hostal Andorra (☎ 531 66 03), Gran Vía 33, is on the 7th floor but has fine rooms with private bath, TV and phone for 5000/6500 ptas.

There are loads of places to stay on Calle de Valverde. *Hostal-Residencia América* (☎ 522 26 14), Calle de Valverde 9, on the 4th floor, is reasonable value at 2100/3800 ptas. *Hostal Medieval* (☎ 522 25 49), Calle de Fuencarral 46, has spacious and bright singles/doubles for 3000/4300 ptas.

Hostal Serranos (☎ 448 89 87), Calle de Fuencarral 95, is spick and span, if a tad pricey at 3500/5500 ptas. In the same building and a floor up, *Hostal Sil* (☎ 595 09 93) charges a little less for equally good rooms with private bath.

Calle de Fuencarral is choked with hostales and pensiones, especially at the Gran Vía end. *Hostal Ginebra* (☎ 532 10 35), Calle de Fuencarral 17, is a fine choice not far from Gran Vía. All rooms have TV and phone, and singles with shower start at 3000

ptas, while doubles with full bathroom cost 5000 ptas. English and French are spoken.

At No 25, *Hostal Palacios* (☎ 531 10 58) is a safe choice with singles/doubles for 2100/3600 ptas. All rooms have private bath.

Hostal Odesa (☎ 521 03 38), Calle de Hortaleza 38, has straightforward rooms with TV and private bathroom for 3000/4000 ptas. This place caters to a primarily gay clientele.

Back on Gran Vía, *Hostal Delfina* (☎ 522 64 23) is up on the 4th floor, putting some distance between you and the traffic noise. Singles/doubles with private bath start at 2600/4000 ptas.

Places to Stay – middle
Around Plaza de Santa Ana & Sol The *Hotel Santander* (☎ 429 66 44), Calle de Echegaray 1, is not a bad mid-level choice. At 5000/7000 ptas for singles/doubles, about all it really offers that other places for 2000 ptas less don't, is more space.

For a faint hint of faded elegance, the *Hotel Inglés* (☎ 429 65 51; fax 420 24 23), Calle de Echegaray 8, is OK at 7000/10,000 ptas. *Hotel Moderno* (☎ 531 09 00; fax 531 35 50), Calle del Arenal 2 (just off Puerta del Sol), has rather faded but comfortable rooms for 6500/9900 ptas plus IVA.

A better but more expensive option is *Hotel Regina* (☎ & fax 521 47 25), Calle de Alcalá 19. Singles/doubles with private bath, phone and TV come in at 9050/11,900 ptas.

Around Gran Vía *Hotel Regente* (☎ 521 29 41), Calle de los Mesoneros Romanos 9, has decent mid-range rooms with private bath, TV, air-con and telephone for 6600/8700 ptas.

Hostal Laris (☎ 521 46 80), Calle del Barco 3, is slightly cheaper at 5800/7900 ptas. *Hotel Los Condes* (☎ 521 54 55; fax 521 78 82), Calle de los Libreros 7, is a comfortable, modern option with rooms starting at 7000/9500 ptas plus IVA.

Hotel California (☎ 522 47 03; fax 531 61 01) is a smart choice at Gran Vía 38, with attractive rooms going for 5900/7900 ptas.

Salamanca & North Those wanting to mix it in the smarter parts of town could try the *Hostal Don Diego* (☎ 435 07 60) for size. It's at Calle de Velázquez 45, and comfortable singles/doubles with private bath, TV, minibar and phone cost 6300/8500 ptas plus IVA.

In the Chamberí area north of Malasaña, another perfectly good mid-range possibility is *Hotel Trafalgar* (☎ 445 62 00; fax 446 64 56), Calle de Trafalgar 35 (map: Madrid). It's in a quiet part of town but close to several metro stops and not a long walk from the Malasaña area. They charge 7900/13,200 ptas plus IVA.

Places to Stay – top end

There is no shortage of bland, all mod cons four and five star hotels scattered across Madrid, particularly along the main drags like Paseo de la Castellana. An attractive alternative to these and just off the Castellana is *Hotel Emperatriz* (☎ 563 80 88; fax 563 98 04), Calle de López de Hoyos 4. Tranquil singles and doubles cost as little as 12,000 ptas plus IVA, depending on the season.

A solid, popular choice is the *Hotel Santo Domingo* (☎ 547 98 00; fax 547 59 95), Plaza de Santo Domingo 13. Rooms here are fine and cost 14,250/19,950 ptas plus IVA in the high season.

Hotel Villa Real (☎ 420 37 67; fax 420 25 47) is right by the Cortes (parliament) at Plaza de las Cortes 10, and has rooms with all the accoutrements you might need for 17,000 ptas plus IVA, regardless of whether you take them as singles or doubles.

Among those with a touch of charm is the *Gran Hotel Reina Victoria* (☎ 531 45 00; fax 522 03 07), at Plaza de Santa Ana 14. The location is great (if noisy for all the nocturnal activity) and good rooms will set you back 17,475/21,900 ptas plus IVA.

More expensive is one of Madrid's old classics, the *Hotel Palace* (☎ 429 75 51; fax 429 82 66), Plaza de las Cortes 7, where comfortable and elegant rooms come in at 31,000/52,000 ptas plus IVA in the high season. Not far away is its old rival, the *Hotel Ritz* (☎ 521 28 57; fax 532 87 76), Plaza de la Lealtad 5. At 37,900/60,500 ptas plus IVA,

this is Madrid's priciest location. It was once a favourite of Mata Hari.

Longer-Term Accommodation

If you are planning on spending a long time in Madrid, you can usually make a deal in the pensiones and smaller hostales to include meals, laundry and so on.

Those thinking in terms of more than a couple of months might find renting a more attractive option. Check the notice boards at the various cultural institutes, university campuses and the Escuela Oficial de Idiomas, and finally in the *Segundamano* magazine. Finding a room in shared flats is generally not too difficult, but look around, as you can be offered some pretty dismal mouse holes for big money. With luck and persistence you can find good-quality rooms in central locations for around 35,000 ptas a month. Your bills will include electricity *(luz)*, water, gas (most places use bottled butane gas, which sells for around 1000 ptas a bottle; you'll probably see trucks loaded up with the orange *bombonas* trailing around the city), phone and *comunidad*. The last is a fixed bimonthly charge for building maintenance, sometimes included in the rent.

Places to Eat

Madrid is riddled with restaurants, snack bars and various kinds of fast-food outlets, so you'll rarely have any trouble finding somewhere to quiet a rumbling tummy. Madrid is also one of the few Spanish cities to have a fair sprinkling of non-Spanish options. They can make a welcome change if you are overdosing on the splendours of Spanish cuisine.

Generally, people eat lunch *(comida* or *almuerzo)* between 2 and 4 pm. Arrive any later and you run the risk of finding the kitchen closed. Dinner *(cena)* is a little more flexible, but most people start to munch between 10 and 11 pm.

Because the line dividing bar and restaurant is often blurred, you will find that some of the places included in the Entertainment section under Bars & Pubs also serve up food. They have been listed as bars because

MADRID

the food can be regarded as an adjunct to the drink.

Asking the average madrileño where you can find a 'tapas bar' may well cause a moment of perplexity. In one sense there is no such thing, since virtually all bars will serve up some kind of *tapa* with a drink. True, in some cases the barman must be prompted and in others the tapa is nothing to write home about. It is equally true that certain places have a justly good reputation for the quality of their bar snacks.

Those doing their own cooking could head to the *mercado* in Plaza de San Miguel, the main fresh produce market just off Plaza Mayor. If you're looking for less likely items, the Marks & Spencer department store's food department carries a range of foodstuffs generally unavailable in Spanish shops. The food departments in the Corte Inglés stores are also good.

Around Sol & Plaza Mayor Plaza Mayor and the immediate area offer plenty of possibilities, but a good number fall into the category of tourist traps, serving up average food at not-so-average prices. A few places, however, are worth looking for.

Calle de la Cava de San Miguel and Calle de Cuchilleros are packed with *mesones* that are not bad for a little tapas-hopping. Among them is *Restaurante Madrid 1600*. A cut above the rest is *Restaurante Sobrino de Botín*, Calle de Cuchilleros 17, where the set menu costs about 3200 ptas. It's popular with those who can afford it.

Restaurante Pontejos, Calle de San Cristóbal 11, is a reliable, stock-standard place where you can often get an acceptable paella. If you're not eating the set menu, about 2500 ptas will cover you for a full meal with wine.

Casa Paco, Plaza de la Puerta Cerrada 11, is a Madrid classic – a place to enjoy madrileño cooking at reasonable prices. Still more of an institution is *Casa Ciriaco*, Calle Mayor 84, a bar and restaurant with loads of character. It was founded in 1917 in a building that had previously been popular with would-be assassins: one threw a bomb from one of the balconies at Alfonso XIII as he passed by with his queen, Victoria Eugenia, on their wedding day in 1906. The attack failed, but 24 people died. On the subject of eating, the set meal costs 2100 ptas.

Casa Marta, Calle de Santa Clara 10, has a nice, intimate atmosphere and is moderately priced with mains for around 1000 ptas.

If it's paella your heart desires, the best advice is to head for Valencia. Failing that, you could try the *Restaurante La Paella Real*, Calle de Arrieta 2. This place does a whole range of rice-based dishes from 1500 ptas a head. It's not cheap, but then even halfway decent paella never is in Madrid.

The *Taberna del Alabardero*, Calle de Felipe V 6, is a fine place for a splurge – expect little change per person from 5000 ptas. Or just try a few tapas at the bar.

La Latina *Restaurante Julián de Tolosa*, where Calle del Almendro runs into Calle de la Cava Baja, has a pleasingly simple brick and timber décor and a rather limited menu. If you feel like a chuletón (huge chop) for two for 4600 ptas, this is the place for you.

Restaurante Gure-Etxea, Plaza de la Paja 12, is a fine Basque place and typically expensive. If you feel like a bit of a splurge, there is a menú de degustación that allows you to sample a range of excellent Basque dishes for 3500 ptas a head. Not as well known, but extremely good and also serving a range of Basque dishes with style, is *Restaurante Alamillo*, on Plaza del Alamillo.

La Tasquita, on the corner of Plaza de Gabriel Miró and Travesía de Vistillas, is an enchanting little spot serving no-nonsense Spanish cuisine at mid-range prices and is recommended by locals.

Nearby, tucked in behind a row of trees, is *Restaurante Rayuela*, Calle de Bailén 33. The building, rebuilt after the civil war, once served as servants' quarters for the Palacio Real. Now you can get pasta dishes for up to 1500 ptas or other mains for around 2000 ptas.

Plaza de Santa Ana & Huertas As well as being loaded with popular bars, the area around Plaza de Santa Ana is also busy with eating possibilities. In and around Calle de la Cruz, Calle de Espóz y Mina and Calle de la Victoria is a cluster of restaurants and bars, many specialising in seafood with a more or less legitimate gallego (Galician) touch.

La Casa del Abuelo, Calle de la Victoria 14, on a back street south-east of Puerta del Sol, is a classic old bar in which to sip a chato (small glass) of the heavy, sweet El Abuelo red wine, made in Toledo province. The food side is heaven – king prawns, grilled or with garlic. (Unfortunately, *El Abuelo II* has opened nearby at Calle de Núñez de Arce 5, and is not a patch on the original.) After this, duck around the corner to *Las Bravas*, Callejón de Álvarez Gato, for a caña and the best patatas bravas you'll ever eat. The antics of the bar staff are themselves enough to merit a pit stop and the distorting mirrors are a minor Madrid landmark.

La Trucha, Calle de Núñez de Arce 6, is one of Madrid's great bars for tapas. It's just off Plaza de Santa Ana, and there's another nearby at Calle de Manuel Fernández y González 3. You could eat your fill at the bar or sit down in the restaurant.

Something of an institution in Madrid is the *Museo del Jamón*. Walk in to one of these places and you'll understand the name. Huge clumps of every conceivable type of ham dangle all over the place. You can eat plates and plates of ham – the Spaniards' single most favoured source of nutrition. There's one on Calle de la Victoria, just east of Sol.

In the pleasant enclosed garden of the *Champagnería Gala*, Calle de Moratín 22, you can enjoy several versions of paella and follow the food with some celebratory cava (the Spanish equivalent of champagne). It's especially suited to groups, for whom food and drink need not cost more than 2000 ptas per head.

Mesón La Casolera, Calle de Echegaray 3, is an unassuming place but a popular hang-out with madrileños for seafood. Ask for a fritura, a mixed platter of deep-fried seafood.

Taberna Toscana, on the corner of Calle de Ventura de la Vega and Calle de Manuel Fernández y González, is a simple old place

for straightforward cooking and a beer or two.

If it's just plain cheap you want, *Restaurante La Sanabresa*, Calle del Amor de Dios 12, has simple main meals starting at about 500 ptas. Another very popular local stop is the *Restaurante Pasadero*, Calle de Lope de Vega 9, which has a solid set lunch menu for 975 ptas.

For a little more you can indulge in Madrid's most inventive salads and some mouthwatering desserts at *Gula Gula*, Calle del Infante 5. The atmosphere is more reminiscent of New York or London and the all-you-can-eat salad buffet for 1200 ptas is hard to beat.

Lavapiés *Manhattan*, Calle de la Encomienda 5, is a busy, no-frills establishment that fills up quickly at lunchtime for the 800 ptas set menu. Across the road at No 2, *Cervecería La Vega* is not so popular but offers a set menu for the same price.

A popular place for barbecue-style grills is the Argentine *Restaurante La Pampa*, Calle del Amparo 61.

Gran Vía, Malasaña & Chueca A bright and popular little place for a quick snack and a beer is *Vía 59*, Gran Vía 59. But if you're in this area, you should plunge into the labyrinth of narrow streets and alleyways north off Gran Vía – you won't need to go far to satisfy your taste buds.

For excellent extremeño food, make for the *Restaurante Extremadura* (well, what else?), Calle de la Libertad 13. An excellent meal with wine can come to around 3000 ptas per person. There is a more modern and less enticing branch at No 31, but on a busy night you could wait for a table in a trio of pleasant bars around No 13.

A simple, down-market eating house is the *Bar/Restaurante Cuchifrito*, Calle de Valverde 9, where the set menu is 900 ptas.

Better still is *Restaurante Veracruz*, Calle de San Leonardo 5, just a couple of blocks off Plaza de España (map: España). The set menu (including a bottle of wine) is 800 ptas and is topped off by wonderful home-made desserts – try the tarta de queso and mousse de limón. Manuel García López has been welcoming locals here since 1961.

For a cheap pizza and beer out of doors, you could try *Restaurante Sandos*, Plaza del Dos de Mayo 8. Better still is *Pizzeria Mastropiero*, Calle de San Vicente Ferrer 34 (corner Calle del Dos de Mayo), a justifiably popular Argentine-run joint where you can get pizza by the slice.

Casa Pablo, also known as *La Glorieta*, Calle de Manuela Malasaña 37, is a polished place with a solid reputation for good, modestly priced food. The set menu is excellent value at 950 ptas. The fried anchovies are the best in Madrid.

El Bistró is a very inner-city style sort of place – the kind of thing you might almost expect to find in London's Soho or somewhere on the lower east side in New York. It's at Calle de Hortaleza 108. In the same building is a pleasant pseudo-Italian alternative, the *Trattoria Nabucco*.

One of the better places in Madrid for paella is *Restaurante Cañas y Barro*, Calle de Amaniel 23. Expect to pay around 2000 ptas a head for the paella alone.

Tucked away unobtrusively at Calle de Santo Tomé 6 is one of Madrid's quality secrets, *El Mentidero de la Villa*. A pleasing selection of imaginative Spanish nouvelle cuisine is served up in intimate surroundings. You'll get little change from 5000 ptas. Also not far from the main law courts (and the park known as Plaza de la Villa de París) is a mid-range lunch spot, *Casa Manolo*, popular with lawyer types for its good 1500 ptas set lunch menu. It's at Calle de Orellana 17.

About the same prices can be expected at *Restaurante La Barraca*, Calle de la Reina 29, which does a fair paella for around 2000 ptas.

Momo, Calle de Augusto Figueroa 41, has an above-average set evening menu for 1500 ptas, including wine. The cuisine tends to be inventive, steering well clear of standard Spanish stuff. It makes a nice change.

Taberna La Bola, Calle de la Bola 5 (map: Central), has been stirring up a storm with its traditional cocido a la madrileña since 1880.

The atmosphere reflects the years, making this a worthwhile once-off in spite of the prices.

A great place for dessert or stomach lining after a round or two of drinks, especially for the sweet teeth among us, is the *Chocolatería Madrid*, Calle de Barbieri 15, off Plaza de Chueca.

Later in the evening, there's nothing better for soaking up alcohol than a crêpe at the *Crêperie Ma Bretagne*, Calle de San Vicente Ferrer 9.

Río Manzanares Area Head down past the Príncipe Pío train station towards the Río Manzanares and turn northwards. At Paseo de la Florida 2 (map: Madrid) is a great old place for chicken and cider. A full roast chook, salad and bottle of cider – plenty for two – at *Casa Mingo* will cost less than 2000 ptas. They've been pouring cider here since 1888. It's right by the Ermita de San Antonio de la Florida.

Prada a Tope, Cuesta de San Vicente 32 (map: Central), is another wonderfully atmospheric place. Señor Prada, from the El Bierzo region in north-western Castilla y León, doesn't often make an appearance here any more, but the food from his home region is as good as ever. Specialities include cecina (a kind of beef jerky), empanada de cacabelos and various chorizos.

Salamanca, Goya & Beyond A great little lunch stop just north of El Retiro is *Alfredo's Barbacoa*, Calle de Lagasca 5 (map: Madrid). On the menu are lightly spicy spare ribs for 935 ptas and some good steaks.

For midday tapas with a clientele leaning towards suits, the *Taberna de Daniela*, Calle del General Pardiñas 2 (metro: Goya), is one of the best known places in the snootier Goya barrio. The tile décor is great, but service can be patchy and you're probably better off at the bar.

Casa Julián, Calle de Don Ramón de la Cruz 10, specialises in grilled meats and, for this part of town, is a no-nonsense and atmospheric place in a down-to-earth fashion.

Grilled meat of various red varieties comes in at 1400 ptas a person.

Restaurante Oter, around the corner at Calle de Claudio Coello 73, is a rather up-market spot for Navarran cuisine. You'll get little change from 5000 ptas but the food is good.

An enticing choice, especially for a Sunday lunch pig-out, is *Moncho's de Madrid*, Calle de Orense 66, near Plaza de Castilla (metro: Tetuán; map: North). Unfortunately the all-you-can-eat buffet for which it was justly famous is a thing of the past, and prices are going up. Still, it offers generous servings of all sorts of meats on a spit as well as seafood.

Not too far off, you can dig into a limited variety of roast meats at the sumptuous-looking *Asador La Tahona*, Calle de Capitán Haya 21. A full meal will cost you around 3000 ptas with wine.

International Cuisines The area around Plaza de España, in particular some of the back streets to the east of the square, is a good hunting ground for non-Spanish foods. But there are other possibilities all over the city.

Restaurante Bali, Calle de San Bernardino 6, is Madrid's only Indonesian restaurant. While your average Madrid Chinese serves up pretty bland versions of Asian cooking, this place has authentic cuisine and is a welcome alternative to Iberian fare. A good meal should come in at 5000 ptas or less for two.

The Thai *Restaurante Siam*, next door to the Bali and run by the same woman, is not as good as its neighbour, although the food is quite all right. The menú de degustación for 3000 ptas includes a cross-section of dishes and all your drinking requirements.

Virtually across the road is about the best Madrid can do in Indian food. The *Adrish*, Calle de San Bernardino 1, does pretty convincing dishes, so expect to pay a minimum of 2000 ptas per person.

Restaurante La Llama, Calle de San Leonardo 3, is a pleasant little Peruvian restaurant where a full meal generally comes in just under 2000 ptas a head.

Gabal Lebnan, Calle de los Dos Amigos 8, puts on a good spread of Middle Eastern cuisine, and chucks in the odd belly dancer as a crowd pleaser – for some, perhaps, as a warm-up for the two risqué nightclubs virtually next door? It's a little pricey, with mains costing around 1500 ptas.

For another Thai alternative, you could try the lavish *Thai Gardens* at Calle de Jorge Juan 5 (map: Sal). Here the menú de degustación costs 3900 ptas.

A great deal more fun are the Middle Eastern and North African eateries and salones de té popping up around Lavapiés. These places are often simple, with tasty Arab food and on weekends more often than not a little belly dancing. *Babilonia*, just off Plaza de Lavapiés on Calle del Ave María (just opposite the Café Nuevo Barbieri; map: Central) is a perfect example. Another bright and attractive version is *Asociación Hispano-Árabe*, Calle de la Magdalena 14 (map: Ana & Hue).

However, for some of the most authentic North African and Middle Eastern food you are likely to find in Madrid, you'll need to head a little out of town to *Al-Manzor* (☎ 326 64 63), a restaurant in the basement of the Centro Cultural Islámico, Calle de Salvador de Madariaga 4. This place is home to a Saudi-financed mosque, and women will be obliged to wear a cloak on their way from the entrance down to the restaurant. The food is, however, of a high standard and the restaurant is popular. Get a taxi, as the centre is off the M-30 ring road heading out to the airport. Given the distance, call ahead to book a table.

Some of the best Italian food in town can be enjoyed at *La Dolce Vita*, Calle de Cardenal Cisneros 58 (metro: Quevedo; map: Madrid). The desserts are sublime. Count on about 3000 ptas per person. Another good place is *Ristorante Sassari*, Avenida del Brasil 26 (map: North), where a full meal could cost around 2500 ptas.

Restaurante Robata, Calle de la Reina 31 (map: Mal & Ch), is reputedly one of Madrid's best Japanese eating houses. You'll end up spending about 3000 ptas a head.

Another popular Japanese place is the *Restaurante Donzoko*, on Calle de Echegaray (map: Ana & Hue).

If it's Chinese you're after, *China Crown*, Calle de la Infanta Mercedes 62, has about the best reputation in town (metro: Tetuán; map: North).

There are several Argentine restaurants scattered about Madrid. One reasonable rep is the *Restaurante La Carreta*, Calle de Barbieri 10. After you've filled up on loads of South American-style meat, you are well placed to drink on into the night in the surrounding Chueca area.

Every city's got one. The *Hard Rock Café*, on the Paseo de la Castellana side of Plaza de Colón, serves up American-style club sandwiches, nachos and cocktails. It's lively and the food is generally good value; helpings are of the American jumbo persuasion. You can eat well for 2000 ptas or even less.

Good Mexican food and excellent margaritas can be had at the *Taquería de Birrä*. There is one on Plaza de las Comendadoras (map: Mal & Ch) with a lovely summertime terraza. Otherwise, head for the branch at Calle de Don Pedro 11, just off Calle de Bailén near the Palacio Real.

Vegetarian Vegetarians generally do not have an easy time of it Spain, but Madrid offers a few safe ports. *Restaurante La Biotika*, Calle del Amor de Dios 3, is a reliable favourite in the Huertas area.

The *Restaurante Integral Artemisa*, Calle de Ventura de la Vega 4 (map: Ana & Hue), is an excellent vegetarian place with a tasty set menu for 1200 ptas. There is another branch off Gran Vía at Calle de las Tres Cruces 4 (map: Central).

Another good one that also offers a non-vegetarian menu is *Restaurante Al Natural*, Calle de Zorrilla 11 (map: Ana & Hue).

Restaurante La Granja II, Calle de San Andrés (just off Plaza del Dos de Mayo; map: Mal & Ch), has a set vegetarian lunch for 900 ptas.

The genre is represented in Lavapiés too, with *El Granadero de Lavapiés*, Calle de Argumosa 10 (map: Central).

Pastries Central Madrid is riddled with pastry shops. A particularly good one is the *Antigua Pastelería del Pozo*, at Calle del Pozo 8 near the Puerta del Sol. In operation since 1830 (and for 20 years before that as a bread bakery), it is the city's oldest dealer in sublime tooth-rotting items.

Cafés There is no shortage of places to get a drink of one sort or another in Madrid, and some areas seem to be pretty much wall-to-wall bars. A feature of many that can take a little getting used to is the habit of dropping all rubbish – from napkins and uneaten bits of tapas through to cigarette ash and coffee dregs – onto the floor by the bar. At one point or another it all gets swept out and there is perhaps some logic to it. If one or two people do it, you have to sweep it up, so you may as well let everyone do it! At tables or outside on the *terrazas* the habit does not apply.

Unlike, say, in Italy, the price difference between drinking at the bar or at a table is not so rigidly enforced, but in some places the price of sitting down may be quite high. Table prices on the terrazas, especially in summer, are always higher than bar prices – some of them extravagantly so.

The neat Anglo-Saxon division between cafés (for coffee or tea and scones) and pubs or bars (for getting plastered) is a feature happily absent from the madrileño approach to drinking in society – absent, indeed, from all of Spain. Nevertheless, some bars are fairly evidently *not* intended for a leisurely *café con leche* and a read of the paper; these are dealt with under Entertainment. Others clearly do lean this way. Following are some suggestions for the latter, which is not to say that some don't fall fairly equally into both camps!

Around Plaza Mayor *Café del Real*, Plaza de Isabel II, is an atmospheric place with a touch of elegance. It gets busy at night but also makes a fine spot for breakfast; head for the low-ceilinged upstairs part.

Just up the cobbled lane next to it is another brilliantly positioned spot for a coffee or something more extravagant, *Café de Madrid*, Calle del Mesón de Paños 10. There are sometimes photo and art exhibitions here too, in case you're seeking more stimulus. Stay away in summer, as it's like being in a hothouse.

Up Calle de Vergara to Plaza de Ramales is a series of fine cafés. *Café Vergara*, at Calle de Vergara No 1, is a good one, and the rather stiff *Café de los Austrias*, on the corner of the same street and Plaza de Ramales, seems almost as imperial as its name suggests. For a more off-the-wall feel, try the *Café-Bar La Gloria*, at Calle de Vergara 10.

Café del Oriente, on the corner of Plaza de Oriente and Calle de Lepanto, feels more like a set out of Mitteleuropa. When all the scaffolding around the square finally comes down, it will reacquire its full majesty.

From Colón to the Prado Along the Paseo de los Recoletos, just near Plaza de Colón (map: Mal & Ch), the *Restaurante El Espejo* also doubles as one of Madrid's best known and most elegant cafés. You could also choose to sit in the turn-of-the-century style *Pabellón del Espejo* outside. Despite appearances, it was only opened in 1990. Both are a little expensive and the latter also forms the nucleus of one of Madrid's more expensive summertime terrazas.

Just down the road is the equally graceful *Gran Café de Gijón*, at Paseo de los Recoletos 21. It also happens to have a good lunchtime set menu.

If you're strolling along the Castellana around here but want something a little more down-to-earth, *Café de la Villa*, in the cultural centre of the same name on Plaza de Colón, is a cheery den for arty types.

Another wonderful old place with chandeliers and an atmosphere belonging to another era is the café at the *Círculo de Bellas Artes*, Calle de Alcalá 42 (map: Central). You have to pay a temporary membership of the club (100 ptas) to drink in here, but it's worth it.

Malasaña *Café Comercial*, Glorieta de Bilbao, is an old Madrid café with a good whiff of its castizo (true-blue) past. The odd foreigner stops in, but it's just far away off

the usual tourist trail to be reasonably genuine.

Café Manuela, Calle de San Vicente Ferrer 29, lies on that borderline between café and bar. It is a young, hip sort of place, with a vaguely alternative flavour. On Monday evening there is usually a tertulia (conversational get-together) for foreigners wishing to improve their Spanish. *Café Isadora*, Calle del Divino Pastor 14, is great for chatting away the early evening over a coffee.

An enchanting teahouse with a whiff of the 1960s is the *Tetería de la Abuela*, Calle del Espíritu Santo 19. Along with the great range of teas you can indulge in scrummy crêpes.

Huertas & Lavapiés Calle de las Huertas (off Paseo del Prado) has a string of cafés and bars to choose from. In an old-fashioned vein, the *Café Principal*, Calle del Príncipe 33, is an attractive stop on your coffee route. If you head to the end of the street to Plaza de Canalejas, you'll strike another fine, old, nameless madrileño *bar*. It does good food if you're peckish, and the people-watching is an attraction in itself.

A wonderful old place, once the haunt of the artistic and hopefully artistic, *Nuevo Café Barbieri* even provides newspapers to browse through while you sip your cortado. It's at Calle del Ave María 45 (metro: Lavapiés; map: Central).

Around Plaza de España A few steps away from several of Madrid's better cinemas, off Plaza de España, is the perfectly appropriate *Café de las Extrellas*, Calle Martín de los Heros 5. It attracts a hip film-going crowd and is plastered with portrait photos of screen greats, Spanish and international. A block away you can nosh up on fabulous crêpes and cheesecake, washed down with one of any number of teas and infusions, at *Café Macaluca*, Calle de Juan Álvarez Mendizabal 4.

Entertainment
Many new arrivals in Madrid, perhaps

expecting an ancient metropolis on the scale of London, Paris or Rome, are a little disappointed by what they first see. You need to scratch below the surface to really get into the place, for what Madrid may lack in grand sights, it surely makes up for in the life of its bars and nightclubs, its cinemas, theatres and cafés. Madrileños take their enjoyment seriously, and there is every opportunity to join them.

The busiest time of year on Madrid's entertainment calendar – from theatre to rock concerts – runs from late September to early December in the Fiesta de Otoño.

You'll want to get hold of some listings help. *El País* has a daily listings section (*cartelera*) that is particularly good for cinema and theatre. Original-language films and where they are shown are clearly indicated (look for movies in *versión original*, or *v.o. subtitulada*). Also listed are museums, galleries, music venues and the like. The competition *El Mundo* publishes a comprehensive weekly magazine insert, *Metropoli*, suspiciously similar to London's *Time Out* and packed with info.

The weekly entertainment bible is, however, the *Guía del Ocio*, available at all newsstands for 125 ptas and packed with everything you're likely to want to know.

Tickets You can generally obtain tickets for plays, concerts and other performances at the theatre concerned, but there are centralised ticketing offices too. Quite a few lottery ticket booths also sell tickets for theatre, football and bullfights. There's a handy one on Plaza de Santo Domingo, Localidades La Alicantina. Or try Localidades Galicia (☎ 531 27 32), Plaza del Carmen 1.

For many bands and popular music acts you can often obtain tickets at the Madrid Rock record store, at Gran Vía 25, Calle Mayor 38 and Calle de San Martín 3. You can only pay for tickets in cash. On occasion, the FNAC store, Calle de Preciados, also sells tickets to major concerts, and not only those in Madrid. Again, cash only. See the Central Madrid map for all these.

Theatre Autumn is a busy season for theatre after the torpor of summer. The city's grandest stage, the *Teatro Real*, is still undergoing an overhaul that often seems threatened by dwindling funds. Although the theatre, music and dance scene is not as diverse or even of as high a quality as in some other European capitals, there is plenty happening and a plethora of venues large and small, of which the following are a representative selection.

The beautiful old *Teatro de la Comedia* (☎ 521 49 31; map: Ana & Hue), Calle del Príncipe 14, is home to the Compañía Nacional de Teatro Clásico and often stages gems of classic Spanish and European theatre. The *Teatro de Bellas Artes* (☎ 532 44 38; map: Central), Calle del Marqués de Casa Riera 2, also tends to lean towards the classics.

At the *Centro Cultural de la Villa* (☎ 575 60 80), under the waterfall at Plaza de Colón, you can see anything from classical music concerts through comic theatre, opera and quality flamenco performances.

Teatro Alfil (☎ 521 15 16; map: Mal & Ch), Calle del Pez 10, is a good little alternative theatre which puts on all sorts of acts, from folk music to French mime duos. Another alternative venue to keep an eye on is the *Teatro Olimpia* (☎ 527 46 22; map: Central), right by the metro on Plaza de Lavapiés.

Classical Music & Opera For musical and operatic performances, at least while the Teatro Real remains out of action, both the Centro Cultural de la Villa and the *Teatro Monumental* (☎ 429 81 19; map: Ana & Hue), Calle de Atocha 65, are the main venues to look out for.

Also important for classical music is the *Auditorio Nacional de Música* (☎ 337 01 00), Calle del Príncipe de Vergara 146 (metro: Cruz de Rayo; map: North). It often plays host to the Orquesta Nacional de España and international performers. On a smaller scale, regular Saturday concerts are held in the *Fundación Juan March* (☎ 435 42 40), Calle de Castelló 77 (metro: Núñez de Balboa; map: Madrid).

The *Teatro de la Zarzuela* (☎ 524 54 00), Calle de Jovellanos 4 (metro: Banco de España; map: Ana & Hue) is the principal venue in Madrid for opera.

Cabaret For those wanting to stray tamely towards the wild side, *Pirandello*, Calle de Ventura Rodríguez 7, near Plaza de España, might do the trick. Paco España (Jack Spain) is the country's best known transvestite performer, and you can sometimes enjoy his/her antics here with a cast of other 'girls'.

Cinema The standard cinema ticket costs around 700 ptas, but many cinemas have at least one day set aside as the *día del espectador* for cut-price tickets (usually about 200 ptas off). Unfortunately, it is not the same day at all cinemas, so it's a little hit-and-miss.

One of the best concentrations of cinemas for films in the original-language version is in and around Calle de Martín de los Heros and Calle de la Princesa (metro: Plaza de España). The *Renoir*, *Alphaville*, *Lumière* and *Princesa* cinema complexes around here all screen such movies.

The *Cine Doré*, which houses the Filmoteca Nacional, is a wonderful old cinema that shows classics past and present, all in the original language. It's at Calle de Santa Isabel 3 in Lavapiés (metro: Antón Martín; map: Ana & Hue), and has a cheap restaurant attached. If you're in Madrid for any length of time, consider getting a bono for cut-price tickets.

You can also see subtitled movies at the *Multicines Ideal* complex on Calle del Doctor Cortezo (map: Central), or the *Renoir* at Calle de Raimundo Fernández Villaverde 10 (metro: Cuatro Caminos; map: North).

In mid-1996, the huge-screen *Cine Imax* opened in the Parque Enrique Tierno Galván, Camino de Meneses s/n, south of Atocha station (metro: Méndez Álvaro). For this 3D cinema experience you pay from 850 to 1500 ptas, depending on what is being screened.

Bars & Pubs Things have calmed down a little since the heyday of the *movida* in the years after Franco's death, but Madrid can

still easily boast a breadth and depth of nightlife without compare anywhere else in Europe. What follows is little more than a taste of the hundreds of bars to tempt you.

Plaza de Santa Ana & Huertas Plaza de Santa Ana is lined with a series of interesting bars. The atmosphere in these places is a slight cut above the average, as is the price of your caña.

The *Cervecería Alemana* is a century-old meeting place, but any of the bars along here makes for a pleasant watering stop, especially when you can sit outside in the warmer months. In summer, *Bar Hawaiano* sets up a terraza in the middle of the square. *La Moderna* has been going since 1994 and attracts a mixed, 30-something and buzzy crowd.

On Calle de la Victoria (No 2) is *La Fontana de Oro*, one of several good Irish-style pubs you'll find scattered about central Madrid, although it has rather a longer history than most. Prior to occupation of the city by Napoleon's troops early in the last century, it was a hotbed of political dissent, as wine and antigovernment talk flowed freely. It's still a popular place, with plenty of seating downstairs and standing room at street level.

Although it gets hellishly crowded at weekends, you should at least poke your head into *Viva Madrid*, Calle de Manuel Fernández y González 7. The tiled décor and heavy timber ceilings make a distinctive setting for drinks earlier in the evening. Equally beautiful, but even more cheekily expensive, is *Los Gabrieles*, Calle de Echegaray 17, just a few steps away. If tiles are your thing, another good choice is *España Cañí*, west off Plaza de Santa Ana at Plaza del Ángel 14.

To step into a time warp, slip into *La Venencia*, Calle de Echegaray 7, for a sherry. This place is the real thing: it looks as though nothing has been done to clean it in many a long year. Ill-lit and woody, it is the perfect place to sample one of six varieties of sherry – from the almost sweet amontillado to the rather biting fino.

A place done up to look as though it's almost as old, with a dimly lit dash of 1930s elegance, music of a similar era and fine cocktails, is *Casa Pueblo* at Calle de León 3. It's an equally wonderful place for an afternoon coffee or a slightly pricey evening drink.

At *Cardamomo*, Calle de Echegaray 15, they usually play flamenco and related music, although there's nothing live. Virtually around the corner on Calle Manuel Fernández y González, *Carbones* is a busy place, open until about 4 am and featuring a good selection of mainstream music on the jukebox.

Cuevas de Sésamo, Calle del Príncipe 7, is a wonderful old cellar bar that specialises in sangría.

Calle de la Cruz is also rather full of marcha, with a few discos and music places. For a warm-up or a break you could pop into *El Trébol*, at No 3. You can get a mean pizza to go with your beer, and it's open late. *Bar Matador*, opposite the Torero disco, is a popular spot for a few drinks before crossing the road for some dance action (see the Discos, Dancing & Nightclubs section later in this chapter).

A modern spot that's not bad for a warm-up into the evening is the *Bar Cuatro Calles* on Plaza de Canalejas.

Casa Alberto, Calle de las Huertas 18, was founded in 1827 in a building where Cervantes did a spot of writing. It's a fine old place for vermouth on tap, and you can also get a meal.

Café Populart, Calle de las Huertas 22, often has music, generally of a jazz or Celtic nature. For more jazz with your drinks, *Café Central*, Plaza del Ángel, is another good choice.

Just beyond the hubbub of Huertas is *El Parnaso*, a quirky but engaging little bar at Calle de Moratín 25. The area around the bar is jammed with an odd assortment of decorative paraphernalia, while out the back you get the feeling you're sitting in an ancient tram-car. The music and crowd are mellow.

Nearby, at Calle de los Desamparados 3, is a quite different atmosphere and crowd at *La Taberna Celta*, one of the city's Gaelic collection. For an old Madrid favourite, head

for *El Ratón*, a block west on Calle de Santa María.

Around Plaza Mayor & the Palacio Real

Although there is no shortage of standard little bars in this area, few stand out. One exception is *Casa Antonio*, Calle de Latrones 10, just south of Plaza Mayor, which is a classic old Madrid watering hole with loads of character and vermouth on tap.

Further to the south-west things get promising again. Calle de la Cava Baja in particular is full of taverns and eating houses. *La Chata*, at No 24, has a spectacular tiled frontage and is nice for a quick caña or two. Don't spend all your time here though. *Taberna Tempranillo*, at No 38, has plenty of character and many bottles of different Spanish wine that you'll be encouraged to sample. Tucked away in the less lively parallel street of Calle de la Cava Alta is *Café del Mono*, at No 19. It's a rather cool hideaway and a favourite with those in the know.

A less touristy place along similar lines to Casa Antonio is *Taberna Almendro 13*, basically a sherry pub that shuts at midnight. It's at (no prizes for guessing) Calle del Almendro 13.

Just by the summertime terrazas of Las Vistillas (see Terrazas below) is a handful of intriguing places. The gaudily coloured *Travesía*, at Travesía de las Vistillas 8, attracts a diverse crowd with its cocktails and South American music. Occasionally it hosts live performances and storytelling. Also popular is *Bar Irreal*, across the road.

Café del Nuncio, Travesía del Nuncio, is a wonderful bar that straggles up a stairway passage from Calle de Segovia. You can drink in the several cosy levels inside or, better still in summer, hang about at the outdoor tables – a delightful spot for a civilised early-evening tipple.

At Plaza de Gabriel Miró 1, the *Champañería María Pandora* is deliciously pretentious – a place to sip your drinks while poring over the books.

Around Lavapiés
This whole barrio is one of the last worker-Gypsy quarters in central

DAMIEN SIMONIS

DAMIEN SIMONIS

DAMIEN SIMONIS

DAMIEN SIMONIS

Top Left: The Tío Pepe sign above Puerta del Sol, Madrid
Top Right: Tile decoration, Villa Rosa, Plaza de Santa Ana, Madrid
Bottom Left: The Iglesia de Santa Bárbara, next to the Palacio de Justicia in Malasaña, Madrid
Bottom Right: *Farmacia* on Calle de San Vicente Ferrer, Malasaña, Madrid

Left: The 1st century AD Roman aqueduct in Segovia, Castilla y León
Top Right: The village of Peñaranda de Duero in eastern Castilla y León, and the countryside beyond, from the ruins of the medieval castle
Bottom Right: Detail from the plateresque main façade of Astorga cathedral, Castilla y León

Madrid, and while the bars are often *cutre* (basic, spit-and-sawdust style), they brim with a raw energy.

The *Taberna de Antonio Sánchez*, Calle de Mesón de Paredes 13, is an old-time drinking place with a slightly conspiratorial air; it serves beer, wine and snacks, and that's about it.

An excellent place for cañas and seafood pinchos (snacks), with a rough-around-the-edges feel and extremely popular with people in the barrio, is *El Boquerón*, Calle de Valencia 14. Round the corner you can hang out in *La Mancha de Madrid*, Calle de Miguel Servet, which attracts a colourful array of local tipplers earlier in the evening.

PakesTeis, Calle del Amparo 81, was opened years ago by a sound technician for rock bands. The name is a corruption of *'para que estéis'*, which means, roughly, 'so you can hang out' and is at the same time a loose rendition of the English 'backstage'. The place has a no-nonsense rock feel, and there are often impromptu sessions in the basement.

Gran Vía, Malasaña & Chueca Along with the Santa Ana and Huertas area, the web of streets and lanes stretching north off Gran Vía is Madrid's other great party paradise, with more bars, pubs, dance places and general drinking potential than you can shake a stick at. The atmosphere of the area is decidedly different, doubtless shaped by the low-life element that is an essential part of it. Whores, pimps, dealers and a general mix of down-and-outs mix it with revellers of all types, ages and sexual persuasions. In particular, damsels of the night haunt Calle de la Ballesta (lined with escort bars and the like), Calle de la Luna and the immediate area.

Cervecería de Santa Bárbara, at No 8 on the plaza of the same name (metro: Alonso Martínez), is a classic old Madrid drinking house and is generally packed early in the night. It is a popular meeting place and as good a place as any to kick off a night in Malasaña. It also has great seafood tapas. If you really want to get as basic as possible, the place marked simply *Vinos* at Calle de

Sagasta 2 is for you; it serves wine and various cheeses. Around the corner at Calle de Fuencarral 102 you can get an Asturian cider and a tapa of empanada for 170 ptas at *Corripio*. Two doors down at No 98, *Patatus* is popular with a young crowd for early-evening beers and saucy potatoes.

The *Bodega de la Ardosa*, Calle de Colón 13, is a wonderful, dimly lit little bar where you can sip on a vermouth drawn from the barrel. If it really must be a Guinness, step around the corner to *The Quiet Man*, Calle de Valverde 44, a fine Irish pub.

On the Irish theme, *Finnegan's*, Plaza de las Salesas 9, has become something of an obligatory stop for aficionados of the dark fluids. It is the only such pub in Madrid fully owned and run by Irish. Calle de San Vicente Ferrer has a fair quota of bars, and on the corner with Corradera Alta de San Pablo is *Triskel*, yet another jolly Irish joint.

La Vía Láctea, Calle de Velarde 18, is a bright, thumping sort of place with a young, *macarra* crowd. There is plenty of mainstream music playing and a good drinking atmosphere. Or you can settle in for a smoky game of pool. The *Kyoto* bar on Calle de Barceló is another popular hang-out.

In *La Taberna del Foro*, Calle de San Andrés 38, the décor of traditional Madrid shop fronts surrounds an intimate stage where you can often hear good live music.

For one of the best mojitos (a delicious and popular Cuban rum-based concoction) in the area, pop into the *Café Magerit*, Calle del Divino Pastor 21. For another version of the same tipple, try *Café Isadora* (see Cafés under Places to Eat earlier in this chapter).

Up on Plaza de las Comendadoras, the lightly Art Deco *Café Moderno* is a cosy place in winter, especially if you're there on a Thursday night for the belly dancing!

Autores, Calle de Campoamor 6, can generally be relied upon to be busy when other bars nearby are thinning out in the wee hours. It occasionally stages theme nights: to get in to these you either have to pay or pick up a flier.

Calle de Campoamor and its continuation Calle de Pelayo, running parallel to Calle de

Hortaleza, are lined with an assortment of places. Heading from north to south they start off as mainly noisy rock bars for the young 'uns and gradually give over to a string of gay bars. At the bottom end of the street you are in the Chueca area, the heart of Madrid's gay nightlife (metro: Chueca).

Acuarela Café, Calle de Gravina 10, is a quiet place for an intimate drink in more of a gay arty atmosphere. Right next door on the corner with the square is *Truco*, one of the city's few predominantly lesbian bars. *Rimmel*, Calle de Luis de Góngora 4, and *Cruising*, Calle de Pérez Galdós 5, are among the more popular gay haunts. The *Leather* bar, at Calle de Pelayo 42, is just one of the many gay bars towards the southern end of this street.

This does not mean that all Chueca's bars are exclusively gay; everyone can enjoy this pleasingly seedy district. Watch out for the wonderful, gloomy old wine bar, the *Sierra Ángel*, at Calle de Gravina 11, overlooking Plaza de Chueca.

Heading towards Gran Vía, *Libertad 8*, Calle de la Libertad 8, was a favoured haunt of the Left around the time of Franco's demise. It still gets an animated crowd to see singer-songwriters or sit in on the odd poetry reading. Another pleasant place with tiled walls and a cosy feel is *Bar La Carmencita*, at No 16.

El Corazón Negro, Calle de Colmenares 5, a meeting place for cinema people and hopefuls, looks as though it's been trashed, but it has a grungy atmosphere worth wallowing in. On Sunday evening from 6 pm it puts on a coffee-and-sticky-buns buffet. You can't miss it: there's a big black heart on the wall outside. The Art Deco *Café del Diego*, Calle de la Reina 12, does a great cubalibre.

Museo Chicote, Gran Vía 12, is another Art Deco special (founded in 1931), long the haunt of Madrid's chic and well connected. It used to be directly connected with *Cock Bar*, Calle de la Reina 16, which once served as a discreet salon for a higher class of prostitution. The ladies in question have gone, but this popular bar retains plenty of atmosphere – even if the name is a little startling.

Around Plaza de Santo Domingo & Ópera
The streets around this square tend to be home to tacky 'clubs' and tawdry strip joints, but you can find a few curios worth an hour or two of your drinking time. One of the better ones is *Calentito*, Calle de Jacometrezo 15 (map: Central), a lively salsa bar with transvestites in skimpy attire shaking their bits for you on the bar.

Around Plaza de España A good spot for cocktails after the movies is *Ambigú 16*, Calle de Martín de los Heros 16. It's good for a mean caipirinha (a Brazilian cocktail) and has all sorts of wonderful hard stuff, including Colombian rum. This is the best of a few bars along this street.

Salamanca, Cuatro Caminos & North
Teatriz, Calle de la Hermosilla 15 (map: Sal), is a chichi hang-out with a difference. The former Teatro Beatriz has an eerily lit bar right on the stage, and several others scattered about the premises. Downstairs is a small and decidedly weird dance area, where in the low light you appear to leave footprints on the floor as you move. Cocktails go for 1100 ptas, imported beers for 600 ptas.

Garamond, Calle de Claudio Coello 10 (map: Madrid), has the air of a medieval parador for an expensive drink. They usually put on some kind of show or open buffet. Definitely for the jacket-and-tie yuppie brigade.

Playing to quite a younger crowd is *Terraza de Serrano*, Calle de Serrano 41 (virtually across the road from Marks & Spencer; map: Sal). This cavernous drinking mall heaves with one of the greatest concentrations of adolescent hormones in the entire city.

Moving north, the Calle de Orense used to be a local hot spot but the action has moved to the parallel Avenida del Brasil, where about half a dozen bars keep a faithful crowd more than occupied until around 6 am. Probably the best of them is the immense and immensely popular *Irish Rover*, at No 7 (map: North). At the northern end of the same street, *Maes* is an uninspiring-looking place that happens to serve a wide variety of imported beers.

East of the Paseo de la Castellana there's another small strip of bars on Calle de Joaquín Costa (metro: Plaza de la República Argentina; map: North). The *Kangarú Australian Bar* at No 27 occasionally sells Coopers, but that's about as Australian as it gets. It vies for custom with *Tex-Mex* next door (owned by the same people) and a few others, good for the early stages of the evening before heading to Avenida del Brasil.

St Andrew's Pub, Calle de Hermanos Bécquer 5 (map: Sal; look for the stag's head over the entrance), is a quirky departure from the standard Madrid drinking trough. It's a fine old dark-wood pub in the best cigar-smoking style. Sink into a studded red-leather couch of the old-boys' club variety on a Saturday night to take in the live accordion music.

Terrazas Many of the places listed above have terrazas – tables set up on the footpath or plaza – most of which spring up like mushrooms in the summer. The season is from about April to October, and the bars that run them pay for a specific extra licence to operate.

Probably the best located one is *Bar Ventorrillo*, Corral de la Morería, just by the Jardines de Las Vistillas. This is a wonderful spot to relax and drink in the views of the Sierra de Guadarrama, especially around sunset. You can eat here too, although the food is a little overpriced. During the Fiestas de San Isidro bands play in the gardens.

Some of the terrazas, such as those that emerge along Paseo de la Castellana and Paseo de los Recoletos, are something of a haunt for *la gente guapa* (the beautiful people) – those who want to be seen spending serious money for their libations. A perfect case in point is *Bolero*, Paseo de la Castellana 33 (map: Sal), where a modest beer costs 600 ptas. *Boulevard*, at No 37, is largely the domain of better-off university students. For a more staid beginning to the evening, *El Espejo*, Paseo de los Recoletos

31 (see also Places to Eat), is hard to beat for elegance.

Less pretentious and considerably more pleasant are the terrazas that set up in Argüelles – more specifically, on Paseo del Pintor Rosales. With parkland on one side and considerably less traffic than on Paseo de la Castellana, these places also exercise a little more control over their prices. *Terraza España* (map: Madrid) is one of several along this strip.

Madrid's squares make perfect locations for outdoor drinking. Several of the bars on Plaza de Santa Ana operate terrazas, as does *Café del Oriente* on Plaza de Oriente (if the construction works around here ever finish). Bars spread summertime liquid satisfaction across such squares as Plaza del Dos de Mayo and Plaza de las Comendadoras, both in the Malasaña area, as well as Plaza del Conde Barajas (just south off Plaza Mayor), and around Plaza de los Carros, just to name a few.

Flamenco There are several *tablaos* or flamenco performance spots in central Madrid, but most are designed for the tourist crowd. They generally feature dinner and flamenco performances of an indifferent quality, much avoided by locals. They all feature in entertainment guides. The best of this poor lot appears to be *Café de Chinitas* (☎ 559 51 35), Calle de Torija 7 (map: Central). You will almost certainly need to book ahead.

To get a feel for the more genuine article, you have several options. Firstly, there is a handful of peñas flamencas, or bars where flamenco music is often played, although not necessarily live.

For some, *La Soleá*, Calle de la Cava Baja 27 (map: Central), is the last real flamenco bar in Madrid, where aficionados enjoy performers who know it all. At *Candela*, Calle del Olmo 3 (map: Central), the gitanos practise their music and dance out the back (and you probably won't be allowed to watch), but the bar is charged with an Andalucían flamenco atmosphere and is a recommended stop for a late drink in any case. Occasionally you'll get lucky and witness impromptu jam sessions. Another fun little place is *Bar Sacromonte*, Calle de la Magdalena 34, which often has flamenco performances from 10 pm to midnight.

Casa Patas, Calle de Cañizares 10, is a little more organised and hosts recognised masters of flamenco guitar, song and dance. Another such place is the *Peña Flamenca Chaquetón*, Calle de las Canarias 39 (map: Madrid). It is worth keeping your eye on the papers for details of upcoming performances.

A less likely venue is *Revólver*, Calle de Galileo 26 (map: España), basically a rock bar that happens to get in some flamenco on the slow night – Monday. Another very pleasant little place to pop in for some flamenco sounds is *Café Latino*, Calle de Augusto Figueroa 47 (map: Mala). Performances on Wednesday night are free, but don't leave it too late to get in.

Not infrequently the bigger names play to packed houses in various of Madrid's theatres; check the papers.

Other Live Music Bands don't usually appear on stage before 10 pm, and often wait until midnight; in most cases they'd have no-one to play to before then. You can dance at some of these venues.

One of Madrid's better known jazz haunts is *Clamores Jazz Club*, Calle de Alburquerque 14 (metro: Bilbao; map: Madrid). It is generally open all week. Usually there is no cover charge, and the place gets quite a good selection of acts. You can also catch the occasional jazz performance at *Café Central* and *Populart*, two bars listed above.

Galileo Galilei, Calle de Galileo 100 (map: Madrid), attracts a mix of Hispanic dance groups and vocalists.

Latin American rhythms have quite a hold of Madrid nightlife. A good place to indulge in salsas, merengues and other Latin grooves is *Vaiven*, Travesía de San Mateo 1 (metro: Chueca; map: Mal & Ch). For years, Thursday has been the big night, with the band La Única working magic with bolero, salsa and cha-cha-chá. There is no cover charge, but a beer costs about 600 ptas.

Suristán, Calle de la Cruz 7 (map: Ana & Hue), gets in a wide variety of music acts, from Cuban to black African. Music usually kicks off at 11.30 pm, and there is sometimes a cover charge of up to 1000 ptas (including a drink).

Swing, Calle de San Vicente Ferrer 23 (metro: Tribunal) in the heart of Malasaña, always has some kind of performance on, from longtime cantautores like Javier Krahe through to Friday pop and soul nights and Caribbean music. Entry hovers around 1000 ptas (including one drink).

Madrid Jazz, on the corner of Calle de San Vicente Ferrer and Calle de San Andrés (map: Mal & Ch), can get extremely packed, but occasionally features some decent live music, more often than not having nothing to do with jazz. *La Taberna Encantada*, Calle de Salitre 2 (map: Central), gets a similar range of acts.

Sala Caracol, Calle de Bernardino Obregón 18 (metro: Embajadores), is a venue designed to accommodate bigger acts, Spanish and foreign. Keep an eye on entertainment guides to see what's coming up here.

Major Concerts Several venues are used for major concerts, whether of Spanish groups or international acts. A common one is the Plaza de Toros Monumental de Ventas (metro: Ventas; map: Madrid), Madrid's main bullring. Others include the former Cuartel del Conde Duque, near Plaza de España, and the Teatro Monumental (metro: Antón Martín; map: Ana & Hue).

Discos, Dancing & Nightclubs On weekends in particular, it is quite possible to continue the 'night' well into the day. In some discos a 9 or 10 am finish is the norm.

Malasaña Morocco, Calle del Marqués de Leganés 7, although some say it has passed its peak, is still a popular stop on the Madrid dance circuit, usually swinging into gear from about 1 am.

From 5 am, a lively and noisy crowd makes for *Bali Hai*, just off Gran Vía in Calle de la Flor Alta, where you can lose weight through sweat expulsion to the pounding of bakalao.

Ya'sta!, Calle de Valverde 10, is another place that doesn't swing into action until the early morning (about 6 am). It has a reputation as a meat market, but is a lot of good sweaty dance fun.

Around Plaza de España *Ku*, Calle de la Princesa 1, is becoming an increasingly popular late-night dance club, offering music for all tastes – funky, house, techno and acid jazz, to name a few.

Around Plaza de Santa Ana & Sol *Villa Rosa*, Plaza de Santa Ana 15, is as remarkable for its décor as anything else, but from about 1 am makes a mellow place to go for a drink and a little shaking of stuff on the small dance floor. The tile decoration outside (pictures of Sevilla, Granada and Córdoba) and within, and the vaguely artesonado-style ceiling, make it a unique spot.

In Calle de la Cruz are a couple of dance spaces. You may well have to queue if you have no passes or fliers for them. *Torero*, at No 26, has two floors, featuring more Spanish music upstairs and international tunes downstairs. The bouncers can be a real pain, so you could opt for the distinctly tacky *La Cartuja* at No 10.

Palacio Gaviria, Calle del Arenal 9 (map: Central), is indeed palatial, divided up into a series of old-style salons to meet most middle-of-the-road tastes, from waltzes to mainstream disco blah, with a couple of small corners scattered about for a quiet drink or snog. The place gets going about 2 am, and entrance can cost up to 2000 ptas. A beer is worth 900 ptas and a mixed drink 1500 ptas. There is often a free buffet on Sunday at about 11 pm.

Just next door is one of Madrid's premier nightspots, *Teatro Joy Eslava* (☎ 366 37 33 for reservations), Calle del Arenal 11. It is similarly pricey.

Amusement Parks Travellers with kids on the leash can let them loose at the Parque de Atracciones, in the Casa del Campo area west of the city centre (metro: Batán). It opens daily except some Mondays from May to mid-September, but opening times vary considerably (usually from noon until midnight or later, but generally from 6 pm on in late July and August). In winter it tends to open on the weekend and on holidays only, from noon to 7 pm. The cheapest ticket (400 ptas) allows you entry alone. An unlimited all-rides stamp on your hand costs 1550 ptas for adults and 925 ptas for children. Single-ride tickets are available too (most rides cost adults two such tickets).

Spectator Sport

Football Even if soccer (as it is known to some) doesn't interest you, a good match in Spain provides an insight into an essential side of Spanish leisure. Tickets can be bought on the day, starting at around 1000 ptas, although the big fixtures are often sold out. This is especially so if the two local teams, Real Madrid and Atlético de Madrid, clash, or when either meets the enemies from Barcelona.

Real Madrid's home ground is the Estadio Santiago Bernabéu (☎ 344 00 52; metro: Lima; map: North), while Atlético is based at the Estadio Vicente Calderón (☎ 366 47 07), south-west of the centre at Calle de la Virgen del Puerto (metro: Pirámides).

You can get tickets in advance from the grounds or from ticket offices (more expensive) at Calle de la Victoria, near Puerta del Sol.

Bullfighting You either love it or you loathe it, but many people will want to see at least one bullfight to draw their own conclusions. In spite of the Hemingway-inspired fame of the Pamplona fiesta, connoisseurs would rather get a front seat in Madrid's huge Plaza Monumental de Las Ventas (☎ 356 22 00), Calle de Alcalá 237 (metro: Ventas; map: Madrid), for a good fight. The ring is the biggest in the bullfighting world. The best fiesta begins in mid-May, marking the holiday for Madrid's patron saint, San Isidro Labrador (see also Special Events), and lasts well into June. It is in fact considered the most important bullfight season in the world, making or breaking *toreros* and bull breeders alike. Otherwise, *corridas* are organised regularly on weekends over the summer. Madrid has a second, smaller bullring near Vista Alegre metro station.

Tickets *(entradas)* start at a little under 2000 ptas for a basic seat in the sun *(sol)*, and rise steadily from there. A more comfortable position in the shade *(sombra)* can come in at anything from 3000 to 5000 ptas, depending on where the seat is in the ring.

You can purchase tickets at the rings, from the ticket offices on Calle de la Victoria (the same offices as for football tickets), or other places selling theatre tickets and the like (see Tickets under Entertainment earlier in this chapter). It is wise to buy tickets in advance, although you may be able to get basic seating in the sun on the day. Scalpers also operate outside the rings and ticket offices. During the San Isidro feria booking is mandatory.

Things to Buy

On Sunday morning, the Embajadores area of Madrid seems to contain half the city's population as all and sundry converge on El Rastro, the city's flea market. Starting from Plaza de Cascorro, its main axes are Calle de Ribeira de Curtidores and Calle de Embajadores (map: Central). A good deal of what's on sale is rubbish, but the atmosphere alone is worth the effort, and you can turn up interesting items. There are a good many junk and antique stores sprinkled about here, and more contemporary shops in the Mercado Puerta de Toledo, just west of the Rastro area.

On the subject of antiques, Calle del Prado is a good place to look for a higher class of furniture and other antique items.

Those looking to do some shopping in a more chichi environment should head for Calle de Serrano, the city's premier shopping street, in Salamanca. Of interest to those hanging around Madrid for the long haul is Marks & Spencer, whose food department carries all sorts of goodies otherwise unavailable in Madrid. Also well worth exploration is Calle de Almirante, just east of Plaza de Chueca, considered the city's best fashion showcase.

Madrid's, and indeed Spain's, best known department store chain is El Corte Inglés. There's one located just off the Puerta del Sol on Calle de Preciados.

For specialist purchases you need to look elsewhere. Hunt around along Calle Mayor, especially towards its western end, for guitars and other instruments. For leather try the shops along Gran Vía, or Calle de Fuencarral for shoes.

There are plenty of kitsch souvenirs of Madrid to be had around Plaza Mayor and Sol, along Gran Vía or around the Prado. A popular item is a bullfighting poster with your name inscribed as lead torero.

If you're looking for nice gifts of quality Spanish wines and foodstuffs, there are quite a few shops in the Salamanca area. Mallorca, on the corner of Calle de Velázquez and Calle de Don Ramón de la Cruz, is a good one. Smaller but also worth a look is Max 63, at Calle de Claudio Coello 64.

CDs and cassettes are not especially cheap in Spain, but if you're looking for local music you find hard to come by at home, try the music sections of El Corte Inglés or FNAC, on Calle de Preciados. Madrid Rock (see Tickets under Entertainment for addresses) probably has the broadest general music selection and competitive prices.

For late-night munchies and other emergencies, there is a sprinkling of stores across central Madrid. Vips, 7-Eleven and Bob's each have several branches and remain open when everything else but the discos have shut their doors.

Getting There & Away

Air Regular and charter flights from all over the world arrive at Madrid's Barajas airport (☎ 305 83 44), 13 km north-east of the city. There is a left-luggage centre *(consigna;* ☎ 305 61 12) outside the international arrivals hall. It opens daily from 7 am to midnight. You will find several banks with ATMs, a post office, tourist information, hotel booking stand, and general information office. Buses and taxis link the airport with the centre of Madrid.

Internal flights are in general not particularly good value unless you are in a burning hurry. Nor is Madrid exactly the budget airfare capital of Europe. That said, bargains can be found to popular destinations such as London, Paris, New York and the Canary Islands.

For hints on good travel agents, see Information earlier in this chapter. See the Air sections in the Getting There & Away and Getting Around chapters for more information on flights and airfares.

All airlines have representatives at the airport, as well as in Madrid itself. The latter include:

Aerolíneas Argentinas
    Calle de la Princesa 12 (☎ 547 47 00)
Air France
    Torre de España, Plaza de España 18
    (☎ 330 04 00)
American Airlines
    Calle de Pedro Teixeira 8 (☎ 597 20 68;
    901-10 00 01)
British Airways
    Calle de Serrano 60 (☎ 431 75 75)
Delta Airlines
    Calle de Goya 8 (☎ 577 06 50)
Iberia
    Calle de Goya 29 (☎ 587 81 09, 587 87 87;
    InfoIberia ☎ 329 57 67; map: Sal)
Lufthansa
    Calle del Cardenal Marcelo Spínola 2
    (☎ 383 17 64)
Qantas
    Calle de la Princesa 1 (☎ 541 97 36)
Singapore Airlines
    Calle de Pinar 7 (☎ 563 80 01)
Thai
    Calle del Príncipe de Vergara 185 (☎ 411 64 11)

Bus There are as many as eight bus stations dotted about Madrid with companies servicing different parts of the country. The tourist offices can provide detailed information on where you need to go for your destination.

The Estación Sur de Autobuses, near Atocha train station at Calle de las Canarias 17 (metro: Palos de la Frontera; map:

Madrid), is the city's principal bus station. It serves most destinations to the south and many in other parts of the country. Most bus companies have a ticket office here, even if their buses depart from elsewhere. You can get information on ☎ 468 42 00.

The station is big and operates a consigna which is open from 6.30 am to midnight. Each piece of luggage costs 100 ptas per day. There are cafés and a couple of shops, as well as direct access to the No 3 metro line to Sol and Plaza de España.

Of the companies operating from other points around the city, some useful ones include:

Continental-Auto
    Calle de Alenza 20 (☎ 533 04 00; map: North).
    This company runs buses north to Burgos, Soria,
    Logroño, Navarra, the País Vasco and Santander.
    They also run buses to Toledo from the Estación
    Sur and to Alcalá de Henares and Guadalajara
    from Avenida de América 34 (near metro: Car-
    tagena; map: Madrid). There is a Granada service
    from the Calle de Alenza station.
AutoRes
    Calle de Fernández Shaw 1 (☎ 551 72 00, 501 75
    92; map: Madrid). Operates buses to Extrema-
    dura, western Castilla y León (eg Salamanca,
    Zamora and Tordesillas) and Valencia via eastern
    Castilla-La Mancha (eg Cuenca). The nearest
    metro station is Conde de Casal.
La Sepulvedana
    Paseo de la Florida 11 (☎ 467 00 96; map:
    Madrid). Operates buses to Navacerrada, San
    Rafael (near Cercedilla) and La Granja de San
    Ildefonso. Buses for Talavera de la Reina also
    depart from here. The nearest metro station is
    Príncipe Pío.
Herranz
    These buses to San Lorenzo de El Escorial leave
    from the Intercambiador de Autobuses, a bus
    station below ground level at the Moncloa metro
    station on Calle de la Princesa (☎ 543 36 45;
    map: Madrid). The buses leave from platform 3.
Larrea
    Paseo de la Florida 11 (☎ 530 48 00; map:
    Madrid). Operates two to four daily buses to
    Ávila, and up to 11 to Segovia. The nearest metro
    station is Príncipe Pío.
La Veloz
    Avenida del Mediterráneo 49 (☎ 409 76 02). Has
    regular buses to Chinchón. The nearest metro
    station is Conde de Casal.

Some sample one-way fares include:

Destination	Fare
Alicante	2895 ptas
Barcelona	2880 ptas
Córdoba	1540 ptas
Granada	1875 ptas
Lisbon (Portugal)	4125 ptas
Oviedo	3655 ptas
Salamanca	2210 ptas
Santiago de Compostela	5440 ptas
Sevilla	2680 ptas
Tangier (Morocco)	7000 ptas

Train Trains use two main stations. The more important of them is the new Atocha station south of the city centre. It serves all of southern Spain and many destinations around Madrid. Some services north also depart from here and head via Chamartín, the other station in the north of the city. This is smaller and generally serves destinations north of Madrid, although the rule is not a cast-iron one. Some services to Granada, Algeciras and so forth start in Chamartín, and don't even necessarily stop at Atocha on the way through. Be sure when getting a ticket that you find out which station the train leaves from.

International services to France and Portugal start in Chamartín and do *not* pass through Atocha.

The former Estación del Norte, now known as Príncipe Pío, serves three cercanías lines only.

The main RENFE booking office (☎ 328 90 20), Calle de Alcalá 44, is open Monday to Friday from 9.30 am to 8 pm.

For more details and a sampling of fares see Train in the Getting Around chapter.

Car & Motorcycle Madrid is surrounded by two ring-road systems, the older M-30 and the recently completed M-40, considerably further out. Madrid, like Paris, is a hub from which spokes head out in all directions, and these can be pretty clogged at rush hour (around 8 to 10 am, 2 pm, 4 to 5 pm and 8 to 9 pm). Sunday night, especially on the highways from the south, can also be bad. If you intend to hitch, get well out of town. Choose a town just out of Madrid on the highway of your choice and try from there.

Rental The big-name car rental agencies have offices all over Madrid. Avis, Budget, Europcar, Hertz and Atesa/EuroDollar have booths at the airport. A few central locations include:

Atesa/EuroDollar
  Calle de la Infanta Mercedes 90 (☎ 571 19 31; map: North)
Avis
  Gran Vía (☎ 547 20 48; map: Mal & Ch)
Budget
  Calle de Alcántara 59 (☎ 402 14 80; map: Madrid)
Europcar
  Calle de San Leonardo 8 (☎ 541 88 92; map: España)
Hertz
  Edificio de España, Plaza de España (for reservations ☎ 900-10 01 11; map: España)

You can rent motorbikes from Moto Alquiler (☎ 542 06 57; map: España), Calle de Conde Duque 13, but it's a pricey business. Rates start at 4000 ptas plus 16% IVA per day for a 49 cc Vespino. Rental is from 8 am to 8 pm and you have to leave a refundable deposit of 40,000 ptas. Something like a Yamaha 250 will cost you 10,000 ptas a day plus tax and the deposit is 75,000 ptas.

Car Pooling A good alternative to hitching, and cheaper than buses or trains, is to pre-arrange a ride to your destination. You can do this through Auto Compartido (☎ 522 77 72), Calle de Santa Lucía 15. You tell them where you want to go and approximately when, and they try to match you up with a car. There is an annual membership fee of 1160 ptas, and in addition you pay 5 ptas per km (four to the driver and one to the firm).

Bicycle Karacol Sport (☎ 539 96 33), Paseo de las Delicias 53 (south of Atocha station), rents out mountain bikes. The best offer is a weekend for 4000 ptas from Friday to Monday. There's a refundable deposit of 5000 ptas and you need to leave an original document (passport, driving licence or the like).

Getting Around

Madrid is well served by a decent underground rail system (metro) and an extensive bus service. In addition, you can get from the north to the south of the city quickly by using short-range regional trains (cercanías) between the Atocha and Chamartín railway stations. Taxis are also a viable option and won't do the damage to your pocket you may have come to expect in other European capital cities.

The Airport Barajas airport is linked to the city centre by a special bus leaving from an underground station in Plaza de Colón. You can also pick it up at a stop next to the Avenida de América metro station. Using a combination of this stop and the metro you can dodge much of the city-centre traffic, as well as avoid the five minute walk from the bus terminal to the Colón metro station – a pain if you have a lot of luggage. The fare is 360 ptas and buses leave every 12 to 15 minutes. Allow about half an hour in average traffic conditions.

A taxi from the centre will cost you about 2400 ptas depending on traffic and how much luggage you have.

Bus An extensive bus system operates throughout Madrid and outlying suburbs. Unless you buy season passes, you can get tickets on the bus or at most tobacconists. A single ride costs 130 ptas, or a Bono-bus ticket of 10 rides 645 ptas. The main advantage of the bus is that it lets you see what you are passing while getting about Madrid. For the newcomer, however, the metro (see below) is generally more straightforward.

Monthly or season passes (abonos) only make sense if you are staying long-term and using local transport frequently. You need to get an ID card (carnet) from metro stations or tobacconists (estancos). Take a passport-sized photo and your passport or public transport photocard. A monthly ticket for central Madrid (Zona A) costs 4025 ptas and

is valid for unlimited travel on bus, metro and cercanías.

Twenty night bus lines (búhos) operate from midnight to 6 am. They run from Puerta del Sol and Plaza de la Cibeles.

Information booths can be found at Puerta del Sol, Plaza de Callao and Plaza de la Cibeles. Or call ☎ 409 99 00. Route maps are available from the tourist offices.

Metro The metro is a fast, efficient and safe way to navigate Madrid and generally easier than coming to grips with bus routes. It operates from about 6.30 am to 1.30 am and you can buy tickets from booths or machines. A single ride (as many changes as you like) costs 130 ptas. A ticket for 10 rides costs 645 ptas; you can share these tickets. As noted with the buses, the monthly and other seasonal tickets are only worthwhile if you plan a long stay in the capital. This book contains a colour map of the entire metro system.

If you've been to London, you'll notice an odd point of convergence here: people take their queuing to the right on escalators surprisingly seriously here!

Cercanías The short-range regional trains go as far afield as Toledo, Segovia, El Escorial and so on. They also serve some of the outer Madrid suburbs and the rest of the Comunidad de Madrid, and are handy for making a quick north-south hop between Atocha and Chamartín main-line train stations (with stops at Nuevos Ministerios and in front of the Biblioteca Nacional on Paseo de los Recoletos only). A direct link between Chamartín, Atocha and Príncipe Pío stations, the so-called Pasillo Verde (Green Corridor), opened up in mid-1996. Metro tickets are no good on these lines, even if travelling between Atocha and Chamartín. A cercanías ticket between these stations costs 130 ptas.

Car & Motorcycle As Latin cities go, Madrid is not the most hair-raising to drive in, although there is a fair amount of horn-honking, nippy manoeuvring, sloppy lane recognition and general 'madness' to get used to. Avoid peak hours, when the whole city heaves to the masses struggling to and from work. From about 2 to 4 pm the streets are dead. Once in the city, search for a car park or, if you are not fazed by the likelihood of getting a fine, the nearest likely-looking parking space. Driving from sight to sight within Madrid is pointless.

Most of central Madrid is governed by the Operación de Regulación de Aparcamiento (ORA) parking system. This means that, apart from designated loading zones, no-parking areas and the like, all parking positions that appear legitimate in fact are only so for people with yearly permits, or coupons obtainable from tobacconists. Some 300 parking officers stick about 12,000 fines on cars without permits every day. However, action is taken only on about 2500 and fines are rarely paid. Few locals bother buying the permits or coupons any more. The authorities are at a loss what to do about central Madrid's parking congestion – double-parking is as common as the wheel itself – so you can get away with quite a lot. However, if you park in a designated no-parking area, you risk being towed. Double-parking is also risky in this way if you intend to wander far from your vehicle. Should your car be disappeared, call the Grúa Municipal (city towing service) on ☎ 345 00 50. Recovering the car can cost around 10,000 ptas.

If you wish to play it safe, there are plenty of parking stations across the city, starting at about 200 ptas an hour and a little less for each subsequent hour.

For details on vehicle rental, see Getting There & Away above and the Getting Around chapter.

Taxi By European standards, taxis are inexpensive and well regulated. You can pick up a cab at ranks throughout town or simply flag one down. Flag fall is 170 ptas, and you should make sure the driver turns the meter on. The fare from Barajas airport to Plaza de Colón should be no more than 2000 ptas, while the trip from Chamartín train station to the same square will be about 1000 ptas. There are several supplementary charges, usually posted up inside the taxi. They include 350 ptas for going to the airport, 150 ptas for running to rail or bus stations, 150 ptas between 11 pm and 6 am and also on public holidays, as well as 50 ptas for each piece of luggage.

Warning If you have a rental car in Madrid, take extra care. Groups of delinquents are known to zero in on them occasionally, puncturing a tyre and then robbing the driver when s/he acts to change it. This is reportedly a particular problem on the road from the airport to the centre of town.

Comunidad de Madrid

Covering an area of about 8000 sq km, the region around Madrid counts some two million people. Sealed off to the north and west by the Sierra de Guadarrama, it can effectively be considered a part of what was once known as Castilla la Nueva (New Castile).

The capital itself continues to spread into the Comunidad, converting former villages into drab suburbs or simply creating new ones. Through that growing urban sprawl radiate highways to the rest of the country, passing a handful of interesting places within easy one-day striking distance.

To the south lie Aranjuez and Chinchón. The former is the site of one of the great royal palaces that Madrid's rulers created for themselves; Chinchón is a charming village centred on a classic old Castilian plaza.

Heading east towards Guadalajara on the Autovía de Aragón, the old university of Alcalá de Henares is a quick train ride away from Madrid. A slower journey by train (but quick enough by car on the road to Ávila) is the magnificent royal residence town of El Escorial. Nearby is the more dubious monument to Franco, the Valle de los Caídos. Both lie in the Sierra de Guadarrama, a low mountain range that runs from south-west to north-east, marking the length of the Comunidad's border with Castilla y León. Further north there is plenty of scope for walking – and in winter, with luck, a bit of low-grade skiing.

The telephone code for the Comunidad de Madrid is ☎ 91, the same as for the capital itself.

SAN LORENZO DE EL ESCORIAL & AROUND

Sheltering against a protective wall of the Sierra de Guadarrama, the majestic palace-and-monastery complex of San Lorenzo de El Escorial serves today for ordinary *madrileños* as a focal point for escape from the pressure-cooker atmosphere of the

HIGHLIGHTS

- Spending a day at the splendid El Escorial
- Long lunch with suckling pig at Mesón Cuevas del Vino in Chinchón
- A ride on the Strawberry Train (Tren de la Fresa) to Aranjuez
- Walks – or even a little skiing! – in the Sierra de Guadarrama

capital, just as it once did for kings and sycophants of old. At just over 1000 metres above sea level, and protected from the worst of the winter's icy northern winds, the site enjoys a mild and exceptionally healthy climate.

Kings and princes have a habit, before they enter important battles, of promising rather extravagant offerings to God, the angels and saints in return for their help in winning said encounter. Felipe II was no different before the Battle of St Quentin against the French on St Lawrence's day, 10 August 1557. Felipe's victory was decisive, and in thanks he ordered the construction in the saint's name of the San Lorenzo complex, above the little town of El Escorial. A huge monastery, royal palace, and mausoleum for Felipe's parents, Carlos I and Isabel, were raised, largely under the watchful eye of the architect Juan de Herrera. The austere style reflects Felipe's own severe outlook on

life and desire not to be distracted by over-ornamentation. To the academics, El Escorial is a key to understanding developments in Spanish architecture over the subsequent two centuries.

The palace-monastery soon became known as an important intellectual centre, with a burgeoning library and art collection and even a laboratory where local and foreign scientists could dabble in a little alchemy. Felipe II himself died in El Escorial on 13 September 1598. Various additions were made in the following centuries. In 1854 the monks of the Hieronymite order

which had occupied the monastery from the beginning were obliged to leave, to be replaced 30 years later by Augustinians.

The tourist office (☎ 890 15 54) is at Calle de Floridablanca 10 and is open Monday to Friday from 10 am to 2 pm and 3 to 4.45 pm, and Saturday from 10 am to 1.45 pm.

The Monastery

The main entrance lies on the west side. Above the gateway a statue of St Lawrence stands watch, holding a symbolic gridiron, the instrument of his martyrdom. Indeed, the overall shape of the monastery complex recalls the same object. By this gate you enter the austere **Patio de los Reyes**, so-called for the statues of the six kings of Judah. Directly ahead lies the equally restrained **basílica**. As you enter, look up and you'll notice the highly unusual flat vaulting below the choir stalls before the entrance to the main body of the church. Once inside, head off left to view Benvenuto Cellini's beautiful white Carrara marble statue of Christ crucified, carved in 1576.

The marble and bronze reredos behind the high altar is rich in decoration, largely the work of Italian artists. Leone and Pompei Leoni are among them, and they also did the bronze statue groups on either side of the altar. On the left are Carlos I and family; to the right, Felipe II, three of his wives and his eldest son Prince Don Carlos.

When you exit the church, follow the signs to the ticket office *(taquilla)* for the remainder of what is open to the public. You will

have little choice about the order in which you visit the monastery and palace quarters, so just follow the arrows.

After buying your tickets, you first head downstairs in the north-eastern corner of the complex, the general area of the Palacio de los Austrias, to inspect the **Museo de Arquitectura** and, subsequently, the **Museo de Pintura**. The former covers in some detail (in Spanish) the story of how the complex was built, while the latter contains a range of largely Italian, Spanish and Flemish art of the 16th and 17th centuries.

At this point you are obliged to head upstairs again into a gallery around the eastern protuberance of the complex known as the Palacio de Felipe II. These apartments are richly decorated with all manner of paintings, maps and exquisite woodcarvings (some of the doorways and furniture are particularly fine).

From here you descend to the 17th century

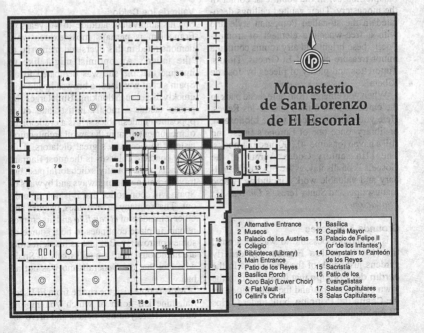

Monasterio de San Lorenzo de El Escorial

1 Alternative Entrance	11 Basílica
2 Museos	12 Capilla Mayor
3 Palacio de los Austrias	13 Palacio de Felipe II
4 Colegio	(or 'de los Infantes')
5 Biblioteca (Library)	14 Downstairs to Panteón
6 Main Entrance	de los Reyes
7 Patio de los Reyes	15 Sacristía
8 Basílica Porch	16 Patio de los
9 Coro Bajo (Lower Choir)	Evangelistas
& Flat Vault	17 Salas Capitulares
10 Cellini's Christ	18 Salas Capitulares

Panteón de los Reyes, where almost all Spain's monarchs since Carlos I lie interred with their spouses. The royal corpses lie in magnificent gilded marble coffins in rather subdued baroque magnificence. It appears there is not a lot of room left to add to their number.

Backtracking a little, you find yourself heading into the **Panteón de los Infantes**, whose nine vaults were built in the 19th century. Here lie buried *infantes* (an infante is the second son of the monarchs), princes and childless queens. Don Juan de Austria (better known to Anglo-Saxon ears as Don John of Austria), victor over the Turks at the Battle of Lepanto, lies beneath a magnificent memorial in the fifth vault. Maria Teresa of Austria is buried in the third vault. Perhaps most intriguing – tasteless even? – is the carousel-style mausoleum for princes who died as infants.

Stairs lead up from the Patio de los Evangelistas up to the **Salas Capitulares** (chapterhouses) in the south-east corner of the monastery. Their vaulted ceilings decorated in the so-called Pompeian style and with a free-wheeling element of trompe-l'oeil, these bright and airy rooms contain a minor treasure chest of El Grecos, Titians, Tintorettos and plenty of pieces by José de Ribera.

When you emerge from here, head back to the entrance before the Patio de los Reyes. Here you can gain access to the **biblioteca**, or library, once one of Europe's finest and still a haven for some 40,000 precious books. The 11th century Codex Aureus of the Gospels is on display, as are other extraordinary and valuable works, including Arabic manuscripts and Santa Teresa's *Libro de las Fundaciones*.

Grounds & Annexes

It is sometimes possible to wander around the **Huerta de los Frailes**, the orderly gardens just south of the monastery. In the **Jardín del Príncipe** that leads down to the town of El Escorial (and the train station) is the **Casita del Príncipe**, built under Carlos III for his heir.

Following Paseo de Carlos III, the road to Ávila, out of town, you pass first on the left the entrance to La Herrería, in the grounds of which stands La Silla de Felipe – a seat, carved of stone, from which Felipe would observe the construction of his monastery. A little further on is the **Casita de Arriba**, another 18th century neoclassical gem from the hands of Juan de Villanueva, who was also responsible for the Casita del Príncipe.

Opening Times & Tickets

San Lorenzo is open Tuesday to Sunday from 10 am to 6 pm (to 5 pm from October to 31 March). Entry costs 850 ptas (350 ptas for students). Only the basilica can be visited free of charge. The price includes a guided tour of the *panteones* and the Palacio de los Austrias if you want to tag along.

The Casita de Arriba and Casita del Príncipe generally open to the public only in August and over Easter, from 10 am to 6.45 pm. Even then they are closed on Monday.

Valle de los Caídos

Spain's ambivalent attitude to 40 years of Francoism is perhaps most expressively demonstrated in this oversized memorial to 'the fallen'. An optimist might like to imagine that the site was dedicated to all Spain's civil war dead; a browse inside will quickly dispel such thinking. Built largely by prison labour – mostly leftists and other opposition undesirables – it is a crude piece of monumentalism in the awful architectural taste of this century's great dictators. This flaky concrete colossus is the most flagrant reminder of the country's dictatorial past, but travellers along the highways and byways of Spain will soon notice that it is not the only one. That so many street names, plaques and other reminders of *el caudillo* and his cronies remain in place continues to be a source of some controversy. But just as his detractors are numerous, there are still many in Spain who feel that the Generalísimo was not all bad.

Most people visit the shrine from El Escorial, nine km north of which you hit the turn-off. Here you buy tickets and drive six km more to the shrine. You are not supposed to stop en route. There is something frankly spooky about the subterranean basilica, and little, artistically, to recommend it. By the altar lies Franco himself. Also buried here is 'José Antonio', a name once known to all Spaniards. Before the civil war, José Antonio Primo de Rivera, son of the 1920s dictator Miguel Primo de Rivera, led the Falange, the party that later formed the fascist political component of Franco's Nationalist movement. Executed in Alicante by the Republicans in late 1936, he became a martyr figure for the Nationalists.

You can also drive up to the base of the enormous cross above the basilica, or catch a cable car (funicular) if it's in operation. The views are splendid.

The site is open daily from 10 am to 6 pm. Entry is 650 ptas per person. The funicular normally operates from 10.30 am to 2.10 pm and 4 to 5.40 pm, but was out of action at the time of writing. About the only way there if you don't have a vehicle is to get the daily Herranz bus from El Escorial (see below).

Places to Stay & Eat

There is really no need to stay in El Escorial, although it's a pleasant enough overnight stop. About the cheapest place to stay is *Hostal Malagón* (☎ 890 15 76), Calle de San Francisco 2, with singles/doubles going for 2000/3500 ptas. In much the same category and located on a pretty square is the *Hostal Vasco* (☎ 890 16 19), Plaza de Santiago.

There are a few places along Calle de Juan de Toledo, the road for El Valle de los Caídos. The best value is *Hostal Cristina* (☎ 890 19 61), at No 6, where you are looking at about 4000/5500 ptas.

Calle de Floridablanca is lined with a trio of rather expensive upper mid-level places, while the top establishment is the *Hotel Victoria Palace* (☎ 890 15 11; fax 890 12 48), at Calle de Juan de Toledo 4. Doubles here cost around 15,000 ptas in summer.

The eating is not the greatest in San Lorenzo de El Escorial. With no permanent local clientele to please, most places have a rather slack attitude to quality but an all-too-

keen eye for your coppers. Keep well away from the places along Calle de Floridablanca, generally a tourist rip-off par excellence. *Restaurante El Candil*, on the corner of Calle de Reina Victoria and Plaza de Jacinto Benavente, does a pretty good menú del día. It's especially pleasant when they set up tables outside overlooking the lower half of the square.

Getting There & Away

Bus The Herranz bus company runs up to 30 services a day from the Intercambiador de Autobuses at the Moncloa metro station in Madrid to San Lorenzo de El Escorial. Only about 10 run on Sunday and holidays. The same company (office on Calle de Reina Victoria) runs a bus to El Valle de los Caídos (see below) at 3.30 pm from El Escorial, returning at 5.30 pm. This bus does not run on Monday.

Train Up to 20 sluggish *cercanías* trains (line C-8a) serve El Escorial from Atocha station (via Chamartín) in Madrid. Seven of these go on to Ávila and one to León. The station is in the town of El Escorial itself, quite a hike from San Lorenzo and its hamlet. You can walk (about two km uphill) or catch a local bus linking the two.

Car & Motorcycle From Madrid take the A-6 and follow the exits. From El Escorial, the M-505 winds its way across the low western ranges of the Sierra de Guadarrama to Ávila – a pretty drive. There are some wonderful views back across San Lorenzo de Escorial shortly before you top the rise.

SOUTH OF MADRID
Aranjuez

A refreshing patch of lively green in sun-drenched central Spain, Aranjuez still plays its centuries-old role as a natural haven from the capital, 48 km to the north. The main difference is that it's no longer a private royal playground and the privilege has been extended to all and sundry. The area is also an important breeding ground for butterflies – so important that when the N-IV *autovía* was built, the engineers diverted it in a dogleg around the heart of the breeding ground!

Information The tourist office (☎ 891 04 27), at Plaza de San Antonio 9, opens Monday to Friday from 10 am to 2.30 pm. It has useful information posted in the window too. You'll find several banks in the town centre. The postcode for Aranjuez is 28039.

Palacio Real When Felipe II built his summer palace here on the lush banks of the Tajo in the late 16th century, there had already been a country residence on the site since the 14th century. What was in Felipe's day a modest 20 room affair, much of it later destroyed by fire, was to become under his successors the exorbitant 18th century conceit that stands today – with more than 300 rooms. Inspired in part by Versailles – an ever-popular model with monarchs throughout Europe – it is filled with a cornucopia of ornamentation. Of all the monarchs who spent time here, Carlos III and Isabel II left the greatest mark.

It appears Carlos III had a new portrait done of himself every year (one hangs in an apartment here); unwilling, however, to waste time on the exercise, he had court painters copy the first one each year. He seems to have taken more interest in interior decorating. The Sala de Porcelana (Porcelain Room) is an extravagant affair, its walls covered in individually hand-crafted porcelain figures in the Japanese style (more than vaguely reminiscent of a similar chamber in Madrid's Palacio Real). It took two years to complete the decoration. The Sala Fumadora is almost as remarkable – a florid imitation of an Alhambra interior, complete with Arabic inscriptions in stucco and an intricate stalactite ceiling carved in wood.

Gardens After the compulsory guided tour of the palace, a stroll in the gardens makes for a relaxing antidote; the English elms that predominate are a reminder that the gardens are more than just a happy accident. The **Jardín de la Isla**, right by the palace and

forming a tranquil island in a bend in the Tajo, is nice enough, but the more extensive **Jardín del Príncipe** along the road to Chinchón is more appealing.

Within its shady perimeter lie two other man-made attractions. The **Casa de Marinos** contains a few royal pleasure boats of days gone by. Further away in the direction of Chinchón is the **Casa del Labrador**, a rather tasteless royal jewellery box crammed to the rafters with gold, silver, silk and some second-rate art. Built for Carlos IV in 1805, it is the final Versailles touch, an attempt to emulate the Petit Trianon.

Entry The Palacio Real and the other attractions are open Tuesday to Sunday from 10 am to 6.25 pm (an hour less in winter). Entry to the palace (guided tours only) costs 650 ptas. It's free for EU citizens on Wednesday. The Casa del Labrador costs 425 ptas and the Casa de Marinos 325 ptas (or 600 ptas for both). The gardens (the palace ticket covers all the gardens) open from 8 am to 8.30 pm in summer (to 6.30 pm in winter). Should you be feeling weary, you can pay 500 ptas to be taken around the grounds on a Disney-style mini-train. You can get on and off wherever you want.

Places to Stay & Eat There is no need and little temptation to stay in Aranjuez, but there are six hotels and a camping ground. The latter, *Camping Soto del Castillo* (☎ 891 13 95), is located between the N-IV and the Río Tajo. It opens from March to October and they charge 750 ptas per person, tent space and car. The cheapest of the hotels is *Hostal Rusiñol* (☎ 891 01 55), Calle San Antonio 26, a couple of blocks from the tourist office and with singles/doubles for 1750/2600 ptas. It also has a bar and restaurant. On the food front, many restaurants are cheekily expensive. The unlikely-sounding *Frankfurt II*, Calle de Almíbar 58, has an OK set meal for 900 ptas. *La Rana Verde*, Calle de la Reina 1, on the Tajo, is the town's best-known restaurant, and a full meal will set you back at least 3000 ptas.

Getting There & Away The easiest way to reach Aranjuez is by cercanías train (line C-3) from Madrid's Atocha station. There are up to 42 runs a day. You can also get here by train from Toledo. If you want to use the bus, the AISA company has up to 17 daily services from the Estación Sur de Autobuses in Madrid. Empresa Samar also has a few. There are two buses a day to Chinchón.

Tren de la Fresa A delightful option available from mid-April through to October is the Strawberry Train. This day excursion sees you seated aboard a nicely done-up steam train with attendants in period dress serving you up free wads of – you guessed it – strawberries. The 2900 ptas price tag includes the return trip from Atocha station in Madrid, a bus transfer to the centre of Aranjuez and admission to monuments. Information and timetables are available at Atocha station.

Chinchón

Home of a well-known brew of *anís*, the aniseed-based heart-starter favoured by not a few Spaniards at breakfast, Chinchón is an agreeable little settlement 50 km south-east of Madrid. The focal point is the pretty Plaza Mayor, ringed by centuries-old two and three-tiered balconies, most of which now accommodate dining madrileños. The plaza also doubles as the town's bullring. Just to the north of the plaza lies the 16th century Iglesia de la Asunción, containing what is said to be an *Assumption* by Goya. A few steps south of the square on Calle del Generalísimo is what was an Augustinian monastery. This building went up in the 18th century, and now serves as a *parador* (☎ 894 08 36). A couple of km south of the town centre you can see castle ruins – for a long time you could go and taste the Chinchón anís in a couple of distilleries here, but they are now closed. A couple of distilleries operate on the eastern edge of town. If you want to buy a bottle of the real McCoy, head for the Alcoholera de Chinchón on Plaza Mayor.

Semana Santa sees Chinchón convert itself into the set for lavish Easter processions, to the extent that Roman soldiers end up by far outnumbering the Guardia Civil.

The *Hostal Chinchón* (☎ 893 53 98), Calle de José Antonio 12, is a pleasant old place with an internal patio just off Plaza Mayor. Singles/doubles with own bath and TV cost 4000/6000 ptas. They also serve up modestly priced raciones. You can scout around the several restaurants right on Plaza Mayor, or head away from the centre. A special but pricey option is the *Mesón Cuevas del Vino*, Calle de Benito Hortelano 13. This cavernous bodega, lined with huge wine barrels and extremely popular with weekenders from Madrid, serves solid Castilian food, but you won't get away for less than 3000 ptas per person.

Buses regularly run between Chinchón and Madrid (No 337 from Calle del Conde de Casal). There are two a day to Aranjuez.

ALCALÁ DE HENARES

A little way north of the Roman town of Complutum (of which nothing remains) and 35 km east of Madrid on the N-II to Zaragoza, Alcalá de Henares entered a period of greatness when Cardinal Cisneros founded a university here in 1486. Now centred on a much-restored Renaissance building in the centre of what is virtually a satellite of Madrid, the university was long one of the country's main seats of learning. In 1836, however, Alcalá was dealt a heavy blow with the transfer of the Universidad Complutense to the capital. The rot was only arrested with the reopening of the university in 1977. The town is also dear to the hearts of many Spaniards as the birthplace of the country's literary figurehead, Miguel de Cervantes Saavedra.

A small tourist office (☎ 889 26 94) is just off Plaza de Cervantes, the town's main square, at Callejón de Santa María 1. It opens daily from 10 am to 2 pm and 4 to 6.30 pm.

You can wander through parts of the **universidad** at pretty much any time, but to visit properly you need to turn up between 11 am and 2 pm or 4 and 6 pm. The ornate entrance, facing on to Plaza de San Diego, is in the plateresque style. Of particular interest inside are the Paraninfo (auditorium), with a fine *mudéjar* ceiling, and the Capilla de San Ildefonso, just to the right of the main university entrance. The latter contains the tomb of Cardinal Cisneros. Guided visits take place at regular intervals and cost 200 ptas.

Predictably, Cervantes' birthplace has been 'found' – at Calle Mayor 48, on the corner of Calle de la Imagen. A relatively new building, the **Museo Casa Natal de Miguel de Cervantes** is nicely enough filled with period furniture and bits and pieces relating to the life of Don Quijote's creator. It opens Tuesday to Friday from 10.15 am to 1.45 pm and 4.15 to 6.45 pm, and on Saturday and Sunday from 10.15 am to 1.45 pm only. Calle Mayor is a pleasant, arcaded boulevard.

Being so close to Madrid, you should have no need to stay, but the *Hostal Jacinto* (☎ 889 14 32), Paseo de la Estación 2, is handy for the train and charges 2000/3600 ptas for singles/doubles with shower.

Those with rumbling tummies could try *El Gran Mesón*, next door to the tourist office on Callejón de Santa María. Housed in the former Convento de Santa Catalina, it is one of several such atmospheric *mesones* scattered about the centre of town. The *Hostería del Estudiante* is an expensive but charming restaurant backing onto the Paraninfo in the main university building.

The easiest way to get to Alcalá from Madrid (or Guadalajara) is by one of the frequent cercanías trains shuttling between Madrid (Chamartín) and Guadalajara.

South of Alcalá

Those with cars might be tempted by a quick excursion to **Nuevo Baztán**, 21 km south. In the early 18th century, José Benito Churriguera was instructed to lay out a village and design its main buildings in an early Spanish attempt at town planning. It's virtually a ghost town now, and Churriguera's church and neighbouring palace are in poor shape. He did the *retablos* inside the church, which is usually closed.

Empresa Argabus (☎ 433 91 49) runs

buses (No 261) to and from Calle del Conde de Casal in Madrid (three a day, Monday to Friday; two on Saturday; and one on Sunday). The same company also has a daily bus to Alcalá de Henares at 7 am and from Alcalá (Calle de Luis Vives) at 3.15 pm.

The mobile might consider heading east along the M-219 via Olmeda de las Fuentes to cross over the regional border with Guadalajara province. Here you are near La Alcarria and its principal town Pastrana (see the Castilla-La Mancha chapter).

SIERRA DE GUADARRAMA

The hill country of the Sierra de Guadarrama forms a getaway for madrileños but is little frequented by foreign visitors. Longer-term visitors to the capital may care to explore it a little, popping into the odd *pueblo* and doing a little walking to relieve some of the big-city stress.

Colmenar Viejo

There's not an awful lot to see in this town of 25,000 people, now virtually a satellite of Madrid. But if you happen to be in Madrid in the first days of February, you might want to get up here to witness the colourful Vaquilla, a fiesta with pagan origins dating back to the 13th century and vaguely reminiscent of some Chinese festivals. A highly ornamental 'heifer' is made each year to be pranced about the town before being 'slaughtered' by 'toreros' dressed in Andalucían style. Dropped during the sober Franco years, it is an increasingly popular festival.

Manzanares El Real

Not far from Colmenar Viejo, before the granite mountain backdrop of La Pedriza, lies the charming little 15th century Castillo de los Mendoza in the town of Manzanares El Real. The castle is open Tuesday to Sunday from 10 am to 2 pm and 4 to 7 pm (10 am to 5 pm in winter). The area is a pretty and popular escape hatch for weekenders.

There are several trails into the nearby Pedriza park, at least one of which leads to cool freshwater pools. Rock climbers have a wealth of options here, with some 1500 climbing routes scattered throughout the park and catering to most levels. For advice, try the information booth in the park or the Federación Madrileña de Montaña (☎ 593 80 74), Calle de Apodaca 16, in Madrid.

The cheapest place to stay in Manzanares is the rather pricey *Hostal El Tranco* (☎ 853 00 63), Calle del Tranco 4, which has good singles/doubles for 5500/7700 ptas. Buses run from Plaza de Castilla in Madrid.

Cercedilla

The mountain town of Cercedilla and the area surrounding it are a popular weekend base for hikers and mountain bikers. Several trails are marked out through the Sierra, the main one known as the Cuerda Larga or Cuerda Castellana. This is a forest trail that takes in 55 peaks between the Puerto de Somosierra in the north and Puerto de la Cruz Verde in the south-west. It would take days to complete, but shorter walks include day excursions up the Valle de la Fuenfría and a climb up Monte de Siete Picos.

Mountain bikers could take their bikes up on the local train to Puerto de los Cotos (a lovely ride in itself), ride across to the Bola del Mundo (in good winters the top end of Guadarrama's best ski piste) and pedal downhill to Cercedilla via the well-known Camino de Schmit.

You can get more information at the Centro de Información Valle de la Fuenfría (☎ 852 22 13), a couple of km from Cercedilla train station.

If you prefer not to strike out on your own, you can participate in group hikes, mountain bike rides or rock-climbing trips. These can be organised through the Puerto de Navacerrada ski-lift and sports operators, Deporte y Montaña, by calling ☎ 852 14 35. Alternatively approach their reps at Gran Vía 42 (☎ 580 27 31) in Madrid. A word of warning: this organisation was slated for privatisation in late 1996, so all could change.

Accommodation is scarce in this area, so you are best attacking this as a day trip from Madrid. Otherwise, be prepared to camp along the trail if you are doing the Cuerda Larga.

Northern Guadarrama

If you want to avoid the crowds that tend to congregate around Cercedilla, the more adventurous could try for quieter walking further north along the Sierra. One possibility is a nice 10 km plateau trail that connects Canencia with Garganta de los Montes (Valle de Lozoya). You're looking at about three hours hiking each way. Continental Auto has buses from Plaza de Castilla in Madrid to Canencia (655 ptas). You could stay at *Hostal Colorines* (☎ 868 74 71), Calle Real, in Canencia.

Skiing in the Guadarrama

Skiing just 60 km from Madrid? Not the first image that springs to mind when one contemplates the idea of central Spain, perhaps, but when the snow falls, as it did with a vengeance in the winter of 1995-96, you can shoot down the pistes of Navacerrada and Cotos, just on the border with Segovia province, north-west of Madrid. Snowless years are common and the available pistes not extensive, but it's a popular business with madrileños on the weekend, when the area should be avoided. Navacerrada is the main centre and there are 13 km of mostly easy – and frustratingly short – runs. The best is the Bola del Mundo, but on the weekend the 40 year old ski lift is overwhelmed. A daily ski-lift pass costs 3200 ptas.

You're not likely to want to stay, especially as the place is not fully equipped as a resort. There are a few hotels in the town of Navacerrada and also at the Puerto de Navacerrada if you really want to hang around more than a day.

It's possible to reach Navacerrada by train from Cercedilla or bus from Madrid (station at Paseo de la Florida 11) and neighbouring towns. If driving, note that available parking is generally full by 9 am on weekends when the snow is good.

NORTH OF MADRID
Palacio Real de El Pardo

Just north of Madrid is the nearest of several regal escape hatches from the pressure cooker of the capital. This one in fact ended up as Franco's favoured residence, although the present building served Felipe II in the same fashion as far back as 1558. Carlos III used to rotate between El Pardo, El Escorial, Aranjuez and La Granja de San Ildefonso, assigning a season to each and pursuing his passion for hunting. Of the art displayed inside, the several hundred tapestries stand out, particularly those based on cartoons by Goya.

About 500 metres away from the palace is the **Casita del Príncipe**, a rather elaborate 'cottage' built for Carlos IV in 1786, while he was still heir apparent. At the time of writing it was closed for restoration.

The palace is open Monday to Saturday from 10.30 am to 6 pm, and Sunday and holidays from 10 am to 1.40 pm. Admission, which also covers the Casita del Príncipe, is 650 ptas (250 ptas for students); it's free for EU citizens on Wednesday.

An outing to El Pardo could be neatly combined with a lunch stop. You'll find no shortage of busy restaurants around Plaza del Caudillo (just to remind you of the great man).

The palace and grounds are out along the Carretera de El Pardo, about 15 km north-west of central Madrid. Bus No 601 leaves every 10 minutes from a stop on Paseo de Moret, near the Moncloa metro station in Madrid.

Alcobendas

At Alcobendas, just 17 km north of Madrid along the N-I to Burgos, the only thing of interest is the Museo Interactivo de la Ciencia Acciona, in the Parque de Andalucía. Although not the greatest interactive museum in the world, this could be a good one for the kids, especially if you fork out another 200 ptas for the *piscina de la ciencia* (science pool), where little 'uns get wet while learning a few basic science lessons. It opens daily from 11 am to 7 pm (an hour earlier in winter) and entry costs 700 ptas (children 500 ptas). Bus Nos 151, 152, 153, 154 and 157 go to Alcobendas from Plaza de

Who Do You Think You're Kidding, Mr Marshall?

In the unassuming village of Guadalix de la Sierra, seven km west of the Burgos highway and 50 km north of central Madrid, are set some of the most memorable scenes of the 1952 classic movie *Bienvenido Mr Marshall*, directed by Luis García Berlanga. Guadalix starred as the archetypal Spanish pueblo with the name Villar del Río and whitewashed in the Andalucían manner. The townspeople gathered on the great day to greet progress and the Americans, who simply drove straight through town without stopping. These days a *caña* in *Bar La Central* on Plaza Mayor is worthwhile: the walls sport photos from the days when the filming was done. The square looked rather different then – half real and half movie set.

If Berlanga cast a sympathetic eye on the sufferings of the poor towns of 1950s Spain, Guadalix still has plenty of problems. With a population of 4000, the penniless town cannot afford to repair streets and the sewerage system, and the dairy business from which it survived is now in deep crisis, unable to absorb the blows dealt by EU agriculture quotas. ■

Castilla just near Madrid's Chamartín train station.

Buitrago & the Valle de Lozoya

About 15 km short of the Puerto de Somosierra and just off the N-I highway to Burgos stand the picturesque walls of Buitrago, surrounded by a pretty reservoir. The Iglesia de Santa María del Castillo was built in 1321, but largely destroyed in 1936. Now restored, it displays mudéjar and Romanesque elements. There is a modest castle and you can walk along part of the walls. The Museo Picasso contains various autographed bits and pieces given by the artist to his barber, who lived here. You could stay, if need be, at *Hostal Madrid París* (☎ 868 11 26), which has singles/doubles for 2000/3500 ptas. The *Cervecería Plaza* has a huge range of seafood. Regular buses run between Buitrago and Plaza de Castilla in Madrid.

Castilla y León

Roughly taking in the territories of the former kingdom of León and Castilla la Vieja (Old Castile), this vast region offers a string of more or less important cities dotted across often desolate plains. Among the 'musts' are Salamanca, León, Segovia, Ávila and Burgos.

As if to confirm the adage that the exception proves the rule, however, fringe areas provide an enormous contrast to the monotony of 'deep Castilla'. The Leonese side of the Picos de Europa mountains (see the Cantabria & Asturias chapter for details), the Sierra de la Peña de Francia (near Extremadura), the Sierra de Gredos (bordering Castilla-La Mancha) and the Sanabria area (just short of Galicia) are just some of the more obvious such exceptions. Searing summer heat and bitter winter cold further characterise the tendency to extremes in this old heartland of Spain.

For this guide, the region has been roughly divided into four zones, with some of the routes described radiating away from a theoretical starting point of Madrid.

As with most of central Spain, centuries of poverty have left their mark in the area's cuisine. The nippy winter climate and local peasant produce have favoured the development of a variety of meat dishes, and Spaniards readily recognise the region as the best to hunt out roast everything, with *cochinillo* (suckling pig) a particular speciality, above all in Segovia. Roast lamb (*cordero asado*) and kid (*cabrito*) are also reliable favourites. The better wines are produced along the Río Duero; Vega Sicilia is probably the best-known wine label of the whole region.

The South-West

Starting from Madrid and passing through El Escorial, an obvious route suggests itself across the most southerly tract of Castilla y

León, taking in the towns of Ávila, Salamanca and Ciudad Rodrigo, from where the road continues west into Portugal. Along the way, you could detour to the Sierra de Gredos for some mountain walks and the timeless villages of the Sierra de la Peña de Francia, 40 km east of Ciudad Rodrigo.

ÁVILA

Huddled behind its hefty walls at an altitude of 1130 metres, Ávila must be one of the chilliest cities in Spain. Known for its long and bitter winters, it is a remarkable sight for the visitor, and particularly pleasant in summer. Although it's not as captivating as Toledo or even Segovia, day-trippers from

Bay of Biscay

Castilla y León

0   50   100 km

ASTURIAS

Gijón

Costa Verde

Santander

N634

Oviedo

N634

Cangas de Onís

Pola de Lena

Oseja de Sajambre

Espinama

CANTABRIA

Carranza

Bilbao

San Sebastián

A8

Puerto de Somiedo

Riaño

Alto Campóo

Balmaseda

Pedrafita do Cebreiro

A66 N630

Portilla de la Reina

Reinosa

Medina de Pomar

Orduña

PAÍS VASCO

Ponferrada

León

Cervera de Pisuerga

Oña

Miranda de Ebro

Vitoria

NI

O Barco de Valdeorras

Astorga

San Miguel de la Escalada

N611

N627 N623

Nájera

N111

A Rúa

N601

Sahagún

Carrión de los Condes

N120

Burgos

Cartuja de Miraflores

Santo Domingo de la Calzada

Navarrete

Calahorra

LA RIOJA

Ribadelago de Franco

Frómista

Arnedillo

Arnedo

La Puebla de Sanabria

A52

Paredes de Nava

Monzón de Campos

NI

Covarrubias

Salas de los Infantes

Benavente

N610

Palencia

Lerma

PORTUGAL

N122

N630

NVI

Medina de Rioseco

Baños de Cerrato

Santo Domingo de Silos

N111

Zamora

Toro

Simancas

N620

Valladolid

Peñaranda de Duero

N234

Calatañazor

Numancia

Tordesillas

N122

Peñafiel

Aranda de Duero

El Burgo de Osma

Soria

Ledesma

N601

Cuéllar

Ayllón

San Esteban de Gormaz

Berlanga

Almazán

Medina del Campo

Coca

Sepúlveda

Riaza

Salamanca

Peñaranda de Bracamonte

Turégano

Pedraza de la Sierra

Atienza

Medinaceli

Santa María de Huerta

N620

Alba de Tormes

N501

Segovia

La Granja de San Ildefonso

Sigüenza

N211

Ciudad Rodrigo

Valle de Las Batuecas

N630

Ávila

Riofrío

A6

NII

Torija

Cifuentes

Béjar

El Barco de Ávila

N110

Navarredonda

Colmenar Viejo

Alcobendas

Brihuega

Guadalajara

Beteta

CASTILLA-LA MANCHA

Arenas de San Pedro

El Pardo

MADRID

Alcalá de Henares

Pastrana

CASTILLA-LA MANCHA

Escalona

Illescas

COMUNIDAD DE MADRID

NV

Maqueda

Chinchón

History

Madrid should nonetheless arrive early or consider staying overnight to do Ávila justice.

History

One of Hercules' sons, according to myth, supposedly founded Ávila, but the more prosaic truth gives the honour to obscure Iberian tribes, who were soon assimilated into Celtic society and later largely Romanised and Christianised. For almost 300 years, Ávila changed hands regularly between Muslims and Christians, until the fall of Toledo to Alfonso VI in 1085.

In the following centuries, 'Ávila of the Knights' became an important commercial centre. Its well-established noble class was not averse to a skirmish in the wars with the Muslims or, later, in the imperial escapades in Flanders and South America. The edict issued in 1492 expelling all Jews from Spain, followed a century later by moves to get rid of the Moriscos (Christianised Muslims), robbed the city of much of its lifeblood. Meanwhile, Fray Tomás de Torquemada was busy at the end of the 15th century organising the most brutal phase of the Spanish Inquisition. He ended his days in Ávila.

Decades later, Santa Teresa began her difficult mystical journey and the unwelcomed campaign to reform the Carmelites in the same city. By the time Teresa died in 1582, Ávila's golden days were over, as indeed were those of most of Castilla, and the city has only recently begun to shake off the deep slumber of neglect and decay that ensued.

Orientation

The old centre is enclosed by a rough quadrangle of robust walls at the western end of town, with the *catedral* butting into the walls at their eastern extremity. The RENFE train station is about a 10 minute walk east of the cathedral, while the bus station is a little closer, just off the Avenida de Madrid. There are several *hostales* clustered around the cathedral area, and a few others near the train station. The tourist office, post office, telephones and banks are all near the cathedral.

Information

Tourist Office The helpful tourist office (☎ 21 13 87), Plaza de la Catedral 4, has reasonable information on the city and province, and opens Monday to Friday from 10 am to 2 pm and 5 to 8 pm; Saturday from 9 am to 2.30 pm and 4.30 to 8.30 pm; on Sunday from 11 am to 2 pm and 4.30 to 8.30 pm. A municipal tourist information kiosk (☎ 35 71 26) also operates just outside the Puerta de San Vicente.

Money There are several banks in the centre of the old town, most with user-friendly ATMs.

Post & Communications The Correos (post office) and Telefónica (phone office) are nearly next to one another, just in from the Puerta de los Leales. The latter opens Monday to Saturday from 9 am to 2 pm and 5 to 10 pm (closes an hour earlier on Saturday). Ávila's postcode is 05080. The telephone code is ☎ 920.

Medical & Emergency Services The local number for the police is ☎ 25 10 00. In a medical emergency, call the Cruz Roja on ☎ 22 22 22.

Catedral

The double vocation of Ávila's cathedral is symbolised in its menacing granite apse, which actually forms the central bulwark in the east wall of the town, the most open to attack and hence the most heavily fortified.

Around the west side, the main façade betrays the Romanesque origins of what is essentially the earliest Gothic church built in Spain. It also betrays some unhappy 18th century meddling in the main portal. The 13th century northern entrance was transferred to its present position in the 15th century. Inside, the red and white limestone employed in the columns stands out. Worth inspecting is the finely worked walnut of the choir stalls, while the Capilla Mayor boasts a retablo mainly carried out by Pedro de Berruguete in the mid-15th century. Behind the main altar lies buried El Tostado, a 15th century bishop and intellectual, who apart from being of dark complexion (hence the name 'the toasted one'), was apparently a rather short chap. Told in audience by the pope to rise from his knees, El Tostado replied: *'Santidad, no soy más'* ('Your Holiness, there's no more of me').

The Museo Catedralicio contains the usual collection of religious art, including an El Greco and a huge monstrance by Juan de Arfe, grandson of the great monstrance maker Enrique de Arfe.

The cathedral is open daily from 8.30 am to 2 pm and 4 to 7 pm, but the museum opens later and closes a little earlier. Entrance to the museum costs 200 ptas.

Basílica de San Vicente

Lying outside the great fortified gate of the same name, the Romanesque basilica is striking in its subdued elegance. A series of largely Gothic modifications in sober granite contrast with the warm sandstone of the Romanesque original. Work started in the 11th century, supposedly on the site where three martyrs, Vicente and his sisters, were slaughtered by the Romans in the early 4th

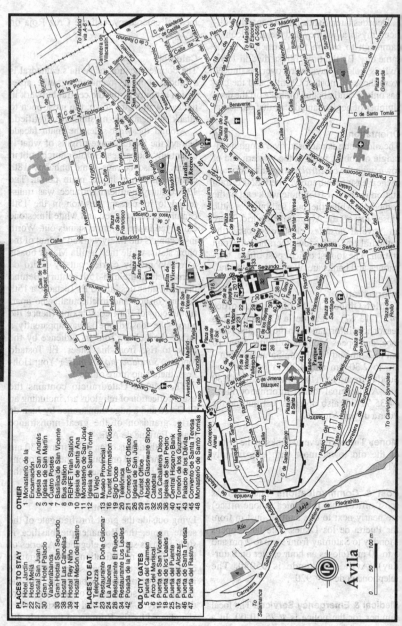

CASTILLA Y LEÓN

PLACES TO STAY
17 Hotel Jardín
22 Hotel Meliá
27 Hostal San Juan
30 Gran Hotel Palacio
     Valderrábanos
33 Gran Hostal San Segundo
39 Hostal Las Cancelas
39 Hostal Rey Niño
44 Hostal Mesón del Rastro

PLACES TO EAT
14 Telepizza
23 Restaurante Doña Guiomar
24 La Alacena
28 Restaurante El Ruedo
34 Restaurante Los Leales
42 Posada de la Fruta

OLD CITY GATES
5 Puerta del Carmen
6 Arco del Mariscal
15 Puerta de San Vicente
18 Puerta de San Pedro
25 Puerta del Puente
37 Puerta del Alcázar
46 Puerta de Santa Teresa
47 Puerta del Rastro

OTHER
1 Monasterio de la
     Encarnación
2 Iglesia de San Andrés
3 Iglesia de San Martín
4 Cuatro Postes
7 Basílica de San Vicente
8 RENFE Train Station
9 Bus Station
10 Iglesia de Santa Ana
11 Iglesia de San José
12 Iglesia de Santo Tomé
     El Viejo
13 Museo Provincial
16 Tourist Information Kiosk
19 Siglo Doce
20 Telefónica
21 Correos (Post Office)
26 Iglesia de San Juan
29 Tourist Office
31 Caside Glassware Shop
35 Los Caballeros Disco
36 Iglesia de San Pedro
40 Central Hispano Bank
41 Torreón de los Guzmanes
43 Palacio de los Dávila
45 Convento de Santa Teresa
48 Monasterio de Santo Tomás

Ávila

0   50   100 m

century. Their sepulchre is a nice piece of Romanesque work. The church is open daily from 10 am to 2 pm and 4 to 7.15 pm. Entry costs 50 ptas. The Parque de San Vicente across the road was, by the way, once the Roman cemetery.

El Real Monasterio de Santo Tomás

A grandiose combination of monastery and royal residence put up in haste by the Reyes Católicos (Catholic Monarchs) Fernando and Isabel in 1482, this is formed by three interconnecting cloisters and the church. The first and smallest of the cloisters is in the so-called Tuscan style, and is the simplest of the three. The church and second cloister (Claustro del Silencio) are Gothic, while the Claustro de los Reyes, where the royal family often resided in summer, is halfway between Gothic and Renaissance in style.

From the Claustro del Silencio you can climb up to the fine if dusty walnut choir stalls in the adjacent church. In the grand tomb in the transept lies Don Juan, son of the Catholic Monarchs, while the retablo by Pedro de Berruguete behind him depicts scenes from the life of St Thomas Aquinas. It is thought the Inquisitor Torquemada is buried in the sacristy. The monastery

---

Torquemada & the Inquisition

In 1483, Fray Tomás de Torquemada was put in charge of the Inquisition in Castilla, Aragón, Cataluña and Valencia. He chose for his head-quarters the Real Monasterio de Santo Tomás in Ávila. Born in Valladolid in 1420, Torquemada was the son of well-placed Jewish *conversos* (converts to Christianity). Converts are sometimes more militant than their co-religionaries, and so it was to prove with this Dominican friar. Nominated by Pope Sixtus IV, Torquemada reorganised the Inquisition's tribunal and embarked on a campaign of terror, cheerfully sending off about 2000 people to burn at the stake and running some 100,000 trials in the 15 years before his death in 1498. Although he often acted in the interests of the Spanish state, his power became so great that he was virtually independent of both the state and the Vatican, and was universally feared. ■

---

complex, about half a km south-east of the cathedral in the new town, is open from 8 am to 1.30 pm and 4 to 8 pm. Entry costs 50 ptas.

In Santa Teresa's Footsteps

The 16th century mystic and ascetic has left her mark all over the city. Born in 1515, she joined the Carmelites 20 years later. Shaken by a vision of hell in 1560 and supported by several spiritual directors, she undertook to reform the Carmelites, an arduous task that led her to found convents of the Carmelitas Descalzas across Spain. She also coopted San Juan de la Cruz (St John of the Cross) to begin a similar reform in the masculine order, a task that earned him several stints incarcerated by the mainstream Carmelites and a good portion of his life in fear of persecution. Santa Teresa's writings were first published in 1588 and proved enormously popular, perhaps partly for the earthy style in which they were composed.

The **Convento de Santa Teresa** was built over the saint's birthplace in 1636, and one of the church's chapels shows what is said to have been the saint's little playground. In the tiny museum next door (through the souvenir shop) are a few bits of memorabilia and relics, including Teresa's ring finger and bone fragments of San Juan de la Cruz. The museum is open from 9.30 am to 1.30 pm and 3.30 to 7.30 pm, while the church stays open about half an hour longer in the morning and evening. Nearby, the **Iglesia de San Juan** on Plaza de la Victoria contains the baptismal font in which Teresa was baptised.

A five minute walk east of the cathedral lies the **Convento de San José** (Convento de las Madres), the first convent Teresa founded (1562). Its museum is replete with Teresian memorabilia, and is open daily from 10 am to 2 pm and 4 to 7 pm (shorter hours in winter). Entry costs 50 ptas.

North of the city walls, the **Convento de la Encarnación** is where Santa Teresa fully took on the monastic life and launched her reform movement. A Renaissance complex modified in the 18th century, the convent contains further mementos of her life.

City Walls

With its eight monumental gates and 88 towers, Ávila's *muralla* (city wall) is one of the best preserved medieval defensive perimeters in the world. Raised between the 11th and 12th centuries on the remains of earlier efforts by the Muslims and Romans, the wall has been much restored and modified with various Gothic and Renaissance touches. The most impressive gates, the Puerta de San Vicente and Puerta del Alcázar, are flanked by towers more than 20 metres high and stand either side of the cathedral's apse, which forms the central defensive point of the eastern walls. It is possible to climb up on to the walls at the Puerta del Alcázar. In the off season you can do this from 10.30 am to 2.30 pm only, but from April to September they are accessible from 11 am to 1.30 pm and 5 to 7.30 pm. Admission costs 100 ptas.

Churches & Mansions

Ávila is besprinkled with churches of interest. The Iglesia de Santo Tomé El Viejo on Plaza de Italia is a small Romanesque church built in the 12th century, and long since fallen out of use. Built a little later and since subjected to several less than fortunate alterations is the Iglesia de San Pedro on Plaza de Santa Teresa. North of the old city is the Iglesia de San Andrés, built in the 11th century and the oldest church in Ávila. Most churches open daily from about 10 am to 2 pm and 4 to 7 pm.

The city also has its fair share of noble mansions, some of which now serve as upper-end hotels. The Palacio de los Velada and Palacio de los Valderrábano, on Plaza de la Catedral, fall into this category. The Palacio de los Dávila, near the Puerta del Rastro, belonged to one of the city's most illustrious fighting noble families.

In the Palacio de los Deanes, on Plaza de Nalvillos, you'll find the Museo Provincial, with mainly archaeological displays from the region. The museum is open Tuesday to Saturday from 11 am to 2 pm and 5 to 7.30 pm, and on Sunday from 11 am to 2 pm only. Entry costs 200 ptas.

Los Cuatro Postes

Just north-west of the city on the road to Salamanca, this spot not only affords fine views of Ávila's walls, but marks the place where Santa Teresa and her brother were caught by their uncle as they tried to run away from home. They were hoping to achieve martyrdom at the hands of the Moorish infidels.

Organised Tours

Guided tours of the town in Spanish are organised, usually at the weekend, by Ávila Monumental (☎ 25 30 97), Calle de Rufino Martín 1. The tourist office can tell you the latest programme.

Special Events

Ávila's principal festival (15 October) takes place, not surprisingly, in memory of Santa Teresa. The early-morning Good Friday procession of *pasos* (sculpted figures depicting the passion of Christ) is equally noteworthy, and Easter in general is marked by a stream of solemn marches and other events.

Places to Stay – bottom end

Camping & Hostel The nearest camping ground is *Camping Sonsoles* (☎ 25 63 36), a couple of km south of town on the N-403 to Toledo. It opens from June to September. Rates are 300 ptas each per person, car and tent. The *Albergue de la Juventud Profesor Arturo Duperier* (☎ 22 17 16), Avenida de la Juventud, is by no means a great choice, and in any case is open only in July and August. A bed costs 850 ptas for members under 26 and 1200 ptas for those above the magic age.

Hostales & Hotels Among the cheaper places near the cathedral, *Hostal Las Cancelas* (☎ 21 22 49), Calle de la Cruz Vieja 6, has simple singles/doubles for 2500/3500 ptas. *Hotel Jardín* (☎ 21 10 74), Calle de San Segundo 38, is a fairly scruffy place with rooms starting at 2500/3500 ptas (heading up to 3500/4600 ptas with private bath). A good choice is the *Hostal San Juan* (☎ 21 31 98), Calle de los Comuneros de Castilla 3. Rooms with telephone and TV cost 3600/6300 ptas.

Better still is the *Hostal Mesón del Rastro* (☎ 21 12 18), Plaza del Rastro 1. Full of character and with a good restaurant, it has rooms starting at 3200/4000 ptas. *Hostal Rey Niño* (☎ 21 14 04), Plaza de José Tomé 1, has adequate rooms for up to 3200/5400 ptas.

Places to Stay – middle
Just outside the Puerta de los Leales, the *Gran Hostal San Segundo* (☎ 25 26 90), Calle de San Segundo 28, is heading into the more expensive bracket, with decent rooms costing 4500/6000 ptas in the low season, and an exaggerated 6000/8000 ptas from June through to October.

Places to Stay – top end
Top of the tree is the *Gran Hotel Palacio Valderrábanos* (☎ 21 10 23; fax 25 16 91), in the Palacio de los Valderrábano, Plaza de la Catedral 9, where rooms cost 8500/13,000 ptas plus IVA. In a similar price league is the *Hotel Meliá* (☎ 25 51 00; fax 25 49 00), across the square at No 10 and housed in the equally splendid old Palacio de los Velada.

Places to Eat
For a cheap, decent pizza in a hurry, you could do worse than the *Telepizza* chain, on the corner of Avenida de Portugal and Calle de San Segundo. *Restaurante Los Leales*, Plaza de Italia 4, has a solid set menu for 900 ptas.

La Alacena is a cosy little place where a full meal can cost less than 2000 ptas. A good moderately priced choice is the *Hostal Mesón del Rastro*, Plaza del Rastro 1. The 1400 ptas set meal is good value and the comedor, with its dark wood beams and wrought-iron work, exudes Castilian charm. It does a tasty ternera del Valle de Amblés, a hearty beef dish typical of the region. Also good and with alfresco dining is the *Posada de la Fruta*, Plaza de Pedro Dávila 8. *Restaurante El Ruedo*, Calle de Enrique Larreta 7, is an unassuming place but offers a good if pricey set meal for 1600 ptas.

Restaurante Doña Guiomar, Calle de Tomás Luis de Victoria 3, has a touch of class and main meals that won't come in under

2000 ptas. On the other hand, it has a special kids' meal (menú niños) for 800 ptas.

Don't miss the local sweet tooth speciality – yemas, a scrummy, sticky business made of egg yolk and sugar.

Entertainment
Ávila is not exactly the most happening town in Spain, but *Siglo Doce*, just inside the Puerta de los Leales, is not a bad little café where you can also get a bite to eat. Otherwise, Plaza de la Victoria and Plaza de Santa Teresa are the places to look for bars, tapas and front-row people-watching seats. Later in the evening, you'll find some marcha (action) along Calle de Vallespín and west to the Puerta del Puente. The *Caballeros* disco, on the corner of Plaza de Italia and Calle de San Miguel, is one dancing possibility.

Things to Buy
If you are interested in glassware, pop into Ábside, Calle de Alemania 1. There is a glass-blowing factory in Ávila and this shop sells some nice wares. Market day, by the way, is Friday in Plaza de la Victoria and Plaza de Santa Teresa.

Getting There & Away
Bus Buses are OK for getting to nearby and out-of-the-way destinations, but the main cities are generally more easily reached by train. A bus leaves at 3.15 pm (Monday to Friday) for Arenas de San Pedro in the Sierra de Gredos. It's an all-stops job and costs 210 ptas. A daily bus leaves for Valladolid at 7.30 am (no services on Sunday), and there are two to four buses daily for Madrid and Salamanca.

Train Up to 17 trains run to Madrid (mostly to Chamartín) daily (755 ptas; up to two hours). Plenty also head west to Salamanca and cost the same. At least a couple of trains a day head for cities such as Bilbao, Santander and Málaga.

Car & Motorcycle From Madrid, you need to get onto the N-VI. You can follow this or the parallel A-6 tollway as far as Villacastín,

****

Toros de Guisando

A curiosity just inside Castilla y León's boundary with the Comunidad de Madrid, a good 70 km east of Arenas de San Pedro, is the so-called Toros de Guisando (*not* the Guisando in the Sierra de Gredos). Four weather-beaten animal statues lined up behind a wall on a narrow country lane off the N-403 between Ávila and Toledo are said to have stood there since pre-Roman times. One theory claims they mark a border between Celtic tribes. At this spot, or perhaps in what remains of a monastery halfway up the hill west of the road, Isabel (as in Fernando and Isabel, the Catholic Monarchs) was supposedly sworn in as heir to the Castilian throne on 19 September 1468. ■

****

where you need to bear south-west along the N-110. You could also take the M-505 (which later becomes the C-505) via El Escorial, which branches off the N-VI just before Las Rozas.

Getting Around

Local bus No 1 (red line; 70 ptas) runs past the RENFE train station to Plaza de la Catedral.

SIERRA DE GREDOS

Virtually taking over where the Sierra de Guadarrama outside Madrid trails off, the Sierra de Gredos is a mighty mountain chain that effectively marks the natural dividing line between the two Castiles – in modern terms, Castilla y León and Castilla-La Mancha to its south. The chain spreads across into Extremadura.

Arenas de San Pedro

This straggly town is the hub around which huddles an assortment of villages lending access to the mountains. You will almost definitely pass through, but may not necessarily want to stay. It's a popular summer escape hatch for sun-stunned Castilians and *madrileños*, where the new overshadows the old.

Still, right on the Río Arenal squats the stout 15th century **Castillo de la Triste**

Condesa and close by is the sober 14th-century Gothic **Iglesia de Nuestra Señora de la Asunción**. A few minutes south, a **medieval bridge** still provides a secure river crossing, while the north end of town is dominated by the neoclassical **Palacio del Infante Don Luis de Borbón** – a gilded cage for Carlos III's imprisoned brother.

Of the half-dozen places to stay, three are gathered near the castle and old centre. *Hostal El Castillo* (☎ 920-37 00 91), Carretera de Candeleda 2, has spartan singles/doubles for 1500/2500 ptas. *Pensión Yeka* (☎ 920-37 21 87), next door, has some decent rooms with private bathroom for 2500/4000 ptas. The *Hostería Los Galayos* (☎ 920-37 13 79), Plaza de Condestable Dávalos 2, offers solid if unexciting food and also has some cheap rooms.

At least four daily buses run from Madrid. One a day heads south for Talavera de la Reina. Most of the surrounding towns are connected at least once a day by bus to Arenas. Buses from Madrid and Ávila to Candeleda also pass through Arenas and Mombeltrán.

Mombeltrán

Just 10 km north of Arenas, this quiet backwater is fronted by the powerful turrets of its low-slung **castillo**, set against an impressive mountain backdrop but closed to visitors. There are two small hotels here and a camping ground a few km out.

El Hornillo, El Arenal & Guisando

Pleasant enough but showing signs of the money that has gone into filling them with new holiday homes, these villages make possible starting points for walks into the Gredos. A bus for the first two leaves Arenas at 12.15 pm on weekdays. A separate one serves Guisando. Of the two places to stay at El Arenal, the *Hostal Isabel* (☎ 920-37 51 48), Calle de las Angustias, has comfortable rooms with loo for 2300/3300 ptas. There are a couple of places at Guisando too. All three towns are within a 10 km radius north or north-west of Arenas and are far more attractively placed in the sierra.

Walks in the Sierra de Gredos

The most popular walks in the area are best undertaken in June or September – midsummer is stifling. Most walkers with limited time aim for the Laguna Grande, in the shadow of the sierra's highest peak, Almanzor (2592 metres), and continue westwards to the Circo de Cinco Lagos. Possible starting points include El Hornillo and Guisando. Coming from the north side of the range, a road also leads south from Hoyos del Espino to the Plataforma, the jumping-off point for the lakes. If you are walking from Guisando or El Hornillo, reckon on taking the better part of the day coming up the steep granite slopes to reach the Plataforma.

From here a well-defined trail heads south-west to the Laguna Grande de Gredos, where there is a *refugio* (often full) and good camping. A couple of hours further west along Alfonso XIII's specially laid hunting track, the Cinco Lagos are spread out before you. The descent is a little wearying but worthwhile. From there you can head back whence you came (you could try hitching a lift north to Hoyos del Espino from the Plataforma). If you are too late to make a bus out of Hoyos, there are three places to stay.

An alternative exit is north along the Garganta (gorge) del Pinar towards the town of Navalperal de Tormes.

Readers of Spanish who are planning serious exploration of the area should get hold of *Gredos*, by Miguel A Vidal and Carlos Frías, which contains 37 suggested walks and information on activities like rock climbing. It's available in Arenas.

Along the Northern Flank of the Sierra de Gredos

Following the southern flank of the mountain chain, the C-501 offers a pretty drive from Arenas towards Cándeleda and on into Extremadura's La Vera valley.

Within Castilla y León, the northern flank is, if anything, a more picturesque proposition. From Arenas, the N-502 climbs high to the Puerto del Pico and heads on to Ávila. However, you can turn west about five km

after the pass on a route that, followed almost directly westward, would take you to the Peña de Francia and on to Portugal via Ciudad Rodrigo. The *Parador de Gredos* (☎ 920-34 80 48), a few km east of Navarredonda de Gredos, has front-row rooms overlooking the mountains for 8000/10,500 ptas in the high season. The more modest *Hostal Almanzor* (☎ 920-34 80 10), just short of the same town, is a reasonable but pricey alternative with singles/doubles for 5000/6200 ptas.

El Barco de Ávila, on a crossroads with the N-110 between Ávila and Plasencia, has a proud if ruinous castle. Another 30 km west, **Béjar** is somewhat more interesting, its old quarters lined up at the west end of a high ridge, partly walled. Most eye-catching is the 16th century Palacio Ducal, just west of the Plaza Mayor and now serving as a college. There's plenty of accommodation in Béjar, including the *Hostal Casa Pavón* (☎ 923-40 28 61), Plaza Mayor 3. It has rooms for 2000/3500 ptas. Buses run frequently to Salamanca and various other destinations, including Madrid and Plasencia.

See later in this chapter for information on the Peña de Francia and Ciudad Rodrigo.

SALAMANCA

The rich copper hues of Salamanca's great university and churches are without equal in Spain. Although a shadow of its medieval self, the university has regained a degree of prestige in the past decades, particularly with its language programmes for foreigners. A compact and busy student town, Salamanca attracts many young people from abroad who elect to carry out their Spanish studies here.

While in Salamanca, see if you can get your teeth into the local speciality, *chanfaina*, a rice dish with various meats in a lightly spicy sauce.

History

As long ago as 220 BC, Celtiberian Salamanca found itself besieged by Hannibal. Later, under Roman rule, it was an important staging post along the Via Lata (Ruta de la

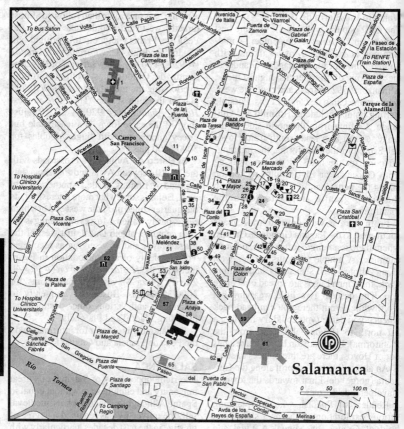

Salamanca

Plata, or Silver Route, from the mines in northern Spain to the south), and it changed hands repeatedly for four centuries after the Muslim invasion of Spain. Possibly the greatest turning point in the city's history was the founding of the university in 1218. It became the equal of Oxford and Bologna, and by the end of the 15th century was the focal point of some of the richest artistic activity in the country. In few other places will you witness the virtuosity in plateresque and Renaissance work that is on hand in Salamanca. The city followed the rest of Castilla into decline in the 17th century,

aggravated by the Napoleonic invasion (la francesada) at the beginning of the 19th century. The city suffered considerable damage before and during the Battle of Los Arapiles in 1812 between Marmont and Wellington.

Orientation

As so often in Spanish cities, the old centre is fairly compact and easily negotiated on foot. At its heart lies Spain's grandest Plaza Mayor, and the whole lies north of the Río Tormes. A fair range of accommodation can be found between Plaza Mayor and the river,

PLACES TO STAY		29	Mesón El Botón Charro	30	Iglesia de San Cristóbal
4	Pensión Cantábrico	38	El Patio Chico	31	Potemkin
8	Hotel Las Torres	53	Restaurante El Trigal	33	Iglesia de San Martín
15	Pensión Robles			34	MusicArte Café
17	Hostal Orly	54	Café El Ave Turuta	35	Tiempo Café
20	Hotel El Toboso			37	Café El Corrillo
26	Pensión Los Angeles & Campus Cibermático	**OTHER**		42	Bar Bennys
		1	Hospital Santísima Trinidad	43	El Gran Café Moderno
32	Gran Hotel			44	Palacium
36	Pensión Lisboa	2	Iglesia de San Juan de Barbados	47	Torre del Clavero
39	Pensión Las Vegas			48	Taberna La Rayuela
40	Hostal Tormes	3	Teatro de la Caja	50	Casa de las Conchas & Tourist Office
41	Hostal La Perla Salamantina	5	Correos (Post Office)		
		6	Torre del Aire	51	Real Clericía de San Marcos
45	Hostal Laguna	7	O'Neill's Irish Pub		
46	Hotel Clavero	9	Morgana (Disco)	52	Palacio de Congresos
49	Pensión Estefanía	10	Casa de las Muertes	55	Museo de Salamanca
62	Pensión Peña de Francia	11	Convento de las Úrsulas	56	Patio de las Escuelas Menores
64	Pensión Feli	12	Colegio de Arzobispo Fonseca	57	Universidad Civil
				58	Catedral Nueva
PLACES TO EAT		13	Palacio de Monterrey	59	Convento de las Dueñas
14	Bambú	16	Museo Taurino		
18	Restaurante El Candil Viejo	19	Tío Vivo	60	Convento de Santa Clara
		22	Iglesia de San Julián		
21	Restaurante Llamas	24	Mercado Central	61	Convento de San Esteban
23	Restaurante El Clavel	25	Telephones		
		27	Oficina Municipal de Turismo	63	Catedral Vieja
28	Mesón Cervantes			65	Casa de Lis

an area that encompasses most of the university buildings. The train and bus stations are about equidistant from the centre, the former to the north-east and the latter to the north-west. If the 20 or so minutes walk from either doesn't appeal, buses connect both to the centre.

Maps The tourist office hand-out maps are OK, but the most detailed and accurate is that contained in the free two-monthly hand-out *En Salamanca*.

Information

Tourist Office The Oficina Municipal de Turismo (☎ 21 83 42), right on Plaza Mayor, concentrates on the city and opens daily from 9 am to 2 pm and 4.30 to 6.30 pm. For information on the remainder of the province, go to the tourist office (☎ 26 85 71) in the Casa de las Conchas, Calle de la Compañía 2. It's open Monday to Friday from 10 am to 2 pm and 5 to 8 pm, and on

Saturday from 10 am to 2 pm. Offices also open at the train and bus stations in summer.

Money There is no shortage of banks around the centre. American Express is represented by Viajes Salamanca (☎ 26 77 31), Plaza Mayor 11.

Post & Communications You'll find the main post office at Gran Vía 25 and a telephone office (locutorio) on Plaza Mayor, near the tourist office. The latter opens daily from 8.30 am to 11.30 pm. The postcode is 37080. The telephone code is ☎ 923. If you need to send e-mail, try Campus Cibermático (☎ 27 11 31), Plaza Mayor 10.

Travel Agencies TIVE (☎ 26 77 31), Paseo de las Carmelitas 83, can help with student travel.

Medical Services A couple of hospitals are located close to the centre. You could try the Hospital Clínico Universitario (☎ 29 11 00),

Paseo de San Vicente 58-182, or Hospital Santísima Trinidad.

Emergency There is a police station *(comisaría)* at Ronda de Sancti Spiritus 8. In a medical emergency, call ambulances at the Cruz Roja (☎ 22 22 22), Plaza de San Benito s/n.

Plaza Mayor

Built between 1729 and 1755, Salamanca's grand square is considered, pretty much unanimously, Spain's most engaging central plaza. Designed by Alberto Churriguera, it is a remarkably harmonious and controlled display of baroque. Bullfights were held here well into the 19th century, and the medallions placed around the plaza bear the busts of sundry famous figures, including the regularly defaced one of a certain Generalísimo Franco. He's the one at the top (north) end of the east flank.

Just off the square, on Plaza del Corrillo, the 12th century Iglesia de San Martín lies wedged into a huddle of houses. It is one of several nice examples of Romanesque religious architecture dotted about the city centre.

Catedrales

The tower of the late Gothic **Catedral Nueva** lords over the centre of Salamanca, its churrigueresque dome visible from almost every angle. It is, however, the magnificent Renaissance doorways, particularly the Puerta del Nacimiento on the west face, that stand out as one of several miracles worked in the city's sandstone façades. Inside, the most notable feature is the highly elaborate baroque choir stalls. The cathedral is open daily from 10 am to 1 pm and 4 to 6 pm.

The Catedral Nueva was raised abutting its largely Romanesque predecessor, which is predictably known as the **Catedral Vieja**. Begun as early as 1120, this church is a bit of a hybrid, with some elements of Gothic. The unusual ribbed cupola (Torre del Gallo) betrays a Byzantine influence, and the *retablo mayor* in the apse of the Capilla Mayor is a sumptuous work depicting scenes

from the life of Christ and the Virgin Mary, topped by a representation of the Final Judgment. The cloister was largely ruined in the 1755 Lisbon earthquake, but in the Capilla de San Bartolomé you can still admire one of Europe's oldest organs. The Catedral Vieja opens daily from 10 am to 12.30 pm and 4 to 5.30 pm. Entry costs 300 ptas.

Universidad Civil & Around

Little can prepare you for the visual feast of the façade constituting the entrance to Salamanca's university. Founded initially as the Estudio General in 1218, the university proper came into being in 1254 and reached the peak of its renown in the 15th and 16th centuries. These were heady times for Spain, fully 'reconquered' from the Muslims in 1492 and later bent on expansion in the Americas. The university's façade, more a tapestry in sandstone, simply bursts with images of mythical heroes, religious scenes and coats of arms, and is dominated in the centre by busts of Fernando and Isabel, the Catholic Monarchs (encircled by an inscription in Greek).

Among the small lecture rooms disposed around the courtyard inside the building, the Aula de Fray Luis de León (named after the celebrated 16th century theologian and writer who taught here and whose statue stands in the Patio de las Escuelas outside) is perhaps the most interesting, conserving the original benches and lectern from Fray Luis' day. Upstairs, the university library boasts fine Late Gothic features and a beautiful *techumbre* (carved wooden ceiling). Some 2800 ancient manuscripts lie in the custody of this, one of the oldest university libraries in Europe.

The university can be visited Monday to Friday from 9.30 am to 1.30 pm and 4 to 7.30 pm (7 pm on Saturday), and on Sunday and on holidays from 10 am to 1.30 pm. Tickets cost 300 ptas (half-price for students) and include entrance to the Museo de la Universidad (see below).

Patio de las Escuelas Menores Head out of the university again and walk over to the

Top: A *toro bravo*, or fighting bull, in pastures south of Salamanca, Castilla y León
Bottom Left: The Romanesque cloister known as Las Claustrillas, in the Monasterio de las Huelgas,
    Burgos, Castilla y León
Bottom Right: Fields of Soria province from the castle ruins in Gormaz, Castilla y León

Don Quixote's old foes, the windmills of Campo de la Criptana, Castilla-La Mancha

✿✿✿✿✿✿✿✿✿✿✿✿✿✿✿✿✿✿✿✿✿✿✿✿✿

Frog Spotting

A compulsory task facing all visitors to the Universidad Civil in Salamanca is to search out the frog sculpted on to the façade. Once pointed out, it is easily enough seen, but you can expend considerable time in vain searching otherwise. Why bother? Well, they say that those who detect it without outside help can be assured of good luck and even marriage (if you consider that good luck) within a year. Some hopeful students see an assured examinations victory in it. If you believe all this, stop reading now. If you do want help, look at the busts of Fernando and Isabel. From there, swing your gaze to the largest column on the extreme right of the façade. Slightly above the level of the busts are sculpted a series of skulls, atop the leftmost of which sits our little amphibious friend. ■

✿✿✿✿✿✿✿✿✿✿✿✿✿✿✿✿✿✿✿✿✿✿✿✿✿

south-west corner of the little square, off which opens the cloister of the Escuelas Menores. In among the arches lies the **Museo de la Universidad**, where you can see the zodiacal ceiling that once graced the university's chapel, along with a fairly standard collection of clerical art. It is open daily from 9.30 am to 1.30 pm and 4 to 6.30 pm. Check out the Sala de Exposiciones, where you can admire two techumbres – one clearly *mudéjar* and the other with Renaissance Italian influences.

Museo de Salamanca Also known as the Museo de Bellas Artes, this modest gallery is as interesting for the building (notable are the little patio and the techumbre ceiling in *sala* 1) as its contents. It is open Tuesday to Friday from 9.30 am to 2 pm and 4.30 to 8 pm, on Saturday from 10 am to 2 pm and 4.30 to 7.30 pm, and on Sunday from 10 am to 2 pm. Entry costs 200 ptas (half for students).

Casa Museo de Unamuno Housed next to the university's main entrance, this small museum dedicated to the writer Miguel de Unamuno is a bit of a travesty, since he never lived here in the house. It is, in any case, closed.

Real Clerícía de San Marcos Seat of the Universidad Pontificia and formerly a Jesuit college and seminary, this building across Plaza de San Isidro from the university is no longer open to visitors except for the monumental baroque cloister – and that only in the

half-hour before Mass, for which times are normally posted.

Casa de las Conchas Across the road is one of the most distinctive buildings in Salamanca, named after the scallop shells carved across its façades.

Convento de San Esteban & Around
Standing proud in the south-east corner of the old city, the façade of this monastery's church is another breathtaking example of the city's plat3resque marvels. It is in effect a huge retablo in stone, with the stoning of St Stephen (San Esteban) its central motif. Inside, the church's centrepiece is also a retablo – this time an ornate masterpiece by José Churriguera. Through the Gothic-Renaissance cloister you can climb upstairs to the church's choir stalls. The monastery is open daily from 9 am to 1 pm and 4 to 7 pm. Entry to the cloister costs 200 ptas.

Convento de las Dueñas Easily the most beautiful cloister in the city is the irregular, pentagonal one that graces this convent of Dominican nuns, who still make and sell a range of traditional pastries. The convent is open daily from 10.30 am to 1 pm and 4.15 to 5.30 pm. Entry costs 100 ptas.

Torre del Clavero If you walk north a couple of blocks along Gran Vía, you will notice a block away to your left this defensive tower, a 15th century octagonal fortress on a square base adorned with smaller cylindrical towers. You can then turn off right for the Convento de Santa Clara.

Convento de Santa Clara The best part of a visit to this convent, which started life as a Romanesque building but has been rebuilt on several occasions, is the chance to climb to inspect at close quarters the 14th and 15th century mudéjar *artesonado* ceilings, hidden from view for almost three centuries by the lower baroque ceiling erected as part of a churrigueresque conceit in the 18th century. Ramps have been placed just below the ceiling. You can only visit this part of the convent with a guide, and will get more out of it if you understand Spanish. It is open Monday to Friday from 10 am to 2 pm and 4 to 7 pm, and on the weekend from 9 am to 3 pm (closed on holidays). Entry costs 100 ptas.

Colegio del Arzobispo Fonseca & Around
A short stroll west of Plaza Mayor brings you to another series of Salamantine monuments. Also known as the Colegio de los Irlandeses (College of the Irish), this one was built in the 16th century in a sober plateresque style. Of particular note are the main entrance and courtyard. You can visit daily from 10 am to 2 pm and 4 to 6 pm. The antique clock collection is open Tuesday to Friday from 3 to 7 pm, and on the weekend and on holidays from 11 am to 2 pm.

Convento de las Úrsulas Nearby, this late Gothic nunnery was founded by Archbishop Alonso de Fonseca in 1516 and now contains his magnificent marble tomb, sculpted by Diego de Siloé. The nunnery is open daily from 10 am to 1 pm and 4.30 to 7 pm. Entry costs 100 ptas.

Palacio de Monterrey A 16th century holiday home of the Duques de Alba, the palace is a seminal piece of Spanish Renaissance architecture. The dukes pop in every now and then, and visitors are not permitted inside.

Other Museums
Casa de Lis Fans of Art Nouveau and Art Deco will probably get a kick out of the gallery devoted to both in this *modernista* house on Calle de Gibraltar, built in 1905. It is open Tuesday to Friday from 11 am to 2 pm and 5 to 9 pm (4 to 7 pm in winter), and on the weekend and on holidays from 10 am to 9 pm (11 am to 8 pm in winter). Entry costs 300 ptas (200 ptas for students).

Museo Taurino Salamanca province is bull-breeding territory, one of the more important sources of *toros* for the country. Those interested can learn a little more at this museum, just north of Plaza Mayor. It is open Tuesday to Saturday from 6 to 9 pm only; also noon to 2 pm on the weekend. Entry costs 200 ptas.

Language Courses
Salamanca is popular with foreigners wanting to learn the lingo. Most go to the university. For information contact Cursos Intensivos de Lengua y Cultura Españolas (☎ 21 83 16; fax 26 24 56), Universidad Pontificia de Salamanca, Calle de la Compañía 5, 37080 Salamanca.

Places to Stay – bottom end
Camping There are four camping grounds around Salamanca, all outside town. Probably the best is *Camping Regio* (☎ 13 88 88), four km out along the N-501 to Madrid. It opens all year and charges 425 ptas per person, tent, car and for electricity.

Pensiones & Hostales It is hard to beat a room in one of the little places on Plaza Mayor, provided you can snag a room looking onto the square. *Pensión Los Ángeles* (☎ 21 81 66), at No 10, has rather basic singles/doubles with washbasin for 1500/2800 ptas. *Pensión Robles* (☎ 21 31 97), No 20, has perfectly adequate rooms for 2200/3300 ptas. The quadruple overlooking the square can be had for the price of a double.

Hostal La Perla Salamantina (☎ 21 76 56), Calle de Sánchez Barbero 7, charges

2000/3500 ptas for bright and clean singles/doubles with bath.

Calle de Meléndez has a few places. *Pensión Lisboa* (☎ 21 43 33), at No 1, offers little rooms starting at 1500 ptas for singles and ranging upwards to doubles for 3200 ptas with private bath. Mildly better value is the *Pensión Las Vegas* (☎ 21 87 49), at No 13, where clean doubles with bath cost 3000 ptas and singles without come in at just over 1000 ptas.

Pensión Estefanía (☎ 21 73 72), Calle de Jesús 3-5, has simple but decent singles/doubles starting at 1750/3000 ptas. More awkwardly placed but a possibility if the others are filling up is the *Pensión Peña de Francia* (☎ 21 66 87), Calle de San Pablo 96, charging 2500/3500 ptas for rooms with bath and a little less for those without.

Hostal Tormes (☎ 21 96 83), Rúa Mayor 20, is OK if a touch drab. The most expensive rooms go for 2500/3500 ptas and have private bath.

Down the road from the main university building is the *Pensión Feli* (☎ 21 60 10), Calle de los Libreros 58. It has cheerful rooms for 2000/2800 ptas.

There are several pensiones by the train station, and about halfway between the station and the centre you could stop at the *Pensión Cantábrico* (☎ 26 29 81), Calle del Pozo Hilera 7, where you'll pay 1500/2300 ptas for rooms with washbasin.

Places to Stay – middle

Hostal Laguna (☎ 21 87 06), Calle del Consuelo 19, has rooms with and without own bath ranging from 3000 to 4200 ptas in the high season. The *Hotel Clavero* (☎ 21 81 08), at No 21, is in much the same class and charges 3000/5000 ptas for singles/doubles.

Hostal Orly (☎ 21 61 25), Calle del Pozo Amarillo 5-7, offers reasonable if unexciting rooms with private bath, TV, telephone and heating for 4000/5000 ptas plus IVA.

A much better deal if you can afford the extra is the *Hotel El Toboso* (☎ 27 14 62), Calle del Clavel 7. The attractive timber and tile reception is no front, and the rooms with private bath, TV and telephone are worth the 4500/6000 ptas charged.

Hotel Las Torres, (☎ 21 21 00), Calle de Concejo 4, has comfortable rooms with all the mod cons for 9000/12,000 ptas plus IVA.

Places to Stay – top end

The *Gran Hotel* (☎ 21 35 00; fax 21 35 01), Plaza del Poeta Iglesias 5, is the city's most expensive and, as the name suggests, grandest place to stay. Rooms cost 14,000/18,500 ptas plus IVA. Otherwise you could try the *Parador de Salamanca* (☎ 26 87 00; fax 21 54 38), south of the river. It is a modern place with a swimming pool and singles/doubles cost 11,200/14,000 ptas plus IVA.

Places to Eat

El Patio Chico, Calle de Meléndez 13, is a lively place to sit around for beers and filling tapas for around 400 ptas a throw. For Spanish-style takeaways, bocadillos and absolutely no atmosphere, *Bambú*, just off Plaza Mayor in Calle del Prior, is the place to go – or the *Burger King* next door if you insist.

At Calle de los Libreros 24, you can get a respectable set meal for a mere 800 ptas at *Café El Ave Turuta*. Vegetarians should head for *Restaurante El Trigal*, at No 20. There are a couple of other reasonably priced eateries on the same street.

Right on Plaza Mayor near the tourist office, the *Mesón Cervantes*, with attractive upstairs dining, serves good-quality set lunches for 1200 ptas.

Restaurante Llamas, Calle del Clavel 9, is a pretty basic place where a tasty set lunch can be had for 950 ptas. For a walk on the expensive side, try the *Restaurante El Clavel*, at No 6. You're looking at about 4000 ptas a head for a full meal.

Restaurante El Candil Viejo, Calle de Ventura Ruiz Aguilera 10, is another popular stop but, at around 2000 ptas for mains, is a little pricey. Not far off is the much recommended *Mesón El Botón Charro*, Calle de Hovohambre 6. The set lunch costs 2750 ptas and average mains around 2000 ptas. Try the escalopines de solomillo al oporto.

Entertainment
Try to get hold of *En Salamanca*, a free booklet that appears every two months. It contains information on bars, cultural events, theatre and the like.

Cafés & Bars If you don't mind paying 250 ptas for your coffee, it is hard to beat sipping your way through the morning at one of the cafés around Plaza Mayor. Just a few steps outside the grand square, *MusicArte Café*, Plaza del Corrillo 20, is a hip place for coffee (at half that price) and cake.

Taberna La Rayuela, Rúa Mayor 19, is a popular place early on in the evening that, when not too crowded, is pleasantly low-lit and intimate.

Café El Corrillo, Calle de Meléndez 8, is a great place to catch a beer and some live jazz.

A drink in *Tío Vivo*, Calle de Clavel 3, is nearly obligatory, if only to experience the peculiar décor, which ranges from carousel horses to old cinema cameras and other oddball antiquities.

O'Neill's Irish Pub, Calle de Zamora 14, is part of a growing chain of popular Irish-style pubs increasingly in vogue in Spain, and is always busy.

A good area to look for *marcha* lies just east of the Mercado Central. Calle de San Justo, Calle de Varillas and Calle del Consuelo in particular are loaded with bars. A good little place is *Bar Bennys*, Calle del Consuelo 20. Later in the night you can head for *Potemkin*, a block north on Calle del Consuelo, for live music. Another popular place for drinks and live music is *Tiempo Café*, at Calle de Doctrinos 3.

Gran Vía itself is another good hunting ground. *El Gran Café Moderno*, at No 75 or 77, depending on which sign you believe, is a Salamanca classic. Across the road, *Palacium* (No 68) is a loud haunt for the juvenile; the bar next door is rather more laid-back.

Discos & Nightclubs To dance away the wee hours on a weekend, try *Morgana*, a disco on the corner of Cuesta del Carmen and Calle de Iscar Peyra.

Theatre The *Teatro de la Caja* on Plaza de Santa Teresa is a frequent scene for concerts and theatre of all sorts.

Getting There & Away
Bus The bus station is north-west of the town centre on Avenida de Filiberto Villalobos. AutoRes has frequent services for 1690 ptas (2210 ptas express) to Madrid. About six buses also serve Valladolid. Plenty of buses go to Alba de Tormes (180 ptas), and there is at least one a day, Monday to Saturday, for La Alberca (365 ptas). Regular buses run to Ciudad Rodrigo (715 ptas) and there are services also to Béjar, Ledesma and throughout the province.

The ALSA company runs buses as far afield as Galicia, Asturias, Cantabria and Cádiz.

Train At least five trains leave daily for Madrid's Chamartín station (three hours; 1560 ptas) via Ávila (1¾ hours; 805 ptas). A train for Lisbon leaves at 4.55 am.

Car & Motorcycle The N-501 leads east to Madrid via Ávila and west to Portugal via Ciudad Rodrigo, while the N-630 heads north to Zamora. For the Sierra de la Peña de Francia, take the C-512.

Getting Around
Bus No 4 runs past the bus station and round the old town perimeter to Gran Vía. From the train station, the best bet is a No 1, which heads down Calle de Azafranal. Going the other way, it can be picked up along Gran Vía.

AROUND SALAMANCA
Ledesma & Embalse de Almendra
Following the Río Tormes north-west, you reach the small town of Ledesma, a grey, partly walled settlement. A medieval bridge still spans the river, and there are a few churches of minor interest, including the Gothic Iglesia de Santa María la Mayor in Plaza Mayor. You can also see remains of the castle of the Duques de Alburquerque. A couple of buses serve the town each day from

Salamanca (275 ptas), and if you get stuck there are a couple of pensiones. If you have transport, you might want to keep trailing the river, which feeds the Embalse de Almendra, a huge reservoir not far short of the Portuguese border.

Alba de Tormes
Resting place of Santa Teresa, Alba de Tormes is a mildly interesting and easily accomplished half-day excursion from Salamanca. Apart from the stout and highly visible **Torreón**, which is all that remains of what was the castle of the Duques de Alba, people come to visit the remains of Santa Teresa, buried in the Convento de las Carmelitas she founded in 1570. There are plenty of buses from Salamanca.

CIUDAD RODRIGO
Less than 30 km short of the Portuguese frontier, Ciudad Rodrigo is a sleepy but attractive walled town and a pleasant final stop on the way out of Spain. From the time the Romans departed after several centuries of occupation, little is known of the city until Count Rodrigo González arrived in the 12th century to refound the settlement as Civitas Roderici. It has always been something of a front-line city with Portugal, but never did Ciudad Rodrigo suffer as much as under siege during the Peninsular War against Napoleon. The city fell in 1811, but a year later Wellington turned the tide and dislodged the French.

Information
The tourist office (☎ 46 05 61), Plaza de las Amayuelas 5, is open Monday to Friday from 9.30 am to 2 pm and 4 to 7 pm, and Saturday from 9.30 am to 2 pm. The post office is at Calle de Dámaso Ledesma 12. The postcode is 37500 and the telephone code is ☎ 923.

Things to See
The **catedral**, begun in 1165, is doubtless the city's outstanding sight. The Puerta de las Cadenas, giving onto Plaza de San Salvador, with its Gothic reliefs of Old Testament

figures, is impressive. More striking, though, is the elegant Pórtico del Perdón. Some of the great windows inside are jewels of Romanesque design, while the cloister is part Romanesque, part Gothic.

The town is liberally strewn with interesting minor palaces, mansions and churches. Among the latter is the **Iglesia de San Isidoro**, with Romanesque-mudéjar elements. Pay a visit to the **correos** (post office) to admire the artesonado ceilings. The 1st floor gallery of the **ayuntamiento** (town hall) is a good spot to shoot film of Plaza Mayor, and the 16th century **Palacio de los Castro**, on Plaza del Conde, boasts one of the town's most engaging plateresque façades. You can climb up onto the city walls and follow their length around the town.

Special Events
Carnaval in February is a unique time to be in Ciudad Rodrigo. Apart from the outlandish fancy dress and festivities, you can witness (or join in) a colourful *encierro* (running of the bulls) and *capeas* (amateur bullfights). It is one of the earliest events in the Spanish bullfighting calendar and fascinating for those not put off by this kind of spectacle.

Places to Stay & Eat
There is a pair of adequate pensiones in the heart of the old town. *Pensión Madrid* (☎ 46 24 67), Calle de Madrid 20, has doubles with washbasin for 2500 ptas, which they let out for 1500 ptas to loners. *Pensión París* (☎ 46 13 72), Calle del Toro 10, offers fairly basic singles/doubles for 1500/3000 ptas. There are a good dozen cheap to mid-range places in the new part of town too.

For a minor splurge, try out the venerable *Hotel Conde Rodrigo* (☎ 46 14 08; fax 46 14 08), Plaza de San Salvador 9. Tastefully appointed rooms go for 5000/6200 ptas in the high season. For sheer luxury in a castle, head for the *Parador Enrique II* (☎ 46 01 50; fax 46 04 04), Plaza del Castillo, where singles/doubles will set you back 10,000/13,500 ptas.

CASTILLA Y LEÓN

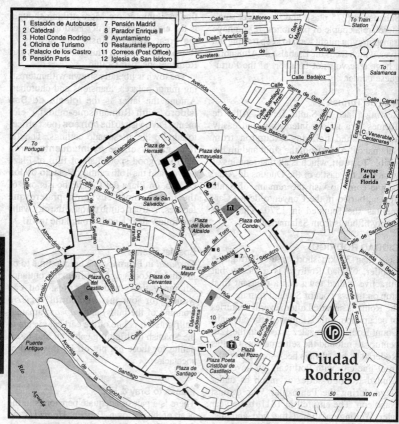

1 Estación de Autobuses	7 Pensión Madrid
2 Catedral	8 Parador Enrique II
3 Hotel Conde Rodrigo	9 Ayuntamiento
4 Oficina de Turismo	10 Restaurante Peporro
5 Palacio de los Castro	11 Correos (Post Office)
6 Pensión Paris	12 Iglesia de San Isidoro

Ciudad
Rodrigo

For a tasty set menu, try the *Restaurante Peporro*, Calle de los Gigantes 5.

Getting There & Away

At least 10 buses a day run to Salamanca (715 ptas). There are no direct buses into the Sierra de la Peña de Francia – you need to return to Salamanca. A daily train to Lisbon passes through at 6 am. At 1 am it heads the other way to Irún and destinations in between.

SIERRA DE LA PEÑA DE FRANCIA

Pretty much a northern extension of Extremadura's Las Hurdes, this compact mountain range could not be more different from the plains around Ciudad Rodrigo, only 40 km west. Here a sprinkling of introspective villages seem even today caught in a time warp, protected, even cut off, by the cool of this craggy, grey-green oasis. However, what may seem a quaint reminder of the idyllic good old days was until not so long ago one of the most godforsaken parts of Spain. It was ridden with malaria until the turn of the century, and things hadn't improved much in 1932 when Buñuel came to film the locals' 'lifestyle' in *Las Hurdes – Terre Sans Pain*,

he first part of which was shot here. Scenes
include a competition among young towns-
men about to be wed. This involved riding
on donkey-back down the main street and
attempting to rip the head off a live chicken
strung up for the purpose across the road.
When King Alfonso XIII visited in June
1922, the only milk available for his coffee
was human! Touched by the abject misery
people lived in, he was supposedly responsible for the introduction of the area's first
cows; malaria hadn't been greatly conducive
to raising them before.

La Alberca & Around

Easily the most extraordinary of the towns
here, La Alberca is a claustrophobic huddle
of gloomy alleys fronted by a hotchpotch of
houses built of heavy stone, wood beams and
plaster – some a couple of centuries old.
Tourism has arrived, but many of the townspeople still seem to live in the traditional
way: donkeys remain a not uncommon transport mode. In winter the dark, dimly lit bars
and cafés around Plaza Mayor are a cosy
retreat from the season's rigours. It is the
logical choice of base for the area, with half
a dozen places to stay.

About a km out of town on the road south,
Hospedaje Las Eras (☎ 923-41 51 13) offers
simple singles/doubles for 2000/3000 ptas.
Right by the entrance to town are a couple of
mid-range hotels and the comfortable *Hostal
La Alberca* (☎ 923-41 52 37), Plaza Padre
Arsenio, which offers modern rooms with en
suite bathroom for 3300/4500 ptas in the
high season.

If you have a vehicle, or time and a hitching thumb, the surrounding villages are more
authentically caught up in the past than La
Alberca. **Mogarraz**, to the east, and **Miranda
del Castañar**, further east again, are among
the more intriguing.

Valle de las Batuecas

The drive south into Extremadura is one of
the more seriously spectacular in Castilla y
León. After you crest the Puerto del Portillo,
a seemingly infinite phalanx of lower mountain ranges stretches south before you. A

series of switchbacks quickly descends
towards the Río Alagón in Extremadura.
About 10 km down is a small Carmelite
monastery (tourist visits not desired), past
which rushes a babbling brook that you can
follow on foot up into the surrounding hills.
About two hours walk brings you to some
caves with rock carvings. It rains a lot here,
so be warned: a sudden downpour could
make your descent to the monastery difficult
to say the least.

Those without transport could try renting
a **mountain bike** at the Hospedaje Las Eras
in La Alberca. If you're interested in horse
riding, contact Caballos Peña de Francia
(☎ 923-45 40 98), Carretera de la Alberca
s/n, just outside the town of the same name.

Peña de Francia

Head north from La Alberca along the SA-
202 and you soon strike the turn-off to the
highest peak in the area, the Peña de Francia
(1732 metres), from which you have sweeping views east to the Sierra de Gredos, south
into Extremadura and west across the plains
to Portugal.

The Central Plateau

With Valladolid, the regional capital, in its
geographical heart, the central plateau of
Castilla y León is dotted with towns and
cities of varying interest. With the exceptions
of Segovia and Zamora, few cry out for an
overnight stay, which places a premium on
mobility. Great sweeps of niggardly rural
plains, wrinkled by often less than breathtaking sierras, provide further incentive to move
fast, although there are exceptions to the
rule: the approaches to Galicia around the
Lago de Sanabria and some of the hill
country around Segovia provide a welcome
contrast.

What follows is an arbitrarily traced route
supposing a starting point in Segovia, just
across from the Comunidad de Madrid. To
make the most of what there is to see, especially if time is limited, a vehicle to chew up

km is a handy asset. That said, it is quite feasible to follow much of this or a similar route with public transport. Where it becomes especially tricky is with small villages. Castilla y León is liberally sprinkled with castillos, *ermitas* (hermitages), monasteries and great churches. It is astonishing just how frequently they pop up on distant horizons as you barrel down an autovía – and this is when independent transport comes into its own.

SEGOVIA

To some, the ridge-top city of Segovia resembles a man-of-war ploughing through the sea of Castilla around it, the base of its prow formed by the confluence of the Río Eresma and Río Clamores. Its arms are a surprising array of monuments, and those contemplating visiting Segovia as a day trip from Madrid will have a full programme if they are to do the town justice. The lofty city walls and Roman aqueduct largely protect the city from any incursion by the characterless modern urban tangle spread out below it to the south-east, and this sets it apart from many other cities across Castilla y León, flat and besieged by new development.

History

The Celtic settlement of Segobriga was occupied by the Romans in 80 BC and rose to some importance in the imperial network. As Christian Spain recovered from the initial shock of the Muslim blitzkrieg, Segovia became something of a front-line city until the invaders were definitively evicted in 1085. The Muslims left behind them a flourishing wool and textile industry, which only began to decline in the mid-16th century. A favourite residence of Castilla's roaming royalty, the city backed Isabel and saw her proclaimed queen in the Iglesia de San Miguel in 1474. In 1520, the rebellious Comuneros found unequivocal support in Segovia, led by Juan Bravo. From then on it was all downhill for the town until the 1960s, when tourism and the introduction of some light industry helped it pull itself up by the bootstraps.

Orientation

The old town of Segovia is strung out along a ridge, rising in the east and peaking in the fanciful towers of the Alcázar to the west. If you arrive by train or bus, the local bus will take you to Plaza Mayor, the heart of the city. Drivers will reach the same square by following the 'Centro Ciudad' signs. The cathedral, tourist office, several hotels and plenty of restaurants and bars are all on or handily close to Plaza Mayor. The main road leading downhill from Plaza Mayor to the *acueducto* and the new town is a pedestrian thoroughfare that changes name several times along the way (Calle de Isabel la Católica, Calle de Juan Bravo and Calle de Cervantes); locals know the length of it simply as Calle Real.

Information

Tourist Office The main tourist office (☎ 43 03 34), Plaza Mayor 10, has a decent free map and accommodation list. It's open Monday to Friday from 10 am to 2 pm and 5 to 8 pm, on Saturday from 10 am to 2 pm and 4.30 to 8.30 pm, and on Sunday from 11 am to 2 pm and 4.30 to 8.30 pm. There is a municipal tourist office (☎ 44 03 02) at Plaza del Azoguejo 1.

Money There are plenty of banks with exchange facilities on or near the so-called Calle Real. Many have ATMs and some, like the Caja de Ahorros de Segovia at Calle Juan Bravo 2, have machines for exchanging foreign cash.

Post & Communications The main post office is at Plaza de los Huertos 5. The postcode is 40080. The main Telefónica locutorio is on the same square, and opens daily from 10 am to 2 pm and 5 to 10 pm. The telephone code is ☎ 921.

Medical & Emergency Services If you need the police, call ☎ 091. Otherwise, the *comisaría*, or main police station, is on the corner of Paseo Ezequiel González and the Carretera de Ávila, in the new part of town.

Segovia

PLACES TO STAY
23 Fonda Aragón & Fonda Cubo
25 Hostal Plaza
30 Hostal El Hidalgo
34 Hotel Infanta Isabel
40 Hotel Juan Bravo
41 Hotel Las Sirenas
56 Hostal Don Jaime

PLACES TO EAT
16 Cuevas de San Esteban
17 Bar El Antiguo Buscón
22 Mesón Mayor
24 Mesón José María
31 Restaurante El Campesino
35 Confitería El Alcázar
36 Restaurante Tasca La Posada
45 Restaurante Narizotas
48 Restaurante El Abuelo
49 Cafetería Castilla
51 Restaurante & Cuevas El Duque
54 Restaurante Cándido
58 Bar Yiyo's
60 Restaurante La Codorniz

OTHER
1 Convento de los Carmelitas Descalzos
2 Iglesia de la Vera Cruz
3 Monasterio de El Parral
4 Casa de la Moneda
5 Alcázar
6 Museo de Holografía
7 Iglesia de San Andrés
8 Casa-Museo de Antonio Machado
9 Iglesia de San Esteban
10 Convento de los Oblatas
11 Iglesia de San Nicolás
12 Iglesia de la Trinidad
13 Torre de Hércules
14 Iglesia de San Quirce
15 Palacio Episcopal
18 Casa del Sol
19 Puerta de San Andrés
20 Catedral
21 Rubi Bar
26 Correos (Post Office)
27 Iglesia de San Juan de los Caballeros
28 Iglesia de San Sebastián
29 Telefónica
32 Iglesia de San Miguel
33 Tourist Office
37 Bodega de Isaac
38 Convento de Corpus Cristi
39 Caja de Ahorros de Segovia
42 Antigua Cárcel
43 Iglesia de San Martín
44 Bar Gimnasio
46 Bar El Ojo
47 Torreón de Lozoya
50 Casa de los Picos
52 Municipal Tourist Office
53 Acueducto
55 Iglesia de San Justo
57 Bars
59 Iglesia de San Clemente
61 Iglesia de San Millán
62 Estacionimiento Municipal de Autobuses
63 Comisaría de Policía

For an ambulance, call the Cruz Roja (☎ 43 01 00) or ☎ 061. The Hospital General (☎ 43 63 63) is about 1.5 km south-west of the acueducto on the Ávila highway.

Things to See

There are three key sights not to be missed in Segovia, and a warren of others worth investigation for the less time-conscious. In the first category are the aqueduct, cathedral and Alcázar. Student discounts are available on entry to some sights.

Acueducto & Around The 1728 metre granite block bridge you see today, made up of 163 arches, is the most extraordinary element of the engineering effort that went into the once 15 km Roman aqueduct raised here in the 1st century AD. Not a drop of mortar was used to hold the thing together – just good old Roman know-how. For almost 2000 years it has withstood the elements, but the modern civilisation that so prizes such antiques is on the verge of toppling it. Pollution and heavy traffic have so weakened the structure that it might just collapse like a house of cards. A delicate billion-peseta restoration programme is aimed at preventing this, but until the flow of traffic on its east side is permanently diverted, the single main cause of the problem will remain unresolved.

While at this end of town, you could inspect a few churches. The **Iglesia de San Millán** stands off Avenida de Fernández Ladreda in what looks akin to an abandoned building site. It is a worn example of the Romanesque typical of Segovia, with porticoes and a mudéjar bell tower. A couple of other late Romanesque churches around here are the **Iglesia de San Justo** and the **Iglesia de San Clemente**.

To the Catedral From the Plaza de Azoguejo beside the acueducto, Calle Real climbs into the innards of Segovia. About a quarter of the way up to Plaza Mayor, you strike the **Casa de los Picos** on the right, a Renaissance mansion named for the diamond-shaped bosses that cover its walls. A little further on and you emerge in one of the most captivat-

ing little squares in Segovia, Plaza de San Martín. It is presided over by a statue of Juan Bravo, a 15th century mansion and the 14th century **Torreón de Lozoya**, which is used for exhibitions. The *pièce de résistance* is however, the Romanesque **Iglesia de San Martín**, with the Segovian touch of mudéjar tower and arched gallery. The interior boasts a Flemish Gothic chapel. Next door is the former **cárcel** (prison). Shortly before Plaza Mayor, the Convento de Corpus Cristi is in the middle of the old *judería* (Jewish quarter) and used to be a **synagogue**.

The shady **Plaza Mayor** is the nerve centre of old Segovia, lined by an eclectic assortment of buildings, arcades and cafés. The **Iglesia de San Miguel**, where Isabel was crowned Queen of Castilla, recedes humbly into the background before the splendour of the cathedral across the square.

Catedral Completed in 1577, 50 years after its Romanesque predecessor had burned to the ground in the revolt of the Comuneros, the cathedral is a last, powerful expression of Gothic art in Spain. At the time of writing it was partly under restorers' scaffolding.

The austere interior contains an imposing choir in the centre and is ringed by 20-odd chapels. Of these, the Capilla del Cristo del Consuelo houses a magnificent Romanesque doorway preserved from the original church. Through here you can get to the Gothic cloister and the rooms of the Museo Catedralicio, with a varied collection of predominantly religious art. The cathedral's museum and cloister are open on weekdays from 9.30 am to 1 pm and 3 to 6 pm; at the weekend from 9.30 am to 6 pm. The weekend timetable operates all week in spring and summer. Entry is 250 ptas.

Around the Catedral The obvious way to the Alcázar is down Calle de Daoíz. About halfway along you pass yet another Romanesque church, the **Iglesia de San Andrés**. Virtually next door at No 9, suffering kids might perk up in the **Museo de Holografía**, open Tuesday to Sunday from 10.30 am to

2.30 pm and 4.30 to 8.30 pm. Entry is 200 ptas.

Before getting this far, you could turn right down Calle de los Desemparados for the **Casa-Museo de Antonio Machado**, at No 5. It opens Tuesday to Sunday from 4 to 7 pm (to 6 pm in autumn and winter). Machado, one of Spain's pre-eminent 20th century poets, lived in this house from 1919 to 1932. A few paces further down the road rises the six level tower of the 13th century Romanesque **Iglesia de San Esteban**.

The scenic way around to the Alcázar along Ronda de Don Juan II passes the **Casa de Sol**, at Calle de Socorro 11. It houses the Museo de Segovia, but only ever displays limited exhibits. It opens from 10 am to 2 pm and 4 to 7 pm from Tuesday to Saturday and 10 am to 2 pm on Sunday.

Alcázar Walt Disney liked it so much he made one in California. Blessed with unrestricted views right around, the site of Segovia's Alcázar has been fortified since Roman days. It takes its name from the Arabic *al-qasr* (castle) and was rebuilt and expanded in the 13th and 14th centuries. Felipe II added the touch of the slate witch's hats, but the whole lot burned down in 1862 and was subsequently painstakingly rebuilt.

The techumbre, or ceiling in the form of an inverted ship, in the Sala de la Galera, is a remarkable reconstruction of the original, while the grand Sala de los Reyes, crowned with an intricate frieze depicting 52 monarchs and another superb ceiling, is also the work of restorers' hands. Before you leave, climb the Torre de Juan II for the magnificent views. The Alcázar opens daily from 10 am to 6 pm (7 pm in summer) and entry costs 350 ptas.

Churches & Convents The rich smorgasbord of religious buildings to be discovered in Segovia goes well beyond what has been cited so far. A string of them stretches across the luxuriant valley of the Río Eresma to the north of the city – a pleasant area for a wander in the shadow of the walls, and a favourite with local picnickers.

Although the most self-effacing of Segovia's churches, the **Iglesia de la Vera Cruz** is one of the most curious. It was built in the 13th century by the Knights Templar, and its polygonal form is offset by a square-based bell tower and simple Romanesque doors. The church long housed what was said to be a piece of the True Cross (Vera Cruz). The church is open Tuesday to Sunday from 10.30 am to 1.30 pm and 3.30 to 7 pm (to 6 pm in autumn and winter). Entry costs 150 ptas. Nearby, San Juan de la Cruz lies buried in the **Convento de los Carmelitas Descalzos**.

The **Monasterio de El Parral** opens from 10 am to 12.30 pm and 4 to 6.30 pm. Ring the bell to get in and be shown part of the cloister and church, the latter a proud Gothic-mudéjar structure, even if the façade was never finished.

On the other side of the city, just off Avenida de Padre Claret (which becomes the N-601), the **Convento de San Antonio El Real** is also worth a look, although it's a bit of a hike. Once the summer residence of Enrique IV, it includes a Gothic-mudéjar church with a splendid artesonado ceiling. The convent is open weekdays from 4 to 6 pm only, and entry costs 250 ptas.

Special Events

Segovians are on the whole a sober lot, but they do let their hair down for the Fiestas de San Juan y San Pedro, which is celebrated on 24-29 June with parades, concerts and bullfights.

Places to Stay – bottom end

Camping & Hostel The nearest camping ground to the city, *Camping Acueducto* (☎ 42 50 00), is about two km south-east of town. Take bus No 2 from Plaza Mayor to where the road to La Granja forks with Avenida de Juan Carlos I. From here you can walk it, following the CN-601. It opens from April to September and charges 400 ptas per person, tent and car.

The youth hostel, such as it is, is only open in July and August. Called the *Albergue de*

CASTILLA Y LEÓN

Juan Bravo & the Comuneros

The ascension of Carlos I to the throne in 1516, uniting under his sceptre Spain and Austria, was not at all a welcome sign to many a Castilian noble family. It soon became clear that the newcomer's absolutist ways were bad news for local overlords unimpressed by the wave of foreigners suddenly entering key positions of power. When Carlos I left for the Netherlands in May 1520, confirming the fears of many that from here on Spanish interests would be subordinated to the needs of the Holy Roman Empire, the core Castilian cities, including Segovia, Toledo, Salamanca, León and Burgos, rose up in revolt. Thus began the Guerra de las Comunidades (War of the Communities).

In Segovia, Juan Bravo became one of the main leaders of the movement, which in July assumed the powers of state for itself. Although often depicted as a popular uprising, it was more about maintaining local privilege in the face of central, absolute and, to top it all, foreign control.

Segovia was soon under siege, but although Juan de Padilla, marching from Toledo, was unable to help, Bravo managed to keep the Royalists out. The Royalists then sacked Medina del Campo, which served only to push the undecided into the rebel Comunero camp. By September, the Comuneros seemed to have the backing of the queen, Juana la Loca, and the Royalists were in deep trouble. Now they pulled out some stops, declaring that they would prohibit the outflow of Spanish cash and halt the nomination of non-Spaniards to positions of power. By this time the rebel camp was coming asunder, with the moderates beginning to back-pedal. In the following months, although the Comuneros won several indecisive battles, the Royalists gained the upper hand after taking Tordesillas (where Queen Juana la Loca was confined). Finally, Padilla was defeated at the Battle of Villalar on 23 April 1521. He, Juan Bravo and other leaders of the revolt were promptly rounded up and executed. Toledo, under Padilla's wife María Pacheco, held out for a while, but soon had to throw in the towel. Absolute imperial rule had arrived in Spain. ■

la Juventud Emperador Teodosio (☎ 42 00 27), it's a fair way out of town (although handy for the train station) at Avenida del Conde de Sepúlveda s/n. A bed costs 850 ptas for under-26s and 1200 ptas for the rest.

Fondas & Hostales A box seat over Segovia's main square, *Fonda Aragón* (☎ 46 09 14), Plaza Mayor 4, on the 1st floor, has rambling old rooms for 1200/2500 ptas. There is no central heating and a shower costs 200 ptas – if there's hot water. Upstairs, *Fonda Cubo* (☎ 46 09 17) is in much the same category, but may charge a couple of hundred pesetas less.

If you have no luck with either of the above, *Hostal Juan Bravo* (☎ 43 55 21), Calle de Juan Bravo 12, will often have a room. Rooms with private bath cost 4000/4200 ptas and are adequate. There are a couple of dingy doubles without bath for 3300 ptas. More pleasant is *Hostal Plaza* (☎ 46 03 03), Calle del Cronista Lecea 11, which also offers a range of rooms starting at 3000/4000 ptas without private bath.

If you don't mind being further away from the centre, about the best deal is the spick-and-span *Hostal Don Jaime* (☎ 44 47 87), Calle de Ochoa Ondategui 8. Singles/doubles with TV cost 3000/5000 ptas.

Places to Stay – middle & top end
In the centre, another good choice is *Hostal El Hidalgo* (☎ 42 81 90), Calle de José Canalejas 3-5, with rooms for 4100/5350 ptas.

Climbing the scale somewhat, *Hotel Las Sirenas* (☎ 43 40 11; fax 43 06 33), Calle de Juan Bravo 30, has reasonable rooms with TV and telephone for 5000/7500 ptas plus IVA.

Top of the tree and in a prime location just off Plaza Mayor, *Hotel Infanta Isabel* (☎ 44 31 05; fax 43 32 40), Calle de Isabel la Católica 1, has all the comforts you require at 7000/10,900 ptas plus IVA.

Places to Eat
Segovians seem obsessed with roasts. Every second restaurant proudly boasts its roasts (*horno de asar*), and they say that 'pork has 40 flavours – all of them good'. Here the speciality is *cochinillo asado* (roast suckling

pig). This and *judiones de la Granja* (a bean dish) are the two big culinary offerings, and it has to be said the kitchen cliché is a little overdone: there isn't a restaurant, no matter how unlikely, that won't do its best to serve up piglets. The town's dessert is a heavy, sweet affair made with *ponche*, a popular Spanish spirit, and hence known as *ponche segoviano*.

Snacks & Breakfast The obvious place to sit down for a morning coffee and pastry is Plaza Mayor. It's lined with cafés, so you'll have no trouble... but they're expensive. If you're not troubled by views, you could head for *Bar El Antiguo Buscón*, Calle del Marqués del Arco 32. A breakfast of juice, coffee and toast will cost 200 ptas.

An excellent place to pick up a pastry for breakfast, or some ponche segoviano, is the *Confitería El Alcázar* at Plaza Mayor 10.

The *Cafetería Castilla*, Calle de Juan Bravo 56, is a popular spot with locals and good for baguettes with various fillings – glorified but good bocadillos. They cost around 400 ptas, depending on what you have on them. *Bar Yiyo's*, Calle de Doctor Sánchez 3, has hamburgers and the like and also one of the cheapest set lunches you're likely to find in Segovia – 875 ptas.

Restaurants A well-respected favourite with Segovians is *Mesón José María*, Calle del Cronista Lecea 11, where mains are about 1500 to 2000 ptas. A set meal featuring cochinillo comes in at 2100 ptas.

Restaurante Narizotas, Plaza de Medina del Campo 1, is ideal if only for its location – especially in summer when you can eat outside. You could eat well for about 2000 ptas. The nearby *Restaurante El Abuelo*, Calle de la Alhóndiga 9, has a rough-around-the-edges feel and serves solid meals for comparatively moderate prices.

Restaurante Tasca La Posada, Calle de la Judería Vieja 5, offers various set meals for lunch, including the predictable cochinillo and judiones for 2000 ptas a head.

North off Plaza Mayor, *Cuevas de San Esteban*, Calle de Valdeláguila 15 (you can

also get in from Calle de los Escuderos) serves a similar double role as eatery and decent bar.

More pricey is *Mesón Mayor*, Plaza Mayor 3, popular and recommended for traditional dishes. Ducking into another lane off Plaza Mayor, *Restaurante El Campesino*, Calle de la Infanta Isabel 12, is an equally well-known and reliable place.

At *Restaurante La Codorniz*, Calle de Aniceto Marinas 3, you can expect to pay about 1500 ptas for a good main meal.

Restaurante El Duque, a short way up Calle de Cervantes from the acueducto, has been going since 1895 and is Segovia's oldest dining establishment. For less formality, try its *Cuevas*, in the same building but entered at Calle de Santa Engracia 10. This is a snug place for a drink, and you can have anything on the restaurant menu as well. For a full meal you'll be lucky to get much change from 4000 ptas.

In the same price bracket and another Segovian old favourite is *Restaurante Cándido*, Plaza del Azoguejo 3.

Entertainment
Cafés & Bars In summer, *Bar Gimnasio* and *Bar El Ojo* spread out over Plaza de San Martín – a pleasant spot for coffee and an alternative to the obvious choice for a drink and people-watching – the cafés lining Plaza Mayor.

For those quirky enough to like the fast-disappearing spit-and-sawdust wine bars of old, *Rubi*, at Calle de los Escuderos 4, is the place to go.

The single best street for atmospheric bars and snacking is Calle de la Infanta Isabel. You'll also find a few decent watering holes on Calle de la Judería Vieja. The above mentioned Restaurante Tasca La Posada can get quite lively, and *Bodega de Isaac*, Puerta del Sol 1, is a cosy retreat. For a few discos, try Calle de los Escuderos. Or there is a small but loud collection of young people's bars along Calle de Ruiz de Alda, under the arches of the acueducto – the thumping music must do it a world of good...

CASTILLA Y LEÓN

Getting There & Away

Bus The Estacionamiento Municipal de Autobuses (☎ 42 77 07) is just off Paseo Ezequiel González, near the junction with Avenida de Fernández Ladreda. There are up to 16 departures a day to Madrid (Paseo de la Florida 11). Regular buses also link Segovia with La Granja, Valladolid and Cuéllar. AutoRes has up to four daily services to Salamanca (1340 ptas) and there is one to Ávila. Sepúlveda, Pedraza and Coca are also served by bus. On Sunday many services do not operate at all.

Train Up to nine trains run daily to Madrid (Chamartín and Atocha), but they are pretty slow.

Car & Motorcycle Of the two main roads down to the N-IV that links Madrid and Galicia, the N-603 is the prettier. The alternative N-110 cuts south-west across to Ávila, and north-east to the main Madrid-Burgos highway.

Getting Around

Bus No 3 runs between Plaza Mayor and the train station (passing the bus station on the way). Apart from this, walking is about the best way to get about, although it can involve some steep climbs if you intend to explore places like the Iglesia de la Vera Cruz.

AROUND SEGOVIA
La Granja de San Ildefonso

It is not hard to see why the Bourbon king Felipe V chose this site, nestling in the western foothills of the Sierra de Guadarrama about 10 km east of Segovia, to create his French version of Versailles, the palace of his French grandfather Louis XIV, the Sun King. In 1720 French architects and gardeners, with some Italian help, began laying out the elaborate gardens. The latter connection reminds one of another Bourbon extravaganza – Carlos III's later palace at Caserta, in southern Italy. El Real Sitio de la Granja de San Ildefonso remained a favourite

summer residence with Spanish royalty for the next couple of centuries – and is now a popular weekend destination for stressed madrileños.

La Granja's centrepiece is the garden's fountains. There are some 28 in all, of which about 10 stand out. Various of them are switched on from about 5 pm on Wednesday, Saturday and on Sunday (subject to change). The gardens open from 10 am to 9 pm daily and entry is free except when the fountains are on, when you have to get a 325 ptas ticket.

The Palacio Real, badly damaged by fire in 1918 and subsequently restored, is impressive but perhaps the lesser of La Granja's jewels. You can visit about half of the palace, including its Museo de Tapices (tapestry museum). Between June 1 and September 30 the palace opens Tuesday to Sunday from 10 am to 6 pm. The rest of the year it opens from 10 am to 1.30 pm and 3 to 5 pm, and Sunday from 10 am to 2 pm. It is closed on Monday. Entry is 650 ptas (250 ptas for students).

Around the palace sprang up a busy village that today caters mostly to the passing tourist trade. There are several bars, restaurants and hotels in the area around Plaza de los Dolores, the central square.

Pensión Pozo de la Nieve (☎ 921-47 05 98), Calle de los Baños 4, is one of the cheaper places to stay, with adequate rooms (bathroom outside) for 2000/3300 ptas. Similarly priced, and just where the road to Segovia begins, is the *Pensión El Parque* (☎ 921-47 09 59). *Hostal Madrid* (☎ 921-47 00 69), Plaza de la Fruta 1, is a big, brash sort of place with rooms for 4000/7000 ptas plus IVA. Right by the entrance to the palace and with a little more personality is *Hotel Roma* (☎ 921-47 07 52), Calle de Guardas 2. Rooms start at 4000/6500 ptas plus IVA.

There are plenty of restaurants to choose from. *Los Siros*, in the same building as Pensión Pozo de la Nieve, serves up filling set lunches for about 900 ptas. More expensive and occasionally more adventurous is *Restaurante Zaca*, Calle de los Embajadores 6 – try the almond chicken (pollo con almendras). Several of the bars liven up on the weekend. Try *Rey de Copas* and *El Gallo de Oro* on Calle de Carral.

Riofrío

About the nicest thing about the Palacio de Riofrío, 10 km south of Segovia along a private road, is the park around it. Teeming with deer, it has a vaguely untouched feel, and this is for good reason: security guards make sure people driving through it do not stop. The rather gloomy palace houses a hunting museum, and at 650 ptas per person is hardly worth the effort. From 1 June to 30 September, it opens Tuesday to Sunday from 10 am to 6 pm. The rest of the year it opens from 10 am to 1.30 pm and 3 to 5 pm (on Sunday from 10 am to 2 pm). EU citizens get in free on Wednesday. If you just want to drive (there's no bus) through the park, you pay a toll of 325 ptas per car.

A CASTLE TRAIL
Pedraza de la Sierra

The 400 or so inhabitants of this walled village, about 35 km north-east of Segovia, live in rough-hewn brown stone houses huddled together on a hefty rock platform. It is quite a captivating place, but more an open-air museum than a living community. During the week it is quite dead, but the considerable number of restaurants and bars come to life with the arrival of weekend swarms from Madrid and Segovia.

At the far end stands a lonely **castillo**, open at the weekend. Otherwise, they hang out a battered old sign: 'Hoy no se visita' (No visitors today). At the opposite end of town, by the only town gate, is the 14th century prison, which can also be visited on the weekend. The uneven, porticoed Plaza Mayor has a particular charm. You might be tempted to stop and eat at *El Soportal* or *El Yantar de Pedraza*, joined on the square by a couple of bars.

Turégano

About 30 km north of Segovia, Turégano is dominated by a unique 15th century castle-church complex built by the then archbishop of Segovia, Juan Arias Dávila, who decided to make a personal fortress of the town. The castle walls are built around the façade of the Iglesia de San Miguel, lending the whole its singular aspect.

Coca

A typically dusty, inward-looking Castilian village, Coca is presided over by a castillo that is anything but ordinary. A virtuoso piece of Gothic-mudéjar architecture and made entirely of brick, it was built in 1453 by the powerful Fonseca family. Surrounded by a deep moat, the beautiful exterior was once matched by an equally breathtaking Renaissance interior, which was nearly stripped of its ornamentation in the 19th century. Now belonging to a forestry school, the castillo has uncertain visiting hours, although it merits the effort just to see the exterior. Guided visits are possible on weekdays from 10.30 am to 1.30 pm and 4.30 to 6 pm, or on the weekend and on holidays from 11 am to 1.30 pm and 4.30 to 7 pm. If there's no-one about, try calling ☎ 921-58 63 59 or 58 66 47.

The town is just over 50 km north-west of Segovia and about 60 km south of Valladolid. Up to three buses a day run between Segovia and Coca.

Cuéllar

Located 60 km north of Segovia on the CL-601 to Valladolid, Cuéllar is yet another dusty Castilian settlement, where the harsh summer light seems even more blinding than usual. Perhaps that impression is in part due to the whitish grey stone of its massive 15th century castillo-cum-palace, which is what makes the place interesting. Displaying a mix of mudéjar style and Renaissance flair, it can only be visited on the weekend, from 11 am to 2 pm and 4 to 7 pm. Stretches of the town's defensive walls remain, and there are several churches (mostly deconsecrated) dating from as far back as the 12th century. The Iglesia de San Martín, near the castillo, combines mudéjar with Romanesque touches. Six buses run daily from Valladolid to Cuéllar.

CASTILLA Y LEÓN

VALLADOLID

Once the de facto capital of imperial Spain and a flourishing centre of the Spanish Renaissance, Valladolid is now a modern giant in which hints of former greatness are parsimoniously scattered about. With a population of some 350,000 (more than double that of 1950), Valladolid has known a rapid and unlovely expansion, buttressed by heavy industry and its position as a transport crossroads. The isolated splendours that remain of the old city repay exploration; early birds could stretch a point and make a day trip of it from Madrid.

History

Little more than a hamlet in the early Middle Ages, Valladolid had become a major centre of commerce, education and art by the time Fernando of Aragón and Isabel of Castilla discreetly contracted matrimony here in 1469. As Spain's greatest-ever ruling duo, they carried Valladolid to the heights of its splendour. Its university was one of the most dynamic in the peninsula, and things only got better under Carlos I, who based the Consejo Real here and so made Valladolid the seat of imperial government. A sad and unrewarded Christopher Columbus (Cristóbal Colón to the Spaniards) ended his days here in 1506 – about as far from the sea as he could get! The seeds of Valladolid's decline were sown here too, with the birth of Felipe II in 1527. Thirty-three years later he chose to make Madrid the capital, to the displeasure not only of Valladolid, but several other contenders too (such as Toledo).

Orientation

The centre of Valladolid lies east of the Río Pisuerga. At its southern edge are the Estación del Norte (trains) and the nearby bus station. From these it's about a 2.5 km walk to the Museo Nacional de Escultura, as far north as you're likely to want to go. The tourist office is at the northern tip of the Campo Grande, Valladolid's central park. Spread out between the museum and tourist office is the rest of what you are likely to

want to see, as well as hotels, restaurants and banks.

Information

Tourist Office The tourist office (☎ 35 18 01), Plaza de Zorrilla 3, opens Monday to Friday from 10 am to 2 pm and 5 to 8 pm. On Saturday it opens from 9 am to 2 pm and 4.30 to 8.30 pm, and on Sunday from 11 am.

Money There are plenty of banks with ATMs around Plaza de Zorrilla.

Post & Communications The main Correos y Telégrafos (post office) is on Plaza de la Rinconada and the postcode is 47080. There's a Telefónica office at Plaza Mayor 7. Valladolid's telephone code is ☎ 983.

Medical & Emergency Services The most central police comisaría is at Calle de Felipe II. Next door is the Hospital de la Cruz Roja Española (☎ 22 22 22).

Museo Nacional de Escultura & Around

No sober testament to modern museum-making, Spain's premier showcase of sculpture is housed behind a flamboyant example of Hispano-Flemish Gothic glory – the façade of what was once the Convento de San Gregorio, at the northern end of the town centre. Classic works of Spanish sculpture from the 13th through to the 18th centuries are on show. The first three rooms are devoted to Alonso de Berruguete and in particular an enormous retablo commissioned from him in 1526. The retablo was taken apart in order to fit it into the three rooms and is the star attraction of the ground floor, itself gathered around a pleasing Gothic patio.

The move towards the Renaissance is embodied in works by Diego de Siloé and Juan de Moreto (rooms 11 and 12), while the work of Juan de Juni (room 15) takes up more fluid Mannerist themes. His *Entierro de Cristo* rates a special mention. Don't fail to look over the *capilla* (chapel), left of the main entrance, which also contains interesting works, including another retablo by Berruguete.

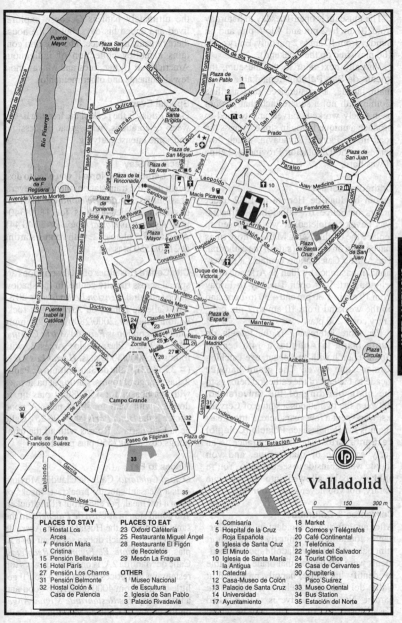

Valladolid

0   150   300 m

PLACES TO STAY

6 Hostal Los Arces
7 Pensión María Cristina
15 Pensión Bellavista
16 Hotel París
27 Pensión Los Charros
31 Pensión Belmonte
32 Hostal Colón & Casa de Palencia

PLACES TO EAT

23 Oxford Caféteria
25 Restaurante Miguel Ángel
28 Restaurante El Figón de Recoletos
29 Mesón La Fragua

OTHER

1 Museo Nacional de Escultura
2 Iglesia de San Pablo
3 Palacio Rivadavia
4 Comisaría
5 Hospital de la Cruz Roja Española
8 Iglesia de Santa Cruz
9 El Minuto
10 Iglesia de Santa María la Antigua
11 Catedral
12 Casa-Museo de Colón
13 Palacio de Santa Cruz
14 Universidad
17 Ayuntamiento
18 Market
19 Correos y Telégrafos
20 Café Continental
21 Telefónica
22 Iglesia del Salvador
24 Tourist Office
26 Casa de Cervantes
30 Chupitería Paco Suárez
33 Museo Oriental
34 Bus Station
35 Estación del Norte

The museum is open Tuesday to Saturday from 10 am to 2 pm and 4 to 6 pm, and on Sunday from 10 am to 2 pm only. Entry costs 400 ptas (free on the weekend).

Virtually next door to the museum, the **Iglesia de San Pablo** is remarkable for its main façade, a masterpiece of Isabelline Gothic with not a square inch that has not been finely worked, carved and twisted to produce a unique fabric in stone. Across the road in the Palacio Rivadavia, which now serves as the Diputación Provincial, Felipe II was born.

Cathedral Zone

Begun by Juan de Herrera in 1582 under orders of Felipe II, Valladolid's cathedral was never completed. It was supposed to replace the Gothic Santa María, whose ruins can be seen on the north side of the cathedral. The Museo Catedralicio contains a processional monstrance by Juan de Arfe and other religious art. It is open Tuesday to Friday from 10 am to 1.30 pm and 4.30 to 7 pm, and on the weekend from 10 am to 2 pm only. Entry costs 250 ptas.

Far more interesting is the **Iglesia de Santa María la Antigua**, a 14th century Gothic church with an elegant, eye-catching Romanesque tower. The grand baroque façade to the east of the cathedral belongs to the main building of the **universidad**. Between the two stands a statue of Cervantes, who spent a few years here. Further east again is the Renaissance **Palacio (Colegio) de Santa Cruz**. The main entrance is an early example of plateresque, and you should wander inside to see the patio. You're unlikely to be allowed into the baroque library, but you never know your luck.

Cervantes & Columbus

After an unfortunate incident in which Cervantes found himself unjustly doing a short stint behind bars in Valladolid, police documents were left behind that made it possible to identify his house, happily preserved at Calle del Rastro 7 behind a quiet little garden. Not so attractive is the so-called Casa-Museo de Colón. This may be where

the ultimately hapless Genoese explorer lived and ended his days, but of the house there remains not a trace. The museum contains a motley collection of indigenous American art (Aztec, Inca and Maya) and a few documents and other mementos.

Special Events

Good Friday is the peak of the frenetic Easter week celebrations, with great processions and some intense partying.

Places to Stay

Near Estación del Norte If you need to doss down near the train station, there are several possibilities. *Pensión Belmonte* (☎ 30 01 79) has basic singles/doubles for 1800/3400 ptas. A step up is *Hostal Colón* (☎ 30 40 44), Acera de Recoletos 22, with rooms starting at 2150/3550 ptas.

City Centre Hostelries of all descriptions are spread across the city centre. In the shadow of the cathedral, *Pensión Bellavista* (☎ 20 81 33), Calle de Núñez de Arce 1, has rock-bottom digs for 2000/2800 ptas. A more salubrious option is *Pensión María Cristina* (☎ 35 69 02), Plaza de los Arces 3, with rooms for 3000/4000 ptas. *Hostal Los Arces* (☎ 35 38 53), Calle de San Antonio de Padua 2, has a range of rooms, starting at basic ones with washbasin for 1500/3000 ptas up to doubles with bath for 4500 ptas. A good choice is the *Hotel París* (☎ 37 06 25), Calle de la Cebadería 2. Rooms with all the trimmings cost 5200/7550 ptas plus IVA.

Places to Eat

Oxford Cafetería, Calle de Claudio Moyano 4, is a pleasant spot for breakfast, snacks or even a full meal. For cheap but filling tucker, you could stop in at *Casa de Palencia*, in the same building as the Hostal Colón, Acera de Recoletos 22, which does a set menu for 850 ptas. *Restaurante El Figón de Recoletos*, Calle de Mantilla 2A, is one of the town's top restaurants and prices reflect this – you'll get little change from 4000 ptas. Also good and a little cheaper is *Restaurante Miguel Ángel* on the corner of Calle de Mantilla and Calle de M Escobar. There are a few others around here. *Mesón La Fragua*, on the west side of Campo Grande at Paseo de Zorrilla 10, has fine food, with mains coming in at around 1500 to 2000 ptas.

Entertainment

Cafés & Bars Plaza Mayor is a good place to seek out your morning coffee haunt. *Café Continental*, on the corner of Calle de Jesús, is especially good – they give you a free orange juice with your sticky bun. Another excellent bar-café and very popular is *El Minuto*, Calle de Macias Picavea 15. There are a few other bars for late-night drinking on the same street.

For a younger, louder scene, Calle de Padre Francisco Suárez, just west of the bottom end of Campo Grande, remains the main centre of late-night drinking action. The *Chupitería Paco Suárez* is just one of many favourites here.

Getting There & Away

Air There is one flight a day on weekdays to Paris and another to Barcelona. Otherwise the odd charter flight serves Palma de Mallorca and Tenerife (Canary Islands). The airport is 12 km west of town and there is no bus.

Bus There are regular buses to Madrid (Estación Sur), about a dozen to Palencia and about the same to Zamora via Tordesillas. Others run to Bilbao, Burgos, Barcelona (two a day), Logroño, Zaragoza, Segovia (five a day) and Salamanca.

Train Up to eight trains daily run between Valladolid and Madrid (Chamartín and most also to Atocha). The 2nd class one-way standard fare is 1455 ptas and the trip takes 2¾ hours. A similar number run to León (1095 ptas; two hours). A few head north to Burgos, Vitoria and Santander. All but the Madrid-bound trains pass through Palencia.

Car & Motorcycle The N-620 motorway passes Valladolid en route from Burgos to Tordesillas, where it picks up with the N-VI

between Madrid and La Coruña. The N-601 heads north-west to León and south to hit the N-VI and A-6 west of Segovia.

Getting Around

Local bus Nos 2 and 10 pass the train and bus stations on their way in to Plaza de España, while No 19 passes the stations and terminates in Plaza de Zorrilla.

AROUND VALLADOLID
Simancas

Simancas was an important junction in Roman times and a linchpin on the Duero defensive line in the early days of the Reconquista. The Castillo de Simancas has housed the Archivo Real (royal archive), which is still used by researchers, since the 16th century. It retains its medieval profile, but at the time of writing could not be visited. About the only other building of any note is the Late Gothic Iglesia del Salvador, and there are nice views over the Río Duero and its medieval bridge. Frequent buses (80 ptas) run the 13 km south from Valladolid.

Medina de Rioseco & Around

Much ignored, Medina de Rioseco is a trip of a different kind. From Plaza Mayor, the old Calle de Lázaro Alonso winds up a slope past the bulky but unattractive 16th century Iglesia de Santa Cruz. Peep into the shops and bars along this porticoed street, its pillars made of twisted wood, and you can't help feeling you are time-warping back to another era. Turn off for the Iglesia de Santa María de la Mediavilla, a grandiose Isabelline Gothic work with a pleasing baroque belfry. Down the hill, the Iglesia de Santiago is worth visiting for its pretty but neglected plateresque portal. Neglected is the word – some of Medina de Rioseco looks as though an earthquake just hit – but the place is interesting. *Hostal Duque de Osuna* (☎ 983-70 01 79), Avenida de Castilviejo 16 (not far from the end of Calle de Lázaro Alonso), has rooms ranging from 1500 to 2800 ptas. *Restaurante Pasos*, Calle de Lázaro Alonso 44, has loads of atmosphere and a set meal for 1600 ptas. At

CASTILLA Y LEÓN

least two buses connecting Valladolid, 40 km to the south-east, and León call in here.

Urueña For an off-the-beaten-track diversion, head 20 km south-west from Medina de Rioseco down the C-519 and take the turn-off south-east for Urueña (signposted). Judging by its powerful walls, this minuscule backwater must once have been an important place. Now you can stare out from the stout defences across the endless patch-work plains of the Tierra de Campos, and wonder at glories past. Urueña is equally accessible from Tordesillas and Toro on the road to Zamora – by car, that is.

PALENCIA
As sluggish as the Río Carrión that struggles through it, Palencia has little to divert you apart from the Gothic cathedral. Known to the Romans as Pallantia and later an important Visigothic centre, Palencia reached its zenith, as did so many other Castilian towns, in the Middle Ages, only to decay rapidly after the 15th century.

Orientation & Information
The bus and train stations are adjacent in the north-east corner of the town centre. From nearby Plaza de León, Calle Mayor forms the main north-south axis through Palencia, part of it pedestrianised. Several hotels lie near or just off it, as do most of the offices, banks and so on you may need.

The tourist office (☎ 74 00 68), Calle Mayor 105, opens Monday to Friday from 10 am to 2 pm and 5 to 8 pm, and slightly different hours on the weekend. There are several banks along the same street, while the Correos (post office) is on Plaza de León. A Telefónica office is situated on the corner of Calle del Patio de Castaño and Calle de Menéndez Pelayo. The postcode is 34080, and the telephone code is ☎ 979.

Catedral
Of the cathedral's otherwise austere exterior, the ornate Puerta del Obispo (Bishop's Door) is the most striking element, but you really

need to get inside the church and pay for a guided tour in Spanish (if you can stand it) to appreciate its riches.

The screen behind the choir stalls, or *trascoro*, is a masterpiece of bas-relief attributed to Gil de Siloé; it is considered the most beautiful trascoro in all Spain. The plateresque stairwell leads down beneath the choir stalls to the crypt, actually remnants of the original Visigothic church and a later Romanesque replacement. The crypt is known as the Cueva de San Antolín because King Wamba supposedly had the French martyr's remains moved here from Narbonne. In the Museo Catedralicio, you'll see some fine Flemish tapestries and a *San Sebastián* by El Greco. Along the tour, the guide lights up various other corners of the cathedral and takes you to the partly restored cloister. The cathedral is open Monday to Saturday from 10 am to 1.30 pm and 4 to 6.30 pm; the tour costs 300 ptas and starts every hour or so in the sacristy.

Other Attractions
Of the half-dozen or so other churches around town, it is worth seeking out the Iglesia de San Pablo, in the convent of the same name near the bus station, and the Iglesia de San Miguel. The former bears a Renaissance façade and in its Capilla Mayor you can see an enormous plateresque retablo. San Miguel stands out for its tall Gothic tower and, according to the legend, El Cid was betrothed to his Doña Jimena here. Just outside town, the 20-metre-high Cristo del Otero statue was erected in 1930 and dominates, Rio-style, the surrounding plains.

Places to Stay & Eat
There are about 20 hotels in Palencia. *Pensión Comercio* (☎ 74 50 74) is handily located at Calle Mayor 26, and singles/doubles cost 1300/2300 ptas. Nearby, *Pensión Eduardo* (☎ 74 29 48), Calle de Valentín Calderón 5, is a little better and charges 2000/3000 ptas. Better still is *Pensión El Hotelito* (☎ 74 69 13), Calle del

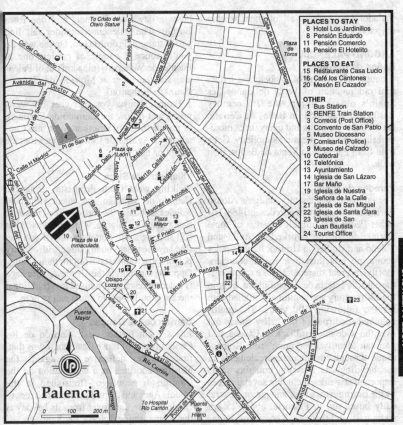

PLACES TO STAY
6 Hotel Los Jardinillos
8 Pensión Eduardo
11 Pensión Comercio
18 Pensión El Hotelito

PLACES TO EAT
15 Restaurante Casa Lucio
16 Café los Cantones
20 Mesón El Cazador

OTHER
1 Bus Station
2 RENFE Train Station
3 Correos (Post Office)
4 Convento de San Pablo
5 Museo Diocesano
7 Comisaría (Police)
9 Museo del Calzado
10 Catedral
12 Telefónica
13 Ayuntamiento
14 Iglesia de San Lázaro
17 Bar Maño
19 Iglesia de Nuestra
    Señora de la Calle
21 Iglesia de San Miguel
22 Iglesia de Santa Clara
23 Iglesia de San
    Juan Bautista
24 Tourist Office

Palencia

0   100   200 m

CASTILLA Y LEÓN

General Amor 5. The better doubles with private bath cost 3500 ptas. For a little more class, try *Hotel Los Jardinillos* (☎ 75 00 22), Calle de Eduardo Dato 2, with rooms at 4200/6000 ptas.

The *Mesón El Cazador*, Calle del Obispo Lozano 7, is a cosy little restaurant with a set meal for 900 ptas. *Restaurante Casa Lucio*, Calle de Don Sancho s/n, is a more elegant alternative, with a varied menu and main meals costing around 1000 to 1400 ptas. There are also several restaurants on Plaza Mayor. For drinks and tapas, *Café Los Cantones*, Calle Mayor 43, is a pleasant spot. *Bar*

Maño, Calle del General Franco 5, is an atmospheric old place.

Getting There & Away

Buses and trains run frequently to Valladolid and other main cities. Two buses a day go to Aguilar de Campóo via Frómista. One goes to Sahagún and several head for Paredes de Nava.

From Palencia roads fan out in a northerly arc. The N-611 heads up into Cantabria, the N-620 peels off east to Burgos, and the N-610 heads west to pick up the N-601 from

Valladolid to León – all of them worthy objectives.

AROUND PALENCIA
Baños de Cerrato
A couple of km west of the belching industrial rail junction of Venta de Baños lies Spain's oldest church, the 7th century Basílica de San Juan, in Baños de Cerrato. Built by the Visigoths and many times modified since, it has a pleasing simplicity. Get a train from Palencia to Venta de Baños, then walk.

Paredes de Nava
The eminent 16th century sculptor Alonso Berruguete was born in Paredes in 1488. His father Pedro was himself an artist of some distinction, having worked in Ávila and Toledo and studied in Urbino, Italy. Paredes counts no less than four major churches, mostly in great disrepair. The exception is the eclectic Iglesia de Santa Eulalia, built in the 13th century and continually fiddled with for the following 300 years. The multi-coloured tiled roof of the belfry stands out over the wide uneven Plaza de España, and you can identify everything from Romanesque through to Renaissance elements in the building. Its museum contains some important artworks, including several pieces by the Berruguetes senior and junior. Several daily buses run to Palencia, about 25 km south-east, and there are a couple of *fondas* if you need to stay.

Frómista
The exceptional Romanesque Iglesia de San Martín is the main reason for calling in here (apart from resting blistered feet if you are doing the Camino de Santiago walk). Long left to decay, it was faithfully restored towards the end of the last century, and the exterior is lined with a menagerie of human and zoomorphic figures. Inside, the capitals are also richly decorated. You can enter from 10 am to 2 pm and 4 to 7 pm. *Pensión Marisa* (☎ 979-81 00 23), Plaza de Obispo Almaraz 2, offers good clean rooms for 2200/3300 ptas. It also provides meals. There are two

buses a day from Palencia and one from Burgos. The Palencia-Santander rail line passes through Frómista too. On the way up you'll notice a couple of castles, one at Fuentes de Valdepero (nine km out of Palencia) and the other at Monzón de Campos (four km further on).

From Frómista you can veer off westwards and follow the Camino de Santiago, or pursue the N-611 further north into Cantabria via Aguilar de Campóo (see Montaña Palentina below).

Villalcázar de Sirga
Striking west from Frómista along the Camino de Santiago, the wheat village of Villalcázar boasts the fortress-like Iglesia de Santa María La Blanca, with a neglected but still striking south portal. Inside (if you can find anyone to let you in), three 13th century polychrome tombs stand out for their beauty. Opposite the church, the *Mesón de Villasirga* is a decent restaurant housed in a traditional medieval building. No buses call in here.

Carrión de los Condes
Just six km further west, Carrión de los Condes is one of those Castilian towns that, first as a key defensive post against the Muslims and then as a way station on the Camino de Santiago, flourished in the Middle Ages and then collapsed into irrecoverable decline. Left over from its heyday is the Romanesque Iglesia de Santiago, of which only the intricately decorated main façade survived destruction during the Peninsular War in 1811. More intact is the Iglesia de Santa María del Camino, begun in the 12th century, but with the odd Gothic and even baroque touch. The frieze above the main entrance purportedly depicts scenes from a legend according to which for a time 100 local women constituted the town's regular tribute to its Muslim overlords.

Across the Río Carrión, the former Monasterio de San Zoila is being turned into a luxury hotel, but you can still visit the 16th century cloister, which houses a handful of Romanesque tombs.

There is a camping ground, and *Pensión*

Estefania (☎ 979-88 01 60), Calle de Esteban Collantes 7, has rooms for 2000/3000 ptas.

From here, the road heads west on the pilgrim route across the Tierra de Campos (Land of Fields) – treeless since the area was deliberately cleared of all vegetation in a kind of medieval scorched earth policy during the Reconquista. The next major stop on the Camino is Sahagún (see the Around León section). A bus leaves Monday to Saturday at midday for León, and one for Burgos leaves around 5 pm. Ask at the Bar España.

MONTAÑA PALENTINA

The hills straddling the northern fringe of the province of Palencia are collectively known as the Montaña Palentina, and are an attractive and little-visited foretaste of the massive Cordillera Cantábrica that divides Castilla from Spain's northern Atlantic regions.

Aguilar de Campóo

The squat form of Aguilar de Campóo's medieval castillo stands watch over this quiet northern town, the historic heartland of Spanish biscuit production. You'll smell the biscuits if you approach from the east. Set a

---

El Camino de Santiago

The Camino de Santiago pilgrim route's principal path across Castilla y León is the so-called Camino Francés, which skims the top of the region. After leaving Logroño behind and traipsing the length of La Rioja, the route enters Castilla y León 54 km east of Burgos at the tiny settlement of Redecilla del Campo.

The pilgrim has plenty to keep him or her occupied along the way. Apart from the great cities of Burgos and León, several other important towns are distributed along the 390 km that the Camino covers in Castilla y León. At Frómista, the Romanesque Iglesia de San Martín has long been a must on the pilgrim's list of things to see, and the churches of San Tirso and San Lorenzo in Sahagún are two more gems. The *catedral* and Palacio de Gaudí of Astorga mark a unique juxtaposition of the very best of classic religious architecture and modern flights of fantasy. Other Camino stops covered in this chapter are Carrión de los Condes, Villafranca del Bierzo and Villalcázar de Sirga. The country across this northern strip of Castilla y León is largely typical of Castilla, with plains of cereal crops interrupted at intervals by low rises and winding streams. It is well protected from the capriciousness of Atlantic weather by the rock barrier of the Cordillera Cantábrica, but still uncomfortably cold throughout the long, dark months of winter. Only in its latter stages, as the *meseta* gives way to the mountains of Galicia, do real changes appear, setting the tone for what awaits those determined to pursue the Camino to the end.

You can pick up several brochures and a small guidebook to the Camino in Castilla y León from most tourist offices in the region. The latter lists *albergues* (refuges) for pilgrims and other accommodation possibilities in towns right along this stretch of the Camino.

For a general introduction to the Camino de Santiago, see the boxed aside in the Galicia chapter. A further aside in the País Vasco, Navarra & La Rioja chapter introduces the Camino's route across that part of Spain. ■

few km east of a big dam and about 15 km short of the regional boundary with Cantabria, the town makes a pleasant base for exploring the region, which is dotted with Romanesque churches and cool hilly countryside, presaging the beauty of the Cordillera Cantábrica to the north.

Tourist, post and telephone offices are all on or just off the elongated Plaza de España, which is capped at its eastern end by the majestic **Colegiata de San Miguel**, a 14th century Gothic church with a fine Romanesque entrance and small museum. Downhill from the castillo is the graceful Romanesque **Ermita de Santa Cecilia**, and just outside town on the road to Cervera de Pisuerga is the **Monasterio de Santa María la Real**, where the 13th century cloister is a masterpiece.

You'll find plenty of accommodation, including a few places right on Plaza de España. *Hostal Siglo XX* (☎ 979-12 29 00), at No 11, has perfectly good singles/doubles from 2000/3700 ptas. The square is swarming with cafés and bars and a couple of restaurants.

Regular buses link Aguilar de Campóo with Palencia, and at least one a day goes to Burgos and Santander.

Romanesque Circuit

The area around Aguilar is studded with little villages and churches of interest. One circuit for those with their own transport would take you south along the N-611 towards Palencia. At **Olleros de Pisuerga** is a little church carved into the living rock, while further south on a back road the Benedictine **Monasterio de Santa María de Mave** has an interesting 13th century Romanesque church. The prize in this area lies to the south-west, along the P-222. The **Monasterio de San Andrés de Arroyo** is an outstanding Romanesque gem, especially its cloister (one side of which was later restyled in a mixture of plateresque and Gothic).

The C-627 highway to **Cervera de Pisuerga** is lined with still more little churches dating from as far back as the 12th century. Cervera de Pisuerga itself is dominated by an imposing Late Gothic church, the Iglesia de Santa María del Castillo. There are several places to stay, including the homely *Hostal Cervera* (☎ 979-87 02 34), Plaza Mayor 16, with singles/doubles going for 3000/4000 ptas.

From Cervera you could complete the circle and return to Aguilar. Alternatively, a narrow mountain road winds west along the so-called *ruta de los pantanos* (dams route), describing an arc to Guardo, just short of the provincial frontier with León. The N-621 north from Cervera is a lovely road into Cantabria and to the south face of the Picos de Europa mountains (see the Cantabria & Asturias chapter).

THE ROAD TO ZAMORA

Castilla is at its least flattering around Valladolid, and the road to Zamora is no exception. But while you won't want to hang around for the parched, featureless countryside, there are several worthwhile stops en route.

Tordesillas

Commanding a rise on the north flank of the Río Duero, this originally Roman town became part of the front line between the Christians and Muslims after the latter had been thrown back from the north in the 9th century.

There is a tourist office in Las Casas del Tratado, near the Iglesia de San Antolín. It opens Wednesday to Saturday from 10.30 am to 2 pm and 5 to 8 pm, and on Sunday and holidays from 10 am to 2 pm.

Convento de Santa Clara Much of the history of Tordesillas has been dominated by this convent, still home to 14 Franciscan nuns living in almost total isolation from the outside world. What started as a palace for Alfonso XI, much of it built in the mudéjar style, was later turned into a convent by Pedro I. In its heyday, more than 70 nuns lived here. It is commonly held that the mad queen, Juana la Loca, was locked up here for many years before her death in 1555. She was in fact buried here for 19 years before her body was exhumed and transferred to Granada (as she had wished). Her place of confinement, a nearby castle, no longer exists. Juana was shunted aside after her husband Felipe I died in 1506, although she remained officially queen and treated with the Comuneros during their uprising (see the boxed aside 'Juan Bravo & the Comuneros' earlier in this chapter).

The guided tour takes in some remarkable rooms, including a wonderful mudéjar patio left over from the palace, and the church, whose stunning ceiling, or techumbre, is a masterpiece of woodwork.

The convent is open Tuesday to Saturday from 10 am to 1.30 pm and 3.30 to 7 pm, and on Sunday and holidays from 10.30 am to 2 pm and 3.30 to 6 pm. Hours are slightly shorter from October to March. Entry to the convent is 425 ptas, and a separate guided tour of the Arab baths is 225 ptas.

Around Town The deconsecrated Gothic **Iglesia de San Antolín** houses a religious art museum, open Tuesday to Saturday from 10

am to 2 pm and 4 to 8 pm, and on Sunday from 10 am to 2 pm. Entry is 250 ptas.

The heart of town is formed by the pretty, arcaded Plaza Mayor, whose deep yellow paintwork contrasts with dark brown woodwork and black *rejas* (grilles).

Places to Stay & Eat All Tordesillas' hotels are on or near the highways to Madrid, Valladolid and Salamanca, and many are on the expensive side. One characterless but quiet, clean place is the *Hostal Bastida* (☎ 983-77 08 42), Avenida de Valladolid 38. You can get rooms for 1300 ptas per person, and it's handy for buses. Nearby, *Hotel Los Toreros* (☎ 983-77 19 00) has comfier rooms with TV and private bath for 4500/ 6500 ptas. *Bar Ruski*, on Calle Garabato, off Calle de Santa María, is a cheap and cheerful place to eat. The cafés on Plaza Mayor are great for a morning coffee.

Getting There & Away Buses for Valladolid and Zamora leave regularly from Avenida de Valladolid, near Calle de Santa María.

Medina del Campo
A mostly morose stop 25 km south of Tordesillas, Medina del Campo does have one or two redeeming features, apart from being a major rail junction. You'll find a tourist office (☎ 983-81 13 57) at Plaza Mayor 27.

The dignified **Castillo de la Mota**, just outside town across the railway line to Madrid, is another fine example of the mudéjar brickwork species in Castilla y León. It's closed for restoration, but there wasn't much to see inside anyway. In town, make for the huge rambling Plaza Mayor de la Hispanidad (Plaza de España). Queen Isabel dictated her last will and testament in the **Palacio Real**, an unassuming edifice on the west side of the square.

There are quite a few places to stay in Medina. *Pensión Medina* (☎ 983-80 26 03), Plaza Mayor 36, has very basic rooms for 2000 ptas. For something better, try *Hostal El Orensano* (☎ 983-80 03 41), Calle Claudio Moyano 20 (out towards the train station), where singles/doubles start at

CASTILLA Y LEÓN

❋ ❋ ❋ ❋ ❋ ❋ ❋ ❋ ❋ ❋ ❋ ❋

The Treaty of Tordesillas
Only two years after Columbus had sailed the ocean blue, Spain's Catholic Monarchs and Portugal sat down at the negotiating table in Tordesillas to hammer out a treaty regulating who got what in the New World. The Spanish-born Borgia pope, Alexander VI, had earlier simply pronounced that everything west of the Azores Islands belonged to Spain, something Lisbon considered slightly lopsided. The Tordesillas deal pushed the limiting line 370 leagues (a little less than 1800 km) further west, after which Portugal claimed Brazil. The French monarch, François I, asked himself whether this rather pompous division of the planet (a separate treaty dividing up Africa was also signed) was part of some secret clause in Adam's last will and testament. Later on, Spain and Portugal began to recognise that more than one demarcation line for America, or at least the southern half of it, was required, and they thrashed it all out again in the Treaty of Zaragoza in 1529. ■

❋ ❋ ❋ ❋ ❋ ❋ ❋ ❋ ❋ ❋ ❋ ❋

2300/3000 ptas. Restaurants abound in the vicinity of Plaza Mayor, and Calle de Ángel Molina is loaded with bars.

Buses run from various points around the town, but for most destinations you are better off with the trains. More than 20 a day run to Madrid (1215 ptas). Other regular services include: Salamanca (one hour; 450 ptas); Valladolid (50 minutes; 290 ptas) and Ávila (45 minutes).

Toro

The drama of Toro's position north of the Río Duero, a 37 km sprint west of Tordesillas, only becomes clear when you get into the centre of this higgledy-piggledy place. Coming from Zamora, the wandering English writer Laurie Lee was quite unprepared for the 'ancient, eroded, red-walled town spread along the top of a huge flat boulder', which to his surprise, 'half-ruined though it certainly was – was ... buzzing with life'. His account, from *As I Walked Out One Midsummer Morning*, would not be totally out of place today. Having seen the whole historical parade – Celts, Romans, Visigoths, Muslims et al – Toro reached the height of its glory between the 13th and the 16th centuries. Fernando and Isabel cemented their primacy in Christian Spain at the Battle of Toro in 1476. The tourist office (☎ 980-69 18 62) is in the ayuntamiento building in Plaza de España.

Partly inspired by the Catedral Vieja in Salamanca, the **Catedral de Santa María Mayor** boasts a fine Romanesque doorway in the north façade and the still more magnificent Romanesque-Gothic Pórtico de la Majestad, which is being restored. The church opens from 11 am to 1.15 pm and 5 to 7.30 pm. From behind the cathedral you have a superb view south across fields to the Romanesque bridge over the Duero. The nearby 10th century Alcázar conserves its walls and seven towers.

The 13th century Romanesque-mudéjar **Iglesia de San Lorenzo el Real**, north-west of the Alcázar, is worth a look. South-west of town, the **Monasterio Sancti Spiritus** features a fine Renaissance cloister and the

striking alabaster tomb of Beatriz de Portugal, wife of Juan I. It is open from 9.30 am to 2 pm and 4 to 7 pm, and it has a small museum too.

Most of the accommodation is out of town, but there is an adequate fonda, *Pensión Castilla* (☎ 980-69 03 81), at Plaza de España 19. It has rooms for 1400/2600 ptas. For more style, go for the *Hotel Juan II* (☎ 980-69 03 00), Paseo Espolón 1, near the cathedral. Singles/doubles start at 3500/5000 ptas. There are plenty of little places to eat around Plaza de España.

Forget the train – the station is two km downhill and few trains stop here anyway. Regular buses to Zamora and Valladolid leave from near the junction of Avenida de Carlos Pinilla and Calle de la Corredera, while Madrid buses leave from the edge of town at Calle de Santa Catalina de Roncesvalles. All these services stop in at Toro en route from bigger centres. There are two direct services to Salamanca on weekdays.

ZAMORA

Another fortress town on the north bank of the natural defensive line of the Río Duero, Zamora is far enough away from other major Castilian cities not to figure highly on travellers' itineraries. It's a middle-ranking town that in the past 30 years has slowly expanded as the surrounding rural area empties its labour force into the city. The already subdued casco antiguo in the western half of the city gets quieter and quieter as the people move into the growing modern *barrios* (suburbs) to the east.

History

Roman Ocelum Durii was a significant way station along the Ruta de la Plata (silver route) from Astorga to southern Spain. The Romans were replaced by the Visigoths, who in turn collapsed before the Muslim invasion. Zamora was twice laid waste by the Muslims, and it was not until the 11th century that the Christians began serious reconstruction. By the 12th and 13th centuries, when a fever of church-building formed

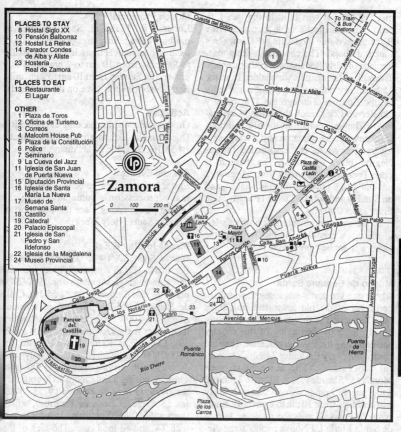

PLACES TO STAY
8 Hostal Siglo XX
10 Pensión Balborraz
12 Hostal La Reina
14 Parador Condes
    de Alba y Aliste
23 Hostería
    Real de Zamora

PLACES TO EAT
13 Restaurante
    El Lagar

OTHER
1 Plaza de Toros
2 Oficina de Turismo
3 Correos
4 Malcolm House Pub
5 Plaza de la Constitución
6 Police
7 Seminario
9 La Cueva del Jazz
11 Iglesia de San Juan
    de Puerta Nueva
15 Diputación Provincial
16 Iglesia de Santa
    María La Nueva
17 Museo de
    Semana Santa
18 Castillo
19 Catedral
20 Palacio Episcopal
21 Iglesia de San
    Pedro y San
    Ildefonso
22 Iglesia de la Magdalena
24 Museo Provincial

Zamora

CASTILLA Y LEÓN

the architectural core of what you see today,
Zamora had reached its zenith as a commercial centre.

Orientation

The bus and train stations are a good half-
hour walk roughly east of the town centre,
from where it's another 15 minutes west to
the cathedral and the heart of the casco
antiguo. Accommodation is spread out
roughly between Plaza Mayor and Calle
Alfonso IX, which marks the eastern boundary of the city centre.

Information

The tourist office (☎ 53 18 45), Calle de
Santa Clara 20, opens Monday to Friday
from 10 am to 2 pm and 5 to 8 pm, and 9.30
am to 2.30 pm on Saturday.

The Correos (post office) is at Calle de
Santa Clara 15. The postcode is 49080.
Zamora's telephone code is ☎ 980. There are
plenty of banks on and around Plaza de
Castilla y León.

Catedral

Crowning medieval Zamora's highest point,
the largely Romanesque cathedral is an odd

mix. Most of it was built in the late 12th century, and its most notable aberration is the Byzantine dome (recalling Salamanca's Catedral Vieja). The choir stalls are a masterpiece of early Renaissance craftsmanship. The bulk of the chapels were added from the 15th century on, some showing a markedly Gothic flourish. Through the 17th century cloister you can reach the Museo Catedralicio. The museum has mainly religious treasures, but the star attraction, for tapestry-lovers at any rate, is the so-called Tapices Negros (black tapestries). The museum is open Tuesday to Saturday from 11 am to 2 pm and 5 to 8 pm (4 to 6 pm in winter), and on Sunday and holidays from 11 am to 2 pm. Entry costs 200 ptas.

In the grounds outside stands what's left of the city's **castillo**, and this is where the city walls are best preserved.

Museo de Semana Santa

About one km north-east along the northern perimeter of the old town, this museum's main attraction is the *pasos*, statues dating mostly from the beginning of this century and depicting the Passion of Christ. They are hauled out every Easter for Zamora's colourful processions. The museum is open Monday to Saturday from 10 am to 2 pm and 4 to 8 pm (to 7 pm in winter), and on Sunday and holidays from 10 am to 2 pm only. Entry costs 200 ptas. Across the road, the Iglesia de Santa María La Nueva retains some elements of the 12th century Romanesque original.

Churches

Zamora is dotted with churches built in the 12th century, but in most cases they have been much altered. Among those retaining some of their Romanesque charm are the Iglesia de San Pedro y San Ildefonso (with Gothic touches), Iglesia de la Magdalena (look at the south doorway, considered the city's best), and Iglesia de San Juan de Puerta Nueva. They open from 10 am to 1 pm and 5 to 8 pm, and are closed on Monday.

Museo Provincial

Located on Plaza de Santa Lucía, the museum has a mildly engaging collection of local archaeological finds. It is open Tuesday to Saturday from 10 am to 2 pm and 4 to 9 pm, and on Sunday from 10 am to 2 pm only. Entry costs 100 ptas (free on the weekend).

Activities

Groups interested in canoeing along the Río Duero might like to approach Turisnautic (☎ 51 10 53), Calle de la Amargura 2.

Special Events

Easter is a good time to be in Zamora, with many processions, some involving the unique pasos, taking place through most of Semana Santa (Holy Week).

Places to Stay & Eat

Hostal Siglo XX (☎ 53 29 08), Plaza del Seminario 1, is in a pleasant, quiet spot and has simple singles/doubles for 1950/2980 ptas. *Pensión Balborraz* (☎ 51 55 19), Calle de Balborraz 25-29, offers more spacious rooms for 1000/1900 ptas. More attractive than either is the *Hostal La Reina* (☎ 53 39 39), Calle de la Reina 1, with rooms for 1800/2600 ptas with washbasin only, and doubles with private bath for 3500 ptas. Those requiring a little more style could try the *Hostería Real de Zamora* (☎ 53 45 45; fax 53 45 22), Cuesta de Pizarro 7, which starts at 5000/6500 ptas plus IVA for rooms with TV and all mod cons. The pick of the crop is the *Parador Condes de Alba y Aliste* (☎ 51 44 97; fax 53 00 63), Plaza Viriato 5, where princely rooms start at 13,000 ptas.

Restaurante El Lagar, Calle del Sacramento, is an inviting place to try some cabrito (kid meat).

Entertainment

For a relaxing coffee or beer and a bit of people-watching, the cafés on Plaza Mayor are fine. If it's late-night drinking you're after, head off the square down the narrow Calle de los Herreros, which is jammed with pubs and bars. A little more sedate is *La Cueva del Jazz*, Cuesta del Piñedo 5.

Getting There & Away

Bus The bus station is a good half-hour's walk from the centre and there are no local buses. Still, bus is generally the best way to get to Zamora. Regular services link it with Salamanca (475 ptas; 13 a day), Valladolid (seven a day), Benavente (eight a day), León (five a day) and Madrid (3¼ hours; six a day). A couple of buses run to places as far away as Santiago de Compostela and Sevilla, as well as into Portugal.

Train The train station is just down the hill from the bus station. There are up to six trains a day to Madrid (Chamartín). A couple of these go via Ávila, and one goes on to Zaragoza and Barcelona. Two trains head for Galicia (Vigo, Pontevedra and La Coruña).

Car & Motorcycle See below for routes out of Zamora.

BEYOND ZAMORA
North to León

The N-630 heads directly north from Zamora to León. There is little to hold you up on the way, but in **Benavente** a *parador* has been built around the impressive Torre del Caracol, a squat 15th century castle tower. About 30 km before, just south of the village of Granja de Moreruela, lie the ramshackle ruins of a 12th century **monastery** in a perfect state of bucolic abandon, four km down a track west of the highway.

From Benavente you could skew west along the N-525 for La Puebla de Sanabria and on to Galicia (see below), or keep bearing north for León or north-west towards Astorga and on to pick up the Camino de Santiago at Villafranca del Bierzo. Major roads also run east to Palencia and Valladolid.

Buses run to Benavente and on to León from Zamora.

To Portugal

Even if Portugal is not on your itinerary, if you have a vehicle it is worth considering heading west to the fascinating northern Portuguese town of **Bragança**. From there you

can also easily head on to Galicia. With border controls all but nonexistent, the trip is as hassle-free as travelling within Spain, and the city is a worthwhile stop.

To Galicia

An alternative route to Galicia runs north-west from Zamora between the Sierra de la Culebra and Sierra de la Cabrera.

La Puebla de Sanabria Here a captivating little web of medieval alleyways unfolds around the 15th century castle built with an eye to nearby Portugal by the fourth Conde de Benavente. You can enter the castle at will and wander around the walls. The transition from Castilla to Galicia is already manifest here in the increasingly hilly country, the stone houses with their slate roofs, lower bar prices and even in the way people speak – a pleasing lilt peculiar to the far west of Spain.

There are several hotels at the foot of the old town. *Hostal Galicia* (☎ 980-62 01 06), Calle de las Ánimas 22, has basic singles for 1600 ptas, while the nearby *Hotel Victoria* (☎ 980-62 00 12), Calle del Arrabal 29, has doubles for 5000 ptas. *Cervecería Veti*, just off Plaza Mayor near the castle, has cheap tapas and wine.

By car you can follow the N-525 west from La Puebla over the Portilla de la Canda on the way to Verín, in Galicia. From there you could swing northwards to Orense or push on for the Rías Bajas on the Atlantic. There are buses between La Puebla and Benavente.

Lago de Sanabria About 15 km north of La Puebla de Sanabria, this lake is a peaceful spot with some pleasant walking possibilities in the surrounding *parque natural*. You will find camp sites dotted around the lake, which was originally formed by glaciers. Otherwise, there are a couple of hostales in Ribadelago de Franco, where the road on the lake's southern shore peters out. The best is the brand-new *Hostal San Martín* (☎ 980-62 03 37), Plaza de España 1, where the spotless rooms have en suite bath and TV. Singles/doubles/triples cost 3900/5000/7000 ptas.

San Martín de Castañeda, a small village with a monastery high up above the northern flank of the lake, has no accommodation.

Detour through Portugal Incurable dawdlers heading between Galicia and La Puebla de Sanabria might consider going the long way. Just 19 km south of La Puebla lies the Portuguese frontier, and a mere 22 km beyond it is Bragança. You could make this a Portuguese lunch stop (if you have the flexibility of your own vehicle), or extend the process still further by following the serpentine N-103 between Bragança and Chaves, to the west, from where Galicia lies about 10 km to the north. It's a longish drive, but much of it has you up on a ridge with rewarding views away on both sides.

León & the North-West

Once the centre of Christian Spain, León now stands like a sentinel at the rim of the great Castilian heartland. The last major city on the Camino de Santiago before it climbs west into the sierras that separate Castilla from Galicia, León is also the final staging post on the road north towards the Cordillera Cantábrica and Asturias – a lush, green idyll worlds away from these sun-drenched expanses. For all that, even before you cross into Galicia, Asturias or Cantabria, you can feel the coming changes in climate, landscape, language and people. And even the Picos de Europa mountains (see the Cantabria & Asturias chapter) spill over here into Castilla y León's most northerly reaches.

LEÓN

For a couple of centuries the flourishing capital of the expanding Christian kingdom of Asturias and León, the city of León retains a powerful hold over its visitors. In possession of two jewels of Spanish Romanesque and Gothic creativity, the city is also liberally sprinkled with less exalted reminders of its glory days, and blessed with a bustling city centre, itself a successful marriage of medieval inheritance and thoughtful modern town planning.

History

In 70 AD a Roman legion made camp where later the city of León would rise. The imperial troops were based here to control the gold mines of Las Médulas, further west. A residual settlement muddled along until the Asturian King Ordoño II decided to move his capital here from Oviedo in the 10th century. Later sacked by Al-Mansour, León was nevertheless maintained by Alfonso V as the capital of his growing kingdom, a role it continued to play until the union with Castilla in 1230. It was in this period that the city reached its zenith. Centuries of decline followed, but mining brought León back to life in the 19th century. In this respect, the city has more in common with its Asturian neighbours across the Cordillera to the north than with its Castilian sister cities to the south and east, and during the Second Republic León's workers joined their Asturian comrades in the bloody, and ultimately futile, October revolt of 1934.

Orientation

The train and bus stations lie on the west bank of the Río Bernesga, while the heart of the city is concentrated on the east side. Cross the river at the bridge nearest the train station and head east along Avenida de Ordoño II. From the river to the cathedral it's about a km, with Plaza de Santo Domingo marking the halfway point. There are plenty of banks, hotels and pensiones on or off this axis, and a good number of the restaurants and bars are within a short walking distance of the cathedral.

Information

Tourist Office The tourist office (☎ 23 70 82), Plaza de la Regla 3 (opposite the cathedral), is open Monday to Friday from 10 am to 2 pm and 5 to 8 pm, on Saturday from 9 am to 2.30 pm and 4.30 to 8.30 pm, and on Sunday from 11 am to 2 pm and 4.30 to 8.30 pm.

Money There are any number of banks along

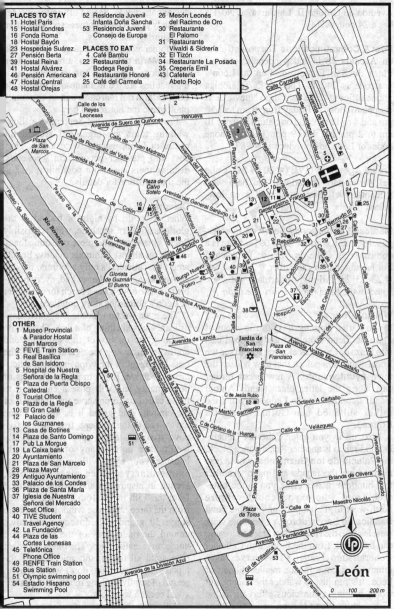

PLACES TO STAY
11 Hotel París
15 Hostal Londres
16 Fonda Roma
18 Hostal Bayón
23 Hospedaje Suárez
27 Pensión Berta
39 Hostal Reina
41 Hostal Alvárez
46 Pensión Americana
47 Hostal Central
48 Hostal Orejas
52 Residencia Juvenil
   Infanta Doña Sancha
53 Residencia Juvenil
   Consejo de Europa

PLACES TO EAT
4 Café Bambu
22 Restaurante
   Bodega Regia
24 Restaurante Honoré
25 Café del Carmela
26 Mesón Leonés
   del Racimo de Oro
30 Restaurante
   El Palomo
31 Restaurante
   Vivaldi & Sidrería
32 El Tizón
34 Restaurante La Posada
35 Crepería Emil
43 Cafetería
   Abeto Rojo

OTHER
1 Museo Provincial
   & Parador Hostal
   San Marcos
2 FEVE Train Station
3 Real Basílica
   de San Isidoro
5 Hospital de Nuestra
   Señora de la Regla
6 Plaza de Puerta Obispo
7 Catedral
8 Tourist Office
9 Plaza de la Regla
10 El Gran Café
12 Palacio de
   los Guzmanes
13 Casa de Botines
14 Plaza de Santo Domingo
17 Pub La Morgue
19 La Caixa bank
20 Ayuntamiento
21 Plaza de San Marcelo
28 Plaza Mayor
29 Antiguo Ayuntamiento
33 Palacio de los Condes
36 Plaza de Santa María
37 Iglesia de Nuestra
   Señora del Mercado
38 Post Office
40 TIVE Student
   Travel Agency
42 La Fundación
44 Plaza de las
   Cortes Leonesas
45 Telefónica
   Phone Office
49 RENFE Train Station
50 Bus Station
51 Olympic swimming pool
54 Estadio Hispano
   Swimming Pool

CASTILLA Y LEÓN

León

0   100   200 m

Avenida de Ordoño II. La Caixa, at No 11, has a 24 hour ATM.

Post & Communications The post office is on Avenida de la Independencia, just off Plaza de San Francisco. Central León's postcode is 24080. There is a Telefónica phone office at Calle del Burgo Nuevo 15. It is open Monday to Friday from 9 am to 2.30 pm and 4 to 11 pm, and on Saturday from 10 am to 2 pm and 4 to 9 pm. The telephone code for León and province is ☎ 987.

Travel Agencies TIVE (☎ 20 09 51), Calle del Arquitecto Torbado 4, can help with student travel information and even low-priced tickets.

Medical & Emergency Services In emergencies, call the police on ☎ 091 – there is a comisaría on Calle de Villa de Benavente. For an ambulance call either ☎ 24 24 24 or ☎ 23 23 23. All-night pharmacy rotas are listed in the local paper, *Diario de León*.

Walking Tour

If you started from the busy traffic circus of Plaza de Santo Domingo and dropped east into Plaza de San Marcelo, you would see the Renaissance-era palace that now houses the town **ayuntamiento**. A few paces further east along the latter plaza stands Antoni Gaudí's contribution to León's skyline, the rather subdued neo-Gothic **Casa de Botines**.

Next up as you enter Calle del Generalísimo Franco is another Renaissance block, the **Palacio de los Guzmanes**, whose best features are the façade and patio. Another few hundred metres bring you to the **catedral**, from where you could venture north-west to the equally unmissable **Real Basílica de San Isidoro**. A 15 minute walk west leads to the **Hostal San Marcos**, or you can backtrack from the basilica to Calle del Generalísimo Franco. This serves as a jumping-off point for the medieval heart of León. It's fun just to wander the streets, but worth making a conscious effort for is the 17th century **Plaza Mayor**, or former Plaza del Ayuntamiento. Sealed off on three sides by shady porticoes, it comes especially alive on Saturday, market day.

Another captivating square is **Plaza de Santa María del Camino**, a broad, uneven cobblestone expanse whose most outstanding features are the Romanesque **Iglesia de Santa María del Mercado** and an extremely photogenic old house and bar.

From mid-June to mid-September, official walking tours are organised around the centre of León, usually twice a day. They cost 400 ptas per person. On weekends, evening tours are also a possibility. Ask at the tourist office for details.

Catedral

Whether spotlit by night or bathed in the glorious northern sunshine, what is possibly Spain's greatest masterpiece of Gothic fancy exudes an almost luminous quality. People aren't the cathedral's only admirers, for day and night, good weather or bad, every possible pinnacle doubles as a perch for a member of León's numerous stork populace.

The main western façade is at once magnificent and something of a flop. There is no doubting the quality of the sculpture and craftwork in among the ogival arches – the Last Judgment in the tympanum is particularly evocative. Problem is, the stone is of poor quality and will pose a challenge to those called on to preserve the grandeur of the church. And grand it is. Inside, three naves lead to the transept, from which five naves pass on to the apse. You probably won't have noticed any of this though, because your eyes will be glued to the extraordinary stained-glass windows, French in inspiration and mostly executed from the 13th to the 16th centuries. Aside from the three huge rose windows, there are some 30 grand kaleidoscopic windows around the main body of the church, and numerous smaller ones. The one discordant note amid all the artistic splendour is the piped Gregorian chant; don't waste time in search of saintly-looking monks giving their vocal cords a work-out.

Adjoining the church proper is an unusully florid cloister, off which a series of rooms show off what remains of the cathedral's riches, mostly religious art ranging from early Romanesque through to the baroque. A good deal of the cathedral's once exceptional wealth in gold and silver was melted down to finance the good fight against Napoleon in the Peninsular War.

The cathedral and its museum are open Monday to Saturday from 9.30 am to 1 pm and 4 to 6.30 pm, and Sunday morning. Entry to the museum and cloister costs 400 ptas. Or you can visit the cloister alone for 100 ptas. The bad news is that the guided tour of the museum and cloister (in Spanish) is unavoidable: the guide opens and closes each room as s/he goes.

Real Basílica de San Isidoro

A step back further in history, San Isidoro is as seminal a work of Romanesque as the cathedral is a gem of Gothic. The right-hand entrance (Puerta del Perdón) has been attributed to Maestro Mateo, the genius of the cathedral at Santiago de Compostela.

The real attractions, however, lie beyond the souvenir desk. You first enter what was initially a portico in front of the original main entrance to the basilica. The entrance was later sealed off and the portico became a burial place for early Leonese and Castilian royalty, later known as the **Panteón Real**. More than 40 kings, queens, princes, infantes and counts were buried here – you can see a roll posted up next to the former church entrance.

Napoleon's troops sacked San Isidoro in the early 19th century, leaving behind them only about five sarcophagi. What they couldn't take remains today as one of the greatest treasures in Romanesque art in Spain, if not all Europe. The frescos that cover the vaults and arches of the Panteón represent the cream of 12th century art, depicting a range of Biblical scenes, among them the Annunciation, to the right of the former church entrance; King Herod's slaughter of the innocent infants; and the Last Supper, on the main central vault. One vault back is a particularly striking represen-

tation of Christ Pantocrator. Also worth noting is the medieval agricultural calendar inside an arch to the left of the church entrance.

The heavily restored Romanesque wall of the otherwise Hispano-Flemish Gothic main cloister was originally the external wall of the church. Much of the gold and jewellery held as part of the church treasures was stolen by Napoleon's troops. What remains can be seen in the rooms constituting the basilica's museum.

The museum is open daily from 10 am to 1.30 pm and 4 to 6.30 pm. In July and August the timetable is 9 am to 2 pm and 3 to 8 pm. On Sunday it only opens for the morning session. Entry costs 300 ptas. The church remains open night and day by historical royal edict. Entry to the Panteón and other parts of the museum entails joining a guided tour.

Hostal de San Marcos

Back in the 12th century, the Knights of Santiago took up residence at this pilgrimage way station, but the bulk of what stands today was remodelled in the 16th century, and the façade is largely platersque. It is now getting some much needed restorative treatment, and behind lie the church and Museo Provincial (to the right), and the former monastery, now one of the country's better parador hotels. The museum is housed in the *sala capitular* (chapterhouse) and boasts an admirable artesonado ceiling. From the museum, given over mostly to archaeology, you pass into the cloister.

It has to be said that you can wander into the cloister from the foyer of the parador, although strictly speaking you ain't supposed to. To observe the artesonado ceiling, you could enter the parador and look through the glass doors immediately to the right.

The museum is open Tuesday to Saturday from 10 am to 2 pm and 5 to 8.30 pm (or 4.30 to 8 pm from October to April), and on Sunday from 10 am to 2 pm only. Entry costs 200 ptas.

Swimming

There are a couple of municipal swimming pools for hot summer afternoons. The

Olympic pool is just south of the bus station on Paseo del Ingeniero Sáez de Miera. The other pool, by the Estadio Hispano, is next to one of the youth hostels.

Special Events
Although not known for the splendour of its fiestas, León does stir for Semana Santa and, more so, from 21 to 30 June for the Fiestas de San Juan y San Pedro.

Places to Stay
Hostels León's two youth hostels are open only in July and August, and are fairly uninspiring buildings. The *Residencia Juvenil Consejo de Europa* (☎ 20 02 06), Paseo del Parque 2, and the *Residencia Juvenil Infanta Doña Sancha* (☎ 20 34 14), Calle de la Corredera 2, offer beds for 850 ptas for HI members under 26, or 1200 ptas for older members.

Hotels *Pensión Berta* (☎ 25 70 39), Plaza Mayor 8, has basic singles/doubles for 1500/2200 ptas. The position is unbeatable. *Hospedaje Suárez* (☎ 25 42 88), Calle del Generalísimo Franco 7, has similar rooms for 1500/2500 ptas, if you can get in.

A little more expensive is the *Hostal Central* (☎ 25 18 06), Avenida de Ordoño II 27, with reasonable rooms for 1800/2700 ptas. *Pensión Americana* (☎ 25 16 54), at No 25, has rooms for 1300/2500 ptas.

Hostal Bayón (☎ 23 14 46), Calle del Alcázar de Toledo 6, is run by a friendly woman who keeps clean rooms for 2500/3300 ptas.

The *Fonda Roma* (☎ 22 46 63), Avenida de Roma 4, is in an attractive old building. The rooms are dirt cheap at 900/1500 ptas. The owner of *Hostal Álvárez* (☎ 25 20 02), Calle de Burgo Nuevo 3, is on the pushy side but has acceptable doubles/triples for 2800/4500 ptas.

At the *Hotel Reina* (☎ 20 52 12), Calle de Puerta de la Reina 2, you can get rooms with basin for 1800/3000 ptas or with private bath for 4200/4500 ptas.

Hostal Orejas (☎ 25 29 09), Calle de Villafranca 8, is a pretty good deal. Singles/doubles with TV and telephone cost 2900/4700 ptas. Also with TV and more spacious rooms is *Hostal Londres* (☎ 22 27 74), Avenida de Roma 1. It has doubles only for 5000 ptas.

A much better deal is the *Hotel París* (☎ 23 86 00; fax 27 15 72), Calle del Generalísimo Franco 20, a wonderful old hotel with moderate prices at 4000/6000 ptas.

Parador Hostal San Marcos (☎ 23 73 00; fax 23 34 58), Plaza de San Marcos 7, has rooms fit for royalty at 17,500 ptas plus IVA.

Places to Eat
There is any number of places to try out for breakfast, but *Cafetería Abeto Rojo*, Calle de Burgo Nuevo 26, has a decent deal. Coffee, juice and toast costs 275 ptas at the bar until midday.

At the end of the day, *Café Bambú*, behind the cathedral on Avenida de los Cubos, is a sedate vantage point for gazing on the floodlit apse of the cathedral.

The lifeblood of León's nocturnal activity flows most thickly through the aptly dubbed Barrio Húmedo (Wet Quarter), a heavy concentration of bars and restaurants packed into the crowded tangle of lanes leading south off Calle del Generalísimo Franco. Plaza de San Martín, for instance, is a particularly pleasant part of the centre for eats and drinks. *Restaurante El Tizón*, at No 1, is good for wine and meat dishes, and offers an abundant set meal for 1600 ptas. There are a few decent pizzerias and bars on the same square.

Restaurante Honoré, Calle de los Serradores 4, has a good-value set lunch for 750 ptas, while the *Café del Carmela*, at No 7, has a very inviting and relaxed atmosphere for snacks and coffee.

Mesón Leonés del Racimo de Oro, Calle de Caño Badillo 2, is a long-established restaurant and reputable place where most mains cost around 1500 ptas. In a similar price league, *Restaurante Bodega Regia*, Calle del General Mola 5, is a good spot for outdoor eating in summer. *Restaurante La Posada*, Calle de la Rúa 31, is another popular leonés restaurant.

Restaurante El Palomo, on the tiny Calle de la Escalerilla off Plaza Mayor, is a quality stablishment with a set lunch for 1300 ptas. Next door is the *Restaurante & Sidrería Vivaldi*, also popular, and one of the few places in León where you can get an Asturian cider.

For dessert, you might like to try *Crepería Emil*, Calle de la Misericordia 8, with a pretty good imitation of the French original.

Entertainment

Bars Away from the traditional Barrio Húmedo area, a series of streets heading north of Calle del Generalísimo Franco is lined with bars to suit most tastes. *El Gran Café*, Calle de Cervantes, is a classy and popular spot for a drink, but there are plenty of other possibilities along Calle de Cervantes, Calle de Fernando Regueral and Calle del Sacramento.

Discos There are a few possibilities for dancing until dawn. Friday nights are the best for this sort of thing at *Pub La Morgue*, a noisy place for the young *bakalao* scene on the corner of Avenida de Roma and Calle del Cardenal Lorenzana. A more mixed crowd and music can be had until 6 am at *La Fundación*, just off Burgo Nuevo. It is one of a couple of discos and bars in the same area.

Getting There & Away

Bus Empresa Fernández has as many as eight buses to Madrid a day. The trip takes 4½ hours. Frequent buses also run to Astorga. Other destinations include Bilbao, Oviedo, Zamora, Salamanca and Valladolid.

Train Up to 10 trains a day leave for Madrid. A one-way, 2nd class ticket costs 2550 ptas. Plenty of trains head west to Astorga (405 ptas), north to Oviedo (820 ptas) and Gijón, and south to Valladolid (1095 ptas). There are three to Barcelona and up to five to La Coruña and other destinations in Galicia.

FEVE trains run only as far as Guardo on this private line which links León with the País Vasco. These trains leave from a separate station at the north end of the city centre.

Car & Motorcycle The N-630 heads north to Oviedo, although the A-66 tollway paralleling it to the west is faster. The N-630 also continues south to Sevilla via Salamanca. For Galicia take the N-120. The N-601 heads south-east for Valladolid.

EAST OF LEÓN
Iglesia de San Miguel de Escalada

In simplicity often lies a potent beauty, and this restored and somewhat out-of-place treasure is a fine demonstration of the thought. Originally built in 930 by refugee monks from Córdoba, it displays the horseshoe arch typical of Muslim-inspired architecture but not often seen so far north in Spain. The graceful exterior porch is balanced by the impressive marble columns within. It is open Tuesday to Saturday from 10.30 am to 1.30 pm and 4 to 7 pm, and on Sunday from 10.30 am to 1.30 pm only. Entry is free. You really need your own vehicle, as there is no nearby accommodation and the two buses from León seem timed to render a visit impossible.

Sahagún & Around

An unremarkable place today, Sahagún was once home to one of Spain's more powerful abbeys, so much so that angry locals took to sacking the place towards the end of the Middle Ages. Virtually nothing remains today. Testimony to the strong Mozarabic community that once lived here are the two charming Romanesque-mudéjar churches, San Tirso next to the remains of the abbey and San Lorenzo, just north of Plaza Mayor. The former (open Tuesday to Saturday from 10.30 am to 1.30 pm and 4 to 7 pm, and on Sunday morning) was built in the 12th century and the latter 100 years later. Both have unusually fat bell towers laced with arches. San Lorenzo only opens its doors for Mass on Sunday. Near San Tirso, Benedictine nuns have a small museum containing a monstrous monstrance by Enrique de Arfe (he and his son Antonio and grandson Juan seem to have left them scattered all over Spain), but more often than not the place is closed and not a nun is to be seen.

Pensión La Asturiana (☎ 987-78 00 73),

CASTILLA Y LEÓN

Plaza de Lesmes Franco 2, is the cheapest place in town, with singles/doubles going for 1400/2300 ptas. There are four hostales scattered about too, all with rooms for around 3000/4500 ptas. *Restaurante Luis*, on Plaza Mayor, is one of the better eateries. The occasional bus comes through from León, and one from Valladolid, but you're better off with a train along the León-Palencia-Valladolid line.

Grajal de Campos Six quick km down the C-613 from Sahagún (there is an occasional bus and train from Sahagún), this dusty rural hamlet is fronted by a squat, white stone castillo dating from the 16th century that belonged to the local Marqués de Grajal. If you can find Pablo, he'll let you inside to climb onto the walls.

HEADING WEST
From León the old pilgrim road gradually climbs over the Montes de León and beyond into El Bierzo country – an area that displays greater similarities with Galicia than with Castilla. Finally, after Villafranca del Bierzo and one last rest, the real ascent into the Galician highlands begins. On the way the town of Astorga, with its grand cathedral, Roman remains and splash of Gaudí, is an obvious place to call in. Further on, Ponferrada's castle and the former Roman gold mines of Las Médulas are also worth detours before resting up in Villafranca and moving on into Galicia.

Astorga
It was the Romans who put Asturica Augusta on the map, at the head of the Ruta de la Plata, although for a long while the material being transported south from this region was the gold of Las Médulas. The traffic in precious metals under the Romans gave way to that in pilgrims in the Middle Ages, and by the 15th

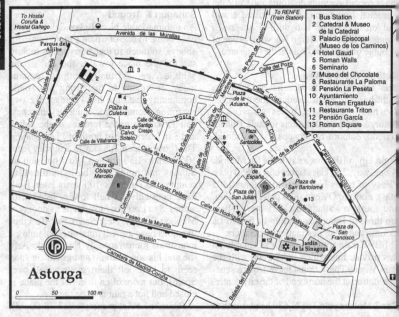

1 Bus Station
2 Catedral & Museo de la Catedral
3 Palacio Episcopal (Museo de los Caminos)
4 Hotel Gaudí
5 Roman Walls
6 Seminario
7 Museo del Chocolate
8 Restaurante La Paloma
9 Pensión La Peseta
10 Ayuntamiento & Roman Ergastula
11 Restaurante Triton
12 Pensión García
13 Roman Square

Astorga

entury the town had reached its apogee. The athedral was raised at this time, and the usy town was liberally sprinkled with hosices for pilgrims on the Camino de antiago. Astorga's 3rd century walls were lso rebuilt then but it was not until the 19th entury that the cathedral acquired its disinctive neo-Gothic neighbour, Gaudí's 'alacio Episcopal.

Astorga lies in a zone known as the Maraatería. Many claim that the Maragatos, who vith their mule trains long dedicated themelves almost exclusively to the carrying rade, were descendants of the first Berbers o enter Spain in the Muslim armies in the th century. Local historians dismiss such ssertions as pure fantasy.

Orientation & Information Astorga's old entre is compact and simple to navigate. he cathedral and Palacio Episcopal huddle ogether in the north-western corner of the asco, and the tourist office (☎ 61 68 38) lies etween the two on Plaza de Eduardo de Castro. The office is open Monday to Saturay from 10 am to 2 pm and 4 to 6 pm, and junday from 11 am to 2 pm. The telephone ode is ☎ 987.

Catedral & Palacio Episcopal Work on the athedral, begun in 1471 on the site of its Romanesque predecessor, proceeded in stop-start fashion over three centuries. This led to a predictable mix of styles, with the lavishly worked plateresque main façade standing in stark contrast to the more severe Flemish Gothic elements exemplified in the apse area. Inside, the 16th century retablo behind the main altar monopolises the visitor's gaze. The museum attached to the cathedral has a varied collection of the usual religious art, documents and curios.

It was Gaudí's flair that gave Astorga its unique skyline, and in some respects the more conventional cathedral seems to fade before the Catalan's extravagance. Built for the local bishop from the end of the 19th century, the Palacio Episcopal (or Palacio de Gaudí) nevertheless is a much simpler piece of work. For all the eccentricity of its exterior, it is bereft of interior detail. Perhaps for this reason the so-called Museo de los Caminos has been installed. You'll find local Roman artefacts and coins on the bottom floor, religious art on the ground and 1st floors, and temporary exhibitions on the top floor.

The cathedral and the Palacio Episcopal are open in summer from 10 am to 2 pm and 4 to 8 pm. The cathedral closes on Sunday, except during August. In winter, opening times are noon to 2 pm and 3.30 to 6.30 pm. Note that entry to the Palacio Episcopal and the Museo de la Catedral each cost 250 ptas,

CASTILLA Y LEÓN

The First Chocolatiers

Hernán Cortés, they say, first sipped a bitter chocolate drink in the palace of Moctezuma back in the 16th century. It was a while before the idea started to get around that it tasted much better if mixed with sugar, and by that stage the odd new beverage had begun to spread across Europe. When the first loads were landed in Spain's Galician ports, not a few of the Maragatos who were to transport it around the country saw some business potential and were quick to introduce it in the main town of their home turf – Astorga. Here the townsfolk began to produce chocolate in commercial quantities, and by the early 17th century Astorga was one of the country's main centres of chocolate making. The process used in Astorga was much the same as it had been in Mexico. The cocoa beans were toasted over a wood fire, hand-peeled, and the grains ground over a small fire together with sugar and often cinnamon. The liquid mixture was then poured into wooden or zinc moulds and left to cool – simple.

Things started to go sour in the late 19th century, however, as greater mechanisation and competition forced the price of chocolate in Spain to drop drastically. As chocolate factories closed, foreign brands flooded the Spanish market. The industry was virtually dead by the 1950s, although a handful of people still churn out the real *chocolate de Astorga*, a bar of which you can pick up in the town's little Museo del Chocolate. ■

or you can pay 400 ptas for both – you must ask specifically for the latter ticket.

Museo del Chocolate This small private collection, at Calle de José María Goy 5, of old chocolate-making implements, advertising and the like could be one for the kids. Astorga was once the capital of Spanish chocolate production. It is open daily from noon to 2 pm and 6 to 8 pm. You can leave a coin for upkeep of the museum.

Roman Traces Those interested in the city's Roman origins can join a free guided tour from the tourist office (once or twice daily) to visit the Roman walls (rebuilt in medieval times), the ancient *ergastula* (prison, located in the basement of the 17th century ayuntamiento) and several other minor excavation sites.

Special Events The last week of August is the most exciting time to be in Astorga, when the city celebrates the Festividad de Santa Marta with fireworks, dances and bullfights.

Places to Stay There are several small pensiones on the highways out of Astorga. Of these, the most convenient are *Hostal Coruña* (☎ 61 50 09), Avenida de Ponferrada 72, and *Hostal Gallego* (☎ 61 54 50), Avenida de Ponferrada 78. The first is slightly cheaper, with doubles only at 4000 ptas. The latter charges 3800/6800 ptas.

Try, if possible, to get a room in the town itself. *Pensión García* (☎ 61 60 46), Bajada Postigo 5, has simple rooms for 2000/3000 ptas. Much better is the *Pensión La Peseta* (☎ 61 72 75), Plaza de San Bartolomé 3, but it costs 4800/6900 ptas. The pick of the crop is the *Hotel Gaudí* (☎ 61 50 40), Calle de Eduardo de Castro 6, with doubles for 9500 ptas plus IVA (less out of the high season).

Places to Eat *Pensión García* has a solid restaurant, while the kitchen at *Pensión La Peseta* is known well beyond the limits of Astorga. For tapas, *Restaurante La Paloma*, Calle de Pío Gullón 16, is good. Another pleasant little place is *Restaurante Triton*,

Plaza de San Julián. At the *Hotel Gaudí*, yo can dine in elegance with a set lunch for 130 ptas.

Getting There & Away By far the mos convenient way in and out of Astorga is b bus – the station is nearly across the roa from the cathedral. There are regular buse to León and Ponferrada. If you do arrive b train, the station is a couple of km north c town.

Around Astorga
Whatever you make of the stories surround ing the Maragatos, the five km detour t **Castrillo de los Polvazares**, one of thes villages, is a pleasant diversion. The hamle is built of a vivid orange stone, made all th more striking by the brilliant green paint jo on the doors and window frames. In late Jul the place livens up with the Fiestas de l Magdalena.

Ponferrada
Climb the Montes de León west of Astorg and you drop down into what is definitely no one of the region's more enticing towns Despite a long history, Ponferrada has bee largely unsuccessful in maintaining its heri tage. From the early 20th century, with th arrival of the train line from Madrid and robust steel industry, perhaps the tow fathers had little time to worry about the pas preoccupied as they were by urban spraw and keeping the wheels of industry turning Named after an iron bridge *(pons ferrata* built in 1082 as the then village's importanc grew as a way station on the pilgrim route Ponferrada is worth a look-in for its castl and what remains of the old centre, but you' be better off looking for somewhere else t stay.

Information The tourist office (☎ 42 42 36) Calle de Gil y Carrasco 4, lies in the shadow of the castle walls. Ponferrada's telephon code is ☎ 987.

Castillo Templario The castle is an unmis takable landmark, its somewhat crumbl valls rising high over the sluggish Río Sil elow. Take the old bridge from the town entre over the river and head right for the astle and Plaza de la Virgen de la Encina. he entry is round the other side, near the nore modern bridge to the west. The Knights 'emplar raised this fortress-monastery in the 3th century, and it remains an imposing difice despite considerable deterioration. It s open Tuesday to Saturday from 10.30 am o 1.30 pm and 4 to 7 pm, and on Sunday rom 10.30 am to 1.30 pm only. This seems o be interpreted flexibly.

Around Town At the foot of the castle ntrance lies the baroque **Iglesia de San Andrés**. Further up the hill past the tourist ffice, the spire of the Renaissance **Basílica le la Virgen de la Encina** dominates the quare of the same name. Otherwise there is recious little of old Ponferrada. Following :alle del Reloj to the gateway that gives the treet its name, you enter Plaza del Ayunta- niento – a grave disappointment. The only uilding of any significance is the baroque :asa consistorial (town hall), which was overed in scaffolding at the time of writing.

Places to Stay Ponferrada is not the nicest place to stay (Astorga is preferable). If you nust, there should be no problem. There are a few hostales near the train station if you need to make a quick getaway. Otherwise, *Pensión Mondelo* (☎ 41 14 84), Calle de Flores Osorio, is the only option in the old part of town, just off Calle del Reloj. It has asic rooms for 1500/2600 ptas.

In the new town, *Hostal San Miguel* (☎ 41 0 47), Calle de Luciana Fernández 2, is a comfortable option fairly close to the old entre, but only has doubles. The rooms with 'V and telephone cost 4000 ptas. The same people run the slightly more expensive *Pensión San Miguel II* (☎ 42 67 00), Calle le Juan de Lama 14, virtually across the ntersection.

Places to Eat *Mesón Mosteiro*, Calle del Reloj 10, does cheap set meals and is about he only place where you'll get a full meal in the old town. *Mesón El Quijote*, Calle de Gregoria Campillo 3, just across the river in the new town, is also OK, and there is a pair of cheap places on Calle Matachana, an alley a couple of blocks further away from the river.

Getting There & Away The bus station is awkwardly located at the northern end of town (local bus No 3 runs into the centre and to Plaza del Ayuntamiento). ALSA has five daily buses from Ponferrada to Madrid. Heading west, there are buses to most main Galician cities, with six to Lugo and five to Santiago de Compostela. ALSA also has a couple of buses to Bilbao. Regular buses run through Ponferrada between Villafranca del Bierzo and León (via Astorga).

The train station is on the west side of the centre. Eight trains a day run to León via Astorga, and four or five eastwards into Galicia. Two trains run daily to Madrid and three to Barcelona.

Around Ponferrada
A unique excursion, but one most easily done with your own transport (a daily bus runs from Ponferrada to Carucedo) would take you to the ancient Roman gold mines at **Las Médulas**. You can drive beyond Las Médulas village (four km south of Carucedo and the N-536 highway, about 20 km south-west of Ponferrada) into the heart of the former quarries, from where several trails weave away among the chestnut patches and weird orange formations left behind by the miners. The Romans honeycombed the area with canals and tunnels through which they pumped water to break up the rock and free from it the gold they were after. The result is a singularly unnatural natural phenomenon.

There are a few unremarkable mesones in the village if you get really hungry. Another vantage point you could make for is **Orellán** (signposted). If you have to walk it from Carucedo, you should set aside four or five hours.

About 15 km along the N-536 from Ponferrada to Carucedo (for Las Médulas), you'll notice the ruins of the **Castillo de**

CASTILLA Y LEÓN

Cornatel, another Templar fortress high up on a precipice.

Villafranca del Bierzo
By the time you reach Villafranca you might just as well have left Castilla. Lying at the foot of the Galician hills, the slate tile roofs and heavy stonework reek of Galicia. Indeed, the Bierzo district, cradled between Galicia and the Montes de León, is something of a transitional zone between the Castilian *meseta* and the Atlantic country of the Spanish north-west. Judging by the graffiti and the local tongue, the people of the Bierzo feel they have more in common with the Galicians than Castilian Spaniards, and the town was even named capital of the short-lived Bierzo province in 1822.

For many pilgrims, this was the last stop on the Camino de Santiago. Daunted by the climb into Galicia, they would appear at the Puerta del Perdón (Door of Pardon) of the 12th century Romanesque Iglesia de Santiago to claim the same spiritual gains they would have received in Santiago de Compostela. Since the 15th century, the church has looked onto the massive turrets of the castillo, which can't be visited. It is suggested the Convento de San Francisco, just back from Plaza Mayor, was founded by Francis of Assisi.

Hostal Comercio (☎ 987-54 00 08) is a basic old place in a 15th century building at Calle del Puente Nuevo 2 and has rooms for 1800/2500 ptas. A restaurant with a good reputation is *La Charola*, on the highway just before you enter the town, by the parador. It's an unprepossessing-looking place, but you can eat well for about 3000 ptas. A speciality in this area is *sopa de ajo*, garlic soup – which is better than it sounds.

Eastern Castilla y León

BURGOS
A mighty chilly place in winter, with a distinctly northern European feel, Burgos makes the ideal location for Spain's greatest Gothic cathedral. The massive churc entirely dominates the elegant old tow centre, its houses characterised by th glassed-in balconies or *galerías* more readil associated with seaside towns in Galicia. O the eastern and western limits of the town ar a couple of admirable monasteries.

History
Like so many Castilian towns, Burgo started life as a strategic fortress – mos historians believe, in 884 – facing off bot the Muslims and the rival kingdom o Navarra. Around it was grouped a series o little villages, or *burgos*, which eventuall would melt together to form the basis of new city. Centuries later, Burgos was thriv ing as a way station on the Camino d Santiago and as a trading centre between th interior and the northern ports. Until wel into the 17th century, the city's wealth cam in from wool exports, mostly throug Bilbao, which in turn sold Burgos muc needed iron. Franco made Burgos hi 'capital' during the civil war, and the indus trial development he encouraged here in th 1950s and 60s brought a degree of prosperit to the city.

Orientation
The heart of old Burgos, dominated by th cathedral, is ensconced between the Rí Arlanzón and the hill to the north-west tha still bears remnants of the town's old castle South of the river, in the newer half of town you'll find the bus and train stations. Th former is handily placed for some budge hotels and a quick walk from the cathedral You'll find a couple of tourist offices on th north bank, one right by the cathedral.

Information
Tourist Offices The main regional touris information office (☎ 20 31 25), at Plaz Alonso Martínez 7, has a good range o information on the city and province o Burgos in particular. It is open Monday t Friday from 10 am to 2 pm and 5 to 7 pm and on Saturday from 10 am to 2 pm. There' another booth (☎ 27 94 32) at Calle de l

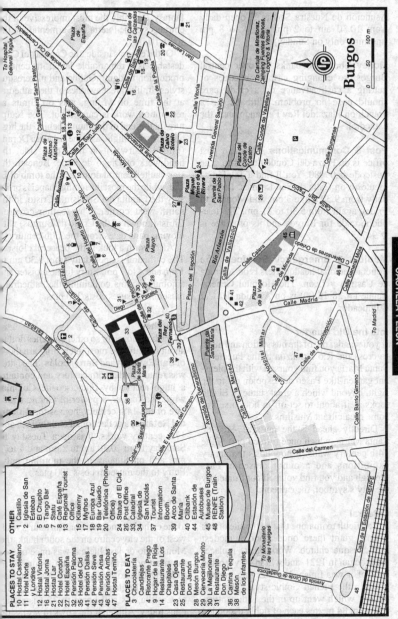

Burgos

0   50   100 m

CASTILLA Y LEÓN

PLACES TO STAY
10 Hostal Castellano
11 Hotel Norte
    y Londres
12 Hostal Victoria
16 Hostal Joma
21 Hostal Lar
27 Hotel Cordón
27 Hotel España
35 Pensión Paloma
36 Hotel del Cid
41 Pensión Dallas
42 Pensión Seve
43 Pensión Ansa
46 Pensión Arribas
47 Hostal Temiño

PLACES TO EAT
3   Chocolatería
    Candilejas
4   Ristorante Prego
9   Hogar de la Rioja
14 Restaurante Los
    Chapiteles
23 Casa Ojeda
25 Restaurante
    Don Jamón
28 Mesón Burgos
30 Cervecería Morito
31 La Mejillonera
31 Restaurante
    Don Diego
38 Cantina Tequila
38 Mesón
    de los Infantes

OTHER
1   Castillo
2   Iglesia de San
    Esteban
5   El Chupito
6   Tango Bar
7   Statu
8   Café España
13 Regional Tourist
    Office
15 Kilkenny
17 Mythos
18 Europa Azul
19 Bar Guedio
20 Telefónica (Phone
    Office)
24 Statue of El Cid
26 Post Office
33 Catedral
34 Iglesia de
    San Nicolás
37 Tourist
    Information
    Booth
39 Arco de Santa
    María
40 Citibank
44 Estación de
    Autobuses
45 Museo de Burgos
48 RENFE (Train
    Station)

Asunción de Nuestra Señora 3, open daily from 10.30 am to 2 pm and 4 to 8 pm (morning only on Sunday).

Money There are banks all over central Burgos, so changing cash or cheques or getting a cash advance on a credit card should pose no problem. Citibank has a branch on Plaza del Rey Fernando, near the cathedral.

Post & Communications The main post office is on Plaza del Conde de Castro. The postcode is 09080. You'll find a Telefónica locutorio on Calle de San Lesmes. It opens daily from 9.30 am to 3 pm, and Monday to Friday again from 5.30 to 11 pm. The telephone code for Burgos and its province is ☎ 947.

Medical & Emergency Services The Policía Nacional headquarters is on Avenida de Castilla y León. The Hospital General Yagüe (☎ 28 18 00) is on Avenida del Cid Campeador.

Into the Old Quarter

If you wander out of the bus station and north to cross the Río Arlanzón at the Puente de Santa María you find yourself with the pleasant garden-like Paseo del Espolón off to the right, beyond which a great statue of El Cid looks as if about to set off in hot pursuit of some recalcitrant Muslims.

Directly ahead is the massive Arco de Santa María, which once formed part of the 14th century walls. It now hosts temporary exhibitions and a minor museum. Pass through and you find yourself confronted by the city's symbol, the cathedral.

Catedral

It is difficult to imagine that on the site of this Gothic giant there once stood a modest Romanesque church. Work on its replacement began in 1221, and within 40 years the bulk of it was finished, a dizzying masterpiece in the French Gothic style. The twin towers, which went up in the 15th century, represent 84 metres each of richly decorated

fantasy. Probably the most impressive of th entrances is the Puerta del Sarmental, on th south flank.

Of the chapels inside, the Capilla del Con destable is a remarkable late 15th centur production bridging Gothic and plateresqu styles. It, like great swathes of the cathedra at the time of writing, was off limits a restoration work is carried out. The sculp tures at this end of the church behind the hig altar are a highlight, as is the Escalera Dorad (gilded stairway) on the north side, th handiwork of Diego de Siloé. Beneath th star-vaulted central dome lies the tomb of E Cid, while the most intriguing chapel is prob ably the Capilla del Santísimo Cristo, in th south-west corner. The leather-covere Christ (known as the Cristo de Burgos) wit moving parts dates from the 13th century.

Also worth a look is the peaceful cloister The cathedral is open daily from 9.30 am t 1 pm and 4 to 7 pm. Entry to the cloister an adjoining rooms containing the cathedral' museum treasures costs 350 ptas.

Churches

Of the half-dozen or so other churches dotte about the city, the most interesting are thos of **San Esteban** and **San Nicolás**. The latte was rebuilt in the 15th century and contain a huge retablo by Francisco de Colonia while the former, a powerful Gothic struc ture of the 14th century, houses the **Muse del Retablo**, a collection of mainly 16th anc 17th century works. It is open Tuesday tc Saturday from 10.30 am to 2 pm and 4 to 7 pm, and on Sunday in the morning only Entry to the museum costs 200 ptas.

Monasterio de las Huelgas

Second in importance among Burgos' sights to the cathedral and about half an hour's walk west of the city centre on the south bank, the Monasterio de las Huelgas was once one ol the most powerful in all Spain. Founded in 1187 by Eleanor of Aquitaine, daughter of Henry II of England and wife of Alfonso VIII of Castilla, it's still home to 35 Cistercian nuns today. Although the vows of seclusion nd silence have been relaxed a little, they till mark the life of the convent.

Your compulsory tour in Spanish starts, ddly enough, in the apse with its five hapels. The main body of the church was valled off in the 16th century when the closed order moved in. This way the nuns could hear Mass without being seen by the general public, who had to crowd into the apse. A curious movable pulpit allowed the priest to address both halves.

It is impossible to appreciate the austere beauty of the church fully, since its three naves are also partly walled up. Some 32 tombs of the great and powerful lie here, including those of Alfonso and Eleanor. Most of the rest are infantes and abbesses; of the latter it was often said that only they, by virtue of their power, would be worthy of marriage to the pope – were he the marrying kind.

The highlight is probably the delicately composed smaller cloister known as Las Claustrillas, a Romanesque gem.

The monastery is open Tuesday to Saturday from 10.30 am to 1.15 pm and 4 to 5.45 pm, and on Sunday from 10.30 am to 2.15 pm (shorter hours in winter). Entry costs 650 ptas except on Wednesday, when it's free for EU citizens.

Not far from the convent is the **Hospital del Rey**, once a hospice for pilgrims on the Camino de Santiago and now the law faculty. Of interest is the plateresque Puerta del Romero.

Cartuja de Miraflores

You can only visit the church of this strict Carthusian monastery, located in peaceful woodlands 3.5 km east of the city centre. But it is worth the effort for a trio of master works by Gil de Siloé, the most dazzling of which is without doubt the ornate star-shaped tomb of Juan II and Isabel of Portugal, commissioned by Isabel la Católica only a few years before the fall of Granada. Gil de Siloé also did the tomb for their son, the Infante Alfonso, and helped with the giant retablo that forms a worthy backdrop to the royal mausoleum. The church itself, while simple enough, betrays a distinct Isabelline flavour – the main entrance being a perfect illustration.

It is open Monday to Saturday from 10.15 am to 3 pm and 4 to 6 pm. On Sunday and on holidays it opens an hour later in the morning and also closes for half an hour at 12.30 pm. Entry is free.

The Cartuja is about an hour's walk from the centre, or you can catch bus No 26 hourly from Plaza de Miguel Primo de Rivera in summer *only* from 11 am to 9 pm. Get off at the fork in the road, from where it's about a 500 metre walk.

Museo de Burgos

The archaeological section of the museum, housed in the Casa de Miranda, contains some fine Gothic tombs and other artefacts covering a wide period. In the Casa de Ángulo is an art collection, including some modern pieces. The museum is open Tuesday to Friday from 9.45 am to 2 pm and 4.15 to 7 pm, and on Saturday and Sunday from 10 am to 2 pm. Entry costs 200 ptas during the week and is free on the weekend.

Special Events

Burgos' big fiestas take place in the last days of June and the first two weeks of July to celebrate the Festividad de San Pedro y San Pablo (Feast of SS Peter and Paul). There are bullfights, pilgrimages and much merrymaking, particularly on the first Sunday of July, the Día de las Peñas. Other feast days include the Festividad de San Lesmes, for the city's patron saint, on 30 January and Las Marzas, celebrated on the first Sunday of March, a veritable rites of spring fiesta.

Places to Stay – bottom end

Camping & Youth Hostels The nearest camping ground, *Camping Fuentes Blancas* (☎ 48 60 16), is about four km from the centre on the same road as the Cartuja de Miraflores. Bus No 26 leaves hourly from Plaza de Miguel Primo de Rivera in summer *only* from 11 am to 9 pm.

The *Albergue de la Juventud Gil de Siloé* (☎ 22 03 62) is inconveniently located well east of the town centre on Avenida del General Vigón and is only open from July to mid-August.

Convent Women who fancy a stint with the Cistercian nuns in the Monasterio de las Huelgas can stay for up to eight days, paying a voluntary contribution. Call ☎ 20 16 30.

Pensiones & Hostales There's a fair sprinkling of down-market places on both banks of the river. Virtually around the corner from the bus station and dirt cheap is *Pensión Arribas* (☎ 26 62 92), Calle de los Defensores de Oviedo 6, with simple singles/ doubles (and nearly no heating in winter) for 1500/2800 ptas. The rooms at *Pensión Ansa* (☎ 20 47 67), Calle de Miranda 9 (opposite the bus station), are nicer at 2000/3000 ptas, but some of the singles are tiny.

Plaza de la Vega is not a bad position, right by the river. There are a couple of places here. *Pensión Seve* (☎ 26 81 05), at No 8, and *Pensión Dallas* (☎ 20 54 57), at No 6, both have rooms with views for about 1800/3000 ptas. The latter is marginally better.

Require something in this area with one or two modern conveniences? You could do worse than the *Hostal Temiño* (☎ 20 80 35), Calle de la Concepción 14, with comfortable if uninspiring doubles ranging from 3000 to 4250 ptas. Single occupancy of the same rooms is cheaper.

Moving into the old centre, you also have a few budget possibilities. *Hostal Victoria* (☎ 20 15 42), Calle de San Juan 3, has OK singles/doubles with sink for 2000/3000 ptas. *Pensión Paloma* (☎ 27 65 74), Calle de la Paloma 39, has doubles starting at 2400 ptas, but you should be able to negotiate a lower rate for single occupancy. Any closer to the cathedral and you'd be in the belfry. *Hostal Joma* (☎ 20 33 50), Calle de San Juan 26, is basic but in the heart of the action. Rooms go for 1500/2500 ptas.

Heading up the scale and further from the centre, *Hostal Lar* (☎ 20 96 55), Calle de Cardenal Benlloch 1, offers singles/doubles with private bath for 3200/5300 ptas. *Hostal Castellano* (☎ 20 50 40), Calle de Laín

Calvo 48, only seems to want to rent ou doubles at 4000 ptas, but they are decer enough.

Places to Stay – middle
Wilting a little, the old *Hotel España* (☎ 2(63 40), Paseo del Espolón 32, charges 500C 7500 ptas for singles/doubles with privat bath, TV and telephone in the high season.

Hotel Norte y Londres (☎ 26 41 25), Plaz de Alonso Martínez 10, is in a rather charm ing old building. Comfy rooms with privat bath, TV and telephone cost 5300/8500 pta in the high season plus IVA.

If you can spare a little more dough, yo can make a quantum leap in quality by staying at the *Hotel Cordón* (☎ 26 50 00; fa: 20 02 69), Calle de la Puebla 6, where fin rooms cost 6000/10,000 ptas in the higl season plus IVA.

Places to Stay – top end
One of the city's best establishments is th *Hotel del Cid* (☎ 20 87 15; fax 26 94 60) Plaza de Santa María 8, where good room cost 8000/14,000 ptas plus IVA.

Or, if you want to head over the top, mak for the *Landa Palace* (☎ 20 63 43; fax 26 4(76), on the N-I to Madrid, a few km out o town, where you'll shell out a fantasti 14,000/30,000 ptas plus IVA in the higl season.

Places to Eat
A good place for tapas and a beer is the *Restaurante Don Jamón*, on Plaza del Conde de Castro.

In the heart of the old town, try around Calle de la Paloma. *La Mejillonera Restaurante*, at No 33, specialises in seafood snacks, while *Mesón Burgos*, Calle de la Sombrerería 8, is a simple, homely place where you can eat a filling meal for around 1000 ptas. For more beer and good patatas bravas, the *Cervecería Morito*, just opposite. is popular with locals. Nearer the cathedral. *Restaurante Don Diego*, Calle de Diego Porcelos 7, has a hearty set menu for 95C ptas.

CASTILLA Y LEÓN

Hogar de la Rioja, Calle de Lain Calvo 37, has a higher standard and more varied menu, and a full meal will cost you about 2000 ptas. Try the escalopines de ave al oporto. Leaning a little more to the tourist trade, but solid nonetheless, is the *Mesón de los Infantes*, Calle del Corral de los Infantes, where again you won't get much change from 2000 ptas.

For a change, eat Mexican at *Cantina Tequila*, Calle de Santa Agueda 10. It has a set meal for 1400 ptas. Better still, the Italian cooking is the genuine article at *Ristorante Prego*, Calle del Huerto del Rey 4. There is a set meal for 1700 ptas as well as scrummy pizzas.

A Burgos institution is *Casa Ojeda*, Calle de la Victoria 5, with a fine old upstairs closed terrace looking across Plaza de Calvo Sotelo. Or you can just snack at the bar downstairs. Another up-market eating house is the *Restaurante Los Chapiteles*, Calle del General Santocildes 7. You won't get much change from 3000 ptas.

For dessert, head for *Chocolatería Candilejas*, Calle de Fernán González 36, where you can get sticky buns, churros or milk shakes (batidos).

Entertainment

Cafés Burgos has a few pleasant little cafés to hang around in, one of the better ones being *Café España*, Calle de Lain Calvo 12.

Bars & Discos If you want a night on the tiles, ease into it in the bars along Calle de San Juan. Among popular haunts along this drag are *Mythos* (No 31), *Bar Guedio* (No 30) and *Europa Azul* (No 32). Or for a Guinness try *Kilkenny* at No 23.

From here the marcha migrates to the area around Calle del Huerto del Rey, locally known as *las Llanas*. The area is fairly crammed with noisy music bars to suit many tastes, including *Statu*, *Tango Bar* and *El Chupito*, all on Calle del Huerto del Rey.

There are few decent discos in Burgos, but the last stage of the pub-crawl scene is the Bernardos area, around Calle de las Calzadas, where you'll find more than your fill of alcohol and truly loud music.

Getting There & Away

From Burgos, roads stretch off west towards León or Palencia, south to Madrid and along several axes into Cantabria, the País Vasco and east into La Rioja.

Bus The bus station is at Calle de Miranda 3. Continental-Auto runs up to 11 buses a day to Madrid, more on Fridays. Tickets cost 1970 ptas. The same company also services Santander. Regular buses also go to San Sebastián (1825 ptas), Vitoria (940 ptas), Bilbao, Pamplona, Logroño and Zaragoza via Soria.

There are also services to most towns in Burgos province, and international buses to destinations as far-flung as London and Agadir (Morocco).

Train As a rule the trains are more expensive than the bus. Main routes include north-south runs from Irún and Bilbao to Madrid and on to Alicante. From east to west, other trains run through Burgos from Barcelona to Salamanca or into Galicia.

Car & Motorcycle For Madrid, take the N-I directly south. The N-234 branches off south-east to Soria and on to Zaragoza and ultimately Barcelona. The N-623 north leads to Santander, while the A-1 autopista goes most of the way to Vitoria and hooks up with the A-68 to Bilbao. The latter two are both tollways.

AROUND BURGOS

The country south-east of Burgos offers some welcome relief from the bleak plains immediately south and to the west. It is also a haven for some intriguing spots.

Quintanilla de las Viñas

If you take the Soria road (N-234) out of Burgos, a worthwhile stop some 35 km out is the 7th century Ermita de Santa María de

CASTILLA Y LEÓN

Lara. This modest Visigothic hermitage preserves some fine bas-reliefs around its external walls, one of the better examples of Visigothic religious art to survive in Spain. If you want to get inside, track down the guardian in the village of Quintanilla de las Viñas, although the hermitage is supposed to be open Wednesday to Sunday from 9.30 am to 2 pm and 5 to 8 pm in summer; from 9 am to 4 pm in winter.

Covarrubias

This pretty hamlet struggles to digest the tourist influx in summer and on the weekend. Spread along the banks of the Río Arlanza, it is made up of a cluster of attractive wood-beam houses with porticoes fronting onto a network of little squares. More solid is the squat 10th century **Torre de Doña Urraca**, towering over the remains of Covarrubias' medieval walls. A little further along the river, the Late Gothic **Colegiata de San Cosme y Damián** rises up. Its cloisters are of the same era, and inside you can also see the stone tomb of Fernán González, founder of Castilla in the 10th century. In various annexes and side rooms are kept the artistic treasures constituting the former abbey's museum, among them a triptych attributed to Gil de Siloé. The Colegiata is open to Sunday and other holidays from 10.30 am to 2 pm and 4 to 7 pm. It closes altogether on Tuesday, and visits of at least four people can be organised on other days by agreement with the parish priest (enquire at No 3 on the same square). Entry costs 200 ptas.

Covarrubias is a charming spot to stay. *Casa Galín* (☎ 947-40 30 15), Plaza de Doña Urraca 4, has comfortable doubles with private bathroom which go for 3400 ptas, or half for single occupancy. There are a few cheaper rooms without their own bath. The fancier *Hotel Arlanza* (☎ 947-40 30 25), nearby at Plaza Mayor 11, charges 5000/8600 ptas in the high season. The staff there also organise such tourist delights as medieval feasts. Casa Galín has a comedor; the oven-baked trout is good.

Autobuses Arceredillo runs two buses from Burgos to Covarrubias on weekdays,

and one on Saturday. A road leads west to Lerma and east to hook up with the Burgos Soria highway.

Salas de los Infantes

Although much of its medieval lines have long since been obscured by modern development of questionable taste, the area around the Iglesia de Santa María is interesting, i only for the houses with their curious conica chimneys, typical of this part of the country If for any reason you needed a room, there are several hostales here. Salas is connected by fairly regular buses to Burgos and Soria

Santo Domingo de Silos

This is the monastery whose monks made the pop charts a couple of years ago, in Britain and elsewhere, with recordings of Gregorian chants. It appears probable that, as long ago as the 7th century, the Visigoths had a religious centre here, but it is not until the arriva of Santo Domingo (St Dominic) in 1040 tha a surer light penetrates the swirling mists o our Dark Age ignorance. He began construc tion of the Benedictine abbey, still inhabited by 26 Benedictine monks today (after a period of disuse in the wake of the grea confiscation of church property in the 19th century).

The jewel is the cloister, a treasure chest of some of the most remarkable and varied Romanesque art in all Spain. As you proceed around the courtyard, you are confronted with a rich series of sculptures depicting everything from lions to Harpies, intermingled with occasional floral and geometrical motifs betraying the never distant influence of Islamic art in Spain. More important still are the pieces executed on the corner pillars, representing episodes from the life of Christ. At least two masters, anonymous as was so often the case with medieval craftsmen, were responsible for this work, and the dividing line can be divined from comparing the style of the pillars. The first master raised columns that widen in the middle while those of the second, who probably worked into the early 12th century, do not. The galleries are covered by mudéjar artesonado ceilings from the 14th century. In the north-east corner sits a 13th century image of the Virgin Mary carved in stone, and nearby is the original burial spot of Santo Domingo.

The guide you will compulsorily have at your side will also show you inside the 17th century *botica*, or pharmacy. You may also be shown around other annexes making up the museum – with the predictable collection of religious artworks, Flemish tapestries and the odd medieval sarcophagus. The 18th century church is considerably less interesting, and much of the monastery is off limits to visitors.

The visitable parts are open Tuesday to Sunday from 10 am to 1 pm and 4.30 to 6 pm. Monday and on holidays it opens only for the evening session. Entry costs 200 ptas and there is an extra charge of 150 ptas for photography.

Men can take a heated room here for 2000 ptas with meals included, but it's a popular thing to do and you'll need to book well ahead. Call the Padre Hospedero between 11 am and 1 pm on ☎ 947-38 07 68. You can stay for a period of three to 10 days.

Those just passing through have a choice of at least five spots. The cheapest is *Hostal Cruces* (☎ 947-39 00 64), Plaza Mayor 2, with decent singles/doubles for 2500/4000 ptas. Rooms come with private bath. There are two other dearer hotels on the same square. *Hotel Arco de San Juan* (☎ 947-39 00 74), Pradera de San Juan 1, is nearby and has good rooms with TV and en suite bathroom for 2850/5650 ptas.

Autobuses Arceredillo runs two buses from Burgos to Santo Domingo de Silos on weekdays and one on Saturday.

Desfiladero de Yecla

A couple of km down the back road (BU-911) to Caleruega from Santo Domingo, the spectacular Desfiladero de Yecla, a magnificent gorge, opens up. It is easily visited thanks to the installation of a walkway. There is a small office in Santo Domingo de Silos, nearly opposite Hostal Cruces, where you can get information on the gorge.

ROUTES NORTH OF BURGOS

Most people heading north from Burgos do just that – belt up the highway until they reach Cantabria, the Picos de Europa mountains or the País Vasco. Brits in particular, heading for the UK ferry from Santander, tend to pass through without stopping to look around. Although at least a bus a day serves most towns from Burgos on weekdays, getting around these parts is laborious without your own transport.

Valle de Sedano & North

The N-623 highway carves a pretty trail from Burgos, particularly between the mountain passes of Portillo de Fresno and Puerto de Carrales. About 15 km north of the Portillo de Fresno, a side road takes you through a series of intriguing villages in the Valle de Sedano. The town of the same name has a fine 17th century church, but more interesting is the little Romanesque one above Moradillo de Sedano; the sculpted main doorway is outstanding.

Plenty of villages flank the highway on the way north, but **Orbaneja del Castillo** is the area's best-kept secret. Take the turn-off for Escalada and follow the bumpy road until you reach the waterfall. Park where you can and climb up beside the waterfall to the village, completely hidden from below. A dramatic backdrop of strange rock walls lends this charming spot a uniquely enchanting air. It is perfect for lunch, with two places to choose from. *El Arroyo* serves fine menús for 1500 ptas per person.

Back Roads to Bilbao

About 20 km north of Burgos, the C-629 forks north-east as the first stage in a winding route to Bilbao. You will be rewarded mainly around the Puerto de la Mazorra, some 65 km north of Burgos. Once over the pass you wind down into a pretty valley. A couple of towers and churches dot the area around Valdenoceda, but your main objective should be the Romanesque **Iglesia de San Pedro de Tejada**. Built early in the 12th century, the church stands in open fields just outside the hamlet of Puentearenas. To the

CASTILLA Y LEÓN

north-east (on the C-629 road), the rather desolate town of **Medina de Pomar** still retains an impressive twin-towered castle and city walls, built in the 14th century by the Velasco family that long ruled the city and surrounding countryside, known as the Merindades.

SOUTH TO THE RÍO DUERO

The road south from Burgos to Madrid crosses some particularly bleak Castilian country, and most people chew up km as fast as their motors can carry them. Still, there are some worthwhile places to check out off the motorway, and at Aranda de Duero you could convert your north-south flight into a riverside excursion from east to west along the Río Duero, the third-longest and second-biggest river in the Iberian Peninsula.

Lerma

An ancient settlement, Lerma hit the big time in the first years of the 17th century, when Grand Duke Don Francisco de Rojas y Sandoval launched an ambitious project to create another El Escorial. He clearly failed, but the cobbled streets of the old town retain a degree of charm today. Pass through the **Arco de la Cárcel** (Prison Gate) off the main road to Burgos and you climb up the long Calle del General Mola to the enormous Plaza Mayor. This is fronted by the sober **Palacio Ducal**, notable inside for its courtyards. To the right off the square is the Dominican nuns' **Convento de San Blas**. Heading downhill from Plaza Mayor at the opposite end from the palace, there opens up a pretty *pasadizo-mirador*, a passageway and viewpoint over the Río Arlanza whose arches connect with the 17th century Convento de Santa Teresa on Plaza de Santa Clara.

Pension Martín (☎ 947-17 00 28), Calle del General Mola 23, has cheap, simple singles/doubles for 1000/2000 ptas. For more comfort, *Hostal Docar* (☎ 947-17 10 73), Calle de Santa Teresa de Jesús 18, charges 3600/5000 ptas for rooms with private bathroom. The *Mesón del Duque*, just off Plaza Mayor, is not a bad choice of restaurant. There are regular buses from Burgos, and some buses coming north from Aranda de Duero or Madrid also stop in here. The same can be said for trains running between Madrid and Burgos.

Aranda de Duero

Considerably less attractive than Lerma, Aranda de Duero is more interesting as a crossroads on the north-south and east-west routes across this half of Castilla y León. The main attraction is the main portal of the Late Gothic **Iglesia de Santa María**. This remarkably rich sculptural flourish was executed in the 15th and 16th centuries and incorporates scenes ranging from the Three Kings at Bethlehem to the death of Christ. The nearby earlier-Gothic **Iglesia de San Juan** is also worth a look.

There's precious little to keep you here overnight, but should you choose to stay, there are a quite a few places. Closest to the old part of town is the *Hostal Sole* (☎ 947-50 06 07), with singles from 3200/5000 ptas with own bath, or a little less without.

For classic Castilian cooking – roast lamb – several reasonable restaurants compete for trade on and around Plaza del Arco Isilla. Look for the 'Asador' signs.

Buses connect Aranda with most major cities in Castilla y León and some beyond. About four buses daily serve Madrid (Estación Sur) for 1200 ptas, and about seven head north to Burgos. Soria, Almazán and El Burgo de Osma are connected to the east, as are Peñafiel and Valladolid to the west and Segovia to the south-west.

One daily regional train stops here en route from Madrid to Burgos. A couple of more expensive Talgos connecting the País Vasco with Alicante also call in.

Aranda is right on the N-I for Burgos or Madrid, or you can branch off east or west on the N-122 to follow the Río Duero (see below).

Peñaranda de Duero

About 20 km east of Aranda along the C-111, the village of Peñaranda de Duero is a much more interesting stop. It was a Celtic fortress village in origin, and it is the central Plaza Mayor that encompasses its surviving riches. The **Palacio de los Zúñiga y Avellaneda** is a grand Renaissance palace with a fine plateresque entrance and artesonado ceilings inside. The 16th century Iglesia de Santa Ana is also impressive. For superb views of the village and surrounding country, walk up to the medieval castle ruins. The *Hotel Señorío de Vélez* (☎ 55 22 01), Plaza de los Duques de Alba 1, is right in the heart of town and charges 4000/6500 ptas for singles/doubles.

If you are driving around this area and have time to kill, there are modest Roman ruins at **Clunia**, about 15 km north-east, and an interesting monastery at **Vid**, just seven km south on the N-122 between Aranda and Soria.

Sepúlveda

Its houses staggered along a ridge carved out by the gorge of the Río Duratón, Sepúlveda is one of many weekend escape hatches for stifled madrileños, but retains a little more life of its own than places such as nearby Pedraza, which tend to be virtual ghost towns from Monday to Friday. Nevertheless, you'll be about the only stranger in town during the week. The town, known under the Romans as Septempublicam, lies about 50 km south of Aranda de Duero, west of the N-I.

The warm ochre tones of Sepúlveda's public buildings, fronting the central Plaza de España, are an enviable setting for a hot Sunday roast; the town is considered one of the best in Spain for roast lamb. The ayuntamiento houses a tourist office and backs onto what remains of the old castle. High above it all rises impassive the 11th century **Iglesia del Salvador**, considered the prototype of this variant of Castilian Romanesque, marked by the single arched portico. It opens on the third Sunday of every month.

Hostal Postigo (☎ 921-54 01 72), Calle del Conde Sepúlveda 22, charges 3500/6000 ptas for singles/doubles, while *Hostal Hernanz* (☎ 921-54 03 78), at No 4, charges 5000/6000 ptas. Both places are just off Plaza de España. There are several restaurants around Plaza de España, among them

Restaurante Filka, at No 4. Here, as in the others, a huge dish with a quarter of a lamb (more than enough for two) well roasted in a wood-fired oven will cost about 3500 ptas.

At least two buses link Sepúlveda daily with Madrid, one via the N-I highway, the other via the Puerto de Navacerrada, southeast of Segovia. There is at least one bus a day to Segovia from Monday to Saturday, and another east to Riaza.

Parque Natural del Hoz del Duratón

A good chunk of land north-west of Sepúlveda has been constituted as a natural park. The centrepiece is the Hoz del Duratón (Duratón gorge), in particular where it widens out behind the dam just south of Burgomillodo. A dirt track leads five km west from the hamlet of Villaseca to the **Ermita de San Frutos**. In ruins now, the hermitage was founded in the 7th century by San Frutos and his brother and sister, San Valentín and Santa Engracia. They lie buried in a tiny chapel nearby. This is a magic place, overlooking one of the many serpentine bends in the gorge. Come in the middle of the afternoon and you'll be accompanied by squadrons of buzzards and eagles. Stay away at the weekend though, as a surprising number of people crowd in, pretty much wrecking the atmosphere for those who want to be as alone as possible with the canyon. Some people take kayaks up to Burgomillodo to launch themselves down the waters of the canyon.

Duratón

About six km east of Sepúlveda, just outside the village of Duratón, the **Iglesia de Nuestra Señora de la Anunciación** is a fine example of Romanesque church-building in rural Castilla.

Castilnovo

Some 12 km south of Sepúlveda, this rather cute little castle has more the air of a private conceit by some moneyed eccentric. Originally built in the 14th century and largely mudéjar, it has undergone a lot of alterations. It's open from 10 am to 2 pm, Monday to

Friday; 10 am to 1 pm and 5 to 7 pm on the weekend. Entry costs 400 ptas and a half-hour guided tour is obligatory.

WEST ALONG THE RÍO DUERO
Peñafiel

Riding high above the medieval Castilian stronghold of Peñafiel stands what must be about the longest and narrowest castle in Spain. Its crenellated walls and towers stretch over 200 metres, and were raised and modified over a period of 400 years from the 11th century. The sight of it in the distance alone is worth the effort of getting here. It opens Tuesday to Sunday, from 11 am to 2 pm and 4 to 7 pm (it may close earlier in winter). Entry costs 150 ptas.

In the town itself, the Iglesia de San Pablo is a curious mix of mudéjar, Gothic and plateresque decoration. The Plaza del Coso is another oddity, an ample square contained by the wooden balconies and houses that front onto it. It is still used for bullfights today. The Río Duratón winds its way through the town in the home stretch of its course to join the Río Duero just north of the town.

Right in the centre is the *Hostal Chicopa* (☎ 983-88 07 82), Plaza de España 2, with basic rooms for 2500/3200 ptas. Just off the square is the small, pedestrianised town centre, and on Calle de José Antonio Girón de Velasco you'll find several bars and the *Restaurante El Bodegón*, at No 14, where you can dig into a moderately priced meal. Four or five buses (455 ptas) run daily west to Valladolid.

EAST ALONG THE RÍO DUERO

From Aranda, you can follow the Río Duero east towards Almazán, or take the N-122 direct for Soria, Castilla y León's eastern-most provincial capital. Both routes are dotted with curious little *pueblos* (villages) and plenty of worthwhile detours. Apart from what is mentioned below, it is worth heading off on your own tangent down the rural byways. Some of the hamlets you encounter in this area really give the impression that time has stopped still for centuries.

In a sense, you can measure the enormous changes and modernisation in Spain over the past 20 years against the rough edge of life in these bucolic backwaters.

San Esteban de Gormaz

This dusty little town contains hidden away in its centre a couple of little Romanesque gems, the 11th century churches of San Miguel and Del Rivero. Both sport the porticoed side galleries that characterise the Romanesque style of the Segovia and Burgos areas, and indeed San Miguel is thought by some to have served as a model for other churches. There are three places to stay here if you need to.

El Burgo de Osma

Some 12 km east of San Esteban de Gormaz and veering away from the Duero, this is a real surprise packet. Once important enough to host its own university, El Burgo de Osma is an elegant if somewhat rundown little old town which is dominated by a quite remarkable cathedral.

El Burgo really only got going in the 12th century as a commercial extension of the town of Osma, which it came to overshadow. Nearby lies the partly excavated Celtiberian castro of Uxama, the area's first settlement.

Begun in the 12th century as an essentially Romanesque building, the cathedral was continued in a Gothic key and finally topped with a weighty baroque tower. Apart from the 16th century main retablo and some interesting odds and ends in the museum rooms around the cloister, the jewel in the crown is the so-called Beato de Osma, a precious 11th century codex that can be seen in the sacristy. The cathedral and museum are open from 10.30 am to 1 pm and 4 to 6 pm, although from November to February they only open on Sunday and on holidays. Entry to the museum and cloister costs 250 ptas.

From Plaza de San Pedro, where the cathedral stands, Calle Mayor, its portico borne by an uneven phalanx of stone and wooden pillars, leads into Plaza Mayor. This is fronted by the 18th century ayuntamiento and the more sumptuous Hospital de San

Agustín, now a cultural centre. Outside the main approach to the town is the 16th century Renaissance former university. If you exit El Burgo from near Plaza de San Pedro, take a left for the village of Osma and high up on a hill you'll see the ruins of the Castillo de Osma.

Of the half-dozen places to stay, *Pensión El Arco* (☎ 975-36 04 62), Calle del General Álvarez de Castro 3, is about the closest to the centre, with simple rooms for 2500 ptas. In summer, they double to 5000 ptas. At that price you're much better off at *Hostal La Perdiz* (☎ 975-34 03 09), Calle de la Universidad 33, where singles/doubles with TV cost 3000/5500 ptas. *Casa Agapito* (☎ 975-34 02 12), Calle de la Universidad 1, has nondescript rooms for 1300/2500 ptas. The discerning traveller with dosh will go for the *Hotel Il Virrey* (☎ 975-34 13 11; fax 975-34 08 55), Calle Mayor 2-4. Charming, comfortable rooms go for 7000/11,000 ptas in the high season. Apart from a couple of hotels, the restaurant choices are limited. For simple, solid meals, try *Mesón Luis*, Calle de la Universidad 2.

From early February to March, Spaniards from as far off as Madrid flock here at the weekend to 'pig out', as it were. A pig is ritually slaughtered in the morning and then diners at the Hotel Il Virrey indulge in an all-you-can eat foodathon, eating all the pork they can fit in. At about 5000 ptas a head it's not the cheapest feed you'll ever have, but the experience is quite unique.

Buses link El Burgo with Soria and places as far afield as Valladolid. Minor roads lead south to Berlanga de Duero and north to the Cañón del Río Lobos (see below).

Gormaz

Some 14 km south of El Burgo you can rejoin the Río Duero at the virtual ghost town of Gormaz. The great castle with 21 towers was built by the Muslims in the 10th century and altered in the 13th century. Its ruins still convey enormous dignity and the views alone justify the effort of getting here. There's nowhere to stay in Gormaz, but in nearby Quintanas de Gormaz you'll find the

delightful *Casa Grande de Gormaz* (☎ 975-34 09 82). This grand old house has seven rooms, which at their most expensive cost 5000/6500 ptas.

Berlanga de Duero

Another 15 or so km east, Berlanga is lorded over by a powerful but ruinous castle. Down below, the Colegiata de Santa María del Mercado is a fine Late Gothic church, with the star-shaped vaulting inside perhaps its most pleasing aspect. The area around the pretty Plaza Mayor, with the occasional Renaissance house, is equally charming. Outside the old town centre on a desolate open plot is the Picota – to which petty criminals were tied in the good old days. The *Hotel Fray Tomás* (☎ 975-34 30 33), Calle Real 16, has comfortable but overpriced rooms for 4000/6500 ptas.

Beyond Berlanga de Duero

About eight km south-east of the town stands the **Ermita de San Baudelio**. The simple exterior belies a remarkable 11th century Mozarabic interior – a real gem. A great pillar in the centre of the only nave opens up at the top like a palm tree to create horseshoe arches. Some invaluable Mozarabic wall paintings and 12th century Romanesque frescos have been preserved. It is open Wednesday to Saturday from 10.30 am to 2 pm and 4 to 7 pm, and on Sunday and holidays from 10.30 am to 2 pm. Another 17 km south, **Rello** still retains much of its medieval defensive walls.

To push on to Almazán you can retrace your steps and pick up the C-116 highway. More adventurously, you could follow the C-101 from Baraona or strike out down the back roads for Medinaceli to the south-east, or to Atienza and eventually Sigüenza in the province of Guadalajara to the south (see the Castilla-La Mancha chapter).

Calatañazor

As you round a tight bend in the road, the grave stone walls and odd modest turret of this one-time Muslim fort (the name comes from the Arabic Qala'at an-Nassur, 'the vulture's citadel') present a timeless face. Climb the uneven cobbled street through the town gate, and you step back hundreds of years into a mournful medieval village. Virtually empty and little cared for, some of the old ochre adobe and stone houses look ready to tumble into one another. The only building that seems to be holding its own is the Iglesia de Santa María del Castillo, with a small museum and Romanesque façade. Look up to the rooftops too; many of the houses are equipped with strange-looking conical chimneys. Believe it or not, scenes for the movie *Doctor Zhivago* were shot here. Lying along a minor road off the N-122 to Soria, the village is certainly an original place to hang out. The *Hostal Calatañazor* (☎ 975-34 05 70), Calle Real, with singles/doubles for 3000/4000 ptas, would be great for an overnight kip. Check beforehand, because at the time of writing it was shut.

Cañón del Río Lobos
Some 15 km north of El Burgo de Osma, the Parque Natural del Río Lobos not only presents some rather bizarre rockscapes, but is home to vultures and various other birds of prey. Just outside the park is an information centre, and about four km in from the road, along the tiny river, stands the Romanesque Ermita de San Bartolomé. You can hike deeper into the park but free camping is forbidden.

If you want to stay in the area, the best choice is El Burgo de Osma, although there are several hostales in the drab village of San Leonardo de Yagüe to the north of the park. *Camping Cañón del Río Lobos* (☎ 975-36 35 65), near Ucero, is open from June to the end of August.

A Route to Madrid
For those wanting to maintain a vaguely southerly trajectory from this part of Castilla y León, the N-110 winds south-west from San Esteban de Gormaz to join up with the N-I highway between Madrid and Burgos just short of the Puerto de Somosierra mountain pass. Along the way, stop in at Ayllón and Riaza.

Ayllón This village lies about 50 km south-west of El Burgo de Osma and bathes in the same orange glow that characterises El Burgo's townscape. You enter by a medieval archway and immediately are confronted on the right by the ornate façade of a late 15th century noble family's mansion in Isabelline style. The uneven, porticoed Plaza Mayor is capped at one end by the Romanesque Iglesia de San Miguel (being restored), and nearby stands the Renaissance-era Iglesia de Santa María la Mayor. Turn right behind this and follow the narrow street for about half a km and you will come to the extensive remains of another Romanesque church, now oddly incorporated into a rambling private residence.

There are two *hostales* should you get stuck. A side road leads 44 km northwards to Aranda de Duero from here. Along the way you can't miss the rather brooding walled town of Maderuelo, perched on a ridge overlooking the Linares dam.

Riaza About 20 km south of Ayllón, Riaza's main claim to fame is its charming old circular Plaza Mayor. The sandy arena in the centre is still used for bullfights. If you want to stay, about the cheapest place is the *Hostal Las Robles* (☎ 921-55 00 54), where singles/doubles cost 1200/1900 ptas. Bull fans might like to eat at the *Restaurante Matimore*, on Plaza Mayor. It is a mini-museum for bullfight posters, and the walls also support four rather large stuffed bulls' heads.

Six km away is the local ski resort of **La Pinilla**. It's nothing superb, but if there have been good falls and you happen to have your skis handy...

SORIA
A rather diminutive provincial capital, Soria cannot boast of the great towering cathedrals or soaring citadels emblematic of many other Castilian capitals. For all that, it does have a pleasant enough old centre and a few monuments worth a glance. Try to stay away in winter, as the city is rather chilly.

Although possibly populated before

Roman times, Soria only appears in the history books with the arrival of the Muslims. Until the crowns of Castilla and Aragón were united at the end of the 15th century, Soria was a hive of commercial and political activity, straddling the frontier territory between Old Castilla, Aragón and Navarra. From the 16th century on, however, it lost importance and, with the expulsion of the Jews, much of its business drive. It has never really recovered.

Information

Tourist Office The tourist office (☎ 21 20 52), Plaza de Ramón y Cajal, is open Monday to Saturday from 10 am to 2 pm and 4 to 7 pm, and on Sunday from 10 am to 2 pm. These hours vary somewhat between summer and winter.

Money There are several banks in the centre near the tourist office.

Post & Communications You'll find the main post office on Calle El Espolón, and a small locutorio on Calle de la Aduana Vieja. The postcode is 42080. The telephone code for Soria and its province is ☎ 975.

Medical & Emergency Services In a medical emergency you can try the Cruz Roja (☎ 21 26 36), Calle de Santo Domingo de Silos. You can call an ambulance on ☎ 22 11 03 or 22 15 54.

Casco Viejo & Around

The modern centre of Soria is uninspiring to say the least, so head for the casco viejo (old town centre) first to get a bit of a tonic. Although there's not an awful lot to it, the few narrow streets around Plaza Mayor are characterful enough, and the square is fronted by the attractive Renaissance-era ayuntamiento and Iglesia de Santa María la Mayor, which has a Romanesque façade.

Overlooking the town a block north is the majestic ochre **Palacio de los Condes Gomara**. Raised in the late 16th century, it is with little doubt the most impressive piece of secular architecture in the city. Further

north again, on Calle de Santo Tomé, is Soria's most beautiful church, the **Iglesia de Santo Domingo**. The blind arches and exquisite sculptures that grace the main portal, together with the rose window, come together in a particularly harmonious display of Romanesque art.

Among other churches worthy of some time is the **Iglesia de San Juan de Rabanera**, built in the 12th century and restored early in the present one. Hints of Gothic and even Byzantine art gleam through the mainly Romanesque hue of this building. Heading east towards the Río Duero you pass the **Concatedral de San Pedro**. Its incomplete Romanesque cloister is its best feature.

To the south-east of the centre, past the cemetery where the wife of the great early 20th century poet Antonio Machado lies buried, you can climb up to the remains of Soria's **castle**.

Museo Numantino

Prehistory buffs with a passable reading knowledge of Spanish should enjoy this well-organised museum dedicated to finds from ancient sites across the province of Soria, especially Numancia (see the Around Soria section for more). Starting with bones of mammoths found south of Soria in what appears to have been a prehistoric hunting ground and swamp, the displays go through important Celtiberian settlements and their Roman successors. Ceramics, tools, jewellery – the standard stuff of archaeological collections – are accompanied by detailed explanations of the historical developments in various major settlements.

It is open Tuesday to Saturday from 10 am to 2 pm and 5 to 9 pm (in winter supposedly from 9.30 am to 7.30 pm, but in reality it seems to close for a couple of hours from 2 pm). On Sunday and on holidays it opens from 10 am to 2 pm. Entry costs 200 ptas.

Beside the Río Duero

With little doubt the most striking of Soria's sights is the 12th century **Monasterio de San Juan de Duero**, just over the bridge and to the left (north). What most catches the eye

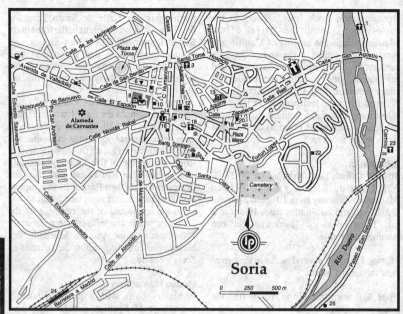

Soria

is the now open porticoes of what was the cloister. Each side displays a different style, underlining the unique mix of Romanesque and Oriental ideas fused together by mudéjar artists. It is open Tuesday to Saturday from 10 am to 2 pm and 4 to 7 pm. On Sunday and on holidays it opens from 10 am to 2 pm.

A walk south for a couple of km takes you first past the 13th century church of the former Templar **Monasterio de San Polo**, and then the baroque **Ermita de San Saturio**, its odd-looking octagonal chapel built over the cave where Soria's patron saint spent a good portion of his life.

Special Events
Since the 13th century, the 12 barrios of Soria have celebrated with some fervour the Fiestas de San Juan y de la Madre de Dios in the second half of June. The main events occur on Jueves (Thursday) La Saca, when each of the barrios presents a bull to be fought the next day. The day following the

fight some of the meat is auctioned, after which dancing and general carousing go on into the wee hours of Sunday. Hangovers an' all, the *cuadrillas* or 'teams' representing the 12 districts parade in all their finery and stage folk dances and the like. If you can find a room, this is the time to be in Soria.

Places to Stay
There are several cheap possibilities in the centre of Soria. *Pensión Sol* (☎ 22 72 02), Calle Ferial 8, has simple but adequate singles/doubles for 1300/2600 ptas. In much the same league is *Pensión Casa David* (☎ 22 00 33), Calle del Campo 6. It charges a bit more at 1800/3600 ptas, and has a decent little restaurant. In an older building behind the tourist office is the *Pensión Carlos* (☎ 21 15 55), which charges the same as the Sol, although in the off season you might score a single for 1000 ptas.

Although austere-looking from the outside, the *Hostal Viena* (☎ 22 21 09), Calle

PLACES TO STAY
- 5 Hostal Viena
- 7 Pensión Casa David
- 10 Pensión Sol
- 16 Hostal Alvi
- 17 Pensión Carlos

PLACES TO EAT
- 6 Restaurante Casa Garrido
- 19 Mesón Castellano

OTHER
- 1 Monasterio de San Juan de Duero
- 2 Concatedral de San Pedro
- 3 Iglesia de Santo Domingo
- 4 Estación de Autobuses
- 8 Museo Numantino
- 9 Post Office
- 11 Lazaro Perez
- 12 Phone Office
- 13 Palacio de los Condes de Gomara
- 14 Local Bus for Train Station
- 15 Tourist Office
- 18 Iglesia de San Juan de Rabanera
- 20 Café Hispano
- 21 Cruz Roja
- 22 Parador Antonio Machado
- 23 Monasterio de San Polo
- 24 Train Station RENFE
- 25 Ermita de San Saturio

de García Solier 5, comes with some recommendations. Rooms have TV, telephone and air-conditioning. Singles/doubles with their own bathroom cost 2100/5500 ptas in the high season. Closer to the centre is the *Hostal Alvi* (☎ 22 81 12), Calle de Alberca 2, with reasonable rooms for 3500/5800 ptas in the high season.

Top of the range is the modern *Parador Antonio Machado* (☎ 21 34 45; fax 21 28 49). Room rates range up to 8200/12,500 ptas.

Places to Eat
On the western edge of the old centre you'll find several bars and restaurants on Plaza de Ramón Benito Aceña. Three more are lined up on Plaza Mayor, including the very reasonable *Mesón Castellano*, where you can eat well for around 1500 ptas. Up behind the post office, the *Restaurante Casa Garrido* is a cosy spot, all dark wood and solid, meaty Castilian cooking.

Entertainment
The spit-and-sawdust crowd should look in at the *Lázaro Pérez* wine bar, at Calle del Collado 52. It's a bit of a man's world though. For something more genteel, head for the *Café Hispano*, on Plaza San Gil just north off Plaza Mayor.

No Spanish city is complete without its zone of noisy bars and discos. In this case the bulk of them are concentrated in the area north-west of the Alameda park and Avenida de Valladolid.

Getting There & Away
The bus station (☎ 22 51 60) is about a 15 minute walk from the centre on the road to Valladolid. There are regular services to Valladolid, Madrid, Logroño, Almazán and a host of small towns. Trains leave from the station (☎ 22 28 67) south-west of the centre (local buses connect with Plaza de Ramón y Cajal). Trains run north to Pamplona and beyond and connect up with the main Madrid-Barcelona line at Torralba. Roads in all directions head from Soria like spokes on a wheel, with straightforward routes to Burgos, Logroño, Valladolid, Madrid, Zaragoza and Teruel.

AROUND SORIA
Numancia
The mainly Roman ruins left today at Numancia, eight km north of Soria, suggest little of the long history of this city. Inhabited as early as the Bronze Age, Numancia would much later prove one of the most resistant cities to Roman rule. Several attempts by the Romans to take control of it were frustrated until finally Scipio, who had crushed Carthage, managed to starve the city into submission in 134 BC. Under Roman rule, Numancia was an important stop on the road from Caesaraugustus (Zaragoza) to Asturica (Astorga). Ceramics unearthed here have revealed an advanced artistic tradition among not only the Romanised inhabitants of the city, but also their Celtiberian forebears. The site is open Tuesday to Saturday, from 10 am to 3.30 pm and 4 to 6 pm (4 to 7 pm in April, May, September and October; 5

to 9 pm in July and August). On Sunday and on holidays it opens from 10 am to 2 pm. Entry costs 200 ptas.

Sierra de Urbión

Some of the most surprisingly green and unspoilt country in all of Castilla y León lies to the north-west of Soria. The Sierra de Urbión stretches north into La Rioja and is a popular weekend excursion destination with the people of Soria. The focal point is the **Laguna Negra**, 18 km north of the pretty village of Vinuesa. The glacial lake lies still like a mirror at the base of brooding rock walls. The road is not in great shape, but the objective is well worth the battering to your shock absorbers (there are no buses). It is possible to hike to the Laguna de Urbión in La Rioja, or to the summit of the Pico de Urbión, above the village of Duruelo de la Sierra, and then on to a series of other tiny glacial lakes.

In **Vinuesa**, a good base for the area, there are two hostales. The *Hostal Urbión* (975-37 84 94) has singles/doubles for 2000/3000 ptas (or doubles with private bath for 4000 ptas), and a popular if somewhat pricey restaurant. Alternatively you could try for a room at the *Casa del Cura* (☎ 975-27 04 64), Calle de la Estación, in Herreros, a hamlet just off the N-234 highway to the south-east of Vinuesa. The nearest camping ground to the Laguna is *Camping El Cobijo* (☎ 975-37 83 31). It opens from March to mid-October.

SOUTH OF SORIA
Almazán

Three of this small town's massive gates remain to testify to a past more illustrious than the present in this quiet backwater. It frequently changed hands between the Muslims and Christians, and for a short three months was chosen by Fernando and Isabel as their residence.

On Plaza Mayor you can see the Romanesque **Iglesia de San Miguel**, with a slightly jarring octagonal cupola-cum-bell tower. It seems usually to be closed. The prettiest face of the **Palacio de los Condes de Altamira**

is actually the loggia looking out over the river, which can be seen only when approaching the town from the river side.

If you want to stay, *Pensión Ochea* (☎ 975-30 04 07), Calle de los Caballeros 19, is just up from Plaza Mayor and has reasonable singles/doubles for 1250/2500 ptas a head. Better is the *Hostal El Arco* (☎ 975-31 02 28), Calle de San Andrés 5-7, by one of the three city gates. *Restaurante Puerto Rico*, Calle de los Caballeros 12, is a good cheap restaurant in the old town. There are frequent bus and train connections with Soria, 35 km north.

Medinaceli

Entering Medinaceli along a slip road just north of the N-II motorway, you find a modern one-horse town. The old Medinaceli is actually draped along a high, windswept ridge three km to the north. Its most incongruously placed landmark is a 2nd century **triumphal arch**, all that remains of the Roman settlement. Little is left to remind you of Medinaceli's Muslim occupiers; its empty streets are redolent more of the noble families that lived clustered around the La Cerda family, pretenders to the Castilian crown, after the town fell to the Reconquista in 1124. The Plaza Mayor has a dilapidated grandeur, but the town as a whole has a distinctly ghostly feel.

There is a Centro de Iniciativa y Turismo at Plaza Mayor 16, in the old town, for information. The *Hostal Medinaceli* (☎ 975-32 61 30) has singles/doubles for 3000/4800 ptas and the newer *Hostería El Mirador* (☎ 975-32 62 64) offers rooms for 3000/4000 ptas. Add IVA to both. You'll find several more hostales in the new town. There are a few restaurants, including those in the hotels, but arguably the town's best known is *Las Llaves*, Plaza Mayor 14.

The odd bus leaves for Guadalajara and Madrid from in front of the ayuntamiento in the new town, and the occasional slow train calls in on the Madrid-Zaragoza line. There is no transport between the old and new towns – it's quite a hike.

Santa María de la Huerta

This dusty, insignificant village, off the N-II and just short of the Aragonese frontier, contains a jewel in the form of a Cistercian monastery founded in 1162. Monks lived here until 1835, when the monastery was expropriated. The order was allowed to return in 1930, and 18 Cistercians now live here. Before entering the monastery, you will see ahead of you the impressive 12th century façade of the church with its rose window (now being restored).

Inside the monastery, you pass through two cloisters, the second of which is by far the more beautiful. Known as the Claustro de los Caballeros, it is Spanish Gothic in style, although the medallions on the 2nd floor bearing coats of arms and assorted illustrious busts, such as that of Christopher Columbus, are a successful plateresque touch. Off this cloister is the *refectorio*, or grand dining hall. Built in the 13th century, it is remarkable especially for the absence of columns to support the vault. The monastery is open daily from 9 am to 12.45 pm and 3 to 6.30 pm, and entry costs 300 ptas.

Pensión Santa María (☎ 975-32 72 18), at the turn-off to the monastery, is a basic place with singles/doubles for 1300/2500 ptas. A couple of km east, near the slip road onto the N-II, is the *Hotel Santa María de Huerta* (☎ 975-32 70 11), with bed and breakfast for 7000/11,000 ptas plus IVA. A couple of buses connect the village with Almazán and Soria, and slow trains on the Madrid-Zaragoza line stop in.

Castilla-La Mancha

The modern autonomous community of Castilla-La Mancha is a post-Franco creation with Toledo as its capital. It covers roughly what was known as Castilla la Nueva (New Castile), the territory south from Toledo that was added to the Corona de Castilla (Castilian Crown) as the Reconquista progressed through the Middle Ages. The boundaries of the region's five provinces are those drawn up in 1833, when La Mancha – the harsh, dry southern plateau that served as a front-line buffer zone against the last of Spain's Muslim rulers after the Battle of Las Navas de Tolosa in 1212 – ceased to exist as an administrative unit. Embodied by its literary hero Don Quixote, La Mancha (which comes from an Arabic expression meaning 'dry, waterless land') has nevertheless remained very much alive in the Spanish imagination.

With the exception of Toledo, however, little of this region – one of the country's biggest – is seen by the millions of foreigners who pour into Spain each year. The empty expanses alone are quite unique in Western Europe, reminiscent of some of the more monotonous stretches of rural Australia or Mid-West America. Many people simply end up crossing Castilla-La Mancha from Madrid or Toledo en route to somewhere else, and those with only limited time are probably right to skip the bulk of this dispiriting, hot land of treeless plains and glum, bald hills. A closer look, however, reveals a wide smattering of pretty villages, medieval castles (of which there are many) and, on occasion, some surprisingly varied and fertile landscape. The absence of busloads of camera-clicking tour groups presents an opportunity to see some of Spain as it really is. Given the distances involved in reaching any place of interest, however, having your own vehicle is a greater asset here than in most other parts of Spain.

The cuisine of Castilla-La Mancha, like that of much of Spain, is firmly based in peasant tradition. In and around Toledo,

HIGHLIGHTS

- The medieval splendour of the imperial city of Toledo
- Participating in the Corpus Christi festivities in Toledo
- Coffee on Almagro's fine Plaza Mayor, and perhaps some theatre at the unique El Corral de Comedias
- Tilting at windmills around Consuegra
- Washing down a good meal of game with some Valdepeñas wine

where *la caza* (hunting) has long been a big contributor to the local table, venison and partridge figure largely. The plains are hot but not unproductive. The strong *queso manchego* (La Manchan goat and/or sheep cheese) is sold everywhere and appreciated by gourmets. Among the odder manchego dishes are *migas*, which are basically fried breadcrumbs mixed with garlic and other ingredients. They are better than they sound.

Traditionally, La Mancha has long been given over to intense wine production. Next to olive groves, the grape vine is one of the most common agricultural sights across the country. Quality always came second to quantity, but with EU quotas forcing drastic cutbacks, growers are now concentrating more on producing a good drop. Although not Spain's greatest, La Mancha and Valdepeñas from this area are DO wines.

Toledo

They still call it La Ciudad Imperial – and for a while Toledo indeed looked set to become the heart of a united Spain. The Iberian Peninsula's Rome and something of an army town, this remarkable medieval city bristles with monumental splendour.

By the time El Greco arrived here from Italy in 1577, Toledo's chances of becoming the permanent capital had already all but evaporated. Sixteen years earlier, Felipe II had moved the court to the relatively undistinguished location of Madrid, a site that, unlike the claustrophobic Toledo, lent itself to rapid expansion in all directions as might befit a great empire. Toledo's city elders were slow to realise that, partly owing to an earlier revolt against Carlos I, they had missed the boat, and until the end of the century the city continued to enjoy one of its greatest moments of economic and artistic development. When the penny finally dropped, artists, nobles, courtesans and sycophants left in droves, leaving Toledo to sink slowly into provincial disrepair.

Like a creaky museum, now much spruced up but not without problems, *la ciudad de la tres culturas* (the city of the three cultures) has survived as a unique centre where Romans and Visigoths once ruled, and for a time Jews, Muslims and Christians – and all those who converted from one religion to another – lived in comparative harmony. The artistic legacy is a complex cross-breeding of European and Oriental values that can be seen elsewhere in Spain, but rarely of the intensity found here.

The seat of the head of the Catholic church in Spain for most of its Christian history, Toledo exerts a strange and sometimes dark fascination over people who stay around long enough to get over the initial monument shock and the summer crowds. To see the city in the gloomy depths of winter, shrouded in fog and even more introverted than usual, is in some ways to get a truer measure of its character.

Toledo's twisting lanes and blind alleys, the extraordinarily decorated internal patios hidden by grim façades looking onto steep, cobbled streets, and its sheer architectural diversity make it worthy of more attention than most visitors give it. Travellers who have passed through Damascus, Cairo or Fés will recognise the labyrinth of the *medina*, but in none of those cities will they also be confronted by the Gothic grandeur of a cathedral or the grim composure of Toledo's oft-remodelled Alcázar.

The sad part of Toledo's story is taking place almost unnoticed. People are abandoning the old city for the new, characterless but comfortable suburbs sprawled out beneath it, leaving behind only public servants, students and the rent-protected elderly. If this continues, the shops and businesses will also decline, leaving only a motley collection of souvenir stalls and eateries to satisfy summer tourist crowds. The old city is dying and appears more than ever destined to become an empty open-air museum – a place without soul.

History

Its strategic position made ancient Toletum an important way station in the days of Rome's domination of the Iberian Peninsula. In the 6th century, long after Rome had ceased to have any influence on the affairs of Hispania, the Visigothic king Atanagild moved the site of his capital from Sevilla to Toletum. At once, the city also became the religious heart of the Visigothic kingdom, with no less than 18 councils solemnly held here to deal with such problems as the conversion of the Visigoths to Catholicism, the faith of the majority of the subjugated Hispano-Roman populace. But Toledo also became the scene of endless feuds between Visigothic nobles, which so weakened their state that when the Muslims crossed the Strait of Gibraltar in 711, they had little problem in taking Toledo on their lightning-fast march north.

Toledo was the main city of central Muslim Spain, and after the collapse of the caliphate in Córdoba in 1031 it became the capital of a vast and independent Arab *taifa* (kingdom). For the following 50 years the city was unrivalled as a centre of learning and arts in Spain, and for a brief time its power ranged across all modern Castilla-La Mancha, and to Valencia and Córdoba itself.

Alfonso VI marched into Toledo in 1085, a significant victory on the long and weary road of the Reconquista. Shortly thereafter, the Vatican recognised Toledo as seat of the church in Spain, and in the following centuries the city was also one of the most important of several temporary residences of the Castilian monarchy. Since the Archbishop of Toledo was a vocal proponent of the Reconquista and the monarchs' right-hand man at this time, Toledo's position as a flourishing power base was assured. Christians, Jews and Muslims managed to rub along tolerably well for a period, but by 1492, when Granada fell to the Catholic Monarchs, the situation had changed, and shortly afterwards Spain's Muslims and Jews were compelled to convert to Christianity or flee.

Carlos I looked set to make Toledo his permanent capital in the 16th century, in spite of the revolt against him that began in the city and degenerated into the so-called Guerra de las Comunidades (see the boxed aside 'Juan Bravo and the Comuneros' in the Castilla y León chapter for more on this civil conflict). His successor, Felipe II, dashed any such ideas with his definitive move to Madrid, and Toledo began to recede into the background.

In the early months of the 1936-39 civil war, Nationalist troops (and some civilians) were kept under siege in the Alcázar, but were eventually relieved by a force from the south in a move that some claim cost Franco a quick victory. By diverting his units to Toledo, he missed an opportunity to get to Madrid before the arrival of the International Brigades – one of those 'what if?' scenarios that so intrigue historians. In 1986 UNESCO declared the city a monument of world interest to humanity.

Orientation

Toledo is built upon a hill around which the Río Tajo (Tagus) flows on three sides; modern suburbs continue to spread rapidly well beyond the river and walls of the old town.

The bus station lies just to the north-east of the old town (*casco antiguo*), and the train station a little further east across the Tajo. Both are connected by local bus to the centre.

Whether you arrive on foot or by local bus, you are bound to turn up sooner or later at Plaza de Zocodover (known as Zocodover or Zoco to the locals), the main square of the casco. There are plenty of banks around the square, and other useful offices are a short walk away. The bulk of the hotels and a good number of bars and restaurants are spattered around the nearby labyrinth of medieval alleyways – which can be quite confusing on arrival.

Information

Tourist Offices The main tourist office (☎ 22 08 43) is just outside Toledo's main gate, the Puerta Nueva de Bisagra, at the northern end of town. Apart from a map and hotel list, it has precious little to offer. It opens from 9 am to 2 pm and 4 to 6 pm

Monday to Friday, from 9 am to 3 pm and 4 to 7 pm on Saturday, and from 9 am to 3 pm on Sunday. An information booth is open on Zocodover from 10 am to 6 pm on weekdays, until 7 pm on Saturday and until 3 pm on Sunday.

Money There is no shortage of banks in central Toledo. You can use most credit/debit cards in at least some of the ATMs. The Caja Rural, Plaza de Zocodover 14, has an ATM and automatic cash-changing machine.

Post & Communications The main post office is at Calle de la Plata 1. It is open Monday to Friday from 8 am to 9 pm for most services, and on Saturday from 9 am to 2 pm. The postcode for poste restante in central Toledo is 45080 and the telephone code is ☎ 925.

Books Apart from the usual tourist books, Spanish readers wanting a quality guide and account of the city should consider *Rutas de Toledo* (4000 ptas), published by Electa and available all over town.

Youth Affairs The Delegación Provincial de Educación y Cultura, Calle de la Trinidad 8, can give you a full list of youth hostels, university residences and camp sites throughout Castilla-La Mancha. It is open Monday to Friday from 9 am to 2 pm.

Medical & Emergency Services There is a *comisaría* (police station) in the old city on Plaza Ropería. For an ambulance or urgent medical help, the Cruz Roja (Red Cross) is on ☎ 22 22 22. You'll find a Centro de Salud (clinic; ☎ 21 50 54) at Calle de la Sillería 2. Night pharmacies change daily on a rotational basis; the week's *farmacias de guardia* are posted up in most pharmacies.

Things to See & Do

Take the time to wander and soak up some of the most distinctive architectural combinations in Spain. The Arab influence on all you see, from church bell towers to arches in city gates, is a singular expression of Spain's

CASTILLA-LA MANCHA

CASTILLA-LA MANCHA

Toledo

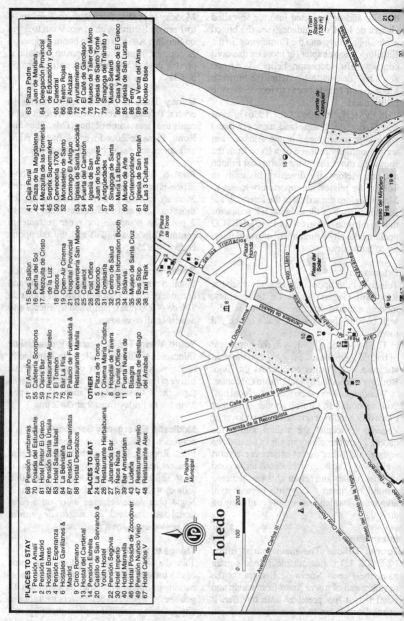

PLACES TO STAY
1 Pensión Amalí
2 Pensión Madrid
3 Hostal Boxes
4 Pensión Esperanza
6 Hostales Gavilanes & Madrid
13 Circo Romano
14 Pensión Estrella
20 Castillo de San Servando & Youth Hostel
22 Pensión Segovia
30 Hotel Imperio
40 Hotel Maravilla
46 Hostal Posada de Zocodover
49 Pensión Nuncio Viejo
67 Hotel Carlos V
68 Pensión Lumbreras
70 Posada del Estudiante
81 Hotel Pintor El Greco
82 Pensión Santa Ursula
83 Hotel Santa Isabel
84 La Belviseña
87 Hostal El Diamantista
88 Hostal Descalzos

PLACES TO EAT
24 La Abadía
26 Restaurante Hierbabuena
27 Jacaranda Bar
37 Naca Naca
39 Bar Amsterdam
43 Ludeña
47 Restaurante Aurelio
48 Restaurante Alex
51 El Amiño
59 Cafetería Scorpions
55 Osiris Bar
73 Restaurante Aurelio
75 El Torreón
76 Bar La Ría
78 Palacio de Fuensalida & Restaurante Manila

OTHER
5 Plaza de Toros
7 Cinema María Cristina
8 Hospital de Tavera
11 Tourist Office
12 Puerta Nueva de Bisagra

15 Bus Station
17 Puerta del Sol
44 Mezquita de Cristo de la Luz
18 Discos
19 Open-Air Cinema
21 Cervecería San Mateo
23 Camelot
28 Post Office
29 Macondo
31 Comisaría
32 Centro de Salud
33 Tourist Information Booth
34 Sildavia
35 Museo de Santa Cruz
36 Bus Stop
38 Taxi Rank
41 Caja Rural
42 Plaza de la Magdalena
45 Serjux Supermarket
50 Cervecería 1700
52 Monasterio de Santo Domingo El Antiguo
53 Iglesia de Santa Leocadia
54 Puerta del Cambrón
56 Iglesia de San Juan de los Reyes
57 Antigüedades
58 Sinagoga de Santa María La Blanca
60 Museo de Arte Contemporáneo
61 Iglesia de San Román
62 Las 3 Culturas
63 Plaza Padre Juan de Mariana
64 Delegación Provincial de Educación y Cultura
65 Catedral
66 Teatro Rojas
69 El Alcázar
72 Ayuntamiento
74 El Café de Garcilaso
76 Museo de Taller del Moro
77 Iglesia de Santo Tomé
79 Sinagoga del Tránsito y Museo Sefardí
80 Casa y Museo de El Greco
85 Iglesia de San Lucas
86 Ferry
89 La Venta del Alma
90 Kiosko Base

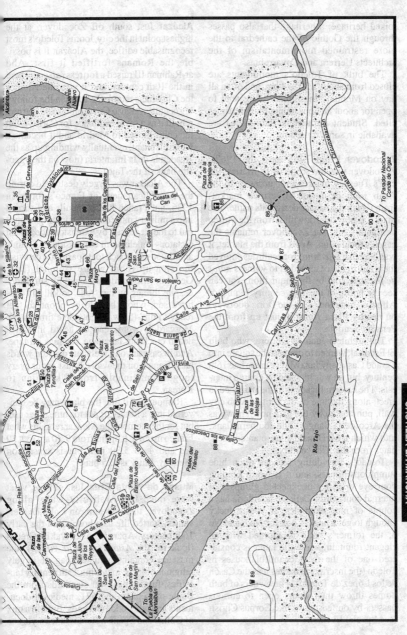

mixed heritage, a heritage that also passes through the Gothic of the cathedral to the more restrained monumentalism of the architects Herrera and Covarrubias.

The bulk of Toledo's monuments are closed from about 1.30 to 4 pm, and often all day on Monday. In summer, they tend to open for about an hour longer than the times cited. Student reductions (half-price) are available in some museums.

Zocodover From 1465 until the 1960s, Zocodover was the scene of El Martes, the city's Tuesday market and successor to the Arab *souq ad-dawab* (livestock market) from which the square derives its name. The market is now held downhill from the Museo de Santa Cruz, but Zocodover remains the casco's focal point. Apart from the market, it was here that *toledanos* for centuries enjoyed their bullfights or crowded to witness *autos de fe* carried out by the Inquisition. You can see the house of the 16th century Inquisitor Alfonso Castellón (with the Doric doorway) on nearby Plaza Agustín, just up from the Pensión Segovia.

The architect Juan de Herrera, who built El Escorial, wanted to convert the square into a grand Castilian Plaza Mayor in the late 16th century, but he was blocked by church interests. The eastern façade is all he managed to erect, along the line of the former Arab city wall, punctuated by the gate now known as the Arco de la Sangre. The southern flank, into which a McDonald's has planted itself, dates from the 17th century.

Toledo's forbidding façades often hide sumptuous houses, and it is worth keeping your eye open for unexpected glimpses of internal courtyards. Calle de la Sillería has a couple of nice examples, if you're lucky enough to get a peek. Look for No 6 and No 3; the former's patio is adorned with an elegant fountain, while the latter is considered one of the most beautiful houses in Toledo (the inscription names it as the Casón de los López de Toledo). The owners of both homes throw their doors open to curious passers-by on feast days like Corpus Christi (see Special Events).

Alcázar Just south off Zocodover, at the highest point in the city, looms Toledo's most recognisable edifice, the Alcázar. It is possible the Romans fortified it first. Abd ar-Rahman III raised a fortress *(al-qasr)* here in the 10th century, and it was altered after the Christians retook the town in the following century. Alonso Covarrubias and Herrera rebuilt it as a royal residence for Carlos I, but the court moved to Madrid and it became a white elephant, eventually winding up as the Academia de la Infantería (now on the opposite bank of the Tajo).

The Alcázar was largely destroyed during the Republican siege of Franco's forces in 1936, but Franco had it rebuilt and turned into a military museum, a fascinating memorial to the siege and, by extension, the fascist dictator – an eloquent expression of Spain's ambiguous approach to its past. You can visit the shot-up room where Colonel (later General) Moscardó refused to surrender despite threats by the 'reds' to kill his captured son, whom he told by phone to 'get ready to die' (he was shot some time later). Moscardó's words can be heard in half a dozen crackling language versions on tape. And in case anyone feels left out, the words hang framed on the walls in just about every tongue imaginable from Ukrainian to Korean.

Rumour has it that the place may be converted into a library or put to some other use, but for the moment the Alcázar remains what Franco made it. It opens from 9.30 am to 1.30 pm and 4 to 5.30 pm, but is closed on Monday. Entry is 125 ptas.

Museo de Santa Cruz Just outside what were once the Arab city walls along Zocodover, this museum, on Calle de Cervantes, started life as a hospital in the early 16th century. Apart from several El Grecos (look for the *Asunción de la Virgen*), the museum contains a mixed bag of largely religious objects, including 15th century tapestries, furnishings, war standards from the Battle of Lepanto in 1571, medieval documents and other odds and ends. Built in a mix of Gothic and Spanish Renaissance styles on a Greek-cross floor plan, the former hospital is flanked by a pleasant cloister. It opens from 10 am to 6.30 pm (2 pm on Sunday), sometimes closing for lunch. Entry is 200 ptas (free on Saturday afternoon and Sunday).

Catedral From the earliest days of the Visigothic occupation of the ancient Roman Toletum, the modern site of the cathedral has been the centre of worship in the city. In 646, Toledo's archbishop was first recognised as the primate of the Catholic Church in Spain. Three centuries of Muslim rule saw the Visigoths' basilica converted into Toledo's central mosque. Alfonso VI promised, in the instruments of surrender signed by Christians and Muslims in 1085, that the mosque would be preserved as a place of worship for Toledo's considerable Muslim population. Predictably enough, the promise was broken and the mosque destroyed to make way for a cathedral. The construction of a new house of worship began in the 13th century and proceeded slowly over the following centuries. Essentially a Gothic structure, the cathedral nonetheless is a hotchpotch of styles peculiar to a city with such a mixed history. *Mudéjar* elements are plain to see in the interior decoration and the Spanish Renaissance makes itself felt in various chapels that line the church naves. Behind the main altar lies a masterpiece of churrigueresque baroque, the Transparente. A lavish 18th century embellishment, it also serves to remedy the lack of light in the cathedral.

Entering by the **Puerta del Mollete** under the Arco de Palacio that links the cathedral to the Palacio Arzobispal (Archbishop's Palace), you enter the cool and pretty cloister typical of the greater churches in the Iberian Peninsula. For centuries the city's destitute would line up at this entrance for daily bread distribution; now tourists do much the same for tickets to various chapels inside the church.

The centre of the cathedral is dominated by the highly unusual **coro** (choir stalls), a feast of sculpture and carved wooden stalls. The lower tier was carved in the 15th century in late Gothic style and depicts the conquest

Catedral de Toledo

1 Puerta del Mollete
2 Claustro
3 Puerta del Reloj
4 Sacristía
5 Sala Capitular
6 Puerta de los Leones
7 Puerta Llana
8 Coro
9 Capilla Mayor
10 Capilla de la Torre o del Tesoro

of Granada, while the upper, Renaissance level features images of saints and apostles, many by Alonso de Berruguete.

Opposite is the **Capilla Mayor**, too small to accommodate the choir stalls as originally planned, but an extraordinary work of art. In its present state it dates back to 1498, and serves in part as a mausoleum for Cardinal Mendoza (prelate and adviser to Fernando and Isabel), and several kings. The masterpiece is the retablo in Flemish Gothic style, depicting scenes from the life of Christ and culminating with a *Calvario* and an *Asunción de la Virgen*. Of the magnificent stained glass, the oldest is in the rose window above the Puerta del Reloj.

All the chapels and rooms off the main church body are worth visiting. Among the 'don't misses' are the **Capilla de la Torre**, in the north-west corner, and the **sacristía**. The latter contains what amounts to a small gallery of El Greco (for more on whom, see below), while the former houses what must be one of the most extraordinary monstrances in existence, the Custodia de Arfe, by the celebrated 16th century goldsmith Enrique de Arfe. With 18 kg of pure gold and 183 kg of silver, this 16th century conceit

CASTILLA-LA MANCHA

bristles with some 260 statuettes. Its big day is the feast of Corpus Christi (see Special Events), when it is paraded around the streets of Toledo on a special vehicle that prevents it tipping over in spite of the medieval ups and downs.

The cathedral is open to visitors daily from 10.30 am to 1 pm and 3.30 to 6 pm (7 pm in summer). Tickets (500 ptas; no student discount) can be bought at a souvenir stand in the cloister. They entitle you to enter the Capilla de la Torre, sacristía, coro and also the *sala capitular* (chapterhouse), which boasts a remarkable *artesonado* ceiling in the so-called Cisneros style, Renaissance murals depicting the life of Christ and the Virgin Mary, and other artworks.

El Greco Trail It's easy to guess what the tour buses are in Toledo for. Hordes pile down the city's narrow streets with one thing in mind – the 16th century painter El Greco First stop is the **Iglesia de Santo Tomé** Plaza del Conde, which contains his masterpiece, *El Entierro del Conde de Orgaz* (The Burial of the Count of Orgaz). When the count, a 14th century benefactor of the church, was buried in 1322, SS Augustine and Stephen supposedly descended from heaven to attend the funeral. El Greco's work depicts the miracle, along with a series of his chums in the lower, terrestrial part of the painting. The church, in the south-west of the town, is open from 10 am to 1.45 pm and 3.30 to 5.45 pm. Entry costs 150 ptas.

Afterwards you can follow the tourist stream past rows of souvenir shops to the **Casa y Museo de El Greco**, in Calle de Samuel Leví. This was set up as a museum by a noble chap, Don Benigno de Vega-Inclán, in 1910, but it is unlikely that El Greco actually ever lived here. Inside are about 20 of the Cretan's minor works and the

El Greco in Toledo

After a long apprenticeship in Crete, where he was born in 1541, Domenikos Theotokopoulos moved to Venice in 1567 to be schooled as a Renaissance artist. He learned to extract the maximum effect from few colours, concentrating the observer's interest in the faces of his portraits and leaving the rest in relative obscurity, a characteristic that remained one of his hallmarks. From 1572 he learned from the mannerists of Rome and the work left behind by Michelangelo.

He came to Toledo in 1577 hoping to get a job decorating El Escorial. Things didn't quite work out, and Felipe II rejected him as a court artist. In Toledo, itself recently knocked back as permanent seat of the royal court, the man who came to be known simply as El Greco felt sufficiently at home to hang around, painting in a style different from anything local artists were producing. He even managed to cultivate a healthy clientele and command high prices. His rather high opinion of himself and his work, however, did not endear him to all and sundry. He had to do without the patronage of the cathedral administrators, the first of many clients to haul him to court for his obscenely high fees.

El Greco liked the high life, and with things going well in the last decade of the 16th century, he rented rooms in a palace on the Paseo del Tránsito, where he often hired musicians to accompany his meals. As Toledo's fortunes declined, so did El Greco's personal finances, and although the works of his final years are among his best, he often found himself unable to pay the rent. He died in 1614, leaving his works scattered about the city, where many have remained to this day. ∎

more important *Vista y Plano de Toledo*. You'll also find a small collection of minor works of the 17th century Toledo, Madrid and Sevilla schools. It's open from 10 am to 2 pm and 4 to 6 pm (closed on Sunday evening and all day Monday). Entry is 400 ptas (half for students).

If you want to develop your own El Greco trail, other places in Toledo where you can see his works include the Museo de Santa Cruz, the sacristía of the cathedral, the Monasterio de Santo Domingo El Antiguo and the Hospital de Tavera.

Jewish Quarter Toledo still considers itself the 'city of the three cultures', and near El Greco's supposed house is what was once the *judería* or Jewish quarter. 'Once' because, as a huge plaque in the cathedral proudly proclaims, the bulk of Toledo's Jews, like those elsewhere in Spain, were expelled in 1492. In the centuries prior to that black day, Toledo's Jews worshipped in 11 synagogues.

Of the two synagogues that survive, the **Sinagoga del Tránsito**, Calle de los Reyes Católicos, is the most interesting. Built in 1355 by special permission of Pedro I (construction of synagogues was by then prohibited in Christian Spain), its main prayer hall is in an impressive state of restoration. The mudéjar decoration – yet another reminder of the unique cultural mix of the city – is particularly striking. Academics are still puzzling over the full meaning of the Hebrew inscriptions that line the walls, but less attention seems to have been paid to those in Arabic in the ceiling. From 1492 until 1877 it was variously used as a priory, hermitage and military barracks. The modern **Museo Sefardi** it now houses affords enlightening insights into the history of Jewish culture in Spain, although the explanations are all in Spanish only. Entry is 400 ptas (free on Saturday afternoon and Sunday). The complex is open from 10 am to 2 pm and 4 to 6 pm (morning only on Sunday, and closed all day Monday).

A short way north along Calle de los Reyes Católicos, the **Sinagoga de Santa María La Blanca** is characterised by the horseshoe arches that delineate the five naves – a classic of Almohad architecture. Entry costs 150 ptas, and opening times are similar to those for El Tránsito.

San Juan de los Reyes A little further north lies one of the city's most visible sights, the Franciscan monastery and church founded by Fernando and Isabel to demonstrate the power of the crown over the nobles and the supremacy of the Catholic faith in Spain – for how else could you interpret the decision to erect such an edifice in the heart of the Jewish *barrio*? The rulers had planned to be buried here, but when they took Granada in 1492, they opted for the brilliance of the southern city's Muslim palace. Begun by the Breton architect Juan Güas in 1477, San Juan de los Reyes was finished only in 1606. Throughout the church and two-storey cloister the coat of arms of Fernando and Isabel (or in other words of the united Spain) dominates, and the chains of Christian prisoners liberated in Granada hang from the walls. The prevalent late Flemish-Gothic style is tarted up with lavish Isabelline ornament and counterbalanced by unmistakable mudéjar decoration, especially in the cloister, where typical geometric and vegetal designs stand out. The church and cloister are open daily from 10 am to 1.45 pm and 3.30 to 5.45 pm. Entry is 150 ptas.

Muslim Toledo Although many of Toledo's great buildings betray the influence of its medieval Muslim conquerors, expressed in the mudéjar style adopted in churches, synagogues, city gates and other edifices, little that is specifically Muslim remains. On the northern slopes of town you'll find the **Mezquita de Cristo de la Luz**, a modest mosque built at the turn of the millennium that suffered the usual fate of being converted to a church – as the religious frescos soon make clear. The narrow, steep Calle de Cristo de la Luz continues past the mosque and its charming gardens, and under a gate the Muslims knew as Bab al-Mardum (also the original name of the mosque). The city wall here marked the boundary between the

Muslim medina proper and Ar-Rabal, the 'outer suburbs'. Entry to the mosque is free, but only when the guardian is around (forget it from about 1 to 4 pm). If you can't see him, try calling at No 11.

The remnants of another modest mosque, the **Mezquita de las Tornerías**, in the street of the same name, now house an arts and crafts display.

Museums Around the corner from the Iglesia de Santo Tomé and the adjoining 15th century Palacio de los Condes de Fuensalida is the 14th century **Taller del Moro** in Calle del Taller del Moro. Formerly part of a noble family's residence, it now houses a modest museum with a small collection of mudéjar decorative items, ceramics, wood architraves and stucco work. Entry is 100 ptas. It opens from 10 am to 2 pm and 4 to 6.30 pm (closed on Monday, and Sunday afternoon).

The **Museo de Arte Contemporáneo**, housed in the restored 16th century mudéjar Casa de las Cadenas, in the lane of the same name, is home to a modest collection of Spanish modern art, including a couple of pieces by Joan Miró and some turn-of-the-century Toledo landscapes by Aureliano de Beruete. Opening hours and entry are as for the Taller del Moro.

The Iglesia de San Román, an impressive hybrid of mudéjar and Renaissance styles, houses the **Museo de los Concilios y Cultura Visigótica**. The documents, jewellery and other items are perhaps less interesting than the building itself, located up Calle de San Román from Plaza de Padre Juan de Mariana. Opening hours and entry are as above.

Further north, below Plaza de Padilla, the **Monasterio de Santo Domingo El Antiguo** is one of the oldest convents in Toledo, dating from the 11th century. It houses some of El Greco's early commissions (most are copies) and an eclectic display of religious artefacts. It's open from 11 am to 1.30 pm and 4 to 7 pm. Entry is 100 ptas.

Outside the city walls on the road to Madrid, the one-time **Hospital de Tavera**, built in 1541, contains an interesting art collection, including some of El Greco's last works. Entry is 500 ptas, and it opens daily from 10.30 am to 1.30 pm and 3.30 to 6 pm

Around the City Walls Large portions of the old city walls remain intact, and for many people the first sight of old Toledo is the hefty turrets of the 16th century **Puerta Nueva de Bisagra**, emblazoned with Carlos I's coat of arms and as imposing now as they must have appeared to visitors approaching from Madrid down the Camino Real de Castilla.

You can follow the walls around to the west until you reach the equally solid **Puerta del Cambrón** (Buckthorn Gate), also known as Puerta de los Judíos (Jews' Gate) for its proximity to the judería. A short walk from here past San Juan de los Reyes brings you down to one of the two remaining medieval bridges in Toledo – the **Puente de San Martín**, several times rebuilt and altered since its initial construction in the 14th century. Another symbol of the city is the **Puente de Alcántara**, east of Bisagra.

Outside the City After scurrying about the sometimes claustrophobic lanes of the casco, head out of town to the south bank of the **Río Tajo** for some air and the best views of the

CASTILLA-LA MANCHA

❋ ❋ ❋ ❋ ❋ ❋ ❋ ❋ ❋ ❋ ❋ ❋ ❋

Bitter Tears & Peaceful Strolls
Most day-trippers to Toledo follow a well-defined and restricted route through the city, and it is quite easy to flee the crowds by diving off into less explored barrios. The medieval labyrinth that spreads south of the cathedral and the Alcázar was, and to an extent remains, a largely working-class district, and reading the various explanatory plaques in the streets (unfortunately, in Spanish only) adds flavour to an otherwise uncluttered stroll. The waters of the Pozo Amargo (Bitter Well), in the centre of this area, are said to have gone bad after a young Jewish woman's Christian lover was murdered by her father, for in her grief she spent much of the remainder of her life crying tears of bitterness into the well. ■

❋ ❋ ❋ ❋ ❋ ❋ ❋ ❋ ❋ ❋ ❋ ❋ ❋

city. From the Puente de Alcántara you're looking at about a two-km walk. Alternatively, you can get the tiny cable-ferry from near the Casa del Diamantista, in the south end of the casco, and hike up the opposite bank. See also Cafés & Drinks below for suggestions on places to drink in the views. Scattered about this hinterland are the *cigarrales*, country estates of wealthy toledanos. If you own one of these, you've more than made it.

Swimming Midsummer in Toledo is scorching, and several pools open in the hot months. The best of them is the Piscina Municipal on the roundabout at the northern end of Avenida de la Reconquista (take bus No 1 from Zocodover to the roundabout).

Special Events

The Feast of Corpus Christi (or of the Body of Christ) falls on the Thursday after Trinity Sunday, a week after Pentecost, and is by far the most extraordinary on Toledo's religious calendar. For convenience's sake, the feast day, which is preceded by several days of processions and festivities, is celebrated on the following Sunday, when the massive Custodia de Arfe (see Catedral above) is paraded around the city. It is preceded by hundreds of people marching in traditional dress in the name of countless religious fraternities *(cofradías)* and other groups, as well as the army (the troops always get a big hand in this traditionally military town).

Easter is also marked by several days of solemn processions by masked members of cofradías, several held around midnight in the key days of Holy Week. The Feast of the Assumption is 15 August. On this day of the Sagrario de la Virgen, you can drink of the cathedral's well water. The water is held by many to have miraculous qualities; the queues for a swig from an earthenware *botijo* can be equally astonishing.

Places to Stay

Camping & Youth Hostel There are three camp sites around Toledo. Closest to the old city is *Circo Romano* (☎ 22 04 42), Avenida

de Carlos III 19. Charges are 500 ptas per person, tent and car. Better and marginally cheaper, but more awkward for those without their own vehicle, is *El Greco* (☎ 22 00 90). It's a couple of km south-west of town, on the road to La Puebla de Montalbán, and has good views of Toledo from the pool. The *Toledo* (☎ 35 30 13) is well out of town on the highway to Madrid.

The HI *youth hostel* (☎ 22 45 54) is exceptionally well located in the Castillo de San Servando, a castle that started life as a Visigothic monastery and later belonged to the Knights Templar. B&B costs 1100 ptas (under 26) or 1500 ptas per person. A membership card is necessary.

Pensiones, Hostales & Hotels – Old City

The fair range of accommodation is offset by the number of people looking for a bed, especially from about Easter to September, so arrive early. Lower-end places generally skimp on heating in winter, and have only communal showers. Some of the middle and top-end hotels discount rooms in January and February.

Toledo's cheapest place lies in the maze of alleys directly south of the Alcázar, an area little visited by tourists, which retains the air of the medieval working-class quarter it once was. *La Belviseña* (☎ 22 00 67), Cuesta del Can 5, is a basic affair at 1000/2000 ptas for singles/doubles. Showers are 100 ptas. The *Pensión Virgen de la Estrella* (☎ 25 31 34), Calle Real del Arrabal 18, just inside the Puerta Nueva de Bisagra, is in the same class and has rooms for 1500/3000 ptas.

A good deal further into the tangle of the casco is the charming old *Pensión Segovia* (☎ 21 11 24), in a cosy old house at Calle de Recoletos 2. It only has doubles, but they are spotless and cost 2100 ptas. Virtually on Zocodover is the *Hostal Las Armas* (☎ 22 16 68), Calle de las Armas 7. Several hundred years old, it is a little less well kept than the Segovia, and rooms cost 1900/3000 ptas plus IVA.

Near the Alcázar is the *Pensión Lumbreras* (☎ 22 15 71), Calle de Juan Labrador 9. It has reasonable rooms around a pleasant courtyard for 1600/2500 ptas. The *Pensión Nuncio Viejo* (☎ 22 81 78), Calle del Nuncio Viejo 19, has unexceptional doubles for 2900 ptas, or 3200 ptas with own bathroom. The *Posada del Estudiante* (☎ 21 47 34), Callejón de San Pedro 2, has simple student accommodation for 1500 ptas a head. There may be a spare room going.

Moving up the scale, *Hotel Imperio* (☎ 22 76 50), Calle de las Cadenas 7, is a pleasant place and a quick walk from Zocodover. It charges 3590/5350 ptas plus IVA. Similarly priced, but a little out of the way, is the *Pensión El Diamantista* (☎ 25 14 27), Plaza Retama 5, down by the Río Tajo in the south of the casco. Closer to the centre is *Hostal Descalzos* (☎ 22 28 88), Calle de los Descalzos 30. It has comfortable doubles only for up to 5600 ptas plus IVA. The *Pensión Santa Úrsula* (☎ 21 09 63), Calle de Santa Úrsula 14, has decent doubles with bathroom for 5300 ptas. Another good place at this price is the *Posada de Zocodover* (☎ 21 43 75), a short walk from the cathedral at Calle de las Cordonerías 6.

The *Hotel Maravilla* (☎ 22 83 17), Plaza de Barrio Rey 7, is in an enchanting spot off Zocodover. Rooms with private bath cost 3750/6000 ptas. The *Hotel Santa Isabel* (☎ 25 31 36), Calle de Santa Isabel 24, is another good choice. Rooms cost 3673/5720 ptas plus IVA.

Pricier is the *Hotel Pintor El Greco* (☎ 21 42 50; fax 21 58 19), Calle de Alamillos del Tránsito 13. Singles/doubles cost 8000/10,000 ptas plus IVA. *Hostal del Cardenal* (☎ 22 49 00; fax 25 28 77), Paseo de Recaredo 24, is just down from Puerta Nueva de Bisagra and has a popular restaurant. Singles/doubles go for 6300/10,200 ptas plus IVA. *Hotel Carlos V* (☎ 22 21 00; fax 22 21 05), Calle de Trastámara 1, has rooms for 7600/10,900 ptas.

Pensiones, Hostales & Hoteles – outside the Old City If all else fails, there is a cluster of places near the Plaza de Toros, a five-minute walk north along the Carretera de Madrid from Puerta Nueva de Bisagra. They are much of a muchness. *Hostal Boxes* (☎ 22

06 11), Calle de Covarrubias 4, has rooms for 2700/3800 ptas. The *Pensión Amalí* (☎ 22 70 18), Calle de Alonso Berruguete 1, charges 3800 ptas for doubles. The *Pensión Madrid* (☎ 22 11 44), Calle del Marqués de Mendigorría 7, has rooms for 2900/4000 ptas plus IVA (less from October to March). It has a branch across the road at No 14. Also at No 14 is *Hostal Gavillanes* (☎ 21 16 28), which has slightly more up-market rooms for 5600 ptas. *Pensión Esperanza* (☎ 22 78 59), Calle de Covarrubias 2, has only doubles for 4600 ptas.

On the south bank of the Tajo and boasting magic views of the city is Toledo's premier establishment, the *Parador Nacional Conde de Orgaz* (☎ 22 18 50; fax 22 51 66). Rooms cost 8500/16,500 plus IVA. Without a car it's awkward to reach, although bus No 7 from Zocodover goes close.

Places to Eat

For your own supplies, there is a mediocre *produce market* on Plaza Mayor. The *Serprix supermarket* at Calle del Comercio 4 is about the most central.

The cuisine of Toledo and indeed the whole region is based on simple peasant fare. Partridge, cooked in a variety of fashions, is probably the premier dish and particularly representative of Toledo. *Carcamusa*, a meat dish, is also typical, as is *cuchifritos*, a kind of potpourri of lamb, tomato and egg cooked in white wine with saffron.

Old City Toledo is predictably full of restaurants, many serving up average food for not-so-average prices.

For excellent bocadillos – great after a round of the bars – it is hard to beat *Ñaca Ñaca* on Zocodover (skip McDonald's across the road!). If you just want to pick at a pâté and cheese platter over a beer, try the *Jacaranda Bar*, Callejón de los Dos Codos 1. It's a cosy place and you could eat the equivalent of a full meal for about 1000 ptas.

About the cheapest lunch you'll find in Toledo is to be had at the *Posada del Estudiante*, Callejón de San Pedro 2. The home-cooked set menu costs 600 ptas, plus 100 ptas for wine.

Restaurante Manila, in the Palacio de Fuensalida at Plaza del Conde 2 (near the Iglesia de Santo Tomé), has loads of atmosphere, and the set lunches for about 1100 ptas are usually good value. For food of similar quality and price, the *Osiris Bar* on the shady Plaza de Barrio Nuevo is a decent choice. Another outdoor option is the *Restaurante Alex* on Plaza Amador de los Ríos.

La Abadía, Plaza de San Nicolás 3, as well as being a popular bar, offers good downstairs dining with typical Toledan dishes such as perdiz estofada (stewed partridge). The set lunch menu, at about 1200 ptas, is reliable.

An excellent little place for a full meal (set lunch for 1200 ptas) or simply a beer and tapas is *Ludeña*, Plaza de la Magdalena 13.

For slow service but good food (including a selection of tolerable pizzas), the family-run *El Armiño*, Calle de las Tendillas 8, is solid.

For Toledo's best seafood, *Bar La Ría*, Callejón de los Bodegones 6, is hard to beat. The place, allegedly run by Galicians, has a wide menu. Problem is, it's popular and tiny. A good meal will cost about 2000 ptas a head. Have a shot at the mariscada, a cold and hot seafood platter.

Among the best known of Toledo's more expensive restaurants is *Restaurante Aurelio*, Calle de la Sinagoga 1. You will eat very well for about 5000 ptas a head. There is an extension across the road at No 6, and the proprietors have another restaurant at Plaza del Ayuntamiento 4. Better still is the *Restaurante Hierbabuena*, Calle de Cristo de la Luz 9. The food is expensive but imaginatively classy – a considerable step up from the usual traditional fare.

Outside the Old City In summer, several delightful places open up in the hills around Toledo. They are only practical for those with wheels. The *Ermita de la Bastida* exudes a haphazard barbecue atmosphere and is popular with groups. Follow the road to La Puebla de Montalbán and at the first roundabout take the C-401 for Navahermosa and follow it for two km; the badly signposted dirt track to the Ermita is off to the right.

Cafés & Drinks The cafés on Zocodover are pleasant for a morning coffee or lunchtime beer over a paper, but prices reflect the predominantly tourist clientele – that is, you pay double the usual.

Bar Amsterdam is in the same league, but occupies an irresistibly sunny position on Plaza de la Magdalena. Another nice coffee stop is *El Torreón*, Plaza del Consistorio 3.

Cafetería Scorpions, Calle del Pintor Matias Moreno 10, is a trendier place to while away a Sunday afternoon. They have board games too.

Just outside Toledo is a charming old roadside hostelry, *La Venta del Alma*, Carretera de Piedrabuena 25. Cross the Puente de San Martín and turn left up the hill – it's a couple of hundred metres up on your left.

For splendid views of the city, head out of town. Where the Carretera de Circunvalación (ring road on the south bank of the Tajo) forks for the parador there is a small roadside drink stop, the *Kiosko Base*. Or you could enjoy still more sweeping views and more expensive drinks from the *parador* itself. Further up again, *Hotel Doménico* has a beer terrace with views – about the only place you'll get a breeze in the stifling midsummer months.

Entertainment
Bars & Nightclubs Toledo is not known for outstanding nightlife, but there are enough watering holes and noisy discos bursting with the city's young student population to keep you happy for a couple of days.

Start on a sedate note at *1700*, a pleasant cervecería on Plaza de Tendillas. A couple of places serve a variety of Spanish and foreign beers – a decent one is *La Abadía*. In the streets around here, particularly Calle de los Alfileritos and Calle de la Sillería, are many of the old city's busier bars. They jump with largely adolescent hormones from about Thursday on. For a South American touch,

Macondo, Calle de los Alfileritos 28, is lively. *Camelot*, Calle de Cristo de la Luz 10, is a standard late-night watering hole. A little lighter is the new *Cervecería San Mateo*, Calle de la Sillería 5.

At *Sildavia*, Calle de Santa Fe 12, go downstairs and ask for your favourite cocktail in a *porrón*, the glass version of a wine pouch – stained shirts inevitable.

For more old-fashioned dancing and a decidedly more refined atmosphere, *El Café de Garcilaso*, Calle de Rojas 5, is a unique spot that doesn't get moving until quite late. Back in the early 1970s it was about the only place young toledanos could let their hair down – and was much disapproved of by the Church.

Most of the young people finish the night in one of the discos down by the Miradero (a terrace overlooking the northern end of town), on the road from Zocodover to Puerta Nueva de Bisagra.

In summer, the focus shifts elsewhere. The *terrazas* outside the Puerta del Cambrón become a series of open-air bars, and *disco-piscinas* (discos with swimming pools you are often *not* supposed to swim in!) with such predictable names as *Splash* open up in the countryside or in small towns around Toledo; ask at the tourist office.

Theatre & Cinema *Teatro Rojas* (☎ 22 39 70), Plaza Mayor, often has an interesting programme of theatre and dance, sometimes with prestigious Spanish and foreign companies. Tuesday nights are reserved for film cycles, often foreign pictures in the original language. Check for weekend kids' matinees. Otherwise there is the *María Cristina cinema complex*, at Calle del Marqués de Mendigorría 10, near the Plaza de Toros. In summer an open-air cinema functions at the Miradero.

Bullfighting Aficionados can occasionally indulge their whims at the Plaza de Toros (built in 1866) on the road to Madrid. Quality *corridas* are more the exception than the rule.

Things to Buy

For centuries, Toledo was reputed for the excellence of its swords. Few people need such weapons these days, but toledanos keep forging them, along with all sorts of other metalwork. A little less ostentatious are the innumerable objects bearing damascene (*damasquinado*) decoration. A clear descendent of Arab artistic traditions, the fine encrustation of gold and/or silver onto everything from sword sheaths to lighters can make a decent souvenir. Another Arab bequest is the art of ceramics, which the whole region churns out in all imaginable forms. Toledo is bursting with stores selling this stuff, so shop around.

Among all the souvenir shops, there are a few places of a more original bent and higher quality. The Antigüedades shop at Calle de los Reyes Católicos 8, near the Sinagoga de Santa María La Blanca, has good antiques – among them a lot of Jewish religious items – and attractive lithographs. For hand-painted copies of mainly medieval art on solid wood bases, you might like to have a peek at Las 3 Culturas, Calle de San Román 3, off Plaza de Padre Juan de Mariana.

Toledo is also famed for its marzipan (*mazapán*), which city merchants flog to all and sundry. There is good and bad. The Santo Tomé brand is reputable. You could also try El Convento, made by Dominican nuns at the Monasterio de Jesús y María. Take bus No 4 from Zocodover along Avenida Europa to Buenavista. At the roundabout, turn right up the hill, and the new monastery (the nuns used to live in the casco) is to your left after another roundabout. When you enter, you'll see a kind of antique rotating dumbwaiter. Hit the buzzer and tell the nuns what you want. They don't want to see or be seen, so you put the money in the dumb waiter, and they rotate the marzipan out.

Getting There & Away

For most major destinations, you will need to backtrack to Madrid (or at least as far as Aranjuez), as most transport from Toledo is local and regional.

Bus Galiano Continental buses run every half-hour between Madrid (Estación Sur) and Toledo's bus station (☎ 21 58 50) from about 6 am to 10 pm (to 11.30 pm on Sunday and holidays). Direct buses (50 minutes) run roughly every hour; the remainder call at all *pueblos*. The fare is 550 ptas. The same firm runs buses to Talavera de la Reina (675 ptas). Other companies run to most surrounding towns and villages, such as Orgaz, Ocaña, Alcázar de San Juan and La Puebla de Montalbán. The Aisa bus company has a service to Cuenca at 5.30 pm from Monday to Friday, and daily buses to Albacete via Ciudad Real at 3.30 pm.

Train Built in 1920 in neo-mudéjar style, Toledo's train station (☎ 22 12 72) is a pretty introduction to the city. Although the *cercanías* operating to Madrid (Atocha) via Aranjuez are more pleasant than the bus, there are only nine of them per day (the first at 7 am, the last at 9.30 pm). From Madrid, the first leaves at 7.20 am and the last at 7.55 pm, and a one-way ticket costs 565 ptas. Toledo's mayor is talking of deviating the high-speed Madrid-Sevilla AVE line to Toledo, which could make the 70-km journey a cinch – but that's a long way off yet.

If you are heading south for Granada, Córdoba and beyond, you can usually change at Aranjuez rather than go all the way back into Madrid.

Taxi Those in a fix could take a taxi from Toledo to Madrid. This luxury will set you back 7000 to 8000 ptas.

Car & Motorcycle The N-401 connects Toledo with Madrid. Heading south, you can take the same road to Ciudad Real, from where it becomes the N-420 to Córdoba. If you want the N-IV Autovía de Andalucía, the main motorway running south from Madrid to Córdoba and Sevilla, take the N-400 for Aranjuez. The N-403 heads north-west for Ávila and continues as the N-501 for Salamanca.

Getting Around

You're unlikely to want wheels while exploring the nooks and crannies of Toledo's casco, but buses do circulate through it and connect with outlying suburbs. Handy ones run between Zocodover and the train station (Nos 5 & 6) or the bus station (No 5).

There is a taxi rank just up from Zocodover in the shadow of the Alcázar, and another at the bus station. Or you can call one on ☎ 25 50 50.

If you're driving, Toledo's winding one-way lane system can be nightmarish for the inexperienced. It is possible to park, but not easy. The desperate could try one of the car parks, which charge around 150 ptas an hour.

AROUND TOLEDO
Orgaz

About 40 km south of Toledo on the N-401 to Ciudad Real, this cheery village boasts a modest 15th century **castle**. It's in good nick but only open every second Wednesday from April to November. According to a rather enigmatic plaque, El Cid's wife, Doña Jimena, 'played here'. The leafy Plaza Mayor is flanked by attractive buildings with heavy wood-beam arcades and an 18th century church built by Alberto Churriguera. Buses run fairly regularly from Toledo.

If you have a vehicle, a more interesting way of reaching Orgaz is via the C-400 road. About 20 km out of Toledo, the ruined Arab castle of **Almonacid de Toledo** rises up directly in front of you. Some legends suggest El Cid lived here, but the lonely ruins have long been abandoned. A few km further down the road is another, smaller castle, in the centre of the village of **Mascaraque**. On reaching Mora, turn west for Orgaz, from where you can pick up the N-401 for Ciudad Real and Andalucía.

Castle Circuit

Castilla-La Mancha is littered with castles in varying states of upkeep; a few have already been cited south of Toledo, and several more are mentioned later in this chapter. Aficionados of *castillos* who have their own wheels could undertake a tour of several of them

CASTILLA-LA MANCHA

west and south-west of Toledo. What follows is a round trip of about 250 km – feasible but perhaps a little tiring as a one-day trip.

Take the C-401 for Navahermosa. After about 15 km you turn right for **Guadamur**, which sports an impressive, privately owned 15th century castle that has played host to all sorts of VIPs, from Pedro I (the Cruel) and Juana la Loca (the Mad) to Carlos I. During the civil war, its once beautiful grounds and much of the library and furnishings were destroyed by Republican militia. It opens a few days each month (check with the Toledo tourist office).

Back on the C-401, head south-west to the junction with the C-403, and follow the latter north towards La Puebla de Montalbán. About 10 km up (a little way north of San Martín de Montalbán) and off to your left lie the ruins of the **Castillo de Montalbán**, standing majestically over the Río Torcón valley. Historians believe it to be a 12th century Templar castle. Officially it's open on Saturday morning from May to January only, but there seems little to stop you wandering around at pretty much any time.

Continue to La Puebla de Montalbán and turn west along the C-502. At **Malpica de Tajo** is a well-preserved castle, parts of which date from the 10th century. From here you cut north across back roads (head for Santa Olalla) to pick up the N-V and head 10 km east for **Maqueda**. The Romans first saw the strategic use of the site, and Isabel I figures among the long line of its subsequent guests. It now houses the Guardia Civil. You might want to break the circuit here and drive 13 km north along the N-403 to **Escalona**, where you'll find the ruins of a castle of Arab origin prettily located on the banks of the Río Alberche. Finally, turn heel and take the same road back to Toledo (or continue north-west to Ávila – see the Castilla y León chapter), stopping en route if you like at **Barcience**, with its abandoned 14th century castle built by the Portuguese Silva family, supporters of Juan I's notions of Iberian union. The shell is impressive, but there is nothing inside.

If you do opt for Ávila, the insatiable could pop into **San Martín de Valdeiglesias**, 26 km north of Escalona and actually just inside the boundaries of the Comunidad de Madrid. It boasts a much-restored castle and a handful of old mansions.

The West

TALAVERA DE LA REINA

Scene of a key battle between Wellington and the French in 1809, and overrun by the Muslim Almoravid dynasty seven centuries earlier, Talavera betrays little evidence of its long and varied history. Though the town was the birthplace of Fernando de Rojas, whose *Celestina* (published in 1499) is judged by some as Europe's first great novel, the only evidence of artistic activity of any sort today lies in the ubiquitous ceramics for which the town has long been justly famed. A fine example of their use is the façade of the recently restored **Teatro Victoria**, just off Plaza de Juan de Mariana. Otherwise you can see stretches of the city walls (there were once three cordons) and a couple of churches in need of restoration. One day the **Museo de Ruiz de Luna** (probably to be dedicated mostly to ceramics) might open. It is on an unnamed square near Plaza de San Pedro. The road leading north to the N-V motorway is lined with ceramics factories and shops.

There is no particular reason to stay here, but there are a few hostales around if you need them. *Hostal Edan* (☎ 925-80 22 50), Calle de General Yagüe 24, has doubles for 3400 ptas.

The bus station is in the centre of town. Regular buses between Madrid and Badajoz stop here, and 10 a day go to Toledo (about 90 km to the east). You can also reach Mérida, Cáceres, Plasencia and Guadalupe (twice a day). A daily bus to Barcelona leaves at 8.45 pm. Talavera is on the Madrid-Lisbon train line – not one of the peninsula's fastest.

AROUND TALAVERA DE LA REINA

Much more pleasant than Talavera is the village of **Oropesa**, 34 km west along the

N-V. Its 14th century **castle** (open daily from 10 am to 2 pm and 4 to 8 pm, and on Sunday and holidays from 10 am to 8 pm; entry 100 ptas) looks north across the plains to the Sierra de Gredos and also hosts a *parador* (☎ 43 00 00), which has comfortable doubles for 13,500 ptas plus IVA.

Another 13 km south, **El Puente del Arzobispo** is another well-known ceramics centre. There are plenty of places where you can inspect the town's wares. The bridge after which the town is named was built in the 14th century. From here you could follow the slender TO-702 south for another 40-odd km to the regional frontier with Extremadura, crossing at Puerto de San Vicente and heading on west to Guadalupe (see the Extremadura chapter). Of some interest about 10 km south-east of El Puente del Arzobispo are the scanty ruins of **Vascos**, probably a Roman settlement: after the bridge, take the first left and head towards Aldeanueva de Barbarroya. The site is south of the road.

MONTES DE TOLEDO

Beginning as the low foothills that lie south of Toledo astride the road to Ciudad Real, the Montes de Toledo rise westwards towards Extremadura. Exploring the Montes takes you into the heart of some of the most sparsely populated country of Spain's interior. You can't get much further away from the tourist routes, but you could make a slow trip through the mountains on the way from Toledo to Guadalupe (or vice-versa). Most towns are served by the occasional bus – often no more than one a day on weekdays – from Toledo.

If you have a vehicle, the most straightforward road is along the C-401 (see also Castle Circuit above), which skirts the northern slopes of the Montes. Eleven km short of Navahermosa, a trail leads south to the **Embalse de Torcón**, a popular lakeside picnic spot.

Beyond Navahermosa you have several options for branching south and exploring the villages and hills as you choose. Some of the more heavily wooded areas offer unexpectedly charming vistas, and apart from the odd tiny pueblo, you will hardly see a soul. One longish route that gives a taste of the area would see you dropping south off the C-401 at Los Navalmorales. Take the TO-752 for the small village of Los Navalucillos. A few km further on there is a peaceful *bar* right on the banks of the lively little Río Pusa. From here you keep heading south past villages like Robledo del Buey and Los Alares until you hit a T-junction (just inside Extremadura). Turn right (west) and about 35 winding km on you will pass the northern reaches of the huge Embalse de Cijara, part of a chain of reservoirs fed by the Río Guadiana. After the tiny village of Cijara, swing north towards Puerto Rey, a mountain pass from where you can branch off west along a back road to the C-401 and the last curvy stretch towards Guadalupe (see the Extremadura chapter).

Yet another alternative is to head for the **San Pablo de los Montes** area. You can take the TO-781 via Argés south of Toledo, and onward via Las Ventas con Peña Aguilera (renowned for its venison). San Pablo de los Montes is an average hill town, but the drive or walk about eight km further south is rewarding. It brings you to **Baños de Robledillo**, where there are thermal springs. The youth hostel, *Albergue Juvenil Baños de Robledillo* (☎ 925-41 53 00), has baths using the spring water. B&B is 1100 ptas for those under 26, and 1500 ptas for the rest. The hostel is closed from 1 July to 30 September.

The South

CIUDAD REAL

Just 110 km down the road from the Imperial City of Toledo lies its royal counterpart, Ciudad Real. Before you get too excited, about the only things the two cities have in common are their grandiose titles. Founded by Alfonso X in 1255 to check the power of the Knights of Calatrava, who were based in nearby Almagro, Ciudad Real quickly became an important provincial capital, although only finally eclipsing Almagro in the 18th century. Little remains today of the old city, and you'd not be missing much by following the ring road around it and continuing on your way.

Information

The Oficina de Información Turística (☎ 21 29 25), Avenida Alarcos 31, opens Monday to Friday from 9 am to 2 pm. It has a reasonable stock of information on the province. The main post office is on Plaza de la Constitución. The postcode for poste restante is 13080. The telephone code is ☎ 926.

Things to See

Coming from the north, you enter Ciudad Real by the **Puerta de Toledo**, a 14th century defensive gate built in mudéjar style by Alfonso XI.

Inside the largely modern city, the pick of the crop is the **Museo Provincial**, Calle del Prado 4, which offers a reasonable display of archaeological finds dating from Palaeolithic times, along with a collection of artworks, mostly provincial, covering the past four centuries. It opens from 10 am to 2 pm daily (except Monday, when it closes) and 5 to 8 pm from Tuesday to Saturday. Entry is free.

Of the few churches to be seen, the most striking is the 14th century Gothic **Iglesia de San Pedro**.

Places to Stay & Eat

Accommodation is a little sad, so try not to be caught in Ciudad Real. Just outside the southern end of the city centre is a cluster of three undistinguished places. Cheapest and most spartan is the *Pensión Villa Oriente* (no phone), Carretera de Valdepeñas 12, with rooms for 1200/2200 ptas (communal bathroom). A little better is the *Pensión Angelo* (☎ 22 85 92), Calle de Galicia 49, which charges 1450/2500 ptas. The *Pensión Escudero* (☎ 25 23 09), Calle de Galicia 48, has rooms starting at 2200/3300 ptas with shared bathroom; a double with bathroom is 4200 ptas. Bus No 5 from the train station

```
PLACES TO STAY          OTHER
 9 Hotel Santa Cecilia   1 Puerta de Toledo
                         2 Post Office
PLACES TO EAT            3 Museo Provincial
 4 Restaurante Villa Real 4 Parque de Gasset
11 Cafés                 5 Oficina de Información
15 Restaurante Masther     Turística
16 Horchatería La Fama   7 Cines Castillo
                         8 Bus Station
                        10 Plaza del Pilar
                        12 Plaza Mayor
                        13 Ayuntamiento
                        14 Iglesia de San Pedro
```

Ciudad Real

0   100   200 m

runs past all these places. Visitors with more expensive tastes could try the *Hotel Santa Cecilia* (☎ 22 85 45), Calle de Tinte 3, which has singles/doubles for 6300/7880 ptas.

For all your food and drinking requirements, head for Avenida del Torreón del Alcázar and the parallel Calle de los Hidalgos. The former is lined with cafés and a couple of restaurants, such as the *Masther* at No 5, where you can get a reasonable set menu for 975 ptas. The nearby *Horchatería La Fama* does decent ice creams. In Calle de los Hidalgos you can snack well on tapas while imbibing cañas in the string of bars.

The Battle of Alarcos

On 19 July 1195, the greatest of all the Almohad rulers, Yacoub Al-Mansour (the Victorious), drew his forces up near the settlement of Alarcos, about five km south-west of Ciudad Real, to face the Castilian army of Alfonso VIII. Unwilling to wait for the arrival of reinforcements marching from the north, Alfonso decided to unleash his cavalry at the Muslim forces, recently arrived from Morocco to restore Muslim control over Spain. Alfonso's horsemen crushed Al-Mansour's vanguard but quickly found themselves surrounded. A promising start thus turned into a rout.

According to the Almohad chronicler Ibn Idari: 'Allah granted [us] victory and the defeated Christians turned their backs and abandoned their swords. The tyrant's camp was sacked and swept as in a harvest with [the Christians'] deaths – said to be around 30,000...Alfonso, the enemy of God, escaped to Toledo...' Some say only 300 soldiers survived the disaster.

A Christian observer saw Alfonso's role a little differently: 'The noble king advanced and, plunging in amongst the enemy, felled with manliness many Moors...but as his men realised that Spain was in imminent danger, pulled him from the battle. He later arrived in Toledo with a few soldiers, aggrieved by the great misfortune.'

Al-Mansour never really capitalised on his victory, and 17 years later it was made irrelevant by the crushing Christian victory in the Battle of Las Navas de Tolosa. Today there is little to see at the battleground except a chapel dedicated to Our Lady of Alarcos. ■

Otherwise, the *Restaurante Villa Real*, Calle de las Postas 12, does platos combinados from 600 ptas. The *cafés* on Plaza Mayor are pleasant for a morning coffee and a sticky bun.

Getting There & Away

Bus The bus station is south of the town centre, off Ronda de Ciruela. There's a bus to Toledo at 8 am, another to Córdoba at 11 am and five a day to Madrid. Most surrounding towns can be reached by bus.

Train The bulk of trains linking Madrid with Andalucía, including the high-speed AVE to Sevilla, call in at Ciudad Real (☎ 22 02 02; the station is east of the town centre). Trains also head east to Albacete, Valencia and Alicante, as well as to Badajoz in Extremadura. Local bus Nos 5 and 2 run to the station from Plaza del Pilar in the centre.

CIUDAD REAL PROVINCE
Almagro

It may have come second in the struggle for local supremacy with Ciudad Real, but Almagro has retained a charm long lost in its competitor. De facto medieval capital of what even today is still known as the Campo de Calatrava, Almagro underwent a unique face-lift in the 16th century after the arrival of several German families, including the Fuggers of Augsburg, bankers to Carlos I. It is largely to them and their successors that Almagro's porticoed **Plaza Mayor** owes its present distinctive appearance.

At No 18 you'll find **El Corral de Comedias**, a 17th century theatre still often used, especially for the annual Festival Internacional de Teatro Clásico in July. It is open from Tuesday to Friday from 10 am to 2 pm and 4 to 7 pm (shorter hours on the weekend; closed on Monday); buy tickets (400 ptas) at the small Museo del Teatro (same hours) across the square. A smattering of churches, convents and public buildings around the town make Almagro a pleasant spot for a little exploration. The Infotur tourist office (☎ 86 07 17), Calle Mayor de Carnicerías 5, has information. The telephone code is ☎ 926.

Almagro is preferable to Ciudad Real for an overnight stop. *Fonda Peña* (☎ 86 03 17), Calle de Emilio Piñuela 10 (near the Ermita de San Blas), is a good, clean deal at 1300/2300 ptas for singles/doubles. The *Hospedería Municipal* (☎ 88 20 87), Calle de Ejido de Calatrava s/n, has doubles for 3200 ptas with shower or 3500 ptas with full bath. Nearby, *Hotel Don Diego* (☎ 86 12 87), Calle de Ejido de Calatrava 1, charges 3800/

6500 ptas for singles/doubles (more in the high season).

If you want to do it in a little more style, the *parador* (☎ 86 01 00), Ronda de San Francisco, could be the way to go. Rooms in this former convent cost 12,000/15,000 ptas plus IVA.

There are several restaurants on Plaza Mayor, and bars like *El Gordo*, No 12, will do you tapas and raciones.

Two to three trains a day go to Madrid, Ciudad Real and Jaén. You can also get to Alicante. Buses run from near the Hotel Don Diego to Ciudad Real, but there are none on Sunday.

Castillo de Calatrava

About 30 km south of Almagro, the brooding walls of the castle-and-monastery complex of Calatrava La Nueva (signposted as Castillo de Calatrava) command magnificent views across the sierra of the same name. Once a forward base of the medieval order of knights that long controlled this frontier area of La Mancha during the Reconquista, the complex is open from Tuesday to Sunday from 10 am to 2 pm and 4 to 6 pm (5 to 8 pm in summer). Entry is 200 ptas. Even if closed it merits a visit for the site alone. From Calzada de Calatrava, it's seven km south along the CR-504, and is accessible only with your own vehicle.

Parque Nacional de Las Tablas de Daimiel

You get used to a steady diet of olive-studded red plains and forbidding plateaus while traversing much of southern Castilla-La Mancha, but a couple of exceptions prove the rule.

The reedy lakes of Las Tablas, 11 km north of Daimiel, are no great inspiration, but an early-morning stroll here in spring or autumn can be profitable for the bird-watcher. The park's information centre opens daily from 8 am to dusk. There is no public transport to the park, and years of near drought have taken their toll. Fortunately, heavy rains in late 1995 and a subsequent deal to transfer water from the Río Tajo arrested the slow but steady decline.

Parque Natural de las Lagunas de Ruidera

A more unexpectedly green patch in the middle of parched Castilla-La Mancha is the Parque Natural de las Lagunas de Ruidera. Surrounding a series of small lakes, with the odd waterfall and diverse bird life, it is a favoured summer retreat for hot and bothered Castilians. There is an HI youth hostel on the Laguna Colgada, the *Albergue Juvenil Alonso Quijano* (☎ 967-21 50 12 for reservations). Beds go for 945 ptas if you're under 26, and meals are available. You need a membership card. Among several other options further around the lakes is the *Hostal El Molino* (☎ 926-69 90 73), which has doubles for 2500 ptas, or 3000 ptas with own bath.

You really need wheels to get into and around the park. The town of Ruidera and the lakes are about halfway between Ciudad Real and Albacete on the N-430 highway, and buses connect with Albacete.

Valdepeñas

When it comes to wine, the people of Castilla-La Mancha generally stick to the produce of their own province. One exception seems to be the fruit of the Valdepeñas area's vines, which finds its way round not only the region, but the whole country. For those weary of long, dusty drives between the odd castle and provincial pueblos, a spot of wine tasting in one of this town's several *bodegas* might be just the ticket. The best are north of town on the road to Madrid. If that's not your scene, don't bother stopping in this surprisingly large and uninviting place.

Villanueva de los Infantes

About 30 km east of Valdepeñas along the C-415 road to Alcaraz (see below) in Albacete province lies Villanueva de los Infantes, fruit of a repopulation campaign in La Mancha as the Muslims fell back into Andalucía after the Battle of Las Navas de Tolosa in 1212. Like Almagro, the town's **Plaza Mayor** offers its most pleasing aspect, although the deep ochre-coloured buildings and heavy wooden balconies are altogether in a different style. On the square stands the **Iglesia de San Andrés**, with two doors and a pulpit in plateresque style. The 16th century poet Francisco Gómez Quevedo y Villegas was buried here. Like Almagro, Villanueva is studded with old nobles' houses and rewards a bit of a wander. You could do worse than stay a night in the *Hostal Imperio* (☎ 926-36 00 77), Calle de las Monjas Franciscanas 14, where rooms start at 2000/4000 ptas. Buses head west to Ciudad Real.

SOUTH-EAST TO ALBACETE
The highways leading south-east from Madrid to Albacete and on into Valencia take you through arguably some of the most depressing examples of Spanish countryside. The shrivelled, treeless expanses of La Mancha soon weary all but the most enthusiastic lovers of scorched earth. If you're heading to the Valencian costas from Madrid, about all you can do is scream down the road as fast as your wheels will carry you. Offerings along the way are sparse, but there are a few potential stops to break the journey.

Windmills & More Castles
Following the C-400 out of Toledo (see Around Toledo above), you arrive at the village of Mora. Instead of making southwest for Orgaz, follow the C-400 (signs for Madridejos) to the south-east.

Tilting at Life
Time and again as you march across the glum stretches of La Mancha you are reminded by roadside plaques and signs that you are in the territory of Don Quixote (Don Quijote to the Spaniards). The potty and idealistic *manchego* knight, or rather his creator, Miguel de Cervantes, could not have chosen a more challenging territory for his character's search for a new individualism, unfettered by the rigidity of 16th century Spanish society.

But Cervantes, however well he may have known La Mancha, sensibly spent most of his years elsewhere, painting his life on a much vaster canvas than he allows his hapless but tenacious hero. A brief look at Cervantes' CV reveals an equally tenacious and perhaps even more accident-filled existence. Having passed his younger years between Valladolid, Salamanca, Madrid and Sevilla, the 19-year-old writer and soon-to-be adventurer fled to Italy in 1568 to escape a prison sentence for assault. Three years later he was wounded at the Battle of Lepanto. In 1573 he participated in the seizure of Tunis, and in 1575 he hopped on a galley for Spain from Naples. It seems natural that Cervantes, ever in trouble, should have been on board the boat that was separated from the convoy and taken by corsairs. Sold as a slave in Algiers, he only managed to escape, after four failed attempts, in 1580. After trying unsuccessfully to get passage to America, he married and almost settled down in Sevilla. Vexation was never far from Cervantes' door, however, and in 1602 he ended up in chains for his involvement in a bank's collapse. He did time again a few years later under an unproved charge of murder, and subsequently moved to Madrid, where in the years until his death in 1616 he wrote the bulk of his work, of which *El Ingenioso Hidalgo Don Quijote de la Mancha* was the jewel in his literary crown. ∎

CASTILLA-LA MANCHA

Consuegra First stop along the way, 32 km south-east from Mora, Consuegra is in classic La Mancha country. The tumbledown village huddles below a hill topped by a 13th century castillo that once belonged to the Knights of Malta. Fans of Don Quixote will be delighted to know that the castle is flanked by a dozen restored windmills. The site is well chosen: it gets quite blowy. The tourist office (☎ 925-47 57 31) in the Bolero mill (they all have names) opens from 9 am to 2 pm and from 4 pm for a couple of hours. The much-restored castle is open daily from 9 am to 2 pm and 4 to 7 pm (200 ptas) and is worth a quick look. The guy in the tourist office can open up some of the mills for you, and you can see at least one in action during the annual Fiesta de la Rosa del Azafrán, held on the last weekend of October.

The only place to stay is the *Hotel Las Provincias* (☎ 925-48 03 00), not a great option, out on the Toledo-Alcázar de San Juan highway. Singles/doubles cost 3500/6000 ptas. If you haven't got wheels to get away on, there are up to eight daily buses between Consuegra and Toledo (three at weekends), and a couple to Madrid.

Campo de la Criptana & Around Don Quixote thought he might do battle here, mistaking for enemies the windmills that are the only interesting feature in this otherwise dispiriting place. The Infotur tourist office (☎ 926-56 22 31) in the Poyatos mill opens from 10 am to 2 pm and 4 to 7 pm (5 to 8 pm in summer). There are a few small hotels in town, including the *Fonda Los Molinos* (☎ 926-56 02 90), Calle de la Soledad 1, with acceptable rooms for 1500 ptas per person (250 ptas extra for a shower).

The odd train and regional bus calls in, but options are greater from **Alcázar de San Juan**, seven km west of Campo de la Criptana (about five buses a day run between the two). In fact, if you're travelling around this area without your own wheels, you could wind up in Alcázar, a major rail junction. Apart from the 18th century Iglesia de Santa María (it is thought Cervantes was baptised

here) in the square of the same name, and the nearby Torreón (tower) de Don Juan de Austria, there is nothing to draw you to Alcázar but its transport options. If you get stuck, the *Hostal Numancia* (☎ 926-54 11 47), Avenida de Criptana 11, has decent rooms for 2000/3800 ptas. You can get a filling meal for 900 ptas at the *Mesón Don Quijote*, Avenida de Doctor Bonardell 32. Trains leave for destinations throughout the country, including Madrid, Ciudad Real, Albacete, Barcelona, Cádiz, Málaga and Sevilla. Occasional buses serve Toledo, Cuenca and Belmonte.

The windmill-obsessed can see still more at **Mota del Cuervo**, 29 km north-east of Campo de la Criptana, at the junction with the N-301.

Belmonte About 25 km north-east of Mota del Cuervo is one of the better preserved Castilian castles. Set on a low knoll above the village of the same name, the 15th century Castillo de Belmonte, with its six round towers, was for a while home to France's Empress Eugénie after her husband Napoleon III lost the French throne in 1871. It's open Tuesday to Sunday from 9 am to 1 pm and 4 pm to sunset. Entry is 200 ptas, although there's not an awful lot to see inside. Also worth a visit if you can find the curate is the Iglesia Colegial de San Bartolomé, or **Colegiata**, with an impressive retablo. If you need to stay, try *La Muralla* (☎ 967-17 10 45). Rooms cost 1500/3000 ptas.

To continue on towards Albacete or beyond into Valencia, you can drop south to the N-301 or head north-east for the N-III autovía; both go to Albacete.

ALBACETE
Named after its location (*al-basit*, in Arabic, refers to the plains), this dull provincial city expanded rapidly after malarial swamps were drained in the 19th century – too late to create anything of great interest. At best, it

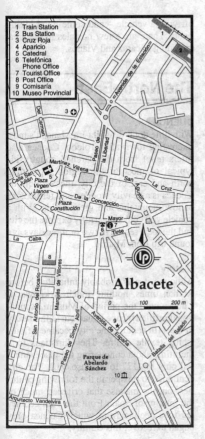

1 Train Station
2 Bus Station
3 Cruz Roja
4 Aparicio
5 Catedral
6 Telefónica
  Phone Office
7 Tourist Office
8 Post Office
9 Comisaría
10 Museo Provincial

Albacete

0   100   200 m

may serve as a transport junction for people wandering about this part of the country.

Information

The tourist office (☎ 58 05 22), in the Consejería de Industria y Turismo, Calle Mayor 46, is open from 9 am to 2 pm, Monday to Friday only. The post office is on Calle de Dionisio Guardiola, and the Telefónica phone office at Calle Mayor 42. The postcode for central Albacete is 02080 and the telephone code for the province is ☎ 967.

Things to See

Set in the leafy Parque de Abelardo Sánchez, the **Museo Provincial** is the best place to kill an hour or two. It has a reasonable archaeology section and opens Tuesday to Saturday from 10 am to 2 pm and 4.30 to 7 pm, and on Sunday and holidays from 9 am to 2 pm; it's closed on Monday. Entry is 200 ptas (half for students). In the centre of town, you could take or leave the 17th century **catedral** with its four Ionic columns.

Places to Stay

There is a ton of accommodation if for reasons beyond your control you end up needing to stay here. The *Aparicio* (☎ 21 78 90), at Calle de los Zapateros 20 in the centre, has simple rooms for 1300/2500 ptas.

Getting There & Away

A good thing to do in Albacete is leave. The bus station, next to the train station, is at the north-eastern end of town. Enatcar buses serve Madrid, Barcelona, Alicante, Valencia and Benidorm. There's a bus to Toledo at 5.30 am and to Cuenca at 6 am and 3 pm (nothing to either on Sunday). Buses run to most destinations in the province, including Chinchilla de Monte Aragón, Alcaraz and other villages in the Sierra, Ruidera and Almansa.

Trains serve Madrid, Ciudad Real, Alicante and Valencia. You can go to Toledo via Aranjuez.

AROUND ALBACETE

Bereft of interest itself, the town of Albacete is also surrounded by some of Spain's least attractive country. There are several interesting little places scattered about, however, and at its more distant margins the scenery changes quite unexpectedly for the better.

Chinchilla de Monte Aragón

Rising above the desolate plains, this white-washed village 13 km east of Albacete is topped by yet another **castle** (open weekends only), although for some the pretty

CASTILLA-LA MANCHA

Plaza de la Mancha will be more attractive, with its **ayuntamiento** (the main 18th century façade features an unflattering relief of Carlos III) and the 15th century **Iglesia de Santa María del Salvador**. Buses run between here and Albacete.

Almansa

About 60 km further on, just short of Valencia province, a square-turreted **castle** built by the Muslims stands high above the town; to get the keys, go to the police at Calle de Corredera 120.

Río Júcar

Cutting a deep, tree-filled gorge to the north-east of Albacete, the Río Júcar makes for a pleasant back-road drive. About halfway along the east-west route, **Alcalá del Júcar** is impossible to miss – its 15th century castle tower is an unmistakable landmark. The village houses are piled crazily one above the other up the steep bank of the Júcar. At the foot of the town, the *Hostal Hermanos Plaza* (☎ 967-47 30 29), Calle de Batan 46, has doubles for 2500 ptas. Just opposite, the *Hotel Júcar* (☎ 967-47 30 55) has clean, small rooms for 2500/4500 ptas.

Sierra de Alcaraz

Stretching across the southern strip of Albacete province, the cool, green peaks of the Sierra de Alcaraz are laced with small, intensively farmed plots and dotted with villages, and are a great escape from the dusty plains around Albacete. The Río Mundo begins its life as a waterfall near Riópar, and Alcaraz is itself an attractive little place with a pretty Plaza Mayor. You can follow a circuit passing through or past Alcaraz, Vianos, Riópar, Ayna (one of the better scenic lookouts, the **Mirador del Diablo**, is nearby) and Bogarra. Donkey-mounted shepherds still watch over their small flocks of sheep in the remoter corners of this low mountain territory. The odd bus gets to some of these towns, but you really would be better

off with a vehicle – and some good hiking boots. There are a few hostales in the area, including Alcaraz and Vianos.

The North-East

CUENCA

With little doubt Castilla-La Mancha's most interesting town after Toledo, Cuenca also offers relief from the parched countryside typical of most of the region. Spreading north and east of the city, the Serranía de Cuenca is a heavily wooded and fertile zone of low mountains and green fields. With a vehicle you could cheerfully explore the city and the local region in two or three days as a round trip from Madrid.

History

Although it was probably inhabited before Roman times, nothing much is known of Cuenca until the period of Muslim occupation. Fortified by one Ismail bin Dilnun early in the 11th century, the city became a flourishing textile centre. The Christians took their time about conquering the place, and it fell only in 1177 to Alfonso VIII. The city continued to prosper in the following centuries, but the malaise that crippled much of the interior of Spain from the 16th century led to a decline from which Cuenca only began to recover this century.

Orientation

Cuenca is relatively small, its old centre a narrow rise high up at the northern end of the city between the river gorges of the Júcar and Huécar. The train and bus stations are virtually opposite each other near the centre of the new town, and a 10-minute walk from the foot of the casco antiguo. It's a long climb to Plaza Mayor, the main square in the casco. Most of the hotels and offices are in the new part of town.

Information

Tourist Office The main office of the Dele-

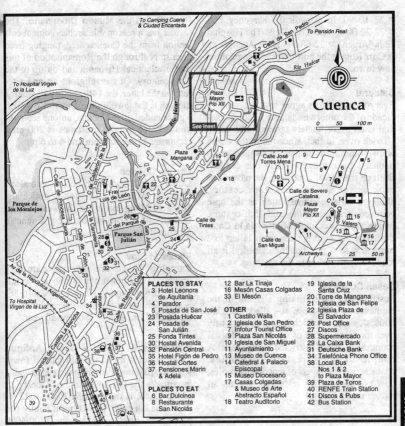

Cuenca

PLACES TO STAY
3 Hotel Leonora
de Aquitania
4 Parador
5 Posada de San José
23 Posada Huécar
24 Posada de
San Julián
25 Fonda Tintes
30 Hostal Avenida
32 Pensión Central
35 Hotel Figón de Pedro
36 Hostal Cortes
37 Pensiones Marin
& Adela

PLACES TO EAT
6 Bar Dulcinea
8 Restaurante
San Nicolás

12 Bar La Tinaja
16 Mesón Casas Colgadas
33 El Mesón

OTHER
1 Castillo Walls
2 Iglesia de San Pedro
7 Infotur Tourist Office
9 Plaza San Nicolás
10 Iglesia de San Miguel
11 Ayuntamiento
13 Museo de Cuenca
14 Catedral & Palacio
Episcopal
15 Museo Diocesano
17 Casas Colgadas
& Museo de Arte
Abstracto Español
18 Teatro Auditorio

19 Iglesia de la
Santa Cruz
20 Torre de Mangana
21 Iglesia de San Felipe
22 Iglesia Plaza de
El Salvador
26 Post Office
27 Discos
28 Supermercado
29 La Caixa Bank
31 Deutsche Bank
34 Telefónica Phone Office
38 Local Bus
Nos 1 & 2
to Plaza Mayor
39 Plaza de Toros
40 RENFE Train Station
41 Discos & Pubs
42 Bus Station

CASTILLA-LA MANCHA

gación Provincial de Industria y Turismo (☎ 17 88 00), Glorieta de González Palencia 2 (3rd floor), is in the new town and open 9 am to 2 pm and 5 to 7 pm from Monday to Friday. Of greater use is the Infotur office (☎ 23 21 19) at Calle de San Pedro 6, just off Plaza Mayor. It opens from 9 am to 2 pm and 4 to 7 pm, but closes on Sunday afternoon and all day Monday.

Money There are plenty of banks in the new town, especially around Calle de la Carretería.

Post & Communications The main post office is on the corner of Calle del Parque de San Julián and Calle de Leming. It opens from 9 am to 2 pm Monday to Saturday, and the postcode for central Cuenca is 16080. The main Telefónica phone office is at Calle de Cervantes 2 and opens Monday to Saturday from 9.30 am to 1.30 pm and 5 to 10 pm. The telephone code is ☎ 969.

Medical & Emergency Services If you need the police in a hurry, call ☎ 091 (or the Guardia Civil on ☎ 062). In case of fire, call

☎ 22 10 80. In a medical emergency, call ☎ 22 22 00 for the Cruz Roja. The Hospital de la Virgen (☎ 22 68 51) is off Avenida de la Cruz Roja at the north-western edge of the new town.

Catedral
Everyone seems to agree that the western façade of the otherwise largely Gothic cathedral is an unfortunately tasteless aberration – twice over, in fact, since the initial errors were committed in the 1600s and compounded by restoration early this century. Built on the site of a mosque, the nave dates back as far as the early 13th century, although other elements such as the apse were constructed in the mid-15th century. Inside, there is a small **Museo de la Catedral**. The museum is open from 11 am to 2 pm and 4 to 6 pm, but the cathedral itself tends to open earlier in the morning.

Casas Colgadas
Possibly the most striking element of the medieval city is these so-called 'hanging houses', some of which jut out precariously over the steep defile of the Huécar. This is economical use of restricted living space! A couple of much-restored examples, characterised by layers of wooden balconies, now contain a posh restaurant and an art museum (see below).

Museums
All the museums are closed on Sunday afternoon and Monday. Depending on your taste in art, the star of the Cuenca line-up may be the **Museo de Arte Abstracto Español**. The setting, one of the casas colgadas, sports a fine *artesonado* coffered ceiling, and the artists represented include Zobel, Sempere, Millares and Chillida. Initially a private initiative of Fernando Zobel to unite works by fellow artists of the 1950s Generación Abstracta, it now includes works up to the present day. Entry is 300 ptas, and the museum opens from 11 am to 2 pm and 4 to 6 pm (to 8 pm on Saturday).

Virtually opposite each other on Calle del Obispo Valero are the **Museo de Cuenca** (No 12) and the **Museo Diocesano**. The former has a reasonable archaeological collection from the Cuenca area, ranging from prehistory through the Romanisation of this part of classical Hispania and on up to the 12th century. Of the religious art and artefacts in the latter, the 14th century Byzantine diptych is the jewel in the crown. How such a piece ended up in Cuenca, no-one seems to know. Entry to both museums is 200 ptas. Hours are 11 am to 2 pm and 4 to 6 pm.

Muslim Cuenca
Down the hill from the casco antiguo along Calle de Alfonso VIII, you'll notice the **Torre de Mangana** off to the west, all that remains of a fortress built by Cuenca's Muslim rulers.

Places to Stay
Camping There are several camping grounds in the area around Cuenca. The relatively new *Camping Cuenca* (☎ 23 16 56) is eight km out of town on the road towards the Ciudad Encantada. It opens all year.

Pensiones & Hotels – Casco Antiguo
There is not a lot in the old part of town. Right up past the crumbling old castle walls, in virtually the last house in the highest part of the casco, is the *Pensión Real* (☎ 22 99 77), Calle Larga 99. It is a typical family-run place with singles/doubles for 1700/4000 ptas. *Posada Huécar* (☎ 21 42 01), Paseo del Huécar 3, is a quiet, comfortable mid-range place in the Huécar valley at the foot of the old city. Singles range from 2000 to 3000 ptas and doubles from 3800 to 5000 ptas, depending on room quality and season. For a little more, the *Posada de San José* (☎ 21 13 00), Ronda de Julián Romero 4, is better still. This lovely 16th century residence is in the heart of the Casco Antiguo. The only other possibility is the *Hotel Leonora de Aquitania* (☎ 23 10 00), Calle de San Pedro 60, a classy but less characterful place. Singles/doubles cost 5000/8500 ptas plus IVA. Doubles with views are 2000 ptas more. Breakfast is included.

Pensiones & Hotels – New Town Cuenca's new part of town is littered with places to stay. The *Fonda Tintes* (☎ 21 23 98), Calle de Tintes 3, has basic rooms for about 1300 ptas a head in summer (otherwise it is full with students in permanent residence). It is just outside the old town, as is the *Posada de San Julián* (☎ 21 17 04), Calle de las Torres, a cavernous old place with doubles only for 2400 ptas (3300 ptas with own bathroom).

A spartan sort of a place is the *Pensión Central* (☎ 21 15 11), Calle de Doctor Chirino 9, with rooms for 1390/2550 ptas.

There are two no-frills pensiones in the same building at Calle de Ramón y Cajal 53, a short walk from the train station. *Pensión Adela* (☎ 22 25 33) has rooms for 1250 ptas per person, plus 200 ptas for use of a shower. The *Pensión Marín* (☎ 22 19 78) upstairs is marginally better value at 1300/2400 ptas for singles/doubles.

A couple of doors up at No 49, *Hostal Cortes* (☎ 22 04 00) is more comfortable but equally characterless. It also has a garage (885 ptas a day). Rooms with bath, TV and phone cost 3430/5350 ptas.

Other mid-range hotels include the *Hotel Figón de Pedro* (☎ 22 45 11), Calle de Cervantes 17, with decent rooms for 3700/5000 ptas plus IVA. The *Hostal Avenida* (☎ 21 43 43), Calle de la Carretería 39, has basic singles for 1800 ptas and others with bathroom for 3000 ptas. Doubles with bath are 4200 ptas. Add IVA to all prices.

Parador The top of the tree is the *parador* (☎ 23 23 20), in the converted Dominican Convento de San Pablo on the south bank of the Río Huécar. Rooms cost 16,500 ptas plus IVA. A footbridge connects the parador with the old town across the Huécar gorge.

Places to Eat
There are several restaurants scattered around Plaza Mayor in the heart of the casco – easily the nicest part of town to eat in. The city's star is the rather expensive *Mesón Casas Colgadas*, Calle de los Canónigos 3, next to the Museo de Arte Abstracto Español. It is a wonderful location, but you won't get

away for much less than 6000 ptas. Another decent establishment for solid manchego food is the *Restaurante San Nicolás*, Calle de San Pedro 15. A full meal will come in at around 5000 ptas.

If you're not fussed about eating in the casco, your choices expand down the hill. A popular local favourite with loads of atmosphere is *El Mesón*, Calle de Colón 56. It opens for lunch, and Friday and Saturday evenings only for dinner. The set meal of 1300 ptas is good value.

Cafés The cafés on Plaza Mayor are perfect for a relaxing drink and people-watching. *Bar La Tinaja*, Calle del Obispo Valero 4, is a good one. *Bar Dulcinea*, Calle de San Pedro 10, is a pleasant and popular place for a drink.

Entertainment
Bars & Discos You can join the young set that crowds together along Calle de San Miguel for loads of noisy evening *copas*. There are a couple of bars here, but many of the locals just bring their own.

If you're looking for a bit more excitement, you'll find some discos across the road from the train station, and a few others in the slightly less tacky Calle de Doctor Galíndez.

Things to Buy
You might want to pick up a special bottle of the local firewater, Resoli, made in the shape of the casas colgadas – an unusual souvenir idea.

Getting There & Away
The bus and train stations are virtually next to one another, about a 10-minute walk to the foot of the casco. Local bus Nos 1 and 2 for Plaza Mayor leave from near the train station. There is a *consigna* (left-luggage counter) at both train and bus stations.

Bus Up to nine daily runs (two express) with AutoRes serve Madrid (2½ hours; 1260 ptas). Other companies run buses to Valencia (up to three a day) and Albacete (up to two a day), and one to Barcelona (nine hours; 4030 ptas) via Teruel. This last one leaves at 9.30 am. There is a bus a day to Aranjuez, Beteta and Belmonte (3 pm, Monday to Saturday).

Train Cuenca lies on a line connecting Madrid to Valencia. Five trains a day go to Madrid (Atocha). They take 2½ hours and a 2nd-class ticket costs 1215 ptas. Three go to Valencia (3¼ hours; 1335 ptas).

Car & Motorcycle From Madrid, the quickest route to Cuenca is the N-III, turning east onto the N-400 at Tarancón.

SERRANÍA DE CUENCA

The rivers Júcar and Huécar flow through Cuenca from the high hinterland to the north-east of the city known as the Serranía de Cuenca. If you have transport, the area is worth a day or two of exploration, if only to convince yourself that not all Castilla-La Mancha is mind-numbing plains, olive groves and sad plateaus.

From Cuenca, take the CU-921 (follow the Ciudad Encantada signs). About 22 km north is the **Ventano del Diablo**, a marvellous lookout towering over the Júcar gorge. Not far on, and six km off to the right, is the so-called **Ciudad Encantada**, or Enchanted City. Extremely popular with locals, this series of rocks eroded into some quite fantastical shapes have been lent equally outlandish names by human observers. Still, it is possible to see a boat on its keel, a dog and a Roman bridge if you let your imagination carry you away. The site opens daily from 9.30 am to sunset, and entry is 200 ptas. There is a hostal opposite the entrance with a restaurant and bar. From Cuenca, the only transport is by taxi. You'd be looking at around 6000 ptas return, with an hour to see the place.

Those with their own wheels could head back to the CU-921 and proceed east. The country is pleasant, dotted by a couple of sleepy villages and the clear blue lake of the **Embalse de la Toba**. About six km on from

Huélamo, a turn-off to the right leads across the Montes Universales to Albarracín (see the Aragón chapter) – a perfect place to end the day's drive and stay overnight.

Alternatively, the CU-921 swings north to the **Nacimiento del Río Cuervo**, a pretty enough spot with a couple of small waterfalls where the Río Cuervo rises. From here you could loop around towards **Beteta** and the gorge of the same name, or cross the provincial frontier into Guadalajara to make for the pleasant if unspectacular **Parque Natural del Alto Tajo**. To the west lies La Alcarria, about which see the Guadalajara section below.

SOUTH OF CUENCA

If castles are your thing, there are a couple of decent examples of the species south of Cuenca. For Belmonte, about 100 km south-west down the N-420, see the South-East to Albacete section earlier in this chapter. **Alarcón** lies about 100 km south of Cuenca, and for those with a little money it could make an ideal way station. The town's *parador* (☎ 969-33 03 15) has been accommodated in the triangular-based Muslim castle. Singles/doubles here cost 13,200/16,500 ptas plus IVA.

GUADALAJARA

Founded as Roman Arriaca and today a grubby provincial capital, Guadalajara (from the Arabic *wad al-hijaara*, or 'stony river') was in its medieval Muslim heyday the principal city of a large swathe of northern Spain under the green banner of Islam. At that stage, Madrid was no more than a military observation point. In 1085, however, the Castilian king Alfonso VI finally took Guadalajara as the Reconquista moved ponderously south. Under the Mendoza family, the city experienced its most prosperous era from the 14th to the 17th centuries, but from then on it was repeatedly sacked during the War of the Spanish Succession, the Napoleonic occupation and the Spanish Civil War.

Information

The tourist office (☎ 22 06 98) is in the basement of the ayuntamiento building at Plaza Mayor 7. It opens from 10 am to 2 pm and 4 to 6 pm (mornings only on the weekend). The post office is at Calle de Teniente Figueroa 5, and the postcode is 19080. The main Telefónica phone office is on Plaza Mayor. Guadalajara's phone code is ☎ 949. The police comisaría (☎ 22 15 00) is on Paseo de Dr Fernández Iparraguirre, and in a medical emergency you can call the Cruz Roja on ☎ 22 17 88.

Things to See

Little remains of the city's glory days, but definitely worth some of your time is the much-restored **Palacio de los Duques del Infantado**, where the Mendoza family held court. Its striking façade is a fine example of Gothic-mudéjar work. The heavily ornamental patio is equally admirable. The local art museum is housed here too, for what that's worth. It opens Tuesday to Saturday from 10 am to 2 pm and 4.15 to 7 pm (morning only on Sunday), and entry is 200 ptas. Of the city's churches, the mudéjar **Iglesia de Santa María** is the most interesting, with its horseshoe-shaped arches and slender bell tower. At the time of writing it was covered by restorers' scaffolding.

Places to Stay & Eat

Guadalajara is a simple day trip from Madrid, but you can stay if need be. A cheap, no-frills possibility is the *Hostal Venecia* (☎ 21 13 52), Calle de Dr Benito Hernando 12. Rooms cost 1600/3000 ptas. The *Restaurante Miguel Ángel*, Calle de Alfonso López de Haro, just off Calle Mayor, has a pleasant atmosphere. A full meal will cost about 2000 ptas.

Getting There & Away

Bus The bus station is on Calle de Dos de Mayo, a short walk from the Palacio de los Duques del Infantado. About 20 buses daily connect Guadalajara with Madrid (Avenida de América) and cost 460 ptas one way. Buses from Madrid stop here en route to Zaragoza (three a day), Soria (at least one a day) and Teruel (one a day). Sigüenza, Pastrana and Brihuega get two connections daily on weekdays, one on Saturday and none on Sunday.

Train The train station is several km out of town, but the train is the best way to reach Guadalajara from the bigger cities. Regular cercanías go to Madrid (Chamartín) from about 5 am to 11.30 pm. Up to eight regional trains go to Sigüenza, beyond which occasional trains go on to Soria and Zaragoza.

Car & Motorcycle Guadalajara is on the N-II highway that links Madrid with Zaragoza (and continues to Barcelona).

LA ALCARRIA & BEYOND

Those with an unbridled loathing for autovías who find themselves heading east towards Aragón can undertake diversions to stay off the N-II pretty much all the way to the border between Castilla y León and Aragón.

The N-320 south-east from Guadalajara (it soon becomes the C-200) takes you towards the so-called Mar de Castilla, a collection of lakes formed by dams built in the late 1950s. The lakes lie in an area known as La Alcarria. Hardly a touristic goal of the first order, it was nevertheless immortalised in an enchantingly simple account of a walking trip made there in 1946 by Camilo José Cela, *Viaje a La Alcarria*.

Pastrana

Of the many pueblos Cela called in at, Pastrana is the most worthwhile for a brief stop. Forty-two km south of Guadalajara along the C-200, it is a small, quiet medieval town. The area closest to the main road, Albaicín, was once populated mainly by Moriscos, converts from Islam to Christianity. Passing through here you arrive at Plaza de la Hora, an airy and somewhat uncared-for square fronted by the impressive and equally unloved Palacio Ducal, where the one-eyed

CASTILLA-LA MANCHA

Princess of Eboli, Ana Mendoza de la Cerda, was confined in 1581 for a love affair with Felipe II's secretary. She died here 10 years later.

Proceed from the square along the main street and you soon reach the massive, gloomy **Iglesia de Nuestra Señora de la Asunción**. Inside is a small museum containing jewels and other personal effects of the Princess of Eboli. There are also some interesting 15th century Portuguese tapestries. Entry is 300 ptas, if the guy with the keys is around.

You can stay and eat at the *Hostal Moratín* (☎ 911-37 06 28), a decent place on Calle de Moratín, just in from the main highway. Singles without bath cost 1500 ptas, and doubles with private bath 3500 ptas. A bus leaves early in the morning for Madrid, and two a day (on weekdays) go to Guadalajara.

On from Pastrana

Following the C-204 (later N-204) up the west bank of the Embalse de Entrepeñas, the area's main reservoir, you could push on north to **Cifuentes**, with its 14th century castle. From here the N-204 proceeds to the N-II, which you take for a few km before branching off north again for Sigüenza.

There are other alternatives. From Guadalajara you could put up with 19 km of autovía heading north-east and turn off at **Torija**, which has a rather impressive, if empty, castle. Take the C-201 for La Alcarria's second town after Pastrana, **Brihuega**, a leafy village that preserves stretches of its medieval walls. The drive east along the Río Tajuña is one of the more pleasant in this part of Castilla-La Mancha. The road forms a T-junction with the N-204, from where you can head north for Sigüenza or south to the great lake of the Embalse de Entrepeñas (see above).

Yet another possibility from La Alcarria is to head east from the lake towards the **Parque Natural del Alto Tajo**, which also makes for some unexpectedly nice drives. Combined with the Serranía de Cuenca (see Cuenca above) further south and east, the

area is a popular weekend escape hatch for *madrileños* fleeing their hectic city lives.

SIGÜENZA

This tranquil medieval town, built on a low hill cradled by the Río Henares and a slender tributary, disguises a less peaceful past. Fighting here during the civil war was heavy and it was a long while before most, but not all, of the scars of the conflict could be removed.

Originally a Celtiberian settlement, Segontia became an important Roman and, later, Visigothic military outpost. The arrival of the Muslims in the 8th century changed the town's strategic situation, putting it in the front-line provinces facing the Christians. In fact Sigüenza remained in Muslim hands for considerably longer than towns further to the south-west such as Guadalajara and Toledo (which fell in 1085), resisting until the 1120s. It was occupied by the Aragonese and later ceded to the Castilians, who turned Sigüenza and its hinterland into a vast church property. The bishops remained complete masters, material and spiritual, of the town and land until the end of the 18th century. About this time things began to go downhill, as Sigüenza found itself repeatedly in the way of advancing armies, from the War of the Spanish Succession until the civil war.

Information

There is no tourist office as such, but the information desk of the town hall library has a few brochures. Look for the *biblioteca* on the ground floor of the ayuntamiento building on Plaza Mayor. It's open from 9 am to 2 pm, Monday to Friday. The post office is housed in what was the old university on Calle de la Villa Viciosa, but may be replaced by another planned for a site across the road. The postcode is 19250 and the telephone code ☎ 949. There are several banks (some with ATMs) where you can change money on and near Calle del Cardenal Mendoza. In a medical emergency call the Cruz Roja on ☎ 22 22 22.

To Atienza (32 km)

To Medinaceli & Zaragoza

Calle de Ramón y Cajal

Sigüenza

0   50   100 m

Alameda

Río Henares

Camino Viejo

Plaza de Hilario Yaben

Plaza del Obispo Don Bernardo

Plaza Mayor

Plaza del Castillo

To Madrid (130 km)

Arroyo del Vadillo

PLACES TO STAY
7 Hostal Venancio
9 Hostal El Doncel
11 Hostal El Mesón

PLACES TO EAT
15 Mesón Las Tapas
24 Restaurante Medieval Segontia
29 Restaurante Calle Mayor

OTHER
1 RENFE Train Station
2 Buses
3 Iglesia de Nuestra Señora de los Huertos
4 Discos & Pubs
5 Iglesia de las Ursulinas
6 Palacio de los Infantes
8 Ermita del Humilladero
10 Seminario de San Bartolomé
12 Farmacia
13 Catedral
14 Puerta de la Torre
16 Ayuntamiento
17 Museo Diocesano
18 Cubo del Peso
19 Present Post Office (Correos)
20 Projected Post Office
21 Palacio Episcopal & Antigua Universidad
22 Iglesia de Santa María
23 Arco del Portal Mayor
25 Puerto del Hierro
26 Plaza de la Cárcel
27 Iglesia de San Vicente
28 Casa del Doncel
30 Iglesia de Santiago
31 Alcazaba (Parador)

CASTILLA-LA MANCHA

Catedral

The heart of the old town is made up of the combination of the cobbled Plaza Mayor and Plaza del Obispo Don Bernardo. Rising up on their north flank is the centrepiece of the city, the cathedral. It was begun as a Romanesque structure in 1130, and work continued for four centuries as the church was expanded and adorned. The largely Gothic result is laced with elements of other styles, from Renaissance through plateresque to mudéjar. The church was heavily damaged during the civil war, and subsequently restored.

For 300 ptas, you can be guided around the church's chapels, sacristy and neglected Gothic cloister. The guide rattles off his speech with enormous lack of interest, but even if you don't understand Spanish, the tour is good value. First up you will probably be shown the **Capilla Mayor**, a chapel containing the reclining marble statue of El Doncel, aka Don Martín Vázquez de Arce, who died fighting the Muslims in the final stages of the Reconquista. Of particular beauty is the **Sacristía de las Cabezas**, whose ceiling is covered with hundreds of heads sculpted by Covarrubias. His intention was to represent all humanity, and his characters, Christian and Muslim, range from knights to knaves. The **Capilla del Espíritu Santo** boasts a doorway combining platersque, mudéjar and Gothic styles. Inside you'll see a remarkable dome and an *Anunciación* by El Greco. The church can be visited daily from 11 am to 1.30 pm and 4 to 7 pm.

Museo Diocesano

Across the square from the cathedral, this museum houses a fairly extensive collection of religious art from Sigüenza and the surrounding area, including a series of mainly 15th century retablos. Entry costs 200 ptas and the museum is open from Tuesday to Sunday from 11.30 am to 2 pm and 5 to 7.30 pm.

Alcazaba

Calle Mayor heads south up the hill from the cathedral to what was once the archbishops' castle, originally built by the Muslims and still known as the Alcazaba. There has probably been some kind of fort here since pre-Roman times, but what you see today is the much-restored residence erected by the archbishops. It now functions as a parador.

Places to Stay & Eat

There is a only a handful of accommodation possibilities in Sigüenza. *El Palomar* youth hostel (☎ 39 12 99), Calle de Santa Bárbara, is open from 1 July to 30 September. B&B is 1100 ptas (under 26) or 1500 ptas.

You can probably forget the *Hostal El Mesón* (☎ 39 06 49), Calle de Román Pascual 14, a cheapish place almost always full with permanent guests. *Hostal Venancio* (☎ 39 03 47), Calle de San Roque 1, has simple singles/doubles without bathroom for 2000/3000 ptas. *Hostal El Doncel* (☎ 39 10 90), across the road at Calle de General Mola 1, has rooms with shower, TV and telephone starting at 3500/4600 ptas plus IVA. A real treat, the *parador* (☎ 39 01 00) has doubles for 13,500 ptas plus IVA.

For snack food, the *Mesón Las Tapas*, Plaza Mayor 1, is a good spot. The *Restaurante Medieval Segontia*, Calle del Portal Mayor 2, offers solid meals for 2000 ptas, while the more expensive *Restaurante Calle Mayor*, Calle Mayor 21, has a good set meal for 2500 ptas.

Getting There & Away

Bus Buses mostly serve towns around Sigüenza, and are far from frequent. They stop on Avenida de Alfonso VI, near the train station.

Train From Madrid (Atocha and Chamartín) there are up to 13 regional trains, the quickest taking about 1½ hours. Some go on to Zaragoza and Soria (and vice versa).

Car & Motorcycle Sigüenza lies north of the N-II highway. The main exits are the C-204 coming from the west and the C-114 from the east. The C-114 then heads north towards Almazán or Soria in Castilla y León.

AROUND SIGÜENZA
Palazuelos & Carabias

About 10 km north of Sigüenza, the sleepy little villages of Palazuelos and Carabias retain neglected remnants of their more distant past, the former with walls and a castle and the latter with a Romanesque church.

Atienza

Those travelling between Sigüenza and Almazán or Soria to the north might consider a trip to Atienza, 32 km north-west of Sigüenza. A charming little walled medieval village dominated by the inevitable castle ruins, Atienza is jammed with half a dozen largely Romanesque churches. There is a small museum in the Iglesia de San Gil. If you come by bus you'll have to stay, and the only option is the *Fonda Molinero* (☎ 949-39 90 17), Calle de Héctor Vázquez 11, with singles/doubles for 1500/3000 ptas. It is often full in summer and on the weekend. A couple of buses leave early in the morning for Madrid, Guadalajara and Sigüenza.

Towards Aragón

From Sigüenza, you can get back onto the N-II, which briefly crosses Castilla y León's Soria province before heading into Aragón. Minor roads also follow this route, and a couple of worthwhile stops for those with vehicles are Medinaceli and, just south of the N-II on Castilla y León's border with Aragón, Santa María de Huerta. See the Castilla y León chapter for details.

CASTILLA-LA MANCHA

Barcelona

Barcelona is, some say, the most southerly city of northern Europe. The phrase spotlights not just its nearness to France and its age-old links with other countries, but also its industrious (and industrial) character, its densely packed urban centre, its obeisance to cool and chic – not exactly the fiesta-and-siesta image of more southerly Spanish regions.

Actually, Barcelona shares the good and bad of the south *and* the north. It's buzzing, glittering, at times spectacular, probably Spain's most cosmopolitan, forward-looking and stylish city, and certainly one of its richest. With 1.7 million people in the city proper and some four million if you include its satellite towns, it can be a hard city too: respect and friendship have to be earned; image and appearance are vital; wealth and poverty face each other daily on its streets.

Barcelona is the capital of a region, Cataluña, that has its own language, its own very distinct character and turbulent history, and in many ways thinks of itself as a separate country. This gives the city a rather self-absorbed aspect which sits oddly with the openness that you'd expect of a major Mediterranean port on the most important corridor between the Iberian Peninsula and the rest of Europe.

Set on a plain rising gently from the Mediterranean to a range of wooded hills, Barcelona enjoys fine vistas, lovely and unusual parks, and a fascinating medieval core dotted with pearls of Gothic architecture. There's also spectacular, more recent, architecture outside this core – notably Antoni Gaudí's La Sagrada Família church, perhaps Spain's most famous building.

The atmosphere is always lively, often exciting. Barcelona has great nightlife, some superb restaurants, and top-class museums (with more opening all the time, it seems). It has been breaking ground in art, architecture and style for at least a century now – from the turn-of-the-century *modernista* architects led by Gaudí to the adventurous

HIGHLIGHTS

- Rambling along La Rambla, Spain's most famous street
- Exploring the Barri Gòtic, a classic medieval quarter
- The Museu Picasso, Spain's best collection of the work of its major modern artist, in the city where he spent his formative years
- La Sagrada Família, Spain's most spectacular building
- A day on Montjuïc, the hill of parks, museums, funfairs and stadiums that hosted the 1992 Olympics
- A first class Catalan meal at *Senyor Parellada*
- An absinthe or two in the *Bar Marsella*
- *Cava* (Catalan champagne) at *El Xampanyet*
- Dancing the night away at stylish *Otto Zutz*

redevelopments on the waterfront and Montjuïc hill catalysed by the 1992 Olympics; from Pablo Picasso and Joan Miró, whose spirits still haunt the city, to the weird postmodern concoctions of contemporary artists and nightclub designers. Barcelona's continuing devotion to style is shown not least by its people themselves – from the near-bald haircuts lately *de rigueur* for men to the care taken with the mode of even the most casual clothes and footwear.

History

Barcelona and Cataluña have a history which

for long periods was distinct from the rest of Spain's and is in large measure responsible for their independent-mindedness today. It's worth a bit of a look.

Early Barcelona Barcelona was probably founded by the Carthaginians in about 230 BC, and probably derives its name from Hannibal's father Hamilcar Barca. Roman Barcelona covered an area within today's Barri Gòtic and was overshadowed by Tarraco (Tarragona), 90 km to the south-west. Under the Visigoths, and then under the Muslims who took it in 713 AD, Barcelona remained a modest place.

The Counts of Barcelona Frankish armies, soon pushing the Muslims back from present-day France, set up a buffer zone along the south of the Pyrenees known as the Frankish March, which included Barcelona. Thus it was that for many centuries Cataluña looked more to France than to the Iberian Peninsula – one result of which today is the Catalan language, whose closest relative is said to be the *langue d'oc*, the old tongue of southern France. As the Frankish empire fractured in the 9th century, one Guifré el Pilós (Wilfrid the Hairy – so named because he had hair where most people don't) managed to gain control of several of the counties composing the march. In 878 he founded the house of the Counts of Barcelona, which by the late 10th century ruled, from Barcelona, an independent principality covering most of modern Cataluña except the south, plus Roussillon, which today lies across the border in France. This was the only Christian state on the Iberian Peninsula not to fall under the sway of Sancho III of Navarra in the early 11th century.

Like Iberia's other Christian states, Cataluña – especially Barcelona – grew rich on pickings from the collapse of the Muslim caliphate of Córdoba in the 11th century. Count Ramon Berenguer I was able to buy the counties of Carcassonne and Béziers, north of Roussillon, with Muslim gold bounty. Barcelona would maintain ambitions in France for two more centuries – at one point it held territory as far east as Provence. Under Ramon Berenguer III (1082-1131) Cataluña launched its own fleet and sea trade developed. This was the era of great Catalan Romanesque art, with its masterly church frescos.

The Golden Age In 1137 Ramon Berenguer IV was betrothed to Petronilla, heiress of Cataluña's western neighbour Aragón, creating a joint state and setting the scene for Cataluña's golden age. He took southern Cataluña from the Muslims in the 1140s. His son Alfonso I and his successors styled themselves monarchs of Aragón, even though Cataluña was the stronger partner in the joint state and Barcelona its chief city. They faced frequent power struggles with the Aragonese nobility, however.

Meanwhile Castilla was laying sole claim to the reconquest of Muslim territory in the southern Iberian Peninsula – a claim recognised by Aragón's Alfonso II in a treaty in 1179. Suffering reverses in France too, Cataluña turned to the Mediterranean instead. Jaume I (1213-76) took the Balearic Islands and the Valencia region from the Muslims in the 1230s. Barcelona finally grew too big for its Roman walls and Jaume I built new walls. These enclosed an area 10 times bigger, ending on the west side at La Rambla, then still a river.

Jaume I's son Pere II conquered Sicily in 1282. Then followed a spectacular expansion of Cataluña's Mediterranean trade-based empire, albeit hampered at home by divisions in the ruling family, the odd war with Castilla, and trouble with the aristocracy in Aragón. Malta (1283), Athens (1310), Corsica (1323), Sardinia (1324) and Naples (1423), as well as several ports in North Africa, all fell, for varying periods, under Catalan control or dominance. Cataluña also controlled the gold trade between Sudan and Europe, and its merchants were powerful in Alexandria and Constantinople.

Cataluña's Corts, an early form of parliament, first met under Jaume I. Committees formed by the Corts in 1289 to control taxes were the origin of the Generalitat, a council with powers over how taxes should be spent and over law, order and Cataluña's armed forces. The Generalitat functioned until the 18th century.

Barcelona's trading wealth paid for the great Gothic buildings which still bejewel the city. The cathedral, the Capella Reial de Santa Àgata and the churches of Santa Maria del Pi and Santa Maria del Mar were all built in the late 13th or early 14th century. King Pere III (1336-87) created the wonderful Reials Drassanes (Royal Shipyards) and extended the city walls again, this time to include the El Raval area west of La Rambla.

Decline & Castilian Domination Like many empires, Cataluña's came to exhaust its homeland. Sea wars with Genoa, resistance in Sardinia, the rise of the Ottoman empire and the loss of the gold trade all drained the coffers. The Black Death and famines killed about half Cataluña's population in the 14th century. Barcelona's Jewish population suffered a pogrom in 1391.

After Martí I, the last of Guifré el Pilós' dynasty, died heirless in 1410, a special council elected Fernando de Antequera, a Castilian prince, to the Aragonese throne. This was engineered by the nobility in Aragón, who saw a chance to reduce Catalan influence over their affairs. Fernando and his successors were soon at daggers drawn with their Catalan subjects, who felt they were being exploited for Castilian interests. A rebellion which began in 1462 against King Joan II ended in a siege in 1473 that devastated Barcelona.

Joan II's son, who succeeded to the Aragonese throne in 1479, was Fernando, whose marriage to Isabel, queen of Castilla, united Spain's two most powerful monarchies. Cataluña effectively became part of the Castilian state, but was excluded from the exploitation of the Americas which brought such riches to 16th century Castilla. Impoverished and disaffected by growing demands from the crown, Cataluña revolted again in the 17th century and declared itself an independent republic, under French pro-

tection, in the War of the Reapers (1640-52). Countryside and towns alike were devastated, and Barcelona was finally besieged into submission.

Cataluña saw the War of the Spanish Succession (1702-13) as another chance to win its freedom, and sided with Britain and Austria against Felipe V, the French Bourbon contender for the Spanish throne. But Cataluña ended up fighting alone, and Barcelona fell in 1714 after a 14 month siege. Felipe V abolished the Generalitat, built a huge fort, the Ciutadella, to watch over Barcelona, and banned writing and teaching in the Catalan language.

Economic Development & the Renaixença The late 18th and 19th centuries finally brought new economic growth. From 1778 Cataluña was permitted to trade with America, boosting the shipping industry and launching an industrial revolution – Spain's first – based on American cotton. Wine, cork and iron industries also developed. So did working-class poverty, overcrowding, disease and unrest. To ease the crush, Barcelona's medieval walls were demolished in 1854, and in 1869 work began on l'Eixample, an extension of the city beyond Plaça de Catalunya which was then its limit. The flourishing bourgeoisie paid for lavish, ostentatious buildings, many of them in the unique, Art Nouveau-influenced *modernista* or Catalan modernist style, whose leading exponent was Antoni Gaudí.

Modernisme was the most visible aspect of the Catalan Renaixença (renaissance) – a movement for the revival of Catalan language and culture in the late 19th century. The Catalan language was readopted by the middle and upper classes and a new Catalan literature emerged. By the turn of the century Barcelona was also Spain's hotbed of avant-garde art, with close links to Paris, and it was here that the young Picasso spread his artistic wings and drank in the famous artists' hangout Els Quatre Gats.

Barcelona's 1888 Universal Exhibition pulled in over two million visitors. The speedy construction of exhibition sites gave birth to the city's modern reputation for dynamic hard work.

The Renaixença's political sibling was Catalanism, a new-found Catalan nationalism which was intensified by Spain's loss of Cuba in 1898. Many Catalans had prospered in Cuba, so the loss – blamed on Madrid's incompetence – brought a new wave of poverty.

Mayhem Neither the Renaixença nor Catalanism cut much ice with Barcelona's exploited workers, whose numbers were rising fast. The city's population grew from 115,000 in 1800 to over 500,000 by 1900 and over one million by 1930, boosted by poor immigrants from rural Cataluña in the early 19th century, and from other regions of Spain later. The decades around the turn of the 20th century were ones of wild mayhem in Barcelona, which became a swirling vortex of anarchists, Republicans, bourgeois regionalists, gangsters, police terrorists, political gunmen called *pistoleros*, and political meddling by Madrid. (Have a read of Gerald Brenan's *The Spanish Labyrinth* or Eduardo Mendoza's novel *City of Marvels* if you want a taste of some of the unbelievable things that went on: in one episode related by Brenan, gangsters in police pay planted 2000 bombs at or near the bourgeoisie's factories so that the police could find an excuse for arresting anarchists.)

One genuine anarchist bomb at the Liceu opera house on La Rambla in the 1890s killed 20 people. Anarchists were also reckoned to be behind the Setmana Tràgica (Tragic Week) in 1909 when, following a military call-up for Spanish wars in Morocco, mobs wrecked 70 religious buildings and workers were shot on the streets in reprisals.

In the post-WWI slump, unionism took hold, led by the anarchist CNT, which embraced as many as 80% of the city's workers. During a wave of strikes in 1919-20, employers hired assassins to eliminate union leaders. The 1920s dictator Primo de Rivera opposed both bourgeois Catalan nationalism and working-class radicalism,

banning the CNT and even closing Barcelona football club, a potent symbol of Catalanism. But he did support the staging of a second world fair in Barcelona, the Montjuïc International Exhibition of 1929.

Catalan Nationalism Rampant Rivera's repression only succeeded in uniting, after his fall in 1930, the pent-up fervour of Cataluña's nationalists and leftists. Within days of the formation of Spain's Second Republic in 1931, leftist Catalan nationalists led by Francesc Macià and Lluís Companys proclaimed Cataluña a republic within an imaginary 'Iberian Federation'. Madrid quickly pressured them into accepting a unitary Spanish state, but Cataluña got a new regional government, with the old title of Generalitat. Macià, its first president, died in 1933 and was succeeded by Companys, who in 1934 tried again for near-independence, proclaiming 'the Catalan State of the Spanish Federal Republic'. The Madrid government responded with an army bombardment of the Generalitat offices and Barcelona's city hall. The Generalitat was closed and its members given 35-year jail terms.

But they were released, and the Generalitat restored, when the leftist Popular Front won the February 1936 Spanish general election. Now, briefly, Cataluña gained genuine autonomy. Companys, its president, carried out land reforms and planned an alternative Barcelona Olympics to the official 1936 games in Nazi Berlin.

The Civil War On 17 July, the day before the Barcelona games were to start, an army uprising in Morocco began the Spanish Civil War. Barcelona's army garrison attempted to take the city for Franco but was defeated by armed anarchists and police loyal to the government. The civil war broke the Catalan class alliance. For nearly a year Barcelona was run by anarchists and the POUM Trotskyist militia, with Companys president only in name. Factory owners and rightists fled the city. Unions took over factories and public services, hotels and mansions became hospitals and schools, everyone wore workers' clothes, bars and cafés were collectivised, trams and taxis were painted red and black, private cars vanished from the streets, and even one-way streets were ignored as part of the old system.

The anarchists were a disparate lot ranging from gentle idealists to hardliners who drew up death lists, held kangaroo courts, shot priests, monks and nuns (over 1200 of whom were killed in Barcelona province during the civil war), and burnt and wrecked churches – which is why so many Barcelona churches are today oddly plain inside.

But the revolutionary atmosphere waned as anarchists began to join the Catalan and Spanish Republican governments and, under Soviet influence, the Catalan communist party PSUC grew more powerful. In May 1937 Companys ordered police to take over the anarchist-held telephone exchange on Plaça de Catalunya. After three days of street fighting, chiefly between anarchists and the PSUC, in which at least 1500 died, the anarchists asked for a cease-fire. They and the POUM were soon disarmed.

Barcelona became the Republicans' national capital in autumn 1937 after the government fled Valencia. The city was first bombed from the air in March 1938. In the first three days 670 people were killed; after that, the figures were kept secret. In the end, after the Republicans' defeat in the Battle of the Ebro – the last big set piece of the war – in southern Cataluña in summer 1938, Barcelona was not defended. Fighters and the Catalan and Spanish Republican governments joined civilians fleeing to France – around 500,000 in all – and the city fell to the Nationalists on 25 January 1939. Up to 35,000 people were shot in the ensuing purge, with executions continuing into the 1950s. Lluís Companys was arrested in France by the Gestapo, handed over to Franco, and shot in secret on Montjuïc hill with the words *'Visca Catalunya!'* ('Long live Cataluña!') on his lips.

The Franco Era Franco banned public use of Catalan, and castilianised town, village and street names. Book publishing in Catalan was allowed from the mid-1940s, but education, radio, TV and the daily press remained in Spanish. There were some anarchist shootings and bombings in Barcelona in the 1940s but by the 1950s opposition had turned to peaceful mass protests and strikes. In 1960 an audience at the city's Palau de la Música Catalana concert hall sang a banned Catalan anthem in front of Franco. The ringleaders included a young Catholic banker, Jordi Pujol, who spent two years in jail as a result. Pujol was to become Cataluña's president in the post-Franco era.

The big social change under Franco was a flood of immigrants from poorer parts of Spain, chiefly Andalucía, attracted by economic growth in Cataluña. Some 750,000 came to Barcelona in the 1950s and 1960s, and almost as many to the rest of Cataluña. Many lived in appalling conditions.

After Franco The 1978 Spanish constitution bowed to Catalan nationalism by creating the autonomous community of Cataluña, with Barcelona as its capital. The Generalitat, its parliament, has wide powers over matters like education, health, trade, industry, tourism and agriculture. Education is now nearly all in Catalan, which at Franco's death had been in some danger not only because of the immigration of Castilian-speakers but also because many Catalans, though they spoke Catalan, could no longer read or write it.

Jordi Pujol's moderate nationalist Convergència i Unió (CiU) party has controlled the Generalitat ever since the first elections in 1980, though CiU lost its overall majority in 1995. CiU does not want full independence from Spain but constantly seeks to strengthen Catalan autonomy. On broader issues, CiU is right of centre. Barcelona itself has favoured the Partit Socialista de Catalunya (PSC), which is aligned with the national PSOE and headed by a younger generation than CiU.

Politics aside, the big event in post-Franco Barcelona was of course the successful 1992

BARCELONA

Antoni Gaudí's Barcelona
Top: The façade and roof of Casa Batlló, which represent Sant Jordi (St George) and the dragon
Bottom Left: The still unfinished Temple Expiatori de la Sagrada Familia
Bottom Right: A mosaic-roofed fantasy near the entrance to Parc Güell

BETHUNE CARMICHAEL

JOHN NOBLE

BETHUNE CARMICHAEL

Top: A street corner in l'Eixample, Barcelona
Bottom Left: Sculpture by Josep Subirachs on the Passion Façade, La Sagrada Família, Barcelona
Bottom Right: A living statue on La Rambla, Barcelona

Olympics, which spurred a burst of public works bringing new life to areas like Montjuïc, where the major events were held, and the once-shabby waterfront, which is now strung with promenades, beaches, marinas, restaurants, leisure attractions and new housing. The Olympics also focused world attention on Barcelona's prosperity and cultural, entertainment and tourist attractions. Since then, Catalans who travel abroad no longer face the dilemma, when asked where they're from, of whether to answer 'Spain' (which many of them don't like to admit being part of) or 'Cataluña' (which many foreigners haven't heard of). They simply say 'Barcelona'.

Orientation

Barcelona's coastline runs roughly from north-east to south-west, and many streets are parallel or perpendicular to this. So there are few simple north, south, east or west alignments.

La Rambla & Plaça de Catalunya The focal axis is the famous La Rambla, a 1.25 km boulevard running north-west and slightly uphill from Port Vell (the Old Harbour) to Plaça de Catalunya. The latter is a wide square which marks the boundary between the old part of the city, the Ciutat Vella, and the more recent parts further inland.

Montjuïc & Tibidabo Two good pointers to which way you're facing are the hills of Montjuïc and Tibidabo, visible from many places in the city. Montjuïc, the lower of the two, begins about 700 metres south-west of the bottom of La Rambla. Its assembly of parks, sports complexes and museums is well worth some of your time. Tibidabo, with its landmark TV tower and golden Christ statue, is six km north-west of the top of La Rambla. It's the high point of the range of wooded hills forming a backdrop to the whole city. You can ride to the top by funicular for a change of air and fine views.

Catalanism 1990s-Style

Modern Cataluña is engaged in an ongoing struggle for more autonomy within Spain, but full independence is a dream dreamt only by a few. The pro-independence party Esquerra Republicana de Catalunya (ERC; Republican Left of Cataluña) has won only 8% to 10% of the vote in recent elections. ERC is avowedly nonviolent and there's no Catalan equivalent of the Basque ETA. But there's still a deep antipathy among many Catalans to the Spanish state and its influence over Cataluña. A survey in 1995 found that 38% of people in Cataluña considered themselves either more Catalan than Spanish, or not Spanish at all.

Catalans remain strongly aware of Cataluña's historic rivalry with Castilla and are infused with the sense that Cataluña enjoyed its golden ages when it was independent or under minimal Castilian influence. They have a tendency to think of themselves as more civilised, less insular, more diplomatic and more worldly than other Spaniards. These notions have probably been reinforced since the 1940s by the arrival of around two million people from poorer parts of Spain, chiefly Andalucía, seeking work in Cataluña. Meanwhile the rest of Spain looks on Catalans as somewhere between irritatingly quirky and provocatively arrogant.

The cliché is that Catalans are harder-working, more sober and more commercially minded than other Spaniards. They certainly seem to be less addicted to noise, colour and flamboyance – compare the sedate Catalan national dance, the *sardana*, with Andalucian flamenco – though Catalan *festes* (fiestas) can still be riotous.

Because of immigration from other parts of Spain, today probably less than half the almost four million people in Barcelona and its satellite towns speak the Catalan language, though the figure is around two-thirds in Cataluña as a whole, and nearly everyone claims to understand it.

Everyone in Barcelona *does* speak Spanish, though; French is fairly widely understood and English less so. Though you'll find all street names, and many signs and menus, in Catalan, you'll have no greater language difficulty here than anywhere else in Spain. If you know some Spanish and/or French you can make sense of much written Catalan (see the Language section in Facts about the Country for some useful words and phrases, and the 'Catalan Cuisine' aside in the Cataluña chapter for help with Catalan menus). ■

Barcelona

Ciutat Vella The Ciutat Vella (Old City), a warren of narrow streets, antique buildings, and a lot of bottom-end and mid-range accommodation, spreads either side of La Rambla. Its heart is the lower half of the section east of La Rambla, called the Barri Gòtic (Gothic quarter). West of La Rambla is El Raval, whose lower half is the seedy Barri Xinès (Chinese quarter, though there's nothing Chinese about it). The area between the Barri Xinès and Montjuïc, beyond the edge of the Ciutat Vella, is called Poble Sec.

Watch your pockets and bags anywhere south of Plaça Reial in the Barri Gòtic or in the Barri Xinès – and indeed on La Rambla itself.

The Ciutat Vella continues north-east of the Barri Gòtic, across Via Laietana, to the area called La Ribera, location of several major sights and some good restaurants and bars. East of La Ribera, 1.25 km from La Rambla, is pretty Parc de la Ciutadella.

Waterfront The waterfront from Port Vell to the north-east has been attractively cleaned up and redeveloped in a renewal programme inspired by the Olympics. Port Vell itself has an excellent modern aquarium and two

BARCELONA

PLACES TO STAY		12	Guinardó	17	Savannah
7	Alberg Mare de Déu	13	Camp de l'Arpa	20	Hospital Creu Roja
	de Montserrat	14	Navas	22	Temple Expiatori de la
42	Alberg Studio	16	Sagrera		Sagrada Família
51	Alberg Pere Tarrès	19	Clot	23	Els Encants Flea
60	Hostal Sofia	21	Hospital de Sant		Market
66	Hostal Sans		Pau	25	Plaça Braus
		24	Monumental		Monumental
PLACES TO EAT		26	Glòries	29	Zeleste
4	Mirablau Terrazza	27	Poblenou	31	Estació del Nord Bus
		28	Llacuna		Station
TRAIN STATIONS		30	Marina	34	American Institute
1	Peu del Funicular	32	Lesseps	38	British Council
5	Avinguda de Tibidabo	46	Maria Cristina	44	Museu-Monastir de
15	Sagrera	50	Palau Reial		Pedralbes
18	Clot	53	Les Corts	45	Sarrià Stadium
33	Sant Gervasi	54	Plaça del Centre	47	Finca Güell Gate
35	Pàdua	55	Entença	48	Palau Reial de
36	El Putxet	62	Sants-Estació		Pedralbes (Museu
37	Muntaner	64	Hostafrancs		de Ceràmica &
39	La Bonanova	65	Plaça de Sants		Museu de les Arts
40	Les Tres Torres	67	Mercat Nou		Decoratives)
41	Sarrià	68	Badalè	49	Jardins del Palau
43	Reina Elisenda	69	Collblanc		Reial
57	Estació de França	70	Torrassa	52	Camp Nou & Museu
63	Estació Sants	71	Santa Eulàlia		del Futbol Club
72	Ildefons Cerdà				Barcelona
73	Gornal	OTHER		56	Catedral
		2	Tibidabo Funicular	58	Estació Marítima N-1
METRO STATIONS			Lower Station	59	Viva Travel Agency
6	Penitents	3	Mirablau	61	Estació d'Autobuses
8	Vallcarca	9	Casa Museu Gaudí		de Sants
10	Alfons X	11	Hospital de Sant Pau	74	Estadi Olímpic

marinas. At its north-east end is La Barceloneta, the old sailors' quarter, from where beaches and a pedestrian promenade stretch one km north-east to the Port Olímpic, a harbour built for the Olympics and now surrounded by lively bars and restaurants.

L'Eixample Plaça de Catalunya at the top of La Rambla marks the beginning of l'Eixample (el Ensanche in Spanish, meaning 'the Enlargement'), the grid of straight streets into which Barcelona spread in the 19th century. Ranging one to 1.5 km north, east and west from Plaça de Catalunya, l'Eixample is where you'll find most of Barcelona's famous *modernista* architecture – including La Sagrada Família – as well as its glossiest shops and most of its expensive hotels. The main avenues are Passeig de Gràcia and Rambla de Catalunya, running parallel to the north-west from Plaça de Catalunya.

Gràcia Beyond l'Eixample you're in the suburbs – some of which have plenty of character as they began life as villages outside the city. Gràcia, beyond the wide Avinguda Diagonal on the north edge of central l'Eixample, is a net of narrow streets and small squares with a varied population, and can be a lively place to spend a Friday or Saturday night. Just north of Gràcia is Gaudí's famous Parc Güell.

Main Transport Terminals The airport is 14 km south-west of the centre at El Prat de Llobregat. The main terminus for domestic trains is Estació Sants (metro: Sants-Estació), 2.5 km west of La Rambla, on the western fringe of l'Eixample. International trains usually terminate at Estació de França, one km east of La Rambla, near Barceloneta metro station. The main bus station, Estació del Nord (metro: Arc de Triomf), is 1.5 km north-east of La Rambla.

BARCELONA

Maps Tourist offices hand out free city and transport maps which are OK for basics, though poor on detail of the Ciutat Vella. If you're staying in Barcelona a while, it's worth getting the Michelin *Barcelona* map, widely available for around 1900 ptas, which comes with a comprehensive street index.

Information

Tourist Offices The main tourist office, the Catalunya Oficina de Turisme (☎ 301 74 43) at Gran via de les Corts Catalanes 658 (L'Eixample), has info on the rest of Cataluña and Spain as well as Barcelona. It has lots of give-away material and is open Monday to Friday from 9 am to 7 pm, and Saturday from 9 am to 2 pm; in summer it may stay open till 8 pm Monday to Saturday, and open on Sunday from 9 am to 2 or 3 pm. In busy seasons there can be queues: avoid going between 2 and 4 pm, when most staff take lunch.

Turisme de Barcelona (☎ 412 91 71) in Estació Sants covers Barcelona only. It's open Monday to Friday from 8 am to 8 pm, and Saturday, Sunday and holidays from 8 am to 2 pm (8 am to 8 pm daily in summer). There's also a tourist office (☎ 478 47 04) in the airport arrivals hall, open Monday to Saturday from 9.30 am to 8 pm, Sunday from 9.30 am to 3 pm.

In summer up to 20 temporary information booths are placed at handy points around the city. You can also ring ☎ 412 20 01 for Barcelona tourist information.

Foreign Consulates Consulates in Barcelona, most of which are open Monday to Friday from 9 or 10 am to 1 or 2 pm, include:

Belgium
 Carrer de la Diputació 1 (☎ 417 82 10)
Denmark
 Carrer del Comte d'Urgell 240 (☎ 419 04 88)
France
 Passeig de Gràcia 11 (☎ 317 81 50)
Germany
 Passeig de Gràcia 111 (☎ 415 36 96)
Italy
 Carrer de Mallorca 270 (☎ 488 02 70)
Japan
 Avinguda Diagonal 662-664 (☎ 280 34 33)
Netherlands
 Avinguda Diagonal 601 (☎ 410 62 10)
Sweden
 Carrer de Mallorca 279 (☎ 488 25 01)
Switzerland
 Gran via de Carles III 94 (☎ 330 92 11)
UK
 Avinguda Diagonal 447 (☎ 419 90 44)
USA
 Passeig de la Reina Elisenda de Montcada 23-25 (☎ 280 22 27)

Money In many places the more money you change, the better the rate. The best rates are in banks, which are everywhere, including several around Plaça de Catalunya and more on La Rambla and on Plaça de Sant Jaume in the Barri Gòtic. Bank hours are usually Monday to Friday from 8 am to 2 pm. There are a few exchange offices along La Rambla and elsewhere, open longer hours – some on La Rambla stay open till midnight every day – but giving worse rates. The one on the ground floor of El Corte Inglés on Plaça de Catalunya gives better rates. American Express (☎ 415 23 71; fax 415 37 00) at Passeig de Gràcia 101 (the entrance is round the corner on Carrer del Rosselló) has a currency exchange desk with good rates and a machine giving cash on American Express cards. The office is open Monday to Friday from 9.30 am to 6 pm, and Saturday from 10 am to noon.

Most banks have permanently open ATMs. La Caixa, with a blue star logo designed by Joan Miró, is one bank with ATMs all over the place giving cash on Visa, MasterCard, Eurocard, Eurocheque, Cirrus, Plus, American Express, JCB and other cards.

Post & Communications The main post office (☎ 318 38 31) is on Plaça d'Antoni López opposite the north-east end of Port Vell. It's open for stamp sales, poste restante (window No 36) and information Monday to Friday from 8 am to 9 pm, and Saturday from

9 am to 2 pm. The poste restante address here is as follows:

your name
Poste Restante
08080 Barcelona
Spain

The post office also has a public fax service, as do many shops and offices around the city.

Another useful post office is at Carrer d'Aragó 282, just off Passeig de Gràcia, open Monday to Friday from 8.30 am to 8.30 pm, and Saturday from 9 am to 1 pm. American Express (see Money) holds mail for American Express card and travellers' cheque holders.

There are telephone and fax offices at Estació Sants (open daily except Sunday from 8.30 am to 9 pm) and the Estació del Nord bus station.

You can use the Internet for 600 ptas a half-hour if you're a customer at El Café de Internet, near the main tourist office at Gran via de les Corts Catalanes 656 (see Places to Eat – L'Eixample).

The Barcelona telephone code is ☎ 93.

Travel Agencies Viva (☎ 483 83 78; fax 483 83 70) at Carrer de Rocafort 116-122 (metro: Rocafort) is Cataluña's equivalent of TIVE, the Spanish youth travel organisation, and sells youth and student air, train and bus tickets. It's open Monday to Friday from 10 am to 8 pm, Saturday from 10 am to 1.30 pm. Viajes Wasteels at Catalunya metro station has similar youth and student airfares, and other discounted tickets.

For other cheap international flights try Halcón Viatges, with several branches including one at Avinguda del Paral.lel 93 (☎ 443 43 43).

Press & Bookshops Many newsstands, especially on La Rambla, carry a wide range of foreign newspapers. Here's a selection of Barcelona's many good bookshops:

Barri Gòtic
Cómplices, Carrer de Cervantes 2 – gay and lesbian books

Documenta, Carrer del Cardenal Casañas 4 – novels in English and French, maps
Próleg, Carrer de la Dagueria 13 – women's bookshop
Quera, Carrer de Petritxol 2 – specialist in maps and guides, including for hiking and trekking

L'Eixample
Altaïr, Carrer de Balmes 71 – great travel bookshop with maps, guides and travel literature in several languages on every corner of the world including Spain
BCN, Carrer d'Aragó 277 – excellent selection of literature and travel guides in English; some French literature; good for dictionaries
Come In, Carrer de Provença 203 – specialist in English-teaching books; also plenty of novels and books on Spain, in English and French
Laie, Carrer de Pau Claris 85 – novels and books on architecture, art and film in English, French, Spanish and Catalan
Librería Francesa, Passeig de Gràcia 91 – lots of novels and guidebooks in French, English, Spanish and Catalan

Gràcia
Bookstore, Carrer de la Granja 13 – second-hand English-language books

For some recommended books on Barcelona, see the Books section in the Facts for the Visitor chapter.

Cultural Centres There are English libraries at the British Council (☎ 209 63 88) at Carrer d'Amigó 83, near Muntaner suburban train station, and the American Institute (☎ 200 75 71) at Via Augusta 123, near Plaça Molina suburban train station. The Institut Français de Barcelona (☎ 209 59 11) at Carrer de Moià 8 (metro: Diagonal) puts on films, concerts and exhibitions.

Laundry Lavandería Tigre at Carrer d'En Rauric 20 in the Barri Gòtic will wash and dry three kg in a couple of hours for 750 ptas (five kg for 1075 ptas, seven kg for 1175 ptas). Doing it yourself saves 100 to 150 ptas. It's open daily except Sunday from 8 am to 6.30 pm.

Medical Services Hospitals with emergency service include the Hospital Creu Roja (☎ 235 93 00), Carrer del Dos de Maig 301

BARCELONA

(metro: Hospital de Sant Pau); and Hospital de Sant Pau (☎ 347 31 33), Carrer de Sant Antoni Maria Claret 167 (metro: Hospital de Sant Pau).

For an ambulance, call ☎ 061, ☎ 329 97 01 or ☎ 300 20 20; for emergency dental help, ☎ 415 99 22; for information on duty chemists, ☎ 010.

Emergency The Guàrdia Urbana (City Police) has a special office (☎ 301 90 60) at La Rambla 43, opposite Plaça Reial, to help tourists who are victims of crime. It's open from 7 am to midnight (to 2 am on Friday and Saturday nights) and can help with consulate or family contact, cancellation of stolen credit cards and so on. There's always an English-speaker on duty, and usually a French-speaker.

The general police numbers are ☎ 091 for national police, ☎ 092 for city police. For the fire brigade call ☎ 080. The city lost-and-found (objetos perdidos) office is on ☎ 301 39 23.

Gay & Lesbian Information Sextienda, a gay sex shop at Carrer d'En Rauric 11 in the Barri Gòtic, has a give-away map of gay Barcelona showing lesbian and gay bars, discos and restaurants. Casal Lambda (☎ 412 72 72) at Carrer Ample 5 in the Barri Gòtic is a gay and lesbian social, cultural and information centre. Coordinadora Gai-Lesbiana (☎ 237 08 69) has a daily lesbian and gay telephone information service (☎ 237 70 70) from 6 to 10 pm. Some lesbian groups are to be found at Ca la Dona (☎ 412 71 61), Carrer de Casp 38, which houses over 20 women's organisations – open Monday to Friday from 10 am to 2 pm and 4 to 8 pm.

Dangers & Annoyances Watch your pockets, bags and cameras like a hawk on the train to/from the airport, on the metro – especially when these are crowded – on La Rambla, in the Barri Gòtic south of Plaça Reial, and in the Barri Xinès. These last two areas, once very seedy, have been somewhat cleaned up in recent years but there are still some pickpockets, bag-snatchers and intimi-dating beggars about. It's best not to go walking alone down dark alleyways at night.

La Rambla

Spain's most famous street is the place to head for a first taste of Barcelona's atmosphere, and a place you're bound to come back to. Though there are narrow traffic lanes at each side, the middle of La Rambla is a broad, tree-lined pedestrian boulevard, crowded every day until midnight or 1 am (later on the weekend) with a cross-section of Barcelona's varied populace – and a heavy slice of its visitors – strolling to or from somewhere in the Ciutat Vella, or just strolling. Dotted with cafés, restaurants, kiosks, and newsstands sporting reams of international press as well as pornography, and enlivened by buskers, pavement artists, mimes and living statues, La Rambla rarely allows a dull moment. It's impossible to imagine Barcelona without it.

La Rambla gets its name from a seasonal stream (raml in Arabic) which once ran here. It was outside the city walls until the 14th century, and built up with monastic buildings and palaces in the 16th to 18th centuries. Unofficially, it's divided into five sections, with their own names, though street numbers are in a single sequence, going up from the bottom (south-east) end.

Rambla de Canaletes This first section going down from Plaça de Catalunya is where you'll probably encounter the first of La Rambla's living statues: these are people decked out in weird garb, maybe covered in silver or gold paint, holding some tricky pose almost long enough to make you believe they *are* statues – and always with a receptacle for your coins at their feet.

A block off to the east along Carrer de la Canuda is Plaça de la Vila de Madrid, with a sunken garden where some **Roman tombs** have been exposed.

Rambla dels Estudis This second stretch of La Rambla, from below Carrer de Santa Anna to Carrer de la Portaferrissa, is also called Rambla dels Ocells (birds) because of its twittering **cage bird market**.

Rambla de Sant Josep This section from Carrer de la Portaferrissa to Pla de la Boqueria is lined with verdant **flower stalls** which give it the alternative name Rambla de les Flors (flowers). The **Palau de la Virreina**, La Rambla 99, is a grand 18th century rococo mansion housing an arts/entertainment information and ticket office run by the *ajuntament* (city hall).

The next building down is La Rambla's most colourful – the **Mercat de la Boqueria**, a large covered food market with brilliant displays of fruit, vegetables and seafood. Pla de la Boqueria, where four side streets meet just north of Liceu metro station, is your chance to walk all over a Miró – the colourful **Mosaïc de Miró** in the pavement, with one tile signed by the artist.

Rambla dels Caputxins Also called Rambla del Centre, this stretch runs from Pla de la Boqueria to Carrer dels Escudellers. On the west side is the intact façade of the **Gran Teatre del Liceu**, Barcelona's famous 19th century opera house, which was gutted in 1994 by a fire started by a welder's spark. The Liceu, which launched such famous Catalan opera singers as José Carreras and Montserrat Caballé, was not just Spain's only real opera house, but one of the biggest and most beautiful in the world. It had extraordinary acoustics which carried even the quietest note to the top of the audience. Politicians pledged it would be rebuilt in record time after the fire – a promise they could hardly keep since the Liceu had been rebuilt in a single year after a previous fire in 1861. It will probably reopen in 1998.

On the east side of Rambla dels Caputxins, further south, is the entrance to the large Plaça Reial (see the Barri Gòtic section). Just below Plaça Reial, La Rambla gets seedier, with a few strip clubs and peep shows reflecting the former status of surrounding streets as Barcelona's chief red-light area.

Rambla de Santa Mònica This final stretch of La Rambla widens out to approach the Columbus monument overlooking Port Vell. On the east side, at the end of narrow Passatge de la Banca, is the **Museu de Cera** (Wax Museum), which has tableaux of a Gypsy cave, a bullring medical room and a hall of horror as well as wax figures of Cleopatra, Franco etc – not bad as wax museums go. It's open daily from 8 am to 8 pm in summer, 10 am to 1.30 pm and 4 to 7.30 pm otherwise (750 ptas).

Monument a Colom The bottom of La Rambla, and the harbour beyond it, are supervised by the tall Columbus monument, built in the 1880s. You can ascend by lift (225 ptas) daily from 10 am to 6.30 pm, except for a 2 to 3.30 pm break from Monday to Friday.

Museu Marítim West of the Monument a Colom on Avinguda de les Drassanes stand the Reials Drassanes (Royal Shipyards), a wonderful and rare work of nonreligious Gothic architecture. They now house the Museu Marítim, which, together with its setting, forms a fascinating tribute to the seaborne contacts that have shaped so much of Barcelona's history. The shipyards, first built in the 13th century, gained their present form – a series of long bays divided by stone arches – a century later. Extensions in the 17th century made them big enough to accommodate the building of 30 galleys. In their shipbuilding days (up to the 18th century) the sea came right up to them. Inside

***

Barcelona Museums
Every Barcelona museum has its own concoction of opening days and hours, sometimes with seasonal variations. Many have a range of prices too, with students and pensioners often paying half-price and under-16s getting in for free. Some are free to everyone on the first Sunday of the month and/or half-price on non-holiday Wednesdays. Where only one price is given in this chapter, that's the normal full adult price. ■

***

Central Barcelona

0   250   500 m

Passeig de Gràcia
Carrer de Pau Claris
Carrer de Roger de Llúria
Carrer de Casp
Carrer d'Ausiàs Marc
Carrer d'Ali Bei
Ronda de Sant Pere
To Estació
del Nord
Bus Station

Rambla de Catalunya
Rambla de Catalunya
Carrer de Balmes

Urquinaona
Carrer   de
Plaça
d'Urquinaona
Carrer d'Ortigosa
Trafalgar
Ronda de Sant Pere

Carrer d'Enric Granados
Carrer de Pelai
Ronda de la Universitat
Les Corts Catalanes

Catalunya
23
Plaça de
Catalunya
Carrer de Sant Pere mes alt
Carrer de Sant Pere mes baix
La   Ribera

22
21
20
Carrer   del Rec   dels Cadens

Gran via de
Universitat
Carrer dels Tallers
Carrer de Pelai
Catalunya
Rambla de
Canaletes
Av del Portal de l'Àngel
Cr de Comtal
24   26
25
27
Cr de Montsió
19
18
17

37
36
38
40
39
42
43
30
32
34
33
31
35
29   28
See Barri Gòtic Map
51
62
61

41
44
45
Fernàndina
Plaça
dels
Àngels
46   47
50
49
48
Rambla dels Estudis
Cr de la Canuda

Jaume
Carrer de l'Argenter

See Montjuïc & Poble Sec Map
See L'Eixample & Gràcia Map

Carrer de Valldonzella
Carrer de Montalegre
Carrer d'Elisabets

66
67
Carrer del Carme
Carrer de Jerusalem

Barri
Gòtic

Carrer   d'Avinyó

68
l'Hospital
Liceu
Rambla dels Caputxins
Rambla de Santa Mònica

El   Raval
69
70
Barri   Xinès
72
71
Carrer de la Riera Alta
Carrer de la
Sant
Carrer Nou de la Rambla
L'Arc del Teatre
73
79
74
77
76
Carrer de les Flors
78
Avinguda de les Drassanes
Drassanes
80
81

65
Carrer de la Mercè
Passeig de Colom

Carrer del Parlament
Ronda de Sant Pau
75

85
Avinguda   del   Paral·lel
Paral·lel
Carrer Nou de la Rambla
86
87
Plaça del
Portal de
la Pau

Dàrser
Nacion
Rambla de M

Moll de la Fusta
Moll de les Drassanes

86

Avinguda   del   Paral·lel
Carrer de Blai
Carrer del Roser
Carrer d'En Fontrodona
Carrer de Vila i Vilà
Passeig de Josep Carner
Carrer de les Tàpies
Carrer Nou de la Rambla

BARCELONA

PLACES TO STAY
2 Hostal de Joves
11 Hotel Arts Barcelona
22 Hostal Fontanella
24 Residencia Victoria
26 Hostal Lausanne
28 Hotel Colón
30 Pensión Estal
31 Nouvel Hotel
35 Hotel Continental
36 Pensión Noya &
    Restaurant Nuria
39 Hotel Lloret
41 Hotel Mesón Castilla
48 Le Meridien
54 Hostal Nuevo Colón
69 Hotel San Agustin
70 Hotel Segura
81 Hostal Marítima

PLACES TO EAT
7 La Taverna del Cel Ros
8 Cafè Museu Tardà Rock
10 Planet Hollywood
14 Pla de la Garsa
18 Lluna Plena
25 Bocatta
27 Els Quatre Gats
29 Cerveceria Edelman
32 Self-Naturista
33 Santa Ana
34 Bocatta
37 Xaica Pizzeria
38 Pastafiore
40 Restaurant Tallers

43 Pans & Company
47 Restaurante Riera
49 Simago Supermarket
50 Viena
55 Can Busto
56 Cal Pep
58 La Cuina
60 Granja Xador
62 Senyor Parellada
63 Restaurant Set Portes
65 Bar Celta
76 Restaurant Ca L'Isidre
84 El Pati, Pans & Company &
    Maremagnum Shopping Centre

OTHER
1 Arc de Triomf
3 Cascada
4 Museu Nacional d'Art
    Modern de Catalunya
5 Parlament de Catalunya
6 Torre Mapfre
9 Peix Sculpture
12 L'Umbracle (Arboretum)
13 Museu de Geologia
14 L'Hivernacle
    (Arboretum)
15 Museu de Zoologia
16 Teatre Malic
19 Mercat Santa Caterina
20 La Cuina Concert Hall
21 Palau de la Música
    Catalana
23 El Corte Inglés
42 L'Ovella Negra

44 Centre de Cultura
    Contemporània de Barcelona
45 Museu d'Art Contemporàni
    de Barcelona (MACBA)
46 Casa Almirall
51 Museu Textil i
    d'Indumentària
52 Museu Picasso
53 Galeria Maeght
57 Església de Santa Maria
    del Mar
59 El Xampanyet
61 El Nus
66 Post Office
67 Mercat de la Boqueria
68 Antic Hospital de la
    Santa Creu
71 The Quiet Man
72 Bar Marsella
73 Barnastop
74 Teatre Llantiol
75 Mercat de Sant Antoni
77 Teatre Arnau
78 Escola Oficial d'Idiomes
    de Barcelona
79 Bar Pastís
80 Museu de Cera
82 Imax Port Vell
83 L'Aquàrium
85 Monument a Colom
86 Reials Drassanes
    (Museu Marítim)
87 Golondrina Quay
88 Estació Marítima N-1

BARCELONA

is an impressive array of boats, models, maps, paintings and more, with sections including the port and city of Barcelona, the Reials Drassanes themselves, ships' figureheads, Columbus and Magellan, and 16th century galleys (the full-scale replica of Don Juan of Austria's royal galley from the battle of Lepanto is a highlight). The museum is open Tuesday to Sunday from 10 am to 7 pm; entry is 800 ptas.

Barri Gòtic

Barcelona's 'Gothic quarter', east of La Rambla, is a classic medieval warren of narrow, winding streets, quaint little plazas and wonderful structures from the city's golden age. It also has most of the city's best budget accommodation and plenty of good bars, cafés and restaurants. It's probably unique among Europe's old cities in that few of its great buildings date from after the early 15th century – the decline Barcelona went into at that time curtailed grand projects for several centuries.

The Barri Gòtic stretches from La Rambla in the west to Via Laietana in the east, and roughly from Carrer de la Portaferrissa in the north to Carrer de la Mercè in the south. Carrer de Ferran and Carrer de Jaume I, cutting across the middle, form a kind of halfway line: these streets and those to their north tend to be strung with chic little shops and feel 100% safe, while those to their south become darker and, below Carrer de Ferran, seedier – though they still contain several good and perfectly respectable places to eat, drink and stay.

Plaça de Sant Jaume This square at the east end of Carrer de Ferran has been Barcelona's political hub on and off since the 15th century and is a good place to start an exploration of the Barri Gòtic. Facing each other across it are the Palau de la Generalitat (the seat of Cataluña's government) on the north side and the ajuntament on the south. Both have fine Gothic interiors – which, unhappily, the general public can only enter at limited times.

The **Palau de la Generalitat**, founded in the early 15th century to house Cataluña's parliament of the time, is open only on 23 April, the Dia de Sant Jordi (St George, Cataluña's patron saint), when it's decked out with roses and very crowded. At any time, however, you can admire the original Gothic main entrance on Carrer del Bisbe Irurita.

It's a similar story with the **ajuntament**. The original, now disused, Gothic entrance on Carrer de la Ciutat is the only feature of note except when the public is allowed inside on Saturday and Sunday. On those days, you could take your passport and ask permission to see the Saló de Cent, a fine arched hall created in the 14th century for the medieval city council, the Consell de Cent (but since remodelled).

Catedral & Around You can reach Barcelona's cathedral, its most magnificent Gothic structure, by following Carrer del Bisbe Irurita north-west from Plaça de Sant Jaume. The narrow old streets around the cathedral are beautifully traffic-free, and are dotted with buskers playing classical guitar or Catalan folk songs.

At the north end of Carrer del Bisbe Irurita poke your head into the courtyards of the 16th century **Casa de l'Ardiaca** (archdeacon's house) and the 13th century **Palau Episcopal** (bishop's palace). On the outside of both buildings at the very end of Carrer del Bisbe Irurita you can make out the bottom parts of the rounded **Roman towers** which guarded a Roman gate here. The lower part of the Casa de l'Ardiaca's north-west wall was part of the **Roman walls**.

The best view of the cathedral is from Pla de la Seu beneath its main **north-west façade**. Unlike most of the building, which dates from between 1298 and 1460, this façade was not created till the 1870s, though it is closely based on a 1408 design, itself much more intricate and pointy than the rest of the cathedral.

The interior – open from 8 am to 1.30 pm and 4 to 7.30 pm (5 to 7.30 pm on Saturday and Sunday) – is a broad, soaringly high space divided into a central nave and two aisles by lines of elegant, thin pillars. Unlike many much-visited cathedrals, this one maintains a truly serene atmosphere, at its height as hushed worshippers gather for evening mass. The cathedral was one of the few Barcelona churches spared by the anarchists in the civil war, so its ornamentation, which was never over-lavish, is intact.

In the first chapel on the right from the north-west entrance, the main Crucifixion figure above the altar is the **Sant Crist de Lepant**, said to have been carried on the prow of the Spanish flagship at the battle of Lepanto. Further along this same wall, past the south-west transept, are raised the wooden **coffins of Count Ramon Berenguer I and Almodis**, his wife, founders of the 11th century Romanesque predecessor of the present cathedral.

The **crypt** beneath the main altar contains the tomb of Santa Eulàlia, one of Barcelona's patron saints, a good Christian lass of the 4th century who suffered terrible tortures and death at the hands of the then-pagan Romans. Her alabaster sarcophagus was carved by an Italian in 1327. If you put 100 ptas in the slot by the gate, the crypt will light up.

You can visit the cathedral's **roof and tower** by a lift (ascensor) which rises every half-hour from 9.30 am to 12.30 pm and 4.30 to 6.30 pm from the Capella de les Animes del Purgatori near the north-east transept. Tickets (200 ptas) are sold in the choir (coro), the enclosed section in the middle of the nave.

From the south-west transept, exit to the lovely **claustre** (cloister), with its trees, fountains and flock of geese (there have been geese here for centuries). One of the cloister chapels commemorates 930 priests, monks and nuns martyred in the civil war.

Opposite the south-east end of the cathedral, narrow Carrer del Paradis leads back down towards Plaça de Sant Jaume. Inside No 10 are four columns of Barcelona's main **Temple Romà** (Roman temple), built for emperor worship in the 1st century AD. You can visit (free) Monday to Saturday from 10 am to 2 pm and 4 to 8 pm, and Sunday from 10 am to 2 pm.

Plaça del Rei & Around Just a stone's throw east of the cathedral, Plaça del Rei is the former courtyard of the Palau Reial Major, the palace of the counts of Barcelona and monarchs of Aragón. It's surrounded by tall, centuries-old buildings, most of which are now open to visitors as the **Museu d'Història de la Ciutat** (City History Museum). This is one of Barcelona's most fascinating non-art museums, combining large sections of the palace with a subterranean walk through Roman and Visigothic Barcelona.

The museum has several sections and a number of entrances; at any one, you get a ticket good for all sections. It's open Monday to Saturday from 10 am to 2 pm and 4 to 8 pm, and Sunday from 10 am to 2 pm. Entrance is normally 500 ptas (250 ptas for students under 26, pensioners and unemployed, free for under-16s). A fan-shaped stairway in the north corner of Plaça del Rei leads up to the Saló del Tinell, on the left, and the Capella Reial de Santa Àgata on the right. The **Saló del Tinell** was the royal palace's throne hall, a masterpiece of the strong, unfussy Catalan Gothic style, built in the mid-14th century with wide, rounded arches holding up a wooden roof. The **Capella Reial de Santa Àgata**, also from the 14th century, whose spindly bell tower rises from the north-east side of Plaça del Rei, was the palace's chapel. It's plain inside except for its 15th century altarpiece, painted wood roof and stained glass (which is not old). Follow the staircases up inside either of its side walls and you'll come out on the multi-tiered **Mirador del Rei Martí** (Lookout Tower of King Martin), built in 1555. The tower dominates Plaça del Rei and gives excellent views over the city.

The main entrance to the Roman and Visigothic part of the museum is through the **Casa Padellàs** on Carrer del Veguer just south of Plaça del Rei. Casa Padellàs, built for a 15th century noble family, has a courtyard typical of Barcelona Gothic mansions, with an outdoor staircase up to the 1st floor. Today the staircase leads to a restored Roman tower and a section of Roman wall. Below ground is a remarkable walk through

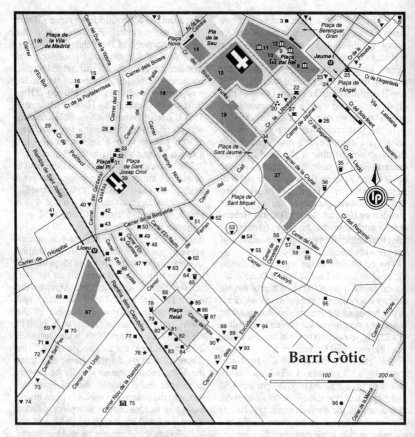

Barri Gòtic

0   100   200 m

excavated **Roman and Visigothic Barcelona** – complete with sections of Roman street, Roman baths, remains of a Visigothic basilica (church), and a Visigothic baptismal pool. The route extends underneath the cathedral, where there are traces of the earlier Romanesque cathedral.

The south-west side of Plaça del Rei is taken up by the **Palau del Lloctinent** (viceroy's palace), built in the 1550s as the residence of the Spanish viceroy of Cataluña. A short distance down Carrer dels Comtes is the **Museu Frederic Marès**, in another part of the Palau Reial Major. Marès was a rich 20th century Catalan sculptor, traveller and

obsessive collector. He specialised in medieval Spanish sculpture, huge quantities of which are displayed on the ground and 1st floors – including some lovely coloured wood sculptures of the Crucifixion and the Virgin. The top two floors, known as the Museu Sentimental, hold a mind-boggling array of other Marès knick-knacks, from toy soldiers and cribs to scissors and tarot cards. The museum is open Tuesday to Saturday from 10 am to 5 pm, Sunday and holidays from !0 am to 2 pm. Entrance is 300 ptas.

Roman Walls From Plaça del Rei it's worth a little detour to see the two best surviving

PLACES TO STAY					
3	Hostal Layetana	22	Bon Mercat	**OTHER**	
6	Pensión Lourdes	23	La Colmena	1	Roman Tombs
15	Hostal-Residencia	25	Il Caffe di Roma	8	Casa Padellàs (Museu
	Rembrandt	27	Mesón del Café		d'Història de la
16	Pensión-Hostal Fina	29	Granja La		Ciutat)
24	Hotel Suizo		Pallaresa	9	Capella de Santa
28	Hostal Galerias	33	Xocolateria La Xicra		Agata
	Maldà	34	Bocatta	10	Palau del Lloctinent
32	Hotel Jardi	38	Mesón Jesús	11	Museu Frederic Marès
43	Hostal Paris	40	Sandvitxeria	12	Saló del Tinell
44	Pensión Dalí		Entrepaipa	13	Catedral
45	Hotel Internacional	41	Bocatta	14	Casa de l'Ardiaca
49	Pensión Bienestar	46	Cafè de l'Òpera	18	Palau Episcopal
50	Pensión Europa	47	Les Quatre	19	Palau de la Generalitat
51	Pensión Fernando		Barres	20	Temple Romà
54	Hostal Levante	48	Can Culleretes	26	Próleg Bookshop
58	Casa Huéspedes	53	El Gran Café	30	Quera Bookshop
	Mari-Luz	55	El Gallo Kiriko	31	Bar del Pi
59	Alberg Juvenil	56	Bar-Restaurant	35	Bodega La Palma
	Palau		Cervantes	36	Bar L'Ascensor
68	Hostal Residencia	57	Cal Kiko	37	Ajuntament
	Opera	63	Pans & Company	39	Església de Santa
70	Hotel España	66	Les Quinze Nits		Maria del Pi
71	Hotel Peninsular	69	Bar Restaurante	42	Documenta
77	Hotel Oriente		Romesco		Bookshop
80	Pensió Colom 3 &	72	Restaurante Els Tres	52	CIAJ
	Disco-Bar Real		Bots	60	Harlem Jazz Club
83	Hotel Cuatro Naciones	73	Restaurante Pollo Rico	61	Cómplices Bookshop
84	Youth Hostel Kabul	74	Kashmir Restaurant	62	Sextienda
86	Hotel Roma Reial		Tandoori	64	Lavandería Tigre
95	Pensión Avinyó	88	Restaurante Senshe	65	Bar Malpaso
			Tawakal	67	Gran Teatre del Liceu
PLACES TO EAT		89	Buen Bocado	75	Palau Güell
2	Pans & Company	90	Restaurante Rincón de	76	Guàrdia Urbana
4	Comme-Bio		Ríos Baixos	78	Glaciar
5	Restaurant El Cid	91	Bar Comercio	79	Barcelona Pipa Club
7	Bar-Restaurant	92	La Fonda	81	Sala Tarantos
	Nervion		Escudellers	82	Jamboree
17	Croissanterie del Pi	93	Los Caracoles	85	Karma
21	Santa Clara	94	Felafel & Kebab	87	Bar Reixas
			Takeaway	96	Casal Lambda

stretches of Barcelona's Roman walls. One is on the south-west side of Plaça de Berenguer Gran, with the Capella Reial de Santa Agata atop them. The other is a little further south, by the north end of Carrer del Sots-tinent Navarro. They date from the 3rd and 4th centuries, when the Romans rebuilt their walls after the first attacks by Germanic tribes from the north.

Plaça de Sant Josep Oriol & Around This small plaza not far off La Rambla is the prettiest in the Barri Gòtic. Its bars and cafés attract buskers and artists and make it a lively place to hang out for a while. It's surrounded by some of the Barri Gòtic's quaintest little streets, many of them dotted with other appealing cafés, restaurants and shops. The plaza is dominated by the **Església de Santa Maria del Pi**, a Gothic church built in the 14th to 16th centuries, open daily from 8.30 am to 1 pm and 4.30 to 9 pm. The beautiful rose window above its entrance on Plaça del Pi is claimed to be the world's biggest. The inside of the church was gutted by fire in 1936 and most of the stained glass is modern. The third chapel on the left is dedicated to Sant Josep Oriol, with a map showing spots in the church where he worked numerous miracles.

BARCELONA

The area between Carrer dels Banys Nous and Plaça de Sant Jaume is known as the Call, and was Barcelona's **Jewish quarter** – and centre of learning – from at least the 11th century till anti-Semitism saw Jews expelled from it in 1424.

Plaça Reial & Around Just south of Carrer de Ferran, near its La Rambla end, is Plaça Reial, a large, traffic-free plaza surrounded by eateries, bars, nightspots and budget places to stay. The plaza's 19th century neo-classical architecture looks as if it would be at home in some elegant quarter of Paris, but before its 1980s cleanup, this area had a fearsome reputation for poverty, crime and drugs. The plaza is still a place with a restless atmosphere where respectable tourists, ragged buskers and down-and-outs come face to face. The lampposts by the central fountain are Antoni Gaudí's first known works.

The whole area between Carrer d'Avinyó and La Rambla was once a red-light zone and a notorious den of low life. It's now a lot less dangerous than it once was, and you needn't be put off from exploring it or using some of its good bars and restaurants – but still watch your pockets and bags along Carrer dels Escudellers and nearby streets, and avoid dark alleys.

This southern half of the Barri Gòtic is imbued with the memory of Picasso, who lived as a teenager with his family in Carrer de la Mercè, had his first studio in nearby Carrer de la Plata, had a later studio in Carrer dels Escudellers Blancs near Plaça Reial, and was a regular visitor to a brothel at Carrer d'Avinyó 27 which may have inspired his famous 1907 painting *Les Demoiselles d'Avignon*.

El Raval

El Raval is the part of the Ciutat Vella west of La Rambla – stretching to Ronda de Sant Antoni, Ronda de Sant Pau and Avinguda del Paral.lel, which together trace the line of Barcelona's 14th century walls. It contains one of the city's poorest areas, the so-called Barri Xinès (Chinese quarter) south of

Carrer de l'Hospital, the traditional haunt of the lowest of Barcelona's low life. Despite attempts to clean up the Barri Xinès, you still need to take care there: streets like Carrer d'En Robador and Carrer de Sant Ramon remain cheap red-light zones and are pretty sordid.

Museu d'Art Contemporani & Around One area that's seeing ambitious renewal is around Plaça dels Àngels in the north of El Raval. Here the vast, white Museu d'Art Contemporani de Barcelona (MACBA) opened in 1995. Initially, its collection is mainly of Catalan and non-Spanish art from the 1950s and 1980s, plus some important antecedents. Artists include Joan Miró, Antoni Tàpies, Paul Klee and Alexander Calder. Opening hours are Tuesday to Friday from noon to 8 pm, Saturday from 10 am to 8 pm, and Sunday and holidays from 10 am to 3 pm. Entry is 600 ptas (400 ptas on non-holiday Wednesdays).

On Carrer de Montalegre behind the museum is the **Centre de Cultura Contemporània de Barcelona**, a complex of auditoriums and exhibition and conference halls created in the early 1990s from an 18th century hospice. The big courtyard, with a vast glass wall on one side, is spectacular.

Antic Hospital de la Santa Creu Two blocks south of Plaça dels Àngels is an architectural masterpiece from another age. Founded in the early 15th century as the city's main hospital, the Antic Hospital de la Santa Creu today houses the Biblioteca de Catalunya (Cataluña's national library) and the Institut d'Estudis Catalans. You can walk through its beautiful courtyards, stretching between Carrer del Carme and Carrer de l'Hospital and surrounded by stone buildings from the 15th, 17th and 19th centuries.

Palau Güell A few steps off La Rambla at Carrer Nou de la Rambla 3-5, the Palau Güell is the only Gaudí house open to the public in Barcelona, and one of the few *modernista* buildings in the Ciutat Vella. Gaudí built it in the late 1880s for his most important patron, the industrialist Eusebi Güell, as a guest wing and social annexe to Güell's main mansion on La Rambla. The Palau Güell lacks some of Gaudí's later playfulness but is still a characteristic riot of styles – Gothic, Islamic, Art Nouveau – and materials. After the civil war it was in police hands and political prisoners were tortured in its basement. Today, with its austere street frontage and dark, medieval-feeling interior, it maintains a heavy, almost doom-laden atmosphere.

Features to look out for include the carved wooden ceilings and fireplace, the stonework, the use of mirrors, stained glass and wrought iron, and the main hall with its dome reaching right up to the roof. There's little colour until you come out on the roof with its spectacularly tiled, fantastically shaped chimney pots. The Palau Güell is open Monday to Saturday from 10 am to 2 pm and 4 to 8 pm. Entry is 300 ptas (students 150 ptas).

Picasso – who hated Gaudí's work – began his Blue Period in 1902 in a studio across the street at Carrer Nou de la Rambla 10.

La Ribera

La Ribera is the area of the Ciutat Vella north-east of the Barri Gòtic, from which it's divided by noisy Via Laietana, driven through this part of the city in 1907. La Ribera has intriguing, narrow streets, some major sights and good bars and restaurants, and lacks the seedy character of some parts of the Barri Gòtic.

Palau de la Música Catalana This concert hall at Carrer de Sant Pere mes alt 11 is one of the high points of *modernista* architecture. It's not exactly a symphony, more a series of crescendos in tile, brick, sculptured stone and stained glass. Built between 1905 and 1908 by Lluís Domènech i Montaner for the Orfeó Català musical society, with the help of some of the best Catalan artisans of the time, it was conceived as a temple for the Catalan Renaixença.

You can see some of its splendours – such as the main façade with its mosaics, floral capitals, and sculpture cluster representing Catalan popular music – from outside, and glimpse lovely tiled pillars inside the ticket office entrance on Carrer de Sant Francesc de Paula. Best, however, is the richly colourful auditorium upstairs, with its ceiling of blue and gold stained glass and, above a bust of Beethoven, a towering sculpture of Wagner's Valkyries (Wagner was No 1 in the Renaixença charts). To see this, you need to attend a concert or book yourself on one of the regular free building tours (☎ 268 10 00 or, better at busy times, go to the building a few days ahead).

Museu Picasso & Carrer de Montcada Barcelona's most visited museum, the Museu Picasso, occupies three of the many fine medieval stone mansions on narrow Carrer de Montcada. The street was cut through the southern part of La Ribera in the 14th century as an approach to the port, which was then further east than it is today. The mansions belonged to nobles and merchants who grew rich off Mediterranean trade. Today the street is the city's most concentrated stretch of medieval masonry. The Museu Picasso, at Carrer de Montcada 15-19, can't claim to have a representative collection of Picasso's life's work but it is very good on his Barcelona periods. It shows clearly how the young Picasso learned to handle a whole spectrum of subjects, styles and treatments before developing his own forms of expression. The museum is open Tuesday to Saturday from 10 am to 8 pm, and Sunday from 10 am to 3 pm (closed on Monday and on 1 January, Good Friday, 1 May, 24 June, 25 and 26 December). Entry is normally 500 ptas (250 ptas for students under 26 and pensioners; free for under-16s), but it's 250 ptas for everyone except under-16s on non-holiday Wednesdays, and free on the first Sunday of each month. There are additional charges for special exhibitions.

On the 1st floor are ceramics and 1890s paintings from Málaga, Barcelona and Madrid – religious scenes, portraits and self-portraits, still lifes, city, land and seascapes, academic works like *Science and Charity* (done at the age of 16) and works clearly

✦ ✦ ✦ ✦ ✦ ✦ ✦ ✦ ✦ ✦ ✦ ✦

Picasso & Barcelona

Pablo Picasso, born in Málaga in 1881, came to Barcelona in 1895 when his father got the job of professor at the city's fine-arts college. The amazingly precocious Pablo soon excelled as a student at the college, gaining an academic grounding which, together with Barcelona's contacts with Paris, formed the key to his early artistic development. Picasso stayed in Barcelona – mainly amid the poverty and bohemian life of the Barri Gòtic and Barri Xinès – most of the time till 1900, constantly drawing, painting and keeping company with other artists, especially at Els Quatre Gats, the famed gallery, tavern and artists' hang-out. (See Places to Eat for more on Els Quatre Gats, and the Plaça Reial & Around section earlier in the chapter for more on some of Picasso's other haunts.)

Picasso quickly showed he could work in any number of different styles, including impressionism and symbolism. He left for Paris in 1900, returning to Barcelona from December 1901 to 1904. This was his Blue Period, and works from this time show his first really personal style, strong on intense portrayals of city poverty and low life. In 1904 he settled permanently in France, and thereafter made only occasional visits to Barcelona.

Picasso opposed Francoism and refused to visit Spain under the Generalísimo, dying in France in 1973. But he felt differently about Cataluña and in 1962 agreed to his old Barcelona friend and secretary Jaume Sabartés' idea of founding a Picasso museum here. Sabartés' Picasso collection was combined with works already owned by the city. Later Picasso himself made large donations (including many early works and a bequest of graphics) to the museum, and in 1981 his widow, Jacqueline Roque, gave 141 ceramics. ■

✦ ✦ ✦ ✦ ✦ ✦ ✦ ✦ ✦ ✦ ✦ ✦

are a complex technical series, *Las Meninas*. These consist for the most part of studies on Diego Velázquez's masterpiece of the same name (which hangs in the Prado, Madrid), but also include eight appealing treatments of *Pichones* (Young Doves).

Almost across the street is the **Museu Textil i d'Indumentària** (Textile & Costume Museum) in the 14th century Palau dels Marquesos de L/ió at Carrer de Montcada 12. Its 4000 items range from 4th century Coptic textiles to 20th century local embroidery, but best is the big collection of clothing from the 16th century to the 1930s. Hours are Tuesday to Saturday from 10 am to 5 pm, Sunday and holidays from 10 am to 2 pm. Entrance is 300 ptas. There's a nice café in the old courtyard.

Several other mansions on the street are now commercial art galleries where you're welcome to browse (they often stage exhibitions). The biggest is the **Galeria Maeght** at No 25 in the 16th century Palau dels Cervelló. Barcelona has dozens of other art galleries, by the way; you'll find listings in *Guía del Ocio* (see Entertainment later in this chapter).

Església de Santa Maria del Mar Carrer de Montcada opens at its south-east end into **Passeig del Born**, a plaza where jousting tournaments took place in the Middle Ages and which was Barcelona's main square from the 13th to 18th centuries. At the south-west end of Passeig del Born stands one of Barcelona's finest Gothic churches, Santa Maria del Mar. Built in the 14th century, Santa Maria was lacking in superfluous decoration even before anarchists gutted it in 1909 and 1936. This only serves to highlight its fine proportions, purity of line and sense of space. There's a beautifully slim arcade in the apse, and some lovely 15th to 18th century stained glass. The church is open Monday to Saturday from 9 am to 12.30 pm and 5 to 8 pm, and on Sunday from 9 am to 2 pm and 5 to 8 pm.

Parc de la Ciutadella

East of La Ribera and north of La Barceloneta, Parc de la Ciutadella is easily reached

influenced by Cézanne and Toulouse-Lautrec. The 2nd floor starts with work of 1900-04 from Barcelona and Paris, with more impressionist-influenced paintings like *Waiting* and Blue Period canvases like *The Defenceless*. There's also the haunting *Portrait of Senyora Canals* (1905) from the following Pink Period. The collection then jumps to 1917, when Picasso visited Barcelona with the Ballets Russes, which inspired his *Harlequin* of that year, a work reckoned to mark the start of his classical phase (which followed his cubist period!). The museum's main later works, all done in Cannes in 1957,

from the city's central areas. It's perfect if you just need a bit of space and greenery, but also has a couple of more specific attractions.

The park occupies the site of a huge, much-loathed fort (La Ciutadella) built by Felipe V to watch over Barcelona after the War of the Spanish Succession. Later, the fort was used as a political prison before a friendlier government in Madrid permitted it to be knocked down in 1869. The site was turned into a park and used as the main site for the Universal Exhibition of 1888. It's open daily from 8 am to 8 pm (to 9 pm from April to September). Arc de Triomf and Barceloneta, both about half a km away, are the nearest metro stations.

The single most impressive thing in the park is the monumental **Cascada** near the Passeig de Pujades entrance, created in 1875-81 by Josep Fontsère with the help of the young Gaudí – a dramatic combination of classical statuary, rugged rocks, greenery and thundering water.

South-east of here, in the fort's former arsenal, are the **Museu Nacional d'Art Modern de Catalunya** and the **Parlament de Catalunya**, where the Generalitat meets. The museum, despite its title, is devoted to Catalan art from the mid-19th century to the 1920s, the era of *modernisme* and its classicist antithesis, Noucentism. Look for the works by the two leading lights of *modernista* art, Ramon Casas and Santiago Rusiñol, among them Casas' drawings of the habitués of Els Quatre Gats and Rusiñol's landscapes; Picasso's portrait of Casas; paintings by later impressionist-influenced artists like Nicolau Raurich, Joaquim Mir and Isidre Nonell; and Dalí's portrait of his father in the section on the avant-garde of the 1910s and 1920s. The museum is open Tuesday to Sunday from 10 am to 7 pm; entry is 300 ptas (students 200 ptas).

The south end of the park is occupied by a large **Parc Zoològic** (zoo), which is best known for its albino gorilla Copito de Nieve (Snowflake), orphaned by poachers in Africa in the 1960s. The zoo also has numerous other big beasts, good dolphin shows three times daily and a children's section with farm animals. It's open daily from 10 am to 5 pm (950 ptas).

Along the Passeig de Picasso side of the park are several buildings constructed for, or just before, the Universal Exhibition. These include two arboretums, the specialised Museu de Geologia, and the **Museu de Zoologia** or Castell dels Tres Dragons (open Tuesday to Sunday from 10 am to 2 pm, 300 ptas). The contents of this museum are less interesting than the building itself, by the *modernista* Lluís Domènech i Montaner, who put medieval-castle trimmings on a pioneering steel frame.

North-west of the park along Passeig de Lluís Companys is the imposing *modernista* **Arc de Triomf**, designed by Josep Vilaseca as an entrance to the Universal Exhibition, with unusual, almost Islamic-style brickwork.

Port Vell

Barcelona's old port at the bottom of La Rambla, once such an eyesore that it caused public protests, has been transformed since the 1980s into an attractive, people-friendly environment with some excellent leisure developments.

For a view of the harbour from the water, you can take a **Golondrina** excursion boat from Moll de les Drassanes in front of the Monument a Colom. A 35 minute trip to the breakwater *(rompeolas)* and lighthouse *(faro)* on the seaward side of the harbour is 380 ptas (200 ptas for children aged four to 10); a two hour trip to Port Olímpic is 1210 ptas (less for under-19s). Breakwater trips normally go at least hourly in the daytime, Port Olímpic trips at least three times daily. North-east from the Golondrina quay stretches the palm-lined promenade **Moll de la Fusta**.

At the centre of the redeveloped harbour is the **Moll d'Espanya**, a former wharf linked to Moll de la Fusta by a wave-shaped footbridge, the **Rambla de Mar**, which rotates to let boats enter the marina behind it. At the end of Moll d'Espanya is the glossy Maremagnum shopping and eating complex, but the major attraction is **L'Aquàrium**

(☎ 221 74 74) behind it – an ultra-modern aquarium which opened in 1995. It's claimed to be Europe's biggest aquarium and to have the world's best Mediterranean collection. A highlight is the 80 metre long shark tunnel. Entry is a steep 1300 ptas (950 ptas for four to 12-year-olds and pensioners). It's open daily, all year, from 10 am to 9 pm (to 10 pm on Saturday, Sunday and holidays). Beyond L'Aquàrium is the Imax Port Vell big-screen cinema.

The **cable car** (*telefèric* or *funicular aéreo*) strung across the harbour to Montjuïc was closed, seemingly long-term, at the time of research.

La Barceloneta & Port Olímpic

It used to be said that Barcelona had 'turned its back on the sea', but an ambitious Olympics-inspired redevelopment programme has returned a long stretch of coast north-east of Port Vell to life.

La Barceloneta, at the north-east end of Port Vell, is an old sailors' quarter now mostly composed of dreary five or six storey apartment blocks. It's known for its seafood restaurants, though some of the most characteristic ones were knocked down in the redevelopment. In the Palau de Mar building facing the harbour is the new **Museu d'Història de Catalunya** (History of Cataluña Museum), a 4500 million peseta (US$35 million) affair opened in 1996. It's an almost Disneyesque sort of place incorporating lots of technological wizardry, with audiovisuals and interactive information points galore – but nearly all labelling is in Catalan. Running from prehistory to 1980, the museum includes re-creations of things like a Roman house and a civil war air-raid shelter. You can stick your hand in a machine to feel how cold it was during the ice ages, or climb on a medieval knight's horse. Entry is 500 ptas and the museum is open Tuesday to Thursday from 10 am to 7 pm, Friday and Saturday from 10 am to 8 pm, and Sunday and holidays from 10 am to 2.30 pm.

Barcelona's fishing fleet ties up along the Moll del Rellotge, south of the museum. On La Barceloneta's seaward side are the first of Barcelona's **beaches**, once dirty and unused, but now cleaned up and popular on summer weekends. **Passeig Marítim**, a 1.25 km promenade from La Barceloneta to Port Olímpic – through an area formerly full of railway sidings and warehouses – is pleasant.

Port Olímpic itself is a harbour built for the Olympic sailing events and now surrounded by bars and restaurants which get very lively on spring and summer nights. An eye-catcher on the approach from La Barceloneta is the giant copper *Peix* (Fish) sculpture by Frank Ghery, one of a series of modern sculptures dotted around this part of town. The area behind Port Olímpic – dominated by Barcelona's two tallest skyscrapers, one of which is now the luxury Hotel Arts Barcelona, the other the Torre Mapfre office block – is the Vila Olímpica, the living quarters for the Olympic participants, now mostly sold off as expensive apartments. To the north-east stretch more beaches.

L'Eixample

L'Eixample (the Enlargement) is the area stretching one to 1.5 km north, east and west of Plaça de Catalunya. This was Barcelona's 19th century extension beyond the overcrowded medieval city.

A competition to design l'Eixample was held in 1859 but work didn't start till 1869, largely because of wrangling between Barcelona and the government in Madrid, which eventually overrode Barcelona's own preference. The design chosen was the Pla Cerdà, whose architect Ildefons Cerdà specified a grid of wide streets with plazas formed by their cut-off corners. Cerdà also planned numerous green spaces but these didn't survive the intense demand for Eixample real estate.

L'Eixample has been inhabited from the start by the city's middle classes, many of whom still think it's the best thing about Barcelona. Along its grid of straight streets are the majority of the city's most expensive shops and hotels, plus a range of eateries and several nightspots. The main sightseeing objective is *modernista* architecture, the best of which – apart from La Sagrada Família –

is clustered on or near l'Eixample's main avenue, Passeig de Gràcia. But don't expect to find an entire quarter of colourful tiles, Art Nouveau curves and neo-Gothic towers: the really imaginative buildings are widely separated by dull ones – and disappointingly, since interior decoration is one of the most exotic features of *modernisme*, you can't actually look round most of these buildings.

Manzana de la Discordia The so-called 'Block of Discord' on the west side of Passeig de Gràcia, between Carrer del Consell de Cent and Carrer d'Aragó, gets its name from three houses remodelled in highly contrasting manner between 1898 and 1906 – one by each of the three leading *modernista* architects. You can't normally go inside any of the rooms, but the concierges will let you peep into the hallways and up the stairs.

At No 35, on the corner of Carrer del Consell de Cent, is **Casa Morera**, Domènech i Montaner's contribution, with Art Nouveau carving outside and a bright, flower-tiled lobby. Apparently the chief glories – mosaics, stained glass, sculpture – are in the Patronat de Turisme offices upstairs.

Casa Amatller at No 41, by Puig i Cadafalch, combines Gothic window frames with a stepped gable reminiscent of Amsterdam. The pillared entrance hall and the staircase lit by stained glass are like the inside of some romantic castle.

Casa Batlló, next door at No 43, is one of Barcelona's gems. Of course it's by Gaudí. The façade, sprinkled with bits of blue, mauve and green tile and studded with wave-shaped window frames and balconies, rises to an uneven blue-tiled roof with a solitary tower. Though the roof may represent Sant Jordi and the dragon, the whole building's effect is, if anything, of an underwater castle. In the lobby and on the stairs are more curves, and white and light-blue tiles.

Fundació Antoni Tàpies Round the corner from the Manzana de la Discordia, at Carrer d'Aragó 255, this is both a pioneering *modernista* building of the early 1880s and the major collection of a leading 20th century Catalan artist. The building, designed by Domènech i Montaner for his brother's publishing firm, combines a brick-covered iron frame with Islamic-inspired decoration. Antoni Tàpies, whose abstract, experimental art has often carried political messages – he opposed Francoism in the 1960s and 70s – launched the Fundació in 1984 to promote contemporary art, donating a large collection of his own work. He has also topped the façade with a 'sculpture' resembling, perhaps, an unravelled pan scourer. The Fundació is open Tuesday to Sunday from 11 am to 8 pm. Entry is 500 ptas (250 ptas for students under 26 and pensioners, free for under-16s).

La Pedrera Back on Passeig de Gràcia, 450 metres up at No 92, is another Gaudí masterpiece, built between 1905 and 1910 as a combined apartment and office block. Formally called the Casa Milà after the businessman who commissioned it, it's better known as La Pedrera (the quarry) because of its uneven grey stone façade, which ripples round the corner of Carrer de Provença. The wave effect is emphasised by elaborate wrought-iron balconies.

Signs forbid you from stepping more than a few paces inside the entrances on the ground floor. The only part of the building open to visitors is the roof, with its giant chimney pots looking like multicoloured

---

❋ ❋ ❋ ❋ ❋ ❋ ❋ ❋ ❋ ❋ ❋ ❋ ❋

Manzana de la Discordia
Despite the catalanisation of most Barcelona names in recent decades, the Manzana de la Discordia has kept its Spanish name to preserve a pun on *manzana*, which means both 'block' and 'apple'. According to Greek myth, the original Apple of Discord was tossed on to Mt Olympus by Eris (Discord) with orders that it be given to the most beautiful goddess, sparking jealousies that helped start the Trojan War. The pun won't transfer into Catalan, whose word for block is *illa*, and for apple *poma*. ■

❋ ❋ ❋ ❋ ❋ ❋ ❋ ❋ ❋ ❋ ❋ ❋ ❋

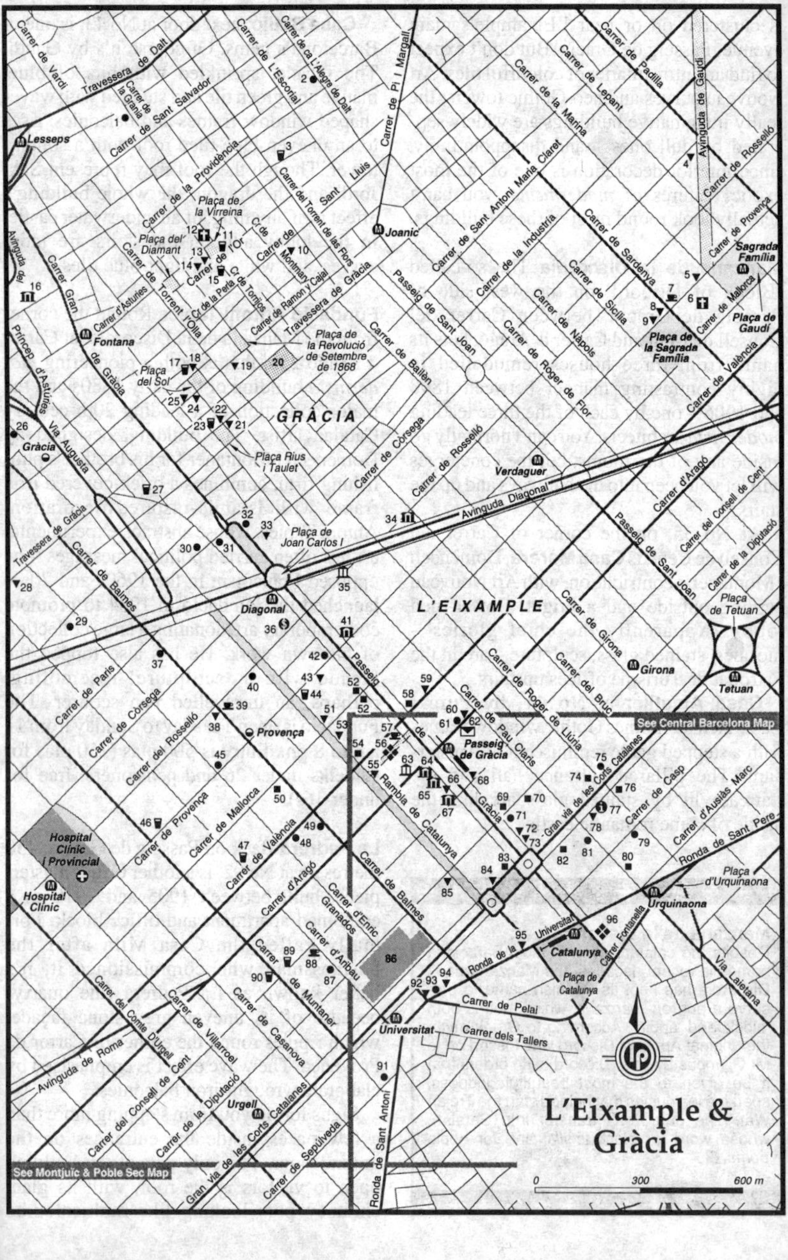

L'Eixample & Gràcia
GRÀCIA
L'EIXAMPLE
Carrer de Vardi
Travessera de Dalt
Carrer de la Granja
Carrer de Sant Salvador
Carrer de L'Escorial
Carrer de ca L'Alegre de Dalt
Carrer de Pi I Margall
Carrer de Padilla
Carrer de Lepant
Carrer de la Marina
Avinguda de Gaudí
Carrer de Rosselló
Carrer de Provença
Lesseps
Carrer de la Providència
Carrer del Torrent de las Flors
Sant Lluis
Plaça de la Virreina
Plaça del Diamant
Carrer de l'Or
Cr de Montmany
Carrer de Torrent l'Olla
Cr de la Perla
Cr de Torrijos
Carrer de Ramon y Cajal
Travessera de Gràcia
Carrer de Sant Antoni Maria Claret
Joanic
Carrer de la Indústria
Carrer de Sardenya
Sagrada Família
Carrer de Mallorca
Plaça de Gaudí
Plaça de la Sagrada Família
Carrer de Sicília
Carrer de Nàpols
Carrer de Roger de Flor
Passeig de Sant Joan
Carrer de Bailèn
Carrer de València
Avinguda del Príncep d'Astúries
Carrer Gran de Gràcia
Carrer d'Asturies
Fontana
Plaça de la Revolució de Setembre de 1868
Plaça del Sol
Plaça Rius i Taulet
Gràcia
Via Augusta
Carrer de Còrsega
Carrer de Rosselló
Verdaguer
Carrer d'Aragó
Carrer del Consell de Cent
Carrer de la Diputació
Avinguda Diagonal
Travessera de Gràcia
Carrer de Balmes
Plaça de Joan Carlos I
Diagonal
Passeig
Plaça de Tetuan
Tetuan
Carrer de Girona
Girona
Carrer del Bruc
Carrer de Roger de Llúria
Carrer de Pau Claris
Carrer de París
Carrer de Còrsega
Carrer del Rosselló
Provença
Passeig de Gràcia
See Central Barcelona Map
Gran via de les Corts Catalanes
Carrer de Casp
Carrer d'Ausiàs Marc
Rambla de Catalunya
Carrer de Provença
Carrer de Mallorca
Carrer de València
Hospital Clínic i Provincial
Hospital Clínic
Carrer d'Aragó
Carrer d'Enric Granados
Carrer d'Aribau
Carrer de Balmes
Ronda de Sant Pere
Plaça d'Urquinaona
Urquinaona
Ronda de la Universitat
Catalunya
Carrer Fontanella
Plaça de Catalunya
Via Laietana
Carrer de Muntaner
Carrer de Casanova
Carrer de Villarroel
Carrer del Comte D'Urgell
Avinguda de Roma
Carrer del Consell de Cent
Carrer de la Diputació
Urgell
Carrer de Sepúlveda
Universitat
Carrer de Pelai
Carrer dels Tallers
Ronda de Sant Antoni
See Montjuïc & Poble Sec Map
0
300
600 m

BARCELONA

PLACES TO STAY
50 Hotel Balmes
52 Comtes de Barcelona Hotel
54 Hotel Regente
58 Hotel Majestic
69 Hostal Oliva
70 St Moritz Hotel
74 Hostal Palacios
76 Hotel Ritz
80 Hostal Goya
82 Hotel Gran Via
83 Hotel Avenida Palace

PLACES TO EAT
4 Bar Bon Punt
5 Bar Sin Nombre
7 La Baguetina Catalana
8 Pil-Pal Sandwichería
9 Restaurante La Palmera
10 Taverna El Glop
13 Cal Majó
14 Casa de Pizzas
18 Equinox Sol
19 El Tastavins
21 Bar Candanchu
22 Punto Pizza
24 La Botiga del Sol
25 Tetería Jazmín
28 Pastafiore
33 La Miel
38 La Gran Tasca
39 La Baguetina Catalana
43 Pastafiore & Pans & Company

47 Bar Ariño 2
51 Capitán Cook
53 Bocatta
55 Pizza del Arte
57 Cafè Torino
59 Fresc Co
60 L'Hostal de Rita
66 Pans & Company
68 Cerveseria Tapa Tapa
72 Ba-Ba-Reeba
73 Quasi Queviures
78 El Café de Internet
84 Botiga-Restaurant Les Corts Catalanes
85 Pastafiore & Pans & Company
88 La Flauta
92 Bar Estudiantil
94 Pans & Company
95 Pizza del Arte

OTHER
1 Bookstore
2 KGB
3 La Nostra Illa
6 Temple Expiatori de la Sagrada Família
11 Café La Virreina
12 Església de Sant Josep
15 Café Salambó
16 Casa Vicenç
17 Café del Sol
20 Market
23 Bar Chirito de Oro
26 OttoZutz
27 Café de la Calle
29 Institut Français de Barcelona

30 Bahía
31 Members
32 Martin's
34 Casa de les Punxes
35 Palau Quadras (Museu de la Música)
36 American Express
37 Velvet
40 Nick Havanna
41 La Pedrera
42 Librería Francesa
44 La Bodegueta
45 Come In Bookshop
46 La Fira
48 Café de las Artes
49 Altaïr Bookshop
56 Boulevard Rosa
61 BCN Bookshop
62 Post Office
63 Fundació Antoni Tàpies
64 Casa Batlló
65 Casa Amatller
67 Casa Morera
71 Iberia
75 Pullmantur
77 Catalunya Oficina de Turisme
79 Ca la Dona
81 Laie Bookshop
86 Universitat de Barcelona
87 Satanassa
89 Este Bar
90 Punto BCN
91 Metro Disco
93 Julià Tours
96 El Corte Inglés

medieval knights. Gaudí wanted to put a tall statue of the Virgin up here too: when the Milà family said no, fearing it might make the building a target for anarchists, Gaudí resigned from the project in disgust and left its completion to others. To see the roof you must book a free guided tour through the Fundació Caixa Catalunya office (☎ 484 59 80) on the ground floor of the Carrer de Provença side of the building. Tours go from Tuesday to Saturday (except holidays) at 10 and 11 am, noon and 1 pm. In winter book a day or two ahead; in busy tourist periods the waiting list may be 10 days long.

Palau Quadras & Casa de les Punxes
Within a few blocks north and east of La

Pedrera are two of Puig i Cadafalch's major buildings. The nearer is the Palau del Baró de Quadras at Avinguda Diagonal 373, created between 1902 and 1904 with detailed neo-Gothic carvings on the façade and fine stained glass. This is one building that you can see inside, since it houses the Museu de la Música, with a collection of international instruments from the 16th century to the present. It's open Tuesday to Sunday from 10 am to 2 pm.

The Casa Terrades is on the other side of Avinguda Diagonal, 1½ blocks east at No 420. This apartment block of 1903-05, like a castle in a fairy tale, is better known as the Casa de les Punxes (House of the Spikes) because of its pointed turrets.

The Modernistas

Most visitors to Barcelona will have heard of Antoni Gaudí ('gow-DEE'), whose La Sagrada Família church is one of the city's major drawing cards. But Gaudí (1852-1926) was just one – albeit the most spectacular – of a whole generation of inventive architects who left their mark on Barcelona between 1880 and 1910. These were the *modernistas*, or Catalan modernists.

Modernisme is usually described as a version of Art Nouveau, and certainly derived its taste for sinuous, flowing lines and decorative artisanry from that movement. Art Nouveau also inspired *modernisme*'s adventurous combinations of materials like tile, glass, brick, and iron and steel (which provide the unseen frames of many buildings). But Barcelona's *modernistas* used an astonishing variety of other styles too – Gothic and Islamic, Renaissance and Romanesque, and Byzantine. Some of their buildings

BETHUNE CARMICHAEL

The sinuous roof line of the Casa Milà, better known as La Pedrera (the quarry), one of Antoni Gaudí's *modernista* masterpieces, on the corner of Passeig de Gràcia and Carrer de Provença

look like fairy-tale castles. They were trying to create a specifically Catalan architecture, often looking back to Cataluña's medieval golden age for inspiration. It's significant that the two other leading *modernista* architects, the tongue-twisting Lluís Domènech i Montaner (1850-1923) and Josep Puig i Cadafalch (1867-1957), were also prominent in the Catalan nationalist political movement. Gaudí too was a Catalan nationalist, though he turned increasingly to spiritual concerns as he grew older.

L'Eixample, where most of Barcelona's new building was happening during the *modernista* period, is home to many of the *modernista* creations. Others in the city (with the sections of this chapter where you'll find them covered) include Gaudí's Palau Güell (El Raval) and Parc Güell (Parc Güell); Domènech i Montaner's Palau de la Música Catalana (La Ribera), Castell dels Tres Dragons (Parc de la Ciutadella) and Hotel España restaurant (Places to Stay); and Puig i Cadafalch's Els Quatre Gats (Places to Eat). There are many, many more. Nor was *modernisme* confined to architecture: you can explore its painting and drawing side at the Museu Nacional d'Art Modern de Catalunya (Parc de la Ciutadella). ■

La Sagrada Família If you only have time for one sightseeing outing in Barcelona, this should probably be it. La Sagrada Família inspires awe by its sheer verticality, and leaves you wondering how anyone dared to work on its pinnacles. And in the true manner of the great medieval cathedrals it emulates, it's still not half built, after more than 100 years. If it's ever finished, the topmost tower will be more than half as high again as those standing today.

The Temple Expiatori de la Sagrada Família (Expiatory Temple of the Holy Family) was the project to which Antoni Gaudí dedicated his life. It stands in the east of l'Eixample (metro: Sagrada Família). It's open to visitors daily – May to September from 9 am to 9 pm, March, April and October from 9 am to 7 pm, November to February

from 9 am to 6 pm. The entry charge of 750 ptas for everybody – the money goes towards the building programme – includes a good museum in the crypt. What you're visiting is a building site, but the completed sections and the museum can be explored at leisure.

The entrance is by the south-west façade fronting Carrer de Sardenya and Plaça de la Sagrada Família. Inside is a bookstall where you should invest 500 ptas in the *Official Guide* if you want a detailed account of the church's sculpture and symbolism. To get your bearings, you need to realise that this façade, and the opposite one facing Plaça de Gaudí, each with four skyscraping towers, are at the *sides* of the church. The main façade, as yet unbuilt, will be at the southeast end, on Carrer de Mallorca. The 170 metre central tower will be above the crossing, halfway between the two existing façades.

Nativity Façade This, the north-east façade, is the building's artistic pinnacle, mostly done under Gaudí's personal supervision and much of it with his own hands. You can climb high up inside some of the four towers by a combination of lifts (when they're working) and narrow spiral staircases – a vertiginous experience. The towers are destined to hold tubular bells capable of playing complicated music at great volume. Their upper parts are decorated with mosaics spelling out *'Sanctus, Sanctus, Sanctus, Hosanna in Excelsis, Amen, Alleluia'*. When asked why he lavished so much care on the tops of the spires,

which no-one would see from close up, Gaudí answered: 'The angels will see them'.

Beneath the towers is a tall three part portal on the theme of Christ's birth and childhood. It seems to lean outward as you stand beneath looking up. Gaudí used real people and animals as models for many of the sculptures: a friend of Picasso's called Opisso fainted with cramp when covered with plaster in an angel pose; a kicking donkey used for the flight into Egypt was hoisted into mid-air so that it would calm down enough to be cast.

The three sections of the portal represent, from left to right, Hope, Charity and Faith. Among the forest of sculpture on the Charity portal, you can make out, low down, the

---

Gaudí & La Sagrada Família

The idea for La Sagrada Família came from a rich publisher, Josep Maria Bocabella, who was worried about the growth of revolutionary ideas in Barcelona and set up a religious society dedicated to Sant Josep, patron saint of workers and the family. Construction of the society's church (it's not a cathedral) began in 1882 under Francesc de Villar, who planned a relatively conventional neo-Gothic structure. Villar fell out with Bocabella and was replaced, in 1883, by the 31 year old Antoni Gaudí.

Gaudí, born into an artisan family in Reus, southern Cataluña, and originally trained as a metalsmith, was already a successful *modernista* architect. Up to 1909 he worked on other projects in Barcelona and elsewhere as well as La Sagrada Família. After that he devoted himself entirely to La Sagrada Família, attending to every detail and becoming increasingly single-minded, spiritual, ascetic and unkempt. When he was run over by a tram on Gran via de les Corts Catalanes in 1926, he had been living in a workshop at La Sagrada Família. His clothes were held together by pins and at first no-one recognised him. He died in hospital three days later.

As he worked on La Sagrada Família, Gaudí had evolved steadily grander and more original ideas for it. Though he stuck to the basic Gothic cross-shaped ground plan with an apse, he eventually devised a temple 95 metres long and 60 metres wide, able to seat 13,000 people, with a central tower 170 metres high and 17 others of 100 metres or more. With his characteristic dislike for straight lines (there were none in nature, he said), Gaudí gave his towers swelling outlines inspired by the weird peaks of the holy mountain Montserrat outside Barcelona, and encrusted them with a tangle of sculpture that almost seems an outgrowth of the stone.

At Gaudí's death only the crypt, the apse walls, one portal and one tower had been finished. Three more towers were added by 1930 – completing the north-east (Nativity) façade – but in 1936 anarchists burned and smashed everything they could in La Sagrada Família, including the workshops, models and plans. Work restarted in the 1950s using restored models and photographs of drawings, with only limited guidance on how Gaudí had thought of solving the huge technical problems of the building. Today the south-west (Passion) façade, with four more towers, isn't very far off completion, and the nave, started in 1978, is coming along nicely.

Constant controversy has dogged the building programme. There are those who say the quality of the new work and its materials – concrete instead of stone for the new towers – are inferior to the earlier parts; others who say that in the absence of detailed plans, the shell should have been left as a kind of monument to Gaudí; and yet others who simply oppose the spending of large amounts of money on a new church (even though all the funds come from private sources). The chief architect Jordi Bonet and his supporters, aside from their obvious desire to see Gaudí's mighty vision made real, argue that their task is a sacred one – that it's not just any old building, but a church intended, as its 'Temple Expiatori' title indicates, to atone for sin and appeal for God's mercy on Cataluña. ■

manger surrounded by an ox, an ass, the shepherds and kings, with angel musicians above. Directly above the blue stained-glass window is the Archangel Gabriel's Annunciation to Mary. Further up, in the centre, is Mary's symbolic coronation as queen and empress. Still higher, a group of angels surround a cross so highly ornamented that it's almost unrecognisable. At the top is a green cypress tree, symbolic refuge in a storm for the white doves of peace dotted over it.

Lower sculptures on the Hope portal show the flight into Egypt and the massacre of the innocents, with Jesus and Joseph in their carpenters' workshop just above. Higher up is the marriage of Mary and Joseph. Sculpture on the Faith portal includes, in the centre of the lower group, the child Jesus explaining the Scriptures to the temple priests.

Interior The semicircular apse wall at the north-west end of the church was the first part to be finished (in 1894). From the altar steps you can look down the nave at work in progress, with the walls and columns near completion and the roofs begun. The main Glory Façade on the south-east end will, like

La Sagrada Família

0   20   40 m

the north-east and south-west façades, be crowned by four towers – the total of 12 representing the 12 apostles. Further symbolism will make the whole building a microcosm of the Christian church, with Christ represented by the massive central tower above the crossing. Four other towers surrounding this will stand for the four evangelists, while another above the apse will symbolise the Virgin.

Passion Façade This south-western façade, on the theme of Christ's last days and death, has been constructed since the 1950s with, like the Nativity Façade, four needling towers and a large, sculpture-bedecked portal. The sculptor, Josep Subirachs, has not attempted to imitate Gaudí's work but has produced strong images of his own. The sculptures, on three levels, are in an S-shaped sequence starting with the Last Supper at bottom left and ending with Christ's burial at top right.

Museu Gaudí Open the same times as the church, the museum includes interesting material on Gaudí's life and other work, as well as models, photos and other material on La Sagrada Família.

Gràcia

Gràcia is the area north of the middle of l'Eixample, two to four km from Plaça de Catalunya. Once a separate village, then in the 19th century an industrial barrio famous for its republican and liberal ideas, it became fashionable among radical and bohemian types in the 1960s and 70s. Though now a bit more sedate and gentrified, it retains much of its style of 20 years ago, with a mixed-class population. Gràcia's interest lies less in specific sights than in the atmosphere of its narrow streets, small plazas and the bars and restaurants on them. An evening or night-time wander is the best way to savour these. Diagonal and Fontana are the nearest metro stations to central Gràcia.

The liveliest plazas are **Plaça del Sol**, **Plaça Rius i Taulet** with its clock tower, and **Plaça de la Virreina** with the 17th century Església de Sant Josep. Three blocks east of Plaça Rius i Taulet there's a big covered market. West of Gràcia's main street, Carrer Gran de Gràcia, there's an early Gaudí house, the turreted, vaguely *mudéjar* **Casa Vicenç** at Carrer de les Carolines 22.

Montjuïc

Montjuïc, the hill overlooking the city centre from the south-west, is home to some of Barcelona's best museums and leisure attractions, some fine parks and the main group of 1992 Olympics sites. It's well worth a day or two of your time.

The name Montjuïc means Jewish Mountain, indicating that there was once a Jewish settlement here. Before Montjuïc started being turned into parks in the 1890s, its woodlands had long provided food-growing and breathing space for the people of the cramped Ciutat Vella. Montjuïc also has a darker history: its castle was used by the Madrid government to bombard the city after political disturbances in 1842, and as a political prison right up to the Franco era. The first main burst of building on Montjuïc came in the 1920s when it was chosen as the stage for Barcelona's 1929 World Exhibition. The Estadi Olímpic, the Poble Espanyol and some museums all date from this time. Montjuïc got a face-lift and more new buildings for the 1992 Olympics.

Abundant roads and paths, with occasional escalators, plus buses and even a chair lift allow you to visit Montjuïc's sights in any order you choose. Probably the five main attractions – which would make up a pretty full day – are the Poble Espanyol, the Museu Nacional d'Art de Catalunya, the Estadi Olímpic, the Fundació Joan Miró and the views from the castle.

Getting There & Away There are several ways to approach Montjuïc. One is to walk from the Ciutat Vella (the foot of La Rambla is 700 metres from the east end of Montjuïc). Also convenient is bus No 61, which runs every 15 to 30 minutes until 8.15 pm (to 9.40 pm on Sunday and holidays) from Avinguda

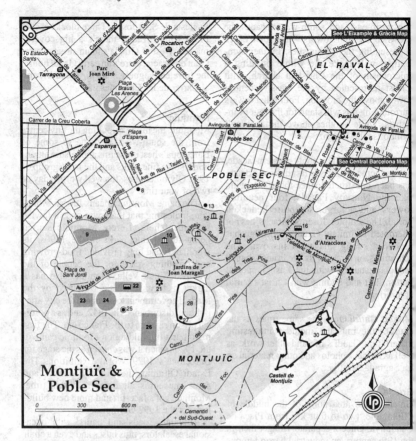

Montjuïc & Poble Sec

POBLE SEC

MONTJUÏC

Castell de Montjuïc

Cementiri del Sud-Ouest

0   300   600 m

de la Reina Maria Cristina, just off Plaça d'Espanya at the northern foot of the hill (metro: Espanya). This goes to the Estació Parc Montjuïc funicular and chair-lift station via the Poble Espanyol, the Estadi Olímpic and the Fundació Joan Miró. The Bus Turístic, No 100 (see Getting Around), also makes several stops on Montjuïc.

Another way of saving your legs is the funicular railway up from Paral.lel metro station to Estació Parc Montjuïc. From mid-June to the end of September this goes daily from 11 am to 10 pm; in October and the Christmas and Semana Santa holiday periods, daily from 10.45 am to 8 pm; the rest of the year, only on Saturday, Sunday and holidays from 10.45 am to 8 pm. The fare is 185 ptas one way, 325 ptas return.

From Estació Parc Montjuïc, the Telefèric de Montjuïc chair lift will carry you yet higher, to an upper entrance of the Parc d'Atraccions (Mirador stop) and then the castle (Castell stop). From mid-June to the end of September this operates daily from 11.30 am to 9.30 pm; in October and the Christmas and Semana Santa periods, daily from 11 am to 2.45 pm and 4 to 7.30 pm; the rest of the year, only on Saturday, Sunday

1	Dona i Ocell Sculpture
2	Halcón Viatges
3	Teatre El Molino
4	Paral.lel (Funicular)
5	Teatre Victoria
6	Club Apolo
7	Elche Restaurant
8	La Font Màgica
9	Poble Espanyol
10	Palau Nacional de Montjuïc
	(Museu Nacional d'Art de Catalunya)
11	Museu Etnològic
12	Museu d'Arqueologia
13	Mercat de les Flors
14	Fundació Joan Miró
15	Estació Parc Montjuïc (Funicular &
	Telefèric)
16	Piscina Municipal de Montjuïc
17	Jardins de Costa i Llobera
18	Jardins del Mirador
19	Mirador (Telefèric)
20	Jardins de Mossén Cinto
21	Jardí d'Aclimatació
22	Piscines Bernat Picornell
23	INEFC
24	Plaça de Europa
25	Torre Calatrava
26	Palau Sant Jordi
27	Galería Olímpica
28	Estadi Olímpic
29	Castell (Telefèric)
30	Museu Militar

and holidays, from 11 am to 2.45 pm and 4 to 7.30 pm. The adult fare is 375 ptas one way, 575 ptas return.

Around Plaça d'Espanya The approach to Montjuïc from Plaça d'Espanya gives you the full benefit of the landscaping on the hill's north side and allows Montjuïc to unfold for you from the bottom up. On Plaça d'Espanya's north side is the big **Plaça Braus Les Arenes** bullring, built in 1900 but no longer used for bullfights. The Beatles played here in 1966. Behind the bullring is the **Parc Joan Miró**, created in the 1980s – worth a quick detour mainly for Miró's giant, highly phallic sculpture *Dona i Ocell* (Woman and Bird) in the north-west corner.

Fountains & Museu Nacional d'Art de Catalunya Avinguda de la Reina Maria Cristina, lined with modern exhibition and congress halls, leads from Plaça d'Espanya

towards Montjuïc. On the hill ahead of you is the Palau Nacional de Montjuïc, and stretching up a series of terraces below it are Montjuïc's fountains, starting with the biggest, La Font Màgica. These come most alive with a lights-and-music show on summer evenings; the show lasts about 15 minutes and happens from late June to late September, on Thursday, Friday and Saturday, every half-hour from 10 to 11.30 pm.

The Palau Nacional, built in the 1920s for displays in the World Exhibition, today houses the Museu Nacional d'Art de Catalunya. At the time of writing, the museum's Romanesque section had only just reopened after many years of reconstruction work. The section consists mainly of 11th and 12th century murals, woodcarvings and altar frontals (painted, low-relief wooden panels which were forerunners of the elaborate *retablos* that adorn later churches). These works, gathered from decaying country churches in northern Cataluña early in the 20th century, constitute probably Europe's greatest collection of Romanesque art. The museum's other main section, Gothic, was due to reopen in late 1996.

Thanks to its contacts with France, Cataluña was, in the 10th century, the first part of the Iberian Peninsula to experience a flowering of Romanesque art and architecture – a kind of attempt to recreate classical Roman styles but with influences from Byzantium via Lombardy in northern Italy. Some work also shows the colourful touch of Mozarabic Christians, who had lived under Muslim rule in the south of the peninsula but fled north in the 9th and 10th centuries.

As you enter the museum, it's well worth forking out 100 ptas on a guide booklet in your own language, as the museum's labelling is mostly in Catalan. Highlight works to look out for include the murals from the church of Sant Pere in La Seu d'Urgell, and the bright, rather modern-looking altar frontals from La Seu d'Urgell and Ix, in hall No 1; the murals from the church of Sant Joan de Boí, displayed in a space recreating the shape of the church they came from (hall No

BARCELONA

2); some fine crucifixion carvings and altar frontals in hall No 4; the murals from the church of Sant Climent de Taüll, which rank among the masterworks of all Romanesque art, in hall No 5; and a fascinatingly varied group of coloured Virgin Mary woodcarvings in hall No 8. The museum is open Tuesday to Saturday from 10 am to 7 pm (Thursday to 9 pm), Sunday and holidays from 10 am to 2.30 pm (closed Monday and on 1 January, 1 May and 25 December). Entry is 500 ptas (students 250 ptas).

Poble Espanyol This 'Spanish Village' in the north-west of Montjuïc – 10 minutes walk from Plaça d'Espanya or the Museu Nacional d'Art – is both a tacky tourist trap and an incredible scrapbook of Spanish architecture. Built for the Spanish crafts section of the 1929 exhibition, it's composed of plazas and streets lined with surprisingly good copies of characteristic buildings from all the country's regions.

You enter from Avinguda del Marquès de Comillas, beneath a towered medieval gate from Ávila. Inside, to the right, is an information office with free maps. Straight ahead from the gates is a Plaza Mayor, or town square, surrounded with mainly Castilian and Aragonese buildings. Elsewhere you'll find an Andalucían *barrio*, a Basque street, Galician and Catalan quarters and even – at the east end – a Dominican monastery. The buildings house dozens of moderate to expensive restaurants, cafés, bars, craft shops and workshops, and a few tacky tourist shops.

The Poble Espanyol is open from 9 am daily (Monday to 8 pm; Tuesday to Thursday to 2 am; Friday and Saturday to 4 am; Sunday to midnight). Entry is 950 ptas (450 ptas with a student card or for children aged seven to 14). After 9 pm on days other than Friday and Saturday, it's free; at night, the restaurants, bars and discos become a lively corner of Barcelona nightlife.

Museu Etnològic & Museu d'Arqueologia
Down the hill east of the Museu Nacional d'Art, these are worth a visit if their subjects interest you, though neither is very excitingly presented and most explanatory material is in Catalan.

The Museu Etnològic on Passeig de Santa Madrona has extensive displays covering a range of cultures from other continents, and puts on some interesting temporary exhibitions – open Tuesday to Sunday from 10 am to 2 pm (Tuesday and Thursday to 7 pm, except in summer) for 300 ptas.

The Museu d'Arqueologia, at the corner of Passeig de Santa Madrona and Passeig de l'Exposició, covers Cataluña and related cultures elsewhere in Spain. Items range from copies of pre-Neanderthal skulls to lovely Carthaginian necklaces and jewel-studded Visigothic crosses. There's good material on the Balearic Islands (rooms X to XIV) and Empúries (Emporion), the Greek and Roman city on the Costa Brava (rooms XV and XVI). Hours are Tuesday to Saturday from 9.30 am to 1.30 pm and 3.30 to 7 pm, Sunday from 9.30 am to 2 pm (200 ptas, free on Sunday).

Nice gardens climb the hill from here to the Fundació Joan Miró.

Anella Olímpica The 'Olympic Ring' is the group of sports installations where the main events of the 1992 Olympics were held, on the ridge above the Museu Nacional d'Art. Westernmost is the **Institut Nacional d'Educació Física de Catalunya** (INEFC), a kind of sports university, designed by the best-known contemporary Catalan architect, Ricardo Bofill. Past a circular arena, the Plaça de Europa, with the **Torre Calatrava** telephone tower behind it, is the **Piscines Bernat Picornell** building, where the swimming and diving events were held – now open to the public (see the Swimming & Gym section later in this chapter).

Next comes a pleasant little park, the Jardí d'Aclimatació, followed by the **Estadi Olímpic**, the main stadium of the games. It's open daily, free, from 10 am to 6 pm; enter at the north end. If you saw some of the Olympics on TV, the 65,000 capacity stadium may seem surprisingly small. So may the Olympic flame-holder rising at the north end, into which a long-range archer spectacularly deposited a flaming arrow in the opening ceremony. The stadium was opened in 1929 but completely restored for 1992. At the south end of the stadium (enter from outside) is the **Galería Olímpica**, which has an exhibition, including videos, on the 1992 games – open Tuesday to Saturday from 10 am to 1 pm and 4 to 6 pm (to 8 pm in summer), Sunday and holidays from 10 am to 2 pm (350 ptas).

West of the stadium is the 17,000 capacity **Palau Sant Jordi**, an indoor sports, concert and exhibition hall opened in 1990 and designed by the Japanese architect Arata Isozaki.

Cementiri del Sud-Ouest On the hill top south of the Anella Olímpica you can see the top of a huge cemetery, the Cementiri del Sud-Ouest or Cementiri Nou, which extends right down the south side of the hill. Opened in 1883, it's an odd combination of elaborate architect-designed tombs for rich families and small niches for the rest. It includes the graves of numerous Catalan artists and politicians.

Fundació Joan Miró Barcelona's gallery for the greatest Catalan artist of the 20th century, Joan Miró (1893-1983), is 400 metres east, downhill, from the Estadi Olímpic.

Miró gave 379 paintings, sculptures and textile works, and almost 5000 drawings, to the collection, only a selection of which is displayed at one time. The displays tend to concentrate on Miró's more settled last 20 years, but there are some important exceptions. The ground-floor Sala (room) Joan Prats shows the younger Miró moving away, under surrealist influence, from his *relatively* realistic early style, then starting to work toward his own recognisable style. This section also includes the 1939-44 Barcelona Series of tortured lithographs, Miró's comment on the Spanish Civil War.

The Sala Pilar Juncosa, upstairs, also displays works from the 1930s and 1940s. Another interesting section is devoted to the

***

Joan Miró

Miró was born and grew up in the Barri Gòtic, and lived at least one-third of his life in Barcelona. A shy man, he practised and studied art from childhood but had no natural ability for lifelike drawing, being more attracted to art lacking perspective. He was deeply drawn to the Catalan countryside and coast, and divided his time from 1919 to the early 1930s between winters in Paris and summers at his family's farmhouse at Mont-roig on the southern Catalan coast. In Paris he mixed with Picasso, Hemingway, Joyce and co and made his own mark, after several years of struggle, with an exhibition in 1925. In the early 1930s he went through an artistic crisis, temporarily rejecting painting in favour of collage and other techniques. He had gained wide international recognition by the mid-1930s.

By the 1940s Miró's characteristic style had emerged – arrangements of lines and symbolic figures in primary colours, with shapes reduced to their essence. Among his most important images are women, birds (the link between earth and the heavens), stars (the unattainable heavenly world, source of imagination), and a sort of net entrapping all these levels of the cosmos. In the 1960s and 70s Miró devoted more and more time to sculpture and textiles. From 1956 he lived in Mallorca, home of his wife Pilar Juncosa.

An anti-Francoist, Miró had a stormy relationship with Barcelona after the civil war, but in the early 1970s he set up the Fundació Joan Miró for display of his own work and promotion of avant-garde art. Miró was supported in the project by two close Barcelona friends, the art patron and hat-shop owner Joan Prats – to whom Miró had given many paintings in exchange for hats – and the architect Josep Lluís Sert. Sert designed the building, which is notable for its abundant natural light. ∎

***

'Miró Papers' which include many preparatory drawings and sketches, some on bits of newspaper or cigarette packets. 'A Joan Miró' is a collection of work by other contemporary artists, donated in tribute to Miró. There's also a compelling little group of photos of Miró at different stages of his life, by Man Ray and others. Out on the upstairs roof are a number of sculptures that Miró put together from things like dustbin lids and footballs.

The Fundació also has a contemporary art library open to the public, a good specialist art bookshop and a café, and stages exhibitions and recitals of contemporary art and music. It's open Tuesday to Saturday from 11 am to 7 pm (Thursday to 9.30 pm), and Sunday and holidays from 10.30 am to 2.30 pm. Entry is 600 ptas (300 ptas for students). All areas are wheelchair-accessible.

Parc d'Atraccions, Castell de Montjuïc & Around The south-east of Montjuïc is dominated by the big Parc d'Atraccions funfair and the Castell (castle) de Montjuïc on the hill top above it. Near the bottom of the Parc d'Atraccions are the Estació Parc Montjuïc funicular/telefèric station, the big open-air Piscina Municipal de Montjuïc (see Swimming & Gym), and the ornamental **Jardins de Mossén Cinto**.

The two main entrances to the Parc d'Atraccions are by the bottom (Parc Montjuïc) and middle (Mirador) telefèric stations. In summer – usually early June to mid-September – the park is open Tuesday to Friday from 5 to 10 pm, Saturday from 6 pm to 1 am, and Sunday from noon to 11 pm. The rest of the year it's only open on Saturday, Sunday and holidays from 11.30 am to 8 pm. Entry is 600 ptas, then you pay more for each ride. From the **Jardins del Mirador** opposite the Mirador telefèric station there are fine views over the port of Barcelona.

The Castell de Montjuïc dates in its present form from the late 17th and 18th centuries. For most of its existence it has been used to watch over the city and as a political prison and execution ground. Anarchists were executed here around the turn of the century, fascists during the civil war and Republicans after it – most notoriously Lluís Companys in 1940. It was finally given by the army to the city in 1960. The castle is surrounded by a network of ditches and walls, and today houses the **Museu Militar** with a section on Catalan military history, plus old weapons, uniforms, maps, castle models and so on (open daily except Monday from 9.30 am to 7.30 pm). The best thing is the excellent views from the castle area of the port and city below.

Towards the foot of this part of Montjuïc, above the thundering traffic of the main road to Tarragona, the **Jardins de Costa i Llobera** have a good collection of tropical and desert plants; they're open from 10 am to sunset.

Parc Güell
North of Gràcia and about four km from Plaça de Catalunya, Parc Güell is where Gaudí turned his hand to landscape gardening. It's a strange, enchanting place where Gaudí's passion for natural forms really took flight – to the point where the artificial almost seems more natural than the natural.

The simplest way to Parc Güell is to take the metro to Lesseps, then walk 10 to 15 minutes: follow the signs north-east along Travessera de Dalt then left up Carrer de Larrard, which brings you out almost at the park's two Hansel and Gretel-style gatehouses on Carrer d'Olot. The park is open daily from 10 am: May to August to 9 pm, April and September to 8 pm, March and October to 7 pm, other months to 6 pm (free). It's extremely popular, and its quaint nooks and crannies are irresistible to photographers – who on busy days have trouble keeping out of each other's pictures.

Parc Güell originated in 1900 when Count Eusebi Güell bought a tree-covered hillside (then outside Barcelona) and hired Gaudí to create a miniature garden-city of houses for the wealthy in landscaped grounds. The project was a commercial flop and was abandoned in 1914 – but not before Gaudí had created three km of roads and walks, steps and a plaza in his inimitable manner, plus the two gatehouses. In 1922 the city bought the estate for use as a public park.

The steps up from the entrance, guarded by a mosaic dragon/lizard, lead to the **Sala Hipóstila**, a forest of 84 stone columns (some of them leaning), intended as a market. To the left from here curves a gallery whose twisted stonework columns and roof give the effect of a cloister beneath tree roots – a motif repeated in several places in the park. On top of the Sala Hipóstila is a broad open space with the famous **Banc de Trenadis**, a lovely tiled bench, curving sinuously round its entire perimeter.

The spired house over to the right is the **Casa Museu Gaudí**, where Gaudí lived for most of his last 20 years (1906-26). It contains furniture by Gaudí and other memorabilia and is open Sunday to Friday from 10 am to 2 pm and 4 to 6 pm (250 ptas).

Much of the park is still wooded but full of pathways. The best views are from the cross-topped **Turo del Calvari** in the south-west corner.

Tibidabo

Tibidabo (542 metres) is the highest hill in the wooded range that forms the backdrop to Barcelona. It's a good place for a change of scene, some fresh air and, if the air's clear, views over the city and inland as far as Montserrat. The top of Tibidabo is often several degrees colder than the city. Tibidabo gets its name from the devil, who, trying to tempt Christ, took him to a high place and said, in fluent Latin: *'Haec omnia tibi dabo si cadens adoraberis me'* ('All this I will give you if you will fall down and worship me').

Getting There & Away This is half the fun if you go the traditional way. First get a suburban train to Avinguda de Tibidabo from Catalunya station on Plaça de Catalunya – a 10 minute ride for 125 ptas, every six to 15 minutes from 6 am to 11 pm (to 12.30 am on Friday, Saturday and holiday nights). Outside Avinguda de Tibidabo station, hop on the *tramvia blau*, Barcelona's last surviving tram line, which runs up between fancy turn-of-the-century mansions to Plaça del Doctor Andreu for 175 ptas or 300 ptas return. The tram runs daily in summer, and on Saturday, Sunday and holidays the rest of the year, every 15 or 30 minutes from 9 am to 9.30 pm. On other days a bus serves the route at the same times. From Plaça del Doctor Andreu the Tibidabo funicular railway climbs through the woods to Plaça de Tibidabo at the top of the hill for 300 ptas (400 ptas return), every 15 to 30 minutes

from 7.15 am to 9.45 pm, daily. If you're feeling active, you can walk up or down through the woods instead.

The cheaper alternative is bus No T2, the 'Tibibús', from Plaça de Catalunya to Plaça de Tibidabo (225 ptas). This runs on Saturday, Sunday and holidays year round, every 30 minutes from 11.30 am. From late June to early September it runs Monday to Friday too, every hour from 11.30 am. The last bus down leaves Tibidabo 30 minutes after the Parc d'Atraccions closes.

Temple del Sagrat Cor The Church of the Sacred Heart, looming above the top funicular station, is meant to be Barcelona's answer to Paris' Sacré Coeur. It's certainly equally visible, and even more vilified by aesthetes. It's actually two churches, one on top of the other. The top one is surmounted by a giant Christ and has a lift to the roof (100 ptas).

Parc d'Atraccions The reason most Barcelonese come up to Tibidabo is for some thrills in this funfair, which is also close to the top funicular station. Entry is around 2000 ptas with access to most rides, or you can pay 500 ptas to enter, then pay for individual rides. For a further 600 ptas you can enjoy seven minutes in the Hotel Krueger, an *hospedaje* of horrors inhabited by actors playing out their Dracula, Hannibal Lecter and other fantasies. The funfair's opening times change with the season, so check with a tourist office: in summer it's usually open daily until late at night; in winter it may open on Saturday, Sunday and holidays only, from about noon to 7 pm.

Torre de Collserola From the top of the funicular it's a few minutes walk west to the 288 metre Torre de Collserola telecommunications tower, built in 1990-92. The external glass lift to the visitors' observation area, 115 metres up, is as hair-raising as anything at the Parc d'Atraccions. It operates Monday to Friday from 11 am to 2.30 pm and 4 to 6 pm; Saturday, Sunday and holidays from 11 am to 7 pm (500 ptas). On a clear day, they say, you can see 70 km.

BARCELONA

Camp Nou

Hard on the heels of the Museu Picasso among Barcelona's most visited museums comes the Museu del Futbol Club Barcelona at the club's giant Camp Nou stadium, 3.5 km west of Plaça de Catalunya (metro: Collblanc). Barça, as it's known, is one of Europe's top clubs, having carried off the Spanish championship a couple of dozen times and the European Cup more than once. Barça has also been described as Cataluña's unarmed army: the club was banned for a while in the 1920s because the Spanish government feared its potential for focusing Catalan nationalism, and today its annual matches with Real Madrid act as a modern safety-valve for the age-old rivalry between Cataluña and Castilla. The many world greats who have worn Barça's blue and red stripes include Johann Cruyff and Diego Maradona. Cruyff was also the club's coach for several years until he was sacked in 1996 when the team 'only' finished third in the league and lost the Spanish cup final and a European semifinal.

Camp Nou, built in the 1950s and enlarged for the 1982 World Cup, is one of the world's biggest stadiums, holding 120,000 people, and the club has a world record membership of over 100,000. Soccer fans who can't get to a game (see Entertainment) should find the museum – on the Carrer d'Aristides Maillol side of the stadium – worthwhile. The best bits are the photo section, the goal videos, and the visit to the directors' box overlooking the pitch. It's open Monday to Saturday (Tuesday to Saturday from October to March) from 10 am to 1 pm and 3 to 6.30 pm (400 ptas).

Pedralbes

This is a wealthy residential area north of Camp Nou.

Palau Reial Right by Palau Reial metro station, across Avinguda Diagonal from the main campus of the Universitat de Barcelona, is the entrance to the **Jardins del Palau Reial**, a verdant park open daily. In the park is the Palau Reial de Pedralbes, an early 20th century building which has served variously as a residence for Gaudí's patron Eusebi Güell, king Alfonso XIII, the president of Cataluña and General Franco. Today it houses the **Museu de Ceràmica**, with a good collection of Spanish ceramics from the 13th to 19th centuries including work by Picasso and Miró, and the **Museu de les Arts Decoratives**. Both museums are open Tuesday to Sunday from 10 am to 3 pm (500 ptas for both).

Over by Avinguda de Pedralbes are the Gaudí-designed stables and porter's lodge for the **Finca Güell**, as the Güell estate here was called. They were done in the mid-1880s, when Gaudí was strongly impressed by Islamic architecture. They're not open to the public but you can admire Gaudí's weird wrought-iron dragon gate.

Museu-Monestir de Pedralbes This lovely old convent building, now a museum of monastic life also housing part of the famous Thyssen-Bornemisza art collection, stands at the top of Avinguda de Pedralbes, 700 metres from Finca Güell. Bus Nos 63 and 114 run occasionally along Avinguda de Pedralbes.

The convent, founded in 1326, still houses a community of nuns who inhabit separate closed quarters. The museum entrance is on Plaça del Monestir, a lovely quiet corner of Barcelona; opening hours are Tuesday to Friday and Sunday from 10 am to 2 pm, Saturday from 10 am to 5 pm (500 ptas).

The architectural highlight is the large, elegant, three storey cloister, a jewel of Catalan Gothic architecture built in the early 14th century. Off this is the Capella de Sant Miquel with fine 14th century murals, plus a restored refectory, a kitchen and a reconstruction of the old infirmary – all giving a good idea of old convent life.

The Col.lecció Thyssen-Bornemisza, also here, is part of a fabulous art collection acquired by Spain in 1993. Most of the collection has gone to the Museo Thyssen-Bornemisza in Madrid; what's here is mainly religious work by European masters including Titian, Rubens and Velázquez.

Top: The Monestir de Montserrat, one of Cataluña's most important shrines
Bottom: Costa Brava blue, Tossa de Mar, Cataluña

DAMIEN SIMONIS

View over the valley of the Río Nansa from east of Carmona, Cantabria

Swimming & Gym

The Olympic pool on Montjuïc, the Piscines Bernat Picornell, is open to the public daily from 7.30 am, till 10 pm Monday to Friday, 9 pm Saturday, and 2.30 pm Sunday. Entry is 1000 ptas and includes use of the good gym inside. To swim, you must rent a cap if you don't have one. The large open-air Piscina Municipal de Montjuïc is open from about early June to early September – from 11 am to 6 pm daily, for 550 ptas (400 ptas for under-14s and over-65s).

Language Courses

Some of the best-value Spanish courses are offered by the Universitat de Barcelona, which runs one-month intensive courses (80 hours tuition, 40,000 ptas) about four times a year. Longer Spanish courses, and courses in Catalan, are also available. For more information you can ask at the university's Informació office at Gran via de les Corts Catalanes 585 (metro: Universitat), open Monday to Friday from 9 am to 1 pm and 4 to 8 pm, or (for Spanish) its Instituto de Estudios Hispánicos (☎ 318 42 66 ext 2084; fax 302 59 47), or (for Catalan) its Servei de Llengua Catalana – both in the same building as Informació.

The university-run Escola Oficial d'Idiomes de Barcelona (☎ 329 24 58; fax 441 48 33) at Avinguda de les Drassanes s/n (metro: Drassanes) is another place offering economical 80-hour summer Spanish courses, as well as longer part-time courses in Spanish and Catalan.

The tourist office at Gran via de les Corts Catalanes 658, the CIAJ youth information service at Carrer de Ferran 32 in the Barri Gòtic (open Monday to Friday from 10 am to 2 pm and 4 to 8 pm), and the British Council at Carrer d'Amigó 83 have further information on courses. There are also notice boards with ads for courses and private tuition at the above-mentioned university building, Come In bookshop at Carrer de Provença 203, and the British Council. Also advertised at Come In are some jobs for English teachers.

Organised Tours

The Bus Turístic (see the Getting Around section later in this chapter) is better value than conventional tours for getting around the sights, but if you want a guided trip, Julià Tours (☎ 317 64 54) at Ronda de la Universitat 5 (metro: Universitat) and Pullmantur (☎ 318 02 41) at Gran via de les Corts Catalanes 635 (metro: Girona) both do daily city tours by coach, plus out-of-town trips to Montserrat, Vilafranca del Penedès, the Costa Brava and Andorra. Their city tours are about 4000 ptas for a half-day, 10,000 ptas a full day.

Special Events

Barcelona's main festivals include:

24 April
: *Dia de Sant Jordi* – the day of Cataluña's patron saint and also the Day of the Book – men give women a rose, women give men a book; publishers launch new titles, La Rambla and Plaça de Sant Jaume (where the Generalitat building is open to the public) are filled with book and flower stalls

23 June
: *Verbena de Sant Joan* – midsummer celebrations with bonfires, even in the squares of l'Eixample, and fireworks (a big display on Montjuïc)

28 June
: *Dia per l'Alliberament Lesbià i Gai* – gay and lesbian festival and parade

Late June to August
: *Grec arts festival* – music, dance, theatre at many locations

Around 15 August
: *Festa Major de Gràcia* – big local festival in Gràcia; decorated streets, dancing, music

11 September
: *La Diada* – Cataluña's national day marking the fall of Barcelona in 1714 – a holiday in Barcelona

Around 24 September
: *Festes de la Mercè* – the city's major festival; several days of merrymaking including concerts, dancing, a swimming race across the harbour, *castellers* (human castle builders), a firework display synchronised with the Montjuïc fountains, dances of giants on the Saturday, and *correfocs* – a parade of firework-spitting dragons and devils from all over Cataluña – on the Sunday

Late October to late November
: *Festival Internacional de Jazz de Barcelona* – jazz and blues around the city

You can check at tourist offices or the ajuntament information office in the Palau de la Virreina, La Rambla 99, for more details of these festivals and numerous others.

Places to Stay – bottom end

Camping The nearest camp site is the big *Cala Gogo* (☎ & fax 379 46 00), nine km south-west of the centre at Carretera de la Platja s/n, El Prat de Llobregat, near the airport. It's open from about mid-March to mid-October and charges 1800 ptas per site plus 560 ptas per person. You can get there by bus No 65 from Plaça d'Espanya, or by suburban train from Plaça de Catalunya to El Prat, then a 'Prat Playa' bus.

There are some better – but still vast – sites a few km further out to the south-west on the coastal C-246 road, the Autovía de Castelldefels (*not* the A-16 autopista heading for Sitges, and *not* the C-245 through central Viladecans and Gavà). All are reachable by bus No L95 from the corner of Ronda de la Universitat and Rambla de Catalunya. They include (with prices for a car, a tent and two adults):

El Toro Bravo (☎ & fax 637 34 62), Carretera C-246, Km 11, Viladecans; open all year; 2500 ptas
Filipinas (☎ & fax 658 28 95), Carretera C-246, Km 12, Viladecans; open all year; 2500 ptas
La Ballena Alegre (☎ & fax 658 05 04), Carretera C-246, Km 12.5, Viladecans; open Easter to end September; 3500 ptas
La Tortuga Ligera (☎ 633 06 42), Avenida Europa 69, Gavà; open all year except December; 2500 ptas
Albatros (☎ 633 06 95), Carretera C-246, Km 15, Gavà; open May to September; 2900 ptas

Eleven km north-east of the city there's *Camping Masnou* (☎ 555 15 03), open all year at Carretera N-II, Km 639.8, El Masnou. It's 200 metres from El Masnou train station (reached by suburban trains from Catalunya station on Plaça de Catalunya) and charges 2370 ptas for a car, tent and two adults.

Youth & Backpacker Hostels
Barcelona has four HI hostels and two non-HI hostels. All require you to rent sheets – 150 to 350

ptas for your stay – if you don't have a sleeping bag or sheets, and some lock their gates in the early hours so aren't suitable if you plan to party on very late in the city. Except at the Kabul, which doesn't take bookings, it's very advisable to call ahead in summer.

The non-HI *Youth Hostel Kabul* (☎ 318 51 90; fax 301 40 34) is at Plaça Reial 17 in the Barri Gòtic. It's a very rough-and-ready place but does have, as its leaflets say, a 'great party atmosphere' and no curfew. If sleep is your priority, though, you're better off somewhere else. The price is 1300 ptas, plus 1000 ptas key deposit. Security is not great but there are safes available for valuables. There's room for about 150 people in bare and basic bunk rooms holding up to 10 each. There's a small restaurant, and washing machines (500 ptas to wash and dry a load). In July and August you should be there by 10 am to get a place.

The biggest and most comfortable hostel is the 180 place *Alberg Mare de Déu de Montserrat* (☎ 210 51 51; fax 210 07 98), four km north of the centre at Passeig Mare de Déu del Coll 41-51. It's a 10 minute walk from Vallcarca metro or a 20 minute ride from Plaça de Catalunya on bus No 28, which stops almost outside the gate (the last bus leaves Plaça de Catalunya at 1.30 am). The main building is a former private mansion with a wonderful mudéjar-style lobby. Most rooms sleep six. A hostel card is needed: if you're under 26 or have an ISIC or FIYTO card, B&B is 1500 ptas; otherwise it's 2075 ptas. There's a laundry (500 ptas to wash and dry), but no cooking facilities. The gate is open from 7 am to midnight and is opened again for one minute at 1, 2 and 3 am. This is one of the few Spanish hostels in HI's International Booking Network (IBN), which enables you to book through about 200 other HI hostels and booking centres around the world. You can also book through the central booking service of Cataluña's official youth hostels organisation, the Xarxa d'Albergs de Joventut (☎ 483 83 63; fax 483 83 50). (Note: the other Barcelona hostels, even the HI ones, are not in the Xarxa.)

Alberg Juvenil Palau (☎ 412 50 80) at Carrer del Palau 6 in the Barri Gòtic (metro: Liceu) has a friendly atmosphere and just 40 places in separate-sex bunk rooms. Cost is 1200 ptas, including breakfast. It's non-HI, so it doesn't matter whether you have a hostel card. There's a kitchen and a good common room-cum-eating room.

Hostal de Joves (☎ 300 31 04) at Passeig de Pujades 29 faces the north end of Parc de la Ciutadella, a few minutes walk from the Estació de França and Arc de Triomf metro station. It has 68 bunk places in small dorms, and a kitchen with a sociable dining area. A hostel card is only needed during the six peak summer weeks. The price – 1300 ptas including breakfast – is the same for all. The hostel closes at 2 am on Friday and Saturday nights, 1 am other nights.

Alberg Pere Tarrès (☎ 410 23 09; fax 419 62 68) at Carrer de Numància 149, one km north of Estació Sants and 600 metres from Les Corts and Maria Cristina metro stations, has 90 places in bare dorms with four to eight bunks. B&B is 1300 ptas for under-26s, 1550 ptas for others; add 250 ptas if you don't have a hostel card. The building is basic and functional but there's a guest kitchen, open from 4 to 10.30 pm, a washing machine and a courtyard. The gates are shut from 10 am to 4 pm and from 11.30 pm to 8.30 am (they're opened briefly to let guests in at 2 am).

The small *Alberg Studio* (☎ 205 09 61; fax 205 09 00) at Carrer de la Duquessa d'Orleans 58, four km north-west of Plaça de Catalunya, is open only from 1 July to 30 September, and has about 40 places. It stays open 24 hours and charges 1300 ptas. Bus No 66 from Plaça de Catalunya stops nearby, and suburban trains run to Reina Elisenda station, 200 metres away, from Catalunya station.

Hostales, Pensiones & Hotels Finding a room should be easy from mid-September to early July. In the busier periods it's worth ringing ahead to book at the smaller places. Many of these places are constantly adjusting their prices according to demand. Some raise the prices given in what follows by 100

to 500 ptas in summer – which means from some time in April, May or June to some time in September. In winter you may pay less. Some charge 100 to 350 ptas extra for a shower if you don't have a room with its own. Many places have three or four-bed rooms which are little dearer than a double.

Bathrooms in these places are shared unless it's stated otherwise.

La Rambla Little *Pensión Noya* (☎ 301 48 31) at Rambla de Canaletes 133 (the top of La Rambla, above Restaurante Nuria) has 15 smallish but clean rooms at 1500/2800 to 1600/3000 ptas for singles/doubles. Front rooms overlooking La Rambla can be noisy (metro: Catalunya).

Down near the bottom of La Rambla at No 4, the friendly *Hostal Marítima* (☎ 302 31 52) is a time-honoured backpackers' lodging with a dozen worn but adequate singles/doubles/triples/quads at 1500/2500/3600/4800 ptas, and doubles with shower cubicle for 3500 ptas. There's a washing machine (800 ptas a load). The entrance is on Passatge de la Banca leading to the Museo de la Cera (metro: Drassanes).

Barri Gòtic This area has many of the better bottom-end places and is atmospheric and central. Places are covered in approximate north-to-south order. The first few are not strictly speaking in the Barri Gòtic but are within a couple of minutes walk of it.

Pensión Estal (☎ 302 26 18) at Carrer de Santa Anna 27 is a friendly place on a quiet street with 12 clean, good-sized rooms, which cost 2000/3000 ptas, or 4000 ptas for doubles with private bath (metro: Catalunya).

Hostal Lausanne (☎ 302 11 39) at Avinguda del Portal de l'Àngel 24 is a friendly, helpful place with good security. It takes about 25 people in good, very clean rooms at 2000/3200 ptas, or around 4000 ptas for doubles with private bath. There's a TV lounge and an open-air rear terrace (metro: Catalunya).

Residencia Victoria (☎ 318 07 60, 317 45 97) at Carrer de Comtal 9 has decent rooms for 2000/3000 ptas plus a guest kitchen, washing machine, sitting room with TV, and outdoor terrace. It's run by a friendly couple and used by some foreigners and Spaniards studying in Barcelona; monthly rates are 45,000/60,000 ptas (metro: Urquinaona).

Hostal Fontanella (☎ & fax 317 59 43) at Via Laietana 71 is a friendly, immaculately cared-for little place, with just 10 rooms costing 2700/4200 ptas, 3500/5900 ptas with bathroom, or 4800 ptas for doubles with shower (metro: Urquinaona).

Pensión-Hostal Fina (☎ 317 97 87) at Carrer de la Portaferrissa 11 – another quiet street – has 28 plain, clean rooms for 2200/3300 ptas, or 4300 ptas for a double with private bath. At off-peak periods they'll often cut these rates by 500 ptas if you stay four days, which is good value (metro: Catalunya or Liceu).

Hostal-Residencia Rembrandt (☎ & fax 318 10 11) at Carrer de la Portaferrissa 23 has good rooms at 2500/3600 ptas, or 3000/4500 ptas with shower and toilet. Breakfast is available (metro: Catalunya or Liceu).

Hostal Paris (☎ & fax 301 37 85) at Carrer del Cardenal Casañas 4 has 42 mostly large rooms for 2000/3300 ptas, or 3000/4000 ptas with private bathroom. Prices can go down a couple of hundred ptas at quiet times. There's a TV room (metro: Liceu).

Hostal Galerias Maldà (☎ 317 30 02), upstairs in the arcade by Carrer del Pi 5, is a rambling family house with 24 rooms, some of them really big. It's one of the cheapest places in town, at 1000/2000 ptas, with no charge for showers. The few singles are usually full, however. The rooms and communal areas are clean but the shared bathrooms not always so (metro: Liceu).

Pensión Dalí (☎ & fax 318 55 80) at Carrer de la Boqueria 12 has 60 ordinary but adequate rooms, all with phone, for 1700/2900 ptas, or 2700/3900 ptas with private bath. There are large sitting and TV rooms (metro: Liceu).

Pensión Europa (☎ 318 76 20) at Carrer de la Boqueria 18 has around 40 plain, reasonably sized rooms at 1600/3200 ptas, 2100/3400 ptas with private shower, or 2600/3700 ptas with bathroom. Some of the bathrooms are nicely modernised. There's a big sitting room with TV, too (metro: Liceu).

Pensión Bienestar (☎ 318 72 83) at Carrer d'En Quintana 3 has around 30 clean, ordinary rooms, at 1300/2400 or 1500/2600 ptas depending on size (metro: Liceu).

Pensión Fernando (☎ 301 79 93) at Carrer de la Volta del Remei 4, between Carrer de la Boqueria and Carrer de Ferran, has around 100 plain but quite adequate rooms, mostly doubles and all with shared bathrooms, at 1500 ptas per person. Some rooms are to be converted to dormitories which may be a bit cheaper. The entrance may move round the corner on to Carrer de Ferran (metro: Liceu).

Hostal Layetana (☎ 319 20 12) at Plaça de Berenguer Gran 2 is friendly and very well kept, with 20 good-sized rooms at 2200/3500 ptas, or 4900 ptas for doubles with bathroom (metro: Jaume I).

Pensió Colom 3 (☎ 318 06 31) at Carrer de Colom 3 on Plaça Reial is rather dreary and very basic, with dormitory beds for 1200 ptas and rooms for 2300/3600 ptas, or 2600/4200 ptas with bath (metro: Liceu).

Hotel Roma Reial (☎ 302 03 66, 302 04 16; fax 301 18 39) at Plaça Reial 11 has 105 decent rooms, all with private bath, at 3200/5300 ptas, but the lobby lounge is the only public space.

Hostal Levante (☎ 317 95 65) at Baixada de Sant Miquel 2 is a large, very clean hostal, popular among travellers, charging up to 2500/4000 ptas, or 5000 ptas for doubles with private bath (metro: Liceu).

The ever-popular *Casa Huéspedes Mari-Luz* (☎ 317 34 63) at Carrer del Palau 4 has friendly management, a sociable atmosphere, and room for 52 people in doubles and bunk dorms holding up to six people. All cost 1200 to 1300 ptas per person. You can use a small kitchen at certain times. Go up three flights of stairs on the right from the courtyard (metro: Liceu or Jaume I).

Pensión Avinyó (☎ 318 79 45; fax 315 26 52) at Carrer d'Avinyó 42 is better than it looks from outside – a friendly place with 38 rooms that are mostly good-sized if a little faded. Singles/doubles go for 1500/2000 ptas, doubles with shower for 2500 ptas, doubles with bathroom for 2800 ptas (metro: Liceu or Jaume I).

El Raval *Hotel Peninsular* (☎ & fax 302 31 38) at Carrer de Sant Pau 34 is a bit of an oasis in this rather dark area on the fringe of the Barri Xinès. Once part of a convent, it has a plant-draped atrium extending the full height and most of the length of the hotel. The 80 rooms are clean, fairly spacious, and all with private bathroom, though furniture and fittings are a bit aged in some. They cost 3620/5565 ptas, with continental breakfast included (metro: Liceu).

Hostal Residencia Opera (☎ 318 82 01) at Carrer de Sant Pau 20 is a bit tatty but with around 80 rooms it's worth trying if other places are full. Rooms are 1700/2600 ptas, or 2500/3000 ptas with private bath (metro: Liceu).

Hotel Segura (☎ 302 51 74; fax 318 36 64) at Carrer de Junta de Comerç 11 is another big hostal, with 50 basic but fairly well kept rooms costing 1500/2500 ptas (2000/3000 ptas with shower). There's a TV room (metro: Liceu).

La Ribera *Pensión Lourdes* (☎ 319 33 72) at Carrer de la Princesa 14 has about 20 clean rooms for 1500/2400 ptas. A shower is 300 ptas (metro: Jaume I).

Hostal Nuevo Colón (☎ 319 50 77), opposite Estació de França at Avinguda del Marquès de l'Argentera 19 has nice, recently decorated rooms for 2000/3200 ptas, or 3200/4500 ptas with private bath (metro: Barceloneta).

L'Eixample There are only a few cheapies in this up-market part of town north of Plaça de Catalunya.

Hostal Goya (☎ 302 25 65) at Carrer de Pau Claris 74 has just 12 nice, good-sized rooms at 2200/3000 ptas or 2700/3800 ptas with private shower, 2900/4000 ptas with bath. There's a good sitting/TV room (metro: Urquinaona).

Hostal Palacios (☎ 301 37 92) at Gran via de les Corts Catalanes 629 bis, almost opposite the main tourist office, has 28 decent rooms costing 2700/3900 ptas, 3700/4800 ptas with shower, or 4300/5000 ptas with bath, all plus IVA. The public areas, including a sitting room, are good and bright, and the bathrooms are attractively tiled (metro: Catalunya or Urquinaona).

Hostal Oliva (☎ 488 01 62, 488 17 89) on the 4th floor at Passeig de Gràcia 32 is a friendly little place, very clean and well kept. Some of the 14 or so varied rooms are refurbished and modern, others are older but still fine. Singles/doubles are 3000/5000 ptas, doubles with private bath are 6000 ptas (metro: Passeig de Gràcia).

Near Estació Sants *Hostal Sofia* (☎ 419 50 40) at Avinguda de Roma 1-3 is just across the square in front of the station. The 12 very nice, sparkling clean rooms cost 3500/4500 ptas, or 5500 ptas for doubles with private bathroom (metro: Sants-Estació).

Hostal Sans (☎ 331 37 00, 331 37 04), a five minute walk south-west of the station at Carrer de Antoni de Capmany 82, is a modern place with rooms for 2100/3100 ptas, or 3100/4700 ptas with private bathroom. Use of communal showers is 350 ptas (metro: Plaça de Sants).

Places to Stay – middle
All rooms in this range have attached bathrooms.

La Rambla These places are in north-south order. The *Hotel Continental* (☎ 301 25 70; fax 302 73 60), at Rambla de Canaletes 138, has 35 pleasant, well-decorated rooms, all with cable TV, microwave, fridge, safe and fan. Prices – 6950/8650 ptas for standard singles/doubles, 9550/9900 ptas overlooking the Rambla, both plus IVA – include a good continental buffet breakfast and free coffee or tea at any time. There's a pleasant, small lounge (metro: Catalunya).

Hotel Lloret (☎ 317 33 66; fax 301 92 83) at Rambla de Canaletes 125 has 50 varied rooms; some are rather worn and not very big, though still adequate. All have air-con

BARCELONA

and TV. They cost from 3500/6000 to 4000/6300 ptas (500 ptas more from April to September). There's a breakfast room (continental buffet breakfast 350 ptas) and lounge areas (metro: Catalunya).

Hotel Internacional (☎ 302 25 66; fax 317 61 90) at La Rambla 78-80 on Pla de la Boqueria has 60 simple, clean rooms with TV at around 6000/7600 ptas plus IVA. There's a breakfast room (breakfast 475 ptas) and bar with a balcony over La Rambla. You can book by calling the free number ☎ 900-10 12 25 (metro: Liceu).

Hotel Oriente (☎ 302 25 58; fax 412 38 19) at La Rambla 47 is famous for its *modernista* design and has a fine sky-lit restaurant and other public rooms, but staff can be offhand. The 150 bedrooms are slightly past their prime but still comfortable, with tiled floors and bathrooms, safes and TV. Singles/doubles are 7150/9000 ptas plus IVA (metro: Liceu).

Hotel Cuatro Naciones (☎ 317 36 24; fax 302 69 85) at La Rambla 40 has about 40 adequate rooms, with TV, for 4280/6420 ptas. It was built in 1849 and was once – a long time ago – Barcelona's top hotel. Breakfast is 450 ptas (metro: Liceu).

Barri Gòtic The *Nouvel Hotel* (☎ 301 82 74; fax 301 83 70), at Carrer de Santa Anna 18 & 20, has some elegant *modernista* touches and good air-con rooms with satellite TV for 7600/12,100 ptas plus IVA. There are also some unrenovated 4th floor doubles for 7700 ptas plus IVA. Prices include breakfast (metro: Catalunya).

Hotel Jardi (☎ 301 59 00, 301 59 58; fax 318 36 64) at Plaça de Sant Josep Oriol 1 has 40 clean rooms, but they're plain, and some are small. Unrenovated rooms are 3800/5000 ptas, or 5500 ptas overlooking the street; renovated rooms, all overlooking the street, are 6000 ptas single or double. Continental breakfast is 650 ptas (metro: Liceu).

Hotel Suizo (☎ 315 41 11, 315 04 61; fax 310 40 81) at Plaça de l'Àngel 12 is recently modernised and has a restaurant and snack bar. Rooms – comfortable if unspectacular –

are about 9600/12,000 ptas plus IVA (metro Jaume I).

El Raval *Hotel Mesón Castilla* (☎ 318 21 82; fax 412 40 20) at Carrer de Valldonzella 5 has some lovely *modernista* touches – stained glass and murals in its public rooms. Gaudíesque window mouldings – and 60 good, quaintly decorated rooms for 7000/10,550 ptas plus IVA. There's easy parking too (metro: Universitat).

Hotel San Agustín (☎ 318 16 58, 318 16 62; fax 317 29 28) at Plaça de Sant Agustí 3 is a modern place on a quiet square, with rooms for 6300/8500 ptas plus IVA, including breakfast. All rooms have air-con and satellite TV (metro: Liceu).

Hotel España (☎ 318 17 58; fax 317 11 34) at Carrer de Sant Pau 9 & 11 is famous for its two marvellous dining rooms designed by the *modernista* architect Lluís Domènech i Montaner – one with big sea-life murals by Ramon Casas, the other with floral tiling and a wood-beamed roof. The 60-plus comfortable rooms are 5136/9801 ptas including breakfast (metro: Liceu).

L'Eixample A good choice for a bit of old-fashioned style is the *Hotel Gran Via* (☎ 318 19 00; fax 318 99 97) at Gran via de les Corts Catalanes 642, with 54 good-sized rooms at 7000/8000 ptas plus IVA (8000/10,000 ptas plus IVA in the high season) and a big, elegant lounge opening onto a good roof terrace. Breakfast is available for 600 ptas (metro: Catalunya).

Places to Stay – top end

You can get top-end quality at mid-range prices in Barcelona by taking advantage of some swingeing price cuts for double rooms – 50% or even more – at these hotels' off-peak times when business travellers are absent. Such offers come and go but at the time we researched this book, such price cuts were being offered from Friday to Sunday nights all year by the Le Meridien, Comtes de Barcelona, Avenida Palace, St Moritz, Regente and Majestic hotels. The last four named were doing the same over the Christmas and Semana Santa holiday periods, and for the whole of August and chunks of July and/or September.

La Rambla The top hotel on La Rambla is the elegant *Le Meridien* (☎ 318 62 00) at No 111. Its top-floor presidential suite (200,000 ptas a night) is where the likes of Michael Jackson, Madonna and Julio Iglesias stay. Normal singles/doubles are 21,000/29,000 ptas plus IVA (metro: Catalunya or Liceu).

Barri Gòtic *Hotel Colón* (☎ 301 14 04; fax 317 29 15) is a good choice for its location at Avinguda de la Catedral 7 facing the cathedral. The 150 comfortable and elegant rooms are 13,750/20,500 ptas plus IVA. There's a restaurant and piano bar (metro: Jaume I).

L'Eixample The 164 room *Hotel Ritz* (☎ 318 52 00; fax 318 01 48) at Gran via de les Corts Catalanes 668 is the top choice for old-fashioned elegance, luxury, individuality and first-class service. It has been going since 1919. Singles/doubles are 29,500/43,000 ptas or, with tiled step-down 'Roman baths', 41,500/52,000 ptas, all plus IVA. There are suites up to 200,000 ptas-plus (metro: Urquinaona).

A less expensive choice for old-fashioned elegance is the recently renovated *Hotel Avenida Palace* (☎ 301 96 00; fax 318 12 34) at Gran via de les Corts Catalanes 605. Standard singles/doubles are 15,400/22,700 ptas plus IVA (metro: Catalunya).

The *St Moritz Hotel* (☎ 412 15 00; fax 412 12 36), at Carrer de la Diputació 262 bis, is another up-market hotel with 92 rooms at 16,200/25,500 ptas plus IVA. It has a restaurant and a pleasant terrace bar (metro: Catalunya or Passeig de Gràcia).

The *Hotel Majestic* (☎ 488 17 17; fax 488 18 80) at Passeig de Gràcia 70 is a big, very comfortable place with a nice line in modern art on the walls and a rooftop swimming pool. The 300-plus rooms, all air-con with satellite TV, are 13,000/22,900 ptas plus IVA (metro: Passeig de Gràcia).

The modern-style *Hotel Regente* (☎ 487 59 89; fax 487 32 27), at Rambla de Catalunya 76, is being renovated, but gradually, so most of its 78 rooms, all with air-con and satellite TV, remain open. Singles/doubles are 12,500/19,200 ptas plus IVA. Both the renovated rooms and the older ones are nice; you get wood panelling and retiled bathrooms in the renovated ones. There's an open-air pool but the restaurant is closed during the renovations (metro: Passeig de Gràcia).

The *Comtes* (or *Condes*) *de Barcelona Hotel* (☎ 488 22 00; fax 488 06 14) at Passeig de Gràcia 73-75 is one of Barcelona's best hotels. It has two separate buildings facing each other across Carrer de Mallorca. The older one occupies the Casa Enric Batlló, built in the 1890s but now stylishly modernised. There are 183 air-conditioned, sound-proofed rooms with marble bathrooms and all the usual top-end touches. Singles/doubles are 23,000/29,000 ptas plus IVA (metro: Passeig de Gràcia).

Hotel Balmes (☎ 451 19 14; fax 451 00 49) at Carrer de Mallorca 216 is a good, 100 room modern hotel with white bricks much in evidence in the interior. Standard rooms – not huge but with air-con, nice tiled bathrooms and satellite TV – are 12,000/16,500 ptas plus IVA. There's garage parking, a coffee shop, a garden with bar and swimming pool, and a restaurant (metro: Passeig de Gràcia).

Port Olímpic Barcelona's most fashionable modern hotel is the *Hotel Arts Barcelona* (☎ 221 16 60; fax 221 10 70) at Carrer de la Marina 19-21 in one of the two sky-high towers that dominate the Port Olímpic. It has over 450 rooms and charges around 27,500 ptas plus IVA for a double (metro: Ciutadella).

Longer-Term Accommodation
The Universitat de Barcelona at Gran via de les Corts Catalanes 585 (metro: Universitat), the Viva youth and student travel agency at Carrer de Rocafort 116-122 (metro: Rocafort) and the British Council at Carrer d'Amigó 83 (near Muntaner suburban train

station) all have notice boards advertising flat shares and rooms to let.

Places to Eat

Barcelona is packed with good places to eat. Menus may be in Catalan or Spanish, or both; some places have foreign-language menus too. Specifically Catalan food tends, for some reason, to be a bit expensive in Barcelona, but you won't regret having at least one Catalan meal while you're here (see the boxed aside 'Catalan Cuisine' in the Cataluña chapter for a rundown on some typical dishes and words you'll encounter on Catalan menus).

Barcelona folk usually eat lunch between about 1 and 3 pm, and don't start a dinner out till 9 or 10 pm. Most restaurants stop serving at 11 pm to midnight. Many have a weekly closing day and some stay shut throughout August, when natives abandon the city in droves. Telephone numbers are given for places where it may be worth booking ahead.

Chains There are a few good local restaurant chains where you can get a quick, decent snack or meal with minimum effort.

Bocatta – hot and cold baguettes with a big range of fillings, mostly 300 to 400 ptas; at La Rambla 89; Carrer de Santa Anna 11, Plaça de Sant Jaume, and the corner of Carrer de Comtal and Carrer de N'Amargòs (all Barri Gòtic or near); Rambla de Catalunya between Carrer de Mallorca and Carrer de València (l'Eixample); most branches open daily from 8 am to midnight

Pans & Company – similar fare and prices to Bocatta; at La Rambla 123; Carrer de Ferran 14, and on Carrer dels Arcs off Plaça Nova (both Barri Gòtic); the Maremagnum building (Port Vell); Ronda de la Universitat 7, Passeig de Gràcia 39, Rambla de Catalunya 29 and Carrer de Provença 278 (all l'Eixample); most branches open Monday to Thursday from 9 am to 11 pm, Friday and Saturday from 9 am to midnight, Sunday from 10 am to 11 pm

Pastafiore – pizza and pasta: a half *(media)* pizza is 395 to 575 ptas but you'll need a whole *(entera)* one for 550 to 865 ptas if you're hungry; pasta is around 475 to 675 ptas but tends to be less appetising; at Rambla de Canaletes 125; Rambla de Catalunya 29 and Carrer de Provença 278 (all l'Eixample); Travessera de Gràcia 60 (Gràcia)

La Rambla *Restaurant Nuria* at Rambla de Canaletes 133, just down from Plaça de Catalunya, is a big, busy place doing pasta from 500 ptas, fish and meat courses from 700 ptas. There's a three course menú for 1100 ptas.

Viena at Rambla dels Estudis 115 is a popular café with stools round a central counter and good barretas (baguettes) for 300 to 500 ptas.

Cafè de l'Òpera at La Rambla 74, opposite the Liceu opera house, is La Rambla's most interesting café, with elegant 1920s décor. It gets very busy at night (see Bars), but is quieter for morning coffee and croissants. There are also bocadillos, from 350 ptas, and tapas.

Barri Gòtic This area is peppered with good eateries, some of them excellent value.

Restaurants These are described in approximate north-to-south order. *Santa Ana* at Carrer de Santa Anna 8 is a bright, friendly place with quick service. Pizzas and sizeable platos combinados are 700 to 900 ptas, baguettes 300 to 400 ptas, all plus IVA. It's open daily from 8 am to midnight.

Self-Naturista at Carrer de Santa Anna 13 is a self-service vegetarian restaurant with a four course lunch menú for 810 ptas which pulls in the crowds.

Els Quatre Gats (☎ 302 41 40) at Carrer de Montsió 3 bis is the famous turn-of-the-century artists' hang-out (see the boxed aside), now a fairly expensive restaurant. It was restored a few years ago to its original appearance, with reproductions of its old customers' portraits of each other (including one of Ramon Casas swinging on a chandelier). Starters/snacks such as esqueixada, or escalivada amb torrada, are close to 1000 ptas, and main fish and meat dishes 1100 to 2700 ptas – but you can stick to a drink if you just want to sample the atmosphere (open Monday to Saturday from morning to 2 am, plus Sunday evening only).

Cervecería Edelman at Avinguda del Portal de l'Àngel 6 is a bright, friendly bar-cum-restaurant with platos combinados from

✿ ✿ ✿ ✿ ✿ ✿ ✿ ✿ ✿ ✿ ✿ ✿ ✿

Cool Cats of the 1900s

Els Quatre Gats was opened in 1897 by four Barcelonese who had spent time in Paris artistic circles: the *modernista* artists Ramon Casas and Santiago Rusiñol, and their friends Miquel Utrillo and Pere Romeu who, among other things, were deeply interested in shadow puppetry. Romeu, the manager, was a colourful character equally devoted to cabaret and cycling. The name Els Quatre Gats is Catalan for 'the four cats', and alludes both to the café's four founders and to Le Chat Noir, an artistic café in Montmartre, Paris. Idiomatically, it means 'a handful of people, a minority' – no doubt how its avant-garde clientele saw themselves. Situated in the first Barcelona creation of the *modernista* architect Josep Puig i Cadafalch, Els Quatre Gats quickly became an influential meeting, drinking and cavorting place of young artists, writers, actors, musicians and their circles. It published its own magazine and staged exhibitions, recitals and, of course, shadow puppet shows. Picasso's first exhibition was here, in 1900, and included drawings of many of the customers. Els Quatre Gats closed in 1903. Later it was used as an art gallery, before its present incarnation as a restaurant. ∎

✿ ✿ ✿ ✿ ✿ ✿ ✿ ✿ ✿ ✿ ✿ ✿ ✿

around 500 ptas, and good, crisp filled baguettes called bocadillos en xapata. There's a good range of beers but they can be expensive.

Sandvitxeria Entrepaipa at Carrer del Cardenal Casañas 5 also does reasonably priced platos combinados – eg eggs, bacon, chips and tomato for 550 ptas.

Can Culleretes (☎ 317 30 22) at Carrer d'En Quintana 5 is Barcelona's oldest restaurant, founded in 1786. It's still going strong, with old-fashioned décor and good Catalan food. A three course menú including half a bottle of wine is 1600 or 2000 ptas. Opening times are 1.30 to 4 pm and 9 to 11 pm, closed Sunday night and Monday.

Les Quatre Barres (☎ 302 50 60) at Carrer d'En Quintana 6 serves up more excellent Catalan food – 3000 or 4000 ptas for a meal with drinks, open the same hours as Can Culleretes.

Mesón Jesús at Carrer dels Cecs de la Boqueria 4, between Plaça de Sant Josep Oriol and Carrer de la Boqueria, is a cosy little place with a rustic ambience, doing a good 1000 ptas three course lunch menú including a drink – open from 1 to 4 pm and 8 to 11 pm.

El Gran Café (☎ 318 79 86) at Carrer d'Avinyó 9 is classier, with *modernista* décor and good Catalan/French food. À-la-carte main dishes are 1200 to 3000 ptas, but there's an entire lunch menú for the same price. It's open daily except Sunday and holidays from 1 to 4 pm and 9 to 11.30 pm.

El Gallo Kiriko at Carrer d'Avinyó 19 is a friendly, inexpensive Pakistani restaurant popular with travellers. A good tandoori chicken with chips or salad, or couscous with chicken, beef or vegetables, is just 450 ptas. Curries with rice are 600 ptas. It's open daily from noon to 1 am.

Little *Bar-Restaurant Cervantes* at Carrer de Cervantes 7 does a good three course lunch menú with plenty of choice, plus a drink, for 900 ptas. The basic *Cal Kiko* at the corner of Carrer de Cervantes and Carrer del Palau does a four course menú for 725 ptas.

Les Quinze Nits (☎ 317 30 75) at Plaça Reial 6 is a stylish bistro-like restaurant on the borderline between smart and casual, with a long menu of good Catalan and Spanish dishes at reasonable prices. Three courses with wine and coffee typically come to about 2000 ptas. All this makes it highly popular and can mean long queues in summer and on Friday night, Saturday and Sunday all year. It's open Tuesday to Sunday from 1 to 3.45 pm and 8.30 to 11.45 pm.

Facing each other across Carrer del Vidre off the south end of Plaça Reial are two very cheap, busy little places: *Restaurante Senshe Tawakal*, which serves lentils and vegetables or chicken and chips for 450 ptas and couscous for 550 ptas, and *Restaurante Rincón de Ríos Baixas* with economical daily dishes such as paella for 500 ptas. Both stay open till 2 or 3 am – by which time people use them pretty much as bars.

La Fonda Escudellers (☎ 301 75 15) at the corner of Carrer dels Escudellers and Passatge dels Escudellers is run by the same people as Les Quinze Nits on Plaça Reial, and has very similar menu, prices, hours,

BARCELONA

ambience and standards – and is every bit as popular.

Bar Comercio, across Carrer dels Escudellers from La Fonda, is a much plainer affair but will do you a decent feed – salads 300 to 400 ptas, mussels 475 ptas, chicken or rabbit 500 to 550 ptas.

Los Caracoles (☎ 302 31 85), a block along at Carrer dels Escudellers 14, is one of Barcelona's best-known restaurants – though more so now among tourists than among the celebrities whose photos adorn it. It's still good and lively, and offers a big choice of seafood, fish, rice and meat; a typical full meal is 3000 or 4000 ptas, though you could get away with less. The snails after which the place is named are a starter for 975 ptas. Hours are 1 to 11 pm daily.

Pastry Shops & Coffee Bars There are tempting pastry and/or chocolate shops, often combined with coffee bars, all over the Barri Gòtic – some of them all too tempting if your budget is limited. There's a special concentration along Carrer and Baixada de la Llibreteria, north-east off Plaça de Sant Jaume – among the least resistible pastry/chocolate places are *Santa Clara* at Carrer de la Llibreteria 21 and *La Colmena* on the corner of Baixada de la Llibreteria and Plaça de l'Àngel. Three places with particularly good coffee in this area are the *Mesón del Café* at Carrer de la Llibreteria 16, the *Bon Mercat* on the corner of Baixada de la Llibreteria and Carrer de la Freneria, and *Il Caffe di Roma* on Plaça de l'Àngel.

Up at Plaça de Sant Josep Oriol 2, *Xocolateria La Xicra* is a cosy little café with great cakes, various coffees, teas and hot chocolate (xocolata, 210 ptas) so thick that it's listed under postres (desserts) on the menu. Two other good places nearby to sit down for a coffee and croissant or pastry are *Granja La Pallaresa* at Carrer de Petritxol 11 and *Croissanterie del Pi* at Carrer del Pi 14.

Tapas Bars Down on Carrer de la Mercè and nearby streets near the bottom end of the Barri Gòtic is a cluster of old-fashioned tapas

bars which can get very lively, especially on weekend evenings. *Bar Celta* at Carrer de la Mercè 16 is a good one, specialising in seafood. These places are fun but not cheap: if you don't establish in advance just what your order will cost – not always easy with waiters giving every appearance of being rushed off their feet – you may be in for a shock. Try to specify, among other things, whether you want a tapa (saucerful) or a ración (plateful). At Bar Celta, tapas of sepia (cuttlefish) and patatas bravas, with a beer, come to around 800 ptas.

Takeaway Felafel & Kebabs *Disco-Bar Real* on the corner of Plaça Reial and Carrer de Colom has a takeaway counter doing good felafel for 250 ptas. *Buen Bocado* at Carrer dels Escudellers 31 has felafel for 300 ptas, shwarma kebab for 400 ptas. It's open evenings only, till 2 am. Another, nameless, *felafel & kebab takeaway* on Escudellers, just east of Carrer dels Obradors, charges 100 ptas less for each.

El Raval These restaurants are listed in north-south order.

One of Barcelona's best-value meals is the 695 ptas four course menú at the *Restaurante Riera*, Carrer de Joaquín Costa 30. Servings are generous and the food is good, despite the workaday surroundings. There's a choice of five or six items for each course, with a good paella nearly always among them. You can wash it down with a litre of wine for just 235 ptas. The Riera is open from 1 to 4 pm and 8.30 to 11 pm (closed Friday night and Saturday) and the menú is served at night too.

Xaica Pizzeria at Carrer de Jovellanos 7 does good-sized one person pizzas for 485 to 825 ptas, platos combinados for 600 to 700 ptas, and a three course menú for 835 ptas.

Restaurant Tallers (☎ 318 96 42) at Carrer dels Tallers 6 is a clean, modest place with an adequate four course lunch menú for 850 ptas – open from 1 to 4 pm and 8 to 10 pm.

Bar Restaurante Romesco on Carrer de l'Arc de Sant Agustí, just off Carrer de San Pau, is a no-frills, almost hole-in-the-wall joint serving up good portions of home-style cooking at great prices – such as chicken and chips for 375 ptas, or squid, cuttlefish or baby octopus dishes for 475 to 550 ptas.

Restaurante Els Tres Bots at Carrer de Sant Pau 42 is grungy but cheap, with a menú for 750 ptas, or single dishes like chicken and chips for 350 ptas, pork chop and chips for 450 ptas, fish from 350 ptas. Along the same street at No 31, *Restaurante Pollo Rico* has a downstairs bar where you can get a quarter chicken, an omelette or a veal steak, with chips, bread and wine, for 300 to 400 ptas; and a more salubrious but only slightly more expensive upstairs restaurant. There's fish too. *Kashmir Restaurant Tandoori* at No 39 does tasty curries and biryanis from around 750 ptas.

Restaurant Ca L'Isidre (or *Can Isidre* or *Casa Isidro*, ☎ 441 11 39) at Carrer de les Flors 12, off the western end of Carrer de Sant Pau, is a small, old-fashioned and classy place with a long menu of fresh Catalan and Spanish food. A typical three course meal with wine is around 6000 or 7000 ptas. You might, for example, start with grilled rovellon mushrooms with botifarra sausage (rovellones con butifarra a la brasa), followed up by prawns, onion and tomato in white wine (cigalitas con cebolla y tomate al vino blanco). Booking is advisable. It's open daily – except Sunday, holidays and the whole of August – from 1.30 to 4 pm and 9 to 11.30 pm.

Poble Sec *Elche Restaurant* (☎ 441 30 89) at Carrer de Vila i Vilà 71 does some of Barcelona's best paella. Several varieties are on offer, mostly around 1400 to 1700 ptas per person (minimum two people). Elche is open daily (except Sunday night) from 1 to 4 pm and 8.30 to 11.30 pm.

La Ribera *Comme-Bio* (signs also say *La Botiga*) at Via Laietana 28 is a modern, chemical-additive-free vegetarian restaurant and wholefood shop, with a good four course 1100 ptas daily menú which includes a help-yourself salad bar. Many à-la-carte dishes, including pizzas and spinach-and-Roquefort

crêpes, are around 900 ptas, or there are tofu and seitán (a vegetable protein) dishes for 1200 to 1450 ptas. It's open daily from 8 am to 11.30 pm.

The small, garish *Bar-Restaurant Nervion* at Carrer del Princesa 2 does a three course menú with wine for 875 ptas, plus pizzas and good-value platos combinados from around 500 ptas. *Restaurant El Cid* at Carrer de la Princesa 11 has a slightly cheaper menú and slightly dearer platos combinados.

Lluna Plena at Carrer de Montcada 2 (just north of Carrer de la Princesa) is a brick-walled, cellar-style place with good Catalan and Spanish food, open Tuesday to Saturday. It's packed for its four course 1070 ptas lunch menú, and often in the evenings too. À la carte you could go for escalivada or esquei-xada (around 450 ptas), followed by a quarter-chicken (295 ptas) or rabbit (500 ptas) a la brasa.

Pla de la Garsa (☎ 315 24 13), nearby at Carrer dels Assaonadors 13, is an old-style Catalan restaurant with attractive tiles, lamps and paintings. The 1150 ptas menú gives you three courses plus good wine and cheese. Pâtés are a speciality too. It's open daily from 1 to 4 pm and 8 pm to 2 am.

For a bit of a splurge on superb, mainly Catalan and French cooking, you can't do much better than *Senyor Parellada* (☎ 310 50 94), an informally chic restaurant at Carrer de l'Argenteria 37. You should book for dinner. A typical three course meal with wine is around 3500 ptas. You might start with mushroom and fish crêpes or monkfish soup, followed by duck breast with cherry vinegar, or sole with almonds, hazelnuts and pine nuts, and round it off with a crema Catalana or mel i mató. (If your mouth isn't watering by now, give the place a miss.) The long menu is in seven languages, but it's also worth asking the waiter if they have any seasonal specialities such as calçots amb Romesco or rovellon mushrooms. It's open daily, except Sunday and holidays, from 1 to 3.30 pm and 9 to 11.30 pm.

Granja Xador at Carrer de l'Argenteria 61-3, round the corner from Santa Maria del Mar, is a bright, modern place with a big choice of platos combinados from 475 to about 700 ptas.

La Cuina on Carrer dels Sombrerers right by Santa Maria del Mar does a decent three course menú for 900 ptas, including half a bottle of wine. It's a pleasant place with ceramics and paintings on the walls – closed Sunday night and Monday.

There are several more little restaurants on and around Passeig del Born and Plaça de les Olles east of Santa Maria del Mar – among them the cheap and speedy *Can Busto* at Carrer de Rera Palau 3, with a three course menú for 875 ptas and many individual items for 350 to 500 ptas. *Cal Pep* (☎ 310 79 61), across the way at Plaça de les Olles 8, has great tapas and a small dining room with good seafood, where a three course Catalan meal with drinks will be around 3500 ptas. It's open from 1 to 4.45 pm and 8 pm to midnight but closed Sunday, Monday lunchtime, holidays and all of August.

Port Vell & La Barceloneta In the Maremagnum building on the Moll d'Espanya is *El Pati*, an economical fast-food hall where you can buy anything from Tex-Mex or Chinese to pizza or chicken and chips from counters at the side, then sit with the crowds at long tables in the middle. Pizza slices, bocadillos and nachos are all around 275 ptas.

Restaurant Set (7) Portes (☎ 319 30 33) at Passeig d'Isabel II 14, beyond the northeast end of Moll de la Fusta, is a classic and excellent Barcelona restaurant, founded in 1836. The atmosphere is old-fashioned with wood panelling, tiles, mirrors, and plaques naming some of the famous – such as Orson Welles and the ubiquitous Picasso – who have eaten here. Paella (1200 to 2200 ptas) is the speciality but there's other fish, seafood and meat at similar prices. Portions are good. It's open daily from 1 pm to 1 am. It's near-essential to book.

La Barceloneta has some good seafood restaurants, many on Passeig de Joan de Borbó facing Port Vell. The most economical is *Restaurant Nazca* at No 31, with a four course menú for 1100 ptas (not including drinks). The most prominent is *El Rey de la Gamba*, which encompasses Passeig de Joan de Borbó 46, 48 and 53. Most main dishes here are 1000 to 2000 ptas plus IVA. *Paco Alcalde* (☎ 221 50 26) is a more homely, tiled, little place at Carrer de l'Almirall Aixada 12, with a big range of good fresh seafood and fish dishes from 600 to 1600 ptas – also paella.

Port Olímpic The harbour here is lined on two sides by dozens of restaurants and tapas bars, extremely popular in spring and summer. None is cheap but some are very good. The north side is less expensive than the east and one of the more economical places here is *La Taverna del Cel Ros*, which has a three course menú for 975 ptas plus IVA. On the upper level of the north side is *Cafè Museu Tardà Rock* (☎ 221 39 93). Foodwise, this is a straightforward burger, salad and Tex-Mex joint (600 to 950 ptas for most things); what makes it different is that it's kitted out with Barcelona disc jockey Jordi Tardà's rock memorabilia collection. You'll find Kurt Cobain's guitar, a bottle of Jack Daniels emptied by Keith Richards during a 1982 Madrid concert, and a contract committing the 'Jimmy Hendricks Experience' to play in a club in England one afternoon in 1967 for £125. Rock videos too, of course. Hours are 1 pm to 2 am daily.

Just west of the Port Olímpic, beneath the giant copper *Peix* (Fish) sculpture, is Tardà Rock's cinematic sibling, *Planet Hollywood* (☎ 221 11 11), one of a chain part-owned by Arnold Schwarzenegger and Silvester Stallone. Here you can eat pasta and pizza as well as burgers and Tex-Mex (900 to 1500 ptas for most things) and admire décor of Hollywood costumes, props and stills. The Cyborg used in *Terminator 2: Judgement Day* revolves revoltingly in a glass cylinder at the restaurant's upper entrance. Hours are 1 pm to 1 am daily.

L'Eixample This is another area with loads of good places to eat. A good place to start an Eixample visit is the 9th floor cafeteria at *El Corte Inglés* department store on Plaça de

Catalunya. It's reasonably priced and has tremendous views.

Restaurants These are in approximate south-to-north order.

Pizza del Arte at Ronda de la Universitat 37 and Rambla de Catalunya 66 is bright and popular, with pizzas that will satisfy one hungry person, or two not-so-hungry ones, for 760 to 925 ptas – open daily from 8 am to 1 am. Monday to Friday from 1 to 5 pm they offer a lunch deal of pizza, salad, dessert, drink and coffee for 1150 ptas.

Bar Estudiantil on Plaça de la Universitat does economical platos combinados – eg chicken, chips and aubergine (berenjena), or botifarra, beans and red pepper, each for around 500 ptas.

Botiga-Restaurant Les Corts Catalanes at Gran via de les Corts Catalanes 603, near Rambla de Catalunya, is a good vegetarian restaurant open Monday to Saturday from 9 am to midnight, and Sunday and holidays from noon to midnight. The four course lunch menú is 1100 ptas (including a salad bar), or there are à-la-carte salads for 650 to 850 ptas, and pasta, pizza, moussaka and tofu dishes for 825 to 1250 ptas.

El Café de Internet at Gran via de les Corts Catalanes 656 has a double bill of food and the Internet: before, during or after your meal or snack, you can use one of 11 Internet terminals upstairs for 600 ptas a half-hour (with guidance from staff if you're a novice). Downstairs, there's a lunch menú for 850 or 950 ptas, or you can just go for a bocadillo and coffee. It's open Monday to Saturday from 1 to 4 pm and 8.30 pm to midnight.

The restaurant of the classy *Hotel Ritz* (☎ 318 52 00) at Gran via de les Corts Catalanes 668 has particularly good seafood – the daily menú is 3250 ptas.

L'Hostal de Rita, on Carrer d'Aragó a block east of Passeig de Gràcia, is an excellent mid-range restaurant, under the same ownership – and in the same mould – as Les Quinze Nits and La Fonda Escudellers in the Barri Gòtic. It's open from 1 to 3.45 pm and 8.30 to 11.30 pm and busy most of the time. The 950 ptas four course lunch menú is a

good deal. À-la-carte mains are 500 to 1000 ptas.

Fresc Co at Carrer de València 263, half a block east of Passeig de Gràcia, packs 'em in with its all-you-can-eat buffet of salads, soups, pizza, pasta, fruit, ice cream and drinks for 975 ptas Monday to Friday at lunchtime or 1250 ptas at other times. It's open from noon to 5 pm and 8 pm to 1 am daily.

Bar Ariño 2 at Carrer d'Aribau 82 is one of the more economical eateries in l'Eixample. The three course menú – eg macaroni or soup, a meat dish and dessert – is 800 ptas.

La Gran Tasca (☎ 451 54 00), at Carrer de Balmes 129 bis, is a big, bright restaurant-cum-tapas bar, busy in the evening with people heading for a night out. Tapas are 275 ptas-plus, main dishes range upwards from a quarter-chicken or rabbit, or meat brochette, for 500 to 600 ptas.

Tapas, Snacks & Coffee There are a number of glossy but informal tapas places near the bottom end of Passeig de Gràcia. At No 24 is *Quasi Queviures (Qu Qu)*, with a big choice from sausages and hams to pâtés and smoked fish – many of them Catalan specialities. Many tapas are over 400 ptas but portions are decent. At No 28 is *Ba-Ba-Reeba*, similar but less Catalan, and serving baguettes too. *Cerveseria Tapa Tapa* at No 44, on the corner of Carrer del Consell de Cent, is another big, bright place with a great range of tapas from 250 ptas. All these are open from 8 am to 1 or 1.30 am.

La Flauta over at Carrer d'Aribau 23 is well known for its tasty baguettes with a range of cheese, ham and sausage filings, from around 300 ptas. It has good tapas too.

For an excellent coffee on Passeig de Gràcia pop into *Cafè Torino* at No 59, on the corner of Carrer de València – a small, neat, friendly place, popular with a mildly chic young clientele.

Another busy, modern tapas bar is *Capitán Cook* at Rambla de Catalunya 92 – 250 ptas or more per item.

La Baguetina Catalana at the corner of

Carrer de Balmes and Carrer del Rosselló does good baguettes for 300 to 400 ptas.

Around La Sagrada Família *Bar Sin Nombre*, across Carrer de Provença from La Sagrada Família, has economical platos combinados such as omelette, chips, tomato and green pepper for 500 ptas. On the corner of Carrer de Provença and Carrer de Sardenya, *La Baguetina Catalana* does good baguettes for 300 to 400 ptas, while *Restaurante La Palmera* and *Pil-Pal Sandwichería* both have outdoor tables and platos combinados: the Pil-Pal is cheaper – eg sausage, eggs and chips for 600 ptas – but its fare can be greasy.

There are other economical options a block or two away, including several along Avinguda de Gaudí, where *Bar Bon Punt* at No 45, two blocks from La Sagrada Família, does a three course menú with wine and bread for 850 ptas.

Gràcia *La Miel* at Carrer de Bonavista 2 is popular for its good waffles (gofres) from 225 ptas and pancakes (crepas) from 350 to 500 ptas. There are salads and platos combinados, too, for 700 ptas or so.

Bar Candanchu at Plaça Rius i Taulet 9 has a restaurant with many platos combinados and meat or fish main dishes for 600 to 800 ptas. *Punto Pizza* on the same square does whole pizzas for 500 to 800 ptas.

At Plaça del Sol 14, *Equinox Sol* does a good trade in felafel for 300 ptas and shwarma kebabs for 375 ptas – also babaghanug, hummus and shish kebabs at similar prices. Don't be put off by the bright plasticky décor. You can stock up on wholefoods in *La Botiga del Sol* on Carrer de Maspons at the corner of Plaça del Sol, then take a few steps west on Maspons to sip tea and herbal infusions in a youthful, Granada-like ambience at *Tetería Jazmín*.

El Tastavins (☎ 213 60 31) at Carrer de Ramon y Cajal 12 does good home-style cooking in a bright, neat environment. Starters such as spinach with Roquefort are mainly 600 to 700 ptas, meat main courses are 900 to 1500 ptas. There's a big choice of wine too. It's open daily from 9 am to 5 pm and 8.30 pm to 1.30 am (closed Sunday night and Monday lunchtime).

Taverna El Glop (☎ 213 70 58) at Carrer de Sant Lluís 24 is a rustic but classy – and busy – sort of place specialising in good torrades, grilled meats and salads. A meal with drinks costs about 2500 to 3000 ptas. It's open Tuesday to Sunday from 1 to 4 pm and 7 pm to 1 am.

Two good, inexpensive small restaurants just off Plaça de la Virreina are *Cal Majó* at Carrer de l'Or 21 and *Casa de Pizzas* at Carrer de l'Or 19. Cal Majó's dishes of the day will probably include such Catalan specialities as escalivada, fricandó and mandonguilles amb sipia for 700 to 900 ptas.

Tibidabo Plaça del Doctor Andreu at the foot of the Tibidabo funicular is a good place to halt on your way to or from Tibidabo. The best views are from the *Mirablau Terrazza*, an open-air café by the tramvia blau stop, and the *Mirablau* bar next door. There's a line of more expensive restaurants across the street.

Markets & Supermarkets There's great fresh food of all types at the *Mercat de la Boqueria* on La Rambla, open Monday to Saturday from 8 am to 8 pm. In La Ribera, *Mercat Santa Caterina* is open Monday to Saturday from 7 am to 2 pm. In Gràcia there's a big *covered food market* at the corner of Travessera de Gràcia and Carrer de la Mare de Déu dels Desemparats.

Simago near the north end of La Rambla is a convenient central supermarket.

Entertainment

Barcelona's entertainment bible is the weekly Spanish-language magazine *Guía del Ocio* (125 ptas), which comes out on Thursday and lists almost everything that's on in the way of music, film, exhibitions, theatre and more. You can pick it up at most newsstands.

Bars Whole books have been written on Barcelona's bars, which run the gamut from wood-panelled wine cellars to bright waterfront places and trendy haunts sporting gimmicky modern design ('designer bars'). Each is its own different scene – some very local, some full of foreigners, some favoured by students, others by the well-dressed middle classes. Some play great music, others are places for a quiet talk. Most are at their liveliest from about 10 pm to 1 am, especially on Friday and Saturday, as people meet for the beginning of a night out. Here are a few places to start.

La Rambla *Cafè de l'Òpera* at La Rambla 74, opposite the Liceu opera house, is the liveliest place on the strip. It gets packed with all and sundry at night, and stays open to 3 am.

Barri Gòtic *Bar del Pi* on Plaça de Sant Josep Oriol is a characterful little local bar with a mixed Barri Gòtic clientele. You can drink outside on one of the Barri Gòtic's nicest little plazas.

Glaciar in a corner of Plaça Reial gets very busy with a young crowd of foreigners and locals in the evening and stays open till 2 or 3 am (beer 250 ptas-plus). The more basic *Bar Reixas* in the opposite corner of the square is also popular.

Tiny *Bar Malpaso* at Carrer d'En Rauric 20, just off Plaça Reial, is packed at night with a young, casual crowd and plays great Latin and African music. It stays open till about 3 am (beer around 250 ptas).

Bar L'Ascensor at Carrer de Bellafila 3, off Carrer de la Ciutat east of the ajuntament, is a cosy little place with good taped music and a young clientele. The entrance – as the name might suggest – is a demounted lift (beer 300 ptas).

Bodega La Palma round the corner at Carrer de la Palma de Sant Just 7 is a relaxed, old-fashioned, backstreet wine bar, with big barrels and a few tapas – cava (Catalan champagne) by the glass, too.

El Raval This area still has a number of old Marseille-harbour-style bars – dark, wood-panelled and bare except for the odd mirror and vast arrays of bottles behind the bar.

These tend to be Bohemian hang-outs rather than dens of real low life now, but are still atmospheric places to drink. One not to miss is *Bar Marsella* at Carrer de Sant Pau 65 which specialises in absinthe (absenta in Catalan), a beverage hard to find in Spain – and apparently illegal in France – because of its supposed narcotic qualities. Your glass of absinthe (400 ptas) comes with a lump of sugar, a fork and a little bottle of mineral water (100 ptas). Hold the sugar on the fork, over your glass, and drip the water onto the sugar so that it dissolves into the absinthe, which turns yellow. The result should be a warm glow in you and a mellow atmosphere in the bar. If you go too far, you may find your brain won't work too well the next day. The Marsella is open from 6 pm to 1 am nightly.

Nearby is *The Quiet Man*, a relaxed Irish pub at Carrer del Marquès de Barberà 11, attracting both locals and foreigners (500 ptas for a pint of Guinness). There's live music some nights.

Another good place is *Casa Almirall*, which has been at Carrer de Joaquín Costa 33 since the 1860s; it's dark and intriguing, with *modernista* décor and a mixed clientele (beer 300 ptas). Little *Bar Pastís* down at Carrer de Santa Mònica 4 is a grade sleazier, complete with records by Edith Piaf. It's open from 7.30 pm to 2.30 am (closed Tuesday) and sometimes has live music.

L'Ovella Negra (The Black Sheep) at Carrer de les Sitges 5 is a noisy, fun, barn-like tavern with a young crowd and pool and fútbol games. It opens at 9 pm; there's beer by the jug if you like.

La Ribera *El Xampanyet* at Carrer de Montcada 22 is the city's best-known cava bar – a small, cosy place with nice tiled walls and good tapas as well as cava, which is around 500 ptas for a typical bottle but also available by the glass. It's open from noon to 4 pm and 6.30 to 11.30 pm (closed Sunday night and Monday).

El Nus at Carrer dels Mirallers 5 is a small, dim, chic bar in the narrow, old streets near the Església de Santa Maria del Mar, done out with pictures of its Maharishi-lookalike owner – good for a quiet drink after dinner.

Port Olímpic Just wander round the harbour here and take your pick of the many bright and busy spots, all with open-air tables out front; some have good music inside too.

L'Eixample *La Bodegueta* is a classic wine cellar at Rambla de Catalunya 100. Bottles and barrels line the walls, and stools surround marble tables.

La Fira (The Fair) at Carrer de Provença 171 is a designer bar with a difference. You enter through a hall of distorting mirrors, and inside everything is fairground paraphernalia. It sounds corny but the atmosphere is real fun – open daily from 7 pm to 3 am (to 4 am on Friday and Saturday nights).

Gràcia *Café del Sol* and *Eldorado* are the lively bars on Plaça del Sol. The former has a vaguely Bohemian crowd, tapas, and tables outside too; it's open from noon to 2 am (beer 200 ptas before 7 pm, 300 ptas afterwards). The main bar on Plaça Rius i Taulet is *Bar Chirito de Oro*.

Café Salambó at Carrer de Torrijos 51 is a gentle kind of designer bar, imitating some village bars with benches at low tables, and has an upper level with pool tables. It's a favourite of writers, being owned by Carme Balcells, literary agent of Gabriel García Márquez, Milan Kundera and others who have spent time in Barcelona. It's open daily from noon to 2.30 am (3 am on Friday and Saturday nights). There's food too – 1150 ptas for a three course menú (beer 350 ptas).

A bit further up the hill, there are several bars and cafés with potential around the corner of Carrer de Torrijos and Carrer de la Perla. A block north, *Café La Virreina* on Plaça de la Virreina is a relaxed place with a mixed-ages crowd, 1970s rock music, good cheap hot bocadillos, and tables outside (beer 200 ptas).

Montjuïc The Poble Espanyol has several bars that get pretty lively. The most original is *Torres de Ávila*, inside the tall entrance towers themselves. Created by the top Barcelona designer Javier Mariscal, it has several levels and all sorts of surreal touches, including an egg-shaped room and glass lifts that you fear will shoot you through the roof. It's open from 10 pm to 4 am.

Gay & Lesbian Bars Two of the best gay bars are *Punto BCN* at Carrer de Muntaner 63-65 in l'Eixample and *Este Bar* round the corner at Carrer del Consell de Cent 257 – both relaxed places where people meet and talk before maybe moving on to a disco. Punto BCN has pool tables too. A favourite lesbian bar-café is *La Nostra Illa* at Carrer de Reig i Bonet 3, Gràcia – it has good bocadillos. *Café de la Calle* at Carrer de Vic 11, Gràcia, is a cosy meeting place for lesbians and gay men of mixed ages, open from 6 pm to 3 am.

Live Music There's now a good choice most nights of the week. Most places with live music also have bars (a beer is usually between 300 and 600 ptas); many also have dance space, with the bands playing before or between disco sessions, for which you won't have to pay any extra. Starting times are rarely before 10 pm, more often midnight or 1 am. Normal entry charges range from nothing to 1500 ptas or so – the higher prices usually include a drink or two. You may pay more for visiting 'name' bands. Really big touring bands often play in the 17,000 capacity Palau Sant Jordi on Montjuïc.

To find out what's on, look in *Guía del Ocio*'s 'Música' section, and check posters and leaflets in places like Glaciar bar on Plaça Reial. Here are some of the most dependable places, both for music and for general liveliness:

Barri Gòtic

Barcelona Pipa Club, Plaça Reial 3: jazz Thursday to Saturday around midnight (usually 500 ptas plus drinks); open from 10 pm (ring the bell to get in) to 2 or 3 am; like someone's flat inside

Harlem Jazz Club, Carrer de la Comtessa de Sobradiel 8: music from around 11 pm to 2 am nightly except Monday – often jazz, but also some rock and Latin (entry free, a drink compulsory)

Jamboree, Plaça Reial 17: varied jazz nightly, usually at 9 pm and midnight (1000 to 1500 ptas); disco later

Sala Tarantos, next door to the Jamboree: class flamenco some nights – most often Friday and Saturday at midnight (around 1500 ptas)

Poble Sec

Club Apolo, Carrer Nou de la Rambla 113: world music – chiefly African, Latin and Spanish – several nights a week around 10.30 pm (2000 ptas for big names), followed by live salsa or (on Friday and Saturday) a disco

Port Vell

Blue Note, Maremagnum, Moll d'Espanya: varied jazz, usually Wednesday to Saturday around midnight (anywhere from free to 2000 ptas); open all day from 1 pm to the early hours

Western Gràcia/Avinguda Diagonal
These are all within a few blocks of Avinguda Diagonal; the nearest stations are Diagonal (metro), Hospital Clínic (metro) and Gràcia (suburban train).

La Antilla Cosmopolita, Carrer de Muntaner 244: full of Latin Americans and Caribbeans dancing salsa; live bands at 12.30 am or later several nights a week (normally 1500 ptas)

La Boîte, Avinguda Diagonal 477: jazz or blues – sometimes jams – several nights a week at midnight (1200 to 2500 ptas); disco later

La Tierra, Carrer d'Aribau 230: live bands every night at midnight, mostly Latin and rock/pop (1500 ptas); disco later

Luz de Gas, Carrer de Muntaner 246: live soul, country, salsa, rock, jazz or pop most nights at midnight or 1 am (usually 1500 ptas)

Other Areas

Savannah, Carrer de la Muntanya 16 in the El Clot area (metro: Clot): rock or punk bands a few nights a week, often around 10.30 pm (usually 1000 to 1300 ptas); disco later

Zeleste, Carrer dels Almogàvers 122, Poble Nou (metro: Marina): huge club converted from a warehouse, regularly hosting visiting rock and pop bands – as does its smaller neighbour Zeleste 2 round the corner at Carrer de Pamplona 88; name bands are usually on around 10 pm, for 1500 to 2500 ptas

Discos Barcelona's discos come alive from about 2 or 3 to 5 or 6 am, and are best on Friday and Saturday nights. Some have live bands, often starting at midnight or so to fill the place up a bit before the real action. (Places where the bands are likely to be an attraction in their own right are listed in the Live Music section). Disco cover charges range from nothing to as much as 3000 ptas: they depend partly on how busy the place is and whether the bouncers like the look of you (which puts women at an advantage). If you go early, you'll often get in cheaper. Drinks are expensive, of course: anywhere from 300 to 800 ptas for a beer. Some discos are fairly smart and won't let you in in sneakers or runners.

Guía del Ocio lists many discos in its 'Tarde & Noche' section: those described as *multiespacio* will probably have spaces for a quiet drink, a game of pool or other diversions as well as dancing. Where's hot (or should we say cool?) changes as fast as it does everywhere, but these will give you a start:

Barri Gòtic

Jamboree, Plaça Reial 17; from around 1.30 am, after the nightly jazz (see Live Music), a lively disco with two spaces – one for Latin rhythms, one for Western disco and rock – till 5 am or so; entry can range from nothing to 1500 ptas

Karma, Plaça Reial 10: youngish, studenty basement place with good music; open from around 11 pm to 4 am; usually 1000 ptas including a drink

Poble Sec

Club Apolo, Carrer Nou de la Rambla 113: ethnic/funk/house/soul/R&B disco Friday and Saturday at 1.30 am, live salsa Wednesday and Thursday at 12.30 am, following main live band (see Live Music); 1000 ptas including a drink (free if you stay on after the main band)

L'Eixample

Café de las Artes, Carrer de València 234: relaxed bar-cum-disco with standard disco music and a mixed-ages, fairly clean-living crowd; entry free, beer 350 ptas

Nick Havanna, Carrer del Rosselló 208: big 1980s 'designer bar' with a video bank at one end of the dance space and glass-backed urinals flushed by veritable cascades of water; attracts a rather respectable crowd these days; open nightly from 11 pm to 4 or 5 am, often with bands or salsa/merengue classes at midnight; free entry, beer 650 ptas

Satanassa, Carrer d'Aribau 27: 'antidesign' haunt of androgynous people of both sexes, with gaudy erotic murals; open from about 11 pm to 4 or 5 am; free entry

Velvet, Carrer de Balmes 161: smallish designer bar and disco inspired by the film *Blue Velvet*, with 1960s music; busy with a fairly straight crowd from 2 or 3 to 5 or 6 am; free entry, beer around 400 ptas

Western Gràcia/Avinguda Diagonal

La Antilla Cosmopolita, Carrer de Muntaner 244: salsa scene, popular with Latin Americans and Caribbeans, often live bands on late; usually 1500 ptas including a drink

La Boîte, Avinguda Diagonal 477: disco after the nightly jazz or blues (see Live Music); beer 600 ptas

Nitsa, Plaça Joan Llongueras 1-3: thumping bastion of techno and its relatives

Otto Zutz, Carrer de Lincoln 15, west of Via Augusta: as its blurb says, 'where the beautiful people go ... 2000 ptas. Worth it'; fills from 3 to 5 or 6 am; three levels with bars on each, cool crowd but great atmosphere – just don't wear runners, and if in doubt, do wear black; often bands at midnight with no cover – you can stay after the band finishes without paying; beer 800 ptas

Other Areas

Mirablau, Plaça del Doctor Andreu, at the foot of the Tibidabo funicular: bar with great views and a small disco floor; open daily from 11 am till 4.30 or 5 am; entry free, beer around 450 ptas

Savannah, Carrer de la Muntanya 16 in the El Clot area (metro: Clot): good dance music nightly from 8 pm, Sunday till midnight, Tuesday to Thursday to 3 am, Friday and Saturday to 5 am (closed Monday)

Zeleste, Carrer dels Almogàvers 122, Poble Nou (metro: Marina): vast ex-warehouse on several levels including huge dance space and a long, quiet bar with waiter service; best from around 2.30 to 5 am, Friday and Saturday nights; legendary name thanks to its predecessor near Santa Maria del Mar church, a gathering place for young new musicians and the 1970s alternative scene

Late-Night Venues

KGB, Carrer de ca l'Alegre de Dalt 55: hard rock warehouse-type multiespacio; open from 10 pm to 4.30 am, then again from about 5.30 to 8 am for cool all-night boogiers

Gay & Lesbian Venues

The two top gay discos are *Metro* at Carrer de Sepúlveda 185 near Plaça de la Universitat, and *Martin's* at Passeig de Gràcia 130. Metro attracts some lesbians and heteros as well as gay men; it's packed for its regular Monday-night cabarets.

Martin's is gay men only. Both are open from midnight to 5 am and have 'dark rooms'.

Members at Carrer de Seneca 3 and *Bahía* at Carrer de Seneca 12, both in Gràcia, are relaxed little bars with dance space and a predominantly female crowd.

Classical Music, Theatre & Dance

There's plenty to choose from in these fields too. *Guía del Ocio* has ample listings. The monthly *Informatiu Musical* leaflet has the best classical music listings: you can pick it up at tourist offices and the Palau de la Virreina arts info and ticket office at La Rambla 99, which also sells tickets for many events.

Though Barcelona's great opera house, the Gran Teatre del Liceu, is out of action until probably 1998 (following its 1994 fire), there's still opera at one or two places in the city such as *La Cuina* at Carrer de Sant Pere mes baix 7 and the *Teatre Malic* at Carrer de la Fusina 3, both in La Ribera.

The chief venue for classical and choral music is the *Palau de la Música Catalana* at Carrer de Sant Pere mes alt 11 in La Ribera, which has a busy and wide-ranging programme. Attending a concert here is also a way to see the gorgeous interior of this *modernista* building (see the earlier La Ribera section). The *Palau Sant Jordi* on Montjuïc is used for some really big concerts. The *Mercat de les Flors* at Carrer de Lleida 59, at the foot of Montjuïc, is an important venue for dance and drama as well as music. The *Teatre Victòria* at Avinguda del Paral.lel 67-69 often stages ballet and contemporary dance.

Theatre is nearly all in Catalan or Spanish (*Guía del Ocio* specifies which). More meaningful to the average visitor than straight drama might be Barcelona's music hall/cabaret scene, a tradition dating from the turn of the century and still alive and well at theatres on and near Avinguda del Paral.lel like the *Arnau*, Avinguda del Paral.lel 60, the *Llantiol*, Carrer de la Riereta 7, and *El Molino*, Carrer de Vila i Vilà 99.

Sardana

The *sardana*, Cataluña's national dance, is danced every week – except sometimes in August – on Pla de la Seu in front of the cathedral at 6.30 pm on Saturday and noon on Sunday, and in Plaça de Sant Jaume at 6 pm on Sunday. These are not shows for tourists, but ordinary Catalans doing something they enjoy and which expresses their Catalanity. The dancers join hands to form ever-widening circles, placing their bags or coats in the centre. The dance is intricate but, in true Catalan style, not flamboyant. The steps and the accompanying brass and reed music are rather sedate, at times jolly, at times melancholy, rising to occasional crescendos, then quietening down again.

Cinema Foreign films shown with subtitles and original soundtrack, rather than dubbed, are marked 'v.o.' *(versión original)* in movie listings. Cinemas to check for these include the *Alexis*, *Arkadín*, *Capsa*, *Casablanca*, *Filmoteca*, *Maldà* and *Verdi*. A ticket is usually 600 to 700 ptas but most cinemas have a weekly *día del espectador* (viewer's day; often Monday) when they charge 400 to 500 ptas. The Maldà, at Carrer del Pi 5 in the Barri Gòtic, is good value as each programme includes two feature films.

Spectator Sport

Football Barcelona football club has not only one of Europe's best teams but also one of its best stadiums, the 120,000 capacity Camp Nou in the west of the city (metro: Collblanc). Games here against any opposition good enough to fire up the home team and the crowd are quite an occasion. Check the daily press for upcoming games. Tickets normally cost 2200 to 8200 ptas – the cheapest are in the one small standing section, a long, long way above the pitch. See the earlier Camp Nou section for more on the club. The city's other club, Espanyol, based at the Sarrià stadium (one km from Maria Cristina metro station), traditionally plays a quiet second fiddle to Barça, though it has enjoyed some better-than-usual times in the mid-1990s.

Bullfights Bullfighting to the death is not a favourite Catalan pastime, but there are some fights on summer Sunday afternoons at the Plaça Braus Monumental, at the corner of Gran via de les Corts Catalanes and Carrer de la Marina, 500 metres from Glòries metro station.

Things to Buy

Barcelona's obsession with style is, needless to say, reflected in its shops. There are enough chic – and expensive – little boutiques and trendy shoe shops to keep the fashion-conscious happy (or worried) for weeks. The best hunting areas are Passeig de Gràcia and the streets to its west (including the Boulevard Rosa arcade just north of Carrer d'Aragó), and Barri Gòtic streets such as Carrer de la Portaferrissa, Carrer de la Boqueria, Carrer del Call, Carrer de la Llibreteria and Carrer de Ferran, and around Plaça de Sant Josep Oriol. Also in these areas you'll find some interesting shops specialising in Latin American, African and other crafts.

The best single place to look for anything you need is the El Corte Inglés department store on Plaça de Catalunya – nine floors of everything, open Monday to Saturday from 10 am to 9.30 pm. Here's a small sample of other shops that caught our eye:

Shoes There's a gaggle of relatively economical shoe shops on Avinguda del Portal de l'Àngel, off Plaça de Catalunya. Camper at Carrer de València 249 just off Passeig de Gràcia has a good range of Doc Marten-type boots, mostly around 10,000 ptas a pair.

Music Virgin Megastore at Passeig de Gràcia 16 (corner of Gran via de les Corts Catalanes) and Planet Music at Carrer de Mallorca 214 near Carrer d'Enric Granados, both in l'Eixample, have vast selections of all types of music on CD, tape and vinyl disc. There are several small shops specialising in indie and other niche music on Carrer de les Sitges and nearby on Carrer dels Tallers (El Raval).

Design Vinçon, next door to La Pedrera at Passeig de Gràcia 96, has the slickest designs in furniture and household goods, both local and imported; it's open Monday to Saturday from 10 am to 2 pm and 4.30 to 8.30 pm.

Clothes & Fabrics Jeanne Weis at Carrer d'En Rauric 8 north of Carrer de Ferran (Barri Gòtic) is a tiny shop with some very nice lines in African printed fabrics, cushions and shirts. Jacquard du Monde at Avinguda del Portal de l'Àngel 5 (Barri Gòtic) has some great, very colourfully patterned sweaters from around 8000 ptas. Holala! at Carrer d'Aribau 75 (l'Eixample) sells second-hand leather, suede and denim jackets from 4500 ptas.

Crafts & Antiques Carrer de Banys Nous in the Barri Gòtic is lined with antique shops. Casa Miranda at No 15 has woven baskets of all shapes and sizes.

Nature Selection at Carrer del Consell de Cent 304 between Passeig de Gràcia and Rambla de Catalunya (l'Eixample) has a big stock of ethnic bags (leather and cloth), jewellery, pots, drums, carvings, glass, baskets, tablecloths, rugs and more.

Condoms Barcelona even has an exotic condom shop on one of the prettiest squares of the Barri Gòtic – La Condoneria at Plaça de Sant Josep Oriol 3. Here you can purchase condoms of every colour and shape you could dream of (and some you never could).

Markets The large Els Encants flea market is held every Monday, Wednesday, Friday and Saturday from 8 am to 6 pm (8 pm in summer) next to Plaça de les Glòries Catalanes (metro: Glòries). In the Barri Gòtic, there's a crafts market in Plaça de Sant Josep Oriol on Thursday and Friday, an antiques market in Plaça Nova on Thursday, and a collectors' coin market in Plaça Reial on Sunday morning. On the western edge of El Raval, the Mercat de Sant Antoni dedicates Sunday morning to old maps, stamps, books and cards.

Getting There & Away

See the Travel Agencies section earlier in this chapter for some agents offering cheap airfares and youth and student train and bus tickets.

Air The airport is 14 km south-west of the centre at El Prat de Llobregat. For information in English call ☎ 481 12 99, in Spanish ☎ 481 13 00, in French ☎ 481 02 99. Barcelona is a big international as well as domestic destination, with direct flights from North America as well as many European cities. You can get one-way flights to London from around 17,000 ptas, or to New York from 35,000 ptas (a bit less for under-26s and students). Iberia uses Barcelona as an international hub and flies direct to eight Spanish cities. Aviaco serves a further 14 direct. For cheaper domestic flights try Air Europa (including to Madrid, Málaga and Sevilla) and Spanair (to Madrid, Palma de Mallorca and Santiago de Compostela).

Tickets can be bought at almost any travel agency. Iberia and Aviaco (☎ 412 56 67) are at Passeig de Gràcia 30; Spanair (☎ 478 66 91) and Air Europa (☎ 412 77 33) are at the airport. Other airline numbers include Air France ☎ 487 25 26, Lufthansa ☎ 487 03 00, TWA ☎ 215 84 86, Alitalia ☎ 416 04 24, KLM ☎ 379 54 58 and British Airways ☎ 487 21 12.

Bus The main intercity bus station is the modern Estació del Nord at Carrer d'Alí Bei 80, 1.5 km north-east of La Rambla and 1½ blocks from Arc de Triomf metro. It has a bus information desk (☎ 265 65 08) open daily from 7 am to 9 pm, a luggage *consigna* out by the platforms, a currency exchange office (with poor rates), a La Caixa ATM, and a telephone and fax office.

A few services – most importantly some international buses and the few buses to Montserrat – use Estació d'Autobuses de Sants beside Estació Sants train station.

International The main services are run by Eurolines/Julià Via (☎ 490 40 00) from Estació d'Autobuses de Sants, and by Eurolines/Linebús and Starbus (both ☎ 265

07 00) from Estació del Nord. Services include:

London – three to five times weekly, 24 hours, 14,450 ptas, Eurolines/Julià Via or Eurolines/Linebús
Marseille – daily except Sunday, 11½ hours, 6100 ptas, Eurolines/Julià Via
Milan – three to six times weekly, 17½ hours, 10,750 ptas, Eurolines/Julià Via
Paris – daily except Sunday, 15 hours, 11,125 ptas, Eurolines/Julià Via or Eurolines/Linebús

Eurolines/Julià Via also has services at least three times weekly to Amsterdam, Brussels, Florence, Geneva, Montpellier, Nice, Perpignan, Rome, Toulouse, Venice and Zürich, and twice a week to several cities in Morocco.

Domestic There are buses to most large Spanish cities. Telephone numbers of bus companies at Estació del Nord include: Alsina Graells ☎ 265 68 66; Aratesa ☎ 245 88 56; Barcelona Bus ☎ 232 04 59; Enatcar ☎ 245 25 28; Grupo Alsa ☎ 231 04 01; SARFA ☎ 265 11 58; and Zatrans ☎ 231 04 01. You can also get schedule information on ☎ 265 65 08.

Departures from Estació del Nord include the following, with journey time, fare and bus company (where frequencies vary, the lowest figure is usually for Sunday):

Andorra – five or six daily, four hours, 2500 ptas, Alsina Graells
Burgos – two to four daily, eight hours, 4960 ptas, Zatrans
Granada – four daily, 13 to 15 hours, 7540 ptas, Bacoma
Madrid – six daily, seven or eight hours, 2690 to 3450 ptas, Enatcar
Pamplona – two to six daily, 5¼ hours, 2065 ptas, Irbarsa
San Sebastián – three daily, 6½ hours, 2450 ptas, Irbarsa
Santiago de Compostela – one daily, 17 hours, 7695 ptas, Enatcar
Sevilla – one daily, 16 hours, 8975 ptas, Bacoma
Valencia – five to 10 daily, 4½ hours, 2650 ptas, Enatcar
Zaragoza – nine daily, 4½ hours, 1640 to 1985 ptas, Aratesa

For buses to other places in Cataluña, see the relevant sections in the Cataluña chapter.

Train The two main stations are Estació Sants, on Plaça dels Països Catalans, 2.5 km west of La Rambla (metro: Sants-Estació); and Estació de França on Avinguda del Marquès de l'Argentera, one km east of La Rambla (metro: Barceloneta).

All trains within Spain (except some Barcelona suburban services) use Estació Sants. Most trains to/from France or beyond use Estació de França. Some trains stop at both stations.

Other useful stations for long-distance and regional trains are Catalunya on Plaça de Catalunya (metro: Catalunya), and Passeig de Gràcia, at the corner of Passeig de Gràcia and Carrer d'Aragó, 700 metres north of Plaça de Catalunya (metro: Passeig de Gràcia).

Information & Tickets It's advisable to book at least a day or two ahead for most long-distance trains, domestic or international. There's a RENFE information and booking office in Passeig de Gràcia station, open daily from 7 am to 10 pm (9 pm on Sunday). At Estació Sants, the Informació Largo Recorrido windows give information on all except suburban trains. Ticket window Nos 1 to 21 are for long-distance trains; Nos 22 to 30 are for trains around Cataluña *(trens regionals)* and suburban trains *(rodalies)*. The station has consigna lockers open from 5.30 am to 10 pm (400 or 600 ptas for 24 hours), a tourist information office, a telephone and fax office, a hotel reservations office, currency exchange offices open from 8 am to 10 pm daily, and ATMs.

Estació de França has a train information office and consigna lockers (600 ptas for 24 hours).

For information on international trains you can call ☎ 490 11 22, for domestic trains ☎ 490 02 02.

International Services Direct trains from Estació de França include those to Paris (11¼ hours), Zürich (13 hours) and Milan

(13 hours), all overnight. The Paris train is daily; the others are either daily or three times weekly, depending on the season. These trains have connections for numerous other cities. Sleeping berths to Paris, Zürich or Milan all cost from 16,500 to 40,400 ptas. Seats to Zürich or Milan are 11,000 ptas; there are no seats on the direct Paris train.

From Estació Sants there are two daily trains to Perpignan (three hours) and Montpellier (4½ hours). Montpellier is 5220/8230 ptas in 2nd/1st class.

You can also reach a variety of destinations, in some cases several times a day, by changing trains just across the French border at Cerbère (opposite Portbou) or Latour-de-Carol (opposite Puigcerdà), or at Montpellier. From Estació Sants there are about 10 trains a day to Cerbère (2½ hours) and three to Latour-de-Carol (3½ hours). This way, Paris is nine to 16 hours from Barcelona for 11,795 to 13,420 ptas in 2nd class seats, Marseille is 7½ to 9½ hours (6925 ptas), Nice 10 to 12 hours (9255 ptas), Venice 17¼ to 22¼ hours (from 13,500 ptas), Florence 16½ to 22 hours (from 12,505 ptas) and Rome 18½ to 23 hours (14,145 ptas).

Domestic Long-Distance Services There are trains to most large Spanish cities, with the usual huge range of seat and sleeper accommodation, day and night trains, and a mind-boggling array of fares. Daily direct departures from Estació Sants (some also stopping at Estació de França and/or Passeig de Gràcia), with typical 2nd class seat fares, include :

Burgos – three or four daily, 8 to 9½ hours, 5000 ptas
Granada – one or two daily, 12¾ hours, 6800 ptas
Madrid – seven or eight daily, 6½ to 9½ hours, 4800 ptas
Pamplona – one or two daily, 6½ to 10 hours, 4000 ptas
San Sebastián – one or two daily, 8¼ to 10 hours, 4500 ptas
Sevilla – four daily, 11 to 13½ hours, 6600 ptas (9100 ptas via Madrid)
Valencia – 10 or 11 daily, 4 to 4½ hours, 3000 ptas
Vigo – one or two daily, 16 to 17½ hours, 7800 ptas
Zaragoza – 11 or 12 daily, 3½ to 4½ hours, 3000 ptas

Barcelona & Cataluña Services For suburban trains around Barcelona, see Getting Around in this chapter and relevant destination sections. Regional trains within Cataluña all go from Estació Sants; some also stop at Catalunya or Passeig de Gràcia. See the destination sections for more detail.

Car & Motorcycle Autopistas head out of Barcelona in most directions you'd want to go, including the A-19 to the southern Costa Brava; the A-16 to Sitges; the E-9 and the A-18 both to Manresa (with a turn-off for Montserrat); and the A-7 north to Girona, Figueres and France, and south to Tarragona and Valencia (turn off along the A-2 for Lleida, Zaragoza and Madrid). All these have tolls (over 1700 ptas to La Jonquera near the French border, for instance) but the toll-free alternatives, such as the N-II north to Girona, Figueres and France, and west to Lleida and beyond, or the N-340 to Tarragona, tend to be busy and slow.

Rental If you haven't organised a rental car from abroad, local firms such as Gestvi, Ifasa, Julià Car, Tot Car and Vanguard are generally cheaper than the big international names. From these a typical small car like a Ford Fiesta or Renault Twingo, with minimum compulsory insurance, should cost around 2500 ptas a day plus 25 ptas a km, plus IVA. For unlimited km, they're around 20,000 ptas for three days or 40,000 ptas a week, plus IVA. Special low weekend rates (from Friday lunchtime or afternoon to Monday morning) are worth looking into. Rental firms include:

Avis, Carrer d'Aragó 235, l'Eixample (☎ 487 87 45)
Europcar, Carrer del Consell de Cent 363, l'Eixample (☎ 488 23 98)
Gestvi, Gran via de Carles III 14, Sants (☎ 490 97 63)
Hertz, Carrer de Tuset 10, Gràcia (☎ 217 32 48)
Ifasa, Avinguda de Madrid 6, Les Corts (☎ 448 13 35)
Julià Car, Ronda de la Universitat 5, l'Eixample (☎ 317 64 54)
Tot Car, Carrer de Berlín 97, Sants (☎ 419 34 88)
Vanguard, Carrer de Londres 31, l'Eixample (☎ 439 38 80)

Vanguard also rents motorcycles at around 4000 ptas a day.

Hitching Barnastop (☎ 443 06 32) at Carrer de Sant Ramon 29 in the Barri Xinès matches travellers with drivers who have spare places for long trips. You pay around 3500 ptas to Madrid, 6000 ptas to Paris. Opening hours are Monday to Friday from 11 am to 2 pm and 5 to 8 pm, Saturday from 5 to 8 pm.

Boat Passenger and vehicular ferries to the Balearic Islands, operated by the Trasmediterránea line, dock at the Estació Marítima N-1 on the Moll de Barcelona wharf in Port Vell. Information and tickets are available from Trasmediterránea (☎ 443 25 32; fax 443 27 81) there, or from travel agents.

For information on schedules and fares, see the introductory Getting There & Away section in the Balearic Islands chapter.

Getting Around

The metro is the easiest way of getting around and reaches most places you're likely to visit (though not the airport). For a few trips you need buses or suburban trains (rodalies). The main tourist office at Gran via de les Corts Catalanes 658 gives out the comprehensive *Guia d'Autobusos Urbans de Barcelona*, with a metro map and all bus routes. For public transport information you can call ☎ 010 or ☎ 412 00 00, or ☎ 205 15 15 for suburban trains only. For info on disabled facilities call ☎ 412 44 44.

The Airport Trains run from the airport to Estació Sants and Catalunya station on Plaça de Catalunya every 30 minutes from 6.10 am to 10.40 pm daily. It's 16 minutes to Sants, 21 minutes to Catalunya, for 300 ptas to either place (335 ptas on Saturday, Sunday and holidays). Departures from Sants to the airport are from 5.45 am to 10.15 pm; from Catalunya they're five minutes earlier.

The A1 Aerobús bus service runs from the airport to Plaça de Catalunya and Estació Sants Monday to Friday every 15 minutes from 6 am to 11 pm, and Saturday, Sunday and holidays every 30 minutes from 6.45 am to 10.45 pm. Departures from Plaça de Catalunya (corner of Passeig de Gràcia) are Monday to Friday from 5.30 am to 10 pm, Saturday, Sunday and holidays from 6 am to 10 pm. The trip is about 40 minutes – depending on traffic – for 435 ptas.

A taxi to/from the centre – a half-hour ride – is about 2000 ptas.

Targetas Targetas are multiple-trip city transport tickets, offering worthwhile savings. They are sold at most city-centre metro stations. Targeta T-1 (700 ptas) gives you 10 rides on the metro, buses or suburban trains; Targeta T-2 (680 ptas) gives 10 rides on the metro or suburban trains; Targeta T-DIA (500 ptas) gives unlimited metro, bus or suburban train travel in one day.

Bus Buses run along most city routes every few minutes from 5 or 6 am to 10 or 11 pm. Many routes pass through Plaça de Catalunya and/or Plaça de la Universitat. After 11 pm, a reduced network of yellow *nitbusos* (night buses) runs till 3 or 4 am. All nitbus routes pass through Plaça de Catalunya and most run every 30 to 45 minutes. A single fare on any bus is 130 ptas.

Bus Turístic This bus service, No 100, runs from mid-June to the end of October around a circuit linking virtually all the major tourist sights. Tourist offices and many hotels have leaflets explaining the system. Tickets, available on the bus, are 1200 ptas for one day's unlimited rides, or 1700 ptas for two consecutive days. Service is about every 20 minutes from 9 am to 9.30 pm. Tickets entitle you to discounts of 100 to 500 ptas on entry fees and tickets at 12 stops along the route, which don't *have* to be used on the day(s) you use the bus.

Metro The metro has five lines, numbered and colour-coded, and is efficient and easy to use. A single ride is 130 ptas and tickets are easily available from machines at most stations. At interchange stations, you just

BARCELONA

need to work out which line and which direction you want. The metro runs Monday to Thursday from 5 am to 11 pm; Friday and Saturday from 5 am to 1 am; Sunday from 6 am to midnight. See the colour metro map facing page 17.

Train Suburban trains (rodalies) are useful for reaching some places within the city as well as some outside it. Most run Monday to Thursday from 5 am to 11 pm, and Friday to Sunday from 5 am to 1 am. Rides within the city are 130 ptas. The main city-centre stations for suburban trains, all with metro stations on the spot, are Catalunya (on Plaça de Catalunya), Passeig de Gràcia, Espanya (on Plaça d'Espanya), Arc de Triomf and Estació Sants. See sections that refer to suburban destinations for detail on services. You can call ☎ 205 15 15 for information on suburban trains. They're operated by Ferrocarrils de la Generalitat de Catalunya (FGC), not by the national network RENFE.

Car & Motorcycle An effective one-way system makes traffic flow fairly smoothly, but you'll often find yourself flowing the way you don't want to go – unless you happen to have an adept navigator and the Michelin *Barcelona* map (see Orientation earlier in this chapter), which shows one-way streets. Parking can also be tricky, and expensive if you choose a parking garage. It's better to leave your car alone while you're here and use Barcelona's excellent public transport.

Taxi Taxis are black-and-yellow and cost 270 ptas plus 92 ptas per km (107 ptas per km from 10 pm to 6 am and all day Saturday, Sunday and holidays). A further 300 ptas is added for all trips to/from the airport, and 100 ptas for luggage bigger than 55 by 35 by 35 cm. The trip from Estació Sants to Plaça de Catalunya, about three km, is 550 to 600 ptas. You can call a taxi on ☎ 225 00 00, 481 10 85 or 490 22 22 (☎ 358 11 11 for disabled-adapted taxis).

Cataluña

North, south and west of Barcelona spreads a land of such diverse fascination that, even though its furthest-flung corner is no more than 200 km (six hours by bus) from Barcelona, you could spend weeks exploring it and still feel you'd barely begun. The Costa Brava, for all its dreary concrete pockets of mass tourism, still has all the wild and varied beauty that brought visitors there in the first place, and in many places remains little touched by the tour operators. Indeed some parts are so rugged that they're literally unpackageable. Inland, the Pyrenees rise to mighty 3000 metre peaks from a series of green and often remote valleys, dotted with villages and small towns which retain a palpable air of the middle ages. These mountains provide some magnificent walking and, in winter, good skiing.

Excitement runs thinner in the flatter far west and south, but even here there's enough to keep you happily exploring for a few days, from the bleak wetlands of the Ebro delta to the historic cities of Tarragona and Lleida. Throughout Cataluña (Catalunya in Catalan, often written Catalonia in English) the sense of difference from the rest of Spain is intense, not only in the use of the Catalan language (though everyone speaks Castilian too), but in the unusual festivals, the distinctive cuisine, the fertile, mostly green landscape, and the constant presence of the region's unique history. This last is maintained most forcefully by the wealth of superb Romanesque and Gothic stone buildings from Cataluña's medieval golden age. It doesn't take long to understand why so many people here think of themselves as Catalans first, and as Spaniards, if at all, a distant second.

Accommodation

Room and camping ground prices in this chapter are for the high season – July and August, plus about January to March in ski resorts – when it's advisable to ring ahead to ensure a room in many towns. Most estab-

HIGHLIGHTS

- Exploring the coves and beaches near Palafrugell or Begur
- Cadaqués, a magical Costa Brava village haunted by the memory of Salvador Dalí
- Sunrise or sunset at beautiful Cap de Creus, the easternmost point of mainland Spain
- The Teatre-Museu Dalí in Figueres, a voyage through one of the 20th century's strangest minds
- Riding the Cremallera narrow-gauge railway up to the Vall de Núria
- Walking in the sublimely beautiful Parc Nacional d'Aigüestortes i Estany de Sant Maurici
- A visit to the weird rock-pillar mountain of Montserrat
- A night or two on the town at Sitges, Spain's most outrageous resort

lishments charge around 10% or 20% less at other times.

Don't forget that Cataluña has a wide network of *cases de pagès*, the local name for *casas rurales*, which often provide economical and good accommodation in country areas.

Youth Hostels The 24 member hostels of Cataluña's official youth hostel network, the Xarxa d'Albergs de Joventut, all share a central booking service (☎ 93-483 83 63; fax 93-483 83 50) at the Oficina de Turisme

CATALUÑA

Juvenil, Carrer de Rocafort 116-122, Barcelona (metro: Rocafort). Nearly all hostels in Cataluña outside Barcelona are Xarxa (and REAJ and HI) hostels.

At Xarxa hostels you need an HI card. With a few minor exceptions, all have the same price structure: if you're under 26 or have an ISIC or FIYTO card, B&B is 1275 ptas in the low season and 1500 ptas in the high season; otherwise it's 1750 ptas low season, 2075 ptas high season. There's no cheaper rate for bed without breakfast. High and low seasons vary from hostel to hostel and are specified where hostels are men-

tioned in this chapter. The Christmas and Semana Santa holidays and all long weekends are high season everywhere. If you don't have a sleeping bag or sheets, hostels charge 350 ptas to rent sheets for your stay.

Getting Around

Cataluña has a good network of RENFE *trens regionals* (regional trains) fanning out from Barcelona. Useful lines go north-east to Girona, Figueres and Portbou; north to Ripoll and Puigcerdà; west to Lleida (with a branch via Montserrat); and south to Tarragona and beyond. There are three types of tren regional: a Catalunya Exprés is the fastest, with limited stops and 1st as well as 2nd-class carriages; a Delta stops more often and is 2nd class only; and a plain Regional, also 2nd class only, stops everywhere. Catalunya Exprés fares are about 15% higher than the others.

The Portbou, Lleida and Tarragona lines are also served by RENFE long-distance trains, with fares around twice those on trens regionals.

For some places fairly close to Barcelona, such as Montserrat, Sant Sadurní d'Anoia and Sitges, the best services are often *rodalies*, the Catalan version of *cercanías*.

Places off the railways are served by buses, often including direct services from Barcelona. In general there are more buses in summer than winter, and more from Monday to Friday than at the weekend and on holidays. On some routes fares go up by around 15% at the weekend and on holidays.

The Costa Brava

The Costa Brava, stretching from Blanes, 60 km north-east of Barcelona, to the French border, ranks with the Costa Blanca and Costa del Sol as one of Spain's three great holiday 'costas'. Don't let that put you off. Though it has its share of awful concrete development, packed beaches, traditional English breakfasts and *Konditoreien*, it also has, as its name – 'Rugged Coast' – indicates, just as many spectacular stretches strung with picturesque headlands and inlets, waters of unbelievably inviting shades of blue, and a number of coastal villages which have retained much of their old charm.

Nestling in the hilly and handsome country behind the coast – green and covered in umbrella pine in the south, barer and browner in the north – are a number of attractive small, often very old, country towns. A little further inland are the bigger towns of Girona (Gerona in Castilian), which has a sizeable medieval centre, and Figueres

(Figueras), famous for its bizarre Teatre-Museu Dalí, the foremost of a series of sites associated with the eccentric surrealist artist Salvador Dalí.

The Costa Brava *does* get packed with visitors in the second half of July and August and at these times you should ring ahead to avoid a lengthy room search in many places. June and September are a pleasant couple of degrees cooler than July and August, while May and October are nicely warm. Sea temperatures hold up well through September, too.

Visiting the Costa Brava is made all the more enjoyable by the fact that the people who work in the tourist business here are among the most friendly and helpful in Spain. The telephone code for everywhere in this section is ☎ 972.

Diving

The ruggedness of the Costa Brava continues under the sea to provide some of the best diving in Spain. There are approved tourist diving centres with certified instructors and experienced guides at a dozen or more places along the coast. The Illes Medes off L'Estartit are a group of protected islets with probably the most diverse sea life anywhere along the Spanish coast. Other top Costa Brava diving spots include the Illes Formigues, rocky islets with waters down to 45 metres, off the coast between Palamós and Calella de Palafrugell; and Els Ullastres, three underwater hills off Llafranc, with some sheer walls and depths down to 54 metres.

At the Illes Medes, surface water temperatures average around 21°C from July to September, 18°C or 19°C in June and October, and 15°C in May and November.

Getting There & Away

There are direct buses from Barcelona to most towns on and near the Costa Brava. The railway between Barcelona and the coastal border town of Portbou runs inland most of the way, through Girona and Figueres. From Girona and Figueres there are fairly good bus

CATALUÑA

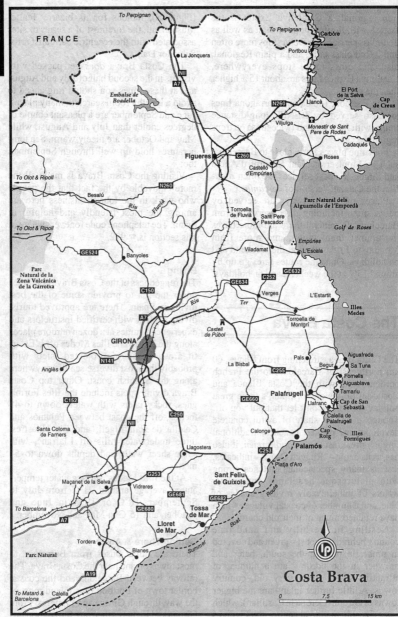

Costa Brava

0   7.5   15 km

services to the coast. Bus services up and down the coast itself are mostly reasonable, but on a few stretches they don't exist at all.

In summer an alternative approach to the southern Costa Brava from Barcelona is by a combination of suburban *rodalia* train and boat (see the Tossa de Mar Getting There & Away section).

The A-7 *autopista* and the toll-free N-II highway both run from Barcelona via Girona and Figueres to the French border a few km north of La Jonquera. Other roads run up the coast itself and inland to Girona and Figueres. The beauty of having your own wheels in this part of Spain is that, thanks to its relatively compact scale, you can reach a wide range of places in day trips from any single base on or near the coast.

TOSSA DE MAR

Curving round a boat-speckled bay guarded by a headland strung with medieval defensive walls and towers, Tossa de Mar is a little old white village of crooked, narrow streets onto which tourism has tacked a larger, modern extension of straighter, wider ones. Though in July and August it's hard to reach the water's edge without tripping over oily limbs, this is a far less packaged and more relaxed resort than its bigger neighbour 12 km south-east, Lloret de Mar – which is a *real* concrete and neon jungle of Piccadilly pubs, *Bierkeller* and soccer chants.

Tossa was one of the first places on the Costa Brava to attract foreign visitors, with a small colony of artists and writers gravitating here in the 1930s. The painter Marc Chagall spent the summer of 1934 in Tossa and dubbed it the 'Blue Paradise'.

Orientation & Information

The bus station is beside the GE-682 road where it leaves Tossa for Lloret de Mar, fronting a roundabout with the unmistakably Catalan name Plaça de les Nacions sense Estat (Stateless Nations Plaza). Almost next door, at Avinguda El Pelegrí 25, is the helpful tourist office (☎ 34 01 08), open June to August, Monday to Saturday from 9 am to 9 pm, Sunday 10 am to 1 pm; in other months

hours are shorter and it's closed on Sunday. The main beach, Platja Gran, and the older part of town, are a 10 minute walk to the south-east.

You'll find banks, many with ATMs, along such streets as Avinguda Costa Brava and Carrer Pou de la Vila, and around Plaça d'Espanya. The post office is on Carrer Maria Auxiliadora, one block east of Avinguda El Pelegrí. The postcode is 17320.

There's a police station (☎ 34 01 35) in the *ajuntament* (town hall) at Carrer Església 4 in the old town. The Centre Mèdic Tossa (☎ 34 14 48) at Carrer Sant Sebastià 2 is a private-practice medical clinic. The state clinic is the Ambulatori (☎ 34 18 28) in the Casa del Mar at Avinguda Catalunya s/n, about one km north-west of the old town. It has emergency and ambulance services.

Old Tossa

The **walls and towers** on the pine-dotted headland, Mont Guardí, at the end of the main beach, were built in the 12th to 14th centuries. The area they girdle is known as the **Vila Vella** (old town). You can walk up on Mont Guardí, where there are also vestiges of a castle, and a lighthouse (*far* in Catalan), at any time of the day or night. In the lower part of the Vila Vella is the interesting **Museu Municipal** in the 14th and 15th century Palau (palace) del Batlle, open Tuesday to Sunday from 10 am to 6.30 pm (200 ptas). In the museum are mosaics and other finds from a Roman villa off Avinguda El Pelegrí, and Tossa-related art including *El Violinista* by Chagall. Behind the musician in question, a Tossa window opens on to a landscape of Chagall's homeland Belarus.

The so-called **Vila Nova** (new town) is actually that part of the old town that stands outside (north of) the walled Vila Vella. Much of its tangle of lanes dates from the 18th century. The real new town stretches a lot further north, north-west and north-east from here.

Beaches & Coves

The main town beach, **Platja Gran**, which begins at the foot of Mont Guardí, is a broad

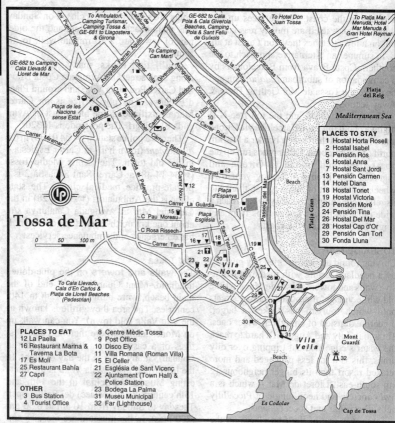

Tossa de Mar

0   50   100 m

Mediterranean Sea

Platja
del Reig

Beach

Platja Gran

Beach

Vila
Vella

Mont
Guardí

Es Codolar

Cap de Tossa

To Ambulatori,
Camping Turismar,
Camping Tossa &
GE-681 to Llagostera
& Girona

GE-682 to Cala
Pola & Cala Giverola
Beaches, Camping
Pola & Sant Feliu
de Guíxols

To Hotel Don
Juan Tossa

To Platja Mar
Menuda, Hotel
Mar Menuda &
Gran Hotel Reymar

GE-682 to Camping
Cala Llevadó &
Lloret de Mar

To Camping
Can Martí

Av Puerto Rico

Av de Catalunya

Avinguda Ferran Agulló

Carrer Pola

Carrer Giverola

Avinguda Costa Brava

Avinguda Auxiliadora

Carrer Enric Granados

Carrer Barcelona

Avinguda de la Palma

Plaça de les
Nacions
sense Estat

Carrer Miramar

Carrer Miramar

Carrer Pintora Barber

Carrer Martín

C Nou

Carrer Pola

Carrer C Bernats

Avinguda el Pelegrí

Carrer Sant Miquel

Carrer Nou

Plaça
d'Espanya

Carrer La Guàrdia

Plaça
Església

C Pau Moreau

C Rosa Rissech

Carrer Tarull

C Sant Telm

Passeig del Mar

Carrer La Guàrdia

C Enric

C Socors

C Estret

Vila
Nova

Carrer Sant Josep

C Portal

PLACES TO STAY
1 Hostal Horta Rosell
2 Hostal Isabel
5 Pensión Ros
6 Hostal Anna
7 Hostal Sant Jordi
13 Pensión Carmen
14 Hotel Diana
18 Hostal Tonet
19 Hostal Victoria
20 Pensión Moré
24 Pensión Tina
26 Hostal Del Mar
28 Hostal Cap d'Or
29 Pensión Can Tort
30 Fonda Lluna

PLACES TO EAT
12 La Paella
16 Restaurant Marina &
Taverna La Bota
17 Es Molí
25 Restaurant Bahía
27 Capri

8 Centre Mèdic Tossa
9 Post Office
10 Disco Ely
11 Villa Romana (Roman Villa)
15 El Celler
21 Església de Sant Vicenç
22 Ajuntament (Town Hall) &
Police Station
23 Bodega La Palma
31 Museu Municipal
32 Far (Lighthouse)

OTHER
3 Bus Station
4 Tourist Office

and busy sweep of yellow sand. Further
along the same bay are the little **Platja del
Reig** and then **Platja Mar Menuda** at the end
of Avinguda Sant Ramon Penyafort, which
tends to be less crowded. The coasts north-
east and south-west of Tossa are strung with
rocky coves, some with small beaches
(sometimes sandy, more often stony). You
can walk cross-country from Tossa to the
small **Cala Llevadó** and **Cala d'En Carlos**
beaches, three km south-west, or the longer
Platja de Llorell (3.5 km), or drive down to
Platja de Llorell from the GE-682. To the
north-east, you can walk down from the GE-

682 to small beaches such as **Cala Pola** (four
km), **Cala Giverola** (five km), **Cala Salions**
(eight km) and **Platja Vallpregona** (11 km).
In summer, glass-bottomed boats run every
hour or so to some of these north-eastern
beaches from Platja Gran, calling in at a few
sea caves on the way (around 900 ptas
return).

Places to Stay

Tossa has over 80 hotels, *hostales* and *pensiones*. You'll find plenty of them open from
Semana Santa to October, but only a handful
outside those months. Some of the best-

value places get booked up weeks, even months, ahead for high summer.

Places to Stay – bottom end

Camping There are five camping grounds around Tossa, each holding between 800 and 1700 people, but you're unlikely to find any of them open between mid-October and Semana Santa. Nearest to town, and one of the cheapest, is *Camping Can Martí* (☎ 34 08 51) on Rambla Pau Casals, one km back from the beach. Here two adults with a car and tent pay 2700 ptas. *Camping Turismar* (☎ 34 04 63) and *Camping Tossa* (☎ 34 05 47) are about one and 2.5 km further out, respectively, on the GE-681. *Camping Pola* (☎ 34 10 50), four km out on the GE-682, is very well sited in a shady valley which leads down to a picturesque cove. *Camping Cala Llevadó* (☎ 34 03 14) is three km out on the GE-682 to Lloret de Mar.

Pensiones & Hostales In July and August it's easier to find rooms in the streets just down from the tourist office and bus station than in the older part of town or on the seafront. Even so, you might want to start looking in the more atmospheric older area. One of the cheapest places here is *Pensión Moré* (☎ 34 03 39) at Carrer Sant Telm 9, which has good-sized singles/doubles for 1300/2600 ptas; bathrooms are shared. *Fonda Lluna* (☎ 34 03 65), also called *Can Lluna*, at Carrer Roqueta 20, is good value at 1700/3400 ptas for small rooms with private bath, and breakfast included.

Pensión Can Tort (☎ 34 11 85) on the corner of Carrer Portal and Carrer Pescadors has sizeable doubles with breakfast for 4400 ptas with bath, or 4000 ptas without. It's open from mid-March to the end of October. *Pensión Tina* (☎ 34 01 44), Carrer dels Tapers 4, has doubles with bath and breakfast for 4000 ptas. This is one place that's open all year. Another is the *Hostal Tonet* (☎ & fax 34 02 37) on Plaça Església, where doubles with bath cost up to 4900 ptas.

On the beachfront, *Hostal Victoria* (☎ 34 01 66), Passeig de Mar 23, is plain but adequate with singles/doubles facing Platja Gran for 3100/4900 ptas, and rear rooms for 2300/3500 ptas. All have private bathroom.

There are a dozen or so pensiones and hostales within three blocks of the tourist office – though none seems to be open from November to April. *Pensión Ros* (☎ 34 02 11) right by the tourist office at Avinguda El Pelegrí 27 has good rooms with bath for up to 3000/4500 ptas. The friendly *Hostal Sant Jordi* (☎ 34 01 34) at Carrer Giverola s/n, open July to September, has small but decent rooms with bath for around 2500/3800 ptas. Comparable places in this area include *Hostal Isabel* (☎ 34 03 36), Carrer Sant Vicenç 3; *Hostal Anna* (☎ 34 06 44), Carrer Tomàs Barber 17, which also has rooms without bath for 1500/2600 ptas; and *Hostal Horta Rosell* (☎ 34 04 32), Carrer Pola 29.

A few blocks towards the old town, *Pensión Carmen* (☎ 34 05 26) at Carrer Sant Miquel 10, with signs also saying *Pensión Pepi* and, for good measure, *Pensión Carmen-Pepi*, has decent doubles only, with shower, for 4000 ptas.

Places to Stay – middle & top end

Two comfortable beachfront hostales are *Hostal Del Mar* (☎ 34 00 80), Passeig de Mar 13, with doubles for 6500 ptas, and the attractive *Hostal Cap d'Or* (☎ & fax 34 00 81), right in front of the old town walls at Passeig de Vila Vella 1, with doubles for 7200 ptas. They're both open from May to October. *Hotel Diana* (☎ 34 18 86; fax 34 11 03), Plaça d'Espanya 6, is a relaxed, small-scale, older hotel fronting Platja Gran. It has a Gaudí fireplace in the lounge and a nice interior courtyard. It's open from April to November, with singles/doubles for around 7500/10,400 ptas.

On Platja Mar Menuda, the 40 room *Hotel Mar Menuda* (☎ 34 10 00; fax 34 00 87) has high standards of comfort and service at 10,200 ptas for doubles. It's open from April to September. The 285 room *Hotel Don Juan Tossa* (☎ 34 07 62; fax 34 17 61), Carrer Barcelona 22, has rooms at 6600/10,000 ptas

Catalan Cuisine

Catalans love their food, and with good reason, for it nudges Basque cuisine for the title of Spain's best. Its variety and originality stem mainly from Cataluña's geographical diversity, which is the source of fresh, high-quality seafood, meat, poultry, game, fruit and vegetables. These can come in some unusual and delicious combinations – meat and seafood (a genre known as *mar i muntanya*, sea and mountain), poultry and fruit, fish and nuts. You'll probably eat more truly Catalan food away from Barcelona, where for some reason it tends to be a bit expensive in restaurants.

The essence of Catalan food lies in its sauces for meat and fish. These sauces may not be mentioned on menus as they're so ubiquitous. There are five main types: *sofregit*, of fried onion, tomato and garlic; *samfaina*, sofregit plus red pepper and aubergine or zucchini (courgette); *picada*, based on ground almonds, usually with garlic, parsley, pine or hazel nuts, and sometimes breadcrumbs; *allioli*, pounded garlic with olive oil, often with egg yolk added to make more of a mayonnaise; and *romesco*, an almond, tomato, olive oil, garlic and vinegar sauce, also used as a salad dressing.

Catalans find it hard to understand why other people put mere butter on bread when *pa amb tomáquet* – bread sliced then rubbed with tomato, olive oil and salt – is so easy. They eat it with almost everything and prefer their *entrepans* (bocadillos) this way too.

Most main courses are meat or fish with a sauce and potatoes. There are some good stews too. And there's good Catalan wine, including *cava*, the inexpensive local version of Champagne, to wash it all down with. Here are some typical Catalan dishes:

Starters

amanida Catalana – Catalan salad; almost any mix of lettuce, olives, tomatoes, hard-boiled eggs, onion, chicory, celery, green pepper and garlic, with fish, ham or sausage, and mayonnaise or an oil-and-vinegar dressing

calçots amb romesco – calçots are a type of long onion, delicious as a starter with romesco sauce

escalivada – red peppers and aubergines (sometimes onions and tomatoes too), grilled, cooled, peeled, sliced and served with an olive oil, salt and garlic dressing

esqueixada – salad of shredded salted cod *(bacallà)* with tomato, red pepper, onion, white beans, olives, olive oil and vinegar

Main Dishes

arròs a la cassola or *arròs a la Catalana* – Catalan paella, cooked in an earthenware pot, without saffron

botifarra amb mongetes – pork sausage with fried white beans

---

in July and August but half that from November to March.

The 166 room *Gran Hotel Reymar* (☎ 34 03 12; fax 34 15 04) on Mar Menuda oeach is the top place in town, with doubles at 23,000 ptas plus IVA in July and August. It's closed from November to April.

Places to Eat

Tossa has a lot of bland, overpriced eateries. The al fresco restaurants lining Carrer Portal are nicely sited and do some good fish and seafood, but are expensive for what you get.

On the beachfront Passeig de Mar, the *Capri* serves up some of the better value, offering a bit of almost everything – salads

from 500 ptas, pizzas, pasta, meat or seafood from around 850 ptas. Servings are generous and in the high season it's open 24 hours. *Restaurant Bahía*, Passeig de Mar 19, does some of Tossa's best food, with lots of seafood and Catalan offerings. Most main dishes are 1500 ptas or more.

On Carrer Tarull, beside the church in the old town, *Restaurant Marina* at No 6 and *Taverna La Bota* both offer two-course menús with wine and bread for 950 ptas. The Marina also does an 800 ptas version with beer, and some economical specials such as chicken, chips, salad and beer for 500 ptas. *Es Molí* at No 3 on the same street serves up classier local cooking, including good *cargols* – snails, a religion in parts of Cataluña; popular stewed with rabbit *(conill)* and chilli

escudella – a meat, sausage and vegetable stew whose liquid, mixed with noodles or rice, is served as a soup, followed by the rest as a main course known as *carn d'olla*

fricandó – a pork and vegetable stew

mandonguilles amb sipia – meatballs with cuttlefish, a subtly flavoured land-sea combination

pollastre amb escamerlans – chicken with shrimps, another amphibious event

sarsuela (zarzuela) – mixed seafood cooked in sofregit with seasonings, a Barcelona invention

Desserts

crema Catalana – a cream custard with a crisp burnt sugar coating

mel i mató – honey and fresh cream cheese – simple but delicious

Other good things to look out for include duck *(ànec)*, goose *(oca)* and canalons (Catalan cannelloni). *Fideuas* (noodles) are usually served with tomato and meat/sausage or fish sauces. Wild mushrooms are a Catalan passion – people disappear into the forests in autumn to pick them. There are many, many types – the large succulent *rovellons* are a favourite. Here are more words to help you with Catalan-only menus:

ametller – almond	*llet* – milk
anyell – lamb	*llonganissa* – salami-type sausage
bou – beef	*oli* – oil
caldereta – a seafood stew	*orxata* – horchata
carxofe – artichoke	*ostra* – oyster
castanya – chestnut	*ous* – eggs
ceba – onion	*pastis* – cake
costella – cutlet	*pebre* – pepper
cranc – crab	*peix* – fish
entrepan – bocadillo	*pernil de la comarca* – country-cured ham
farcit – stuffed	*pops* – octopus
formatge – cheese	*rap* – monkfish
fregit – fried	*suquet* – seafood stew
fuet – salami-type sausage	*torrada* – open toasted sandwich
gelat – ice cream	*truita* – omelette/tortilla, or trout
llagosta – lobster	*xai* – lamb
llenties – lentils	

prawns and fideuas, and has a nice garden patio. There are menús for 2000 and 3000 ptas.

La Paella, Carrer Nou 12, is one of the cheaper places in town, with a menú for 900 ptas, or fish and chips for 450 ptas.

Entertainment

The old town's lively bars, some with music, are along and near Carrer Sant Josep. *Bodega La Palma* is one that manages to maintain an old-fashioned wine-cellar atmosphere. *El Celler* on Carrer Nou just off Carrer La Guàrdia plays some funky music too.

La Tortuga on Avinguda Sant Ramon de Penyafort is a relaxed pub-style bar, often

with live jazz. *Disco Ely* off Avinguda Costa Brava is the in place to carry on at later.

Getting There & Away

Bus SARFA runs to/from Barcelona's Estació del Nord six to 10 times daily. The trip takes 1¼ hours and costs 925 ptas.

There are fairly frequent buses to/from Lloret de Mar (140 ptas): in summer they go every 30 minutes from 8.45 am to 8.45 pm.

Buses don't travel the 23 km stretch of the GE-682 north-east to Sant Feliu de Guíxols. In July and August only, three daily SARFA buses go to/from Sant Feliu via Lloret de Mar and an inland route, taking one hour. From Sant Feliu there are SARFA buses to Girona,

Palafrugell, Torroella de Montgrí and L'Escala (most several times daily). In June, July or August you can also reach Sant Feliu by one of the six daily boats from Tossa (see Boat below).

Two or three buses daily run direct between Tossa and Girona in July and August, and one daily in the first half of September, taking one hour. In other months, there are three or four buses daily from Lloret de Mar to Girona, from where you could reach Palafrugell and points north.

Car & Motorcycle From Barcelona, the 460 ptas of tolls on the A-19 autopista, which takes you almost to Blanes, save a weary trudge on the toll-free N-II. To the north, the 23 km stretch of the GE-682 to Sant Feliu de Guíxols is a great drive, winding its way up, down and around some very picturesque bays. On this road Rose Macaulay, author of *Fabled Shore* (1950), 'met only one mule cart, laden with pine boughs, and two very polite *guardias civiles*'.

Boat In June, July and August two boat services offer a scenic way of reaching Tossa, or of taking an outing from it. Cruce-tours (☎ 34 03 19 in Tossa, ☎ 36 44 99 in Lloret, ☎ 33 01 78 in Blanes) and Viajes Marítimos (☎ 908-93 64 76) both run several times a day between Blanes, Lloret de Mar and Tossa (one to 1½ hours), with stops at a few in-between points. A few of the services continue to/from Calella, 12 km south of Blanes (*not* Calella de Palafrugell further north), and/or Palamós, north of Tossa, again with intermediate stops (including Sant Feliu de Guíxols). You could catch one of the frequent suburban rodalia trains from Barcelona's Catalunya station to Calella (one hour; 345 ptas one way) or Blanes (1¼ hours; 440 ptas), then transfer to the boat. A return boat ticket to Tossa is 1400 ptas from Calella, or 1050 ptas from Sant Feliu de Guíxols. In many places the boats simply pull up at the beach (in Tossa, at Platja Gran) and tickets are sold at a booth there. Tourist offices are the best source of up-to-date schedules and information on landing points.

Getting Around
Scooter, Moped & Bicycle Rental Road Runner (☎ 34 05 03) on Avinguda de la Palma rents mopeds for 3900 ptas a day, scooters for 4900 ptas, mountain bikes for 2000 ptas and other bikes for 1100 ptas.

PALAFRUGELL & AROUND
The 21 km reach of coast from Sant Feliu de Guíxols to Palamós is unattractively built up all the way, but north of Palamós begins one of the most beautiful stretches of the Costa Brava. The town of Palafrugell, five km inland, is the main access point for a cluster of attractive beach spots.

East of Palafrugell are Calella de Palafru-gell, Llafranc and Tamariu, one-time fishing villages squeezed into small bays and now three of the Costa Brava's most charming low-key and low-rise little resorts. Even in July and August they remain relatively laid-back, though accommodation is on the expensive side (Palafrugell itself has some cheaper rooms). Begur, seven km north-east of Palafrugell, is a slightly shabby village of 2700 souls, with a cluster of less developed beaches nearby.

Palafrugell
Palafrugell, a pleasant enough town of 17,000, is the main transport, shopping and service hub for the area.

Orientation & Information The C-255 Palamós-Girona road passes through the west side of Palafrugell, a 10 minute walk from the central square, Plaça Nova. The tourist office (☎ 30 02 28) is at Carrer del Carrilet 2 beside the C-255. It's open Monday to Saturday from at least 10 am to 1 pm and 5 to 7 pm, Sunday and holidays from 10 am to 1 pm. In July and August Monday-to-Saturday hours are 9 am to 9 pm.

The SARFA bus station is at Carrer de Torres Jonama 73-79, five minutes walk from the tourist office and 10 minutes from Plaça Nova. Banks, many with ATMs, and telephones and shops cluster on and around Plaça Nova. The post office is at Carrer de Torres Jonama 16. The postcode is 17200.

The local police (☎ 092 or ☎ 61 31 01) are in the ajuntament at Carrer de Cervantes 4, two blocks south of Plaça Nova.

Things to See & Do A busy morning **market** (selling mainly food) is held daily except Monday on Carrer de Pi i Margall, north off Plaça Nova. The **Museu del Suro**, dedicated to the important local cork industry, is one block east of Carrer de Pi i Margall at Carrer de la Tarongeta 31. It's open Tuesday to Saturday from 5 to 9 pm, and in summer also Tuesday to Sunday from 10 am to 1 pm.

Places to Stay *Fonda L'Estrella* (☎ 30 00 05) at Carrer Quatre Cases 13-17, 1½ blocks west of Plaça Nova, is a pleasant, cool, old-fashioned house where singles/doubles with shared bathrooms are 1800/3400 ptas. It's closed from October to March.

Two blocks in the opposite direction from the plaça, *Residència Familiar* (☎ 30 00 43) at Carrer de Sant Sebastià 29 is a more ordinary but good and clean place with rooms at 1950/3900 ptas. It closes between mid-November and mid-March. The good *Hostal Plaja* (☎ 30 05 26) across the street at No 34 has a nice courtyard, and rooms with bath for 3000/4500 ptas. It's open all year.

Getting There & Away SARFA (☎ 30 06 23) runs buses to/from Barcelona's Estació del Nord (two hours; 1350 to 1535 ptas) four to 11 times daily, and to/from Girona (one hour) up to 14 times daily. SARFA also has a few daily services north to Begur, Torroella de Montgrí, L'Escala and Figueres (1½ hours), and in July and August only two daily buses to Lloret de Mar and Tossa de Mar (two hours).

Calella de Palafrugell

The southernmost of the three Palafrugell resorts, Calella is also the most spread out. Its low buildings are strung almost Aegean-style around a bay of rocky points and small beaches, with a few fishing boats still hauled up on the sand. The tourist office (☎ 61 44 75), down near the seafront at Carrer de les Voltes 6, is open from April to September,

Monday to Saturday from 10 am to 1 pm and 5 to 8 pm, Sunday and holidays from 10 am to 1 pm.

Things to See & Do Apart from picking your place on one of the beaches and cooling off in the sea from time to time, there are nice footpaths to stroll along the coasts north-east to Llafranc (20 or 30 minutes), or south to Platja del Golfet beach close to Cap Roig (about 40 minutes). Atop Cap Roig is the **Jardí Botànic de Cap Roig**, a beautiful garden of 1200 Mediterranean species, set around the early 20th century castle/palace of Nikolai Voevalsky, a tsarist colonel who fled the Russian Revolution. The garden is open daily, from 8 am to 8 pm in summer and 9 am to 6 pm in winter (200 ptas).

Special Events Calella stages probably the Costa Brava's biggest summer *cantada de havaneres* sing-song. Havaneres are strangely melancholy songs from the Caribbean which became popular among Costa Brava sailors in the 19th and early 20th centuries as a result of Cataluña's connections with Cuba at that time. Like several other Catalan traditions, they are enjoying a revival today. Havaneres are traditionally accompanied by the drinking of *cremat*, a rum, coffee, sugar, lemon and cinnamon concoction which must be set alight for a few minutes before you quaff it. Traditionally, Calella's cantada has been in August, but in 1996 it was on the first Saturday of July, following hard on the heels of the *festa major*, held around 29 June.

Places to Stay & Eat *Camping Moby Dick* (☎ 61 43 07), in the village at Carrer de la Costa Verde 16-28, has room for 470 people. *La Siesta Camping* (☎ 61 51 16) has a shady site by the Palafrugell road 1.25 km back from the beach, and space for 2000. Both open from April to September. Moby Dick charges 2040 ptas plus IVA for two adults, a tent and a car; at La Siesta it's 2760 ptas plus IVA.

Hostería del Plancton (☎ 61 50 81) at Carrer de Codina 16 (follow the signs to

Església de Sant Pere) has the best-value rooms in any of three Palafrugell resorts. Unfortunately it's only open from June to September. Good, clean little rooms, some with balconies and all sharing bathrooms, are 1800 ptas per person.

Hotel Batlle (☎ 61 59 05), Carrer de les Voltes 2, just back from the beach, has doubles with bathroom and breakfast for 9000 to 10,000 ptas, depending what they look out on. *Hotel Mediterrani/Mediterráneo* (☎ 61 45 00), overlooking the bay at Carrer de Francesc Estrabau 34, has good rooms with similar prices but is only open from mid-May to September.

Restaurant Tony's on the beach offers some of the better eating value, with platos combinados from 650 ptas. *La Clova*, a friendly and sometimes lively bar at Carrer de Codina 6 near the Hostería del Plancton, has platos combinados from 500 ptas.

Getting There & Away Buses from the SARFA station in Palafrugell run to La Siesta Camping, then Calella, then Llafranc, then back to La Siesta and Palafrugell, a round trip of 30 minutes. They go every half-hour or so from 7.40 am to 8.30 pm in July and August; the rest of the year, service is progressively reduced, to three or four buses a day from November to February.

Llafranc

Barely two km north-east of Calella de Palafrugell and now merging with it along the roads back from the rocky coast between them, Llafranc has a smaller bay but a longer stretch of sand, is a bit more fashionable and lively, and gets more crowded. The tourist office (☎ 30 50 08), a kiosk on Carrer de Roger de Llúria just back from the west end of the beach, is open June to September, the same hours as Calella de Palafrugell's.

Things to Do From the **Far de Sant Sebastià** lighthouse and **Ermita de Sant Sebastià** hermitage, up on Cap de Sant Sebastià, the cape to the east of the town, there are tremendous views in both directions along the coast. It's a 30 or 40 minute walk to get up there;

head up the steps from the harbour, then follow the road up to the right. You can walk on to Tamariu, too: check with the tourist office about the most scenic of the several routes available.

Places to Stay & Eat *Camping Kim's* (☎ 30 11 56) is in a pine wood on Camí de la Font d'en Xeco, about 750 metres back from the beach. It's open from April to September and charges 2700 ptas, plus IVA, for two adults, a tent and a car.

The cheapest rooms are at *Residencia Montaña* (☎ 30 04 04; fax 61 20 64) at Carrer de Cesària 1, off Plaça del Promontori, the square towards the east end of the main beachfront drag, Passeig de Cipsela. It's fraying slightly at the edges, but has clean, basic singles/doubles with breakfast for 2400/4500 ptas, or 2650/5100 ptas with private shower – all plus IVA. It closes from October to March. *Pensió Celimar* (☎ 30 13 74) at Carrer de Carudo 12 – also off Plaça del Promontori – is more modern, stays open all year, and has doubles with private bath for 5000 ptas plus IVA. Its restaurant offers some of the better value in town, with salads from 425 ptas and seafood dishes from 750 ptas.

Hotel Montecarlo (☎ 30 04 04; fax 61 20 64) at Carrer de Cesària 14 has clean singles/doubles with balcony, TV, private bath and breakfast for 4350/8500 ptas plus IVA in the high season. It closes from December to March. *Hotel Llafranc* (☎ 30 02 08 or 30 52 59) on Plaça del Promontori is a good bet if you want somewhere classier. It's open all year with doubles at 11,100 ptas plus IVA in the high season.

La Pasta at the west end of Passeig de Cipsela is popular for its pasta, pizzas and salads from 700 ptas. *Restaurant Bella Costa*, a bit further along the seafront on Carrer Francesc de Blanes, has reasonable-value three course menús for 1100 and 1500 ptas, plus IVA.

Getting There & Away See the Calella de Palafrugell section for information on bus services. The Llafranc stop is on Carrer de la Sirena, up the hill on the Calella side of town.

Tamariu

Three or four km north up the coast from Llafranc as the crow flies, and nearly twice as far by road, Tamariu is smaller and attracts a quieter, more select Catalan crowd. Its beach has some of the cleanest waters on Spain's Mediterranean coast. The tourist office (☎ 62 01 93), in the middle of the village on Carrer de la Riera, is open the same months and hours as Llafranc's.

Places to Stay & Eat *Camping Tamariu* (☎ 62 04 22), about one km back from the beach on Carrer de la Riera, opens from May to September and charges 2100 ptas plus IVA for two adults, a tent and a car.

Hotel Sol d'Or (☎ 62 01 72), 500 metres nearer the beach at Carrer de la Riera 18, is open from June to September. Doubles with private bath are 5250 ptas plus IVA.

The modern *Hotel Es Furió* (☎ 62 00 36), just one block from the beach at Carrer del Foraió 5-7, is open all year and has comfortable rooms for 7400 ptas a double, plus IVA. Its restaurant does a decent 1300 ptas three course menú. *Hotel Tamariu* (☎ 62 00 31) is right on the beach at Passeig del Mar 3, and has doubles at 7500 ptas (closed October to mid-May), and a good but expensive Catalan restaurant, with few main dishes under 1200 ptas. The beachfront is strung with seafood eateries, and *Restaurant Royal* is one of the best.

Getting There & Away SARFA buses from Palafrugell run to Tamariu (15 minutes) three or four times daily, from mid-June to mid-September only.

A rough road will take you on to Aiguablava (see Beaches near Begur).

Begur

The **castell**, dating from the 10th century, on a rock above the village, is still pretty much in the state in which it was left by Spanish troops who wrecked it in 1810 to impede the advance of Napoleon's army. Dotted around the village are half a dozen towers built for defence against 16th and 17th century pirates. There's a tourist office (☎ 62 40 20)

on Plaça de l'Església, in the ajuntament facing the church.

Places to Stay The pine-shaded *Camping Begur* (☎ 62 32 01), open from April to September, is about two km south on the road from Palafrugell. *Hotel Rosa* (☎ 62 30 15) at Carrer Pi i Ralló 11, a few steps towards the castle from the church, has nice rooms with bath; singles/doubles with breakfast are 3425/6650 ptas plus IVA. It's open for Semana Santa and from May to September. Just up the hill and on the first street to the right, *Habitacions Sant Isidre* (☎ 62 25 39), Carrer Metge Pi 3, is the cheapest place, with doubles only, and shared baths, for 3500 ptas.

Getting There & Away SARFA (☎ 62 24 26), at Plaça Forgas 6, runs two or three daily buses to/from Barcelona's Estació del Nord (2¼ hours) via Palafrugell. There's one SARFA bus, Monday to Friday, to/from Girona.

Beaches near Begur

You can reach a series of smallish beaches, on a very pretty stretch of coast, by turning east off the Palafrugell road two km south of the centre of Begur. About two km down is a turning to the black sand beach of **Platja Fonda** (one km). Half a km further on is the turning to **Fornells** (one km), a small village on one of the most picturesque bays of the whole Costa Brava, with a small marina, a small beach and incredibly blue waters. The large but friendly *Hotel Aiguablava* (☎ 62 20 58; fax 62 21 12) overlooking most of this has doubles for 12,000 ptas plus IVA (closed mid-November to mid-February). *Hotel Bonaigua* (☎ 62 20 50; fax 62 20 54), back up the street a little, charges 9900 ptas plus IVA (closed October to March). Back up at the Fornells turning, *Restaurant Ondina* (☎ 62 20 52), open April to October, has four rooms at 7000 ptas a double, plus IVA.

One km on from the Fornells turning is **Aiguablava**, with a slightly bigger and much busier beach, and the *Parador de Aigua-blava* (☎ 62 21 62) enjoying lovely views back across the Fornells bay. Doubles are 18,000 ptas plus IVA in the high season.

Another road from Begur leads a couple of km east to the small beach of **Aiguafreda** on a lovely cove backed by pine-covered hills, and, a bit further south, the slightly more built-up **Sa Tuna** beach. If you fancy staying, try *Hostal Sa Rascassa* (☎ 62 28 45) at Aiguafreda.

Getting There & Away A Bus Platges (beach bus) service runs from Plaça Forgas in Begur from late June to mid-September. It serves Fornells and Aiguablava eight times a day, Aiguafreda and Sa Tuna three times. The fare is 150 ptas one way.

CASTELL DE PÚBOL

Opened to visitors in 1996, the Castell de Púbol at La Pera, just south of the C-255 and 22 km north-west of Palafrugell, is a major addition to north-east Cataluña's 'Salvador Dalí trail', which already included the Teatre-Museu Dalí in Figueres and the Cadaqués area where the artist spent much of his life. It was here that Dalí was almost burnt to a crisp in a 1984 fire.

Dalí bought the Gothic and Renaissance castle – which includes a 14th century church – in about 1970 and gave it to his wife Gala, who lived here without him until she died in 1982. Local lore has it that the notoriously promiscuous Gala was still sending for young village men right up to the time she died in 1982, aged 88. On her death, Dalí himself moved into Púbol, but abandoned it after the fire which nearly cost him his life, to live out his last years at Figueres.

The castle was done up by Dalí in his inimitable style, with lions' heads staring from the tops of cupboards, statues of elephants with giraffes' legs in the garden, and a stuffed giraffe staring at Gala's tomb in the crypt. The strength of the artist's passion for Gala is shown by motifs and reminders of her all over the castle. A visit is in effect a tour of the couple's tortured relationship. The blue bedroom in which Dalí nearly burnt to death now has a bright red fire extinguisher standing ready in the corner. There are many other sumptuous beds in other rooms. In the garage is the blue Cadillac in which Dalí took Gala for a last drive round the estate – after she died.

Check with nearby tourist offices for the castle's current opening times. SARFA buses between Palafrugell and Girona run along the C-255.

GIRONA

The largest city of northern Cataluña, Girona (Gerona in Castilian, population 75,000) sits in a valley 36 km inland from Palafrugell. Its impressive medieval centre, climbing a hill above the Riu Onyar, makes it well worth a visit.

The Roman town of Gerunda lay on the Via Augusta, a road which ran from Rome to Cádiz (Carrer de la Força in Girona's old town follows part of the line of the Via Augusta). Taken from the Muslims by the Franks in 797, Girona became capital of one of Cataluña's most important counties, falling under the sway of Barcelona in the late 9th century. Its wealth in medieval times produced many fine Romanesque and Gothic buildings, which have survived repeated attacks and sieges in wars down the centuries.

Orientation

The narrow streets of the old town climb above the east bank of the Riu Onyar. The old town is little more than one km from end to end, and easy to explore on foot. Several road and foot bridges link it to the new town across the river. The train station is one km to the south-west, on Plaça d'Espanya off Carrer de Barcelona, with the bus station behind it on Carrer Rafael Masó i Valentí.

Information

The tourist office (☎ 22 65 75) is towards the south end of the old town, at Rambla de la Llibertat 1. It's open Monday to Friday from 8 am to 8 pm, Saturday from 8 am to 2 pm and 4 to 8 pm, Sunday from 9 am to 2 pm.

There are branches of La Caixa bank, with ATMs, on Carrer Abeuradors off Rambla de la Llibertat, and on Carrer Nou just across

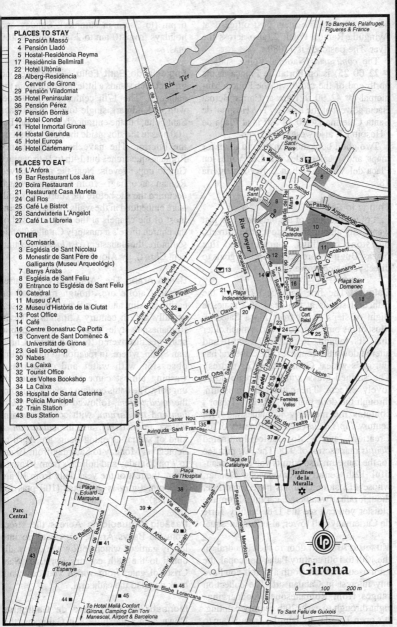

PLACES TO STAY
2   Pensión Massó
4   Pensión Lladó
5   Hostal-Residència Reyma
17 Residència Bellmirall
22 Hotel Ultònia
28 Alberg-Residència
    Cerverí de Girona
29 Pensión Viladomat
35 Hotel Peninsular
36 Pensión Pérez
37 Pensión Borràs
40 Hotel Condal
41 Hotel Inmortal Girona
44 Hostal Gerunda
45 Hotel Europa
46 Hotel Carlemany

PLACES TO EAT
15 L'Anfora
19 Bar Restaurant Los Jara
20 Boira Restaurant
21 Restaurant Casa Marieta
24 Cal Ros
25 Café Le Bistrot
26 Sandwixteria L'Angelot
27 Café La Llibreria

OTHER
1   Comisaría
3   Església de Sant Nicolau
6   Monestir de Sant Pere de
    Galligants (Museu Arqueológic)
7   Banys Àrabs
8   Església de Sant Feliu
9   Entrance to Església de Sant Feliu
10 Catedral
11 Museu d'Art
12 Museu d'Història de la Ciutat
13 Post Office
14 Café
16 Centre Bonastruc Ça Porta
18 Convent de Sant Dòmenec &
    Universitat de Girona
23 Geli Bookshop
30 Nabes
31 La Caixa
32 Tourist Office
33 Les Voltes Bookshop
34 La Caixa
39 Hospital de Santa Caterina
39 Policia Municipal
42 Train Station
43 Bus Station

Girona

0   100   200 m

the Riu Onyar. The main post office is at Avinguda Ramon Folch 2, also across the river. The postcode is 17080.

The *comisaría* (National Police station, ☎ 22 00 25) is on Portal de França at the north end of the old town; the Policia Municipal (☎ 41 90 92) are at Carrer Bernat Bacià 4, west of the Riu Ter. The Hospital de Santa Caterina (☎ 20 14 50) is at Plaça de l'Hospital 5, also west of the river.

Two good bookshops in the old town for maps and local guides are Les Voltes on Plaça del Vi, and Geli at Carrer Argenteria 18.

Things to See

Part of the pleasure of the old town is in just wandering among the narrow, shady streets, old stone buildings, stairways and fine plazas. But there are several special goals to direct your steps towards.

Catedral The fine baroque façade of the cathedral stands at the head of a majestic flight of steps rising from Plaça Catedral. Most of the building, however, is much older than its façade. Repeatedly rebuilt and altered down the centuries, the cathedral has Europe's widest Gothic nave (23 metres). The stained-glass windows create some lovely effects. The cathedral's museum, through the door marked 'Claustre Tresor', contains the masterly Romanesque 11th century *Tapís de la Creació* (Tapestry of the Creation), and a Mozarabic illuminated *Beatus* manuscript of 975. The 300 ptas fee for the museum also admits you to the beautiful 12th century Romanesque cloister, whose 112 stone columns have some fine, though rather weathered, carving. From the cloister you can see the 13th century Torre de Carlemany bell tower, also Romanesque.

Museu d'Art Next door to the cathedral, in the 12th to 16th century Palau Episcopal, the art museum is well worth a visit if you have any interest in Catalan art. The collection ranges from Romanesque woodcarvings right through to early 20th century painting. It's open Tuesday to Saturday from 10 am to 6 pm (to 7 pm in summer), Sunday and holidays from 10 am to 2 pm. Entry is 100 ptas.

Església de Sant Feliu Girona's second great church stands a little downhill from the cathedral. The 17th century main façade, with its landmark single tower, is on Plaça Sant Feliu, but the entrance is at the side. Put 100 ptas in the slot inside the door to light up the interior. The nave has 13th century Romanesque arches but 14th to 16th century Gothic upper levels. Near the altar, carved Roman sarcophagi – from a cemetery which occupied the site before the church was built – are embedded in the walls. In the northernmost of the chapels at the far (west) end of the church there's a masterly Catalan Gothic sculpture, the alabaster *Crist Jacent* (Recumbent Christ), by Aloi de Montbrai.

Banys Àrabs The 'Arab baths' on Carrer Ferran Catòlic are, though modelled on earlier Muslim and even Roman bathhouses, actually a 12th century Christian affair in Romanesque style. They're the only public baths yet discovered from medieval Christian Spain, where, in reaction to the Muslim obsession with water and cleanliness, washing almost came to be regarded as ungodly. The baths contain a changing room, the *apodyterium*, followed by the *frigidarium* and *tepidarium*, with cold and warm waters, respectively, and the *caldarium*, a kind of sauna. Opening hours are April to September Monday to Saturday from 10 am to 7 pm, Sunday and holidays from 10 am to 2 pm; the rest of the year daily from 10 am to 2 pm. Entry is 200 ptas (100 ptas for students).

Passeig Arqueològic Across the street from the Banys Àrabs, steps lead up into lovely gardens which follow the city walls uphill to the 18th century Portal de Sant Cristòfol gate, from which you can walk back down to the cathedral.

Monestir de Sant Pere de Galligants Down across the little Riu Galligans, this

11th and 12th century Romanesque monastery has another lovely cloister with some marvellous animal and monster carvings on the capitals of its pillars. The monastery houses Girona's Museu Arqueològic (archaeology museum), which ranges from prehistoric to medieval times and includes Roman mosaics and medieval Jewish tombstones. Opening hours are Tuesday to Saturday from 10 am to 1 pm and 4.30 to 7 pm, Sunday and holidays from 10 am to 2 pm. Entry is 200 ptas.

Església de Sant Nicolau This pretty little Lombard-style 12th century Romanesque church in front of the Monestir de Sant Pere de Galligants is unusual in having an octagonal tower, and three apses laid out in a trefoil plan.

Call Girona had Cataluña's second most important medieval Jewish community (after Barcelona), and the Jewish quarter, the Call, was centred on Carrer de la Força. The Jewish presence in Girona lasted from at least the 9th century until 1492. For an idea of medieval Jewish life and culture here, visit the Centre Bonastruc Ça Porta, entered from a narrow alley off the upper side of Carrer de la Força. Named after Jewish Girona's most illustrious figure, a 13th century Cabbalist philosopher and mystic, the centre – a warren of rooms and stairways around a courtyard – has exhibitions and a café and is a focus for studies of Jewish Spain. It's open Monday to Saturday from 10 am to 8 pm, Sunday and holidays from 10 am to 3 pm (200 ptas).

Passeig de la Muralla You can walk along a good length of the top of the city walls – the Passeig de la Muralla – from Plaça de Josep Ferrater i Mora, just south of the Universitat de Girona building at the top of the old town, down to Plaça General Marvà near Plaça de Catalunya. This southern part of the old town dates from the 13th century onwards – a bit younger than the more northerly area centred on the cathedral, where the Roman and early medieval towns stood.

✦ ✦ ✦ ✦ ✦ ✦ ✦ ✦ ✦ ✦ ✦ ✦ ✦ ✦

Catalan Romanesque Architecture

Cataluña, through its contacts with southern France and northern Italy, was the first part of Spain to receive the wave of Romanesque architecture and art that rippled across western Europe from about the 10th century.

A blend of ancient Roman traditions and experiments from the Frankish Carolingian empire, the Romanesque style was at first disseminated chiefly by master builders from Byzantine-influenced Lombardy in northern Italy. Typical features of the simple early Romanesque churches were massive masonry to support barrel vaults; tall, square bell towers; aisles separated by lines of pillars which are joined by semicircular arches; semicircular arches round doors and windows; semicircular apses; and blind arcades and pilasters on outside walls.

From the end of the 11th century stonemasons began to deck Catalan churches with increasing amounts of sculpture (notably on the capitals of columns), and bigger churches started to appear, with up to five aisles and apses, transepts, and some fine cloisters.

Cataluña has over 2000 surviving Romanesque buildings. They're much more numerous in what's known as Catalunya Vella (Old Cataluña) – roughly north of a line from Sitges to Tremp – which was taken from the Muslims in the 9th century, than in the southern Catalunya Nova (New Cataluña), which remained in Muslim hands till the mid-12th century. ■

✦ ✦ ✦ ✦ ✦ ✦ ✦ ✦ ✦ ✦ ✦ ✦ ✦ ✦

Places to Stay – bottom end

The nearest camping ground is *Camping Can Toni Manescal* (☎ 47 61 17) at Fornells de la Selva, seven km south. It only holds 140 people but is open all year.

Girona has a good modern youth hostel, the *Alberg-Residència Cerverí de Girona* (☎ 21 81 21), well placed in the old town at Carrer dels Ciutadans 9. From October to June it's virtually full with students but in the other months there are 100 places available. High-season rates are charged all year.

There are several pensiones and hostales in the old town. In July and August the better ones fill up fairly quickly. *Pensión Pérez* (☎ 22 40 08) on quiet little Plaça Bell.lloc has a gloomy entrance stairway but clean, adequate singles/doubles for 1400/2700 ptas, and is friendly. The owners have another cheap place, the *Pensión Borràs* (same ☎), round the corner at Travessera Auriga 6, and might be found there if no-one answers at the Pérez.

Pensión Lladó (☎ 21 09 98) at Carrer Barca 31 has singles/doubles with bath for 2000/3000 ptas. They're ordinary but OK for the price. Nearby at Plaça Sant Pere 12, *Pensión Massó* (☎ 20 71 75) has rooms with shared baths for 2500 ptas a double; the sign just says 'Habitacions'.

One of the nicest cheaper places in the old town is the *Pensión Viladomat* (☎ 20 31 76), Carrer dels Ciutadans 5. Comfortable singles/doubles with bath are 1800/3600 ptas, but there are only eight of them. *Hostal-Residència Reyma* (☎ 20 02 28), Pujada del Rei Martí 15, has 18 good rooms, some with balcony, at 3745 ptas a double, or 5350 ptas with private bathroom.

The fairly modern *Hotel Peninsular* (☎ 20 38 00), just west of the Riu Onyar at Carrer Nou 3, has 68 rooms at 2000/3000 ptas with shared bath, or 3600/5600 ptas with private bath, all plus IVA. *Hostal Gerunda* (☎ 20 22 85) at Carrer de Barcelona 34 near the train station has doubles with private bath for 3600 ptas.

Places to Stay – middle & top end

The attractive little *Residència Bellmirall* (☎ 20 40 09) at Carrer Bellmirall 3 is in a lovely medieval stone building with singles/doubles for 4100/6460 ptas, or 4300/7000 ptas with bath, including breakfast.

Everywhere else in this price range is in the new town west of the Riu Onyar. The *Hotel Inmortal Girona* (☎ 20 79 00), Carrer de Barcelona 31 near the train station, the *Hotel Condal* (☎ 20 44 62), Carrer de Joan Maragall 10, and the *Hotel Europa* (☎ 20 27 50), Carrer Julí Garreta 21, all have doubles for 5000 to 6000 ptas. The *Hotel Ultònia* (☎ 20 38 50), Gran Via de Jaume I 22, is ugly outside but has very comfortable, well-equipped rooms at 9900 ptas plus IVA for doubles.

Top of the tree are the modern *Hotel Melià Confort Girona* (☎ 24 32 33), Carrer de Barcelona 112, and the *Hotel Carlemany* (☎ 21

12 12), Plaça Miquel Santaló, both with doubles for around 13,000 ptas plus IVA.

Places to Eat

The cafés under the arcades on Rambla de la Llibertat and nearby Plaça del Vi are good places to soak up a bit of atmosphere. Several of those on Rambla de la Llibertat offer decent paellas for 850 ptas or more.

The bright *Sandwitxeria L'Angelot* at Carrer Cort Reial 3 is popular for its pancakes and salads from 375 ptas, and pizzas from 550 ptas, and stays open late.

Cafè Le Bistrot on Pujada de Sant Domènec, one of the most picturesque stairways in the old town, is a treat. Cool, relaxed and vaguely bohemian, it serves salads, pizzes de pagès (good little bread-base pizzas) and crêpes all for between 400 and 625 ptas. Also nice is the calm *Cafè La Llibreria* on Carrer Ferreires Velles, doing light meals such as lasagne or escalivada for 600 ptas, or green salads for 350 ptas.

Bar Restaurant Los Jara at Carrer de la Força 4, and *L'Anfora* just up the hill at No 15, both have good-value four course menús for 1000 ptas.

Plaça Independència in the new town, just across one of the Riu Onyar footbridges, has a few fairly economical eateries. Busy *Boira Restaurant* does a three course self-service meal for 890 ptas; *Restaurant Casa Marieta* has a respectable four course menú for 1000 ptas plus IVA.

For a more expensive meal it's hard to beat the veteran *Cal Ros* at Carrer Cort Reial 9, serving excellent Catalan specialities such as chicken with crayfish (cigalas), oxtail with olives, esqueixada, or, if you're adventurous, snails with pig trotters! A meal will set you back around 2500 to 3000 ptas.

Entertainment

Things are livelier when the students are in town – basically from October to June. The old town has lots of good bars and cafés for evening copas along Rambla de la Llibertat, Plaça del Vi and Carrer Carreras Peralta, among other places. The seemingly nameless *café* at Carrer de les Ballesteries 23, which stays open longer than some, is a popular spot overlooking the river. You can keep going to 3 am or so near the river just north of the old town, where streets such as Carrer Palafrugell and Ronda de Pedret harbour several lively and varied music bars. *Fashion* at Carretera de Barcelona 161 in the south of the town is about the best disco.

Getting There & Away

Air Girona's airport (☎ 18 66 00), 11 km south of the centre just off the A-7 and N-II, is more or less devoted to summer charter flights for Costa Brava tourists. Flight-Line (☎ 47 33 00) at the airport sells flights to several British, Irish and German airports.

Bus Barcelona Bus (☎ 20 24 32) runs to/from Barcelona's Estació del Nord (1¼ hours) and Figueres (50 minutes) three to seven times daily. SARFA (☎ 20 17 96) runs buses to/from most parts of the Costa Brava; see other town sections for information on services. TEISA (☎ 20 02 75) runs eight services daily (four on Sunday) to/from Besalú (50 minutes) and Olot (1¼ hours; 580 ptas). Most international buses between Barcelona and France, Italy, London etc stop in Girona.

Train Girona (station ☎ 20 70 93) is on the railway between Barcelona, Figueres and Portbou on the French border. There are around 18 trains a day to/from Figueres (30 to 40 minutes; 310 to 360 ptas in 2nd class) and Barcelona (1¼ hours; 735 to 845 ptas), and about 10 to/from Portbou and/or Cerbère. A few trains a day go through to Montpellier in France, or beyond.

Getting Around

There's no airport bus service. You can call a taxi on ☎ 20 33 77 or ☎ 22 23 33.

It is almost impossible to find parking in the old town.

BESALÚ

This very picturesque medieval village beside the Riu Fluvià, 33 km north-west of Girona, could be a stop on the way to Olot

(see the Pyrenees section of this chapter) or a day outing from Girona, Figueres or the coast.

In the 10th and 11th centuries Besalú was the capital of an independent county which stretched as far west as Cerdanya, before it came under Barcelona's control in 1111. Most picturesque of all is the view of the village across the tall, crooked 11th century **Pont Fortificat** (fortified bridge), with its two tower-gates, from the south side of the Fluvià. The tourist office (☎ 59 12 40) on the arcaded central square, Plaça de la Llibertat, is open only from June to mid-October, from 10 am to 2 pm and 4 to 7 pm daily. It hands out a decent map/brochure, sells 50 ptas tickets for the **Miqvé**, a 12th century Jewish purification bathhouse by the river, and does worthwhile guided visits to the Miqvé, the bridge and the Romanesque **Església de Sant Vicenç**, which is otherwise normally closed. Also have a look at the 11th century Romanesque church of the **Monestir de Sant Pere**, with an unusual ambulatory (walkway) behind the altar, and the **Casa Cornellà**, a 12th century Romanesque mansion.

Places to Stay & Eat

There are three good little places to stay. *Habitacions Venència* (☎ 59 12 57) at Carrer Major 8 just off Plaça de la Llibertat, and *Fonda Siques* (☎ 59 01 10) at Avinguda del President Lluís Companys 6 (on the main road passing through the north of the village) both have doubles with bath at around 3000 ptas. *Residència Marià* (☎ 59 01 06) at Plaça de la Llibertat 15 is a little dearer at 4000 ptas.

Restaurant Can Quei facing the Església de Sant Vicenç has good-value platos combinados from 500 ptas, and a three course menú for 1100 ptas including wine. Or you can eat at a couple of places on Plaça Llibertat (*Residència Marià* is good), or at the *Fonda Siques*, which has menús of good home-style food for 1000 and 1100 ptas, or at the more expensive *Restaurant Pont Vell* by the bridge, which has mainly Catalan fare and a menú for 2000 ptas plus IVA.

Getting There & Away

The N-260 road from Figueres to Olot meets the C-160 from Girona at Besalú. See the Girona and Figueres sections for information on TEISA bus services to Besalú and on to Olot. The stop in Besalú is on the main road just west of the Fonda Siques.

TORROELLA DE MONTGRÍ

On the Riu Ter about 30 km north-east of Girona and 15 km north of Palafrugell, the agreeable old town of Torroella de Montgrí (population 7000) is the funnel through which travellers to the coastal resort L'Estartit must pass.

There's a tourist office (☎ 75 83 00) at Avinguda Lluís Companys 51, on the main east-west (L'Estartit-Girona) road through town and a stone's throw from the main church, the Església de Sant Genis. It's open Monday to Saturday from 10 am to 2 pm, plus Tuesday and Thursday from 4 to 7 pm.

Things to See & Do

About 100 metres south of the porticoed central square, Plaça de la Vila, in an old mansion at Carrer Major 28, the **Museu del Montgrí** will tell you about local history and archaeology, and a bit about the Illes Medes off L'Estartit. It's free, and open Monday to Friday from 10 am to 2 pm and 5 to 8 pm, Sunday and holidays from 11 am to 1 pm (closed Tuesday and holidays from October to March). Three blocks north of Plaça de la Vila is the **Església de Sant Genis**, mainly 15th century Gothic (with fine ceiling tracery) but with an 18th century baroque main façade at the west end.

Overlooking the town from the top of the 300 metre limestone Montgrí hills to the north, the impressive-looking **Castell de Montgrí** was built between 1294 and 1301 for King Jaume II in his efforts to bring to heel the disobedient counts of Empúries, to the north. The castle was never actually finished, which is why all there is to see when you get up there – apart from superb panoramas – is the four-square walls with their battlements and round corner towers. There's no road and by foot it's about a 40 minute climb from Torroella. Head north from Plaça del Lledoner along Carrer de Fàtima, at the end of which is a sign pointing you to the castle. About 50 metres before the castle you can take a marked detour to the **Cau del Duc**, a cave once occupied by prehistoric hunter-collectors.

Places to Stay & Eat

Pensió Mitjà (☎ 75 80 03), open all year at Carrer de l'Església 14, a block north of Plaça de la Vila, has bare but decent singles/doubles with bath for 2400/4800 ptas, and a restaurant with a four course menú for 925 ptas. Four blocks west of Plaça de la Vila, *Pensión Marin* (☎ 75 87 74) at Plaça Quintana i Combis 12 has doubles only, with shower, for 3950 ptas plus IVA. The cafés on Plaça de la Vila are the best place for people-watching.

Getting There & Away

AMPSA (☎ 75 82 33) at Plaça d'Espanya 19 (three blocks west, then two south, from Plaça de la Vila) runs buses about hourly to L'Estartit (120 ptas) and three or four daily to Girona. SARFA (☎ 75 90 04) at Passeig de Catalunya 61 (three blocks east, then one north, from Plaça de la Vila) has three or four daily buses to/from Barcelona's Estació del Nord (1¾ hours), four to/from Palafrugell, and three or four to/from L'Escala (155 ptas) and Figueres (1¼ hours; 530 ptas).

L'ESTARTIT & THE ILLES MEDES

L'Estartit (El Estartit in Castilian), six km east of Torroella de Montgrí, has a very long, wide beach of fine sand but really nothing over any other Costa Brava package resort – except for the Illes Medes (Islas Medes), a group of rocky islets barely one km offshore, which are home to some of the most abundant marine life on Spain's Mediterranean coast.

Orientation & Information

The main road in from Torroella de Montgrí is called Avinguda de Grècia as it approaches the beach; the beachfront road is Passeig Marítim. The tourist office (☎ 75 89 10) is towards the north end of Passeig Marítim. Its summer hours are Monday to Saturday from 9.30 am to 2 pm and 4 to 9 pm, Sunday from 10 am to 1 pm.

Illes Medes

The shores and waters around these seven islets, an offshore continuation of the limestone Montgrí hills, have been protected since 1985 as a Reserva Natural Submarina (underwater natural reserve), which has brought a proliferation in their marine life and made them Spain's most popular goal for snorkellers and divers. Some 1345 vegetable and animal species have been identified here. There's a big bird population too; one of the Mediterranean's biggest colonies of yellow-legged gulls, 8000 pairs, breeds here between March and May.

A series of kiosks by the harbour at the north end of L'Estartit beach offer snorkelling and glass-bottomed boat trips to the islands. Other glass-bottom trips go to a series of caves along the coast to the north, or combine these with the Medes. A two hour snorkelling trip to the Illes Medes costs about 1400 ptas including equipment. Trips go frequently every day from June to September, and depend on demand in April, May and October.

Diving

The range of depths (down to 50 metres), and the number of underwater cavities and tunnels around the Illes Medes contribute much to their attraction for divers. On and around rocks near the surface are colourful algae and sponges as well as octopuses, crabs and some large and small fish. Below 10 or 15 metres, cavities and caves harbour lobsters, scorpion fish and large conger eels and groupers. Some groupers and perch may feed from the hand. Below 20 metres there are encrustations of coral, mussels, and other skeletal creatures forming a maze of openings inhabited by some 600 different animal species. If you get down to the sea floor you may see angler fish, thornback rays or marbled electric rays.

At least half a dozen outfits in L'Estartit

can take you out scuba diving, at the Medes or off the mainland coast – the tourist office has lists of them. It's worth comparing a few to get an idea of their standards and experience before taking the plunge. If you're already a qualified diver, a single two hour trip usually costs between 2500 and 4000 ptas per person. If you need to rent all the gear, the extra cost will be somewhere between 2000 and 3500 ptas. Night dives are possible too. If you're a novice, you can do a one day introductory course for around 6000 ptas, or a full five day PADI Open Water Diver course for 50,000 to 60,000 ptas. Diving centres can usually offer accommodation packages too.

Places to Stay

Apart from the eight camping grounds in and around the town (none open from November to March), budget accommodation doesn't really exist unless you're on a package. Some of the better options are opposite the harbour at the north end of the beach. Here *Hostal Santa Clara* (☎ 75 87 67), Passeig Marítim 18, and *Hostal La Sirena* (☎ 75 77 22), Passeig Marítim 19, have front rooms with balconies overlooking the water. The Santa Clara has singles/doubles with bath for 2600/4650 ptas and is open from May to September; La Sirena charges 3200/6400 ptas and is open from April to October. *Pensión Xumetra* (☎ 75 85 96), nearby at Carrer de Les Illes 55, has no sea view and charges 2900/3500 ptas plus IVA with bath. *Hotel Les Illes* (☎ 75 82 39), next door at the same address and open March to October, has rooms with bath for 3675/6300 ptas and an in-house diving centre. Several pensiones and hostales with doubles around 4500 ptas are dotted around streets behind the tourist office such as Carrer del Port, Carrer de Santa Anna, Carrer de l'Església and Carrer Roca Maura; all of them close from at least November to February.

Places to Eat

Restaurant Montserrat at Passeig Marítim 33, by the roundabout at the north end of the beachfront, does all sorts of plain things at reasonable prices, such as omelette, chips and tomato for 475 ptas. Carrer de Santa Anna, running inland from the same roundabout, has some economical options too. *Restaurant Can Cervera* at No 25 will do you half a chicken and chips for 400 ptas, or other meat and seafood dishes from 800 ptas. *Restaurant Vila* at No 34 has a three course menú for 725 ptas, and a four course one for 925 ptas. Among the fancier restaurants, *La Gaviota*, Passeig Marítim 92, has good fish and seafood. Expect to pay around 3000 ptas per person.

Getting There & Around

Bus AMPSA buses to Torroella de Montgrí (about hourly) and Girona (three or four daily, one hour, 475 ptas) go from Passeig Marítim, 150 metres south of the tourist office. SARFA (☎ 75 77 14) at Plaça Dr Fleming 4, a block inland, runs to Barcelona (two hours; 1665 ptas) three or four times daily.

Bicycle Josep Bicicletas on Avinguda de Grècia, 500 metres back from the beach, rents out mountain bikes for 1500 ptas a day, 5000 ptas a week, or 9000 ptas for two weeks.

L'ESCALA & EMPÚRIES

L'Escala (La Escala in Castilian), on the coast 11 km north of Torroella de Montgrí, is a pleasant medium-sized resort of 5000 people on the south shore of the Golf de Roses. It's of older vintage than places like L'Estartit and attracts mostly Spanish and French family visitors. What makes it a particularly worthwhile stop is its closeness to the ancient Greek and Roman town of Empúries (Ampurias in Castilian) and, a few km further north, the wetlands of the Parc Natural dels Aiguamolls de l'Empordà.

Orientation & Information

If you arrive by SARFA bus, you'll alight on L'Escala's Plaça de les Escoles, where you'll find the tourist office (☎ 77 06 03) at No 1, and the post office a couple of doors along.

The tourist office's summer hours are Monday to Saturday from 9 am to 8.30 pm, Sunday 10 am to 1 pm and 4 to 7 pm.

From Plaça de les Escoles, head downhill (north) on the narrow Carrer Pintor Joan Massanet, Carrer Enric Serra or Carrer Santa Màxima (not the busy Avinguda Ave Maria), to reach the heart of town and the small central beach, La Platja.

Empúries is one km round the coast to the north-west of the town centre.

Empúries

Empúries was probably the first, and certainly one of most important, Greek colonies on the Iberian Peninsula. The first Greeks here were traders who, pushing on from a trading post at Marseille (France), set up a new post around 600 BC at what's now the village of Sant Martí d'Empúries, then an island. Soon afterwards they founded a mainland colony nearby, which forms part of the site you visit today. The colony came to be called Emporion (literally, 'market') and remained an important trading centre – and conduit of Greek culture to the Iberians – for centuries.

Empúries was also the place where, in 218 BC, Roman legions first set foot on the peninsula, to cut off Hannibal's supply lines in the Second Punic War. In about 195 BC the Romans set up a military camp here as they set about consolidating their hold over the Iberian Peninsula. Around 100 BC they added a town, which about a century later was united with the Greek one. Emporiae, as the place was then known, was abandoned in the late 3rd century AD, after raids by Germanic tribes. Later, an early Christian basilica and cemetery stood on the site of the Greek town, before the whole place, after over a millennium of use, disappeared altogether, to be rediscovered by archaeologists around the turn of the 20th century.

Many of the ancient stones now laid bare don't rise more than knee-high. You need a little imagination – and perhaps the aid of a taped commentary (600 ptas from the ticket office) – to make the most of it.

The Site From mid-June to mid-September the site is open from 10 am to 7 pm, with a pedestrian entrance from the seafront promenade in front of the ruins – just follow the coast from L'Escala to reach it. At other times opening hours are 10 am to 5 pm, and the only way in is the vehicle approach from the Figueres road, about one km from central L'Escala. Entry is 400 ptas.

The Greek town lies in the lower part of the site, closer to the shore. Main points of interest include the thick southern defensive walls; the site of the Asklepion, a shrine to the god of medicine, with a copy of his statue found here; the Agora, an open space which was the town square, with remnants of the early Christian basilica and the Greek Stoa, or market building, beside it. In the Stoa, wrote Rose Macaulay in *Fabled Shore* (1950), 'buyers and sellers walked, chaffering and bartering in Greek, Iberian, Latin, all the dialects of the Middle Sea. And through the city the winds from this sea, and the sound of it, murmured always'.

A small museum (the Museu d'Arqueologia in Barcelona has a bigger and better Empúries collection) separates the Greek town from the larger Roman town on the upper part of the site. Highlights of the Roman town include the mosaic floors of a 1st century BC house; the Forum, the town's main square, surrounded by remains of official buildings, a few reconstructed; and the strong 1st century BC walls, said to have been built by Julius Caesar, with chariot wheel ruts clearly visible beneath the gate, as is the phallic carving (apparently a symbol of general potency) carved into the wall nearby. Outside the walls is an oval amphitheatre.

Outside the Site A string of brown sand beaches stretches along in front of the site. On one stands a Greek stone jetty. Some 300 metres north of here is the medieval hamlet of Sant Martí d'Empúries, site of the first Greek settlement, now with a Gothic church and a huddle of pleasant enough tourist restaurants where you can enjoy a pizza for 700 to 800 ptas or an exotic ice cream or pancake for not much less.

Places to Stay

Camping The nearest camping ground to the centre of L'Escala is the small *Camping La Escala* (☎ 77 00 84) at Camí Ample 21, about 700 metres south of La Platja, charging 2725 ptas for two adults with a car and tent. There are five other sites two to four km east of the centre in the Riells and Montgó areas of town, and a further half-dozen or so along or near the beach within a few km north of Empúries.

Youth Hostel The *Alberg d'Empúries* (☎ 77 12 00), Les Coves 41, is just south of the Empúries ruins. It has room for about 60 people, in dorms of six or more. High-season rates are charged from April to September.

Hostales, Pensiones & Hotels Two of the best bets, though often booked up in the high season, are *Hostal Mediterrà/Mediterráneo* (☎ 77 00 28) at Carrer Riera 22-24, a block west of Carrer Pintor Joan Massanet, about halfway down the hill from Plaça de les Escoles, and *Pensió Torrent* (☎ 77 02 78) a few doors up the street at No 28. Both are basic, clean, friendly and open virtually all year. The Mediterrà has a range of rooms from singles/doubles for 1750/3425 ptas to doubles with bath for 5375 ptas. The Torrent has singles/doubles with shower for 2200/3400 ptas and doubles with bath for 3600 ptas. *Hostal Poch* (☎ 77 00 92) at Carrer de Gràcia 10, one block back and a few steps west from La Platja, has doubles only, with bath, for 3700 ptas.

A step up in quality but not much more in price is *Hostal El Roser* (☎ 77 02 19; fax 77 09 77) at Carrer de l'Església 7, in the first street on the right as you go down Carrer Santa Màxima from Plaça de les Escoles. Good-sized modern rooms with TV and bath are 3200/4700 ptas plus IVA; there are also some slightly cheaper older rooms in an annexe next door. This hostal is open all year and has its own very handy car park. *Hostal Garbí* (☎ 77 01 65), Carrer Santa Màxima 7 facing La Platja, has rooms with bath for 4000/6000 ptas but closes from October to April.

On Passeig Lluis Albert, 10 minutes walk east along the seafront from La Platja, *Hotel Voramar* (☎ 77 01 08) at No 2 has rooms for 3975/7940 ptas, and *Hotel Bonaire* (☎ 77 00 68) at No 4 has singles for 4550 ptas and doubles at 7225 or 8425 ptas.

Places to Eat

L'Escala is famous for its anchovies *(anchoas)* and good fresh local fish, both of which are likely to crop up on menús.

The seafront restaurants are mostly expensive, but if your wallet is fat enough try *Els Pescadors* on Port d'En Perris, the next bay west from La Platja (five minutes walk), which does superb baked and grilled fish and seafood, suquet, and rice dishes. You won't get away with much under 3000 ptas per person for a meal. There are also two good, reasonably priced pizzerias, *L'Olla* and *Volanti*, on Port d'En Perris. Both do pizzas for 700 to 800 ptas and menús at 1250 ptas.

Some of the hostales have good restaurants. *Hostal Poch* will do you half a roast chicken with chips for 650 ptas, and other meat and fish dishes from 800 ptas. *Hostal Mediterrà* has an excellent four course menú for 1175 ptas. *Hostal El Roser* has a quite classy restaurant with a very good menú for 1200 ptas plus IVA, and more expensive à-la-carte fare.

Getting There & Away

SARFA has its office on Avinguda Ave Maria at the corner of Carrer Germans Masferrer, but its main stop is up at the top of Avinguda Ave Maria on Plaça de les Escoles. Buses run to/from the following places three to five times daily: Barcelona's Estació del Nord (1½ hours; 1700 ptas), Figueres (50 minutes; 390 ptas), Girona (one hour; 495 ptas), Palafrugell (35 minutes; 325 ptas), Sant Pere Pescador and Torroella de Montgrí.

PARC NATURAL DELS AIGUAMOLLS DE L'EMPORDÀ

This natural park preserves the remnants of the marshes which used to cover the whole coastal plain of the Golf de Roses, an important site for migrating birds. Bird-watchers have spotted over 100 species a day in the March-to-May and August-to-October migration periods, which bring big increases in the numbers of wading birds, and even the occasional flamingo, glossy ibis, spoonbill or rare black stork. There are usually enough birds around to make a visit worthwhile at any time of year.

The best place to head for is the El Cortalet information centre (☎ 25 03 22 or 45 42 22), one km off the Sant Pere Pescador-Castelló d'Empúries road. The centre is open daily from 9.30 am to 2 pm and 4.30 to 7 pm (in October to March, from 3.30 to 6 pm). Marked paths lead to a two km stretch of beach and a number of hides *(aguaits)* where you can view saltwater marshes and their bird life. The paths are always open; morning and evening are the best times for watching birds (though also for mosquitoes!).

The nearest places to El Cortalet that you can reach by bus are Sant Pere Pescador, six km south (served by four or five SARFA buses daily from L'Escala and Figueres), and Castelló d'Empúries, four km north.

CASTELLÓ D'EMPÚRIES

This old town of 4000 people was the capital of Empúries, a medieval Catalan county which maintained a large degree of independence right up to the 14th century. At the heart of the narrow streets in the old part of town you'll find Plaça dels Homes, with a tourist office (☎ 15 62 33) in a building which dates back to the 14th century. Pick up the office's useful map detailing the main points of interest, all of which are within a few minutes walk. The finest monument is the **Església de Santa Maria** on Plaça Jacint Verdaguer, a large 13th and 14th century Gothic church with a superb sculpted doorway and a fine Romanesque bell tower remaining from an earlier church on the site. If the doors are open, check the 15th century alabaster main altarpiece, and the tomb of Count Ponç Hug VI, both further superb examples of medieval carving.

Places to Stay & Eat

Hotel Canet (☎ 25 03 40; fax 25 06 07), a modernised 17th century mansion in the centre at Plaça del Joc de la Pilota 2, has elegant singles/doubles with bath for 4500/6000 ptas plus IVA, and a swimming pool in an interior courtyard. Its restaurant is reasonably priced.

In the newer part of town to the south there are three decent places close together on and just off Carrer Santa Clara, with rooms around 3000/4500 ptas: the modern *Hotel Emporium* (☎ 25 05 93) next to the bus stop, *Hostal Ca L'Anton* (☎ 25 05 09), and *Pensió/Fonda Serratosa* (☎ 25 05 08). All have restaurants, with menús ranging from 860 ptas (at the Ca L'Anton) up.

Just off Castelló's southern bypass, *Hotel Allioli* (☎ 25 03 20), Urbanització Castell Nou s/n, is an attractively modernised old farmstead with pool, garden, a fine array of Jabugo hams in the bar, and simple but comfortable wood-beamed rooms with bath – for 6000/11,500 ptas plus IVA in August, but little more than half that most of the rest of the year. Dinner in the good Catalan restaurant will set you back around 2500 ptas.

Getting There & Away

SARFA (☎ 25 05 93) runs up to 20 buses a day to/from Figueres, up to eight to/from Cadaqués (50 minutes), three daily to/from Girona (45 minutes), and up to four to/from Barcelona's Estació del Nord (1½ hours). The stop is beside the Hotel Emporium.

CADAQUÉS & AROUND

If you have time for only one stop on the Costa Brava, you can hardly do better than Cadaqués. Still not very much more than a whitewashed village straggling round a rocky bay, it and the surrounding area have a special magic – some fusion of wind, sea, light, rock and barren isolation – which isn't dissipated even by the throngs of mildly fashionable visitors who crowd in every July and August.

A portion of that magic owes itself to Salvador Dalí, who spent family holidays in Cadaqués – then little more than a fishing village – in his youth, and lived much of his later life at nearby Port Lligat. The empty, moon-like landscapes, odd-shaped rocks and barren shorelines that litter Dalí's paintings weren't just a product of his fertile imagination. They're strewn all round the Cadaqués area in what Dalí termed a 'grandiose geological delirium'.

As your road twists through the cork-oak-dotted hills towards Cadaqués you quickly realise you're in a barer, drier country than anywhere further south on the Costa Brava. This sparseness of vegetation continues all the way to dramatic Cap de Creus, eight km north-east of Cadaqués, lending itself to some coastscapes of almost (if you'll permit us, Sr Dalí) surreal beauty.

Thanks to Dalí and other artists who came here in the 1910s and 1920s, Cadaqués pulled in an artistic, offbeat and celebrity crowd for decades. One visit by the poet Paul Éluard and his Russian wife Gala in 1929 caused an earthquake in Dalí's life; he broke with his family, ran off to Paris with Gala (who was to become his lifelong obsession and, later, his wife), and joined the surrealist movement. In the 1950s, after Dalí's success in the USA, the crowd he attracted here was more jet-setting: Walt Disney, the Duke of Windsor, Stavros Niarchos. In the 1970s Mick Jagger and Gabriel García Márquez turned up. Today the crowd is neither so creative nor so famous – and a lot bigger – but Cadaqués' atmosphere remains. It's still a fishing village, too.

Orientation

Cadaqués straggles round its bay for one km or so and stretches back uphill about the same distance. The old part of town rises behind the western half of the central beach. The SARFA bus stop and office are at the top end of the village, by the road in from Figueres. From here, walk on down the main street, Avinguda Caritat Serinyana, to reach the central beachfront square Plaça Frederic Rahola. There's a car park near the bus stop if you can't find a spot nearer the heart of things, but it costs 185 ptas an hour. Port

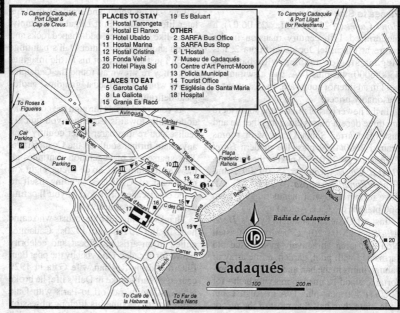

PLACES TO STAY
1 Hostal Tarongeta
4 Hostal El Ranxo
9 Hotel Ubaldo
11 Hostal Marina
12 Hostal Cristina
16 Fonda Vehí
20 Hotel Playa Sol

PLACES TO EAT
5 Garota Café
8 La Galiota
15 Granja Es Racó

19 Es Baluart

OTHER
2 SARFA Bus Office
3 SARFA Bus Stop
6 L'Hostal
7 Museu de Cadaqués
10 Centre d'Art Perrot-Moore
13 Policia Municipal
14 Tourist Office
17 Església de Santa Maria
18 Hospital

Cadaqués

Badia de Cadaqués

Lligat is about 1.25 km north-east of Cadaqués, on a separate inlet.

Information

The tourist office (☎ 25 83 15) is just off Plaça Frederic Rahola at Carrer des Cotxe 2. A couple of banks with ATMs are on or near Plaça Frederic Rahola. The Policia Municipal (☎ 15 93 43) are a few steps behind the tourist office, on Carrer Vigilant. There's a hospital (☎ 25 88 07) on Carrer Guillem Bruguera, just west of the church.

In the Town

Cadaqués is perfect for just wandering – around the town or along the coasts – and relaxing. The 16th and 17th century **Església de Santa Maria**, with a gilded baroque *retablo* (100 ptas to light it up), is the focus of the older part of town with its narrow hilly streets.

There are a number of art galleries and interesting boutiques around town, and two

art museums well worth visiting: the **Centre d'Art Perrot-Moore** off Carrer Vigilant, founded by Dalí's secretary and focusing on Dalí and Picasso, and the **Museu de Cadaqués** at Carrer Narcís Monturiol 15, which includes Dalí among many other local artists. Both are open daily from around 11 am to 1.30 pm and 5 to 8.30 pm; each costs 600 ptas.

Beaches

Cadaqués' main beach, and several others along the nearby coasts, are small, with more pebbles than sand, but their picturesqueness and beautifully blue waters make up for that. Overlooking Platja Llaner on the south side of the bay is Dalí's parents' holiday home, with a statue by Josep Subirachs dedicated to Federico García Lorca, in memory of Lorca's 1920s stay there, in front of it.

Port Lligat

Port Lligat, a walk of about 1.25 km from

Cadaqués, is a tiny settlement around another lovely bay, with fishing boats pulled up on its beach. The **Casa Dalí** here began as a fisherman's hut and was steadily altered and enlarged by Dalí, who lived here – apart from a dozen or so years abroad during and around the Spanish Civil War – from 1930 to 1982. It's the house with a lot of little white chimney pots and two egg-shaped towers, overlooking the west end of the beach. It's due to be opened as a museum at some stage but in the meantime is firmly locked up.

Cap de Creus
Eight km by road north-east of Cadaqués, Cap de Creus (Cabo de Creus in Castilian) is the most easterly point of the Spanish mainland and a place of sublimely rugged beauty, with a steep, rocky coastline indented by dozens of lovely, turquoise-watered coves. It's an especially wonderful place to be at dawn or sunset. Atop the cape stand a lighthouse and a single good, middle-priced restaurant. No buses run here.

Walks
There are infinite possibilities: out along the promontory between Cadaqués and Port Lligat; to Port Lligat and beyond; along the south side of the Cadaqués bay to the Far de Cala Nans lighthouse; or over the hills south of Cadaqués to the coast east of Roses. For a full day's outing you could walk to the Monestir de Sant Pere de Rodes and back, possibly via El Port de la Selva (see the Cadaqués to the French Border section later in this chapter); the Cadaqués tourist office can give you directions.

Paths marked on the tourist office map which seem to show a short cut to Cap de Creus are not reliable. Be prepared for them to disappear and for you to do some backtracking if you want to try to find your way cross-country to Cap de Creus. You may be able to scramble down to some lovely isolated coves along the way, however.

Places to Stay
Camping Cadaqués (☎ 25 81 26), about one km from central Cadaqués on the road to Port Lligat, has room for about 500 people and can get pretty crowded. Two adults with a tent and a car pay 2200 ptas plus IVA. It opens for Semana Santa and from June to September.

Fonda Vehí (☎ 25 84 70) at Carrer de l'Església 6 near the church has rooms with shared baths for 2000/3500 ptas, but it's only open in summer and tends to be booked up for July and August.

Hostal Cristina (☎ 25 81 38) on Carrer Riera has doubles only, for 3000 ptas, or 4000 ptas with private bath. Security isn't great here, as the reception is in a pizzeria a couple of minutes round the bay. *Hostal Marina* (☎ 25 81 99) next door at Carrer Riera 3 is probably a better bet, with singles/doubles at 3000/6000 ptas plus IVA, all with private bath. It usually closes from January to March. Some rooms in both places have balconies.

Hotel Ubaldo (☎ 25 81 25; fax 25 83 24) at Carrer Unió 13, towards the back of the old part of town, has good doubles with bath, some with balcony, for 6200 ptas plus IVA. *Hostal El Ranxo* (☎ 25 80 05) at Avinguda Caritat Serinyana s/n may have a room when others haven't. Pleasant doubles with bath are 6000 ptas plus IVA.

Hotel Playa Sol (☎ 25 81 00; fax 25 80 54) on the east side of the bay at Platja Pianc 3 has singles for 9900 ptas and doubles for 13,900 to 16,900 ptas, plus IVA. Rooms have air-con, satellite TV and bath. There's a nice pool area too.

In Port Lligat, *Residencia/Aparthotel Calina* (☎ 25 88 51) near the small beach, has a range of pleasant modern rooms and one-room apartments from 6100 to 10,250 ptas a double. Its middle-priced restaurant opens on to an excellent pool area. It's closed from November to February. *Hotel Port Lligat* (☎ 25 81 62) just back up the hill has doubles from 8300 ptas.

The magnificently sited *Restaurant Cap de Creus* (☎ 15 92 71), out at Cap de Creus, has a few rooms for 7000 to 10,000 ptas a double. They get booked up in high summer but the place is open all year.

Places to Eat

The eastern part of the central beachfront is lined with uninspired menús at 900 to 1200 ptas, or pizzas for 700 or 800 ptas. *Granja Es Racó* at Carrer Dr Callis 3 does things like sausage/eggs/steak and chips for 500 to 775 ptas, and bocadillos. Its balcony overlooking the western half of the beach catches some breeze. *Fonda Vehí's* 2nd-floor restaurant does three-course menús for 1000 to 1200 ptas plus IVA.

Check *Garota* café on Avinguda Caritat Serinyana for offers such as a quarter-chicken with chips and a glass of cava for 500 ptas.

Es Baluart, Carrer Riba Nemesi Llorens 2, is several steps up in quality (and cost). A good full Catalan and/or seafood meal costs around 3000 ptas. *La Galiota*, Carrer Narcís Monturiol 9, is the favoured haunt of (non-penniless) art types, with good baked fish and mar i muntanya combinations. There's a menú for 1500 ptas; à la carte, you're looking at 4000 ptas.

Entertainment

L'Hostal facing the beachfront Passeig has live music many nights. Press clippings posted outside proclaim that one night in the 1970s Dalí called it the *'lugar más bonito del mundo'*. The beachfront *Marítimo* and *Melitón* bars have fine terrazas but prices to match. *Cafè de la Habana* and the *Es Porró* disco-pub get lively too.

Getting There & Away

SARFA (☎ 25 87 13) has buses to/from Castelló d'Empúries and Figueres (one hour) up to eight times daily (fewer in winter), to/from Girona (1½ hours) three times daily, and to/from Barcelona's Estació del Nord (2¼ hours; 1820 ptas) up to five times daily.

CADAQUÉS TO THE FRENCH BORDER

If you want to prolong the journey to/from France, **El Port de la Selva**, **Llançà** and the border town **Portbou** are all pleasant enough minor beach resorts cum fishing towns. There's a range of accommodation in each.

A more spectacular stop in this area is the **Monestir de Sant Pere de Rodes**, a classic piece of Romanesque architecture looming 500 metres high in the hills south-west of El Port de la Selva, with great views. Founded in the 8th century, it later became the most powerful monastery anywhere between Figueres and Perpignan in France. The great triple-naved, barrel-vaulted basilica is flanked by the fine square Torre de Sant Miquel bell tower and a two-level cloister. These are surrounded by numerous other monastery buildings. The fortress-like nature of the place is the result of local power struggles in medieval times. The monastery (entry 300 ptas, students 150 ptas) is open daily (closed Monday) and in July and August, hours are 10 am to 6.30 pm; in other months call ☎ 38 75 59 or check with a tourist office for the times.

Getting There & Away

The monastery is on a back road over the hills between Vilajuïga, eight km to its west, and El Port de la Selva, five km north-east. Each town is served by three or four SARFA buses to/from Figueres daily, but there are no buses up to the monastery itself. The walk from Vilajuïga is about 1½ hours. Vilajuïga is also on the railway between Figueres and Portbou.

FIGUERES

Twelve km inland from the Golf de Roses, Figueres (Figueras in Castilian) is a humdrum town of 35,000 people which there'd be little reason to visit if it weren't for – once again – Salvador Dalí. In the 1960s and 70s Dalí created here, in the town of his birth, the extraordinary Teatre-Museu Dalí – now Spain's second most visited museum (after the Prado in Madrid). Whatever feelings (or lack of them) you have about old Salvador, this is worth every minute you spend on getting to, into and around it.

Orientation

From the bus and train stations, on Plaça Estació, it's about a 600 metre walk northwest to the central boulevard, the Rambla.

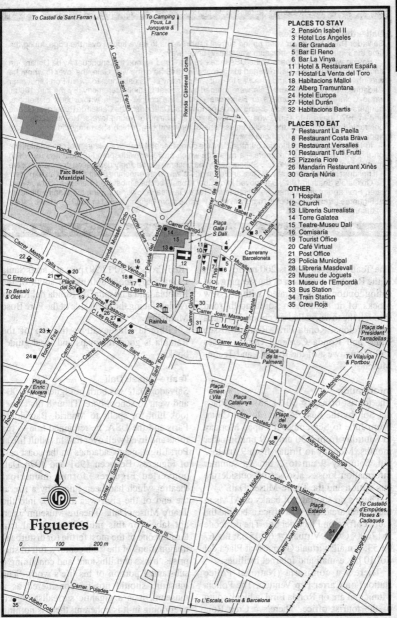

PLACES TO STAY
2 Pensión Isabel II
3 Hotel Los Ángeles
4 Bar Granada
5 Bar El Reno
6 Bar La Vinya
11 Hotel & Restaurant España
17 Hostal La Venta del Toro
18 Habitacions Mallol
22 Alberg Tramuntana
24 Hotel Europa
27 Hotel Durán
32 Habitacions Bartis

PLACES TO EAT
7 Restaurant La Paella
8 Restaurant Costa Brava
9 Restaurant Versalles
10 Restaurant Tutti Frutti
25 Pizzeria Fiore
26 Mandarin Restaurant Xinès
30 Granja Núria

OTHER
1 Hospital
12 Church
13 Llibreria Surrealista
14 Torre Galatea
15 Teatre-Museu Dalí
16 Comisaría
19 Tourist Office
20 Café Virtual
21 Post Office
23 Policia Municipal
28 Llibreria Masdevall
29 Museu de Joguets
31 Museu de l'Empordà
33 Bus Station
34 Train Station
35 Creu Roja

Figueres

0   100   200 m

Dalí – the Last Decades

Salvador Dalí's life, never short on the surreal itself, seems to have tipped over the edge during the time the Figueres theatre-museum was getting under way.

Having won huge success in the USA in the 1940s – and earned the sobriquet Avida Dollars, an anagram of his name – Dalí returned to his roots. In 1948 he came with Gala, the lover to whom he was obsessively devoted and who was the subject of many of his paintings, to live at Port Lligat near Cadaqués. In 1958 Dalí and Gala were married in a secret Catholic ceremony. By the late 1960s, wrote Colm Tóibín in *Homage to Barcelona* (1990), the couple had 'a whole court of helpers, hangers-on, advisers, secretaries and sexual performers'. Dalí bought the Castell de Púbol near Girona and in 1970 gave it to Gala, who was now enjoying a string of young lovers. He masochistically contracted never to visit the castle unless she summoned him, which she rarely did (though she apparently talked to him by phone daily).

In 1975 Dalí, ever a glutton for outrage, sent the dying General Franco a telegram of congratulations on the execution of five prisoners – a message which provoked widespread disgust and for which many people never forgave Dalí. Subsequently, he became increasingly depressed and inaccessible – a prisoner himself, some say, of Gala and/or 'minders' who were enriching themselves at his expense.

On Gala's death in 1982, Dalí moved into Púbol himself, but he almost died there in a fire two years later. Frail and malnourished, he retired to the Torre Galatea, a tower adjoining the theatre-museum at Figueres (and now part of it), hardly ever leaving his room before he died in 1989. His tomb is part of the theatre-museum. ■

The Teatre-Museu Dalí is 200 metres north of the Rambla, with most of the sleeping and eating options concentrated within a few blocks of it. The main south-north road through the town, called successively Ronda de Barcelona, Ronda Firal, Ronda Mossèn Cinto and Ronda Cardenal Gomà, passes 150 metres west of the Rambla and Teatre-Museu.

Information

The tourist office (☎ 50 31 55) is on Plaça del Sol, by the busy Ronda Mossèn Cinto. From June to September it's open Monday to Saturday from 8.30 am to 9 pm; in other months, Monday to Friday from 9 am to 7 pm, Saturday 9 am to 1 pm. In summer information kiosks also set up outside the bus station and the Teatre-Museu Dalí.

There's no shortage of banks or ATMs in the central area. The post office is behind the tourist office on Plaça del Sol. The postcode is 17600. C@fè Virtual (☎ 67 45 33; fax 67 03 53; e-mail: virtualc@grn.es) at Plaça del Sol 10 has e-mail and Internet facilities.

There's a comisaría (National Police station) on Carrer Pep Ventura. The Policía Municipal are on Ronda Firal, a block south of the tourist office. There's a Creu Roja

(Red Cross; ☎ 50 17 99) post at Carrer Santa Llogaia 67, about 800 metres south of the Rambla, and a hospital on Ronda del Rector Aroles, facing the north side of the Parc Bosc Municipal.

Llibreria Masdevall at the top of the Rambla is good for maps and local guide-books.

Teatre-Museu Dalí

Salvador Dalí was born in Figueres in 1904 and went to school here. Though his career took him for spells to Madrid, Barcelona, Paris and the USA, he remained true to his roots and lived well over half his adult life at Port Lligat, near Cadaqués on the coast east of Figueres. Between 1961 and 1974 Dalí converted Figueres' former municipal theatre, which had been ruined by a fire at the end of the civil war in 1939, into the Teatre-Museu Dalí. 'Theatre-Museum' is an apt label for this multi-dimensional trip through one of the most fertile (or disturbed) imaginations of the 20th century, full of surprises, tricks and illusions, and containing a substantial portion of his life's work. 'The museum should not be considered as a museum, it is a gigantic surrealist object, everything in it is coherent, there is nothing which escapes my net of understandings,' explained its creator with characteristic modesty.

Even outside, the building aims to surprise, from the collection of bizarre sculptures outside the entrance on Plaça Gala i Salvador Dalí, to the pink wall along Pujada del Castell, topped by a row of Dalí's trademark egg shapes and what appear to be female gymnast sculptures. From July to September the museum is open from 9 am to 7.15 pm daily and for most of this period there are night sessions from 10 pm to 12.30 am. There are long queues on summer mornings. From October to June it's open from 10.30 am to 5.15 pm daily, but closed Monday and on 1 January and 25 December. Entry is 1000 ptas (700 ptas for students), and 1200 ptas for the summer night sessions. You can take photos inside, but only without flash.

Inside, the ground floor (Level 1) includes a semicircular garden area on the site of the original theatre stalls. In its centre is a classic piece of weirdness called *Taxi Plujós* (Rainy Taxi), composed of an early Cadillac – said to have belonged to Al Capone – and a pile of tractor tyres, both surmounted by statues, with a fishing boat balanced precariously above the tyres. Put a coin in the slot and water washes all over the inside of the car. The Sala de Peixateries (Fish Shop Room) off here holds a collection of Dalí oils including the famous *Autoretrat tou amb tall de bacon fregit* (Self-Portrait with Fried Bacon) and *Retrat de Picasso*. Beneath the former stage of the theatre is the crypt, with Dalí's own plain tomb.

The stage area (Level 2), topped by a glass geodesic dome, was conceived as Dalí's Sistine Chapel. The large egg/head/breasts/rocks/trees backdrop was part of a ballet set, one of Dalí's many ventures into the performing arts. If proof were needed of Dalí's acute sense of the absurd, the painting *Gala mirando el Mar Mediterráneo* (Gala looking at the Mediterranean Sea) appears from the other end of the room, with the help of coin-operated viewfinders, to be a portrait of Abraham Lincoln. Off this room is the Sala del Tresor, where paintings such as *La panera del pa* (The Breadbasket) show that Dalí was a master draughtsman too.

One floor up (Level 3) you come across the Sala de Mae West, a living room whose components, viewed from the right spot, make up a portrait of Ms West – a sofa for her lips, two fireplaces for nostrils, two impressionist paintings of Paris for eyes. On the top floor (Level 5) is a room containing works by other artists from Dalí's own collection, including El Greco's *Sant Pau* (St Paul).

Other Attractions

The **Museu de l'Empordà** at Rambla 2 combines archaeological finds from Greek, Roman and medieval times with a sizeable collection of art – mainly by Catalan artists but also some works lent by the Prado in Madrid. It's free, and its convoluted opening hours include Tuesday to Saturday from 11 am to 1 pm and 4 to 7 pm.

The **Museu de Joguets**, Spain's only toy museum, at Rambla 10, was due to reopen in spring 1997 after expansion works. It has more than 3500 Cataluña and Valencia-made toys from the pre-Barbie, pre-video, pre-plastic 19th and early 20th centuries.

The shady **Parc Bosc Municipal** just north of the tourist office is a nice place to relax by day.

The large 18th century **Castell de Sant Ferran** stands on a low hill one km northwest of the centre. In its dungeons Spain's Republican government held its final meeting of the civil war, on 1 February 1939, having abandoned Barcelona. It's in military use but parts were due to be opened to the public in late 1996.

Places to Stay – bottom end

Camping Pous (☎ 67 22 66), north of the centre on the N-II towards La Jonquera, is small (210 people) but is open all year. Don't be tempted to sleep in the Parc Bosc Municipal: people have been attacked there at night.

The *Alberg Tramuntana* youth hostel (☎ 50 12 13) is two blocks west of the tourist office at Carrer Anicet de Pagès 2. It holds only 56 people (in dorms of four to 24) but is open nearly all year; high-season rates are charged from April to September.

Habitacions Bartis (☎ 50 14 73) at Carrer Méndez Núñez 2, on the way into the centre from the bus and train stations, has adequate singles/doubles for 1200/1900 ptas plus IVA.

Bar La Vinya (☎ 50 00 49), Carrer Tins 18, three short blocks east of the Teatre-Museu Dalí, has bare rooms up the street on Carrer Muralla for 1000/2000 ptas. They're getting flaky but are just about OK for the price. *Bar Granada* and *Bar El Reno*, also in Carrer Muralla, have rooms too.

Much better is the *Hotel España* (☎ 50 08 69), at Carrer de La Jonquera 26 just down the steps east of the Teatre-Museu Dalí, which has decent rooms for 1500/3000 ptas, or 2000/4000 ptas with shower, and spacious, even elegant, public areas.

Pensión Isabel II (☎ 50 00 04) at Carrer Isabel II 16 has reasonable rooms with bath for 2000/3500 ptas. *Hostal La Venta del Toro* (☎ 51 05 10), Carrer Pep Ventura 5, has bare but adequate rooms for 2000/4000 ptas – though there's only one shower for all 11 of them. *Habitacions Mallol* (☎ 50 22 83) along the street at No 9 charges 1750/3050 ptas.

Places to Stay – middle

Hotel Los Ángeles (☎ 51 06 61; fax 51 07 00) at Carrer Barceloneta 10 is good value with roomy singles/doubles for 3445/5165 ptas. *Hotel Europa* (☎ 50 07 44), Ronda Firal 18, is another respectable mid-range hotel. Rooms with bath are 3200/5500 ptas plus IVA. *Hotel Durán* (☎ 50 12 50; fax 50 26 09) at Carrer Lasauca 5, just off the top end of the Rambla, is a very good bet if you're looking for somewhere with a bit more style. Comfortable, homely singles/doubles are 5300/7700 ptas plus IVA.

Places to Eat

Carrer de La Jonquera, just down the steps east of the Teatre-Museu Dalí, is lined with restaurants – among them *Restaurant España*, *Restaurant Tutti Frutti*, *Restaurant* *Versalles* and *Restaurant Costa Brava* – offering reasonable three-course menús for 700 to 900 ptas. *Restaurant La Paella*, two short blocks east on Carrer Tins, does likewise.

The 750 ptas (plus IVA) menú turístico at *Granja Núria*, nearby at Carrer Girona 9, is in fact one plato combinado plus dessert and bread, though the way the menu is set out it looks more substantial. Still, it's not bad value.

For food of a different nationality, *Mandarin Restaurant Xinès*, Carrer Lasauca 11, has a Chinese menú for 900 ptas, and *Pizzeria Fiore* across the street at No 16 has an Italian one for 850 ptas. The excellent restaurant of the *Hotel Durán* at Carrer Lasauca 5 is a big step up, serving Catalan and Spanish specialities like suquet de peix, baked fresh fish, duck leg and turnips (muslo de pato con nabos) and, in season, wild asparagus (espárragos silvestres). You won't get much change from 3500 ptas for a full meal.

Things to Buy

Dalí prints, posters and cards seem to fill half Figueres' shop windows. Llibreria Surrealista next to the Teatre-Museu Dalí has one of the best selections.

Getting There & Away

Bus Barcelona Bus (☎ 50 50 29) runs to/from Girona (50 minutes) and Barcelona's Estació del Nord (2¼ hours; 1350 ptas) three to seven times daily.

SARFA (☎ 67 42 98) serves Castelló d'Empúries 10 to 20 times daily, and Cadaqués (one hour) up to eight times. It also runs a few times a day to numerous other places including L'Escala (50 minutes; 390 ptas), Palafrugell (1½ hours), Sant Pere Pescador, Torroella de Montgrí and Vilajuïga.

TEISA runs to/from Besalú (320 ptas) and Olot (535 ptas) two or three times daily.

Most international buses between Barcelona and France, Italy, London etc stop in Figueres.

There's a left-luggage *consigna* at the bus station, costing 300 ptas.

Train Figueres (station ☎ 50 46 61) is on the railway between Barcelona, Girona and Portbou on the French border. There are around 18 trains a day to/from Girona (30 to 40 minutes; 310 to 360 ptas in 2nd class) and Barcelona (1¾ to 2¼ hours; 1040 to 1195 ptas in 2nd class), and about 10 to/from Portbou and/or Cerbère on the French side of the border. A couple of daily trains go through to Montpellier in France or more distant destinations.

The Pyrenees

The Pyrenees in Cataluña don't reach quite as high as further west in Aragón, but this eastern end of the range still throws up some awesomely beautiful mountains and valleys. There are also many fine spots in the foothills reaching up to the main range, which runs along the French border and through Andorra.

If you have time to sample only one area of the Catalan Pyrenees, try to make for the Parc Nacional d'Aigüestortes i Estany de Sant Maurici, a jewel-like area of lakes and dramatic peaks in the north-west. Aside from the natural beauty of the mountains and valleys and the obvious attractions of walking, skiing and other activities, the Catalan Pyrenees and their foothills also have a rich cultural heritage, notably many lovely Romanesque churches and monasteries, often tucked away in surprisingly remote valleys. These are mainly the product of a time of prosperity and optimism in these regions in the 11th and 12th centuries, after Cataluña had broken ties with France in 988 and as the Muslim threat from the south weakened. The distant past also remains alive in the distinctly medieval atmosphere of some of the mountain towns and villages, and in the region's rich folklore. This is an area where Gothic is almost modern.

Activities
Walking The Pyrenees provide magnificent walking and trekking areas and this chapter suggests numerous routes, ranging from strolls of a couple of hours to day hikes that can be strung together into treks of several days. Nearly all of these can be done without camping gear, with nights spent in villages or in *refugis*, mountain refuges which offer basic dormitory accommodation and often meals. If you're relying on a refuge, however, you should try to reserve places or at least establish that it's not going to be full. Contact numbers are given for most of those mentioned in this chapter, and tourist offices can often tell you whether a booking is needed. Nearly all the refuges mentioned in this chapter are run by two Catalan alpine clubs based in Barcelona, the Federació d'Entitats Excursionistes de Catalunya (FEEC; ☎ 93-412 07 77 or 93-302 64 16), and the Centre Excursionista de Catalunya (CEC; ☎ 93-315 23 11 Monday to Thursday

❋❋❋❋❋❋❋❋❋❋❋❋❋

Walking in the Pyrenees
The best season for walking in the high Pyrenees mountains is late June to early September. Earlier than that, snow can make things difficult, and there's a potential avalanche danger. Later, the weather can turn poor. It *can* get very hot even at high altitude in high summer, but nowhere in the Pyrenees is the weather reliable; even in July and August you can get plenty of rainy days, cloud – and cold at high altitude.

The Pyrenees are very much mountains to be respected, and anyone heading into the hills should be properly equipped for any condition. Though this book suggests a number of walks, of varying length and toughness, it is not a trekking or walking guide.

For detailed route descriptions and advice on equipment and preparation, consult other sources such as those mentioned under Maps, Books and Activities in the Facts for the Visitor chapter. Local advice, from tourist offices, mountain refuges and other walkers, is also invaluable. You should ensure before you set off that you have adequate information on routes and conditions, and are suitably fit, equipped and experienced. ■

❋❋❋❋❋❋❋❋❋❋❋❋❋

from 7.30 to 9.30 pm). A night in a refuge usually costs 900 to 1100 ptas; meals, where available, are around 650 ptas for breakfast and 1700 ptas for lunch or dinner. Normally FEEC refuges allow you to cook, CEC ones don't.

The coast-to-coast GR-11 long-distance footpath traverses the entire Pyrenees from Cap de Creus on the Costa Brava to Honda-rribia on the Bay of Biscay. Its route across Cataluña goes by way of La Jonquera, Albanyà, Beget, Setcases in the upper Ter valley, the Vall de Núria, Planoles, Puig-cerdà, Andorra, south of Cataluña's highest peak Estats (3143 metres), over to the Parc Nacional d'Aigüestortes i Estany de Sant Maurici, then on to the south flank of the Vall d'Aran and on into Aragón.

Skiing Baqueira-Beret in the Vall d'Aran is one of Spain's biggest and best ski resorts. La Molina near Puigcerdà is also good, and there are several other smaller ones, plus a number of Nordic skiing centres.

Other Activities The Riu Noguera Pallaresa around Llavorsí and Sort has some of Spain's most exciting white water and is a centre not just for rafting, canoeing and hydrospeed (water-tobogganing) but for several other adventure sports too.

You can go horse riding almost anywhere – there are *hípicas* (riding stables) all over the place. Mountain bikes are, by Spanish standards, relatively easy to rent in the Pyrenees area. Another sport that's taking off here is *parapente*, a cross between hang-gliding and parachuting. And of course there's boundless scope for climbers – Pedraforca in the Serra del Cadí offers some of the most exciting ascents.

Getting There & Away

The only railway into the Pyrenees runs from Barcelona to Ripoll, Ribes de Freser and Puigcerdà, then across to Latour-de-Carol in France, where you can pick up onward trains.

The main Spanish roads into the Pyrenees tend to follow river valleys northward. These are the N-152 from Barcelona to Ripoll, Ribes de Freser and Puigcerdà; the A-18 and C-1411 from Barcelona to Puigcerdà via the Túnel del Cadí, with a branch west along the N-260 for La Seu d'Urgell; the C-1313 and N-260 from Lleida to La Seu d'Urgell; and the N-230 from Lleida to Vielha. There are a few lesser south-north routes, plus a series of east-west roads linking the main valleys. South-north roads tend to be better served by buses than east-west ones. The roads from Ribes de Freser to Puigcerdà and from La Seu d'Urgell to Sort are among those with no bus service, though the railway parallels the former.

Three main roads cross the Catalan Pyrenees into France: the C-151 north-east of Ripoll, the N-260 just east of Puigcerdà, and the N-230 north-west of Vielha. The N-145 heads north from La Seu d'Urgell to Andorra.

In this section we follow an overall east-to-west trajectory across northern inland Cataluña.

OLOT

Olot is only 450 metres above sea level and the hills around it are little more than pimples, but the pimples are the volcanoes of the Parc Natural de la Zona Volcànica de la Garrotxa – extinct or dormant volcanoes admittedly, but one erupted as recently as 11,500 years ago. Olot, if not the world's prettiest place, is a lively town of 28,000 people and an obvious base for the natural park.

Orientation

At the heart of town is a small grid of old streets centred on Plaça Major, with the parish church, the Església de Sant Esteve, three blocks west of the plaça. The main road through the centre, Carrer Bisbe Lorenzana, runs east-west three blocks south of Plaça Major, changing its name to Carrer Mulleres a short distance west. At the west end of Carrer Mulleres is Plaça Clarà, with a nice little park in the middle. The bus station is at Carrer Bisbe Lorenzana 20. Olot's 'Rambla',

An International Language

The Catalan language *(català)* is not confined to Cataluña. As a result of Cataluña's role in the Reconquista in the middle ages, it's also the first language of a majority of people in the Balearic Islands and nearly half those in the Valencia region – areas that were taken from the Muslims by Cataluña in the 13th century.

Catalan is also spoken in a narrow strip of Aragón bordering Cataluña – and in the French district of Roussillon, a wedge spreading east from Andorra to the Mediterranean, including the city of Perpignan (Perpinyà in Catalan). Roussillon was ruled from Barcelona for most of the middle ages until the Treaty of the Pyrenees in 1659, which set the current French-Spanish border. Further afield, the town of Alghero in Sardinia (L'Alguer in Catalan) speaks Catalan too – a remnant of Cataluña's medieval empire. And so, back in the Pyrenees, do the people of Andorra, always closely connected with Cataluña. Much to Catalans' delight, Andorra's recent entry to the United Nations has meant that Catalan is now heard there too.

Like all languages, Catalan has its dialects. The main distinction is between western and eastern Catalan – the former being used in Andorra, western and far southern Cataluña and the Catalan-speaking parts of Aragón and Valencia, the latter in the rest of the Catalan world. Expert ears go on to subdivide these into a total of 12 sub-dialects! Valencians prefer to call their sub-dialect *valencià* rather than català, while in the Balearic Islands you may hear of languages called *mallorqui, menorqui* and *eivissenc* – actually the Catalan sub-dialects used in Mallorca, Menorca and Ibiza, respectively. ■

Passeig d'En Blay, heads north-west from the Església de Sant Esteve.

Information

Tourist Offices Olot has three. The best town map is given out by the Patronat Municipal de Turisme (☎ 26 01 41) at Carrer Bisbe Lorenzana 15 opposite the bus station. It's open Monday to Friday from 9 am to 2 pm and 3 to 7.30 pm, and on the weekend and holidays from 10 am to 2 pm. The Centre d'Iniciatives Turístiques (☎ 27 02 42) is along the street at Carrer Mulleres 33. The Casal dels Volcans (☎ 26 62 02) concentrates on information about the Parc Natural de la Zona Volcànica de la Garrotxa. It's in the Jardí Botànic on Avinguda Santa Coloma de Farners, one km south-west of Plaça Clarà. Hours are Wednesday to Monday from 10 am to 2 pm, plus 4 to 6 pm (5 to 7 pm from July to September) every day except Tuesday, Sunday and holidays.

Other Services There are lots of banks on Carrer Bisbe Lorenzana west of the bus station, and a couple on Plaça Major. The main post office is at Carrer Joaquim Vayreda 4. The postcode is 17800. The Policia Municipal (☎ 27 91 33) are on Carrer Mira-

dor: from the top of Passeig d'En Blay go one block straight on, then one to the left. The Hospital de Sant Jaume (☎ 26 18 00) is at Carrer Mulleres 15. Drac bookshop on Plaça Rector Ferrer is good for maps and local guidebooks.

The telephone code is ☎ 972.

Things to See

The interesting **Museu Comarcal de la Garrotxa**, at Carrer Hospici 8, covers Olot's growth as an early textile centre and includes an excellent Catalan art collection focusing on the 19th century Escola Olotina (Olot school) of artists, who were inspired by the local landscape. It's open from 11 am to 2 pm and 4 to 7 pm (closed Tuesday, Sunday and holiday afternoons).

The **Jardí Botànic**, a botanical garden of Olot area flora, contains the interesting **Museu dels Volcans**, covering local flora and fauna as well as volcanoes and earthquakes. Also here is the Casal dels Volcans information centre for the natural park (see Information). The garden and museum have the same opening hours as the Casal dels Volcans.

There are four **volcanoes** on the fringes of Olot itself. Head for Volcà Montsacopa, 500 metres north of the centre, or Volcà La

Garrinada, one km north-east of the centre. Both have paths climbing to their craters.

Places to Stay

Camping Les Tries (☎ 26 24 05) at Avinguda Pere Badosa s/n, just off the N-260 on the east edge of town, has room for 180 people and is open from Semana Santa to October, at 1800 ptas for two people with a car and tent. The *Torre Malagrida* youth hostel (☎ 26 42 00), at Passeig de Barcelona 15, is an unusual early 20th century modernist building, renovated in 1994, with room for 70 people in dorms of up to 10. The high season, price-wise, is April to September.

Hostal Stop (☎ 26 10 48), 500 metres west of Plaça Major at Carrer Sant Pere Màrtir 29, has ageing but adequate rooms with shared baths for 2400 ptas a double. *Hostal Residència Garrotxa* (☎ 26 16 12), very central at Plaça Mora 3, offers bare but clean and quite big singles/doubles with private shower for 1500/3000 ptas. *Pensión Narmar* (☎ 26 98 07) right in the centre on Plaça Major has good, modern rooms at 3500 ptas a double, or 4300 ptas with bath.

Aparthotel Perla D'Olot (☎ 26 23 26; fax 27 04 74), 1.3 km from Plaça Clarà at Avinguda Santa Coloma de Farners 89, has 30 rooms with kitchen, bathroom and TV for 5900 ptas a double, plus IVA. *Hotel La Perla* (same ☎ & fax), just behind at Carretera de la Deu 9, has well-renovated rooms with shower/bath for 3500/3900 ptas plus IVA. The two share a restaurant.

Places to Eat

It's hard to beat the good, popular and cheap *Restaurant Can Guix* at Carrer Mulleres 3-5 for value. A wide range of Catalan and Spanish fare includes salads from 135 ptas, esqueixada for 185 ptas, and fish from 375 ptas. You can come for a good filling breakfast too; it's open Monday to Saturday from 8 am to 10.30 pm. For a lighter breakfast, try the friendly unnamed *café* with a cow sign outside, on Carrer Sant Roc off Plaça Major. It has good pastries and teas as well as the usual bread and coffee.

The restaurant of the *Pensión Narmar* on Plaça Major is economical, with main dishes (which include trout and chicken) from 450 ptas. Across the plaça, *La Plaça dels Gegants* is a haven for vegetarians, with a veggie menú del día for 1200 ptas, entrepans from 250 ptas, and drinks such as fruit lassi.

Fet al Gust at Passeig d'En Blay 49 has average pizzas from 800 ptas, and pasta dishes from 600 ptas.

Getting There & Away

Bus TEISA (☎ 26 01 96) runs buses to/from: Barcelona two to five times a day (2¼ hours; 1385 to 1660 ptas); Girona via Besalú eight times daily (four on Sunday; 1¼ hours; 580 ptas); Figueres via Besalú two or three times daily (1¼ hours); Ripoll three or four times daily (one hour; 495 ptas), most via Sant Joan de les Abadesses; and Camprodon once or twice daily (45 minutes; 390 ptas).

Car & Motorcycle The easiest approach from Barcelona is by the A-7 and C-152. The N-260 runs west to Ripoll and east to Besalú and Figueres, passing Olot on a northerly ring road. For Sant Joan de les Abadesses and Camprodon, the C-153 leaves Olot in a north-easterly direction along Avinguda de Girona, then Carretera de la Canya, but turns west at La Canya, rising through thickly forested hills, then passing through the Túnel de Capsacosta shortly before striking the C-151 four km north-east of Sant Joan. The main route to Girona follows the N-260 east to Besalú, then the C-150; an alternative, through the best parts of the Parc Natural de la Zona Volcànica de la Garrotxa, is the GE-524 via Santa Pau to Banyoles, on the C-150 18 km from Girona.

PARC NATURAL DE LA ZONA VOLCÀNICA DE LA GARROTXA

The natural park surrounds Olot on all sides but the most interesting area is between Olot and the village of Santa Pau, 10 km south-east.

Volcanic eruptions began here about 350,000 years ago and the most recent one, at Volcà del Croscat, happened 11,500 years ago. In the park are about 30 volcanic cones, up to 160 metres high and 1.5 km wide. Together with the lush and varied vegetation – a result of fertile soils and a damp climate – these create a landscape of unusual beauty. Three-quarters of the park, including most of the volcanic cones, is covered in trees. Between the woods are crop fields, a few hamlets, and scattered old stone farmhouses.

Information
The main information office for the park is the Casal dels Volcans in Olot. There are two others: the Centre d'Informació Can Serra (☎ 19 50 74), beside the GE-524 Olot-Banyoles road, 4.5 km from the middle of Olot, and the Centre d'Informació Can Vayreda (☎ 68 03 49) on Plaça Major in Santa Pau. Their hours change with the wind; in July and August you can expect them to be open daily from 10.30 am to 2 pm and 5 to 7 pm. You can pick up useful free walking itinerary leaflets, or buy the good *plànolguia* map of the whole park for 500 ptas.

The phone code is ☎ 972.

Things to See & Do
Walks The heart of the park encompasses the Fageda d'en Jordà beech wood and two of the biggest volcanoes, Volcà de Santa Margarida and Volcà del Croscat, all of which are included in the marked walking route No 1, an 11 km, four hour circuit from Can Serra. In summer the beech wood, on the south side of the GE-524, is filled with light so green it's almost intoxicating. Moving east from the wood to the Volcà de Santa Margarida, you pass the little 11th century Romanesque Església de Sant Miquel de Sacot. You then ascend 100 metres to the 330 metre-wide crater of Santa Margarida, containing a small Romanesque hermitage. From Santa Margarida you head north across the GE-524 and around the Volcà del Croscat, part of which has been quarried, enabling you to see its lava strata.

For a shorter walk, you could follow route No 2, a half-hour circuit through the Fageda d'en Jordà from Can Serra, or walk up Volcà de Santa Margarida from the car park on its north side on the GE-524.

Walking route No 3, also well marked, leads from Olot to the Fageda d'en Jordà by paths and tracks in about an hour, and on to Can Xel on the GE-524 between the fageda and Volcà de Santa Margarida. You can start this route at various places in Olot including the Patronat Municipal de Turisme and the Casal dels Volcans. You can link up with route No 1 at the Fageda d'en Jordà. From Can Xel, route No 4 continues east to Santa Pau.

Santa Pau The old part of the village, perched picturesquely on a rocky outcrop, contains a pretty, porticoed plaza, the Romanesque Església de Santa Maria, and a locked-up baronial castle.

Castellfollit de la Roca This village on the N-260 eight km north-east of Olot stands atop a crag composed of several layers of petrified lava – most easily viewed from the road north of the village.

Places to Stay & Eat
Just off the GE-524 and close to the most interesting parts of the natural park are two pleasant, small country camping grounds, open all year: *Camping La Fageda* (☎ 27 12 39), four km from the middle of Olot, and *Camping Lava* (☎ 68 03 58), seven km out. *Restaurant Can Xel*, about halfway between the two on the GE-524, does meals. Wild camping is banned throughout the Garrotxa district, which stretches from east of Besalú to west of Olot, and from the French border to south of Sant Feliu de Pallerols.

In Santa Pau, there are 10 quaint old rooms with bath at *Bar-Restaurant Cal Sastre* (☎ 68 04 21), Cases Noves 1 on Placeta dels Balls in the old part of the village. Doubles are about 4500 ptas. The less attractive *Restaurant Bellavista* (☎ 68 01 03) is at Carrer Sant Martí s/n, north of the GE-524. Both do meals. *Cal Sastre* has excellent Catalan food but isn't cheap. There are more economical cafés in the village centre.

Getting There & Away
A TEISA bus runs along the GE-524

between Olot and Banyoles on Wednesday and non-holiday Saturdays only, departing Olot at 7.15 am and Banyoles at 12.45 pm. Banyoles has buses about hourly to/from Girona.

RIPOLL

Ripoll, 30 km from Olot in the next valley west, is a shabby industrial town of 12,000 people. But it can claim, with some justice, to be the birthplace of Cataluña, and at its heart, in the Monestir de Santa Maria, is one of the finest pieces of Romanesque art in Spain.

Back in the 9th century Ripoll was the power base from which the local strongman, Guifré el Pilós (Wilfred the Hairy), succeeded in uniting several of the counties of the Frankish March along the south side of the Pyrenees. Guifré went on to become the first Count of Barcelona, effectively founding Cataluña in the process. In 879, to encourage repopulation in the Pyrenees valleys, he founded the Monestir de Santa Maria, which grew into the most powerful monastery of medieval Cataluña.

Orientation & Information

The tourist office (☎ 70 23 51) is on Plaça Abat Oliba, by the Ribes de Freser-Sant Joan de les Abadesses road which runs through the north of town. It's open from 10 am to 1 pm and 4 to 7 pm. The Monestir de Santa Maria is virtually next door. You'll find plenty of banks around Plaça Sant Eudald, a couple of blocks south. The Creu Roja (☎ 70 06 01) faces the tourist office on Plaça Abat Oliba. The Policia Municipal (☎ 71 44 14) are across the street at Plaça Ajuntament 3.

The telephone code is ☎ 972.

Monestir de Santa Maria

Following its founding in 879, the monastery grew rapidly richer, bigger and more influential, and from the mid-10th to mid-11th centuries, under famous abbots such as Arnulf and Oliba, it was Cataluña's spiritual and cultural heart, a centre for theology, manuscript copying and translation of scientific works from Arabic. A great five-naved

basilica was built, and was adorned in about 1100 with a fabulous carved stone portal which ranks among the high points of all Romanesque art. Decline set in after Ripoll was replaced as the burial place of Catalan royalty by Poblet, in the south, in the 12th century. The monastery lived on in gradual decay until the monks were evicted during 19th century anticlerical reforms. Two fires left the basilica in ruins by 1885, after which it was restored in rather gloomy imitation of its former glory. The most interesting feature of the interior now is the restored tomb of Guifré el Pilós.

You can visit the basilica and its great portal, now protected from atmospheric decay by a wall of glass, daily from 8 am to 1 pm and 3 to 8 pm (free). A chart near the portal – in Catalan – helps interpret the feast of sculpture on the portal's central pillars, the semicircular arches above them, and the seven levels of carving to either side. The whole is a vision of the medieval universe from God the Creator, in the centre at the top to the month-by-month scenes of daily rural life on the innermost pillars. Look for the crossing of the Red Sea (panel No 15 on the chart), Cain and Abel (Nos 60 to 66), Daniel (Nos 50 to 54; the lions' den is No 50), Jonah (Nos 55 to 59; he's swallowed by the whale in No 56), and St Peter and St Paul (Nos 38 to 49).

Down a few steps to the right of the doorway is the monastery's beautiful cloister (claustre), which is open daily from 10 am to 1 pm and 3 to 7 pm (100 ptas). It's a two storey affair, created in the 12th to 15th centuries. The lower level is embellished by some fine, though often badly weathered carved capitals.

Museu Etnogràfic de Ripoll

Next door to the Monestir de Santa Maria this museum, housed in part of the medieval Església de Sant Pere, covers local crafts industries (including firearms, once important here), and religious art.

Places to Stay

The friendly Hostal Paula (☎ 70 00 11)

Carrer Pirineus 6, is barely a stone's throw from the Monestir de Santa Maria. Its 11 rooms, modernised with sparkling bathrooms, are 4000/5500 ptas plus IVA for a double/triple. The decaying *Hotel Payet* (☎ 70 02 50), Plaça Nova 2, has singles/doubles for 3000/4000 ptas with bath, or 1800/3500 ptas without. *Hostal del Ripollès* (☎ 70 02 15), opposite at Plaça Nova 11, is better but can get full. Closer to the train and bus stations, *Hostal La Trobada* (☎ 70 23 53) at Passeig Honorat Vilamanyà 4 has good rooms at up to 7500 ptas a double.

Places to Eat
Reasonable cafés near the Monestir de Santa Maria include *Bar El Punt*, across the road on Plaça Ajuntament, and *Bar Stop* on Plaça Tomàs Raguer, which has a 925 ptas menú. *La Piazzetta* restaurant at the Hostal del Ripollès does reasonably priced pizzas, pasta, and meat and fish dishes. Next door, lively *Cafè Canaules* is more a place to drink than eat.

Getting There & Away
The bus and train stations are almost side by side on Carrer Progrés, 600 metres southeast of the centre. Connections with Barcelona, Ribes de Freser and Puigcerdà are all much better by train than bus.

Bus Buses run to/from Barcelona once daily (1½ hours); Olot three or four times daily (one hour; 495 ptas); Ribes de Freser two or three times a day Monday to Friday, once on Saturday; Gombrèn, La Pobla de Lillet and Guardiola de Berguedà once or twice daily Monday to Saturday.

Train About 12 trains a day run to/from Barcelona (two hours), and six a day to/from Ribes de Freser (20 minutes) and Puigcerdà (1¼ hours). For information you can call ☎ 70 06 44.

VALL ALTO DEL TER
From Ripoll, this upper part of the Riu Ter valley reaches north-east to the pleasant small towns of Sant Joan de les Abadesses

and Camprodon (950 metres), then north-west up to the small Vallter 2000 ski centre (2150 metres) just below the French border. The area is a more pleasant overnight stop than Ripoll, and from the upper reaches there are some excellent hikes across the mountains west to the Vall de Núria.

The C-151 road leaves the Ter valley at Camprodon to head over the 1513 metre Collado d'Ares pass into France.

Information
There's a tourist office in Sant Joan de les Abadesses (☎ 72 05 99), and there are two in Camprodon (☎ 74 09 36, 74 00 10). Salvat bookshop at Carrer del Beat Miró 8 in Sant Joan stocks Editorial Alpina map/guides and other guidebooks. The telephone code is ☎ 972.

Things to See
Well worth a look in Sant Joan de les Abadesses are the 12th century **bridge** (restored after damage in the civil war) soaring over the Ter, and the **Museu del Monestir** on Plaça Abadessa. This monastery, another Guifré el Pilós foundation, began life as a nunnery but the nuns were expelled in 1017 for supposed licentious conduct. Its elegant 12th century church contains the marvellous *Santíssim Misteri*, a 13th century polychrome woodcarving of the descent from the cross, composed of seven life-size figures. It's open daily from at least 11 am to 2 pm and, except Monday to Friday from November to mid-March, 4 to 6 pm (200 ptas).

Walks
For the fit and properly equipped, there are some excellent full-day hikes west from the topmost part of the Ter valley to the Vall de Núria, 10 to 12 km away as the crow flies. The Editorial Alpina *Puigmal* map/guide is the one for this area.

One route takes you through Tregurà de Dalt (1400 metres) north-west over the Coll dels Tres Pics pass (2400 metres), down to the FEEC's small Coma de Vaca refuge (2000 metres, recently closed for renovation) at the top of the steep Gorges del Freser

CATALUÑA

valley, then north-west up to the Coll de Torreneules (2585 metres), and down to the Vall de Núria (1970 metres).

A stiffer route follows a stretch of the GR-11 from Setcases to Núria, via lengths of the main Pyrenean ridge. This is a 20 km hike taking you up from 1265 metres to 2800 metres, then down to 1970 metres at Núria. You can shorten it to 13 km and save a lot of ascent by starting from the Xalet-Refugi d'Ull de Ter, at 2220 metres.

There's a great variety of shorter walks down in the valley or higher up.

Skiing

Lying at 2150 metres in an impressive mountain bowl just one km from the French border, **Vallter 2000** is the easternmost ski resort in the Pyrenees and snow can be unreliable (☎ 13 60 57 or 74 01 04 for information). It has 12 pistes of all grades, ranging from 2535 down to 1950 metres, seven lifts and a ski school. A day's lift pass is about 2800 ptas. You can rent gear at the resort itself or in Setcases or Camprodon. The nearest accommodation is the Xalet-Refugi d'Ull de Ter (see Places to Stay & Eat).

In summer, the Telecadira Jordi Pujol chair lift opens from late July to early September from 11 am to 4 pm. It rises to the Cafeteria Les Marmotes at 2535 metres, from where on a good day there are magnificent views.

Places to Stay & Eat

There are numerous accommodation options, including camping grounds near Sant Joan and Camprodon and the good *Camping Conca de Ter* (☎ 74 06 29) at Vilallonga de Ter, five km north-west of Camprodon, which is open all year at 2595 ptas plus IVA for two adults with a car and tent.

Good bets in Sant Joan are *Hostal Ter* (☎ 72 00 75) at Carrer Vista Alegre 2 overlooking the river, with singles/doubles for 2100/3600 ptas, and doubles with bath for 4000 ptas; and *Hostal Janpere* (☎ 72 00 77) at Carrer Mestre Andreu 3, which has

singles/doubles at 1500/3000 ptas plus IVA, or 2500/5000 ptas plus IVA with private bath.

Camprodon is a popular base for walkers and skiers. *Can Ganansi* (☎ 74 01 34) at Carrer Josep Morera 11, 100 metres south of the central Plaça d'Espanya, has singles/doubles with bath and TV for 2200/4400 ptas, and a restaurant with a menú for 1200 ptas; trout – a good thing to eat in Camprodon – is 1000 ptas. *Hostal La Plaçeta* (☎ 74 08 07), nearby at Plaça del Carme 9, has pleasant singles/doubles for 2500/5000 ptas with breakfast. *Restaurant Núria* on Plaça d'Espanya has good Catalan country cooking, with a three course menú for 1150 ptas; à la carte you could go for snails at 700 ptas. *Bar La Tinaja*, nearby on Carrer Catalunya, does platos combinados from 475 ptas. The village shops are flush with local sausages, hams and cheeses. *Cal Xec* on Carrer d'Isaac Albèniz just north of the Pont Nou bridge has a particularly impressive selection.

North-west up the valley from Camprodon, the villages of Vilallonga de Ter, Tregurà de Dalt (five km up a steep side road, 12 km from Camprodon) and Setcases (11 km) have at least one pensión or hostal each. Setcases has half a dozen: *Hostal Nova Tiranda* (☎ 13 60 37), at Carrer Núria 3 in the centre, is one of the better ones and has doubles for 3360 ptas without bath or 3885 ptas with, plus IVA.

Up near Vallter 2000, *Xalet-Refugi d'Ull de Ter* (☎ 93-867 93 61) is a decent CEC mountain refuge with 80 bunk places, a bar and meals. It's a 20 minute uphill walk from its car park on the road about one km below the ski station, and is open from late June to late September, and on the weekend and in holiday periods during the rest of the year.

Getting There & Away

Güell i Güell (☎ 74 02 95) runs around seven buses daily from Ripoll to Sant Joan de les Abadesses and Camprodon. The single daily bus north-west from Camprodon, as far as Setcases, leaves in the early afternoon and comes back down soon after.

❋ ❋ ❋ ❋ ❋ ❋ ❋ ❋ ❋ ❋ ❋ ❋ ❋

The Legend of Comte Arnau

Sant Joan de les Abadesses is one of many places in the country north of Ripoll that's involved in perhaps the strangest of Pyrenean legends – that of Comte Arnau, the wicked medieval Count of Mataplana, who cheated his workers of their due payments of wheat and had more than his quota of lust for local womanhood. The insatiable count, it seems, came by tunnel to Sant Joan from Campdevànol, 10 km west, for covert trysts with the abbess and nuns. When the abbess, his favourite, died, her pious replacement barred him from the convent, but he still got in, and carried on, thanks to help from the devil.

Eventually Arnau fell in love with a local lass, whose only refuge was the nunnery at Sant Joan. Arnau forced his way into the convent to find his beloved dead – from fear and misery, it's surmised. Her corpse, however, revived just long enough to give the count a good ticking-off for his misdeeds. Overcome by remorse, Arnau retired to the Serra de Mogrony, where, condemned to eternal misery for his sins, his tortured soul still wanders, returning on thundery nights (some say full-moon nights) to the convent at Sant Joan – a horrific vision on horseback with a pack of balefully howling dogs.

If you visit Sant Joan or other villages in the region in summer, you might be lucky enough to catch one of the occasional re-enactments of bits of the Arnau legend. Or you can look at his supposed residence, the Castell de Mataplana, at Gombrèn, about 11 km north-west of Ripoll on the GE-401. ■

❋ ❋ ❋ ❋ ❋ ❋ ❋ ❋ ❋ ❋ ❋ ❋ ❋

TEISA (☎ 20 48 68) runs a couple of buses daily from Olot to Sant Joan de les Abadesses and Camprodon.

VALL DE NÚRIA & RIBES DE FRESER

Around 700 AD, the story goes, Sant Gil (St Giles) came from Nîmes to live as a hermit in a cave in an isolated mountain valley 26 km north of Ripoll, preaching the Gospel to shepherds. Before he departed four years later, apparently fleeing Visigothic persecution, Sant Gil hurriedly hid away a wooden Virgin-and-child image that he had carved, a cross, his cooking pot, and the bell which he had used to summon the shepherds. They stayed hidden till 1079, when an ox miraculously led some shepherds to the spot. The

statuette, the Mare de Déu de Núria, became the patron of Pyrenean shepherds, and Núria's future was assured. The first historical mention of a shrine here was made in 1162.

Sant Gil would probably recoil in shock if he were to come back today. The large, grey, modern sanctuary complex squatting at the heart of the valley, 1960 metres above sea level, is a bit of an eyesore to many tastes, and the crowds of visitors would make anyone with hermitic leanings run a mile. Despite all this, however, Núria remains an almost pristine place, a wide, green bowl, ringed by mountains, that is the starting point for numerous fine walks. And getting there is fun, either on foot up the Gorges de Núria – the steep, green, rocky valley of the thundering Riu Núria – or by the exciting little 'Cremallera' railway from Ribes de Freser, which rises over 1000 metres in its 12 km journey up the same valley.

Bring warm clothes as the altitude can mean quite a temperature drop.

Orientation

Unless you're hiking to Núria across the mountains, you must approach from the small town of Ribes de Freser, on the N-152 14 km north of Ripoll. The Cremallera starts at Ribes-Enllaç station, just off the N-152 at the south end of Ribes, and makes two stops on the way to Núria: at Ribes-Vila station, near the north end of Ribes after one km, and at the village of Queralbs (1200 metres) after six km. There's a road from Ribes to Queralbs, but from there on it's the Cremallera or your feet.

The N-152 passing through Ribes is called Carrer Sant Quintí. The town's main street, Carrer Major, turns east off this, 750 metres north of Ribes-Enllaç station.

Information

Núria's tourist information and reservations office (☎ 73 20 20), open daily from 9 am to 8 pm, is in the Núria station of the Cremallera, beside the sanctuary complex.

Ribes de Freser's main tourist office (☎ 72 77 28) is at Plaça de l'Ajuntament 3 on

Carrer Major. The telephone code for everywhere in this section is ☎ 972.

Santuari de Núria

The large 19th and 20th century building dominating the valley contains a hotel, restaurants and exhibition halls as well as the *santuari* itself, which holds the sacred *símbols de Núria*. The santuari is open daily from 9 to 11.50 am and 1 to 8 pm. The Mare de Déu de Núria sits behind a glass screen above the altar and is in the Romanesque style of the 12th century, so either Sant Gil was centuries ahead of his time or this isn't actually his work! Steps lead up to the bell, cross and cooking pot (all dated back to at least the 15th century). To have a prayer granted, put your head in the pot and ring the bell while you say it.

Walks

Get hold of Editorial Alpina's *Puigmal* booklet/map before you come to Núria if you plan on some walking. If you want to walk up to Núria, you can avoid the first relatively unexciting six km from Ribes de Freser by taking the Cremallera (or road) to Queralbs, saving your energies for the steepest and most spectacular part of the approach – about three hours up the good (and sometimes very busy) track climbing the Gorges de Núria. Another idea, of course, is to take the Cremallera up, and walk down! In early summer the wild flowers are spectacular on this route.

From the Vall de Núria (where you're advised to fill in a route sheet at the information office before you head off), you can cap several 2700 to 2900 metre peaks on the main Pyrenees ridge in about 2½ to three hours walking each.

Skiing

In winter Núria is a small-scale ski resort, with 10 runs of all grades, totalling just seven km, and limited lift capacity, going up to only 2252 metres. It's cheap, however; a one day lift ticket is 1275 to 1600 ptas. You can rent full equipment for 1950 ptas a day. Off-piste skiing is good here.

Places to Stay & Eat

Wild camping is banned in the whole Ribes de Freser-Núria area.

Núria There's a *zona d'acampada* (camping area with limited facilities) behind the sanctuary. It's cheap – 200 ptas a tent and 150 ptas a person – but space is restricted and it's advisable to book on ☎ 73 20 20.

The *Alberg Pic de l'Àliga* youth hostel (☎ 73 20 48) is up at the top of the cable car (telecabina) on the east side of the valley. It has 138 places in dorms of four to 14. High-season prices apply all year except October and November. The cable car runs daily from 9 am to 8.15 pm, and also on Friday and Saturday from 9.30 to 10 pm.

The *Hotel Vall de Núria* (☎ 73 20 00) in the sanctuary building has 65 comfortable singles/doubles with bath and TV ranging from 4550/6850 ptas (from Monday to Friday most of the year) to 8175/12,300 ptas in August, breakfast included. There are also good apartments (same ☎) for up to five people, costing 6650 to 10,850 ptas. In the sanctuary building, the *Autoservei* self-service cafeteria and the *Bar Finistrelles* both have starters in the 450 ptas region and main courses around 700 ptas. The hotel restaurant has a menú for 2000 ptas. There's also a shop in the sanctuary building that sells food.

Ribes de Freser *Fonda Vilalta* (☎ 72 70 95) at Carrer de Cerdanya 6 off Carrer Major has a variety of basic but clean rooms at 2800, 3800 or 4800 ptas a double. The most expensive have private bath. *Hotel Fanet* (☎ 72 70 77), at Carrer Balandrau 24 near Ribes-Vila station, has singles/doubles with bath and TV for 2675/5350 ptas, and a good restaurant with main courses from 700 ptas. There are three lower mid-range hotels, with doubles at 6000 to 7000 ptas, on Carrer Sant Quintí.

Getting There & Away

Bus Transports Mir (☎ 70 02 97) runs between Ripoll and Ribes de Freser, with two or three buses a day Monday to Friday and one on Saturday. There's no bus service west of Ribes on the N-152.

Train About six RENFE trains a day run to Ribes-Enllaç from Ripoll (20 minutes), Barcelona (2¼ hours) and Puigcerdà (one hour). The café at the station will look after luggage.

The Cremallera (☎ 72 70 31), a narrow-gauge electric-powered cog-wheel railway operating since 1931, runs from Ribes-Enllaç to Núria and back six to 12 times a day depending on the season. Current timetables find their way to tourist offices all over Cataluña. Some services connect with RENFE trains at Ribes-Enllaç.

The Cremallera ride is about 45 minutes one way and all trains stop at Ribes-Vila and Queralbs. It's an exciting and spectacular trip, particularly after Queralbs as the train winds carefully up the precipitous side of the Gorges de Núria. The one-way/return fare from Ribes to Núria is 1300/2075 ptas.

PUIGCERDÀ

Just a couple of km from the French border, Puigcerdà (pronounced 'puh-cher-DA'; population 6000) is not much more than a way station or stepping-off point, but it's a jolly little one, particularly in summer and the ski season. There are a dozen Spanish, Andorran and French ski resorts within 45 km.

At a height of 1200 metres, Puigcerdà is capital of the district of Cerdanya which, with the French Cerdagne district across the border, occupies a low-lying basin between higher reaches of the Pyrenees to the east and west. Cerdanya and Cerdagne, once a single Catalan county, were divided by the Treaty of the Pyrenees in 1659 but still have a lot in common. It's in areas like this that one has the strongest sense of being neither in Spain nor in France, but in Cataluña.

Orientation & Information

Puigcerdà stands on a small hill, with the train station at the foot of its south-west side. A few minutes climb up flights of steps takes you to Plaça Ajuntament, off which is the tourist office (☎ 88 05 42) at Carrer Querol 1. You'll find plenty of banks on the main plaças. The post office is at Avinguda Coronel Molera 11 and the postcode is 17520. The Guàrdia Urbana (municipal police; ☎ 88 19 72) are in the ajuntament on Plaça Ajuntament. The Hospital de Puigcerdà (☎ 88 01 50) is very central at Plaça Santa Maria 1. The telephone code is ☎ 972.

Things to See

Despite serious damage in the civil war, the town centre still retains a pleasant, relaxed and old-fashioned air which is Puigcerdà's greatest attraction. Of the 17th century parish church, the **Església de Santa Maria**, only the tower remains; the rest fell victim to the civil war. The 13th century Gothic **Església de Sant Domènec** on Passeig 10 d'Abril was also wrecked in the war, but rebuilt. It contains 14th century Gothic murals which somehow survived. The **Estany** (lake) in the north of town, created back in 1380 for irrigation, is surrounded by turn-of-the-century summer houses built by wealthy Barcelona families.

Places to Stay

Camping Stel (☎ 88 23 61) on the Llívia road is open from late June to late September and charges about 3000 ptas for two adults with a car and tent.

Right outside the train station, *Hostal Estación* (☎ 88 03 50), Plaça Estació 2, has plain but quite adequate rooms for 2000/3600 ptas, or 2500/4300 ptas with private bath, all plus IVA, and a handy café downstairs.

Up in the town, *Pension Llorens* (☎ 88 04 86) at Carrer Alfons I 1 has small but nice, clean rooms for 3000 ptas a double, with shared bathrooms. The friendly *Hostal Alfonso* (☎ 88 02 46), Carrer Espanya 5, is a bit better at 2000/4000 ptas for large singles/doubles with bath. *Hostal La Muntanya* (☎ 88 02 02), Avinguda Coronel Molera 1, is also good at 2500/5000 ptas with bath. *Hostal Núria* (☎ 88 17 56), Plaça Cabrinetty 18, has nice doubles with bath and balcony for 5000 ptas.

Hotel Maria Victoria (☎ 88 03 00), Carrer

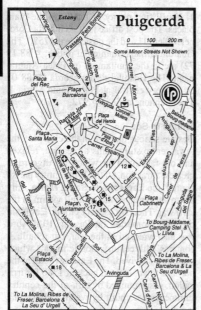

Puigcerdà

0   100   200 m
Some Minor Streets Not Shown

PLACES TO STAY
1   Hotel Del Lago
3   Hostal La Muntanya
12 Hostal Alfonso
13 Hotel Maria Victoria
14 Pensión Llorens
15 Hostal Núria
18 Hostal Estación

PLACES TO EAT
2   Pizzeria Casa Clemente
4   Pizzeria Frankfurt
6   Restaurant Kennedy
7   Granja Fran Ros
11 El Niu

OTHER
5   Post Office
8   Església de Sant Domènec
9   Tower of Església de Santa Maria
10 Hospital de Puigcerdà
16 Tourist Office
17 Guàrdia Urbana
19 Train Station

Querol 7, has some fine views, with doubles at 8100 ptas. *Hotel Del Lago* (☎ 88 10 00), near the Estany at Avinguda Dr Piguillem s/n, has old-fashioned style and comfort and a nice garden, for 11,000 ptas a double plus IVA.

Places to Eat

One of the best-value places is *El Niu* at Carrer Alfons I 15, where the 975 ptas menú appears to be just two courses but is actually three – one of which is usually trout – with wine thrown in too. There's also a range of tapas from 250 ptas, and raciones and torrades from 400 ptas.

At *Granja Fran Ros*, Plaça dels Herois 8, you can get platos combinados for around 700 ptas, chicken and chips for 550 ptas, or a green salad for 275 ptas.

Restaurant Kennedy, Plaça dels Herois 2, with tables on the square, is very popular and has a good three course menú with wine for 1450 ptas. The two best-priced of several pizzerias are *Pizzeria Frankfurt* at Carrer Major 54, with most pizzas from 700 ptas, and *Pizzeria Casa Clemente*, Avinguda Dr Piguillem 6 (from 800 ptas).

Getting There & Away

Bus Alsina Graells runs two daily buses (one at weekends) to/from Barcelona (three hours) via the Túnel del Cadí; three to/from La Seu d'Urgell (one hour); and one to/from Lleida (four hours). They stop at the train station. The tourist office has timetables.

The quickest way to Andorra is by train to Latour-de-Carol, then by bus, a total journey of 2¼ to 2¾ hours. See the Andorra chapter for information on the bus connections. You can also reach Andorra la Vella by changing buses in La Seu d'Urgell.

Train About six trains a day run to/from Ribes de Freser, Ripoll and Barcelona (3¼ hours; 1040 ptas). Just three or four in each direction make the seven minute hop over the border to/from Latour-de-Carol in France (which in Spain you may see spelt La Tor de Querol or variations on that theme). These connect at Latour-de-Carol with trains to/from Toulouse or Paris, and with the narrow-gauge Train Jaune down the Têt valley to Perpignan. Puigcerdà station (☎ 88 01 65) has details on the French trains.

Car & Motorcycle From Barcelona, the A-18 autopista feeds into the C-1411, which approaches Puigcerdà through the five km Túnel del Cadí (1330 ptas toll for cars). Bicycles are not allowed in the tunnel.

The N-152 from Ribes de Freser climbs west along the north flank of the Rigard valley, with the pine-covered Serra de Mogrony rising to the south, to the 1800 metre Collado de Toses pass, then winds down to Puigcerdà.

The main crossing into France is at Bourg-Madame, immediately east of Puigcerdà, from where roads head to Perpignan and Toulouse.

AROUND PUIGCERDÀ
Llívia

Six km east of Puigcerdà across flat farmland, the little town of Llívia is a piece of Spain in France. Under the 1659 Treaty of the Pyrenees Spain ceded 33 villages to France, but Llívia was a 'town' so, together with the 13 sq km of its municipality, remained a Spanish possession.

The interest of Llívia's tiny medieval nucleus, near the top of the town, centres on the **Museu Municipal** at Carrer dels Forns 4, and the 15th century Gothic **Església de Nostra Senyora dels Àngels**, just above the museum. There's a tourist office (☎ 972-89 63 13) in the museum and both museum and church open Tuesday to Saturday (and Monday in July and August) from 10 am to 1 pm and 3 to 6 pm, and on summer Sundays from 10 am to 2 pm. The museum (150 ptas) is in what's claimed to be Europe's oldest pharmacy, the Farmacia Esteva, which was founded in 1415. The church, open daily (except winter Mondays) from 10 am to 1 pm and 3 to 6 pm, contains an 18th century baroque retablo and a processional cross given to Llívia by Carlos I. From the church you can walk up to the ruined **Castell de Llívia**, where, during the short-lived period of Islamic dominion in the Pyrenees, the

Muslim governor Manussa enjoyed secret dalliance with Lampègia, daughter of the Duke of Aquitaine (or so legend has it).

At the time of writing, an Alsina Graells bus leaves Puigcerdà train station for Llívia Monday to Friday at 11.50 am, returning from Llívia at 1.30 pm. If these times don't suit, it's not a long walk, and the road is fairly quiet. You only cross about two km of France before entering the Llívia enclave, and apart from an abandoned border post just past Camping Stel and a couple of French road signs, you'd hardly know you'd left Spain.

La Molina & Masella

These two ski resorts lie either side of 2537 metre Tosa d'Alp, about 15 km south of Puigcerdà. La Molina is one of Cataluña's biggest and most popular ski centres, though the temporary closure of its Tosa d'Alp slopes for remodelling has recently deprived it of some of its longest runs. Altogether it has 27 pistes of all grades, totalling 38 km, at altitudes of 1600 to 2537 metres. There's a fairly good lift system though, even so, queues build up at peak times. A one day lift pass costs from 2600 to 3250 ptas depending on the season. The resort straggles about four km up the hill from La Molina proper, where the train station is, to 'Supermolina', where some lifts start and you'll find the information and bookings office (☎ 972-89 20 31).

Recently modernised Masella (☎ 972-14 42 01) has some long forest runs among its 29 pistes totalling 46 km. The majority are blue or red. The lift system is more limited than La Molina's. A one day pass is 2700 to 3400 ptas.

Both resorts offer equipment rental and ski schools (La Molina has three).

Places to Stay There's a youth hostel, the *Alberg Mare de Déu de les Neus* (☎ 972-89 20 12) in the bottom part of La Molina near the train station. It has 148 places in rooms ranging from doubles to a 38-person dorm. High-season prices are charged from December to March and in July and August.

Other accommodation is mostly on the expensive side and many skiers stay in

Puigcerdà or even further afield. *Hostal 4 Vents* (☎ 89 20 97), Carrer Afores s/n, about halfway up the hill to Supermolina, has doubles from 6000 to 8000 ptas, some with bath. *Hotel Solineu* (☎ 14 50 16) in Supermolina is a bit cheaper. If you're coming for more than a day's skiing, you're probably best booking a package through the La Molina booking centre. A two day weekend deal including accommodation, lift pass and some meals costs from 11,000 ptas per person.

Getting There & Away La Molina is on the Barcelona-Ribes de Freser-Puigcerdà railway, with about six trains a day each way. In the ski season there's some kind of bus service from Puigcerdà. Most people come by car; the easiest route from Barcelona is by the A-18 autopista and the C-1411 through the Túnel del Cadí. Roads also wind down to La Molina and Masella from the N-152 west of the Collado de Toses.

SERRA DEL CADÍ

The N-260 runs west along the wide Riu Segre valley from Puigcerdà to La Seu d'Urgell, with the Pyrenees climbing away northward towards Andorra, and one of the finest pre-Pyrenees ranges, the Serra del Cadí, rising steep and high along the south side. Though this face of the Cadí – rocky and fissured by ravines known as *canales* – looks daunting enough, the range's most spectacular peak is Pedraforca (2497 metres), a southern offshoot with probably the best rock climbing in Cataluña. Pedraforca and the main Cadí range also offer some excellent mountain hiking for those suitably equipped and experienced. Together with the dramatic scenery, attractive villages, and some unpaved roads in among the hills which are passable for non-4WD vehicles in dry conditions, this all adds up to an area that's well worth turning your steps towards.

Orientation

The area around Pedraforca is most easily approached from the C-1411, along the B-400, which heads west 1.5 km south of Guardiola de Berguedà. Pedraforca looms mightily into view about halfway to the village of Saldes, which sits 1215 metres high at its foot, 15 km from the C-1411. The main Cadí range runs from east to west about five km north of Saldes. The Refugi Lluís Estasen (see Places to Stay & Eat) is under the north face of Pedraforca 2.5 km northwest of Saldes. You can reach it by footpath from Saldes or by a partly paved road which turns north off the B-400 about one km west of Saldes. Park at the Mirador de Gresolet, from where it's 10 minutes walk up to the refuge.

Information

The Parc Natural del Cadí-Moixeró's main Centre d'Informació (☎ 93-824 41 51) is in Bagà, a village on the C-1411 four km north of Guardiola de Berguedà. Open Monday to Friday from 9 am to 1.30 pm, Saturday from 10 am to 2 pm and 4 to 6.30 pm, and Sunday and holidays from 10 am to 2 pm, the office is a mite inconveniently placed at Carrer de la Vinya 1, on the Gisclareny road on the western edge of Bagà. Some information on the park is also available from the tourist offices at the service area at the north end of the Túnel del Cadí (☎ 973-51 02 33), in Bellver de Cerdanya (☎ 973-51 04 12), in Tuixén (☎ 973-37 00 30) and in La Seu d'Urgell.

In Saldes, the Centre d'Informació Massís del Pedraforca (☎ 93-825 80 05), open daily from 11 am to 2 pm and 5 to 7 pm, has information on the Saldes and Pedraforca area only. Saldes has a post office but no bank or ATM.

Editorial Alpina's *Serra del Cadí – Pedraforca* map/guide covers the Saldes-Tuixén route, Pedraforca, the main Cadí range and its northern slopes. For areas east of Saldes you need *Moixeró – Tosa d'Alp*, and for the Segre valley you need *Cerdanya*.

Pedraforca

The name means 'Stone Fork' and the approach from the east makes clear why, with the two separate rocky peaks – the

Puigcerdà & Serra del Cadí Area

0   5   10 km

northern Pollegó Superior (2497 metres) and the southern Pollegó Inferior (2400 metres) – divided by a saddle called L'Enforcadura. The north face, rising near-vertically for up to 600 metres, has several great classic rock climbs, while the south face has a wall which sends the modern school of alpinists into raptures.

Pedraforca is also quite possible for walkers, but certainly exhilarating. From the Refugi Lluís Estasen you can reach the summit of the Pollegó Superior in about three strenuous hours – either southward from the refuge, then up the middle of the fork from the south-east side (a path from Saldes joins this route); or westward up to the Collada del Verdet, then south and east to the summit. The latter route has some particularly hairy precipices and requires a good head for heights, but *is* classed as a walk rather than a climb; it's not suitable for coming down, however: for that you must use the first route.

Other Hikes

Hikers can ascend Comabona (2530 metres), towards the east end of the main Cadí ridge, in about four or five hours from the Refugi

Lluís Estasen. Puig de la Canal del Cristall (2563 metres) and Puig de la Canal Baridana (2647 metres, the highest in the range) are longer walks which may require a night in the hills.

There are various routes of one to two days right across the Cadí, from Saldes, the Refugi de Lluís Estasen or Gósol, to the Segre valley. If you want to overnight in the mountains, the FEEC's small *Refugi Prat d'Aguiló*, at 2037 metres on the northern slopes, has room for 20 and a kitchen.

Gósol

The B-400 continues paved from Saldes to the pretty stone village of Gósol, 12 km further west. Pedraforca looks slightly less daunting from here. The original Gósol (the Vila Vella), which dated back to at least the 9th century, is now abandoned on the hill south of the present village and worth a look. Picasso spent some of 1906 painting in Gósol, and the village has a museum just off the Plaça Major with a section devoted to him.

Tuixén & Beyond

An unpaved road west from Gósol climbs the 1625 metre Coll de Josa pass then descends past the picturesque hamlet of Josa del Cadí to Tuixén (1206 metres), another attractive village on a small hill. From Tuixén very scenic paved roads lead north to La Seu d'Urgell (36 km) and south to Sant Llorenç de Morunys (28 km) which is on a beautiful cross-country road from Berga to Organyà.

Places to Stay & Eat

Saldes & Around There are at least four camping grounds along the B-400 between the C-1411 and Saldes, some open year round. In Saldes, *Cal Manuel* (☎ 93-825 80 41) on the plaza has singles/doubles from 1000/2000 to 1250/2500 ptas, and economical food. *Fonda Carinyena* (☎ 93-825 80 25) near the church is cheap too. *Cal Xic* (☎ 93-825 80 81), Carrer Els Serrats s/n, is a good casa de pagès just off the road up to the Mirador de Gresolet. It has singles/doubles with bath for 2000/3600 ptas, or half-board

for 3500 ptas per person. Saldes has a couple of food stores.

The FEEC's *Refugi Lluís Estasen* (☎ 93-822 00 79) near the Mirador de Gresolet (see Orientation) is open year round with 100 places, meals and a warden in summer, and about 30 places in winter. When the refuge is full you can sleep outside, but not in a tent.

Gósol There are two decent hostales here. *Hostal Cal Francisco* (☎ 973-37 00 75), by the road at the east end of the village, has singles/doubles for 2200/4400 ptas. The smaller *Hostal Can Triuet* (☎ 973-37 00 72), in the centre at Plaça Major 4, requires you to take at least half-board, at 3900 ptas per person.

Tuixén *Albergue Can Cortina* (☎ 973-37 01 96), next to the tourist office, is a youth hostel run by the local municipality, with about 50 places in small bunk rooms. Cost is 1100 ptas, or 1600 ptas for B&B. Sheet rental is 350 ptas. It's open all year but you need to book at busy times. The friendly *Can Farragetes* (☎ 973-37 00 34), nearby at Carrer Coll 7, has six rooms with bath (doubles 3000 ptas), and food in the bar. There are a couple of other places nearby. The small *Camping Molí de Fòrnols* (☎ 973-37 00 21), open all year, is about four km north of Tuixén, down by the Riu de la Vansa off the La Seu d'Urgell road.

Elsewhere There are pensiones and/or hostales in Bagà, Guardiola de Berguedà and Sant Llorenç de Morunys, and at Martinet in the Segre valley.

Getting There & Away

At about 5.30 pm from Monday to Friday in school terms – mid-September to mid-June, with about a fortnight's break over both Christmas-New Year and Easter – ATSA (☎ 93-822 15 00) runs a bus to Saldes and Gósol from the central bus stop in Berga, on the C-1411, 17 km south of Guardiola de Berguedà. The downward bus stops at Saldes about 7 am.

Berga, Guardiola de Berguedà and Bagà

are all on the Alsina Graells bus routes from Barcelona to Puigcerdà and La Seu d'Urgell via the Túnel del Cadí. There's a bus between Guardiola de Berguedà and Ripoll once or twice daily from Monday to Saturday.

Hitching along the B-400 is feasible as far as Saldes or Gósol in July or August, or on the weekend during the other summer months, but there won't be much traffic at other times.

The only transport to Tuixén is run Monday to Friday by Transportes Nadal (☎ 973-35 06 42) from La Seu d'Urgell bus station. This is a truck with a compartment for about eight passengers, leaving La Seu at about 2 pm and Tuixén in the morning.

Martinet is on the Puigcerdà-La Seu d'Urgell bus route.

For a taxi you can call ☎ 973-37 00 65 (Gósol) or ☎ 93-822 71 30 (Guardiola de Berguedà).

There's a petrol station on the B-400 a couple of km east of Saldes.

LA SEU D'URGELL

The lively valley town of La Seu d'Urgell (pronounced 'la SE-u dur-ZHEY'; population 10,400) is Spain's gateway to Andorra, nine km north. It's a pleasant place to spend a night, with a very fine medieval cathedral. The Castilian version of its name is Seo de Urgel.

When the Franks evicted the Muslims from this part of the Pyrenees in the early 9th century, they made La Seu both the seat of a bishopric and capital of the counts of Urgell. It has been an important market and cathedral town since the 11th century, and has also played an important role in the history of Andorra (see the Andorra chapter).

Orientation & Information

The main axis runs north-south under the names Avinguda de Pau Claris, Carrer de Sant Ot and Passeig de Joan Brudieu, with the old part of town to its east.

The tourist office (☎ 35 15 11) is in the Sala de Cultura de Sant Domènec on Plaça dels Oms just north of the cathedral; it's open Monday to Saturday from 9 am to 9 pm,

Sunday and holidays from 10 am to 2 pm and 3 to 9 pm.

The telephone code is ☎ 973 and the postcode 25700. The Policia Municipal (☎ 35 04 26) are in the Casa de la Ciutat (Town Hall) at Plaça dels Oms 1. There's a hospital (☎ 35 00 50) at the south end of Passeig de Joan Brudieu.

Llibreria Ribera de Antich on Carrer de Sant Ot is a good source of maps and local guides.

Catedral de Santa Maria & Museu Diocesà

Looming on the south side of Plaça dels Oms, the 12th century cathedral (or *seu*) is one of the outstanding Romanesque buildings in Cataluña despite having undergone various remodellings over the centuries. The fine west façade, through which you enter, is decorated in typical Lombard style. The inside is dark and fairly plain but still impressive, with five apses, some murals in the south transept, and a 13th century Virgin-and-child sculpture in the central apse. The cathedral is open daily from 9.30 am to 1 pm and Monday to Saturday from 4 to 6 pm.

From inside the cathedral, or from Plaça del Deganat to its south, you can enter the good Museu Diocesà. This encompasses the cathedral cloister and the 12th century Romanesque Església de Sant Miquel, as well as some good medieval Pyrenees church murals, sculptures and altarpieces and a rare 10th century Mozarabic *Beatus* (illustrated manuscript of the Apocalypse). From June to September the museum is open daily from 10 am to 1 pm and (except Sunday and holidays) from 4 to 7 pm. In other months it's open only from noon to 1 pm! Entry is 300 ptas.

Places to Stay

Camping En Valira (☎ 35 10 35) in the north of town on Avinguda del Valira has room for 1200 people at 1900 ptas for two adults with a car and tent. It's open all year.

The modern *Alberg La Valira* youth hostel (☎ 35 38 97) at Carrer de Joaquim Viola

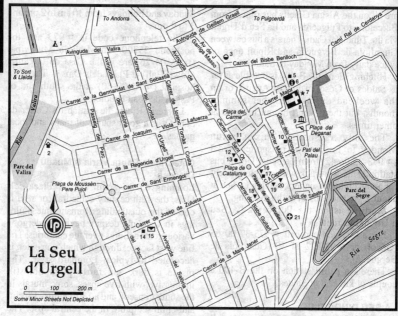

La Seu
d'Urgell

0   100   200 m
Some Minor Streets Not Depicted

Lafuerza 57, 800 metres west of the centre, has spacious public areas and 100 places in eight-bunk dorms. The high season is July, August, and December to March. There's little other cheap accommodation. *Habitacions Palomares* (☎ 35 21 68) on Carrer dels Canonges has small, dingy singles/doubles for 1500/2500 ptas and a couple of slightly brighter doubles for 3000 ptas.

By contrast there are lots of good lower mid-range hotels. *Hotel Avenida* (☎ 35 01 04), Avinguda de Pau Claris 24, is a good bet, with bright singles/doubles from 2500/4500 ptas plus IVA. *Residència Duc d'Urgell* (☎ 35 21 95), Carrer de Josep de Zulueta 43, has nice modern rooms with TV and bath, on a fairly quiet street, for 3500/5000 ptas. *Hotel Andria* (☎ 35 03 00, 35 14 25) at Passeig Joan Brudieu 24 has sizeable rooms with a certain antiquated charm, but seems a bit expensive at 4500/5500 ptas with bath. The bigger 56-room *Hotel Nice* (☎ 35 21 00), Avinguda de Pau Claris 4-6, is a slight step up, with smart rooms for 4200/6500 ptas.

La Seu's *parador* (☎ 35 20 00), built around the restored cloister of the 14th century Sant Domènec convent, at Carrer de Sant Domènec 6, is suitably luxurious with doubles at 15,000 ptas plus IVA.

Places to Eat

About the cheapest lunch you'll find is the 750 ptas menú at the rather gloomy *Bar Frankfurt* on Carrer de l'Orri. Much more convivial is *Bar La Mina* at Passeig Joan Brudieu 24, which does good pizzas for around 700 ptas, crêpes for 400 ptas and salads for 500 ptas. Its outside tables are a fine place to watch the world go by, but you pay 100 ptas extra per dish to sit at them. *Restaurant-Pizzeria Canigó* at Carrer de Sant Ot 3 has a reasonable four course lunch menú for 925 ptas, pizzas, pasta and salads for 475 to 675 ptas, and à-la-carte Catalan dishes for 550 to 1400 ptas.

PLACES TO STAY

1	Camping En Valira
2	Alberg La Valira
4	Hotel Avenida
5	Parador
10	Habitacions Palomares
11	Hotel Nice
14	Residència Duc d'Urgell
17	Hotel Andria

PLACES TO EAT

12	Restaurant-Pizzeria Canigó
16	Bar La Mina
18	Bar Frankfurt
19	Bar Montserrat
20	Burguer Chips

OTHER

3	Bus Station
6	Sala de Cultura de Sant Domènec & Tourist Office
7	Policia Municipal
8	Catedral de Santa Maria
9	Museu Diocesà
13	Llibreria Ribera de Antich
15	Post Office
21	Hospital

On Carrer de Fra Andreu Capella, *Burguer Chips* has reasonably priced salads and platos combinados from 450 ptas (quarter-chicken, chips and salad) to 775 ptas, and *Bar Montserrat* does platos combinados from 575 to 850 ptas.

The *Hotel Avenida* and *Hotel Nice* offer Catalan and Spanish food, with menús at 1150 and 1350 ptas, respectively.

Getting There & Away

Bus The bus station is on the north edge of the old town. Alsina Graells (☎ 35 00 20) runs four or five buses daily to/from Barcelona (3½ hours; 2300 ptas; two each via Solsona and Ponts, and one, which does not run on Sunday, via the Túnel del Cadí); three to/from Puigcerdà (one hour); and two to/from Lleida (2½ hours). La Hispano Andorrana runs up to seven buses daily to/from Andorra la Vella (30 minutes; 315 ptas). Hispano Igualadina has one bus daily to/from Tarragona (3¼ hours). There's no bus service west to Sort.

Car & Motorcycle The N-260 heads six km south-west to Adral, then turns off west over

the hills to Sort. The C-1313 carries on south to Lleida, threading the towering Tresponts gorge about 13 km beyond Adral.

VALL DE LA NOGUERA PALLARESA

The Riu Noguera Pallaresa, running south down a dramatic valley about 50 km west of La Seu d'Urgell, is Spain's best-known white-water river. The main centres for white-water sports are the town of Sort and the villages of Rialp and Llavorsí, upstream, each of which has several firms which will take you rafting, hydrospeeding, canoeing, kayaking – or, when you feel like getting out of the river, canyoning, trekking, climbing, mountain biking, horse riding or *ponting* (which seems to involve dangling by rope from bridges).

There's a tourist office (☎ 62 10 02) on Sort's main street at Avinguda Comtes del Pallars 21. The telephone code for Sort, Rialp and Llavorsí is ☎ 973.

Activities

The Noguera Pallaresa has no drops of more than grade four (on a scale of one to six), but it's exciting enough to attract a constant stream of white-water fans from April to August. It's at its best in May and June. The best stretch is the 12 km or so from Llavorsí to Rialp, on which the standard raft outing lasts two to 2½ hours and costs around 4000 ptas per person. A seven km hydrospeed ride is around 5000 ptas.

The Vall de Cardós and Vall Ferrera heading back into the hills north-east of Llavorsí lead to some remote and, in parts, tough mountain hiking country along and across the Andorran and French borders, including Pica d'Estats, the highest peak in Cataluña. Lonely Planet's *Trekking in Spain* and Editorial Alpina's *Pica d'Estats* and *Montgarri* will help you find your way around this area.

Places to Stay

Llavorsí is the most pleasant base, still much more of a mountain village than Rialp or Sort. *Camping Riberies* (☎ 62 21 51) has a good riverside site and charges 425 ptas per

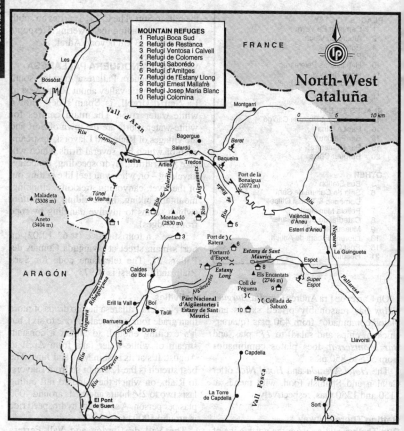

MOUNTAIN REFUGES
1 Refugi Boca Sud
2 Refugi de Restanca
3 Refugi Ventosa i Calvell
4 Refugi de Colomers
5 Refugi Saboredo
6 Refugi d'Amitges
7 Refugi de l'Estany Llong
8 Refugi Ernest Mallafrè
9 Refugi Josep Maria Blanc
10 Refugi Colomina

North-West Cataluña

0   5   10 km

person, per tent and per car, but is only open from mid-June to mid-September. *Camping Aigües Braves* (☎ 62 21 51), about one km north by the river, is slightly dearer. *Hostal de Rey* (☎ 62 20 11), *Hostal Noguera* (☎ 62 20 12) and *Hotel Lamoga* (☎ 62 20 06) all overlook the river. They charge 4000, 4700 and 6900 ptas, respectively, for doubles with bath.

Getting There & Away

Alsina Graells runs one daily bus (at 7.30 am) from Barcelona to Sort, Rialp, Llavorsí (5½ hours) and Esterri d'Àneu. From June to October it continues to the Vall d'Aran. The return bus leaves Llavorsí at 1.55 pm. Alsina Graells also has a daily bus (except on Sunday) between Lleida and Esterri d'Àneu via Sort, Rialp and Llavorsí.

PARC NACIONAL D'AIGÜESTORTES I ESTANY DE SANT MAURICI & AROUND

Cataluña's only national park extends just 15 km from east to west, and no more than nine km from north to south, but it packs in more beauty than most areas 100 times its size. The product of glacial action over the past two million years, it's essentially two east-west valleys at 1600 to 2000 metres altitude lined by jagged and precipitous 2600 to 2900 metre peaks of granite and slate. Against this backdrop, the park's pine and fir forests and open bush and grassland – decked with wonderful wild flowers in spring and early summer – combine with some 200 small lakes (estanys) and countless streams and waterfalls to create a wilderness of rare splendour. Nor does this stop at the park boundaries: there's some magnificent high country to the north and south too.

Though the park's main valleys are easily accessible and there are numerous marked walking routes, off the main trails it's not hard to lose your way, and the peaks themselves are mainly for mountaineers only. The whole park is normally under snow from December to April, and some snow lingers on the crests right through summer.

Chamois are relatively abundant in the park. Though in summer they prefer to stick to high altitudes, you may still spot some lower down when they come out to feed in the early morning and evening. Deer are more common at the lower altitudes. Spectacular birds include the capercaillie and the golden eagle.

Apart from its natural wonders, the region also contains a cluster of Cataluña's most charming Romanesque churches, in the Boí and Taüll area south-west of the park.

Orientation

Approaches One main approach to the park is from the village of Espot (1320 metres), four km east of its eastern boundary. An eight km paved road leads west up to Espot from the C-147 road 12 km north of Llavorsí (see the Vall de la Noguera Pallaresa section).

The other main approach – and in summer the easier one if you're dependent on buses (see Getting There & Away) – is from the L-500, which heads north-east off the N-230 Lleida-Vielha road two km north of El Pont de Suert. From this turning it's 15 km to the turning for the village of Boí (one km east), then a further 1.5 km to the turning for the park, which begins four km east.

Walkers can also enter the park by passes

from the Vall Fosca to the south and the Vall d'Aran to the north.

The Park The two main valleys are those of the Riu Escrita in the east, and the Riu de Sant Nicolau in the west. The Escrita flows out of the park's largest lake, one km-long Estany de Sant Maurici. The Sant Nicolau's main source is Estany Llong, four km west of Estany de Sant Maurici across the 2423 metre Portarró d'Espot pass. Three km downstream from Estany Llong, the Sant Nicolau runs through a particularly beautiful stretch known as Aigüestortes (Twisted Waters).

Apart from the valley openings at the east and west ends, virtually the whole perimeter of the park is mountain crests, with numerous spurs of almost equal height reaching in towards the centre. One of these, from the south, ends in the twin peaks Els Encantats (2746 and 2733 metres), towering over Estany de Sant Maurici – a scene so much photographed that it has almost become the emblem of the park.

Information

Tourist Offices National park information offices in Espot (☎ 62 40 36) and Boí (☎ 69 61 89) are open daily from 9 am to 1 pm and 3.30 to 7 pm. The tourist office (☎ 69 40 00) in Barruera, on the L-500 10 km up from the N-230, is a good source of information on the area around the west side of the park. It's open Monday to Saturday (closed on holidays) from 10 am to 2 pm and 4 to 7 pm. There are other tourist offices south of the park in El Pont de Suert (☎ 69 06 40), La Torre de Capdella (☎ 66 30 01) and La Pobla de Segur (☎ 68 02 57).

Money Espot has no bank or ATM, but the Hotel Roya will change money. Boí has a Caixa de Catalunya ATM just up the road from the Pensió Pey. In Barruera there's a La Caixa bank on the main road.

Post & Communications The telephone code for this whole area is ☎ 973.

Maps & Guides Editorial Alpina's map-guides are adequate, though they don't show every single trail. *Sant Maurici – Els Encantats* covers the eastern half of the park and its approaches; *Vall de Boí* covers the western half and its approaches; *Montsent de Pallars* covers the Vall Fosca and *Vall d'Aran*, naturally, covers the Vall d'Aran.

Park Rules Private vehicles cannot enter the park. From Espot, they can go to the park entrance; on the west side they must stop about 2.5 km short of the park on the approach from the L-500. Jeep-taxis, however, offer easy transport into the park from Espot and Boí (see Getting Around).

Wild camping is officially not allowed in the park, nor are swimming or other 'aquatic activities' in the lakes and rivers.

Romanesque Churches
The Vall de Boí south-west of the park is dotted with some of Cataluña's loveliest little Romanesque churches. Two of the finest are at Taüll, three km east of Boí. **Sant Climent de Taüll** at the entrance to the village, with its slender six storey bell tower, is a gem, not only for its elegant, simple lines but also for the art which graced its interior until transferred to museums earlier this century. The central apse contains a copy of a famous 1123 mural that now resides in Barcelona's Museu Nacional d'Art de Catalunya. At its centre is a Pantocrator whose rich Mozarabic-influenced colours, and expressive but superhuman features, have become a virtual emblem of Catalan Romanesque art. Other art from this church has found its way to museums as far away as Boston, USA! The church is open daily from 10.30 am to 2 pm and 4 to 8 pm (75 ptas).

Santa Maria de Taüll, up in the atmospheric old village centre with a five storey tower, is also well represented in the Barcelona museum, but lacks the *in situ* copies which add to the interest of Sant Climent. However, it's another elegant building and, as the only one of this group of churches – apart from Sant Climent – that's open daily,

worth a visit. It's open the same times, and with the same ticket, as Sant Climent.

Other Romanesque churches in the area are at Boí, Barruera, Durro, Erill la Vall, Cardet and Coll. Erill la Vall's has a slender six storey tower that rivals Sant Climent's in elegance. All of these, however, can only be entered on (free) guided tours at fixed hours two or three times a week – the tourist office in Barruera has the timetable.

Walks & Treks
The park is crisscrossed with plenty of paths – ranging from well marked to unmarked – enabling you to pick routes and circuits to suit yourself.

East-West Traverse You can walk right across the park in one day. The full Espot to Boí (or vice-versa) hike is about 25 km and takes nine hours, but you can shorten this by using jeep-taxis to/from Estany de Sant Maurici and/or Aigüestortes. Espot (1300 metres high) to Estany de Sant Maurici (1900 metres) is eight km, about two hours walk. A path then climbs to the Portarró d'Espot pass (2423 metres), where there are fine views over both of the park's main valleys. From the pass you descend to Estany Llong and Aigüestortes (1820 metres; about 3½ hours from Estany de Sant Maurici). Then you have around 3.5 km to the park entrance, four km to the L-500, and 2.5 km south to Boí (1260 metres) – a total of about three hours.

Shorter Walks Numerous good walks of three to five hours return will take you up into spectacular side valleys from Estany de Sant Maurici or Aigüestortes.

From the east end of Estany de Sant Maurici, one path heads south 2.5 km up the beautiful Monastero valley to Estany Monastero (2171 metres), passing Els Encantats on the left. Another goes three km north-west up by Estany de Ratero to Estany Gran d'Amitges (2350 metres). From Planell Gran (1850 metres), one km up the Sant Nicolau valley from Aigüestortes, a path climbs 2.5 km south-east to Estany Gran de

Dellui (2370 metres). You can descend to Estany Llong (three km) – about four hours from Aigüestortes to Estany Llong.

A good walk of three to four hours one way from Espot goes south-west up the Peguera valley to the Refugi Josep Maria Blanc (2350 metres) by Estany Tort. A marked turning to the right just out of Espot on the road up to the small ski resort of Super Espot points the way. This walk is the first half of the route to the Refugi Colomina (see Other Traverses).

Other Traverses Serious hikers and trekkers have many options for extended trips in and out of the park. Several of these are detailed in Lonely Planet's *Trekking in Spain*.

One of the most attractive areas to head to or from is the lake-rich basin south of the middle part of the park. The Refugi Colomina here is about four hours from the Refugi Josep Maria Blanc via the 2630 metre Collada de Saburó pass, or about seven hours from Estany de Sant Maurici by the more difficult Coll de Peguera (2726 metres). You can reach the Refugi Colomina from the south by a half-day walk up from the village of Capdella at the head of the Vall Fosca, 20 km north off the N-260 La Pobla de Segur-El Pont de Suert road. (Capdella, sometimes spelt Cabdella, is not to be confused with La Torre de Capdella, which is eight km further south.) From July to September you can shorten the walk by taking a *telefèric* (cable car) from the Sallente reservoir to Estany Gento.

The most obvious route between the park and the Vall d'Aran to the north is via Estany de Ratera and the Port de Ratera pass (2530 metres) over to the Refugi de Colomers (2125 metres), in a fine lake-strung valley – a not-too-long day from Estany de Sant Maurici. From the Refugi de Colomers it's about 10.5 km down the Vall de l'Aiguamotx, mostly by a partly paved road, to Tredòs. A slightly longer alternative, diverging at Port de Ratera, is via the Refugi de Saborèdo (2310 metres) and the Ruda valley (east of the Aiguamotx). There are also good,

more westerly routes using the Refugi Ventosa i Calvell at the head of Vall de Boí and the Refugi de la Restanca on the Aran side. See the Vall d'Aran section for more on some of these routes.

Places to Stay

Camping At Espot the small *Camping Solau* (☎ 62 40 68), at the top of the village, and *Camping Vorapark* (☎ 62 41 08), one km up towards the park entrance, are open all year. Two bigger camping grounds below the village have summer-only seasons. At Taüll, *Camping Taüll* (☎ 69 61 74) is open all year. There are three camping grounds on the L-500 between El Pont de Suert and Boí. All these places charge around 500 ptas per person, per tent and per car.

Mountain Refuges Four refuges in the park and others outside its boundaries provide accommodation for hikers. In general they tend to be staffed from early or mid-June to September, and for some weeks in the first half of the year for skiers. At other times several of them leave a section open where you can stay overnight.

In the Park You don't usually need to book for these except in August. The Espot park office can contact the Mallafré, Amitges and JM Blanc refuges for you to check on availability.

Refugi Ernest Mallafré, sometimes called *Refugi Sant Maurici*, near the east end of Estany de Sant Maurici (1885 metres), is run by the FEEC and has 36 places, with meals available. *Refugi d'Amitges* (☎ 93-318 15 05 for reservations) at Estany Gran d'Amitges in the north of the park (2380 metres), is run by the CEC and has 80 places (16 when unstaffed). Meals are available.

Refugi de l'Estany Llong (☎ 69 62 84 for reservations) near Estany Llong (2000 metres) is run by the national park, with 40 places and a kitchen. *Refugi Josep Maria Blanc* (☎ 93-423 23 45 for reservations) near Estany Tort (2350 metres) is run by the CEC, with 30 places and meals available when staffed.

Outside the Park *Refugi Colomina* (☎ 68 10 42 for reservations), south of the park by Estany de Colomina (2395 metres), is run by the FEEC and has 40 places, and meals available, when staffed.

Refugi Colomers, north of the park in the lovely Circ de Colomers (2125 metres), is run by the FEEC, with 30 places, and meals available when staffed. *Refugi Saborèdo* (☎ 93-329 97 36 for reservations), north of the park in the lake-strewn Circ de Saborèdo (2310 metres), is run by the FEEC and has 21 places.

North-west of the park, the CEC's *Refugi Ventosa i Calvell* has 80 places (12 when unstaffed); the FEEC's *Refugi de la Restanca* has 80 places (16 when unstaffed). Both have meals available when staffed.

Espot The following places are all near the centre of this small village. The friendly, family-run *Residència Felip* (☎ 62 40 93) has nice clean singles/doubles, with shared bathrooms, for 2000/4000 ptas including breakfast. *Casa Palmira* (☎ 62 40 72) has rooms with bath for 2200/4400 ptas. *Hotel Roya* (☎ 62 40 40; fax 62 41 44) has singles/doubles with shower or bath for 3500/5700 ptas. The big *Hotel Saurat* (☎ 62 41 62) has doubles for 7365 ptas plus IVA.

Boí *Hostal Fondevila* (☎ 69 60 11), on the right as you enter the village, and *Pensió Pey* (☎ 69 60 36) on the small village square, both have doubles with breakfast for 5500 ptas plus IVA.

Cases de pagès have cheaper rooms with shared baths. To find *Casa Cosan* (☎ 69 60 18) and its nice garden, head down into the village from the square, bear right and ask. The seven rooms are 1500 ptas per person. *Casa Guasch* (☎ 69 60 42) charges 1300 ptas per person; take the lane along the right side of the Pensió Pey, then fork right down the hill.

Taüll Though three km uphill from Boí, Taüll is more picturesque and a nicer place to stay. *Restaurant Sant Climent* (☎ 69 60 52), on the road into the village from Sant Climent

church, is a new stone building with singles/doubles for 1500/3000 ptas, or 2000/4000 ptas with private bath.

Casa Chep (or *Xep*; ☎ 69 60 54), up in the village on Plaça Santa Maria, has singles/doubles for 1400/2800 ptas, and a kitchen available. *Casa Llovet* (☎ 69 60 32), an atmospheric old four storey stone house on Plaça Franc, has the same prices. Follow Carrer L'Església up from Santa Maria church to find it.

Elsewhere There are hostales and/or cases de pagès in Barruera, El Pont de Suert, Capdella and La Torre de Capdella.

Places to Eat
Espot has a couple of supermarkets and Boí one small one. Espot's best-value meals seem to be at *Restaurante Ivan*, up the lane past Casa Palmira, then down to the left. A good three course Catalan menú, including beer or wine, is yours for 1100 ptas. There are lighter options too, such as torrades or eggs with ham or sausage, and a drink, for 400 ptas. *Casa Palmira's* restaurant is also popular. *Restaurant Bintureta* has an interesting Catalan menú for 1200 ptas.

In Boí *Pensió Pey* does meals, but more economical is *Pizzeria Els Arenys* up on the road out towards Taüll – pasta and pizzas are from 550 ptas, salads from 450 ptas. In Barruera, *Hostal Noray* does a good menú for 1300 ptas.

Getting There & Away
Bus La Pobla de Segur, a staging post on some approaches, can be reached by bus from Barcelona (twice daily), and by bus or train from Lleida. For further information you can ring tourist offices or the Alsina Graells bus company (in La Pobla de Segur ☎ 68 03 36).

Espot Daily Alsina Graells buses from Barcelona, Lleida and La Pobla de Segur to Esterri d'Àneu (and in summer to the Vall d'Aran) will stop at the Espot turning on the C-147, from where you have an eight km uphill walk (or hitch) to Espot.

Boí From June to mid-September, an Alsina Graells bus from La Pobla de Segur and El Pont de Suert stops daily at Barruera and at the Boí turn-off (el Cruce de Boí) on the L-500. The rest of the year it runs on Friday only. At the time of writing the bus leaves La Pobla de Segur at 9.30 am, and El Pont de Suert at 11.15 am. The southbound return bus stops at the Boí turn-off about 2 pm. Both buses connect at El Pont de Suert with Alsina Graells buses from/to Lleida. You can also get from Boí to Vielha, or vice versa, in one day with a change at El Pont de Suert.

Capdella At the time of writing an Alsina Graells bus leaves La Pobla de Segur for Capdella at 5.15 pm, Monday to Friday in school terms – roughly mid-September to mid-June, with a fortnight's break over both Christmas-New Year and Easter – and on Monday, Wednesday and Friday at other times. The trip is about one hour. The downward bus leaves Capdella at 8 am.

Taxi For a taxi in Boí call ☎ 69 60 15.

Getting Around

Once you've got close to the park, the easy way of getting inside it is by jeep-taxi from Espot or Boí. Fleets of these things – whose drivers congregate loudly in local bars in their off-duty moments – run a more or less continuous shuttle service between Espot and Estany de Sant Maurici, and between Boí and Aigüestortes, saving you, respectively, eight and 10 km walking. The one-way fare for either trip is 500 ptas per person, and they run from outside the park information offices in Espot and Boí – July to September from 8 am to 7 pm, other months from 9 am to 6 pm. In July or August you may have to queue for a while.

VALL D'ARAN

This famously green valley – Cataluña's northernmost outpost – is almost entirely surrounded by spectacular 2000 metre-plus mountains. Its only natural opening is northward to France, to which it gives its river, the Riu Garona (Garonne), flowing down to

Bordeaux. Thanks to this geography, Aran's native language is not Catalan but Aranese (aranés), a dialect of Occitan or the langue d'oc, the old Romance language of southern France (still spoken colloquially in some areas there). Most Aranese people, however, can switch equally happily into Catalan, Castilian or French.

Despite this northward orientation, Aran has been tied politically to Cataluña since 1175, when Alfonso II took it under his protection to forestall the designs of rival counts on both sides of the Pyrenees. In 1312, following one of many French take-over bids, the Aranese voted by popular referendum to stay with Cataluña – perhaps because in practice this meant a large degree of independence. The major hiccup came with a Napoleonic occupation from 1810 to 1815.

For all its intriguing past, however, the Vall d'Aran today is in danger of being overrun by tourism, which since the opening of the Baqueira-Beret ski resort in 1964 has replaced farming and herding as the economic mainstay. A valley that 30 years ago probably was still a pocket of scattered stone villages centred on quaint, pointy-towered Romanesque churches is being swamped by unsympathetic ski-apartment development, and its 'capital', the town of Vielha, almost resembles Andorra la Vella in its garish sprawl. That said, most of the villages retain an old-fashioned core and there are some good outings up Aran's side valleys – from which hikers can continue over the mountains in any direction, notably southward to the Parc Nacional d'Aigüestortes i Estany de Sant Maurici.

The Vall d'Aran (population about 7000) is some 35 km long and is considered to have three parts: Naut Aran (Upper Aran), the eastern part, aligned east-west; Mijaran (Middle Aran) around Vielha; and Baish Aran (Lower Aran), where the Garona flows north-east to France. Despite Baqueira-Beret, Naut Aran is still the most attractive area, and the pleasant village of Salardú is a base for some of the best outings.

Editorial Alpina's Vall d'Aran is a useful

aid here. The telephone code for the Vall d'Aran is ☎ 973.

Walks & Treks
One nice shortish walk, if you have a vehicle to get to Beret (some eight km north up a hairpin road from Baqueira), is the five km from Beret along the headwaters of the Riu Noguera Pallaresa to the abandoned village of Montgarri, with a 16th century shrine.

More spectacular routes head south up into the mountains on the northern fringes of the Parc Nacional d'Aigüestortes i Estany de Sant Maurici. The following three can all be done partway by vehicle, and end at mountain refuges for those who want to linger or head on over into the national park.

From the village of Tredòs, slightly east of and below Salardú, a road ascends the valley of the Riu d'Aiguamotx. You can get a car about eight km up, to a level of about 1850 metres. From there it's a 2.5 km walk up to the Refugi de Colomers at 2125 metres, set in a beautiful lake-strewn bowl. From the refuge there are easy marked circuit walks of two and four hours.

Or from Tredòs you could head south-east up the valley of the Riu de Ruda to the Refugi Saborèdo, some 12 km up at 2310 metres, in another fine lake-dotted cirque. This route is motorable about two-thirds of the way.

From Arties, three km west of Salardú, it's eight km up the Riu de Valarties valley to the Refugi de la Restanca. It's driveable for about the first 4.5 km; from there you must walk the steeper part – about 3.5 km – up to the refuge at 2000 metres. From the refuge you can walk for about one hour south-west up to the lake Estany de Mar, amid extremely rugged scenery at 2250 metres, or spend a day climbing and descending 2830 metre Montardó (to the east), with magnificent views.

The Refugi de Colomers and Refugi de la Restanca are a short day's walk from each other, on the GR-11. From Restanca the GR-11 heads about five hours west to the *Refugi Boca Sud* (☎ 64 28 90), near the south end of the Túnel de Vielha. From there it's two days (with a night's camping) past the

Maladeta massif over to Benasque in Aragón.

Getting There & Away
The N-230 from Lleida and El Pont de Suert reaches Aran through the 5.25 km Túnel de Vielha (built in the 1940s and showing its age), then heads north from Vielha to the French border at Eth Pont de Rei. Continuing as the French N-125, it reaches the Toulouse-Pau road at Montréjeau, 46 km from the border.

From the Vall de la Noguera Pallaresa, the C-147 crosses the 2072 metre Port de la Bonaigua pass – which may be closed in winter – into Nautaran, where it becomes the C-142, meeting the N-230 at Vielha.

Two Alsina Graells buses daily run between Lleida and Vielha via El Pont de Suert, taking three hours. At Lleida there are connections to/from Barcelona. From June to October there's a daily Alsina Graells bus between Barcelona and Vielha, taking seven hours via La Pobla de Segur, Llavorsí, the Espot turning on the C-147, Port de la Bonaigua and Salardú. At the time of writing the southbound departure from Vielha is at 11.59 am.

There are a couple of daily buses between Vielha and Salardú and Eth Pont de Rei. In the ski season there's some kind of service between Vielha and Baqueira.

Vielha
Vielha is Aran's junction town, at an altitude of 975 metres. The Aranese spelling of its name is more common than the Catalan and Castilian Viella.

Orientation The Alsina Graells bus stop and ticket office are by the roundabout in the west of town where the N-230 meets the C-142. The centre is south-east of the roundabout along the C-142, which is at first called Avenguda Castièro, then, from the central square Plaça déra Glèisa onward, Avenguda deth Pas d'Arró.

Information The Vall d'Aran's main tourist office (☎ 64 01 10), at Carrèr Sarriulèra 10

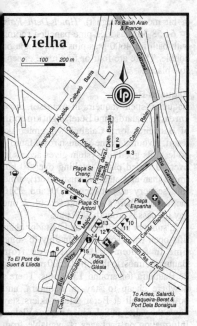

Vielha

0   100   200 m

To Baish Aran & France

PLACES TO STAY
2 Casa Vicenta
3 Pensión Puig
4 Hostal El Ciervo
5 Hotel Urogallo
6 Hotel Arán
7 Hotel Riu Nere

PLACES TO EAT
10 Restaurante Papa
11 Ñam Ñam Burguer
12 Sidreria Eth Plaça

OTHER
1 Alsina Graells Bus Stop
8 Musèu déra Val d'Aran
9 Hospital
13 Post Office
14 Tourist Office
15 Mossos d'Esquadra
16 Glèisa de Sant Miquèu

facing Plaça déra Glèisa, is open daily from at least 10 am to 1 pm and 5 to 7.30 pm. There are banks along Avenguda Castièro and Avenguda deth Pas d'Arró. The post office is at Carrèr Sarriulèra 6. The postcode is 25530. The Mossos d'Esquadra (Cataluña regional police; ☎ 64 20 44) are on Carrèr Sarriulèra too. There's a hospital (☎ 64 00 56) on Carrèr Espitau off Avenguda deth Pas d'Arró.

Things to See The small old quarter is around Plaça déra Glèisa and across the little Riu Nere just west of the square. The **Glèisa de Sant Miquèu** church on Plaça déra Glèisa is a mix of 12th to 18th century styles, with a 13th century main portal. It contains some notable medieval artwork, especially the 12th century *Crist de Mijaran*, an almost life-size wooden bust thought to have been part of a Descent from the Cross ensemble. The **Musèu déra Val d'Aran** at Carrèr Major 11 tells the interesting tale of Aran's history

up to the present day. It's open Tuesday to Friday from 5 to 8 pm, Saturday from 10 am to 1 pm and 5 to 8 pm, and Sunday from 10 am to 1 pm. Entry is 200 ptas.

Places to Stay For some of the cheaper places, head down Passeig déra Llibertat, north off Avenguda Castièro just west of Plaça déra Glèisa. *Hostal El Ciervo* (☎ 64 01 65) at Plaça Sant Orenç 3, just off Passeig déra Llibertat, has ageing but adequate singles/doubles for 1500/3000 ptas, or 2500/5000 ptas with private bath. On Camin Reiau, a north-eastward extension of Passeig déra Llibertat, *Pensión Puig* (☎ 64 00 31) at No 4, with no sign except a 'P', has doubles for just 1400 ptas; *Casa Vicenta* (☎ 64 08 19) at No 3 is much better at 4600 ptas for doubles with bath and breakfast.

For a bit more comfort, *Hotel Urogallo* (☎ 64 00 00) at Avenguda Castièro 7, *Hotel Arán* (☎ 64 00 50) at Avenguda Castièro 5, and *Hotel Riu Nere* (☎ 64 01 51) at Carrèr Major 1 all have doubles with bath ranging from around 5000 to 9500 ptas depending on the season.

Places to Eat *Sidreria Eth Plaça* has pleasant outside tables on Plaça déra Glèisa and good-value platos combinados (meat or squid with salad, chips and two eggs) from 750 ptas – also torrades for 450 ptas. In the arcade across Avenguda deth Pas d'Arró from here, *Restaurante Papa* does pasta from 450 ptas and pizzas from 500 ptas, and *Ñam Ñam Burguer* has burgers from 400 ptas and platos combinados from 550 ptas.

Salardú

Nine km east of Vielha and 1270 metres high, Salardú's little nucleus of old houses and narrow streets has undergone relatively little modern sprawl. If you happen to come in May, June, October or November, however, you'll find only a few accommodation places open. There's a tourist office (☎ 64 40 30) by the car park near the middle of the village, open in summer from 10.30 am to 1.30 pm and 4.30 to 8 pm. In the apse of the village's 12th and 13th century church you can admire the 13th century *Crist de Salardú* crucifixion carving.

Places to Stay & Eat *Xalet-Refugi Juli Soler Santaló* (☎ 64 50 16), just above the main road towards the east end of the village, has dormitory places for 800 ptas and bunk rooms at 1500 ptas a person, plus a kitchen and cafeteria. The large *Alberg Era Garona* youth hostel (☎ 64 52 71) nearby has room for 180 people, at 100 ptas more than the normal Cataluña rates; the high season is December to April and July and August. *Refugi Rosta* (☎ 64 53 08; fax 64 58 14), in the centre at Plaça Major 1, is a characterful 18th century place with dormitory bunks for 1800 ptas a person, and double rooms for 4600 ptas in July and August or 5600 ptas in the ski season (prices include breakfast). It's closed at most other times. There's a great wood-panelled bar where you can eat sausage, pâté or pancakes (crèps) for 500 to 700 ptas, and a dining room with a four course menú (vegetarian version available) for 1800 ptas.

Pensión Montaña (☎ 64 41 08), Carrèr Major 4, has doubles for 3000 ptas. *Residència Aiguamòg* (☎ 64 54 96), near the centre at Carrèr Sant Andrés 14, has quaint singles/doubles with bath for 2000/4000 ptas

(a bit more in August). *Hotel Deth Païs* (☎ 64 58 36) has nice pine-panelled rooms with bath for 4600 ptas plus IVA, single or double. There are four or five more expensive places.

Baqueira-Beret

Baqueira (spelt Vaquèira in Aranese), three km east of Salardú, and Beret, eight km north of Baqueira, form Cataluña's premier ski resort, favoured by the Spanish royal family, no less! Its good lift system gives access to over 40 varied pistes totalling over 70 km (more than any other Spanish resort), amid fine scenery at between 1500 and 2510 metres, and there's a big ski school. A one day lift pass is around 3900 ptas.

In summer the Bosque and Mirador chair lifts open from some time in July to some time in September to carry you from Baqueira almost to the top of 2500 metre Cap de Baqueira for around 1300 ptas. There's nowhere cheap to stay in Baqueira, and nowhere at all at Beret. Many skiers stay down the valley in Salardú, Arties or Vielha. Information on packages is available from Baqueira-Beret's Central de Reservas (☎ 64 44 55; fax 64 44 88), Apartado 60, 25530 Vielha. The cheapest five day room-only apartment packages range from around 18,000 to 30,000 ptas per person depending on dates.

West of Barcelona

The mountain and monastery of Montserrat and the Penedès wine-growing area are both within day-trip distance of Barcelona. From Montserrat you could continue north to the Pyrenees, and from Vilafranca del Penedès you can reach the coast to the south. From either place you could head on west to Lleida, a transport hub with enough history to detain you briefly, and Aragón.

MONTSERRAT

Montserrat (Serrated Mountain), 50 km north-west of Barcelona, is an amazing 1236 metre mountain of truly weird rock pillars, shaped by wind, rain and frost from a conglomeration of limestone, pebbles and sand which once lay under the sea. With the historic Benedictine Monestir de Montserrat, one of Cataluña's most important shrines, perched at 725 metres on its side, it makes a great outing from Barcelona, easily accomplished in one day with an early start.

The most dramatic approach is by the cable car which swings high across the Llobregat valley from Aeri de Montserrat station, served by regular trains from Barcelona. From the mountain, on a clear day, you can see as far as the Pyrenees, Barcelona's Tibidabo and even, if you're really lucky, Mallorca. Bear in mind that it can be a lot colder up on Montserrat than in Barcelona.

Orientation & Information

The cable car from Aeri de Montserrat arrives on the mountain just below the monastery. Just above the cable-car station is a road. To the left is the information office (☎ 835 02 51, ext 586), open daily from 9 am to 6 pm, with a good free leaflet-map on the mountain and monastery. Past here, a minor road doubles back up to the left to the lower station of the Funicular de Sant Joan. The main road curves round and up to the right, passing the blocks of cel.les (see Places to Stay & Eat), to enter Plaça de Santa Maria at the centre of the monastery complex.

The Montserrat telephone code is ☎ 93.

Monestir de Montserrat

The monastery was founded in about 1025 to commemorate an apparition of the Virgin on the mountain. Wrecked by Napoleonic troops in 1811, then abandoned as a result of anticlerical legislation in the 1830s, it was rebuilt from 1858 on. Today there is a community of about 80 monks. Pilgrims still come from far and wide to venerate its Black Virgin (La Moreneta), a 12th century Romanesque wooden sculpture of Mary with the infant Jesus, who has been Cataluña's official patron since 1881.

The two-part **Museu de Montserrat**, on Plaça de Santa Maria, has an excellent collection ranging from an Egyptian mummy and Gothic retablos to art by El Greco, Monet, Degas and Picasso. It's open daily from 10.30 am to 2 pm and 3 to 6 pm, for 400 ptas (students 200 ptas).

From Plaça de Santa Maria you enter the courtyard of the 16th century **basilica**, the monastery's church. The basilica's façade, with its carvings of Christ and the 12 Apostles, dates from 1900-01 despite its 16th century plateresque style. Daily from 8 to 10.30 am and noon to 6.30 pm, you can file past the image of the Black Virgin, high above the basilica's main altar: follow the signs to the Cambril de la Mare de Déu, to the right of the main basilica entrance.

The famous **Montserrat Boys' Choir** or Escolania, reckoned to be Europe's oldest music school, sings in the basilica every day at 1 and 7 pm, except in July. The church fills up quickly, so try to arrive early.

On your way out have a look in the room across the courtyard from the basilica entrance, filled with gifts and thank-you messages to the Montserrat Virgin from people who give her the credit for all manner of happy events. The souvenirs range from plaster casts to wedding dresses.

The Mountain

You can explore the mountain above the monastery on a web of paths leading to some of the peaks and to 13 empty and rather dilapidated hermitages. The **Funicular de Sant Joan** (475/775 ptas one way/return) will carry you up the first 250 metres from the monastery. If you prefer to walk, the road past the funicular's bottom station will lead you up and round to its top station in about one hour (three km).

From the Sant Joan top station, it's a 20 minute stroll (signposted) to the **Sant Joan hermitage**, with fine westward views. More exciting is the one hour walk north-west along a path marked with occasional blobs of yellow paint to Montserrat's highest peak, **Sant Jeroni**, from which there's an awesome sheer drop on the north side. The walk takes you across the upper part of the mountain, with a close-up experience of some of the weird rock pillars. Many have been given names: on your way to Sant Jeroni look over to the right for La Prenyada (the pregnant woman), La Mòmia (the mummy), L'Elefant (the elephant), the phallic Cavall Bernat, and El Cap de Mort (the death's-head).

Places to Stay & Eat

If you want to stay over, there are several options (all ☎ 835 02 51) at the monastery. A small camping ground 300 metres along the road past the lower Sant Joan funicular station is open from Semana Santa to October. The cheapest rooms are in the *Cel.les de Montserrat*, three blocks of simple apartments for two to 10 people. A two person apartment is 2360 ptas, or 2555 to 3155 ptas with kitchen. Overlooking Plaça de Santa Maria are the *Hotel El Monestir*, open from Semana Santa to October with singles/doubles from 2050/3535 ptas with toilet to 3045/5100 ptas with bath; and the comfortable *Hotel Abat Cisneros*, which charges 4365/7385 ptas with shower, or 4785/8000 ptas with bath, from April to October and at Christmas-New Year, but little more than half that at other times. Add IVA to both hotels' prices.

The *Snack Bar* near the top cable-car station has platos combinados from 875 ptas and bocadillos from 325 ptas. *Bar de la Plaça* in the Abat Oliva cel.les building has similar prices. *Cafeteria Self-Service* near the car park has great views but is dearer. *Hotel Abat Cisneros* has a four course menú for 2900 ptas.

Getting There & Away

Bus There's a daily bus to the monastery from Estació d'Autobuses de Sants in Barcelona at 9 am (plus 8 am in July and August) for a return fare of 1090 ptas (1240 ptas at the weekend).

Train & Cable Car Trains run from Plaça d'Espanya station in Barcelona to Aeri de Montserrat every two hours daily from 7.10 am to 9.10 pm – a 1½ hour ride. One-way/return tickets for 1015/1560 ptas include the

cable car between Aeri de Montserrat and the monastery. The cable car goes about every 15 minutes, Monday to Saturday from 10 am to 5.45 pm, Sunday and holidays from 10 am to 6.45 pm.

From Aeri de Montserrat, trains continue north to Manresa, from which there are three trains daily west to Lleida and one or two Alsina Graells buses daily north to Berga, Guardiola de Berguedà, Puigcerdà and (except on Sunday) La Seu d'Urgell.

Car & Motorcycle Probably the most straightforward route from Barcelona is by Avinguda Diagonal, Via Augusta, the Túnel de Vallvidrera and the E-9. Turn on to the BP-1213 just past Terrassa and follow it 18 km north-west to the C-1411. Then head a couple of kilometres south on this road to Monistrol de Montserrat, from which a road snakes about seven km up the mountain to the monastery.

SANT SADURNÍ D'ANOIA & VILAFRANCA DEL PENEDÈS

Cataluña's best wine – among the best in Spain – comes from the area centred on these two towns. Sant Sadurní d'Anoia, a half-hour train ride west of Barcelona, is the capital of cava, Spanish 'champagne'. Vilafranca del Penedès, 12 km on down the track, is the heart of the Penedès DO, which produces some of the country's best still wines, notably light, fruity whites. Visitors are welcome at numerous wineries; there'll often be a free glass or two included in the tour, and plenty more for sale, but if you fancy a full-scale tasting you should ring ahead. The telephone code for this region is ☎ 93.

Sant Sadurní d'Anoia

A hundred or so wineries around Sant Sadurní produce 140 million bottles of cava a year – something like 85% of the entire national output. Cava is made by the same method as French Champagne, it's just that it's not allowed to be called Champagne. Freixenet (☎ 818 32 00), the best-known cava company, is conveniently based right next to the train station at Carrer Joan Sala 2. Free tours are given Monday to Friday (and Saturday and Sunday in December) at 9, 10 and 11.30 am and 3.30 and 5.30 pm. Codorníu (☎ 818 32 32) is at Can Codorníu, at the entry to the town by road from Barcelona. Josep Raventós, head of this firm back in 1872, was the first Spaniard to successfully produce sparkling wine by the Champagne method. The Codorníu headquarters, a modernist building which has been declared a national monument, is open for free visits Monday to Friday from 9 am to 12.30 pm and 3 to 4.30 pm, Saturday and Sunday from 10 am to 1.30 pm.

Vilafranca del Penedès

Unlike Sant Sadurní, Vilafranca is a reasonably attractive and interesting town for reasons other than wine. The helpful tourist office (☎ 892 03 58) on Plaça Vila is open Monday to Friday from 10 am to 1 pm and 4 to 7 pm, and Saturday from 10 am to 1 pm. In summer it also opens on Saturday from 5 to 8 pm and Sunday from 10 am to 1 pm. A block north, the mainly Gothic **Basílica de Santa Maria** faces the combined **Museu de Vilafranca** and **Museu del Vi** (Wine Museum) across Plaça Jaume I. The museum, itself a fine Gothic building, covers local archaeology, art, geology and bird life and also has an excellent section on wine, at

Of Giants, Dragons & Human Castles

As befits a people of such independent traditions, Catalans get up to all sorts of unusual tricks at *festa* (festival) time.

Fire and fireworks play a big part in many Spanish festivals, but Cataluña adds a special twist with the *correfoc* (fire-running), in which devil and dragon figures chase through the streets spitting fireworks at the crowds. (Wear protective clothes if you intend to get close!) Correfocs are often part of the *festa major* – a town or village's main annual festival. Many of these are in July or August. Also usually part of the festa major fun are the *sardana* (Cataluña's national round-dance), all sorts of costumed local dances, and *gegants*, splendidly attired and lifelike five metre high giants who parade through the streets or dance in the squares to the sound of old-fashioned instruments. Giants usually come in male-and-female pairs – a medieval king and queen, a Muslim sultan and a Christian princess. Almost every town and village has its own – sometimes just one pair, sometimes five or six. They're usually accompanied by an entourage of grotesque 'dwarfs'.

On La Nit de Sant Joan, 23 June, big bonfires burn at crossroads and on town and village squares in a combined midsummer and St John's Eve celebration. Fireworks go on all night. But Cataluña's supreme fire festival is the Patum in the otherwise unexceptional Pyrenean foothill town of Berga. A whole evening of dancing and firework-spitting angels, devils, mule-like monsters, dwarfs, giants, and men covered in grass culminates in a kind of mass frenzy of fire and smoke which has been likened to a medieval vision of hell. The 'real' Patum happens on Corpus Christi – the Thursday following the eighth Sunday after Easter Sunday – though there are watered-down versions on the next two or three days.

An activity demanding rather more calm and order, but still emotive, is the building of *castells*, human castles. This tradition is strongest in southern and central Cataluña: Valls, Vilafranca del Penedès and Terrassa have three of the most famous groups of *castellers*. Since the 1980s the practice has experienced a revival that is threatening to break all-time records for the difficulty of some of the towers built. The golden age was the 1880s when castells of *tres de nou* and *quatre de nou* (three of nine and four of nine, ie nine storeys of three people and nine storeys of four people) were achieved. There are all sorts of permutations in the construction of the castell: those built without a *pinya*, *folre* or *manilles* – extra rings of support for the first, second and third storeys – are particularly tricky and are termed *net* (clean). A completed castell is signalled by the small kid at the top (the *anxaneta*) raising his arm – a cue for tumultuous applause and cheering from the onlookers. If the castell manages to dismantle itself without collapsing it's termed *descarregat*. Especially difficult is a *pilar*, a tower of only one person per storey. The best pilar ever done was eight storeys, a *pilar de vuit*.

Building castells is a sort of sport and competitions are held, often at festes majors. Festivals where you can expect to see castellers include: Vilafranca del Penedès, at the end of August; Tarragona, in the last week of September; El Vendrell, around 16 October; and Valls, on the first Sunday after 21 October. ■

the end of which you're treated to a free *copa*. It's open Tuesday to Saturday from 10 am to 2 pm and 4 to 7 pm (9 am to 9 pm in summer), Sunday and holidays from 10 am to 2 pm. Entry is 400 ptas. A statue on Plaça Jaume I pays tribute to Vilafranca's famous *castellers*, who do their thing during Vilafranca's lively festa major at the end of August.

Vilafranca's premier winery is Torres (☎ 817 74 87), three km north-west of the town centre on the BP-2121 road near Pacs del Penedès. The Torres family revolutionised Spanish wine-making back in the 1960s by introducing new temperature-controlled stainless-steel technology and French grape varieties which helped produce much lighter wines than the traditional heavy Spanish plonk. Torres is open for visits Monday to Friday from 9 am to noon and 3 to 5 pm, Saturday and Sunday from 9 am to 1 pm. Most other Penedès wineries are, like Torres, out of town. One in Vilafranca itself that you can visit if you ring ahead is Mascaró (☎ 890 16 28) at Carrer Casal 9, which produces brandy too.

Getting There & Away

Up to three rodalies trains an hour run from Barcelona Sants to Sant Sadurní and Vilafranca. By car, take the A-2, then the A-7. From Sitges, both places are a short drive inland, or a longer train journey involving a change at Coma-ruga.

LLEIDA

Western Cataluña is fairly flat and drab, but if you're not in a hurry Lleida (Lérida in Castilian), Cataluña's second city with 144,000 people, is a likeable place with a long, varied history. As the starting point of several routes towards the Pyrenees, it's a place you may find yourself in anyway.

Orientation

The centre spreads around the southern side of the hill dominated by the old cathedral, La

Seu Vella, with Carrer del Carme, Carrer Sant Joan, Plaça de Sant Joan and Carrer Major forming a mainly pedestrianised axis from north-east to south-west. The train station is at the north-east end of Rambla de Ferran, with the bus station 1.25 km away on Carrer Saracibar, off Avinguda de Madrid.

Information

The tourist office (☎ 27 09 97) is at Avinguda de Madrid 36. The main post office is on Rambla de Ferran (postcode 25080). The telephone code is ☎ 973. If you're heading for the Pyrenees, Caselles at Carrer Major 46 and Ramon Fregola at Carrer Sant Joan 18 stock maps and local guidebooks.

La Seu Vella

Lleida's Old Cathedral towers above all else in both position and grandeur. It stands within a compound *(recinte)* of defensive walls erected between the 12th and 19th centuries. The main entrance to the recinte (open daily from 8 am to 9 pm, free) is from Carrer de Monterey on its west side, but during the cathedral's opening hours you can use a lift *(ascensor)* from above Plaça de Sant Joan. The cathedral was built in sandy-coloured stone in the 13th to 15th centuries on the site of a former mosque (Lleida was under Muslim control from 719 to 1149). It's a masterpiece of the Romanesque-to-Gothic Transitional style, though only recently recovered from 241 years use as a barracks which began as Felipe V's punishment for the city's opposition in the War of the Spanish Succession. A 70 metre octagonal bell tower rises at the south-west end from the cloister, whose windows have exceptionally fine Gothic tracery. The spacious but rather austere interior – used as stables and dormitories during the military occupation – has a forest of slender columns with carved capitals. The cathedral is open Tuesday to Saturday from 10 am to 1.30 pm and 3 to 5.30 pm (4 to 7.30 pm from June to September) and on Sunday and holidays from 10 am to 1.30 pm. Entry is 300 ptas.

Lleida

0   150   300 m

To Camping Les
Basses & Huesca

To El Pont de
Suert & Vielha

To Barcelona &
Huesca

To Barcelona
(via N-II) & La
Seu d'Urgell

To Barcelona &
Zaragoza (via A-2)

To Zaragoza
(via N-II)

PLACES TO EAT
3 Pizzeria San Siro
4 Pizzeria Trastevere
5 Toc Casolà
15 Cafeteria Triunfo
19 El Celler del Roser

OTHER
1 Train Station
6 Police Station
7 La Seu Vella
9 Post Office
10 Ramon Fregola Bookshop
11 Lift
12 Market
16 La Paeria
18 Antic Convent del Roser
    & Museu d'Art Jaume Morera
20 Caselles Bookshop
22 La Seu Nova
24 Hospital de Santa Maria
    & Museu Arqueològic
25 Bus Station
26 Tourist Office

PLACES TO STAY
2 Hotel Ramon Berenguer IV
8 Hotel La Canonja
13 Hostal Mundial
15 Hotel Principal
17 Alberg Sant Anastasi
    & Universitat
21 Hotel Real
23 Residència Andreu

Above the cathedral are remains of the Islamic fortress and residence of the Muslim governors, known as the Castell del Rei.

Carrer Major & Around

A 13th century Gothic mansion, **La Paeria**, has housed the city government almost ever since it was built. The 18th century neoclassical **Seu Nova** on Plaça de la Catedral was built when La Seu Vella was turned into barracks. Opposite is the **Hospital de Santa Maria**, with a Gothic courtyard, now housing the **Museu Arqueològic**, which includes Iberian and Roman finds from the Lleida

region – open Tuesday to Saturday from noon to 2 pm and 6 to 8.30 pm.

Carrer del Caballers and Carrer de la Palma climb from Carrer Major up through the old part of town. The **Antic Convent del Roser** at Carrer del Caballers 15, with an unusual three storey cloister, houses the **Museu d'Art Jaume Morera** and its collection of work by Lleida-associated artists.

Places to Stay

Camping Les Basses (☎ 23 59 54) at Km 5 on the N-240 to Huesca charges 525 ptas per person, per tent and per car. Lleida's youth hostel, *Alberg Sant Anastasi* (☎ 26 60 99) at Rambla d'Aragó 11, has room for 120 and no high season – but it's used as a student residence from mid-September to June so you may have trouble getting in then.

The friendly *Hostal Mundial* (☎ 24 27 00), Plaça de Sant Joan 4 – the entrance is on Carrer Major – is hard to beat with a range of worthy rooms from 1000/2000 ptas to 1600/3200 ptas with private bath. It offers free overnight use of a nearby underground car park. *Residència Andreu* (☎ 27 12 25), Carrer Canonge Brugulat 2, has doubles with shared baths around 2600 ptas. From mid-September to June it's a student residence too, so ring first.

Convenient for the train station are *Hotel La Canonja* (☎ 23 80 14), Carrer General Britos 21, and *Hotel Ramon Berenguer IV*, Plaça de Ramon Berenguer IV 3. Doubles with bath are 3800 ptas and 5000 to 5500 ptas, respectively.

If you're looking for a bit more style, two good central options are the *Hotel Principal* (☎ 23 08 00), at Plaça de la Paeria 7 on Carrer Major, with doubles from 6500 ptas, and the modern *Hotel Real* (☎ 23 94 05), Avinguda de Blondel 22, at around 8000 ptas.

Places to Eat

Despite the many pleasant cafés around Plaça de Sant Joan and elsewhere, the downtown options for an actual meal are extremely limited, especially in the evening. *Cafeteria Triunfo*, on Carrer Major just off Plaça de Sant Joan, has overpriced platos combinados from about 1000 ptas. Or you might try *Pizzeria San Siro* at Carrer Magdalena 22. Even these two places close on Sunday.

Lleida is Cataluña's snail-eating capital, and so many *cargols* are swallowed during the annual Aplec del Cargol snail feast, held on a Sunday in early May, that some of them have to be imported. *El Celler del Roser* at Carrer del Caballers 24 serves the creeping things a la llauna (baked on tin over hot coals), as well as other Catalan fare. It's closed Sunday night and Monday.

A less central hunting ground is the area around Plaça de Ricard Vinyes, north-west of La Seu Vella, where you'll find good places like *Pizzeria Trastevere*, Carrer Camp de Mart 27, with pasta and pizzas from 700 ptas, and *Toc Casolà*, down the street, with meaty main dishes from 675 ptas and salads for two at 1500 ptas. This area is also the heart of Lleida's nightlife.

Getting There & Away

Bus Daily services by Alsina Graells (☎ 27 14 70) include up to 13 buses to/from Barcelona (2¼ to 2¾ hours); two to/from El Pont de Suert and Vielha (2¾ hours); one (except Sunday) to/from La Pobla de Segur, Sort, Llavorsí and Esterri d'Àneu (three hours); two to/from La Seu d'Urgell (2½ hours); and one to/from Puigcerdà (four hours). Other buses go to Tarragona (three daily), and westward to Zaragoza (four or five daily from Monday to Saturday, but only one on Sunday), and Barbastro and Huesca (four daily).

Train Lleida (station ☎ 22 02 02) is on the main Barcelona-Zaragoza-Madrid line. Up to 20 trains daily run to/from Barcelona, most taking about two hours though some dawdle for four. Second-class fares range from 1170 to 2200 ptas. There are up to 12 daily trains to/from Zaragoza (1¾ hours; 1700 to 2300 ptas) and up to eight to/from Madrid. Other direct services run to/from Tarragona (nine daily; 1¼ hours; from 605 ptas), La Pobla de Segur (three daily; two hours), Valencia, San Sebastián, and as far afield as Galicia, Andalucía and Cerbère (France).

Car & Motorcycle The quickest routes to Barcelona, Tarragona and Zaragoza are by the A-2, but you can avoid tolls by taking the N-II to Zaragoza or Barcelona or the N-240 to Tarragona. The main northward roads are the C-1313 to La Seu d'Urgell, the N-230 to Vielha, and the N-240 to Barbastro and Huesca.

Southern Cataluña

Sitges, 35 km south-west of Barcelona, is the wildest resort on the Catalan coast. From there to the Valencian border stretches the Costa Daurada (Golden Coast), a series of far less exciting resorts along a mainly flat coast varied only by the delta of the Río Ebro, which protrudes 20 km out into the Mediterranean. Along the way, however, are the old Roman capital of Tarragona and the modern extravaganza of Port Aventura, Spain's successful answer to EuroDisney.

SITGES

Sitges attracts everyone from jet-setters to young travellers, honeymooners to weekending families, Barcelona night owls to a big international gay crowd – in short, anyone who's after a good time. The beach is long and sandy, the nightlife thumps till breakfast, and there are lots of groovy boutiques if you need to spruce up your wardrobe. In winter Sitges can be pretty dead, but it wakes up with a vengeance for *carnaval*, when the gay crowd puts on an outrageous show.

Sitges has been fashionable in one way or another since the 1890s, when it became an avant-garde art world hang-out. It has been Spain's most anticonventional, anything-goes resort since the 1960s. One thing it isn't, though, is cheap.

Orientation

The main landmark is the Església de Sant Bartomeu i Santa Tecla parish church, atop a small rocky elevation which separates the two km long main beach, to the south-west, from the smaller, quieter Platja de Sant Sebastià to the north-east. The old part of town climbs gently inland from the church area, with the train station some 500 metres back, at the top of Avinguda Artur Carbonell.

Information

The tourist office (☎ 811 76 30) is at Carrer Sínia Morera 1 just off the top end of Passeig de Vilafranca, a traffic-busy plaza at the foot of Avinguda Artur Carbonell. In July and August it's open daily from 9 am to 9 pm; in other months, from 9.30 am to 2 pm and 4 to 6.30 pm. You can pick up a free map of gay-oriented bars, hotels, restaurants and shops, the *Plano Gay de Sitges*, at several spots around town including Parrots Pub on Plaça Industria.

There are several banks and ATMs on and around Plaça Cap de Vila in the old town. The post office is on Plaça Espanya. The postcode is 08870 and the telephone code ☎ 93. The Policia Local (☎ 811 76 25) are on Plaça Ajuntament behind the parish church. The Hospital Sant Joan (☎ 894 00 03) is on Carrer Hospital in the upper part of town above the railway.

Sitges tap water tastes salty but is drinkable.

Museums

The **Museu Cau Ferrat** on Carrer Fonollar behind the parish church was built in the 1890s as a house-cum-studio by Santiago Rusiñol, a co-founder of Els Quatre Gats in Barcelona, and the man who attracted the art world to Sitges. In 1894 Rusiñol reawakened the world to the then unfashionable work of El Greco by parading two of the Cretan's canvases in solemn procession from Sitges railway station to Cau Ferrat. These are now on show in the museum along with the remainder of Rusiñol's large art and crafts collection which includes paintings by the likes of Picasso, Ramon Casas, and Rusiñol himself.

Next door on Carrer Fonollar is the **Museu Maricel** with art and artisanry from the middle ages to the 20th century. The museum is part of the Palau Maricel, a stylistic fantasy built around 1910 by Miquel Utrillo. The **Museu Romàntic** at Carrer Sant Gaudenci 1 recreates the lifestyle of a 19th century Catalan landowning family, and contains a collection of several hundred antique dolls.

From late June to early September all three museums are open Tuesday to Sunday from 10 am to 9 pm; at other times, Tuesday to Sunday from 9.30 am to 2 pm, plus Tuesday

CATALUÑA

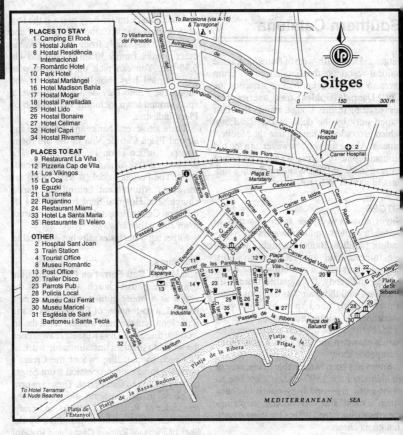

Sitges

0   150   300 m

PLACES TO STAY
1 Camping El Rocà
5 Hostal Julián
6 Hostal Residència Internacional
7 Romàntic Hotel
10 Park Hotel
11 Hostal Mariàngel
16 Hotel Madison Bahía
17 Hostal Mogar
18 Hostal Parelladas
25 Hotel Lido
26 Hostal Bonaire
27 Hotel Celimar
32 Hotel Capri
34 Hostal Rivamar

PLACES TO EAT
9 Restaurant La Viña
12 Pizzeria Cap de Vila
14 Los Vikingos
15 La Oca
19 Eguzki
21 La Torreta
22 Rugantino
24 Restaurant Miami
33 Hotel La Santa Maria
35 Restaurante El Velero

OTHER
2 Hospital Sant Joan
3 Train Station
4 Tourist Office
8 Museu Romàntic
13 Post Office
20 Trailer Disco
23 Parrots Pub
28 Policia Local
29 Museu Cau Ferrat
30 Museu Maricel
31 Església de Sant Bartomeu i Santa Tecla

MEDITERRANEAN SEA

to Saturday from 4 to 6 pm. Entry is 200 ptas at each.

Beaches
The main beach is divided by a series of breakwaters into sections with different names. A pedestrian promenade runs its whole length. In high summer, especially on the weekend, the end nearest the parish church gets jam-packed. Crowds thin out slightly towards the south-west end. Sitges also has two nude beaches – one exclusively gay – about 20 minutes walk beyond the

Hotel Terramar at the far end of the main beach. To reach them, you have to walk along the coast past a sewage plant, over a hill and along the railway a bit.

Special Events
Carnaval in Sitges is a week-long riot of the extravagant, ambiguous and exhibitionist, capped by an outrageous gay parade on the last night. June sees the Sitges International Theatre Festival, with a strong experimental leaning. Sitges' festa major in late August features a huge firework show on the 23rd,

Early October is the time for Sitges' International Fantasy Film Festival.

Places to Stay

Sitges has over 50 hotels and hostales, but many of them close from around October to April, then are full in July and August. If you haven't booked ahead, it's not a bad idea, especially if you arrive late in the day, to ask the tourist office to ring round for you.

Camping *Camping El Rocà* (☎ 894 00 43), Avinguda de Ronda s/n, is in the upper part of town north of the railway, one km from the beach. It has room for 600 people, at 565 ptas per adult, per car and per tent. It's open from April to September. *Camping El Garrofer* (☎ 894 17 80) and *Camping Sitges* (☎ 894 10 80) are out of town off the C-246.

Hostales Two friendly places popular with travellers, both on the central Carrer de les Parellades, are *Hostal Mariàngel* (☎ 894 13 57) at No 78 and *Hostal Parelladas* (☎ 894 08 01) at No 11. The Mariàngel has 19 varied rooms from 2000/3750 ptas to 3000/5000 ptas (with shower). The Parelladas has four singles for 2200 ptas and eight doubles with shower for 4900 ptas.

Hostal Juliàn (☎ 894 03 06), Avinguda Artur Carbonell 2 near the train station and tourist office, has garishly wallpapered but good-sized rooms, with shared baths, for 3000/4750 ptas. Close by, *Hostal Residència Internacional* (☎ 894 26 90), Carrer Sant Francesc 52, has eight sizeable and clean doubles for 4500 ptas (5000 ptas with private shower).

One place open all year is *Hostal Bonaire* (☎ 894 53 26), Carrer Bonaire 31, where doubles are 4000 ptas with washbasin or 5000 ptas with bathroom. *Hostal Mogar* (☎ 811 00 09), Carrer Bonaire 2, has similar prices. *Hostal Rivamar* (☎ 894 34 08) is right on the seafront at Passeig de la Ribera 46. Doubles with bathroom, if you're lucky enough to get one, are 6000 ptas plus IVA.

Hotels *Hotel Lido* (☎ 894 48 48), Carrer Bonaire 26, a popular gay haunt, has good

doubles with bathroom for 6000 ptas plus IVA.

Hotel Madison Bahía (☎ 894 00 12), Carrer de les Parellades 31-32, has friendly management and singles/doubles with bath at 7100/8000 ptas including breakfast. All 25 rooms have exterior windows. The *Park Hotel* (☎ 894 02 50), Carrer Jesús 16, is a slight step up with doubles at 10,800 ptas plus IVA.

The *Romàntic Hotel* (☎ 894 83 75), Carrer Sant Isidre 33, comprises three adjoining 19th century villas, sensuously restored in period style, with a leafy dining courtyard. It's popular with gay visitors though not exclusively so. There are about 60 rooms with shower from 7600/10,500 to 8700/11,600 ptas, including breakfast.

On the seafront near the parish church, *Hotel Celimar* (☎ 811 01 70), Passeig de la Ribera 20, has rooms for 7920 to 13,200 ptas plus IVA. *Hotel Capri* (☎ 811 02 67), Avinguda de Sofia 13-15, is a good family-run place with just 22 doubles at 13,400 ptas plus IVA, including breakfast. Its *Residència Veracruz* annexe across the street is much less appealing.

Places to Eat

You'll be lucky to find a menú del día for less than 1200 ptas. The self-service *Los Vikingos*, in the thick of the action at Carrer Marques de Montroig 7-9, does tolerable pasta, pizzas and seafood from 600 ptas. *La Oca*, round the corner on Carrer de les Parellades, is popular for its pizzas from 585 ptas and grilled chicken at 340 ptas for a quarter-bird. Out on Passeig de la Ribera, the *Hotel La Santa Maria*, No 52, has a vast and incredibly busy Catalan and Spanish restaurant, partly open-air, with starters like xató (a local fish salad in piquant dressing), escalivada and esqueixada, and a full range of meat and fish mains, all from 775 ptas. *Restaurante El Velero* along the street is a classier fish and seafood joint with most mains at 1500 ptas or more.

Carrer Sant Pau has a string of good restaurants including the Basque *Eguzki* at No 3, concentrating on seafood from 650 ptas and good for tapas too, and *Restaurant Miami*, No 11, which has a decent four course menú for 1250 ptas. Nearby, the popular *Pizzeria Cap de Vila* on Plaça Cap de Vila does pizzas and pasta from 800 ptas. *Restaurant La Viña*, Carrer Sant Francesc 11, has a range of generous tapas for 375 ptas. A calmer area to eat is over on Platja de Sant Sebastià, where *Rugantino* does pizza, pasta, and meat and vegetarian dishes from 800 ptas, and the classy *La Torreta* deals mainly in seafood, from 1300 to 2000 ptas a main course.

Entertainment

A large portion of Sitges' nightlife happens on one short pedestrian strip that's packed with humanity right through the night in summer: Carrer 1er de Maig, Plaça Industria and Carrer Marques de Montroig, all in a short straight line off the seafront Passeig de la Ribera. Carrer 1er de Maig – or Calle del Pecado (Sin Street) – vibrates to the volume of 10 or so disco-bars all trying to outdo each other in decibels. They start to fill at about midnight. Plaça Industria and Carrer Marques de Montroig have the bars and cafés where people sit, drink and watch other people. All you have to do is cruise along, see what takes your fancy – and try not to bust your budget. If you're in need of a change of location, head round the corner to Carrer de les Parellades, Carrer Bonaire or Carrer Sant Pere, where there's a bit more of much the same. Carrer Sant Bonaventura has a string of gay bars, mostly behind closed doors. *Trailer*, Carrer Àngel Vidal 36, is a popular gay disco.

Getting There & Away

Four rodalies trains an hour, from about 6 am to 10 pm, run from Barcelona Sants to Sitges, taking 30 minutes and costing 290 ptas. Several trains a day leave Sitges for Tarragona (one hour), where you can change for Port Aventura, Valencia and beyond.

The best road from Barcelona is the A-16, which carries a 645 ptas toll on the Túnels de Garraf stretch approaching Sitges. In Sitges

itself, the traffic usually makes it quicker to walk than drive.

TARRAGONA

Tarragona was first occupied by the Romans who called it Tarraco, in 218 BC. In 27 BC Emperor Augustus made it capital of his new Tarraconensis province – in other words most of what's now Spain – and lived here till 25 BC while directing campaigns in Cantabria and Asturias. It would not have been long afterwards that Tarragona's most famous son, Pontius Pilate, was born here. Tarragona was abandoned when the Muslims arrived in 714 AD, but reborn as the seat of a Christian archbishopric in 1089. Today, with 111,000 people, it's a mainly modern city, but its rich Roman remains and very fine medieval cathedral make it an absorbing place.

Orientation

The main street is Rambla Nova, which runs roughly north-west from a clifftop overlooking the Mediterranean. A couple of blocks to the east, and parallel, is Rambla Vella, which marks the beginning of the old town – and incidentally, follows the line of the Via Augusta, the Roman road from Rome to Cádiz.

The train station is some 600 metres south-west of Rambla Nova, near the seafront, and the bus station is about 1.75 km inland, on Plaça Imperial Tàrraco at the end of Rambla Nova.

Information

The main tourist office (☎ 24 50 64) is at Carrer Major 39 in the old town; it's open Monday to Friday from 10 am to 2 pm and 4 to 7 pm, Saturday, Sunday and holidays from 11 am to 2 pm (and extra hours from July to September). There's also a Cataluña regional tourist office (☎ 23 34 15) at Carrer Fortuny 4. There are many banks on Rambla Nova; the main post office (postcode 43080) is on Plaça Corsini. The telephone code is ☎ 977.

The Guàrdia Urbana (municipal police; ☎ 092 or 24 03 45) are at Carrer Pare Palau

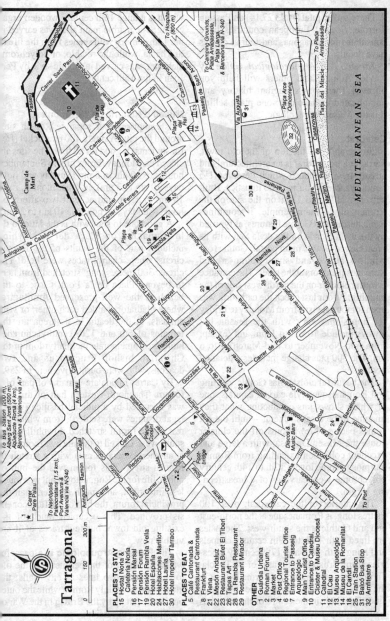

Tarragona

0   150   300 m
0   150   300 m

PLACES TO STAY
15 Hostal Noria &
    Cafetería Noria
16 Pensión Marsal
17 Pensión Forum
19 Pensión Rambla Vella
20 Hotel España
24 Habitaciones Mariflor
27 Hotel Lauria
30 Hotel Imperial Tárraco

PLACES TO EAT
5   Café Cantonada &
    Restaurant Cantonada
21 Viena
22 Mesón Andaluz
23 Restaurant Bufet El Tiberi
26 Tapas Art
28 La Rambla Restaurant
29 Restaurant Mirador

OTHER
1   Guàrdia Urbana
2   Roman Forum
3   Market
4   Post Office
6   Regional Tourist Office
7   Entrance to Passeig
    Arqueològic
9   Main Tourist Office
10 Entrance to Catedral,
    Cloister & Museu Diocesà
11 Catedral
12 El Cau
13 Museu Arqueològic
14 Museu de la Romanitat
18 El Candil
25 Train Station
31 Balcó Bus Stop
32 Amfiteatre

7. There's a hospital (☎ 23 27 14) on Passeig Torroja. Several European countries have consulates in Tarragona, and tourist offices have details.

Tarraco, An Archaeological Guide by Xavier Aquilué and others will help you unravel Tarragona's ancient history and complicated archaeology; one place selling it is the Museu Arqueològic.

Catedral

Sitting grandly at the top of the old town, Tarragona's cathedral is an architectural and artistic treasure house which deserves 1½ hours or more if you're to do it justice. Built between 1171 and 1331 on the site of the Roman city's main temple, it combines Romanesque and Gothic features, as typified by the main façade on Pla de la Seu with its great carved Gothic main portal, Gothic rose window above and small round-arched Romanesque doors at the sides. The entrance is by the cloister on the north-west side of the building. At our last check the cathedral was open for tourist visits from Monday to Friday for hours that vary with the season but always include 10 am to 1 pm and (except from mid-November to mid-March) 4 to 6 pm. The 300 ptas charge includes a detailed booklet.

The beautiful cloister has Gothic vaulting and Romanesque-style carved capitals, one of which shows rats conducting what they imagine to be a cat's funeral – until the cat comes back to life! Rooms off the cloister house the Museu Diocesà, with a large and excellent collection extending from Roman hairpins to some lovely 12th to 14th century polychrome woodcarvings of a breastfeeding Virgin.

The interior of the cathedral, over 100 metres long, is Romanesque at the north-east end and Gothic at the south-west. The aisles are lined with 14th to 19th century chapels and hung with 16th and 17th century tapestries from Brussels. The arm of St Thecla, Tarragona's patron saint, is normally kept in the Capella de Santa Tecla on the south-east side. The choir in the centre of the nave has 15th century carved walnut stalls, above which is a huge 16th century wooden organ casing. The marble main altar was carved in the 13th century with scenes from the life of St Thecla, while the retablo, of polychrome alabaster, was carved in Gothic style by Pere Joan in the 15th century.

Museu d'Història de Tarragona

This comprises four separate Roman sites around the city. A single 400 ptas ticket (free for students) is good for all four. The sites are closed on Monday. From July to September hours are 10 am to 8 pm (Sunday and holidays 10 am to 3 pm); in other months, from 10 am to 1 pm and at least two afternoon hours (Sunday and holidays 10 am to 2 pm).

A good one to start with is the **Museu de la Romanitat** on Plaça del Rei, which includes part of the vaults of the Roman circus, where chariot races were held. The circus, 300 metres long, stretched from here to beyond Plaça de la Font. Close to the beach is the well-preserved **Amfiteatre** where gladiators battled each other, or wild animals, to the death. In its arena are the remains of 6th and 12th century churches built to commemorate the martyrdom of the Christian bishop Fructuosus and two deacons, who were burnt alive here in 259.

By Carrer Lleida are remains of part of a **forum**. The north-western half of this site was occupied by a judicial basilica (where legal disputes were settled), from which the rest of the forum stretched downhill to the south-west. Linked to the site by a footbridge is another excavated area with a stretch of Roman street. This forum was the hub of public life for the Roman town but was much less important, and much smaller, than the provincial forum, the hub of all Tarraconensis province. This occupied much of the existing old town, but few traces of it are visible now.

The **Passeig Arqueològic** is a peaceful walk round part of the perimeter of the old town between two lines of city walls; the inner ones are mainly Roman while the outer ones were put up by the British in the War of the Spanish Succession.

Museu Nacional Arqueològic de Tarragona

This carefully presented museum on Plaça del Rei gives further insight into Roman Tarraco, though most explanatory material is in Catalan or Castilian. Exhibits include part of the Roman city walls, frescos, sculpture and pottery. A highlight is the large, almost complete *Mosaic de Peixos de la Pineda* showing fish and sea creatures. In the section on everyday arts you can admire ancient fertility aids including an outsize stone penis, symbol of the god Priapus. The museum is open Tuesday to Saturday from 10 am to 1 pm and 4.30 to 7 pm, Sunday and holidays 10 am to 2 pm. Entry is 100 ptas, free on Tuesday.

Other Attractions

The **Necròpolis Paleocristians** on Passeig de la Independència on the western edge of town is a large Christian cemetery of late Roman and Visigothic times with some surprisingly elaborate tombs. It was closed for 'remodelling' at the time of research. Outstanding among several Roman sites outside the town is the **Aqüeducte Romà**, some four km inland on the N-240 Lleida road. This fine stretch of two-tiered aqueduct is 217 metres long and 27 metres high. Bus No 5 to Sant Salvador from Plaça Imperial Tàrraco (on the opposite side of this roundabout from the bus station), every 10 to 20 minutes, will take you there.

Beaches

The town beach, Platja del Miracle, is reasonably clean but can get terribly crowded. Platja Arrabassada, one km north-east across the headland, is longer, and Platja Llarga, beginning two km further out, stretches for about three km. Bus Nos 1 and 9 from the Balcó stop on Via Augusta go to both.

Places to Stay

There are seven camping grounds on or close to the beach within 11 km north-east of the city along the N-340. Nearest is *Camping Tàrraco* (☎ 23 99 89) behind Platja Arrabassada, but others, such as *Camping Las Palmeras* (☎ 20 80 81) at the far end of Platja Llarga, are better. These two close from October to March but others stay open all year.

The *Alberg Sant Jordi* youth hostel (☎ 24 01 95) at Avinguda President Lluís Companys 5, about 300 metres north-west of the bus station, has 192 beds but during the academic year 150 of them are taken up by students. The high season is from April to August.

Plaça de la Font in the old town has three good pensiones. *Pensión Marsal* (☎ 22 40 69) at No 26 has clean singles/doubles with short beds and shower for 1650/3300 ptas (or 1400/2800 ptas if you can make it up to the 5th floor). The better *Pensión Forum* (☎ 23 17 18) at No 37 charges 2750/4800 ptas, also with shower. *Hostal Noria* (☎ 23 87 17) at No 53 is a bit better value at 2600/4500 ptas but is often full.

Habitaciones Mariflor (☎ 23 82 31) in a drab block at Carrer General Contreras 29, near the train station, has clean rooms with shared baths for 1700/3250 ptas. *Pensión Rambla Vella* (☎ 23 81 15), Rambla Vella 31, has small, clean rooms for 1870/3750 ptas, or 2140/4280 ptas with bathroom.

Hotel España (☎ 23 27 12), Rambla Nova 49, is an unexciting but well-positioned one star hotel where rooms with bath cost 3300/6000 ptas plus IVA. The three star *Hotel Lauría* (☎ 23 67 12), Rambla Nova 20, is a worthwhile splurge at 5250/10,000 ptas plus IVA, with a good location and a pool. *Hotel Imperial Tàrraco* (☎ 23 30 40) at Rambla Vella 2 is the best in town, with a great position overlooking the Mediterranea and rooms for 12,675/16,200 ptas plus IVA. Several of the better hotels offer big discounts on Friday, Saturday and Sunday nights.

Places to Eat

The *Pensión Marsal* has a respectable four course lunch or dinner menú for just 700 ptas. For Catalan food, head for the stylish *Restaurant Bufet El Tiberi*, Carrer Martí d'Ardenya 5, which offers an all-you-can-eat buffet for 1390 ptas per person. It closes Sunday night and Monday. Nearby *Mesón Andaluz*, upstairs at Carrer de Pons d'Icart 3, is a backstreet local favourite, with a good three course menú for 775 ptas including wine, and main courses from 350 ptas. *Café Cantonada* at Carrer Fortuny 23 is another popular place and has a lunch menú for 900 ptas; next door, *Restaurant Cantonada* has pizzas and pasta from 575 to 700 ptas.

Frankfurt at Carrer Major 30 is one of the better-value cafés in the old town, doing good platos combinados from 500 ptas and a big range of bocadillos, hot and cold, from 170 to 270 ptas. *Cafeteria Noria*, Plaça de la Font 53, has similar fare and prices.

Rambla Nova has several good places, either for a snack or a meal. *Viena*, No 50, has good croissants and a vast range of entrepans from 250 ptas. *Tapas Art*, No 26, has good tapas from 200 ptas. Two good restaurants are *La Rambla* at No 10 and, almost directly opposite, *Restaurant Mirador*. Both have menús for about 1400 ptas and you can eat well à la carte for 2500 to 3000 ptas.

Entertainment

El Candil, Plaça de la Font 13, is a popular, relaxed bar-café with a studenty clientele. *El Cau*, in a Roman circus vault on Carrer Trinquet Vell, is similar, but with music. *Café Cantonada* at Carrer Fortuny 23, with its pool table, is nice for a drink or two. A few louder music bars, and discos, cluster on Carrer Pau del Protectorat near the train station.

Getting There & Away

Lying on main routes south from Barcelona, Tarragona is well connected. Train is the easiest way to/from Barcelona.

Bus Services include: to Barcelona (1¾ hours), 10 buses Monday to Friday, one or two on the weekend, for 805 ptas; Valencia, nine daily (3½ hours); Lleida, two or three daily (two hours); Zaragoza, up to six daily (2¾ hours); La Seu d'Urgell (3¼ hours) and Andorra la Vella, one daily. Other buses run daily to Madrid, Alicante, Pamplona, the main Andalucían cities and the north coast. There are also services to France and beyond, and to Morocco.

Train About 40 regional and long-distance trains a day run to/from Barcelona Sants (one to 1½ hours; 650 to 1400 ptas in 2nd class). Around eight of them stop at Sitges (one hour from Tarragona). There are about 12 trains daily to/from Valencia (three to 3½ hours; 2500 ptas in 2nd class), and at least eight a day to Lleida (one to 1½ hours) and Zaragoza (three to 3½ hours). To Madrid, there are four trains each day – two via Valencia in seven hours and two via Zaragoza in six hours – with fares ranging from 3700 to 5600 ptas. Other trains run to just about every corner of Spain, and as far as Montpellier in France.

Boat In summer (1 June to 8 September in 1996) Trasmediterránea (☎ 22 55 06) runs a 'Fast Ferry' service to/from Palma de Mallorca, taking just 3¾ hours one way, four days a week. Passenger fare is 7500 ptas and a car is 18,000 ptas.

PORT AVENTURA

Port Aventura (☎ 902-20 22 20), which opened in 1995 seven km west of Tarragona, near Salou, is Spain's newest, biggest and best funfair-adventure park. If you have 3900 ptas to spare (3000 ptas for children aged from five to 12), it makes a real fun day out with never a dull moment – though it only opens from Semana Santa to October. Apart from hair-raising experiences like the Dragon Khan, claimed to be Europe's biggest roller coaster (with eight loops and speeds up to 110 km/hour), and the Tifon, which simulates a tropical typhoon, there are gentler rides and areas especially for children. Port Aventura also has a hectic street life that includes Wild West shoot-outs, Polynesian dance troupes, and theatres with Chinese acrobats. The park is divided into five theme areas: China, a Mediterranean fishing village, the American Far West, Polynesia and ancient Mexico.

Port Aventura is open daily during its season from 10 am to 8 pm, and from around mid-June to mid-September it stays open to midnight. Night tickets, valid from 7 pm to midnight, are 2300 ptas.

Trains run to Port Aventura's own station, about a one km walk from the site, several times a day from Tarragona and Barcelona. By road, take exit 35 from the A-7, or the N-340 from Tarragona. Parking is 500 ptas.

EBRO DELTA

The delta of the Río Ebro (Delta de l'Ebre in Catalan), formed by silt brought down by the river, sticks 20 km out into the Mediterranean near Cataluña's southern border. Dotted with reedy lagoons and fringed by dune-backed beaches, this flat and exposed wetland is northern Spain's most important water-bird habitat. The October-November migration season sees the peak bird population, with an average of 53,000 ducks and 15,000 coots on the delta, but they're also very numerous in winter and spring. Ten per cent of all water birds wintering on the Iberian Peninsula do so here.

Nearly half the delta's 320 sq km are given over to rice growing. Some 77 sq km, mostly along the coasts and around the lagoons, form the Parc Natural Delta de l'Ebre.

Orientation

The delta is a seaward-pointing arrowhead of land with the Ebro flowing eastwards across its middle. The town of Deltebre straggles about five km along the north bank of the river at the centre of the delta. Deltebre's western half is called Jesús i Maria and the eastern half La Cava. Facing Deltebre on the south bank of the river is the smaller town of Sant Jaume d'Enveja. Roads crisscross the delta to Deltebre and beyond from the towns of L'Ampolla, Amposta and Sant Carles de la Ràpita, all on the N-340. Three ferries (transbordadors), running from early morning till nightfall, link Deltebre to Sant Jaume d'Enveja. They cost around 40 ptas per pedestrian and 200 ptas for a car with two people.

Information

The tourist office (Centre d'Informació) at Carrer Ulldecona 22, Jesús i Maria (☎ 48 96 79), is open Monday to Friday from 10 am to 2 pm and 3 to 6 pm, Saturday from 10 am to 1 pm and 3.30 to 6 pm, Sunday and holidays from 10 am to 1 pm. Adjoining is an Ecomuseu with examples of delta environments and an aquarium-terrarium of delta species.

There's another information office, with a bird museum, at Casa de Fusta, by L'Encanyissada lagoon about 10 km southwest of Deltebre. It's open the same hours as the one at Deltebre but closed Monday. Other tourist offices are in Sant Jaume d'Enveja, Sant Carles de la Ràpita, Amposta and L'Ampolla.

There are several banks on and off the main street in the centre of La Cava. The telephone code for the whole delta region is ☎ 977.

Things to See & Do

A good way to explore the delta is by bicycle and there are several places in Deltebre where you can rent one for around 1000 ptas a day. Early morning and evening are the best times for bird-watching, and good areas for this include L'Encanyissada and La Tancada lagoons and Punta de la Banya, all in the southern part of the delta. L'Encanyissada has two observation towers and La Tancada one. La Tancada and Punta de la Banya are generally the best places to see the greater flamingoes which are the delta's most spectacular birds. Punta de la Banya is joined to the delta by a five km sandspit with the very wide, long and sandy Platja de l'Eucaliptus beach at its north end. Vehicles can normally get at least some way along the sandspit.

The Garriga (☎ 48 91 22) and Olmos (☎ 48 04 73 or 48 05 48) companies run daily tourist boat trips from Deltebre to the mouths of the Ebro and the Illa de Buda at the delta's tip. Trips last 1½ hours and cost 500 ptas a person. They go daily, but frequency depends on the season: in summer both companies do several trips a day.

Places to Stay

Camping Mediterrani Blau (☎ 46 81 46) on Platja de l'Eucaliptus is open from April to September with room for 240 people in a small eucalyptus wood, at 425 ptas plus IVA per adult, per car and per tent. It has a restaurant. There are two more camping grounds, open all year, at Riumar, 10 km east of Deltebre.

Habitacions Cal d'Àngela (☎ 48 07 62), Carrer Pompeu Fabra 4, Jesús i Maria, has very basic rooms at 1000 to 1500 ptas, or 1300 to 2000 ptas with bath. It's a short walk from the tourist office. *Restaurant Can Salat* (☎ 48 02 28) at Carrer Ramon i Cajal 14 in the centre of La Cava has a few adequate singles/doubles for 1500/3000 ptas, or 1700/3400 ptas with private bathroom. The *Delta Hotel* (☎ 48 00 46) at Avinguda del Canal, Camí de la Illeta s/n, on the north edge of Deltebre by the road to Riumar, has nice modern singles/doubles at up to 5400/8600 plus IVA, and a good restaurant.

Restaurant 21, Avinguda Goles de l'Ebre 273, on the main road through the middle of La Cava, has a three course menú for 1200 ptas and seafood main dishes from 600 ptas. It'll do you arròs a la banda, the local variant

of paella, for 1000 ptas (minimum two people). Other delta delights include eels (anguilas), baby eels (angules), and shellfish.

There are several places to stay in Sant Carles de la Ràpita, which is a pleasant town with a marina and fishing harbour.

Getting There & Away

The delta is certainly easiest to get to with your own wheels, but you *can* reach it by bus or a train-bus combination.

Autocars Hife (☎ 44 03 00) runs to Jesús i Maria and La Cava from the inland town of Tortosa (one hour) five times daily (twice on Saturday, Sunday and holidays), and from Amposta (30 minutes) once or twice daily. Some Hife buses from Barcelona, Tarragona, Lleida and Valencia connect with these services.

Tortosa is also served by numerous trains from Tarragona (1¼ hours), Barcelona and Valencia.

Andorra

The Catalan-speaking princedom of Andorra (population 65,000), whose mountainous territory comprises only 468 sq km, nestles in the Pyrenees between Cataluña and France. Though it *is* tiny, this political anomaly contains some of the most dramatic scenery, and best skiing, in the Pyrenees. And in summer there's plenty of good walking in the higher, more remote parts of the princedom, away from the overdevelopment and heavy traffic that plagues Andorra's towns. There's relatively little of cultural or historical interest other than a number of Romanesque parish churches and a few simple but elegant stone bridges.

Facts about the Country

HISTORY

By tradition, Andorra's independence is credited to Charlemagne, who captured the region from the Muslims in 803. His son, Louis I (the Pious), presented the area's inhabitants with a charter of liberties. The earliest known document concerning Andorra is an order of 843 by Charlemagne's grandson, Charles II, granting the Valls d'Andorra (Valleys of Andorra) to Sunifred, Count of Urgell, whose base was La Seu d'Urgell, Cataluña. From the counts, Andorra later passed to the bishops of Urgell, also based in La Seu. In 1278 and 1288, following a succession dispute between the bishops and the French counts of Foix, to the north, Andorra's first constitutional documents, the Pareatges (Acts of Joint Overlordship), established a system of shared sovereignty between the bishops and the counts. This feudal setup created a peculiar political equilibrium that saved Andorra from being swallowed up by its powerful neighbours despite recurrent tension down the centuries between the co-princes.

Since the 1950s Andorra has developed as

a centre for skiing and duty-free shopping – the latter a business which grew out of the smuggling of French goods to Spain during the Spanish Civil War and Spanish goods to France in WWII (Andorra remained neutral in both wars). These activities have brought not only wealth, foreign workers and eight million visitors a year, but also some pretty unsightly development, and thick traffic, for several km either side of the capital, Andorra la Vella.

GEOGRAPHY

Andorra consists of a group of valleys and their surrounding mountains in the midst of the Pyrenees. It measures 25 km from north to south at its maximum and 29 km from east to west. Most of its 40 or so towns and hamlets – some with just a few dozen people – are in the valleys. The main river, the Riu Gran Valira, is formed near the capital,

ANDORRA

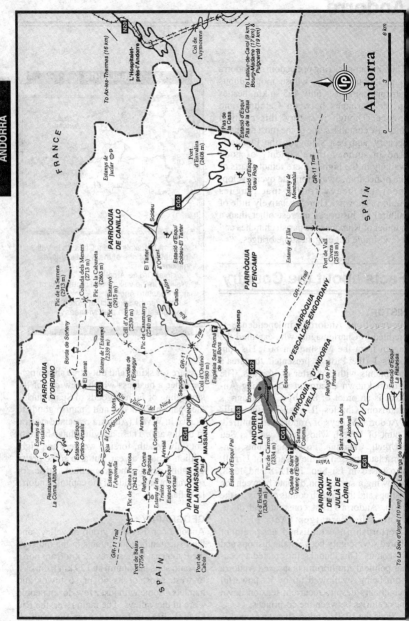

Andorra la Vella, by the confluence of the Valira d'Orient and the Valira del Nord.

Pic de Coma Pedrosa (2942 metres) in western Andorra is the princedom's highest mountain. The lowest point, which is on the Spanish frontier at La Farga de Moles, is 838 metres above sea level. Andorra's mountain peaks remain snowcapped until early July or later.

GOVERNMENT & POLITICS
For seven centuries until 1993, Andorra had a unique form of government known as a 'co-princedom' with its sovereignty vested in two 'princes': the president of the French Republic, who inherited the job from France's pre-Revolutionary kings (who in turn had taken it over from the Counts of Foix), and the bishop of La Seu d'Urgell. In March 1993, about 75% of the 9123 native Andorrans who were eligible to vote (less than one-sixth of the population) cast ballots in a referendum that established Andorra as an independent, democratic 'parliamentary co-princedom'. Under the new constitution, which placed full sovereignty in the hands of the Andorran people, the French and Spanish co-princes continue to function as joint heads with much-reduced powers.

The country's elected parliament is the Consell General (Council General); its forerunner, the Consell de la Terra (Council of the Land), was established in 1419. The 28 members of the Consell General – four from each of the seven parishes – are elected for four-year terms. The Consell General meets three or four times a year and is chaired by two presiding officers called *síndics*. It appoints a *cap de govern* (prime minister), who chooses ministers; their programmes have to be approved by the Consell General. The liberal Marc Forné replaced Óscar Ribas as cap de govern in 1994. New elections for the Consell General were scheduled for early 1997.

Women were given the vote in 1970, and all Andorran citizens over 18 now have it. Andorra is a member of the United Nations, but not of the EU.

For administrative purposes, Andorra is divided into seven parishes (*parròquies* in Catalan). Six of the parishes have existed since at least the 9th century; a seventh, Escaldes-Engordany, was created in 1978 by lopping off part of the parish of Andorra la Vella.

ECONOMY
The Andorran economy is based on cheap shopping, tourism (eight million people pass through the princedom every year) and banking. The most important components of the agricultural sector, which makes up only 1.2% of total economic activity, are tobacco growing and cattle raising.

POPULATION & PEOPLE
Only about a quarter of Andorra's 65,000 inhabitants, almost two-thirds of whom live in Andorra la Vella and its suburbs, are Andorran nationals. The rest are Spaniards (about 30,000), Portuguese (5000), French (5000) and others. Until the 1950s Andorra's population was only 6000 or so.

LANGUAGE
The official language is Catalan, but nearly everyone speaks Spanish too (see the Language section in this book's Facts about the Country chapter for some useful words and phrases in Catalan). Local lore has it that everyone in Andorra speaks Catalan, Spanish and French, but there are plenty of people who can't understand more than 10 words of French, and some Spanish residents who speak little Catalan. Very few people speak English. Trilingual restaurant menus provide a good opportunity to compare Catalan with Spanish and French.

Facts for the Visitor

TOURIST OFFICES
There are two tourist offices in Andorra la Vella and several others around the country (see relevant sections of this chapter). Andorra's tourist offices or tourism representatives abroad include the following:

ANDORRA

ANDORRA

Belgium
10 Rue de la Montagne, 1000 Brussels
(☎ 02-502 12 11; fax 02-513 39 34)
France
26 Ave de l'Opéra, 75001 Paris
(☎ 01 42 61 50 55; fax 01 42 61 41 91)
Germany
Finsterwalder Strasse 28, 13435 Berlin
(☎ 030-415 49 14)
Spain
Carrer de Marià Cubí 159, 08021 Barcelona
(☎ 93-200 07 87; fax 93-414 18 63)
UK
63 Westover Road, London SW18 2RF
(☎ 0181-874 48 06)
USA
6899 N Knox Avenue, Lincolnwood, IL 60646
(☎ 708-674 30 91; fax 708-329 94 70)

VISAS & DOCUMENTS

Visas are not necessary to visit Andorra; the authorities figure that if Spain or France let you in, that's good enough for them. But you must carry your passport or national identity card, which may be checked at the border and has to be presented when you check into a hotel so the management can register you with the police.

EMBASSIES

Andorra does not have any diplomatic legations abroad, but Spain and France maintain embassies in Andorra la Vella.

France
Carrer Les Canals 38-40 (☎ 82 08 09)
Consulate: Carrer de la Sobrevia (☎ 86 91 96)
Spain
Carrer Prat de la Creu 34 (☎ 82 00 13)

CUSTOMS

Duty-free allowances, per adult, for goods entering Spain or France from Andorra include: five bottles of still wine; either 1.5 litres of spirits of 22% or higher alcohol content, or three litres of lighter spirits or sparkling wine; 300 cigarettes; four kg of cheese; and 525 ecus (about 81,000 ptas) worth of industrial products such as electronic goods, shoes, clothes and jewellery. If you need to know more, ask a tourist office for the leaflet *Franquícies dels Viatgers*.

MONEY

Andorra, which has no currency of its own, uses both the peseta and the French franc (FF). Except in Pas de la Casa on the French border, prices are usually noted in pesetas. It's best to use pesetas: the exchange rate for francs in shops and restaurants is seldom in your favour.

Exchange Rates

Australia	A$1	=	97 ptas	= 4.04FF
Canada	C$1	=	92 ptas	= 3.83FF
France	1FF	=	24 ptas	
Germany	DM1	=	82 ptas	= 3.42FF
Japan	¥100	=	113 ptas	= 4.71FF
New Zealand	NZ$1	=	86 ptas	= 3.58FF
Portugal	P100$00	=	87 ptas	= 3.62FF
Spain			100 ptas	= 4.17FF
UK	UK£1	=	195 ptas	= 8.12FF
USA	US$1	=	125 ptas	= 5.21FF

POST & COMMUNICATIONS
Post

Andorra has no post office of its own; France and Spain each operate a separate postal system with their own Andorran stamps. Those printed, issued and sold by La Poste (France) are in francs while the Spanish ones are in pesetas. Andorran stamps of both types are valid only for items posted within Andorra and are necessary only for international mail; letters mailed to destinations within the country are free and do not need stamps. Regular French and Spanish stamps cannot be used in Andorra.

International postal rates are the same as those of the issuing country, with the French tariffs slightly cheaper. Andorrans say that you are better off routing all international mail (except letters to Spain) through the French postal system. There are two kinds of postboxes, but should you use the wrong one your letter will be transferred.

Letters to Andorra la Vella marked 'Poste Restante' are sent to the town's French post office. There's a charge of about 3FF for each letter you pick up. American Express card or travellers' cheque holders can also receive mail via the American Express agent in Andorra la Vella. The best way to get a letter to Andorra (except from Spain) is to address it to 'Principauté d'Andorre via FRANCE'.

Telephone

International Andorra's country code is ☎ 376. Thus to call Andorra from Spain, dial 07-376 before the six-digit local number. From France, dial 00 (the international access code) followed by 376 and the local number. To call Andorra from other countries, dial the international access code, then 376 and the local number.

To call Spain from Andorra, dial 00-34 followed by the area code and local number. To call France, dial 00-33 (00-33-1 for the Paris area), then the local number. To call other countries, dial 00, then the country code, area code and local number. To call directory assistance, dial ☎ 111; operators speak Catalan, Spanish and French. The international operator can be reached by dialling ☎ 82 11 11. To Spain and France, telephone rates are 50% cheaper between 10 pm and 8 am and all day on Sunday and holidays. Reverse-charge (collect) calling is not available in Andorra.

Public Telephones Public telephones take pesetas (francs in Pas de la Casa) or an Andorran *teletarja*, which operates on the same principle as the *tarjeta telefónica* used in Spain (see Post & Communications in the Facts for the Visitor chapter). Telephone cards worth 50 and 100 units are sold at post offices, tourist offices, tobacconists and some other shops for 500 ptas and 900 ptas. One unit is good for a local call of about three minutes and for a far shorter international one.

MEDIA

There are two radio stations in Andorra: the government-run Radio Nacional Andorra (RNA) and the privately run Radio Valira, which broadcasts at 93.3 MHz and 98.1 MHz on the FM band. The two daily newspapers in Catalan are the mass-circulation *Poble d'Andorra* and the more conservative *Diari d'Andorra*.

TIME

Andorra, like Spain, is two hours ahead of GMT/UTC from the last Sunday in March to the last Sunday in October, and one hour ahead at other times.

ELECTRICITY

The electric current is either 220V or 125V, both at 50 Hz.

HEALTH

Visitors must pay for all medical attention and care in Andorra.

USEFUL ORGANISATIONS

For information on weather and snow conditions in winter, call ☎ 84 88 52 (Spanish), ☎ 84 88 53 (French) or ☎ 84 88 51 (Catalan). Ring ☎ 84 88 84 for information about road conditions in Spanish, French and Catalan.

DANGERS & ANNOYANCES

The country's minimal legislation to protect the consumer often goes unenforced, so that hotels and petrol stations sometimes neglect to post their prices, and restaurants are free to refuse to serve tap water with meals. The road system is underdeveloped, leading to long traffic jams in towns amidst unsightly buildings erected with very little regard for aesthetics.

Emergency telephone numbers include:

Police ☎ 110
Medical emergency ☎ 116
Fire or ambulance ☎ 118
Mountain rescue service ☎ 112
Car assistance & towing ☎ 86 99 86

BUSINESS HOURS & PUBLIC HOLIDAYS

Shops in Andorra la Vella are open daily from 9.30 am to 1 pm and 3.30 to 8 pm, except (in most cases) Sunday afternoon, 1 January, Good Friday, 8 September (a national holiday) and 25 December.

ACTIVITIES
Hiking
The tranquillity of Andorra's beautiful and relatively unspoiled back country begins only a few hundred metres from the bazaar-like bustle of the towns. The country's north-west region (see the North-Western Andorra section later in this chapter) has some especially good areas for hiking. All told, Andorra has over 50 lakes hidden among the soaring mountains.

The best season for hiking is June to September, when temperatures climb well into the 20s in the day, though they drop to around 10°C at night. June can be wet.

The GR-11 trail, which traverses the Spanish Pyrenees from the Mediterranean to the Atlantic, crosses Andorra from the Port de Vall Civera pass (2518 metres) in the south-east to the Port de Baiau pass (2756 metres) in the north-west.

Hikers can sleep for free in over 20 mountain refuges dotted around Andorra's high country (see the Accommodation section following). A 1:25,000 government *mapa topogràfic* of the country costs 1200 ptas in bookshops and some tourist offices. The country is also covered in 19 *Valls d'Andorra* sheets at 1:10,000 (275 ptas each).

Tourist offices give out a useful booklet available in several languages (it's called *Sport Activities* in English), with 52 recommended walks of 15 minutes to eight hours duration and 17 mountain bike routes. It gives further detail on several of the walks suggested in this chapter.

Skiing
Downhill Andorra has the best inexpensive skiing and snowboarding in the Pyrenees. All the country's five downhill ski resorts (*estaciós d'esquí*), are covered in this chapter. For further information enquire at one of the capital's two tourist offices or contact Ski Andorra (☎ 86 43 89; fax 86 59 10) at Avinguda Carlemany 65 in Escaldes.

The biggest, best (and most expensive) resorts are Pas de la Casa-Grau Roig and Soldeu-El Tarter, both in the east. Arinsal, Pal and Ordino-Arcalís are in the north-west.

The skiing is mainly good for beginners and intermediates, with little of interest for experts. The ski season normally lasts from December to April, depending on snow conditions, which in the last decade have not been reliable. All the Andorran resorts have ski schools – the biggest are at Soldeu-El Tarter and Pas de la Casa-Grau Roig – and snow-making machines for their main pistes.

Prices for lift passes, ski school and, often, accommodation rise at the following 'high-season' times: all Saturdays and Sundays; the Spanish long weekend around the 6 and 8 December public holidays; the Christmas-New Year period from about 23 December to 7 January; from 10 February to early March; and Semana Santa. Low and high-season lift pass prices are given for each individual resort in this chapter; it's also possible to get a combined five-day pass for all five resorts for around 14,000 ptas (low season) or 16,500 ptas (high season). Ski school costs from 3200 to 3600 ptas an hour for individual tuition, 2200 to 2900 ptas for three hours of group classes, or 9000 to 11,000 ptas for 15 hours of group classes.

Ski Touring There are many variations of a circular ski trip, and many shorter ones, that can be done around Andorra. The princedom's plentiful mountain shelters allow the option of not having to take a tent, but an all-seasons sleeping bag is essential, as are an ice axe, food and a camping stove (some huts lack cooking facilities). One of the popular routes, taking about six days, starts in Aixirivall, just east of Sant Julià de Lòria in southern Andorra, from where it goes anticlockwise around the country to the Pal ski station. This should only be attempted by experienced ski tourers.

There's also a Nordic skiing centre at La Rabassa in the south, with 15 km of marked forest trails.

ACCOMMODATION

Almost all of Andorra's hotels stay open year round. They are fullest in July and August and from December to March – when some places put prices up a bit – but since turnover is high (except in winter, most people stay just long enough to do a bit of shopping), rooms are almost always available in the morning.

There are no youth hostels in Andorra. The 26 *refugis* – mountain huts for the use of both shepherds and hikers (one room for each) – do not require reservations, and all except one are unstaffed and free. Most have bunks, fireplaces and sources of drinkable water but no cooking facilities. Tourist offices have brochures and maps indicating the location of the shelters.

Tourist offices can provide information on apartments and chalets *(xalets)* available for short-term rental.

THINGS TO BUY

Because customs duties and taxes are very low in Andorra, and because some EU products attract subsidies when exported from the EU (making them cheaper in non-EU countries such as Andorra), Andorra has become famous as a bazar for cheap electronic goods, photographic equipment, shoes, clothing, perfume, petrol and, above all, alcohol, cigarettes and French dairy products. Shops selling these goods cluster in Andorra la Vella and its suburbs, Encamp, Pas de la Casa and near the Spanish road border. These are what many visitors from Spain and France come to Andorra for, even though potential savings are no longer what they once were.

If you're after a particular piece of photographic or electronic equipment, you can probably find it (or something similar from among last year's models). But if you don't know what you want, Andorra is not such a great place to shop since most places sell a little bit of everything (a few car radios, some watches etc), and salespeople know very little about the merchandise on offer and usually can't produce more than a few roughly similar models for comparison.

If you search out the best price (pricing varies widely from shop to shop) and bargain a bit – ask for the *'precio último'*, the final price – you'll find that the prices for most cameras and electronic goods are about 20% or 30% less than in Spain or France.

Some shops add a surcharge of 4% if you pay by credit card. If you're buying something that comes with a warranty, make sure to have the store fill in the card and rubber-stamp it. Some warranties are valid only in the country of purchase, so it's a good idea to read the fine print. Beware of confusion – unintentional or otherwise – that may result from going back and forth between pesetas, francs and your home currency.

Getting There & Away

The only way into Andorra – unless you trek across the mountains – is by road. One of the two roads into the country comes from La Seu d'Urgell in Spain, 20 km south of Andorra la Vella. The other enters Andorra at Pas de la Casa on the eastern border with France, then crosses the spectacular 2408 metre-high Port d'Envalira (the highest pass in the Pyrenees, occasionally closed by snow in winter) en route to Andorra la Vella. It's approached along the French N-22 from the N-20 Bourg-Madame-Toulouse road, which begins just across the French-Spanish border from Puigcerdà. Both routes have bus services.

Petrol in Andorra is about 15% cheaper than in Spain and 25% cheaper than in France. There are a number of petrol stations near the borders.

The nearest major airports are at Barcelona (225 km south), Toulouse, France (180 km north) and Perpignan, France (166 km east). All three cities are linked to Andorra by bus or train-bus combinations.

Schedules of some of the following buses are subject to minor changes from time to time. You can check timetables by ringing the companies or the English-speaking municipal tourist office in Andorra la Vella.

Spain

La Hispano Andorrana (☎ 82 13 72) runs five or more buses daily between La Seu d'Urgell bus station and Plaça Guillemó in Andorra la Vella (30 minutes; 315 ptas).

Alsina Graells (☎ 82 73 79 in Andorra, ☎ 93-265 68 66 in Barcelona) runs five or six buses a day between Barcelona's Estació del Nord and Andorra la Vella's Estació de Autobusos on Carrer Bonaventura Riberaygua (four hours; 2500 ptas). Viatges Relax, the American Express agent in Andorra la Vella (see Money in that section) runs minibuses to/from Barcelona airport for 4500 ptas a person, one way. At the time of writing departures from the airport were at 1 and 5 pm, and from Andorra la Vella at 5 and 8 am.

Other buses to/from the Estació de Autobusos are by the Hispano Igualadina line to/from Tarragona (four hours; 1260 ptas) once daily; by Samar/Andor-Inter (☎ 82 62 89 in Andorra, ☎ 91-468 41 90 in Madrid) to/from Zaragoza and Madrid three times a week, and to/from Murcia and Cartagena once a week; and by Andor-Inter/Nort-Bus (☎ 82 62 89 in Andorra, ☎ 986-63 03 75 in Tuy) to/from Logroño, Valladolid, Orense, Pontevedra and Tuy (Galicia) twice weekly.

An interesting alternative approach is by train from Barcelona, Ripoll, Ribes de Freser or Puigcerdà to Latour-de-Carol in France. The 9.18 am train from Barcelona Sants (12.35 pm from Puigcerdà) connects with the 12.50 pm bus from Latour-de-Carol to Andorra la Vella – a total journey from Barcelona of 5½ hours for about 2400 ptas. An additional evening bus from July to late September connects with the 3.16 pm train from Barcelona Sants (6.17 pm from Puigcerdà). In the reverse direction the connections don't work quite so well and the trip takes 6¾ or 7¾ hours: it's no slower to get the 8.05 am bus from Andorra la Vella to La Seu d'Urgell, then the 9.30 am bus to Puigcerdà, then the 11.14 am train from Puigcerdà to Barcelona. See the Puigcerdà section of the Cataluña chapter for more on these trains, and the France section, following, for more on the Latour-de-Carol bus service.

France

Samar/Andor-Inter (☎ 82 62 89 in Andorra, ☎ 05 61 58 14 53 in Toulouse) runs a bus on Saturday morning from Andorra la Vella's Estació de Autobusos to the *gare routière* (bus station) in Toulouse, taking four hours for 2400 ptas. It returns from Toulouse on Sunday morning.

Otherwise you can take a train from Toulouse to one of three French stations near Andorra from which there are buses to Plaça Guillemó in Andorra la Vella via Pas de la Casa. The three stations are Ax-les-Thermes (☎ 05 61 64 20 72; 1½ to 1¾ hours from Toulouse; 97FF), L'Hospitalet-près-l'Andorre (☎ 05 61 05 20 78; 2¼ to 2¾ hours; 110FF) and Latour-de-Carol (☎ 04 68 04 80 69; 2½ to 3¼ hours; 122FF). The following buses all connect with trains from or to Toulouse, with waits varying from a couple of minutes on some Andorra-bound journeys to 2½ hours on some downward trips. If you're picking them up in mid-route – at Soldeu or Pas de la Casa, for instance – get to the stop in good time, as they sometimes go through earlier than scheduled.

From Ax-les-Thermes, Société Franco-Andorrane de Transports (SFAT; ☎ 82 13 72 in Andorra) runs a bus at 4.15 pm from May to October, with another at 12 noon from mid-July to mid-September, taking just over two hours to Andorra la Vella for 45FF (about 1100 ptas). Return buses leave Plaça Guillemó at 8.15 am (May to October), taking 2½ hours, and 11 am (mid-July to mid-September), taking 3¼ hours.

From L'Hospitalet-près-l'Andorre there's a daily bus all year, at some time between 5 and 6.30 pm depending on the season, run by La Hispano Andorrana (☎ 82 13 72 in Andorra), taking 1¾ hours to Andorra la Vella for 37FF (about 900 ptas). The return bus leaves Plaça Guillemó at 5.45 am.

From Latour-de-Carol, buses of Autos Pujol Huguet (☎ 82 13 72 in Andorra) leave at 12.50 pm all year and at 6.50 pm from July to late September, taking about two hours to Andorra la Vella for 45FF (about 1100 ptas). Return buses leave Plaça Guillemó at 7.45 am daily and 2.30 pm from July to late

September. These all connect at Latour-de-Carol with the narrow-gauge Train Jaune to/from Villefranche-de-Conflent, where there are further connections for Perpignan.

Getting Around

BUS

Cooperativa Interurbana (☎ 82 04 12) runs eight bus lines along the three main roads from Andorra la Vella, and Autobus Parroquial de La Massana i d'Ordino operates a few services from La Massana. See individual destination sections for detail on services, but bear in mind that schedules can change; the municipal tourist office in Andorra la Vella has current timetables.

CAR & MOTORCYCLE

Andorra has just four main roads. The CG1 (CG stands for Carretera General) runs 10 km from Andorra la Vella via Sant Julià de Lòria to the Spanish border, from where it's a further 10 km to La Seu d'Urgell. The CG2 runs 33 km from Andorra la Vella to Escaldes, Encamp, Canillo, Soldeu, Port d'Envalira – which has something in common with the road from Kashmir to Ladakh – and Pas de la Casa on the French border. The CG3 heads north from the capital via La Massana, Ordino and Llorts to the Ordino-Arcalís ski area. The CG4 branches west off the CG3 at La Massana up to the Pal ski area.

The speed limit in populated areas is 40 km/h. With all the traffic and twists and turns, it's almost impossible to reach the inter-hamlet speed limit of 90 km/h. Using a seat belt isn't compulsory, but motorcycle helmets are.

The biggest problems for drivers are Andorra la Vella's horrendous traffic jams – barely alleviated by the many police directing traffic at rush hour – and the ever-vigilant parking police. If you do not buy one of the coupons available from machines everywhere and place it on the dashboard, you will be fined for sure.

Andorra la Vella

Andorra la Vella (Vella – 'old' – is pronounced 'VEY-yah'), the capital of the princedom and its largest town (population 22,000), lies on the Riu Gran Valira in a valley just over 1000 metres above sea level, surrounded by mountains of up to 2400 metres. The town is given over almost entirely to the retailing of duty-free electronics and luxury goods. With the mountains, constant din of jackhammers and 'mall' architecture, you could almost be in Hong Kong, were it not for the snowcapped peaks and the lack of noodle shops!

Orientation

Andorra la Vella is strung out along one main street, whose name changes from Avinguda Príncep Benlloch to Avinguda Meritxell at Plaça Rebés. The little Barri Antic (historic quarter) stretches from the Església de Sant Esteve to Plaçeta del Puial. The town merges with the once-separate villages of Escaldes and Engordany to the east and Santa Coloma to the south-west.

Information

Tourist Offices The helpful municipal tourist office (Oficina d'Informació i Turisme; ☎ 82 71 17), on Plaça de la Rotonda, is open daily from 9 am to 1 pm and 3.30 to 8 pm (7 pm on Sunday). In July and August, it's open from 9 am to 9 pm (7 pm on Sunday). The office has maps, all sorts of brochures, stamps and telephone cards.

The national tourist office (Sindicat d'Iniciativa Oficina de Turisme; ☎ 82 02 14) is on Carrer Doctor Vilanova just down from Plaça Rebés. It is open Monday to Saturday from 10 am (9 am from July to September) to 1 pm and 3 to 7 pm, and on Sunday morning.

There's a tourist information kiosk (☎ 82 09 63) on Plaça dels Co-Prínceps, about one

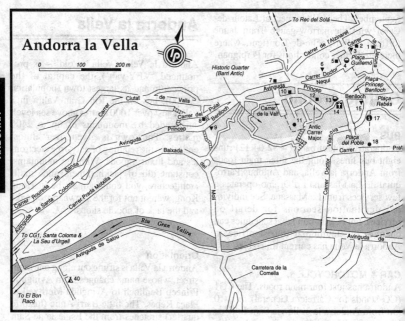

Andorra la Vella

km east of the STA telephone office in Escaldes.

Money Banks are open Monday to Friday from 9 am to 1 pm and 3 to 5 pm and on Saturday from 9 am to noon. Very few charge a commission, but rates vary. There are banks every 100 metres or so along Avinguda Meritxell and Avinguda Príncep Benlloch in the town centre, most with ATMs. Crèdit Andorrà, next to the river at Avinguda Meritxell 80, has a 24-hour banknote exchange machine that accepts 15 different currencies.

American Express (☎ 82 20 44; fax 82 70 55) is represented by Viatges Relax, a travel agency at Carrer Roc dels Escolls 12. It is open Monday to Friday from 9.30 am to 1 pm and 3.30 to 7 pm and Saturday from 9.30 am to 1 pm. The office cannot change money (you have to go to a bank for that), but it can reissue a lost or stolen American Express card, provide a reimbursement for lost or stolen travellers' cheques, and sell travellers' cheques against card-holders' personal cheques.

Post & Communications La Poste (☎ 82 04 08), the main French post office, is at Carrer Pere d'Urg 1. It is open weekdays from 8.30 am to 2.30 pm and Saturday from 9 am to noon. During July and August, weekday hours are 9 am to 7 pm. All purchases must be made with French francs and almost no one here speaks Spanish.

Correus i Telègrafs (☎ 82 02 57), the main Spanish post office, is three blocks away at Carrer Joan Maragall 10. It is open weekdays from 8.30 am to 2.30 pm and Saturday from 9.30 am to 1 pm. It accepts pesetas only.

You can make international telephone calls from street pay phones or from the Servei de Telecomunicacions d'Andorra (STA; ☎ 82 10 21) at Avinguda Meritxell 110, daily from 9 am to 9 pm. STA also has

ANDORRA

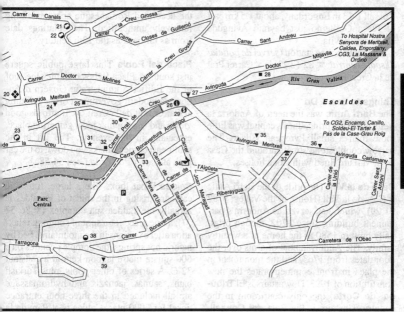

PLACES TO STAY

1 Hotel Florida
2 Residència Benazet
5 Hotel Les Arcades
7 Hôtel Pyrénées
8 Habitacions Baró
10 Pensió La Rosa
12 Hostal Calones
16 Hotel Galaxia
25 Hotel Costa &
   Restaurant Martí
28 Hotel Residència Albert
32 Novotel Andorra
40 Camping Valira

PLACES TO EAT

3 El Timbaler del Bruch
6 Pizzeria Primavera

9 Tex-Mex Café
15 Pans & Company
24 Kentucky Fried
   Chicken & Pizza Hut
27 Pizzeria La Mossegada
35 Pans & Company
36 McDonald's
39 McDonald's

OTHER

4 Plaça Guillemó Bus
   Stop
11 Casa de la Vall
13 Plaça Príncep Benlloch
   Bus Stop
14 Església de Sant
   Esteve
17 National Tourist Office

18 Public Lift to Plaça del
   Poble
19 Viatges Relax/
   American Express
20 Pyrénées Department
   Store
21 French Embassy
22 French Consulate
23 Spanish Embassy
26 Municipal Tourist
   Office
29 Crédit Andorrá
30 Casa del Llibre
31 Police Station
33 French Post Office
34 Spanish Post Office
37 STA
38 Estació de Autobusos

a fax service Monday to Friday from 9 am to 5 pm.

Travel Agencies Viatges Relax (see the Money section) is a full-service travel agency. It can issue French and Spanish rail tickets, and air tickets.

Bookshops Casa del Llibre on Carrer Fiter Rossell has a good selection of books, some in English.

Medical & Emergency Services The modern Hospital Nostra Senyora de Meritxell (☎ 86 80 00) is at Avinguda Fiter i

Rossell 1-13 in Engordany, about 1.5 km east of Plaça Guillemó just beyond Avinguda Doctor Mitjavila.

The main police station (*servei de policia/despatx central*; ☎ 82 12 22) is at Carrer Prat de la Creu 16.

Things to See & Do

The **Barri Antic** was the heart of Andorra la Vella when the princedom's capital was little more than a small Pyrenean village. The narrow cobblestone streets around the Casa de la Vall are lined with stone houses.

Casa de la Vall The pride of the Barri Antic is Casa de la Vall (House of the Valley; ☎ 82 91 29), which has served as Andorra's parliament building since 1702, though originally built in 1580 as the home of a wealthy family. The Andorran coat of arms over the door dates from 1763, and the monument in the plaça in front commemorates the new constitution of 1993. Downstairs is **El Tribunal de Corts**, the only courtroom in the country. Upstairs is the **Sala del Consell**, which has to be one of the cosiest parliament chambers in the world. The 28 members of the Andorran parliament sit along the walls, the government ministers sit in the blue chairs in the middle, while the three red chairs at the end of the room are for the two síndics and the parliamentary secretary. The **Chest of the Seven Locks** (Set Panys) once held Andorra's most important official documents and could be opened only if a key-bearing representative from each of the parishes was present.

Free guided tours of the Casa de la Vall (sometimes in English) are given about once an hour on weekdays from 9 am to 1 pm and 3 to 7 pm: they're very popular and you're advised to book a week ahead to ensure a place, but individuals can sometimes join a group at the last minute.

Església de Sant Esteve Andorra la Vella's parish church is at the edge of the Barri Antic across the street from Plaça Príncep Benlloch. It dates from the 11th century, though the interior is now mainly modern, with only

the decorated Romanesque apse remaining relatively unmodified. The paintings date from as far back as the 13th century.

Plaça del Poble This large public square just south of Plaça Rebés occupies the roof of the Edifici Administratiu Govern d'Andorra, a modern government office building at Carrer Prat de la Creu 64. It affords good views and is a popular local gathering place, especially in the evening. The lift in the south-east corner whisks you down to the car park at Carrer Prat de la Creu 54-58.

Caldea What looks like a large, futuristic cathedral rising in the midst of Escaldes is actually the Caldea spa complex (☎ 86 57 77), a fine place for a spot of soothing relaxation after exertions in the mountains. Fed by natural hot springs, the complex centres on a 600 square metre lagoon kept at a constant 32°C. A series of other pools, plus Turkish baths, saunas, jacuzzis and hydromassage are all included in the three-hour entrance ticket for 2000 ptas. Caldea is at Parc de la Mola 10, just east of Avinguda Fiter i Rossell, the continuation of Avinguda Doctor Mitjavila, and about a two-km walk from Plaça Guillemó. It is open daily from 10 am to 11 pm (last entry at 9 pm).

Places to Stay – bottom end

Camping *Camping Valira* (☎ 82 23 84), open all year at the southern edge of town on Avinguda de Salou, charges 500 ptas per person and the same for a tent or car. There's a small indoor swimming pool. Telephone reservations are accepted; during July and August, they are accepted a maximum of 24 hours in advance. *Camping Riberaygua* (☎ 82 66 99) and *Camping Santa Coloma* (☎ 82 88 99), both in Santa Coloma about 2.5 km south-west of Plaça Guillemó, are also open all year, with marginally lower prices.

Pensiones, Hostales & Hotels The helpful, 15-room *Residència Benazet* (☎ 82 06 98) at Carrer La Llacuna 21 (1st floor), just off

Plaça Guillemó, has large, serviceable rooms with washbasin, for up to four people at 1300 ptas a person. Bathrooms are shared. Nearby at Plaça Guillemó 5, *Hotel Les Arcades* (☎ 82 13 55) has singles/doubles with shower and toilet from 2000/3000 to 3000/5400 ptas depending on the season.

In the Barri Antic, *Pensió La Rosa* (☎ 82 18 10), Antic Carrer Major 18, has nondescript singles/doubles for 1700/3000 ptas and triples/quads for 3900/5200 ptas. The quiet *Hostal Calones* (☎ 82 13 12) at Antic Carrer Major 8 has unadorned and slightly dilapidated singles/doubles with large bathrooms for 2800/3700 ptas. *Habitacions Baró* (☎ 82 14 84) at Carrer del Puial 21 is one of the cheapest places in town, with rooms for 1300/2600 ptas, or 1800/3600 ptas with bath. It's worth ringing first as sometimes it's left unattended. To find it, climb the steps opposite Avinguda Príncep Benlloch 53.

Hotel Costa (☎ 82 14 39) at Avinguda Meritxell 44 has basic but clean rooms for 1300 ptas per person. Reception is on the 3rd floor; take the stairs on the right of the ground-floor shopping arcade. The 21 room *Hotel Residència Albert* (☎ 82 01 56), east of the centre at Avinguda Doctor Mitjavila 16, has singles/doubles with shower for 1500/3000 ptas, or doubles with shower for 3500 ptas.

Places to Stay – middle & top end

The *Hotel Galaxia* (☎ 82 69 75) is at Avinguda Meritxell 9 on the 3rd floor. As you walk into the arcade, take the lift or stairs on the right. Large, plain singles and doubles with shower, toilet, TV and video are 3500 ptas; singles/doubles with a view are 4000/5000 ptas. Reception is open daily from 12.30 to 7 pm.

The 74 room *Hotel Pyrénées* (☎ 86 00 06; fax 82 02 65) at Avinguda Príncep Benlloch 20 is only one block from Casa de la Vall. It has a tennis court and a swimming pool behind it. Singles/doubles cost from 5300/8700 to 5900/9900 ptas including breakfast. Ask for a room away from the street if you want a good night's sleep.

The delightful *Hotel Florida* (☎ 82 01 05;

fax 86 19 25) at Carrer La Llacuna 15 (one block from Plaça Guillemó) has modern doubles for 6500 ptas (including breakfast) in the low season. The price jumps to 7500 or 8500 ptas on the weekend, around Christmas and Easter, in August and at the height of the ski season.

The *Novotel Andorra* (☎ 86 11 16; fax 86 11 20) on Carrer Prat de la Creu is devoid of character but has all the mod cons you could hope for. Singles/doubles start at 10,500/13,000 ptas.

Places to Eat

El Timbaler del Bruch on Plaça Guillemó is a good spot for breakfast or a light meal at any time of day. Excellent torrades (open toasted sandwiches), with generous toppings, cost from 375 ptas. On the same square, the restaurant at the *Hotel Les Arcades* has a decent three course Spanish menú for 800 ptas. *Pizzeria Primavera*, round the corner at Carrer Doctor Nequi 4, has pizzas and pasta for 500 to 750 ptas and a menú for 900 ptas. It closes on Wednesday. In the Barri Antic, *Hostal Calones* has a much better menú for 1500 ptas. Fancy Mexican in Andorra? *Tex-Mex Café* at Avinguda Príncep Benlloch 49 has tacos with chilli (850 ptas) and Mexican spare ribs (1200 ptas).

The restaurant of the *Hotel Pyrénées* at Avinguda Príncep Benlloch 20 serves Catalan, French and Spanish dishes amidst sparkling chandeliers and two-tone tablecloths. The menú costs 2500 ptas, and meat and fish dishes are 1500 to 2500 ptas, but there are much cheaper platos combinados – from 475 ptas. This place is open from 1 to 3 pm and 8 to 10 pm.

Pans & Company at Plaça Rebés 2 and Avinguda Meritxell 91 is good for hot and cold baguettes with a range of fillings for 300 to 400 ptas.

Restaurant Martí (☎ 82 43 84), upstairs at Avinguda Meritxell 44, has a rather ordinary menú for 935 ptas, a better one for 1425 ptas, and platos combinados from 590 ptas. It's open daily from noon to 3.30 pm (4 pm on the weekend) and 8 to 10 pm (10.30 pm on the weekend).

Pizzeria La Mossegada overlooks the river at Avinguda Doctor Mitjavila 3. Pizzas cost between 750 and 875 ptas, or there are burgers and grilled meat dishes from 850 to 1800 ptas. It's closed on Wednesday.

If you find that all the corporate products on sale in Andorra la Vella are making you hungry for multinational food, *McDonald's*, on Avinguda de Tarragona opposite the bus station, and at Avinguda Meritxell 105, is open weekdays to 11 pm and to 1 am on the weekend. Or there's *Kentucky Fried Chicken* and *Pizza Hut* together at one convenient location: Avinguda Meritxell 26.

The best place for real Catalan cooking is the up-market *El Bon Racó* at Avinguda de Salou 86 in Santa Coloma, about a km west of Camping Valira. Meat – especially xai (lamb) – roasted in an open hearth is the speciality (1200 ptas), but you might also try escudella, a Catalan stew of chicken, sausage and vegetables (650 ptas).

The big supermarket on the 2nd floor of the *Pyrénées* department store at Avinguda Meritxell 21 is open Monday to Saturday from 9.30 am to 8 pm and on Sunday to 7 pm.

Entertainment
Cultural events sometimes take place at Plaça del Poble, where you'll find Andorra la Vella's theatre and its music academy. Contact the tourist office for details of festivals, dance performances etc.

Things to Buy
Most of Andorra la Vella's duty-free shops are strung along the eastern part of Avinguda Príncep Benlloch, the length of Avinguda Meritxell and on into its continuation, Avinguda Carlemany in Escaldes.

Getting There & Away
Buses to Sant Julià de Lòria, La Seu d'Urgell and France leave from Plaça Guillemó. Buses to other places in Spain use the Estació d'Autobusos on Carrer Bonaventura Riberaygua, south of the river. Buses to other places in Andorra leave from the Plaça Príncep Benlloch stop near the Església de Sant Esteve. For details of Spain and France services, see this chapter's introductory Getting There & Away section; for services within Andorra, see the relevant destination sections.

Taxi You can order a taxi in Andorra la Vella by ringing ☎ 86 30 00.

AROUND ANDORRA LA VELLA
Església de Santa Coloma
The Church of Santa Coloma, mentioned in documents from the 9th century, is Andorra's oldest, but its pre-Romanesque form has been modified over the centuries. The four-storey, almost-round bell tower was built in the 12th century, apparently in two stages. All the church's 12th-century Romanesque murals, except one entitled *Agnus Dei* (Lamb of God), were taken to a museum in Berlin for conservation in the 1930s and are still there. The church is 2.5 km south-west of Plaça Guillemó along the road to La Seu d'Urgell.

Hiking
The **Rec del Solà** (altitude 1100 metres) is an almost flat, 2.5-km path that follows a small irrigation canal running along the hillside just above the north side of Andorra la Vella. Another option is to hike south-eastward from Andorra la Vella's Carretera de la Comella up to the **Refugi de Prat Primer** mountain refuge (2250 metres), where it's possible to stay overnight. The walk up takes about three hours from Andorra la Vella.

From Carrer dels Barrers in Santa Coloma, a path leads north-west up the hill to the **Capella de Sant Vicenç d'Enclar** (20 minutes), which was the site of an important castle before the Pareatges of the 13th century, which banned castles in Andorra. Nowadays, in addition to the view, you'll see a recently reconstructed church, a cemetery, several silos and some ruins. A trail continues up the valley to **Bony de la Pica** (2405 metres) on the Spanish border, from which ou can follow the crest north-east to **Pic l'Enclar** (2383 metres) and **Pic de Carroi** 2334 metres), which overlooks Santa Colona from the north – a day's walk there and back.

North-Western Andorra

La Massana, six km north of Andorra la Vella, is the gateway to the ski centres of Arinsal and Pal. From La Massana the CG3 continues north into the mountainous Parròquia d'Ordino, arguably the country's most beautiful parish, with slate and fieldstone farmhouses, gushing streams and picturesque stone bridges. It has plenty of fine walks and, in winter, skiing at the Ordino-Arcalís ski area.

LA MASSANA

The town of La Massana (population 2164; altitude 1252 metres) is much less attractive than its smaller neighbours a few km north in the Parròquia d'Ordino, but it has a number of hotels and some good restaurants.

Orientation & Information

The tourist office (☎ 83 56 93) is at Plaça de la Caseta d'Informació, on La Massana's main street, the CG3.

Places to Stay

Camping Santa Catarina (☎ 83 50 65 at the proprietors' home), in a grassy field next to a rushing stream, just outside La Massana by the CG3 to Ordino, is open from late June to late September. Charges are 350 ptas per person and 300 ptas per tent and per car. Buses to Ordino stop a bit down the hill from the camping ground opposite the Hotel Les Costes de Giberga.

Hotel Naudi (☎ 83 50 95), near the tourist office in the centre of town on the CG3, has singles/doubles from 2800/3300 ptas including breakfast. The *Hotel Palanques* (☎ 83 50 07), on the corner of the CG3 and Carrer Major, which leads up the hill to the church

and police station, has rooms for about 2400/3600 ptas.

Places to Eat

The pizzeria-restaurant on the ground floor of the *Hotel Naudi*, with pizzas from 700 to 1300 ptas, is open daily from 12.30 to 3 pm and 7.30 to 10.30 pm (or later). It's closed on Wednesday in November, January, May and June. The *Restaurant El Siurell*, nearby on the CG3, has inexpensive plats combinats (combination platters).

Two of Andorra's better restaurants, *La Borda de l'Avi* and *La Borda Raubert*, are a couple of km north of La Massana on the road to Arinsal. Both are 'country-style' places with open hearths and have lots of grills, Andorran specialities and good wine selections.

Getting There & Away

Buses from Andorra la Vella to La Massana (105 ptas) run daily about twice an hour from 7.30 am to 9 pm. The same buses continue to Ordino.

ESTACIONS D'ESQUÍ ARINSAL & PAL

Arinsal (☎ 83 58 22; fax 83 62 42), five km north-west of La Massana, has good skiing and snowboarding for beginners and intermediates, and a lively après-ski scene. Pal (☎ 83 62 36; fax 83 62 42), nine km from La Massana, has gentler slopes which make it an ideal ski resort for families.

Skiing

Arinsal has 14 lifts, 28 km of pistes and a vertical drop of 1010 metres. Pal has 14 lifts, 30 km of pistes and a vertical drop of 578 metres. Lift passes at either cost 2600/6475 ptas for one/three days in the low season, and 3000/7475 ptas in the high season. Combined tickets for Arinsal, Pal and Ordino-Arcalís are also available: the cheapest are two days in the high season for 6100 ptas, five days in the low season for 12,200 ptas, or five days in the high season for 14,000 ptas. There's also a free bus system that takes skiers and snowboarders between the three ski resorts, giving access to a total 82 km of pistes.

Hiking

From the bottom of the Arinsal ski slopes, a trail leads north-west then west to a 2260 metre-high lake called **Estany de les Truites**. The walk up takes around 1½ hours. The *Refugi de Coma Pedrosa*, Andorra's only staffed mountain refuge, is just above the lake. Cost per night is 900 ptas, and meals are available (dinner 1500 ptas). The refuge is normally open from June to late September, but you should confirm this with a tourist office or by ringing ☎ 83 50 93 or the Spanish number ☎ 908-14 55 17 (from Andorra ☎ 00-34-08-14 55 17). From the lake, it's about a further 3½ hours to the highest point in Andorra, 2942-metre **Pic de Coma Pedrosa**.

Other Activities

From July to mid-September, chair lifts open at Pal and Arinsal and mountain bikes are available at Pal for 750/1900/2600 ptas an hour/half-day/whole day. Horse riding costs 1600 ptas an hour.

Places to Stay

The large *Camping Xixerella* (☎ 83 66 13) between Pal and Arinsal is open all year and has an outdoor swimming pool. Charges are 425 ptas per adult, per tent and per car.

In Arinsal the basic *Hotel Baró* (☎ 83 51 75) has rooms for 4000 ptas, single or double. One of the more popular top-end places is the *Hotel Solana* (☎ 83 51 27; fax 83 73 95), which has large rooms with bath and toilet for 5500/8000 ptas. There's no accommodation at Pal.

Entertainment

A late-night bar in Arinsal that's popular with English skiers and occasionally has live music is *Quo Vadis*. The *Pub Solana* at the Hotel Solana is the place for dancing.

Getting There & Away

Buses leave Andorra la Vella for Arinsal (175 ptas) via La Massana at 9.30 am and 1 and 6 pm. The last one back from Arinsal is at 3 pm. In the ski season there are seven buses daily from La Massana to the Arinsal ski slopes and four to Pal.

ORDINO

Ordino (population 1008; 1304 metres) is large as Andorran villages go, but despite recent development (holiday homes and English-speaking residents abound), it remains peaceful and Andorran in character, with most building still in stone.

Orientation & Information

The tourist office (☎ 83 69 63), on Highway CG3, is open Monday to Saturday from 9 am to 1 pm and 3 to 7 pm and on Sunday from 9 am to noon. The Banc Agricol i Comercial d'Andorra, with an ATM, opposite the tourist office, is open weekdays from 9 am to 1 pm and 3 to 5 pm. Saturday hours are 9 am to noon. For the central Plaça Major, which has more banks, turn right 50 metres up the hill from the tourist office. Ordino has French and Spanish post offices.

Museu d'Areny i Plandolit

The ancestral home of one of Andorra's most illustrious families, the Areny Plandolits, built in the 17th century and modified in the mid-19th century, is now a museum (☎ 83 69 08). The family's most illustrious member was Don Guillem, síndic and leader of the political reform movement of the 1860s. The house has furnished rooms (the library and dining room are particularly fine) and is of typically rugged Andorran design. Half-hour guided visits cost 200 ptas. It is open Tuesday to Saturday from 9.30 am to 1.30 pm and 3 to 6.30 pm, and on Sunday morning.

Hiking

From the hamlet of Segudet, just east of Ordino, a path goes up through fir woods to the **Coll d'Ordino** (1980 metres), about 1½ hours from Ordino. **Pic de Casamanya** (2740 metres), which has fine long-distance views, is about two hours walk north from Coll d'Ordino.

Places to Stay & Eat

Just off Plaça Major, in the alley behind the Crèdit Andorrà bank, is the *Hotel Quim* (☎ 83 50 13), which is run by a friendly older woman. Doubles/triples with shower cost 3000/3500 ptas. Much more expensive is the *Hotel Santa Bàrbara de la Vall d'Ordino* (☎ 83 71 00) on Plaça Major, which has doubles from 6000 ptas.

The *Restaurant Armengol* on Plaça Major has an excellent menú of Catalan dishes for 1650 ptas. The *Quim* restaurant next door has menús for 1350 and 1500 ptas. A small grocery, *Comerç Fleca Font*, just opposite, is open from 7 am to 2 pm and 4 to 8 pm daily except Sunday afternoon. Spring water flows from two spouts right outside the door.

Getting There & Away

The bus from Andorra la Vella (125 ptas) runs daily about every 30 minutes from 7.30 am to 8.30 pm.

LLORTS

The tiny mountain hamlet of Llorts (population 105; 1413 metres), on the CG3 six km north of Ordino, has traditional architecture set amidst tobacco fields and a near-pristine mountain setting. This is one of the most unadulterated spots in the whole country. Llorts is pronounced 'yorts'.

Hiking

A trail leads west from the village up the valley of the Riu de l'Angonella to a group of lakes, the **Estanys de l'Angonella**, at about 2300 metres. Count on about three hours to get there.

From slightly north of the village of El Serrat (population 60; 1600 metres), which is about three km up the CG3 from Llorts, a secondary road leads four km east to the Borda de Sorteny mountain refuge (1969 metres), one of the largest in the princedom with space for 30. From there, a trail goes south-east to **Estany de l'Estanyó** lake (2339 metres). Another heads east up to the Collada dels Meners pass (2713 metres; about 1½ hours), from which you can go north to **Pic de la Serrera** (2913 metres; 30

minutes) or a couple of hours south and west via **Pic de la Cabaneta** (2863 metres) to **Pic de l'Estanyó** (2915 metres), Andorra's second-highest. In about eight hours from Borda de Sorteny you could bag all three peaks and continue via the Coll d'Arenes pass (2539 metres) and Pic de Casamanya to the Coll d'Ordino (see the Ordino section), enjoying many great panoramas along the way.

From Arans (population 80; 1385 metres), a village two km south of Llorts, a trail goes north-eastward to **Bordes de l'Ensegur** (2180 metres), where there is an old shepherd's hut.

The tiny, partly Romanesque **Església de Sant Martí** in La Cortinada, one km south of Arans, has 12th-century frescos in remarkably good condition. They were only discovered in 1968.

Places to Stay

Some 200 metres north of Llorts, *Camping Els Pardassos* (☎ 85 00 22), one of the most beautiful camping grounds in Andorra, is surrounded by forested mountains and has its own spring. Open from July to the middle of September, it costs 275 ptas per person, per tent and per car. Bring your own provisions.

Hotel Vilaró (☎ 85 02 25), 200 metres south of the village limits, has singles/doubles with washbasin and bidet for 2100/3925 ptas. It is open all year. Up at El Serrat, the *Hotel Subirà* (☎ 85 00 37) has fabulous views of the valley and surrounding mountains. It is open all year, with rooms at 4500/6000 ptas.

Getting There & Away

Buses to Llorts and El Serrat (215 ptas) leave Andorra la Vella at 1 and 8.30 pm. Downward buses leave El Serrat at 7.45 am and 2.45 pm. In summer a few minibuses a day from Ordino to the Estació d'Esquí Ordino-Arcalís go through Llorts and El Serrat.

ESTACIÓ D'ESQUÍ ORDINO-ARCALÍS

The Ordino-Arcalís ski area (☎ 85 01 21; fax 83 73 00) is in Andorra's far north-western corner. Though the slopes are mostly good for beginners and intermediates, experts can have some fun on a mogul run, and there are good prospects for ski touring in the area. A number of the rugged peaks in this beautiful mountainous area reach 2800 metres.

Orientation & Information
Lifts start from three car parks along the road. Restaurant La Coma Altitude at the end of the paved road near the uppermost car park at an altitude of 2200 metres is a useful landmark. The Telecadira La Coma chair lift rises opposite it.

The closest accommodation is at El Serrat and Llorts. There are more hotels, as well as banks and post offices, in Ordino.

Skiing
In winter, Ordino-Arcalís has enough snow and a decent selection of runs, but it can be rather cold and is often windy. There are 12 lifts (mostly drag lifts) covering 24 km of pistes at altitudes between 1940 and 2600 metres. A lift ticket costs 2650/6700 ptas for one/three days in the low season, or 3300/8200 ptas in the high season. See the Estaciós d'Esquí Arinsal & Pal section for information on combined tickets with those two resorts. Ski equipment can be rented for about 1500 ptas, and snowboards with boots for 2500 to 3000 ptas.

Hiking
The trail behind the Restaurant La Coma Altitude leads eastward across the hill, then north and over the ridge to a group of beautiful mountain lakes called **Estanys de Tristaina**. The walk to the first lake takes about 30 minutes.

In summer, you can also start walking from the 2700 metre top of Telecadira La Coma, which operates daily from late June to early September from 10 am to 6 pm. Summer fees are 425/750 ptas one way/return.

Other Activities
The souvenir kiosk opposite the Telecadira La Coma's lower station rents mountain bikes from late June to early September

(daily from 10 am to 6 pm; closed Monday in June and July). Charges are 625 ptas for one hour, 1775 ptas for a half-day and 3100 ptas for a full day.

Places to Eat
Restaurant La Coma Altitude, with both snacks and a full menu, is open from December to early May. From late June to early September, it's open daily from 10 am to 6 pm (closed Monday in June and July).

Getting There & Away
In the ski season there are five shuttle buses a day between Arinsal, La Massana and the first car park. There are also four minibuses daily from Ordino to the ski station, passing through Llorts and El Serrat, some of which operate in summer too.

Eastern Andorra

The best skiing in Andorra is here, at Soldeu-El Tarter and Pas de la Casa-Grau Roig.

ENCAMP
The town of Encamp (altitude 1266 metres) has one of the few museums in Andorra: the **Museu Nacional de l'Automòbil** (National Automobile Museum; ☎ 83 22 66). Located at Avinguda Príncep Episcopal 64, it has about 100 cars dating from 1898 to 1950 as well as 50 antique motorcycles and 100 bicycles. It is open Tuesday to Saturday from 10 am to 1 pm and 4 to 7 pm, Sunday from 10 am to 1 pm. Visits are by guided tour only (200 ptas).

Most of the **Església Sant Romà de les Bons**, a km or so north of Encamp, dates from the 12th century. The Romanesque frescos in the apse, however, are reproductions of the originals, which are now in the Museu Nacional d'Art de Catalunya in Barcelona.

Buses run from Andorra la Vella to Encamp (105 ptas) every 20 or 30 minutes from 7.30 am to 9.30 pm.

ANDORRA

ESTACIÓ D'ESQUÍ SOLDEU-EL TARTER

The Soldeu-El Tarter ski area (☎ 85 11 51; fax 85 13 37) is 19 km north-east of Andorra la Vella, midway between the town of Canillo, which has a splendid Romanesque church (Sant Joan de Caselles) dating from the 11th century, and Port d'Envalira. Soldeu and El Tarter, both popular with British and French skiers, are separate villages two km apart, but their ski lift systems interconnect.

Information

The Crèdit Andorrà bank just up the road from the Soldeu bus stop has an ATM and is open Monday to Friday from 9 am to noon and 3 to 6 pm. The post office across the road is open Monday to Saturday from 10 am to noon and Monday to Friday from 4 to 5 pm.

Skiing

The 21 lifts, which are mostly tow lines, connect 60 km of runs with a vertical drop of 850 metres. The skiing is similar to that at Pas de la Casa except that the black runs into the villages are steeper and more picturesque. Soldeu, higher than El Tarter at 1826 metres, has the bulk of the accommodation and facilities.

There are plenty of shops renting ski equipment from about 1500 ptas a day (a snowboard and boots go for about 2500 ptas). Lift tickets for a half-day/day/three days cost 2100/3100/7650 ptas in the low season, 2600/3600/8700 ptas in the high season.

Other Activities

From mid-July to the end of August, chair lifts operate up to 2400 metres (900 ptas return or 2000 ptas for a day pass). Mountain bikes, which can be taken aboard and ridden down, rent for 650/1900/2600 ptas for an hour/half-day/day.

Places to Stay & Eat

Most of the accommodation and restaurants are along the main road, the CG2. In Soldeu, *Hotel Soldeu* (☎ 85 10 35; fax 85 29 29) is not bad for the price with doubles for 2850 ptas. *Residència Supervalira* (☎ 85 10 82;

fax 85 10 62) has better-value rooms – 2400 ptas single or double – but is two km up the road from Soldeu towards Pas de la Casa. A more up-market place to stay is the popular *Sport Hotel* (☎ 85 10 51; fax 85 15 93), which has singles/doubles for 8500/14,000 ptas.

Snack-Bar Bonell on the way down to the Soldeu ski lifts has reasonable platos combinados from 750 ptas, and pizzas. The restaurant at the *Hotel Soldeu* has tasty menús for 1200 or 1500 ptas. *Restaurant Espiolets* up on the Soldeu ski slopes, open from December to April, has also been recommended.

Entertainment

There is a lively night scene at Soldeu-El Tarter in winter. A popular bar is *Hardrock Soldeu*. *Piccadilly Pub* by the Sport Hotel is a typically British pub which occasionally has bands. The small (and crowded) *Disco Z* by the Soldeu bus stop plays dance music late into the night.

Getting There & Away

Buses run from Andorra la Vella to El Tarter and Soldeu (325 ptas; 40 minutes) hourly from 9 am to 8 pm. Both places are also on the routes of buses between Andorra la Vella and the French railheads of Ax-les-Thermes, L'Hospitalet-près-l'Andorre and Latour-de-Carol (see this chapter's introductory Getting There & Away section). You can check bus times at the Soldeu post office.

ESTACIÓ D'ESQUÍ PAS DE LA CASA-GRAU ROIG

Pas de la Casa and Grau Roig are linked ski stations either side of the Port d'Envalira pass, boasting the highest skiing in Andorra at 2050 and 2600 metres, with the country's most reliable snow conditions. Grau Roig, with just one hotel, is on the west side of the col, two km south of the CG2; Pas de la Casa, on the French border, is a large, unattractive village with numerous shops catering to French visitors.

Information

Pas de la Casa's tourist office (☎ 85 52 92) is on the other side of the road from the Andorran customs station. Hotel reservations can be made by calling the accommodation service (☎ 86 20 00).

The Crèdit Andorrà bank at Carrer Sant Jordi 7 is open Monday to Friday from 9.30 am to 1 pm and 2 to 4 pm. It changes major currencies and travellers' cheques and gives cash advances on credit cards. The post office, opposite Carrer de les Abelletes 4, is open Monday to Friday from 10 am to 1 pm and Saturday until noon.

Skiing

The combined ski area (☎ 85 56 92) has a network of 27 lifts and 75 km of pistes. The skiing and snowboarding are well suited to beginners and intermediates. Ski touring is also possible in the area. Several ski rental shops hire complete ski equipment for around 1500 ptas and snowboards for around 2500 ptas a day. Lift tickets are 2300/3300/7900 ptas for a half-day/day/seven days in the low season, and 2650/3800/9100 ptas in the high season.

Places to Stay & Eat

There is plenty of accommodation in Pas de la Casa, most of it with a wide seasonal price range. One of the least expensive places is

Hotel Llac Negre (☎ 85 51 98; fax 85 51 37) at Carrer Sant Jordi 43. Its basic singles/doubles are from 3000/3750 to 5000/6250 ptas. A reasonable mid-range place is *Hotel Les 4 Estacions* (☎ 85 53 29) at Avinguda d'Encamp 9, with rooms from 4000 to 9000 ptas, single or double. At the top end, *Hotel Residència Envalira* (☎ 85 50 95; fax 85 53 71) at Carrer Bearn 8 has singles/doubles from 3840/5880 to 5985/ 10,170 ptas.

Many people stay for a week or longer in Pas de la Casa on full or half-board basis at their hotel. A popular place for breakfast is the bar at *Hotel Els Cims* at Carrer Major 4-6. *Restaurant Les Neus* at Carrer Comte de Foix offers inexpensive menús from 1300 ptas. At the top end, the *Restaurant Marseillais* at Carrer Bearn 10 has à-la-carte meals for about 1800 ptas.

Getting There & Away

From Andorra la Vella, there is one bus a day at 9 am to Pas de la Casa (560 ptas). It returns at 11.30 am. In winter there are an extra three buses daily to/from Andorra la Vella and Soldeu-El Tarter. Pas de la Casa is also on the routes of the buses between Andorra la Vella and the French railheads of Ax-les-Thermes, L'Hospitalet-près-l'Andorre and Latour-de-Carol (see this chapter's introductory Getting There & Away section).

Aragón

Little explored by foreign tourists, sparsely populated Aragón is caught between several worlds, flanked by France, Cataluña, the Basque territory of Navarra and the north-eastern reaches of Spain's Castilian heartland.

Aragón's northern strip, taking in some of the best of the Spanish side of the Pyrenees, offers a wealth of walking and skiing possibilities that could easily be carried over to the French side of the frontier. Along the valleys and down into the lower pre-Pyrenees hills further south is a surprising mix of pretty villages, lonely castles and venerable monasteries.

The bigger cities are certainly not among the country's most enticing, but lovers of monuments are in for a treat in places like Teruel and Zaragoza, where you can admire samples of a particularly striking version of *mudéjar* architecture.

Central Aragón consists mainly of a forlorn series of treeless depressions and high, bald plateaus. It was the scene of some of the nastiest fighting in the Spanish Civil War, and the two sides could hardly have chosen a more comfortless place to do combat. Just when you think you have a measure of the land, however, you come up against the mysterious mountain region of El Maestrazgo in the south, peppered with isolated hamlets and little-known villages, many of which are of more than passing monumental interest.

Although various local culinary specialities are much touted, there is little to differentiate average Aragonese cooking from the efforts of its Castilian neighbours. *Ternasco*, basically lamb's ribs, is a standard local dish, and ham shavings make an occasional appearance as the one-million-and-first variation on the Spanish pig theme.

Overshadowed by the fame of neighbouring La Rioja and Navarra in the wine production game, Aragón doesn't produce a bad drop. Of the four areas at work, wines

HIGHLIGHTS

- Skiing in the Pyrenees (Candanchú, Astún, Panticosa & El Formigal)
- Summertime hiking in the Parque Nacional de Ordesa y Monte Perdido in the Pyrenees
- Eating & drinking in El Tubo, the heart of Zaragoza
- Villages of stone houses in the Valles de Ansó & Hecho
- The *mudéjar* towers of Teruel
- The brick-red medieval town of Albarracín
- Getting well off the beaten track in the hill *pueblos* of El Maestrazgo

from the Cariñena zone just south of Zaragoza are among the best.

Though Aragón gave its name to one of the Iberian Peninsula's great medieval kingdoms, the so-called Crown of Aragón was actually dominated by Cataluña, with which Aragón itself united in the 12th century. Territories ranging from Valencia and the Balearic Islands to Sicily and Sardinia were conquered in the name of Aragón, but this was actually the work of the more commercially minded and cosmopolitan Catalan half of the joint kingdom. The feudal nobility of Aragón proper took some revenge on the Catalans in 1412 when they engineered the election of a Castilian, Fernando of Antequera, to the vacant throne. This set the scene for the union of Aragón and Castilla later in

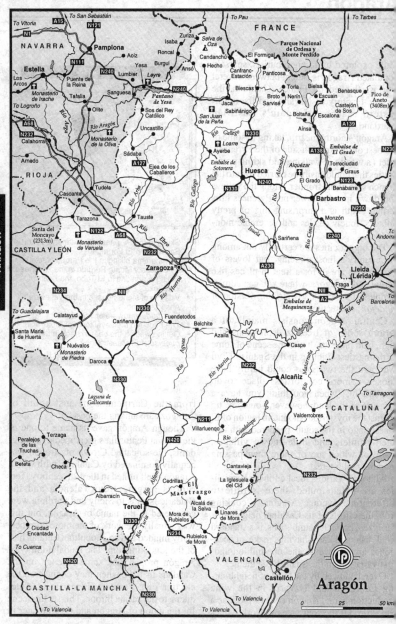

Aragón

he century under their respective monarchs 'ernando and Isabel, which effectively gave irth to the entity we now know as Spain.

Those planning to spend any length of ime in Aragón are advised to get hold of the *Guía de Servicios Turísticos de Aragón*, published by the Aragonese tourism department. It contains complete lists of hotels, camping grounds, casas rurales, mountain refuges and other information.

Activities

Skiing Aragón is well endowed with ski resorts, mainly strung out along the Pyrenees in the north. The tourist offices in Zaragoza, Huesca and Jaca have plenty of information on the subject, but as in most of Europe, you are generally better off arranging a package deal rather than simply turning up under your own steam. The downhill version is the most popular, but cross-country skiing is also gaining a higher profile. See also the individual entries throughout the chapter.

Walking The mountains are, if anything, more popular in summer than in winter, with innumerable options for walking – anything from gentle rambles of a few hours to long-distance hikes taking up to a week. A network of long-distance trails (Grandes Recorridos, GRs) are marked throughout the northern strip of Aragón and overlap into neighbouring regions and France. The GR-1 pretty much follows the mountain line just south of France, beginning on the coast of Cataluña and heading on west to Navarra and the coast of the País Vasco, but there are plenty of others.

The optimum time to head for the hills with your hiking boots is late June to early September. Even then the weather can be unpredictable, so serious hikers need to come prepared for most contingencies. Mid-July to mid-August is peak summer holiday period in Spain, when the more popular parks and hiking routes can become intensely crowded.

The Federación Española de Montañismo (☎ 91-445 13 82) in Madrid can be contacted for guidance on routes, refuges and specialist equipment shops. Or you can try the Federación Aragonesa de Montañismo in Zaragoza (☎ 976-23 63 55). Editorial Alpina publishes a series of maps of the entire Aragonese Pyrenees at a scale of 1:40,000 and 1:25,000. They come accompanied with small information booklets roughly outlining walking routes and providing other background information. Keep an eye out for this series of red (in some cases orange) booklets, which generally cost from 450 to 600 ptas.

Walkers should refer to the boxed aside 'Walking in the Pyrenees' in the Cataluña chapter.

Adventure Sports Rock climbing, paragliding and white-water rafting are all potential options in Aragón, mainly in the Pyrenees area. Tourist offices have more information on local firms that organise these activities.

Central Aragón

ZARAGOZA

With more than 600,000 inhabitants, Zaragoza (Saragossa) is like an outsize head on the rather frail body of an otherwise thinly populated Aragón, which totals some 1.2 million people. Long an important crossroads on one of Spain's most important waterways, it is today a centre of industry, producing iron, steel, chemicals, plastics, canned food and electrical goods.

A couple of rather spectacular monuments aside, there is really not a helluva lot to see in Zaragoza, but the lively old centre is definitely worth a day or two's exploration, if only to sample the atmosphere in the bars and restaurants.

On a bad day it can get quite blowy, and locals call the north wind that can seem to tear right through you El Cierzo. Fortunately, it is not a permanent phenomenon, and perhaps for this reason Zaragoza has avoided that unfortunate sobriquet of 'the Windy City'.

ARAGÓN

ARAGÓN

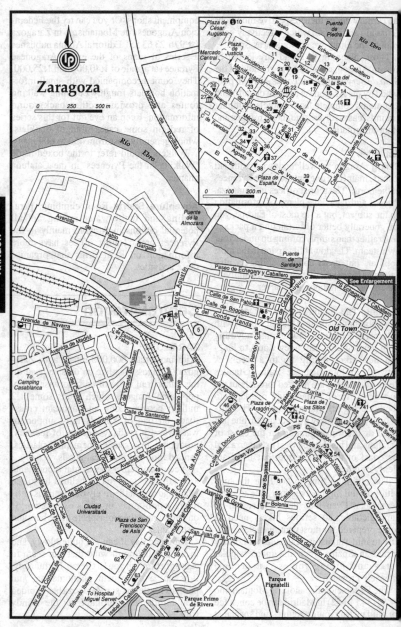

Zaragoza

0   250   500 m

PLACES TO STAY
7 Posada de las Almas
16 Hotel Via Romana
17 Hostal Ambos Mundos
18 Hostal Plaza
20 Hotel Las Torres
21 Hostal Santiago
23 Fonda Manifestación
32 Hostal España
33 Fonda Madrileña, Fonda Borja, Fonda Haro
36 Fonda Peña
48 Albergue de la Juventud Baltasar Gracián
55 Pensión La Dama

PLACES TO EAT
3 Restaurante Casa Emilio
4 Café Madrid
24 Café de Orfeo
26 Crêperie Flor
28 Casa Juanico
29 Café Praga
34 Pascualillo
38 Casa Lac

50 Restaurante La Alcarabea
52 Risko Mar
53 Restaurante El Mangrullo
54 Churrasco
57 Los Borrachos
59 Casa Tena
60 Casa Martín
61 Café Universal

OTHER
1 Cinco Villas Buses
2 Aljafería
5 Plaza de Toros
6 Iglesia de San Pablo
8 Casa Perdiguer
9 Oasis
10 Torreón de la Zuda & Regional Tourist Office
11 Basílica de Nuestra Señora del Pilar
12 Ayuntamiento
13 La Lonja
14 Roman Forum
15 La Seo
19 Oficina Municipal de Turismo

22 Palacio de los Pardo & Museo Camón Aznar
25 Bar Corto Maltés
27 Museo de Pablo Gargallo
30 Café El Prior
31 Chastón
35 Bar Plata
37 Iglesia de San Gil
39 Roman Theatre
40 Iglesia de Santa María Magdalena
41 Iglesia de San Miguel
42 Museo de Zaragoza
43 Iglesia de Santa Engracia
44 Post Office
45 Airport Bus
46 Agreda Bus Company
47 El Portillo RENFE Train Station
49 Loctel Phone & Fax Office
51 TIVE
56 American Express
58 Marqués
62 Policía Local
63 KWM

ARAGÓN

History

Although inhabited beforehand, this Ebro town really only gained importance when refounded by the Romans as Caesaraugusta (hence the modern corruption of its name). As many as 25,000 people came to live in the prosperous city, which in 380 AD played host to a synod of the Christian church. From 714 it remained in the hands of the Muslim invaders for three centuries, falling to the Aragonese king Alfonso el Batallador in 1118.

Centuries later, as Napoleon's troops marched all over the country, Zaragoza put up unusually stiff resistance under siege, although it was finally compelled to capitulate in 1809. Its growth late in the 19th century as an industrial city made it a centre of militant trade unionism, but in 1936 the Republicans had no time to organise themselves and Zaragoza was quickly put under Nationalist control. The country's main military academy had been set up in Zaragoza under a chap known as General Franco in 1928.

Orientation

The core of old Zaragoza lies on the south bank of the Río Ebro, the outline of its former walls marked by Avenida de César Augusto and El Coso. Much of what there is to see and a good choice of hotels, restaurants and bars lie within the old city limits. To the south, several great avenues stretch into the city that has grown up over the past hundred years, capped by the extensive Parque Primo de Rivera. The train station is about a 15 minute walk west of the old centre, and most regional and national buses depart from a station halfway between the two.

In the old centre, Plaza del Pilar, a kind of open arcade dominated by Zaragoza's great basilica, gives way to a maze of busy lanes and alleys, the heart of which is known as El Tubo. The seedy area east of Calle de San Vicente de Paul is probably best avoided at night.

Information

Tourist Office The main regional tourist office (☎ 39 35 37) is in the Torreón de la

Zuda, Glorieta Pío XII, at the western end of Plaza del Pilar. It opens Monday to Friday from 8.15 am to 2.45 pm and 4 to 6 pm, and Saturday from 10 am to 1 pm. For more ample information on the city alone, you could try the Oficina Municipal de Turismo (☎ 20 12 00) virtually opposite the basilica. It opens Monday to Saturday from 9.30 am to 1.30 pm and 4.30 to 7.30 pm, and Sunday from 10 am to 2 pm. A summer tourist office opens at El Portillo train station.

Money Banks abound all over the city, most with ATMs that accept a wide range of foreign credit cards.

American Express (☎ 38 39 11), officially at Paseo Sagasta 47, is actually in the Turopa travel agency around the corner on Camino de las Torres.

Post & Communications The main post office (Correos) is at Paseo de la Independencia 33. The postcode for central Zaragoza and poste restante is 50080. Telefónica has no telephone office, but if you really need one, the private Loctel company at Calle de Tomás Bretón 26 offers a telephone and fax service. The telephone code for the city and province is ☎ 976.

Travel Agencies Students and young people can get international student ID cards and discount travel advice at the TIVE office hidden away in the Residencial Paraíso, off Calle de León XIII. Its office number is 40.

Medical Services One of the bigger and better public hospitals is the Hospital Miguel Servet (☎ 35 57 00) on Paseo de Isabel la Católica, south of the city centre.

Emergency The Policía Local is based at Calle de Domingo Miral. Otherwise, there are several stations throughout the city centre. Call ☎ 092 in case of emergency. For an ambulance, call ☎ 35 85 00.

Lost & Found It's a long shot, but if you have lost something, you might try ☎ 55 91 76, at the Policía Local headquarters.

Basílica de Nuestra Señora del Pilar

One day while preaching in Spain, St John i supposed to have beheld a vision of th Virgin Mary, descended from the heaven atop a marble pillar. This she left behin when returning, and around it was built chapel. At least that's the story of the *pila* around which was later built the rather ove whelming baroque edifice you see today o Plaza del Pilar. Designed in 1681 by Fran cisco de Herrera, the building was late altered by Ventura Rodríguez and Jos Ramírez. The towers were not complete until the early 20th century. The main dom is accompanied by 10 smaller ones, all deco rated with tiles of blue, green, yellow an white.

The Capilla Santa, the oval chapel i which the supposed pilar is enshrined, is rather sumptuous pink marble structure the eastern end of the church. The painting in the cupola above it were carried out b Antonio González Velázquez. Goya als worked here, his most important contribu tion being the painting inside the cupol above the Capilla de San Joaquín.

A small portion of the supposed pillar i accessible at the rear of the Capilla Santa and for centuries pilgrims have come to kis and touch it. Another few centuries of thi and they'll kiss a hole right through it!

The single greatest piece of fine art is th alabaster high altar piece by Damián For ment, actually done in the early 16th century well before the present church was started.

In the north flank is the **Museo Pilarista** which has a small collection of jewellery 'capes of the Virgin' and a planning mode of the chapel built for the holy pillar.

The basilica opens daily from 5.45 am t 9.30 pm (8.30 pm in winter). The museum to which entry costs 150 ptas, opens daily from 9 am to 2 pm and 4 to 6 pm.

Plaza del Pilar

Roman Forum The trapezoid thing squat ting at the east end of Plaza del Pilar in fron of La Seo, the city's second church, appear for all the world like the fevered flourish o ome enlightened contemporary artist. It is in fact the exterior of a remarkable structure built to house ancient Caesaraugusta's forum, well below the present city's ground level, and opened in 1996.

What you see are the remains of shops, porticoes, the great *cloaca* (sewerage system) built in Tiberius' time and a limited collection of artefacts. Perhaps most interesting are sections of lead pipes used to channel water to the city's populace – they look much like modern piping and are a reminder of the Romans' genius for engineering. All of this dates from between the 1st century BC and the 1st century AD.

What the forum lacks in artefacts, it makes up for in imaginative presentation, with a 'cyclorama' show of slides, music and commentary breathing life into the old crockery. It's done well, but it's done in Spanish. Still, if you are interested in ancient history it's probably worth the effort anyway. Apart from the sparse remains of the Roman wall at the western end of the square and traces of the theatre, the forum is the most substantial reminder of the empire's presence here.

The forum is open Tuesday to Saturday from 10 am to 2 pm and 5 to 8 pm. On Sunday and holidays it opens from 10 am to 2 pm. Entry costs 400 ptas (200 ptas for students). The presentation begins on the hour and, strictly, you are not meant to stay beyond the hour into the next session.

La Seo Once the main church in Zaragoza, and built over the site of what had been the central mosque, the Catedral de San Salvador, known to all as La Seo, is a smorgasbord of styles. From its 12th century Romanesque apse to its 16th century Late Gothic additions, there's a bit of everything.

If you circle around this ponderous and brooding building, you will be stopped in your tracks by the north-western façade, an Aragonese mudéjar masterpiece, combining the classic dark brickwork and ceramic decoration. The main colours are a restrained mix of greens, blues and white deployed in a series of eye-pleasing geometrical patterns.

Opposite this extraordinary façade lies the low and, in comparison, humble Palacio Arzobispal, or seat of the archbishop.

There are several admirable works inside the cathedral, but it has been closed for some time while excavation and restoration work are carried out.

La Lonja The fairly plain building between the Palacio Arzobispal and the *ayuntamiento* (town hall) was built in the mid-16th century in the Renaissance style and is now only open when there's an exhibition.

Torreón de la Zuda This is all that remains of the Muslim governors' palace, located at the western end of the square. The tower was modified in the 15th century.

Aljafería

For all the changes it has undergone, the Aljafería remains the greatest Muslim-era edifice outside Andalucía. Built as a kind of pleasure dome for Zaragoza's Muslim rulers, much along the lines of the 'castles' strung out across the desert in modern Syria and Jordan, it was never intended as a serious defensive installation. From the 12th century, Zaragoza's Christian rulers made various alterations to the palace, and in 1486 the Inquisition moved into the main square tower, the Torre del Trovador. At the end of the 15th century, Fernando and Isabel tacked on the new palace. From then on it found various uses as a hospital and barracks, at the same time being allowed to decay. From the late 1940s serious restoration was carried out and in 1987 the Aragonese parliament *(cortes)* established itself in the palace. Restoration and other work continue today.

Once you pass through the main gate, cross the courtyard into a second, known as Santa Isabel's courtyard. Here you are confronted on the northern and southern flanks by the opulence and geometric mastery of Muslim architecture, with its arches like fine lacework. Opening off the northern porch is the small oratory. A magnificent horseshoe arched doorway leads inside, where you find

ARAGÓN

the *mihrab*, or prayer niche indicating the direction of Mecca. The finely chiselled floral motifs, inscriptions in Arabic from the Qur'an and pleasingly simple inner side of the cupola are impressive examples of high Muslim art.

As though by way of a riposte, the Catholic Monarchs' new palace, upstairs, also has treasures of decoration to boast, especially the *artesonado* ceilings – beautiful mudéjar work that, whether the Christians like it or not, also took much of its original inspiration from Oriental sources.

The Aljafería is open Monday to Saturday from 10 am to 2 pm and 4 to 8 pm (4.30 to 6.30 pm in winter). On Sunday and holidays it opens from 10 am to 2 pm. Entry is free.

Churches

Apart from the two great houses of worship that dominate Plaza del Pilar, several minor churches dotted in and around the centre are also worth a quick look. The **Iglesia de Santa María Magdalena**, at the east end of Calle Mayor, is remarkable for its mudéjar tower, reminiscent of the magnificent Torre de San Salvador in Teruel to the south.

The **Iglesia de San Pablo**, too, boasts an impressive mudéjar tower and a retablo by Damián Forment. Much the same story applies to the **Iglesia de San Miguel**. The tower of the **Iglesia de San Gil** underwent something of a baroque transformation, but remains largely faithful to its 14th century mudéjar origins. The main doorway is all that remains of the 16th century version of the Iglesia de Santa Engracia, the rest having been rebuilt after destruction during Napoleon's Iberian adventures.

Museums

Museo de Zaragoza The Archaeology and Fine Arts section is the main part of the museum, on Plaza de los Sitios. On display are artefacts from prehistoric to Muslim times on the ground floor, and an important collection of Gothic art, as well as contributions from Damián Forment and Goya (including a self-portrait). There is also an Ethnology section in the Parque Primo de

Rivera, south of Paseo de Fernando e Católico. Both sections are open Tuesday t Saturday from 9 am to 2 pm (10 am to 2 pr on Sunday and holidays). Entry to each cost 200 ptas.

Museo Camón Aznar Housed in the Palaci de los Pardo, this eclectic collection o Spanish art from the 15th to the 20th centu ries is spread out over the three stories of th Renaissance mansion at Calle de Espoz Mina 23. It is open Tuesday to Friday from 10 am to 2 pm, on Saturday until 1 pm an on Sunday from 11 am to 2 pm. Entry cost 50 ptas.

Museo de Pablo Gargallo This is a good representative display of bronze sculpture by Pablo Gargallo, possibly Aragón's mos gifted artistic son after Goya. The works most of which he did in the first decades o this century, are housed in a mid-17t century mansion built in late Renaissanc style. It is open Tuesday to Saturday from 10 am to 1 pm and 5 to 9 pm. On Sunday an holidays it opens from 11 am to 2 pm. Entry is free.

Modernisme

Although many have disappeared, ther remain in Zaragoza some fine examples o late *modernista* architecture. The Mercad Central is one, but the pick are on Paseo d Sagasta. Look out in particular for stree numbers 11, 13, 19, 40 and 76.

El Rastro

Sunday morning is the best time to hun around in markets. A good flea market take place by the Plaza de Toros.

Organised Tours

The Oficina Municipal de Turismo organise free tours on Sunday (in Spanish) of some o the salient sights of the old town. Enquire about times and itinerary.

Special Events

The Fiesta de San Valero, the day of the city' patron saint, is celebrated in rather muted fashion throughout the province on 29 January. Most things shut on this day, and the big treat is the *roscón*, a rich cake loaded with cream in the shape of a doughnut – a super-human one is placed in Plaza del Pilar if weather permits.

In the last days of February, Zaragoza joins most other cities throughout Spain to celebrate Carnaval. But the city's big event is the Fiestas del Pilar, a week of celebrations around 12 October.

In November, the city hosts an international jazz festival.

Places to Stay – bottom end

Camping & Hostel The city's only camping ground, *Camping Casablanca* (☎ 33 03 22), is a few km out of town to the south-west, off the Autovía de Madrid towards Valldefierro. They charge 540 ptas per person, tent place and car.

The *Albergue de la Juventud Baltasar Gracián* (☎ 55 13 87), Calle de Franco y López, is open all year except August. Beds cost 700 ptas (or 500 ptas if you're a member under 26) from May to October, and 100 ptas more during the rest of the year.

Fondas, Hostales & Pensiones Zaragoza is full to bursting with fondas, hostales and hotels of most categories.

An excellent choice in the heart of El Tubo is *Fonda Peña* (☎ 29 90 89), Calle de Cinegio 3, with beds for 1100 ptas per person. There is a decent little *comedor* here, too.

For cheap, you can't go much further down-market than the *Fonda Madrileña* (☎ 29 81 49), Calle de Estébanes 4, with basic rooms at 1000 ptas per person. In the same building you'll also find the *Fonda Haro* (☎ 29 39 63) and the *Fonda Borjano* (☎ 39 48 75). They are pretty much the same, but all are worth checking out to see if you can find an appreciably better room.

Another reasonable cheap dive is the *Fonda Manifestación* (☎ 29 58 21), Calle de la Manifestación 36, with singles/doubles for 1500/3000 ptas.

Hostal España (☎ 29 88 48), Calle de Estébanes 2, is OK but a little overpriced for what you get at 2500/3500 ptas with en suite bathroom.

Pensión La Dama (☎ 22 39 99), Calle de Doctor Casas 20, is a good-value cheapie in the new part of town. Quiet, clean rooms with outside shower cost 2000/2800 ptas.

If you want to be right on Plaza del Pilar and have the chance of views of the basilica, try *Hostal Plaza* (☎ 29 48 30) at No 14. It has quite reasonable singles/doubles for 2000/3300 ptas. *Hostal Ambos Mundos* (☎ 29 97 04), at No 16, is perhaps a little more tatty, but also has fairly good rooms for 2000/3500 ptas with bath (doubles without own bathroom go for 3000 ptas).

Close by and with slightly better rooms is the *Hostal Santiago* (☎ 39 45 50), Calle de Santiago 3. Rooms with TV, phone, en suite bathroom and heating cost 3000/4000 ptas, but there is no view.

Places to Stay – middle

The *Posada de las Almas* (☎ 43 97 00), Calle de San Pablo 22, has been going since 1705 and has an atmospheric restaurant. The rooms are good but few have any of the character you might have expected. Singles/doubles cost 4000/5500 ptas. The same people run the *Hotel San Blas* across the road.

A comfortable if also fairly characterless option for views of the basilica is the *Hotel Las Torres* (☎ 39 42 50; fax 39 42 54), with singles/doubles for 4000/6500 ptas. The latter are fine, but the former can be pokey. Not all rooms come with views.

Places to Stay – top end

Hotel Via Romana (☎ 39 82 15; fax 29 05 11), Calle Don Jaime I 54-56, is not the steepest-priced hotel in Zaragoza, but it is a comfortable place overlooking Plaza del Pilar. Singles/doubles cost around 6000/9000 ptas.

Places to Eat

There are several zones to look for restaurants. For the cheaper, inner-city end of the

ARAGÓN

scale, El Tubo, the labyrinth of lanes at the heart of the old town, is the place to start. In the new town, the area around Calle de Francisco Vitoria is also good, and there's a clutch of mid-range spots on Plaza de San Francisco de Asís.

In the heart of El Tubo -- around Calles de la Libertad, del Cuatro de Agosto and the like – is clustered a huddle of restaurants and bars. At *Pascualillo*, Calle de la Libertad 5, you can get a good set-menu meal for under 1000 ptas. More up-market with a touch of fading class is *Casa Lac*, Calle de los Mártires 12, which has been going nonstop since it received its licence in 1825 during the reign of Fernando VII. *Casa Juanico*, Calle de la Santa Cruz 21, is a popular old-style tapas bar with comedor out the back. The solid set menu costs 1100 ptas. A great dessert of crêpes can be had in the *Crêperie Flor*, just off Plaza de San Felipe.

Outside this area but in a similar vein is the *Restaurante Casa Emilio*, Avenida de Madrid 5, a simple sort of place with low-priced, home-cooked meals; they'll win no cuisine medals, but it's wholesome stuff and you'll find no tourists about.

At Plaza de San Francisco de Asís 9, *Casa Martín* is a bright place. Set menus cost from 1300 to 3000 ptas. Try the leek and prawn pie (pastel de puerros y gambas) as a starter. *Casa Tena*, at No 16, has mains for 1000 to 1500 ptas.

Risko Mar, Calle de Francisco Vitoria 16, is one of the city's best known fish restaurants, but it's pricey. An excellent set meal for two will cost 5000 ptas. Across the road, you could try *Restaurante El Mangrullo*, at No 17, for Argentine food. Main meals go for about 1000 to 1500 ptas. Next door, *Churrasco* is another Zaragoza mainstream institution, with a slightly taverny feel to it. You'll be up for as much as 3000 ptas for a full meal. They have a wide variety of meat and fish dishes.

For vegetarian food, try *Restaurante La Alcarabea*, Calle de Zumalacárregui 23. Not far away is a Zaragoza establishment restaurant, *Los Borrachos*, Paseo de Sagasta 64. It ain't cheap though.

Cafés In keeping with its profile as a burgeoning metropolis, Zaragoza is blessed with some particularly pleasing and elegant cafés. It also has some great classic working-class dives, like *Café Madrid*, Avenida de Madrid 1.

In the old town, *Café de Orfeo*, Calle de Santa Isabel 3, is an old-fashioned bar, but not as evocative as the *Gran Café Nike* next door, which unfortunately appears to have been closed for good.

Café Praga, Plaza de Santa Cruz, is bare, blue and trendy.

Café Universal, Paseo de Fernando el Católico 32, is a long-standing Zaragozan institution. You almost feel as though you should dress up to be there.

Of course, Plaza del Pilar is lined with cafés, most of them quite good.

Entertainment

Bars Drinking is as serious a business in Zaragoza as in any other big Spanish city, and there are several zones to do some prospecting in. One is the area around the university, obviously with a fairly young student crowd. Closer to where most travellers are likely to hang out, there is no shortage of options in El Tubo or the adjacent Mercado Central area. Calle de Doctor Cerrada and the immediate vicinity is another place to try.

Bar Corto Maltés, Calle del Temple 23, is one of a string of rather cool places on this lane near the Mercado Central. All the barmen seem to sport the 'corto maltés' – the cut of the sideburns in the theme picture.

In El Tubo itself, *Chastón*, Plaza de Ariño 4, is a relaxing little jazz club.

In the new town, *Marqués* is a cosy, soft-lit bar with almost a UK pub atmosphere, except that from 11.30 pm there's a piano. It's on Plaza de San Francisco de Asís (next to Casa Tena) but it is not the cheapest bar around.

Nightclubs & Discos *Bar Plata*, Calle del Cuatro de Agosto, is smack in the heart of El Tubo, and is a 'bar cantante', where you get cabaret with your drinks. Another oddity is

Oasis, Calle de Boggiero 28. Founded in 1909 as a concert hall, it underwent various transformations until it became Oasis in 1942. This one leans more to variety shows.

For some dancing in the earlier stages of a big night out, *Café El Prior*, just near Plaza de Santa Cruz, on Calle de Contamina, is a good place to start.

KWM, Paseo de Fernando El Católico 70, is a popular mainstream disco open until about 5 am.

Torreluna is a favourite, built inside a severe-looking old mansion out of town on Calle de Miguel Servet 193. Catch bus No 38 from Plaza de España (and a taxi back!).

Gay nightspots include a place called *Sphing* on Calle de Ramón y Cajal.

Things to Buy

Shops in and around El Tubo sell the usual kitsch as well as ceramics from various parts of Aragón. For something a little different, wine-lovers should drop in at Casa Perdiguer, Calle de San Pablo 39, purveyors of fine wines in bottles and huge wooden vats.

Getting There & Away

Air Zaragoza is linked by air to Madrid, Barcelona and, for some reason, Jerez. There is also the occasional direct flight to London and Paris.

Bus A dozen or so companies serve Zaragoza, with offices all over the city – there is no central station. The Agreda company operates buses to most major Spanish cities from Paseo de María Agustín 7. The one-way trip to Madrid costs 1750 ptas and to Barcelona 1640 ptas. La Oscense also operates from here to Huesca and Jaca. The tourist office has a full list of bus company addresses and destinations.

Train All trains use the shiny El Portillo station. Zaragoza is an important junction and there are connections to most destinations. Up to 14 serve Madrid (2450 ptas in ordinary 2nd class) daily and a similar number run to Barcelona (2235 ptas). Trains travel as far afield as Galicia, Valencia and

even Cádiz. Closer to home, the trip south to Teruel costs 1300 ptas, as does the voyage to Jaca (via Huesca; 650 ptas).

Car & Motorcycle Zaragoza is on a major junction of highways. The A-2 motorway autopista hooks up with the A-7 for Barcelona, and the N-II heads south-west for Madrid. The N-330 will take you north to Huesca and the Pyrenees and south towards Teruel. The A-68 autopista heads north-west through Navarra and La Rioja to Bilbao.

Getting Around

The Airport If you need to get a flight, Ebrobus (☎ 32 40 09) runs buses from Plaza de Aragón to link with flights. They leave up to five times a day.

Bus Bus No 22 links the El Portillo train station to Plaza de España, which almost all routes serve.

AROUND ZARAGOZA

The pickings are pretty slim in the immediate vicinity of Zaragoza, but the further you get away, particularly to the south and southeast, the more little gems you'll run into. Although most of the following places can be reached by bus, your own transport is ideal for hopping between them en route to or from Zaragoza.

Cartuja de Auli

This Carthusian monastery about 10 km north of Zaragoza contains a series of frescos by Goya depicting the lives of Christ and the Virgin Mary. That they look OK today is the result of careful repainting carried out in past decades. They had suffered badly since the monastery was suppressed early in the 19th century. In fact, the whole monastery suffered, and restoration work continues. At the time of writing it was closed, so check at the tourist office in Zaragoza. Until now only men have been allowed in, but women in Zaragoza have recently started a campaign to have access opened to both sexes. Again, check with the tourist office. The occasional Agreda bus goes past the monastery.

ARAGÓN

Muel & Cariñena

Winos heading south for Teruel could do worse than pass through Cariñena country – home of the best viticulture you'll find in Aragón. The depressing little town of Muel has an 18th century church housing a Roman fountain and some paintings by Goya. Another 19 km south and you're in Cariñena itself. There ain't much to see – so head to one of the many *bodegas* on the main road into town and see if you can scrounge a free sample.

If you decide to linger, the *Hostal Iliturgis* (☎ 976-62 04 92), Plaza de Ramón y Cajal 1, has comfortable singles/doubles with bathroom and TV for 2000/3600 ptas. A few steps away is the *Restaurante La Rebotica*, a popular stop with main meals for around 1000 ptas. Try the pollo a la abuela – 'chicken grandmother-style'! Agreda buses leave from Avenida de Valencia 20 in Zaragoza for Muel and Cariñena.

Fuendetodos

Some of the biggest start small. This couldn't be much truer than in the case of Francisco Goya y Lucientes, who was born in this insignificant Aragonese hamlet in 1746. His house stayed in the family until the beginning of the 20th century, when the artist Ignacio Zuloaga found and bought it. Partly destroyed during the civil war, the humble three storey house has been restored. About 100 metres down the road, the Museo del Grabado de Goya contains an impressive collection of the painter's etchings, and is well worth a visit. Entry to both is Tuesday to Sunday from 11 am to 2 pm and 4 to 7 pm. The combined ticket costs 300 ptas. The Samar Buil company runs daily buses to Zaragoza (Calle de Borau 13).

Belchite

This town, or rather the twin towns that constitute Belchite, must be one of the most eloquent reminders of the destruction wrought in the civil war. The ruins of the old town, replaced by a new village next door, have been left standing as a silent memorial. A few km west stands the 18th century **Santuario de Nuestra Señora del Pueyo**, a strangely neglected church complex topped by five squat spires above tiled domes.

Azaila

The tiny pueblo of Azaila, directly on the N-232 between Zaragoza and Tarragona, is not going to stop any crowds, but ancient history buffs might like to steer off 1.5 km along the back way to **Vinaceite** to inspect the remains of an ancient Celtic-Roman castro. It has been far too lovingly restored, but is interesting nonetheless. The streets and houses are clearly laid out, and the hilltop is circumscribed by a water channel. The views over the surrounding country seem limitless.

Lest We Forget

In the summer of 1937, Republican forces fought a savage battle with Franco's troops for control of the small town of Belchite. By the time they had finished, the elegant houses along the Calle Mayor, along with the town's two churches, mostly built of the narrow bricks typical of *mudéjar* architecture, had been thoroughly blasted. The Torre del Reloj (clock tower) was left leaning precariously, the clock face blasted away. In March of the following year, Nationalist forces marched back in as the seesaw war in this heavily fought-over part of Spain moved back in Franco's favour. By now the town's populace lived in a labyrinth of wreckage, struggling to keep life going in the midst of disaster. The Franco government judged the town too far gone to be rebuilt, and decided to build it afresh next door. That plan was not completed until 1954 – a long wait for people living in such misery. Today, it is an eerie experience to wander past the shell-shocked buildings down silent streets, where for a time life and death led a tragic coexistence. ■

Along the Río Ebro

If you end up at Azaila, one option to keep you far from the highways is to proceed 46 km east along the A-1404 to **Caspe**. This hilltop town was also heavily damaged during the civil war, as the 13th century Colegiata church in the centre still shows. Caspe is known to lovers of Spanish history for the Compromiso de Caspe (Caspe Compromise), signed in 1412 to settle the Aragonese succession by putting a Castilian from the Trastámara house on Aragón's throne. Here the dams built on the Río Ebro are at their most magnificent. You can follow the river north-east to **Mequinenza**, dominated by a medieval castle that saw action in the War of Succession and as late as 1938 during the civil war. Virtually destroyed then, it was later rebuilt. From here it is 20 km north to **Fraga** (see the next section).

EAST OF ZARAGOZA

The often disconsolate plains that stretch east of Zaragoza, sliced up at intervals by waves of bare plateaus, are for all their spartan appearance not entirely empty of interest, and a couple of short stops along the way to or from Cataluña suggest themselves.

Monasterio de Sigena

Lying in a quiet clearing off the A-131 Fraga-Sariñena road, this monastery was first raised in the 12th century, and for some 800 years occupied by the Order of St John of Jerusalem. Since 1985 the order has been replaced by a handful of nuns living in isolation under a vow of silence. The Romanesque church is the focal point, or rather its main doorway is – blessed with no fewer than 14 graceful arches. It appears you can wander in at any time during the day, but try not to disturb the nuns' peace.

Fraga

The old core of this town seven km short of Aragón's border with Cataluña is just interesting enough to warrant a stop. The much restored and remodelled 12th century **Iglesia de San Pedro** is the centrepiece, seemingly growing out of the steeply sloping streets,

but the main attraction is simply strolling around. *Cobertizos*, the galleries that allow passage between houses above the streets, cast deep shadows over the dishevelled and uncared-for maze below. Head up Calle de Dr Barraquer from the Plaza de San Pedro (where the church is) and on for Calle del Castillo, from where you have unlimited views across the *casco histórico*, the wide Río Cinca valley and the chain of parched hills beyond to the west.

The *Hostal Flavia* (☎ 974-47 15 40), Paseo Barrón 13, is in the heart of the old town and has basic rooms for 1300/2500 ptas. Calle Mayor links this square with Plaza de San Pedro. Otherwise, there are a few places on Avenida de Aragón and Avenida de Madrid in the new part of town. The Flavia serves food too, and some of the town's more happening bars are on the same square – which may prove a little noisy.

The bus station is just on the west bank of the river on Avenida de Aragón. Up to 10 a day head east to Lleida (Lérida), three to Zaragoza and two to Huesca. Some take roundabout routes, and there is hardly a bus to anywhere on Sunday.

TARAZONA

Moving westwards from Zaragoza, you could take the N-II for Madrid (via Calatayud: see the Roads to Teruel section later in this chapter) and then swing south for Teruel, make a more north-westerly drive into Navarra, or follow the setting sun towards Soria in Castilla y León. If you opt for the latter, make time for Tarazona, a remarkable leftover of the Muslim occupation that is often likened to Toledo. This is overdoing it, although perhaps it bears some resemblance to the Toledo of 20 years ago – its dimly lit serpentine streets see few tourists, and the town has a way to go in providing restaurants and other excitements.

Turiaso, as the town was then known, went down in the Roman military annals as the scene of a famous victory by a small band of intrepid imperial soldiers over a far greater Celtiberian army. Later it was a Visigothic bishopric before being taken by the Muslims. By 1118 it was again in Christian hands.

Information

There is a tourist office (☎ 64 00 74) next to the cathedral at Calle de las Iglesias 5. It opens Monday to Friday from 9 am to 1 pm and 4 to 7 pm; Saturday from 10 am to 1 pm and 4 to 6 pm; and Sunday from 10 am to 1 pm. The telephone code is ☎ 976.

Things to See

The **catedral**, closed for restoration, is something of a mixed bag of Romanesque, Gothic, mudéjar and Renaissance. The mudéjar cloisters are particularly pretty, while the prime oddity is a brick dome, fashioned by Juan Botero.

Nearby, the old **Plaza de Toros** is one of the more original bullrings in Spain. The octagonal ring is made up of 32 houses and was built at the end of the 18th century as a kind of private housing initiative – with entertainment thrown in.

Though Tarazona is quite a deal smaller than Toledo, you can still manage to get yourself temporarily lost in the twisting cobbled ways that constitute the bulk of the medieval 'high part' of the town. From all around can be seen the tall, slender mudéjar tower of the **Iglesia de Santa María Magdalena**. The **Palacio Episcopal** opposite started life as a Muslim fortified palace. Further north on Plaza de España is the richly decorated 16th century ayuntamiento, among whose reliefs is supposedly one of Hercules.

Places to Stay & Eat

You can stay in one of three places. The cheapest is the *Hostal María Cristina* (☎ 64 00 84), Carretera de Castilla 3, which looks like it's been going for a century but is quite OK. If you want a single room, ask very specifically for it, as they may well place you in a discounted double otherwise. In the high season, singles/doubles cost 1500/3000 ptas. They charge an extra 300 ptas for a hot shower.

On the opposite way out of town is the *Hotel Brujas de Becquer* (☎ 64 04 04), Carretera de Zaragoza s/n, with rooms for 4000/5700 ptas. The luxury joint is right on the Río Queiles in town. *Hotel Ituri Asso* (☎ 64 31 96), Calle de la Virgen del Río 3, has good rooms with en suite, TV and phone for 5000/8000 ptas. Both these hotels have decent restaurants. Otherwise you could try *El Galeón*, close to the centre, at Avenida de la Paz 1. Ask for the ternasco (lamb ribs).

Getting There & Away

The main bus station is on Avenida de Navarra, although for the Monasterio de Veruela you need to go to a different stop on Calle de la Carrera Zaragoza.

AROUND TARAZONA

The fortified walls of the **Monasterio de Veruela** are more reminiscent of a Castilian castle than a monastery, and yet from its founding in the 12th century, that is precisely what it was. Starting off in the hands of Carthusians, it was long inhabited by Jesuits. It now belongs to the Zaragoza provincial government. The cold Gothic church is flanked by a charming cloister, whose lower Gothic level is counterbalanced by a Renaissance upper gallery. It is open Tuesday to Saturday from 10 am to 2 pm and 4 to 6 pm (7 pm in summer). Entry is 200 ptas for non-Spaniards, although you might well slip in for free. There are a couple of good homy restaurants, one on the premises and the other across the road. The nearest hostal is a few km down the road in Vera de Moncayo. Several buses come here from Tarazona.

If you have a car and time, go for a spin in the nearby **Parque Natural de la Dehesa del Moncayo**.

Pyrenees & the North

As you leave the multiple sierras and parched depression of Zaragoza province behind you to head north, a gradual change comes over

Borgia by Another Name

About 25 km east of Tarazona, you pass through a small town with yet another castle. 'So what?', you might think. After all, there's hardly a town in central Spain that *doesn't* have a castle. True, but this is a piddly *pueblo* with a difference. Borja is not only at the centre of one of Aragón's four main wine-growing districts, it is also the ancestral stamping ground of one of the most notorious families in *Italian* history! Borja, written in Italian, comes out as Borgia, and the crumbly castle of Borja was once home to the colourful crew of that name.

Rodrigo Borgia, as Alexander VI, became Rome's most talked-about pope in history – a wheeler-dealer philanderer who was nothing if not irreligious. And his offspring (he did little to hide his paternity), Cesare and Lucrezia, have had a bad press ever since they romped across the world stage in the first half of the 16th century. Cesare probably deserved every ounce of his reputation as a vicious and cynical murderer, prepared to do anything to fulfil his grandiose plans for secular rule over much of Italy. Whether or not Lucrezia was the husband-poisoner she was made out to be is less certain; nor is it clear whether the rumours that she had an incestuous relationship with her father the pope are true.

Of course, the little old town of Borja had long been forgotten, and picked up not a ray of reflected 'glory'. For Rodrigo's ancestors upped sticks and moved to the more salubrious climes of Valencia in the early 14th century. One can only guess at what the upright citizens of 15th and 16th century Borja made of their one-time neighbours' doings. ■

the territory. A hint of green tinges the landscape, and although the town of Huesca lies in a little-comforted basin, the first of the hilly ranges preceding the Pyrenees are not far off.

The Aragonese section of the Pyrenees is among the most rewarding on the Spanish side of the border with France, with half a dozen decent ski resorts and some good walking and trekking to be done, especially in the eastern Parque Nacional de Ordesa y Monte Perdido. There are numerous ways of approaching the area, with several main routes clawing up through the valleys and some crossing into France.

A few things are worth bearing in mind

when you reach the Pyrenees. Maintenance on walking tracks seems haphazard at best. Some designated paths are in good shape. Others marked on maps are little more than goat trails; even stretches of what might be considered main routes are often impossible to make out. Reference is made to some mountain refuges in what follows, and there are others. They are generally basic and, to many people's minds, overpriced. They are also often fully booked by clubs well in advance. The moral of the story is that you should always go prepared to camp.

HUESCA

Known to the Romans as Osca and to its Muslim masters of nearly four centuries as Washka, Huesca today is still largely a depressed sort of place. The surprisingly interesting medieval centre has that down-at-heel, crumbling feel common to quite a few Aragonese towns, giving the impression that time has stopped still. That has its charm, but the new town spreading beyond this nucleus shows little sign of any thought beyond cut-price functionality. It is, however, not a bad starting point for exploring the north.

As occurred in many centres across Spain at the end of the 15th century, the decision to expel the Jews and the subsequent dispersal of the remaining Muslims and Moriscos (Muslims converted to Christianity) struck a blow from which the once flourishing trading town never really recovered. During the civil war it was for a long time held under siege by Republican forces, but never taken.

Orientation & Information

Huesca is seated on a slight rise, to the north-east of which flows the modest Río Isuela. The bus station is just off Plaza de Navarra in the heart of town and a short walk from the old town and tourist office. The train station is a few hundred metres further south.

The helpful tourist office (☎ 22 57 78) is at Calle del Coso Alto 23, and opens daily from 9 am to 2 pm; also Monday to Saturday from 5 to 8 pm.

There are plenty of banks in the centre.

ARAGÓN

Banesto and Banco Santander on Plaza de Navarra have ATMs.

The post office is on the corner of Calle del Coso Alto and Calle de Moya. Send poste restante mail to Huesca 22080. The telephone code is ☎ 974, and there is a Telefónica phone office at Calle de Caspe 3. It opens Monday to Friday from 9 am to 1 pm and 5 to 10 pm. The main police station (☎ 091) is on Plaza de Luis Buñuel. For an ambulance, call ☎ 22 92 92.

Plaza de la Catedral & Around

At the heart of the casco antiguo, this pleasant leafy square is presided over by a venerable Gothic cathedral, unfortunately showing its age a little more than you might wish. The main portal actually belongs to an earlier 13th century church, and is topped by typically Aragonese eaves (alero). Next door is the Museo Diocesano, with a collection of mainly religious art. It opens Monday to Saturday from 10 am to 1 pm. The 16th century ayuntamiento across the square is another Aragonese gem, again with the characteristic alero. A little way north, the octagonal Museo Provincial (closed for renovation) was once the Palacio de los Reyes de Aragón (Palace of the Kings of Aragón).

Iglesia de San Pedro El Viejo

Directly south of Plaza de la Catedral is Huesca's real masterpiece, an understated 12th century Romanesque wonder. The cloister in particular is worthy of a close look. The sculpture on the capitals of its columns is remarkably well preserved, or in some cases, restored. The bell tower is a graceful, six sided addition. Begun in 1134, the church was not finished until well into the following century.

Parque Municipal Miguel Servet

The newer part of town has few saving graces apart from this unusually well manicured, shady park.

Places to Stay & Eat

All the following tend to raise prices in August. Pensión Bandrés (☎ 22 47 82), Calle de Fatás 5, has adequate singles/doubles for 1500/2500 ptas (bathroom outside). Hostal El Centro (☎ 22 68 23), Calle de Sancho Ramírez 3, has pleasant rooms with shower and TV for 2700/3800 ptas, or 3000/4100 ptas with loo included. Hostal San Marcos (☎ 22 29 31), Calle de San Orencio 10, has good rooms for 4000/5775 ptas. Hotel Pedro I de Aragón (☎ 22 03 00; fax 22 00 94), Calle del Parque 34, is the top-end spot with rooms for 8500/13,700 ptas.

Restaurante Os Danzantes, Calle de Sancho Ramírez 18, is an understated place that does a set evening meal for 1500 ptas; try the rabbit and mushrooms. Restaurante San Voto, on the corner of the plaza of the same name and Calle del Olmo, is a good grill restaurant. Classier is Restaurante El Molinero, below Hostal San Marcos. You won't get much change from 3000 ptas a head.

For late-night drinking, Calle de San Lorenzo and the surrounding area are loaded with bars. Or you could try Rincón Musical, Calle de San Jorge 29, for live music.

Getting There & Away

Bus The bus station is at Calle del Parque 3, just back from Plaza de Navarra. Six buses run to Zaragoza (Paseo de María Agustín 7) daily (about an hour), four to Lleida (Lérida; two hours) and Jaca (one hour), and up to three each to Pamplona (about three hours) and Barcelona (2½ hours). Six leave for Barbastro, and other destinations with at least one daily service include Fraga, Benasque, Biescas and Panticosa (for skiing).

Train The RENFE train station is a couple of blocks further south of the bus station, and is of little use. One daily train connects with Madrid. A couple of other trains from Madrid and Barcelona run to Tardienta, well south of Huesca and difficult to reach.

Car & Motorcycle The N-330 passes Huesca on the way from Zaragoza to Jaca and France. The N-240 heads south-east to Lleida (Lérida) in Cataluña.

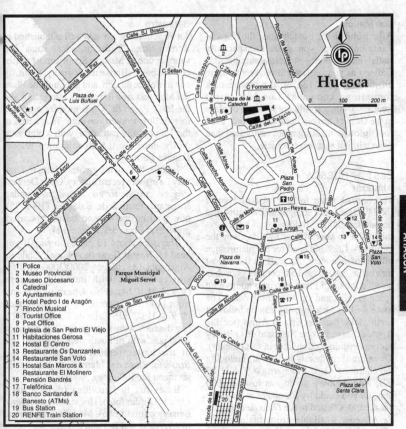

MAP KEY

1 Police
2 Museo Provincial
3 Museo Diocesano
4 Catedral
5 Ayuntamiento
6 Hotel Pedro I de Aragón
7 Rincón Musical
8 Tourist Office
9 Post Office
10 Iglesia de San Pedro El Viejo
11 Habitaciones Gerosa
12 Hostal El Centro
13 Restaurante Os Danzantes
14 Restaurante San Voto
15 Hostal San Marcos &
   Restaurante El Molinero
16 Pensión Bandrés
17 Telefónica
18 Banco Santander &
   Banesto (ATMs)
19 Bus Station
20 RENFE Train Station

ARAGÓN

NORTH OF HUESCA
Castillo de Loarre

Rambling and haughty on its rocky perch just south of the Sierra de Loarre, the *castillo* of the same name could not have been better placed as a lookout for Muslim raiders bolting up across the wheat plains to the south.

Built in and around the living rock, the labyrinthine string of dungeons, tunnels and towers has been left in just enough of a state of partial restoration to lend it a suitably untamed feeling. Put up in the 12th century by Sancho VII of Navarra, it is uncannily reminiscent of the Crusader castles that sprang up in the Holy Land.

You can climb two of the towers for magnificent views and get to the Romanesque church's crypt via trapdoors before the altar. Entrance to the castillo is free. It opens daily from 10 am to 1.30 pm and 4 to 7 pm (closed Monday).

A couple of buses run to Loarre from Huesca (40 minutes; 330 ptas). That's the easy part. It's then a long five km walk or hitch up to the castle. Beware also that there is nowhere to stay in Loarre or Ayerbe, seven km away on the Huesca-Pamplona road.

Los Mallos

After a quite boring patch along the Huesca-Pamplona road, you quite unexpectedly round into a pretty stretch along the Río Gallego as you push north of Ayerbe. Here on the east bank rise up the bizarre rock formations known as Los Mallos (or 'mallets') – they would not look out of place in the Grand Canyon. For a closer look, head for **Riglos**, something more easily said than done without your own vehicle.

EAST OF HUESCA
Alquézar

The normal route to take east of Huesca (N-240) takes you straight to Barbastro and on into Cataluña. Aficionados of back ways might like to veer off northwards along the narrow A-1229 and head for the picturesque village of Alquézar. As well as the almost inevitable castle, the 16th century church is worth a look and Plaza Mayor is an inviting space to relax and sip a soothing *caña*. The route itself is pleasing, and can be followed north along the Río Ena to Aínsa (see the Approaches to Parque Nacional de Ordesa y Monte Perdido section later in this chapter). There are three hotels to stay at, including the charming *Casa Jabonero* (☎ 974-31 83 99), with doubles starting as low as 2000 ptas. Or you could try for one of at least five casas rurales (listed in the *Guía de Servicios de Aragón*, available from main tourist offices throughout the region).

Monasterio El Pueyo

Six km short of Barbastro on the main highway from Huesca, the hilltop Monasterio El Pueyo commands unlimited vistas in all directions, and for that alone is worth a stop if you're motorised. The main attraction is the Camarín de la Virgen, added to the small Gothic church in the 18th century to house a figure of the Virgin and containing fine paintings thought to have been executed by Francisco Bayeu. In July 1936, 20 monks were shot here by Republican militiamen. It's open daily from 10 am to 1 pm and 4 to 8 pm.

Barbastro

An ancient town already well established in Roman times, Barbastro spent some 350 years as one of Muslim Spain's most northerly outposts. Barbastro is really a scruffy sort of a place though, and although the Plaza del Mercado area is vaguely interesting and the leafy Paseo del Coso nice for a coffee, there is little to keep you here. Take a look at the 16th century cathedral, with a high altar partly done by the Renaissance master Damián Forment.

In time, the town's greatest claim to fame may lie in more recent history. Opus Dei fans may be curious to know that its founder, Josemaría Escrivá de Balaguer (1902-75), now well on the way to being canonised, grew up at Plaza del Mercado 11.

There are about 10 places to stay if you need to. *Hostal Goya* (no phone), Calle de Argensola 13, charges 2000/3000 ptas for singles/doubles with bath. *La Sombra* (☎ 974-31 10 64), at No 9, has simple rooms from 1400 to 2000 ptas. *Fonda San Ramón* (☎ 974-31 02 50), Calle de San Ramón 28, has doubles with shower for 2200 ptas or 3000 ptas with full bathroom. It is also one of the better restaurants in town. *La Brasería*, Plaza del Mercado 9, has a solid set menu for 1000 ptas.

Buses run to Barcelona (three a day), Lleida (Lérida; four), Huesca (up to seven), Benasque (up to two), Monzón (six), Fraga (one), Aínsa and Boltaña (one).

Monzón

Potential enemies riding against this small town must have been given pause for thought by the seemingly impregnable walls of the Templar castle that stands proudly over the jumble of Monzón. Once there was the core of a Celtiberian settlement here, but it was the Muslims who built Monzón's first great fortress, taken by Sancho Ramírez in 1089. The Knights Templar took it over in 1143, and used it mostly as a convent and centre of education. Later, after the order of knights fell, the fortress gradually decayed under the effect of several sieges over the 16th to 19th centuries, during which time most of the

ARAGÓN

brickwork sections at the eastern end were added. Part of the castle is being restored, as is the 12th century town church, the **Colegiata de Santa María del Romeral**, below it. The castle is open daily from 11.30 am to 1 pm and 3 to 5 pm, and entry costs 100 ptas.

About the nearest place to the centre of the old town is the *Pensión del Pilar* (☎ 974-40 12 27), Calle de Manuel Serrano Albors 3 (off Avenida del Pilar), with simple rooms for about 1000 ptas per person. The place is one of a series of low-level blocks of modern flats – not an inspiring environment. Virtually in front of the train station, the *Fonda Nueva* (☎ 974-40 09 84), Calle de Miguel Cervantes 2, has serviceable little singles/doubles for 1100/2400 ptas. On the same street, *Pensión Rech* (☎ 974-40 22 41) is in much the same category. Or try the bar cum *Pensión Venecia*, virtually next door. Several other better and more expensive places are a few km out of town on the road to Lleida (Lérida), and the *Hotel Vianetto* (☎ 974-40 19 00), Avenida de Lérida 25, is the premier choice with rooms costing from 3500/5400 ptas.

Apart from the usual bar food, you could choose to eat in greater style at *Jairo*, Calle de Santa Bárbara 10. They specialise in seafood and the cheapest set menu starts at 1500 ptas. If splurging is not on your agenda, the pizzeria on the same street is not bad either. Their salads are huge. *Café La Aurora*, Calle de Joaquín Costa 15, is an urbane, lowlit place for a cosy coffee or stronger beverage.

Although buses connect with Barbastro and Huesca, as well as Fraga to the south, you may find the train more convenient. Monzón lies on the Barcelona-Zaragoza line, and so gets numerous through trains. The buses stop near the Cafetería Acapulco on the Huesca-Lleida highway.

Torreciudad
North-east of Barbastro, this spiritual heart of modern Catholicism's most controversial movement, Opus Dei, keeps a watchful eye above the grand Embalse de El Grado (El Grado reservoir). A modern religious complex of questionable artistic taste, the Santuario de Torreciudad was opened for business in 1975, the year of the death of Opus' founder, Josemaría Escrivá.

Much ink has been spilled on Opus Dei, most of it either in vitriolic attack or in an equally steady defence of what is without doubt a highly conservative and secretive body. With nearly 80,000 followers worldwide, this curious group, a personal prelature responsible to the pope alone for its actions, has fewer than 1000 clergy. The core text by which Opus members lead their spiritual lives is contained in the 999 aphorisms of Escrivá's *El Camino* (The Way), an odd assortment of puritanical exhortations. Enthusiastic members indulge in a little good old-fashioned medieval mortification of the flesh, and several people who have left the order have kicked up quite a stink about Opus' doings. Elitist, it attracts high-flying professionals and encourages them to continue their careers rather than become clerics – making them useful contributors to the Opus coffers, by all accounts said to be quite substantial. Beatified in 1992 (with unusual haste, it has to be added), Escrivá may soon become a fully fledged saint, giving Opus Dei (Latin for 'the work of God') a credibility boost that would undoubtedly only further frustrate the critics.

The site is accessible daily from 9 am to 8.30 pm, but the Santuario building itself is open from 10 am to 2 pm and 4 to 8.30 pm. Buses from Huesca or Barbastro run to El Grado. You have to get a taxi or otherwise make your own way from there.

BENASQUE & THE NORTH-EAST
Even in midsummer the peaks of this extreme north-eastern corner of Aragón can be covered in a blanket of snow and ice. Climbers have a choice of peaks to attack, while walkers can join the long-distance GR-11 trail in this area – just one of several hiking options.

Through Benabarre to France
The easternmost corner of the Aragonese Pyrenees can be most easily reached from

Huesca or from Lleida (Lérida) in Cataluña. Most directly, the route from Huesca takes you east via Barbastro (see above) and on towards Graus and Benabarre. The latter makes a pleasant stop if you intend to head into France following the highly picturesque river route up the Río Noguera Ribagorçana (N-230). A couple of reservoirs, the Embalse de Escales and the Embalse de Baserca, are among the highlights along this way. The road hugs and crisscrosses the boundary with Cataluña until finally leaving Aragón to enter the Vall d'Aran in Cataluña and thereafter France.

Graus to Benasque

To get to the Reserva Nacional de Benasque, you would more likely follow the A-139 up the Río Ésera from Graus. The drive up is particularly pleasant as you pass through the narrow defile of the Congosto de Ventamillo to reach **Castejón de Sos**. There is little to note about the place, but the location is pleasant and offers a wealth of accommodation if you have trouble further north. Five hostales, with singles/doubles starting at around 2000/3000 ptas and rising according to type of room and season, are supplemented by the refuge-style *Albergue Pájaro Loco* (☎ 974-55 30 03) and a camping ground. You'll also find shops and banks here. There are a few places to stay in **El Run** too, a few km before Castejón de Sos.

A nice drive eastwards brings you to the N-230 to France, while the A-139 north proceeds to Benasque. Along the way, you'll encounter more accommodation in Eriste (four hostales) and Villanova (one pensión and a camping ground).

Benasque

In this happening nerve-centre of the Valle de Benasque, the typical greystone and raggedy slate tile roofs of old Benasque (also known locally as Benás) have been swamped by new construction, albeit mostly more or less in keeping with the style of the area. Walkers and climbers in summer and skiers in winter flock here for a little weekend nightlife when the outdoors have lost their appeal. It makes a convenient if unprepossessing base for the area.

The Els Ibons shop on Calle Mayor, next door to the Pensión Barrabés, sells a range of books and maps dealing with the Benasque area. Vit's shop on Plaza Mayor rents out crampons and other climbing equipment, as well as mountain bikes.

Accommodation is abundant, with more than a dozen possibilities. One of the better budget choices is the *Pensión Barrabés* (☎ 974-55 16 54), Calle Mayor 5, with singles/doubles starting at 1800/2500 ptas in the off season. They are also home to the Compañía de Guías de Benasque, which can organise trekking in the area. Another fairly cheap deal is *Pensión Solana* (☎ 974-55 16 19), Plaza Mayor 5. They have a range of rooms costing up to 5500 ptas for a double with private bath. Another cheapie is *Hostal Valero* (☎ 974-55 10 61), Carretera Anciles s/n, with rooms at similar prices.

There are also two camping grounds outside town on the road north of Benasque between the turn-off to Cerler and the one for Estós. Of these *Camping Aneto* (☎ 974-55 11 41) is open all year.

If the idea of a good pizza for around 1000 ptas appeals, try out *Pizzeria La Pirenaica*, Carretera de Francia. Another fun place to eat and hang out is *Pepe & Company*, across the road from Pensión Barrabés. They serve up pizzas, Spanish food, snacks and ice creams.

One or two buses run daily (nothing on Sunday) to Benasque via Castejón de Sos from Barbastro.

Skiing in Cerler

Six km east of Benasque lies Aragón's easternmost ski resort, based on the Pico de Cerler (2409 metres). On offer are 26 varied runs totalling 34 km, and there are ski hire outlets in the town. The only drawback is that there are only two mid-range hotels – so if you have a vehicle you are better off down in Benasque.

Hiking & Climbing around Benasque

There are plenty of walking options of four

or so hours or less (one way) in the area around Benasque. Among the more exacting ones is a piste setting out from Hospital de Benasque (about 15 km north-east of Benasque) for the French frontier. The trail heads north-east and upwards to the Peña Blanca and from there winds steeply to the Portillón de Benasque on the frontier. This should take fit walkers about 2½ hours. Another three to 3½ hours north would take you past the Boums del Port (lakes) to the French town of Bagnères-de-Luchon.

The GR-11 runs right across this area. From Benasque head about 3.5 km north along the surfaced road to the Puente de Cuera. You could cross the river and follow the piste north along the Río Ésera, and then drop east along the Ballibierna valley. The wide trail as far as the Refugio de Pescadores involves about 2½ hours walking. There it narrows on its long way into Cataluña. You'll need a tent and supplies if you are considering a trek into Cataluña, as the Refugio de Llausets remains uncompleted.

Alternatively, heading west from Puente de Cuera, make first for the Refugio de Estós (open all year), about a three hour walk. Another five or so hours brings you to Viadós, where a refuge *may* be open. Call ahead (☎ 974-50 60 82) to be sure. This is a good base for ascents of the **Pico de Posets** (3371 metres), or could be an intermediate stop along the GR-11, which continues west to Bielsa and beyond into the eastern reaches of the Parque Nacional de Ordesa y Monte Perdido. Bielsa itself is a good place to recharge batteries, with several hotels and hostales.

Experienced climbers will find the challenge of the glacial **Macizo de la Maladeta** hard to resist. This forbidding line of icy peaks, culminating in the **Pico de Aneto** (3408 metres), is the highest in the entire Pyrenees system, and still contains glaciers suspended from the higher crests. From the Refugio de la Renclusa (which can be reached in a car by following the Río Ésera), you can tackle Aneto in a minimum of five hours. You'll need crampons, ropes and ice axes. The massif offers other peaks to

explore as well, including Pico de la Maladeta (3308 metres) and the Cresta del Medio (3355 metres). Get hold of the Editorial Alpina map and guide entitled *Maladeta Aneto*, but bear in mind that they are not completely accurate.

APPROACHES TO PARQUE NACIONAL DE ORDESA Y MONTE PERDIDO

From mid-1995, a ceiling was placed on the number of visitors allowed into this park – 1500 at any one time – in an attempt to reduce the damage caused by hordes of people descending on the area. The easiest way to enter the park is from Torla, to which there are several approaches.

A long loop east and then north from Huesca would allow you to take in Barbastro, Torreciudad (see the East of Huesca section) and Aínsa before making for the park. Or you could simply head straight north via Sabiñánigo and hang a right at Biescas. You would go via the same towns from Jaca too.

Aínsa

The wide cobblestone plaza that occupies a good portion of this attractive hilltop settlement is what draws a disconcerting number of tourist buses in the course of a day; there's nothing for it though, as it is one of the prettiest towns in the area.

The tourist office (☎ 974-50 07 67), Avenida Pirenaica 1, is open in summer only, or you could try the Turismo Rural office on Plaza Mayor (open 9 am to 2 pm).

Just back from the eastern corner of the square rises the town **Colegiata**, a well-restored Romanesque church, with a pleasing little cloister and a belfry you can climb. The latter served as part of the town defences during the civil war when the whole area suffered heavy damage. The western end of town is dominated by what remains of defensive walls, inside which you can now park your car.

The place to stay of choice is just across the road from the east door of the church. Look for the 'Habitaciones' sign or call ☎ 974-50 07 50 (mobile ☎ 908-39 97 90).

ARAGÓN

Spotless rooms cost 3000/4500 ptas. Otherwise, there is a hive of hostales and pensiones at the foot of the town. If you feel like splashing out on food, *Restaurante Bodegas del Sobrarbe* is recommended. It's just off Plaza Mayor, and you're looking at about 3000 ptas per person.

One bus a day runs between Barbastro and Boltaña, passing Aínsa on the way. It leaves Barbastro at 7.45 pm.

If you're driving, you might elect to continue north towards the Reserva Nacional de los Circos and France along the A-138, or cut north-west through the Valle de Solana for Torla, along the N-260, and the most common approach to the Parque Nacional de Ordesa y Monte Perdido.

Aínsa to Torla

At the time of writing, the N-260 from Aínsa to Torla and on to Biescas was in pretty bad shape along some stretches, although being improved. First stop, about five km out of Aínsa, is the pretty stone village of **Boltaña**. Once a Celtic settlement, it has a church and many houses which date from the 16th century. Unfortunately, the old town is well on the way to being engulfed by the new town. The tourist office (☎ 974-50 20 43) on the main road is open all year round. *Fonda Alegría* (☎ 974-50 21 83), Avenida de Ordesa 20, is the cheapest deal here at 2000/3000 ptas for singles/doubles.

From Boltaña the road winds through gorges and up the Valle de Solana towards **Broto** and the valley of the same name. This town is nothing special, but has accommodation that you may need when things get crowded. Much the same can be said for **Sarvisé**, a few km south. **Oto**, off the main road and two km south-west of Broto, is a little more pleasing to the eye. Broto has at least four hotels, and you may find one or two private houses offering rooms too. The high season is summer, and you'll probably only get doubles. The cheapest at 4000 ptas is *Hostal Español* (☎ 974-48 60 07), Avenida de Ordesa 20. In Sarvisé, try the cosy *Casa Frauca* (☎ 974-48 63 53), on the main road. It has a variety of rooms starting

at 3500 ptas for a double without private bath. In Oto, there are two *casas rurales* along Calle de la Peña, both charging 3500 ptas for doubles (you may get less for single occupancy).

From Broto, it's a few serpentine km north to **Torla**, the last hamlet on the way in to the Parque Nacional de Ordesa y Monte Perdido. A bus runs Monday to Saturday from Aínsa to Torla.

Aínsa to Torla via Escalona

A more dramatic route suggests itself for people with wheels. From Aínsa head 11 km north to Escalona and turn west along the HU-631, a minor road that links up with Sarvisé. The road now passes via the all-but-deserted villages of Buerba and Vió, shortly after which you get spectacular views over the Garganta de Añisclo gorge. There is a small *albergue* (basic refuge-style accommodation) in Nerín (☎ 974-48 61 38) and a couple more small places in Fanlo, the last town before Sarvisé.

Sabiñánigo to Torla

Those approaching Torla from Jaca will pass through the tawdry town of Sabiñánigo. You'll need to change buses here to get to Torla, but it's possible you'll only make it as far as **Biescas** in the same day with public transport. Biescas is not a bad little spot to get stuck, and *Pensión Las Heras* (☎ 974-50 27), Calle de Agustina de Aragón 35, is the cheapest place for a bed with singles/doubles starting at 2000/3000 ptas. Hitch-hikers trying their luck along the 25 km to Torla should note that there is a handful of places to stay in Gavin and Linas de Broto too.

Torla

The location remains enchanting, but holiday-boom building is increasingly obscuring this stone village's charm. There is an information office for the national park (summer only), and you can stock up on supplies in supermarkets open seven days a week. If you need to change money or pull some out of an ATM, do it here. You can also ferret out Editorial Alpina maps of the park area (600 ptas).

With so many places to stay, getting a bed for the night gets tricky only in the monster season of July-August, when booking well ahead is mandatory. There are four camping grounds in and around Torla.

In the *Refugio L'Atalaya* (☎ 974-48 60 22), in the town itself, a dormitory bed costs 900 ptas, or half-board 2700 ptas. The nearby *Refugio Lucien Briet* (☎ 974-48 62 21) has beds for 1000 ptas per person. Otherwise, the *Fonda Ballarín* (☎ 974-48 61 55), Calle de Capuvita 11, charges around 1800/3000 ptas for singles/doubles. The same people also run the more expensive *Hostal Alto Aragón* (☎ 974-48 61 72), at the same address. Doubles with private bathroom cost up to 4500 ptas. A little classier is the *Hotel Villa de Torla* (☎ 974-48 61 56), Plaza Nueva 1. Rooms cost up to 4500/6000 ptas plus IVA in the high season.

Bar Brecha, which runs the Refugio Lucien Briet, has a good menú del día for 1400 ptas.

A bus a day connects Torla with Aínsa, and another with Sabiñánigo.

PARQUE NACIONAL DE ORDESA Y MONTE PERDIDO

Some seven km north-east of Torla the road ends in a car park marking the entrance to the national park. The Casa de Recepción, when it's open, can help with information on walking trails through the park. You will also find a restaurant and souvenir shop. The range of walking possibilities in and beyond the park is great enough to keep walkers of most levels well occupied for days. Indeed, for some the first walk may be from Torla itself to the park proper, as there are no buses. A path leads across the Río Ara from the Hostal Bella Vista (on the main road in Torla) northwards for a few km before hitting the GR-11 long-distance path, and then east along the Río Araza.

Those planning to undertake walks into France should be sure to have their passports with them.

Circo de Soaso

Once in the park, one of the easier walks leads seven km east along the gorge of the Valle de Ordesa to the Circo de Soaso, a rocky balcony whose centrepiece is the Cascada (waterfall) de la Cola de Caballo. Follow the signs through the beech woods for 'Cascada' and 'Gradas'. Along the way you pass the little stone Refugio de Pastores, and several other waterfalls along the north bank of the Río Araza, including the charming Cascada del Abanico (not quite halfway). Most hikers elect to return along the south bank on the so-called Senda de los Cazadores (hunters' trail). From this side you get a better impression of the grandeur of the northern flank of the gorge. The whole circuit takes about seven hours.

Monte Perdido

Fitter trekkers, having climbed by a series of steep switchbacks to the top of the Circo de Soaso, strike out north for the *Refugio de Góriz* (or *Delgado Úbeda*; ☎ 974-50 02 45). This refuge is open all year and makes an ideal base for attempting the ascent of Monte Perdido, although the facilities are nothing great. You'll need climbing gear to bag the peak, one of the highest in the Pyrenees (3355 metres).

Circo de Cotatuero

Another interesting walk sees you veering north from the gorge shortly after leaving the car park. Follow the signs for Cotatuero and after a couple of hours and a fairly steep hike you reach yet another impressive waterfall. The sturdy-hearted may elect to climb the wall of the Circo by the series of iron pegs installed way back in 1881. From here you are about 2½ hours march from La Brecha de Rolando – a gap in the mountainous wall forming the frontier with France.

To France via Valle de Bujaruelo

A long but rewarding route into France starts about three km north of Torla, where the GR-11 trail forks north from the asphalt road. The GR-11 describes a long six km arc along the Valle de Bujaruelo to San Nicolás

ARAGÓN

de Bujaruelo, where there is a camping ground. From there you strike out on a three hour hike to the north-east along the Piñarroya valley. The path forks but rejoins about half an hour later at the Refugio de los Pastores. From here you push on to the Puerto de Bujaruelo, on the border with France. You are now in the French Parc National des Pyrénées, and in about two hours can descend to the village of Gavarnie (the direct walking trail branches off to the right after a short stretch down the asphalt road). Another possibility from San Nicolás is to strike out westwards for Panticosa. This is a long haul for which you should reckon on a minimum of eight hours walking.

Southern Gorges

South of Monte Perdido, the gaping wound of the **Garganta del Añiscolo** stretches away, a tectonic fracture in the mountain fabric. Although more adventurous walkers may want to descend the gorge from the Refugio de Góriz (see the Monte Perdido section) and so stay up high above the bottom, it is probably easier to make a day trip of it along the bottom from the south end – quite feasible if you have your own vehicle. Driving east from Sarvisé along the minor HU-631 road, take the left fork after Nerín (the right fork leads to Buerba and ultimately Escalona). This leads down to an opening in the gorge. It is possible to hike up as far north as La Ripareta and back in one day. Although the Editorial Alpina map only shows one trail, there are in fact two.

The less spectacular but pleasing **Gargantas de Escuain** over to the east can be approached from several points, so again it helps to have your own chariot. Narrow roads lead to the hamlets of Tella, Puértolas and Revilla. From the latter it is a short walk to Escuain, from where you head north-west up the gorge and return at leisure. This is an easy day trip that could be extended greatly by exploring the area south of Escuain.

JACA

In among Jaca's urban sprawl beats the heart of an ancient city. Occupied by the Muslims and later the Franks, Jaca became capital of the nascent kingdom of Aragón under Ramiro I in 1035, a state of affairs that lasted for 60 years until Huesca picked up the baton. It knew the rigours of occupation again when Napoleon's troopers moved in for five years in 1809. The military continues to play a role here, with an army academy housed in the citadel. More importantly, tourism and skiing further north have brought prosperity to the town. On winter weekends especially it is a kind of aprés-ski-cum-lager-lout fun town.

Information

The tourist office (☎ 36 00 98), Calle del Regimiento de Galicia 2, opens Monday to Friday from 9 am to 1.30 pm and 4.30 to 7 pm; Saturday from 10 am to 1 pm and 5 to 7 pm. There are plenty of banks, including a couple on Calle Mayor. The telephone code in Jaca (as in the rest of Huesca province) is ☎ 974.

For information on organising mountain activities and mediocre ski hire you could try Alcorce (☎ 36 39 72), Calle de la Salud 5.

Things to See

Spare some time to give the town a look over. The **catedral**, although still a fine building, has seen much of its original French-style Romanesque grace obscured by later tinkering. The real attraction lies in the **Museo Diocesano**, housed in what was the church cloister. A remarkable collection of frescos, gathered from churches throughout the region, has been brought together under one roof, allowing a rare chance to observe the evolution of religious art from 12th century Romanesque through to 15th century Late Gothic. The museum opens daily but Monday from 11 am to 1.30 pm and 4 to 6.30 pm. Admission is 200 ptas, and well worth it. Addicts of all things Romanesque may want to see the tomb of Doña Sánchez, Ramiro I's daughter, which lies in the **Iglesia de San Salvador y San Ginés**.

The 16th century star-shaped **ciudadela** (citadel) can only be visited as part of a guided tour from 11 am to noon and 5 to 6

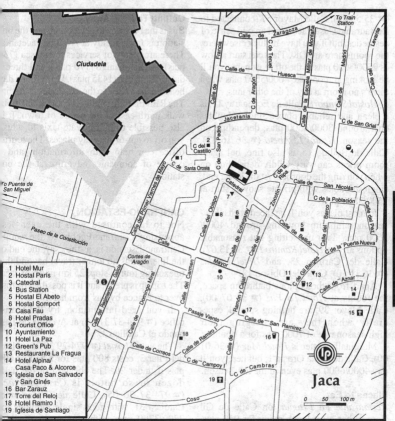

1 Hotel Mur
2 Hostal París
3 Catedral
4 Bus Station
5 Hostal El Abeto
6 Hostal Somport
7 Casa Fau
8 Hotel Pradas
9 Tourist Office
10 Ayuntamiento
11 Hotel La Paz
12 Green's Pub
13 Restaurante La Fragua
14 Hotel Alpina/
   Casa Paco & Alcorce
15 Iglesia de San Salvador
   y San Ginés
16 Bar Zarauz
17 Torre del Reloj
18 Hotel Ramiro I
19 Iglesia de Santiago

ARAGÓN

...m, when the soldiers briefly drop their
...uard. West of the citadel, the well-preserved
...edieval **Puente de San Miguel** spans the
...ío Aragón.

pecial Events

...ca puts on its party outfit for the week-long
...iesta de Santa Orosia, the town's patron
...int, which starts on June 23. If you want to
...e medieval jousts, try to be around on the
...rst Friday of May, when Jaca celebrates a
...mous victory over the evil Muslim hordes
... 760.

Places to Stay

There are few truly cheap options in Jaca,
and the place can fill up easily in peak
periods, particularly summer, Easter and
holiday weekends.

Camping Peña Oroel (☎ 36 02 15), a few
km out on the road to Sabiñánigo, is open for
Easter and from mid-June to mid-September.

In town, *Hostal París* (☎ 36 10 20), Plaza
de San Pedro 5, is one of the few places
suitable for a low budget, although the reception can be crotchety. Singles/doubles with
private shower start at 1800/2600 ptas.

The interior decorators at the *Hotel Alpina*

(☎ 35 53 69), Calle Mayor 57 (connected to Restaurante Casa Paco), had an odd sense of aesthetics, but if you have no luck elsewhere, the rooms here are OK. They can start as low as 2500/3000 ptas in the off season, but you'll be looking at more like 4000/5600 ptas when there's no room at any of the other inns.

Hostal Somport, Calle de Echegaray 11, is a clean and reliable place. Singles/doubles cost around 3000/4500 ptas, depending on the season. *Hostal El Abeto* (☎ 36 16 42), Calle de Bellido 15, is also fine, but again room prices can vary wildly depending on when you ring the doorbell. At the lower end, singles/doubles with private shower start at 2500/3800 ptas.

In most places you'll be faced with a low-season minimum hovering around 4000/5500 ptas. Two unexciting but reasonable options are the *Hotel Ramiro I* (☎ 36 13 67), Calle del Carmen 23, and *Hotel Pradas* (☎ 36 11 50), Calle del Obispo 12.

Apart from the copious bathroom space, the rooms at *Hotel La Paz* (☎ 36 07 00), Calle Mayor 39, are nothing special, especially when they are charging their high-season rate of 7000 ptas for a double.

Marginally better is *Hotel Mur* (☎ 36 01 00), Calle de Santa Orosia 1, but here you'll pay 4000/6000 ptas even in the low season.

Places to Eat
Restaurante La Fragua, on Calle de Gil Berges, has a set lunch menu for 950 ptas. They seem to be especially fond of ham. *Casa Fau*, on Plaza de la Catedral, as well as being a lively place to hang out for a drink, has a mouthwatering array of food items draped along the bar.

Entertainment
About the only conceivable reason for hanging about in Jaca longer than a day is to detox a little from all the bucolic delights in the nearby mountains and hit the bars. A bevy of them lines Calle de Gil Berges, off Calle Mayor, and trickles off into the neighbouring lanes. One that seems particularly popular is *Green's Pub*. For a slicker, less boisterous crowd, try *Bar Zarauz*, on Plaza del Pilar 10.

Getting There & Away
Bus is the best way to get around, and the bus station is fairly handy at Avenida Jacetania. There are plenty of services to Huesca (735 ptas) and Sabiñánigo (170 ptas), and three a day to Zaragoza (1435 ptas). Up to four a day head up the valley to the ski slopes at Astún. The RENFE train station is about a half-hour walk north-east of the centre of town. It is also possible to hire private taxis to whisk you off to out-of-the-way places. The tourist office can help with information, and a couple of companies advertise at the bus station.

CANFRANC-ESTACIÓN
Not to be confused with the even less appetising Canfranc-Pueblo to the south, Canfranc-Estación is, as they say, the end of the line. Trains no longer travel beyond this unexciting tourist stop, 25 km north of Jaca. The trip up is pretty, and it is possible to cross over to France by bus from here.

If you need information, try the tourist office (☎ 974-37 31 41) at Avenida de Fernando el Católico 3.

The *youth hostel* (☎ 974-29 30 25), Plaza del Pilar 3, costs 800 ptas for a bed or 600 ptas if under 26. The cheapest of the half-dozen or so hotels is *Casa Marracó* (☎ 974-37 30 05), Calle de Fernando el Católico 31, with good singles/doubles for 2200/3200 ptas with shower in the low season, or more with full private bathroom.

SKI RESORTS NORTH OF JACA
Candanchú & Astún
Just 34 km north of Jaca is Aragón's westernmost and longest-established ski resort. Some 40 km of widely varied pistes make the area appealing to most grades of skiers. Although there are only four hotels, you can organise alternative accommodation in apartments and the like by calling ☎ 974-37 32 63. The small town is reasonably well equipped with general stores and ski hire shops.

One advantage of Candanchú is that there

Tunnel Vision

Candanchú is just inside Spain's border with France, and is reached along a steep, winding road loaded with switchbacks and plenty of great views. A controversial project to bypass all this inefficient meandering with a tunnel has raised local hackles. Ecologists claim that construction of the nine km that will constitute the Somport Tunnel will cause untold damage. The last few bears *(osos pardos)* living in the Pyrenees (estimates range from as few as two on the Spanish side to 15 on both sides of the border) call this area home, but will be endangered by the massive excavation and heavy truck traffic that the construction presupposes. Various species of eagle and other birds may leave the area for good, and much of the teeming river life in the Río Aragón and Río Aspe will be affected. Opponents say that for the 200,000 million ptas the project is expected to cost, the average time-saving for vehicles on this route will be 16 minutes. ■

is another good resort, Astún, just three km o the east. The 33 km of pistes there are argely for reasonably capable skiers. The only place to stay is the rather expensive *Hotel Europa* (☎ 974-37 33 12) in town, which charges up to 13,000 ptas per double in the high season.

Panticosa & El Formigal

Good things come in pairs, and the comparatively small Panticosa ski resort has a bigger counterpart about 10 km further north, El Formigal. The runs at Panticosa aren't too distressing, and the long, pretty Mazarrahuala is a must for everyone. If you want to book accommodation in advance, call ☎ 974-48 81 26. Cross-country skiing is also an option in the area.

El Formigal, a regular host for ski competitions, is a livelier place with far more extensive infrastructure than Panticosa. Here you have the full range of facilities, including restaurants, bars, discos, saunas and the ike at your disposal, as well as 50 km of ski uns.

WEST OF JACA
San Juan de la Peña

A much recommended excursion from Jaca, but difficult to undertake without some form of independent transport, is to the mountain eyrie of one of Aragón's more memorable monasteries, San Juan de la Peña. The first 11 km you could cover by Jaca-Pamplona bus, getting off at the turn-off for **Santa Cruz de la Seros** (four km), a tumbledown village gathered in under the skirts of its sparsely decorated Romanesque parish church. The church is open daily from 10 am to 1 pm and 4 to 6 pm. Entry costs 100 ptas, except on Mondays, when it is free. The snug and cosy *Hostelería Santa Cruz* (☎ 974-36 19 75) has beds for 1500 ptas per person and good food.

From here you can walk up a marked path to San Juan de la Peña (about 50 minutes), or follow the circuitous road if you have a vehicle (hard work on a good bicycle but possible). The views from vantage points higher up on this road are magnificent, taking in the Pyrenees to the north and several peaks to the east and west.

You come quite suddenly upon the original monastery, sheltering below an overhanging lip of rock in a bend in the road. Established in the 9th century, it has suffered all that history could throw at it, sacked and rebuilt repeatedly until Napoleon's troops had a last go at it in 1809. It is said to have once held the Holy Grail (now in Valencia) and the lower level of the monastery, with its Mozarabic church, is thought to have been built in the 10th century. The Romanesque cloister has, in a loose sense, the living rock for a roof.

A couple of km further up is the more recent baroque monastery, founded in the 17th century. It can't be visited, but you can drop into the restaurant and bar next door.

Valle de Hecho

Less spectacular than the territory further to the east, the Valle de Hecho nonetheless boasts some charming old stone villages and culminates, at its northern end, in the beautiful Selva de Oza.

A bus leaves Jaca daily except Sunday at

ARAGÓN

ARAGÓN

4.45 pm for Hecho. There are no buses further up the valley.

Hecho The biggest village in the valley, Hecho (Echo) is a surprising warren of silent stone houses and winding lanes. Unlikely though it may seem today, it was briefly the seat of what was to become the Kingdom of Aragón in the 9th century. The only 'sight' is the Museo Etnológico, something of a genre in these parts with odds and sods supposedly characteristic of rural life in the area. It's near the church.

You could not do better than stay at *Pensión Casa Blasquico* (☎ 974-37 50 07), Plaza del Palacio 1, almost totally obscured by batteries of exotic flora. The charming rustic lodgings are attached to an equally tempting restaurant. Singles/doubles cost 2500/3500 ptas. If it's full, there are two other bland hostales and a hotel to choose from.

Siresa A couple of km up the road to the north, Siresa is another hamlet typical of the region and is dominated by the formidable Iglesia de San Pedro. *Fonda Pirineos* (☎ 974-37 51 13), Plaza Mayor, is the cheaper of two places here, where basic singles/doubles without bathroom go for 2000/3000 ptas. A few km north on the road to the Selva de Oza, the *Hospedería Usón* (☎ 974-37 53 58) lies in splendid isolation with fine singles/doubles equipped with TV for 4000/5500 ptas in the high season. The *asador* here is a popular food stop.

Selva de Oza The main attraction of the valley lies at the top end. From Siresa the road follows Río Aragón Subordán another 12 km and ends at the sprawling but beautifully located *Camping Selva de Oza* (☎ 974-37 51 68; open June to September). The GR-11 trail passes a few km north of the camping ground, and at least half a dozen mountain peaks offer themselves in an arc to the north and east for strenuous day assaults.

Valle de Ansó
As with the Valle de Hecho, the main interest

for walkers only begins at the northern end of the valley, but the village of Ansó is an enticing stop on the way up.

The bus from Jaca to Hecho continues to Ansó (arriving at 6.35 pm). There are no buses further up the valley. The Editorial Alpina map entitled *Ansó-Echo* is very useful for this area.

Ansó The rough-hewn stone houses here repeat the pretty picture of Hecho, but on a smaller scale. Like its bigger brother in the next valley, it could make an ideal base for exploring the region, especially if you have the freedom of movement your own transport can provide. The local Museo Etnológico is in the church but does not seem to stick rigidly to the posted timetable. If interested, call at the house opposite the church. Admission is 200 ptas.

The *Posada Magoria* (☎ 974-37 00 49) is a superb country cottage – the rooms even have old porcelain hand basins. Singles/doubles cost 3000/4600 ptas, and downstairs you can savour the delights of good vegetarian cooking.

Hostal Kimboa (☎ 974-37 01 30) has simple clean rooms with little character, but private bathroom, for 3500/5500 ptas. Three other hostales also compete for trade, with singles/doubles starting at a minimum 2500/3500 ptas with private shower. They all have restaurants, and a sprinkling of bars for a beer and a snack complete the entertainment picture here.

Zuriza Walkers head north 15 km from Ansó to Zuriza, basically little more than a camping ground and glorified refugio. *Camping Zuriza* (☎ 974-37 01 96) is popular, so you should try to book ahead if you plan to stay there in peak periods and weekends. If you don't want to camp, there is also a handful of double rooms here starting at 4000 ptas without private bath, or 5500 ptas with. A rough but drivable track leads five km further north to the *Refugio Linza*, open all year and equipped with a bar.

The GR-11 long-distance walking route passes right through Zuriza, so you could follow it west to Isaba (Navarra), a hike for which you should set aside at least six hours. Eastwards, the path meanders on via the Selva de Oza (see above) to Candanchú. This involves at least 10 hours legwork. A couple of peaks right on the border with France – Sobarcal (2249 metres) and Petrechema (2360 metres) – attract a lot of attention. Both can be done as day excursions from the Linza refuge (or even from Zuriza), calculating a couple of extra hours for the walk to and from Linza from Zuriza). The latter is a trickier ascent than the former.

Other walks of varying duration and difficulty abound, as do opportunities for rock climbing and caving.

NORTH-WESTERN ARAGÓN
Sos del Rey Católico & the Cinco Villas
Just inside the border with Navarra and about 150 km north-west of Zaragoza, or 85-odd km west of Jaca, Sos del Rey Católico takes its name from a son of whom any town would be proud, Fernando II of Aragón, born here in 1452. He went on to marry Isabel I of Castilla and together, known as Los Reyes Católicos (the Catholic Monarchs), they finished off the Reconquista and united all Spain. The old medieval town, which could perhaps do with a little more tender loving care, is nevertheless a fascinating little spider's web of twisting, cobbled lanes and claustrophobic houses smothered atop a hill rising on the northern rim of the Aragonese wheat plains.

While wandering, worth pointing out are the Castillo de la Peña Feliciano and the Gothic Iglesia de San Estéban. The great man is said to have been born in one of several mansions scattered about the centre, the Palacio de Sada. Apart from the expensive *parador*, the only place to stay is the *Fonda Fernandina* (☎ 976-88 81 20), which has basic singles/doubles for 1000/1700 ptas.

If you have a car, a little-travelled back route (A-1601) connects Sos with the N-240 east of the Embalse de Yesa. **Urriés** is a crumbling, near-abandoned village that invites exploration. If you really want aban-

doned, push on 14 km east of Urriés for what is virtually a ghost town, where the only signs of life are in the recently reopened pilgrim *Albergue Ruesta*. It is not even marked on most maps.

A zigzag route south from Sos towards Zaragoza takes you through the remaining four of the Cinco Villas, which were declared towns *(villas)* by Felipe V in the 18th century. A minor road bearing south-east leads to **Uncastillo**, seemingly little touched by the passage of time and dominated by the Gothic tower of the otherwise mainly Romanesque Iglesia de Santa María. There is a castle. Follow the Río Riguel 16 km south-west into the plains and you reach **Sádaba**, which has a 13th century castle and remains of a synagogue. From Sádaba the A-127 proceeds south to **Ejea de los Caballeros**, by far the largest of the Cinco Villas and once a walled town. If you need to stay, there are four hotels. From here the road drops another 26 km south to **Tauste**, about 50 km short of Zaragoza to the south-east, and sporting a mudéjar-style church. *Hostal Casa Pepe* (☎ 976-85 58 32), Calle de Santa Clara 7, has singles/doubles for 2600/4000 ptas.

Cinco Villas buses run daily from Avenida de Navarra 81 in Zaragoza to all these towns. The Sangüesa company also runs a daily service to Sos del Rey Católico from next to Zaragoza's El Portillo train station.

The South

Although vast sweeps of the country immediately south of Zaragoza are made up of dreary plains or a lunar landscape of bald, uninviting ridges, there are several exceptions to the rule. Teruel, the capital of Aragón's southernmost province of the same name, is a storage house of some of the best examples of mudéjar craftsmanship you will find anywhere, and the nearby ochre town of Albarracín is a medieval Muslim treat. To the east of Teruel stretch the uplands of El Maestrazgo, a rugged and sparsely populated mountain area where vivid green fields and valleys alternate with hostile gorges and at times snowbound slopes.

ROADS TO TERUEL

If starting in Zaragoza, you could opt for a couple of routes south. The N-330 takes you south 184 km to Teruel via Daroca – a pleasant stop en route. Alternatively, following the N-II south-west (towards Madrid) will bring you to Calatayud, which makes a vaguely interesting launch pad for an excursion to the Monasterio de Piedra, 30-odd km further still south-west. Back in Calatayud, the N-234 heads south-east to meet the N-330 just north of Daroca.

Calatayud

There is really very little to keep you in this rather nondescript and much-neglected town, but if you happen to be hanging around, there are a few points of interest. Head into the maze of narrow streets at the heart of the old town and search out the Iglesia de Santa María, with a fine platteresque portal and breathtaking mudéjar bell tower. The 15th century Iglesia de San Andrés has a similarly impressive bell tower. The castle ruins are not among the country's best. The Iglesia de San Pedro's tower, on Rua de Eduardo Dato, looks as though it's about to topple into the street.

Should you have to stay, there are several cheap and very basic fondas to choose from. *Pensión La Perla* (☎ 976-88 13 40), Calle San Anton 17, has singles/doubles/triples for 1500/2700/3600 ptas. The *Pensión Casa Sixto* (☎ 976-88 32 94) next door is in the same league, as is the *Fonda El Comercio* (☎ 976-88 11 15), Rua de Eduardo Dato 33, which has singles/doubles for 1300/2400 ptas.

There are regular buses from the bus station, in the centre of town, to Zaragoza (Calle de Almagro 18), and three a day to Madrid.

Monasterio de Piedra

Set in the soothing park of the same name, the one-time Cistercian Monasterio de Piedra tends a little to the Disneyesque. Founded in 1194 and moved to its present site in 1218, the monastery was abandoned in the 1830s. Now in private hands and partly restored to house a posh hotel, much of it remains a shell. The park around it, with its waterfalls and caves, is pleasant enough, but somehow the whole reeks of the artificial. It's not exactly cheap either. If you want to see the monastery and wander around the park, you're looking at 900 ptas. Or you can get separate tickets for each if you want do only one or the other (800 ptas for the park and 250 ptas for the monastery). The monastery is open for (generally guided) visits from 10 am to 1.30 pm and 3 to 7 pm. The park is open until dusk.

If you want to stay around here, there are a few hostales in nearby Nuévalos and on the road between the two. The *Hostal San Sebastián* (☎ 976-87 04 96), about three km short of the monastery when coming from Nuévalos, has decent rooms for 2000 ptas per person. *Las Truchas* (☎ 976-84 90 40) is closer to the monastery, but rooms cost from 3000/5000 ptas up. Singles and doubles at the hotel in the monastery (☎ 976-84 90 11; fax 84 90 54) start at 6995/9095 ptas.

There are one or two daily buses between Nuévalos and Calatayud, but nothing to the monastery. In summer, the Automovil Zaragoza company runs direct buses to the monastery from its office in Calle de Almagro 18, Zaragoza. Otherwise, they run a couple on weekends.

Daroca

An attractive possibility for an overnight stop, Daroca lies low in a valley through which the highway runs south to Teruel. On the hills to either side rise the crumbling remnants of the once-extensive city walls. Some of the original 114 towers have been restored, but most have disappeared. Calle Mayor, the main street, is marked at either end by monumental gates – the Puerta Baja (Low Gate) at the southern end is the more imposing of the two. Off to the right (when looking south towards the Puerta Baja) lies the main square, Plaza de España, dominated by the Iglesia Colegiata de Santa María. Restructured in the 16th century, it is largely a Renaissance building, although the bell tower is mudéjar. Its Museo de los Sagrados Corporales, containing a modest display of religious art, opens Tuesday to Saturday from 11 am to 1 pm and 5.30 to 7.30 pm. Entry is a rather steep (for what you see) 300 ptas.

The best place to stay is the *Pensión El Ruejo* (☎ 976-80 11 90), Calle Mayor 88. It has singles/doubles without private bath for 2000/4000 ptas and for 3000/5600 ptas with. Just outside the northern entrance to town is the *Hostal Legido* (☎ 976-80 01 90), with functional rooms for 2800/4600 ptas.

Buses stop outside the Mesón Felix, Calle Mayor 104. There are at least three a day to Zaragoza (Agreda Automovil company at Avenida de Valencia 20) and five to Teruel. An early morning service goes to Calatayud.

There is little to hold you up on the way south to Teruel, although some of the villages along the N-330 boast the odd mudéjar church or Roman bridge (Luco de Jiloca and Calamocha).

TERUEL

A compact provincial capital of 30,000, Teruel is a largely modern town. It does, however, contain a handful of some of the most ornate and striking mudéjar monuments in the country, which merit a couple of hours of your time at least. Teruel makes a decent stopover if you are travelling between Zaragoza and Valencia, or indeed for those making their way eastwards to the coast from Cuenca (Castilla-La Mancha).

History

Although the region has been inhabited since prehistoric times, the town of Teruel only really began to become significant under the Muslims. Retaken by the Christians in 1171, the city became something of an operational base for Jaume I of Aragón in his campaign to wrest Valencia from Muslim hands.

Orientation & Information

They say there are no distances in Teruel, and you can get around easily on foot. The train station is downhill on the western side of the town, and the bus station on the other side of town, to the east. From either it is a short walk into the centre. There's a small cluster of hotels quite close to the cathedral, in the northern, older half of town.

The tourist office (☎ 60 22 79) is at Calle Tomás Nogués 1, and in summer opens Monday to Saturday from 9 am to 9 pm. Throughout the rest of the year it opens from 9 am to 2.30 pm and 5 to 8.30 pm (5 to 7.30 pm on Saturday). It's closed on Sunday. The post office is on Calle de Yagüe de Salas, and the Telefónica locutorio at Calle de San Andrés 13. The latter is open Monday to Friday from 9 am to 1.30 pm and 5 to 9.30 pm. It opens on Saturday morning too. The postcode for Teruel is 44080 and the telephone code is ☎ 978.

If you need an ambulance, call the Cruz Roja on ☎ 60 22 22. The Hospital General Obispo Polanco (☎ 64 66 00) is on Calle de Ruiz Jarabo 7. There are plenty of banks around Plaza Torico. The local police can be found in the basement of the ayuntamiento.

Catedral

Viewed from outside, the cathedral is like a complicated brickwork wedding cake, decorated in part with brightly coloured ceramic tiles – a rich example of the mudéjar imagination at work. First begun in 1176, work continued on the church until it was raised to cathedral status in the 16th century. The bell tower is perhaps its most appealing feature, but then beautiful bell towers are a hallmark of Teruel. It was erected in the 12th and 13th centuries and the mainly mudéjar style is tinged with a little Romanesque.

Inside the church, it is the artesonado ceiling, again a testament to the genius of the mudéjar style, that draws your attention. You can pop 100 ptas into a machine to light up the ceiling, in which are depicted saints, kings, Moors and battles in among the more standard geometric designs. Behind the church, the Museo Diocesano has some religious art. It opens daily except Monday from 10 am to 2 pm, and entry costs 150 ptas.

ARAGÓN

ARAGÓN

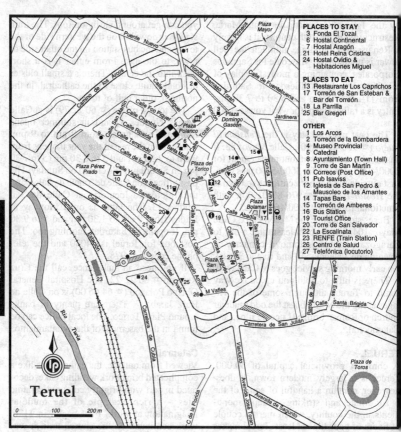

PLACES TO STAY
3 Fonda El Tozal
6 Hostal Continental
7 Hostal Aragón
21 Hotel Reina Cristina
24 Hostal Ovidio &
   Habitaciones Miguel

PLACES TO EAT
13 Restaurante Los Caprichos
17 Torreón de San Esteban &
   Bar del Torreón
18 La Parrilla
25 Bar Gregori

OTHER
1 Los Arcos
2 Torreón de la Bombardera
4 Museo Provincial
5 Catedral
8 Ayuntamiento (Town Hall)
9 Torre de San Martín
10 Correos (Post Office)
11 Pub Isaviss
12 Iglesia de San Pedro &
   Mausoleo de los Amantes
14 Tapas Bars
15 Torreón de Amberes
16 Bus Station
19 Tourist Office
20 Torre de San Salvador
22 La Escalinata
23 RENFE (Train Station)
26 Centro de Salud
27 Telefónica (locutorio)

Teruel

0   100   200 m

Mudéjar Monuments

Of the other mudéjar monuments around
Teruel, the tower of the Iglesia de San Salvador, a 13th century fantasy of brick and
ceramics, is the most impressive. You can
climb to the top of the Torre de San Salvador
from 5 to 8 pm.

Closer to the northern end of the old town
at the end of Calle de los Amantes is the Torre
de San Martín, much the same in dimensions
and style, but a little more worn around the
edges. If you head out of the Torre de San
Salvador and down towards the train station,
you pass down La Escalinata, an equally

obviously mudéjar-inspired brick and
ceramic staircase.

Iglesia de San Pedro

More or less a block east from Plaza Torico,
another mudéjar church, the Iglesia de San
Pedro, watches over the **Mausoleo de los
Amantes**. The church is now covered in
scaffolding, but for most people the main
interest lies next door in the mausoleum
anyway. There, supposedly, lie buried the
remains of Isabel and Diego, 13th century
star-crossed lovers who died of grief at
seeing their love frustrated. The mausoleum

s open daily except Monday from 10 am to
? pm and 5 to 7.30 pm, and entry is 50 ptas.

Museo Provincial

Housed in the 16th century Casa de la Comunidad, the Museo Provincial is on Plaza
Padre Polanco. The building is Teruel's best
example of Aragonese Renaissance, and was
completely restored in the 1970s and 80s. It
contains mainly archaeological exhibits and
entry is free. It opens Tuesday to Friday from
0 am to 2 pm and 4 to 7 pm, but mornings
only on weekends. It is closed on Monday.

Los Arcos & Walls

At the northern end of the town stands an
aqueduct built in 1533 and known as Los
Arcos (the arches). Little remains of the
city's medieval walls, but a couple of turrets
still stand along the eastern side of town, one
of them now converted into a snack bar.

Special Events

On the Sunday and Monday closest to St
Christopher's Day (Día de San Cristóbal; 10
July), fall Las Fiestas de la Vaquilla del

✦✦✦✦✦✦✦✦✦✦✦✦

Diego & Isabel
After years seeking fame and fortune in war
and peace across Spain, Diego returned to
Teruel to claim the hand of the woman for whom
he had done it all, Isabel. He was a little late,
though, arriving after the expiry of the time limit
imposed by Isabel's parents, right on the day
of her marriage to a nobleman from Albarracín.
The two had been lovers since adolescence,
and the grief-stricken Diego managed to see
Isabel that night and asked for one last kiss.
Seeing his request refused, he promptly
expired at her feet. At his funeral in the Iglesia
de San Pedro the following day, Isabel, still in
her wedding finery, stepped forward to give
Diego the kiss he had so pined for in life, and
she, too, promptly died. So astounded were the
townspeople by all of this that they decided to
bury the two lovers together in the church
where Isabel had died. The bodies, it is said,
were later transferred to what is now their
mausoleum. ■

✦✦✦✦✦✦✦✦✦✦✦✦

Ángel, in celebration of the foundation of the
town.

Places to Stay

A good, cheap place with a little character is
the *Fonda El Tozal* (☎ 60 10 22), Calle del
Rincón 5. Singles/doubles cost 1300/2500
ptas in rooms with low, wood-beam ceilings.
Nearby, the *Hostal Aragón* (☎ 60 13 87),
Calle de Santa María 4, has ordinary rooms
without own bath for 1620/2750 ptas and
2775/4450 ptas with private bath. The
Hostal Continental (☎ 60 23 17), Calle de
Juan Pérez 9, has rooms for 2000/3200 ptas
without private bath and 2800/4500 ptas
with.

If you prefer to be near the train station,
there are a couple of simple but acceptable
options. *Hostal Ovidio* (☎ 60 28 66), Calle
de la Estación 6, has singles/doubles without
own bath for 1300/2400 ptas (1500/2800
ptas in peak season). On the 2nd floor of the
same building, *Habitaciones Miguel* (☎ 60
04 31) has four rooms for 2000/3000 ptas.

For something classier, you could stay at
the modern *parador* (☎ 60 18 00; fax 60 86
12), a few km to the north of town. Rooms
there cost from 10,000 to 12,000 ptas. Close
to the Torre de San Salvador is the *Hotel
Reina Cristina* (☎ 60 68 60), Paseo del
Óvalo 1, the most expensive place in town
with singles/doubles for 9400/13,700 ptas.

Places to Eat

Spain is pretty obsessed with all things
porcine, and Teruel is no exception, going to
great lengths to promote its local version of
jamón. Virutas de jamón – ham shavings –
are one form in which it sometimes arrives
at your table.

Bar Gregori, Paseo del Óvalo 6, is a
popular spot for tapas and raciones, and there
are a couple of tapas bars on Plaza de la
Judería too. For something more substantial,
try *Bar El Torreón*, Ronda de Ambeles 28.
It's in one of the turrets (Torreón de San
Esteban) of what were the city walls, and
offers a filling set lunch for 800 ptas. *La
Parrilla*, Calle de San Esteban 2, is a good

ARAGÓN

place to get a hearty meal in the heart of Teruel's bar zone.

A brighter, more genteel sort of place is the *Restaurante Los Caprichos*, a block behind the Iglesia de San Pedro on Calle de Hartzembusch.

Entertainment

Most of the late-night excitement takes place in the bars of Calle de San Estéban and the immediate area. For a more relaxed drink or coffee, *Pub Isaviss*, on the corner of Calle del Salvador and Calle de Yagüe de Salas, is a good choice.

Getting There & Away

Bus Services depart from the bright new bus station terminal on Ronda de Ambeles for many destinations including Zaragoza, Valencia, Cuenca, Barcelona, Alicante, Madrid (2215 ptas one way), Alcañiz and Ademuz. Be aware that in most cases there are only a few departures per day.

Train Teruel is about equidistant from Zaragoza and Valencia on the train line linking the two. There are three services a day, and the trip in either direction can take up to three hours.

Car & Motorcycle The main road north to Zaragoza is the N-330. It continues to the south-east as the N-234, leading to Sagunto on the Valencian coast and thence to Valencia itself.

RINCÓN DE ADEMUZ & BEYOND

A picturesque drive into one of those anomalous corners of Spain – in this case a piece of Valencia inside Aragón – leads virtually south from Teruel along the N-330 towards the so-called Rincón de Ademuz – the 'Ademuz corner'. The road follows the heavily cultivated green valley of the Río Turia, closed in by arid, table-top mountains, and gradually dips into a narrow ravine as far as Villel, where it opens up again before entering the little enclave of Valencia province.

The Rincón's main town is Ademuz, a steep and unremarkable little place, beyond

which the road winds its way south through two small villages – Casas Altas (High Houses) and Casas Bajas (Low Houses) – that appear not to have changed much in centuries. The road continues to trail the deepening gorge of the Alto Turia before crossing into Cuenca province (Castilla-La Mancha) in quite spectacular fashion. At Santa Cruz de Moya the road forks. You can take the scenic but slow C-234 into Valencia or follow the faster N-330 around the long way to Valencia city via Requena.

Back at Ademuz, a secondary road (the N-420) cuts west towards Cuenca (see the Castilla-La Mancha chapter), skirting the southern hills of the Serranía de Cuenca.

If you need to stay in this area, about the only choice is the *Hostal Casa Domingo* (☎ 978-78 20 30), Avenida Valencia 1, in Ademuz. Decent rooms cost 2350/3725 ptas.

A bus leaves Ademuz daily for Teruel at 8 am and one or two per day go to Valencia. Buses stop in Ademuz outside the Hostal Casa Domingo.

ALBARRACÍN

The crenellated walls overshadowing the brick-red medieval town of Albarracín dramatically announce the hillside town's presence even before you have arrived. For four years from 1009 it was the seat of the tiny Islamic statelet of Ibn Razin, and subsequently an independent Christian kingdom in the hands of the Azagra family sandwiched between Castilla and Aragón from 1170 to 1285.

The cool, narrow lanes of Albarracín even today are in the best tradition of the Arab medina, and are vaguely reminiscent of Toledo – albeit on a much smaller scale. Centuries-old buildings lean and bulge alarmingly over some streets, but there is none of the mucky chaos of the true medina. If there were such a thing, Albarracín would win the world's Tidy Medina awards. It has been proposed as a UNESCO monument of worldwide interest.

Information

The tourist office (☎ 71 02 51) is in the Casa

le la Sierra on Calle de la Excma Diputación Provincial, just off Plaza Mayor. You'll find he post office and a couple of banks on or ust off Plaza Mayor. The postcode is 44100 und the telephone code is ☎ 978.

Things to See

There are few specific sites. The cathedral, with its cupola typical of the Spanish Levant, s closed for restoration, and not far off lie he ruins of a castle erected by the Muslims. The city walls that climb the slopes above the sity have been much restored, but for all that are imposing. Best of all, walk the lanes and enjoy the play of colour – the earthy red of he town's buildings and green of its gardens.

Hiking

f you fancy hiking in the Montes Universales to the south or the Sierra de Albarracín to the north, you could try contacting Lobetania (☎ 71 00 72). They also ake people around in 4WDs.

Places to Stay & Eat

The cheapest place to stay would be the HI Albergue Juvenil (☎ 71 00 05), Calle de Santa María 5, down from the cathedral. About three km out of town on the road to Teruel is another youth hostel, the Aben-Racin (☎ 60 18 19). Both were closed for renovations at the time of writing. A bed at either costs 1400 ptas a night, or 1000 ptas for those under 26. Breakfast is another 200 ptas.

Otherwise, the most cost-effective option s the reasonable Mesón del Gallo (☎ 71 00 32), Calle Los Puentes 1, on the main road ust beyond the tunnel. Rooms with TV and phone cost 2000/4000 ptas. They have a restaurant and bar too.

Possibly the most attractive deal is the Casa de Santiago (☎ 70 03 16), Subida a las Torres 11. This cosy place has just five charmingly appointed rooms, and lies a short way off Plaza Mayor. Singles/doubles cost 4000/6300 ptas (the latter are 7000 ptas in the high season). The Hotel Albarracín (☎ 71 00 11), Calle Azagra s/n, is a comfy hotel with singles/doubles/triples for 6000/

10,500/12,125 ptas (plus 7% IVA). Prices rise in the high season.

There are several restaurants in the streets off Plaza Mayor, although none are remarkably cheap. La Taberna, on the square itself, does good raciones and tapas. The nearby Bar Aben Razin is an atmospheric place for a drink.

Getting There & Away

A daily bus connects the town with Teruel, 38 km east. It stops near the Mesón del Gallo.

WEST INTO CASTILLA-LA MANCHA

For those with a vehicle, a couple of routes suggest themselves if you plan to head west via Albarracín into Castilla-La Mancha. The TE-903, west from Albarracín, forks after seven km. The way to the left leads into Cuenca province of Castilla-La Mancha, through varied and often pretty countryside (the road is in bad shape from the fork until you hit the CU-921 in Cuenca province, from where it follows the Río Júcar gorge to the city of Cuenca).

The right fork takes you through the picturesque Reserva Nacional de los Montes Universales and into Guadalajara province in Castilla-La Mancha. You could follow several routes, but perhaps the one that passes Checa, Terzaga and Peralejos de las Truchas across the mountains of the Serranía de Cuenca, and then down the Hoz de Beteta (Beteta Gorge) towards the Alcarria area of Cuenca and Guadalajara provinces, is the most scenic. See also the Castilla-La Mancha chapter.

EL MAESTRAZGO

The series of sierras that stretches east of Teruel across southern Aragón and into the province of Castellón de la Plana in Valencia present a smorgasbord of bleak rocky peaks, dramatic gorges and verdant fields. The highest peaks just top 2000 metres and the area is littered with small pueblos, seemingly abandoned to their own devices. Unless you have a lot of time, you really need your own vehicle to explore El Maestrazgo in any depth. Buses link most places, but rarely

ARAGÓN

more than once a day, and forward connections are virtually impossible on the same day. What follows is a somewhat serpentine route from Teruel to Alcañiz, with a selection of interesting villages and scenic roads. The weather can be cold and unpredictable in winter – you can be coasting along in pleasant sunshine one minute, fogged in and poured upon the next. Roads are being upgraded, but the older ones can be hairy in adverse conditions.

Southern Maestrazgo

The most straightforward approach to the area from Teruel is the TE-800 road, which forks off the northbound N-420 a few km out of the city. A 35 km drive through largely inhospitable country brings you to **Cedrillas**, a dishevelled little spot with castle ruins and a mudéjar church. You can follow this same road west as far as Cantavieja (see below) and on into the Valencia region. The windswept heights gradually give way to quite spectacular scenery, particularly as you wind your way down from the Puerto de Villaroya (1701 metres).

To have a look at the southernmost reaches of El Maestrazgo, take a right instead down the TE-802, 15 km east of Cedrillas. This narrow back road takes you down a few hundred metres and the change in scenery is almost instant, leafy and soothing as you make your way to **Alcalá de la Selva**. Dominated by its castle, the hillside village overlooks the Río Valbona, and in winter it makes a popular base for skiers – if there is enough snow. A few km on, **La Virgen de la Vega** lies in a tranquil riverside meadow and makes a lovely spot to break the trip. There are a few hostales here, and a camping ground. *Hostal Ríos* (☎ 978-80 10 77), Calle Virgen de la Vega 9, has doubles with private shower for 4500 ptas. Some 15 km to the east are the modest ski fields of **Valdelinares**, with a couple of decent medium-level runs.

The next stop, 19 km on, is **Mora de Rubielos**. Little is known about the place before the arrival of the Muslims, and for centuries after they were expelled in 1170, Mora was passed around from one noble family to another until definitively attached to the Aragonese Crown in 1365. The stout castillo and Iglesia Colegiata were built in the 15th century, suffered badly during the civil war, and have since been restored.

Swing south-east along the A-232 to **Rubielos de Mora** (is this some kind of joke?), 14 km away. Possibly one of the most attractive villages on the southern fringe of El Maestrazgo, Rubielos is a tranquil patchwork of narrow lanes whose houses are all adorned with the typically small Aragonese balconies. Franco made Rubielos the headquarters of his Navarran corps in 1938, and it is surprisingly big, considering its population of fewer than 700. There are a few places to stay and for those with some money spare the nicest is the *Hotel Portal del Carmen* (☎ 978-80 41 53), Calle de la Glorieta 2. It has doubles for 6000 ptas (7500 ptas in the high season).

Our route from here turns back north (take the TE-811), heading up into the hills of El Maestrazgo proper, with the Sierra de Nogueruelas to the west. Shortly before crossing one of the highest passes (Puerto de Linares; 1720 metres), you'll pass the small pueblo of **Linares de Mora**, surrounded by mountains. Time seems to have stood still here. *Pensión La Venta* (☎ 978-80 20 18), Calle de Regajo 6, has basic doubles for 2200 ptas.

Northern Maestrazgo

From Linares de Mora the road loses altitude as it heads north for **La Iglesuela del Cid** after briefly crossing into Valencian territory. This plays in with a quick stop for a peek at the old ayuntamiento and the main parish church. The *Casa Amada* (☎ 964-44 33 73), Calle Fuente Nueva 10, has rooms for 2000/3000 ptas. If you are bussing it, the early morning bus to Teruel passes via Cantavieja. Heading east, the bus from Teruel stops here in the afternoon and heads on about 15 km to Villafranca del Cid, from where you can get an onward bus to Castellón the *following* morning.

Some 13 km north-west lies **Cantavieja**, a town the Aragonese seem to be pushing a tourist destination, but which really has no more charm than several other places already mentioned. Hannibal reputedly founded this town in the days when Carthage reigned supreme in Spain. In two of the Carlist wars during the 19th century it was heavily damaged. The best preserved (and partly restored) part of town is the porticoed Plaza del Ayuntamiento. The cheapest of two places to stay here is *Pensión Julián* (☎ 964-8 50 05), Calle García Valiño 2, with no-frills doubles for 1800 ptas. The odd bus runs to Teruel, Alcorisa (to the north, via Villarluengo) and Morella (to the north-east, in Valencia). From Alcorisa and Morella you can connect to Alcañiz, and from Morella to Castellón.

West of Cantavieja, you find yourself on a particularly pretty stretch of the TE-800. You could complete this circuit and return to Teruel via the Puerto de Villaroya, or alternatively tack to the north up the TE-804. This is another particularly attractive drive through the heart of El Maestrazgo, passing the precariously located **Villarluengo** and, a few km further on, the weird rock formations of the **Órganos de Montoro**, which form the river valley walls of the Río Guadalope. A beautifully located place to stay here is the *Hostal La Trucha* (☎ 978-77 30 08), about 10 km north of Villarluengo and right on the river. Singles/doubles cost 6000/9000 ptas.

Another 30 km north and you hit the N-211. If you head west it takes you to the main Zaragoza-Teruel road. Heading north-east you can reach Alcañiz and an alternative, slightly faster route to Zaragoza. **Alcañiz** itself really doesn't warrant going out of your

way for. The country plains here, north of El Maestrazgo's mountainous splendour, are drab and the town overgrown, dusty and unattractive. It *does* lie on the road to Tarragona in Cataluña, 150 km away, and may be a convenient rest stop.

Hasdrubal gave the Romans a drubbing here in 212 BC. It was later known to the Arabs as *al-kenees* (the churches), and the city's castillo (now a parador) came under the control of the Knights of Calatrava in 1179, who for centuries used it as their Aragonese base. The castillo is more impressive from a distance than close up, but is in any case extremely hard to miss. Of equally exaggerated dimensions is the Iglesia de Santa María Mayor, dwarfing all around it in Plaza de España with its huge baroque portal. Also on the square are the 14th century Lonja and adjoining ayuntamiento, which boasts a Renaissance façade.

If you need to stay, *Hotel Guadalope* (☎ 978-83 07 50), Plaza de España 8, is OK and right in the centre. Singles/doubles cost 2000/3000 ptas. Buses run to Barcelona, Zaragoza, Alcorisa (for other connections), Castellón and other destinations, although in most cases only once or twice a day.

About 40 km south-east of Alcañiz, **Valderrobres** is another comparatively pretty riverside pueblo in the foothills of El Maestrazgo. Again, it is the castillo and principal church here that stand out as monuments, although the town's Plaza Mayor is also made appealing by its 17th century ayuntamiento. There is a handful of cheap pensiones here, should you need to stay.

País Vasco, Navarra & La Rioja

The territories of the Basques, which take in the three provinces of the País Vasco (Basque Country) and Navarra, as well as the abutting parts of south-western France, together form a remarkable historical anomaly. Descended from a people who, according to some theories, predate even the earliest Indo-European invasions of Europe in prehistoric times, the Basques have retained a language whose origins still puzzle linguists and a sense of independence and apartness that have been the bane of everyone from the Muslims through Charlemagne to Franco.

A mountainous, green interior, often shrouded in Atlantic mists, presents a soothing and beautiful counterpoint to the rugged coast and its cosmopolitan centres. People are drawn here for all manner of reasons: the sophisticated seaside life of San Sebastián, the surfing, the (in)famous festivities at the running of the bulls in Pamplona, and the striking countryside. The area's proximity to France is also an attraction.

Created as a separate region in 1978, La Rioja is for most people synonymous with wine. Indeed the vineyards of the Ebro valley form a kind of buffer zone between the Basque territories and the broad expanse of Castilla to the south.

Across the País Vasco and, to a lesser extent, in Navarra, the Basque names for towns are gaining the upper hand over the Castilian versions, which in many cases only pose minor variations in spelling anyway. In this guide, Basque has been favoured in all cases except for the provincial capitals, which are still better known by their Castilian names.

País Vasco

Known as Euskadi or Euskal Herri to the Basques, the País Vasco is made up of three provinces: Guipúzcoa (Gipuzkoa in the Basque language), Álava (Araba) and Vizcaya (Bizkaia, and hence Biscay in English).

Just what to call the Basque country presents a smorgasbord of options. In Spanish, País Vasco is the common term used to denote the three provinces of what is officially the Comunidad Autónoma Vasca (CAV).

In Basque *(euskara)*, the nationalists coined the term Euskadi at the end of the 19th century. The classic term is Euskal Herri (or Euskal Herria – the final 'a' means 'the'). Any of these terms can mean: Iparralde (the three Basque provinces in France); Navarra; Egoalde (the three provinces of the CAV); or any combination you like of the above. It all depends on whom you talk to!

HIGHLIGHTS

- Tapas at the bars in San Sebastián
- Surfing the left-hander at Mundaka
- The jazz festival in San Sebastián (also in Vitoria & Getxo)
- The Camino de Santiago, particularly Estella and the pilgrims' bridge at Puente La Reina
- Following the Hemingway trail in Pamplona for the *fiesta* and the world's best-known *encierro* (running of the bulls)
- Searching out a good drop in Spain's premier wine-growing region, La Rioja

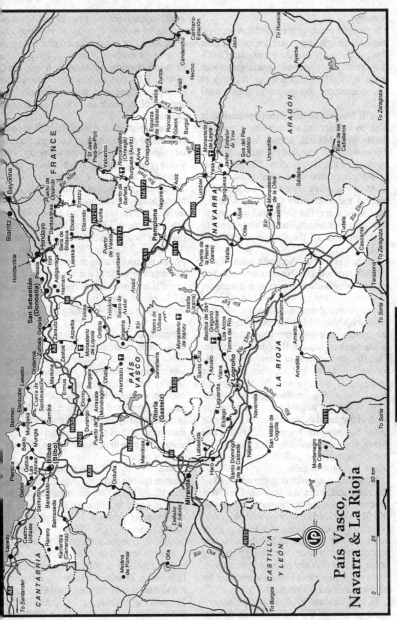

País Vasco,
Navarra & La Rioja

History

Throughout much of the Middle Ages rival warlords fought constantly for control over Basque territory, and the expanding Castilian crown only gained sovereignty with some difficulty. Neighbouring Navarra in fact constituted a separate kingdom until 1512.

Still, Navarra and the three provinces were able to extract broad autonomy arrangements from Madrid, known as the *fueros*. These were first repealed by Napoleon at the opening of the 19th century. The new ideas of the centralised state were anathema to more conservative Basques, who tended to support the reactionary Don Carlos during the Carlist wars. The colour red was associated with the Carlists, and has since come to be emblematic of the Basque assertion to separateness.

At the close of the Second Carlist War in 1876 all provinces but Navarra were stripped of their coveted fueros, although a measure of economic autonomy remained. This of course alienated the many Basques who had sided with liberal Madrid, and by the end of the century their resentment had taken shape in the form of nascent Basque nationalism. The Basque Nationalist Party (PNV) was formed in 1894, but support was never uniform, as Navarra and the province of Álava had a considerable Castilian contingent. When the Republican government in Madrid proposed the possibility of home rule to the Basques, the regions of Navarra and Álava both declined the offer. Navarra in particular, with the bulk of its fuero rights intact, had little to gain.

However, the remaining provinces liked the idea, and when the Spanish Civil War broke out in 1936, they threw in their lot with the Republicans. Conservative, rural Navarra and Álava sided with Franco, so of course it was Vizcaya and Guipúzcoa that paid the heaviest price for backing the wrong horse. In fact Navarra managed to retain its fuero rights in spite of Franco's penchant for ultra-centralised government.

In 1961, a small group of Basque nationalists known as ETA (Euskadi Ta Askatasuna) carried out its first terrorist attack setting in motion a cycle of violence and repression that has continued to this day, i[n] spite of the death of Franco and the granting of wide-ranging autonomy in the earl[y] 1980s. ETA has undergone innumerabl[e] transformations and still commands th[e] support of as much as 15% of the Basqu[e] populace.

The public political wing, Herri Batasuna constitutes a marginal but vocal parliamentary force, but perhaps more worrying is the youth group, Jarrai, from whose rank[s] tomorrow's assassins are often picked[.] Thought to have been all but dismantled afte[r] numerous successful police operations in th[e] early 90s, ETA began to hit back with sur[-] prising vigour in 1994, with bomb attacks i[n] places as far apart as San Sebastián, Madri[d,] Alicante and Sevilla. Now that Spain and France are cooperating more closely and the EU is on the verge of putting a unified anti terrorist and extradition system into place[,] ETA's effectiveness may well dwindle, bu[t] the problem is far from being resolved.

Language

In the modern autonomous region of the Paí[s] Vasco the *ikurriña* (Basque flag) flies every where, and a renewed sense of Basque identity has thankfully not only expresse[d] itself in violence, but in such areas as lan[-] guage. Suppressed by Franco, the idiom i[s] being learned by a growing number of young Basques, although comparatively few people use it as the main language of every day discourse.

You may in fact never hear a word o[f] Basque spoken throughout your stay in the País Vasco, but in Guipúzcoa province especially, the zeal to promote it is leading to the extinction of Spanish in one of its mos[t] useful forms – signs. This can be rathe[r] confusing, especially if you're driving.

Bear in mind that many Castilian words are also written slightly differently in the País Vasco. *Tx* often replaces *ch*, *b* replaces *v*, and *k* takes over from the hard Castilian *c*[.] The letter *g* is always pronounced hard in Basque. For more information on the Basque

Signs in Basque
Basque words which commonly appear on signs include:

ERDIALDEA	CITY CENTRE
ERDIA	CENTRE
JATETXEA	RESTAURANT
KALEA	CALLE (STREET)
KALE NAGUSIA	CALLE MAYOR (MAIN ST)
KOMUNA/K	TOILET/S
KONTUZ!	CAUTION/BEWARE!
NEKAZALTURISMOA	AGROTURISMO/ CASA RURAL
ONGI ETORRI	WELCOME
TURISMO BULEGOA	TOURIST OFFICE

language, turn to the Language section in the Facts about the Country chapter.

Food

Basque cuisine is generally regarded as Spain's finest. Catalans might dispute that, but if you can wangle your way into one of the private Basque gastronomic societies (traditionally all-male affairs), you'll certainly be in food heaven. They emerged mainly in San Sebastián, formed by groups of chefs cooking for each other and friends. San Sebastián is home of the greatest *tapas* in Spain – just entering some bars is enough to get you salivating. Apart from beer and cider, the traditional plonk of the region is a very crisp, slightly tart white wine called *txacoli*.

The classics of Basque cooking are simple enough, and seafood is the main pillar. Famous dishes include *bacalao al pil pil* (salt cod cooked with garlic and chillies), *merluza a la vasca* (hake in green sauce), *chipirones en su tinta* (cuttlefish in their own ink) and *chuletas de buey* (enormous beef chops). What has really brought the area's restaurants to grandeur is the flood of nouvelle cuisine influences that have taken hold in San Sebastián especially. Led by such chefs as Juan Mari Arzak, the Basque country's more imaginative cooks have, since the 1970s, made a name for themselves in Spain

and abroad with what is commonly called the *nueva cocina vasca*, a genre in constant tasty evolution.

Sport

The Basques indulge in a rather odd assortment of sports, ranging from grass-cutting and log-chopping through to caber-tossing and tug-of-war. The most famous is *pelota vasca* (or *jai-alai* in Basque), a form of handball played on a walled court known as a *frontón*. There is also a version involving the use of a *txistera*, a kind of hand-held basket that allows the ball to be hurled with disconcerting velocity at the wall. You can often see local teams whacking away at the town frontón. Teams of two or three a side wear all white and can be distinguished only by the the red and blue sashes worn by each team.

The traditional game is played with the bare hand, but there are up to 20 variants of the sport, now played in one form or other all over the world. Fourteen variants are accepted at world championship level. The bare-hand version, *esku huska*, is played in several different ways, with court and ball sizes, and rules, varying. The Txistera version is the newest, and the French Basques have a variant involving use of a smaller catch-hurl scoop called a *joko garbi*. The five-a-side game *rebot* is supposedly the hardest to score properly. Some export versions are odder still, such as *xari*, an Argentine derivation in which a string racquet is employed.

Emergency

The general telephone number for all emergency situations (police, ambulance, fire) in the País Vasco is ☎ 088. There are also local numbers, some of which are noted in this chapter.

SAN SEBASTIÁN

Forming a half-moon around the beautiful bay of La Concha, this most Basque of Basque cities is at the same time a captivating crossroads. A seaside resort surrounded by the low green hills of Guipúzcoa (Gipuzkoa), the province of which it is the capital, San Sebastián (Donostia) is a stone's throw from France.

Although at first you could be forgiven for drawing comparisons with its French Basque cousin, Biarritz, the two could not be further apart in atmosphere. Where the latter has a rather reserved quality, San Sebastián's Parte Vieja (Old Town) boasts possibly the greatest concentration of bars per square metre in Spain.

If there is one major city where you are likely to hear the Basque language, euskara, spoken, this is it. Although in many people's minds Bilbao has a bad reputation for street confrontations between the police and ETA sympathisers, San Sebastián is, if anything, worse. Bands of young Jarrai members hurling bottles and rocks at the local autonomous police (the Ertzaintza) are not an uncommon sight – although not common enough that it should put you off a visit.

History
Long little more than a fishing village privileged by its position on a protected bay at the mouth of the Río Urumea, San Sebastián was later the Kingdom of Navarra's principal outlet to the sea. By the 16th century, it had become a prosperous trade centre specialising first in the export of Castilian wool and other products to France, the Low Countries and England, and later benefiting from burgeoning commerce with the Americas. Disaster came with the Peninsular War, during which Anglo-Portuguese forces virtually razed the city in 1813 after wresting it from French hands. The city you see today is, hardly surprisingly, largely a product of the years following the withdrawal of Napoleon's troops from Spain.

Orientation
The heart of San Sebastián beats in the Parte Vieja, squeezed together in the narrow grid of lanes below Monte Urgull on the eastern spur of the Bahía de la Concha. This is where you'll find the greatest concentration of bars and restaurants, and some of the cheaper hotels. More hotels are scattered about the newer parts of town to the immediate south,

also known as the Zona Romántica. Just across the river is the RENFE train station, while the main bus station is about a 20 minute walk south of the Parte Vieja.

Information
Tourist Office The Oficina Municipal de Información (☎ 48 11 66), Calle de la Reina Regente s/n, has comprehensive information on the city and the province of Guipúzcoa. In summer (June to September) it opens Monday to Saturday from 8 am to 8 pm, and 10 am to 1 pm on Sunday. Otherwise its hours are Monday to Friday from 9 am to 2 pm and 3.30 to 7 pm, and on Saturday from 9 am to 2 pm (closed Sunday).

For more information on the rest of the País Vasco, try the Oficina de Información Turística del Gobierno Vasco (☎ 42 62 82), Paseo de los Fueros 1. Opening hours are Monday to Saturday from 9 am to 1 pm and 3.30 to 6.30 pm, and on Sunday from 10 am to 1 pm.

Money There are plenty of banks scattered all over the city centre where you can change cash or travellers' cheques or get cash advances on most major credit cards.

Post & Communications The main Correos y Telégrafos (post office) is at Calle de Urdaneta, behind the cathedral, while the Telefónica phone centre is at Calle de San Marcial 29. The latter is open Monday to Saturday from 9.30 am to 11 pm. The postcode for poste restante (lista de correos) is 20080, and the telephone code throughout San Sebastián province is ☎ 943.

Travel Agencies TIVE (☎ 27 69 34), Calle de Tomás Gros 3, can help with student travel arrangements.

Bookshops If you are staying in San Sebastián for any length of time and want to really explore all the entertainment and eating possibilities, you should pick up a copy of El Sabelotodo, available in most bookshops for 590 ptas.

Librería Graphos, on the corner of Calle

Mayor and Alameda del Boulevard, is excellent for travel books and maps.

Laundry Lavomatique, in the Parte Vieja at Calle de Iñigo 14, is a rarity in Spain – a good self-service laundrette.

Medical & Emergency Services There are several hospitals in San Sebastián, including the Hospital de Gipuzkoa (☎ 45 40 00), Alto de Zorroaga s/n. In a medical emergency you can call the Cruz Roja on ☎ 22 22 22. The local police are on ☎ 091.

Things to See

Museo de San Telmo This is the most interesting museum in town. It contains an eclectic assortment of medieval archaeological finds, agriculture and carpentry displays, and paintings ranging from the Renaissance through baroque to the 19th century, with a heavy emphasis on Basque painters. The building itself, and in particular its Renaissance cloister, is worthy of a visit. It is open Tuesday to Saturday from 10.30 am to 1.30 pm and 4 to 7.30 pm (closed Sunday afternoon and Monday). Entry is free.

Aquarium If you want to look at seafood rather than eat it, this could be the place for you. It is open daily from 10 am to 1.30 pm and 3.30 to 7.30 pm (closed on Monday from mid-September to mid-May). Entry costs 450 ptas.

Museo Naval Not far from the aquarium, on Paseo del Muelle, this museum of seafaring history is interesting enough, so long as you can read the Spanish explanations. It is open Tuesday to Saturday from 10 am to 1.30 pm and 4 to 7.30 pm (5 to 8.30 pm in summer), and on Sunday from 11 am to 2 pm.

Churches The city's Catedral del Buen Pastor is of little artistic interest, but in the Parte Vieja are a couple of churches with a little more history. The Iglesia de Santa María del Coro stands out for its churrigueresque façade, while the 16th century Gothic

Iglesia de San Vicente is the city's oldest standing house of worship.

If you are mad keen on all things religious, you could drop into the Museo Diocesano, Plaza de la Sagrada Familia, open Tuesday to Saturday from 4.30 to 8 pm.

Monte Urgull You can walk to the top of Monte Urgull, topped by a grand statue of Christ, by taking a path from Plaza de Zuloaga. The views across the Bahía de la Concha and the city are wonderful.

Monte Igueldo The views from the summit of Monte Igueldo are better still. You can save your legs by catching the funicular to the Parque de Atracciones (amusement park). The four star Hotel Monte Igueldo and Ku disco are also up here.

Activities

Beaches & Isla de Santa Clara The Playa de la Concha and its westerly extension, the Playa de Ondarreta, are among the best city beaches in Spain, although the water can be a touch nippy. Generally the water is placid, as it is shielded from the open sea by the Isla de Santa Clara. You can swim out to the island, or landlubbers can hop aboard the boats that run there every half-hour from 10 am to 8 pm (June to September). The Playa de Zurriola (also known as Playa de Gros), east of the Río Urumea, is polluted and best avoided.

Diving The Scuba Du dive shop (☎ 42 24 26), Paseo del Muelle 23, runs diving courses (CMAS and PADI) and hires out gear.

Swimming If the Atlantic is too chilly for your tootsies, you can have a swim at the Piscinas Anoeta (☎ 48 18 70), Paseo de Anoeta.

Special Events

Among San Sebastián's top drawing cards are the International Jazz Festival in July and the two week Festival de Cine (film festival), which has been held annually in the second

PAÍS VASCO

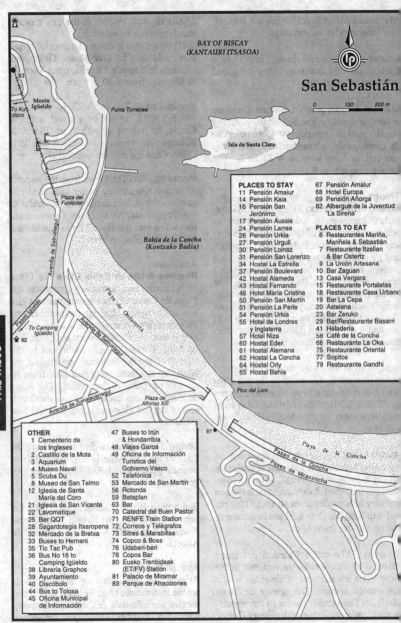

**BAY OF BISCAY
(KANTAURI ITSASOA)**

San Sebastián

0   100   200 m

Monte
Igüeldo

To Kuk
disco

Punta Torrepea

Isla de Santa Clara

Plaza del
Funicular

Avenida de Satrustegui

*Bahía de la Concha
(Kontxako Badia)*

Paseo Igüeldo

To Camping
Igüeldo

Avenida de Satrustegui

Playa de Ondarreta

Avenida de Zumalacarregui

Plaza de
Alfonso XIII

Pico del Loro

Palacio de Miramar

Playa de la Concha

Paseo de la Concha

Paseo de Miraconcha

PLACES TO STAY
11 Pensión Amaiur
14 Pensión Kaia
16 Pensión San
    Jerónimo
17 Pensión Aussie
24 Pensión Larrea
26 Pensión Urkia
27 Pensión Urgull
30 Pensión Loinaz
31 Pensión San Lorenzo
34 Hostal La Estrella
37 Pensión Boulevard
42 Hostal Alameda
43 Hostal Fernando
46 Hotel María Cristina
50 Pensión San Martín
51 Pensión La Perla
54 Pensión Urkia
55 Hotel de Londres
    y Inglaterra
57 Hotel Niza
60 Hotel Eder
61 Hostal Alemana
62 Hostal La Concha
64 Hostal Orly
65 Hostal Bahía

67 Pensión Amalur
68 Hotel Europa
69 Pensión Añorga
82 Albergue de la Juventud
   'La Sirena'

PLACES TO EAT
6 Restaurantes Mariña,
   Mariñela & Sebastián
7 Restaurante Itzalian
   & Bar Ostertz
9 La Unión Artesana
10 Bar Zaguan
13 Casa Vergara
15 Restaurante Portaletas
18 Restaurante Casa Urbano
19 Bar La Cepa
20 Astelena
23 Bar Zeruko
29 Bar/Restaurante Basarri
41 Heladería
58 Café de la Concha
66 Restaurante La Oka
75 Restaurante Oriental
77 Sopitos
79 Restaurante Gandhi

OTHER
1 Cementerio de
   los Ingleses
2 Castillo de la Mota
3 Aquarium
4 Museo Naval
5 Scuba Du
8 Museo de San Telmo
12 Iglesia de Santa
    María del Coro
21 Iglesia de San Vicente
22 Lavomatique
25 Bar QQT
28 Sagardotegia Itxaropena
32 Mercado de la Bretxa
33 Buses to Hernani
35 Tic Tac Pub
36 Bus No 16 to
    Camping Igüeldo
38 Librería Graphos
39 Ayuntamiento
40 Discóbolo
44 Bus to Tolosa
45 Oficina Municipal
    de Información

47 Buses to Irún
   & Hondarribia
48 Viajes Garoa
49 Oficina de Información
   Turística del
   Gobierno Vasco
52 Telefónica
53 Mercado de San Martín
56 Rotonda
59 Bataplan
63 Bar
70 Catedral del Buen Pastor
71 RENFE Train Station
72 Correos y Telégrafos
73 Sitres & Marabillas
74 Copco & Boss
76 Udaberi-beri
78 Copos Bar
80 Eusko Trenbideak
   (ET/FV) Station
81 Palacio de Miramar
83 Parque de Atracciones

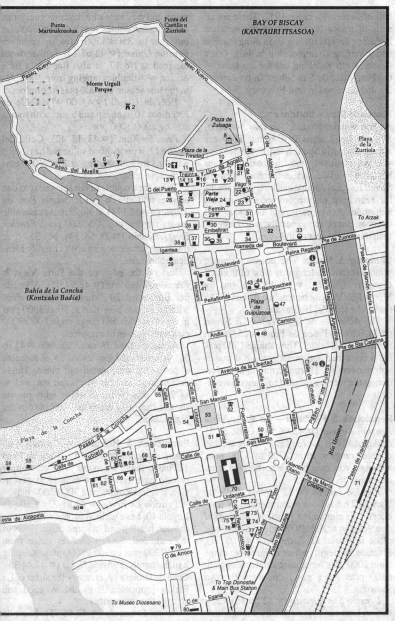

PAÍS VASCO

half of September since 1957. There are all sorts of minor fiestas during the summer, including several rowing and sailing regattas and a surfing championship in July. Other fiestas worth watching out for are those of the Festividad de San Sebastián on January 20, and *carnaval* in mid-February.

Places to Stay – bottom end
As you wander around, you may occasionally see hotel signs in Basque. They are almost always in Spanish too, but just in case you get confused, note that *ostatu* means hostal or pensión. As in much of northern Spain, July and August can be trying months for searching out accommodation in San Sebastián. Arrive early and be aware that summer prices are generally much steeper than during the rest of the year.

Camping & Hostel The nearest camping ground is rather a long way west of the city. *Camping Igueldo* (☎ 21 45 02), out by Monte Igueldo, can be reached by bus No 16 from Alameda del Boulevard.

The *Albergue de la Juventud La Sirena* (☎ 31 02 68), Paseo de Igueldo 25, is San Sebastián's HI hostel. They charge 1500 ptas for a bunk bed and breakfast (1700 ptas if you're over 26). There is a midnight curfew during the week, extended to 2 am on weekends.

Pensiones & Hostales – La Parte Vieja
Pensión Amaiur (☎ 42 96 54), Calle de 31 de Agosto 44, is as pretty as a picture and has doubles ranging from 2700 to 4700 ptas, although you may be able to bargain them down a little.

Pensión Larrea (☎ 42 26 94), Calle de Narrika 21, has been recommended by travellers. It is simple but pleasant and singles/doubles start at 2000/3000 ptas. Another nice place is *Hostal La Estrella* (☎ 42 09 97), Plaza de Sarriegi 1, where room prices range from 2000 ptas for a basic single through to 6500 ptas for a good double with own shower.

Pensión San Lorenzo (☎ 42 55 16), Calle de San Lorenzo 2, is a friendly enough little place, and they have a kitchen that guests can use. Singles/doubles start at 2000/2500 ptas but rise to 3500/4500 ptas in summer. *Pensión Loinaz* (☎ 42 67 14), further down the road at No 17, is also fine but a little pricier, with doubles ranging from 3000 ptas in the low season to 5000 ptas in summer.

Pensión Urgull (☎ 43 00 47), Calle de Esterlines 10, is cheap and basic, with rooms costing 2000/3000 ptas.

Pensión Kaia (☎ 43 13 42), Calle del Puerto 12, is pretty good value and has rooms with private bath starting at 2500/4000 ptas in the low season.

There are a couple of cheapies next to one another on Calle de San Jerónimo. *Pensión Aussie* (☎ 42 28 74), at No 23, has reasonable rooms starting at 2500/3500 ptas. *Pensión San Jerónimo* (☎ 28 64 34), No 25, is in much the same category with virtually identical room rates.

Just on the edge of the Parte Vieja is *Pensión Boulevard* (☎ 42 94 05), Alameda del Boulevard 24, where singles/doubles without private bath start at 2000/3000 ptas in the off season and range up to 5000/8000 ptas with shower in summer.

Across the road, *Hostal Alameda* (☎ 42 16 87), Alameda del Boulevard 23, is a decent if somewhat dilapidated old place. Single occupation of double rooms can start as low as 2000 ptas, while doubles with private shower can be as steep as 7400 ptas in the high season.

Pensiones & Hostales – Centro The *Pensión Añorga* (☎ 46 79 45), Calle de Easo 12, has a range of rooms with or without private bath/shower. At their most expensive, singles/doubles cost 3000/5000 ptas.

Pensión La Perla (☎ 42 81 23), Calle de Loyola 10, has excellent rooms with private shower, heating and in some cases views of the cathedral. Singles/doubles range from 2500/3200 ptas to 3000/5000 ptas. Keeping it in the family, *Pensión Urkia* (☎ 42 44 36), Calle de Urbieta 12, is run by the sister of La Perla's proprietor. It is just as good and charges the same prices.

Hostal Fernando (☎ 42 55 75), Plaza de

Guipúzcoa 2, is not a bad spot on one of the city's more attractive squares. Simple but very clean rooms cost 3000/4200 ptas (a little more in summer).

If Calle de San Martín were a bough it would be bending under the weight of the hotels along it. Towards the eastern end at No 10, *Pensión San Martín* (☎ 42 87 14) has squeaky-clean doubles with private bath for 5200 ptas (6700 ptas in summer), which they will let go for about 4000 ptas to lone travellers.

Most places up on the western end tend to be mid-range jobs, but the *Pensión Amalur* (☎ 46 08 61), at No 43, offers functional rooms without bath for 2000/4000 ptas. They also have more expensive rooms with their own bath.

Hostal La Concha (☎ 45 03 89), No 51, is OK but not great value at 4000/6000 ptas (they'll come down a little out of season). The reception is a little on the gruff side.

Places to Stay – middle
Hotel Niza (☎ & fax 42 66 63), Calle de Zubieta 56, is a pleasant upper mid-range hotel with good rooms just off the waterfront for 5450/11,650 ptas in the low season.

Not far off is the *Hotel Europa* (☎ 47 08 30; fax 47 17 30), Calle de San Martín 52, which has rooms for 8500/11,500 ptas. *Hostal Alemana* (☎ 46 25 44), at No 53, has huge rooms. The bathrooms have hair dryers and you can get drinks and snacks in the salon. It's a friendly place with singles/doubles for 7700/10,400 ptas.

Places to Stay – top end
Hotel Orly (☎ 46 32 00; fax 45 61 01), Plaza de Zaragoza 4, is a very pleasant upper level option in the heart of the centre and a brisk walk from the beach. Smallish but well-appointed singles/doubles come in at 12,125/16,000 ptas, rising by up to 3000 ptas in summer.

Hotel de Londres e Inglaterra (☎ 42 69 89; fax 42 00 31), Calle de Zubieta 2, overlooks the waterfront. Singles/doubles generally cost 12,000/17,800 ptas outside the summer high season.

The truly extravagant could throw their credit cards at the *Hotel María Cristina* (☎ 42 49 00; fax 42 39 14), Paseo de la República Argentina 4, where prices soar into the stratosphere at 20,200/28,000 ptas in the low season.

Places to Eat
Some of the best eating you will ever experience in Spain will be accomplished in San Sebastián. The choice of venues seems virtually limitless, and it is here that the art of the bar snack has been refined, with tray after tray of mouth-watering goodies lining the bars. Snacking in this way is not the cheapest way to fill your stomach, but it's a lot of fun!

If you want to stock up to make your own meals, go where the locals go – the Mercado de la Bretxa. Another option in La Romántica is the Mercado de San Martín on Calle de San Marcial.

For seafood by the sea, there is a string of places down by the fishing harbour. *Restaurante Mariña*, *Restaurante Mariñela* and *Restaurante Sebastián* are side by side on Paseo del Muelle and much of a muchness. They all charge around 1300 to 2000 ptas for main courses. A little further along you can either eat the same at *Restaurante Itzalian* or indulge in snacks and a beer at *Bar Ostertz*.

Casa Vergara, Calle Mayor 21, is a good little place where you dine on a set menu lunch for 1200 ptas.

For those in a financial jam, *Bar Zaguan*, Calle de 31 de Agosto 31, does a set lunch for 950 ptas and platos combinados for as little as 650 ptas.

Bar La Cepa, at No 7 on the same street, is just one of many bars in the Parte Vieja that comes warmly recommended for its tapas, or pinchos.

Restaurante Casa Urbano, at No 17, is a more up-market choice and an old favourite with a well-entrenched reputation for quality seafood. Mains cost around 2500 ptas.

The heavy timber beams that dominate its décor help make the *Restaurante Portaletas*, Calle del Puerto 28, a popular place with the locals. Meat and fish dishes cost around 1300 ptas.

Bar/Restaurante Basarri, Calle de Fermín Calbetón 17, is plain and simple but the cooking is good – worth every one of the 1200 ptas for the set meal. *Bar Zeruko*, Calle de la Pescadería 10, has a menú de noche for 1200 ptas.

Plaza de la Constitución is loaded with atmosphere and a great choice of bars. *Astelena* is one of the city's grand old institutions and something of a must on your culinary and liquid odyssey through San Sebastián. It's not that the food is necessarily better than in the other places, but it goes back a long way.

One of the country's most acclaimed chefs, Juan Mari Arzak, cooks up his world-renowned Basque nouvelle cuisine at *Arzak*, Alto de Miracruz 21. You can sample his goodies in a special menu for 6500 ptas. If you're inspired to do your own cooking, watch for his recipes in the weekend magazine of *El País* newspaper.

If you're after a little variety, you could have Indian at *Restaurante Gandhi*, Calle de Arroca, just off Plaza de Easo. A menú de degustación for two costs 3900 ptas. Very good value too is the Chinese *Restaurante Oriental*, Calle de los Reyes Católicos 6, just south of the cathedral. They use a little more than the usual dose of imagination and even serve vaguely spicy food – in spite of the generally disapproving Spanish palate. Nearby, at Calle de General Prim 30, you can eat Mexican at *Sopitos*.

A fun self-service vegetarian place is *Restaurante La OKA*, Calle de San Martín 43.

For dessert on the run, the *Heladería* at Calle de Hernani 3-5 is a good place to pick up an ice cream.

Cafés For your morning coffee and cake, there are several promenade cafés along Alameda del Boulevard. Considerably more chic is *Café de la Concha*, overlooking the beach. For a smoky, old-style ambience, try *La Unión Artesian*, on the corner of Plaza de Zuloaga and Calle de 31 de Agosto.

Entertainment

Bars – Parte Vieja The Parte Vieja of San Sebastián is, as you will have noticed already, crawling with all sorts of bars. The whole area comes to life from about 8 pm virtually every day of the week, although weekends are predictably more intense. As the tapas bars (often with restaurants attached) begin to shut their doors at around 1 am, certain streets die off, leaving the late-night bars to rock on. Calle de la Pescadería and Calle de Fermín Calbetón are among the busier streets. In case you're wondering, the pudgy little glasses many people drink their beer and wine from are called zurritos. The small quantity of alcohol in a zurrito allows the locals to indulge their custom of fitting in as many drinking establishments as possible in one evening.

It is difficult to single out particular bars – on a weekend they will all be full of merry-makers. The crowd tends to be young. *Bar QQT*, on Calle del Puerto, is a downstairs dance bar that attracts a mixed crowd. Another place to look out for is *Tic Tac Pub* on Calle de Embeltran.

If you'd like to have a swig of Basque cider (sidra), head for *Sagardotegia Itxaropena*, Calle de Embeltran 16. It doesn't stay open much after midnight.

Bars – Calle de los Reyes Católicos The other easily accessible concentration of nocturnal activity is down by Calle de los Reyes Católicos, just south of the cathedral.

Just before you launch into it, have an early evening libation at the great old nameless bar on the corner of Calle de San Martín and Calle de Lezo.

Copos Bar, on the corner of Calle de General Prim and Calle de los Reyes Católicos, has a laid-back pub feel to it. *Udaberi-beri*, corner of Calle de los Reyes Católicos and Calle de Larramendi, has a cool bar upstairs and a rather hysterical Spanish music karaoke scene downstairs. If that's not loud enough, try *Sitres*, Calle de Sánchez Toca 3, for some head-banging heavy metal. *Marabillas*, next door, couldn' be further removed – a great mellow spot for a late-night snack and tipple.

Copco and *Boss* stand side by side on Calle de Larramendi. Girls seem to hang around in the first, a rather metallic and slightly snotty locale, and lads in the latter. Perhaps they mingle later in the night?

Discos & Nightclubs One of the better known discos is *Ku*, a taxi ride away near the Monte Igueldo funicular. It keeps its doors open until around 3 am. Closer to the centre, *Bataplan* and *Rotonda* are both on the beach promenade. *Discóbolo*, on Alameda del Boulevard, is the nearest disco to the Parte Vieja. *Top Donosti* disco is out by the Olympic stadium, one stop along the ET/FV rain line.

Getting There & Away

Air The city's airport (information on ☎ 66 35 00) is 22 km out of town, near Hondarribia. There are regular flights to Madrid and occasional charters to major European capital cities.

Bus The main bus station is basically a car park between Plaza de Pío XII and the river, some 20 minutes walk south of the centre. Ticket offices are spread north of it along Avenida de Sancho el Sabio and Paseo de Vizcaya.

For long-distance services within Spain and abroad, go to the Enatcar (☎ 46 80 87) office on Paseo de Vizcaya. To Barcelona, Ibarsa (☎ 45 75 00) has three buses a day for 2450 ptas (much cheaper than the train). La Burundesa (☎ 46 23 60) runs buses six times a day to Vitoria for 900 ptas. La Roncalesa (☎ 46 10 64) has eight buses a day to Pamplona (750 ptas) and six to Zaragoza (2335 ptas for the fast service). Other lines connect with Logroño (in La Rioja) via Estella (in Navarra).

The PESA (☎ 46 39 74) company runs half-hourly buses to Bilbao along the autopista from 6.30 am to 10 pm for 1030 ptas. It also has twice-daily buses to Biarritz and Bayonne in France, as well as to Durango and Vitoria.

The same company offers weekend services to Lourdes (France) for 2000 ptas from mid-May to mid-September. Tickets are also available from Viajes Garoa, Plaza de Guipúzcoa 16.

Buses depart regularly for Tolosa (195 ptas), Irún and Hondarribia from Plaza de Guipúzcoa.

Train The main RENFE train station is just across the Río Urumea on Paseo de Francia, on a line linking Paris to Madrid. There are six services daily to Madrid, taking anything from six to 8½ hours. The cheapest one-way ticket is 4600 ptas on a night train (200 ptas more on the slower day trains). Trains to Barcelona run a few times each day via Pamplona and Zaragoza. The cheapest one-way fare is 4600 ptas. There is only one direct train to Paris (2nd class, one way costs 10,500 ptas), but you can pick up plenty more from the French border town of Hendaye. About half a dozen trains a day run to Hendaye from San Sebastián and there are plenty to Irún, just on the Spanish side of the frontier.

There are also daily trains going as far afield as Alicante, Algeciras, Salamanca, La Coruña, Vigo, Porto (in Portugal) and Lisbon (one a day). *Cercanías* run to Tolosa and Zumárraga.

A second station is used by the private rail company (international passes not valid) Eusko Trenbideak (ET/FV) south of the town centre near Plaza de Centenario. Rather slow trains head west to Bilbao (590 ptas; change at Ermua) via Durango (275 ptas). Others go east to Hendaye via Irún for 120 ptas.

Car & Motorcycle The A-8 tollway passes through San Sebastián to Bilbao on the west and into France (where it becomes the A-63) to the east. If you are prepared to deal with traffic you can avoid the toll on the virtually parallel N-634. The most picturesque route west is along the minor coast roads. The main route south is the N-I, which runs to Madrid via Vitoria.

Rental Several major companies are represented by agencies in San Sebastián, including Atesa (☎ 46 30 13), Calle de Amézketa 7; Avis (☎ 46 15 27), Calle del Triunfo 2; Europcar (☎ 46 17 17), Calle de San Martín 60; and Hertz (☎ 46 10 84), Calle de San Martín 47.

Bicycle You can rent bicycles and mountain bikes at Comet (☎ 42 23 51), Avenida de la Libertad 6, or Mini (☎ 21 17 58), Calle de la Escolta Real 10.

EAST OF SAN SEBASTIÁN
Pasaia

Pasaia (Pasajes) is asphyxiated by a clot of highway bypasses, industry and a port, so it's unlikely Victor Hugo would want to hang around here at all now, as he did for a summer back in 1843. Coming out from San Sebastián, you'd hardly know you'd entered another town. Still, down by the waterside two of the three constituent bits of Pasaia retain some charm in spite of the surrounding grime. The bus from San Sebastián drops you in Pasai San Pedro, from where you can get a launch across the mouth of the port to the more interesting Pasai Donibane (Pasaje San Juan in Spanish). Calle de San Juan and the area immediately around the central square are lined with some pretty houses vaguely reminiscent of what one can better contemplate in Hondarribia, to the east.

Irún

A more nondescript introduction to Spain you could hardly get, so if you don't arrive too late in the evening, the best advice is to move straight on. Hondarribia, just a few km away, makes an infinitely better first halt.

If you do find yourself obliged to stay, don't despair. Half a dozen relatively cheap places are located within a stone's throw of the trains. *Pensión Los Fronterizos* (☎ 943-61 92 05), Estación Kalea 7, is a perfectly clean and decent little place with rooms for 2500/3500 ptas.

Getting There & Away To shuttle between Irún and Hendaye, take the half-hourly train (known as 'El Topo' – 'the mole') from the ET/FV station on Paseo de Colón (100 ptas). Regular trains to San Sebastián also use this line, or you can take a cercanía from the RENFE station, five minutes walk to the south. Long-distance trains leave from here to Madrid, Barcelona, Alicante, Galicia and other destinations. Long-distance buses also depart from here. Turytrans has regular services along the north coast as far as Gijón. There are five direct services per day to Vitoria with La Burundesa.

Up to 10 trains daily leave the SNCF station in Hendaye for Paris (six of them high-speed TGVs). Other trains serve Pau, Lille and Bordeaux, and there is a daily train to Rome via Ventimiglia.

Hondarribia

Hondarribia (Fuenterrabía in Castilian), founded by the Romans and the scene of several sieges throughout its history, has managed to preserve its charming old city. Although it has a character all its own, the whiff of France, lying just across the bay, is somehow also perceptible in the reserved orderliness of the place.

The tourist office (☎ 64 54 58), Javier Ugarte Kalea 6, is open Monday to Friday from 9 am to 1.30 pm and 4 to 6.30 pm, and Saturday from 10 am to 2 pm. The phone code is ☎ 943.

You can enter the partly intact old town walls through the Puerta de Santa María, traditionally the main gate. To the left and right as you climb Kale Nagusia are the proud houses of Hondarribia's one-time high-fliers. Past the Gothic Iglesia de Santa María de la Asunción you arrive in the expansive Plaza de Armas, dominated by a palace attributed to King Sancho Abarca de Navarra but renovated by Spain's Carlos I. Around the other sides of the plaza spreads a profusion of the engaging wood-beam houses that are a hallmark of the town. The town also has a fine beach.

Places to Stay & Eat There are about 10 places to choose from here. The cheapest option is *Hostal Álvarez Quintero* (☎ 64 22

99), Beñat Etxepare Kalea 2, with singles/doubles at 3100/4300 ptas out of season, and rising by about 1000 ptas in summer. *Pensión Txoko Goxua* (☎ 64 46 58), Murrua Kalea 22, is in a nicer location on the edge of the casco antiguo (old town), but may not offer lower rates for singles. Doubles cost 5300 ptas.

Those with more dosh have a tempting range of options in the casco, starting with the extremely homey and postcard-pretty *Hotel San Nikolas* (☎ 64 42 78), Plaza de Armas 2, with rooms starting at 5500/6500 ptas. At the other end of the scale is the grand *Parador El Emperador* (☎ 64 55 00; fax 64 21 53), housed in the Castillo de Carlos V. Rooms start at 10,000/13,000 ptas plus IVA.

The casco has oodles of eating places, but none are particularly cheap. In the new part of town, *Bar Maitane*, Sabin Arana Goiri Kalea (just behind the tourist information office), is popular with locals, has good bar snacks and serves up low-priced meals.

Getting There & Away Buses leave from near the post office *(correos)* for Irún, San Sebastián and occasionally across the border to Hendaye.

SOUTH OF SAN SEBASTIÁN
Cider Territory
The lush green hinterland just in from the coast, far removed from worldly San Sebastián, has long been home to a liquid tradition most pleasing to the palate. The cider *(sidra)* produced here is like pure apple juice, only with an alcoholic kick. Locals will tell you it's better than that made further west in Asturias, but the jury is out on that one. Although there are a few *sidrerías* (*sagardotegiak* in Basque) in San Sebastián, the best place to look is in and around the towns of Hernani and Astigarraga. Most stay open only from January to the end of April, the season for making the cider. They then bottle the surplus and close the doors to their bars. A few stay open all year, operating restaurants and serving the bottled stuff.

A well-signposted series of half a dozen sidrerías lies along a two km winding, hilly road off the narrow highway connecting Hernani to Astigarraga (three km apart). To get to the area, take a bus from Calle de la Reina Regente in San Sebastián.

If you turn up out of season, head for *Sagardotegia Mendizabal* (☎ 55 57 47), the last of the above mentioned series, or *Sagardotegia Petritegi* (☎ 45 71 88), in Astigarraga itself. Their restaurants get packed out on weekends, so call in advance.

Tolosa
A small medieval nucleus lends this busy industrial town, 22 km south of San Sebastián, some vague interest, but the only time you'd want to go out of your way to visit is for carnaval. These festivities are known particularly for having continued right through the Franco era. Jolly man that he was, he did his best to stamp out such outward demonstrations of merry-making. If you want to stay overnight, try *Hostal Oyarbide* (☎ 943-67.00 17), Plaza Gorriti 1. Rooms cost 2000 ptas per person. Buses run frequently to San Sebastián's Plaza de Guipúzcoa. You can also catch a train.

Ordizia & Monte Txindoki
Ordizia, 30 km south of San Sebastián, is the best base from which to visit the hills to the east. The popular walk up to the top of Monte Txindoki, one of the highest peaks (1341 metres) in the Sierra de Aralar, begins from the village of **Larraitz**, about eight km to the east (follow the signs for Zaldibia). A few buses make the run from Ordizia on weekends *only* – that's the hard bit. A marked trail leads walkers up the slope from Larraitz. At a relaxed pace you should need no more than 1½ hours each way. More ambitious walkers head for other peaks further into the chain and even make for the Santuario de San Miguel in Excelsis – a good day's strong hiking to the south-east in Navarra. Regular buses connect Ordizia with San Sebastián.

Túnel San Adrián
Another 10 km south from Ordizia brings you to **Segura**, just off the main road. Apart

from a few noble houses that once belonged to powerful clans, you'll find precious little to hang around for. Much the same can be said for Zegama, but the drive on this back road is pleasant. If you push on a little, you hit a nice long-distance walking path, for which the hamlet of **Otzaurte** serves as a trailhead.

From Otzaurte, a stretch of the GR-12 trail heads westwards to the Refugio de San Adrián and a natural tunnel of the same name (higher up from the refuge). This important medieval pilgrim route linked the heart of Spain with the rest of Europe. Traces of what may be a Roman road, but more likely an early medieval highway, can still be seen on the approach to the tunnel – inside which rests the small Ermita de San Adrián. The medieval road then emerges from the tunnel and continues southwards.

Most of the five km to the refuge can be driven if you feel so inclined. If you have no transport, you can get a train to Otzaurte from Vitoria, from where you should calculate two hours to get to the refuge, and as long as you want following the ancient road south out of the tunnel. The refuge supposedly opens on weekends and in summer, but it's a little unreliable.

BETWEEN SAN SEBASTIÁN & BILBAO

The coast road out of San Sebastián snakes its way past some spectacular ocean scenes, with cove after cove stretching west and verdant fields suddenly dropping away in rocky shafts to the sea. The stretch between Zumaia and Bermeo is one of the best. The bulk of the towns and fishing villages on the way are, with a few exceptions, an average lot – richer pickings lie further west in Cantabria, Asturias and Galicia.

Zarautz, Getaria & Zumaia

The narrow, straight beach of **Zarautz**, 23 km from San Sebastián, is backed by the serried ranks of holiday flats, hotels and overpriced cafés. There's a section for nudists, but most local nudists head for

Hendaye, across the border in France. It is difficult to imagine why anyone apart from surfers would want to make a special effort to come here, much less stay. The long beach hosts a round of the World Surfing Championship every September. If you do want to stay, there are plenty of expensive hotels and one or two agroturismo places, elsewhere in the country known as casas rurales, on the outskirts. There is also a youth hostel (☎ 943-13 29 10).

Another five km round the coast is **Getaria**, a small medieval fishing settlement huddled in the shadow of El Ratón (the Mouse), the distinctive islet visible long before you enter the town. The sober mass of the 14th century Iglesia de San Salvador stands sentinel over the port, which back in 1522 saw the return of its most illustrious son, Juan Sebastián Elcano, after more than three years spent in the first successful circumnavigation of the globe. He had joined Magellan's (Magallanes to the Spaniards) expedition in 1519 – its aim to find a passage to India across the Atlantic and Pacific. Magellan and most of the fleet perished during the next three years, but Elcano crawled back to Spain, reaching Sanlúcar de Barrameda (in Andalucía) in his vessel, the *Victoria*, with just 18 other survivors.

Again, there is little reason to stay here, but you have a couple of mid-level pensions at your disposal.

What little of beauty there is in **Zumaia** has long been buried in an avalanche of modern construction, with rows of housing blocks spreading out from the centre. Still, the austere Late Gothic Iglesia de San Pedro is admirable, and there are two good beaches. The Playa de Izturun is wedged in among cliffs while, a couple of km east of the town centre, the Playa de Santiago is a more open strand. Just before you reach the beach stands the Museo de Zuloaga, in the Basque artist Zuloaga's one-time house and farm and now containing some of his important works as well as a handful by several other big names, such as Goya and El Greco. The museum opens Wednesday to Sunday from 4 to 8 pm.

Inland to Oñati

Zestoa A few km west of Zumaia, a branch road shoots off southward to the one-time spa resort of Zestoa. This sleepy town, or rather the hotel complex built last century around the thermal baths, came to be known as the Karlsbad of Guipúzcoa in the days when all the right people came to take a 'cure'.

Azpeitia Another 10 km south, the pleasant little town of Azpeitia is interesting above all for what lies outside it – the portentous Santuario de Loyola, dedicated to St Ignatius, the founder of the Jesuit order. This sumptuous baroque spectacle seems a little out of place in its peaceful rural setting. Inside, the circular-plan basilica is laden with dark grey marble and plenty of ornamentation. The house where Loyola was born is conserved in one of the two great wings of the *santuario*. It opens daily from 10 am to 12.30 pm and 3.30 to 7 pm, but you can generally wander into the church any time.

Bergara Bearing south-west from Azpeitia along the Río Urola, a delightful back road (GI-3750) winds up high into the hills to take you to this rather scraggly town. Give it a chance though, as its old centre does preserve quite a number of interesting reminders of a past when perhaps it looked a little more attractive. Among them are the *ayuntamiento* (town hall) and the seminary (both on Plaza Mayor), and the nearby Iglesia de San Pedro, which has a wooden portico characteristic of this area. There are three hotels if you need to stay. Bergara can be reached by bus along the main highways from Bilbao and San Sebastián.

Oñati One of the most enticing towns in the interior of the País Vasco, Oñati is a short hop from Bergara – head down the GI-627 towards Arrasate (Mondragón) and turn off east at the sign to Oñati.

The very helpful tourist office (☎ 943-78 34 53), on Foru Enparantza, is open Monday to Friday from 10 am to 1 pm and 3.30 to 7 pm, and on weekends from 10 am to 2 pm.

A fine example of Renaissance building is the **Universidad de Sancti Spiritus**, where for 350 years alumni were schooled in philosophy, law and medicine until its closure in 1902. The plateresque façade is a gem, as is the courtyard. Virtually across the road stands **Iglesia de San Miguel**, a Late Gothic creation with its cloister built over the river. The church faces onto the main square, Foru Enparantza, with the eye-catching baroque façade of the ayuntamiento on the east side. Keep an eye out too for the plateresque **Monasterio de Bidaurreta** and the many fine noble houses dotted about the place.

You can stay at the *Hostal Echeverria* (☎ 943-78 04 60), Kalebarria Kalea 19, which has rooms for as little as 2200/3500 ptas in the off season. They also have a decent restaurant. For more inventive cuisine, try *Itturitxo Jatetxea*, Atzeko Kalea 32. They have a scrumptious set menu, cheapest if taken in the café. It costs 900 ptas for lunch and 1300 ptas for dinner.

There are frequent buses to San Sebastián, Bilbao and Vitoria.

Arantzazu About 10 km south of Oñati, the modern Santuario de Arantzazu is something of a shrine for Basques, since Nuestra Señora de Arantzazu is Guipúzcoa's patron saint. Various modern artists had a hand in its design, including Eduardo Chillida, who did the entrance doors. The road up and the setting are themselves worth the effort, and the whole area lends itself to some nice walks – the Oñati tourist office can sell you a collection of route maps. That said, it appears *no* buses go to Arantzazu from Oñati, although there is supposed to be a weekend service.

Mutriku

Back on the coast road, the next stop of any note west of Zumaia is the picturesque fishing village of Mutriku. Clamped by a steep rocky vice cut into the coast, its streets wind tortuously down to a small harbour. Up in the town, the main features of interest are several mansions, such as the restored 16th century **Palacio de Zabiel** on Erdiko Kalea.

The town is surrounded by five camping grounds, two of them open all year. The attraction is the fine beach of **Saturrarán**, a few km west of Mutriku.

Restaurante Zumalage, high up on the road heading out from the eastern end of town, has great views of Mutriku and its harbour. Expect to pay about 2000 ptas for lunch.

Buses between San Sebastián and Lekeitio pass through here.

Ondarroa

Ondarroa, too big, modern and sprawling to be all that attractive, is split by a river and has a small beach. Fishing is still big business here, and that's about all there is to say of the place. If for whatever reason you need to stay, *Hostal Vega* (☎ 94-684 29 84), Calle de Antiguako Ama 8, has large clean rooms overlooking the water for 2400 ptas per person. There is no shortage of harbourside eateries and bars.

Inland to Markina

About 10 km inland from Ondarroa, the pretty town of Markina is the home of pelota – the local frontón is known as the Universidad de la Pelota! A few km outside lies the birthplace of Simón Bolívar, the great early 19th century South American independence fighter. A museum here dedicated to his exploits (and more mundane matters closer to home) opens Tuesday to Friday from 10 am to 1 pm, and on weekends from noon to 2 pm. In July and August it opens Tuesday to Sunday from 5 to 7 pm.

Lekeitio

Another 12 km west from Ondarroa brings you to this attractive fishing town. Of the two beaches, the one just east of the river is the nicest. The harbourside is dominated by the Late Gothic **Iglesia de Santa María de la Asunción**. Unfortunately, the hostales here are not cheap and they fill up quickly in summer. Alternatively, in summer you could try *Camping Endai*, on Playa Menedexa, a

few km east. The waterfront and back streets of the old part of town are teeming with bars and snack joints.

Elantxobe

Sticking to the 'coast road' unfortunately does not mean hugging the cliffs, although occasionally you get some great views. The tiny hamlet of Elantxobe is worth a look. It seems to have been glued onto the almost perpendicular rock walls leading down to the sea. There is nowhere to stay in the town, but *Hotel Arboliz* (☎ 94-627 62 83) is just outside it on the road from Lekeitio – although rather expensive. If you're unimpressed, there's an agroturismo place right across the road. At the top end of the steep Calle Mayor in the town itself you'll find some restaurants. A couple of buses run from Gernika every day except Sunday.

The odd bus from Gernika also crawls up the broad Ría de Mundaka to the lovely beaches of **Laga** and **Laida**, a couple of km west of Elantxobe.

Cueva de Santimamiñe

About halfway down the estuary to Gernika is a turn-off to the grotto of Santimamiñe. Apart from some impressive stalactites and stalagmites, you can also see prehistoric cave paintings. You must join a guided tour (no more than 15 people a time), which start at 10 and 11.15 am, 12.30, 4.30 and 6 pm. If you find yourself hanging around fruitlessly, a couple of bucolically nice walks have been signposted away from the car park; at the end of one is a small agroturismo (look for the 'Nekazalturismoa' sign). There is no public transport, although the Gernika-Lekeitio bus can drop you at Kortezubi, from where it's a 40 minute walk. Given the limitations on entry, it might be worth enquiring about organised trips at the Gernika tourist office.

Gernika

The attraction of Gernika (Guernica) lies more in the symbolic than in any specific sights. Here, in April 1937, Hitler's Condor Legion, sent to aid Franco's forces, unleashed the first-ever massive air raid against a civilian target. Almost 2000 people died in the attack, later immortalised in Picasso's nightmare vision entitled *Guernica* (now in the Reina Sofía gallery in Madrid). Sixty years on, the German government has set aside three million Deutschmarks from its 1997 Budget to help to pay for a new sports complex in Gernika; this amounts to about US$1000 for each person killed in the raid.

In the grounds of the **Casa de Juntas** is the Árbol de Gernika, a tree beneath which the Basque parliament traditionally used to meet. Inside the Casa, a huge stained-glass window depicts historic scenes. Down the road, the **Euskal Herriko Museoa** is housed in the 18th century Palacio de Montefuerte. The museum, dedicated to Basque history and culture, opens Tuesday to Saturday from 10 am to 2 pm and 4 to 7 pm, and Sunday from 10 am to 1.30 pm. Behind it extend the gardens of the **Parque de los Pueblos de Europa**, across the road from which you can see a pair of sculptures, one by Eduardo Chillida and the other by Henry Moore.

Gernika is an easy day trip from Bilbao by bus or train (from Atxuri station). There are a few hotels, but you are frankly better off staying in Bilbao or pushing on northward to Mundaka or even Bermeo.

Mundaka

The legend of the world's longest left still attracts surfers the world over to this unassuming little estuary town 10 km north of Gernika. Australians in particular seem drawn to the place. They may well want to track down Craig at his Billabong surf gear shop. He came to Mundaka at the beginning of the 1980s and hasn't been able to drag himself away since. The surf is at its best in September and October.

Aside from *Camping Portuondo* (☎ 94-687 63 68), which is about one km out of the town centre, there is little in the way of cheap accommodation. *Hotel El Puerto* (☎ 94-687 67 25), Portu Kalea 1, has the prettiest location overlooking the town's minute fishing port, but charges anything up to 4500/6500 ptas in the high season. Eating choices are

limited too, and in fact you'd be better off heading up the coast a few km to Bermeo for your meals. The Bilbao bus to Bermeo and Gernika passes through Mundaka. Buses and ET/FV trains from Mundaka run to Bilbao, Bermeo and Gernika.

Bermeo

A few km north-west, Bermeo is a rather sprawling and ugly place, but a better bet for a cheap evening meal and a few drinks than Mundaka. The fishing port is lively enough, and real aficionados could poke their noses into the **Museo del Pescador** (Fishing Museum). Housed in a 16th century *casa-torre*, the style of aristocratic house typical in much of the País Vasco, it is replete with model boats and a great many hooks. The tourist office (☎ 94-618 65 43) is at Askata-sun Bidea 2, on the waterfront.

There are five places to stay. Cheapest are *Hostal Ainhoa* (☎ 94-618 65 61), Calle de Arostegi 25, and *Pensión Talape* (☎ 94-688 16 77), Calle de Garabilla tar José 1, both with singles/doubles for 3000/4000 ptas. There is an agroturismo (☎ 94-688 23 12) at Calle de Artike Auzoa 16, with doubles for 4500 ptas. ET/FV trains run to Bilbao via Mundaka and Gernika. Buses follow the same route.

Ermita de San Juan de Gaztelugatxe

The coast road west from Bermeo offers some tantalising glimpses of the rugged and at times forbidding Basque coast, but none better than where an odd lick of land jutting out from the coast (or, rather, linked to it by a winding stone stairway) a few km north-west of Bermeo plays host to this modest hermitage-chapel.

Bakio

Hardly worth going out of your way for, the minor fishing town of Bakio has a quite attractive little beach but little else to recommend it.

BILBAO

Bilbao (Bilbo), the capital of Vizcaya (Bizkaia) province, has a twin vocation that becomes obvious from whatever angle you approach the city. Maritime commerce and, from a later date, heavy industry have dominated the life of Bilbao since its emergence in the Middle Ages.

Today much of the industry has gone – a chimney stands in the green plain of the Parque de Extebarria as a solitary reminder of what once lay behind the city's prosperity. Shipbuilding, too, is an endangered species, but the port remains busy. In fact, Bilbao has spread out Ruhr valley-style to swallow up the neighbouring towns along both banks of the Ría de Bilbao. Save for the signs announcing you have officially left Bilbao, you would never know, and the recently opened metro runs all the way up the right bank to Plentzia. Central Bilbao retains a business-like and soberly elegant air reminiscent of many a French provincial capital, and the architectural face of the city reflects the bourgeois boom days of the late 19th and early 20th centuries.

Hang around for an evening and any comparisons with stuffy French provincial capitals disappear in a whirlwind of frenzied partying in Las Siete Calles – the nucleus of the medieval Casco Viejo. Here the Spanish propensity for raucous night-long revelry is taken for a serious spin – there is nothing sober about a weekend night out in Bilbao.

History

Bilbao was granted the title of *villa* (a city statute) in 1300, and medieval *bilbaínos* went about their business in the bustle of Las Siete Calles and on the wharves of San Antón and Abando. As the boats got bigger and the business more sophisticated, the quays moved further towards the coast and the city grew. Conquest of the Americas stimulated trade growth and by the late 19th century the area's skyscape was crimped by the slender smoke stacks of furnaces and smelters. Bilbao's golden age lasted from the mid-19th century to the 1920s, when steelworks, shipbuilding yards and chemical plants fed its coffers.

The crises that have affected all of Europe's heavy industries in the past few

decades have also hit Bilbao. Commerce remains buoyant, but the city, easily the largest in the País Vasco, sees itself increasingly as a centre of learning and culture, to which its two universities and the new Museo Guggenheim attest.

Orientation

The nerve-centre of Bilbao, the Casco Viejo, lies bundled up on the right bank of the Ría (estuary) de Bilbao, also sometimes known as the Río Nervión, which it becomes upriver. Many hotels, restaurants and an innumerable concentration of bars are to be found in among Las Siete Calles. The main train stations are just over the river in Abando and many buses also depart from near there. The Museo Guggenheim and Museo de Bellas Artes, west of the centre, and the Basílica de Begoña, to the east, are about the only sights requiring more than a shortish walk from the Casco Viejo.

Information

Tourist Office The Iniciativas Turísticas office (☎ 416 00 22), in the Teatro Arriaga, is one of the more helpful tourist offices in Spain. It opens Monday to Friday from 9 am to 2 pm and 4 to 7 pm, and on weekends and holidays from 10 am to 2 pm. They have a free booklet, updated fortnightly, listing all the cultural happenings throughout Vizcaya province.

Money There is no shortage of banks in central Bilbao and many are armed with user-friendly ATMs.

American Express (☎ 444 48 58) is represented by Viaca, at Calle Alameda Recalde 68.

Post & Communications The central post office, on Alameda de Urquijo, is near Abando train station. The code for poste restante here is 48080. There is a public *locutorio* at Calle de Barroeta Aldamar 7. It opens Monday to Saturday from 9 am to 2 pm and 4 to 9 pm.

Bilbao's telephone code is ☎ 94.

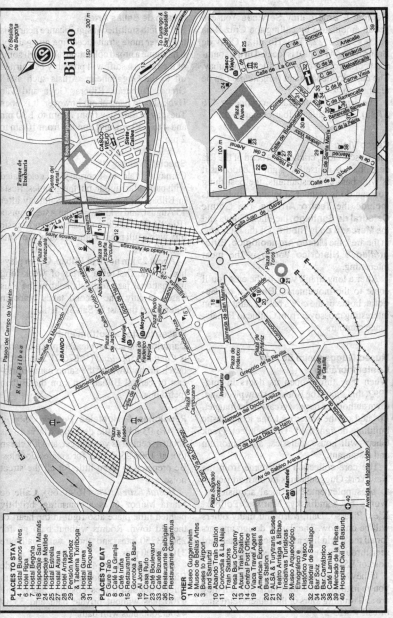

Bilbao

To Basílica de Begoña

To Durango & San Sebastián

See Enlargement

CASCO VIEJO

Siete Calles

Plaza Nueva

Casco Viejo

PLACES TO STAY
4 Hostal Buenos Aires
6 Hotel Ripa
7 Hostal Begoña
18 Hospedaje San Mamés
24 Hospedaje Matilde
25 Hostal Estrella
27 Hostal Arana
28 Hotel Arriaga
29 Pensión Mendez
  & Taberna Txiriboga
30 Hostal Gurea
31 Hostal Roquefer

PLACES TO EAT
5 Gure Talo
8 Café La Granja
9 Café Iruña
15 Restaurante
  Gorroxa & Bars
16 Al Jordan
17 Casa Rufo
23 Café Boulevard
33 Kiskule
36 Restaurante Sabigiain
37 Restaurante Gargantua

OTHER
1 Museo Guggenheim
2 Museo de Bellas Artes
3 Buses to Airport
  and Santurtzi
10 Abando Train Station
11 Termibus & La Naja
  Train Stations
12 Pesa Bus Company
13 Atxuri Train Station
14 Central Post Office
19 Viaca Travel Agent &
  American Express
20 Bus Station
21 ALSA & Turytrans Buses
22 Teatro Arriaga & Bilbao
  Iniciativas Turísticas
26 Museo Arqueológico,
  Etnográfico,
  Histórico Vasco
32 Catedral de Santiago
34 Bar Soiz
35 Bar Cantábrico
38 Café Lamiak
39 Mercado de la Ribera
40 Hospital Civil de Basurto

Medical & Emergency Services You can get an ambulance by calling the Cruz Roja on ☎ 422 22 22. The Hospital Civil de Basurto (☎ 441 87 00) is located in the south-west corner of the city on Calle de Gurtubay. The casualty department *(urgencias)* can be reached on ☎ 442 40 51.

The *ertzainzta*, the Basque police (☎ 476 37 88), are at Calle de Ibarrekolanda 9.

Casco Viejo

The Casco Viejo, cradled in a bend of the Ría de Bilbao, is in itself a 'sight'. Loaded as it is with bars and restaurants, the best thing you can do is wander at leisure. Highlights include the **Teatro Arriaga**, the Gothic **Catedral de Santiago**, the Plaza Nueva and the **Mercado de la Ribera**. Of the museums in the area, the **Museo Arqueológico, Etnográfico e Histórico Vasco** is the most interesting.

After a long uphill walk to the east you'll come to the monumental **Basílica de Begoña**, home of the city's patron saint and an interesting crossover from Gothic to Renaissance contours.

Museo Guggenheim de Arte Contemporáneo

When they throw open its doors in mid-1997, this should be Bilbao's showpiece and, town authorities hope, a great tourist magnet. Located on the waterfront, the iconoclastic building designed by US architect Frank Ghery will house galleries, an auditorium and restaurant.

The core collection will come from the New York Guggenheim's modern art riches, to be supplemented by local acquisitions. Works by Kandinsky, Matisse, Pollock, Klee, Picasso, Dalí, Miró and many others will be on show. The daring design appears for all the world like a huge scrap-metal yard seen through the eyes of someone on a strong dose of LSD.

If they haven't finished construction when you're in town, ask at the tourist office if they are still running tours of the rather weird site, or call ☎ 423 27 99.

Museo de Bellas Artes

Paling into stultified insignificance nearby is the rather more strait-laced fine arts gallery. It has quite a broad collection, although some of the modern stuff will probably be spirited off to the Guggenheim. Artists such as El Greco, Zurbarán, Ribera, Goya and Van Dyck should hang about however. It is open Tuesday to Saturday from 10 am to 1.30 pm and 4 to 7.30 pm, and Sunday from 10 am to 2 pm.

Special Events

Carnaval, held in February, is celebrated with particular vigour, but the grandest fiesta in Bilbao begins on the first Saturday after 15 August, and is known as the Aste Nagusia (Big Week). Traditional parades and music mix with a full programme of cultural events over 10 days.

About 25 km north of Bilbao, Getxo plays host to the first of a series of week-long international jazz festivals held in the País Vasco in July (the second takes place in Vitoria and the last in San Sebastián).

Places to Stay – bottom end

Camping The nearest pleasant place to camp is *Camping Sopelana* (☎ 676 21 20), by the beach in the town of the same name north-east of central Bilbao – it's on the Bilbao metro line.

Pensiones & Hostales *Pensión Méndez* (☎ 416 03 64), Calle de Santa María 13, is about as central as you can get, and it's cheap too, at 1500/2500 ptas for singles/doubles. Be prepared to sleep little for all the street noise.

Hostal Estrella (☎ 416 40 66), Calle de María Múñoz 6, is a charming, brightly painted little place also right in the heart of the old town. Rooms without bath go for 2500/3750 ptas and those with bath are 3100/5000 ptas.

Hostal Gurea (☎ 416 32 99), Calle de Bidebarrieta 14, is another solid choice with singles/doubles/triples costing 2800/3500/4700 ptas without private bath and 3350/4200/5600 ptas with bath.

The friendly *Hostal Roquefer* (☎ 415 07 55), Calle de la Lotería 2, has singles/doubles without own bath starting at 1800/3000 ptas, and doubles with for 4000 ptas.

Hostal Arana (☎ 415 64 11), Calle de Bidebarrieta 2, is a little more expensive than your average hostal but well placed on the edge of the casco – just far enough away to ensure a quiet night's sleep. Rooms with private bath start at 4500/5500/7000 ptas and cost about 1000 ptas less without bath. Pricier still is the *Hospedaje Matilde* (☎ 415 59 28), Calle de Ascao 27.

On the other side of the river, *Hostal Begoña* (☎ 423 01 34), Calle de la Amistad 2, is a reliable if unexciting option. Rooms without private bath start at 2500/4500 ptas.

Close to where many of the intercity buses operate from is *Hospedaje San Mamés* (☎ 441 79 00), Alameda de San Mamés 26. Room prices start at 3500/6500 ptas.

Hostal Buenos Aires (☎ 424 07 65) is in a nicer location at Plaza de Venezuela 1, and somewhat overpriced rooms (some with a view) cost 4500/7000 ptas.

Places to Stay – middle

A charming and moderately priced mid-level option is *Hotel Arriaga* (☎ 479 00 01), right by the theatre at Calle de la Ribera 3. Singles/doubles here are 5000/7000 ptas. *Hotel Ripa* (☎ 423 96 77), just across the river at Calle de Ripa 3, is also fine but can get a little noisy. You pay 5500/7500 ptas.

Places to Eat

If you have moderately loose purse strings and an appetite for an approximation of Basque haute cuisine, pick up the tourist office's guide, *Menú BIT*, to some 20 of Bilbao's better restaurants offering a set menu of this kind. Available for lunch or dinner, the menú BIT allows you to sample some of the city's best without assaulting the bank account. Otherwise, there are plenty of eating options across the centre of town. Many of Bilbao's bars, including some of those listed below under Bars, have a restaurant attached, usually out the back.

Restaurante Saibigain, Calle de Barren-calle Barrena 16, is a good bar/restaurant. They have a tasty set menu for 2100 ptas, or you can pick away at tapas at the bar beneath rows of heavy-hanging hams overhead. Good lunchtime value is the set meal at *Restaurante Gargantua*, Calle de Barren-calle Barrena 3, which costs 1000 ptas.

Gure Talo, Calle del Príncipe 1, is a very earthy place serving up good Basque food and it's popular with bilbaínos. The set meal costs 2000 ptas.

For a trip to the other end of the Med, try *Al Jordan*, Calle de Elcano 26. You can have a mint tea and baklava for breakfast, or an Arabic evening meal with belly dancing.

Casa Rufo (☎ 443 21 72), Calle Hurtado de Amézaga 5, is an extraordinary place – an intimate comedor behind a gourmet food store. Prices for the inventive Basque cooking are moderately expensive, and you should call in advance to be sure of a table.

Restaurante Gorrotxa, Alameda de Urquijo 30, is in an arcade crammed with bars in the new part of town, so after enjoying gourmet nouvelle and traditional Basque cooking (count on about 3000 ptas a head), you need do no more than stumble out the door to continue merry-making into the wee hours.

Cafés Bilbao is graced with a pleasing collection of fine old cafés, of which *Café Iruña*, going strong since 1903 on Calle de Colón Larreátegui, is probably the most celebrated. The décor in one half of the café has its inspiration in the Alhambra – right down to the endlessly repeated carved inscriptions in Arabic declaring 'la ilah illa Allah' – 'There is no god but Allah'. The other side has more the feel of a wine bar in Andalucía.

Café Boulevard, just by the Teatro Arriaga, is another fine spot for a coffee, while *Café La Granja*, on Plaza de España, tends to be a rowdy early evening drinking hole – not wholly in keeping with its more sophisticated past.

In summer, *Café Bizuete* sets up tables in the square next to the cathedral. The porticoed Plaza Nueva is another good spot for coffee and people-watching.

Entertainment

La Ría del Ocio (125 ptas) is a handy weekly what's-on guide to all the bars, concerts, film and theatre in Bilbao; it's sold at all newsagents. The tourist office also puts together a comprehensive listings guide of cultural events in the city and province.

Bars There are several areas to search out nightlife, but the most obvious is the central Siete Calles. That said, it can be extremely crowded, rowdy and adolescent. Calle de Barrencalle is probably the most concentrated scene of drinking and post-tipple lunacy in the country.

Taberna Txiriboga, next to the Pensión Méndez at Calle de Santa María 13, is a curious mix – a kind of Basque nationalist-cum-gay crowd hang out here. It has a cheap set menu for 700 ptas in the comedor out the back.

For a low-lit drink, head for the laid-back *Café Lamiak* and its marble-top tables; it's on Calle de la Merced. *Bar Soiz*, on the corner of Calle de la Torre and Calle de Barrencalle, is a tiny den with a weird and wonderful collection of cocktails. The nearby *Bar Cantábrico* is a popular if more straightforward watering hole.

There is a line of bars along La Ripa, between the Puente del Ayuntamiento and the Puente del Arenal, and a whole arcade of them at Alameda de Urquijo 30. Finally, the zone around the intersection of Calle de Licenciado Poza and Calle de Gregorio de la Revilla is also a fruitful hunting ground.

Getting There & Away

Air Aviaco flies from Bilbao to Madrid and Barcelona, and Iberia puts on a direct flight to London daily, along with several to Paris.

Bus Buses leave from several locations. Long-distance services to Madrid (3245 ptas), Barcelona (4855 ptas), León and other cities depart from the bus station at Calle de la Autonomía 17. Turytrans and ALSA buses leave from the nearby Plaza de Amézola for destinations along the coast to Gijón (west) and San Sebastián (east) – tickets can be purchased in the Viaca travel agent at Alameda de Recalde 68.

The PESA bus company, located near the main train station on Calle Hurtado de Amézaga, runs buses all over the País Vasco, including half-hourly ones to San Sebastián. Other destinations include Irún, Durango, Oñati and even Biarritz (in France).

Train RENFE's Abando train station is in the city centre on the left bank of the river. Three trains daily run to Madrid, and there are two to Barcelona, Alicante and Galicia.

Next door is the rather fancy Concordia train station used by the FEVE private rail company for trains west into Cantabria and Asturias. Below it is La Naja cercanías station, where you can take a train for Santurtzi and the UK ferry.

ET/FV has local Basque services from Atxuri train station, which is across the river and a short way south of Concordia. There is one train to Bermeo via Gernika and Mundaka, and another to San Sebastián (change at Ermua).

Car & Motorcycle The A-68 tollway leads directly south and is the quickest way to make for Vitoria, Burgos and Madrid. The A-8 autopista west to Santander is not a tollway, but you pay heading east to San Sebastián. In all cases there are alternative highways that, in general, are slower but more picturesque.

Boat P&O ferries leave for Portsmouth from Santurtzi, about 14 km north-west of Bilbao's city centre. As a rule there are two sailings a week and the voyage takes about 35 hours from England and 30 hours the other way. There are only two boats in January.

Fares vary according to season, and the standard high-season (late June to September) return ticket costs £181. For this you get a cabin (some with bunk beds) with private shower. If you want a window on the world floating by or something more luxurious still, you can pay from £20 to £85 extra for a double cabin.

The cost of taking a vehicle varies, with the most expensive period being mid-July to mid-August, when the standard return fare for a vehicle up to 6.5 metres long and two metres high is £470, including driver. The low-season return cost is £265. There are special eight and five-day return fares too.

Motorcycles and scooters cost from £150 to £250 (return) in the high season (including rider), while bicycles go free of charge. Ask about special family holiday fares.

The cheapest low-season one-way foot passenger ticket is £45.

Ferries leave Portsmouth at 8.30 pm and Bilbao at 1 pm.

Enquiries and reservations can be made at P&O's office (☎ 423 44 77), Calle de Cosme Echevarrieta 1, or by calling ☎ 0990-980980 in the UK.

Santurtzi can be reached by either cercanía train from La Naja station in central Bilbao or by Bizkaibus bus from La Sendeja, near the Puente del Ayuntamiento.

Getting Around

A measure of the way in which Bilbao has merged with adjacent towns up and down the estuary is the extent of the metro line. It runs right up to the north coast at Plentzia from a number of stations on both sides of the river, and makes getting to the beaches (see below) nearest Bilbao relatively simple.

Bizkaibus operates a regular service to the airport from La Sendeja.

AROUND BILBAO
Beaches

There are better beaches further east and west of Bilbao, but if you want something relatively close to Bilbao, you can try Las Arenas, near Algorta, or the beaches further north outside Plentzia, such as Sopelana. The left end of the Playa Salvaje, in the same area, is for nudists. The Bilbao metro runs to Algorta and Plentzia. A three zone ticket to Plentzia from central Bilbao's Abando train station costs 180 ptas.

Castillo de Butrón

Walt Disney probably would have done it better. This sugary castle a few km west of the village of Gatica (Gatika) and roughly 20 km north-east of Bilbao was first built in the 14th century, but in its present form dates from the 19th century – most of it recently rebuilt. Groups of rowdy school kids romp past sickly looking wax mannequins of soldiers, prisoners and fair damsels in this fanciful place. The scene is completed with audiovisual tall tales and a tacky souvenir stall. That said, the castle – long the bastion of the medieval Basque clan of the Butrón – makes a pleasant little excursion from Bilbao if you have your own transport.

It opens daily from 10.30 am to 8 pm (11 am to 6.30 pm in winter) and entry costs 700 ptas (or 900 ptas if you want a guided tour of the Nobles' Floor included – something you can probably dispense with). Bizkaibus buses from Bilbao run past but are irregular.

Cueva de Pozalagua

Few travellers venture into the Encartaciones, the westernmost district of Vizcaya province, but if you like caves it may be worth your while to head over to Karrantza (Carranza), not far short of Cantabria. Seven km to the north-west, just beyond the village of Ranero, the Cueva de Pozalagua is full of weird and wonderful stalactites. The cave is open on weekends and holidays from 11 am to 7 pm (to 6 pm from October to May) and entry is 500 ptas. You may have to wait for groups of at least six to form before you can enter. If you want to stay in the area, there are several casas rurales in and around Karrantza, which is served by FEVE trains between Bilbao and Santander.

The Road to Burgos

Following the Río Nervión south into Castilla y León (and eventually on to the N-I and Burgos), there is precious little to hold you up on the way. **Orduña**, a little enclave of Vizcaya inside Álava province, is a possible stop of mild interest – in a mouldy sort of way. Look for the Gothic Iglesia de Santa

María, with its thickset tower and portico, down Calle de Burdin off the main square.

Heading East
Durango & Around The industrial town of Durango has few drawcards, although the massive oak portico of the Iglesia de Santa María de Uribarri is quite remarkable. The real attraction is the Duranguesado, the mountainous area around the city. The drive south to the Puerto de Urquiola pass is festooned with spectacular lookouts. Climbers make for the summit of Amboto (1327 metres), about five km east of the pass.

Elorrio, a short bus ride east of Durango, is the best place to stay in the area.

It seems that at one stage just about everyone in Elorrio was a VIP, if the number of mansions bearing family crests is anything to judge by. San Balentin Berrio-Otxoa Kalea in particular is loaded down with the impressive façades of past greatness. It spills into the delightful Plaza Gernikako Arbola, dominated on one side by the austere countenance of the 15th century Basílica de la Purísima Concepción. Opposite is the local frontón, often packed of an evening for the serious business of pelota, while less sports inclined people pass the time in neighbouring cafés.

Apart from an expensive hotel, you could try one of two local agroturismos. *Arabio-Azpikoa* (☎ 94-658 33 42), Arabio Kalea 8, and *Galartza Barrena* (☎ 94-658 27 07), Zenita Kalea 1. Both have double rooms for around 3500 ptas.

For food and drinks, just wander down Erreka Kalea off the main square – there's plenty around.

There are regular buses and trains from Bilbao to Durango.

VITORIA
Capital not only of the southern Basque province of Álava (Araba) but of the entire País Vasco, Vitoria (Gasteiz) is a strange mix of sober, business-like city and ebullient student enclave. This cocktail is of course given that special Basque twist. Although you'll probably never hear a word of Basque spoken here, the place is covered in posters and graffiti that keep a consciousness of the continuing struggle between the ETA and its opponents alive and kicking. And you could easily stumble across a game of pelota down at the frontón on Plaza de los Fueros.

History
Nueva Vitoria was founded in 1181 by the Navarran king Sancho VI (El Sabio) on the site of the old Basque village of Gasteiz. It later swapped hands between the Castilian and Navarran crowns. The expansion that began in the 18th century picked up pace in the 20th with the growth of industry. The city was named capital of the País Vasco in 1979.

Orientation
The old city centre, composed of narrow alleys arranged more or less as a series of concentric circles, is easily distinguishable. A 10 minute walk south brings you to the train station, while the bus station lies a few blocks to the east of the centre. Hotels of all categories are spread out between the two, with a handful in the old city itself.

Information
Tourist Office The tourist office (☎ 13 13 21) in Parque de la Florida is the handiest. It opens Monday to Friday from 8.30 am to 7 pm; Saturday from 9 am to 1 pm and 2 to 7 pm; and Sunday from 10 am to 2 pm. Another office (☎ 16 15 98) with similar hours is located on the corner of Avenida de Gasteiz and Calle de Chile.

Money There is no shortage of banks in the newer part of town between the train station and Plaza de España.

Post & Communications The main post office is on Calle de las Postas and the postcode for poste restante is 01080.

Vitoria's phone code is ☎ 945.

Medical & Emergency Services Hospital de Santiago (☎ 25 36 00) is handily placed on Calle de la Paz. If you need an ambulance,

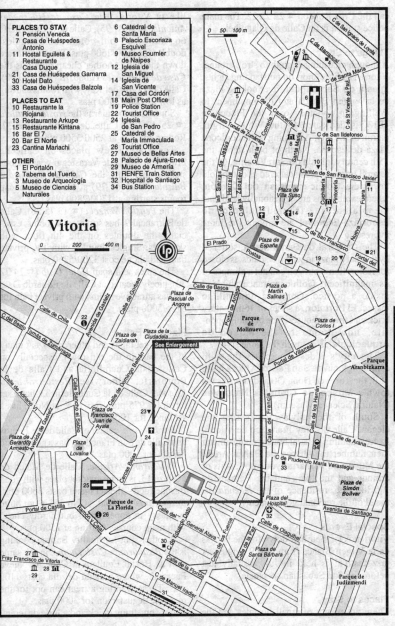

PAÍS VASCO

call the Cruz Roja on ☎ 22 22 22. The main
police station is on Calle de Olaguibel.

Things to See

Although charming enough to stroll around,
Vitoria is a little short on outstanding sights.
Iglesia de San Miguel, overlooking Plaza
de la Virgen Blanca and its monument to
Wellington's victory over the French in
1813, is dedicated to the White Virgin,
patron of the city. Adjoining is the porticoed
Plaza de España. North of both stands the
15th century **Iglesia de San Vicente**. Of the
several noble houses scattered about the old
town, the Gothic-era **Casa del Cordón**,
where exhibitions are occasionally held, and
the plateresque-fronted **Palacio de
Escoriaza-Esquivel** are among the more
interesting.

The **Catedral de Santa María**, softened
by the leafy plaza in which it stands, is closed
for restoration – but you can get a glimpse of
its magnificent Gothic entrance shielded
inside a portico. Continue downhill to
inspect **El Portalón**, a series of 16th century
brick and timber houses. The building opposite, now home to the **Museo de
Arqueología**, is in much the same style.

The city's oldest church is the 14th
century **Iglesia de San Pedro**. A block north
of it, the Torre de Doña Otxanda houses the
town's **Museo de Ciencias Naturales**
(Natural Science Museum).

South of the railway tracks runs the
elegant Calle de Fray Francisco de Vitoria.
Its freestanding palatial houses count among
their number the **Museo de Bellas Artes**,
the **Museo de Armería** (you know, suits of
armour and the like) and the **Palacio de
Ajuria-Enea**, residence of the *lehendakari*
(head of the regional government).

Special Events

Vitorianos let their hair down for the Fiestas
de la Virgen Blanca from 4 to 9 August. A
jazz festival is held in July, usually just
before the San Sebastián spectacle.

Places to Stay

There are plenty of small hostales and the
like in Vitoria. The *Casa de Huéspedes
Antonio* (☎ 26 87 95), Calle de la Cuchillería
66, has small but comfortable singles/
doubles for 1500/2600 ptas. The showers are
down the hall. Another cheap option is the
Casa de Huéspedes Gamarra (☎ 25 40 90),
Calle del Portal del Rey, with rooms starting
as low as 1200/2400 ptas.

Somewhat roomier is the *Hostal Eguileta*
(☎ 25 17 00), Calle de Nueva Fuera 32.
Rooms come in at 2500/3500 ptas.

There are a few places on Calle de
Prudencio María de Verastegui near the bus
station, including the *Casa de Huéspedes
Balzola* (☎ 25 62 79) at No 6, with cheap
rooms starting at 1700/2800 ptas.

The *Pensión Venecia* (☎ 13 75 88), Calle
de Barrancal 9, has some great rooms, especially the doubles on the 4th floor with
skylights. Singles/doubles with TV, private
bath and phone cost 3200/5250 ptas.

The spick and span *Hotel Dato* (☎ 14 72
30), nicely located at Calle de Eduardo Dato
28, has attractive rooms with private bath for
3725/5000 ptas.

Places to Eat

You can get tapas and other snacks at many
of the bars in the old town, especially on
Calle de la Cuchillería and Calle de la
Pintorería. Otherwise, *Restaurante la
Riojana*, Calle de la Cuchillería 33, has a set
lunch for 975 ptas. *Bar El 7*, at No 3, has a
set lunch for 1000 ptas.

Bar El Norte, corner of Calle de los Fueros
and Calle de San Francisco, has a good menú
del día for 1000 ptas.

Restaurante Arkupe, Calle de Mateo de
Moraza 13, is an up-market place with good
Basque food – the set menu costs 3600 ptas.
Restaurante Kintana, at No 15, is not quite
as classy in appearance, but hardly cheap
with main courses starting at 1500 ptas.

Another spot for quality Basque cooking
is the *Restaurante Casa Duque*, in the same
spot as Hostal Eguileta at Calle de Nueva
Fuera 32, where a menú del día costs 1100
ptas. Those wanting a treat can opt for the
menú de degustación for 3000 ptas.

For something quick and a little different,

Cantina Mariachi, Calle de las Cercas Bajas 17, has fast Mexican food.

At *Esquibel*, Calle de Adriano VI 37, you are looking at about 3000 ptas for a full meal. Their arroz Esquibel is a must.

The cafés on Plaza de España are the most atmospheric places for your morning coffee.

Entertainment

Bars The centre of the old town, and in particular Calle de la Cuchillería and Calle de la Pintorería, is wall to wall bars, creating an intense, largely student, nightlife from Thursday into the weekend. A good late-night haunt is *Baco*, Calle de los Fueros 39. In El Portalón there is a bar called *Taberna del Tuerto* where you can get a tattoo with your drinks.

Discos & Nightclubs A popular dance place with thirty-somethings is *Aural*, Paseo de la Senda 2, open until 5 am. A younger set heads to *Círculo*, Calle del General Álava 5 (entry 1000 ptas; includes first drink).

Getting There & Away

Bus Continental-Auto has about six buses daily to Madrid (2800 ptas). Other companies have regular services to Bilbao (640 ptas), Durango, Pamplona (875 ptas), Logroño and Estella.

Train At least six trains a day go to Madrid. The basic one-way fare is 3800 ptas. To San Sebastián you pay 940 ptas.

Car & Motorcycle The N-I highway linking Madrid to San Sebastián passes by Vitoria. Take the N-240 for Bilbao.

AROUND VITORIA
Mendoza & Oppidum de Iruña

About 15 km west of Vitoria (take the N-I for Burgos), the farming village of Mendoza features the Torre de los Mendoza, a castle now converted into the Museo de Heráldica, of interest for those keen to study Basque coats of arms. A few km further south, a medieval bridge at Trespuentes leads to the ancient Roman settlement of Oppidum de Iruña.

Laguardia & Nearby

The prettiest of the Rioja wine-growing towns is undoubtedly Laguardia, about 45 km south of Vitoria along a picturesque road that crosses an enclave of Burgos province located inside Álava. The area has been inhabited since the Iron Age. In the old walled town, look for the Iglesia de Santa María de los Reyes, which features a rare example of a grand Gothic doorway with its polychrome colouring intact. If you are hoping to taste some local wines, pop into the Bodegas Casa Juan and ask for Ángel. If he's around, he will oblige with a drop of his red or white, although the place is not formally set up for tastings. For more on the area's wines, see the Wine Region section in the La Rioja part of this chapter.

Littered with the houses of noble families, Laguardia's laneways are perfect for a post-luncheon constitutional. That lunch should be had at the *Restaurante Pavoni*, Calle Mayor 26. A scrumptious, hearty menú costs 1000 ptas and is worth every peseta. There is a choice of five places to stay, including the *Casa de Huéspedes* (☎ 941-10 01 14) at Calle Mayor 17, where comfortable singles/doubles cost 3500/5000 ptas. Slow buses which connect Vitoria and Logroño pass through Laguardia.

You'll find plenty of interesting little villages if you have a vehicle to tour around the area, including **Elciego**, a few km south of Laguardia, and **Labastida**, just six km short of Haro in La Rioja. Labastida straggles up a small hillside capped by the Ermita del Cristo with its fine Romanesque entrance.

If disappearing into the countryside is your thing and you want a different return route to Vitoria, follow the back roads to the north-east of Laguardia that take in the hamlets of Elvillar, Cripán, Meano, Aguilar and Santa Cruz, where you switch north-west along the A-132 for Vitoria. The prettiest stretch starts in Meano and actually takes you briefly into Navarra.

Navarra

Several Spains intersect in Navarra (Nafarroa in Basque). The fiercely independent traditions of the Basques here have their special flavour in the historical fueros, or autonomous rights long exercised by the Navarrese and resurrected today – the region is in fact officially known as the Comunidad Foral de Nafarroa.

The Navarrese are strong on symbolic points – red dominates the region's coat of arms. The Policía Foral have bright red cars, motorbikes and uniforms. In the Navarran Pyrenees everyone seems to paint doors and window frames red; when villages celebrate local fiestas, half the locals wear the traditional Basque white trousers and tops with red scarves, and red geraniums seem to be the main form of floral decoration in the ubiquitous window box.

The soft greens and bracing climate of the Navarran Pyrenees lie like a cool compress across the sunstruck brow of the south, which is all stark plains, cereal crops and vineyards, sliced up by high, forbidding sierras. Navarra is pilgrim territory – for centuries the faithful have used the pass at Roncesvalles to cross from France on their way to Santiago. Here too armies have crossed to and from Spain, but not always with success: Roland's retreating Frankish forces were harried and decimated by Basques in 778, leaving behind little but one of the great *gestes* of early medieval French literature, *La Chanson de Roland*.

Although many associate Navarra exclusively with the running of the bulls in Pamplona, the region's real charm is in its small towns and villages, many in possession of fine monuments ranging from Romanesque to Renaissance.

The phone code for all Navarra is ☎ 948.

If you're planning to spend any time in or near the Pyrenees of Navarra, pick up a copy of the *Guía de Alojamientos de Turismo Rural*, available from most tourist offices in Navarra, which lists all the private homes and farmsteads in the area that rent out rooms. The standards are often higher than in your average hostal, and they are cheaper too.

PAMPLONA

Pamplona (Iruña, Iruñea), capital of the fiercely independent-minded Navarrese, is an attractive display of centuries-old middle-class wellbeing set behind the remains of its once haughty city walls. A fine cathedral is the jewel in the crown, but the footloose wanderer will get pleasure from simply meandering along narrow streets fronted by tall, elegant apartment houses.

On 6 July, all hell breaks loose as Spain's best known bull fest, the Fiesta de San Fermín (or the Sanfermines) kick-starts the city into a frenzy of drinking and mayhem. The running of the bulls (*el encierro*), made famous by Hemingway, is accompanied by a stampede of visitors from all over the world bent on having such a good time they are unlikely to remember much of it at all.

History

The Romans called the city Pompaelo, after its founder Pompey the Great. They were succeeded by the Visigoths and briefly by the Muslims, but by the 8th century Pamplona formed the nucleus of an independent power – the future kingdom of Navarra. It reached the height of its glory under Sancho III in the 11th century, and its position on the Camino de Santiago assured it prosperity. When Franco did his thing in 1936, Pamplona and indeed the rest of Navarra sided with the Nationalists.

Orientation

The old city centre is extremely compact. It is marked off to the north and east by the Río Arga and what remains of the old defensive walls, and to the west by parks and the former citadel. The main square, Plaza del Castillo, roughly marks the division between old and new in the south. Everything, including the bullring, is a short walk away. Much of the cheaper accommodation is in the streets west of Plaza del Castillo and near the

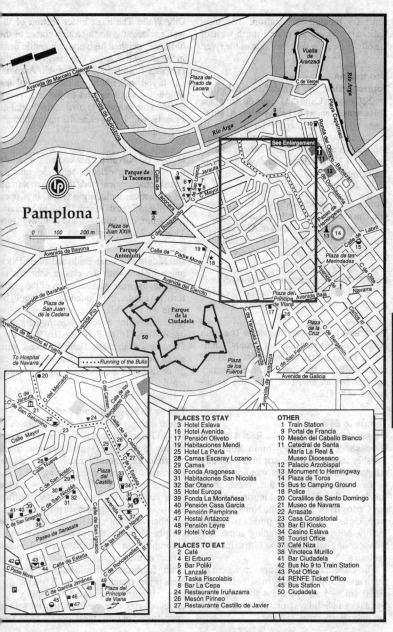

NAVARRA

PLACES TO STAY
3 Hotel Eslava
16 Hotel Avenida
17 Pensión Oliveto
19 Habitaciones Mendi
25 Hotel La Perla
28 Camas Escaray Lozano
29 Camas
30 Fonda Aragonesa
31 Habitaciones San Nicolás
32 Bar Otano
35 Hotel Europa
39 Fonda La Montañesa
40 Pensión Casa García
46 Pensión Pamplona
47 Hostal Artázcoz
48 Pensión Leyre
49 Hotel Yoldi

PLACES TO EAT
2 Café
4 El Erburo
5 Bar Poliki
6 Lanzale
7 Taska Piscolabis
8 Bar La Cepa
24 Restaurante Iruñazarra
26 Mesón Pirineo
27 Restaurante Castillo de Javier

OTHER
1 Train Station
9 Portal de Francia
10 Mesón del Caballo Blanco
11 Catedral de Santa
    María La Real &
    Museo Diocesano
12 Palacio Arzobispal
13 Monument to Hemingway
14 Plaza de Toros
15 Bus to Camping Ground
18 Police
20 Coralillos de Santo Domingo
21 Museo de Navarra
22 Arrasate
23 Casa Consistorial
33 Bar El Kiosko
34 Casino Eslava
36 Tourist Office
37 Café Niza
38 Vinoteca Murillo
41 Bar Ciudadela
42 Bus No 9 to Train Station
43 Post Office
44 RENFE Ticket Office
45 Bus Station
50 Ciudadela

centrally located bus station. The train station is awkwardly placed north-west of the city centre, on the other side of the river.

Information

Tourist Office You'll find the tourist office (☎ 22 07 41) at Calle del Duque de Ahumada 3. It opens Monday to Friday from 10 am to 2 pm and 4 to 7 pm, and Saturday from 10 am to 2 pm. In July and August it opens Monday to Saturday from 9.30 am to 2.30 pm and 4.30 to 7.30 pm, and Sunday from 9.30 am to 2.30 pm.

Money There is no shortage of banks where you can change cash and travellers' cheques or get cash advances (plenty of ATMs around too). Note, however, that throughout the fiesta they open in the morning only.

Post & Communications The post office is at Calle de Estella 10. The postcode for poste restante at the central post office is 31080.

Medical & Emergency Services The main police station is on Calle del General Chinchilla. The Hospital de Navarra (☎ 10 21 00) is on Calle de Irunlarrea. The emergency number for all services, including ambulances, is ☎ 112.

Things to See

Catedral de Santa María La Real & Museo Diocesano Pamplona's main house of worship stands on a rise just inside the city ramparts. Its single most outstanding feature is the Gothic cloister in the French style. Inside the church lie buried in some splendour Carlos III of Navarra (the Noble) and his wife Doña Leonor. The museum houses mainly religious art, including some fine woodcarving dating from the 12th to the 14th centuries.

The cathedral and museum are visited as a unit and are open Tuesday to Saturday from 10.30 am to 1.30 pm and 4 to 6 pm, and Sundays and holidays from 10.30 am to 1.30 pm only. Entry costs 350 ptas.

City Walls The most intact section of the wall encloses the north-eastern corner of the old town, perched high above a gentle bend in the shady Río Arga. You can get up to the ramparts from behind the Palacio Arzobispal. If you walk north past the cathedral and follow the walls around to the left, you'll come to the gateway known as the Portal de Francia, which was once the main entrance to Pamplona.

Museo de Navarra This contains a mildly interesting and eclectic selection ranging from archaeological finds through to a small art collection, including a Goya. It is open Tuesday to Saturday from 10 am to 2 pm and 5 to 7 pm, and Sundays and holidays from 11 am to 2 pm. Admission is 200 ptas.

Ciudadela & Parks Built and remodelled much in line with the classic schemas of Vauban, the walls and bulwarks of the grand fortified citadel, the Ciudadela, can barely be made out for all the grass and trees in what now constitutes a very pleasant park. It's open daily from 7.30 am to 9.30 pm. Pamplona's northern flank is laced with green, and the sculpted gardens of the Parque de la Taconera are also nice for an evening stroll.

Places to Stay – bottom end
There are only a handful of cheap places to stay in Pamplona, and in the first two weeks of July (Sanfermines) some places as much as triple their normal rates. It is next to impossible to get a room during the fiesta without booking well ahead. Touts will often greet you at the train station or tourist office at this time, offering rooms in private houses.

Otherwise you can join the many who simply sleep in the parks. Leave your belongings in the *consigna* (left-luggage office) at the bus and train stations. People opting for the parks should be aware that they are a prime target for thieves. Expert at slitting sleeping bags and whipping out anything you may have stuffed into them apart from yourself, these people have also

Fiesta de San Fermín

The Fiesta de San Fermín, or Sanfermines, has its origins in medieval legend. Fermín, son of a recently Christianised Roman governor of Pamplona, went off to spread the word in Gaul, ending up imprisoned and decapitated in Amiens for his trouble. No-one really knows when he became the patron saint of Navarra and Pamplona, but his feast day was set on 7 July in 1591. A 15th century wooden statue of the saint is hauled around the city in solemn procession at 10 am on 7 July.

The fiesta is an almost nonstop cacophony of music, dance, fireworks, processions and, of course, bullfights. The fights take place at 6.30 pm each day from 7 to 14 July. The day starts early – at 6.45 am bands march around town with the aim of waking everyone from their slumbers to launch them into another day of festivity and abandon. Although the festivities begin on 6 July, the first running of the bulls doesn't take place until the following morning. This is not some one-off tradition peculiar to Pamplona. The running of the bulls, or *el encierro*, always preceded the day's bullfights for the simple reason that you had to get the bulls to the ring somehow. Originally, the *toros bravos* (fighting bulls) were accompanied by *toros mansos* (quiet bulls) and herded from behind. How or when this exercise became a dangerous diversion remains unknown. Nowadays in many cities the bulls are often transported by truck to the *plaza de toros*, but plenty of smaller Spanish towns celebrate the encierro as an integral part of the fiesta.

Every morning from 7 to 14 July, the bulls are let loose from the Coralillos de Santo Domingo and charge across the square of the same name (a good vantage point). They continue up the street, veering into Calle de los Mercaderes from Plaza Consistorial and sweeping right into Calle de la Estafeta for the final charge to the ring. The brave or the foolish, depending on one's point of view, race madly with the bulls, aiming to keep close – but not too close. The total course is some 800 metres long. A little later, *vaquillas* (small cows) are let loose in the ring to chase (or be chased by) other spectators – these are *not* the bulls that have been run from the Coralillos de Santo Domingo.

The entire ethos of the *corrida*, or bullfight, is steeped not only in measuring the valour of man against beast, but also in the skill, some would say art, of the fight. To a certain extent, the same can be said of the encierro. Every year, people are hurt and sometimes killed in encierros, not only in Pamplona but across the country. This is largely because the majority of those who run are full of bravado (or drink or both) but have little idea of what they are doing. It is difficult to recommend this activity, but plenty participate anyway. Try to run with someone experienced, and above all do not get caught near bulls that have been separated from the herd. Keep ahead of the herd and you should be all right. To increase the thrill, some runners try whacking bulls with rolled up newspapers and the like. Not a very nice thing to do, and designed to get one taking a special interest in you. That kind of attention you can well live without!

To participate you must enter the course before 8 am from Plaza de Santo Domingo and take up your position. At around 8 am two rockets are fired. The first announces that the bulls have been released from the corrals. The second lets you know they are all out and running. The first truly dangerous point is where Calle de los Mercaderes leads into Calle de la Estafeta. Here many of the bulls crash into the barriers because of the sheer speed at which they attempt to take the turns, and this is where at least some bulls are likely to be separated from the herd. A bull thus separated and surrounded by charging humans is probably rather more frightened than the people. And 300 to 400 kg of frightened bull make for an unpredictable and dangerous animal. Another particularly dangerous stretch comes towards the end, where Calle de la Estafeta slopes down into the final turn to the Plaza de Toros. A third rocket goes off when all the bulls have made it to the ring, and a final one when they have been rounded up in the stalls where they will await the fight. If you want to watch a fight, and fail to get tickets in advance at the ring, you'll usually find scalpers selling cheaper seats for around 1000 ptas.

The whole shebang is wound up at midnight on 14 July by a candlelit procession, known as the Pobre de Mí, which starts from Plaza Consistorial. ∎

been known to artfully make off with the watch on your wrist.

Alternatively, base yourself outside Pamplona, although you may still have to put up with a night in the park if you are relying on public transport and want to be in Pamplona in good time for the early morning running of the bulls.

Camping The nearest camping ground, *Ezcaba* (☎ 33 03 15), is seven km north of town. It opens from Easter to October, but like just about everything else is full for the fiesta. Basic temporary camping facilities are set up nearby for the fiesta. A bus service runs four times a day from just near the Plaza de Toros. Look for the Montañesa bus to Arre/Oricain.

Fondas, Pensiones & Hostales *Fonda La Montañesa* (☎ 22 43 80), Calle de San Gregorio 2, has basic rooms for 1300 ptas per person. A little better is *Pensión Casa García* (☎ 22 38 93), at No 12. Here rooms go for 1400/2700 ptas. *Camas Escaray Lozano* (☎ 22 76 25), Calle Nueva 24, has small but clean singles/doubles for 1500/ 4000 ptas.

If you have no luck with these, there are a few others in the same category, including the *Fonda Aragonesa* (☎ 22 34 28), Calle de San Nicolás 32; *Habitaciones San Nicolás* at No 13; *Bar Otano* at No 5; and another place with a sign saying *Camas* at Calle del Pozo Blanco 16.

Near the bus station you'll find several places that all look much the same inside. They are clean and comfortable, but none has private bathroom. *Pensión Pamplona* (☎ 22 99 63), Calle de Tudela 5, has small rooms starting at 3500/5000 ptas. *Pensión Leyre* (☎ 21 16 47), Calle de San Ignacio 10, charges 3000/5000 ptas for better rooms with TV. *Pensión Oliveto* (☎ 24 93 21), Calle de Oliveto 3, has virtually the same deal for 3500/4500 ptas. Also by the bus station, *Hostal Artázcoz* (☎ 22 51 64), Calle de Tudela 9, offers small rooms without own bath for 3500/4500 ptas or 4500/5500 ptas with bath.

Habitaciones Mendi (☎ 22 52 97), Calle de las Navas de Tolosa 9, is a particularly good deal. Its rooms have a little character and come with own loo. They cost 3000/ 5000 ptas.

Places to Stay – middle
Hotel Eslava (☎ 22 22 70; fax 22 51 57), Plaza Virgen de la O 7, is a homey little place charging 3500/6000 ptas plus IVA for singles/doubles with TV, phone and en suite bath.

For a touch of slightly faded class, the *Hotel La Perla* (☎ 22 77 06), Plaza del Castillo 1, could be the right place. Rooms start at about 5000/8000 ptas plus IVA.

More expensive and less characterful is the *Hotel Yoldi* (☎ 22 48 00; fax 21 20 45), Avenida de San Ignacio 11, where rooms come in at 5800/9500 ptas plus IVA.

Places to Stay – top end
For a tad more elegance, the *Hotel Europa* (☎ 22 18 00; fax 22 92 35), Calle de Espoz y Mina 11, has singles/doubles starting at 6900/13,500 ptas plus IVA. The *Hotel Avenida* (☎ 24 54 54; fax 23 23 23), Avenida de Zaragoza 5, has a basic rate of 8100/ 14,500 ptas, but offers cheaper deals on weekends.

Places to Eat
Some good places for raciones (bar snacks) are bunched together on Calle de San Lorenzo, including *El Erburo*, at No 19, which has a set menu for 1200 ptas and *Lanzale*, at No 31, which has a set lunch for 1000 ptas. Otherwise you can eat tapas at *Bar Poliki*, No 21, and the *Taska Piscolabis*, No 14. *Bar La Cepa*, at No 2, also serves up food.

Restaurante Iruñazarra, Calle de los Mercaderes 15, offers a tasty set menu for 1200 ptas – try the escalopines al Roquefort.

The cosy, timber-laden atmosphere of the *Mesón Pirineo*, Calle de la Estafeta 41, makes for a nice option and mains are not unreasonable at around 1000 to 1500 ptas. Around the corner at Bajada de Javier 2, *Restaurante Castillo de Javier* is the place to head for up-market Basque food.

If you need to stock up on vast amounts of

good Navarran wine, the Vinoteca Murillo, on the corner of Calle de San Gregorio and Plaza de San Nicolás, will fill five-litre containers for 690 ptas. Or you could buy something with a little more class.

Entertainment

Cafés & Bars The cafés on Plaza del Castillo with their French-style awnings are a great place to start the day, or end it. *Bar El Kiosko* is boisterous, while *Casino Eslava* is more reservedly chic.

Pamplona in fact boasts several rather elegant spots for a coffee or apéritif. *Arrasate*, Calle de Saturnino 16, is one. A little younger and with a busy atmosphere is *Café Niza*, opposite the tourist office on Calle del Duque de Ahumada.

Bar Ciudadela, Calle de la Ciudadela 3, has a great upstairs section where you can sip a beer on the little balconies in summer. Better still is perhaps the *Mesón del Caballo Blanco*, just inside the city walls north of the cathedral.

Although there is no shortage of bars along Calle de San Gregorio and Calle de San Nicolás, the best street to head for is Calle de Jarauta. It is wall-to-wall bars of the loud and late variety.

Getting There & Away

Bus Buses run from the central bus station, on Avenida de Yanguas y Miranda, to most towns throughout Navarra, but in many cases there is no service on Sunday.

Six buses run daily to Bilbao (1510 ptas), about 10 run to Vitoria (875 ptas) and up to 12 run to San Sebastián (700 ptas). Some of the latter are express buses. Other destinations with regular services include Estella, Logroño, Zaragoza, Tafalla, Tudela and Soria.

Train Pamplona is on the San Sebastián-Zaragoza line, but the station is awkwardly situated north of town. If you arrive this way, catch bus No 9 to Paseo de Sarasate.

Car & Motorcycle The A-15 tollway rounds the city and links up other autopistas to Zaragoza to the south and San Sebastián to

the north. Several pretty routes lead north into the Pyrenees and on to France, while the N-240 heads east into Aragón (Jaca) and the N-111 goes south-west to Logroño.

EAST OF PAMPLONA

South-east along the N-240, a handful of interesting towns and a grand monastery lying virtually on the southern rim of the Pyrenees together form a worthwhile excursion or stopover before heading on into Aragón. If you intend to veer north into the Pyrenees, you might want to dash across the frontier to Sos del Rey Católico (see the Aragón chapter) while in the area. This is straightforward with your own transport. If relying on the infrequent buses, you might be tempted to speed up the process by hitching, as all these places are pretty close to one another. The best prospects for a cheap room are Sangüesa or Yesa.

Sangüesa

The biggest town in eastern Navarra and once an important stop on the pilgrim route to Santiago de Compostela for those who chose to cross from France via Somport, Sangüesa still retains an air of importance and a sense of its past unique to this part of Navarra.

Approaching from the north, you cross the Río Aragón and immediately on the left are presented with one of the premier examples of Romanesque religious art in Navarra, the Iglesia de Santa María. Entry is through an exquisite 12th century portal. Simpler, but with its own charm, is the Iglesia de Santiago, a Romanesque church which shows signs of the transition to Gothic. Sangüesa is not a bad place to lay over for the night since it has more life than you'll find in any of the nearby pueblos, and a sufficient assortment of other minor monuments and mansions to keep you interested.

The only place to stay in town is *Pensión Las Navas* (☎ 87 07 00), Calle de Alfonso el Batallador 7 (near the ayuntamiento), with singles/doubles for 3000/4000 ptas. They also do decent food, although you could try

Camino de Santiago

The principal route for pilgrims to Santiago de Compostela enters Navarra, and hence Spain, at the pass through the Pyrenees just north of Roncesvalles. It makes its way through Pamplona and proceeds south-west to Puente la Reina on the Río Arga. A beautiful bridge spans the river at this point, where a secondary *camino* from Aragón joins the main road. From Puente la Reina the Camino de Santiago follows the way to Logroño. Of major interest en route are Estella (Lizarra) and, just beyond, the Monasterio de Irache. Other stops worth a look include Torres del Río and Viana. The Pamplona-Logroño stretch of the Camino is covered in this chapter's West of Pamplona section.

Beyond Logroño (in the modern autonomous region of La Rioja), the Camino heads west to Burgos. You can take or leave Navarrete and Nájera, but make an effort to visit the extraordinary monastery of Santo Domingo de la Calzada (see the Camino de Santiago section of the La Rioja part of this chapter) before continuing the route to Burgos in Castilla y León. Lists of pilgrims' hostels for the whole camino are available in tourist offices at Pamplona and Estella. ■

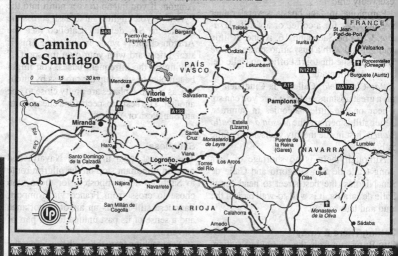

Camino de Santiago

eating at one of the handful of bars in the surrounding streets.

Javier

From Sangüesa, it's 11 km north-east to Javier (or Xavier), where the patron saint of Navarra, San Francisco Xavier, was born in 1506. The town itself, an eminently forgettable grid of dead streets, lies downhill from Javier's *castillo*. Although there may have been a watchtower as early as the 11th century, what you see today is largely the result of extensive restoration in 1890 and 1952. In March each year, it is the object of the Javierada, when thousands of people

descend on the castle and town to commemorate the saint. During the rest of the year, a steady stream of tourist coaches keeps the place busy. Inside, there is a small display devoted to the life of San Francisco, and also a small chapel decorated with macabre figures doing the dance of death. Entry is free.

South of the castle stands a church erected in memory of San Francisco Xavier. The saint is said to have been baptised in the font that is preserved here.

The two hotels have a monopoly on food and beds and are overpriced, but if you must stay, *Hotel El Mesón* (☎ 88 40 35) is the cheaper one at 4200/5500 ptas plus IVA. A bus a day passes through from Pamplona and Sangüesa en route for Huesca, and there is another that heads up the Valle de Roncal.

Yesa

If you have wheels and no luck with rooms in Sangüesa, skip those in Javier and try here. There's not much to the village, but a couple of places rent out rooms, including the *Hostal El Jabalí* (☎ 88 40 42), on the road out to Jaca. Rooms start at about 2500/3800 ptas.

About five km north lies the **Monasterio de Leyre** (or Leire), set in the shadow of the Sierra de Leyre, virtually the last mountain range before the Pyrenees. A religious community was first established here in the 9th century. By the 12th century, it had become a powerful Cluniac bastion, looming large in the religious and cultural life of all Navarra, and pretty much in command of all the pilgrim-route passes from France. By the time the Cistercian reform was introduced in the 13th century, the monastery was beginning to lose influence. In 1836 the monks were turfed out, and over the next 100 years local shepherds used the monastery to shelter themselves and their flocks. In 1954, when the Benedictines moved in, they found themselves confronted by the enormous task of restoration.

The early Romanesque crypt is without doubt the most fascinating part of the complex. It is a three nave structure with a low roof and its squat columns with their outsize base capitals and vaguely horseshoe-shaped arches are unique to the monastery. The Romanesque cloister was destroyed after the expulsion of the Cistercians, but the 12th century main portal of the church is a fine reminder of Romanesque artistry at its most challenging and is rich in symbolism. Much of the church is, however, built in the early-Gothic style.

The monks here sell recordings of themselves performing Gregorian chants. If you can make it to the 5 pm Mass, you can hear the real thing.

The monastery is open roughly from 10 am to 6 pm, but whenever you turn up, you must wait for a group to assemble for the obligatory guided tour in Spanish. This costs 150 ptas.

Apart from the *Hospedería de Leyre* (☎ 88 41 00), which is a little expensive at 4500/6400 ptas for singles/doubles, men could try getting a bed in the monastery itself – ask at the *portería* (reception).

There's a bus a day from Yesa to Pamplona at 8 am and one to Huesca at 7 am. You might also be able to pick up the daily service connecting Pamplona and the Valle de Roncal in north-east Navarra. There are virtually no buses on Sunday, and there are no buses from Yesa to the monastery.

WEST OF PAMPLONA

The main route west out of Pamplona winds gently south-west to Logroño following the Camino de Santiago. This pretty route, dotted with a handful of charming little towns and especially bursting with colour after the spring rains, is one of the more enticing stretches for those walking the Camino. Buses regularly run between Pamplona and Logroño along this route.

Puente de la Reina

It is at Puente de la Reina (Gares) that pilgrims approaching from Roncesvalles to the north and Aragón to the east have for centuries joined forces to take the one main route west. Their first stop here was the late-Romanesque **Iglesia del Crucifijo**, erected by the Knights Templar and still containing one of the finest Gothic crucifixes in existence. From here, those eager to push on would walk down the narrow Calle Mayor past the **Iglesia de Santiago** and its Romanesque portal to the Río Arga. The six arched medieval **Puente de los Peregrinos** at the end of Calle Mayor remains the nicest way to cross the river and pursue the Camino.

Places to Stay & Eat Apart from the *refugio* for pilgrims (summer only), there's no really cheap accommodation. *Hostal Puente* (☎ 34 01 46), Plaza de los Fueros, is central and has singles/doubles with private bath for 3500/5000 ptas. They have a few slightly cheaper rooms without private bath. Prices rise

NAVARRA

steeply in summer. Otherwise, *Hotel Jakue* (☎ 34 10 17), Calle de Irumbidea s/n, offers rooms for 4500/8000 ptas plus IVA in the low season. The *Mesón del Peregrino* (☎ 34 00 75), just outside town on the road to Pamplona, is worse still at 7000/9000 ptas.

You can eat at the *Bar-Asador Joaquín*, Calle Mayor 50.

Estella

Without doubt the highlight on this route is the picturesque little town of Estella (Lizarra), huddled on the bend of the tree-shaded Río Ega. It makes a good base if you intend doing any little excursions in the vicinity, and is certainly the best place to plan to end up for the night.

Seat of the Carlists in the 19th century, the village of Lizarra acquired its Castilian name in 1090 when Sancho Ramírez (king of Navarra and Aragón) made it the primary reception point for the growing flood of pilgrims along the Camino.

The extremely helpful tourist office (☎ 55 40 11), Calle de San Nicolás 1, is right in among the most important monuments on the south-west bank of the river. It opens (April to September) Monday to Friday from 10 am to 2 pm and 4 to 7 pm, and weekends from 10 am to 2 pm only. They also organise guided tours of the town.

The fortified tower of the 13th century **Iglesia de San Pedro de la Rúa** lords it over the town. To see the partly ruined cloister, ask at the tourist office. Next door to the tourist office is a rare example of Romanesque civil construction, the so-called **Palacio de los Reyes**. It now houses the Museo de Gustavo de Maetzu, a small gallery open Tuesday to Saturday from 11 am to 1 pm and 5 to 7 pm; on Sundays and holidays it's open from 11 am to 1.30 pm. Entry is free.

Across the river and overlooking the town is the **Iglesia de San Miguel**. Its most interesting feature is the elaborate Romanesque north door.

Places to Stay & Eat There is a *refugio* where pilgrims can eat. The *Fonda Izarra* (☎ 55 00 24), Calle de la Calderería 20, has basic singles/doubles for 1500/3000 ptas and the *Pensión San Andrés* (☎ 55 04 48), Plaza de Santiago 58, has rooms without private bath for 1600/3200 ptas, or 2500/5000 ptas with bath. Classier is the *Hotel Yerri* (☎ 54 60 34), Avenida de Yerri 35, with rooms for 4400/6600 ptas. The *Hostal Cristina* (☎ 55 07 72), Calle de Baja Navarra 1, charges similar prices. There are several restaurants in the centre.

Monasterio de Irache

Just outside Ayegui, this ancient Benedictine monastery has undergone many changes over the centuries. Now in the process of restoration, its most alluring feature is the slightly tumbledown plateresque cloister, erected in the 16th century. It opens daily from 10 am to 2 pm (Wednesday to Friday also from 5 to 7 pm) and on weekends from 9 am to 2 pm and 4 to 7 pm. Virtually next door you can taste some local reds at the Bodega de Irache.

Los Arcos & Torres del Río

The only point of interest in Los Arcos is the **Iglesia de Santa María** and its Gothic cloister. If you need to stay, the central *Hotel Mónaco* (☎ 64 00 00), Plaza del Coso 22, has rooms from 2500/3650 ptas. At *Hostal Ezequiel* (☎ 64 02 78), Calle de la Serna 14, rooms start at 2200/3600 ptas.

The road on this stretch twists and turns through rolling country to Torres del Río whose little gem is the simple 12th century Romanesque **Iglesia del Santo Sepulcro**.

Viana

Only about 10 km short of Logroño, Viana is a quiet spot with the mansions of noble families peppered around its old centre. The Gothic **Iglesia de Santa María** has an outstanding Renaissance doorway. You can stay in the pilgrims' *albergue* or at *Pensión La Granja* (☎ 64 50 78), Calle de Navarro Villoslada 19, which has rooms for 2000/4000 ptas.

Valle de Lana & Sierra de Aralar

This area, north of the Pamplona-Logroño road, is dotted with minor Romanesque jewels hidden away in little-visited hamlets. With the Sierra de Urbasa, the Valle de Lana marks the changeover from a Mediterranean to Atlantic geography. Interesting spots in this area include the **Monasterio de Iranzu**, near Abárzuza; the **Basílica de San Gregorio Ostiense** at Sorlada; and the town of **Azuelo**. The tourist office at Estella has loads of information on the zone.

Further north again, up towards the N-130 road that sheers off the A-15 to San Sebastián, you find yourself in the Sierra de Aralar. This area is dominated by a series of mountain ridges and was much beloved by Hemingway, an avid trout fisherman. From the area's main town, Lekunberri, you can head 15 km westwards for the **Santuario de San Miguel in Excelsis**, which lies in the shadow of Monte Altxueta (1343 metres).

INTO THE PYRENEES

Remember that Navarra has a particularly well-organised set of casas rurales across its northern strip. These places are often beautifully looked-after houses in mountain villages and are very popular in peak periods. In summer and on weekends it is a good idea to book ahead. There is a central reservations switchboard on ☎ 948-22 93 28. You can recognise the casas rurales by one of two small plaques – one has 'CR' in white on a dark green background; the more modern one, in brown, olive green and white, displays the letter 'C' and the outline of a house.

Walkers should refer to the boxed aside Walking in the Pyrenees' in the Cataluña chapter. Trekkers and skiers alike should note a couple of emergency numbers in case they get into serious trouble on the Navarran or French side of the mountains. Call ☎ 088 in Navarra, or ☎ 17 in Aquitaine (France).

Valle del Baztán & Regata de Bidasoa

If you're headed for San Sebastián, the coast and/or France from Pamplona, you have several options. The quickest dash to San Sebastián can be made up the A-15 autopista, or more picturesquely along the national (N) roads that hug it.

A preferable and dawdling route would, however, see you pushing straight up north along the N-121A (keep alert for the right exit from Pamplona by car as it's a little confusing). The initial stretch is pretty enough, but there's little to stop for until you wind over the **Puerto de Velate** pass. From here you could follow the same highway along the valley known as the **Regata de Bidasoa**.

If you're in no tearing hurry, consider making a detour up the lush Valle del Baztán to the north-east. Minor roads take you past charming little villages like **Ziga** (which has a 16th century church and, about one km further north, a beautiful lookout point) and **Irurita** (with another fine church) before reaching the valley's biggest town, **Elizondo**, on the N-121B. Although not the prettiest of the Baztán pueblos, this can make a convenient base for exploring the area, and there is plenty of accommodation.

There are at least three casas rurales in and around Elizondo. The closest is *Casa Jaén* (☎ 58 04 87), with cute little doubles for 3500 ptas. About 10 km out of town, *Casa Urruska* (☎ 45 21 06) is in a more tranquil, rural setting and offers singles/doubles for 1500/3000 ptas. In town there is also a pensión and a couple of expensive hotels. Bear in mind that most of the valley's villages (and all those mentioned here) have at least one casa rural.

The bus station is on the main road and services go to Pamplona and San Sebastián up to three times daily, stopping in many of the smaller villages up and down the valley on the way.

Beyond Elizondo, a particularly lovely road climbs eastwards through the enchanting villages of **Arizkun** and **Erratzu** to the French border pass of Puerto de Izpegui. Coming the other way, this is without doubt one of the prettiest introductions to Spain from France. You'll find at least six casas rurales in Erratzu and two in Arizkun. Just outside Erratzu, *Camping Baztán* (☎ 45 31 33)

NAVARRA

charges 475 ptas per person and up to 900 ptas per tent.

Back on the N-121B, turn northwards for the Puerto de Otxondo and the border crossing into France at Dantxarinea. Just before the border a minor road veers west to **Zugarramurdi**, whose main claim to fame is its caves. Anyone expecting great winding tunnels dripping with stalactites will be disappointed. Rather, a little trail snakes around and through a huge rock tunnel. For centuries they have been known also as the Witches' Caves, for legends tell of a coven (or *akelarre* in Basque) held in the fields just behind the caves. Entry is 300 ptas. A few km away are more caves, this time with the odd stalactite and stalagmite, at Urdazubi-Urdax.

There are two very welcoming casas rurales in Zugarramurdi, and one bus daily (except Sunday) to Elizondo.

From Zugarramurdi you could now follow a tiny back road south to Mugairi (Oronoz), putting you back onto the N-121A and into the Regata de Bidasoa. The first worthwhile stop from there heading north along the N-121A is a few km off to the east at **Etxalar** (also spelled Echalar). The churchyard is sprinkled with traditional tombstones in the shape of small discs. A little further north and off to the west, **Lesaka** is noted for its Iglesia de San Martín de Tours and the so-called *cascherna*, a medieval tower in the village centre. Last stop before the coast is **Bera (Vera) de Bidasoa**, with an atmosphere virtually indistinguishable from that of French Pyrenees towns. It has a handful of impressive buildings, such as the 15th century Iglesia de San Esteban and the ayuntamiento. You'll find a range of accommodation available, including several casas rurales, in Etxalar, Lesaka and Bera de Bidasoa.

To France via Roncesvalles

As you bear north-east out of Pamplona along the N-135 and ascend into the Pyrenees, the yellows, browns and olive green of lower Navarra begin to give way to a more luxuriant vegetation.

❋ ❋ ❋ ❋ ❋ ❋ ❋ ❋ ❋ ❋ ❋ ❋ ❋

Bewitched

1610 was a lousy year for the wicked witches and warlocks of Zugarramurdi. Fear and loathing on the part of God-fearing locals had prompted Don Juan del Valle Alvarado, an inquisitor from the Tribunal of Logroño, to make the arduous trip to this sodden corner of northern Navarra to investigate reports of rampant witchery. It appears folk from all around were only too willing to denounce anyone they could think of. 'She's a witch!' (or 'He's a warlock!') was a common cry, and no fewer than 300 luckless individuals found themselves accused. Don Juan was anxious to get home, so he picked out those he considered to be the worst offenders, about 40 in all, and carted them off to Logroño for further questioning. Of these, 18 were absolved and 12 were burned at the stake. Well, seven of them were – five had already died in the inquisitorial prison and were burned in effigy. The rest received punishments ranging from the confiscation of their property to life imprisonment.

What did these people get up to? According to the Inquisition they not only worshipped the devil as a god, but practised metamorphosis (which might have come in handy while in prison); caused wild storms in the Bay of Biscay; cast spells on fields, animals and even people; and indulged in vampirism and occasionally tucked into a good meal of corpse.

And the poor sods who had to put up with all this – did they have no remedy? To make a witch disappear, you could make a sign of the cross and hiss the word 'Jesús' at the unwelcome interlocutor. To keep the nasties out of the home, one attached to the door a cross made of two ash-tree branches, and next to it a blessed branch of laurel. ∎

❋ ❋ ❋ ❋ ❋ ❋ ❋ ❋ ❋ ❋ ❋ ❋ ❋

Burguete The bus from Pamplona only goes as far as Burguete (Auritz), a spotlessly pleasant, if rather quiet, mountain village. It was a favourite getaway for Hemingway - worlds apart from its dusty counterparts further south. There is a fair spread of accommodation here, including the *Casa Loigorr* (☎ 76 00 16), which has doubles for 3000 ptas, and *Casa Vergara* (☎ 76 00 44), which charges 4500 ptas. *Hostal Juandeaburre* (☎ 76 00 78) is good value at 1950/3350 ptas for singles/doubles. There are a couple of more expensive hostales on the main road if the others are full, or you could make for *Camping Urrobi* (☎ 76 02 00; open April to

October), a few km south where the NA-172 road leaves the N-135. For a meal out, *Restaurante Tikipolit*, on the main drag, has tasty mains for around 1000 ptas. There is also a supermarket and a bank.

Roncesvalles A few km further north, Roncesvalles (Orreaga) is little more than a monastery complex with a couple of extra buildings thrown in. It is said Roland and the remains of his soldiers were buried here on Charlemagne's orders. The spot is now covered by the 12th century Capilla de Sancti Spiritus. In the 13th century Gothic Real Colegiata de Santa María church, the cloister (rebuilt in the 17th century) is of interest, and more particularly the Sala Capitular off it. This contains the tomb of King Sancho VII (El Fuerte) of Navarra, the apparently 2.25 metre high victor in the Battle of Las Navas de Tolosa, which was fought against the Muslims in 1212.

You can try the *albergue de la juventud* (☎ 76 00 82), housed in the 18th century hospital where pilgrims rested up before proceeding on the long walk to Santiago de Compostela. *Hostal Casa Sabina* (☎ 76 00 12) has doubles only for 4500 ptas, and they may do a deal for single occupancy. *Hostal La Posada* (☎ 76 02 25) has rooms with private bath for 4500/5700 ptas.

Puerto de Ibañeta & Valcarlos From Roncesvalles, the road climbs to the Puerto de Ibañeta, the pass where Roland and his men were attacked – a modern memorial marks the spot. From here you have magnificent views across into France. The last town before the frontier is Valcarlos, a sleepy but pretty spot. Twice a year it comes to life, on Easter Sunday and 25 July, when the colourful Bolantes take over the streets with their folk dances and comic antics.

Casa Etxezuria (☎ 79 00 11), on the main road heading towards France, is a private house with delightful doubles for 3000 ptas. The owner has a couple of other places nearby. Those (with own transport) exploring the Spanish and French sides of this part of the Pyrenees might want to consider this

as a base. *Hostal Maitena* (☎ 79 02 10) has good rooms for 3000/5000 ptas.

From Valcarlos, you'll know you've crossed the border when you pass the Campsa petrol station – it is well worth pursuing the road on to St Jean Pied-de-Port.

Into the Backblocks If little villages and quiet country roads are an attraction, there is plenty of scope for losing yourself in the area east of the main Roncesvalles road. A couple of km south of Burguete, the NA-202 branches off east to Garralda. Push on to **Arive**, a charming little hamlet on the crossroads of several country lanes. You could continue east to the Valle del Salazar (see that section), go south along the Río Irati towards Aoiz (see the Valle de Arce section), or take a loop north-east through the Bosque (forest) de Irati, which again would eventually bring you to the Valle del Salazar, at Ochagavía. The forest, full of elms, beeches and lime trees, is one of Europe's most extensive, inviting you to dump your vehicle and head off for a hike.

Valle de Arce

This little-travelled valley leading due south from Burguete is a pleasant route south from the Pyrenees through the lower sierras and wheat fields of northern Navarra. Just north of Nagore is a fine Romanesque church, the Iglesia de la Purísima Concepción d'Arce. Another 10 or so km south and you reach **Aoiz** (Agoitz), where a Romanesque bridge spans the Río Irati. Above the bridge is the apse of the powerful, squat 15th century Iglesia de San Miguel. The *Hostal Beti-Jai* (☎ 33 60 52), Calle de Santa Agueda 4, has doubles starting at 2400 ptas if you need to stay.

Valle del Salazar

A bus runs the length of the Salazar valley from Pamplona to Ochagavía.

Lumbier About 20 km south-east of Aoiz and a potential launch pad for a trip up the Valle del Salazar, Lumbier is typical of the region, with a small, decaying centre and the odd medieval bridge spanning the gurgling

❀ ❀

Roland's Swan Song

After an unsuccessful foray against the Muslims in northern Spain back in 778, Charlemagne decided it was time to call it a day and pull back from Zaragoza into France. His chosen route via Roncesvalles through the Pyrenees was, although one of the few viable options, not among the safest. He managed to get the bulk of his army across without great incident, but his rearguard under Roland de Bretagne was not so lucky. Caught in the gorge of Roncesvalles, he and his men were ambushed by local Basque (or Gascon) guerrillas and slaughtered to the last man.

Out of this unfortunate incident emerged one of the great medieval *gestes* (epic poems), *La Chanson de Roland*, which gave rather a different slant to the whole story. The essence of it has Roland as the unwitting victim of a nasty plot between another of Charlemagne's lieutenants, Ganelon, and the wicked Saracens. His heroism in the face of overwhelming odds is matched only by the Frankish emperor's almost divine instinct for justice, which he exacts at the expense of the Muslim Emir Baligant near Zaragoza. Ganelon is of course found out and sentenced to death. The geste is thought to have been composed about 1090, although the legend surrounding Roland's death was born shortly after the historical events. The extant version of the *La Chanson de Roland* manuscript, consisting of 3998 Anglo-Norman verses, is held in the Bodleian Library in Oxford. ■

❀ ❀

stream that skirts its lower reaches. About a km to the east, a side road takes you to the head of the Foz de Lumbier. The gorge offers pleasant walks, and your every move will be observed by a squadron of eagles overhead. If you are interested in exploring the region more, contact Mirua, which organises day-long trips, on ☎ 46 48 31 or c/o the Hotel Iru-Bide in town (☎ 88 04 35).

Up the Valley The NA-178 heads north-east and soon crosses paths with a still more extraordinary gorge, the Foz de Arbayún. Just after you see the sign, swing right for the platform that affords splendid vistas across the gorge. Those with binoculars will be able to see a flurry of eagles.

Many of the hamlets that line the road north contain some gem of medieval handiwork, and in some cases their quiet cobbled streets and little plazas are equipped with the odd bar or café. Among the candidates are **Güesa**, nearby **Igal**, **Sarriés** and particularly **Esparza de Salazar**, with its mansions, medieval bridge and restored Iglesia de San Andrés.

Ochagavía Busier than the rest of the valley, this Pyrenean town lying astride the narrow Río Zatoya sets itself quite apart from the villages further south. Grey stone and slate are the main building materials in the old

centre and the place has a sober dignity reinforced by the looming presence of the Iglesia de San Juan Evangelista.

There are several banks here and at least one ATM, so you might want to stock up on cash. This is a popular base for walkers and even skiers, so many local families have opened up their homes as casas rurales. There are no less than 14 of these places (refer to the *Guía de Alojamientos de Turismo Rural*, or ask around), in addition to a couple of hostales and pensiones. There is also a camping ground, *Camping Osate* (☎ 89 01 84).

A lively place for a meal or drink is *Iratxo Bar*, the first place to the left on the main drag when you arrive from the south.

Heading North The smaller of the two roads north from Ochagavía winds 24 km over the Pyrenees into a dead end in the Bosque de Irati, where you can embark on some pleasant, solitary walks.

For France you take the N-140 north-east from Ochagavía into the Sierra de Abodi and cross at the Puerto de Larrau (1585 metres), a majestically bleak pass where you won't even realise you've crossed the frontier north until you're already over. Four km short of the border is a restaurant and bar for skiers. Day-trippers come here to ski, but there are no lifts or other facilities.

Valle del Roncal

This easternmost valley in the Navarran Pyrenees is in most respects also the region's most attractive. Its mountain territory is Navarra's most spectacular, although for skiing and alpine splendour, neighbouring Aragón has more to offer.

Burgui The gateway to this part of the Pyrenees is Burgui. Its Roman bridge over the Río Esca, combined with its huddle of stone houses, is an evocative introduction to the rural Pyrenean towns further upstream. Nice as it is, you should really push on upriver for Roncal or Isaba. Be warned, however, that these can get crowded in summer. If you need to stay here, *Pensión El Almadiero* (☎ 47 70 86), Calle Mayor s/n, has singles/doubles for 2000/3500 ptas.

Roncal This brooding, tightly knit village boasts a 16th century parish church, but it is the cobblestone alleyways twisting between dark stone houses that lend the village its charm.

The valley's only tourist office (☎ 47 51 36), on the main road towards the Isaba exit from town, can provide photocopies of walking maps. It is open Monday to Saturday, in summer only, from 10 am to 2 pm and 4.30 to 7.30 pm, and on Sunday from 10 am to 2 pm only. There is one bank and even a ski-hire outlet here.

Although Isaba, further north, makes a better base, you could do a lot worse than to choose one of the four casas rurales in the centre of Roncal as a place to stay. *Casa Pily* (☎ 47 51 35) and *Casa Txarpa* (☎ 47 50 68) are both traditional houses in the centre of the village and charge 3200 ptas for a double. There are a couple of hostales too if you get stuck.

The daily bus between Pamplona and Uztárroz leaves Roncal at 7 am for Pamplona and 5 pm for Isaba. There is no bus on Sunday.

Isaba The village of Isaba, a popular base for walkers and skiers, is in a similar vein to Roncal, lying on the confluence of the Río Belagua and Río Uztárroz, which together flow into the Río Esca. There are a few banks, a couple of them with ATMs.

An indication of the popularity of the place is the number of casas rurales offering rooms – 11 at last count. Just look around the town centre. Among the better ones are *Casa Catalingarde* (☎ 89 31 54) and *Casa Federico Mayo* (☎ 89 31 66). If none appeal, there are plenty of pensiones and hostales all over the village, or you can try *Camping Asolaze* (☎ 89 30 34).

A good restaurant is the *Tapia*, just out of the old centre on the road to Roncal. You can eat well for 1500 ptas a head or even less. For the morning after, the *Cafetería Marruzuri Goxotegi*, at the northern end of town on the main road, is great for breakfast.

North of Isaba The *Refugio Belagua*, 19 km north of Isaba, is a handy base for trekkers in summer and skiers in winter. They operate a restaurant and bar, and have some bunks to throw a sleeping bag onto. There is no bus up this way.

Uztárroz Another potential base, this little hamlet lies about three km north-west of Isaba. There are a few casas rurales, or you could try the *Fonda Ekia* (☎ 89 30 20), which has doubles for 3100 ptas. They also organise hikes and canyoning expeditions.

Across the Top

As already hinted, there are numerous walking trails in the Navarran Pyrenees. For those with more time, it is possible to follow the GR-12, a trail well marked with red and white signs, across the best Navarra has to offer. You will need a sleeping bag and even in summer you should have all-weather gear. Starting in Burguete, you head north to Roncesvalles, cross the Puerto de Ibañeta and steer eastwards to Fábrica de Orbaitzeta. You may need to head south to the town of Orbaitzeta proper to get a bed (there are three casas rurales).

The next day would take you through the Bosque de Irati to Las Casas de Irati; you can stay in the *Casa del Guarda* (a kind of warden's house) but will more likely end up free camping. The following stage sees you climbing to the bare heights of the Puerto de Larrau (ask at the restaurant/bar four km south of the French border about bunk beds). The trail then cuts across the Sierra de Abodi and you can reach the Belagua refugio in about five hours march.

The final trek takes you to the highest mountain in Navarra, La Mesa de los Tres Reyes (2438 metres), from where the easiest thing to do is descend to the town of **Zuriza** at the top end of the Valle de Ansó, in Aragón (see the Valle de Ansó section of the Aragón chapter).

SOUTH OF PAMPLONA
Tafalla
This town, with a rambling old centre, is not unpleasant but there's not an awful lot to detain you here. Right in the heart of the old town is the huge **Iglesia de Santa María**, which boasts a grand *retablo*.

The cheaper of an expensive pair of lodgings is the *Pensión Arotza* (☎ 70 07 16), Plaza de Navarra 3. Spacious rooms with bath, TV and phone cost 3000/5000 ptas plus IVA. You can eat good bar snacks at *Bar Tubal* on the same square.

Regular buses run to Pamplona, and Tafalla is on the train line to Zaragoza.

Olite
The extensive medieval defensive complex known as the **Palacio Real**, which completely dominates the small town of Olite, was built on the site of what was originally a fortified Roman *praesidium* (garrison). The bulk of what you see today was built by Carlos III of Navarra in the early 15th century, and its centrepiece is the Gran Torre, one of a straggle of towers and annexes. Opening times vary by season. In winter it opens daily from 10 am to 2 pm and 3.30 to 5.30 pm; in summer, a little later. Admission costs 300 ptas.

There is no cheap accommodation here. The *Hotel Carlos III El Noble* (☎ 74 06 44), Rúa de Medios 1, has singles/doubles starting at 4500/5800 ptas plus IVA. *Hotel Casa*

Zanito (☎ 74 00 02), Rúa Revillas, charges 6000/8500 ptas plus IVA. Top of the tree is the stylish *Parador Príncipe de Viana* (☎ 74 00 00; fax 74 02 01), Plaza de los Teobaldos 2. In the low season its singles/doubles begin at 10,800/13,500 ptas plus IVA. There are several bars for snacks around the palace and there are regular bus connections to Pamplona.

Ujué
Just 19 km east of Tafalla (there is another back road from Olite too, via San Martín de Unx), this tiny medieval village clings to the summit of a hill dominating the plains around it. The icing on the cake, as it were, is the hybrid Iglesia de Santa María, a fortified church of mixed Romanesque-Gothic style.

Monasterio de la Oliva
Off another side road to the east of the main Pamplona-Zaragoza highway lies the quiet backwater of **Carcastillo**. Two km further on is another of the fine monasteries with which Navarra is richly blessed. The formidable Monasterio de Santa María de la Oliva was begun by the Cistercians in the 12th century. Its austere church was built during the 12th and 13th centuries and gives onto a particularly pleasing Gothic cloister.

There are two or three buses daily between Pamplona and Carcastillo.

Tudela
Tudela is little more than 20 km in from the neighbouring region of Aragón, and even closer to La Rioja and Castilla y León. You might easily forget you are in Basque territory here, except for the ETA graffiti smeared liberally over just about every available surface in the old town. For those emerging from the south for the first time, this can come as something of a shock.

The unpleasantness lurking below the surface of the whole ETA issue pushed to one side, Tudela's old town is well worth a wander. An ancient city that was in Muslim hands for some 400 years, its twisting street layout serves as a reminder of the Islamic past. Most people set out to explore the town from Plaza de los Fueros. There is a tourist office (☎ 82 15 39) on the brightly decorated old square.

Things to See From Plaza de los Fueros, take Calle de Yanguas y Miranda through the arch and at the next square take a left into Calle de las Carnicerías. This leads to the **catedral**, a sober 12th century Gothic structure built of stone and brick. The west door is particularly striking, its many sculpted figures looking decidedly uneasy about their participation in the Last Judgment. There are some good retablos inside. In 1993, traces of the central mosque that had preceded the cathedral were identified adjacent to it. On the same square is the 18th century ayuntamiento. Perhaps the quirkiest of Tudela's attractions is its 13th century **bridge** over the Río Ebro. To get to it, follow Calle del Portal eastwards (downhill) from the cathedral to the Iglesia de la Magdalena and then head out the scruffy town gate (topped by the railway line). The Spaniards call a botch job a *chapuza*, and this bridge, with its arches all different shapes and sizes, seems to fit the bill perfectly. Yet seven centuries later, it still works fine! The Ebro flows mightily by, quite unperturbed by the lack of symmetry above it.

Of the other churches in Tudela, the **Iglesia de San Nicolás** still sports a fine tympanum featuring lions above one of its doors. It's at the end of Calle Rúa. Take time to wander the streets, as there are some fine old mansions, many with Aragonese-style awnings *(aleros)* jutting out from the roof; the **Palacio del Marqués de San Adrián**, at Calle de Magallón 10, is an impressive example.

Places to Stay & Eat If you want a room in the old town, try *Bar La Estrella*, at Calle de las Carnicerías 13. They may have beds. Otherwise, there are some rather expensive places along the main road from Plaza de los Fueros out into the depressing wastelands of the new sprawl. Closest to the square is the *Hostal Remigio* (☎ 82 08 50), Calle de

Gaztambide Carrera 2. Singles/doubles cost 2500/4700 ptas and they also have a venerable old dining room.

Getting There & Away Tudela is on the Pamplona-Zaragoza train line and buses operate from next to the train station.

Cascante

Dawdlers with wheels who are heading south from Tudela (it's worth crossing into Aragón to have a peek at Tarazona) could call in at Cascante. Look for the old covered walkway that leads uphill to the 17th century town church.

La Rioja

Mention the word Rioja and thoughts turn to some of the best red wines produced in Spain. The bulk of the vineyards line the Río Ebro around the town of Haro and extend into neighbouring Navarra and the Basque province of Álava (Araba). Logroño, the capital, lies on the Camino de Santiago, which constitutes the area's other main attraction, although the handful of pilgrim stops through here on the road to Burgos are not among the most awe-inspiring.

The telephone code throughout La Rioja is ☎ 941.

LOGROÑO

Although Logroño is an important agricultural, industrial and commercial centre, it also owes some of its wealth to its position on the Río Ebro and the Camino de Santiago. There is not a helluva lot to see, but the centre of town is pleasant enough for a wander and not a bad place for an overnight stop and a little bar-hopping.

History

It was the Muslim armies in the 8th century that gave Logroño its name. In the Middle Ages Logroño was the object of a dispute between the crowns of Castilla and Navarra,

LA RIOJA

but its fortunes declined in the 18th century. By 1861, when the walls were torn down to permit expansion, things were looking up and La Rioja's agricultural riches were reflected in the prosperity of the capital.

Orientation

If you arrive at the train or bus station, south of the town centre, head up Calle del General Vara de Rey until you reach the big square known as the Espolón. The tourist office is here and the old town starts on the north side of the square. A bed, food and drink can all be easily had in the old city.

Information

Tourist Office The tourist office (☎ 29 12 60), at Calle Miguel Villanueva 10, opens Monday to Friday from 9 am to 2 pm.

Money There are plenty of banks with user-friendly ATMs around the Espolón.

Post & Communications The main post office is in the old quarter on Calle de Portales. The postcode for central Logroño poste restante is 26080.

Things to See

The cathedral, the **Iglesia de Santa María Redonda**, started life as a Gothic church, a fact easily overlooked when your eyes are held by the voluptuousness of the churrigueresque towers added in the 18th century. Closer to the river and sitting right on the pilgrims' route through the city is the predictable **Iglesia de Santiago**. Above one of the portals is a somewhat uncared for equestrian statue of the church's patron saint. Take a look at the impressive main entrance to the **Iglesia de San Bartolomé** too.

A stroll around the old town and down to the river is a pleasant diversion, or you could pop in to see the art exhibits in the **Museo de la Rioja**. Entrance is free and it is open Tuesday to Saturday from 10 am to 2 pm and 4 to 9 pm (Sunday from 11.30 am to 2 pm).

Special Events

Try to be in Logroño for the Fiesta de San

1 Iglesia de Santiago
2 Iglesia de San Bartolomé
3 Iglesia de Santa María Redonda
4 Hostal Marqués de Vallejo
5 Hostal La Numantina
6 Hostal París
7 Tourist Office
8 Bus Station
9 Café Eldorado
10 Restaurante Navarrería
11 Lorenzo
12 Fonda Blanca
13 Museo de la Rioja
14 Post Office
15 Hostal Niza
16 Fonda Bilbaína
17 RENFE Train Station

Logroño

Mateo on September 21. This also doubles as a harvest festival, for which all of La Rioja comes to town to celebrate and to watch the grape-crushing ceremonies in the Espolón. Another day to watch is 11 June, when the Fiesta de San Bernabé is held.

Places to Stay

At the bottom end you can choose from a few fondas. *Fonda Bilbaína* (☎ 25 42 26), Calle del Capitán Gallarza 10, has quite decent singles/doubles for 2000/3500 ptas. *Fonda Blanca* (☎ 22 41 48), Calle de Laurel 24, is also quite OK, with a variety of rooms from shoe-box-size (1500 ptas) up to a triple (4500 ptas).

For something a little more comfortable, the *Hostal La Numantina* (☎ 25 14 11), Calle de Sagasta 4, is reasonable at 3000/4700 ptas for rooms with private bath. A little more expensive are the equally handy *Hostal París* (☎ 22 87 50), Avenida de la Rioja 8, and *Hostal Niza* (☎ 20 60 44), Calle del Capitán Gallarza 13. They charge 3900/6300 ptas and 4500/6200 ptas respectively for good rooms with TV and private bath. Another jump up the scale in the old quarter is *Hostal Marqués de Vallejo* (☎ 24 83 33), at Calle del Marqués de Vallejo 8.

Places to Eat

The area around Calle de San Agustín and Calle de Laurel is jammed with tapas bars and restaurants. You can get great pinchos morunos (the Spanish version of kebabs) for 85 ptas a stick at *Lorenzo*, on Calle de Laurel. There's no shortage of rather dear eating houses, but *Restaurante Navarreria*, Calle de San Agustín 17, has a set meal for 975 ptas.

Café Eldorado, Calle de Portales 80, sometimes provides live music to accompany your beer.

Getting There & Away

Bus Up to five buses leave daily for Burgos (835 ptas) via Santo Domingo de la Calzada (360 ptas). Four buses a day head north for Bilbao (1410 ptas), while six services daily go to Madrid (2485 ptas). Other destinations such as Vitoria, Pamplona, Haro and Calahorra are regularly served.

Train Logroño is connected by train to Zaragoza, and to Burgos and Vitoria. Generally, buses are cheaper and more frequent.

Car & Motorcycle The A-68 tollway from Zaragoza to Bilbao skirts Logroño to the south. The N-111 heads north-east to Pamplona and south to Soria, while the N-120 reaches west for Burgos.

WINE REGION

Spain's best known wines come from La Rioja – the vine has been exploited here since Roman times. When talking wine, the name 'La Rioja' really refers to the banks of the Río Ebro. Much is in fact produced on the País Vasco side of the river, known as La Rioja Alavesa (from the southern Basque province of Álava). Reds, rosés and whites are all produced in La Rioja.

The bulk of the reds are designed to be aged and some of the best years include 1994, 1982 and 1964. Around Laguardia on the Basque side some nice drops are also made. They are fruity and soft, and can only be grown in this part of La Rioja because the area has a unique microclimate. Protected by the Sierra de Cantabria from the worst of the bitter northern cold and blessed with an ochre soil different from the red earth of the south bank, the vine produces quite a distinct result from elsewhere in the region.

As is the case throughout the country, most of the wine produced in La Rioja is bought up and marketed by big concerns, but small family *bodegas* are reasserting themselves. Wine tasting for passing tourists is not a very common phenomenon in Spain. Most bodegas reserve such activity for people in the business. Here again, though, things are changing a little, and some smaller bodegas will open their doors to curious passers-by.

Exploring the Rioja region will almost inevitably take you across the border into the País Vasco and La Rioja Alavesa. See Around Vitoria in the País Vasco section earlier in this chapter.

Haro

The rather dull town of Haro is considered the capital of La Rioja's wine-producing region. There's not a whole lot of interest here, although the compact old quarter leading off Plaza de la Paz is pleasant enough for a little wander. The tourist office (☎ 31 27 26), on Plaza de Florentino Rodríguez, is open Monday to Saturday from 10 am to 2 pm and 4.30 to 7.30 pm (mornings only on Sunday).

LA RIOJA

The Museo del Vino (or Estación Enológica), near the bus station on Calle de Cira Anguciana, houses a detailed display on how wine is made. It is open Tuesday to Saturday from 10 am to 2 pm. Entry costs 300 ptas (free on Wednesday).

Of the many bodegas in and around Haro, the only one offering visits to the public is the Bodega Muga, just after the railway bridge on the way out of town. Guided visits start at 10.30 am and noon, and with luck you should get to taste a drop or two at the tail end of your inspection.

Places to Stay & Eat There are a few budget places to stay. *Hostal Aragón* (☎ 31 00 04), Calle de la Vega 9, has acceptable rooms without bath for 1800/3000 ptas. Getting to some rooms requires negotiating a tight spiral staircase. A couple of places rent out rooms on the same street. Bright, clean rooms above the *Restaurante La Peña* (☎ 30 41 01), at No 1, cost 2000/3000 ptas and some overlook Plaza de la Paz. The restaurant itself is not bad, with a set menu for 900 ptas.

For a classier meal washed down with fine Rioja wines, try *Restaurante Beethoven*, Calle de Santo Tomás 10. Mains cost from about 1500 to 2000 ptas.

Getting There & Away Regular trains and buses connect Haro with Logroño and Vitoria.

CAMINO DE SANTIAGO

The road west from Logroño to Burgos follows the ancient Camino de Santiago. The route can be covered by bus.

Navarrete

A mere eight km out of Logroño, you can still see the well-preserved Romanesque doorway of what was once the Hospital de San Juan de Arce, a pilgrims' hostel. It now fronts the cemetery.

Nájera

This town, sitting on the Río Najerilla, still manages to retain some of its medieval

charm, but the main attraction is the Gothic Monasterio de Santa María la Real, and in particular its fragile-looking early 16th century cloisters. Inside the church you can see a pantheon of tombs containing the remains of kings of Castilla, León and Navarra. It is open Tuesday to Sunday from 10 am to 12.30 pm and 4 to 6 pm (closing times are a little earlier on Sunday). Entry costs 200 ptas.

There are a few places to stay here, but there's little need to do so, as buses leave frequently for Logroño (210 ptas).

San Millán de Cogolla

If you have a vehicle, hit the back roads south-west of Nájera to take in the Monasterio de San Millán de Cogolla. First built in the 10th century to house the remains of the 6th century hermit San Millán, the original Mozarabic structure has undergone many changes. They say that the 43 words scribbled into a Latin codex by a monk in the 10th century here were the first-ever Castilian words committed to paper.

In the same valley is the 16th century church complex of San Millán de Yuso, known a little optimistically as El Escorial de la Rioja. From here you can veer back north-west to pick up the highway again and head on to Santo Domingo de la Calzada.

Santo Domingo de la Calzada

The baroque bell tower of the cathedral stands tall above what little is left of this scrappy town's old centre. Back in the 11th century, a hermit later known as Santo Domingo took pity on the poor pilgrims struggling along a Roman road that had seen better days. He undertook some improvements – including a 24 span bridge.

The cathedral is undergoing some serious restoration, but is worth a look nonetheless. Among notable artworks is a retablo done by Damián Forment in 1550. The most curious bits of 'decoration', however, are the white rooster and hen kept in a special niche and swapped for new ones every month. The tall tale is that a young German pilgrim, wrongly hanged for theft whilst staying here, was

✱✱✱✱✱✱✱✱✱✱✱✱✱✱✱✱✱✱✱✱✱✱✱✱✱✱✱✱✱✱✱✱

In the Footsteps of Big Feet
Dinosaurs tramped about most of Spain, but far and away their favourite stomping ground was La Rioja – long before wine was an attraction. Hikers looking for something a little different could choose to follow a route dotted with traces of this prehistoric passing trade. The section of the long-distance walking route GR-93 between the villages of Enciso, about 10 km south of the spa village of Arnedillo, and Muro de Aguas, about 15 km east of Enciso, has eight fossil prints of dinosaurs along the way, signposted and with explanations posted in Spanish. In Valdecevillo, for example, you can see the footprints left by an enormous carnivorous biped. Other such fossils can be seen scattered about the area along different tracks. You'll also be accompanied overhead by Leonado (griffon) vultures along the 20 km route, which lies about midway between Logroño and Soria (Castilla y León). The most attractive place to stay around here is Arnedillo. ■

✱✱✱✱✱✱✱✱✱✱✱✱✱✱✱✱✱✱✱✱✱✱✱✱✱✱✱✱✱✱✱✱

saved by the intercession of Santo Domingo and survived. When told of this, the disbelieving local ruler *(corregidor)* exclaimed that the lad was about as alive as the roast chook he was about to tuck into. The hen and rooster on his plate then sprouted feathers and began to leap about the table!

A cheap and pretty average place to put your head down is *Hostal Río* (☎ 34 00 85), Calle de Echegoyen 2. Singles/doubles with washbasin cost 2000/3200 ptas. A little better is *Hostal Santa Teresita* (☎ 34 07 00), Calle del General Mola 2, with rooms for 2800/5300 ptas. The pick of the crop is the attractively presented *parador* (☎ 34 03 00; fax 34 03 25), a former pilgrims' hospice where St Francis of Assisi is said to have stopped over while on pilgrimage. *Restaurante Albert's*, just off Plaza de San Jerónimo Hermosilla, also has a couple of cheap rooms and serves a hearty set meal for 1200 ptas. For a little noisy music and late drinking, try Calle de Madrid, just off the same plaza.

Buses leave the square for Burgos (66 km west) and Logroño (48 km east).

SOUTH OF LOGROÑO
A couple of picturesque routes suggest themselves if you're heading south for Soria in Castilla y León. The N-111 itself, after a boring start, picks up as it follows deep canyon walls along the Río Iregua into the sierras that mark Soria province off from the flatlands of central La Rioja. Several pretty villages, including Villanueva de Cameros, line the lower half of the route. About

halfway to Soria you could turn west for Montenegro de Cameros and then drop south for Vinuesa and the Laguna Negra (see the Castilla y León chapter).

Calahorra
Calahorra is nicely located in a commanding position overlooking the Río Ebro and its tributary Río Cidacos. The cathedral, near the river, is of moderate interest – to get in you'll have to ask the parish priest in the Palacio Obispal opposite. Although wandering about the steep, straggling lanes of this town is vaguely pleasing, there's not much reason for hanging about.

If you want a good room in the heart of what used to be the medieval labyrinth, try *Fonda López* (☎ 13 14 92), Calle de la Estrella 12, just off Calle Mayor. The latter road links the cathedral with the newer part of town.

A Route to Soria
Another good road to Soria departs from Calahorra and follows the Río Cidacos through quite dramatic country. You can probably do without stopping in the unkempt and surprisingly large Arnedo. Make instead for the small, traditional spa town of **Arnedillo**. Gathered up in a fold of the valley, it is in a pretty location ideal for a night or two if you plan to do a spot of walking in the area. The road starts to climb after entering Soria province and is frequently blocked by snow in winter.

LA RIOJA

Cantabria & Asturias

For all they hold in common, the neighbouring regions of Cantabria and Asturias, stretching west across the northern Spanish seaboard from the Basque territories, throw up some striking differences. Established as a province only late in the 18th century, Cantabria was, until after Franco's demise, merely an extension of Castilla la Vieja (Old Castile). Asturias, on the other hand, has a long history of independence and along with Galicia was exclusively Celtic territory before the arrival of the Romans. Asturians take pride, too, in coming from the sole patch of Spain untouched by the Muslims. Asturias, they say, is the real Spain; the rest is simply reconquered land – *tierra de la Reconquista*.

The two regions share a coastline of alternating sheer cliffs, sandy beaches and tiny protected coves, and the lifestyles and history of both have been in great measure dictated by the chain-mail strip of highlands and mountains that together form the Cordillera Cantábrica. The rich green pastures reaching down from the hills to the sea could not stand in greater contrast to the standard images of a dry, sun-drenched Spain. To cross the cordillera is to taste that contrast. While to the south the broad, parched sweep of the Castilian *meseta* is generally bathed in sunshine, to the north the verdant, undulating hills and meadows are just as likely to be getting a downpour.

Cantabria

The Romans reported having a hard time dealing with the Cantabrians, a people of obscure origins who inhabited coastal and mountain areas beyond the limits of modern Cantabria. From 29 to 19 BC, the fortunes of war fluctuated, but in the end Rome carried the day and the subdued coastal tribes were absorbed into imperial Hispania.

HIGHLIGHTS

- Touring the bars of Santander
- The enchanting towns of Santilla del Mar and Comillas
- Trekking and walking in the Picos de Europa mountains
- The pre-Romanesque churches of Asturias
- Discovering little beaches and coves, especially around Llanes in Asturias
- Hanging around in Asturian *sidrerías* – and trying the cider
- Ancient *castros* (Celtiberian settlements), the best-known of which is near Coaña
- Sitting down to an Asturian *fabada* – the ideal food for the chill mountain climate

Until the constitution of 1978 created the region of Cantabria, the area had, unlike the País Vasco to the east and Asturias to the west, known no separate identity. Rather, it was always regarded as a coastal extension of the Castilian kingdom (later Castilla la Vieja) and as its direct gateway to what was confidently known as the Mar de Castilla (Castilian Sea).

With a few obvious exceptions, Cantabria is not over-endowed with grand monuments. Its main attractions are natural, from the east flank of the Picos de Europa mountains through the evergreen rural hinterland, to the rippled coastline and its sprinkling of pretty beaches and coastal towns. Santander itself boasts fine beaches and a thumping nightlife,

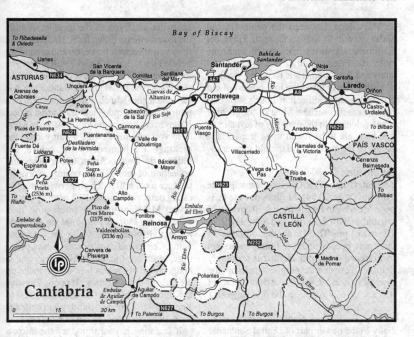

Cantabria

0   15   30 km

while Santillana del Mar and Comillas to the west are among the region's prettiest towns.

The telephone area code is ☎ 942 throughout Cantabria.

SANTANDER

A bustling centre with a clanking port and shapeless suburbs reaching inland, the bulk of modern Santander stands in somewhat drab contrast to its pretty beaches, particularly the haughty old-world elegance of El Sardinero. The old centre, such as it is after a huge fire raged through the city in 1941, is certainly a lively source of entertainment for the palate and liver, but all up Santander is a good deal more staid than its resort cousin, San Sebastián. And if nightlife is low on your list of priorities, you may well want to search out smaller and prettier littoral towns further west in Cantabria or Asturias.

History

When the Romans landed on the beaches here in 21 BC, they had more serious business in mind than sunbathing. They named the place Portus Victoriae (Victory Harbour) and indeed, within two years they had finally vanquished the Cantabrian tribes that had given them so much strife in the previous eight years.

From that time, Santander, as the city eventually became known, led a modestly successful existence as a port. Its heyday came rather late, when the royal family, and especially King Alfonso XIII, began to make a habit of spending summer here in the early 1900s. The locals were so pleased they gave him Magdalena peninsula, upon which he raised a little palace. Everyone who wanted to see and be seen converged on Santander, giving rise to a *belle époque* building boom – most in evidence around El Sardinero.

Orientation

The city spreads long and narrow along the Bahía de Santander out to the Península de la Magdalena. Between the peninsula and Cabo Menor to the north-west, Playa del Sardinero, the city's main beach, faces the open sea. From the city's bus and train stations and ferry port it's a 10 minute walk in a north-easterly direction to the heart of old Santander, and another half-hour's stroll east to the nearest beaches. Most of the cheaper hotels, along with the majority of restaurants and bars, are to be found in a compact area taking in the stations and the old quarter.

Information

Tourist Office The Oficina Municipal de Turismo (☎ 36 20 54), Jardines de Pereda, is open Monday to Friday from 9.30 am to 1.30 pm and 4.30 to 7.30 pm, and Saturday from 10 am to 1 pm. There is another office at the ferry port, open Monday to Friday from 9 am to 1 pm and 4 to 7 pm. Neither is startlingly helpful. You can sometimes pick up the biweekly *Guía Informativa* at the offices, but it is not as informative as the title suggests.

Money You'll find plenty of banks, especially in the newer part of central Santander around Avenida de Calvo Sotelo.

American Express (☎ 31 17 00) is represented by Viajes Altair, Calle de Calderón de la Barca 11.

Post & Communications The main post office is on Avenida de Calvo Sotelo facing the Jardines de Pereda. The postcode for central Santander is 39080.

Medical & Emergency Services The Hospital Marqués de Valdecilla (☎ 20 25 20) is at Avenida de Valdecilla 25. Casualty (*urgencias*) is on ☎ 20 25 76. For an ambulance you can call the Cruz Roja on ☎ 27 30 58. The main police *comisaría* is on the Plaza Porticada.

Things to See & Do

Santander is rather thin on sights, so do what the locals do and head for the beaches. Those on the Bahía de Santander are a little more protected than the main strand, the Playa del Sardinero. The latter is quite a walk from the

centre, so catch one of the local buses from the *ayuntamiento* (town hall). Different lines drop you at various points on and around the beach. Nos 1, 3, 4, 7, 8 and 9 will all get you to the general vicinity. Less crowded are the strands across the Bahía de Santander. You can catch the launch for Somo (325 ptas return) from the quay near the tourist office. It runs every half-hour from 7.30 am to 8 pm.

If you are stuck with a rainy day, the pickings are limited. In the centre, the **Museo de Bellas Artes** has a dusty old collection of mostly 19th century works by obscure local artists. The otherwise uninteresting **catedral** boasts a 13th century Gothic crypt. Marginally more interesting than either is the **Museo Regional de Arqueología y Prehistoria**, Calle de Casimiro Sainz. Copies and photocopies of cave paintings, such as those in Altamira, and a hodgepodge of ancient bric-a-brac make up the bulk of the collection. It opens Tuesday to Saturday from 9 am (10 am in summer) to 1 pm and 4 to 7 pm, and Sunday and holidays from 10 am to 1 pm. Admission is free.

If seafaring is your thing, try the **Museo Marítimo**, near the bay beaches. It has everything from a whale skeleton to sections with models on the history of Cantabrian sea lore. It is open Tuesday to Saturday from 10 am to 1 pm and 4 to 6 pm, and Sunday from 11 am to 2 pm. Entry is free.

The gardens of the Península de la Magdalena, crowned by the former Palacio Real, are popular with picnickers and contain a mini-zoo.

Special Events

Right through the summer, the Palacio Real serves as an international university, a kind of global get-together for specialists in all sorts of academic disciplines. The big cultural event is the Festival Internacional de Santander, a broad, sweeping musical review throughout July and August that covers everything from jazz to chamber music.

Places to Stay

Camping The nearest camping ground open

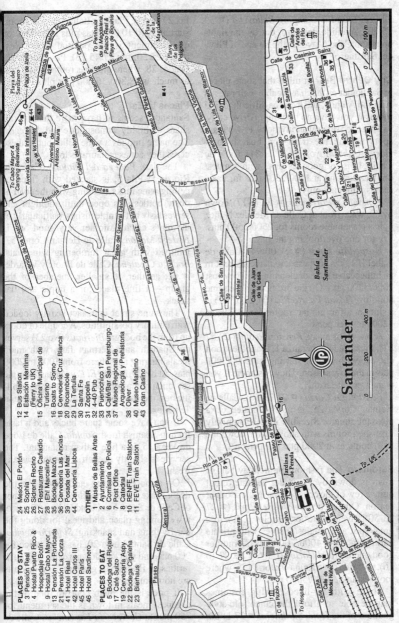

PLACES TO STAY
3 Pensión Real
4 Hostal Puerto Rico &
   Hospedaje Botín
9 Hostal Cabo Mayor
13 Bodega Mazón
21 Pensión La Porticada
   Pensión La Corza
41 Hotel Real
42 Hotel Carlos III
45 Hotel París
46 Hotel Sardinero

PLACES TO EAT
5 Bodega del Riojano
17 Café Suizo
19 Cervecería Aspy
22 Bodega Cigaleña
23 Bierhaus

24 Mesón El Portón
25 Sophia
26 Sidrería Recino
27 Restaurante Cañadío
28 ¡Eh! Marcelino
35 Bodega Mazón
36 Cervecería Las Anclas
39 Posada del Mar
20 Rocambole
29 Santa Fe
30 La Tertulia
   Cervecería Lisboa

OTHER
1 Museo de Bellas Artes
6 Ayuntamiento
7 Comisaría de Policía
8 Post Office
10 RENFE Train Station
11 FEVE Train Station

12 Bus Station
14 Estación Marítima
   (Ferry to UK)
15 Oficina Municipal de
   Turismo
16 Boats to Somo
18 Cervecería Cruz Blanca
31 Zeppelin
32 4-40 Pub
33 Puertochico 17
34 Café/Bar San Petersburgo
37 Museo Regional de
   Arqueología y Prehistoria
38 Oliver
40 Museo Marítimo
43 Gran Casino

Santander

Bahía de
Santander

all year round is *Camping Bellavista* (☎ 39 15 30), Avenida del Faro, out by the lighthouse on Cabo Mayor at the far end of Playa del Sardinero.

City Centre Bear in mind that some places in Santander as much as double their rates in July and August, and it can be difficult to find rooms if you have no booking. Arrive early.

There are several anonymous, low-budget spots around the train and bus stations. *Hostal Cabo Mayor* (☎ 21 11 81), Calle de Cádiz 1, is as good as any, with singles/doubles starting at 1500/2500 ptas for basic rooms with sink only.

Pensión La Porticada (☎ 22 78 17), down by the waterfront at Calle de Méndez Núñez 6, has reasonable rooms for 2500/3500 ptas. Try for one overlooking the bay.

Hospedaje Botín (☎ 21 00 94), Calle de Isabel II 1, has some spacious rooms kept in an impeccable state of cleanliness. They cost 2000/3200 ptas. On the 3rd floor in the same building, *Hostal Puerto Rico* (☎ 22 57 07) is a simpler affair but has rooms for as little as 1200 ptas per person.

A few steps away, *Pensión Real* (☎ 22 57 87), Plaza de la Esperanza 1, is another good choice, with rooms starting at 2000/3000 ptas in the low season. They cost more if you want a private bath.

Pensión La Corza (☎ 21 29 50), Calle de Hernán Cortés 25, is nicely located on a pleasant square. Sizeable if rather quirkily furnished rooms with shower (loo down the hall) come in at 2000 ptas per person.

Sardinero The fashionable holiday part of town is down by Playa del Sardinero, but quite a few of the cheaper places close out of season. One such spot is *Hotel París* (☎ 27 23 50), Avenida de los Hoteles 6. It's in a great spot and singles/doubles with private bathroom cost 4000/7000 ptas. Another good one is *Hotel Carlos III* (☎ & fax 27 16 16), Avenida de la Reina Victoria 135, where rooms start at 4200/5800 ptas.

Those with fur-lined bathing costumes may be able to afford the chichi old-style glamour of the *Hotel Sardinero* (☎ 27 11 00;

fax 27 89 43), Plaza de Italia 1, where rooms start at 8000/10,000 ptas plus IVA. The top establishment is the palatial *Hotel Real* (☎ 27 25 50; fax 27 45 73), Paseo de Pérez Galdós 28, where glorious rooms could cost as much as 28,800/36,000 ptas plus IVA.

Places to Eat

Santander seems to have more than its fair share of highly atmospheric old *bodegas*. The name implies a wine cellar but in these cases they act as restaurants too.

The dark *Bodega del Riojano*, Calle del Río de la Pila 5, is stacked with floor-to-ceiling wine racks creaking with the load of dusty bottles. It's open until midnight and serves tasty but simple dishes, particularly of the day's catch. Another very good one is *Bodega Mazón*, Calle de Hernán Cortés 57, jammed with great lumbering wine vats. *Bodega Cigaleña*, Calle de Daoíz y Velarde, is yet another, if smaller, member of the group – a fine place for a tipple and bar snack.

The same street is in fact heavily loaded with culinary possibilities. A couple of doors up from the bodega, *Bierhaus* (No 23) serves up Spanish and German fare, with main meals ranging anywhere from 1000 to 2000 ptas. At No 29, *Mesón El Portón* has a simple set lunch menu for 850 ptas. Other possibilities on the same strip include Chinese and Tex-Mex.

If you have some spare bucks and a taste for non-Spanish food, *Sophia*, Calle de Lope de Vega 15, is a fine Italian restaurant. The service is slightly eccentric, but the pasta is fresh.

On a more down-to-earth level, the tile décor makes *¡Eh! Marcelino*, on the corner of Calle de Santa Lucía and Calle de Pizarro, a welcoming place and ideal for doing the bar-fly thing and snacking. *Sidrería Recino*, Calle de Santa Lucía 20, has a set lunch for 900 ptas and you can down a cider with such rarities as Hungarian goulash. The desserts are home-made.

If price is the main concern, one of the cheapest meals in town is the set menu for 750 ptas at *Cervecería Las Anclas*, Calle de

Casimiro Sainz, opposite the Museo Regional de Arqueología y Prehistoria.

More expensive, but often crowded out with locals at lunchtime, *Cervecería Aspy*, Calle de Hernán Cortés 20, has a reliable *menú del día* for 1000 ptas.

For a seafood blowout, head for the *Posada del Mar*, Calle de Juan de la Casa 3. A set menu fish feast will set you back 2800 ptas, and the décor, with boat wheels and the like on the walls, is suitably maritime.

One of the most innovative places in town is the *Restaurante Cañadío*, Calle de Gómez Oreña 15. A full meal a la carta would leave you little change from 5000 ptas, but the more modest set lunch menu of 1550 ptas allows you a taste of the exquisite cooking here. Even the bar snacks are a class apart.

Dessert should prove no problem if you like ice cream, as the city seems unusually well endowed with *heladerías*. There's one opposite the Cervecería Aspy.

Cafés The waterside promenades bristle with cafés. *Café Suizo*, Paseo de Pereda 28, is a pricey choice, but it has a great range of sandwiches and ice-cream desserts.

Down near the beach at El Sardinero, *Cervecería Lisboa*, Plaza de Italia, is a bit of an institution.

Entertainment

For an overview of what's happening nocturnally in town, track down a copy of the *Guía Secreta de Santander*. Apart from what is listed below, check out Calle del Río de la Pila and the immediate neighbourhood – it is teeming with bars of all descriptions.

Bars As you move from eating to drinking in the evening, an enjoyable first port of call might be the *Cervecería Cruz Blanca*, on the corner of Calle de Hernán Cortés and Calle de Lope de Vega. It has 32 different non-Spanish beers in bottles and a few more on tap.

The *Santa Fe*, Calle de Valliciergo 2, seems to be the present summertime favourite, with revellers spilling onto the street outside. A quieter one nearby, with a range

of cocktails, is *La Tertulia*, Calle de Santa Lucía 17.

Zeppelin, at the junction of Calle de Valliciergo and Paseo de Menéndez Pelayo, is just one of a half-dozen café-bars around the same junction.

The heavily mood-lit *Oliver*, Paseo de Menéndez Pelayo 14, is the perfect place for a sleek late-night cocktail to mellow jazz tunes.

Another place for a quiet drink is *Puertochico 17*, Calle de Santa Lucía. You'd never know it was here, as it's virtually hidden behind a garage – enter by the 'salida vehículos' sign.

The *Café/Bar San Petersburgo*, Calle de Andrés del Río, is very blue inside and a cross between a bar and a disco.

Discos & Nightclubs The *4-40 Pub*, on a small square off Calle de Santa Lucía, is very clearly a disco of the brash variety. Another popular late-night dance spot is *Rocambole*, Calle de Hernán Cortés.

Getting There & Away

Air The airport is about five km east of town at Parayas. There are a handful of regular flights to Madrid and Barcelona, and one a week to Santiago de Compostela.

Bus Continental-Auto runs up to five buses a day to Madrid via Burgos. Frequent services run south to Reinosa, and less frequently on to destinations in Castilla y León, such as Valladolid (1330 ptas) and Salamanca (1905 ptas). Turytrans buses run along the coast as far as San Sebastián (1790 ptas) and Irún in the east and Gijón/Oviedo (1970 ptas) in the west.

Train There are two train stations. From the main RENFE station there are three daily departures for Madrid. The cheapest one-way fare is 3550 ptas. More than a dozen trains serve Reinosa, and five of them continue south to Valladolid.

The private FEVE line is next door. There are two trains a day to Oviedo (1610 ptas) and four to Bilbao (885 ptas). Surfers report being allowed to transport bicycles and surf-boards in the guards' van.

Car & Motorcycle Heading west, take the A-67 for Torrelavega for a quick getaway. Watch for the turn-off to Santillana del Mar, an obligatory first stop on a coastal tour out of Santander. Two pretty routes take you south – the N-623 to Burgos (and from there the N-I to Madrid) or the N-611 to Palencia and Valladolid.

Boat Brittany Ferries (☎ in the UK 0990-360360), at Milbay Docks in Plymouth, operates a twice weekly car ferry to Santander (24 hours travel time) from mid-March to mid-November. In the remaining months, the service drops to once a week and departs from Portsmouth; from here it takes 30 to 33 hours. There are five fare periods, the highest being from mid-July to mid-August (out-bound), or the whole month of August (from Spain). The standard return for car and driver is £462 in this period, or £595 with one passenger. The cheapest low-season one-way foot passengers' fare is £46.

In addition you will normally be obliged to pay for some form of accommodation, or at least reserve a seat (£6). If you arrive at Santander in the evening, you can generally stay on board until the following morning.

In Santander, tickets can be bought at the Estación Marítima (port) itself, or reserva-tions made by calling ☎ 36 06 11.

AROUND SANTANDER
Dunes
About 10 km west of Santander lies the most extensive stretch of dunes on Spain's north-ern coast. From the Isla de la Virgen del Mar, north-east of Soto de la Marina, a walk of up to 16 km west to the Playa de Valdearenas is tempting, taking in not only dunes but a series of low though nonetheless attractive cliffs. You could take yourself to the town of **Liencres** and head for the coast from there, turning east to the Isla de la Virgen del Mar. The best time to visit is summer and autumn, not only for the weather, but also to avoid

disturbing the fauna that breeds in the dunes area in spring.

Puente Viesgo
The valley town of Puente Viesgo is located downhill from some impressive caves, about 30 km south of Santander on the N-623 highway to Burgos. Of the four caves, two can be visited, including the most spectacu-lar, known as El Castillo. In addition to a labyrinth of stalactites and stalagmites, it contains a series of prehistoric wall paintings that, while not as breathtaking as the ones you probably have *not* seen at Altamira (see West of Santander), are still well worth inspecting. The caves are open Tuesday to Sunday from 10 am to 1 pm and 3 to 7 pm (10 am to 3 pm in winter). Admission to El Castillo costs 225 ptas and the visit takes around 45 minutes, though you may have to wait until a big enough group has been assembled. Admission to the lesser cave known as Las Monedas costs 125 ptas.

The cheapest place to stay is *Hostal La Terraza* (☎ 59 81 02), on the turn-off from the highway to the caves. They charge 2000/3000 ptas for singles/doubles but only open in July and August. The alternative is the expensive *Gran Hotel* (☎ 59 80 61). Regular buses run to Puente Viesgo from Santander.

EAST OF SANTANDER
The stretch of coast between Santander and the industrial city of Bilbao, 95 km east, offers jaded citizens of both cities several seaside escape hatches. Some, such as Noja, are little more than beaches fronted by endless rows of holiday flats. The pick of the bunch is undoubtedly Castro Urdiales, 35 km short of Bilbao.

Santoña
Santoña's people once thought it prudent to add to the defence of their town, which cowers on the protected south side of a head-land, by constructing two forts, the Fuerte de San Martín and, higher up, the Fuerte de San Carlos. You can take a pleasant walk around

these or plonk yourself on the sandy Playa de San Martín.

Buses serve Santander and other towns along the coast, and a ferry links Santoña with the west end of Laredo beach.

Laredo

On a good day, you could almost forgive yourself for thinking you'd landed on a bland stretch of Miami beach. Laredo, with its miles of sandy strand backed by phalanxes of holiday flats, is a pleasantly watery if largely characterless location. The old town at the eastern end awakens mild curiosity, but if you are looking for anything but sand this is really not the place.

Should you want to hang around, there are plenty of places to stay. *Hotel Ramona* (☎ 60 71 89), Alameda de José Antonio 4, is near the buses and a short walk from the beach. It has functional rooms for 3000/5000 ptas in the low season, quickly peaking at 5000/7000 ptas in August. The increase is typical of Laredo's hotels.

Regular buses leave for Bilbao and Santander from Alameda de José Antonio (the ticket office is next to Café Orio), as well as at least seven to Santoña and four to Castro Urdiales via Oriñon.

Oriñon

One of the nicer beaches along this stretch of coast is at Oriñon, seven km east of Laredo. Popular on summer weekends, the broad sandy strip is set deep behind protective headlands, making the water calm and *comparatively* warm. In contrast, you'll find a chill sea and some surfable waves on the windward side of the western headland. All-stops buses between Santander and Castro Urdiales can drop you near Oriñon.

Castro Urdiales

The haughty Gothic **Iglesia de Santa María de la Asunción** stands out like a beacon to the curious traveller, standing high above the tangle of narrow lanes that make up the medieval centre of Castro Urdiales. Equally popular with city folk from Santander and Bilbao, it makes a pleasant overnight stop.

Next to the 13th century church stand the ruins of what was for centuries the town's defensive bastion, now home to a lighthouse. Take time to wander the streets of the old town too. Of the two **beaches**, the westerly Playa de Ostende is the more attractive.

Of the dozen or so places to get a bed, one of the cheapest is the *Hostal La Marina* (☎ 86 13 45), La Plazuela 20 – a nice if rowdy location. Singles/doubles with washbasin cost 2500/3800 ptas. There are several other small spots scattered about the old centre of town, but most tend to open in the summer only. A dependable place is *Hostal La Mar* (☎ 87 05 24), Calle de la Mar 27, with bright, functional rooms for 3000/4500 ptas (a little more in the high season).

If you need a break from Spanish seaside delights, head for *La Pizzeria di Stefano*, at the west end of town on Paseo de Ostende. Thin-crust pizzas, made the way they should be, cost around 1200 ptas, and the menu also includes pasta. There are some great places to snack, including *Fast Food Serman*, Avenida Constitución 4, which does huge sandwiches. Otherwise, more traditional fare abounds in mesones and tabernas all over the old centre. *Bar La Puerta del Sol*, at the junction of Calle de la Mar and Calle de Ardigales, has a wonderful range of bar snacks.

At weekends in particular, Castro is pretty lively, and you'll have no trouble finding late-night drinks in the numerous old town bars.

WEST OF SANTANDER

A trio of charming little towns awaits the westward-bound traveller from Santander, all connected by bus to the capital. Santillana del Mar is the first, down a back road (the C-6316) that runs close to the coast but unfortunately rarely allows more than a glimpse of it.

Santillana del Mar

You could easily drive through this place and never know what lies off the main road. Don't make that mistake. This medieval jewel has been casting its spell over outsiders

CANTABRIA

since it was declared a national monument in 1889, and tourism is an important source of income – many of the townspeople spend time making solid 'Spanish-style' furniture for the more well-lined visitors. Jean-Paul Sartre was among the more illustrious of the town's guests to remark on Santillana, but since all the other guidebooks quote him on the subject, we won't.

Locals themselves have something to say about it: *'Santillana es la villa de las tres mentiras – no es santa, no es llana y no tiene mar'* (Santillana is the city of the three lies – it is neither holy nor flat, nor does it have a sea).

Second to the herds of two-legged animals come the four-legged variety. Santillana still lives for much of the year from its dairy industry, and the ruddy-cheeked people renting you a room in the centre of the town will probably be out in the fields with the cows for much of the day.

Information You'll find a small tourist information office (☎ 81 82 51) on Plaza de Ramón Pelayo (Plaza Mayor), along with a post and telephone office. There are several banks where you can change money.

Things to See A stroll down the cobbled Calle del Cantón past solemn nobles' houses, some with magnificent coats of arms, leads you to the Romanesque **Colegiata de Santa Julia**. Before heading inside, take the time to admire the simple lines of the exterior design, especially in the apse. The drawing card inside is the cloister, a formidable reliquary of Romanesque artisanry, with its lines of twin columns surmounted by variegated reliefs. Santa Julia, who was supposedly tortured by her husband for not wanting to renounce her faith, lies buried in the centre of the church. You can visit daily from 9.30 am to 1.30 pm and 4 to 7.30 pm (shorter hours in winter). Entry costs 300 ptas. The same ticket allows you entry to the **Museo Diocesano**, housed in the Convento Regina Coeli, across the Santander highway from the rest of the old town.

A little way down the main road from the Colegiata, the town has been blessed with a somewhat less elevating display – the **Museo de la Inquisición**, with all sorts of instruments of medieval barbarity on show. It opens daily from 10 am to 10 pm and admission is 600 ptas.

Places to Stay Three or four private houses along the main street and Plaza de las Arenas (behind the Colegiata church) have rooms. Check these out as they can be very good. *Casa Octavio* (☎ 81 81 99), Plaza de las Arenas 4, has particularly charming rooms with timber-beam ceilings for 2500/3500 ptas with own bathroom, or less without. There are a couple more such places on, and also just off, Plaza de Ramón Pelayo.

Otherwise, there must be around 20 other places of varying classes, mostly across the Santander road around the park known as the Campo de Revolgo and out along the road to Santander itself. The latter area should be tried only if all else fails. The three *hospedajes* on Calle de la Robleda, overlooking the park, all have reliable rooms starting at around 2000/3000 ptas.

More up-market and good value is the *Hotel Altamira* (☎ 81 80 25; fax 84 01 36), Calle del Cantón 1. The well-appointed rooms all have private bath, TV and telephone, and start at 5000/6000 ptas plus IVA in the low season. For a classier stay, head for the *parador* (☎ 81 80 00), on Plaza de Ramón Pelayo. Doubles start at 13,500 ptas.

Places to Eat *Casa Cossío*, about the nearest restaurant to the Colegiata, serves wonderful ribs with spicy sauce and a good range of seafood. The *Restaurante Altamira*, attached to the hotel of the same name, has a reliable set lunch for 1100 ptas. There are several snack and burger places too if you want to keep it simple.

Getting There & Away Several buses call in at Santillana en route between Santander and other destinations further west, like Comillas and San Vicente de la Barquera, but more frequent services connect the town with

Torrelavega, itself easily reached by FEVE train from Santander.

Cueva de Altamira & Zoo

Lots of hot air from the mouths and nostrils of the yearly flood of tourists to the prehistoric cave (*cueva*) of Altamira, two km west of Santillana, led to the inevitable result. The extraordinary wall paintings of bison, boar and other beasts have been closed since 1977 to all but 20 visitors a day – to protect the already damaged images from the moisture caused by, well, too much breathing. You need to plan ahead to see the famous paintings, scratched into the cave walls around 12,000 BC. You are supposed to write a year in advance to the Centro de Investigación de Altamira, Santillana del Mar 39330, Cantabria, Spain. Admission is 400 ptas (half for students). For information call ☎ 942-81 80 05. A small museum at the cave contains the fossil of a prehistoric man. It can be visited at any time. It is open Tuesday to Sunday from 9.30 am to 2.30 pm.

About one km away, on the road to Puente de San Miguel, is a modest little zoo, open daily from 9.30 am to sunset.

Comillas

Easily one of the most attractive towns west of Santander, Comillas offers the combination of a genuinely enchanting old town centre, a handful of monuments and a couple of good beaches to choose from nearby. One result is that you can all but forget about trying to find a bed here in midsummer without a reservation.

The tourist office (☎ 72 07 68) is at Calle de María de Piélago 2. It opens from 10 am to 1 pm and 5 to 9 pm Monday to Saturday and 11 am to 1 pm and 5 to 8 pm on Sunday in summer. There are several banks with ATMs around the centre.

Things to See Of the few reminders of his genius that Antoni Gaudí left behind beyond Cataluña, his 1885 **Capricho** in Comillas is easily the most flamboyant, although modest in stature. If he reined in his imagination in Astorga and León, the opposite can be said

here. He definitely let himself go a little, plastering the building liberally with ceramic sunflower motifs on a green background. You can let yourself go too, as it's now an expensive restaurant.

Next door lies the neo-Gothic **Capilla Panteón de los Marqueses de Comillas**, set in lovely gardens dominated by the nearby **Palacio de Sobrellano**. The latter is a majestic piece of neo-Gothic architecture conceived by Joan Martorell Montells, a Catalan modernist like Gaudí. All you can do is admire the buildings and gardens through the garden gates, as they are privately owned. Martorell also had a hand in what was until 1968 the **Universidad Pontificia**. Lluís Domènech i Montaner, another Catalan modernist, contributed a medieval flavour to the elaborate design of the building, which stands on a rise between the Palacio de Sobrellano and the coast. In keeping with the theme, Comillas bristles with what might be unkindly seen as a minor rash of *caprichos* (caprices), the lavish private residences of the town's well-to-do.

Predating it all, Comillas' compact medieval centre is full of its own little pleasures. Plaza del Generalísimo Franco is its focal point, an inclining cobbled square flanked by the ayuntamiento, the Iglesia de San Cristóbal and a series of pleasing old sandstone houses with flower-bedecked timber balconies.

Places to Stay You can pitch a tent at *Camping Comillas* (☎ 72 00 74), a couple of minutes out of town by car on the main road to Santillana.

About the cheapest place to stay if you need a hotel double is *Pensión La Aldea* (☎ 72 10 46), near the tourist office at Barrio Velecio 12, with simple rooms for 3500 ptas. They won't reduce the price for lone travellers at the height of the season. The ramshackle *Hostal Fuente Real* (☎ 72 01 55), in a dead-end lane just behind the Capricho de Gaudí (signposted), has beds for 2000 ptas a person. Back in the centre, *Pensión Tuco* (☎ 72 10 30), Calle de Antonio López 4, is a respectable place offering

CANTABRIA

doubles for 3500 ptas or 4500 ptas with private bath.

The utterly charmless *Hotel Paraíso* (☎ 72 00 25), just off Plaza del Generalísimo Franco at Calle de los Padres Páramo y Nieto, has rooms starting at 3500/4500 ptas in the low season and rising to 5000/7000 ptas in August. They also charge full board (3500 ptas per person) on top in the high season.

There are several options in the middle to expensive bracket, but if you're in the mood to splurge a little, head straight for the *Casal del Castro* (☎ 72 00 36; fax 72 00 61). This period-furnished, 17th century mansion could compete with the better paradores. Singles/doubles with private bath, TV, telephone and breakfast cost 7000/10,000 ptas plus IVA. By comparison, the *Hostal Esmeralda* (☎ 72 00 97), Calle de Antonio López 7, is solid without being exciting. Rooms with similar mod cons cost 7500/10,000 ptas plus IVA, although you can get cheaper ones without private bath for 5500/6500 ptas plus IVA.

Hotel Josein (☎ 72 02 25), Calle de Santa Lucía 27, overlooks the water and rooms cost 7500/12,500 ptas in the high season, dropping to a more reasonable 5500/6500 ptas in the low season. Add IVA to all prices.

Places to Eat For snack food, tapas and the like, *Pensión La Aldea* is a decent bet, or you could try *Bar El Galeón* across the road. You can eat well at either for around 1500 ptas. A cute little place (try for a table by the window upstairs) is the *Restaurante El Pirata*, Calle del Marqués de Comillas. They have a set meal for 1200 ptas. Opposite the park leading to the Palacio de Sobrellano, *Restaurante Martina*, Paseo de Solatorre 6, also has good tapas. At the *Capricho de Gaudí*, you'd be lucky to get away with less than 5000 ptas a head for a full meal.

Getting There & Away Up to eight buses daily head east to Santander and Torrelavega, and west to San Vicente de la Barquera. The bus stop is on Paseo de Solatorre, close to the Palacio de Sobrellano park.

Around Comillas

Although there are a couple of beaches in Comillas (about a 20 minute walk from the centre, signposted from the centre), the **Playa de Oyambre**, five km west, is decidedly superior – so much so that the road is choked on summer weekends. Inland from the beach lie the wetlands of the small Parque Natural de Oyambre. Further west, the **Playa de Merón** is bigger still, a little wild and less crowded. From here you could walk west along the beaches to San Vicente de la Barquera. There are a few hotels on the road from Comillas to Playa de Oyambre, as well as *Camping El Rodero* (☎ 72 20 40), just back from the beach and open all year.

San Vicente de la Barquera

San Vicente fell for a time under Roman control, and was then occupied and expanded by Alfonso I of Asturias in the 8th century. Throughout the Middle Ages it was an important fishing port, and later it became a member of the so-called Cuatro Villas de la Costa – converted by Carlos III into the province of Cantabria in 1779.

Today, streams of lorries and, in summer, holiday traffic, pour through the largely modern town and across the low arches of the originally 15th century Puente de la Maza. Towering above it all is the craggy outcrop that contains what remains of the old town. East of the estuary a string of good beaches begins.

There is a tourist office (☎ 71 07 97) at Avenida del Generalísimo 20 (the main drag), open in summer only, and several banks along the same street.

Apart from a few remnants of the old city walls and former *castillo*, the one outstanding monument is the largely 13th century **Iglesia de Santa María de los Angeles**. Although Gothic, it sports a pair of impressive Romanesque doorways. Inside, the reclining statue of the Inquisitor Antonio del Corro is deemed by those who know to be the best example of Renaissance funerary art in all Spain.

Aside from *Camping del Rosal*, just across the estuary on the beach, there are a handful of hotels in town. About the cheapest is *Hostal La Paz* (☎ 71 08 97), Calle del Mercado 2, with singles/doubles starting at 2600/3900 ptas. A good deal is *Pensión Liébana* (☎ 71 02 11), Calle Ronda 2, a block back from the main square, Plaza de José Antonio. It has doubles starting at 4000 ptas with own bath and TV. If that fails, try *Hospedaje El Nido* (☎ 71 26 28), Calle de Carlos V, with doubles for 6000 ptas. Outside the high season, lone travellers can usually negotiate a reduced rate.

As for food, there is no shortage of choice. *Restaurante Maruja*, Avenida del Generalísimo 22, is a long-established posh seafood spot. A little scruffier and easier on the wallet are two neighbours, *Restaurante Las Redes*, at No 24, and *El Pescador* next door. All these have tables set up out the back looking over the estuary. In the town centre, *Sidrería La Brasa*, at the top of the steps leading up from the square to Calle Ronda, has a wide choice of first and second courses on its 900 ptas set menu.

Up to 15 buses run to Santander, and as many as 13 go on to Bilbao. Several buses head into Asturias, reaching Arriondas, Oviedo and Ribadesella. Autobuses Palomera has a couple of services that link Santander to Potes and Fuente Dé in the Picos de Europa, via San Vicente.

SOUTH OF SANTANDER

Deep river valleys flanked by patchwork quilts of green and high peaks unfold before the traveller penetrating deeper into the Cantabrian interior. Every imaginable shade of green seems to have been employed to set this fairy-tale stage, strewn with warm stone villages and held together by a network of narrow and often poorly maintained country back roads. It is the delight of meandering about here, rather than any extraordinary monuments, that makes an incursion into this country so attractive. Many of the small villages have at least one *casa de labranza* (the Cantabrian equivalent of a *casa rural*) where you can stay.

Western Valleys

Generally ignored by holiday-makers concentrating their attention on the Picos de Europa further west, the valleys of the Río Nansa and, next over to the east, the Río Saja make a soft and beautiful contrast to the craggy majesty of the Picos.

People starting from the Picos might well take the following route. A narrow, winding way snakes up high and eastwards from La Hermida, on the Río Deva. It is a beautiful drive and there is a small *hospedaje* in **Quintanilla**. The village of **Puentenansa** (banks and bars) forms a crossroads. The road south follows the Río Nansa and eventually passes the man-made Laguna (a reservoir) to join the C-627 road back up to Potes (this could be done as a circuit from Potes). Along the way, **Tudanca** (before the Laguna) is probably one of the more attractive hamlets. Its more distinctive houses, or *casonas*, were built by one-time migrants returned from the Americas – known throughout northern-western Spain as *indianos*. You can stay in the *fonda*, where you can also get a hearty meal. The place also acts as a general store.

To proceed east you'll have to retrace your steps to Puentenansa and take the road for Carmona. For a few km after passing Carmona there are some splendid views back over the Nansa valley. When you reach the town of Valle de Cabuérniga and the Río Saja, head south for Reinosa. Again, the views are magnificent and the country is among the least spoiled in the region. **Bárcena Mayor**, about nine km east off the main road, is a popular spot with a couple of places to stay and great mesones where you can eat cheaply and well. Locals often hike there from Reinosa (see the next section) on weekends. Leaving at about 7.30 am gives them ample time to enjoy the trail and arrive at Bárcena Mayor for lunch – *cocido montañés* is the meal most in demand.

CANTABRIA

Reinosa & Alto Campóo

Reinosa, the main town in southern Cantabria, is drab, with little to recommend
stopping in. That said, five km south of the
city in Cervatos is one of Cantabria's finest
Romanesque collegiate churches, the
Monasterio de San Pedro. And if you're
around in winter and have skis itching for a
brief run, you could head 27 km west to the
ski 'resort' of Alto Campóo, which has one,
rather expensive, hotel.

In town, the tourist office, near the bridge
at Avenida del Puente de Carlos III, is open
Monday to Saturday from 9.30 am to 2 pm.

If you get stuck in Reinosa (try not to),
there are several options for a bed. *Hostal
Sema* (☎ 75 00 47), Calle de Julióbriga 14,
is handy to the train and bus stations, and has
singles/doubles for 2000/3000 ptas.

The part of Avenida del Puente de Carlos
III between the bus station and the Río Ebro
is jammed with bars, snack joints and the odd
restaurant. The most atmospheric is *Pepe de
los Vinos*, near the tourist office.

The train and bus stations are adjacent.
Five trains run through Reinosa to Santander
and Valladolid (in Castilla y León). Buses
serve various destinations along the Cantabrian coast and south into Castilla y León, and
several local villages, including Polientes
(three a day), San Martín de Elines and Arija
(along the Embalse del Ebro reservoir).

Along the Río Ebro

The Río Ebro, one of Spain's primary rivers,
rises about 10 km west of Reinosa, spills into
the artificial lake of the Embalse del Ebro
and then meanders, its force much reduced,
south and east into Castilla y León. You can
follow the river course along minor roads out
of Reinosa. Head first towards Arroyo on the
south bank of the lake (you will pass the
minimal ruins of Roman Julióbriga on the
way). Just before Arroyo, make a right
(south). You will pass the Monasterio de
Montes Claros, then descend to Carabeo and
finally hit a T-junction. Turn left and follow
the signs for Polientes. Along the way,
several small churches hewn into the rock
can be visited in the pueblos of Olleros,

Campo de Ebro and **Arroyuelos**. The best
example, the Iglesia de Santa María de
Valverde, is actually about 10 km *west* of the
T-junction. At **Polientes** you'll find a couple
of places to stay, banks and a petrol station.
About 10 km further on, **San Martín de
Elines** has a fine Romanesque church and
marks the end of the line for the daily bus
from Reinosa via Polientes. Those with their
own transport should push on for Orbaneja
del Castillo (see Routes North of Burgos in
the Castilla y León chapter).

Eastern Valleys

Short on specific sights but rich in some of
Cantabria's least spoiled rural splendour, the
little visited valleys of eastern Cantabria are
great for exploring – especially for those
who can get hold of a vehicle. Plenty of route
combinations suggest themselves, so what
follows is by way of an example only.

From Puente Viesgo (see the Around
Santander section), take the S-580 south-east
and make for Vega de Pas. The town is of
minimal interest, but the drive is quite something. If you pass in late spring, you'll see
farmers out collecting hay with time-
honoured methods – scythes and wooden
rakes still predominate, and either farmer
women load the stuff on their backs or the
family horse and cart are dragged out for the
job of taking the hay into storage. The views
from the **Puerto de Braguía** pass in particular are stunning. From Vega de Pas you
could continue south-east, briefly crossing
the territory of Castilla y León, before
turning north again at Río de Trueba and
following the Río Miera up through San
Roque de Riomeira towards Santander.
Another option from Río de Trueba is to take
the BU-571 road up via the Puerto de la Sía
pass towards Arredondo. This road is full of
switchbacks, a couple of mountain passes
and isolated little farmhouses where people
still see few enough strangers passing
through to warrant unembarrassed staring.
The drive along the Río Gandara and Río
Asón, further east again, is just as rewarding.
You'll find places to stay in **Arredondo** and
Ramales de la Victoria.

Principado de Asturias

'Ser español es un orgullo,' the saying goes, *'asturiano es un título'*. If being Spanish is a matter of pride, to be called Asturian is a title, or so some of the locals will have you think. Ever since King Pelayo warded off the Muslims in the Battle of Covadonga in 722 and laid the foundations of Christian Spain's 800 year comeback, Asturians have thought of themselves – or been seen to think of themselves – as being a slight cut above the rest of the peninsula's inhabitants. One can only wonder if this local pride has anything to do with the fact that the region's name appears to be in the plural – a phenomenon for which no-one appears to have a convincing explanation.

Be that as it may, the Reconquista's slow southward progress left Asturias increasingly as a backwater. As a sop, Juan I, king of Castilla y León, made Asturias a principality in 1388, and to this day the heir to the Spanish throne holds the title of Príncipe de Asturias, much as the Prince of Wales is heir to the British throne. Yearly literary and other prizes in the prince's name to personalities of distinction are Spain's rough equivalent of the Nobel.

Although Oviedo and other towns have their moments, the area's real beauty lies beyond the cities. Much of the grand Picos de Europa mountain range is on Asturian territory, and coastal towns such as Llanes and Cudillero make great bases for exploring the coast's riches. For the art and architecture buff, Asturias is the land of pre-Romanesque – modest but unique leftovers of early medieval church-building and decoration.

Asturias' climate is great for growing apples – you'll never eat a better apple anywhere else in Spain. And true to the area's Celtic roots, these apples are put to good use in the production of cider *(sidra)*, which you'll see drinkers and bartenders pouring, bottle held high overhead, more or less successfully into their glasses in *sidrerías* across the region.

Traditional dishes are simple, peasant fare. The best known is the *fabada asturiana*, a hearty bean dish jazzed up with bits of meat and sausage. Mountain streams teem with salmon, always a treat for fish-lovers. Another tasty dish you may come across in

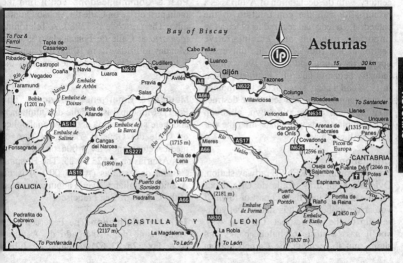

western Asturias is *repollo relleno de carne* – cabbage stuffed with meat.

The telephone code throughout the region is ☎ 98, and the first digit of every phone number (they all have seven digits) is 5. Should you be in doubt about local emergency numbers, call ☎ 006 from anywhere in Asturias for any service.

OVIEDO

Capital of Asturias and in parts a depressingly industrial city of 203,000, Oviedo nonetheless presents a remarkably cosmopolitan face. The modern part of the city centre, with its elegant parks and shopping streets, is agreeably offset by what remains of the *casco antiguo* (old town). Out in the periphery, the hum and heave of factories is a reminder that Oviedo is a key producer of textiles, pharmaceuticals, metal goods, sugar and even chocolate.

History

When the Asturian king Alfonso II El Casto (the Chaste) defeated a Muslim detachment that had all but destroyed the small town of Oviedo, he was sufficiently impressed by the site to rebuild and expand it and move his court there from Cangas de Onís. By the 14th century, with the declaration of Asturias as a principality and the construction of the cathedral, Oviedo had secured its place as an important religious and administrative centre. In the 16th century the university opened its doors, and in the 19th century industry began to take off. A miners' revolt in 1934 and a nasty siege in the first months of the Spanish Civil War led to the destruction of much of the old town, although considerable efforts were made after the war to repair the damage.

Orientation

From the main-line RENFE railway station, Oviedo's main drag, Calle de Uría, leads south-east right into the old part of town. If you arrive at the main bus station, get yourself up to the same street. On your way, you'll pass a string of hotels, banks and shops, not to mention the Campo de San Francisco, a huge shady park with swings and the like to keep ratty kids amused. The cathedral rises up in the north-eastern corner of the old town, a mostly pedestrianised district. A good collection of restaurants, cafés and bars wait to be discovered in the narrow streets around and south of the cathedral, while the biggest concentration of traditional sidrerías lies to the north-west, just outside the historic centre.

Information

Tourist Office The main tourist office (☎ 521 33 85), Plaza de Alfonso II 6, opens Monday to Friday from 9.30 am to 1.30 pm and 4 to 6.30 pm, and Saturday from 9 am to 2 pm. The Oficina Municipal de Información, in the Campo de San Francisco, also has brochures and a good map of Oviedo. It opens Monday to Friday from 10.30 am to 2 pm and 4.30 to 7.30 pm, and from 11 am to 2 pm on weekends.

Money Calle de Uría is lined with banks, most with user-friendly ATMs.

American Express (☎ 522 52 17) is represented by Viaca, Calle de Uría 26, next door to McDonald's.

Post & Communications You'll find the main post office on Calle de Alonso Quintanilla. The postcode is 33080. A Telefónica *locutorio* at Calle de Foncalada 6 is open Monday to Friday from 10 am to 2 pm and 5 to 10 pm. On Saturday it opens in the morning.

Medical & Emergency Services The Policía Municipal is at Calle de Quintana and there's a comisaría of the national police on Calle del General Yagüe. In case of medical emergency, try ☎ 006, or Ambulancias Asturias on ☎ 523 50 25. The Hospital General de Asturias (☎ 523 00 00) is on Avenida de Julián Clavería about a km west of the Campo de San Francisco.

Trekking Information The Federación de Montañismo del Principado de Asturias (☎ & fax 525 23 62), Avenida de Julián

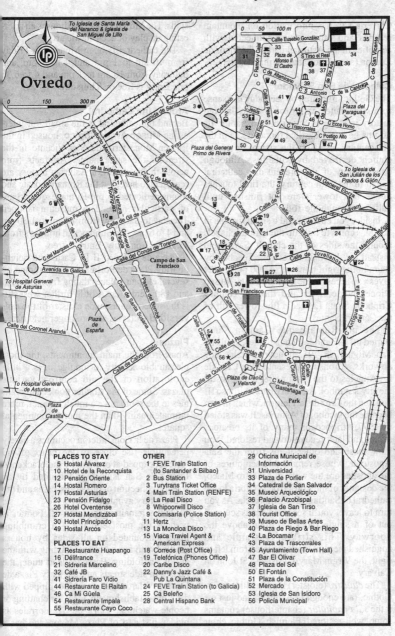

PLACES TO STAY
5 Hostal Álvarez
10 Hotel de la Reconquista
12 Pensión Oriente
14 Hostal Romero
17 Hostal Asturias
23 Pensión Fidalgo
26 Hotel Oventense
27 Hostal Mendizábal
30 Hotel Príncipado
49 Hostal Arcos

PLACES TO EAT
7 Restaurante Huapango
16 Délifrance
21 Sidrería Marcelino
32 Café JB
41 Sidrería Faro Vidio
44 Restaurante El Raitán
46 Ca Mi Güela
54 Restaurante Impala
55 Restaurante Cayo Coco

OTHER
1 FEVE Train Station
  (to Santander & Bilbao)
2 Bus Station
3 Turytrans Ticket Office
4 Main Train Station (RENFE)
6 La Real Disco
8 Whipoorwill Disco
9 Comisaría (Police Station)
11 Hertz
13 La Moncloa Disco
15 Viaca Travel Agent &
   American Express
18 Correos (Post Office)
19 Telefónica (Phones Office)
20 Caribe Disco
22 Danny's Jazz Café &
   Pub La Quintana
24 FEVE Train Station (to Galicia)
25 Ca Beleño
28 Central Hispano Bank

29 Oficina Municipal de
   Información
31 Universidad
33 Plaza de Porlier
34 Catedral de San Salvador
35 Museo Arqueológico
36 Palacio Arzobispal
37 Iglesia de San Tirso
38 Tourist Office
39 Museo de Bellas Artes
40 Plaza de Riego & Bar Riego
42 La Bocamar
45 Plaza de Trascorrales
45 Ayuntamiento (Town Hall)
47 Bar El Olivar
48 Plaza del Sol
50 El Fontán
51 Plaza de la Constitución
52 Mercado
53 Iglesia de San Isidoro
56 Policía Municipal

ASTURIAS

Clavería s/n, has information on mountain refuges and other issues connected with activities in the Asturian part of the Picos de Europa (see section later in this chapter).

Catedral de San Salvador

The Gothic structure you see today in a sense forms the outer casing of a many-layered history in stone of Spanish Christianity. Its origins lie in the basilica founded late in the 8th century, itself on the site of an earlier church destroyed by Muslims. Although construction of the present-day cathedral began in the 14th century, the final touches to the bell tower were not finished until halfway through the 16th.

Inside, you could spend a small fortune in 100 ptas coins to light up the various chapels around the sides of the church. Save them instead for the main attractions, reached by stairs in the right transept. A 300 ptas ticket gives you access to the Cámara Santa, Museo Diocesano, cloister and the 9th century Cripta de Santa Leocadia (the lower half of the Cámara Santa).

The pre-Romanesque Cámara Santa started off as a modest chapel, the Capilla de San Miguel, in 791. It now contains key artworks. Alfonso II presented the Cruz de los Angeles to the city in 808, and it is still the city's symbol. A century later, Alfonso III donated the Cruz de la Victoria, which in turn became the symbol of Asturias. It was stolen in 1977, stripped of many of its precious stones and later recovered and restored. You view these and other items from the Sala Apostolar, whose remarkable sculptures of the apostles are the work of Maestro Mateo, the designer of the Pórtico de la Gloria in the cathedral of Santiago de Compostela. As you turn to leave, you'll see three heads sculpted out of a single block of stone above the doorway. This strikingly simple and anguished piece of work depicts, from left to right, the Virgin Mary, Christ and St John on Calvary.

The *claustro* (cloister) is pure 14th century Gothic, rare enough in Asturias, and just off it the *sala capitular* (chapterhouse) contains some well-restored Flemish Gothic choir stalls. The Museo Diocesano houses an interesting display of ecclesiastic art.

The cathedral is open Monday to Friday from 10 am to 1 pm and 4 to 8 pm, and Saturday from 10 am to 1 pm and 4 to 6.30 pm. Entry is free on Thursday.

Around the Cathedral

Behind the cathedral is the small but interesting **Museo Arqueológico**, housed in the former Monasterio de San Vicente in the street of the same name. Artefacts from across the spectrum of Asturian history are represented here, but the Roman mosaic and rooms dedicated to pre-Romanesque art are of particular note. The museum is open Tuesday to Saturday from 10 am to 1.30 pm and 4 to 6 pm, and Sunday and holidays from 11 am to 1 pm only. Entry is free.

Plaza de Alfonso II El Casto and neighbouring Plaza de Porlier are both fronted by several elegant palaces dating from the 17th and 18th centuries. A little further west still is the sober Renaissance cloister of the **universidad** – classes are no longer held here.

Plazas

Apart from the main monuments, the most pleasurable activity to indulge in is a little exploration of the old centre's various plazas. Some of the smaller nooks and crannies to the south have a much warmer, more intimate quality than the more monumental squares.

Plaza de la Constitución occupies a barely perceptible rise close to the heart of old Oviedo, capped at one end by the blackened Iglesia de San Isidoro and fronted by an eclectic collection of old stores, cafés and the 17th century ayuntamiento.

Of the remaining squares, El Fontán is perhaps the most enticing – a crumbling plaza surrounded on all sides by houses mottled with age and kept standing with the aid of scaffolding. Passages lead under the houses to side streets and the leafy Plaza de Daoíz y Velarde. All are well equipped with drinking establishments ideal for chatting or people-watching. Plaza de Trascorrales is hidden just east of Plaza Mayor, and has a couple of pleasant restaurants (see Places to Eat). Other little squares include Plaza de Riego, Plaza del Sol and the suggestively named Plaza del Paraguas (Umbrella Square).

Pre-Romanesque Churches

For many, Oviedo's key attraction is its pre-Romanesque churches. Closest to the centre is **San Julián de los Prados**, unhappily located by the autovía to Gijón. It is supposed to be open Tuesday to Saturday from 9.30 am to 1 pm and 3 to 6 pm, although you may have to approach the rector to let you in.

Considerably more evocative, if only for their position, are the **Iglesia de Santa María del Naranco** and, a few hundred metres further on, the **Iglesia de San Miguel**

de Lillo. They lie three km out of town (take bus No 6 from Campo de San Francisco) on the slopes of Monte Naranco.

The two monuments are open in summer Monday to Saturday from 9.30 am to 1 pm and 3 to 7 pm, and Sunday from 9.30 am to 1 pm only. In winter the hours are 10 am to 1 pm and 3 to 5 pm. Visits, which are guided, cost 200 ptas, but you can wander in for free (and unguided) on Monday. For more on these, see the boxed aside 'Pre-Romanesque Architecture in Asturias'.

Monte Naranco enjoys commanding views of Oviedo, and there are a few restaurants and cafés along the way to help soak them up. A couple of km on from the churches is a rather ugly concrete statue of Christ.

Pre-Romanesque Architecture in Asturias

More or less cut off from the rest of Christian Europe by the Muslim invasion and occupation of most of Spain, the small, rough-and-tumble kingdom that emerged in the mountains of Asturias gave rise to a style of art and building distinct not only in Spain, but in all Europe.

The 30 or so buildings, mostly churches, that survive from the 150-odd years of the Asturian kingdom take some inspiration from other sources but are unique. The three in Oviedo are representative of the best pre-Romanesque you'll find. Typical of all is their straight profile – no curves and cylinders here. The semicircular arches that abound to a greater or lesser extent in all the pre-Romanesque churches are an obvious forerunner to a style that would later triumph in northern Spain and across much of Europe – Romanesque. Another precursor to the Romanesque style is the complete vaulting of the nave.

Roman and Visigothic elements *are* visible. In many cases the bases and capitals of columns, with their Corinthian or floral motifs, have simply been cannibalised from earlier structures. Another adaption, which owes something more to developments in Muslim Spain, was the use of lattice windows. They appear purely as a design effect, since their eastern progenitors were inspired by the desire to maintain privacy from the outside world – hardly an issue in a church.

The **Iglesia de San Julián** de los Prados, in Oviedo, is the largest remaining pre-Romanesque church, and one of the oldest, built under Alfonso II. It is flanked by two porches – another very Asturian touch – and the inside was once covered

DAMIEN SIMONIS

The Iglesia de Santa María del Naranco, one of three fine pre-Romanesque churches in or near Oviedo

with frescos. The **Iglesia de Santa María del Naranco** and the nearby **Iglesia de San Miguel de Lillo** stem from the reign of Ramiro I, and mark an advance in Asturian art. An outstanding feature of the decoration in the former is the *sogueado*, the sculptural motif imitating rope used in its columns. Other decoration was influenced by Byzantine and Near Eastern art. The large windows are a pointer to later Gothic solutions in church architecture. The tall, narrow Iglesia de Santa María was originally intended as a royal residence, while San Miguel is thought to have started life as Ramiro I's palace. ■

Organised Tours

The Viaca travel agency (☎ 522 52 18), Calle de Uría 26, organises one day bus excursions along several scenic routes in eastern Asturias, including to Covadonga and the Lagos de Enol and de la Ercina, in the Picos de Europa.

Special Events

Oviedo's top fiesta is that of San Mateo, celebrated in the third week of September and climaxing around the 21st. Carnaval, in February or March, is also a good time to sample street festivities.

Places to Stay

Oviedo is liberally sprinkled with hotels of most grades, so finding a bed for the night should prove easy. You'll find any number of places near the RENFE train station and along or off Calle de Uría. Otherwise, the area including Calles de Covadonga, de Foncalada and de Jovellanos also has a fair spread of cheaper spots.

A perfectly good-value cheapie is the *Pensión Oriente* (☎ 521 22 82), Calle de Melquiades Álvarez 24. Singles/doubles start at 1500/2500 ptas, but for 500 ptas more you can get a room looking onto the street.

Hostal Mendizábal (☎ 522 01 89), Calle de Mendizábal 4, has good, clean rooms without private bath for 2000/3500 ptas. It is neatly located just off Plaza de Porlier. A little further off and solid, if unspectacular, is *Pensión Fidalgo* (☎ 521 32 87), Calle de Jovellanos 5. Rooms start at 2000/3500 ptas.

For the same price, *Hostal Arcos* (☎ 521 47 73), Calle de Magdalena 3, is ideally located within stumbling distance of some of the best of central Oviedo's watering holes.

Hostal Asturias (☎ 521 46 95), Calle de Uría 16, is an old-style place with loads of character. Singles/doubles without private bath cost 2500/4000 ptas, while doubles with bath go for 6000 ptas.

Up the road at No 36, *Hostal Romero* (☎ 522 75 91) charges about the same and has decent-sized rooms with TV. *Hostal Álvarez* (☎ 525 26 73), Calle de la Indepen-

dencia 14, is run by the same people and is similar in quality and price.

Of the several more expensive options *Hotel Oventense* (☎ 522 08 40), Calle de San Juan 6, is comfortable and has rooms starting at 4000/6500 ptas. Heading into luxury class is *Hotel Principado* (☎ 521 77 92), Calle de San Francisco 6, with rooms starting at 9500/13,500 ptas plus IVA. Top of the heap is the *Hotel de la Reconquista* (☎ 524 11 00) in the rather opulent former Real Hospital at Calle de Gil de Jaz 16. Doubles go for up to 25,000 ptas plus IVA.

Places to Eat

For lunchtime pinchos (snacks) and a beer locals tend to converge on the bars along Calle del Rosal.

Délifrance, Calle de Uría 20, makes a welcome change to standard Spanish set menus at the lower end of the eating scale on the usual fast-food alternatives. For less than 1000 ptas you can get a decent pizza sub, salad and drink.

Most of the places along Calle de Mon are bars pure and simple, but at one or two you can get food. *Ca Mi Güela*, at No 9, has a straightforward set lunch for 800 ptas.

More is said below about sidrerías, but it's worth noting that you can get a square meal in most of them, as well as tippling on fermented apples. One of the more popular ones for a feed is *Sidrería Marcelino*, Calle de Santa Clara 4. A slightly more up-market option is *Sidrería Faro Vidio*, Calle de Cima-devilla 19.

Restaurante Cayo Coco, Calle de Cabo Noval 8, is worth seeking out. The menu of Cuban specialities (try Pollo Piqui-Chiqui) can be followed up with any one of a number of 300 ptas cocktails. Next door at No 10, *Restaurante Impala* does good Asturian food for reasonable prices. The set lunch is good value at 1000 ptas.

Restaurante El Raitán, Plaza de Tras-corrales 6, is an atmospheric place where a satisfying meal will probably set you back about 2500 ptas. Next door is their rather classy version of a chigre, or traditional tavern. On the same square, at No 14, *La*

Bocamar is in a similar league, and in summer sets up tables in the plaza.

Logos, Calle de San Francisco 10, is a good grill restaurant with a touch of class. The set lunch is 1600 ptas – a little expensive but well prepared.

Back on the Latin American front, *Restaurante Huapango*, Calle del Matemático Pedrayes 16, offers Mexican cuisine.

Lunchers up on Monte Naranco should check out the *Parrilla Buenos Aires*, about a km up the hill from the Iglesia de Santa María. The views over Oviedo from here are unbeatable.

Cafés Plaza de Porlier is speckled with a nice crowd of cafés for your morning coffee. And the dark woodwork of *Café JB*, Calle de Ramón y Cajal 16, makes it a cosy alternative when the sun don't shine; ensconce yourself upstairs. The lacework of squares around the old town is loaded with cafés to suit all tastes. Plaza del Paraguas in particular can be pleasant in summer, when a couple of cafés put out tables and chairs, and later in the evening a tiny unnamed bar fills with a lively thirty-something clientele.

Entertainment

Bars & Sidrerías If you're after no-frills drinking Asturian-style, you need to check out the *sidrerías*. In these places you will often see practised drinkers pouring cider into glasses from a bottle held high overhead. You may just want to have a drink yourself and skip the pouring. This is easily enough done; in most places the bartenders are happy to get themselves wet as they pour, seemingly staring into the middle distance as they do so. Calle de la Gascona is a classic street lined with the old no-nonsense version, but you'll soon start turning them up all over own.

Ca Beleño, Calle de Martínez Vigil 4, is a well-established spot for indulging in Celtic music, whether of Asturian, Galician or Irish extraction – and those of a mind can swig a Foster's. If you are not interested in Celtic music, you could have a stab at *Danny's Jazz*

Café, just next door to *Pub La Quintana*, Calle de la Luna 9.

Calle de Mon is the place to seek out for rowdier and later opening bars, mainly at weekends. *Bar El Olivar*, No 14, is a slightly psychedelic joint, but if it's not your scene there's plenty of choice. Other streets in the area to explore are Calle de Altamirano and Calle de la Canóniga.

Discos & Nightclubs Apart from some sleazy 'clubs', central Oviedo is not richly blessed with discos and all-night dance-till-you-drop joints. One handy place to check out is *Caribe*, Calle de Foncalada 4. Not far off is *La Moncloa*, Calle de Covadonga 28. Further into the new part of the city are *La Real*, Calle de Cervantes 19, and *Whipoor-will*, Calle del Matemático Pedrayes 18.

Getting There & Away

Air The Aeropuerto de Asturias is 43 km north-west of Oviedo, 39 km east of Gijón and 15 km from Avilés. There are flights with Aviaco to main cities within Spain all year round, and the occasional flight, including summer charters, to several European destinations such as London, Paris and Brussels.

Bus The principal bus station is at Plaza del General Primo de Rivera 1, but the entrance is unmarked – look for what appears to be an arcade.

The ALSA company runs buses to destinations over much of Spain, including Madrid (about eight a day; 3530 ptas), Salamanca, Sevilla, Bilbao and various cities in Galicia. The same company has an extensive network covering Asturias too. Direct services charge up the motorway to Gijón (235 ptas) and Avilés (240 ptas) every few minutes from 7 am to 10.30 pm. Each trip takes about 30 minutes.

Intercar has services across northern Spain from Bilbao as far as Tuy in Galicia. You can pick up international services from the same station to places as far afield as Lisbon, Paris, London and Zürich.

Of the half-dozen or so other smaller bus companies, the most important is Turytrans, with offices at Calle de Jerónimo Ibrán 1. Its buses run to Gijón, Llanes and on to Santander (1710 ptas; seven a day) and a string of cities in the País Vasco and Navarra (including Pamplona, San Sebastián (3450 ptas; five a day) and Bilbao. More locally, the same company has buses to Arriondas (635 ptas), Cangas de Onís (630 ptas), Covadonga (725 ptas) and Lago de Enol (930 ptas). Services to the latter two are not too reliable outside summer and can be cancelled when there are adverse weather conditions in the Picos de Europa.

Train The best way to get to Gijón and Avilés is by the frequent *cercanías* trains. They run from 6 am to midnight and take 30 to 45 minutes to either destination. Otherwise, eight daily main-line RENFE trains serve León to the south. A handful of these go on to Madrid, Barcelona and Vigo (Galicia).

Finally, there are two stations for the FEVE trains. The first, just down the road from the RENFE station, has two daily trains for Santander (1575 ptas) and Bilbao via Gijón. For Bilbao you must change in Santander – about a one hour wait. The other station, parallel to Calle de Jovellanos, is for trains heading west to O Ferrol in Galicia.

Car & Motorcycle The main north-south axis through Oviedo is the A-66. If you're going to León, the more picturesque but slower N-630 forks off to the left after 36 km. The N-634 is the main choice east towards the Picos de Europa.

Rental There are about 10 car rental companies in Oviedo. Hertz (☎ 527 08 24) is handy to the train station, at Calle de Ventura Rodríguez 4.

Getting Around
The Airport Up to four buses a day run to the Aeropuerto de Asturias (650 ptas; 55 minutes) from the bus station, timed to coincide with flights.

Bus & Taxi About the only bus you might need is the No 6 from the central park, Campo de San Francisco, to Monte Naranco (for the Iglesia de Santa María). Radio taxis can be called on ☎ 525 25 00.

WESTERN ASTURIAS – THE COAST
Avilés
What may have been good news on the employment front in Avilés has done nothing for the aesthetic appeal of this once small but dignified town of nobles, artisans and fishermen. The 1950s changed all that, and the now ageing steel industry has created a nightmarish landscape of factories and workers' slums. If all that doesn't deter you, the much neglected old centre is worth a visit – easily enough done as a half-day trip from Oviedo or Gijón. There is a tourist office (☎ 554 43 25) at Calle de Ruiz Gómez 21 off Plaza de España.

The Old Centre Just south off Parque del Muelle on Calle de la Ferrería stands the Franciscan **Iglesia de San Nicolás**, whose 12th century Romanesque façade has been much restored. Next door is the Gothic **Capilla de los Alas**.

A few blocks west you can admire the crumbling remains of what once must have been a stylish baroque structure, the **Palacio de Camposagrado**, today sadly neglected Calle de la Ferrería is one of the town's more evocative streets, its porticoes lending shelter from the probable rain – nobly assisted by the range of chigres (old-style watering holes) that line its route to Plaza de España. The plaza is fronted by several 17th century palaces.

Cross the square and make for Calle de San Francisco, whose **Iglesia de San Nicolás de Bari** (formerly Iglesia de San Francisco) is essentially a 17th century structure, but with a hodgepodge of elements dating as far back as the 12th century. From here, the cobbled Calle de Galiana stretches south-west away from the centre, and is Avilés' most atmospheric street. The porticoed walkway on one side shelters various eateries and bars; jutting higgledy-piggledy into the street are the glassed-in balconies of enturies-old houses jammed up hard one against the other.

If you have time, visit the **Iglesia Vieja de Sabugo**, a few blocks north-west of Parque del Muelle, which is an inspired 12th century Romanesque church.

Special Events The time to be in Avilés is for *carnaval* in February or March. It's a pretty frenetic four day celebration of the end of the winter, and the whole event is so big it's known by the plural: carnavales.

Places to Stay Accommodation is scarce on the ground, and little is enticing. Frankly, Oviedo is a much better base and is only a short bus or train ride away. If you need to stay, *Fonda El Norte*, Calle de la Estación 57, is a cheap and cheerless dive across from the RENFE train station with singles/doubles for 2000/3200 ptas.

A better option is *Pensión Conde 2* (☎ 556 93 01), Calle del Doctor Graiño 1, which offers doubles only for 3500 ptas.

For those with a healthy credit card, *Hotel Luzana* (☎ 556 58 40), Calle de la Fruta 9, is the top establishment in the heart of town. Singles/doubles cost 7500/9500 ptas plus IVA.

Places to Eat & Drink For food and drink, the best streets to hunt around in are Calle de la Ferrería and Calle de Galiana. On the former you'll strike some wonderful cavernous old taverns, among them the *Chigre Gorfoli*, No 20. *Casa Alvarín*, tucked away on Calle de las Alas, just off Calle de la Ferrería, is a classic chigre, where you can get simple local meals. *Entre Calles*, Calle le San Francisco 14, is a lively little barum-restaurant.

The pick of the crop is easily the *Restaurante Serrana*, Calle de la Fruta 9, where superb and well-presented meals should not cost more than 2000 ptas a head. Or for something different, head for *Charolita Canina Mexicana*, Calle de Pablo Iglesias 9.

For a drink, the *Queen Maeve*, Calle de la Ferrería 4, comes close to the atmosphere of good UK pub. Maybe it's the weather and

the industry, but not a few of the sidrerías have that 'pub feeling' – only they don't close at 11 pm.

Getting There & Away The main bus company, ALSA, has its office on Calle de la Muralla, on the Parque del Muelle. Regular services leave for Oviedo, Gijón (285 ptas) and Luarca via Cudillero (525 ptas). The only direct rail line to Gijón is FEVE, but services are regular. For Oviedo, get the cercanías trains from the RENFE station.

Cudillero

Cudillero is easily the most picturesque fishing village on the Asturian coast, and it knows it. The houses, freshly painted in pastel colours, cascade down to a tiny protected port, where half a dozen restaurants compete for custom. You could be forgiven for thinking there's a local law that the doors and window frames of each house be a different colour. Despite its touristy feel, Cudillero *is* cute, and pretty laid-back. The nearest beach is the **Playa de Aguilar**, a fine, sandy strand a few km east. Heading west a few km, the pick is probably the small but undeniably pretty **Playa de San Pedro**.

The tourist office (☎ 559 01 18) is on Calle de Suárez Inclán, shortly before you reach the port.

The closest camping grounds are *Camping Cudillero* (☎ 559 06 63), Playa de Aguilar, and *L'Amuravela* (☎ 559 09 95), El Tolombrero, open from 1 June to the middle of September. These and other grounds around are packed in August.

The only accommodation in town itself is the *Hotel San Pablo* (☎ 559 11 55), Calle de Suárez Inclán 36-38. Singles/doubles cost up to 5000/8000 ptas. About two km back on the road towards Avilés (a hefty uphill walk), is the perfectly adequate *Hostal Álvaro* (☎ 559 02 04), Avenida Selgas s/n, with rooms for 3500/5000 ptas. If that fails, you'll get a double for 4000 ptas 50 metres down the road at *Hospedaje El Pino* (☎ 559 05 31), a more rundown but friendly enough place.

There is no shortage of places to eat. A full

ASTURIAS

meal with wine will cost you about 3000 ptas wherever you try. *Restaurante El Remo*, beside the port, and *Mesón El Pescador*, up the hill at Calle de Suárez Inclán 9, are both reliably good seafood places.

Some ALSA buses on the Gijón-Ribadeo (Galicia) route stop in here, as does the occasional FEVE train – the station is about three km out of town.

To Luarca via the Coast

From Cudillero west the road is decent for about 10 km, after which weekenders find themselves trapped in traffic jams most of the way to Luarca. This stretch is slowly being replaced by an autovía – to the distress of those who prefer scenery to asphalt. The pebbly **Playa de Cadavedo** is pleasant, and from nearby Cabo Busto you can get some measure of the Asturian coast's wildness.

To Luarca via Salas

Instead of choosing the coast road the whole way west, a pretty alternative suggests itself in the N-634, which snakes north-west up and down lush valleys from the Asturian capital to meet the N-632 coast road about 10 km east of Luarca. The most significant stop along the way is **Salas**, 45 km from Oviedo. It soon becomes clear that Cardinal Fernando de Valdés Salas, founder of Oviedo's university in the 16th century, was the town's most illustrious son. His **castle**, whose tower next door you can climb, has been converted into a hotel. The venerable clergyman lies buried in the nearby **Colegiata de Santa María**.

There are several pensiones in Salas, and the *Hotel Castillo de Valdés Salas* (☎ 583 22 22) makes an attractive place to stop, with doubles for 5500 ptas plus IVA. It's the best choice of restaurant too. There are regular buses to Oviedo.

Luarca

Larger and more dishevelled than Cudillero to the east, Luarca will appeal to lovers of seaside decay. This is one of those places which, simply because it is carved in two by a murky stream equipped with a handful of

bridges, tourist brochure lyricists like to talk about as the 'Venice of ...' – in this case, of Asturias. It's certainly an interesting enough place to wander around in, and it has a couple of mediocre beaches; Venice, however, it ain't.

For a better beach, head seven km east to the **Playa de Cuevas**, which is set back from a dramatic headland and occasionally throws up some decent surf.

Places to Stay & Eat Those with a taste for the Middle Ages might try the ancient *Pensión El Cocinero* (☎ 564 01 75), Plaza de Alfonso X. The rooms are OK, and cost 2000/3000 ptas for singles/doubles. *Pensión La Moderna* (☎ 564 00 57), Calle del Crucero 2, has rooms for 2000/3500 ptas, as does *Pensión Oviedo* (☎ 564 09 06) across the road at No 3.

Reasonable value is *Hotel La Colmena* (☎ 564 02 78), Calle de Uría 2, with rooms costing 4000/6500 ptas in the high season.

Next to Pensión El Cocinero (which is also a restaurant), the brand new-looking *Hostal Rico* (☎ 547 05 85) has somewhat overpriced doubles only, starting at 4500/7500 ptas without/with private bath in the low season and rising to 6000/10,000 ptas in summer. A more enticing option in this range is the *Hotel Báltico* (☎ 564 09 91), Paseo del Muelle, overlooking the port. Doubles cost up to 10,000 ptas plus IVA. The restaurant has a wide menu.

You should first direct your search for food to the waterfront. *Mesón de la Mar*, at the end of the jetty, is a huge and popular seafood establishment, but there are other options. *Mesón El Ancla*, Paseo del Muelle 15, has tapas and cider. On the central Plaza de Alfonso X, the *Restaurante Leonés* is a reliable mid-range option.

Getting There & Away The easiest way in and out of Luarca is by bus. Regular services run along the coast to Oviedo (2¼ hours) and into Galicia (Ribadeo). The bus station is on Paseo de Gómez, near the centre. FEVE trains leave from a station a couple of km out of town. There are three a day to Oviedo and two direct to O Ferrol (Galicia). The train is less practical, but scenically more pleasing.

Navia

Twenty km further west you strike another busy port town, Navia. Rather than hang about, cross the estuary (a modest version of Galicia's grander rías to the west) and take a sharp left along what becomes the Río Navia towards Coaña (see Western Asturias – Inland Routes).

Tapia de Casariego

A welcoming fishing haven along the west Asturian coast, Tapia de Casariego makes a pleasant lunch stop, but little else. There are a couple of unspectacular beaches nearby, the best of them Playa de Represas, and you may be able to get a wave here. Uluru (☎ 562 86 02), Calle de Santa Rosa, is one of several local surf shops.

The most convenient and cheapest places to stay are *Hotel La Ruta* (☎ 562 81 38), on the main coast road, and *Hotel Puente de los Santos* (☎ 562 81 55), just across the road. In the high season, singles/doubles are about 4000/6000 ptas in the first, and up to 5000/8000 ptas in the latter.

For nutrition, try *Bar Maxin's*, Calle del Arquitecto Villanil 7, which offers a tasty set lunch for 1000 ptas. Otherwise, *La Marina*, down by the port, is popular. If seafood delicacies are your thing, you might have the chance to eat *percebes* (a kind of barnacle), more commonly found in Galicia.

On to Galicia

Castropol The majestic **Ría de Ribadeo** marks the frontier between the Principado de Asturias and Spain's north-westernmost region, Galicia. Spanning the broad mouth of this, the first of the many grand estuaries (*rías*) that slice up the length of Galicia's Atlantic coast, is the Puente de los Santos. Just before you make the move across (or shortly after arriving from Galicia), you could detour a few km down the east side of the Río Eo (which joins the ría here) to visit the small, whitewashed town of Castropol. *Pensión de San Vicente* (☎ 562 30 51) is

nicely situated above the river, and is a tranquil alternative to staying in Ribadeo, just inside Galicia. Singles/doubles cost 3000/5000 ptas. The road south offers itself as a little-travelled back route into Galicia; see the next section.

WESTERN ASTURIAS – INLAND ROUTES

Few visitors to Asturias venture far from the coast or the area's premier natural attraction, the Picos de Europa mountains. Nevertheless the west of the principality offers some magnificent country constituting a series of rewarding routes into Castilla y León and Galicia – all alternatives to the more obvious coastal run or the autovía linking Oviedo and León.

To Ponferrada & León from Cudillero

Head east seven km to Soto del Barco. From here you can pick up the AS-16, opening up several possible roads south. To start with, the most promising takes you along the placid valley of the Río Nalón and then the Río Narcea. Make south-west for Soto de los Infantes on the AS-15. The wooded hills on either side of the valley begin to acquire stature here, and eight km on the dammed **Río Narcea** matches them. The one blemish is the Santianes power station, and nearby quarries.

Just before you cross the misnamed Puente del Infierno (Hell's Bridge), there is a turn-off west to **Pola de Allande**, a peaceful village dominated by the lugubrious 16th century Palacio de Peñalbas. On the way, you could make a detour for **Celón**, with its 11th century Romanesque Iglesia de Santa María, which contains much-damaged 15th century frescos. In Pola, the *Hostal La Nueva Allandesa* (☎ 580 73 12), Calle de Donato Fernández 3, has modern singles/doubles for 4000/6000 ptas overlooking the gurgling stream through the middle of the village. From Pola you could push west to Grandas de Salime and pick up the Río Navia route (see below).

About four km further from Celón,

ASTURIAS

achievers may feel impelled to push on to the partly excavated and overgrown Celtic **Castro de San Luis** (also known as San Chuis). Make for San Martín de Beduledo. Just at the town sign a dirt track cuts off to the left. You can just get a car up here, or walk it in about half an hour. The castro is not as well preserved as its counterpart at Coaña (see below), but it makes up for this in sweeping views and a feeling of being 'undiscovered' – no tourist buses here.

Back on the AS-15, the road to Cangas de Narea passes the **Monasterio de Corias**. Cangas itself is a rather large and modern place, although not without some charm. Of the two roads south into Castilla y León, the AS-213 offers the more spectacular pass across the Cordillera, the Puerto de Leitariegos (1525 metres). From the pass it's about 80 km to Ponferrada.

Via Reserva Nacional de Somiedo Eight km before Soto de los Infantes, you have the option of dropping more or less directly south along the AS-227 through the southern reaches of the Somiedo national hunting reserve. Once in Castilla y León, you are about equidistant from León (south-east) and Ponferrada (south-west).

To Ponferrada from Luarca
If you really want to leave the beaten track between Luarca and Castilla y León, head directly south from Luarca for Pola de Allande along the AS-219, a minor, winding road through the Aristébano country. From Pola de Allande, follow the above routes. The Aristébano country is the territory of the *vaqueiros*, one-time pastoralists who still celebrate La Vaqueirada on the last weekend of July. Brides and grooms are transported up to Braña de Aristébano by bullock-drawn carts for a traditional wedding and much merry-making.

Coaña & the Río Navia
The small town of Coaña lies about four km inland along the Río Navia. There's nothing much there, but a couple of km beyond is one of the best preserved Celtic settlements, or

castros, in northern Spain. It is open Tuesday to Sunday from 11 am to 2 pm and 4 to 7 pm (summer); 11 am to 1.30 pm and 4 to 5 pm in winter. Entry costs 200 ptas.

From the castro, a poor road snakes its way high above the cobalt blue Río Navia on a long, winding journey to Lugo, in Galicia. This route takes you through classic Asturian countryside – meadows alternating with rocky precipices – and on into some of Galicia's least visited and wildest territory, around the town of **Fonsagrada**.

To Lugo from Castropol
Rather than hug the length of Galicia's coast you could proceed south from Castropol along the wooded route via Vegadeo. A busy town but with few substantial monuments to hold you up, Vegadeo marks the beginning of the most attractive part of the road. Take the AS-21 for **Taramundi**, 20 km on, a quiet settlement surrounded by rich meadows. Here you could arrange to stay at the classy *Hotel La Rectoral* (☎ 564 67 67; fax 564 67 77), an 18th century nobleman's house. It's a little pricey at up to 14,000 ptas a double, although there are also separate apartments for less.

EASTERN ASTURIAS – THE COAST
With the magnificent Picos de Europa rising up some 25 km inland, the coast of eastern Asturias attracts a good number of Spanish holiday-makers over the summer. A string of pretty beaches and coves provides a tempting counterpoint to the mountains.

Gijón
Bigger, busier and gutsier than Oviedo, Gijón produces iron, steel, chemicals and oil as well as being the main loading terminal for Asturian coal. Many of its 260,000 inhabitants think it should be the capital, and some go to the trouble of buying cars in Girona (Gerona), Cataluña, to have a 'GI' number plate instead of one with 'O' (for Oviedo). As if that were not enough, Gijón in the local dialect is written Xixón anyway! There's not an awful lot to see here, although not a few

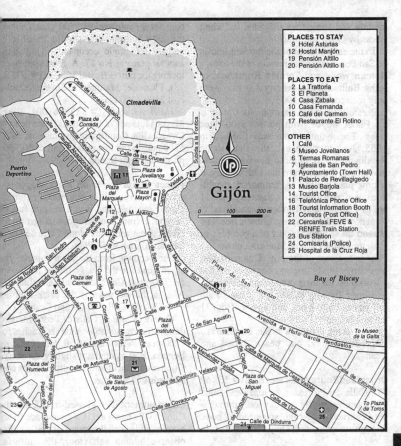

PLACES TO STAY
9 Hotel Asturias
12 Hostal Manjón
19 Pensión Altillo
20 Pensión Altillo II

PLACES TO EAT
2 La Trattoria
3 El Planeta
4 Casa Zabala
10 Casa Fernanda
15 Café del Carmen
17 Restaurante El Rotino

OTHER
1 Café
5 Museo Jovellanos
6 Termas Romanas
7 Iglesia de San Pedro
8 Ayuntamiento (Town Hall)
11 Palacio de Revillagigedo
14 Museo Barjola
14 Tourist Office
16 Telefónica Phone Office
18 Tourist Information Booth
21 Correos (Post Office)
22 Cercanías FEVE &
     RENFE Train Station
23 Bus Station
24 Comisaría (Police)
25 Hospital de la Cruz Roja

Gijón

0   100   200 m

ASTURIAS

paniards are attracted over summer to be by
he sea and mountains and still enjoy what a
arge city can offer.

nformation The main tourist office (☎ 534
0 46), Calle del Marqués de San Esteban 1,
pens Monday to Friday from 9.30 am to
.30 pm and 4.30 to 6.30 pm, and Saturday
rom 9 am to 2 pm only. In summer, another
ooth opens on Playa de San Lorenzo. The
nain post office is on Plaza Seis de Agosto
nd the postcode is 33200. There's a
elefónica office on Plaza del Carmen.

Old Gijón The ancient core of Gijón is concentrated in the headland, known as
Cimadevilla, that juts out into the Bay of
Biscay. Seawards, what used to be a fortified
military zone has now been converted into
something of a park. Wrapped around the
landward side of the hill, descending to the
isthmus which connects the old town with
the rest of the city, is a fine web of narrow
lanes, small squares and dead ends. The
Plaza de Jovellanos is dominated by the 16th
century house of the poet and politician of
the same name, now housing a modest
museum devoted to archaeology, history of

the city and some fine artworks, including works by Goya and Murillo.

To the east, in front of the modern Iglesia de San Pedro, are what remain of the town's **Roman walls** and **Termas Romanas**, or baths. Built in the 1st century AD, they were only rediscovered in 1903.

Possibly the most harmonious square is the **Plaza Mayor**, with porticoes on three sides. The ayuntamiento was finished in 1865. Just to the west, the Palacio de Revillagigedo is Gijón's most noticeable monument. Dating from the 17th century, it is now mainly used for temporary exhibitions. It is open Tuesday to Saturday from 11 am to 1.30 pm and 4 to 9 pm, and Sunday from noon to 2.30 pm only. Entry is free. The **Museo de la Gaita** is part of a complex of museums at the Feria de Muestras, on the Río Piles in the east of the city. This particular museum not only displays bagpipes but has a workshop for their production and repair. It is open Tuesday to Saturday from 10 am to 1 pm and 5 to 8 pm, and Sunday from 11 am to 2 pm only. Entry is free.

For a swim, the Playa de San Lorenzo is a surprisingly good city beach, broad and clean.

Organised Tours Autocares Faro (☎ 538 69 79), Calle del Professor A González Muñiz 13, organises mostly one day tours throughout Asturias. As a rule, you need to book through travel agents. They tend to cram in a lot.

Special Events Carnaval (February or March) is about the first major excuse in the year for fancy-dress partying in the streets, although it's not as big as in Avilés. In July, Gijón hosts a cinema fest and the Festival Internacional de Música.

Places to Stay There are plenty of cheaper-end places scattered about the centre of the new town between the train station and Cimadevilla.

Closer to the Playa de San Lorenzo, *Pensión Altillo* (☎ 534 33 30), Calle de Capua 4, has reasonable doubles with private

bath for a maximum of 5500 ptas. Outside the high season, you should be able to bargain for single occupancy. They have another place at No 17. A good spot over looking the port is *Hostal Manjón* (☎ 535 2. 78), Plaza del Marqués 1. Singles/double cost 2500/4100 ptas.

Hotel Asturias (☎ 535 06 00), Plaz. Mayor 11, is one of two hotels in the heart o Cimadevilla. Comfortable rooms cost 3300 5300 ptas in the low season, but 6500/750(ptas in the high season.

Places to Eat Just in off Plaza Mayor is a series of lively little sidrerías, including *Casa Fernanda*, and if you venture furthe in you'll find another popular group o places to eat and drink along Calle de Osca Olavarría, such as *El Planeta*.

For a change from the local cuisine, yo could head for the classy Italian restauran *La Trattoria*, Cerro de Santa Catalina 10 Also in the old town is the prize-winning *Casa Zabala*, Calle del Campo Grande 2.

Café del Carmen, Calle de Pedro Menén dez 3, offers reasonable-value set lunches fo 1200 ptas. *Restaurante El Rotino*, Calle d(Begoña 28, is a popular if slightly expensiv(Gijón restaurant of long standing. Mains cos upwards of 1500 ptas.

Entertainment The glassed-in café on th(Cimadevilla headland is a great place to si a coffee and watch the waves. If you'd rathe observe human behaviour, the sidrería; already mentioned are the place to be.

On the subject of sidrerías, cafés and bars Calle de San Bernardo and its parallel street. are teeming with them. Check out Calle d(la Corrida and Calle de los Moros too. Th(bars and discos that litter the waterfron streets and spill into the barrio known as L Calzada are good hunting grounds for late night excitements.

Getting There & Away For most destina tions, buses are the best bet. ALSA has a least 12 a day to Madrid (5½ hours); 10 t(León (2½ hours); one to Tuy (Galicia) vi. Santiago de Compostela (3565 ptas); an(

one to Barcelona. Closer to home, there are frequent departures to Oviedo and Avilés. Buses to Cudillero (770 ptas) leave regularly, and three go to Ribadeo (Galicia). The bus station is on Calle de Llanes, near Plaza del Humedal.

There are two train stations. The main one known as Cercanías) is on Plaza del Humedal. FEVE trains leave from here for Oviedo (from where you can connect further on to O Ferrol in Galicia) and eastwards to Santander. FEVE has direct trains to Avilés as well. Regular cercanías trains run to Oviedo. A few long-distance trains also leave from here, although at night they often only depart from the Estación Norte (about half a km west). All trains stop at the Estación Norte anyway, but you're better off arriving at the main station (Cercanías) wherever possible.

The A-8 motorway heads west for Avilés, with the A-68 branching south for Oviedo. Heading east, the narrow N-632 goes to Villaviciosa and Ribadesella.

Villaviciosa & Around

Apart from the Iglesia de Santa María, a 13th century late Romanesque structure with some evident signs of the move to Gothic, this pretty town is mostly a child of the 18th century. Avenida de García Caveda, the main street, is lined with noble houses, mostly in a good state.

The town makes a good base for church-lovers. The surrounding rich pastures and wooded hills are fairly sprinkled with often diminutive places of worship bearing Romanesque or even pre-Romanesque features. Many are for aficionados only, but one example that should not be missed is the pre-Romanesque **Iglesia de San Salvador de Valdediós**, about eight km south along the road to Pola de Siero. It was built in 893 as part of a palace complex for Alfonso III in what Asturians dubbed 'God's Valley', but archaeologists have failed to find any remnant beyond this simple church. Next door are the Romanesque **Iglesia & Monasterio de Santa María**, of the Cistercian persuasion. From May to November

they can all be visited from 11 am to 1 pm and from 4.30 to 6 pm. Otherwise you've got to be there from 11 am to 1 pm. Another fine Romanesque church is the **Iglesia de San Juan de Amandi**, 1.5 km from Villaviciosa.

Facing the open sea on the west side of the Ría de Villaviciosa is the minute port of **Tazones**, where Carlos I supposedly first landed in Spain in 1517. It is quite a popular spot, and in summer gets a little crowded.

The east side of the ría is covered by the golden sands of **Playa Rodiles**.

Places to Stay & Eat Playa Rodiles has a camping ground. There are several cheapish places to stay in Villaviciosa. *Hospedaje Pedro* (☎ 589 00 03), Calle del Deán José Cuesta 3, has singles/doubles for 1500/4000 ptas, while *Café del Sol* (☎ 589 11 30), Calle del Sol, offers them for 2000/3300 ptas. *Hospedaje El Ñeru* (☎ 589 04 22), Calle del General Campomanes 1, is also OK at 2500/4000 ptas. There are several up-market options along Avenida de García Caveda, but for a real treat try *La Casona de Amandi* (☎ 589 01 30), a mid-19th century farmhouse in Amandi, 1.5 km from Villaviciosa. Doubles with their original Isabelline furnishings range up to 13,900 ptas. On the food front, head straight for *Casa Milagros*, next to the Hospedaje El Ñeru. The salmon a la ribereña is delicious.

There are a couple of places to stay in and around Tazones, including the waterfront *Hotel Imperial* (☎ 589 71 16), with singles/doubles for 5000/6000 ptas. Seafood is the speciality in Tazones, although the restaurants are pricey.

Getting There & Away ALSA buses along the coast call in at Villaviciosa on the way to and from Oviedo and Gijón. You can get to Lastres (145 ptas), Ribadesella (325 ptas) and Covadonga (425 ptas) by bus. In summer there are buses to Playa Rodiles. The station is behind Bar El Ancho, off Plaza de Obdulio Fernández.

Villaviciosa to Ribadesella

The only worthwhile stop along this 40 km

ASTURIAS

stretch is the rather precarious cliff-side fishing village of **Lastres**, a scruffier version of Cudillero (see Western Asturias – The Coast) with a couple of 16th century churches thrown in. Try for a room with a sea view at *Hostal Miramar* (☎ 585 01 20), Bajada al Puerto. Doubles in the high season cost 4400 ptas plus IVA. A few km east of Colunga and south off the N-632 is the delightful *La Cabaña del Roble* (☎ 585 30 10), near Caravia, a great Turismo Rural. It's often booked up weeks ahead.

Ribadesella

Unless you've booked ahead, stay well away from here on the first weekend of August, when the place goes mad over the kayak festival down the Río Sella from Arriondas, and more liquid is poured down throats than could ever flow down the river. Otherwise, Ribadesella is a fairly low-key resort, in some vague way not unlike Newquay and similar places in Cornwall. Split by the river, the two halves are joined by a causeway. The westernmost half has a good, fairly clean beach, while the old town and fishing harbour are on the east side of the bridge.

Information The tourist office (☎ 586 00 38) is in an *hórreo* (a traditional grain store; see the Galicia chapter for more on hórreos) just on the western side of the causeway. It opens Monday to Saturday from April to the end of September. The hours are 9.30 am to 1.30 pm and 4.30 to 8 pm.

Cueva de Tito Bustillo Those disappointed about the inaccessibility of the Altamira caves to the public can make up for it a little by visiting the Cueva de Tito Bustillo, on the beach side of Ribadesella (signposted). The cave drawings here, mostly depictions of animals, are roughly 12,000 years old; the best of them are in the western half (Sector Occidental). The site is open from April to September, Tuesday to Saturday from 10 am to 1 pm and 3.30 to 5.15 pm, and Sunday from 10 am to 1 pm only. Entry costs 300 ptas (free on Wednesday). There is a limit of 400 visitors daily, so in August turn up early.

Activities Ribadesella is also a centre for a wide range of adventure sports. Turaventura (☎ & fax 586 02 97), Calle de Manuel Caso de Villa 26, hires out bicycles for 1500 ptas a day and organises white-water canoeing on the Río Sella for 12,000 ptas for two days. Or you could look in at the Centro de Información de Turismo Activo (CITA) at the Albergue Roberto Frassinelli youth hostel (☎ & fax 586 13 80), Calle de Ricardo Cangas. Here you can hire everything from mountain bikes to surfboards and kayaks. They also organise excursions along the coast by kayak, descents of the Río Sella by canoe, mountain bike trips and the like.

Places to Stay & Eat *Camping Los Sauces* (☎ 586 13 12), Carretera de San Pedro, is just in off the west end of Playa de Santa Marina (the main beach) and opens from mid-June to late September. Further inland, *Camping Ribadesella* (☎ 585 77 21), Calle de Sebreño, with its own pool, charges a little more and is open from Easter to 30 September.

A bed (in rooms of two or four) at the *Albergue Roberto Frassinelli* (☎ 586 13 80), Calle de Ricardo Cangas, costs 1500 ptas (1750 ptas in July and August). You don't need a HI card and the hostel is on the beach.

Otherwise, there's not too much in the line of cheap accommodation. *Hostal Varadero* (☎ 586 01 22), Gran Vía 22, has basic doubles for 3500 ptas, but outside the high season you could negotiate. *Hostal Apolo* (☎ 586 04 42), Gran Vía 31, has singles/doubles for 2500/4000 ptas. A friendly option is *Hotel Boston* (☎ 586 09 66), across the causeway from the main part of town (near the beach) at Calle El Pico 7. Doubles cost 5000 ptas from July to September, but out of season prices drop and you can negotiate for a single. A classier choice is *Hotel Covadonga* (☎ 586 02 22), which has rooms from about 3000/4500 ptas without private bath in the low season. In the high season, prices rise to 5500 ptas for a double without own bath and 7000 ptas with; there is no single rate on offer then.

The Gran Vía area of the old part of town is a good place to look for a variety of cafés and places to eat. *Restaurante Rico*, Calle del Infante López Muñiz 27, has set meals for 900 ptas. They also offer eggs and bacon for breakfast for 375 ptas with a cup of coffee – or a glass of wine!

Getting There & Away Up to eight ALSA buses run to Gijón each day. If you want Oviedo, change at Villaviciosa. EASA buses run four times a day to Cangas de Onís, while six a day head east for Llanes. The bus station is just out of the town centre on Paseo del Cobayo. The FEVE train station is further out on the old Carretera de Santander.

To Llanes
There are several little beaches and coves to be discovered on the way from Ribadesella to Llanes, and those with transport and time should always be ready to duck off the main road to see what's about. About 10 km short of Llanes, the **Playa de San Antolín** is an open and comparatively unprotected beach where you might pick up the odd wave. More interesting for some will be the nearby Benedictine **Monasterio de San Antolín de Bedón**, founded in the 11th century. You'll be lucky to find anyone in the surrounding half-dozen houses to let you inside the Romanesque church which is its main feature. The unkempt setting makes up for it though.

Llanes
Inhabited since ancient times, Llanes was long an independent-minded town and whaling port with its own charter awarded by Alfonso IX of León in 1206. Today it is one of northern Spain's more popular holiday destinations and, although pleasant enough, has clearly been marred by the nascent urban spread and construction work around the port. It does make a very handy base for some of the north coast's prettiest beaches, and only a few km inland rise the first rocky walls of the Picos de Europa.

Information The tourist office (☎ 540 01 64), Calle de Nemesio Sobrino (in the casino building), is open Monday to Saturday from 9 am to 2 pm and 5 to 9 pm, and Sunday from 10 am to 3 pm. The street is also known as Calle del Castillo; the ruined tower behind the Turismo is about the only remainder of the town's 13th century defences.

Activities If you are interested in organised walks and trips into the Picos de Europa, caving, canoeing or horse riding, see what Naturas (☎ 540 22 00), Calle Mayor s/n, has to offer. Another group that offers excursions on horseback or by 4WD and canoe trips down the Río Sella is Senda (☎ 540 26 42), Avenida de las Llamas (just outside Llanes on the road to Cué). Of the two town beaches, Playa de Toró to the east is infinitely preferable to the tiny Playa del Sablón.

Places to Stay In July and August finding a room can be next to impossible – and lone travellers will be lucky indeed to get a single.

The nearest camping grounds to Llanes are east of the town. *Camping Entre Playas* (☎ 540 08 88), just near the Playa de Toró, is open from June to the end of September. *Camping Las Bárcenas* (☎ 540 28 87) is just shy of the eastern side of town on the main highway and is also open from June to September.

About a km east of town, the *Albergue de la Portilla* (☎ 540 14 66) has beds (without sheets, which you can hire) for 2000 ptas, or more decent doubles for 6000 ptas. It opens from July to September only. Similarly cheap but a little on the nose is the *Pensión La Guía* (☎ 540 25 77), Plaza de Parres Sobrino 1, which charges 2000 ptas per person. The fonda at *Bar Colón* (☎ 540 08 83) is in a similar category. A good deal is the *Hostal Iberia* (☎ 540 08 91), Calle de Nemesio Sobrino (virtually opposite the tourist office) – but you need to go to the Restaurante La Covadonga, Calle de Manuel Cué 11, for information. Singles/doubles/triples without private bath go for 3000/4500/5500 ptas. *Hospedaje del Río* (☎ 540 11 91), Avenida de San Pedro 3, is a good place with rooms for 4000/5000/6500 ptas.

Places to Eat A series of lively *marisquerías* along the banks of the unimpressive Río Carrocedo (down steps off the main street through the heart of the town, heading away from the port) are the obvious places to look for seafood – raciones start at about 650 ptas. There are a few bars and discos in the side streets too. Otherwise, the narrow Calle de Manuel Cué has some more mainstream restaurants. *Restaurante Siete Puertas*, on Plaza de la Magdalena, is an up-market place where you'll pay around 2000 ptas for a full meal. If it's just a cider and tapas you want, try the big old sidrería, *El Bodegón*, on the same square.

Getting There & Away Buses along the coast to Ribadesella (six a day) and on to Oviedo and Gijón leave from a station about half a km east of the town centre. In summer there is usually a daily service to Covadonga, and one or two to Arenas de Cabrales. The FEVE train station is a five minute walk west of the town centre. Up to four trains head west for Oviedo, while as few as two run east to Santander.

Those driving into the Picos de Europa from the Llanes area might like to get off the main roads and explore the backblocks a little. For one surprisingly picturesque little drive that will bring you out onto the road (AS-114) connecting Cangas de Onís and Arenas de Cabrales, turn off for Parres shortly after heading west out of Llanes. From Parres make for Caldueño and Meré before reaching the AS-114. This route takes you across the Sierra de Cuera, a mild foretaste of the Picos massifs.

Beaches near Llanes

There are plenty of little beaches and coves to either side of Llanes, and together they form one of the most appealing coastal stretches this side of Santander.

Particularly worth noting are Playa Ballota, a longish strand hemmed in by green cliffs and accessible by dirt track. Part of it is for nudists and it lies a few km east of Llanes. About seven km to the west is the village-cum-understated holiday resort of Barro. Its main beach is a little bigger than the average cove and not too badly crowded. There are a few places to stay here, including *Hostal La Playa* (☎ 540 07 66), a friendly little place with singles/doubles for 4000/6500 ptas plus IVA.

On to Cantabria

Apart from continuing your exploration of beaches (Playa de la Franca is a nice one, and there is a camping ground), there is little to hold you up en route into Cantabria. The N-634 passes just to the north of **Unquera**, just inside Cantabria, and through which passes the main route south from the coast into the eastern Picos de Europa. If you're headed east, push on for San Vicente de la Barquera, or even on to Comillas (see the Cantabria section).

Picos de Europa

In May 1995, the Cortes (parliament) in Madrid voted to create what, at 647 sq km, is claimed to be the biggest national park in Europe, the Parque Nacional de los Picos de Europa. Way back in 1918, the Marqués de Villaviciosa had established Spain's first-ever national park, the Parque Nacional de la Montaña de Covadonga – the 170 sq km precursor of the new park. Straddling three regions (Asturias, Cantabria and Castilla y León), the mountains are roughly bounded by the Río Sella to the west, the Cabrales valley (highway AS-114) to the north, and the Río Deva to the east and south. The Picos consist of three *macizos*, or massifs. From west to east they are: the Cornión (or Occidental), Los Urrieles (or Central) and the Andara (or Oriental).

The mostly limestone mountains, although not extraordinarily high (the highest peak, Torre Cerredo, is 2648 metres), offer plenty for walkers, climbers and cavers of all skill levels. Paragliding and whitewater rafting are alternative activities, and the pretty beaches along the Bay of Biscay

Picos de Europa

To Llanes

To Arriondas (5 km),
Ribadesella, Oviedo
& Gijón

Cangas
de Onís

N625

Covadonga

Parque Nacional
de los Picos de
Europa

Sames

Amieva

Mirador de
Ordiales

Torre de
Santa María
(2486 m)

Torre Santa
de Castilla
(2596 m)

Los
Moledizos
(2295 m)

Torre
Bermeja
(2400 m)

Soto de
Sajambre

Oseja de
Sajambre

Soto de
Valdeón

CASTILLA Y LEÓN

Embalse
de Riaño

To Riaño

Sierra

Meré

Benia

Lago de
Enol

Lago de
la Ercina

Vega
de Arlo

Cañada del Cares

Caín

Torre de
Cerredo
(2648 m)

Cordiñanes

Cabaña
Verónica

Teleférico

Posada de
Valdeón

de
Cuera

Carreña

Arangas

Cáraves

Niserías

Panes

Arenas de
Cabrales

ASTURIAS

Oceño

Poncebos

Camarmeña

Bulnes

Vega de
Urriello

Naranjo
de Bulnes
(2519 m)

Peña
Vieja
(2613 m)

Refugio
de Aliva

Fuente Dé

Espinama

Cosgaya

Cordillera

Cantábrica

Cucayo

Tielve

Collado de
Pandébano

Sotres

Vega de
Sotres

Morra de
Lechugales
(2441 m)

Urdón

Treviso

Bejes

Linares

Argüébanes

Turieno

Camaleño

Los Llanos

CANTABRIA

Vega de
Liébana

To
Puentenansa
La
Hermida

Lebeña

Potes

N621

0   5   10 km

are never far away. As a measure of its popularity, mostly with Spaniards, the former Parque Nacional de la Montaña de Covadonga was getting 1.2 million visitors a year by 1995 – mostly in summer and at Easter.

Ecologists were chuffed by the 1995 result, but opposition was fierce from some quarters, particularly inhabitants of various villages inside the park – fearing they would find themselves reduced to exhibits in a reserve.

With some 30 species of reptile and amphibious animal, 130 species of bird and the occasional wolf and bear, the park is a rare enclave of what remains of Europe's once-teeming wildlife.

Information

Outside Easter and summer, activity slows to a trickle, and many tourist offices and the like either close altogether or only open up on long weekends. In an arc from west to southeast, Cangas de Onís, Arenas de Cabrales and Potes are the three principal settlements where you can find tourist information, banks (though ATMs are in short supply, so remember that most banks open from about 8.30 am to 2 pm, Monday to Friday) and good supermarkets. You can get maps for the area in these towns, all of which make reasonable places to base yourself. They are full to bursting in August and you should always try to call ahead, whether you are heading for a hotel or a mountain refuge.

Several operators offering everything from 4WD tours to mountain bike rental are listed throughout this section.

Ecology & Environment
One disconcerting aspect of the massive summer influx of visitors here is the rubbish many people leave behind, especially by the lakes and along the Cares gorge. The opinion seems to prevail that *someone* will come along and tidy it all up; this is to an extent true, but it would be a lot better not to fall into this selfish habit. You transported your rubbish up here, so take it out again.

Flora & Fauna
At first glance, talking of flora in the bald, grey peaks of the Picos may seem hopeful, but of course at lower levels there is plenty. Among native trees thrive oaks, chestnuts, hazelnuts and corks.

Although the odd bear *(oso pardo)* still survives, along with dwindling packs of wolves *(lobo)*, you are highly unlikely to see either. Elsewhere in the Cordillera Cantábrica wolves are occasionally driven down towards the mountain pueblos when snow sets in, but again it is hardly a frequent occurrence. A total of perhaps 50 bears survive across the entire Cordillera Cantábrica. Mountain wildcats *(gato montés)* are also increasingly rare. More common in the Picos is the chamois *(rebeco)*, a kind of cross between antelope and mountain goat. Foxes, squirrels and wild boar abound in more heavily wooded areas, while beavers can be found in the rivers. Lack of space prevents us from considering individually all the frog, lizard and other reptile species that inhabit the Picos.

A variety of eagles, hawks and other raptors fill the skies above the Picos, but you'd be truly lucky to catch sight of the majestic golden eagle *(águila real)* or the huge scavenging griffon vulture *(buitre leonado)*. Various types of owl come out in the night hours.

When to Go
The weather across northern Spain is more like what you'd find in Great Britain, Ireland or Brittany, and in the Picos is notoriously changeable. You could begin a walk in brilliant sunshine, only to find yourself enveloped in a chilly pea-soup fog a few hours later. That said, the south-eastern end of the Picos is generally drier than further north and west, as much of the moist weather coming in off the Atlantic doesn't make it right across the range.

Given that there are no guarantees of pleasant weather at any time of year, the time to avoid is August, when most of Spain is on the move and finding rooms is near impossible. July is not far behind. May, June and September are about the best times to visit – more tranquil and just as likely to be candidates for sunshine as August. In fact, most serious hikers and climbers choose September, as it tends to be the driest month – an important consideration when stuck up in the heights.

Drivers should beware of bad weather. Conditions can become extremely dangerous, especially in winter, when chains are also needed.

What to Take
For the walks mentioned here, you don't need special equipment. However, sun protection (hats, creams, sunglasses) is a good idea, as is a water bottle because sources of water are irregular at best. Proper walking shoes are helpful, if not absolutely necessary, and even on a sunny day you might consider taking some items of warmer clothing and even a raincoat, poncho or the like – you never know. For any treks or climbs off established tracks, you'll need the appropriate gear and experience.

Books & Maps
For more detailed information on the Picos

de Europa, refer to Lonely Planet's *Trekking in Spain*, by Marc Dubin.

One of the better general maps of the whole Picos area is one at a scale of 1:75,000 by Miguel Ángel Adrados. For Spanish-readers there is a detailed accompanying walking guide. The same guy has also written a route guide for mountain bikers that includes the Picos, *Cordillera Cantábrica – Ciclo-Travesías*.

More detailed maps include the set of two published by Editorial Alpina for 500 ptas each (scale 1:25,000) and a series covering an area considerably beyond the boundaries of the Picos and put out by IGN. Each sheet (1:25,000) costs 300 ptas (look for the plain blue covers). Unfortunately, none are free of errors.

The bookshops in Potes and Cangas de Onís are stacked with guidebooks of varying quality to the area, a couple of them in English.

Getting Around

Without your own wheels, getting around can be frustrating if you aim to taste the main delights of Picos without hanging around long enough to crisscross them on foot.

The most frequent transport all year round links Cangas de Onís with Oviedo, Arenas de Cabrales and Ribadesella. In summer, a couple of buses a day run between Arenas and Panes, as well as between Panes and Potes (and on to Fuente Dé). Up to five a day connect Covadonga with the lakes. For the rest of the year, services drop to a trickle, sometimes not even one bus a day. In summer at least, several private operators run 4WDs between less accessible parts of the mountains.

Where you enter the Picos de Europa will largely depend on where you're coming from and what most grabs your fancy. Many visitors combine excursions into the mountains with a stay on or near the coast. Here we can do little more than present an overview, starting in the north-west (which corresponds to Covadonga and the lakes) and taking in the western flank of the Picos.

We then proceed east across the northern rim of the massifs, exploring trails into the mountains. From there we follow the road that descends along the east side of the Picos towards the southern approaches.

Warning

The Picos de Europa are not the highest mountains in Europe, but walkers and climbers should come armed with a dose of respect. In particular, those attempting the tougher walks and climbs must bear several factors in mind: the weather is changeable, and snow, rain and fog are common problems. Higher up, few trails are marked, and there is virtually no animal life or vegetation. Water sources are infrequent. Paying insufficient attention to these details has cost several lives over the years, and you don't want to join the statistics.

WESTERN PICOS & THE LAKES

Arriondas

Eighteen km inland from Ribadesella on the N-634 highway to Oviedo, Arriondas is only interesting as the starting point for whitewater excursions down the Río Sella. There is a camping ground, the *Sella* (☎ 584 09 68), and a youth hostel, the *Arriondas* (☎ 584 03 34), Calle del Barco s/n. The former is open for Easter and from June to September; the latter, all year. Canoasturs (☎ 584 05 72), near the camping ground, and Jaire (☎ 584 14 64), Calle de Juan Carlos I 7, will both send you downriver to Ribadesella. Such a trip can cost 3000 ptas, but shop around and find out what each company throws in – such as equipment, and transport from and to the town you are staying in. The descent takes about four to five hours, and these companies provide all the equipment.

Cangas de Onís

Good king Pelayo, after his victory at Covadonga, moved down the hill about 12 km to settle the base of his nascent Asturian kingdom in Cangas in 722. Though Cangas had been inhabited since well before the

Romans arrived on the scene, this was nevertheless the town's big moment in history, lasting 70 years until the capital was moved to Oviedo.

Its second boom time seems to have arrived with the latter 20th century invasion of tourists. In August especially the largely modern town is full to bursting with trekkers, campers, holiday-makers and not a few people desperately searching for a room – a common story throughout eastern Asturias in high summer.

If you do get a room, Cangas makes a reasonable base, although as usual you'll be better placed if you have a vehicle. The town itself, sitting astride the Río Sella, is not an unpleasant little spot.

Information In summer, the tourist office (☎ 584 80 05), a kiosk on Avenida de Covadonga, opens Monday to Saturday from 10 am to 2 pm and 4 to 9 pm, and 10 am to 1 pm and 4 to 8 pm on Sunday. It is surprisingly bereft of information. There is a fair smattering of banks with ATMs in Cangas; stock up on dosh here.

Things to See With one outstanding exception, Cangas is bereft of historical monuments. The so-called **Puente Romano** spanning the Río Sella is almost certainly medieval, but no less impressive for all that. Not far off, the tiny **Ermita de Santa Cruz** is an entirely modern building standing on what has been a sacred site for several millennia. Walk inside and you can observe a megalithic dolmen in the crypt. The first Christian church was built here in 437 AD, on the remains of a modest Roman temple.

Activities Cangas Aventura (☎ 584 92 61), Avenida de Covadonga s/n, offers a range of activities, including excursions to the Cares Gorge, descents of the Río Sella by canoe (3000 ptas), horse riding (3000 ptas for three hours) and rock climbing (6000 ptas). They hire out mountain bikes for 2000 ptas a day. You could also try Guías de Montaña (☎ 584 89 16), Calle de Emilio Laria 2, for walking and trekking information.

Places to Stay One of the best deals you'll find for a bed is *Pensión El Chofer* (☎ 584 83 05), Calle de Emilio Laria 10, which has doubles only for 3500 ptas in the high season. There are a couple of nameless *pensiones* near the Puente Romano. The first, at Avenida de Castilla 1 (the road to Riaño), is on the 1st floor and has doubles for 3300 ptas. The other, around the corner on the main drag (look for the red 'Pensión' sign) has doubles/triples for 4000/6000 ptas. Even if they were willing to give their telephone numbers, they wouldn't take a booking. If you miss out on these in the high season, you'll be looking at about 4000/6000 ptas minimum for singles/doubles in any one of several hostales. For a little more comfort, try the *Hotel Puente Romano* (☎ 584 93 39), about 50 metres from the bridge on the road to Oviedo, with singles/doubles for 6000/8000 ptas. Note that August is the peak month and prices drop considerably in September and even July.

Places to Eat *Pensión El Chofer* has a popular, no-nonsense restaurant. At Avenida de Covadonga 19, *Restaurante Mario* is another good bet. *Mesón El Puente* is an obvious choice for location alone, with tables spread out in the shadow of the medieval bridge. A set meal costs 1000 ptas.

Getting There & Away There are buses (ALSA and Turytrans) from Oviedo and a few from Gijón, as well as local connections to Ribadesella, Llanes and Arenas de Cabrales. In summer there are up to six buses to Covadonga. The main stop is nearly opposite the tourist office on Avenida de Covadonga. If you have a group, you might consider using Taxitur (☎ 584 87 97) to reach the lakes above Covadonga.

Covadonga
Covadonga's importance lies in what it represents rather than what it is. To many, it symbolises the end of the beginning, for here the Muslims were defeated in battle in 722 by King Pelayo, who set up the Asturian kingdom that proved the nucleus of the first

faltering steps towards the Reconquista – a mere 800 year project. More recently, Covadonga was also the object of much fascist propagandist rot about Spanish unity.

The place is an object of pilgrimage, for in a cave here the Virgin supposedly appeared to Pelayo's warriors before the battle. Subsequently a holy sanctuary *(santuario)* was built, and it still attracts crowds of faithful today. Landslides destroyed much of the zone in the 19th century, so the little chapel and statuette of the Virgin (Nuestra Señora de Covadonga) are comparatively modern, as is the basilica. A magic spring is supposed to assure marriage to those who drink from its waters.

Weekend and summer queues of faithful or superstitious lined up to get into the cave are matched only by the frightening parade of cars crawling past to get up to the Lago de Enol and Lago de la Ercina.

Opposite the basilica is the Tesoro de la Santina, a museum filled with all sorts of items, mostly donations by the illustrious faithful. It opens daily from 10.30 am to 2 pm and 4 to 7.30 pm. Entry costs 50 ptas.

The *Hostal El Peregrino* (☎ 584 60 47) is a pleasant mid-range accommodation possibility, with views across to the santuario. The restaurant here is well overpriced and those who can should dine in Cangas or prepare their own food. There is at least one other mid-range hostal within the town boundaries and several scattered along the road to Cangas de Onís.

In summer up to six buses a day come from Cangas de Onís, and three or so from Oviedo and Gijón.

Lago de Enol & Lago de la Ercina

In summer the almost unbroken line of vehicles crawling up the 12 steep km from Covadonga to the last remaining glacial lakes in the Picos, possibly the most overrun part of the national park, could easily put you off joining the mass lunacy. Don't be deterred. Most of the day-trippers don't make it past patting a few cows' noses near the lakes, so walking here is as pleasant as anywhere else in the Picos.

Lago de Enol is the first lake you strike. There are a *refugio* (☎ 584 85 76; open all year) and a *camping ground* (same ☎) here, and there's another *camping ground* at Lago de la Ercina, further east. When mist descends, the lakes, surrounded by the green pasture and bald rock that characterise this part of the Picos, take on an eerie appearance.

In July and August, five EASA buses a day come up to the lakes from Covadonga.

Walks from the Lakes Two classic and fairly easy trails begin and end at the lakes. The first leads from Lago de la Ercina southeast to the **Vega de Ario**, where there is a *refugio* (for information call ☎ 522 79 75) with room for 40 people (800 ptas for a bunk bed). The last stages around the Vega Robles are marked with splodges of yellow paint, and the reward for about 2½ hours effort is some magnificent views across the Cares gorge to the Macizo Central of the Picos.

The alternative walk takes you roughly south from Lago de Enol to the *Refugio de Vegarronda* (information on ☎ 584 91 54), and on to the **Mirador de Ordiales**, which overlooks a one km sheer drop down into the Valle de Angón. It's about a three hour walk, virtually a stroll along a mule track as far as the refugio, then a little more challenging on up to the mirador.

Up the Río Sella

The road south of Cangas de Onís follows the Río Sella into one of the most extraordinary defiles in Spain, if not all Europe. The Desfiladero de los Beyos road is a remarkable feat of engineering, and links Asturias directly to Castilla y León. The gorge is a dramatic demarcation line of the western extremity of the Picos.

Oseja de Sajambre Once inside the province of León, you soon strike Oseja de Sajambre, an average sort of town in a highly picturesque bend of the road, with magnificent views across the gorge. *Hostal Pontón* (☎ 987-74 03 16), on the main road, charges 3500/4500 ptas for singles/doubles. As well, you can usually find someone renting rooms out privately. There are also a couple of restaurants and grocery shops in the town.

Three days a week in each direction, the Madrid-Llanes bus calls in at Oseja de Sajambre: Sunday, Tuesday and Thursday heading to Llanes via Cangas de Onís and Ribadesella; Monday, Wednesday and Friday to Madrid via Riaño, Sahagún and Valladolid. A separate bus runs to Cangas on Monday, Wednesday and Friday (with extra services in July and August).

Soto de Sajambre For a still better base for walking, you could head six km north-east from Oseja de Sajambre to Soto de Sajambre, considerably higher up and a much prettier village by a freshwater stream. The *Hostal Peñasanta* (☎ 987-74 03 26), Calle Principal, charges 3000/4500 ptas and can organise horse-riding excursions. Here, as in Oseja de Sajambre, you can usually rent a private room.

Various walking possibilities present themselves from Soto de Sajambre, including about a five hour hike north to Amieva, accessible to most walkers, and a more difficult trail eastwards to Posada de Valdeón.

To get from Oseja de Sajambre to Soto de Sajambre without your own vehicle, you hitch.

Embalse de Riaño The road south from Oseja de Sajambre to the beautiful Embalse de Riaño is a worthwhile drive, and the reservoir itself, with its stunning rocky backdrop, is a delight to the eyes. The town of the same name is entirely characterless and, unfortunately, is spreading. The bus between Llanes and Madrid (see Oseja de Sajambre above) stops here, but only runs three times a week in each direction.

MACIZO CENTRAL

The star attraction of the central massif of the Picos is the gorge that divides it from Cornión, its western counterpart. The Garganta del Cares (Cares Gorge) is possibly the most popular walk in the Picos. In summer the trail can be crowded, but the walk is worthwhile, and this part of the Picos has plenty of less heavily tramped walking paths and climbing challenges once you've 'done' the Cares.

You can approach the area from several directions, but for many the easiest will be to come from the north. A good base would be in or near Arenas de Cabrales, if not right up on the trailhead at Poncebos.

Cangas de Onís to Arenas de Cabrales

The AS-114 takes you east out of Cangas along a road that roughly marks off the northern side of the Picos. There are several hotels, hostales and camping grounds along the way.

Carreña Some 25 km along you hit this unassuming town on the Río Casaño, a few km short of the more bustling Arenas de Cabrales and the confluence with the Río Cares. There are a couple of banks in Carreña, but no ATMs. For English-speaking guides to the Picos de Europa, try Spantrek (☎ 584 55 41). Enquire at the Hostal Casa Corro.

There are a few fairly cheap places to stay on the main road here if you have no luck further on in Arenas. *Hostal Cabrales* (☎ 584 50 06) is a friendly little place with singles/doubles for 2500/4000. *Hostal Casa Ramón* (☎ 584 50 39) charges about the same for fairly modern characterless rooms with bath – although in both cases lone travellers will probably pay for double occupancy in the high season. A slight step upwards is the *Hostal Casa Corro* (☎ 584 52 15), which charges 5500 ptas for a double with private bathroom.

Carreña is not the most convenient base if you have no transport, as to reach the Garganta del Cares (the main local attraction) you first have to get to Arenas and then up to the Poncebos trailhead. At least one EASA bus passes through on the way to and from Poncebos. Going up, it calls in at about 11 am coming from Cangas de Onís. The bus back leaves Poncebos at 6.15 pm. Note that this year-round service operates Monday to Friday only. At least three more buses go as far as Arenas de Cabrales from Carreña.

Arenas de Cabrales

Another five km east, Arenas de Cabrales (or just plain Arenas), lies at the confluence of the Río Cares and Río Casaño. The busy main road is lined with hotels, restaurants and bars, and just off it lies a quiet little tangle of tranquil squares and back lanes. Arenas makes as good a base as any for the Picos.

Information The tourist office (☎ 584 52 84), in a kiosk on the main road in the middle of town, opens in summer, at Easter and on long weekends. Opening hours are Tuesday to Sunday from 10 am to 2 pm and 4 to 7 pm, and the staff have quite a lot of information on activities in the area. Albergue de Cabrales (☎ 584 64 45), Plaza del Castañeu, organises 4WD excursions and the like. Its office is open from 8 to 10 am and 6 pm to midnight in summer. Maps of the Picos are available at newsstands. There are a post office and a bank (no ATM) in the main street.

Places to Stay The *Pensión El Castañeu* (☎ 584 65 73), Barrio El Castañeu, is set on a quiet little square just back from the tourist office. Small singles without private bath cost 1500 ptas, and doubles with private bathroom are 4000 ptas. The *Pensión Casa Fermín* (☎ 584 65 66), just around the corner from the tourist office, has doubles for 3000 ptas without private bath and 3500 ptas with. You can bargain for singles outside the high season. *Hotel Naranjo de Bulnes* (☎ 584 65 19), Carretera General s/n, is a comfortable mid-range spot with rooms for 3600/6000 ptas plus IVA.

Places to Eat The *Café San Telmo*, on the main road opposite the *supermercado* in the centre of town, is good for breakfast. You can also get a respectable hamburger there for a main meal. Otherwise, the *Pensión El Castañeu* has a modestly priced restaurant with a varied menu. You could eat well a la carta for less than 2000 ptas. A classier choice is *Casa Victoria*, across the river on the road to Poncebos.

Say Cheese

The Cabrales valley, running along the northern rim of the Picos de Europa and kept fertile by regular rains coming in off the Atlantic, is home to a blue cheese much appreciated by connoisseurs. Untreated cows' milk, particularly that milked over the months of May to July, is mixed with lesser quantities of goats' and sheep's milk. It then takes up to six months for the cheese to mature in caves scattered across the valley. It is the penicillium fungus that gives the cheese its blue hue and a creamy consistency – not to mention a rather strong odour. In this case the bite is every bit as powerful as the olfactory bark, as a good Cabrales cheese tends to have considerable kick. Every August, Arenas de Cabrales hosts a 'cultural week' to celebrate cheese. Apart from the inevitable mutual back-slapping about how great the cheese is, and the predictable cheese tastings, there are exhibitions and folkloric musical performances. Similar cheeses made elsewhere in the Picos include the *picón*, made in Treviso. ∎

For drinks and a little *movida*, the *Sidrería La Palma* at the eastern end of town is one of the best places. *Disco Xana*, across the road from the Café San Telmo, is about the only late-night dancing alternative.

Getting There & Away There are one or two buses in the summer months between Arenas and Llanes on the coast. Otherwise, four regular buses run west to Cangas de Onís (from where you can push on to Oviedo), and two east to Panes (where you can pick up a connection for Potes and Fuente Dé). Buses stop next to the tourist office.

Garganta del Cares

Twelve km of well-maintained track high above the Río Cares between Camarmeña/Poncebos and Caín constitute, perhaps unfortunately, one of the most popular walks in the Picos; in August the experience is akin to London's Oxford Street on a Saturday morning. If you do arrive with the holiday rush, try not to be put off – the walk is a spectacular excursion between two of the Picos' three massifs. If you're feeling fit (or need to get back to your car), it is possible to walk the whole 12 km and back as a (somewhat tiring) day's outing.

Camarmeña A clump of houses barely distinguishable from those belonging to Poncebos up the road, Camarmeña has a fairly decent **mirador** looking out over the Cares valley and surrounding mountainscape. It's signposted, and only a short stroll away.

Poncebos This straggle of buildings is exclusively dedicated to Picos tourism. The closest place to the Garganta del Cares trail for a bed is the *Hostal Garganta del Cares* (☎ 584 50 63), which has doubles without private bath for 3500 ptas and others with for 4600 ptas. Next closest is the *Hotel Mirador de Cabrales* (☎ 584 66 73), with rooms for 6200/7800 ptas plus IVA. Last comes *Hostal Poncebos* (☎ 584 64 47), with adequate rooms for 3500 ptas.

From July to September, an EASA bus runs to Oviedo Monday to Friday at 10.15 am. Another bus leaves at 6.15 pm, doing something of a grand tour to Llanes, Cangas de Onís, Oviedo and other destinations in between. Should you want to, you can get on a 4WD excursion to Caín from Poncebos. The trip takes about 2½ hours and costs 3000 ptas. Ask at the Hostal Garganta del Cares.

Walking up the Cares By doing the walk in this direction, approaching from Poncebos, you save the best until last. The initial stages involve a steady climb upwards through the wide and mostly bare early stages of the gorge. After about 3.5 km you'll hit some abandoned houses and probably a makeshift drinks stand. A little further on you are over the highest point in the walk. Within a km or so you should encounter another drinks stand (they lug the stuff up on horseback).

As you approach the regional boundary with Castilla y León, the gorge becomes narrower and greener, creating greater contrast with the alpine heights above. From the boundary on, the gorge walls are thick with vegetation. The last stages of the walk are

possibly the prettiest, and as you approach the end, descending closer to the valley floor, you pass through a series of low (and wet) tunnels to emerge at the end of the gorge among the meadows of Caín. Along the way, there are several paths – most of them on the slippery side – leading down to the river, which you can follow for stretches.

Caín If coming from the south, the trailhead is at Caín, where the rickety (and picturesque) road from Posada de Valdeón ends. You can stay at *Pensión Casa Cuevas*, which is open all year and charges 2500 ptas for basic rooms with basin. There are at least two other places to stay, plus a couple of bars and restaurants. You'll find further places to stay at the string of villages south of Caín, including Cordiñanes and Posada de Valdeón. No buses make it up to Caín, but you can try Taxi Emiliano Martínez (☎ 987-74 26 09), based in Soto de Valdeón, if you need transport. They operate 4WDs all over the Picos.

Sotres

A side road leads off eastwards at first, then south, from Camarmeña to Sotres, the highest village in the Picos system and the starting point for a number of popular walks. The people at Casa Cipriano arrange 4WD drives to Fuente Dé, the lakes near Covadonga and other destinations, as well as mountain-bike excursions.

Pensión La Perdiz in Sotres (☎ 594 50 11) charges 2500/3500 ptas for singles/doubles with private bath (less without). The two top rooms have balconies and wonderful views. *Casa Cipriano* (☎ 594 50 24), across the road, is a little more expensive. There are two basic *albergues* as well, plus a couple of restaurants and a shop.

You'll need your own car to get here.

Walks around Sotres A common route takes you east to the village of **Treviso** and on to **Urdón**, on the Potes-Panes road. If the fact that this route is paved as far as Treviso reduces its attractiveness, there are options. A path winds off the Treviso trail and snakes down to **La Hermida** in the defile of the same name via the hamlet of Bejes. (If you know what you're up to, you can do it in a 4WD, although the trail is generally only practicable in summer.)

Heading west from Sotres, many walkers choose to march first to **Pandébano** (about 90 minutes) across the open meadows known as the Praderías del Tejo (again, you can actually drive on the rough track). From Pandébano it is possible to see the **Naranjo de Bulnes** (2519 metres), a favourite peak with climbers and one of the highest in the Picos. It is possible to walk from Pandébano to Vega de Urriello, at the foot of the north-west face of the mountain, where there is a refugio. Otherwise, you can continue west to Bulnes (about an hour).

Bulnes is divided into two parts, Barrio del Castillo and La Villa. All the amenities are in La Villa, including a couple of small places to stay and eat. You can also get to Bulnes by walking south-east from Poncebos (about 1¼ hours). Once they get this close, few hikers can resist the temptation of getting even closer to El Naranjo de Bulnes, but be prepared, as the trek from Bulnes is uphill virtually all the way and tough going (it is easier from Pandébano).

From Sotres, another trail can be walked or driven (4WD) south to the Fuente Dé teleférico (see the Fuente Dé & the Teleférico section at the end of this chapter).

From Arenas de Cabrales to Panes

Following the Río Cares eastwards to Panes, there are several alternative places to put up for a night or two. Most of this stretch takes you through a minor but attractive gorge. A particularly pretty spot on a bend in the Cares is *Hostal Casa Julian* (☎ 541 57 79) in Nise-rias, about 15 km east of Arenas. Rooms cost 4000/7500 ptas plus IVA. The restaurant does great salmon dishes. Oviedo-Panes buses call in here.

About eight km further on, you arrive in Panes, something of a minor crossroads on the east-west route from Cantabria across the northern flank of the Picos and the roughly north-south route from the coast to Potes, Fuente Dé and the south-eastern side of the

massifs. It is possibly one of the least inspiring towns in the area, and there is no reason to stay (unless you can't find anything anywhere else).

Autobuses Palomera runs two or three services a day between Santander (Cantabria) and Potes. In Panes these buses stop outside Bar Composta. The trip to Santander takes about 2½ hours. Two EASA buses head from Panes (Bar La Cortina) to Oviedo Monday to Friday. Times are apt to change, but generally there is one each way in the morning and early evening.

EASTERN PICOS
Desfiladero de la Hermida

Things quickly improve when you leave Panes behind and head south along the Río Deva. For about 10 km you remain on Asturian turf, and as the river cuts its way deeper into what quickly becomes a ravine, you cross into Cantabria and arrive at the little hamlet of **La Hermida**, which lends its name to the narrow defile. There's not much here but the bubbling stream of the Deva, the Picos looming to the west and a trio of hostales. A narrow, winding road off east to Puentenansa, deep inside Cantabria, makes for a pretty, alternative route if you are heading away from the Picos by car or motorcycle – or indeed a fine and little-used first approach from the east (see the South of Santander section earlier in this chapter). To the west, a 4WD track (generally only viable in summer) heads to Sotres. Panes-Potes buses stop at La Hermida.

Lebeña About seven km further south from La Hermida, this spot warrants calling in. A couple of km to the east off the N-621 main road lies the 9th century Mozarabic Iglesia de Nuestra Señora de Lebeña. The horseshoe arches in the bell tower are a telltale sign of the architectural style of the place – not often seen this far north in Spain. That the bell tower is separate from the main body of the church also gives it away. Inside, the floral motifs on the columns are Visigothic, while below the main retablo lies a Celtic stone engraving. A couple of wooden sculptures were stolen from the church in 1993. They say the big olive tree outside was planted 1000 years ago.

If you want to stay in this peaceful location, the *Casa de Labranza* (☎ 942-73 09 44), on the main road from Panes to Potes, charges 4900 ptas for good doubles with private bath. Out of season you can negotiate down for single occupancy.

Panes-Potes buses stop in Lebeña.

Potes

A substantial town, somewhat overrun in peak periods but with quite some charm in the old centre (much restored after suffering considerable damage during the civil war), Potes is a popular staging post for walkers at the south-eastern edge of the Picos. Most of its 1500 inhabitants ride on tourism's coat-tails.

Information The tourist office (☎ 73 07 87), Plaza de Jesús de Monasterio, is open daily in summer from 9 am to 2 pm and 4 to 7 pm. There are several banks with ATMs, and a couple of big supermarkets for stocking up on supplies before heading into the mountains. You're in Cantabria here, so the telephone code is ☎ 942.

Things to See Right in the centre of the town, the squat **Torre del Infantado** is impossible to mistake. Built as a defensive tower in the 14th century, it now houses government offices, having served for a long time as a prison. The **Iglesia de San Vicente Mártir**, built at the same time and deconsecrated in the 19th century, is a nice example of rustic Gothic architecture.

Activities Wentura (☎ & fax 73 21 61), Calle de la Independencia 10, can help organise paragliding at Fuente Dé, horse riding, mountain-bike excursions and walks.

Places to Stay *Camping La Viorna* (☎ 73 20 21) is about one km from Potes en route to Fuente Dé (take the turn-off for the Monasterio de Santo Toribio). It has its own bar and pool.

A cheap place in town with spacious rooms, some looking over the Torre del Infantado, is the *Hostal Lombraña* (☎ 73 05 19), Calle del Sol 2. Singles/doubles with private bath cost 2600/3500 ptas, and there are slightly cheaper rooms without their own bathrooms. *Restaurante El Fogón de Cus*, Calle de Capitán Palacios, has a little pensión upstairs with small but spotless, pretty rooms. The three singles and three doubles here cost around 2500/3500 ptas. The pick of the bunch is *Casa Cayo* (☎ 73 01 50), which has tiny but lovely rooms smelling of timber and in some cases overlooking the river. They start at 2800/4000 ptas. *Hostal Rafa* (☎ 73 09 24), around the corner from the post office on the main road, has attractively furnished rooms for 2000/3400 ptas. If you're looking for more class, *Hotel Picos de Valdecoro* (☎ 73 00 25; fax 73 03 15), which was refurbished in 1992, charges 4000/7400 ptas. It's at the entrance to town coming from Panes.

Places to Eat The *Restaurante El Fogón de Cus* has a good-value set menu for 1150 ptas; go for the grilled trout (trucha a la plancha). *Casa Cayo*, Calle Cántabra 6, has an excellent restaurant. You can eat well for about 2000 ptas a head; try the tarta de limón for dessert.

Getting There & Away Up to three Palomera buses run north to Panes and on to Santander. You can get off at Panes and connect for a bus to Arenas de Cabrales, Cangas de Onís or even Oviedo. Take the earliest departure to have a hope of making a connection on the same day. In summer, two daily buses go from Potes to Fuente Dé. A bus between Santander and León passes through daily. Information and tickets can be had at the Hostería Peñasagra, next to the Hotel Picos de Europa.

From Potes to Fuente Dé

Turieno The Liébana area, of which Potes is in a sense the 'capital', was repopulated with Christians from the meseta by Alfonso I, putting it on the front line between Muslim

Spain and what little there was at this stage of its Christian opponent. The **Monasterio de Santo Toribio de Liébana**, in the hamlet of Turieno (signposted off the road to Fuente Dé outside Potes), was built at this time, although the present austere Gothic church dates from 1256. Since the 8th century, the monastery has housed the Lignum Crucis, a purported piece of Christ's cross supposedly transported from Jerusalem by bishop Toribio de Astorga in the 9th century. The relic was inserted in a crucifix of gold-plated silver, and according to the tradition contains the hole left by the nail that passed through Christ's left hand. It remains an extraordinary magnet for the faithful.

Camping La Isla (☎ 942-73 08 96) is just outside Turieno and four km from Potes. There are a few small hostales here too. Further up the road at Quintana, 5.5 km from Potes, you could try *Camping San Pelayo* (☎ 942-73 30 87). It has a swimming pool. Between here and Cosgaya, about 10 km closer to Fuente Dé, you will find several other possible places to bunk down, and it is possible to pitch a tent in Los Llanos.

Potes-Fuente Dé buses call in here.

Cosgaya The small town of Cosgaya, about 16 km from Potes, is a nice spot to rest up. *Hostal Mesón Cosgaya* (☎ 942-73 30 47) has singles/doubles without own bath for 2500/3500 ptas and doubles with bath for 4500 ptas. In a rather classier range are the two hotels *Del Oso* (☎ 942-73 30 18). The two star hotel has rooms for 6400/8000 ptas in July-September, while its three star counterpart over the road charges 7900/8900 ptas. Add IVA. Prices drop 1000 ptas on all rooms during the rest of the year. Potes-Fuente Dé buses call in here.

Espinama This is the last stop of any significance before Fuente Dé, and for most people's money and taste probably makes a more appealing base if you have your own transport. You could follow a trail leading north of Espinama to reach the Refugio de Aliva. It's an 11 km uphill hike.

There's a surprising choice of decent places to stay here, all on or just off the main road through town – you can't miss them. *Hotel Máximo* (☎ 942-73 66 03) has rooms for 3000/5000 ptas and is possibly the pick of the crop; it has a good restaurant. *Hostal Remoña* (☎ 942-73 66 05) has doubles for 4000 ptas. One of the first places you pass on the way in from Potes is *Habitaciones Sebrango* (☎ 942-73 66 15), which offers doubles only for 3500 ptas, or 4000 ptas with private bathroom. There are self-contained apartments for 6000 ptas, which could be good value. Another attractive option is *Hostal Puente Deva* (☎ 942-73 66 58), with rooms for 2700/4000 ptas. *Hostal Nevandi* (☎ 942-73 66 08) has good rooms for 3000/4500 ptas. The latter two and Hotel Máximo all have restaurants.

Potes-Fuente Dé buses call in here.

Fuente Dé & the Teleférico

At 1078 metres, Fuente Dé lies at the foot of the stark southern wall of the Macizo Central. In four minutes the teleférico here whisks people 762 metres to the top of that wall, from where walkers and climbers can make their way deeper into the central massif.

Most day-trippers just like the buzz of heading up and having a bit of a wander once at the top. Be warned that during the peak season (especially August) you can wait for hours at the bottom before your numbered ticket comes up (numbers are called out on a PA system). Coming down again, you simply join the queue and wait – OK on a sunny summer's day, but otherwise a little unpleasant if the queue's long.

Day return tickets cost a hefty 1200 ptas, and the service basically runs from 9 am until shortly before sunset (8 pm in summer).

Walking & Climbing

Walk to the *Hotel Refugio de Aliva* from the top of the teleférico, or catch one of the private 4WD shuttles that do the trip for 250 ptas per person. The refuge has its own restaurant and even a solarium, but opens only from June to

September. From there, two somewhat more exacting trails descend into the valley that separates the central massif from its eastern cousin. The first winds its way 11 km south to Espinama, while the other will get you north to Sotres. On the way you pass through the hamlet of Vegas de Sotres, from where a trail departs westwards to the Naranjo de Bulnes (see under Sotres earlier in this chapter). 4WDs also cover this route if there is a demand.

Other possibilities for the well-prepared include climbing the Peña Vieja (2613 metres) and making your way across the massif to the Naranjo de Bulnes. This requires proper equipment and experience – Peña Vieja has the sad record of having claimed more climbers' lives than any other in the Picos.

Less exacting is the trail leading north-west, passing below the Peña Vieja by marked trails to the Cabaña Verónica *refugio* (about two hours), near the Horcados Rojos. From there hikers can proceed to the Vega de Urriello, at the base of the Naranjo de Bulnes.

Paragliding Alas Cantabria (☎ 942-73 61 25; fax 27 56 12), actually based in Vega de Liébana, organises beginner flights on paragliders. Prices for one/two/four days are 6000/10,000/20,000 ptas plus insurance. Beginners go accompanied by an instructor.

Eagle Show If it looks like you'll have a long wait for the teleférico, check to see if the **Montaña de las Águilas** is in operation. At the time of writing, the people organising this performance by low-flying eagles, buzzards and other birds of prey were putting on a show at 1, 4 and 6.30 pm (entry 500 ptas). It's a rare chance to see these birds, including the majestic golden eagle, trained to swoop in over the audience and pick up their reward of meat. The organisers use the money to promote rehabilitation of injured birds and increase awareness of the dangers many of these species face.

Places to Stay & Eat There is an adequate camping ground, *El Redondo*, about 100 metres from the Montaña de las Águilas, along with refugio-style accommodation for 20. Otherwise there are no cheap choices. *Hotel Rebeco* (☎ 942-73 66 01) has singles/ doubles/triples for 4800/6800/8400 ptas plus IVA. It also has a restaurant. The *Parador de Fuente Dé* (☎ 942-73 00 01; fax 73 02 12) is still more expensive.

Apart from some overpriced tourist cafés and the hotel restaurants, you have no real dining options here either.

Getting There & Away There are two buses daily between Fuente Dé and Potes in summer.

Galicia

If the regions of Spain were identified by their dominating colour, Galicia's might well be green tinged with grey. In the same way that Andalucía wears its dazzling whitewash and Castilla-La Mancha bathes in the burnt red and dusty olive green of its sun-scorched plains, so the characteristic granite and ubiquitous slate rooftops on a verdant rural background seem symbolic of Galicia. Doubtless, the often inclement weather contributes to the impression.

Battered by the Atlantic, the often wild coastline is sliced up and down its length by *rías*, a series of majestic estuaries. Separated from the meseta by the Cordillera Cantábrica in the east, Galicia is bounded to the south by the Portuguese border and the region's main river, the Río Miño. Frenetic deforestation has, unfortunately, stripped the region of its indigenous trees, which have mostly been replaced by eucalyptus.

Inhabited since at least 3000 BC, by the Iron Age Galicia was populated by Celts living in *castros*, villages of circular stone huts surrounded by a defensive perimeter. The arrival in the 1st century BC of the Romans, who seem to have mingled tolerably well with the locals, gave the area its name: Gallaecia. The Muslim invasion barely touched Galicia, and the big event in the area's medieval history was the 'rediscovery' of the grave of St James the Apostle in 813, at what would become Santiago de Compostela. The site became a rallying symbol for the Reconquista, but by the time this was completed, Galicia had become an impoverished backwater in which the centralist-minded Catholic Monarchs Fernando and Isabel had already begun to supplant the local tongue and traditions with Castilian methods and language. The first signs of the Rexurdimento, a reawakening of a Galician consciousness, did not surface until late in the 19th century, and then suffered a 40-year interruption during the Franco era.

HIGHLIGHTS

- Completing the Camino de Santiago walk from the French border to Santiago de Compostela
- The magnificent Catedral de Santiago de Compostela
- Some of Spain's best and most varied seafood, washed down with a crisp Ribeiro white
- Exploring the *rías* (estuaries) along the coast
- Gazing over the Atlantic from the heights of Cabo Ortegal and Cabo Finisterre
- *Pimientos de Padrón*
- Stretching out on the beaches around Cedeira
- Catching a *curro*, or round-up of wild horses
- The pretty town of Tuy, right on the Río Miño and just across a bridge from the Portuguese fortress town of Valença

Rural and still much ignored by the rest of Spain, Galicia remains in many senses another country. Rather than hope for any good from the centre, Galicians have traditionally looked to the sea. Fishing has long been a mainstay, and the region's seamen have cast their nets far and wide, at least until now. With world fish stocks falling and international conflict over fishing rights growing, Galicia's fleet finds itself staring at an uncertain future. Much as in Cornwall, smuggling is an integral part of Galicia's seafaring lore, but the growth of drug-running from South

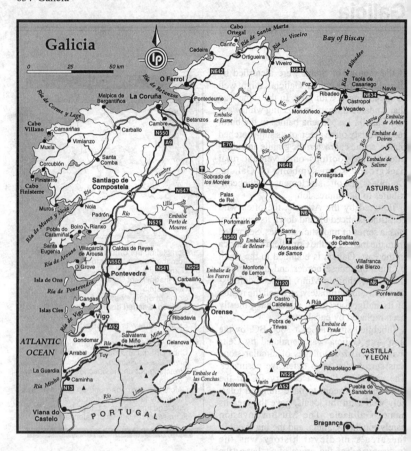

America has led to fears that Galicia is becoming 'another Sicily'.

Most travellers in Galicia make a beeline for Santiago de Compostela, and no-one can blame them. This melancholy medieval city-shrine is surely one of Spain's most engaging urban centres. Beyond it, however, lies plenty more. The popular Rías Bajas and less well known Rías Altas are dotted with coves, beaches and enticing villages, and you'll see some of Spain's wildest coast towards Cabo Ortegal, in the north-west. Of the numerous other towns that could go on to a must list, Pontevedra stands out.

When stomachs grumble in Galicia, thoughts turn to seafood. Although some may feel the quality is higher in Portugal, there is no doubt that you can eat better here than in much of the rest of Spain. And as a rule, eating out is cheaper in Galicia than in much of the rest of the country. *Pulpo* (octopus) is a staple in Galicia, but there are plenty of options (see the boxed aside 'Food Fare' in this chapter). Even more so than in neighbouring Asturias, Galicia's biggest export has traditionally been labour, in particular to Argentina – something reflected in its modern eating habits. Nowhere else in

Travelling in Tongues

Long suppressed during the Franco years (strange, really, since Franco was born in Galicia), the Galician language (*galego* or, in Spanish, *gallego*) sounds much like a cross between Castilian Spanish and Portuguese. It is widely spoken and in recent years has been pushed as the main local language. News broadcasts are often in Galician.

Although the issue of Spanish vs Galician usage is not as politically charged as the parallel debate in Cataluña, it does present difficulties. Increasingly, Galician is used in road signs. Map and atlas publishers, however, all go their own way. A further complication is the existence of apparent discrepancies even in local spelling. Thus the town of La Guardia (Spanish) becomes A Guardia, A Guarda or A Garda. In this chapter we favour Spanish spellings for cities and other geographical features, but not exclusively. For street names and the like we generally follow local usage, leaning towards Galician. As a rule, we name monuments such as churches (*iglesia* in Spanish, *igrexa* in Galician) and monasteries (*monasterio* vs *mosteiro*) in Spanish.

A few clues to those who know Spanish: 'x' in Galician generally replaces 'g' or 'j' (so Junta becomes Xunta and Juan is Xuan), and is pronounced like the 's' in pleasure; 'o' replaces 'ue' (puente becomes ponte); while the ending 'eiro' replaces 'ero' and 'erio'. Common words you'll come across include *praza* (*plaza* in Spanish), *praia* (*playa*) and perhaps *xeral* (*general*) – as in Hospital Xeral. ■

Spain will meat-eaters feel so happy, for this is *churrasco* territory – slabs of grilled meat or ribs accompanied by a slightly tangy sauce.

Galicia produces some fine wines. The Ribeiro wines, mostly from around Ribadavia, count among their number a clean, crisp white and a decent red. Mencia is also a pleasing red. For a robust white, the Condado label is recommended – their grapes are grown around the lower Miño. Rosal is generally a more expensive drop from La Guardia, while the Albariño is considered the prince of Galician tipples. Occasionally you'll be served wine in small, shallow ceramic cups – cute, but potentially wasteful if you've already had a few.

Always served in more conventional glasses is Estrella de Galicia beer, brewed in La Coruña and about the best Spain has to offer. Finally, the Galicians brew several versions of *orujo*, a breath-catching firewater along the lines of *aguardiente* (eau de vie to some).

Galicia has only recently managed to draw Madrid's attention to the poor state of its road network, and EU funds are now being poured into improvements across the region – something you will not fail to notice. Still, opportunities abound for getting lost. Some minor roads and many villages simply aren't marked on even good atlases, and meaningful road signs are as scarce as hen's teeth.

Santiago de Compostela

There can be few cities in the world as beautiful as Santiago founded on the basis of so preposterous a story. The corpse of St James the Apostle (Santiago Apóstol), the myth relates, was transported to the far side of Spain by two disciples after his execution in Jerusalem. They landed at Padrón and, so they say, managed to bury James in a spot about 20 km inland.

In 813 the grave was supposedly rediscovered by a bishop following a guiding star (hence the second part of the city's name, a corruption of the Latin Campus Stellae, or Field of the Star). The saint's purported grave became a welcome rallying symbol for rump Christian Spain, and work began on a church above his remains. The myth gained strength in the following centuries, and so Santiago grew to become a quietly impressive city (it counts about 90,000 inhabitants today), improving with age and the various architectural additions made after the initial wave of enthusiasm for the pilgrimage in the 12th century.

Apart from the undisputed splendour of its gold-tinged (at least when the sun's out) monuments and the charm of its medieval streets, Santiago is a lively place, full of bars and, in summer especially, offering a packed programme of concerts, theatre and exhibitions. This, the city's beauty and a renewed interest in the Camino de Santiago no doubt all helped raise its profile enough for Santiago to be chosen as one of nine Cultural Capitals across Europe for the year 2000.

History

Although the history of Santiago de Compostela virtually begins with the St James the Apostle story, the area had long been inhabited by Visigoths, Romans and Celts. In any event, Alfonso II, the Asturian king, was soon on the spot to have the first church erected in honour of the saintly discovery. By 1075, when the Romanesque basilica was begun and the pilgrimage was becoming a major European phenomenon, Santiago had already been raided and sacked on various occasions by the Normans and Muslims. The worldly-wise Bishop Diego Gelmírez added numerous churches to the city in the 12th century, a period when homage paid to St James brought in a flood of funding, which was used to build much of the present city. The following couple of centuries were marked by internecine squabbling between rival nobles, dampened by the conclusion of the Reconquista and greater attention paid by Fernando and Isabel to internal affairs. After backing the wrong horse and siding with the Carlists in the 1830s, Santiago slipped into the background. Only since the early 1980s has the city, as capital of Galicia and a rediscovered tourist target, really begun to emerge from the shadows.

Orientation

Santiago's compact *casco antiguo* (old town centre) is virtually all pedestrianised. The RENFE train station is about a 15-minute walk downhill from the centre, while the Estación de Autobuses lies about the same distance away to the north-east. Local city buses pass both and take you as far as the main road running along the southern fringe of the old town. Most of the monuments, accommodation, main tourist office, banks and the like can be found in the casco, whose more important streets include Rúa Nova, Rúa do Vilar and Rúa do Franco.

Information

Tourist Office The tourist office (☎ 58 40 81), Rúa do Vilar 43, is open from 10 am to 2 pm and 4 to 7 pm daily. The staff have surprisingly little information. There is also an information kiosk on Praza de Galicia (handy if you arrive by train). It opens daily from 10 am to 2 pm and 5 to 8 pm.

Money There are banks dotted about the centre of town. A handy one is the Central Hispano at Rúa do Vilar 30-32.

American Express (☎ 58 70 00) is in the Ultratur travel agency at Avenida Figueroa 6. It opens Monday to Friday from 9.30 am to 2 pm and 4.30 to 7 pm, and Saturday from 10 am to 12.30 pm.

Post & Communications The main post office (Correos y Telégrafos) lines Travesía de Fonseca, and is open from 8.30 am to 8.30 pm. The postcode is 15700. The telephone office (Telefónica) is in the same building. It opens only Monday to Friday from 8.30 am to 1.30 pm, but there are several other phone offices, and plenty of pay phones, scattered about town. The telephone code is ☎ 981.

Oficina de Acogida del Peregrino People who have walked all or part of the Camino de Santiago as pilgrims (see the boxed aside in this chapter) and want the certificate to prove it can head for this 'pilgrims' reception office' (☎ 56 24 19) in the Casa del Deán Rúa do Vilar 1. It is open daily from 10 am to 2 pm and 4.30 to 7.30 pm.

Medical & Emergency Services The main police station (*comisaría*) is on Avenida Rodrigo de Padrón – call ☎ 092 in an emergency. The Hospital Xeral is north-west of the town centre on Rúa das Galerías. There is a night pharmacy where Rúa das Orfas meets Canton de Toral. If it's not open, the week's rota for night service is posted in most pharmacies.

Santiago de Compostela

Catedral del Apóstol

Those who have chosen to trudge the Camino de Santiago must be assaulted by a great mix of emotions on finally entering Praza do Obradoiro to behold the lavish baroque façade of the Catedral del Apóstol's western flank. Disappointment is rarely one of them. Prior to its construction in the 18th century, the less overwhelming but artistically unparalleled **Pórtico de la Gloria** (Porta da Gloria) was the first scene to greet weary pilgrims. The bulk of the Romanesque cathedral was built from 1075 to 1211. Much of the 'bunting' – the domes, statues, pyramids and endless flourishes – came later.

No doubt, construction of the baroque icing on the essentially Romanesque cake muted the impact of the portico, which was put in place in the 12th century. But it has also been something of a blessing, protecting the sculptures of Maestro Mateo and his team from the elements. The main figure in the central archway is Christ risen, at his feet and hands the four Evangelists, and around them angels with the crown of thorns and other instruments connected with Jesus' passion. Below Christ's feet is represented St James (Santiago), and the tradition says that below him is the figure of Maestro Mateo. Bump your head on it three times and you're supposed to acquire some of his genius; the problem is that his bust appears, if at all, on the other side, facing the altar, while the popular, but mistaken, head belongs to Samson. The other tradition calls for a brief prayer of thanksgiving as you place your fingers in the five holes created near Samson's head by the repetition of this very act by millions of faithful over the centuries.

The remarkably life-like figures that dominate the columns on the right side of the portico are the remaining Apostles, while those to the left represent prophets of the Old Testament. Almost nothing remains of the portico's original colouring.

Approaching the churrigueresque **Altar Mayor**, you may notice an opening and stairs on the left side. Head down here to contemplate what you are assured is the tomb of St James. You emerge on the right side, and a little further on see another entrance with steps going up. Follow the crowds up and embrace the 13th century statue of St James. There was a time when pilgrims would lift a gold crown from the statue's head and put it on their own, exchanging it briefly for their own more humble hats.

With luck, you may catch one of the special masses where the greatest dispenser of incense in the world, the *botafumeiro*, is swung heftily across the length of the transept by an expert team of *tiraboleiros* using an ingenious pulley system – an unforgettable sight.

You really need to make more than one visit to cope with the cathedral's remarkable riches. To the right of the Pórtico de la Gloria is the entrance to the Museo Catedralicio. Entrance costs 400 ptas and includes a visit to the *cripta* (crypt), *tesoro* (treasury) and *claustro* (cloister). The museum is spread over several floors and has an impressive collection of religious art, including Romanesque sculptures, tapestries, a library, and not a few images of St James. The main item of the tesoro (in the Capilla de San Fernando, on the south side of the nave) is the 16th century silver and gold-plated processional monstrance. The cloister replaced the Romanesque original in the 16th century, and is a successful mix of Late Gothic and plateresque.

The cathedral is open all day, but the museum, cloister and so on are open only from 10 am to 1.30 pm and 4 to 7.30 pm; closed in the afternoon on public holidays.

Palacio de Gelmírez

On the cathedral's left flank, the Palacio de Gelmírez was built for the bishop of the same name in 1120 and subsequently altered. There is not an awful lot left to this Gothic adjunct, but worth seeking out is the Sala de Banquetes, the main dining hall. The exquisite little busts around the walls depict happy feasters and musicians, as well as the odd king and juggler. Diego Gelmírez's biggest contribution to Santiago was to resuscitate the myth of the Battle of Clavijo. Supposedly St James appeared to Ramiro I and joined him in this fiesta of Moor-slaying in 844, for which the grateful king promised to dedicate the first fruits of every harvest to the saint. Few historians believe the battle ever took place, but Gelmírez turned the myth into one of the city's biggest revenue sources for centuries after his demise.

The palacio is open daily from 10 am to 1.30 pm and 4 to 7.30 pm; closed in the afternoon on public holidays. Entry costs 150 ptas.

Around the Catedral

However much the cathedral dominates the heart of Santiago and the attention of its visitors, the area around it is rich in other architectural jewels. The northern end of Praza do Obradoiro is closed off by the Renaissance **Hostal de los Reyes Católicos**, built by Fernando and Isabel with some of the loot from Granada to shelter the poor and infirm. It now shelters the well-off instead, as a *parador*, one of the chain of classy hotels. You can walk in, but probably won't get much further than the bar and restaurant. Fronting the west side of the square is the elegant 18th century **Pazo de Raxoi**, in the French neoclassical taste and housing the *ayuntamiento* (city council). In earlier days its various parts served as a prison and a residence for choir boys.

A stroll right around the cathedral takes you through a series of some of the city's most inviting squares. To the south is **Praza das Praterías** (Silversmiths Square), the centre of which is marked by the Fuente de los Caballos (1829), a nice touch. Up the steps is the only original façade of the cathedral, a Romanesque masterpiece. Following the cathedral walls you enter Praza da Quintana, split into two parts by a low staircase. The lower part, 'dos mortos', was once a cemetery. Facing onto it is the Puerta Santa of the cathedral, opened only in Holy Years when the Feast of St James falls on a Sunday. Keep following the walls and you will reach Praza da Azabachería. Rising up on the far side is the huge Benedictine **Monasterio de San Martiño Pinario**. The classical façade hides a couple of extensive cloisters inside, built in the 17th century. Behind them, and best approached from Praza de San Martiño, is the monastery's church, on which construction began in 1611. It is the most captivating church in Santiago after the cathedral, although for some tastes the florid baroque decoration, particularly the 1733 *retablo*, is a little overwhelming. The church's towers were never finished, their construction apparently blocked by officials of the cathedral anxious not to see any shadows cast on its greater glory.

Beyond the Old City

Just north-east of the old city, the former Convento de Santo Domingo stands out, an impressive baroque structure that now houses the **Museo do Pobo Galego**. The most singular feature is the triple spiral staircase, off which lie rooms of the museum. These contain a variety of displays on different aspects of Galician life, tradition and arts, covering everything from the fishing industry through music and crafts to traditional costumes. The museum is open Monday to Saturday from 10 am to 1 pm and 4 to 7 pm. Entry is free. Facing it is the **Centro Galego de Arte Contemporánea**, open Tuesday to Sunday from 11 am to 8 pm. It hosts temporary exhibitions of modern art, and entry is generally free.

About one km south down Rúa do Patio de Madres stands, in precarious fashion (it suffers a pronounced tilt), the Romanesque **Colegiata de Santa María la Real de Sar**. Part of the beautiful cloister, supposedly designed by Maestro Mateo, can still be admired, and there is a small museum containing mainly religious art and Romanesque sculpture.

Organised Tours

One-day bus tours are organised through various hotels and travel agents. They are pretty busy affairs, designed for those with more money than time, covering the Rías Bajas, Rías Altas, Vigo and Portugal, and

GALICIA

Finisterre. Each tour costs 5200 ptas, including lunch. Enquire at Vie Viajes (☎ 56 44 19), Rúa do Hórreo 44.

Special Events

July is the month to be in Santiago. The 25th is the Feast of St James and simultaneously Galicia's 'national' day. The night before, Praza do Obradoiro comes alight with the *fogo do Apóstolo*, a spectacular fireworks display that dates to the 17th century and culminates in the *quemada de la fachada mudéjar*. This spectacular performance's days may be numbered, as fears are growing for the safety of the cathedral's real façade, before which the one to be burned is erected. Apart from the processions and lots of people getting about in traditional costume, the town authorities organise numerous concerts, notably in Praza da Quintana, and other cultural activities.

Places to Stay

Santiago is crawling with accommodation. In the casco, half the bars advertise rooms for rent *(habitaciones)*, and the number of teeny hostelries *(hospedajes)* should be reassuring. Touts frequently intercept new arrivals at the train and bus stations. All this means that you should rarely have trouble finding a place to stay. The preference is to stay in the heart of the casco, but if you have trouble finding something, there are plenty of options on and around Praza de Galicia, between the old town and the train station.

Places to Stay – bottom end

Camping There are several camping grounds on the road to La Coruña, but none of them are close.

Hospedajes & Hostales As you wander into the casco from the train station, a quiet option is *Hospedaje La Tita* (☎ 58 39 81), Rúa Nova 46, with clean singles/doubles for 1500/3000 ptas. For the same price and a view of Praza da Quintana, head for *Hospedaje Lalín* (☎ 58 21 23). The rooms are a little basic and light sleepers might find it *too* central. A quieter and cheaper alternative with better rooms – especially if you can get a top-floor double – is *Hospedaje Fores* (☎ 57 08 11), Callejón de Don Abril Ares 7, with rooms starting at 1300/2400 ptas.

Hospedaje Mera (☎ 58 38 67), Porta da Peña 15, has decent singles/doubles/triples, some with pleasant views, for 3000/4200/5000 ptas. Virtually across the road at No 4, *Hostal Girasol* (☎ 56 62 87) has reliable doubles for 3000 ptas, or 4000 ptas with private bath. *Hostal Real* (☎ 56 66 56), Rúa da Caldererta 49, has good-sized singles/doubles without private bath for 2000/3000 ptas.

A particularly attractive option is the *Hostal Pazo de Agra* (☎ 58 90 45), Rúa da Caldererta 37. Singles/doubles without private bath in this homely and spotless old house start at 2000/4000 ptas. There is also an attic double (watch your head) for 3000 ptas. Rooms with private bath cost 3000/4500 ptas. Enquire at Restaurante Zíngara, Rúa de Cardenal Payá. *Hostal Suso* (☎ 58 66 11), Rúa do Vilar 65, is popular, with rooms for 3000/4200 ptas – less in the low season.

Places to Stay – middle

At *Hostal Barbantes* (☎ 58 10 77), Rúa do Franco 3, you are paying for the lovely position overlooking the little Praza de Fonseca. Singles/doubles/triples cost 3500/5000/6000 ptas.

Hostal Seminario Mayor (☎ 58 30 08), Praza da Inmaculada 5, has somewhat bare rooms but what some might consider a one-off experience – to stay inside the Monasterio de San Martiño Pinario. The rooms cost 3000/5000/6500 ptas, mostly with private bath. Rooms are only available from July to September, when student lodgers are away.

Along the same lines but a step or two up in class and comfort is *Hogar San Francisco* (☎ 58 16 00), in the monastery of the same name, which has doubles starting at 5000/7600 ptas plus IVA.

Cheaper and in a lovely position just below the Carballeira de Santa Susana is the *Hostal Alameda* (☎ 58 81 00) Campo de San Clemente 32, with doubles for 4550 ptas plus IVA, or 6000 ptas with private bath.

Places to Stay – top end

Parador The *Hostal de los Reyes Católicos* (☎ 58 22 00; fax 59 02 87) is itself one of Santiago's prime monuments, closing off the northern flank of Praza do Obradoiro (see Things to See above). In keeping with its exalted past, guests pay rather splendid prices: 23,000 ptas plus IVA for a double – but what a double!

Places to Eat

The do-it-yourself crowd should visit Santiago's majestic *mercado* (market), along Rúa de Santo Agostiño in the south-east of the casco.

It is quite possible to eat well for less than 1000 ptas in one of several little places tucked away around town. The *Restaurante*

O'Rincon, Rúa da Algalia de Arriba 21, is a tiny spot where you'll get simple but filling raciones for a few hundred pesetas. For a full and solid meal with wine and dessert for less than 1000 ptas, try *Restaurante Cuatro Vientos*, Rúa de Santa Cristina 19. Popular with readers of travel guides is *Casa Manolo*, Rúa Travesa 27, which has a good value set meal for 600 ptas without drinks.

A couple of modestly priced places that come up with some good dishes are *Restaurante Entre Rúas* and *Restaurante A Tulla*, next to each other in the tiny square on Entrerúas, a laneway linking Rúa do Vilar and Rúa Nova. You should get away with around 1500 ptas, and while the latter is marginally better, the ternera rellena in the Entre Rúas is very tasty. Likewise the home-made flan for dessert.

For a fresh fish grill (parrillada de pescados), head for *Restaurante El Hispano*, Rúa de Santo Agostiño, just opposite the market – you can't get much closer to the raw materials.

A longtime institution in Santiago de Compostela is *Restaurante Asesino*, Praza da

---

Galician Food Fare
Here is an introductory vocabulary to Galician food:

almejas clams
anguilas small eel fished from the Río Miño
caldo gallego broth with cabbage or turnip, potato and usually a token clump of meat
caldeirada de pescado a hotpot of different types of fish and potato
chinchos various tiny fried fish
chipirones chopped squid cooked in its own ink
chocos/choquitos a variation on the squid theme
cigalas crayfish
empanada/empanadilla something broadly along the lines of a pasty. The most common version is done with tuna and tomato, and is very tasty. *Empanada a la gallega* contains *chorizo* (sausage), onion and occasionally other vegetables. *Empanadilla* is the bite-size snack version.
gambas prawns; most commonly done *al ajillo* (with garlic) and *a la plancha* (lightly grilled)
mejillones orange mussels, mostly bred on the odd web-like platforms you'll see all over most of the rías
pimientos de Padrón small green peppers cooked in loads of garlic, with the occasional seriously hot one thrown in
pulpo a la gallega *the* Galician dish; basically boiled octopus bits
vieiras scallops
xoubas/xoubiñas sardines
zorza a local equivalent of kebabs ■

GALICIA

Universidade 16. There's no sign, and although the food is good, prices have lifted well out of the budget bracket.

A good place to get into a tasty churrasco is *Parrillada La Gaucha*, Rúa da Rosa 42, in the happening area of the new town known as El Ensanche. After your ribs you could hit the tiles in the surrounding pubs.

On a slightly pricier level, *Restaurante Fornos*, Rúa do Hórreo 24 (near Praza de Galicia), has a solid local reputation.

If you want to really splash out, Avenida de Rosalía de Castro is home to a couple of prime targets. *Casa Vilas*, at No 88, is a staunch bastion of the best in Galician cuisine. Various characters, from Fidel Castro to Pope John Paul II, have tucked in here. You're looking at 4000 ptas a head at least. Similarly expensive is the nouvelle cuisine specialist *Toñi Vicente*, at No 24.

For takeaway dessert or a daytime sweet fix, pop in to *Casa Mora*, Rúa do Vilar 60.

Cafés As a general rule, a cup of coffee will not cost you more than about 150 ptas wherever you go, although close to half that price is the going rate in the simple bars. A breakfast of fruit juice, coffee and toast can be had for about 300 ptas in the smaller places. *Café Literarios*, on Praza da Quintana, is a laid-back place in a great location. They do a couple of decent breakfast deals. The brasher sidewalk cafés along Rúa do Franco and Rúa do Vilar and on the main squares charge up to double this just for coffee and juice.

Virtually on the border of the old and new towns, the *Cafetería Derby*, Rúa das Orfas 29, is something of an institution and one of Santiago's oldest cafés.

Entertainment

Try to get hold of *Compostelán*, a local monthly student news rag. It has a fairly comprehensive local listings guide in the back covering restaurants, bars and nightlife in general.

Bars If you want to hear traditional Celtic music, Galician style, head for *Café das Crechas*, Vía Sacra 3. Sometimes it's live,

---

❖ ❖ ❖ ❖ ❖ ❖ ❖ ❖ ❖ ❖ ❖ ❖

Dancing to Their Own Tune

Perhaps it is in Galicia's rich tradition of folk music that the Galicians' Celtic strains come most vividly to the fore. Although the sounds and rhythms differ noticeably from those played by their cousins in Brittany, Ireland and Scotland, the links between them all are impossible to deny. Most readily recognisable is the *gaita* (Galician bagpipes), of which there are several versions. Summertime in Santiago is a good time to catch buskers playing traditional Galician tunes. There is quite an inventory of instruments at the disposal of folk musicians. In addition to the bog-standard gaita, *tamboril* (big drum) and *violín*, there is a range of simple wood instruments, including the *pito* and *penteiro*; the *pandereta* (tambourine); *buguinas* (small ceramic trumpets); the *birrimbao* (Jew's harp); *ferriños* (triangles); *castañolas* and *tarrañolas* (both variations on castanets); and the *zanfona*, a string and key instrument vaguely along the lines of an accordion.

Possibly the best internationally known Galician traditional music group is the very polished Milladoiro. Pallamallada is a Santiago group that does a mix of instrumental and vocal pieces based on traditional popular music. A very middle-of-the-road but lively enough band is Aroda Os Quintos. In a different league altogether is Uxía, a powerful female vocalist very roughly of the Enya genre. Another, more staid chap is Amancio Prada, actually from the province of León, who does his folk interpretations in Galician and Castilian. The group Keltoi, from the Pontevedra area, does Celtic music, but it's mostly of the elevator variety. ■

❖ ❖ ❖ ❖ ❖ ❖ ❖ ❖ ❖ ❖ ❖ ❖

---

other times you'll have to make do with recordings. *Mil y Una Noches* and *Paraíso Perdido* are a pair of bars equally good for a coffee or drinks later in the evening. They are both on the tiny square of Entrealtares, and the latter is one of Santiago's oldest bars.

Discos & Nightclubs You'll possibly get a better feel for the local drinking and dancing scene if you head for the new town. Taking Praza Roxa (Red Square) as your point of reference, cafés, bars and discos fan out along the streets off and near the square. Explore Rúa de Fernando III o Santo, Rúa

Nova and Rúa de Frei Rodendo Salvado. *Black*, Avenida de Rosalía de Castro s/n, is a popular disco. *Maycar*, Rúa do Doutor Teixeiro 5, is apparently one of the last stops on an all-night trek. For more of a Latin American touch, have a look in at *Makumba*, Rúa de Frei Rodendo Salvado 16.

Concerts & Exhibitions *Tunas* – traditionally university students dressed up in medieval garb and busking towards the end of the academic year – seem to be a year-round phenomenon in Santiago. The tradition is an old one and the music, when played well, is entertaining. The hard sell of cassettes and CDs in Praza do Obradoiro is less so.

The modern *Auditorio de Galicia*, north of the city centre, hosts concerts, art exhibitions and other cultural events, especially crammed through the summer months. The ayuntamiento also sponsors similar events elsewhere throughout town, such as in the church of the former *Convento de Santo Domingo*.

Cinema There is a cinema at Rúa do Vilar 53-55, near the tourist office.

Getting There & Away

Air Lavacolla airport is 11 km south-east of Santiago. There are up to six flights a day to Madrid with Iberia and Air Europa. The latter also has several flights to Barcelona, the Canary Islands and Málaga. Possible international destinations include London, Paris, Frankfurt, Rome, New York, Buenos Aires, Cuba and Venezuela.

Bus Along with La Coruña to the north, Santiago is the main bus terminus for Galicia. Castromil runs regular services to Vigo via Pontevedra, south-east to Orense and north to La Coruña. For A Costa da Morte, Transportes Finisterre runs buses to Finisterre, Malpica de Bergantiños. Enatcar has three buses to Barcelona (8½ hours). Dainco has three a day to Salamanca, two to Cádiz and one to Algeciras. International

services connect La Coruña with Paris, Belgium, Holland and various destinations in Germany.

Train There are up to four trains a day to Barcelona (from La Coruña) via León and Zaragoza, and another four to Madrid (Chamartín).

Regular trains run north to La Coruña (about 1½ hours; 450 ptas for a one-way, 2nd class ticket) and south to Vigo (about 2½ hours; 690 ptas) via Pontevedra (one hour; 450 ptas). Less frequent trains connect with Tuy, Orense, León (2550 ptas) and Zamora (2305 ptas).

Car & Motorcycle Santiago is on the A-9 tollway between La Coruña and Vigo. Parallel, slower and free is the N-550.

Getting Around

Santiago is walkable, although it's a hike to the train and bus stations. A public bus system runs *around* the old town. Bus No 10 runs from the bus station to Praza Roxa via Praza de Galicia. You could get out at Rúa de San Roque or Praza de Galicia. The Circular I bus can drop you in the same places. Bus Nos 6 and 9 pass near the train station and go to Praza de Galicia, but unless your bags are unbearably heavy you could probably struggle up on foot.

La Coruña & the Rías Altas

Often more intemperate and certainly much less visited than the southern coast of Galicia (Rías Bajas), the north-western coast is peppered with pleasant surprises. La Coruña is a busy and surprisingly attractive port city with decent beaches. There are plenty of smaller towns and fishing villages worth exploring too, and some of the most impressive coast in all Galicia.

Camino de Santiago

Queen Lupa was more than a little suspicious when two Palestinian refugees landed up in her territory, near Padrón in northern Galicia, with the decomposing and headless body of a Christian martyr called James, and requested permission to bury him. The Apostle St James (Santiago Apóstol), son of Zebedee, is by tradition thought to have preached the Christian faith in Spain, turning up in Zaragoza at one point. Herod Agrippa had him executed on his return to Jerusalem, and his disciples whisked the body to Jaffa, from where they let Providence guide them in a miraculous sea voyage to Spain.

The good queen sent the pair on to the nearest Roman governor, in Finisterre, who promptly incarcerated them. What state James was in at this point is hard to imagine, but before the Romans had a chance to kill off his disciples, they were freed by an angel and returned to Queen Lupa. Impressed by this and other exploits, she eventually converted to Christianity, St James was buried, and a small mausoleum was erected (remains of which are located beneath the Altar Mayor in the catedral in Santiago de Compostela) to mark the spot. St James was then forgotten for about 750 years until his tomb was rediscovered in 813. Things were tough for Spain's Christians in those days, since most of the country was in Muslim hands. Nevertheless, tales abound of St James' spirit appearing on various battlefields and cheerfully cutting down Moors left and right, and he became known as Santiago Matamoros – St James the Moor-Slayer. Understandably, his figure became of prime symbolic importance in Spain, and the word soon spread across Europe. To the 20th century mind, the story takes a lot of swallowing, but swallow it people did, and by the 11th century streams of pilgrims were descending on Santiago, mostly crossing the Pyrenees at Roncesvalles and walking 687 km via Pamplona, Logroño and León.

In the 12th century, the Castilian and Aragonese monarchs upgraded the Camino (Pilgrims' Way) – or in fact several caminos, as there is more than one (see below). At the same time a group of Castilian knights formed a new military order with a religious bent, the Orden de Santiago, which, apart from taking an active part in the Reconquista, also saw as part of its duty to aid and protect pilgrims. The pilgrimage route also became an important commercial conduit across northern Spain, stimulating local trade. The revival of the route today as something more of a touristic activity is no less important for the local economy.

The principal route already mentioned, the Camino Francés, is what most people have in mind when they talk of the Camino de Santiago. Not everyone followed it, however. Other routes include: the Camino del Norte, which passes along the Cantabrian coast and turns inland at Ribadeo; the Camino de Fonsagrada, which crosses the Cordillera Cantábrica and passes via Lugo; the Camino Portugués, which crosses into Galicia at Tuy and heads north; and even a Camino Inglés, from La Coruña and O Ferrol (which presumably entails an initial journey by sea!). Pretty much all the *albergues* (refuges) and information centres for pilgrims are located along the Camino Francés, but signs and references to the Camino de Santiago proliferate all over north-western Spain, making it a collective term for the various caminos.

The Camino Francés is intertwined with asphalted roads, meaning you can drive bits of the old route, and of course all the main towns on the route are linked by road. The Camino is at its most rewarding, however, when it leaves the highway and becomes a minor back road or walkers' track.

You can walk or cycle any part of the Camino as a simple hiking or travel exercise. Plenty, however, still opt to do so in a religious context, and they have the option of staying overnight in pilgrims' refuges. In this case, you can apply for a letter of recommendation in your local parish or at the start of the Camino. You need to keep the letter and a record booklet (which most pilgrim refuges can provide) in

which you collect date stamps as you go. Those who complete at least 100 km on foot or 200 km on bicycle can, on arrival in Santiago, pick up the *compostela*, a document testifying that the bearer has completed at least part of the Camino as a pilgrim (rather than as a tourist). The refuges are free, with priority going to walkers and stays generally limited to one night; it is customary to leave at least a few hundred ptas for maintenance. The greatest distance between refuges along the route is the 23 km from Ponferrada to Villafranca del Bierzo in León province.

There is no shortage of people on the Camino in the warmer months with the telltale staff and scallop shell. The latter was a practical device for sipping water from streams while on the road.

The Camino from O Cebreiro to Santiago

Those pilgrims with true grit – the ones who didn't give up at Villafranca del Bierzo (see the Castilla y León chapter), found themselves faced with the formidable task of climbing to the mountain pass of **Pedrafita do Cebreiro** (1109 metres), the main gateway to Galicia in the Cordillera Cantábrica mountain chain that separates the Castilian *meseta* from Galicia and the northern Atlantic regions.

This achieved, another five km remained to **O Cebreiro**, a tiny, wind-battered settlement of stone houses high above a patchwork quilt of green valleys. In among the huddle of houses and a couple of *pallozas* (traditional circular, thatch-roofed houses), remains an 11th century church. O Cebreiro makes a lovely stop and, apart from a refuge for scallop shell-bearing pilgrims, you can stay in the *Hospedería O Cebreiro* (☎ 982-36 71 25), next to the church. There are comfortable rooms for 3000/4000 ptas, and a great restaurant. Failing that, try *Mesón Antón* (☎ 982-15 13 36), which has a couple of nice rooms for the same price.

About 10 km on, the Camino crosses its highest point in Galicia, the Alto do Poio. Another 14 km brings you to sleepy **Triacastela**, near the Río Oribio. There are a couple of places to stay and eat, a bank and a post office. At this point the route forks. The main road dips south via Samos on the way to Sarriá, 23 km west, while the original Camino takes you along narrow, wooded paths to the north, past small farming hamlets and the odd wayside chapel, meeting the highway at Sarriá.

If you do follow the road, a stop at **Samos** is a must. The imposing Benedictine monastery here is worth visiting, although its history is tragic. The original 6th century monastery was replaced in the 12th century by another, which in turn was destroyed by fire and rebuilt in the Gothic style in the 16th century. Fire struck again in 1951, killing one person and destroying anything not made of stone. Only the 18th century church was unharmed. The place was rebuilt, and the exquisite cloister gardens must be among the most lovingly maintained in all Iberian Christendom. It is open Tuesday to Saturday from 10 am to 1.30 pm and 4 to 7 pm, and Sunday from 10 am to 2 pm only. Entry for the compulsory guided tour costs 200 ptas.

Twelve km on is **Sarriá**, a town grown too big to be charming, although the older hilltop area is vaguely interesting. Sarriá is a transport junction, with regular buses north to Lugo and south to

Monforte de Lemos. Along the Camino, you cannot count on much more than one or two services a day to places like Triacastela, Portomarín and O Cebreiro (6 pm). Remember that few services operate on Sunday.

Better than Sarriá as an overnight halt is **Portomarín**, in spite of the fact that the original village was flooded by the damming of the Río Miño in 1963. The 13th century Iglesia de San Nicolás, with an impressive rose window, was transferred to the new town and dominates the central square. Parts of several other buildings on the square were also salvaged from the old town. You might try for rooms at the *Posada del Camino* (☎ 982-54 50 07), just opposite San Nicolás. Rooms cost 2000/3500 ptas and the restaurant serves up a decent empanada.

There's little to detain you at **Palas de Rei**, the next town on the Camino, but there are several places to stay if you need them. **Melide**, 15 km on, is a little nicer, and is home to the oldest cruceiro (14th century) in Galicia; this stands outside the unassuming Gothic Iglesia de San Pedro on the main road before you reach the centre. One km west of Melide is the Romanesque Iglesia de Santa María. A few km before Melide, you may notice a turn-off to the village of **Furelos**. Pilgrims can pick up a stamp at the local tavern here, and the Romanesque bridge that crosses a tributary of the Río Ulla is a beauty.

If you have the time and inclination, a detour north from Melide recommends itself. The Cistercian monastery of **Sobrado de los Monjes** (Sobrado dos Monxes) that forms the hub of an otherwise humdrum hamlet came close to falling into irrecoverable disrepair in the years following its expropriation in 1834. However, a small band of Cistercians returned in 1954 and much has been restored. The ornate Galician baroque façade of the church belies its comparatively austere, and mouldy, interior. The bare Claustro de los Peregrinos, the first cloister you enter in the complex, was completely rebuilt in 1972. The Claustro de los Medallones, erected in the mid-18th century to replace its 12th century Romanesque forerunner, takes its name from the 'medallions' containing busts that line the porticoes. Off this, the kitchen contains a huge 13th century chimney flue. Possibly the most incongruous element inside the church is the much-neglected choir stalls, jammed in here when it was decided not to lodge them in the Santiago cathedral, as originally intended. The monastery buildings are open Monday to Saturday from 10.30 am to 1 pm and 4.15 to 6.15 pm, and Sunday and holidays from 12.15 to 1 pm and 4.15 to 6.15 pm. Entry costs 100 ptas.

Back on the Camino, there's little of interest until you crest the last hill before Santiago, **Monte do Gozo** (or Monxoi). Pilgrim groups would race to the top, and the first to take in the views of the Catedral de Santiago was proclaimed king of the group. After enjoying (hence the Spanish *gozo*) this satisfaction, only a few km separate weary walkers from that final personal victory. ■

LA CORUÑA

With 250,000 inhabitants, La Coruña (A Coruña) has only in recent years been overtaken by Vigo as Galicia's biggest city. It remains, however, the region's most go-ahead, outward-looking urban centre. It has a liberal-republican tradition at variance with the conservatism of the remainder of Galicia, and its port has kept it open to the rest of the world. It has also been a gateway for those outward bound – everyone from Galician migrants bound for South America to the doomed Armada.

Initially a Celtic port of call on the tin route to the British Isles, the site was later occupied by the Romans, who in the 2nd century AD built the lighthouse known as the Torre de Hércules. Nothing much is known of La Coruña's subsequent history until 991, when the port was put under control of the Church in Santiago. One way or another, Britain looms large on La Coruña's horizon. Felipe II embarked here for England to marry Mary Tudor in 1554, and 34 years later the ill-fated Armada also weighed anchor in La Coruña headed for Britain. The following year, Sir Francis Drake tried to occupy it but was seen off by María Pita, a heroine whose name lives on in the town's main square. Napoleon's troops occupied La Coruña for the first six months of 1809. Their British opponents were able to do a Dunkirk and evacuate, but their commander, General Sir John Moore, died in the covering Battle of Elviña and was buried here.

Orientation

The RENFE train station and the bus station

are a couple of km south-west of the heart of town. La Coruña gets interesting along a fairly narrow isthmus and the large headland to its east. The old part of town (Ciudad Vieja) is huddled together in the southern tip of the headland, while the Torre de Hércules caps its northern extreme. Most offices, hotels, restaurants and bars are in the newer, predominantly 19th century part of town that fills the isthmus. Its northern side is lined with sandy beaches, while to the south lies the port.

Information

Tourist Office The tourist office (☎ 22 18 22), on the Dársena de la Marina, opens Monday to Friday from 9 am to 2 pm and 4.30 to 6.30 pm, Saturday from 10.30 am to 1 pm and 4.30 to 7.30 pm, and Sunday from 10 am to 1 pm only.

Money The Banco Zaragozano on Calle de Durán Loriga is just one of several banks with ATMs on this street and nearby. American Express (☎ 22 99 72), represented by Viajes Amado, is at Calle de Compostela 1.

Post & Communications The central post office is on Avenida de la Marina, and the central postcode is 15080. Phone and fax offices are scattered about the town centre. The phone code is ☎ 981.

Medical & Emergency Services In a medical emergency call ☎ 061 or the Cruz Roja on ☎ 22 22 22. There's a night pharmacy on Calle Fernández Latorre, near the bus station.

Torre de Hércules

One myth says Hercules built the original lighthouse here after slaying the cruel king of a tribe of giants who kept the local populace in terror. All we know is that Romans built a lighthouse here in the 2nd century. It was later used as a fort and restored in 1792. As you enter, you can see the excavated remains of the original Roman base and medieval meddling. Climb to the top for views of the city. It opens daily from 10 am to 7 pm.

Galerías

La Coruña has been dubbed the 'city of glass', and to find out why you need to head down to waterfront Avenida de la Marina. Multistorey houses sport what could almost pass as a uniform protective layer of *galerías* or glassed-in balconies – creating a perhaps unwittingly pleasing effect on the eye.

Ciudad Vieja

The grandiose Plaza de María Pita marks off the western limit of the compact zone that constitutes almost all of that part of La Coruña older than the middle of the 19th century. Sealed off on three sides by porticoes, the city's flamboyant **ayuntamiento** (town hall) is an unmistakable landmark.

The **Iglesia de Santiago**, with its three Romanesque apses backing on to the pretty little Plaza de la Constitución, is the city's oldest church. A short walk through the labyrinth brings you to the slightly unkempt **Jardín de San Carlos**, where General Sir John Moore lies buried. Nearby, war aficionados can look over the **Museo Militar**, which houses arms from the 18th to the 20th centuries. It opens daily from 10 am to 2 pm and admission is free.

Castelo de San Antón

Outside the old town walls and keeping a watch over the port, this 12th century fortress was converted into a prison in the 18th century. It now houses a Museo Arqueológico made up of an eclectic collection of items ranging from Roman and Visigothic artefacts, through some rather incongruous pieces from ancient Egypt and on to items from more recent times. It opens daily from 10 am to 2 pm and 4 to 7.30 pm (Sunday from 10 am to 2 pm only). Entry costs 250 ptas.

Museo de Bellas Artes

Towards the end of 1995, a new art gallery opened in La Coruña on the site of a former Capuchin convent. In addition to works by Rubens and etchings by Goya, there is a

GALICIA

La Coruña

0   150   300 m

Ría de la Coruña

To Torre de Hércules

Paseo Marítimo

Ensenada del Orzán

Calle del Hospital San Roque

Ayuntameinto

Calle de la Maestranza

Plaza de María Pita

Ciudad

Playa de Riazor

Dársena de La Marina

Vieja

Jardines de Méndez Núñez

Puerto de La Coruña

Rosaleda

Parque de Santa Margarita

Estación RENFE Mercancías

Calle Carretera de Acceso al Puerto

Ronda de Nelle

GALICIA

PLACES TO STAY
8 Hospedaje María Pita
   & Hospedaje La Palma
9 Pensión La Alianza
20 Hostal Centro Gallego
21 Hostal La Provinciana
22 Hostal Roma
24 Hostal Santa Catalina
26 Hostal Alameda

PLACES TO EAT
5 Casa Jesusa
6 O' Calexo
10 La Petite Bretagne
11 Farggi

OTHER
1 Museo de Bellas Artes
2 Iglesia de las Capuchinas
3 Iglesia de San Jorge
4 Palacio Municipal
7 Iglesia de San Nicolás

12 Oficina de Turismo
13 Galerías Coruñesas
14 Plaza &
   Convento de Santa Barbara
15 Iglesia &
   Convento de Santo Domingo
16 Iglesia de Santa María
   del Campo
17 Jardín de San Carlos
18 Iglesia de Santiago
19 Post Office (Correos)
23 Telephone and Fax Office
25 Banco Zaragozano
27 American Express
28 Castillo de San Antón
   & Museo Arqueológico
29 Night Pharmacy
30 Estación de Autobuses
31 Local Bus Lines 14 & 17
32 Post Office (Correos)
33 Train Station (RENFE)
34 Local Bus Line 5

representative collection of 16th and 17th century European paintings (taken from the museum's forerunner, virtually next door), as well as contributions from the stores of the El Prado and Reina Sofía museums in Madrid. The building itself is quite innovative, managing to salvage something of the atmosphere of the former convent within the bounds of a modern museum. It opens Tuesday to Sunday from 10 am to 2.30 pm. Entry costs 200 ptas.

Casa de las Ciencias

La Coruña's science museum and planetarium has become one of the country's most popular museums. It's in the Parque de Santa Margarita, and opens Tuesday to Saturday from 11 am to 9 pm in summer and 10 to 7 pm in winter; Sunday from 11 am to 2.30 pm only.

Beaches

Aside from the protected city beaches, Playa de Riazor and Playa del Orzán, several others stretch away along the 30 km sweep of coast west of the city. In summer, RutaBus buses run regularly out to Barrañan, Casón and Baldaio. The last of the them is a long sandy beach.

Places to Stay

There is no shortage of lower-range hotels in La Coruña. Calle de Riego de Agua is a good spot to look, close to the old centre and surrounded by streets with some of the best eating in La Coruña.

Pensión La Alianza (☎ 22 81 14), Calle de Riego de Agua 8, is one of several little places on this street that would see you in the heart of the most interesting part of town. It charges 2000/3500 ptas for average singles/doubles. At No 38 there are a couple of cheap spots. *Hospedaje María Pita*, on the 3rd floor, charges 1200/1800 ptas for basic rooms.

Hostal Roma (☎ 22 80 75), Rúa Nueva 3, is another cheapie, offering basic doubles for 2100 ptas. Virtually round the corner, *Hostal Centro Gallego* (☎ 22 22 36), Calle Estrella 2, has a range of rooms starting at 1500/3000 ptas in high season.

A step up in quality is the *Hostal La Provinciana* (☎ 22 04 00), Rúa Nueva 7-9, which has rooms for 4000/6000 ptas in the high season. In about the same category is the reliable *Hostal Santa Catalina* (☎ 22 66 09), Travesía de Santa Catalina 1.

A little further away from the centre is the extremely pleasant *Hostal Alameda* (☎ 22 70 74), Calle de la Alameda 12. Doubles range from 4500 to 7000 ptas, depending on season and demand.

Places to Eat

The narrow lanes stretching west of Plaza de María Pita are the first place to make for in search of good food. Calle de la Franja in particular is lined with options. *Casa Jesusa*, at No 8, offers a tasty set lunch usually composed of seafood (the empanadillas are especially good) for 1000 ptas. You'll probably have to queue to get into *O' Calexo*, No 34. The reasons are clear, with a great value fish grill (parrillada de pescado) for 2500 ptas for two. Calle de los Olmos and Calle Estrella are also rich hunting grounds – you'll see plenty of octopuses in the windows.

For a dessert with a difference, try the crêpes at *La Petite Bretagne*, Calle de Riego de Agua 13. *Farggi*, at No 5, is good for sticky things and breakfast.

Cafés Although you pay a little over the odds for your coffee, the cafés on Plaza de María Pita are an unbeatable choice for at least one people-watching session. Just as good is the Avenida de la Marina.

Entertainment

Bars & Nightlife Until about midnight, you'll find plenty to drink with your tapas in the central streets already mentioned. If you're more interested in drinking than eating, try one of the more than 50 watering holes crammed into the streets off Playa del Orzán. As the night wears on, Calle de Juan Florez is also worth checking out, as are many of its side streets.

Getting There & Away

Bus There are plenty of buses to most destinations throughout Galicia and several beyond. Castromil runs regular services to

Vigo via Santiago de Compostela and Pontevedra. You can change at Santiago for Orense. IASA has buses to Lugo, O Ferrol and Betanzos. For destinations to the Costa da Morte area, Transportes Finisterre runs up to 30 buses a day to Carballo (420 ptas), four a day to Finisterre (1335 ptas), two to Malpica de Bergantiños. ACP serves Betanzos (285 ptas).

Train Up to 12 trains daily head south to Vigo (1095 ptas) via Santiago de Compostela (450 ptas) and Pontevedra (970 ptas). There are three a day to Madrid (Chamartín), one of which continues to Alicante, and two to Barcelona via Zaragoza. The twice-daily train to O Ferrol (1½ hours; 450 ptas) stops at Betanzos (290 ptas).

Car & Motorcycle The A-9 is the quickest road out of La Coruña. This tollway passes east by Betanzos before heading down to Vigo via Santiago de Compostela and Pontevedra. The N-550 to Santiago is prettier but slower. For Lugo and Madrid, take the N-IV.

Getting Around

Local bus No 5 links the train station with central La Coruña, while Nos 14 and 17 go from the Estación de Autobuses through the centre and out to the Torre de Hércules. To avoid a long walk to the Torre de Hércules, catch No 3A from Plaza de España or Jardín de San Carlos.

RÍAS ALTAS

Less extensive and visited less often than the Rías Bajas, the Rías Altas and surrounding countryside in many respects have quite an edge over them. For starters, they are not nearly as populated, retaining a greater natural attraction. And when the weather is good, many beaches on this stretch are every bit as good as anything you'll find to the south. A handful of enticing little towns like medieval Betanzos and Pontedeume are handsomely accompanied by some of the most dramatic coast you will see in all Galicia, if not the entire country – that of the Serra de la Capelada and Cabo Ortegal.

Betanzos

Just 24 km east of La Coruña, Betanzos could be seen as a small-scale Toledo of the north, decidedly flavoured *a la gallega* with its multistorey houses glassed in by the classic white galerías. Re-sited here in 1219, the medieval walled town's port was long a busy haven until eclipsed by La Coruña.

The Oficina de Información, in the same building as the Museo das Mariñas on Rúa de Emilio Romay, has a map and list of hospedajes. Several banks are located on or near the main sprawling square of the town, Praza dos Irmáns García Naveira. The post office is on Paseo de Alfonso IX, also near the square.

The Celtic settlement (castro) that predated the town was located in what is now Praza da Constitución, flanked notably by the neoclassical ayuntamiento and Gothic Iglesia de Santiago. More interesting is Praza de Fernán Pérez de Andrade. The Gothic churches of **Santa María do Azogue** and **San Francisco** stand opposite each other, separated by the small square. Inside the latter is the tomb of Fernán Pérez de Andrade, supported by the family emblems in stone – a bear and a wild boar.

The **Museo das Mariñas** contains a lot of curios, including fragments of medieval sculpture and a display of traditional Galician costumes. It is open daily from 10 am to 1 pm and 4 to 8 pm. Entry costs 100 ptas.

The Fiesta de San Roque, on August 16, is marked by the sending up of a huge, 'home-made' paper hot-air balloon.

Places to Stay & Eat Of the half-dozen or so places to stay, many are always full with workers on local road-building projects. A last-ditch effort for the desperate is the *Mesón Cortés*, Rúa de Saavedra Meneses 4, just across the Ponte Vello (old bridge) from the medieval town. It has dingy singles/doubles for 1000/2000 ptas. In the centre of things are the rooms above the tapas bar in a lane just off the main square. The unnamed lane is loaded with bars and so it's a noisy option (it leads off the square between Café La Goleta and a pharmacy). Look for the *pensión* at No 17 (☎ 981-77 03 79). Singles/doubles cost 1500/2500 ptas.

Hostal Barreiro (☎ 981-77 22 59), Rúa de Argentina 6, has simple rooms for 1000/2000 ptas. Doubles with private bath are 2500 ptas. *Hotel Los Angeles* (☎ 981-77 15 11), Rúa dos Anxeles 11, charges 4500/6000/8600 plus IVA for singles/ doubles/triples.

The lane referred to above with the pensión is the focus of Betanzos' culinary life. *O' Pote*, at No 9, and the *Mesón O' Progreso* at the end of the lane are decent. The next lane parallel has more tapas bars. The cafés on the main square are popular for breakfast.

Getting There & Away The easiest way in and out of Betanzos is by bus. Regular services to and from La Coruña run from Praza dos Irmáns García Naveira. Less frequent buses head to Lugo and O Ferrol. The closest of the town's two train stations, Betanzos Cidade, is north of the old town, just across the Río Mendo. Two trains daily go to O Ferrol and La Coruña.

Pontedeume
Founded in 1270, this hillside feudal bastion, while scruffier that Betanzos, is an appealing stop with the advantage of having a beach close by the town's fishing port. Rúa Real, the porticoed main street, climbs past a cheerful little square (in front of the *concello*, or town hall) up to the 18th century Iglesia de Santiago. From here numerous lanes wind down the hill, characterised by Galician *galerías*. Down on the waterfront, near the market, rises the **torreón**, or main tower, of what was once the Palacio de Andrade, named after the local feudal lord.

Fonda Martis (☎ 981-43 06 37), Rúa Real 23, has spartan rooms in the heart of things for 1500/2500 ptas. This street is lined with taverns and eateries. At *Bar Cañiza*, No 28, you can try a *queimada* (a kind of hot punch).

Around Pontedeume
Addicts of back roads could head about five km out of town via Campolongo to the remote hilltop tower of what was once the **Castelo de Andrade**, although it's not in great shape. Alternatively, the trip 14 km east to the **Monasterio de San Juan de Caveiro** takes you through a rare stretch of Atlantic forest, rather than the ever-present pines and eucalypts.

O Ferrol
The insignificant fishing village of O Ferrol came into its own when the Bourbon king, Felipe V, established a naval arsenal and shipyard here early in the 18th century. For a town with rather leftist leanings, it is a small irony of history that Franco was born here in 1892. Under his rule the town was known as El Ferrol del Caudillo, and his equestrian statue still dominates Plaza de España. The house he was born in is at Calle María 136. Otherwise there is little to see in a town that has been badly hit by the decline of its shipyards in the past few decades.

If you decide to take a look at the not unpleasant town centre, head for Calle de Pardo Bajo for food and lodgings. *Hostal Aloya* (☎ 981-35 12 31), at No 28, is a reliable place to stay, with doubles for around 4500 ptas in high season. Otherwise, check out some of the cheaper hospedajes on the same street. In between are crammed a selection of restaurants and bars. *Restaurante Côté* is so good there are two of them, at Nos 19 and 24. Oddly enough for a port town, their meat dishes are the best.

Regular buses run to Santiago de Compostela (895 ptas) via Betanzos, Viveiro and Vigo (1725 ptas) via Pontevedra (1415 ptas). A couple of long-distance buses from Galicia to Madrid call in here. Two daily RENFE trains connect O Ferrol with La Coruña (270 ptas) via Betanzos, and up to four FEVE trains head east to Oviedo via Ribadeo.

Cedeira
If possible, give O Ferrol a miss and make for Cedeira, 38 km up the coast and sitting on a stream that spills into the pretty Ría de Cedeira. The older nucleus of this little town fronts the river with traditional glassed-in galerías, while across two bridges on the

GALICIA

modern side of the town is a pleasant, sheltered beach. Better still, head south over to the next estuary, the Ría de Esteiro, where you'll find a still more appealing beach which is popular with free-campers. The local tourist office is at Arriba da Ponte 22, and is open Monday to Saturday from 11 am to 2 pm and 6 to 9 pm, and Sunday from noon to 2 pm.

There are a few hostales to choose from. A cheap alternative is the *unnamed place* on Calle de los Excombatientes 2 (look for the CH sign), which has clean singles/doubles from 1500/2500 ptas. For information, look out for the *Habitaciones El Puente* sign near the second bridge. The *Hostal Brisa* (☎ 981-48 00 85), Calle de Calvo Sotelo-Arriba da Ponte 19, overlooking the stream in the old half of town, has doubles for up to 3700 ptas. A popular place for raciones and a beer is *Mesón Muiños Kilowato*, Avenida a Moreno 12 (further along the waterfront of the old town).

Regular buses connect Cedeira with O Ferrol and Cariño (to the north).

Serra de la Capelada

From Cedeira north things only get better. On the road to San Andrés de Teixido, you exchange the ever-changing horizons of the *rías* for higher, wilder ground. The Serra de Capelada is heavily wooded, and instead of milestones, the winding road is regularly marked by spectacular viewpoints (*miradores*) over some of the sheerest Atlantic coast in Europe. Windy even on a hot summer day, this territory can be downright fear-inspiring in the midst of a winter storm.

Wild horses still mingle here with cattle, and early June tends to be the main time for the *curro*, the festive rounding up and breaking in of these free-spirited animals (see the boxed aside 'Galician Round-Up' later in this chapter).

San Andrés de Teixido Along a particularly pretty stretch of coast, this hamlet is renowned as a sanctuary of relics of St Andrew. Not just a few Spaniards flock to see the sanctuary and fill up a few bottles

with spring water from the so-called Fuente de la Suerte (Lucky Spring). The result of this is a predictable line of tourist kitsch stalls – enough to make you wonder if there's anyone out in the surrounding fields. Don't let this put you off. Anyone with a vehicle should take this route for the views – before, in and after the village. Buses from Cedeira to Cariño occasionally stop in.

Cabo Ortegal Another 20-odd km north, Cabo Ortegal is the mother of Spanish capes. Great stone shafts drop sheer into the ocean from such a height that the waves crashing onto the rocks below seem pitifully – and deceptively – benign. The cape is a few km beyond the soulless fishing town of Cariño. Wheelless travellers can get buses to Cariño from O Ferrol, Cedeira and Ortigueira, and there are a couple of hostales around if you need one. The problem remains thumbing a ride out to the cape.

Cariño to Viveiro

From Cariño, the road roughly follows the contours of the Ría de Ortigueira southwards to the Río Mera. The area is rich in water-bird life, and the only town of any consequence is **Ortigueira**, a not unattractive but hardly captivating fishing town. One time when it is worth being here is during the annual Mundo Celta music festival, usually held in the first week of August.

Otherwise, you'll be happier if you pursue your way north-east to **O Barqueiro**, a Galician fishing village as you might imagine one. White houses capped with slate-tile roofs cascade down to a small protected port. There's little to do but watch the day's catch come in, but that's the point – this is the real thing. There are a couple of places to stay down on the waterfront. Try *Hostal La Marina* (☎ 981-41 40 98), which has doubles only for 3000 ptas, or 4000 ptas with private bath.

Campers should push on up to Porto de Vares (Bares), two km past Vila de Vares. The place is smaller and boasts a pair of beaches, the one closer to town more protected than the other. *Restaurante La*

Marina, with a terrace overlooking the beach, does acceptable seafood and paella. A side road leads to **Cabo Estaca de Vares** (you can't miss the windmills), Spain's most northerly point.

Beaches The coast eastwards to Viveiro is broken up by several decent beaches. It is wise to choose one at least five km short of Viveiro, or you'll have to put up with comparatively built-up strands.

Viveiro

Behind the grand Puerta de Carlos V, the most impressive of Viveiro's three remaining medieval gates, lies a straggle of cobbled lanes and plazas where little seems to have changed since the town was rebuilt after a fire in 1540. There is a small tourist office (☎ 982-56 04 86) inside the gate. Directly up the road past Praza Maior is the **Iglesia de Santa María do Campo**, displaying Romanesque and Gothic features. Nearby is a bad-taste reproduction of Lourdes, while to the north, the 14th century **Iglesia de San Francisco** is the most interesting of Viveiro's buildings.

Fonda Nuevo Mundo (☎ 982-56 00 25), Rúa de Teodoro de Quirós 14, is one of several modest hostelries inside the old town – and a good, clean deal. Singles/doubles cost 1400/2300 ptas. Try for a room in one of the galerías. Just outside the boundaries of the old town, head for *Hostal Vila* (☎ 982-56 13 31), Rúa de Nicolás Cora. It has only one single for 1900 ptas, but the modern doubles with TV are reasonable for 5000 ptas. There are still more hostales and a couple of camp sites on the beaches outside town, particularly at Praia de Covas.

For a decent seafood meal, try *Bar Serra*, Rúa de Antonio Bas 2. The area around Placiña da Herba presents a few appetising options. The pizzeria on the square is good, and *Mesón O'Tunel*, Rúa Fernández Victorio 6, has good tapas. Alternatively, look in at *Mesón A Cepa*, at No 7. For a late-night drink, Rúa Pérez das Mariñas and Rúa Almirante Chicarro are promising.

FEVE line trains call in here between Oviedo and O Ferrol, but buses along the coast here are more frequent. They leave from a station just north of the Puerta de Carlos V, on the waterfront.

Mondoñedo

Compared with the natural spectacles of north-western Galicia's Atlantic coast, the offerings east of Viveiro cut a poor figure. For much of the trip towards Asturias the road lies well inland from the coastline, and what beaches there are pale before their cousins further west and east. The towns of Cervo, Sargadelos, Burela and Foz are all pretty drab and best examined from the comfort of whatever transport you happen to be in.

By contrast, a rewarding detour inland from Foz down the Río Masma brings you to Mondoñedo, first settled in the 5th century by a group of restless migrants from Brittany. An important religious centre and long a provincial capital in the old Kingdom of Galicia, Mondoñedo's slightly down-at-heel appearance in no way diminishes its interest. The tourist office (☎ 982-50 71 77) is just off Praza de España, near the cathedral. Although the cathedral is an impressive Gothic structure, it's not quite pure. The Romanesque main doorway is counterbalanced by baroque towers. Also fronting the old square is the Palacio Episcopal, next to the cathedral, and the porticoed *cantón*. The old fountain (or Fonte Vella) that you can see just south off the square was built in 1548.

The *Pensión La Tropicana* (☎ 982-52 10 08), Rúa de Lodeiro Piñeiroa 8, is the closest place to the centre of town. Singles/doubles cost 2000/3500 ptas. There are several buses to Foz and Lugo.

Into Asturias

Aside from the odd mediocre beach, there is little to keep you waiting along the coast between Foz and **Ribadeo**. The best thing about this frontier town is its ría, a broad expanse and an obvious natural frontier between Galicia and Asturias. The great Puente de los Santos fords the waterway that, in the guise of the Río Eo, continues roughly

GALICIA

to mark the regional frontier for some 30 km south. A busy little place, Ribadeo contains nothing at all to see or do. If you get stuck, the area around the central Praza de España is drowning in hotels of every conceivable category. A more pleasant alternative might be to head for the riverside village of Castropol on the Asturias side (see the previous chapter).

The Costa da Morte

On one of those not-so-frequent hot, sunny days, you could be forgiven for thinking that the tales of danger surrounding this stretch of the Atlantic seaboard – the Death Coast – are greatly exaggerated. But the idyll can undergo a rapid metamorphosis when ocean mists blow in and envelop the whole region.

On the way out of La Coruña, there are a few ocean beaches such as the Playa de Barrañán and Playa de Sorrizo where you must be mindful of the currents. The Costa da Morte begins at the unassuming point of Caión. If travelling by bus, you may find yourself passing inland via Carballo, one of the costa's main transport hubs. Heading south-west along the coast from Caión towards Malpica de Bergantiños, you pass a turn-off for Buño, known for its ceramics.

The telephone code for the Costa de Morte is ☎ 981.

MALPICA DE BERGANTIÑOS

Malpica has a sandy beach on one side and a busy port on the other. The main attraction is the liveliness of the village centre and its bars and eateries, several of which overlook the beach. Off the coast you can see the Islas Sisargas, home to various nesting bird species, mostly various types of seagull. *Hostal JB* (☎ 72 02 66), Rueiro da Praia, has comfortable rooms, some virtually overhanging the beach. Singles/doubles with TV and private bath start at 3000/4000 ptas. *Hostal Panchito* (☎ 72 30 07), Praza de Anselmo Villar Amigo, has decent rooms without the views for about the same price.

To eat, hunt around the various bars squeezed in just back from the beach for tapas and raciones. Buses run from La Coruña to Malpica and on to Corme.

CORME

Climb Corme's steep, winding streets from the waterfront and you'll notice how its fishing port feel gives way to that of the agricultural hinterland (known as Corme Aldea) – quite a complementary arrangement. Although most of the buildings are modern, the place has some of its old pueblo atmosphere and a serviceable nearby beach. If the latter is not good enough for you, move south to the **Praia Hermida**, an attractive and uncrowded ocean beach. Harder to reach without your own transport, but just as pleasant, is **Praia Balarés**. Perhaps not so nice is a growing side industry here, as in other Galician ports. In January 1996 an old fishing vessel was impounded with 2600 kg of cocaine – the biggest haul by Spanish authorities on record.

LAXE & AROUND

If driving down the coast, make first for Ponteceso, a local crossroads. Nearby Laxe has a white sandy beach, but like quite a few of these fishing towns, its mostly modern buildings deprive it of character. For something a little easier on the eye, dare to penetrate the unsignposted maze of roads south of Laxe that should eventually get you to the wilder **Praia de Traba**.

CAMARIÑAS & AROUND

In essence a modern fishing village, Camariñas for some reason attracts a steady trickle of mainly Spanish tourists. The place does have something of a reputation for lacework (*encajes*), and you may see women making the stuff in strategic locations for passers-by. Have a look at prices in one of the shops (the one on the waterfront next to Café Piticlin is a good example) and hunt around – preferably in one of the outlying villages (see below).

Apart from the craftwork, there are really only two reasons for passing through. The first is to take a look at **Cabo Vilán**, an impressive cape five km north-west of the town. The Atlantic storms are put to good use with the modern windmills of the so-called Parque Eólico in the background.

The second is the restaurant at *Hostal La Marina* (☎ 73 60 30), Rúa de Miguel Feixoo 4. For about 2000 ptas, you can taste some of the best value seafood you're likely to encounter in Galicia. The Valencians could learn a thing or two from their version of paella. You can stay overnight too, and add dinner to lunch, for 1900/3500 ptas for singles/doubles in high season. Transportes Finisterre buses connect Camariñas with Santiago and La Coruña.

About 15 km north of Camariñas, **Camelle** is a much less visited fishing village with an average beach. Nearby, **Arou** is still more untouched and has a couple of pleasant swimming areas – especially if you follow the track along the coast. In both these towns you'll find *señoras* working on lace and probably get better prices than in Camariñas.

A lousy track leads off from near Arou towards the not overly visited beach of **Ensenada de Trece**. After 10 km the track passes a cemetery where lie buried 172 English cadets who died in a shipwreck on the Death Coast in 1890.

MUXÍA & AROUND

Getting to and from Camariñas you'll pass through Ponte do Porto, which fords the Río Grande. The coast road south for Os Muiños passes the pretty hamlet of **Cereixo** and heads down a narrow, tree-shaded road. Along here, near Leis, you'll find one of the most inviting beaches along the Costa da Morte, **Praia do Lago**. The sand fronts the ocean and also a quiet river. There are a couple of camping grounds and at least one hostal around it.

From Os Muiños, the road passes the Romanesque **Monasterio de San Xián de Moraime**, built over a Roman settlement. Muxía itself is nothing special, but once here it is worth pushing on to the **Punta da Barca**, which affords good views of the coast. The rocks in front of the baroque Santuario de Nuestra Señora de la Barca are the scene of a popular *romería* in September. *Hostal La Cruz* (☎ 74 20 84), Avenida de Calvo Sotelo 53, has singles/doubles for 4000/6000 ptas in the high season.

Those contemplating a circuit in the area might consider taking in **Vimianzo** on the way. Lying about midway between Carballo and Corcubión on the C-552, Vimianzo's castle is a modest little affair, but lends the town a pleasing silhouette. The present structure dates from the 15th century, and it was a key stronghold in the feudal conflicts that ravaged much of Galicia prior to the end of the Reconquista. It is open Tuesday to Sunday from 10.30 am to 1 pm and 4 to 8 pm; shorter hours in winter. Entry is free, and there is frequently some sort of minor exhibition to inspect. There are several hostales if you want to stay. *Hostal O Castillo* (☎ 71 60 15), on the main road to Finisterre and closest to the castle, has reasonable doubles for 3000 ptas. Buses stop here on the run between La Coruña and Finisterre.

FINISTERRE

Those poking their noses about the Costa da Morte will want to make it to Galicia's version of Land's End, Finisterre, or Fisterra in Galician. From Vimianzo, the road drops south through Corcubión, a largish, unappealing sort of a place although there are a few hostales if you need one. The tree-lined road is appealing, but the towns less so, and Sardiñeiro is hardly much better than Corcubión, only smaller. The nearby *Ruta Finisterre* camping ground (☎ 74 55 85) is not a bad place to stop for the night. There is a reasonable beach a couple of km further on stretching almost to the town of Finisterre. Like most of the towns around here, this is nothing to write home about. For **Cabo Finisterre**, where Spain stops and the Atlantic begins, you have 3.5 km to go. On the way out of town to the right is the 12th century **Iglesia de Santa María das Areas**, a mix of Romanesque, Gothic and baroque. Just opposite once stood the westernmost shelter for pilgrims en route to Santiago – for those approaching *from* the end of the world. The best views of the coast are to be had not from the *faro* (lighthouse), but by climbing up the track to Monte Facho and Monte San Guillermo. The area is laced with myth and superstition, and they say childless couples used to come up here to redouble their efforts to conceive.

Pensión Casa Velay (☎ 74 01 27), just off the main square in the older part of the town, has decent doubles without private bath for 2000 ptas and for 3500 ptas with. They also run a restaurant, or you could hang around *Bar Tito* on the main square for snacks and beer.

TOWARDS THE RÍAS BAJAS

The southernmost stretch of the Costa da Morte, while perhaps not the most stunning of Galicia's coastline, nevertheless has its moments. At **Ézaro**, 27 km from Cabo Finisterre, a steep road climbs two km to a mirador with breathtaking views out over the Atlantic – the power station detracts a little from the atmosphere, but even so it is a stunning piece of country. **O Pindo** (El Pindo), is a cute fishing village set back on a shallow, tranquil bay. *Hospedaje La Morada*

(☎ 85 80 70) has singles/doubles for about 2500/4000 ptas. Another 10 km south and you hit a long, sandy beach, the Playa de Carnota, usually not too crowded, and fine if the wind isn't up. For beaches further on, see Muros below. **Carnota** town, towards the southern end of the beach, is renowned for being home to the longest *hórreo* (grain store; see the boxed aside 'Of Grain Stores and Crossroads' for background) in Galicia – 34.5 metres long, it was built late in the 18th century.

Rías Bajas

The four great estuaries of Galicia's south, the Rías Bajas (Rias Baixas) are doubtless the grandest of all the rías that indent the length of the Galician coast, and they are justly well known. There are plenty of beaches and several relatively low-key resorts, and in summer good weather is a better bet here than further north. Throw in the Islas Cíes, the lovely medieval town of Pontevedra and the more harried centre of

---

Of Grain Stores & Crossroads

Away from the famous façades, Galicia is studded with a wealth of 'popular architecture' quite specific to the region. Most common of all is the *cruceiro*, a crucifix usually bearing a statue of Christ on one side and a distraught Virgin Mary on the other. The more ornate ones represent key scenes from the Bible. In both cases they are most commonly found at crossroads – where they served an orientational function for wayfarers in the days before street signs – and in churchyards. The bulk of them have been erected over the centuries by various religious orders and they are said to possess a protective power, as well as being a subliminal reminder of the religious status of the area in case anyone were in any doubt. As it happens, they frequently became the object for local cult 'worship' of particular saints.

The simple 14th century cruceiro of Melide, along the Camino de Santiago, is the oldest in existence, while the complex 19th century one at Hio (Ría de Vigo), depicting the taking down of Christ from the cross, was carved from a single block of granite and is judged by those in the know to be the most beautiful.

The other odd-looking construction you will see all over the place is the *hórreo*. Generally made of granite, and sometimes partly of wood, this rectangular structure has for centuries served as a grain store. Sitting on squat stilts, the hórreo serves simply to keep grain easily accessible and dry. Some, like the one in Carnota, are extremely long, generally a reflection of the owners' wealth. Your average family hórreo, nowadays more often than not used as a junk shed and clothes line, is of more modest proportions. If you end up in Asturias, you will notice (virtually as soon as you cross the border) that the Asturians have their own version, a square-based wooden affair, sometimes with a tiled roof and quite often a sort of mini-verandah all the way around. ∎

GALICIA

Vigo, and you have a travelling mix that is hard to beat.

RÍA DE MUROS Y NOIA
Muros

A pleasant enough stop along the shores of this ría, Muros is perhaps not quite as wonderful as the literature makes out. Founded in the 10th century, it was long an important port for Santiago de Compostela. Today it lives mainly from fishing and a passing tourist trade. From the main seaside square, dominated by the ayuntamiento building, follow Calle Real vaguely in the direction of Santiago. Along the way are some attractive porticoes, the odd *cruceiro* (crucifix; see the boxed aside 'Of Grain Stores and Crossroads'), a couple of ageing churches and an overly extravagant *mercado* (market). Apart from the potential pleasure of having a beer or meal on the waterfront, that's about all there is to the place.

If you want to stay, there is a series of hostales along the waterfront. *Hostal Ría de Muros* (☎ 981-82 60 56), Avenida de Calvo Sotelo 53, has reasonable singles/doubles for 2000/3000 ptas. However, you might find staying near a beach to the west a more attractive option.

As for food, the ever popular *Don Bodegón*, a couple of hundred metres from the main square on the waterfront, is reliable, or you could poke around in the back lanes. *Mesón Bermeo* and *Tasca Bladio*, at No 4 and No 2 Calle de la Pescadería, are OK for some cheap seafood raciones and a beer.

Beaches Stretching west from Muros are a couple of pretty beaches to choose from. The first worthwhile stop is the popular Ensenada de San Francisco, a protected beach of fine white sand. You can stay at one of a couple of hostales here or at *Camping A' Bouga* (☎ 981-82 60 25), a little way short of the beach. *Hostal Antonio* (☎ 981-82 64 60), just back from the beach, has doubles for 3500 ptas.

Further west you will find Praia de Louro and, beyond the headland, Praia de Lariño stretching for a few km round into the south-

ern extreme of the Costa da Morte. This is a less crowded ocean beach, colder, windier and with waves – all of which gives it potential for windsurfing. Surfing is possible too, but the waves are not top quality.

Noia

Anyone who has been to Florence will no doubt fail to see how anyone came to think of Noia as the Florence of anywhere. Its old centre, however, preserves enough reminders of its glory days in the early Middle Ages to be worth calling in: in particular, the main entrance and rose window of the 15th century Gothic **Catedral de San Martiño**. The entrance is inspired by the masterpieces of Santiago de Compostela, with statues of the 12 Apostles guarding each side of the doors. Nearby is the highly evocative **Casa de Costa**, whose four arches date back to at least the mid-14th century. The former **Iglesia de Santa María La Nova**, a short walk from the old centre, was built in 1327 and today, together with its cemetery, forms a unique museum of headstones and funerary art. It is open Tuesday to Friday from 11 am to 1.30 pm and 6.30 to 8 pm, and Saturday and Sunday from 11 am to 1.30 pm only.

The *Hospedaje Marico* (☎ 981-82 00 09), Rúa de Galicia s/n, on the road to Santiago and near the old part of town, is a good deal at 1000/2500 ptas for rooms without private bath (doubles with own bath cost 3000 ptas). For snacks and drinks, you cannot beat *Tasca Típica*, located right in the Casa de Costa, with tables spilling out under the arches. Several buses call in at Noia en route from Santiago to Muros. A couple also serve Padrón.

South Shore

From Noia you could head east for Santiago or turn down along the southern shore of the ría. The main attraction of the latter option, if the weather is good, is the long series of beaches, such as Arealonga, one of the first you encounter. On a headland near **Baroña** are the remains of a Celtic castro, signposted from the roadside café. The beach nearby is for nudists.

RÍA DE AROUSA

Those hugging the coast and coming from the southern shore of the Ría de Muros y Noia will almost certainly end up in **Ribeira**, the first town of any significance on the Ría de Arousa (Ria de Arosa). A drab and drizzly fishing town, it has virtually nothing to recommend it. There are beaches nearby – but plenty of other places up and down the Rías Bajas suggest themselves as preferable alternatives. There is a handful of hostales here, but you are really better off heading for more pleasant places.

If you are driving in the area, you might just want to make a detour to see the **Dolmen de Axeitos**, a well-preserved megalithic monument. It's signposted off the road between Ribeira and Xuño.

There is little to delay you on the road east. However, a few km past the rather awful town of Boiro is a wonderful place to stay and an ideal country base for exploring the area. The *Casa da Posta de Valmaior* (☎ 981-86 25 48), Cespón Boiro, has a series of lovely rooms ranging from 3000 ptas for a single to 6000 ptas for a double in a country home. It is *turismo rural* at its best, and is well signposted off the N-550 between Boiro and Padrón. You'll need your own transport to get there.

Padrón

The hottest thing to come out of Padrón is peppers. That's right, *pimientos de Padrón*. Shrivelled little green things that taste very good, but beware the odd *very* hot one. Franciscan friars first imported them from Mexico in the 16th century. Now the whole area grows them to meet the high demand. This town of 4000, where St James' corpse supposedly arrived in Galicia, is struggling valiantly to make a tourist attraction of itself, putting most effort into the Galician poet Rosalía de Castro, who died here in 1885. The **Casa y Museo de Rosalía**, just behind the train station, contains memorabilia and is one stop in the so-called Ruta Rosaliana that has been mapped out in various locations throughout this region. It is open Tuesday to Sunday from 9.30 am to 2 pm and 4 to 8 pm (9.30 am to 1.30 pm and 4 to 7 pm in winter).

Hostal del Jardín (☎ 981-81 09 50), Rúa de Salgado Araujo 3, is opposite the park on the road leading to the train station. Singles/doubles in high season start at 2000/3000 ptas.

Catoira

About 15 km down the Río Ulla, which shortly after widens into the Ría de Arousa, stand the Torres (towers) do Oeste, the remainder of the early medieval castle, Castellum Honesti, which was the key in protecting (not always successfully) Santiago de Compostela against Norman landings. On the first Sunday of every August, a Viking landing is staged here as an excuse for a boisterous fiesta.

Villagarcía de Arousa

A busy port in rapid and ugly expansion, Villagarcía (Vilagarcía) de Arousa has developed quite a reputation for itself as a major bridgehead for South American drugs coming into Europe. If you do happen through here, the Convento de Vista Alegre and attached *pazo* (residence) are worth searching out. The immediately surrounding beaches are unattractive and the best thing you can do in Villagarcía is leave – buses connect it with Padrón and Pontevedra.

Caldas de Reyes

An inland diversion from Villagarcía de Arousa, or directly along the road between Pontevedra and Padrón, Caldas de Reyes is an old spa town and something of a curiosity. At one end of the cobbled Calle Real stands a small medieval bridge, while on the Río Umia, the two spa hotels, or *balnearios*, still function. It is worth having a peek inside *Hotel Acuña* (☎ 986-54 00 10), Calle de Herrería 2. You can have a bath if you want to, but generally people here are under medical supervision. The whole place exudes a mouldy 19th-century feeling. The other balneario, *Hostal Dávila* (☎ 986-54 00 12), Calle de Laureano Salgado 11, is even more dilapidated. Just outside it is As Burgas, a small spa water fountain.

Hostal Buceta (☎ 986-54 00 31), Calle de José Salgado 34, is something of an ageing piece as well, where singles/doubles cost 1750/3000 ptas without private bath and 2850/4500 ptas with. *Taberna O' Muiño* is an old, run-down riverside bar and grill. On the way to the tables by the weir, you'll pass some old wine barrels that look as if they have been left to die.

Isla de Arousa

Back by the water, you could drive straight past Vilanova de Arousa (although it has a few reasonable beaches) and make for Isla (Illa) de Arousa, an island connected to the mainland by a long, low bridge. The small town lives mainly from fishing (and smuggling, it appears), and the whole place has a low-key profile. Some of the **beaches** facing the mainland are very pleasant and protected and have comparatively warm water.

A couple of camping grounds open in summer on the island and at Vilanova. The occasional bus runs between here and Pontevedra.

Cambados

Founded by the Visigoths and a victim of constant harrying by Vikings in the 9th and 10th centuries, Cambados is today a peaceful seaside town. Coming from the north you enter by the magnificent **Praza de Fefiñáns**. On two sides it is bordered by a grand 17th century pazo and on another by the 18th century Iglesia de San Benito. Several appealing little streets branch off the square and nearby another pazo has been converted into a parador. There's a small tourist office on Rúa de Novedades. If you have a car, a pretty inland excursion via San Salvador de Meis will take you to the **Monasterio de Santa María de Armenteira**, founded in 1162.

Hostal Pazos Feijoo (☎ 986-54 28 10), Calle de Curros Enríquez 1, is near the waterfront in the newer part of town. Singles/ doubles cost 2500/4000 ptas. At much the

same price there is another hostal a few blocks in, the *Hostal Carisan* (☎ 986-52 01 08). The *Parador El Albariño* (☎ 986-54 22 50; fax 54 20 68), Paseo Cervantes, charges 9200/12,500 ptas plus IVA.

The otherwise unnamed *Café-Bar* on Rúa Caracol is an unpretentious place where you can get a reasonable seafood meal for about 1000 ptas. Cambados is in the heart of Albariño wine country, and Praza de Fefiñáns is swarming with bodegas and bars flogging what can be a very good drop.

Buses to Pontevedra and Santiago de Compostela leave from along the waterfront, near Hostal Pazos Feijoo.

O Grove & A Toxa

How you react to O Grove may well depend on the weather. It's a strange mix of Blackpool and some of Italy's 'family' Adriatic resorts. In summer you'll find little more than hotel blocks, unexciting restaurants, mediocre discos, a fairground and Galicia's unpredictable climate. In winter most of the above, including the weather, is closed.

Still, it could make a lunch stop on your way through the area, and there are several beaches around the little peninsula of which it is a part. As for the island of A Toxa, connected to O Grove by a bridge, this onetime natural beauty spot has been irreparably spoiled by holiday-makers and builders with more money than sense. The place is crawling with 'classy' hotels and holiday apartments.

Should you want to stay, the only potential problem times are August and summer weekends. The tourist office lists 40 hotels, but there are plenty of cheap hostales and other places too. *Hostal María Aguiño* (☎ 986-73 11 87), Rúa de Pablo Iglesias 26, has decent singles/doubles for 1500/3000 ptas. Across the road at No 23, *Residencia Marisé* (☎ 986-73 08 40) has clean singles/ doubles/triples costing 1500/2000/3000 ptas. If hunger strikes, the restaurants around Praza da República Argentina are OK, and *Taberna O' Pescador*, Rúa de Pablo Iglesias 9, is a popular and reasonably priced seafood joint. *O' Peirao*, a basic little bar at Rúa de

GALICIA

Luís Casais 39, is also worth a try for seafood tapas.

Buses run to Sanxenxo, Pontevedra, Padrón and towns in between. In summer, Cruceros Rías Bajas runs boats across to Ribeira. In addition, they sometimes organise trips around the Isla de Arousa.

Around the O Grove Peninsula

There are several little beaches around the peninsula and some of the least touched are on the west side, facing the Atlantic. The problem is that most of this land belongs to the army. Perhaps that's a good thing, as development is sneaking its way around the coast, with a string of still intermittent camping grounds, hotels and holiday homes centred on San Vicente do Grove. **Reboredo** seems to be about the only real fishing and farming village left in the area, although it has no great charm beyond this fact.

RÍA DE PONTEVEDRA (NORTH SIDE)

As you swing around to the south from O Grove you strike the longest beach on offer in the Ría de Pontevedra – **La Lanzada**. There is a string of camping grounds and the odd hostal around here, but the beach is free of the resort feel. Surfers may find the odd decent wave, although it is generally better for windsurfers.

Sanxenxo & Portonovo

A long way from the holiday costas on the Mediterranean, this is about as close as Galicia comes to emulating them. The Praia de Silgar, the best beach Sanxenxo (Sangenjo) has to offer, is fine and sandy, but crowded in summer. The town itself is not nearly as tasteless as places like Benidorm, but is still really about hotels, restaurants and bars, with little to see. In summer, a tourist information kiosk opens seven days a week on Rúa de Madrid from 11 am to 9 pm.

One possible diversion is to take a boat to the **Isla de Ons**, beyond the mouth of the ría. Cruceros Rías Bajas (☎ 986-73 13 43), based at Rúa Reboredo 76, O Grove, organises return trips from Sanxenxo and Portonovo from mid-July to mid-September. In Sanxenxo, buy tickets at the port, just east of the Praia de Silgar.

As far as accommodation goes, late July to early September is the most difficult period, although in practice the main problem is elevated prices. Out of high season, quite a few places have moderately priced rooms. *Hostal Cucos* (☎ 986-72 01 64), Rúa de Carlos Casa 17, is near Praia de Silgar and has singles/doubles for 2000/3500 ptas in the low season. Doubles go for up to 7500 ptas in the high season. Similarly priced is the nearby *Hostal Casa Román* (☎ 986-72 00 31), at No 2. For food and drink, you're best off trekking down the road a couple of km to Portonovo, where you'll find more tapas bars and seafood places than you can poke a stick at. Buses between Pontevedra and O Grove stop here.

Combarro

The road east from Sanxenxo remains fairly liberally laced with hostales and the odd camp site as you head towards Pontevedra. But nothing could stand in greater contrast to the organised amusement of Sanxenxo than the fishing village of Combarro. Although hardly insensitive to the tourist dollar, Combarro has managed to retain some degree of measure. It is best known for the string of hórreos along and near the waterfront Rúa do Mar – a tranquil spot for a leisurely lunch. A tourist office operates Monday to Saturday from 10.30 am to 1.30 pm and 6 to 9 pm.

There are at least three cheapish hostales along the main road from Pontevedra. *Hostal La Parada* (☎ 986-77 01 41) has singles/doubles for 1500/3000 ptas. You could also ask at the *Café Xeito* (☎ 986-77 00 39), about 10 metres away. With a little money, you could enjoy some well-prepared tapas or a full meal at the *Restaurante Alvariñas*, on Rúa do Mar.

La Unión company runs buses by Combarro en route from Pontevedra to O Grove.

Monasterio de San Juan de Poio

Three km east of Combarro and just short of Pontevedra, Poio is dominated by its grand monastery. This was long a Benedictine stronghold – the first church here may have been built in the 7th century – but the Benedictines abandoned the site in 1835, to be replaced 55 years later by the Mercedarios (roughly translated, the Fathers of Mercy). You can visit two cloisters and the church daily from 10 am to 1.30 pm and 5 to 8.30 pm (10 am to 1 pm and 4 to 6 pm in winter). The gardens of the 16th century Claustro de las Procesiones are gathered around a baroque fountain.

PONTEVEDRA

Galicia's smallest provincial capital is perhaps its most striking. With only about 50,000 inhabitants, it has managed to preserve intact a classic medieval centre backing on to the Río Lérez – ideal for simply wandering around and poking one's nose into all sorts of nooks and crannies.

History

Known to the Romans as Ad Duos Pontes, Pontevedra reached the height of its glory in the 16th century, at which time it was the biggest city in Galicia and an important port. The *Santa María*, one of Columbus' caravelles, was built here, and a local legend that the Genoese explorer was born in Pontevedra persists to this day. From the 17th century on, the city began to decline in the face of growing competition in the ría and the silting up of its port. The 1719 sacking of the town by the British did not help matters. In spite of it all, Pontevedra was made provincial capital in 1835 in the face of fierce opposition from Vigo, and tourism is proving a healthy boon.

Orientation

The historic centre, or *zona monumental* as the local authorities refer to it, is clearly confined to a circle formed by Calle del Arzobispo Malvar, Calle de Michelena, Calle de Cobián Raffignac, Calle de Padre A Carballo and the Río Lérez, itself forded by two bridges (not the original *duos pontes* of the Roman name, though they may be in the same place). The walls have gone, but the boundaries remain the same. Inside this area you'll find several hotels, all your eating and drinking needs and much of what you'll want to see. Banks and other offices lie on or near Calle de Michelena, the main drag of the newer town.

Information

Tourist Office The tourist office (☎ 85 08 14), Calle del General Mola 3, is open Monday to Friday from 9.30 am to 2 pm and 5 to 7 pm, Saturday from 10 am to 12.30 pm and 5 to 8 pm, and Sunday from 11 am to 1.30 pm only.

Money There are plenty of banks near the tourist office on Calle de Michelena. They generally open on weekdays from 8.30 am to 2 pm and on Saturday until 1 pm.

Post & Communications The main post office is on Calle Oliva, and opens from 8.30 am to 8.30 pm Monday to Friday. There is a phone office *(locutorio)* at Calle de Oliva 26. The postcode for central Pontevedra is 36080, and the telephone code for the city (as well as the province) is ☎ 986.

Medical & Emergency Services The Policía Municipal are on Praza de Indalecio Armesto. In an emergency, call them on ☎ 092. The comisaría of the Policía Nacional is at Calle de Joaquín Costa 19 (☎ 091). There is a walk-in medical clinic on Calle de la División Azul.

Zona Monumental

Starting on the south-eastern edge of the zona monumental, you can't miss the distinctive curved façade of the **Capilla de la Virgen Peregrina**, an 18th century baroque-neoclassical caprice with a distinctly Portuguese flavour. Virtually across the street lies **Praza da Ferrería** and the immediately adjoining Praza da Estrela. The former, colonnaded on one side and showing off an eclectic collection of buildings dating as far back as the 15th century, was once the scene of the town's bullfights. Set back from

Pontevedra

Ría de Pontevedra

Río Lérez

Puente del Burgo

Praza del Muelle

Calle del Barón

Avenida de Buenos Aires

To Convento de Santa Clara

Praza de Concepción Arenal

Praza do Teucro

Praza de Indalecio Armesto

Praza de Mugartegui

Praza de España

Alameda

Praza de la Estrela

Praza da Ferrería

Praza de Barcelos

Jardines de Vicenti

Jardines de Casto San Pedro

Praza de la Peregrina

Praza de Calvo Sotelo

0   100   200 m

To Avenida de Vigo,
Estación de Autobuses
& Train Station

the square in its own gardens is the **Iglesia de San Francisco**, believed by some to have been founded personally by St Francis of Assisi when on pilgrimage to Santiago. What was the adjacent convent is now the local tax office.

Head down Calle de la Pasantería and you emerge in the Eirado da Leña, one of Pontevedra's most enchanting little corners, partly colonnaded and with a cruceiro in the middle. Just off it lie the main buildings of the **Museo Provincial**, two baroque palaces joined by an arch in 1943. The collection ranges from Bronze Age finds through medi-

eval art and a selection of Spanish painters, including Berruguete and Zurbarán, on to a repertoire of drawings and paintings by Galician modern artist Alfonso Castelao. It is open Tuesday to Friday from 10 am to 2.15 pm and 5 to 8.45 pm, Saturday from 10 am to 12.30 pm and 5 to 8 pm, and Sunday from 10 am to 2 pm only. Entry costs 200 ptas. The museum is closed on Monday.

A block west of the Eirado da Leña is **Praza da Verdura**, so called because of the luxuriant trees that fill what is officially known as Praza de Indalecio Armesto. North-east of the Museo Provincial rises the

PLACES TO STAY

1	Parador Casa del Barón
4	Hospedaje Penelas
10	Fonda
11	Fonda La Lanzada
12	Casa Maruja
13	Casa Alicia
17	Hotel Ruas
26	Hospedaje Margó

PLACES TO EAT

5	O' Noso Bar
6	Casa Fidel – O' Pulpeiro
8	Bar Barrantes
9	Restaurante Agudelo
20	El Menú

OTHER

2	Basílica de Santa María
3	Santuario de las Apariciones
7	Mercado
14	Ayuntamiento
15	Bar
16	Policía Municipal
18	Iglesia de San Bartolomé
19	Museo Provincial
21	Ruins of Iglesia de Santo Domingo
22	Palacio de la Diputación
23	Tourist Office
24	Convento de San Francisco
25	Capilla de la Virgen Peregrina
27	Telephone Office
28	Post Office

baroque façade of the Jesuit **Iglesia de San Bartolomé**.

Further to the west, the area known as **Las Cinco Calles** is a hub of Pontevedra nightlife. The tiny square where the five lanes converge is marked by a cruceiro. From here you can wander north to the Río Lérez and the bustling **mercado** (town market). Take a look at the parador along the way. It's housed in venerable neoclassical **Pazo del Barón de Maceda**.

West up Calle de Isabel II stands the **Basílica de Santa María**, a mainly Gothic church with a whiff of plateresque and Portuguese Manueline influences. It is closed for restoration. On the way up is signposted the **Santuario de las Apariciones**, a chapel and lodgings where Lucía of Fatima resided and the Virgin Mary is said to have appeared to her.

New Town

The elegant Alameda and Jardines de Vicenti spread south-west of the medieval centre and together form modern Pontevedra's green lung. Alongside them are the ruins of the 15th century **Convento de Santo Domingo**, which also house part of the Museo Provincial's archaeological collection.

Places to Stay

There are about half a dozen places in the old town where you could stay. *Fonda La Lanzada*, Calle Paio Gómez de Charino 9, is for the desperate, with dingy rooms for 1000 ptas a head. Considerably better, although hardly the Hilton, is *Hospedaje Penelas* (☎ 85 57 05), Rúa Alta 17. Small but decent singles/doubles cost 2000/3000 ptas. Just outside the old town, *Hospedaje Margó* (☎ 85 26 94), Calle de Riestra 4, is nothing special but the rooms are cheap at 1500/2500 ptas.

Much better located are the *Casa Alicia* (☎ 85 70 79), Avenida de Santa María 5, and *Casa Maruja* (☎ 85 49 01) over the road. The former has homy doubles for around 2500 to 3000 ptas, while the latter charges 3000/4000 ptas for spotless rooms. Best of all for those with a little dosh to fling around is the elegant and popular *Hotel Ruas* (☎ 84 64 16; fax 84 64 11), Calle de Sarmiento 37. Singles/doubles start at 3000/4500 ptas and head up to 4500/8000 ptas plus IVA at the height of the season.

At the top of the tree is one of Spain's more appealing paradores, the *Parador Casa del Barón* (☎ 85 58 00; fax 85 51 00), Calle del Barón 19. Rooms here cost 9800/12,500 ptas plus IVA at the height of the tourist season.

Places to Eat

There is no shortage of places to go hunting for good nosh, and you could do much worse than *El Menú*, an excellent and cheap takeaway place at Calle de Echegaray 7.

The hub of Pontevedra's eating and drinking is, however, the Cinco Calles area in the old town. Converging on Praza de Rogelio Lois, handily marked by a cruceiro, you could keep yourself well occupied here. At

GALICIA

Casa Fidel – O' Pulpeiro, Calle de San Nicolás 7, watch the señoras slaving over a boiling tub of chopped-up octopus. You can also eat cheaply across the road (No 6) at *Bar Barrantes*. Or again at No 5, *O' Noso Bar*. Right on the little square, *Restaurante Agudelo* is a more expensive place, where a fine seafood meal may cost you about 2000 ptas. Other areas to look for restaurants are along Calle de Fifueroa and Calle de la Pasantería, although the area is not quite as lively.

Dessert is important here, and Pontevedra is known for its pastries, particularly its tarta a las almendras, an almond-topped cake you can find in many pastry shops around Calle de Michelena.

Entertainment
The best places for coffee and people-watching are the cafés along the squares. Praza da Ferrería probably wins on this score. For drinking of a more nocturnal kind, head first for the pocket of bars on Calle del Barón, and then, for some heftier *marcha*, up the road to Calle de Charino – you'll soon get a feel for what's right for you. There is a nameless and popular bar – a good atmosphere for that lazy Sunday afternoon tipple – on Praza da Verdura. If it's discos you're after, try Calle de Benito Corbal.

Getting There & Away
Bus The bus station is a couple of km southeast of the centre on Avenida de los Alféreces Provisionales. As many as 20 buses a day head for Santiago de Compostela, some stopping in Padrón, others moving on north to La Coruña. The latter follow the A-9 and are quicker. Other buses serve Vigo, Orense, Lugo and O Ferrol.

Train The train station is right by the bus station. Pontevedra is on the Vigo-La Coruña line, and there are regular connections with those cities and Santiago de Compostela.

Car & Motorcycle The A-9 motorway and N-550 lead south to Vigo and north to Santiago. For Orense, take the N-541 east.

Getting Around
Local circle line buses run from the bus and train stations to Praza de España (the *gobierno civil* building).

RÍA DE PONTEVEDRA (SOUTH SIDE)
Don't be put off by the road from Pontevedra to Marín. It's an ugly business that bears little resemblance to what lies beyond Marín, a foul industrial port and home to the country's naval academy.

Bueu & Around
Side tracks lead off to a series of small beaches on the way to Bueu. A couple of places offer themselves for an overnight stay. *Hostal A Centoleira* (☎ 986-32 08 96), right on the Praia de Beluso, has doubles for 4000 ptas. More expensive but quite nice is *Hotel Playa Agrelo* (☎ 986-32 08 44) by the beach of the same name. Singles/doubles go for 4500/7000 ptas in the high season.

An excursion to the village of **Cela**, three km inland, makes an interesting diversion. The only 'sight' is a small Romanesque church, but watching the locals toiling in the fields so close to the fun and sun of nearby beaches is a sobering spectacle.

A few km west is a track leading off to the windswept **Cabo de Udra**, good for a bracing walk. There is a little beach nearby, although the Atlantic chill will probably keep most out of the drink.

Along the north-south coast from the cape to the village of **Aldán** are cradled a series of pretty, protected **beaches**, among them Praia Vilariño and Areacova.

Hío & Around
A few km south-west of Aldán, the cluster of houses that constitutes Hío has its focal point in Galicia's most remarkable cruceiro. It was sculpted last century from a single block of stone, and the great passages in Christian history, from Adam and Eve's sinful errors through to the taking down of Christ from the cross, are narrated up its length.

A couple of km on are a few tranquil beaches at **Vilanova**, while south of Hío, on the Ría de Vigo, are Praia de Nerga and Praia de Barra. Part of the latter is for nudists, and although both are good, they can get windy. The reward for covering five km of mostly dirt track from Hío to **Cabo de Home** is great views of the Islas Cíes and the Atlantic.

Hío is a peaceful base. *Hostal Stop* (☎ 986-32 94 75), near the famous cruceiro, has rooms for as little as 1000/2000 ptas in winter, but more like 3000/5000 ptas in summer. You can also find rooms in Vilanova.

RÍA DE VIGO (NORTH SIDE)

From Hío you can head for Cangas, which passes for a resort town on the Ría de Vigo and is arguably the ría's least attractive feature. The drive along the north bank of the ría is magnificent in parts, but the surrounding area is not Galicia's best shot at beaches or rural splendour.

Cangas

A bustling but ill-ordered port town, Cangas had its big moment in history, but it was a tragic one. In 1617, a band of several thousand Saracens (possibly Algerians) landed nearby and proceeded to sack the whole area in grand style. Such was the thoroughness of the slaughter, the story goes, that quite a few women went mad and became witches – some good *(meigas)* and others bad *(brujas)*. The Inquisition took things in hand, and so a number of these witches ended up burning at the stake. There is little of specific interest to see, although you could while away an hour or two strolling around the back streets of the port. The nearby Praia de Rodeira is OK, but inferior to those further out beyond Hío. There's a tourist information booth at the port.

Few conceivable reasons for hanging about overnight spring to mind, but if you feel some irresistible urge, head for the east end of Praia de Rodeira (about a two km walk from the bus station and port). *Apartamentos Rodeiramar 2A* (☎ 986-30 17 49), Avenida de Orense 76, right by Cangas' most reasonable beach, has apartments to sleep four with TV, lounge room and kitchen for 7000 ptas. *Hostal Playa* (☎ 986-30 36 74), at No 78, has

rooms for around 4000/6000 ptas in the high season.

There are few places to eat. You might have a go at *Restaurante Casa Juan*, Rúa de Hío 2, which does reasonable seafood tapas.

Buses run regularly from the port to Vigo, Bueu, Hío and other points along the peninsula. There are frequent ferries to Vigo too.

On to Vigo

From Cangas there is little to hold you up before you make the decision about whether to head north to Pontevedra or south to Vigo and beyond. **Moaña** has a modest Romanesque church and an hourly ferry to Vigo; otherwise the best part of the trip along this part of the ría is just that: the trip. You can see serried ranks of *bateas* – platforms that look a little like miniature oil rigs, where mussels *(mejillones)* are grown – and observe Vigo in the distance. If you have wheels, head inland a few km to the **Mirador de Cotorredondo**, a lookout commanding magic views over the Ría de Vigo, with its imposing suspension bridge, the Puente de Rande, and the Ría de Pontevedra.

If you follow the old N-550 down the east side of the ría, you could make a quick diversion east to see the well-preserved **Castillo de Soutomaior**. Back on the main road, you then reach Redondela, characterised by mostly disused railway viaducts. The N-550 proceeds directly south to Tuy and Portugal. Otherwise, stick to the coast for Vigo, which you will need to pass through in order to enjoy the southernmost stretch of Galician coast beyond the rías.

VIGO

Arriving from anywhere else in Galicia, Vigo can come as a shock. With 280,000 inhabitants, this is a big city, traffic-choked and chaotic. Its long port is protected from Atlantic disturbances by the Islas Cíes and once boasted a busy passenger terminal. These days, the furthest you'll get from Vigo by sea is Cangas. The small nucleus of tangled lanes of old Vigo exerts a fascination in a down-and-out sort of way, but in all, this

Vigo

0   100   200 m

city comes as a disappointment given its wonderful setting.

People only started to notice Vigo in the Middle Ages as it began to overtake Bayona. Sir Francis Drake thought it sufficiently interesting to take control for a few days in 1589. In 1702 the English were back with their Dutch allies to sink a galleon fleet bearing gold from the Americas near where the Puente de Rande crosses the narrowest neck of the ría today – so near, yet so far.

Orientation

The RENFE train station is about 1.5 km south-east of the town centre. Between the two you'll find plenty of accommodation although for eating and drinking you are best off hunting around the old town centre. From the station, Rúa Urzaiz and its partly pedestrianised continuation, Rúa do Príncipe, lead you to the centre and port. The Estación de Autobuses is considerably further south again from the centre.

Information

Tourist Offices There are tourist offices all over town. You'll find them at Muelle de Trasatlánticos, by the Estación Marítim

PLACES TO STAY
7   Hotel El Aguila
13   Hostal Princesa
14   Hostal Don Quixote
20   Hotel Pantón
21   Hostal Krishna
22   Hostal Lino
23   Hostal Madrid

PLACES TO EAT
5   Restaurante Fay-Bistes
8   Restaurante Senen
9   Taberna Ramón
10   Patio Gallego
11   Bar Chavols
16   Ristorante Il Tartufo

OTHER
1   Tourist Office
2   Boats to Islas Cíes, Cangas & Moaña
3   Police Station
4   Praza da Pedra & Oyster Market
6   Iglesia Colegiata de Santa María
12   Praza da Constitución
15   Post Office
17   Tourist Office
18   Tourist Office
19   Town Hall (Concello)
24   RENFE Train Station
25   Tourist Office
26   Tourist Office
27   Hospital Xeral

(port); on Praza de España; Praza da Estación (train station); and Paseo de Alfonso XII. All are open Monday to Friday from 10 am to 2 pm and 5 to 9 pm. One opens at the airport for incoming flights, and there is another at Lonja de Concello, open Monday to Friday from 9 am to 2 pm and 4.30 to 6.30 pm, and Saturday from 10 am to 12.30 pm. For information by telephone, call ☎ 43 05 77.

Money There is no shortage of banks, mostly with ATMs, particularly around Rúa do Príncipe. American Express (☎ 43 44 05), represented by Ultratur, is at Calle Cánovas del Castillo 5.

Post & Communications You'll find the main post office (Correos y Telégrafos) on Rúa da Victoria. The postcode is 36200 and the telephone code is ☎ 986.

Medical & Emergency Services   Call ☎ 091 in a police emergency. There is a station at Rúa de Luís Taboada 3. In a medical emergency, try ☎ 47 11 11. The Hospital Xeral, just off Praza de España, is the nearest to the town centre.

Old Town

Praza da Constitución, lined by elegant old houses seated above arcades, marks the entrance into the casco antiguo (old town) from the bustling thoroughfares of downtown Vigo. Take Rúa dos Cesteiros north and you'll stumble upon the **Iglesia Colegiata de Santa María**, a neoclassical construction of 1816. Nearby **Praza da Pedra** hosts a sad-looking off-the-back-of-a-boat market where the *ostreiras* hawk their slithery wares in the morning – oysters. Rúa Real is the old town's main street, on or near which you'll find a fair selection of taverns.

Parque do Castro

Directly south (and uphill) of the casco you can wander in this park for a little peace and quiet, and have a look at the *castillo* that formed part of the town defences built under Felipe IV.

Beaches

The best beaches within reach are the Playa de Samil and another further on at Candido, south-west of Vigo. Local buses run there (see Getting Around below).

Places to Stay

Around the Train Station There is a stack of hotels around the train station, not distressingly far from the centre. *Hostal Madrid* (☎ 22 55 23), Rúa de Alfonso XIII 63, has a variety of rooms, with doubles going for 1800 ptas, 2500 ptas with shower or 3000 ptas with full private bathroom. *Hostal Lino* (☎ 22 42 71), Bajada a la Estación 2, has singles/doubles for 2500/3500 ptas, while *Hotel Pantón* (☎ 22 42 70), Rúa de Lepanto 18, can give you a room with private bathroom and TV for 2500/4300 ptas. Not too far away, *Hostal Krishna* (☎ 22 81 61), Rúa de

Urzaiz 57, has modern if unspectacular rooms for 2000/3000 ptas.

Around the Old Town In the heart of the old town is a sprinkling of generally run-down and poor value *casas de huéspedes* (marked by the blue CH signs) and *fondas*.

Hostal Princesa (☎ 43 37 00), Calle de Fermín Penzol 14, has decent singles/doubles with private bath, TV, phone and heating for 3000/5000 ptas. Rooms at *Hotel El Águila* (☎ 43 13 98), Praza de Compostela 6, start from 3000/3500 ptas and rise to 4500/5000 ptas.

Places to Eat
The winding lanes and blind alleys of old Vigo are laced with tapas bars and eateries of all descriptions – part of the fun is looking around. *Bar Chavolas*, Rúa dos Cesteiros 3, is a cheap, spit-and-sawdust place off Praza da Constitución – itself a pleasant spot for a morning cup of coffee. At No 2A is the *Taberna Ramón*, in much the same league. The *Patio Gallego* at No 7 has a decent set lunch for 1000 ptas. *Restaurante Senen*, Rúa da Palma 3, is similar. *Restaurante Fay-Bistes*, Rúa Real 7, has a set lunch for 850 ptas and good tapas.

If you want a change and have cash to spare, *Ristorante Il Tartufo*, Praza de Compostela 16, is hard to beat for quality Italian food (pasta made on the premises).

Entertainment
At weekends in particular, head for Rúa Real in the old town. Here and in the surrounding lanes is a fair smattering of taverns. Otherwise, you'll find a couple of busy places on Rúa de Churruca, a small lane near the train station. For late-night dancing, El Malecón, Rúa de Taboada Leal, off Rúa de Venezuela, is a Vigo favourite. Another late-night drinking place that attracts a mixed crowd is *74*, at Rúa Areal 74. Don't bother arriving before 2.30 am. In summer, the Playa de Samil area gets busy late at night too.

Getting There & Away
Air Aviaco has flights to Bilbao, Barcelona, Madrid and Las Palmas. In summer you can sometimes get charter flights to the UK. The airport is about 10 km east of town.

Bus From the bus station, well south of town on Avenida de Madrid, you can pick up services to all main Galician destinations, as well as long-distance ones like Madrid, Barcelona and the País Vasco.

Train There are three trains a day to Madrid, two to Barcelona (via Oviedo) and another two to Irún, on the French border. Regular services run to Santiago de Compostela, for which the 2nd class one-way fare is 690 ptas. Pontevedra (295 ptas), La Coruña (1235 ptas), Orense (875 ptas) are also accessible.

Car & Motorcycle The A-9 tollway to La Coruña via Pontevedra and Santiago starts here. The C-550 hugs the coast to La Guardia, the Río Miño and Portugal.

Boat There are regular ferry crossings to the Islas Cíes (see below), as well as to Cangas and Moaña. Either of the latter costs 185 ptas one way. A fast boat to Cangas costs 325 ptas. A boat runs to/from Cangas about every half-hour from 8 am to 9.30 pm.

Getting Around
Vigo has a fairly decent local bus system. From Porta do Sol, Nos 21, 14 and 7 run to the Estación de Autobuses. No 10 goes to the beach at Candido, while Nos 15, 16 and 27 pass Samil beach.

AROUND VIGO
Islas Cíes
The best beaches in the Rías Bajas aren't really in the rías at all. Rather, you need to head out for the Islas (Illas) Cíes. Of the three islands, one has been declared off limits as a national park. The other two, Isla de Monte Faro and Isla de Monte Agudo are linked by a white sandy crescent that also forms a lagoon known as Lago dos Nenos. The little archipelago forms a nine-km breakwater protecting Vigo and its harbour from the Atlantic's fury.

You can only visit the islands from mid-June to the end of September, and numbers are strictly limited. To stay overnight you must book in for the camping ground at the office in the Estación Marítima in Vigo – places are limited. You pay a 1000 ptas reservation fee for the camping voucher. You can then organise a return boat ticket for the day you require. Without the camping voucher, you must get a same-day return ticket. Camping costs 485 ptas per person and per tent plus IVA. At the camping ground, the 1000 ptas reservation fee will be used as a credit towards your overall camping costs. The return boat ticket costs 1700 ptas and the frequency of services depends largely on the weather. While it is also possible to get a boat to the islands from Bayona, you can only arrange camping in Vigo.

The South

THE COAST

Bayona

On 1 March, 1493, the caravel *Pinta* came into view off Bayona, bearing the remarkable news that Columbus had made it to the Indies. In fact, as would later become clear, he and his band had bumped into something quite different – the Americas. In those days Bayona was an important trading port. Later it was eclipsed by Vigo, and its population dropped to 150 in the 17th century. Nowadays it is one of Galicia's premier summer resorts, but understated compared with its Mediterranean counterparts.

There is a tourist information booth just before the gateway to the parador and city walls. It's open daily from 10 am to 8 pm. The telephone code for Bayona is ☎ 986.

The mighty **walls** stretching round the pine-covered west side of town were erected between the 11th and 17th centuries. It costs 100 ptas to walk into the grounds (500 ptas to take a car in), and it is worth it. In the placid harbour, a remake of the Pinta serves as a small **Museo Flotante**. Heading west out of town is the unlovely 15-metre stone statue of the Virgen de la Roca, finished in 1930. You can climb up inside the statue (if it's open) and take in the views from the boat-shaped lookout in her hand.

For beaches, head out on the coast road to Vigo. First up is **Praia Ladeira**, but better is the **Praia América**, a couple of km further on. Most Vigo buses call in at these beaches.

At **A Ramallosa** you'll notice a wonderful old medieval bridge (often mistaken for a Roman one). There was a time when women three months pregnant came here to perform superstitious rites to assure themselves of an easy birth.

A couple of camping grounds open in summer. *Bayona Playa* (☎ 35 00 35) is at Sabaris on Praia Ladeira, but it's pricey – 600 ptas per person, 485 ptas per tent, 610 ptas per car. Only slightly cheaper is *Camping Playa América* (☎ 36 54 04), on the beach of the same name.

About the cheapest place to find a room is *Hospedaje Kin* (☎ 35 56 95), Rúa de Ventura Misa 29 (enquire in the café of the same name at No 53). Basic rooms start at 1500 ptas per person. Next up is the *Hostal Mesón del Burgo* (☎ 35 53 09), Barrio del Burgo (heading out of town on the road to Vigo), with rooms for 3000/4800 ptas in high season.

The cobbled lanes in the centre of town, including Rúa de José Antonio, Rúa do Conde and Rúa de Ventura Misa, are full of restaurants, tapas bars and watering holes. A great place to try is the *Freiduría Jaqueyvi*, Rúa José Antonio 2. They specialise in excellent seafood tapas – and the *tartas* are a treat for dessert.

Frequent buses north for Vigo and south toward La Guardia (A Guarda) leave from near the waterfront at Calle de la Carabela La Pinta. Most of the latter also go to Tuy. In summer you can get boats to the Islas Cíes (see the preceding section).

Oia

About 20 km south of Bayona, a small cove giving shelter to a handful of fishing boats is presided over by the majestic baroque façade of the **Monasterio de Santa María de Oia**.

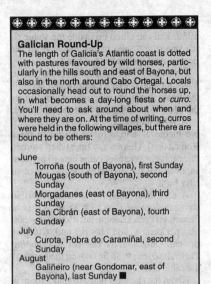

Galician Round-Up

The length of Galicia's Atlantic coast is dotted with pastures favoured by wild horses, particularly in the hills south and east of Bayona, but also in the north around Cabo Ortegal. Locals occasionally head out to round the horses up, in what becomes a day-long fiesta or *curro*. You'll need to ask around about when and where they are on. At the time of writing, curros were held in the following villages, but there are bound to be others:

June
    Torroña (south of Bayona), first Sunday
    Mougas (south of Bayona), second Sunday
    Morgadanes (east of Bayona), third Sunday
    San Cibrán (east of Bayona), fourth Sunday
July
    Curota, Pobra do Caramiñal, second Sunday
August
    Galiñeiro (near Gondomar, east of Bayona), last Sunday ■

Although the present façade went up in 1740, the monastery church dates from the 16th century, when it was remodelled.

La Guardia

A ramshackle and unlovely port, La Guardia (A Guarda, A Garda) nevertheless is in a prime position, sitting just north of where the Río Miño enters the Atlantic. There is a tourist information office on Calle de Rosalía de Castro. The treat here is to head south out of the town centre up Monte de Santa Tecla (100 ptas per person if you drive up). On the way up you can inspect a Celtic castro, where a couple of the primitive circular dwellings have been restored. Once at the top, there's a small museum with some Celtic finds. It's open Tuesday to Sunday from 11 am to 2 pm and 3.30 to 7.30 pm. Entry is free. Better than all that are the wonderful views up the Miño, across to Portugal and out over the Atlantic. A few km from La Guardia you'll find a beach at **Camposancos**, just inside the heads of the Río Miño, although you'd be

much better off on the other side of the river and on an ocean beach in Portugal. The telephone code here is ☎ 986.

Places to Stay & Eat The place to choose is *Hotel Pazo de Santa Tecla* (☎ 61 00 02), up on top of the mountain. Average singles/doubles with private bath cost 3400/4600 ptas. The best feature is the view. There's a restaurant too.

There are several undistinguished cheaper-end hotels in the town itself. *Hostal Celta* (☎ 61 09 11), Calle de Pontevedra s/n has basic rooms for 2000/3000 ptas, and slightly better ones with private bath for 2500/3300 ptas. The *Hostal Martirrey* (☎ 61 03 49), Calle de José Antonio 8, charges up to 2500/4000 ptas in the high season. The modern *Hostal Bruselas* (☎ 61 11 21), Calle de Orense 7, has rooms for 3000/4600 ptas in the high season. Hunt around the centre of town for tapas bars – most of what you eat will have been caught that day.

Getting There & Away ATSA has regular buses to Vigo via Bayona, and some to Tuy. In summer, buses connect La Guardia with the Camposancos beaches. There is supposed to be a ferry from Camposancos to Caminha in Portugal (from where you can get to the first in a string of sandy ocean beaches on the way south to Viana do Castelo). At the time of writing, the ferry still wasn't running.

Around La Guardia

Los Molinos (Os Muiños) de Folón make an off-beat inland objective. You'll need patience to navigate all the back roads to these water mills near Rosal, which were abandoned 40 years ago. It might all seem idyllic now, but the families who kept the mills creaking 24 hours a day to grind up the raw material of their daily bread lived in abject misery.

RÍO MIÑO
Tuy

Tuy (Tui) is a gem, a pretty old town sitting on the Río Miño. Especially popular in summer, when its little bars come alive, it is ideally situated by a bridge across to Portugal's equally interesting Valença. Some of Portugal's best northern beaches are just 35 km away. A fair crowd of Portuguese day-trippers fill Tuy on weekends, and Spaniards reciprocate in Valença.

Roman Tude for a short while hosted the court of the Visigothic king Witiza (702-10). Tuy was subsequently attacked several times by Spain's Muslim invaders and Norman raiders. Later still, the town found itself on the front line during various wars between Spain and Portugal.

The tourist office (☎ 60 17 89), Avenida de Portugal, is housed in a kiosk about a km short of the Portuguese frontier. The telephone code for Tuy is ☎ 986.

Things to See The brooding, fortress-like **catedral** dominates Tuy's small medieval centre. Completed in 1287, it was much altered in the 15th century. The extra stone bracing was added after the Lisbon earthquake. The main 13th century portal is opulently decorated with sculptures in a style typical of so many Galician churches. If you want to visit the claustro (cloister) and Museo Catedralicio, as well as climb the Torre de Sotomayor, the ticket will cost you 250 ptas. The cathedral is open from 9.30 am to 1.30 pm and 4.30 to 9 pm. Opposite the cathedral lies the **Museo Diocesano**, with a modest archaeology collection. It opens Tuesday to Sunday from 10 am to 1.30 pm and 4.30 to 8 pm. Entry costs 100 ptas.

The surrounding steep, narrow lanes, all affording tempting glimpses of Portugal across the Miño, shelter a pair of cruceiros and chapels, including **Capilla de San Telmo** (St Elmo), which contains relics of the patron saint of seamen.

Beyond the old town centre, the pleasant riverside walk around the **Convento de San Domingo** is enticing. The monastery church's baroque façade hides a largely 14th century interior.

While here, take a look at the Portuguese town of **Valença**, just across the century-old Puente Internacional. It is a charming fortress

town and, with border formalities nonexistent, makes a pleasant diversion even if you don't want to go any further into Portugal.

Places to Stay You will find a couple of simple places to stay in the centre of town – but they tend to fill in August. The better of the two is the *O Cabalo Furado* (☎ 60 12 15), Calle de Seijas. Some of the rooms look out on to the cathedral. A little more claustrophobic is *Habitaciones Otilia* (☎ 60 10 62), Calle del Generalísimo 8. Both charge 1000 ptas per person. *Hostal Generosa* (☎ 60 00 55), Calle de Calvo Sotelo 37, is the next closest, with singles/doubles for 1500/2500 ptas. *Hostal Cruceiro do Monte* (☎ 60 09 53), Carretera de Bayona 23, has a good reputation and offers decent singles/doubles with private bath for 2500/3500 ptas. The *Parador de Tuy* (☎ 60 03 09; fax 60 21 63), on the road to Portugal, has rooms for 9800/12,500 plus IVA.

Places to Eat & Drink There are several inviting places to eat in the area immediately around the cathedral. You could try the *Jamonería* on Plaza del Generalísimo, or the *Pizzeria di Marco* on Calle de Seijas. The streets between the cathedral and the river are laced with great drinking establishments. A good one with views of the river is *Pub Zuriza*, on Calle de Cuenca.

Getting There & Away Buses stop along the main road through town. ATSA has regular buses to Vigo and La Guardia, and you can also get to Bayona and Pontevedra from Tuy.

The train station just north of the centre is on the Vigo-Porto (Portugal) line. There are three trains daily each way. If you are headed for Portugal, you could also try getting a train from Valença to Porto (five a day).

For other destinations, such as León, Bilbao, and other cities in Galicia you need to get to the train station at Guillarey (Guillarei), a few km away. It would be easier to make for Vigo first.

Around Tuy
About 20 km south-west of Tuy, Goyán

GALICIA

(Goián) is special only because it has a car ferry to Vila Nova de Cerveira in Portugal every half-hour (280 ptas plus 60 ptas for each passenger). East of Tuy a less reliable car ferry crosses from Salvaterra de Miño.

Ribadavia

In the heart of Ribeiro wine country, Ribadavia was once Galicia's most important Jewish settlement. Even after Their Catholic Majesties decided to expel all Jews in 1492, most managed to hang on, either converting to Christianity or fleeing temporarily to Portugal and returning after the hue and cry had died down.

There is a tourist booth on Praza Maior (☎ 47 12 75), open Monday to Saturday from 10 am to 3 pm and Sunday from 11 am to 3 pm. The telephone code is ☎ 988.

It is a pleasure to wander around the medieval town centre, characterised by a patchwork of uneven little cobbled squares, lined with heavy stone arcades and galerías. The Barrio Judío (Jewish quarter) is signposted and the usually indifferent weather lends the whole a melancholy air. Nearby, Praza de García Boente is fronted by the Casa de la Inquisición. Of the several churches dotted about the town, the Romanesque **Iglesia de Santiago** and **Iglesia de San Juan** stand out. The castle remains date from the 15th century.

There's nowhere much to stay in the centre of this surprisingly big town, unless you get lucky with a cheap room at *Bar Celta*, Praza da Fonte de Prata 8. *Hostal Vista Alegre* (☎ 47 12 86), Avenida Rodríguez de la Fuente 14, is a possibility at 1000 ptas a head, but it is often full with road-workers. The nearest hostal is the *Hostal Evencio* (☎ 47 10 45), out of town at Avenida de Rodríguez Valcarcel 30. Singles/doubles cost 3000/4500 ptas. There are a few places around the town to eat and drink; for a tavern atmosphere, dive into the gloomy and cavernous *Bar O Xudío*, Rúa de Caula 10, between Praza Maior and Praza da Magdaleña.

Six trains a day run to Vigo and Orense,

from a station just over the Río Avia. Regular buses run to Orense from a station nearby.

Ribadavia to Celanova

From Ribadavia, the road to Celanova via Cortegada is a marvel of green – mostly Ribeiro vines – and curves. From Cortegada turn eastwards for Celanova, unless you want to proceed west into Portugal. **Celanova** is a nondescript sort of a place, except for the massive and tatty Benedictine Monasterio de San Salvador, on Praza Maior. Though the place is now partly used as a school, you can generally wander into the two cloisters at any time. At the time of writing, you could peer through the door into the cathedral to see what a pitiful state it's in. From the Claustro de las Procesiones (the mixed Gothic and baroque cloister) there is access to the tiny 10th century Mozarabic Oratorio de San Miguel. You can supposedly get keys for the cathedral and oratorio in the rectory.

The Interior

With the notable exception of the well trodden Camino de Santiago, inland Galicia is much unvisited. Of its cities, Orense has a surprisingly attractive, compact centre while Lugo's main claim to fame is it Roman walls. Away from the towns, nothing humans could produce can match the natural splendour of the Sil valley, which stretches from the border with León to the Río Miño.

ORENSE

Orense (Ourense in Galician) may well be the first Galician city that travellers emerging from neighbouring Castilla or Portugal encounter. With more than 100,000 inhabitants, the first impression is of a uniformly dissatisfying modern sprawl. Give it a chance, as buried deep in the heart of it lies a wonderful old town core bursting with life.

History

Orense was a Roman settlement of some

Rioja vineyards near Laguardia, in Álava province, País Vasco

DAMIEN SIMONIS

DAMIEN SIMONIS

DAMIEN SIMONIS

Top Left: Some of the glassed-in balconies, or *galerías*, that are characteristic of La Coruña, Galicia
Top Right: The picturesque fishing village of Cudillero, Asturias
Bottom: The port of Laxe, on the Costa da Morte, Galicia

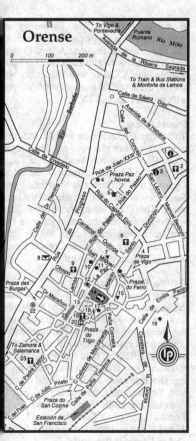

1	Tourist Office
2	Iglesia de San Francisco
3	Tourist Information Kiosk
4	Hostal Lido & Centro de Salud
5	Telephone Office
6	Iglesia de Santo Domingo
7	Restaurante Sanmiguel
8	Post Office
9	Iglesia de Santa Eufemia
10	Hostal Cándido
11	Praza do Cid
12	Police Station
13	Praza Maior
14	Catedral do San Martiño
15	Bar Cazador
16	Claustro de San Francisco
17	Pensión Las Dos Hermanas
18	Praza de Magdalena
19	Iglesia de Santa María Madre
20	Museo Arqueológico
21	Casa Consistorial
22	Fontes As Burgas
23	Iglesia de la Santísima Trinidad

Orientation

The train and bus stations are a few km north of the old town, to which they are linked by local buses. Head straight for the Catedral do San Martiño, around which unfolds the casco antiguo. Rúa do Capitán Eloy marks the northern boundary of this part of town, the life of which is played out in Praza Maior, Praza do Trigo, Praza dos Flores and Praza do Ferro.

Information

The tourist office (☎ 23 47 17), at Rúa de Curros Enríquez 1, opens Monday to Friday from 10 am to 2 pm and 4.30 to 6.30 pm. There's also a little kiosk on the corner of the same street and Rúa do San Lázaro.

There is no shortage of banks along Rúa de Curros Enríquez and its continuation, the pedestrianised Rúa do Paseo.

The post office is at Rúa do Progreso 53, and there is a telephone office just off Praza de Paz Novoa. The postcode is 32080 and the telephone code ☎ 988.

There is a police station (comisaría) just by the cathedral. In an emergency, call ☎ 091 or ☎ 38 81 00. The handiest clinic (centro de salud) is at Rúa de Juan XXIII 6-8.

importance. Later the Visigoths raised a cathedral here before the arrival of the Muslims, who in several raids destroyed the place. Repopulated by Sancho II in 1071, the town eventually began to take off as a trade centre. Orense's considerable Jewish population, having contributed generously to the campaign against Granada, were rewarded in 1492 with expulsion – an order the local branch of the Inquisition was particularly scrupulous in executing. Essentially an ecclesiastical town, it declined for centuries until the arrival of the railway in 1882 put it back on the map.

Puente Romano

Mostly modern, Orense shows its age along the Río Miño, crossed by a bridge that, while its foundations are in part those left behind by the Romans, is otherwise a medieval reconstruction.

Casco Antiguo

A leap of about 1000 years and a walk south into the casco antiguo (old town) brings you to **Catedral do San Martiño**, a rather gloomy 13th century church. Inside the main (western) entrance you'll run up against a Gothic version of the Pórtico de la Gloria, still conserving some of its original colouring. In this case it is known as the Pórtico del Paraíso, and one considerable advantage it has over its counterpart in Santiago is the total absence of tourists. If you want to see the small museum, track down the sacristan.

Around the cathedral unfolds a chain of charming little squares and alleys, inviting exploration by day or night. Praza Maior is the grandest of them, sloping away from the casco antiguo and hemmed in by arcaded walkways, above which stand out the elegant galerías of private houses and the restrained dignity of the *casa consistorial* (town hall). The Museo Arqueológico also backs on to this square, but at the time of writing was closed.

Fontes As Burgas

Since the Romans arrived on the scene, the thermal baths of Orense have been a blessing for the sick and tired, or simply those with sore feet. The steaming mineral waters gush out in fountains on Praza das Burgas, and the water is still used for heating in the immediately surrounding houses. There are always locals around, dipping in weary limbs or filling bottles for takeaway purposes.

Places to Stay

The choice area is around the cathedral. *Hostal Cándido* (☎ 22 96 07), Rúa dos Hermanos Villar 25, faces the delightful Praza do Cid, otherwise crowded with restaurants and bars. Singles/doubles cost 1700/2500 ptas. The *Pensión Las Dos*

Hermanas, Praza do Trigo, is grungy bu costs only 700 ptas per person. There are a few places around Praza do Alférez Provincial. The best is *Hostal Lido* (☎ 21 33 00), Rúa de Juan XXIII 6, with singles/doubles starting at 1500/2500 ptas, or 2900/3500 ptas with private bath and TV.

Places to Eat

The streets and squares around the cathedral are bursting with places to eat. For simple cheap Galician dishes, head for *Bar Caza dor*, Rúa dos Fornos – just near the cathedral Orense's top restaurant is the *Restaurante Sanmiguel*, at No 18 on the street of the same name. There are innumerable tapas bars watering holes and ice-cream joints in thi small area, and plenty of cafés. For the latter try Praza Maior or Rúa do Coronel Ceano Vivas (Calle de Juan de Austria).

Getting There & Away

The bus station is well away from the town centre across the Ponte Nova and has regular services to surrounding towns. At least one a day heads for Verín and Portugal, and a couple head east for the towns along the Sil valley. The RENFE train station is closer to town. At least five trains daily take up to eight hours to reach Madrid. Several connect with Santiago de Compostela (820 ptas in 2nd class regional), Vigo (875 ptas) and L. Coruña (1335 ptas). Local bus Nos 1, 3, 6 12 and 15 run past both stations to the Parque do San Lázaro in the centre.

AROUND ORENSE
South to Portugal

The N-525 south of Orense crosses severa low ranges on the way to the Portuguese border. The only noteworthy stop along th way is **Verín**. An average sort of place wit a vaguely charming Plaza Mayor (in a fade sort of a way), it merits a halt for those wit their own transport for the nearby Castillo d Monterrei. In a commanding position fou km away, the castle's main tower offers spec tacular views on all sides. It is ope Wednesday to Sunday from 10.30 am to 1.3 pm and 5 to 8 pm. Entry is free.

If you have to stay in Verín, there are several cheap places on and around Rúa Lisa and Calle Mayor. Octopus lovers should try *Casa do Pulpo*, Rúa Lisa 14, for a feed. Verín lies on a crossroads, with the Portuguese border 15 km south. The road east takes you to La Puebla de Sanabria (see the Castilla y León chapter), while to the west lie the Rías Bajas. Daily buses run to Orense and Chaves (in Portugal).

Monforte de Lemos

Inhabited before the Romans appeared and later converted into the medieval Mons Forti, this dishevelled place has made its living as Galicia's principal rail junction since 1883, when the Madrid-La Coruña line was completed. It is actually quite interesting if you should be caught between trains.

Long before you reach the town centre you'll see the **Torre del Homenaje**, the most intact part of the 13th century castle remaining at the top of the *monte forte*. Across the river from the town centre stands the proud **Colegio de Nuestra Señora la Antigua**, which once housed a Jesuit seminary.

Should you decide to stay, head for the 16th century bridge over the Río Cabe. *Hostal Puente Romano* (☎ 982-41 11 67), on Paseo del Malecón, has singles/doubles for 1800/3000 ptas. There are a few cafés and eateries around the bridge and river.

Most trains crossing Galicia call in here, and there are plenty of buses (the station is near the centre) heading north to Lugo and south-west to Orense.

ALONG THE RÍO SIL

Take the N-120 north-east out of Orense (the Monforte road) along the Río Miño, a pretty stretch but nothing compared to what's in store if you turn off east at Os Peares. Here the Miño meets the Río Sil, and the ensuing 15 km make for a spectacular drive (or, indeed, hike) along the upper reaches of the **Gargantas del Sil** (Sil Gorges). The Orense-Monforte railway also follows the gorge for about 10 km.

This road ends in a T-junction with another minor road that winds its way about 90 km east before again hitting the N-120 to Castilla y León. Take a right (heading to Orense) at the T-junction and after five km you reach the **Monasterio de San Esteban (San Estevo) de Ribas de Sil**. Some of this huge complex, with three cloisters, dates from the 10th century, although much has been stripped bare. The monastery's opening times seem haphazard; if you turn up within the standard visiting hours (about 10 am to 2 pm, or late in the afternoon), you should be OK. From here you could return to Orense, ending a pleasant loop, or make eastwards for Castilla y León. The road passes through thick woods and high, windswept heath, with the odd village and church off to the sides en route, and the deep gorges of the Río Sil never far away. **Castro Caldelas** and **Pobra de Trives** are among the bigger settlements. The former has a nice castle; shame about the town. But there are a couple of hostales if you need one. After passing A Rúa and O Barco de Valdeorras, the Sil marks the boundary with Castilla y León, with Ponferrada just 31 km away.

The odd bus runs along this route from Orense, but it can be slow going. A bicycle (for the fit) or vehicle of your own is a better bet, although a combination of two feet and a thumb is not impossible for those unconcerned about time.

LUGO

Lugo is not the place to cure depression. Praised in the tourist literature as the city with the most impressive Roman walls in all Spain, it is a sad and neglected city, full of decay and not a little sleaze. It makes an interesting stop for a couple of hours if you're heading elsewhere, but a tantalising place to linger it is not.

The Romans established Lucus Augusti over a Celtic castro in the 1st century AD. The walls went up two centuries later, but were not enough to keep out the Visigoths in the 5th century, or indeed the Muslims 300 years later. Until well into the 19th century the city gates were closed at night and tolls were charged to bring in goods from outside.

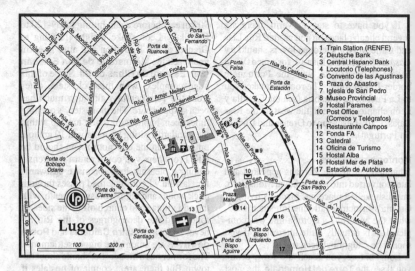

1	Train Station (RENFE)
2	Deutsche Bank
3	Central Hispano Bank
4	Locutorio (Telephones)
5	Convento de las Agustinas
6	Praza do Abastos
7	Iglesia de San Pedro
8	Museo Provincial
9	Hostal Parames
10	Post Office (Correos y Telégrafos)
11	Restaurante Campos
12	Fonda FA
13	Catedral
14	Oficina de Turismo
15	Hostal Alba
16	Hostal Mar de Plata
17	Estación de Autobuses

Orientation & Information

Whether you arrive in Lugo by train or bus (the latter is more convenient), you will end up not too far from the Roman walls. Once inside the city, there are a couple of focal points. The cathedral is near the Porta (gate) de Santiago, where you can climb up onto the city walls. Rúa Nova, the town's main street for bars, tapas and restaurants, stretches more or less east to west from near the cathedral to the Porta Nova. Be aware that the area between the cathedral and the Porta do Carmen is an unsavoury red-light zone.

The tourist office (☎ 23 13 61) is in an arcade at Praza Maior (Plaza de España) 27-29. There are several banks with ATMs around town. The Central Hispano and Deutsche Bank are on Praza de Santo Domingo.

The main post office is just off Praza Maior on Rúa de San Pedro, and there is a phone office (locutorio) on Praza de Santo Domingo. Lugo's central postcode is 27080 and the telephone code is ☎ 982. The local number for the police is ☎ 21 36 40. In a medical emergency call ☎ 061 or the Cruz Roja on ☎ 23 16 88.

Roman Walls

More than two km long and up to 15 metres high, the Roman walls enclosing Lugo are the best preserved of their kind in all Spain, if not the world. You can climb up onto the ramparts and walk right round the town.

Catedral

Back on the ground inside the Porta de Santiago, the imposing grey edifice of the cathedral rises up. It might not seem so at first glance, but it is basically a Romanesque-Gothic structure, begun in 1129 and inspired by the cathedral in Santiago de Compostela. Work went on until the 14th century, and a neoclassical layer was coated on later still. Inside, the walnut choir stalls are a baroque masterpiece. Across Praza de Santa María is the Palacio Episcopal, reconstructed in the early 1990s.

Museo Provincial

Halfway down Rúa Nova, the museum is housed in the former Convento de San Francisco. Apart from the Gothic cloister, old kitchen and refectory of the convent, the museum's religious art collection is housed on the ground floor. Considered Galicia's best museum, the collections also include archaeological finds and works by local artists. It is open Monday to Friday from 11 am to 2 pm and 5 to 8 pm, and Saturday from 10 am to 2 pm only. Entry is 200 ptas.

Places to Stay & Eat

The really desperate could try the *Fonda Fa* (☎ 22 86 21), Rúa Nova 13. For 1000 ptas you get a cell – usually set aside for local whores – and it's real hard-luck stuff. Fork out a bit more. A little more salubrious is the *Hostal Alba* (☎ 22 60 56), Rúa de Calvo Sotelo 31, with simple singles/doubles for 1500/3000 ptas. *Hostal Parames* (☎ 22 62 51), Rúa do Progreso 28, is quite reasonable at 2200/3900 ptas for singles/doubles with private bath. There are a few slightly cheaper rooms without own bath. Near the bus station, just outside the walls, you could try

Hostal Mar de Plata (☎ 22 89 10), Ronda da Muralla 5. Rooms start at 2000/3000 ptas in the low season.

A decent seafood place is the *Restaurante Campos*, Rúa Armaña. You can eat well for 2000 ptas. But before diving straight in here, take a stroll along Rúa Nova, full to bursting with tapas bars and restaurants.

Getting There & Away

Up to fours buses daily connect Lugo with destinations across northern Spain in Asturias, Cantabria and the País Vasco. Four buses also pass through Lugo from Santiago de Compostela and/or La Coruña en route to Madrid (6½ hours). Regular buses run south to Monforte de Lemos and Orense. Up to six trains a day run to La Coruña and Monforte de Lemos.

Valencia

This chapter covers the autonomous community of Valencia and is divided into four sections: Valencia, the Costa del Azahar, Inland Valencia, and the Costa Blanca.

Valencia, the capital, is on the coast roughly in the middle of the region. It's a typically Spanish city and is famed for its exuberant nightlife and the truly wild Las Fallas festival, held in March.

To the north, the Costa del Azahar has a string of low-key coastal resorts and several worthwhile non-coastal attractions, including the historic town of Sagunto and the museums of Castellón de la Plana.

South of Valencia, the Costa Blanca has achieved notoriety as one of Spain's most overdeveloped tourist areas. While it's true that places like Benidorm have become tourism horror stories, quite a few of the smaller resort towns along this coast are surprisingly unspoilt, and places like Calpe, Jávea and Altea are well worth visiting, particularly if you can go on either side of the summer rush.

And should you tire of coastal pursuits or crowds, the inland areas of Valencia offer a wealth of hidden or little-known surprises (not to mention endless orange groves). They include the ancient walled town of Morella; the beautiful scenery of the mountain district known as Els Ports; remote monasteries and charming spa towns; Elx's palm forests and gardens; and the splendid Gothic, Renaissance and baroque architectural monuments of Orihuela and Xàtiva.

Valencia

Spain's third-largest city and capital of the Comunitat Valenciana, Valencia comes as a pleasant surprise to many. Home to *paella* and the Holy Grail, it is also blessed with great weather and the festival of Las Fallas

HIGHLIGHTS

- The Las Fallas festival in Valencia city
- Valencia city's nightlife
- Valencia city's Museo de Bellas Artes
- The medieval fortress town of Morella
- Lunch at the Mare de Déu restaurant in Sant Mateu
- Xàtiva's architectural monuments
- Elx's palm forests and gardens

(in March), one of the wildest parties in the country.

Much of Valencia's appeal lies in what it isn't. It isn't particularly attractive, with perhaps the exception of the city centre and its old quarter. Unlike Barcelona and Madrid, it isn't crammed with must-see museums and world-famous architectural monuments. And unlike much of Spain, it certainly isn't overrun by hordes of foreign tourists.

It's a vibrant, somewhat chaotic and typically Spanish city with friendly inhabitants, an outstanding fine arts museum and one of the most exciting nightlife scenes in Spain. So, instead of rushing around ticking off items on a long itinerary, you can blend in, relax and just enjoy Valencia for what it is (and isn't).

History

The earliest settlements on the banks of the

Valencia

0   30   60 km

Río Turia were built by the Greeks and Carthaginians. The Romans founded a city here in 138 BC and named it Valentia, and began to develop systems of irrigation for the surrounding regions.

Roman rule was ended with the invasion of the Visigoths, but little is known of the subsequent period in the city's history. Then in 709 the Muslims took Valencia. The city prospered under their rule, developing into a rich agricultural and industrial centre. The Muslims redeveloped and improved the irrigation systems the Romans had built and also established ceramics, paper, silk and leather industries, among others.

Early in the 11th century the Muslim world began to fragment into separate *taifa* (small kingdom) states and became vulnerable. In 1094, Valencia and many of the surrounding regions were conquered by the legendary El Cid, a heroic Christian nobleman by the name of Rodrigo Díaz de Vivar. He died in Valencia five years later, and in 1102 the Almoravids retook the city. Muslim rule was finally ended by Jaume I, who led the Reconquista of Valencia in 1238.

Valencia boomed economically during the 15th and 16th centuries and become one of the strongest trading and financial centres on the Mediterranean. This was Valencia's (and Spain's) Golden Age, during which time the arts flourished under the sponsorship of wealthy patrons.

After siding with the losing Habsburg dynasty during the War of the Spanish Succession, Valencia suffered crippling setbacks. After the Bourbons won in 1707, Felipe V abolished the *fueros*, the generous legislative privileges which had been granted to the ancient Kingdom of Valencia.

Valencia was a Republican stronghold during the Spanish Civil War, and was the seat of the Republican government from November 1936 until October 1937.

Orientation

While most of Valencia's street signs are in Castilian, many of the newer signs are now marked in Catalan. This can be confusing, especially when you're standing on a street corner or plaza and can see two different names (eg Plaza del Tosal and Plaça del Tossal).

We have used the Castilian names; you'll find that most maps also use these.

City Centre Plaza del Ayuntamiento marks the centre of Valencia. Surrounded by colourful flower stalls, the plaza is home to the *ayuntamiento* (town hall), tourist office and the main post office. The Estación del Norte (the main RENFE train station) is just 250 metres south of the plaza, but the Estación Central de Autobuses (the main bus station) is almost two km north-west on Avenida Menéndez Pidal.

About 500 metres north of Plaza del Ayuntamiento is Plaza de la Reina (also known as Plaza Zaragoza). Further north again is Plaza de la Virgen, and between these two plazas is Valencia's cathedral.

The areas west of the cathedral and north of the huge Mercado Central food market are the oldest parts of the city. Known as the Barrio del Carmen (or just 'El Carme'), this is Valencia's best nightlife zone.

Valencia's commercial and shopping districts are spread around both sides of Plaza del Ayuntamiento, although the most up-market shops are found in the ritzy areas to the east and north-east of the plaza.

Greater Valencia You'll find that most points of interest are within the city centre. With the exception of a couple of museums and gardens, there isn't much of interest for visitors in Valencia's outer suburbs.

The city centre is actually about four km inland from the Mediterranean beaches, and lies on the southern side of a bend in the Río Turia. This once mighty river is now almost dry, and has been turned into a city-length park and recreation area.

Information

Tourist Offices Valencia's municipal tourist office (☎ 351 04 17) on Plaza del Ayuntamiento is open weekdays from 8.30 am to 2.15 pm and 4.15 to 6.15 pm, and Saturday from 9.15 am to 12.45 pm. This office is run

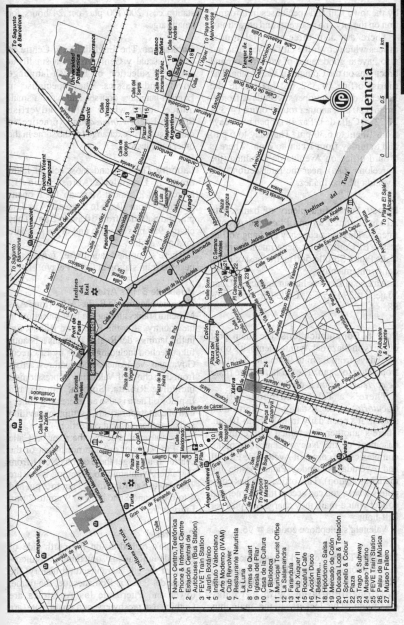

Valencia

1 Nuevo Centro, Telefónica
   Phone & Internet Centre
2 Estación Central de
   Autobuses (Bus Station)
3 FEVE Train Station
4 Jardín Botánico
5 Instituto Valenciano
   Arte Moderno (IVAM)
6 Club Revolver
7 Restaurante Naturista
   La Luna
8 Torres de Quart
9 Iglesia del Pilar
10 Casa de la Cultura
   y Biblioteca
11 Municipal Tourist Office
12 La Salamandra
13 Farandula
14 Pub Xúquer II
15 Rocafull Café
16 Acción Disco
17 Bésame...
18 Hipódromo Salsa
19 Mercado de Colón
20 Década Loca & Tentación
21 Spinello & Colour
22 Plaza
23 Trago & Subway
24 Museo Taurino
25 FEVE Train Station
26 Palau de la Música
27 Museo Fallero

by the town hall and specialises in information on the city and its events and attractions.

There are also three regional tourist offices which cover the city of Valencia but also have a good range of information and brochures on the Comunitat Valenciana. The tourist office (☎ 352 85 73) inside the Estación del Norte opens weekdays from 9 am to 6.30 pm; another tourist office (☎ 394 22 22) at Calle de la Paz 48 is open weekdays from 10 am to 6.30 pm (Thursday to 6 pm) and Saturday from 10 am to 2 pm. There is a third office on Avenida de Cataluña (the Barcelona road), near the intersection with Avenida Blasco Ibáñez.

Money You'll find plenty of banks with ATMs clustered around Plaza del Ayuntamiento. There is a currency exchange office at the El Corte Ingles department store on Calle Pintor Sorolla, 500 metres east of Plaza del Ayuntamiento.

American Express has an agency at Duna Viajes (☎ 374 15 62), Calle Cirilo Amorós 88.

Post & Communications The main post office is on Plaza del Ayuntamiento; it's open weekdays from 8 am to 9 pm and Saturday from 9 am to 2 pm. The poste restante *(lista de correos)* section is on the 1st floor.

There's a Telefónica phone office *(locutorio)* at the Estación del Norte train station; it's open daily from 8 am to 10 pm. There's another Telefónica centre in the basement of the Nuevo Centro shopping complex on the corner of Avenida de Pío XII and Avenida Menéndez Pidal (beside the main bus station). This office also has computers where you can access the Internet and collect your e-mail; they charge 600 ptas per half-hour.

Valencia's telephone code is ☎ 96.

Luggage There are good luggage lockers in the Estación del Norte, halfway along Via 1. They cost 300/400/600 ptas per 24 hours for small/medium/large, with a 15 day maximum. The lockers at the main bus station cost 200/400 ptas per 24 hours for small/large.

Bookshops The English Book Centre at Calle Pascual y Genis 16 has a small but excellent selection of English-language novels and classics. They specialise in English-language courses and have a small notice board where people advertise Spanish-English *intercambio* (practice in one language in exchange for the same in the other) and lessons.

Laundry The best and most central laundrette is Lavandería Autoservicio 'El Mercat', at Plaza del Mercado 12. It opens weekdays from 10 am to 2 pm and 4 to 8.30 pm, and Saturday from 10 am to 2 pm. They charge 950 ptas to wash and dry a standard load of washing.

There's another laundrette, *Lavamatic*, near the train station at Calle Pelayo 11.

Museo de Bellas Artes

Valencia's Museo de Bellas Artes (Fine Arts Museum) ranks among the best museums in the country, after the Prado and Bilbao. Set in the Jardines del Real, it contains a beautiful collection including works by El Greco, Goya and Velázquez, and features artists from the school of Valencian impressionists including Ribalta, Sorolla, Pinazo and Espinosa. There is also an interesting collection of contemporary art, a sculpture pavilion and an archaeological collection.

The museum is across the river on Calle San Pío V, about one km north-east of the centre. You can get there on bus No 11 from Plaza del Ayuntamiento. Opening hours are Tuesday to Saturday from 9 am to 2 pm and 4 to 6 pm, and Sunday from 9 am to 2 pm. Entry is free.

Catedral

Valencia's cathedral, on the north side of Plaza de la Reina, is something of a microcosm of the city's architectural history: the Puerta del Palau is Romanesque; the dome, tower and Puerta de los Apóstoles are Gothic; the presbytery and main gate are baroque; and there are a couple of Renaissance chapels inside.

The cathedral's **museum** claims to be home to the **Holy Grail** (Santo Cáliz), a gold cup purportedly used by Christ during the Last Supper. The museum also contains a collection of religious icons and several works by Goya. It opens Monday to Friday from 10 am to 2 pm and 4.30 to 6 pm and Saturday from 10 am to 2 pm.

On the south-west corner is the **Miguelete**, the cathedral's octagonal bell tower. Its 207 steps wind up a circular staircase to the top of the tower, which has great 360° views of the city rooftops and skyline. The tower opens weekdays from 10 am to 1 pm and 4.30 to 8 pm and weekends from 10 am to 1.30 pm and 5 to 8 pm. Entry costs 100 ptas.

As it has done for the last thousand years, the **Tribunal de las Aguas** (Water Court) meets every Thursday at noon outside the cathedral's Gothic doorway, where the irrigation disputes of the local farmers are settled in Catalan.

A walk-bridge connects the cathedral with the **Real Basílica de Nuestra Señora de los Desamparados**, which houses a small collection of artworks, and a fresco painted by Palomino.

Ayuntamiento

On the plaza of the same name, Valencia's ayuntamiento is a palatial 18th century building and is impressively floodlit by night. Inside are two small museums: the collection of the **Museo Histórico** includes a map of Valencia in 1704, paintings by Sorolla and the sword of King Jaume I (open weekdays from 9 am to 2 pm); and the **Museo Paleontológico** includes a collection of artefacts from South America (open Tuesday to Saturday from 9 am to 1.45 pm and some afternoons). Entry is free to both.

Palacio de Marqués de Dos Aguas

The baroque Palacio de Marqués de Dos Aguas, on Calle Poeta Querol, is a historic palace that was extensively rebuilt during the 18th century. It is fronted by an extravagantly sculpted façade in the churrigueresque style, hand-carved out of alabaster.

The palace houses the **Museo Nacional de Cerámica**, with ceramics from the towns of Manises, Alcora and Paterna. It's currently closed for renovations, but was due to reopen early in 1997.

Torre de Serranos

On the (dry) banks of the Río Turia, this well-preserved 14th century tower was part of the original walls around the Ciutat Vella, Valencia's old quarter. It now houses the **Museo Marítimo** with a collection of model ships and relics rescued from the Mediterranean seabed. The museum opens weekdays from 9 am to 1.30 pm and 4 to 6 pm and Saturday from 9 am to 1.30 pm.

Other Attractions

On the south-west corner of Plaza de la Reina is the Early Gothic **Iglesia de Santa Catalina**. Its beautiful baroque belfry was added in the 18th century and is one of the city's best-known landmarks. Further north on Calle de Caballeros, the lovely **Palau de la Generalitat** is fronted by a garden of orange trees.

The small circular **Plaza Redondo** is well worth a visit. Around the plaza there is an interesting collection of market stalls selling a good range of clothes, souvenirs and locally made crafts and ceramics.

Opposite the Mercado Central is **La Lonja de los Mercaderes**, Valencia's former silk exchange. This Late Gothic structure has a strikingly colonnaded hall that is now used for exhibitions.

The **Estación del Norte** is one of Valencia's most impressive *modernista* buildings. Opened in 1917, its entrance hall is decorated with ceramic mosaics and unusual murals.

Other Museums & Galleries The **Instituto Valenciano Arte Moderno (IVAM)**, northwest of the centre at Calle Guillem de Castro 118, houses an impressive collection of 20th century Spanish art. Its permanent collection features the works of the abstract sculptor

VALENCIA

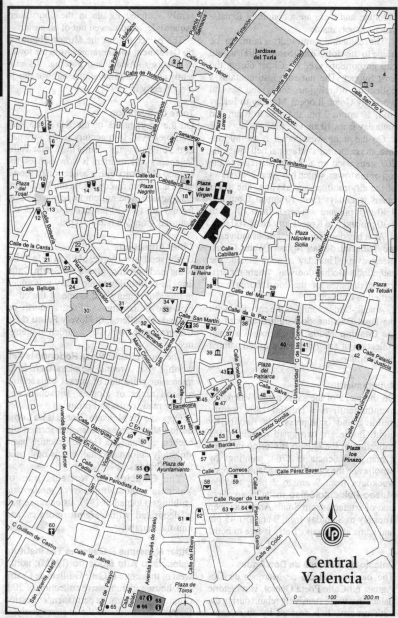

Central Valencia

0   100   200 m

PLACES TO STAY		50	Fosters Hollywood	29	Johann Sebastian
21	Hostal El Rincón	63	Cervecería Pema		Bach
22	Hospedería del Pilar			30	Mercado Central
26	Habitaciones CH Reina	**OTHER**			(Food Market)
32	Hostal El Cid	1	Coyote Bar	33	Plaza Redondo
37	Hotel Inglés	2	Torres de Serranos &	35	Iglesia de San Martín
41	Hostal Comedias		Museo Marítimo	36	Cervecería Madrid
44	Hotel Londres	3	Museo de Bellas Artes	38	Iberia Office
47	Hotel Astoria Palace	4	Jardines del Real	39	Palacio de Marqués
48	Pensión París	5	Bomba Bar		de Dos Aguas &
52	Hostal Moratin	7	Palau de Balia		Museo Nacional de
53	Hostal-Residencia	10	El Café		Cerámica
	Universal	11	Hanax	40	Real Colegio del
57	Hotel Reina Victoria	12	Café Bolsería		Patriarca
59	Hotel Continental	13	Café Infanta	42	Regional Tourist Office
61	Hostal-Residencia	14	Johnny Maracas &	43	Iglesia de San Juan
	Alicante		Charlie Brown's		de la Cruz
62	Hostal Castelar	15	Fox Congo	51	Filmoteca & Teatro
		16	Café-Bar Negrito		Rialto
PLACES TO EAT		17	Palau de la Generalitat	54	Teatro Principal
6	John Silver	19	Real Basílica de	55	Municipal Tourist Office
8	Café de las Horas		Nuestra Señora de	56	Ayuntamiento, Museo
9	Las Cuevas		los Desamparados		Histórico & Museo
18	Restaurante El	20	Cathedral		Paleontológico
	Generalife	23	Lavandería El Mercat	58	Main Post Office
31	Café del Mercat	24	Iglesia de los Santos	60	Iglesia de San Agustín
34	Horchatería de Santa		Juanes	64	English Book Centre
	Catalina	25	La Lonja de los	65	Lavamatic
45	Cezar's Plaza		Mercaderes	66	Estación del Norte
46	Restaurante Nuevo	27	Iglesia de Santa		(Train Station)
	Don Ramón		Catalina	67	Train Information Office
49	Bar-Cafetería Olimpya	28	Finnigan's of Dublin	68	Regional Tourist Office

Julio González, and there are frequent temporary exhibits by modern artists. IVAM opens Tuesday to Sunday from 11 am to 6 pm. Entry costs 350 ptas.

Another museum with works by El Greco, among others, is the **Real Colegio del Patriarca** on Plaza del Patriarca. It opens daily from 11 am to 1.30 pm. Entry costs 100 ptas.

The small **Museo Taurino** behind the Plaza de Toros holds an interesting collection of bullfighting memorabilia.

South-east of the centre on Plaza Monteolivete is the **Museo Fallero**. Dedicated to the Las Fallas festival, the museum houses the best floats from every festival since 1934, as well as posters and photographs from past festivals.

Other places of interest include the **Centro de Artesanía de la Comunidad** (with a collection of the works of Valencian artisans), the **Museo Paleontológico** (great if you're into insects and fossils), the **Casa Museo José Benlliure** (the painter's studio, housing a collection of his paintings and a ceramics collection) and the **Museo Etnológico** (a must-see for agricultural history buffs, if there are any). Check with the tourist offices for addresses and other details.

Parks & Gardens

The dry bed of the Río Turia has been turned into a large municipal park. It's a somewhat patchy collection of dusty playing fields, running paths, plantations, fountains and children's playgrounds. The best areas are those east of the centre around the Palau de la Música, where there are some very pleasant lawns and paths shaded by big old pine trees.

North of the river and the Museo de Bellas Artes are the large **Jardines del Real** (Royal Gardens), on the former site of the Royal Palace. These gardens are a lovely spot for strolling and picnics, and include a beautiful rose garden, a sculpture garden and a zoological park.

North-west of the centre and on the river opposite the main bus station, Valencia's **Jardín Botánico** is said to be Spain's first botanic gardens.

Beaches

Valencia's main city beach is the broad sandy **Playa de la Malvarrosa**. Efforts have been made in recent years to upgrade this beach, although it still isn't as clean as it could be. A string of restaurants, bars and discos line the waterfront, and especially in the warmer weather it's a lively area. Bus No 19 from Plaza del Ayuntamiento will take you there.

A better bet is to take a bus 10 km south to the very pleasant **Playa El Salér**, which is backed by attractive public gardens. You can get there with Mediterráneo Urbano (☎ 349 72 22), whose buses depart from the east side of the train station in Calle Alicante.

Special Events

Las Fallas Valencia's Las Fallas de San José is an exuberant and anarchic blend of fireworks, music, festive bonfires and all-night partying. If you're in Spain between 12 and 19 March, don't miss it.

The *fallas* are huge *papier-mâché* sculptures built by teams of local artists in the months leading up to the festival. Each of Valencia's neighbourhoods sponsors its own fallas, and by festival time more than 350 have been unveiled on local plazas. Reaching up to 15 metres in height, these huge and grotesque effigies satirise celebrities, current affairs and local customs and most are very colourful and very funny.

There are dozens of different events during the week of the festival including street parties, parades, open-air concerts, bullfights and fireworks displays – some organised, some spontaneous. Valencia considers itself to be the pyrotechnics capital of the world, and each day at 2 pm a deafening 10 minute fireworks display is held in Plaza del Ayuntamiento. On the final night each of

the fallas is set alight and burnt, backed by more fireworks of course.

If you haven't booked ahead, hostal and hotel accommodation is all but impossible to find. During the festival there are also rooms for rent in private homes – check with the tourist office on Plaza del Ayuntamiento or haggle with the locals at the train and bus stations.

Other Festivals & Events Valencia celebrates Semana Santa (Holy Week) with elaborate religious processions. Each April 14 the Fiesta de San Vicente Ferrer sees colourful parades with bands and traditional costumes, while on the second Sunday in May locals celebrate the feast day of the Virgen de los Desamparados, patroness of the city.

The festival of Corpus Christi, held during June, was first celebrated here way back in 1355. Each 24 June on the Día de San Juan, thousands of locals spend the evening on the Playa de la Malvarrosa and take part in a traditional cleansing ceremony that involves washing your feet in the ocean, writing your bad habits on a piece of paper and then burning it in a bonfire.

Valencia's Feria de Julio, held during the second week of July, features a packed programme of performing arts, music contests, concerts, bullfights, fireworks and the 'battle of the flowers'.

The Trobada de Música del Mediterrani music festival is held during September, while the Mostra de Valencia Cinema del Mediterrani international film festival is held in October. The Dia de San Dionís on 9 October commemorates the reconquest of Valencia by Jaume I.

In addition to these festivals Valencia's trade organisation, the Feria Muestrario Internacional, hosts more than 40 trade fairs throughout the year.

Places to Stay

Central Valencia's accommodation zones are distinctly different. A few dodgy hostales are clustered around the west side of the train station, but there are better budget options in the Barrio del Carmen north of the Mercado Central, which puts you close to Valencia's best nightlife (and, unfortunately, the red light district). The old quarter is a colourful and lively area to stay in but it can be a little seedy at night.

There's another cluster of hostales around Plaza del Ayuntamiento. These places tend to be a little more expensive – you're paying extra for the central location and better neighbourhood.

Valencia's best hotels and hostales are generally in the more up-market areas to the east and north-east of Plaza del Ayuntamiento.

Places to Stay – bottom end

Camping The nearest camping ground, *Camping del Salér* (☎ 183 00 23), is on the coast 10 km south of Valencia.

Youth Hostels There is a HI hostel, *Albergue La Paz* (☎ 369 01 52), three km east of the centre at Avenida del Puerto 69 – take bus No 19 from Plaza del Ayuntamiento. The hostel is open from July to mid-September and costs 1000 ptas for juniors and 1400 ptas for seniors (HI members only).

Barrio del Carmen *Hospedería del Pilar* (☎ 391 66 00), at Plaza del Mercado 19, is a rambling 45 room hostal with clean singles/ doubles from 1300/2400 ptas, or 1900/3400 ptas with private bathroom. It's well run and has a cosy TV lounge; the front rooms are the brightest but also get more traffic noise.

Nearby at Calle de la Carda 11, *Hostal El Rincón* (☎ 391 79 98) is one of Valencia's oldest and best-known hostales. Most of their 54 rooms are small and dim with a shabby kind of charm; nightly costs are 1300/2400 ptas. They also have three spacious renovated front rooms with modern bathrooms and sound-proofed windows – excellent value at 1900/3600 ptas. Lock-up parking is available at 600 ptas per night.

Hostal El Cid (☎ 392 23 23) is in a narrow side street behind Plaza Redondo at Calle Cerrajeros 13. It's another reasonable budget option, with 12 cosy rooms at 1400/2700

ptas, or 3000/3700 ptas for doubles with shower/bath.

Further north and right on Plaza de la Reina (3rd floor, no lift!), *Habitaciones CH Reina* (☎ 392 18 92) is very basic but well placed. It's also cheap with one single at 1200 ptas and doubles at 2200 ptas.

Around Plaza del Ayuntamiento At Calle Salva 12 (1st and 3rd floors), *Pensión París* (☎ 352 67 66) is one of Valencia's best budget options. It's friendly, in a good area and has 13 freshly painted rooms with white walls, beige-tiled floors and spotless bathrooms. Singles/doubles/triples cost 2000/ 3000/4500 ptas, doubles with shower are 3600 ptas.

Near Plaza del Ayuntamiento at Calle Moratín 15 (5th floor), *Hostal Moratín* (☎ 352 12 20) is quiet, clean and secure. Singles/doubles range from 1900/3250 to 2200/3750 ptas. The hostal has its own small restaurant; *pensión completo* (three meals a day) is available for another 1740 ptas per person per day.

Run by the same family as Pensión Paris (and to similar standards), *Hostal-Residencia Universal* (☎ 351 5384), at Calle Barcas 5, charges 2000/3000/4200 ptas (doubles with shower 3600 ptas).

South of Plaza del Ayuntamiento at Calle de Ribera 1, *Hostal Castelar* (☎ 351 31 99) has rooms from 1900/3200 ptas – they're not particularly flash but the front ones have good plaza views. Across the road at Calle de Ribera 8 (2nd floor) is *Hostal-Residencia Alicante* (☎ 352 74 99). Long, colourfully tiled hallways lead to quaint, oldish rooms with showers and TVs; singles/doubles/ triples cost 2800/3600/5100 ptas.

Places to Stay – middle

Hostal Comedias (☎ 394 1692), at Calle de las Comedias 19, is a warm and inviting hostal with nine excellent rooms from 2500/5000 ptas. The rooms are smallish but stylishly decorated, with modern facilities including heating and private showers. Book ahead.

Just off Plaza del Ayuntamiento at Calle

Barcelonina 1, the popular *Hotel Londres* (☎ 351 22 44) has well-worn but cosy rooms with TV, phone and private bathroom from 4400/7600 ptas including breakfast (3750/6500 ptas on weekends).

Behind the post office at Calle Correos 8, *Hotel Continental* (☎ 351 09 26) is a modern and friendly mid-range hotel with straightforward rooms ranging seasonally from 4750/6600 to 5500/7950 ptas (plus IVA).

Places to Stay – top end

Valencia is more of a business centre than a tourist town. As such the big hotels struggle to fill their rooms on weekends, so they offer fantastic discounts for Friday, Saturday and/or Sunday stays. Take advantage!

Smack-bang in the centre of town at Calle Barcas 4, *Hotel Reina Victoria* (☎ 352 04 87) is a grand old four-star. The rooms have been brightly refurbished and, while some of the facilities are dated, the gracious old-world atmosphere more than compensates. Standard rooms are usually 11,900/19,100 ptas, but on weekends they have singles/doubles from 8000 ptas and triples from 10,000 ptas. A great splurge.

Hotel Astoria Palace (☎ 352 67 37), at Plaza Rodrigo Botet 5, is a classy four star hotel in the most up-market part of town. They have 208 modern rooms costing from 18,600/23,250 ptas (plus IVA), with suites from 30,400 ptas. Their weekend specials are also great value, with rooms from 10,500 ptas.

Hotel Inglés (☎ 351 64 26), Calle Marques de Dos Aguas 6, is an older three star place with 62 comfortably refurbished rooms with all the mod cons. Standard tariffs are from 8000/12,750 ptas (plus IVA) – about 20% cheaper on weekends.

Places to Eat

Valencia is the capital of a fertile agricultural district that is often referred to as Spain's fruit and vegetable bowl. In addition to the world-famous Valencian oranges, the surrounding regions supply the city with a diverse range of fresh produce.

Rice is the cornerstone of Valencian cuisine – it's also the basis of the most famous local dish, *paella valenciana*. Paella appears on the menu of almost every restaurant, but unfortunately what ends up on your plate is often bland, gluggy and spoiled by cheap seafood and bony chicken. It's worth paying a bit more for the real McCoy.

The traditional paella is cooked (as opposed to pre-cooked!) over a wood fire in a flat circular metal dish and contains saffron rice, green and white beans, chicken, snails and lemon wedges for trimming. In practice you'll find plenty of variations – most commonly the addition of shellfish.

You'll also encounter plenty of other rice dishes on local menus, including *arroz a banda* (rice and seafood cooked in a fish stock), *arroz negro* (rice with squid in its ink), *arroz al horno* (rice with pork baked in the oven) and *arroz caldos* (a soup-like version of paella). Then there's *fideuá*, a type of paella made with noodles instead of rice.

While you're here you could also try a glass of *horchata*, a popular local drink that originated in the nearby *pueblo* of Alboraya (five km north of the centre). It's a strange milky substance made from pressed *chufas* (tiger nuts) – definitely something of an acquired taste. The *Horchateria de Santa Catalina*, at Plaza Santa Catalina 6, is a traditional horchata house with colourfully tiled walls and a chessboard floor. They do horchata líquida (225 ptas) or horchata granizada (frozen, 250 ptas), and also have great ice creams and churros y chocolate (425 ptas).

The *Mercado Central* food market is on Plaza del Mercado. Built in the striking *modernista* style of the 1920s, it's one of Europe's biggest markets and houses a great range of produce stalls, plus some good souvenir stalls out the front. It opens Monday to Saturday from 7 am to 2 pm and Friday afternoons from 5 to 8.30 pm.

Across the road from the market, *Café del Mercat* has a downstairs bar with tasty tapas and a mezzanine restaurant with a lunchtime menú for 1200 ptas and a dinner menú for 1800 ptas.

The modern *Bar-Cafetería Olimpya*, at

Calle En Llop 2, is a great spot for a quick bite. They do good breakfasts and also have good tapas and fresh salads as well as 10 different platos combinados (700 to 1200 ptas), bocadillos and burgers (375 to 500 ptas) and an excellent menú (950 ptas). They open daily from 8 am to 11 pm-ish.

Restaurante El Generalife, just off Plaza de la Virgen at Calle de Caballeros 5, has a very pleasant upstairs dining room where you can eat well á la carte for around 2000 ptas a head. They also have a menú for 1000 ptas, with plenty of choices including arroz a banda and paella Valenciana. It's open daily for lunch and Thursday to Sunday for dinner.

Café de las Horas, one block north at Conde de Almodóvar 1, is a wonderful 19th century style salon with mosaic-tiled floors, wax-dripping candelabras, wall tapestries and classical music – very soothing. They serve a wide range of herbal teas, coffees, sandwiches, salads and cakes (great chocky fudge cake!), and host occasional concerts of classical music, plays, exhibitions and tertulias (small discussion groups). Drop in and pick up a programme.

Across the road from here is the popular *Las Cuevas*, a subterranean grotto-like bar-eatery that specialises in tapas, bocadillos and jugs of sangría.

You'll come across quite a few good little budget eateries up in the Barrio del Carmen nightlife zone. One example is *John Silver*, just north of Plaza del Tosal at Calle Alta 8. Named after Long John himself (his wooden leg hangs behind the bar), it's a cluttered bar with an affordable menu that includes salads, bocadillos, bocatas and platos combinados – try the salchichas (550 ptas), a platter piled with frankfurter, sauerkraut, salad and bread.

Restaurante Naturista La Luna, at Calle San Ramón 23, is a well-patronised little vegetarian restaurant deep in the dark heart of the Barrio del Carmen. Good food, good prices. Open Monday to Saturday for lunch and dinner.

Fosters Hollywood, on the corner of Plaza del Ayuntamiento and Calle En Llop, is about as Spanish as Mel Gibson, but if you need something familiar... Part of a restaurant chain, it combines a movie-set décor with an Americanised menu that offers nachos and burgers (700 to 1000 ptas), grilled sandwiches (660 to 750 ptas) and Tex-Mex main courses (750 to 1900 ptas).

Calle de Mosen Femades, a pedestrian-only street one block south-east of Plaza del Ayuntamiento, is home to a cluster of up-market seafood restaurants. If the high-price menus scare you off, head for *Cerveceria Pema* at No 3. The décor is very straightforward but the food, some of which is cooked on a street-front barbecue, is tasty and reasonably priced.

For a splurge, try *Restaurante Nuevo Don Ramón* at Plaza Rodrigo Botet 4. It's a stylish (and somewhat touristy) place with gingham tablecloths and matching curtains. They specialise in paella Valenciana (2500 ptas), with other main courses in the 1000 to 2200 ptas range and a weekday lunch menú for 1100 ptas.

Across the plaza, *Cezar's Plaza* is a good place for a drink or a pre-dinner snack. It's a narrow and cheerful pine-panelled bar with a fine selection of tapas.

Entertainment

Fuelled by a large student population and an overdeveloped sense of competitiveness that manifests itself in a need to outdo Madrid and Barcelona, Valencia has a reputation for one of the best nightlife scenes in the country. For many visitors, Valencia's party-long-and-hard attitude is the primary motivation for coming here in the first place.

The only catch is that you have to know where to go, and when to go there. There are several different nightlife zones, and if you happen to be wandering around the wrong area, or the right area at the wrong time, it can feel as though you're in a shutter-drawn ghost town. So how will you know when you're in the right spot? Don't worry, you'll just know...

The Barrio del Carmen, the old quarter in the city centre, has Valencia's grungiest and grooviest collection of bars all rolled into one. The other major nocturnal zone is the

Ciutat Universitaria, the university area two km east of the centre. Along Avenida Blasco Ibáñez and particularly around Plaza Xuquer are enough bars and discos to keep you busy beyond sunrise.

Also worth checking out is the area around Plaza Cánovas del Castillo (about one km south-east of the centre), and the beach suburbs of Malvarrosa and El Salér which come alive with disco fever over the summer months.

Valencia's 'what's-on' guides, *Que y Donde* and *Turia*, are available from newsstands. Both cost 150 ptas and both give good coverage (in Spanish) of local theatre, cinema, live music, TV, concerts, eats and nightlife.

Bars & Pubs Valencia is well equipped with places to enjoy a *copa* or two.

Barrio del Carmen The maze of narrow streets and alleys of Valencia's old quarter is home to the city's best collection of bars and pubs. Known locally as El Carme, this area has everything from up-market designer bars and yuppie pubs to grungy thrash-metal haunts and psychedelic punk bars.

El Carme doesn't get going until after 11 pm, and most places stay open until 2 am early in the week and until 3 or 3.30 am on Thursday, Friday and Saturday. Calle de Caballeros, which runs from Plaza de la Virgen to Plaza del Tosal, is the main street and is usually crammed with people on *la marcha*, especially later in the week.

It's a reasonably safe area and if you exercise a little caution and common sense you shouldn't have any trouble. Stick to well-lit and busy streets, and don't go wandering too far north of Calle de Caballeros, particularly without company. The areas up around Plaza del Carmen are decidedly seedy, with leather-clad dope dealers on every second corner whispering *'Pssst, ¿quieres fumo?'*.

Plaza del Tosal has some of the most sophisticated bars this side of Barcelona. *Café Bolsería* is a stylish upstairs-downstairs bar that attracts a well-dressed crowd of 30-somethings. On the opposite corner, *Café*

Infanta is a swanky salon-style bar with old stone walls covered with red-velvet wall hangings and old Hollywood posters and photos. On the north side of the plaza, the smaller *El Café* has a quiet upstairs area.

From here you can head east along Calle de Caballeros or north along Calle Alta. Along Calle de Caballeros, look out for *Hanax* at No 36 (see the Live Music section) and *Johnny Maracas* at No 39, a suave Cuban salsa bar and the perfect place to perfect the art of drinking and dancing at the same time. A couple of doors along at No 37, *Charlie Brown's* is a rustic little bar below street level that does tasty crêpes (sweet or savoury) and bocadillos. It's a good place for a quiet drink and a fine place to fall in love with a raven-haired Spanish girl (although she doesn't work here any more). Next door at No 35, *Fox Congo* has an amazing interior with its back-lit marble bar, patchwork suede benches, scrap-metal-montage ceilings and glass-walled toilets.

Just south of Calle de Caballeros on Plaza Negrito, *Cafe-Bar Negrito* is another popular watering hole where the crowd and the music usually spill out onto the plaza.

The bars just north of Plaza del Tosal along Calle Alta are more student-oriented (ie cheaper and grungier!), and most have tables out on the street. At No 8 is *John Silver* (see Places to Eat), while the *Bomba Bar* at No 11 has a pool table downstairs and a narrow mezzanine level from where you can watch the goings-on in the street.

Further north the streets get darker and more dingy, but there are some interesting places to discover – just heed our earlier warnings. The *Coyote Bar*, up at Calle Padre Huérfanos 14, is a popular student hang-out with loud alternative music, a pool table and an Arizona-esque décor. At Calle Ripalda 24, *Club Revolver* has a rock 'n' roll attitude and weird psycho-space-age murals on the downstairs walls.

Other Areas *Finnigan's of Dublin*, an Irish pub on Plaza de la Reina, is a popular meeting place for English-speakers. The music and atmosphere are both good, they have Guinness, Kilkenny Special and Olde English cider on tap, and the kissing booths out the back seem very popular with young Spanish lovers.

Speaking of romantic, *Johann Sebastian Bach* at Calle del Mar 31 is a historic mansion that has been brilliantly converted into a sumptuous salon-bar with a lovely courtyard garden. It's a must-see, if you can afford the cover charge of 1500 ptas per person (the price includes a fruit cocktail; subsequent drinks are 500 ptas). It opens Thursday to Saturday from 10.30 pm to 3 am.

Another busy bar zone is the area around Plaza Cánovas del Castillo, about a km south-east of the centre. This area is tamer and more up-market than El Carme and attracts a younger crowd of teenagers and apprentice bar-crawlers, many of whom are still under parental supervision.

Plaza is a stylish corner bar on the plaza itself. Around the corner there's a string of places along Calle Serrano Morales: *Década Loca* at No 7 does the retro-60s thing with hits and memories from the hippy era, while *Tentación* next door is a salsa dance bar. *Spinello* at No 3 and *Colour* at No 2 are also popular. Further south, Calle Salamanca also has plenty of bars. *Trago* and *Subway*, both on the Calle Conde Altea corner, are worth a quick look.

Live Music Plenty of places around town have live music on a spontaneous basis, especially the bars in the Barrio del Carmen. *Hanax* (☎ 391 81 01), at Calle de Caballeros 36, is an up-market venue for Valencia's beautiful people. Set around an internal courtyard are a disco and pub, a restaurant, an art gallery and a piano bar. Their programme features everything from live jazz, country and folk to opera and classical music. Cover charges are fairly steep.

Cervecería Madrid, at Calle San Martín 10, takes you back in time to the jazz age of the 1920s. It's an atmospheric bar with soft lighting and walls covered with the paintings of local artist Constante Gil. The lounge upstairs has cosy booths around a baby grand

and features live jazz bands Tuesday, Wednesday and Thursday nights from midnight till 3 am. *Club Perdido*, at Calle Sueca 17 (500 metres south of the train station), is another popular jazz venue.

If you're interested in seeing traditional flamenco (as opposed to the contrived shows most tourist venues put on), *Bésame...* at Calle Explorador Andrés 6 (just off Avenida Blasco Ibáñez) has great performances every Tuesday night between October and June. This bar also has jam sessions on Wednesday, live bands on Thursday and DJs on weekends; hours are from midnight to 3 am.

Discos There are a handful of discos scattered around the city centre, but if you really want to experience life after 3 am in Valencia you should head for the Ciutat Universitaria. Two km east of the centre (around 600 ptas in a taxi), this zone is spread for almost a km along and around the broad Avenida Blasco Ibáñez.

Plaza Xuquer is the place to head for early in the night. The plaza is surrounded by dozens of bars and pubs which are in turn packed with students. Crowds spill out onto the streets and, in the great Spanish tradition of bar-hopping, most people just wander from place to place. Bars worth checking out include *La Salamandra*, *Farandula*, *Pub Xuquer II* and the *Rocafull Cafe*.

Around 3 am the stayers (with cash to splash) move on to the big discos along Blasco Ibáñez. Most discos have cover charges of between 600 and 1200 ptas, although discounted passes are often available from local bars.

If you're into the sounds of South American salsa and reggae, head for the funky *Hipodromo Salsa* at Avenida Blasco Ibáñez 146. Most of the other places, including the *Acción Disco* across the road, are dominated by *bacalao* dance music.

During summer there's a big disco scene in Malvarrosa and El Salér, concentrated mainly along the main waterfront roads.

Theatre & Performing Arts The *Teatro Principal* (☎ 351 00 51), at Calle Barcas 15, is Valencia's main venue for theatre, opera and the performing arts. It's an intimate theatre with a lush red velvet interior and steeply rising stalls. Ticket prices range from around 600 to 2000 ptas, depending on seats.

The *Palau de la Música* (☎ 337 50 20), a huge glass-domed concert hall in the Jardines del Turia, hosts more than 200 concerts each year including opera, classical music and solo performances.

Check local guides to find out what's on while you're in town.

Cinemas On the 4th floor of the Teatro Rialto building at Plaza Ayuntamiento 17, *Filmoteca* (☎ 351 23 36) screens classic, art-house and experimental films in their original languages. Session times are Tuesday to Saturday at 6, 8 and 10.30 pm and Sunday at 6 and 8 pm. Filmoteca is subsidised by the Generalitat and tickets are only 200 ptas (150 ptas for students).

There are a couple of other cinemas around town that often screen current-release films in their original language: look for films coded 'v.o. subtitulada' in *Turia* and *Que y Donde*.

Getting There & Away
Air Iberia (☎ 352 05 00) has an office on the corner of Calle de la Paz and Calle Marques de Dos Aguas. Regular flights connect Valencia with Madrid, Alicante, Barcelona, Palma de Mallorca and Ibiza.

Bus The Estación Central de Autobuses is an inconvenient two km north-west of the centre on Avenida Menéndez Pidal. Bus No 8 runs (in a roundabout fashion) between the bus station and Plaza del Ayuntamiento daily between 7 am and 10 pm. Each bus company has its own ticket window at the station; there is also a bus information office (☎ 349 72 22; 24 hours) just inside the front entrance.

Destinations and services for the major bus companies are as follows: Auto Res (☎ 349 22 30) runs 10 to 12 buses to Madrid daily (four to 4½ hour; 2845 to 3145 ptas); Enatcar (☎ 340 08 55) runs six to eight buses to Barcelona daily (4½ hours; 2650 ptas);

and Ubesa (☎ 340 08 55) runs 12 buses daily south along the coast to Alicante (four to 4½ hours; 1825 ptas) via Gandia (675 ptas), Denia (980 ptas), Jávea (1080 ptas), Calpe (1205 ptas), Altea (1300 ptas) and Benidorm (1395 ptas). Ubesa also runs express services to Alicante (2¼ hours; 1890 ptas) via Gandia and Benidorm.

Check with Eurolines (☎ 349 38 22) for destinations further afield including Paris, London and Rome.

Train The RENFE train station, the Estación del Norte, is on Calle de Játiva. There's a train information office at the front of the station (open daily from 7 am to 10.30 pm); otherwise, call RENFE's 24 hour information line (☎ 351 36 12).

There are nine to 10 trains daily between Valencia and Madrid; the trip takes about four hours (or six hours via Cuenca) and costs from 3800 to 4800 ptas one way. A dozen daily trains make the four to five hour haul north to Barcelona (via Tarragona); one-way fares are 2800 to 3800 ptas. If you're heading south, there are eight trains daily to Alicante, taking two to 2½ hours and costing 1800 to 2300 ptas.

Boat Trasmediterránea operates frequent car and passenger ferries from Valencia across to Mallorca, Menorca and Ibiza. They have an office in the city (☎ 367 39 72) at Calle Manuel Soto 15, and another office (☎ 367 65 12) at the Estación Marítima down at the harbour. Tickets can also be booked and bought from any travel agency (see the Balearic Islands chapter for more details).

Getting Around
The Airport The Aeropuerto de Manises is 15 km west of the centre. A taxi into the centre should cost around 1800 ptas.

Bus Local bus services are run by EMT (☎ 352 83 99); bus maps and timetables are available from the municipal tourist office. Buses on most lines run from 5.30 am to 11 pm, with nocturnal services continuing on seven services until 1.40 am.

Points of interest outside the city centre can generally be reached by bus, most of which depart from Plaza del Ayuntamiento. Bus No 19 will take you to Valencia's beach, Malvarrosa, as well as the Balearic Islands terminal. Bus No 81 goes to the university zone, and bus No 11 will drop you off at the Museo de Bellas Artes. Bus No 8 runs to the Estación Central de Autobuses.

Train/Metro Valencia's metro and suburban trains are operated by Ferrocarrils de la Generalitat Valenciana (FGV; ☎ 393 47 71). There are five different lines, although most service the outer suburbs. The closest stations to the centre are Ángel Guimerá (lines two and five), Xàtiva and Colón (both line two) and Pont de Fusta (line four).

Taxi There are taxis aplenty on the streets, but should you need to book one you can call Radio-Taxi (☎ 370 33 33) or Valencia Taxi (☎ 374 02 02).

Car Rental Hertz (☎ 341 50 36), Avis (☎ 152 21 62), Atesa (☎ 152 27 13) and Europcar (☎ 374 15 12) all have rental desks at the airport as well as city offices.

Of the local operators, Cuñat Car Hire (☎ 374 85 61) at Calle Burriana 51 is one of the best-value places, with Ford Fiestas and Opel Corsas from around 6000 ptas a day or around 26,000 ptas a week. Furgo Car (☎ 325 15 38) at Calle Linares 15 is also worth a try.

Around Valencia

Some of the most popular excursions from Valencia include visits to the ancient Roman ruins at Sagunto, the beach resort of Gandia and the inland town of Xàtiva (see the following sections for details of these).

La Albufera About 16 km south of Valencia is La Albufera, a huge freshwater lagoon separated from the sea by a strip of sand dunes and pine forests known as La Devesa. The lake and its surrounding areas are ecologically significant as a breeding area and sanctuary for several hundred species of migrating birds, and have been protected as a natural park. Keen bird-watchers flock to the Parque Natural de La Albufera to count kingfishers, mallards, white herons, coots and red-crested pochards, amongst others.

The unspoiled sections of La Albufera have a serene beauty, and the area is noted for its spectacular sunsets. You can take a boat trip across the lagoon, and temporarily join the local fishers who use distinctive flat-bottomed boats and nets to harvest fish and eels from the shallow waters.

Surrounded by rice fields, La Albufera was the birthplace of paella. The small villages of **El Palmar** and **El Perellonet** both have some excellent restaurants that specialise in paella and other rice and seafood dishes.

You can get to La Albufera, El Palmar and El Perellonet on the same bus as for Playa El Salér (see the earlier Beaches section for details).

Costa del Azahar

Stretching north from Valencia is the Costa del Azahar – the orange-blossom coast. Backed by a green and mountainous hinterland dominated by plantations of orange trees, the region takes its name from the spectacular displays of orange blossom that decorate the countryside each spring.

Benicásim is the best of the popular but low-key resorts along this coast; other attractions include the Roman ruins at the historic town of Sagunto and some interesting museums in the provincial and industrial capital of Castellón de la Plana.

The telephone code for the Costa del Azahar is ☎ 964 (with the exception of Sagunto, which is ☎ 96).

Getting There & Away

Bus Autobuses Vallduxense (☎ 349 37 38) has frequent services between Valencia and Sagunto (30 minutes; 280 ptas). Enatcar (☎ 340 08 55) runs about 10 buses daily between Valencia and Barcelona.

Train RENFE's Valencia-Barcelona train line follows this coast, and regional trains pass through and stop at all the main towns (with the exception of Peñíscola). There are 12 to 15 trains daily between 6 am and 10.20 pm. One-way fares from Valencia to Sagunto are 305 to 350 ptas; to Castellón, 470 to 510 ptas.

SAGUNTO

Sagunto, 25 km north of Valencia, was a thriving Iberian community as early as the 5th century BC, when the settlers fortified their hill town with stone walls and traded with the Greeks and Phoenicians.

In 219 BC the town was besieged by Hannibal for eight months. The inhabitants resisted heroically against overwhelming odds but were eventually wiped out and their town destroyed, an event which led to the Second Punic War between Carthage and Rome. Rome won, named the town Saguntum and set about rebuilding: today the remains of the Roman theatre, castle and Templo de Diana have been declared National Monuments.

Orientation & Information

Sagunto is a town in three parts. The Roman ruins and the old town are atop an inland hill; the new town and its ugly industrial zones flank the main highway; while down on the coast is the resort of Puerto Sagunto with its fine sandy beaches and ritzy boat harbour.

The train station is beside the highway. From there it's a 10 minute walk up to the old town and the tourist office (☎ 266 22 13) on Plaza Cronista Chabret. The office opens Monday from 8 am to 3 pm and Tuesday to Saturday from 8 am to 3 pm and 5 to 8 pm (7 pm out of season). During summer it also opens Sunday from 10.30 am to 1 pm and there's another office at Puerto Sagunto.

From the tourist office another 10 minute walk through the narrow streets of the **judería**, the old Jewish quarter, takes you up to the Roman theatre and castle.

Things to See & Do

You could easily spend a day or so exploring Sagunto's historic monuments. The **Roman theatre** was built into a curve in the hillside during the 1st century AD. Its remains were declared a National Monument 100 years ago, but a highly controversial 'restoration' project saw most of the seating covered with marble and a high cream-brick and bluestone façade tacked onto the front. Still, the acoustics remain outstanding, and it is used as a theatre and musical venue on Sundays between October and June (see also Special Events).

Higher up, the old stone walls of the **castle** wind around the hillside for almost a km. Mostly in ruins, the castle is divided into seven different sections or plazas, each representing a different period in Sagunto's history.

The castle and Roman theatre are open Tuesday to Saturday from 10 am to 2 pm and from 4 to 6 pm (to 7 pm in summer), and Sunday and public holidays from 10 am to 2 pm. Entry is free.

Other monuments include the ruins of the 4th century **Templo de Diana**, the adjacent **Iglesia de Santa María** which features Gothic and baroque doorways, and the 17th century **Ermita de la Sangre**.

Special Events

Sagunto hosts a smaller version of Valencia's Las Fallas festival each year from 15 to 19 March. The Semana Santa celebrations here are famous, and include sacred music concerts, parades and the traditional Calvary processions on Easter Friday.

The Roman theatre is the main venue for Sagunto's Escena each August, a three week open-air festival featuring opera, dance, theatre and orchestral pieces.

Places to Stay

Sagunto is mainly a day-trip destination, and sadly there is no accommodation in the old town.

There are three places down on the highway near the train station if you decide to stay. *Hostal Carlos* (☎ 266 09 02), Avenida País Valencia 43, has clean and straightforward singles/doubles at 1700/

2700 ptas, or 3000/4400 ptas with private bathroom. The modernish two star *Hotel Azahar* (☎ 266 33 68), Avenida País Valencia 8, charges from 4800/6900 to 5900/7900 ptas.

Alternatively, you could head down to Puerto Sagunto which has two camping grounds and a string of beachfront hotels and apartments.

CASTELLÓN DE LA PLANA

Castellón is the provincial capital of northern Valencia. Like many Spanish cities its outskirts are drab and industrial, so the city centre comes as a pleasant surprise to the few tourists who bother to visit.

It's a prosperous commercial centre and university town with an excellent fine arts museum, interesting historic monuments and some fine examples of turn-of-the-century *modernista* architecture.

Orientation & Information

Plaza Mayor marks the centre of Castellón. The train station is almost one km north-west of here, on the far side of the leafy Parque Ribalta; the accommodation hub, Puerta del Sol, is 200 metres south-west; and the tourist office (☎ 22 10 00) is 400 metres north-east at Plaza María Agustina 5. This office opens weekdays from 9 am to 7 pm, Saturday from 10 am to 2 pm; the staff are very helpful and have excellent information on the region.

There are several bus stations. Buses to/from Valencia operate from Plaza País Valenciana (700 metres south-west of Plaza Mayor), while buses to the beaches of El Grau leave from Plaza Juez Bornill (300 metres south of Plaza Mayor).

Things to See & Do

Castellón's under-visited **Museo de Bellas Artes** displays an eclectic collection, with a ceramics section that focuses on this region's major industry, an archaeological collection ranging from early Iberian cultures to medieval times, and a painting section that includes works by Ribalta, Romero de Torres and Sorolla. It's in a modest (and easily missed) building on the corner of Calle

Caballeros and Calle Gracia, and opens weekdays from 10 am to 2 pm and 4 to 6 pm (during summer, 9 am to 2 pm only) and Saturday from 10 am to 12.30 pm.

Also worth visiting are the **Museo Etnológico de la Diputación** at Calle Sanchis Abella 1 (open the same hours as Bellas Artes) and the **Convento de Capuchinas** in Calle Núñez de Arce, which houses 10 fine paintings by Zurbarán and opens daily from 4 to 8 pm.

On Plaza Mayor is **El Fadri** (1604), an octagonal bell tower that is now the symbol of the city. Beside the tower is the reconstructed **Catedral de Santa María**, which was virtually demolished in 1936 during the outbreak of the civil war, while across the plaza is the **ayuntamiento** (1716) with its attractive Tuscan-style façade.

In the centre of the adjacent **Plaza de Santa Clara** is a modernist sculpture by Llorens Poy that depicts the history of Castellón. The **Mercado Central** is between these two plazas.

Four km east of the centre is **El Grau de Castellón**, a huge harbour that handles this industrial region's exports as well as the local fishing fleet. Castellón's beaches start north of here, with long and broad stretches of sand backed by the usual bars, restaurants and mid-rise apartments.

Places to Stay

Castellón has several youth hostels but they are usually booked out by uni students and school groups.

There are three good accommodation options in the centre of town, all within 400 metres of Puerta del Sol: *Fonda La Granadina* (☎ 21 21 41), Calle Navarra 99, has basic but cosy singles/doubles from 1400/2800 ptas. At *Hostal La Esperanza* (☎ 22 20 31), Calle Ximénez 26, an amiable señora rents out spotless rooms above a bar-restaurant at 1700/3100 ptas, or 3200 ptas per person for pensión completo. The two star *Hotel-Residencia Real* (☎ 21 19 44), Plaza del Real 2, has refurbished rooms with 70s décor, TV, phone and air-con from 4200/5900 ptas.

Places to Eat

The restaurant at *Hostal La Esperanza* does a decent menú for 800 ptas. Across the road at Calle Ximénez 7, *Restaurante Labrador* has an agreeable ambience and excellent seafood, specialising in local dishes like arroz negro (900 ptas) and arroz con langosta (1700 ptas); they also have a menú for 950 ptas.

There are some good eateries around Plaza de Santa Clara. *La Taverna Italiana*, Calle Gumbau 11, does delicious pasta, pizzas and salads from 750 ptas and has a menú for 1150 ptas. Across the road at No 18, the stylishly romantic *La Caseta* has starters at 675 ptas and mains from 950 to 1300 ptas.

BENICÁSIM

Benicásim has been a popular resort since the 19th century, when wealthy Valencian families built their summer residences here. It's still the best and most up-market of the Costa del Azahar resorts, despite the addition of all the 20th century trimmings like concrete high-rises, discos, restaurants and minigolf courses.

Unlike the Costa Blanca resorts, it doesn't seem completely overrun by foreigners, and many people from Madrid, Valencia and Castellón keep summer apartments here.

Orientation & Information

Benicásim's beaches and the accompanying development sprawl for six km along the coast. The old town is about one km inland, and is home to the train station and the main tourist office (☎ 30 09 62), inside the ayuntamiento at Calle Médico Segarra 4. This office opens Monday to Saturday from 9 am to 3 pm; during summer there are five other offices along the beachfront.

Things to See & Do

Benicásim's six km of beaches, which have won the EU's Blue Flag for cleanliness, are the main attraction. You can hire windsurfers and other water sports gear; there's also the Aquarama aquatic park and several golf courses nearby.

Backing Benicásim is the mountain range known as the **Desierto de las Palmas**. Back in 1694 the range was purchased by the Order of Barefooted Carmelites, who built a monastery and several chapels here. The area, which is now a natural park, isn't really a desert – the Carmelites used the term to refer to areas suitable for 'mystic withdrawal'. You can visit the monastery and its museum (six km inland) and see the old equipment used by the Barefoots for distilling liqueurs from aromatic mountain plants.

Places to Stay

There are some half a dozen camping grounds here, all within walking distance of the beaches.

Benicásim has a great youth hostel, the *Albergue Argentina* (☎ 386 92 52), opposite the beach on Calle Ferrandis Salvador. It's a whopping whitewashed complex with games rooms, lounges, two pools and 140 bunks. Costs are 715/915 ptas for junior/senior members or 1700/2225 ptas for pensión completo (200 ptas more during summer).

Hostal Almadraba (☎ 30 10 00), in the old town at Calle Santo Tomás 135, has comfy upstairs rooms from 1900/3900 ptas; during summer they charge 3800 ptas per person for media pensión.

Hotel Avenida (☎ 30 00 47), on the corner of Calle Santo Tomás and Calle Cuatro Caminos, is an appealing mid-range hotel with a shady courtyard and a good pool. They have doubles from 4100 ptas; during summer they charge 3000 ptas per person for B&B or 5000 ptas for pensión completo.

Just north of the old town and 300 metres from the beach, *Hotel Vista Alegre* (☎ 30 04 00) on Avenida de Barcelona is a pleasant four storey hotel with a pool, bar and restaurant. Rooms start from 3800/6200 ptas (plus IVA); pensión completo ranges from 4800 to 6200 ptas per person.

Places to Eat

There are plenty of eateries along Calle Santo Tomás (the main street in the old town) with menús ranging from 800 to 1300 ptas.

It's worth searching out *Meson La Llar*, nearby at Calle Santa Agueda 9. This dim, welcoming restaurant specialises in paella and carne a la brasa (char-grilled meat) and has an excellent menú for 950 ptas (plus IVA).

Entertainment
Particularly on weekends and during summer, Benicásim has a vibrant nightlife. Head for the wedge-shaped Plaza de las Dolores in the old town, where you'll find a good collection of bars including *Pay Pay*, *Cactus* and *Mambo*.

OROPESA
It's a fine scenic drive from Benicásim to this small resort, with a narrow road winding around a rocky coastline past a series of coves and small settlements.

Oropesa's development backs the two main beaches of **Morro de Gos** and **La Concha**, named after the similarly shaped bay at San Sebastián. Further south beyond a rocky cove, the town's boat harbour is lined with expensive yachts and cruisers.

The tourist office (☎ 31 00 20), at Avenida de la Plana 4, can help out with accommodation queries.

PEÑÍSCOLA
Perched on a rocky promontory jutting into the sea, Peñíscola's old town is ringed by fortified walls and topped by a castle, with a tight cluster of narrow cobbled streets and whitewashed houses scattered below. The castle was built by the Knights Templar in the 13th century and was the home of Pedro de Luna (the deposed Pope Benedict XIII) from 1411 to 1423.

The old town is as pretty as a postcard and just as commercial, with dozens of souvenir and ceramics shops and clothes boutiques catering to the ascending hordes of tourists. It's also surrounded by an ever-growing collection of modern high-rises, and the main own looks pretty much like any other Spanish coastal resort.

Information
The tourist office (☎ 48 02 08) is at the end of the main road in, on the beach side of Paseo Marítimo.

Things to See & Do
Peñíscola is a busy fishing town, and you can watch the boats unload and auction their catch every afternoon at the port just south of the old town. There is development north along the coast all the way to the town of Benicarlo. The beaches along here are rocky and narrow – more suited to fishing than swimming.

Places to Stay & Eat
The *Chiki Bar* (☎ 48 02 84), near Plaza Ayuntamiento at Calle Mayor 3, is the best deal in the old town. Their modern rooms with tiny bathrooms range from 1600/3200 to 2000/4000 ptas – rooms on the 3rd floor enjoy great views of the sea and town. Downstairs is a small bar and restaurant with an excellent menú for 1200 ptas.

There are a couple of other decent options. *Hostal-Residencia El Torico* (☎ 48 02 02), on the main road 100 metres back from the beach, has reasonable rooms above a grocery shop from 1700/3500 ptas. At *Hotel-Restaurante Simo* (☎ 48 06 20), at the base of the old town at Calle Porteta 5, rooms with sea views and bathroom range from 3440/4300 to 5600/7000 ptas.

For a splurge, book into the *Hosteria del Mar* (☎ 48 06 00), one km north of the old town at Avenida del Papa Luna 18. This sumptuous four star hotel has an outstanding restaurant and rooms with sea views from 5900/7900 to 11,000/14,400 ptas (plus IVA).

Paseo Marítimo, the main waterfront promenade, is lined with restaurants that specialise in local seafood (and high prices).

VINARÒS
Vinaròs is no oil painting – it's a working city with a grim and somewhat dreary appearance. Its only redeeming feature is its sandy and reasonably attractive beaches. The town centre is set back from the coast and is

VALENCIA

chaotic and confusing – expect to get lost if you're driving in.

The tourist office (☎ 64 91 16) is on the main street, Calle de San Cristóbal – opposite the post office and ayuntamiento. Nearby is the **Iglesia Arciprestal**, an interesting baroque church with a tall bell tower and elaborate main doorway decorated with candy-twist columns.

From here, Calle Mayor takes you down to the beaches, via an up-market shopping zone and the excellent Mercado Central on Plaza de San Agustín.

Places to Stay
Pensión Casablanca (☎ 45 04 25), two blocks north of the tourist office at Calle San Pascual 8, is run by a helpful but vague old couple and has presentable budget rooms from 1300/2200 ptas.

Hostal Salom (☎ 45 58 49), 100 metres back from the beach at Plaza de San Antonio 13 (2nd floor), has spotless, slightly prissy rooms from 1800/3000 ptas.

Hostal-Residencia El Pino (☎ 45 05 53), also 100 metres inland at Calle San Pascual 47, is filled with knick-knacks and memorabilia. There's a cosy guest lounge, and pink-and-baby-blue rooms cost from 2140/3500 ptas.

Places to Eat
As befits any fishing town there are some excellent seafood restaurants here. *Restaurante Colon*, on the waterfront at Paseo Colon 13, is one of the more affordable places with menús for 1200 and 1500 ptas; we can recommend their zarzuela de pescado y marisco (1600 ptas).

Inland Valencia

This section covers the diverse regions of inland Valencia, stretching from Morella in the north down to Orihuela in the south. There are plenty of hidden surprises to discover and the few tourists who venture away from the coast are richly rewarded. Obvi-

ously the best way to explore the region is with your own transport, although you can reach most of the main centres by bus or train.

Before heading off we recommend you pick up copies of the parchment-coloured series of fold-out map-brochures produced by the Comunitat Valenciana. Each one covers a distinct geographical region, such as La Tinença de Benifassà, Els Ports, El Alto Palancia and Los Castillos del Vinalopó. The brochures are available (in several languages, including English) from all regional tourist offices.

The telephone code for northern inland Valencia (Sant Mateu to the towns of El Alto Palancia) is ☎ 964; the telephone code for southern inland Valencia (Requena to Orihuela) is ☎ 96.

Activities
The area is particularly popular with cyclists (on-road and off-road) and hikers. Several of Spain's long-distance *senderos de Gran Recorrido* (GR) hiking trails pass through the region, and are linked to each other by the shorter *senderos de Pequeño Recorrido* (PR) trails. GR-7 crosses the Els Ports and La Tinença de Benifassà districts, while the GR-10 and GR-36 pass through the Alto Palancia region.

MORELLA
The fairy-tale town of Morella, in the north of Valencia province, is an outstanding example of a medieval fortress. Perched on a hill top, crowned by a castle and completely enclosed by a wall over two km long, it is one of Spain's oldest continually inhabited towns.

Orientation & Information
The town's fortified walls are broken only by the seven entrance gates. Calle Muralla runs around the inner perimeter, but the rest of the town is a confusing (but compact) jumble of narrow streets, alleys and stairs leading up to the castle.

Pick up a town map from the tourist office (☎ 17 3032) on Plaza Puerta de San Miguel just inside the main entrance gate to the old town. The office opens Tuesday to Saturday from 11 am to 2 pm and from 4 to 6 pm and Sunday from 11 am to 2 pm; during July and August it opens daily.

There's a post office at Calle San Nicolás 13, and you'll find several banks along Calle Blasco de Alagón.

Things to See & Do

Although Morella's wonderful **castle** is in ruins, it is still most imposing. You can almost hear the clashing of swords and clip-clop of horses that were once a part of everyday life in the fortress. A strenuous climb to the top is rewarded by breathtaking views of the town and surrounding country-side. The castle grounds are open daily from 10.30 am until 6.30 pm (7.30 pm between May and August). Entry costs 200 ptas.

The old town itself is easily explored on foot. Three small museums have been set up in the towers of the ancient walls: the **Museo Tiempo de Imagen** has a collection of old B&W photos of Morella; the **Museo Tiempo de Dinosaurios** houses a handful of old bones and a video (in Spanish), although there are great views from the top; and the **Museo Tiempo de Historia** is in three sections devoted to prehistoric relics, the Gothic era and the Carlist Wars.

Morella's major church is the Gothic **Basílica de Santa María la Mayor**, which has two elaborately decorated doorways on the same façade. Inside, the **Museo Arciprestal** (150 ptas entry) houses a collection of religious artefacts and gold and silver pieces.

Also worth looking out for are the 14th century **ayuntamiento**, the **Real Convento de San Francisco** and the numerous, impressive manorial houses such as the **Casa de la Cofradía de Labradores** (Farmer's Guild).

On the outskirts of town stand the arches of a 13th century **aqueduct**.

Special Events

Morella's major festival is the Sexeni, held every six years (the next is in the year 2000)

in honour of the Virgen de Vallivana. A baroque music festival is held every year in August, starring the huge organ in the Basílica de Santa María la Mayor.

Places to Stay

Hostal El Cid (☎ 16 01 25), Puerta San Mateo 2, has reasonable if drab singles/doubles from 1300/2200 ptas and doubles with bathrooms for 3500 ptas – the rooms are heated and the front ones at least have decent views.

A better bet is the friendly *Fonda Moreno* (☎ 16 01 05), Calle San Nicolás 12, with rustic, quaint rooms from 950/1800 ptas. There's a good restaurant here (see Places to Eat); the only drawbacks are the lack of heating and the seven rooms sharing one bathroom.

If you want something more modern, *Hotel La Muralla* (☎ 16 02 43), Calle Muralla 12, has good rooms with private bathroom from 2800/3500 ptas.

At Cuesta Suñer 1 is *Hotel Cardenal Ram* (☎ 17 30 85), set in a wonderfully transformed 16th century cardinal's palace. The hotel opened in 1994 after extensive renovations and combines the best of the old and new; ancient stone floors, high ceilings and antique furniture with modern bathrooms, TV, phone and heating. There's a comfortable guest lounge, a bar and a cavernous dining room with a menú for 1500 ptas (plus IVA). Rooms start from 4000/6500 ptas and suites from 8000 ptas (plus IVA). Highly recommended.

Hotel Rey Don Jaime (☎ 16 09 11), Calle Juan Giner 6, is a modernised three star place with good facilities and rooms from 4500/7500 ptas (plus IVA); you have a choice of castle or countryside views.

Places to Eat

The upstairs restaurant at *Fonda Moreno* does a hearty menú for 850 ptas (drinks and IVA not included).

Restaurante Casa Roque (☎ 16 03 36), Calle Segura Barrera 8, is one of the best restaurants in town. Regional dishes range from 950 ptas up to 2500 ptas for the house speciality, cordero relleno trufado (lamb rolled with truffles). They also offer a four course menú degustación for 1500 ptas. You'll need to book on weekends.

Moralla's nightlife isn't exactly wild, but after dinner you could check out the noisy *Pub Miyagi* at Calle Marquesa del Fuente el Sol 16 and *Bar Xuxo ('Disco Pub')* next door.

There are some interesting little food shops, up-market bakeries and groceries along Calle Blasco de Alagón, and a good street market operates here on Sunday morning.

Getting There & Away

Autos Mediterráneo (☎ 22 05 36) has bus services between Morella and Castellón de la Plana (daily; 1015 ptas) and Vinaròs on the coast (Monday to Saturday; 710 ptas), as well as to Alcañiz in Aragón (Monday, Wednesday and Thursday; 2000 ptas).

Morella is beside the N-232 highway: if you are driving here in winter, check the weather forecast first, as the town is sometimes snowed in for days.

AROUND MORELLA

Morella is an excellent base from which to explore the surrounding regions: rugged mountainous areas scattered with pine forests, lonely hermitages, rocky peaks and peaceful mountain villages.

Els Ports

Morella is the ancient capital of Els Ports, the 'region of the mountain passes'. This northeastern corner of Valencia offers some outstanding scenic drives and strenuous cycling excursions, as well as excellent possibilities for hikers and mountain climbers.

Four km west of Morella at **La Fábrica de Giner**, the *Hotel-Restaurante Fábrica de Giner* (☎ 17 31 42) is an old textile factory and village that has been converted by the Generalitat (regional government) into an impressive (if slightly stark) accommodation complex which includes a swimming pool, playground, walking tracks and a small textile museum. The hotel has modern, stylish rooms from 4500/7350 ptas (plus

IVA) and a very pleasant restaurant with a menú for 1750 ptas (plus IVA).

Nine km further west, **Forcall** is a quiet village set at the meeting place of the stony banks of the Río Caldés and the Río Cantavieja. Forcall is the home of the well-known Fiesta de San Antón (also known as 'La Santantonada'), held over the weekend closest to 17 January. On opposite sides of Plaza Mayor in the centre of the village stand two 16th century Aragonese palaces. One of these has been wonderfully converted into an elegant hotel, the *Hotel-Restaurante Palau dels Osset Miró* (☎ 17 75 24), at Plaza Mayor 16. The rooms retain original features such as heavy ceiling beams and old timber shutters, but also have heating, TV and phone, and are good value from 4500/6500 ptas (plus IVA). There's a cosy guest salon and a restaurant with a menú for 1750 ptas.

Nearby at Plaza Mayor 8, *Mesón de la Vila* has a mock-medieval décor with terracotta-tiled floors, stone arches and whitewashed walls. The food is pretty good, and they offer a filling menú for 1300 ptas.

North of here is the tiny whitewashed village of **Villores**, while to the west is the medieval castle of **Todolella**.

La Tinença de Benifassà

Valencia's northern-most region is a mountainous and remote district that is usually snowbound throughout winter. There are seven small villages here, clustered around the old **Monasterio de Santa María de Benifassà**. The monastery is still in use, and the resident nuns open their church to visitors every Thursday between 1 and 3 pm.

A couple of km south-west of the monastery is the main village of **La Poble de Benifassà**, featuring distinctive local stone houses fronted by timber balconies. On the main street, the small *Hotel Tinença de Benifassà* (☎ (977) 72 90 44), Calle Mayor 50, is set in a restored villa and has 10 rooms with bathroom, heating, TV and phone.

Most of the other villages in the area, including **Bellestar**, **Fredes** and **Coratxá** are uninhabited during the winter months.

Catí

About 35 km south-east of Morella is the well-preserved Gothic village of Catí, famous for its cheeses. Up in the mountains five km from Catí is the tiny spa village of **L'Avellá**, which consists of a dozen buildings, a 16th century hermitage and a plant for bottling the local spring waters, said to be an excellent cure for all skin complaints. *Fonda Miralles* (☎ 76 50 51) is a simple hostal that opens between July and September.

Vallivana

On the N-232 highway 24 km south-east of Morella, Vallivana consists of several lonely stone buildings clustered around the 14th century Santuario de Vallivana (☎ 17 30 27). This slightly neglected complex houses a baroque chapel, a bar-restaurant and a spartan accommodation section with very simple and very cold rooms at 1000 ptas per person. Opposite, the more modern *Casa Forestal* (☎ 16 00 09) is a bunkhouse for bushwalkers (open summer only).

Sant Mateu

Further east and several km south of the N-232 is the town of Sant Mateu. Its impressive mansions and elaborate façades are reminders of the town's more illustrious past. Bars and cafés surround Plaza Mayor in the centre of town, while signposts point you in the direction of several small municipal museums, including the **Museo Paleontológico** and **Museo Arciprestal**.

Sant Mateu's tourist office (☎ 41 61 71) is just off Plaza Mayor at Calle Historiador Beti 4.

Places to Stay & Eat The owners of *Bar-Restaurante Moderno* (☎ 41 62 88) on Plaza Mayor rent out good budget rooms nearby from 1400/2800 ptas.

There are a couple of other places just off Plaza Mayor on Calle Historiador Beti: *Hotel-Restaurante La Perdi* at No 9 has modern and comfy rooms with bathroom, TV and heating at 2500/5000 ptas and a restaurant with a good menú for 900 ptas.

Set on a rocky hillside overlooking Sant Mateu is the wonderful *Restaurante Mare de Déu* (☎ 41 60 44). A monastery up until the outbreak of the civil war, it remains a fairly austere complex with a gilded baroque chapel and several rustic dining areas with whitewashed walls, dark timber furniture and rickety tiled floors. Meals are cooked in a huge old wood-fired oven, and you can choose between rice dishes (750 to 800 ptas) or carne a la brasa (char-grilled meats; 600 to 1300 ptas). The house speciality, pierna de cabritillo (roast leg of baby goat), will set you back 2000 ptas. The restaurant opens for lunch and dinner on Saturday and lunch on Sunday (daily for lunch during summer). From Plaza Mayor in San Mateu, face the *pasteleria* sign, turn left and follow the unnamed tree-lined road out of town.

VILAFAMÉS

Vilafamés, a hillside town 26 km north of Castellón, is topped by the ruins of a Muslim castle. The main attraction is the contemporary art museum.

Vilafamés is in the centre of a region famous for its ceramics industry, but don't expect to find too many artisan-type workshops. Nearby towns like Lucena and Alcora are surrounded by immense factories, most of which mass-produce tiles and pots.

There isn't a tourist office in Vilafamés, although the owner of the souvenir shop near the museum is very helpful and hands out town maps.

Things to See & Do

The **Museo Popular de Arte Contemporáneo**, in the Palacio del Batlle on Calle de Arriba, houses an excellent collection of paintings and sculpture. It opens weekdays from 11 am to 1 pm and 5 to 7 pm and weekends from 11 am to 2 pm and 4 to 7 pm.

It's also worthwhile exploring the old town, a cluttered blend of whitewashed houses and civic buildings built from rust-red stone. The 18th century **Iglesia de la Asunción** features some unique ceramic artworks. From Plaza Sangre, a set of stone steps takes you up to the castle, with its rebuilt circular turret and sensational panoramas of the town and countryside.

Places to Stay & Eat

Hotel El Rullo (☎ 32 93 84), 200 metres below the museum at Calle La Fuente 2, has eight rooms with private bathroom, lurid bedspreads and great views at 2000/4000 ptas including breakfast. If you're after a meal the owners will send you down the road to *Meson El Rullo*, where the menú costs 1000 ptas.

MONTANEJOS

It's a spectacular drive from any direction up to this popular resort town. The main road follows the steep gorges of the Río Mijares and the town is surrounded by craggy mountains clad with pine forests.

The warm spring waters of the nearby **Fuente de Dos Baños** and the cool fresh mountain air attract hordes of (mainly Spanish) visitors during the summer months. The town itself is fairly plain, but it is a popular base for various adventure activities including climbing, abseiling and mountain biking, and there are some fine hiking trails in the surrounding countryside.

Places to Stay

There are about six modernish hotels in town, most of which only open during summer and on weekends. The best budget bet is the three storey *Hostal-Restaurante La Valenciana* (☎ 13 10 62), in the town centre on Avenida de Elvira Peiro, with singles/doubles from 1500/2650 ptas (2000/3900 ptas with bathroom) and pensión completo from 4000 ptas per person.

Another good option is *Hotel Rosaleda del Mijares* (☎ 13 10 79) at Carretera de Tales 28 (the main road). Open year-round, it has comfortable rooms with bathroom from 2300/3600 ptas.

Hostal Casa Ovidio (☎ 13 13 09), on the outskirts on the Jerica road, has plain rooms from 2500/4000 ptas.

EL ALTO PALANCIA

Together with nearby Montanejos, the towns along the upper reaches of the Río Palancia make up the so-called 'route of the mountain springs'. Don't go out of your way, but if you happen to be heading along the N-234 (which links Sagunto with Teruel) there are some worthwhile stopovers along the way.

Thirty km north-west of Sagunto, **Segorbe** is home to an impressive Gothic cathedral with a tranquil patio. Inside one of the alcoves is the small **Museo Catedralicio** (open Tuesday to Sunday from 11 am to 2 pm; 200 ptas entry).

Further north it's worth detouring just off the highway to visit **Navajas**, an attractive village shaded by cypress pines and palm trees and surrounded by almond and olive groves. Navajas has a collection of charming tiled and pastel-painted villas, built during the 19th century by members of the Valencian aristocracy.

On the outskirts, the excellent *Navajas Camping Municipal* is a hillside complex backed by pine trees, with modern facilities including a shop, restaurant and games room. *Hotel Navas Altas* (☎ 71 09 66), Calle Rodríguez Fornos 3, is a three storey modular hotel with a TV lounge, a small pool and rooms with TV and heating from 4100/5200 ptas (plus IVA).

Jerica is dominated by an unusual *mudéjar* tower, but doesn't have much else going for it. A couple of km further on, **Viver** is much more attractive and has a youth hostel and two camping grounds nearby.

REQUENA

On the N-111 highway 71 km west of Valencia, Requena is a bustling commercial centre with wide tree-lined streets, leafy gardens and a fascinating, walled medieval town.

It's at the centre of a grape-growing district which, at almost 700 metres above sea level, specialises in fruity rosé wines and sparkling *cavas*.

Orientation & Information

If you arrive at the train station, the town centre is a five minute walk away: head straight down the tree-lined Avenida de la Estación and turn left at the fountain into the

La Tomatina

If you happen to be in Valencia during the last week in August, you can participate in one of Spain's messiest and most bizarre festivals. Held in the town of Buñol (about 40 km west of Valencia on the N-111 highway and the Madrid train line), La Tomatina is, believe it or not, a tomato-throwing festival.

Buñol is an otherwise insignificant and drab industrial town; its outskirts are dominated by a massive smoke-belching cement factory, while the old town is dominated by a crumbling 12th century stone castle.

The festival's origins are somewhat obscure, but who cares. And while it mightn't last long, it attracts up to 20,000 visitors.

Here's how it goes: just before noon on the day of the festival some half a dozen truckloads of ripe, squishy tomatoes are delivered to (ie thrown at) the waiting crowd, and for the next hour or so everyone joins in a frenzied, cheerful and anarchic tomato war. Apart from being pounded with pulp, you can also expect to have your clothing ripped and torn, be pelted with water bombs and drenched with hoses. Fun, fun, fun!

At 1 pm an explosion signals the end, at which stage the well-prepared participants change into their stash of fresh clothes. Most people just come for the day, arriving on the morning train from Valencia and heading back in the afternoon.

If you decide to stay, *Venta Pilar* (☎ (96) 250 09 23), in the old town just off Plaza Ventas, is a simple family-run workers' *fonda* with rooms around a central courtyard. Doubles cost 2000 ptas (3000 ptas with private bathroom). ∎

broad Avenida del Arrabal (the main street of the new town).

The tourist office (☎ 230 14 00) is in the old town at Plaza de la Villa 14.

Things to See & Do

In the centre of Requena, the old walled town is crammed with elaborate but dilapidated Gothic churches and mansions. As you wander around, look out for the **Iglesia de Santa María**, the **Iglesia Salvador**, the remains of the Muslim **castle**, the Muslim **Arco del Ovejero** and the manorial houses such as the **Casa del Arte Mayor de la Seda** (silk guild house) and **Casa del Corregidor** (magistrate's house).

There are also two museums, the **Museo Municipal** and the adjacent **Convento Carmelito**, both near Plaza Consistorial in the new town.

Places to Stay & Eat

The recently renovated *Pensión Bar Cantarranas* (☎ 230 50 80), at the base of the old town at Calle García Montés 43, has good rooms at 1750/3500 ptas, or 2000/4000 ptas with private bathroom. There's a small bar-restaurant downstairs where you can eat well for 800 ptas.

Hotel Avenida (☎ 230 04 80), just off Avenida del Arrabal at Calle San Agustín 10, has unexciting rooms with bathroom and TV ranging from 2000/3500 to 3000/4500 ptas (plus IVA).

Mesón del Vino Restaurante, Avenida del Arrabal 11, has a cosy little tapas bar flanked by two stylish dining areas decorated with rustic artefacts, and a menú for 1500 ptas.

Getting There & Away

Requena is on the Valencia-Madrid train line. There are six to eight trains daily to Valencia and three trains daily to Madrid.

XÀTIVA

Set at the base of the Serra Vernissa mountain range 50 km south of Valencia, the town of Xàtiva has a fascinating history.

In the nearby Cova Negra (black cave), archaeologists have found relics dating back to the Mousterian period (30,000 BC), along with a Neanderthal skull. Successive Iberian, Roman and Visigoth settlements were followed by the Muslims, who built Europe's first paper-manufacturing plant here during the 11th century.

Xàtiva's importance grew after the Reconquista and it became Valencia's second largest city. Popes Calixtus III and Alexander VI were both born here, but Xàtiva's glory days temporarily ended in 1707 when Felipe V's troops besieged and then set fire to most of the town.

Information

The tourist office (☎ 227 33 46) is on the main road at Alameda Jaume I 50. It opens Monday to Saturday from 10 am to 6 pm and Sunday from 10 am to 2 pm. The post office is nearby at Alameda Jaume I 33.

Things to See & Do

Consider buying a copy of the excellent *Walking Tours Round Xàtiva* book from the tourist office.

Most of Xàtiva's monuments are uphill from the Alameda Jaume I; the further up you go, the older the town is.

The **Museo de l'Almodí** houses a fine collection of archaeological relics and artworks, including the famed portrait of Felipe V that hangs upside down in retribution for his having set fire to the town. Between June and September the museum opens daily (except Monday) from 9 am to 2.30 pm. At other times it's open Tuesday to Friday from

11 am to 2 pm and 4 to 6 pm and weekends from 11 am to 2 pm. Entry is free.

Several of the town's buildings, including the **Iglesia de San Francesc**, are listed as National Monuments.

It's a long and slow climb up to the **castle** on the summit. On the way you can visit the 18th century **Ermita de San José** and the **Iglesia de Sant Feliu** (1269), Xàtiva's oldest church. The climb is rewarded by spectacular panoramas from the top. The castle grounds are open daily (except Monday) from 10.30 am to 2 pm and 4.30 to 7 pm (6 pm in winter). Entry is free.

Places to Stay

Accommodation choices are limited. *Fonda El Margallonero* (☎ 227 66 77), Plaza del Mercado 2, is a rustic family-run place with simple rooms from 1400/2800 ptas.

Hotel Vernisa (☎ 227 1011), in the centre of the new town at Calle Académico Maravall 1, is a classy two star place with modern rooms with air-con, TV and video channels from 4000/5500 ptas.

Getting There & Away

The train station and bus station are both on Avenida Cavaller Ximén de Tovia.

Fiestas de Moros y Cristianos

In a tradition dating back to the 13th century, more than 80 towns and villages throughout Valencia hold their own Fiesta de Moros y Cristianos (Moors and Christians festivals) to celebrate their Arab heritage and to commemorate the Reconquista.

The biggest and best-known festivities are held in the town of Alcoi on 22, 23 and 24 April. Hundreds of local residents dress up in elaborate traditional costumes representing different 'factions' – Muslim and Christian soldiers, slaves, guild groups, town criers, heralds, bands – and march through the streets in spectacular and colourful processions and mock battles.

A wooden fortress is erected in the main plaza, and the various processions converge on the centre from different directions. Tradition dictates who goes where when, but standing in the crowd it all feels incredibly chaotic with processions coming at you from every direction.

It's an exhilarating spectacle of sights and sounds: soldiers clad in shining armour, white-cloaked Muslim warriors carrying scimitars and shields, turban-topped Arabs, scantily clad wenches, brass bands, exploding blunderbusses, fireworks displays and confetti showering down on the crowds from above.

Each town has its own variation on the format of the festival, steeped in traditions that allude to the events of the Reconquista. For example Villena's festival (5 to 9 September) features midnight parades, while in La Vila Joiosa (24 to 31 July) you can see the re-enactment of the landing of Muslim ships on the beaches. Some of the other major festivals are those held in Bocairent (1 to 5 February), Biar (10 to 13 May) and Ontinyent (over four days from the last Friday in August). ■

BETHUNE CARMICHAEL

BETHUNE CARMICHAEL

MARK ARMSTRONG

BETHUNE CARMICHAEL

Top Left: Valley scene from the fine ruined castle of Morella, Valencia
Top Right: Morella's castle seen in the distance through the arches of the town's 13th century aqueduct
Bottom Left: Flower stall on Plaza del Ayuntamiento, Valencia city
Bottom Right: Fortified tower bearing scars of the civil war, Valencia city

MARK ARMSTRONG

MARK ARMSTRONG

MARK ARMSTRONG

Top: Sunset over Pueblo de Pescadores, Menorca
Middle: Beach scene at beautiful Cala Saona, Formentera
Bottom: Banys Àrabs (Arab baths), Palma de Mallorca

Frequent trains connect Xàtiva with Valencia (375 ptas) and Alicante (410 ptas): you can also connect with trains to Madrid from here.

There are also regular bus services to Valencia and Alicante, and Iberbus (☎ 287 41 10) has twice daily services between Xàtiva and Gandia (360 ptas).

VILLENA

Villena, on the N-330 highway between Alicante and Albacete, is an up-beat town with a couple of worthwhile attractions for passing travellers, as well as some fine restaurants and swanky bars.

The **Museo Arqueológico**, housed in the former Palacio Municipal (now the ayuntamiento) on Plaza Santiago, has a small but interesting collection of gold jewellery, bowls, skulls, stone implements, Roman ceramics and Iberian artefacts. It's open weekdays from 9 am to 2 pm. On the other side of Plaza Santiago is the **Iglesia de Santiago**, with a crumbling exterior and an impressively restored interior.

Perched high above the town, the **Castillo de la Atalya** is splendidly lit at night.

Villena's Fiesta de Moros y Cristianos is held each year from 5 to 9 September.

Places to Stay

Hotel-Restaurante Salvadora (☎ 580 09 50), Avenida de la Constitución 102 (the main road in), is a large hotel with pleasant rooms with TV, phone and heating from 3150/4650 ptas.

ELX

Just 20 km south-west of Alicante, Elx (Elche) combines the historic with the industrial and is famed for its extensive gardens of palm trees that date back to Muslim times. The Muslims' irrigation systems were also responsible for converting the region into a rich agricultural district that now produces citrus fruits, figs, almonds, dates and cotton.

Orientation & Information

The town is divided by the Río Vinalopó, with the newer section on the west bank and the older town on the east side. Most of the parks and monuments are in the old town.

The tourist office (☎ 545 38 31) is in a small mock-Muslim palace on the south-east corner of the Parque Municipal. It opens weekdays from 9 am to 2.30 pm and Saturday from 10 am to 1.30 pm.

The train and bus stations are both north of the centre on Avenida de la Libertat, 200 metres apart. From either, exit and take a left, then take the first left down Passeig de la Estació (which leads to the Parque Municipal, tourist office and town centre).

Things to See & Do

There are palm groves all over the city and surrounding areas. Some are pretty dishevelled, but the **Parque Municipal** is very pleasant to stroll through. You should also visit the **Huerto del Cura**, a lovely private garden with tended lawns, colourful flower gardens, towering palm trees and a freakish eight pronged palm tree in the centre. The gardens open daily from 9 am to 8.30 pm; entry costs 300 ptas for adults, 200 ptas for children. Across the road at the Venta de Datiles you can buy a bag of dates fresh off the trees.

The narrow streets of the old Vila Murada (walled city) are also worth a wander. The baroque **Basílica de Santa María** is used for performances of the Misteri d'Elx (see Special Events), while the east wing of the 15th century **Palacio de Altamira** is home to the small **Museo Arqueológico Municipal**. Further south on Calle Major de Raval is the **Museo de Arte Contemporáneo**.

At the L'Alcúdia diggings on the southern outskirts is the excellent **Museo Arqueológico**. It's open Tuesday to Saturday from 10 am to 2 pm and 4 to 7 pm, Sunday from 10 am to 2 pm; entry costs 400 ptas.

Special Events

The town's major festival is the Misteri d'Elx, a two act lyric drama that dates from the Middle Ages. It is performed in the Basílica de Santa María every year on 14 and 15 August (with rehearsals the three previous days).

Places to Stay

Budget choices are fairly limited. *Pensión Juan* (☎ 545 86 09), Calle Pont dels Ortissos 15 (3rd floor), is quirky and grim but cheap at 1000 ptas per person.

Do yourself a favour – save up, come on a weekend and book into the magnificent *Hotel Huerto del Cura* (☎ 545 80 40), at Calle Porta de la Morera 14. Set in lush gardens and shaded by huge palm trees, it has tennis courts, gym, sauna, solarium, a wonderful kidney-shaped pool and spa, bungalow-style rooms – you're right in the city centre but it feels like a tropical island. During the week it's very popular with business people and pricey at 13,500/16,500 ptas (plus IVA). But on Friday, Saturday and Sunday (and for most of August) double rooms are a bargain at 8000 ptas.

Getting There & Away

Elx is on the Alicante-Murcia train line, with 16 to 18 trains daily to both Alicante (225 ptas) and Murcia (310 ptas).

Muvasa (☎ 545 21 68) has nine buses daily to Alicante (355 ptas) and Murcia (475 ptas). Autocares AM Molla (☎ 542 42 42) runs hourly buses to Santa Pola (115 ptas).

ORIHUELA

On the banks of the Río Segura, Orihuela is the provincial capital of the Vega Baja district. The old quarter, set at the base of a barren mountain of rock, houses an extensive collection of Gothic, Renaissance and baroque architectural monuments. Their deteriorated appearance, together with dozens of old palm trees, give the town a slightly decadent feel of bygone splendours.

The tourist office (☎ 530 27 47) is at Calle Francisco Díe 25.

Things to See & Do

Orihuela's old quarter includes half a dozen buildings registered as National Monuments. The 16th century **Convento de Santo Domingo**, which was used as a university until the early 19th century, has lovely Renaissance cloisters inside. Built on the site of a Muslim mosque, the 14th

century Catalan-Gothic **Catedral de San Salvador** houses the **Museo Diocesano de Arte Sacre**, with a religious art collection that includes Velázquez's *Temptation of St Thomas*.

The **Iglesia de las Santas Justa y Rufina** has a Renaissance façade and a Gothic tower decorated with gargoyles. Also noteworthy are the baroque **Palacio Episcopal**, the 14th century **Iglesia de Santiago Apóstol**, and the ruins of a castle dating back to Muslim times further up the mountain.

Places to Stay & Eat

One of the cheapest places is the slightly dodgy *Pensión Versalles* (☎ 530 29 61), Calle San Cristóbal 10 (1st floor), with a couple of rooms in a family apartment at 1000 to 1500 ptas per person. It isn't in the most salubrious of areas.

A better place to stay is the *Hostal-Residencia Rey Teodomiro* (☎ 530 03 49), on the main boulevard in the centre at Avenida Teodomiro 10 (1st floor). It's a renovated two star place with rooms with all the mod cons from 3000/5000 ptas (plus IVA).

While you're here try some of the distinctive local dishes such as cocido con pelotas (meat stew with dumplings) and arroz con costra (a baked rice dish topped with an omelette).

Getting There & Away

The train station is a five minute walk from the centre at the end of the tree-lined Avenida de Teodomiro. Orihuela is on the Alicante-Murcia train line, with two trains daily in either direction to Alicante (370 ptas) and Murcia (145 ptas).

The Costa Blanca

Alicante and the surrounding coastal area, the Costa Blanca, is one of Europe's most heavily visited regions. If you want to find a secluded beach in midsummer, you should keep well away from here. If, however, yo are looking for a lively social life, good beaches and a suntan...

It isn't all concrete and package deals. There are actually some nice little coastal towns along here that haven't been completely overdeveloped, and places like Jávea, Calpe and Altea are well worth a visit, especially out of season. During July and August your chances of finding accommodation anywhere on the coast are limited if you haven't booked ahead.

Note that most accommodation places along the coast adjust their prices according to seasonal demand. Because of these variations, tariffs are quoted here so as to give you an idea of each place's seasonal range. For example, if a hostal's prices for singles/doubles are 2000/4000 ptas in the low season and 3500/7000 ptas in the high season, we'll say something like 'prices range from 2000/4000 to 3500/7000 ptas'.

If you need a break from the coastal pursuits there are some fascinating inland towns worth visiting including Elx, Orihuela, Xàtiva and Villena (see the previous Inland Valencia section for details).

The telephone code for the Costa Blanca is ☎ 96.

GANDIA

Gandia, 65 km south of Valencia, is a tale of two cities. The main town is a large and prosperous commercial centre with a rich history, and was once home to a branch of the Borja dynasty.

Four km away on the coast, Playa de Gandia's amazingly long and broad beaches are groomed daily by a fleet of tractors and backed by swanky medium-rise hotels and apartments. It's a very popular and predominantly Spanish resort with a reputation for great nightlife.

Information
The Playa de Gandia tourist office (☎ 284 24 07), on the waterfront at Paseo Marítimo s/n, opens weekdays from 10 am to 2 pm and 4 to 7 pm and weekends from 10 am to 2 pm. There's another tourist office (☎ 287 77 88)

opposite the train station in the main town. Both will give you a town map – for 100 ptas.

The post office is at Plaza Jaume I 7.

Things to See & Do
Gandia's old town has numerous historic monuments and is worth exploring. The main attraction is the magnificent **Palau Sant Duc**, which in the 15th century became the home of Duke Francisco de Borja. All but derelict 100 years ago, the palace was purchased by the Jesuits and progressively restored and decorated with a collection of the duke's personal belongings. It opens for one-hour tours (250 ptas) on weekdays from 11 am to 5 pm (to 6 pm in summer) and Saturday at 11 am only.

Local authorities have set up an excellent **Ruta Ecoturística Racó del Duc** 'ecotourism route' for walkers and cyclists. The 12 km trail follows an old railway line through unspoiled countryside between the villages of Vilallonga (eight km south of Gandia) and L'Orxa. A brochure covering the route is available from the tourist offices. Allow about 1½ hours by bicycle or three to four hours on foot.

North-west of Gandia is a popular rock-climbing location, the **Penya Roja de Maxuquera**.

Places to Stay
Camping Playa de Gandia has three camping grounds: *Camping Ros* (☎ 284 07 70), on Calle de la Armada Española, is closest to the beach, while *Camping L'Alqueria* (☎ 284 04 70) is one km inland but has a pool in compensation.

Youth Hostel There's an excellent beachfront youth hostel, the *Alburgue Mar i Vent* (☎ 283 17 48) five km south of here in Playa de Piles. A bus from opposite the train station will get you there. Charges are 800/1100 ptas for junior/senior members, or 1900/2400 ptas for pensión completo (closed in winter).

Playa de Gandia *El Nido* (☎ 284 46 40), close to the beach at Calle Alcoy 22, is a friendly two storey hostal with bright rooms from 3500/4500 to 5000/7000 ptas and a restaurant specialising in French cuisine (menús range from 1200 to 1500 ptas). Highly recommended.

On the beachfront at Paseo Marítimo 20, *Hostal Fin de Semana* (☎ 284 00 97) is an attractive little guesthouse with doubles from around 8000 ptas.

The modern *Hotel La Alberca* (☎ 284 51 63), 500 metres back at Calle Cullera 8, has comfy rooms from 2800/4500 to 3500/5800 ptas.

Gandia If you'd rather stay in the main town, *Hotel Ernesto* (☎ 286 40 11), Carretera de Valencia 40, has good rooms with bathroom from 2500/4000 to 3000/5000 ptas (plus IVA).

Entertainment

There's a great summer nightlife scene down at Playa de Gandia, with around a dozen bars including *Paco Paco Paco*, *Mama Ya Lo Sabe* and *Primadona* clustered around Plaza del Castell, 300 metres back from the beach. After they close (around 3 am) you can head for one of the discos that go through till dawn: *Coca Loca* is on the corner of Paseo Marítimo and Calle de Galicia, the huge *Bacarra* is on Calle Navegent, and *Arrassa* and *Matador* are at the back of the town flanking the tennis club.

Getting There & Around

Gandia's train station, on Calle Marqués de Campo in the main town, has trains every half hour to Valencia (one hour; 495 ptas) via Cullera.

The bus station is nearby on the same road. Ubesa (☎ 287 16 54) has frequent buses to Valencia (1½ hours; 650 ptas) and Alicante (three hours; 1100 ptas) via the coast.

Buses to Playa de Gandia depart from opposite the train station about every 15 minutes between 6.30 am and 11.30 pm (105 ptas).

DENIA

Denia is a big, popular and pricey resort town

dominated by a large boat harbour and topped by a ruined castle. Flebasa Lines operates ferry services from here to Palma de Mallorca, Sant Antoni de Portmany and Ibiza City (see the Balearic Islands chapter for more details or ring Flebasa's booking office on ☎ 578 40 11).

Orientation & Information

The tourist office (☎ 642 23 67) is in the town centre and near the waterfront at Calle Glorieta Oculista Buigues 9. The train station and Flebasa terminal are both within 100 metres of the office.

Places to Stay

Conveniently placed in front of the train station at Calle Pintor Llorens 3, *Hotel Costa Blanca* (☎ 578 03 36) has rooms from 3650/5300 to 4850/7150 ptas. Three blocks inland at Calle de La Via 43, *Hostal El Comercio* (☎ 578 00 71) is harder to find but better value, with rooms with bathroom, heating, TV and phone from 2150/3400 to 2700/4650 ptas.

Getting There & Away

Ubesa (☎ 578 05 64) runs frequent buses along the coast in both directions to Valencia and Alicante; see the Alicante section for details of trains.

JÁVEA

Jávea (Xábia) is worth a visit early in the season, when the weather has started to improve but the masses still haven't arrived. This laid-back place is in three parts: the old town (three km inland), El Puerto (the port) and the beach zone of El Arenal, which is lined with pleasant bar-restaurants, all of which are open late in summer. If you have wheels, you might try to get to **Cabo La Nao**, known for its spectacular views, or **Granadella**, with its small, uncrowded beach – both are a few km south of Jávea.

There are three tourist offices here, including one on Plaza Almirante Bastarreche in the centre of El Puerto (☎ 579 07 36).

Places to Stay

Camping There are three camping grounds. *Camping El Naranjal* (☎ 579 29 89) is well set-up and about 10 minutes walk from the beach at El Arenal. Otherwise try *Camping Javea* (☎ 579 10 70) or *Camping Mediterraneo* (☎ 579 12 26).

Other Accommodation The port area is very pleasant and has some reasonably priced accommodation. *Fonda del Mar* (☎ 579 01 17), 100 metres back from the port at Calle Cristo del Mar 12, has clean singles/doubles for 2000/4000 ptas. The front rooms have sea views.

On the foreshore 200 metres south at Avenida de la Marina Española 8, *Hostal La Marina* (☎ 579 31 39) is run by an amiable Scottish family and has bright rooms from 2000/3000 to 3000/4000 ptas and doubles with bathrooms and sea views from 4500 to 5500 ptas (plus IVA).

At Plaza Almirante Bastarreche 12, the large two star *Hotel Miramar* (☎ 579 01 02) has cosy, old-fashioned rooms with bathroom, TV, heating and phone from 3500/6500 to 5000/8000 ptas.

Places to Eat

Hostal La Marina's restaurant has a maritime flavour and offers a diverse selection of both Spanish and Scottish dishes; they have two menús at 1195 and 1695 ptas (plus IVA).

The restaurant on the 1st floor at *Fonda del Mar* has a menú for 1300 ptas.

CALPE

One of the Costa's more pleasant seaside towns, Calpe is dominated by the Gibraltar-esque **Peñon de Ifach**, a towering monolith that juts out into the sea. The rock is now a natural park and there's a popular and strenuous trail leading up to the 332 metre summit; it takes about half an hour to climb to the top, where you can soak up the great views.

There's a small fishing harbour at the base of the rock, and you can watch the local fish auctions here or take a boat cruise around the bays.

Calpe has two large bays on opposite sides of the rock: Playa Arenal on the south side is backed by the old town, while Playa Levante to the north has most of the more recent development.

Information

The tourist office (☎ 583 85 32) on Plaza Mosquit (signposted and 100 metres from Plaza Constitución) opens weekdays from 10 am to 1.30 pm and 5 to 8 pm and Saturday from 10 am to 1 pm. There's another tourist office (☎ 583 69 20) on Avenida Ejércitos Españoles near the base of the rock.

Places to Stay

There are a couple of good places to bed down. Run by the helpful Evelyn, who moved here from England 10 years ago, *Pensión Centrica* (☎ 583 55 28) on Plaza de Ifach has cosy, pretty rooms for 1600 ptas per person. A stone's throw from the beach-front at Calle La Pinta 1, the neat *Hostal Crespo* (☎ 583 39 31) has eight straightforward doubles (four with sea views) ranging from 2500 to 4000 ptas.

There's also an excellent youth hostel here, the modern *Albergue Abargues* (☎ 583 43 96) on Avenida de la Marina on the northern outskirts. It has a pool and is 200 metres from the beach. During summer it's usually booked out by school groups, but out of season they do pensión completo deals for 2700 ptas per person.

Places to Eat

There are plenty of restaurants, bars and bodegas clustered around Plaza Constitución and along Avenida Gabriel Miró. We can particularly recommend the attractive *Restaurante El Pati*, Avenida Gabriel Miró 34. Run by an amiable family, it has a menú for 1550 ptas; if you're ordering à la carte, try the ensalada 'el pati' (600 ptas) and entrecot con pimienta verde (pepper steak, 1500 ptas) – a great combo!

Getting There & Away

Ubesa (☎ 513 01 43) runs buses from here around the coast to Alicante and Valencia.

VALENCIA

You can also get here on the FGV trains between Alicante and Denia.

ALTEA
Altea's beaches may be a blend of pebbles, rocks and sand, but the town beats Benidorm hands down when it comes to character (which, admittedly, isn't saying much). With what's left of the old town perched on a hill top overlooking the sea, Altea is a good place to spend a few days away from the hustle and bustle.

The beaches and boat harbour are backed by a pleasant foreshore promenade and a strip of low-key development. Further back you can explore the up-market boutiques, antique shops and good restaurants scattered around the streets of the whitewashed old town.

Altea's tourist office (☎ 584 4114) is on the beachfront at Calle San Pedro 9; it opens most days from 10 am to 2 pm and 5 to 7 pm.

Places to Stay & Eat
Hotel San Miguel (☎ 584 04 00), on the waterfront at Calle La Mar 65, has pleasant rooms with small bathrooms from 2000/3800 to 3500/6000 ptas (plus IVA); ask for a room with sea views. There are two restaurants downstairs specialising in seafood, rice dishes and paella, with a good menú for 1650 ptas.

BENIDORM
Infamous Benidorm supposedly represents all that is bad about package tourism in Spain. If you're thinking about coming out of sheer curiosity – can it really be that bad? – allow us to save you the trip. It's much, much worse than you could possibly imagine. Five km of white-sand beaches backed by a relentless jungle of concrete high-rise; streets overwhelmed with tourists toting tacky souvenirs and plastic beach toys; and slabs of pasty-white flesh committing outrageous sins in the name of summer fashion.

Despite having been subjected to every derogatory cliché in the (guide) book, Benidorm continues to prosper and grow.

Most of the year it's predominantly a haven for middle-aged and elderly English, German and Scandinavian tourists, but during summer it becomes one of Spain's premier disco hot spots with a club scene that rivals Ibiza's.

The tourist office (☎ 585 32 24) is near the waterfront in the old town at Calle Martínez Alejos 16.

Places to Stay
Almost everyone here is on some kind of package deal, but if you visit and decide to stay, the following hostales and hotels are all on or near the waterfront in the old town.

Hostal La Santa Faz (☎ 585 40 63), Calle Santa Faz 18, has dim and oldish rooms with bathroom from 2850/3500 to 3250/6000 ptas. *Hostal Calpi* (☎ 585 78 48), Costera del Barco 6, has better rooms, also with bathrooms, and charges 2000 to 3000 ptas per person.

Some of the big hotels are good value out of season. The two star *Hotel Colón* (☎ 585 40 63), Paseo Colón 3, has rooms with balcony and sea views ranging from 2700/4400 to 5000/10,000 ptas and pensión completo from 3000 to 5500 ptas per person. *Hotel Bilbaíno* (☎ 585 08 04), on the beachfront at Avenida Virgen del Sufragio, charges from 4000/6500 to 5000/8500 ptas.

ALICANTE
Alicante is a surprisingly refreshing town, with wide boulevards, long white sandy beaches and a number of cultural and historic attractions.

After taking a waterfront stroll beneath the palm trees that shade Explanada de España and enjoying a leisurely drink at one of the open-air cafés, you may well decide to stay the night and experience Alicante's excellent nightlife.

Orientation
Alicante's waterfront is lined with broad, shady boulevards. Set back from the Mediterranean and clustered around the Catedral de San Nicolás are the narrow streets of El Barrio (the old quarter), where you'll find

PLACES TO STAY
10 Hostal Mayor
11 Hostal Portugal
12 Eurohotel Hesperia
21 Pensión Les Monges
26 Pensión
     La Milagrosa
29 Hotel Palas
31 Hotel Sol Alicante

PLACES TO EAT
4 Cafetería Capri
16 Boutique de Mar
17 Restaurante El Refugio
22 Restaurante El Canario
25 Restaurante
     Mixto Vegetariano
32 Restaurante
     Cuidad Imperial

OTHER
1 Estación de Madrid
    (RENFE Train Station)
2 Museo Arqueológico
    Provincial
3 Mercado Central
5 Astoria Cinema
6 Celestial Copas
7 Concatedral de San Nicolás
8 La Naya & Potato-Bar Cafe
9 Jamboree Bar
13 Bus Station, Telephone Office
     & Municipal Tourist Office
14 Cool
15 Post Office
18 Plaza Ayuntamiento
19 Ayuntamiento
     & Tourist Office
20 Plaza Santísima Faz
23 Colección de
     Arte de Siglo XX
24 Iglesia de Santa María
27 Train Ticket Office
28 Regional Tourist Office
30 Telephone Office
     Entrance to lift shaft to
     Castillo de Santa Bárbara
34 Buses to San Juan
35 Boats to Isla de Tabarca

MEDITERRANEAN SEA

Castillo de
Santa Bárbara

Alicante

0   100   200 m

most of the cheapest accommodation places and the best nightlife. El Barrio is bordered by the Rambla de Méndez Núñez; southwest of here in the newer parts of town are the post office and bus and train stations.

Information
Tourist Offices Staffed by two charming and helpful young ladies, the regional tourist office (☎ 520 00 00) at Explanada de España 2 opens Monday to Saturday from 10 am to 7 pm (8 pm during summer), closing between 2 and 3 pm on Saturday.

There are also three municipal tourist offices here. The one next to the bus station on Calle Portugal 17 (☎ 514 92 95) opens weekdays from 9 am to 9 pm and Saturday from 9 am to 7.30 pm; the others are in the ayuntamiento and at the airport.

Post & Communications Alicante's main post office, on Plaza Gabriel Miró, is open weekdays from 8 am to 9 pm and Saturday from 9 am to 2 pm.

There's a public telephone office on the corner of Avenida Juan Bautista Lafora and Calle Bendicho, and another small telephone office in the main bus station.

Things to See & Do
The most obvious of Alicante's attractions is the **Castillo de Santa Bárbara**, a 16th century fortress overlooking the city. There is a lift shaft deep inside the mountain which will take you right to the castle (200 ptas return) – the lift entrance is opposite Playa del Postiguet. The castle opens daily from 10 am to 8 pm (October to March, 9 am to 7 pm); entry is free.

Inside the castle the **Museo de las Hogueras** preserves some of the effigies that have been saved from the flames of the Fiesta de Sant Joan (see Special Events).

The **Colección de Arte del Siglo XX** on Plaza de Santa María houses an excellent collection of modern art including a handful of works by Dalí, Miró and Picasso. It opens daily from 10.30 am to 1.30 pm and 6 to 9 pm (October to April, 10 am to 1 pm and 5

to 8 pm), and closes Monday, Sunday afternoon and public holidays. Entry is free.

On the same plaza, the **Iglesia de Santa María** has an elaborate Gothic façade, which is currently undergoing overdue repairs.

The small **Museo Arqueológico**, in the impressive Diputación Provincial building near the train station on Avenida de la Estación, has well set-up collections of ceramics and paintings.

Kontiki (☎ 521 63 96) runs boat trips most days to the popular **Isla de Tabarca**. The island has quiet beaches and good snorkelling and scuba diving, plus a small hotel. Return fares are 1500 ptas.

A huge industrial port and ritzy boat harbour take up most of central Alicante's foreshore. Immediately north is the main city beach of **Playa del Postiguet**. It's sandy and has been cleaned up in recent years, but gets pretty crowded. You're better off heading further north to the cleaner and less crowded beaches at Playa de San Juan.

Special Events
Alicante's major festival is the Fiesta de Sant Joan, held over the last week of June. On 24 June Alicante stages its own version of Las Fallas, with extensive fireworks displays and satirical effigies going up in smoke.

Places to Stay – bottom end
Camping On the coast seven km north, *Camping Bahía* (☎ 526 23 32) is an unappealing camping ground in the centre of the town of Campello. A little further north on Campello's outskirts, *Camping Costa Blanca* (☎ 563 06 70) is a slightly better bet. It's just 200 metres from the beach and has a good pool and a café, charging between 350 and 500 ptas per car, person and tent.

Youth Hostel *Residencia Universitaria Albergue Juvenil 'La Florida'* (☎ 511 30 44), Avenida Orihuela 59, is an inconvenient two km west of the centre and on a busy main road. Apart from having the longest name in Spain, it has good facilities and 204 beds in single and double rooms. Junior/senior members pay 800/1100 ptas or 1900/2400 ptas for pensión completo.

Hostales & Pensiones There are plenty of cheap hostales in El Barrio – some excellent, some appalling. The old quarter is quaint and charming by day but it can become somewhat grim and seedy by night, especially as you head up towards Plaza del Carmen. Standards and prices generally rise as you move towards the newer parts of town.

At Calle Monges 2, the outstanding *Pensión Les Monges* (☎ 521 50 46) is like a boutique hotel; walls hung with tapestries and artworks, a cosy TV lounge and sitting room for guests, and a charming owner. Each of the eight rooms is different, but they all have heating, TV, hair dryers, wash basins, piped music and air-con (the last two are optional). Singles/doubles are from 1800/3400 ptas (2000/3700 ptas with shower or 2600/4200 ptas with bathroom).

At Calle de Villavieja 8, *Pensión La Milagrosa* (☎ 521 69 18) has basic but clean and bright rooms and a small guest kitchen, and charges 1200 to 1500 ptas per person. Some rooms overlook the Plaza de Santa María.

Hostal Mayor (☎ 520 13 83), Calle Mayor 5, has renovated rooms with modern bathrooms at 2200/4000/5700 ptas for singles/doubles/triples (cheaper out of season).

Opposite the bus station at Calle Portugal 26, *Hostal Portugal* (☎ 592 92 44) is a slightly old-fashioned place with clean, spacious rooms from 2000/3000 ptas, or 3000/3800 ptas with bathroom.

Places to Stay – middle
The three star *Hotel Palas* (☎ 520 93 09), Plaza Puerta del Mar, is a rambling, semigrand hotel with a weird collection of artworks, furniture and mirrors. Their quirky, old-fashioned rooms with mod cons (and a few odd ones) cost 4900/7875 ptas (plus IVA).

A couple of blocks away at Calle Gravina 9, *Hotel Sol Alicante* (☎ 521 07 00) is a modern and stylish three star place with rooms from 8000/9500 ptas; parking costs another 1000 ptas.

Also worth considering is the *Eurhotel Hesperia* (☎ 513 04 40), Calle Pintor Lorenzo Casanova 33. It's a nice hotel although it isn't close to anything much except the bus station. Rooms are 10,450/11,450 ptas midweek or 6250/7520 ptas on weekends.

Places to Eat
If you're self-catering, the huge *Mercado Central* up on Avenida Alfonso X El Sabio is something of a temple to red meat but also has plenty of fresh fruit and veggies.

The glitzy *Restaurante Ciudad Imperial*, Calle Gravina 8, has tasty Chinese tucker with a budget menú at 500 ptas (weekdays only) and banquet menús from 695 to 950 ptas.

There are quite a few budget eateries in the area around Plaza Ayuntamiento: *Restaurante El Refugio*, Calle Rafael Altamira 19, has menús from 1200 to 2400 ptas and, like most places here, their menús come in several different languages.

At Calle Maldonado 25, *Restaurante El Canario* is a no-frills local eatery with a hearty menú for 850 ptas. *Restaurante Mixto Vegetariano*, Plaza de Santa María 2, is a simple low-ceilinged place with vegetarian and carnivorous menús at 980 ptas – you can choose or combine dishes from both menus.

Cafetería Capri, Calle San Ildefonso 6, is a popular indoor/outdoor eatery with a good tapas selection, 22 different platos combinados (600 to 1400 ptas) and a menú for 925 ptas. Opposite the bus station at Calle Portugal 24, *Cafetería Rio* is a good place to hang out while you're waiting for your bus; they have good snacks and a menú for 980 ptas.

You can try local seafood specialities at the stylish *Boutique del Mar* at Calle San Fernando 16. They do arroz negro, arroz a banda or arroz marinara (850 to 950 ptas), seafood dishes (750 to 1500 ptas), and the menú costs 1500 ptas.

Down on the Explanada de España at No 7, the *Boutique de Jamón* features a touristy but appealing mock-Spanish décor and has tables out on the plaza. Try a few of their mini bocadillos or some tapas; they also do sangría by the glass or jug.

Entertainment

Bars & Discos There are a couple of different nightlife areas in Alicante – both geographically and atmospherically.

The best area to start the night is El Barrio, the old quarter around the Catedral San Nicolás. Most of the bars around here open until 2 am early in the week and until 4 or 5 am on the weekends.

The *Jamboree Bar*, Calle San José 10, is a funky stone-walled place with live jazz and blues bands. Around the corner in Calle Labradores (in the moon-shadows of the cathedral) are the *Potato-Bar Cafe* and *La Naya*, a cocktail bar with paintings by local artists.

Nearby on Calle San Pascual, the heavenly (and very weird) *Celestial Copas* has a kitsch collection of religious art/junk and great music. Further up on Calle de Santo Tomás, look out for *Cherokee* at No 8 and the *Desden Cafe Bar* opposite. On the corner of Calle Montengon and Calle Padre Maltes, the tiny *La Llum Pub* is a sweatbox dance-bar that goes wild late in the night.

The area further west in the streets between Rambla de Méndez Núñez and Avenida Doctor Gadea is more up-market. On the corner of Explanada de España and Calle Valdés, *Cool* lives up to its name with a Harley-Davidson mounted above its entrance and hip salsa, jazz and blues bands gracing its small stage. Nearby, people and pounding music spill out of *Pacha* onto its open-air terrace.

There are a couple of sophisticated bars one block back along Calle San Fernando: *Santa Fe Bar*, on the corner of Avenida Doctor Gadea, plays good music and is a good meeting place. Nearby on the Calle Lanuza corner, the stylish *Gran Cafe* features marble columns, timber booths and soft lighting.

At Calle San Fernando 37, the popular *Bugatti* is a slick basement disco with dress regulations and a 1000 ptas cover charge, although you can often pick up free passes from local bars. It's open every night except Monday until dawn (but don't bother turning up before 3 am unless you want to watch the staff set up). Across the roads several 'clubs' of a more dubious nature hide their wares behind red velvet curtains.

During summer there's a great disco scene up at the Playa de San Juan. In fact there are dozens of discos along the coast all the way from Alicante to Denia, and FGV's 'night trains' ferry hordes of party-goers along this notorious section of *la ruta bakalao*. The trains operate every night during July and August with services hourly between 11 pm and 7 am.

Theatre & Cinema Alicante's main venue for the performing arts, the *Teatro Principal* (☎ 520 23 80), is at Calle de Teatro 16.

The *Astoria Cinema* (☎ 521 56 66) 'mini-twin', in El Barrio on Plaza del Carmen, screens v.o. subtitulada films.

Getting There & Away

The Airport El Altet airport is 12 km south-west of the centre. Alcoyana (☎ 513 01 04) has hourly buses between the airport and the bus station.

Air Alicante is the gateway to the Costa Blanca and there are frequent flights to all major centres including Palma de Mallorca, Ibiza City, Valencia, Barcelona and Madrid, as well as to many destinations in Europe.

Bus The bus station (☎ 513 07 00) is on Calle Portugal. Ubesa (☎ 513 01 43) has frequent buses north to Valencia (1890 ptas) via the coastal towns along the Costa Blanca including Benidorm (420 ptas) and Calpe (605 ptas). Enatcar (☎ 513 06 73) handles long-distance hauls to Madrid (five hours; 2950 ptas), Almería (4½ hours; 2500 ptas), Granada (six hours; 3090 ptas) and Barcelona (eight hours; 4300 ptas).

Train Alicante has two train stations. RENFE's Estación de Madrid (☎ 521 02 02) is on Avenida Salamanca. Services include Madrid (10 daily; four hours; 3500 to 4700 ptas); Valencia (eight daily; two hours; 1300 to 2300 ptas) via Villena and Xàtiva; Barcelona (three daily; six hours; 3500 to 5000 ptas); Murcia (1½ hours; 515 to 550 ptas); and Orihuela (one hour; 370 to 400 ptas).

RENFE has a booking office in the centre on the corner of Explanada de España and Calle Cervantes.

The Ferrocarriles de la Generalitat Valenciana (FGV) station (☎ 526 27 31) is at Avenida Villajoyosa 2, on the foreshore at the far end of Playa del Postiguet. Trains operate from here north along the coast as far as Denia (950 ptas) via Playa de San Juan (110 ptas), Benidorm (405 ptas) and Calpe (600 ptas), with services hourly between 6.15 am and 8.30 pm (see the Entertainment section for details of summer night trains).

SANTA POLA

This modern seaside township sprawls around its harbour, which is home to the local fishing fleet and lined with hundreds of pleasure vessels. You can take boat trips from here across to the popular **Isla de Tabarca**, just 3.5 nautical miles offshore.

Most of Santa Pola's beaches are backed by jungles of concrete, but the sandy **Gran Playa**, **Playa Lisa** and **Santa Pola del Este** beaches are still worth a visit.

In the centre of town on Plaza de la Glorieta, the well-preserved 16th century **Castillo-Fortaleza de Santa Pola** fortress stands besieged by 20th century high-rise architecture. Inside there's a sunny courtyard, a bar, a small chapel and the **aquarium and archaeological museum** (open Tuesday to Saturday from 11 am to 1 pm and 4 to 7 pm, Sunday from 11 am to 1.30 pm; entry 100 ptas).

Information

The tourist office (☎ 669 22 76) is at the entrance to town on Plaza de la Diputación (on the northern corner of El Palmeral park). It opens daily from 9 am to 2 pm (Friday until 3 pm) as well as Saturday from 4 to 8 pm.

Places to Stay – bottom end

Camping One km west of town on the C-3317 highway to Elx, the pleasant *Camping Bahia de Santa Pola* (☎ 541 10 12) has a bar-restaurant, pool and shop. During summer they charge 500 ptas per car, tent, caravan and person.

Hostales Most of the budget options are clustered in the streets east of the tourist office, about 500 metres back from the waterfront. The friendly *Hostal Chez Michel* (☎ 541 18 42), Calle Felipe 11, has refurbished rooms with bathroom from 2225/3580 to 2625/4000 ptas and a good restaurant. During summer media pensión costs 6500 ptas a double.

Nearby at Calle Alicante 66, *Hostal-Restaurante Picola* (☎ 541 18 68) is also good, and slightly more expensive.

Places to Stay – middle

Hotel PolaMar (☎ 541 32 00), right on the Playa de Levante beachfront, is a big, bland three star place with rooms from 4500/7800 to 6150/9860 ptas (plus IVA) – ask for a room with sea views.

TORREVIEJA

A heavily developed but not completely unpleasant resort, Torrevieja has good beaches and a lively nightlife, but be warned that you will probably not get to know many, if any, Spaniards here. The tourist office (☎ 571 59 36) is centrally located on the waterfront at Plaza Capdepont.

Places to Stay – bottom end

Camping Four km south beside the N-332 highway, *Camping La Campana* (☎ 670 57 81) is a good camping ground with shady pine trees, a small gym and a heated swimming pool. They charge 500 ptas per car, tent and person.

Hostales & Hotels At Avenida Dr Gregorio Marañón 22 (the main road into town), *Hostal Reina* (☎ 670 19 04) is friendly, cheap and shabby. Rooms with traffic noise, tiny bathrooms and marshmallow beds (and

VALENCIA

a few with ocean glimpses) range from 1500/2400 to 1800/3000 ptas.

A better budget bet is *Hostal Fernández* (☎ 571 00 09), central and 300 metres back from the beach at Calle Ramón Gallud 16. Freshly painted rooms with bathroom are 2000/3000 to 3000/5000 ptas.

Near the bus station at Calle Zoa 53, *Hotel Cano* (☎ 670 09 58) has modern rooms with bathroom from 3000/4500 to 3500/5000 ptas (plus IVA).

Places to Stay – middle

Two blocks back from the tourist office at Rambla de Juan Mateo 19, *Hotel Fontana* (☎ 670 11 25) is a big three star place charging from 3900/6900 to 5500/10,500 ptas (plus IVA).

Places to Eat

There are plenty of restaurants clustered around the waterfront offering cheap meals and international menus. One block back from the beachfront at Calle Pedro Lorca 13, *Restaurante Vegetariano* is a little vegetarian haven run by a Spanish-Australian couple. They do salads and sandwiches (400 to 800 ptas) and good pizzas (around 800 ptas).

Getting There & Away

The bus station is 500 metres inland on Calle Antonio Machado. Enatcar (☎ 571 65 62) runs buses to Madrid (3545 ptas), Albacete (1550 ptas) and Villena (595 ptas). Autocares Costa Blanca (☎ 670 10 68) has frequent buses to Cartagena (490 ptas) and Alicante (410 ptas).

Balearic Islands

Floating out in the blue waters of the Mediterranean off the east coast of Spain, the Balearic Islands (Islas Baleares) are invaded every summer by a massive multinational force of hedonistic tourists. This is not surprising really, when you consider the ingredients on offer – fine beaches, relentless sunshine, wild nightlife and a great range of accommodation and eating options.

What *is* surprising is that despite all this, the four main islands – Mallorca, Menorca, Ibiza and Formentera – have, to a degree, managed to maintain their individuality and strong links with the past. Beyond the bars and beaches are Gothic cathedrals, Stone Age ruins, small fishing villages, some spectacular bushwalks, endless olive groves and orange orchards. It comes as a relief to discover that tourism hasn't *completely* consumed these islands – not yet, anyway.

Place names and addresses are generally given in this chapter in Catalan, the main language spoken in the islands (with slight regional variations). The major exceptions are Ibiza and Ibiza city: although both are called Eivissa in Catalan, we have used the more commonly used and recognised Castilian name Ibiza.

The telephone code for all of the Balearic Islands is ☎ 971.

History

Archaeologists believe that the first human settlements in the Balearics date from around 5000 BC. An abundance of prehistoric relics and monuments uncovered in the islands show that these ancient communities constructed houses of stone, practised basic agriculture, domesticated animals, performed ritual burials and manufactured pottery, tools and decorative jewellery.

The islands were regular ports of call for the ancient Phoenician traders. They were followed by the Carthaginians, who founded Ibiza city in 654 BC and made it into one of

- Trekking in Mallorca's Serra de Tramuntana mountains
- Palma's enormous cathedral, and the old quarter (Mallorca)
- Scenic drives and small villages along Mallorca's north-west coast
- Sunrise at the Sanctuari Puig de Maria (Mallorca)
- Ibiza's amazing discos and bars
- A *bocadillo completo* at Bar Costa in Santa Gertrudis (Ibiza)
- Formentera's beaches and walking and cycling trails
- Menorca's archaeological monuments

the Mediterranean's major trading ports. Next came those compulsive road-builders the Romans, who, in turn, were conquered by the savage Visigoths.

The Muslims, who invaded the islands in the 8th century, left a lasting legacy which is still apparent today – in the appearance and customs of the local people, in their traditional dress, and even in much of the island architecture.

The Muslim domination lasted more than three centuries. The Christian Reconquista was led by Jaume I of Cataluña and Aragón, who took Palma de Mallorca in 1229 and sponsored the invasion of Ibiza in 1235. Menorca was the last to fall when Alfonso III

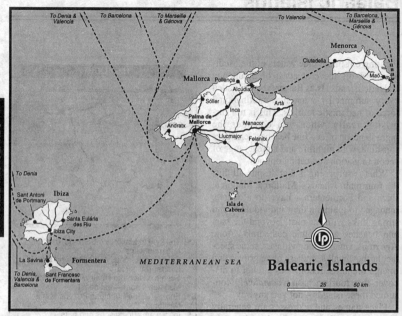

Balearic Islands

MEDITERRANEAN SEA

0   25   50 km

took the island in 1287, completing the incorporation of the Balearics into the Catalan world.

The islands initially prospered as trading centres and Catalan colonies, but by the 15th century they had fallen into economic decline. Isolation from the mainland, famines and frequent raids by pirates all contributed. During the 16th century, Menorca's two major towns were virtually destroyed by Turkish forces, and during this same period Ibiza city's fortified walls were built to protect it from invaders. After a succession of bloody raids, Formentera was completely abandoned.

The Balearics also fared poorly in warfare. After backing the Habsburgs in the Spanish War of Succession, Mallorca and Ibiza were occupied by the victorious Bourbon monarchy in 1715. Menorca, on the other hand, was granted to the British along with Gibraltar in 1713 under the Treaty of Utrecht. British rule lasted until 1802, with the exception of the

Seven Years War (1756-63) when Menorca was occupied by the French.

In subsequent years the islands regained much of their prosperity as important trading and manufacturing centres, but by the early 20th century they had fallen into decline along with the rest of Spain. The advent of mass tourism, which began with a trickle during the 1950s and boomed from the 1970s onwards, became the economic saviour of the Balearics.

When to Go

Summer is certainly the silly season in the Balearics. During July and August you'll have to put up with crowded beaches, higher prices and a shortage of accommodation. On the other hand, you can also expect plenty of sunshine, warm water, great nightlife and opportunities to meet people of all nationalities (especially Brits and Germans).

If you want to avoid these crowds it's worth considering coming during the shoulder seasons of May-June and September-October.

While the winter months can be a peaceful time to visit and get to know the islands, the lack of beach weather keeps most people away. As a result, most tourism-oriented businesses (including hotels and *hostales*) close down between November and April.

Accommodation

While it's true that the majority of beds in the Balearics are in resorts tailored for the package tourism industry, there are still plenty of hostales and hotels willing and able to cater to independent travellers. Most of the places recommended in this chapter fall into the second category – although there are exceptions.

It's also true that accommodation in the islands is generally more expensive than on the mainland – even more so during July and August when tariffs can increase by as much as 100%. Having said that, there are still bargains to be found, especially if you can avoid the peak holiday period.

Because of these substantial variations, tariffs are quoted so as to give you an idea of each place's seasonal range. For example, if a hostal's prices for singles/doubles are 2000/4000 ptas in the low season and 3500/7000 ptas in the high season, we'll say something like 'prices range from 2000/4000 to 3500/7000 ptas'.

Getting There & Away

Air Scheduled flights from the major cities on the Spanish mainland are operated by several airlines, including the domestic airlines Iberia and Aviaco. The cheapest and most frequent flights are from Barcelona and Valencia. Standard one-way fares from Barcelona are 10,600 ptas to Palma, 11,850 ptas to Maó and 12,700 ptas to Ibiza. From Valencia, fares are 10,800 ptas to Ibiza and 12,100 ptas to Palma. Return fares are double the standard one-way fares.

Iberia and Aviaco both offer special fares (on return flights only) but these are very difficult to obtain – in the high season you can forget it. 'Mini Tarifa' fares (you book at least three days in advance) cut the return fare by about 25%, and 'Super Mini Tarifa' (or 'Tarifa Azul') fares cut the standard return fares by 50% (to qualify you must book five days ahead and spend a Saturday night at the destination). Super Mini Tarifa tickets from Barcelona are 12,500 ptas to Ibiza and 11,900 ptas to Maó; from Valencia they are 14,800 ptas to Maó and 10,600 ptas to Ibiza.

Inter-island flights are quite reasonably priced, with Palma to Maó or Ibiza costing 6650 ptas. There are no direct flights from Ibiza to Maó.

There are cheaper flights to the Balearics by other airlines, eg Air Europa flies Barcelona-Palma daily, Barcelona-Maó five days a week and Valencia-Palma five days a week, all for 7500 ptas one way and from 10,500 ptas return; and Barcelona-Ibiza five days a week (8500 ptas one way; from 11,900 ptas return).

Charter flights from Europe are usually sold as a package that includes accommodation deals. If you're looking for a cheap deal it may be worth enquiring at travel agencies, as spare seats on charter flights are often sold at substantially discounted prices.

Boat Trasmediterránea is the major ferry company for the islands, with offices in (and services between) Barcelona (☎ 93-443 25 32), Valencia (☎ 96-367 65 12), Palma de Mallorca, (☎ 40 50 14), Maó (☎ 36 60 50) and Ibiza city (☎ 31 41 73). Trasmediterránea has more than 20 offices throughout Spain and the islands. Tickets can also be booked and purchased through any travel agency.

Trasmediterránea has a 'four seasons' timetable – the warmer it is, the more frequent the sailings. Year-round scheduled services are: Barcelona-Palma (eight hours; seven to eight services weekly); Barcelona-Maó (nine hours; two to six services weekly); Barcelona-Ibiza city (9½ hours; four to six services weekly); Valencia-Palma (8½ hours; six services weekly); Valencia-Ibiza city (seven hours; one to six services weekly); Palma-Ibiza city (4½ hours; two services weekly); and Palma-Maó (6½ hours; two services weekly).

Prices quoted below are the one-way fares during summer; low and mid-season fares are considerably cheaper.

Fares from the mainland to any of the islands are 6300 ptas for a 'Butaca Turista' (seat); a berth in a cabin ranges from 10,500 ptas (four-share) to 15,750 ptas (twin-share) per person. Taking a small car costs 18,000 ptas, or you can buy a 'Paquete Ahorro' (economy package, which includes a car and four passengers sharing a cabin) for 49,500 ptas.

The exception is Valencia-Ibiza city, for which you pay 5040 ptas for a Butaca Turista, 8400 ptas (four-share) to 12,600 ptas (twin-share) for a cabin, 14,400 ptas for a small car and 39,600 ptas for a Paquete Ahorro.

Inter-island services (Palma-Ibiza city and Palma-Maó) both cost 3150 ptas for a Butaca Turista, 9000 ptas for a small car and 24,750 ptas for a Paquete Ahorro.

During summer, Trasmediterránea also operates the following 'Fast Ferry' services (prices quoted are for a Butaca Turista): Tarragona-Palma (3¾ hours; 7500 ptas; four to eight services weekly); Valencia-Palma (5½ hours: 7500 ptas: three services weekly); Valencia-Ibiza city (three hours; 6430 ptas; three services weekly); and Palma-Ibiza city (2¼ hours; 4820 ptas; three services weekly).

Another company, Flebasa (☎ 96-578 40 11 in Denia or ☎ 48 00 12 in Ciutadella), operates services from Denia on the mainland (between Valencia and Alicante) to Sant Antoni on Ibiza, and between Ciutadella on Menorca and Port d'Alcúdia on Mallorca.

See the Formentera section for details on ferries from Ibiza.

Mallorca

Mallorca is the largest of the Balearic Islands. Most of the five million annual visitors to the island are here for the three s's: sun, sand and sea. There are, however, other reasons for coming to Mallorca. Palma, the main population centre, is in itself worth visiting, and the north-west coast is a world away from the concrete jungles on the other side of the island. Dominated by the Serra de Tramuntana mountains, it's a beautiful region of olive groves, pine forests and small villages, with a rugged and rocky coastline.

Most of Mallorca's best beaches are on the north and east coasts, and while most have been consumed by tourist developments there are still exceptions worth searching out.

Orientation

The capital, Palma de Mallorca, is on the south side of the island in a bay famous for its brilliant sunsets. A series of rocky coves and harbours punctuate the short south-west coastline, and offshore from the island's westernmost point is the large uninhabited island of Sa Dragonera.

The spectacular Serra de Tramuntana mountain range runs parallel with the north-west coast and includes the mountain of Puig Major (1445 metres), Mallorca's highest point. The north-east coast is largely made up of two bays, the Badia de Pollença and the larger Badia d'Alcúdia.

The east coast is an almost continuous string of sandy bays and open beaches, and consequently this is where the most intensive tourist developments have been built. In contrast, most of the southern coast is lined by rocky cliffs, and the majority of the Mallorcan interior is made up of the flat plain known as Es Pla.

Activities

Mallorca has some outstanding trekking destinations, particularly in the mountainous north-western region. Note that spring is the best time for walking here as the summers are often unbearably hot and dry. The tourist office's *20 Hiking Excursions on the Island of Mallorca* brochure outlines some of the island's better walks and includes a locater map and brief track notes. For more detailed information see one of the numerous specialist publications, which include Lonely Planet's *Trekking in Spain* by Marc Dubin.

Cycling tours are also particularly popular

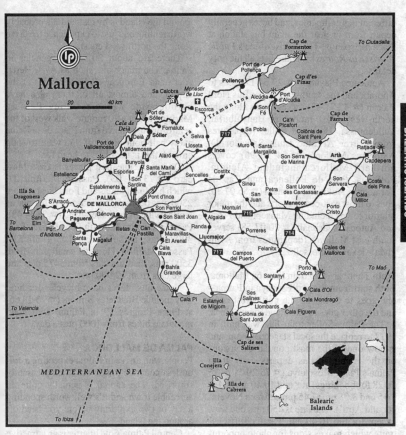

Mallorca

0   20   40 km

MEDITERRANEAN SEA

here, and the handy *Guia del Ciclista* map/brochure (also available from tourist offices) suggests eight different itineraries ranging in length from 50 to 320 km.

Water sports are well catered for, and most beach resorts have a selection of sailboards, catamarans, kayaks and paddle boats for hire. There are also quite a few scuba-diving schools and equipment hire places around the island.

Accommodation

The best of Mallorca's camping grounds is Camping Club Picafort on the north-east

coast (see the Port d'Alcúdia section later in this chapter for details). There's another camping ground near the town of Colònia de Sant Pere.

Budget travellers are pretty well catered for. There are several youth hostels and a couple of quirky old monasteries around the island where you can sleep cheaply, and Palma has a good range of affordable hostales.

Getting Around

Bus Most parts of the island are accessible by bus from Palma. There are around a dozen different bus companies, and buses generally depart from or near the main bus station at Plaça d'Espanya. The tourist office's *Public Tourist Bus Routes* brochure lists all the gory details.

Autocares PlayaSol (☎ 29 64 17) goes to Andratx and the south-east coast; Bus Nord Balean (☎ 42 71 87) serves towns along the north-west coast including Banyalbufar, Valldemossa, Deià and Sóller (departures from Carrer Arxiduc Lluis Salvador 1); Autocares Mallorca (☎ 54 56 96) covers northern Mallorca including Alcúdia, Pollença, Port de Pollença and Cap de Formentor; Autocares Aumasa (☎ 55 07 30) goes to most east-coast resorts and the major interior towns including Manacor and Petra; and Autocares Grimalt (☎ 20 07 58) serves south-east Mallorca (departures from Avinguda Alexandre Rosselló 32).

Train There are two train lines on Mallorca. Both start from Plaça d'Espanya in Palma – one goes to Sóller on the north-west coast and the other goes to the inland town of Inca.

The Palma-Sóller train line was built in 1912 to replace the local stagecoach run, and is now one of the most popular excursions on the island. Trains departs daily from Palma's Plaça d'Espanya (☎ 75 20 51 or 75 20 28 for bookings) at 8 and 10.40 am and 1, 3.15 and 8.05 pm (7.45 pm between November and April). The fare is 450 ptas one way, except for the 10.40 am 'Parada Turística' train, which makes stops for photo opportunities but costs 800 ptas! Trains return from Sóller daily at 6.45, 9.15 and 11.50 am and 2.10 and 7 pm (6.30 pm between November and April), with an extra service at 7.35 pm between May and October.

Boat Palma and the major resorts and beaches around the island are also connected with each other by numerous boat tours and water taxi services. The tourist office's *Excursiones En Barca* brochure details many of these and includes departure times and fares.

Car & Bicycle Rental The best way to get

around the island is by car, and it's probably worth renting one just to experience the drive along the north-west coast.

There are about 30 rental agencies in Palma. The major one such as Avis, Hertz, Alesa and Europcar all have offices at the airport, and almost all of them also have harbour-side agencies along Passeig Marítim (about a 20 minute walk west of the centre, or buses leave from Plaça de la Reina every half-hour or so): if you want to shop around, this is the place to head for.

One of the cheapest places is Casa Mascaro (☎ 73 61 03), Passeig Marítim 21, which has Fiat Pandas and Ford Fiestas from 2300 ptas per day (low season). Other places worth trying include Iber-Auto (☎ 28 54 48), Passeig Marítim 13, with Ford Fiestas from 3900 ptas; and Entercar (☎ 74 30 51), Passeig Marítim 11, with small cars from 3500 ptas, medium cars from 5475 ptas and large cars from 12,900 ptas.

Numerous places have bicycles for hire: they include Bicicletas Bimont (☎ 73 18 66) at Plaça Progrés 19 in Palma, with good mountain bikes from 1000 ptas a day.

PALMA DE MALLORCA

People who arrive in Palma expecting a colourless concrete jungle are often pleasantly surprised. The capital is actually quite an agreeable town and it's well worth spending a day or two exploring before you head off around the island.

Central Palma's old quarter is an attractive blend of tree-lined boulevards and cobbled laneways, Gothic churches and baroque palaces, designer bars and slick boutiques. It's a stylish and prosperous city which buzzes by day and sizzles by night.

That's the good news. The bad news is that it's also crammed to the hilt with tourists and tacky souvenir shops. And you'll have to take a bus to get to the beaches, where you'll discover the endless sprawl of high-rise development that has engulfed the entire bay.

Orientation

Central Palma stretches from the harbour up towards Plaça d'Espanya, a busy and chaotic transport hub. This is where you'll arrive if you come in on the airport bus, and it's also the terminus for Mallorca's two train lines and the main departure point for buses to other parts of the island. There's a tourist office on the plaza, and frequent buses run from here down to the central Plaça de la Reina; otherwise it's about a 20 minute walk.

From the harbour and ferry terminals, Avinguda d'Antoni Maura runs north up to Plaça de la Reina and through the heart of the old quarter. On the west side is Palma's main restaurant and nightlife zone, while on the east side are the Palau de l'Almudaina and the cathedral. The broad boulevard of Passeig d'es Born continues north up to Plaça Rei Joan Carles I; Avinguda Jaume III, which runs west from here, is the heart of the commercial district. Further east is the large open space of Plaça Major, from where another wide boulevard, Passeig de la Rambla, continues north-west.

Information

Tourist Office Palma has four tourist offices. The main office (☎ 72 40 90) can be hard to find: it's in a pedestrian walkway just off the eastern end of Carrer Conquistador at Carrer Sant Domingo 11. It opens weekdays from 9 am to 8 pm and Saturday from 9 am to 1.30 pm. It's usually pretty crowded, and the staff are overworked but helpful, providing decent maps of Palma and the island as well as a good range of pamphlets including transport timetables and details of boat trips and sporting facilities.

There's another convenient office on Plaça d'Espanya (☎ 71 15 27) opposite the bus and train terminals. It's open weekdays from 9 am to 8 pm and Saturday from 9 am to 1 pm. There are other offices on Plaça Major and at the airport.

Money You'll find plenty of banks along Avinguda Jaume III and Passeig d'es Born. American Express has an agency at Viajes Iberia (☎ 72 67 43) at Passeig d'es Born 14.

Post & Communications Palma's post office (postcode 07080) is at Carrer de la Constitució 6. There is a private phone office in front of the post office and a Telefónica centre nearby on Carrer Paraires.

Books Book Inn is a good English-language bookshop just off Passeig de la Rambla at Carrer dels Horts 22.

Laundry There are no decent laundrettes in central Palma, so unless your hostal has washing facilities you might have to hike across to Fast Laundry (☎ 45 46 14) at Avinguda Joan Miró 5.

Catedral

Palma's enormous cathedral, which has often been likened to a huge ship moored at the city's edge, is the first landmark you will see as you approach the island by ferry. Construction work on what was once the site of the main Islamic mosque started in 1230 but wasn't completed until 1600. This awesome structure is predominantly Gothic in form, apart from the main façade (which had to be replaced after an earthquake in 1851) and parts of the interior (which were renovated in *modernista* style by Antoni Gaudí at the beginning of the 20th century).

Entry is via a small, three room museum, which holds a rich collection of religious artwork and precious gold and silver effects, including two amazing candelabras.

The cathedral's interior is stunning in its scope and sense of spaciousness, with a series of narrow columns supporting the soaring ceiling and framing three separate levels of elaborate stained-glass windows. The front altar's centrepiece, a twisting wrought-iron sculpture suspended from the ceiling and periodically lit up with fairy lights, has been widely acclaimed, mainly because it was designed by Gaudí, but some people think it looks awkward and out of place; you can decide for yourself when you visit. The cathedral and museum are open weekdays from 10 am to 6 pm (10 am to 3 pm between November and March) and Saturday from 10 am to 2 pm. Entry is 400 ptas.

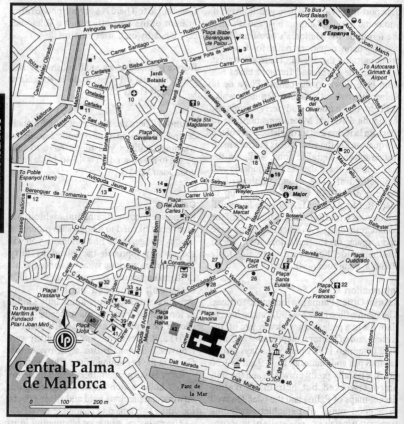

Central Palma de Mallorca

0   100   200 m

Palau de l'Almudaina

In front of the cathedral is the Palau de l'Almudaina, originally built as a Muslim castle and then converted into a residence for the Mallorcan monarchs at the end of the 13th century. It is still occasionally used for official functions when King Juan Carlos is in town, but at other times you can join the hordes and wander through an endless series of cavernous and austere stone-walled rooms and inspect a collection of portraits of Spanish monarchs, Flemish tapestries and antique furniture. The palace opens weekdays from 10 am to 7 pm (10 am to 2 pm and 4 to 6 pm between October and March) and Saturday from 10 am to 2 pm; entry costs 450 ptas, or 225 ptas for students and children.

Museu de Mallorca

A far more interesting way to spend your time and money is to visit the Museu de Mallorca at Carrer de la Portella 5. This converted 15th century palace holds an impressive collection of archaeological artefacts, religious art, antiques and ceramics. Upstairs there is also a great portrait gallery of local identities and painters. Opening hours are Tuesday to Saturday from 10 am

PLACES TO STAY		28	Restaurant	21	Tourist Office
1	Hotel Palladium		Parlament	22	Basílica de Sant
3	Hotel Cannes	36	Vecchio Giovanni &		Francesc
11	Hotel Sol Jaime III		Abaco	23	Iglésia de Santa
12	Hotel Saratoga	38	Taberna de la		Eulalia
13	Hotel Almudaina		Boveda	26	Ajuntament
14	Hotel Born	39	Mario's Cafe	27	Main Tourist Office
17	Hostal Brondo			29	Post Office
18	Hostal Monleon	**OTHER**		32	Bar Flamenco
20	Pensión Costa	4	Tourist Office	35	Cafe-Bar
	Brava	5	Train Stations (to		Barcelona
30	Hostal Pons		Sóller & Inca)	37	Sa Llotja Cafe
31	Hotel San Lorenzo	6	Bus Station & Airport	40	La Llotja
33	Hostal Apuntador		Bus	41	Gotic & Xim's Bar
34	Hostal Ritzi	7	Mercat de l'Olivar	42	Palau de
			(Market)		l'Almudaina
PLACES TO EAT		8	Book Inn	43	Catedral
2	Celler Sa Premsa	9	Santa Magdalena	44	Museu Diocesà
15	La Bodeguilla		Church	45	Museu de
24	Casa Julio	10	Hospital		Mallorca
25	Restaurante Sa	16	Casal Solleric	46	Banys Àrabs (Arab
	Impremta	19	Teatro Principal		Baths)

to 2 pm and 4 to 7 pm and Sunday from 10 am to 2 pm; entry costs 300 ptas, or 150 ptas for students.

Banys Àrabs

The delicate Arab baths, near the Museu de Mallorca, are the only remaining monument to the Muslim domination of the island. All that remains are two small underground chambers, one of which has a domed ceiling supported by columns. Interestingly, each of the columns is topped by a different capital: apparently the Muslims were great recyclers, and the capitals came from demolished Roman buildings. There's a very pleasant adjacent courtyard. The baths are open daily from 9 am to 8.30 pm and entry costs 150 ptas.

Museu Diocesà

Palma's Museu Diocesà, close to the cathedral (and signposted from the exit), houses a collection of religious art including paintings, ceramics and artefacts.

La Llotja

This gorgeous Gothic building, opposite the waterfront on Passeig de Sagrera, was originally built as a merchants' stock exchange and is now used as an exhibition centre. It's

open Tuesday to Saturday from 11 am to 2 pm and 3 to 8 pm, and Sunday from 11 am to 2 pm.

Casal Solleric

This excellent art gallery at Passeig d'es Born 27 has a good café attached. Entry is free and it's open daily from 10 am to 1.30 pm and 5 to 8.15 pm (closed Monday and Sunday afternoons).

Churches

Two of Palma's oldest churches are **Església de Santa Eulalia** and the nearby **Basílica de Sant Francesc**. The latter was begun in 1281 in Gothic style and its baroque façade was completed in 1700. Inside are the tomb of and monument to the 13th century scholar Ramon Llull, while at the front of the church is a statue of Junípero Serra, the Franciscan missionary who founded many Christian missions in California, including those in Los Angeles and San Francisco.

Other Attractions

On the west side of the city, **Poble Espanyol** is a copy of the village of the same name in Barcelona. It displays replicas of Spanish architectural styles as well as famous monuments and palaces, not to mention souvenir shops galore. Further south, the circular **Castell de Bellver** is an unusual 14th century castle set in pleasant parklands.

Also worth visiting is the **Fundació Pilar i Joan Miró**, at Carrer Joan de Saridakis 29 in Cala Major (about four km south-west of the centre). Housed in the artist's Palma studios, it exhibits a permanent collection of those of his works that were here at the time of his death. There are also temporary exhibitions and a shop selling Miró souvenirs, prints etc. Hours are Tuesday to Saturday from 10 am to 7 pm (11 am to 6 pm during winter) and Sunday from 10 am to 4 pm (11 am to 3 pm during winter). Entry costs 500 ptas.

The **Palma-Sóller train** is one of the most popular and spectacular excursions on the island and can easily be done as a day trip – see the earlier Getting Around section for details.

Places to Stay

Central Palma is by far the best area to stay in. As well as being the oldest and most interesting part of the city, most of the major points of interest are within walking distance and the old quarter is also home to Palma's best nightlife and eateries.

Avoid the string of glossy tourist hotels around the waterfront west of the centre: they're a long way from anything (except each other) and are filled with package-deal tourists.

Places to Stay – bottom end

Nothing much seems to have changed at *Hostal Pons* (☎ 72 26 58), Carrer del Vi 8, since the 1880s. The downstairs chambers are cluttered with antiques and artworks, and the quaint bedrooms all have timber bedsteads and rickety tiled floors. Amidst such charm you can almost overlook the spongy beds and queues outside the (solitary) bathroom. Singles/doubles/triples cost 2000/4000/6000 ptas.

If you want somewhere more contemporary, *Hostal Apuntadores* (☎ 71 34 91) at Carrer Apuntadors 8 is an excellent option with firm beds, modern bathrooms and

heating. Singles/doubles range from 1500/2800 to 2000/3600 ptas; doubles with private bathroom are 4100 ptas. Right next door, the friendly *Hostal Ritzi* (☎ 71 46 10) has good security and comfortable singles/doubles at 2300/3300 ptas, or doubles with shower/bath for 3800/4500 ptas.

At Passeig de la Rambla 3, *Hostal Monleon* (☎ 71 53 17) is a big old place with dim rooms from 1900/3600 ptas, or 2500/4300 ptas with private bathroom.

Pensión Costa Brava (☎ 71 17 29), Carrer Martí Feliu 16, is a backstreet cheapie with reasonable rooms from 1300/2300 ptas. On the downside, it's perennially undergoing repairs, and this area is somewhat seedy at night. *Hostal Brondo* (☎ 71 90 43) is in a much better location, just off Plaça Rei Joan Carles I at Carrer Ca'n Brondo 1. It has 10 clean rooms with bathrooms, although they're somewhat overpriced at 3800/5500 ptas (try haggling!).

Palma's youth hostel, the *Albergue Residencia d'Estudiantes* (☎ 26 08 92), is at Carrer Costa Brava in El Arenal, a crowded and heavily developed beach suburb 11 km east of the centre. At present it is only open from June to September – check with the tourist office to see if this has changed.

Places to Stay – middle

Hotel Cannes (☎ 72 69 43), close to Plaça d'Espanya at Carrer Cardenal Pau 8, is a reasonably modern if unexciting two star place with rooms from 4300/6500 ptas – tariffs include breakfast.

The superb *Hotel Born* (☎ 71 29 42), in the heart of the city at Carrer de Sant Jaume 3, is set in an 18th century palace. The entrance foyer is a lovely Mallorcan patio, and the adjacent courtyard is now a marble-clad reception area; the rooms manage to combine elegance and history with all the mod cons. B&B tariffs range from 5500/8000 to 6500/14,500 ptas (plus IVA).

Places to Stay – top end

If you're lucky enough to get a booking and lucky enough to be able to afford to, stay at the outstanding *Hotel San Lorenzo* (☎ 72 82

00), in the backstreets of the old quarter at Carrer San Lorenzo 14. The hotel is in a beautifully restored 17th century building and has its own bar, dining room, and rooftop terrace with swimming pool. There are just six rooms, each with an individual Mediterranean-style décor and modern facilities; tariffs range from 13,400/15,500 to 25,400/29,500 ptas.

Another good bet is the *Hotel-Residencia Almudaina* (☎ 72 73 40) at Avinguda Jaume III 9. It's an oldish hotel that was renovated in 1992. All rooms have air-con, heating, TV and phone, and some have sea views. Tariffs start from 5500/10,750 ptas (plus IVA), including breakfast.

Otherwise, there are three modern three star hotels along Passeig Mallorca that mainly cater to business clients. The best of these is the *Hotel Saratoga* (☎ 72 72 40) at No 6, with 187 stylish rooms, two pools, a restaurant, guest parking etc. Rooms start from 8000/12,000 ptas (plus IVA). At No 14 the refurbished *Hotel Sol Jaime III* (☎ 72 59 43) charges from 8500/10,500 ptas (plus IVA), while the impersonal *Hotel Palladium* (☎ 71 28 41) at No 40 has similar prices.

Places to Eat

For Palma's best range of eateries, wander through the maze of streets between Plaça de la Reina and the port. Carrer Apuntadors is lined with restaurants and should have something to suit everyone – seafood, Chinese, Italian – heck, there's even a few Spanish restaurants along here! Around the corner at Carrer Sant Joan 3 is the deservedly popular *Vecchio Giovanni*, which has a good menú for 950 ptas. After dinner you can pop in to the amazing Abaco next door for a drink (see the following Entertainment section). At *Mario's Café*, on Carrer de la Mar, you can have pizza or pasta from 700 ptas.

The string of tourist restaurants along Avinguda d'Antoni Maura (opposite the Palau de l'Almudaina) are all pretty tacky. You'll know you're in the 'Danger – Insipid and Overpriced Food' zone when you start seeing those prepared platters that show you what your meal will look like – blah.

Just off Plaça Llotja, *Taberna de la Boveda* is a spacious tavern-restaurant with excellent food, reasonable prices and a lively atmosphere. For starters try the delicious pa amb oli – bread smeared with tomato and olive oil and topped with your choice of anchovies (900 ptas), chorizo or cheese (750 ptas).

Restaurant Parlament, beside Palma's parliament building at Carrer Conquistador 11, has a gracious Victorian-era dining room with soaring ceilings and gilt-framed artworks. Main courses range from 875 ptas (roast chicken) to 2400 ptas (Chateaubriand); the Valencian paella (1150 ptas) is pretty good.

There are a couple of good places over near Plaça de Santa Eulalia, both with menús for 800 ptas: The excellent *Casa Julio*, tucked away at Carrer Previsió 4, specialises in local rice dishes and has great home-style cooking at low prices. It's the sort of place people keep coming back to once they've found it (it's open for lunch only, Monday to Saturday). Nearby at Carrer d'en Morey 4, *Restaurante Sa Impremta* is a friendly little bar-eatery which also offers a choice between a menú and ordering à la carte – try the grilled sardines.

The rustic *Restaurant Celler Sa Premsa*, at Plaça Obispo Berenguer de Palou 8, is something of a local institution, and a visit here is almost obligatory. It's a cavernous tavern filled with huge old wine barrels and with faded bullfighting posters covering the walls. The food is hearty but basic. The menú costs 985 ptas (plus IVA) and at the end of your meal you get a complementary glass of cava (sparkling wine). It closes on Sunday.

La Bodeguilla, near the Hotel Born at Carrer de Sant Jaume, is a stylish cellar-bar cluttered with wine bottles, strings of garlic and baskets of nuts and pulses. The specialities are 'La Picada', tapas-style dishes such as morcillo de cebolla and gambas al ajillo (600 to 1500 ptas), and 'Embutidos Ibéricos', platters of local smallgoods and cheeses (700 to 1900 ptas).

Entertainment

Central Palma has really taken off in the last

BALEARIC ISLANDS

few years, and the old quarter is now the city's most vibrant nightlife zone. Particularly along the narrow streets between Plaça de la Reina and Plaça Drassana, you'll find a huge selection of bars and pubs ranging from flashy tourist haunts to stylish bodegas.

Abaco, behind a set of ancient timber doors at Carrer Sant Joan 1, is the bar of your wildest dreams (with the drinks bill of your darkest nightmares). Inside, a Mallorcan patio and candle-lit courtyard are crammed with elaborate floral arrangements, cascading towers of fresh fruit and bizarre artwork, and bow-tied waiters fulfil your wishes while classical music soothes your ears. It ain't cheap – fruit cocktails are 900 ptas and alcoholic cocktails and glasses of champers are 1700 to 2000 ptas – but if your pocket can bear a splurge it's a great experience.

There are plenty of watering holes along Carrer Apuntadors. The atmospheric *Café-Bar Barcelona* at No 5 has live jazz and soul most nights in its somewhat cramped upstairs bar. Further along at No 22, *Flamenco* has a flamenco show every night between 11 pm and 2 am. The standard isn't exactly inspirational, but there's no cover charge.

If you just want a quiet drink there are several stylish bars on Plaça Llotja. *Gotic* and *Xim's Bar* are both fronted by rows of outdoor tables, while on the opposite corner is the smooth and very popular *Sa Llotja Cafè*. Avoid the noisy bars further north around Plaça Drassana, though.

Palma's other supposed nightlife centre is way over on the west side of the harbour, around Avinguda Joan Miró and Plaça Gomila. It's actually a tremendously unexciting area that consists of a string of karaoke bars, music pubs, flamenco shows and, along S'Aigo Doka, a couple of topless bars.

You may find more life down on the waterfront on Passeig Marítim – many of the big tourist hotels along here have their own bars and discos.

Getting There & Away

The airport is eight km east of Palma. Iberia has an office (☎ 72 43 49) in Palma at

Passeig d'es Born 10. Air Europa also has an office on Passeig d'es Born at No 24 (☎ 71 99 78; fax 72 60 76).

Trains and buses to other parts of the island depart from terminals at or near Plaça d'Espanya (see the earlier Mallorca Getting Around section for details).

Getting Around

If you're travelling by air, bus No 17 runs every half-hour between the airport and Plaça d'Espanya in central Palma; the one-way fare is 265 to 295 ptas. Alternatively, a taxi will cost around 1800 ptas.

From the ferry terminal, bus No 1 runs around Passeig Marítim and then left up Avinguda d'Antoni Maura into central Palma.

EMT (☎ 29 57 00) runs some 22 local bus services around Palma and its bay suburbs. Tickets are bought on board. Short trips cost 95 to 140 ptas and the fare to outlying suburbs is 165 ptas.

SOUTH-WEST COAST

A freeway skirts around the Badia de Palma towards Mallorca's south-west coast. Along the way you pass the resorts of Cala Major, Illetes and Palma Nova, which are basically a continuation of Palma's urban sprawl. From the inland town of Andratx, two turn-offs lead down to the coast: one to Port d'Andratx, the other to Sant Elm.

Port d'Andratx

Port d'Andratx is a glamorous little town set on low hills surrounding a narrow bay. The main road around the waterfront is lined with up-market seafood restaurants, many of which have open-air terraces overlooking the harbour.

This is a popular boating and diving centre. Several dive schools are based here, and there are numerous places where you can rent boats and scuba-diving equipment. You can also take boat trips from here around to Sant Elm and the island of Sa Dragonera.

One km south, the **Art Forum** (signposted from Port d'Andratx as 'Cultural Centre') is an interesting series of stone buildings on a hillside above the bay of Cala Llamp. The complex includes apartments, a pool, a café and restaurant, and an open-air art gallery and cinema. The owners hail it as a 'mystic synthesis among nature, humanity and Art...' but it's still worth a look despite such pretentiousness.

Places to Stay On the waterfront at Avinguda Mateo Bosch 12, *Restaurante Las Palmeras* (☎ 67 20 78) rents out good upstairs rooms with singles/doubles from 1500/3800 ptas and doubles with bathrooms and sea views from 4500 ptas.

A couple of hundred metres back from the harbour at Carrer Isaac Peral 63, *Hostal-Residencia Catalina Vera* (☎ 67 19 18) is a lovely guesthouse retreat with rooms set around a tranquil garden courtyard. B&B starts from 3300/5300 ptas.

Places to Eat There's no shortage of good seafood eateries along the waterfront. These places have terrific outlooks but charge accordingly. If you're after somewhere more affordable you could try *Restaurante Es Porteño* a couple of blocks inland at Carrer Isaac Peral 58, which has a lunch menú at 800 ptas and a dinner menú at 1350 ptas.

Sant Elm

The small seaside township of Sant Elm is a popular destination for day trips from Palma. The last part of the drive across from Andratx is a spectacular climb through attractive hills. If you'd rather walk this section, take a bus to Andratx. Walk number two on the tourist office's *20 Hiking Excursions on the Island of Mallorca* brochure starts from here and takes you to the coast via the village of S'Arracó and a ruined 16th century castle.

Sant Elm's sandy beach is pleasant but can get pretty crowded. Just offshore is a small rocky islet – within swimming distance if you've been in training. Further north there's a small dock from where you can join a glass-bottomed boat trip or take a cruise across to the large and imposing island of **Sa Dragonera**, which is uninhabited but has good hiking trails. The *Crucero Margarita*

(☎ 47 04 49) does cruises to the island every day (1100 to 1400 ptas), and also runs a service between Sant Elm and Port d'Andratx (600 ptas).

Places to Stay There are several accommodation places along the waterfront here. *Hostal Dragonera* (☎ 10 90 86), at Avinguda Rei Jaume I 5, is a tidy three storey hostal with a bar and restaurant. Smallish rooms with bathrooms range from 2000/3000 to 5000/6000 ptas – the more expensive rooms have balconies and sea views.

Hotel Aquamarin (☎ 10 90 75), a modern, circular six storey hotel at Carrer Cal Conis 4, has B&B starting from 6500 ptas a double.

Places to Eat Most of the restaurants along the main foreshore road specialise in local seafood and tend to be somewhat pricey. At the rather nondescript *Bar Restaurante*, opposite the beach at Avinguda Rei Jaume I 14, a slow-moving señora serves up a limited but decent menú del día for 800 ptas, or you can snack cheaply on platters of fried local sardines.

NORTH-WEST COAST & SERRA DE TRAMUNTANA

Dominated by the rugged Serra de Tramuntana mountain range, Mallorca's north-west coast and its hinterland are often referred to as 'the other Mallorca'. In stark contrast to Palma and the east coast, there are no sandy beaches and no mass-tourism resorts along this side of the island. The coastline is rocky and largely inaccessible, the towns and villages are mostly built of local stone (as opposed to concrete), and the mountainous interior is much loved by trekkers for its beautiful landscapes of pine forests, olive groves and spring wild flowers.

The main road through the mountains is the C-710, which starts at the town of Andratx and runs roughly parallel with the coast all the way up to Pollença. It's a stunning scenic drive and a particularly popular cycling route, especially during spring when the muted mountain backdrop of browns, greys and greens is splashed with the bright colours of yellow wattles and blood-red poppies. There are plenty of *miradores* (lookout points) along the way where you can stop and appreciate the great views.

Unfortunately the route can be a slow-going traffic nightmare during late spring and summer when it becomes clogged with buses, cars and bikes crawling around the endless bends.

The first section of the C-710 heads north from Andratx, twisting and climbing up into the mountains. It then skirts along the top of the mountain ridges, offering tantalising glimpses of the distant deep blue sea, before finally meeting the coast.

Estellencs

Estellencs is a small and picturesque village of stone buildings scattered around the rolling hills below the mountain of Puig Galatzó (1025 metres). It's a popular base for hikers and cyclists but also a good place to come to if you just want to escape Palma and relax. A rugged walk of about a km leads down to the local 'beach', a rocky cove with crystal-clear water.

Places to Stay & Eat The popular and very stylish *Hotel Maristel* (☎ 61 85 29) has comfortable rooms with all the mod cons, as well as a pool and a restaurant with fine views from its outdoor terrace. Singles/doubles start from 5850/8200 ptas and pensión completo (full board) from 8000/12,500 ptas.

Otherwise, the owner of *Pizzeria Giardini* (☎ 61 85 96) has four rooms in town which he rents out on a casual basis. He charges about 3000 ptas per person: the price varies depending on the time of year and how long you're staying.

Estellencs is also home to the excellent *Restaurant Son Llarg* (☎ 61 85 64), which specialises in cuina mallorquina. Main courses such as faroana amb salsa de prunes (guinea fowl in plum sauce) or calamars amb salsa de ceba (squid casserole Mallorcan-style) range from 1300 to 2000 ptas. You have a choice between the artistic ambience of the upstairs dining room or the open-air terraces out the front.

Banyalbufar

Further north, Banyalbufar is slightly larger but similarly positioned high above the coast. Surrounded by steep, stone-walled terraces carved into the hillside, the town is home to a cluster of bars and cafés and three up-market hotels.

Places to Stay & Eat Fronted by a traditional Mallorcan patio, the family-run *Hotel Baronia* (☎ 61 81 46) has 36 modern rooms with fine views and a great cliff-side swimming pool. The restaurant here serves up hearty home-made meals. B&B costs 6900 ptas a double and media pensión (half-board) is 10,650 ptas.

The *Hotel Mar i Vent* (☎ 61 80 00) has a similar setup but is more formal and a bit more expensive, with B&B at 6950/9800 ptas for singles/doubles and media pensión at 9050/14,000 ptas.

Valldemossa

Valldemossa is an attractive blend of tree-lined streets, old stone houses and impressive new villas. The town owes most of its fame (and subsequent prosperity) to the fact that the ailing composer Frédéric Chopin and his lover George Sand spent their 'winter of discontent' here back in 1838-39.

They stayed in the **Cartuja de Valldemossa**, a monastery which was turned into rental accommodation after its monks were expelled in 1835. Their stay wasn't an entirely happy experience, and Sand later wrote the book *Winter in Mallorca*, which, if nothing else, made her perennially unpopular with Mallorcans.

Tour buses and day-trippers now arrive in droves to visit the monastery. It's a beautiful building with lovely gardens and fine views, and in the couple's former quarters are Chopin's piano (which, due to shipping delays, arrived only three weeks before their departure), his death mask and several original manuscripts. The monastery opens Monday to Saturday from 9.30 am to 1 pm and 3 to 6.30 pm (5.30 pm during winter). The entry price of 1000 ptas includes piano recitals (given eight times daily during summer) and also admits you to the local museum.

The rest of the town is quite charming in a commercialised way, with cobblestone streets lined with stylish bars and souvenir shops. From here it's a torturous seven km drive down to **Port de Valldemossa**, where a dozen or so buildings (including two bar-restaurants) cluster around a rocky cove.

Places to Stay Most visitors make Valldemossa a day trip. There are no cheap places to stay, but those with cash to splash stay at the small and luxurious *Hotel Vistamar de Valldemossa* (☎ 61 23 00), two km south of the town.

Deià

Deià is perhaps the most famous village on Mallorca. Its setting is idyllic, with a cluster of stone buildings cowering beneath soaring mountains and surrounded by steep hillsides terraced with vegetable gardens, vines and fruit orchards.

Such beauty has always been a drawing card for visitors. Many of those who came decided to stay, and Deià became a second home to an international artists' colony of writers, actors, musicians etc. The most famous member was the English poet Robert Graves, who lived here until his death in 1985 and is buried in the town's hillside cemetery.

Now somewhat overrun by pretentious expats, travel writers and tourists, Deià still has something special and is worth experiencing, particularly if you can avoid the summer crowds.

Things to See & Do The C-710 passes though the town centre, where it becomes the main street and is lined with bars and shops, expensive restaurants and ritzy boutiques. There are several pricey **artists' workshops and galleries** flogging locally produced work.

Up beside the church, the small **Museo Parroquial** has an interesting collection of religious effects, icons and old coins; entry costs 100 ptas. There's also a privately run **Archaeological Museum & Research Centre** (open by appointment) with a collection of artefacts that were found in the Valldemossa area.

On the coast, **Cala de Deià** has some popular swimming spots and a couple of bar-restaurants. The steep walking track from town takes about half an hour; you can also drive down, but in the high season this might take almost as long.

There are some fine walks in the area: the gentle **Deià Coastal Path** to Lluc Alcari (three hours return) continues around the coast and on to Sóller, while the **Route of the Olive Trees** (number four on the hiking excursions brochure) takes you south to Valldemossa.

Places to Stay Surprisingly, Deià still has a couple of affordable places to stay. *Pensión Villa Verde* (☎ 63 90 37), at Carrer Ramon Llull 19, has 10 charming rooms with shared bathrooms, a guest lounge and a large sunny terrace. B&B is good value at 2300 ptas per person.

Set on a hillside overlooking the town, *Hostal Miramar* (☎ 63 90 84) is an appealing stone pensión with simple rooms. B&B costs from 3600/6000 ptas, or 7300 ptas for doubles with private bathroom. The summer tariffs (another 1500 ptas per person) include breakfast *and* dinner.

If you want to rub shoulders with the rich and famous, the place to stay is *La Residencia* (☎ 63 90 11), part-owned by Virgin's Richard Branson. A short stroll from the town centre, this former 16th century manor house is now a luxurious resort hotel set in 12 hectares of manicured lawns and beautifully tended gardens. Of course, there's also the pool, tennis court, restaurant and grill-bar. B&B starts from a mere 20,000/30,000 ptas, while suites begin at 51,500 ptas (ouch!).

On the southern outskirts of town, the superbly stylish four star *Hotel Es Molí* (☎ 63 90 00) is a steal in comparison, with B&B from 14,500/23,500 ptas and suites from 21,900 ptas.

Places to Eat The diverse collection of eateries along the main street includes a couple of affordable pizzerias and several expensive restaurants that claim to specialise in cuina mallorquina.

The famous *Christian's Bar*, once the focal point for Deià's expat community, now caters to the tourist trade. It still has a very agreeable ambience and its international menu features dishes like Indonesian chicken (990 ptas) or lemon-chiffon pie (475 ptas).

Café Sa Fabrica is perhaps the least 'affected' of the other bars, and even if you're on a strict budget you'll be able to afford a bocadillo and a beer here.

Lluc Alcari

On the coast three km north of Deià is the secluded *Hotel Costa d'Or* (☎ 63 90 25), a popular mid-range hotel with 32 rooms, a swimming pool, and a sun terrace with fine views of the coast. It's a 15 minute walk through a pine forest down to the hotel's beach. Singles/doubles cost around 4700/6000 ptas, media pensión around 5600/7800 ptas.

Sóller

Sóller's station is the terminus for the Palma-Sóller railway line, one of Mallorca's most popular and spectacular excursions (see Mallorca's Getting Around section for details).

The town sprawls across a flat valley and sits beneath soaring and jagged outcrops of the Serra de Tramuntana. It's a pleasant place with attractive old buildings, lush gardens and open plazas, but be prepared to cope with

Windmills dot peaceful rural Mallorca, where the pace of life remains slow.

thick crowds of visitors during the day. Sóller is also one of the main bases for trekkers and the starting point for some of the island's best walks.

The main square, Plaça Constitució, is 100 metres downhill from the train station. It's surrounded by bars and restaurants and is home to the **ajuntament** (town hall) and the tourist office (☎ 63 02 00), which opens Monday to Saturday from 9.30 am to 1.30 pm. Also here is the large 16th century **Església Parroquial de San Bartolomé**, which has a beautiful Gothic interior and a modernist façade that was added at the start of this century.

Most people who come here also take a ride on one of Sóller's open-sided ex-San Francisco trams, which shuttle two km down to Port de Sóller on the coast (120 ptas). They depart from the train station roughly every half-hour between 6 am and 9 pm.

Places to Stay Beside the train station at Carrer Castañer 2, the family-run *Hotel El Guía* (☎ 63 02 27) is a good place to meet other trekkers. Its bright rooms feature blue bedspreads, timber trim and modern bathrooms. Room tariffs are 4800 ptas for singles (two only) or 6500 ptas for doubles, and the restaurant serves up a good menú for 2000 ptas.

Nearby at Carrer de Reial 3 (past El Guía and turn right), the cosy *Casa de Huéspedes Margarita Thás Vives* (☎ 63 42 14) has just seven rooms with big old beds and shared bathrooms. Doubles/triples/quads cost 2800/3600/5000 ptas and breakfast is another 300 ptas.

Hostal Nadal (☎ 63 11 80), a five minute downhill walk from the centre at Carrer Romaguera 29, is a clean and spacious hostal with singles/doubles from 1700/2600 ptas and doubles with private bathroom from 3400 ptas.

Biniaraix & Fornalutx

From Sóller it's a very pleasant two km drive, pedal or stroll through narrow laneways up to the tiny village of Biniaraix.

From there, another narrow and scenic route continues north up to Fornalutx, taking you through terraced fields crowded with orange and lemon trees. Fornalutx is a pretty village of distinctive stone houses with green shutters, colourful flower boxes and well-kept gardens. Many of the homes are owned by expatriates, and although the village is a popular destination it's still a far cry from the hustle and bustle of Sóller.

The only place to stay here is the small (and pricey) *Hostal Fornalutx* (☎ 63 19 97), a delightfully converted former convent just off the main street at Carrer Alba 22. Singles/doubles with breakfast cost 7000/10,000 ptas.

Port de Sóller

Every day, Port de Sóller is invaded on all fronts by hordes of tourists: they descend from the mountains by the bus load, sail around from Palma in dozens of cruise boats, and the trams trundle them in from nearby Sóller.

Why? Beats us. The harbour itself is quite scenic – the waterfront is lined with cafés and restaurants (and souvenir shops), and a fleet of boats run excursions to Sa Calobra, Deià, Sant Elm and Illa sa Dragonera – but the 'beach' is grubby and any lingering charm has long since been swept away by the flood of tourists. Then again, the tram ride down here can be kind of fun...

Places to Stay If you decide to stay, the large *Hotel Generoso* (☎ 63 14 50), on the waterfront at Carrer Almirante Alberzuza, has rooms with bathrooms from 3100/4800 ptas – you have a choice of sea views or mountain views.

Sa Calobra

The 12 km road from route C-710 across and down to the small port of Sa Calobra is one of the most spectacular and hair-raising scenic drives you'll ever take. This serpentine road has been literally carved through the mountains, skirting over narrow ridges before it twists its way down towards the coast in an eternal series of hairpin bends.

Arriving at the coast is something of an

anticlimax. Three or four big bar-restaurants cluster around a stony black-sand bay, catering to the steady stream of day-trippers who flock here by car, bus and boat. Some lunatics even cycle down here – definitely not recommended!

From the northern end of the road a short walking trail leads around the coast and through a series of long tunnels to a river gorge and small cove with some fabulous (but crowded) swimming spots.

Monestir de Lluc

Back in the 7th century, a local shepherd claimed to have seen an image of the Virgin in the sky. Later, a similar image appeared on a rock, and a chapel was built near the site to commemorate the miracle.

A monastery was established here after Jaume I reconquered Mallorca, and since then thousands of pilgrims have come every year to pay homage to the 14th century statue of the Virgin of Lluc, known as La Moreneta because of her dark-coloured skin.

The current monastery, a huge, stark and somewhat austere complex, dates from the 18th century. Off the central courtyard is the entrance to the **Basílica de la Mare de Déu**, which holds the statue.

Places to Stay & Eat The monastery's accommodation section, the *Santuari de Lluc* (☎ 51 70 25), has 97 rooms and is popular with school groups, trekkers and pilgrims. A double room with bathroom costs 3250 ptas, a quad (two double beds) costs 2600 ptas or 3900 ptas with bathroom, and a room with three double beds and bathroom costs 4300 ptas.

There are three restaurants and two cafeterias to choose from.

Getting There & Away There are frequent trains from Palma to Inca, with twice-daily connecting buses continuing on to the monastery.

Pollença

Next stop on the Mallorcan pilgrimage is the laid-back and pleasant inland town of Pollença. The devout and hardy come here to climb the **steps of Calvary**, 365 stone steps leading from the town up to a hilltop chapel and small shrine; the rest of us drive up the back road. Either way, the views from the top are great.

There isn't much to do when you get back down to town. You can visit a small museum in the town's convent on Tuesday, Thursday and Sunday between 10 am and 2 pm. Otherwise, the central Plaça Major is a good place to relax on a sunny day. *Café Espanyol* has open-air tables shaded by big old plane trees, and an interesting collection of old B&W photos of Mallorcan life inside.

Places to Stay There's no accommodation in Pollença itself, but on a hilltop a couple of km away is the *Santuari Puig de Maria* (☎ 53 02 35). Built during the 14th and 15th centuries, this former monastery was eventually abandoned by the monks and lay deserted for years. It's now a somewhat chaotic retreat – neither the food or accommodation are anything to write home about – but the setting and views are truly spectacular, particularly if you manage to rise at dawn.

The accommodation is suitably spartan, with a choice of spacious upstairs rooms (some with four-poster double beds) or cells out the back. The cost is 1600 ptas for one or two people, then 800 ptas per additional person. Meals such as paella, Mallorcan soup, chicken and chips with salad or tortilla are mostly 700 to 1000 ptas.

From the turn-off (signposted two km south of Pollença on the Palma road), a narrow road leads two-thirds of the way up the hill; from there you'll have a steep 10 minute climb up a rocky path to the monastery. Bring a torch if you're arriving at night!

Port de Pollença

On the northern shores of the Badia de Pollença, this is a fairly slick resort with a growing collection of hotels and apartments alongside English pubs and fish-and-chips shops. Sailboards and yachts can be hired from the beaches, and Lanchas La Gaviota

(☎ 86 40 14) runs frequent ferry services up to the fine beaches of Platja de Formentor (750 ptas return). South of town, the bay's shoreline becomes rocky and the beaches much less attractive.

Places to Stay Three blocks back from the beach at Carrer Joan XXIII 66 (the main road), *Hostal Corro* (☎ 86 50 05) has decent rooms above a bar. Doubles/triples with shared bathroom cost from 3000/3500 ptas. Nearby at Carrer Magallanes 18, *Hostal-Residencia Paris* (☎ 86 40 17) is harder to find but better value with singles/doubles/triples from 2000/3000/3700 ptas (1000 ptas more during summer) all with private bathroom; a buffet breakfast costs 400 ptas extra.

Hostal-Restaurant La Goleta (☎ 86 59 02), on the beachfront at Passeig Saralegui 120, is an impressive small hotel with its own bar and restaurant. Rooms with bathroom cost from 4500/5900/7800 ptas (plus IVA) for B&B. Front rooms have balconies and sea views, and summer prices are about 1000 ptas higher.

Cap de Formentor
It's a splendid drive from Port de Pollença out along this narrow rocky promontory. Midway along (on the south side) is the famous *Hotel Formentor* (☎ 86 53 00), a ritzy five star place which has played host to the likes of Grace Kelly and Winston Churchill since opening in 1926. You can add yourself to the guest-list for a mere 20,000 to 38,000 ptas (33,000 to 55,000 ptas for a suite).

Near the hotel and backed by shady pine forests, the sandy beaches of **Platja de Formentor** are amongst the island's best. There are a couple of exclusive beach bars here, as well as a golf course and horse-riding ranch nearby.

From here it's another 11 km out to the lighthouse on the cape which marks Mallorca's northernmost tip.

BADIA D'ALCÚDIA
This huge bay dominates Mallorca's north-east coast. It has longer and better beaches than the adjoining Badia de Pollença, with broad sweeps of sand that stretch around the coast between the two major resorts of Port d'Alcúdia and Ca'n Picafort.

Alcúdia
Wedged between the two bays, the busy town of Alcúdia was once a Roman settlement. The tourist office here publishes the handy *10 Excursions* booklet, which outlines some good walking and cycling tours to local destinations including the **Parc Natural de l'Albufera** nature reserve and the ruins of the **Roman city of Pollèntia**.

Four km north-east from town on the road to Cap d'es Pinar is the *Albergue Victoria* (☎ 54 53 95) youth hostel, open from mid-June to the end of August.

Port d'Alcúdia
Port d'Alcúdia has two distinct sections. A large harbour dominates the town centre and imparts a chic maritime flavour, with boat trips departing daily to Ca'n Picafort, Platja de Formentor and Port de Pollença. Flebasa (☎ 54 64 54) also has daily ferries across to Ciutadella on Menorca.

South of the harbour, long white-sand beaches are backed by a strip of apartments and hotels that continues for several km around the bay. A good cycling path follows the coast road, so you could always hire a bike and pedal south in search of less crowded beaches.

Places to Stay There are only a couple of budget options here. *Hostal Vista Alegre* (☎ 54 73 47), opposite the harbour and upstairs from the Pizzeria de Raffaele at Passeig Marítim 10, is a friendly place with tidy singles/doubles with showers from 1600/3200 ptas (singles not available during summer). A couple of blocks back on the busy Carrer Teodoro Canet at No 29, the large *Hostal Puerto* (☎ 54 54 47) is a reasonably good alternative with slightly lower prices.

If you're camping, head for *Camping Club Picafort* (☎ 53 78 63), nine km south of Port d'Alcúdia. Across the road from a good beach, it's a large, first-class camping ground with excellent facilities including tennis courts, two pools, a supermarket and a bar. Tent sites range from 600 to 750 ptas, but to this you must add 425 to 525 ptas per person and 525 to 675 ptas per car. Pensión completo is also available for 2200 ptas per person, and there are good bungalows for rent. To get here from Palma, take the bus to Ca'n Picafort. In summer you'll need to book well ahead.

Ca'n Picafort

A smaller version of Port d'Alcúdia, Ca'n Picafort has taken off as a resort in recent years and a growing collection of mid-rise apartments and hotels have sprung up along the coastline. It's a package-tour frontier town and still somewhat raw and soulless, but the beaches are pretty good and there are worse places to end up.

Colònia de Sant Pere

Beyond Ca'n Picafort the road heads inland, but midway to Artà there's a turn-off leading five km north towards the coast. Colònia de Sant Pere is a quiet fishing town with a tiny beach wedged between rocky coves and a few fishing boats bobbing in the sea. Nothing much happens here, which can make for a nice change of pace from some of the resorts.

There are a couple of bar-restaurants along the foreshore. The only accommodation is at the straightforward *Hostal Rocamar* (no phone) at Carrer San Mateo 9, where doubles with bathrooms range from 3500 to 5000 ptas.

Four km around the coast is the sleepy town of Betlem, and close by the third-class camping ground of *Camping Club San Pedro* (☎ 58 90 23). A little way beyond Betlem the road ends; from here, a 15 minute walk/climb leads down to an idyllic and not-so-secret swimming spot, a small rocky bay beneath a spectacular backdrop of towering mountains.

EAST COAST

Most of the fine beaches along Mallorca's east coast have all but succumbed to the ravages of mass tourism. The northern half of this stretch of coastline is home to a series of concrete jungles that rival the very worst excesses of the Costa del Sol.

Further south the coastline is corrugated with a series of smaller coves and ports, and the scale of development is more restrained.

Artà

The inland town of Artà is dominated by the 14th century fortress and church of San Salvador which sit atop the town's highest point. Also of interest is the **Museu d'Artà** on Plaça d'Espanya, which contains a small archaeological exhibition.

On the coast 10 km east of here are the **Coves d'Artà**, which are said to be just as impressive as Porto Cristo's Coves del Drac (see below), and are certainly much less crowded. Tours of the caves are held every half-hour between 10 am and 7 pm; entry costs 750 ptas.

Cala Ratjada

Near the northern tip of the east coast, Cala Ratjada is a heavily developed and glitzy resort that is particularly popular with Germans. The main streets are wall-to-wall with souvenir shops and the beaches are nice but incredibly crowded. The tourist office (☎ 56 30 33), in a glass-sided building on Plaça dels Pins, is highly organised and has a collection of brochures that covers everything from accommodation and cultural activities to guided walks and cycling tours.

Places to Stay Your chances of finding accommodation here in July and August are apparently minimal. At other times, one place worth a try is *Hostal Gil* (☎ 56 41 12) at Carrer Tamarells s/n, overlooking the small bay of Son Moll a couple of km to the south. Set right on the beachfront, it has a pool, sauna, bar and disco, with B&B starting from 2750 ptas per person.

Cala Millor

Stretching along the east coast's largest bay, Cala Millor is a predominantly English resort with white-sand beaches backed by some of Mallorca's blandest and most intensive developments.

Porto Cristo

During the daytime, Porto Cristo teems with day-trippers who flood into town to visit the nearby underground caves. It isn't much fun if you're claustrophobic, but by late afternoon when the hordes have disappeared it can be quite a nice place. The town is centred around a small sandy beach and a very big boat harbour.

The **Coves del Drac** (Caves of the Dragon), on the southern outskirts, are open daily from 10 am to noon and 2 to 5 pm. One-hour tours (800 ptas) are held hourly on the hour, the highlight being the classical music played by boat-bound musicians floating across a large subterranean lake. Nearby you can also visit Porto Cristo's large **aquarium**, which opens daily from 10 am to 7 pm; entry costs 500 ptas.

Places to Stay Opposite the entrance to the caves at Avinguda Joan Servera 11, *Hotel Sol i Vada* (✆ 82 10 74) is a bright and cheerful hostal with a pool, bar-restaurant and tennis court. Rooms with bathroom cost from 2750/4500 ptas for singles/doubles. The main drawback is that it's a long walk from here to the town centre and the beach.

An alternative is to stay at the large and stylish *Hotel Felip* (✆ 82 07 50), on the waterfront at Carrer Burdils 41. B&B starts from 3000/5000 ptas.

Cala d'Or

Once a quaint fishing village, Cala d'Or is now an overblown big-dollar resort. Its sleek new marina is lined with glisteningly expensive boats and the surrounding hills are crowded with blindingly whitewashed villas. Plenty of style but not much substance, as they say.

Porto Petro

Immediately south of Cala d'Or (and virtually joined to it by urban sprawl) is the smaller and more tranquil port town of Porto Petro. Centred around its boat-lined inlet and

surrounded by residential estates, it has a cluster of harbour-side bars and restaurants and a couple of small and quiet beaches nearby.

Places to Stay A mere stone's throw from the inlet, *Hostal Nereida* (✆ 65 72 23) has a pool, a good restaurant and renovated rooms with bathrooms. Singles/doubles/triples range from 4000/5000/6900 to 5500/6500/9000 ptas.

Cala Mondragó

Two km south of Porto Petro, Cala Mondragó is one of the most attractive beaches on the east coast. Sheltered by large rocky outcrops and fringed by pine trees, this protected sandy beach has a solitary beach bar surrounded by deck chairs and thatched umbrellas. Development is limited to a couple of houses and one large hostal, the five storey *Hostal Playa Mondragó* (✆ 65 77 52), which has good facilities including a pool, bar and restaurant. B&B ranges from 3000/5000 to 3900/5800 ptas.

Cala Figuera

The coastline along here is lined with rugged cliffs, broken only by the entrance to the narrow inlet on which Cala Figuera is built. It's a pleasant and relatively unspoiled township with streets shaded by pine trees and yachts moored along the rock-lined inlet. It may not have any beaches (the nearest ones are about two km south at Cala Santanyi), but it does have some good bars and lively nightlife.

Places to Stay & Eat There's a cluster of hostales and restaurants along the southern side of the inlet. *Hostal-Restaurant Ca'n Jordi* (✆ 64 50 35), at Carrer Virgen del Carmen 58, has good rooms with bathrooms, views and balconies from 2500/4200 ptas, as well as studios and apartments for two to five people ranging from 5200 to 8800 ptas. The owners also rent out a couple of houses and villas in town.

The stylish *Hostal-Restaurant Cala* (✆ 64 50 18) next door was being renovated at the time of writing and was due to reopen early in 1997. Nearby, the popular *L'Arcada* has a good range of pizzas, burgers, seafood and salads with meals in the 700 to 1200 ptas range.

Perhaps the cheapest option in town is *Hostal Oliver* (☎ 64 51 27) at Carrer Bernareggi 37 – it's on the right as you enter town. The charge is between 1500 and 2000 ptas per person.

Colònia de Sant Jordi

On the south-east coast, the large resort town of Colònia de Sant Jordi is also popular with Germans. Although it's not a very exciting spot, there are some good quiet beaches nearby, particularly Ses Arenes and Es Trenc, both a few km back up the coast towards Palma.

You can also take boat trips from here to the former prison island of **Cabrera**, where more than 5000 French soldiers died a grisly death after being abandoned in 1809 towards the end of the Peninsular War. Cabrera and its surrounding islets now form the Parc Nacional Archipiélago de Cabrera.

Places to Stay At Carrer Gabriel Roca 9 is the cosy *Hostal Colonial* (☎ 65 52 78). There's a café downstairs, and tariffs are from 2700 ptas per person for B&B or 3200 ptas for media pensión.

THE INTERIOR

East of the Serra de Tramuntana, Mallorca's interior is a flat and fertile plain. Dominated by farmlands and unremarkable agricultural townships, it holds little of interest to the average beach-bound tourist, but for those with time, transport and an interest in discovering the traditional Mallorcan way of life, an exploration of the island's interior can be rewarding.

Several of the major inland towns are well known for the specialised products they sell. **Inca** holds a popular market each Thursday and has numerous factory outlets selling locally produced leather goods, while industrial **Manacor** has a thriving manufactured-pearl industry (including the famous Majo-

rica factory) and is home to many of the island's furniture manufacturers. **Felanitx** is well known for its ceramics showrooms and factories.

Places to Stay

If you're interested in experiencing 'the other Mallorca' there are numerous rural properties, mountain houses and traditional villas around the island which now operate as up-market B&Bs, renting out rooms or apartments to visitors. Twelve of the best of these places are described in the free booklet *Traditional Majorcan Country Homes* which is available from local tourist offices or through the booking agency (☎ 70 60 06 fax 47 09 81) at Carrer Aragó in Palma.

The properties listed are all historic and very stylish country estates, offering outstanding facilities that include swimming pools, tennis courts and organised activities and excursions. Prices for double rooms start from around 12,000 ptas a day.

Ibiza

Ibiza (Eivissa in Catalan) is the most extreme of the islands, both in terms of its landscape and the people it attracts.

The Greeks called Ibiza and Formentera the Islas Pitiusas, or 'islands of pine trees'. The Ibizan landscape is harsh and rocky and the island receives little rainfall. Alongside the hardy pines the most common crops are the traditional Mediterranean ones of olive, fig and almond trees.

A rugged coastline is interspersed with dozens of fine sandy beaches, most of which have now been consumed by intensive tourist developments. There are still a few out-of-the-way beaches that have escaped the concrete sprawl, but during the summer months you won't be doing much solitary swimming.

The island's beaches and its laid-back nature first became a major drawing card during the flower-power heyday of the 1960s: while North America's hippies were

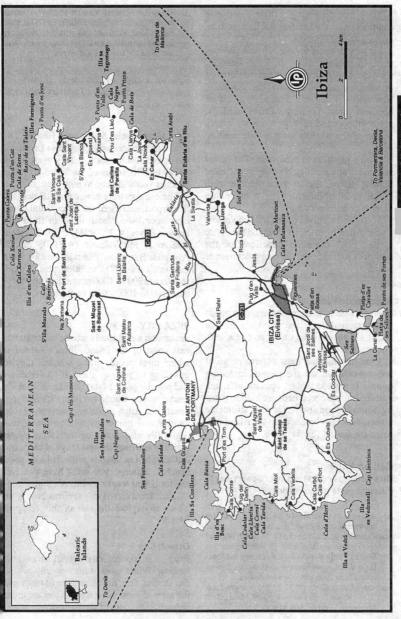

'California dreaming', their European counterparts were heading for Ibiza to tune in, turn on and drop out.

Initially a resort for the hip and fashionable, Ibiza soon discovered the financial rewards of bulk tourism and started shipping in summer sun-seekers by the thousand. Nowadays it attracts a strange blend of hippies, gays, fashion victims, nudists, nightclubbers and package tourists – it truly is one of the world's most bizarre melting pots.

Ibiza's nightlife is renowned. The island is home to some of Spain's biggest and most famous discos, and its great summer club scene is complemented by a huge and diverse collection of bars.

The island receives over a million visitors a year. Apart from the weather and the desire to be 'seen', the main attractions are the notorious nightlife and the many picturesque beaches.

Accommodation

There are half a dozen camping grounds spread around the island: Camping Florida near Cala Nova is the only one of these to open year round.

Ibiza city has the most diverse range of accommodation on the island, including quite a few good budget options, although during summer cheap beds are hard to come by. Santa Eulària also has several affordable places, but elsewhere around the island bargains are few and far between.

Getting Around

Bus Four bus companies operate services to different parts of the island:

Autobuses San Antonio (☎ 34 05 10) operates between Ibiza city and Sant Antoni.
Autobuses Voramar El Gaucho (☎ 34 03 82) operates services from Ibiza city to the airport, Ses Salines, Platja d'en Bossa, Cala Llonga and Santa Eulària. It also services the south and south-west coasts from Ibiza city and Sant Antoni.
Autocares Lucas Costa (☎ 31 27 55) operates from Ibiza city to Santa Gertrudis, Sant Mateu, Sant Miquel and Port de Sant Miquel.

Autobuses Empresas HF Vilas (☎ 31 16 01) operates from Ibiza city to Santa Eulària, Es Canar, Cala Sant Vicent, Portinatx and other beaches along the east and north coasts. This company also does the Santa Eulària-Sant Antoni run.

Pick up a copy of the handy *Horario de Autobuses* (bus timetable) booklet from local tourist offices.

Car, Motorcycle & Bicycle Rental The local bus services will get you to the major towns and beach resorts, but if you are intent on getting to some of the more secluded beaches you will need to rent wheels.

The big operators have car rental desks at the airport, and there are other rental agencies around the island: those in Ibiza city include Ribas (☎ 30 18 11), at Carrer Vicent Cuervo 3, and Valentin (☎ 31 08 22), at Avinguda Bartomeu Vicent Ramon 19. Both hire out cars (4000 to 6000 ptas a day), scooters (2500 to 4000 ptas a day) and bicycles (700 to 1000 ptas a day).

IBIZA CITY

Set around a protected harbour on the southeast coast of the island, Ibiza's capital is where most people arrive whether they're travelling by ferry or plane. It's a vivacious and popular place to stay: unlike most of the tourist resorts around the island it's a living, breathing town with an interesting old quarter and numerous worthwhile attractions. It's also home to the island's best nightlife and most diverse range of cafés and restaurants. On the downside, it lacks good beaches, although you don't have to travel too far if you want a swim. All things considered, Ibiza city is an excellent base from which to explore the rest of this compact island.

Orientation

Ibiza is a modern city spread around its harbour. While most of the new city lies on the western side, the older parts of town and the areas of most interest to visitors are those immediately south of the harbour.

PLACES TO STAY
2 Hostal-Residencia Ripoll
5 Hostal Sol y Brisa
6 Hotel Montesol
9 Casa de Huéspedes Navarro
14 Hostal-Restaurante La Marina
16 Casa de Huéspedes La Peña
21 Casa de Huéspedes Vara de Rey
23 Hostal-Residencial Parque
30 Hotel El Corsario
31 Hotel El Palacio

PLACES TO EAT
3 Restaurante Hong Kong
4 Pizzería da Franco er Romano
8 Restaurant Victoria
10 Ca'n Costa
19 Chi Chi's
20 Comidas Bar San Juan
25 Restaurante El Olivo

OTHER
1 Lavandería Master Clean
7 Ca'n Pou Bar
11 Tango
12 Bar La Biela
13 Pub Tenesse
15 Bar Mambo & Flash
17 Samsara & Capricho Bar
18 Mercat de Verdures
22 Tourist Office
24 Café del Parque
26 Museu d'Art Contemporani
27 La Plaza
28 El Portalon
29 La Scala
32 Museu Arqueológic
33 Catedral

BALEARIC ISLANDS

The old walled town, D'Alt Vila, is perched high on a hilltop overlooking all. Between D'Alt Vila and the harbour lies the area known as Sa Penya (although the area close to the harbour is also known as Sa Marina), a jumble of narrow streets and lanes lined with whitewashed shops, bars and houses. As well as being the nightlife centre, Sa Penya also contains many restaurants and also has quite a few accommodation options.

Passeig Vara de Rey, a broad avenue divided by a central plantation, is a favourite spot for the traditional sunset promenade. It runs westwards from Sa Penya to Avinguda d'Espanya, which in turn takes you out of the city towards the airport, seven km south-west.

Information

Tourist Office Ibiza city's main tourist office (☎ 30 19 00) is at Passeig Vara de Rey 13. The staff are friendly, multilingual and very professional, and can provide excellent information on a wide range of topics. Opening hours are weekdays from 9.30 am to 12.30 pm and 5 to 7 pm, and Saturday from 10.30 am to 1 pm. There's another tourist office at the airport (open summer only).

Post & Communications The post office (postcode 07800) is at Carrer Madrid 23, and there is a Telefónica phone centre opposite the Formentera ferry terminals at Avinguda Santa Eulària 17.

Laundry You'll find a good laundrette, Lavandería Master Clean, at Carrer Felipe II 12. The owners are efficient and helpful: they charge 1000 ptas to wash and dry a 5 kg load, and can also do repairs and alterations. The laundrette is open weekdays from 9 am to 1.30 pm and 4.30 to 9 pm, and Saturday from 9 am to 1.30 pm.

Sa Penya

Perhaps the best thing to do when you first arrive is to take a stroll and familiarise yourself with Sa Penya (the port area) and D'Alt Vila (the old quarter). These are Ibiza city's most interesting areas and both can easily be covered on foot in an hour or two.

There's always something going on in Sa Penya. Day and night, crowds of visitors promenade along the harbour and the narrow streets, and if you're into people-watching you'll be right at home here: this small pocket must have one of the highest concentrations of exhibitionists and weirdos in all of Spain.

Shopping seems to be a major pastime in Ibiza city, and Sa Penya is crammed with dozens of funky and trashy **clothing boutiques**. The range of clothing on offer is amazingly diverse, with everything from the wildest designs from Europe's fashion capitals to the worst excesses of the retro-hippy look. It's actually a surprisingly good place to shop for clothes: the intense competition between the locally made gear and the imports keeps prices at an almost reasonable level, and the constant flow of customers ensures that shops stay open until late in the evening.

Sa Penya is also home to Ibiza city's so-called **'hippy markets'**. Rows of street stalls crowd along Carrer d'Enmig and the adjoining streets, selling just about everything under the sun including watches, sunglasses, souvenirs, T-shirts, jewellery, hash pipes and leather jackets. There aren't too many hippies in sight – most stalls are operated by canny locals cashing in on the steady stream of cash-laden tourists – but the stalls that specialise in locally made arts and crafts are particularly worth checking out.

D'Alt Vila

From Sa Penya you can wander up into D'Alt Vila, the old walled town. The Romans were the first to fortify this hilltop, and the current walls were constructed by Felipe II during the 16th century to protect against invasion by the combined French and Turkish forces. A steep road leads from Plaça de sa Font in Sa Penya up to the **Portal de ses Taules** gateway, the main entrance to the old town. Above the arched gateway hangs a commemorative plaque bearing Felipe II's coat of arms and an inscription recording the 1585 completion date of the fortification, which consists of seven artillery bastions joined by thick protective walls up to 22 metres in height.

Immediately inside the gateway is the expansive **Plaça de la Vila**, with its collection of up-market restaurants, galleries and shops. Up behind the plaza you can walk along the top of the walls and enjoy great views of the city, its harbour and the coast. Nearby, the **Museu d'Art Contemporani** is housed in an 18th century powder store and armoury and features constantly changing exhibitions of contemporary art.

A steep and well-worn route leads from Plaça de la Vila through the narrow streets of the old town up to the **catedral**, which overlooks all from the very top of the hill. Its construction manages elegantly to combine several periods: the original structure was built in the 14th century in the Catalan Gothic style, the sacristy was added in 1592 and major renovation work took place during the 18th century in baroque style.

Beside the cathedral, the **Museu Arqueológic** houses a fine collection of ancient relics, mainly from the Phoenician, Carthaginian and Roman periods. It opens Tuesday to Saturday from 10 am to 1 pm and 4 to 7 pm (5 to 8 pm during summer), and on

Sunday from 10 am to 2 pm; it is closed on Monday and public holidays.

Beaches

The closest beach to Ibiza city is the heavily developed **Platja de Figueretes**, about a 20 minute walk south-west of Sa Penya. The beach itself isn't great – a string of modernish high-rise hotels overlook crowded strips of sand and rocks, and the water tends to be murky – but it's quite a pleasant walk along the waterfront and if you work up an appetite there are plenty of restaurants and cafés to choose from.

In the next bay around to the north-east of Sa Penya is **Platja de Talamanca**. These beaches are okay for a quick dip, although if you have time you'd be better off heading south to the beaches at **Ses Salines** (see that section later in this chapter for details).

Places to Stay – bottom end

There are quite a few reasonably priced hostales in the streets around the port, although in midsummer cheap beds are as scarce as hen's teeth.

The Sa Penya area can get pretty hectic and noisy at night; if you don't like the idea of staying in the heart of the nightlife zone there are a couple of quieter options a little way to the west. The friendly *Hostal Sol y Brisa* (☎ 31 08 18), Avinguda Bartomeu Vicent Ramon 15, has good clean singles/ doubles with shared bathrooms from 1800/ 3400 ptas. Nearby at Carrer Vicent Cuervo 14, *Hostal-Residencia Ripoll* (☎ 31 42 75) has similar rooms: its prices vary seasonally, with singles/doubles ranging from 1200/ 2000 in winter to 2500/4500 in summer. The owners also have 16 excellent studio apartments in a nearby building, each with its own bathroom, lounge (with TV) and kitchenette (with stove, bar fridge, crockery and cutlery). Nightly costs are 2000 ptas in winter, 4000 ptas in mid-season and 9000 ptas in July and August.

On the waterfront at Andenes del Puerto 4, *Hostal-Restaurante La Marina* (☎ 31 01 72) has good doubles with harbour views from 2600 to 3200 ptas, and sleepless singles

with disco views from 1400 to 1800 ptas. If you want your own bathroom the owner also rents out a few doubles in another building and charges between 4000 and 4700 ptas.

One of the most popular low-budget options is the long-running and friendly *Casa de Huéspedes La Peña* (☎ 19 02 40), at the far end of Sa Penya at Carrer de la Virgen 76. There are 13 simple and tidy rooms with shared bathrooms at 1800/2900 ptas; the top rooms have great harbour views.

Casa de Huéspedes Navarro (☎ 31 08 25), in the thick of things at Carrer Cruz 20 (3rd floor), has 10 rooms at the top of a long and narrow flight of stairs. The front rooms have harbour views and the interior rooms are quite dark (but cool in summer), and there's a sunny rooftop terrace. This place charges between 1200 and 1600 ptas per person.

Another reasonable budget option is the well-located *Casa de Huéspedes Vara del Rey* (☎ 30 13 76), one block along from the tourist office at Passeig Vara de Rey 7 (3rd floor, no lift!). Rooms with shared bathrooms range from 1400/2800 to 1800/3200 ptas.

Places to Stay – middle

With perhaps the prime position in Ibiza, *Hotel Montesol* (☎ 31 01 61), Passeig Vara de Rey 2, is a comfortable one star place. Rooms have their own bathroom, TV and phone – and most have views of the harbour or the old town. Singles/doubles range from 4000/6000 to 5000/8000 ptas (plus IVA). This is one of Ibiza's best-known hotels, so you'll need to book ahead during summer.

Another place with private bathrooms is *Hostal-Residencia Parque* (☎ 30 13 58) at Carrer Vicent Cuervo 3. It's quieter and a bit more up-market than most of the other hostales, and the rooms overlook the pleasant Plaça del Parque from above the café of the same name. Rooms range from 2400/ 4700 to 3100/6200 ptas.

There are a couple of interesting hotels up in D'Alt Vila: *Hotel El Corsario* (☎ 30 12 48), at Carrer de Ponent 5, has plain and straightforward rooms with private bathrooms and spectacular views of the town and harbour below. Singles/doubles range from 4000/6500 to 5000/8500 ptas, which includes breakfast in the hotel's courtyard restaurant.

Another possibility is to stay in Platja de Figueretes. Most of the hotels in this area cater for package tourists, and while the beach is nothing special it's a reasonable compromise if you need to be close to both beaches and nightlife. *Hotel-Apartamentos Lux-Mar* (☎ 30 14 58), at Carrer de Ramon Muntaner 79, has stylish and modern studio apartments (sleeping up to three people) ranging seasonally from 5000 to 12,000 ptas, and four-bed apartments from 7000 to 15,000 ptas (plus IVA). *Hotel Marítimo* (☎ 30 27 08), right on the waterfront at Carrer de Ramon Muntaner 48, is a decent two star place with singles/doubles from 4000/6000 to 7000/9000 ptas.

Places to Stay – top end

Another option if you want to stay in D'Alt Vila is *Hotel El Palacio* (☎ 30 14 78) at Carrer de la Conquista 2. Subtitled the 'Hotel of the Movie Stars', this is perhaps the most bizarre place on the island. The hotel is something of a private movie museum with a collection of signed photos, original movie posters and film awards, and each of the seven rooms pays homage to a different Hollywood star – the Greta Garbo suite, the Marilyn Monroe suite, the James Dean suite and so on. It's pretty glitzy but very comfy at the same time. The views are great, and there's a private courtyard with a bar and swimming pool. Tariffs range from a mere 27,000 to 46,000 ptas a double.

Places to Eat

There are plenty of bland and overpriced restaurants scattered along the streets of Sa Penya. Most of these places serve up uniformly tasteless food and offer a similar selection – pizza, pasta, paella and seafood dishes – and many have touts who stand out the front thrusting menus at passers-by to try and lure them in.

Fortunately, there are a few exceptions worth searching out. *Comidas Bar San Juan,*

at Carrer de Guillem de Montgri 8, is a simple, family-run operation with two small dining rooms. The décor ain't flash but the food is outstanding value, with main courses all between 400 and 800 ptas – for dessert try the manzana al horno, a delicious baked caramelised apple. Note that the kitchen only operates between the hours of 1 and 3.15 pm and 8 and 10.15 pm.

The friendly *Ca'n Costa*, a basement eatery at Carrer Cruz 19, is another no-frills concern with good food at reasonable prices. It has a two-course menú for 900 ptas (fruit and a drink included), and most main courses are between 500 and 900 ptas – the grilled sardines (475 ptas) and mixed salad (325 ptas) make a tasty combo.

Another good budget bet is *Restaurant Victoria* on the corner of Carrer Riambau and Carrer de Guillem de Montgri. The dining room is somewhat stark, with its linoleum floors, brown checked tablecloths and a couple of token paintings on the walls, but the food is hearty and cheap with all main courses in the 400 to 850 ptas range. It's open Monday to Saturday for lunch and dinner.

The restaurant downstairs at the *Hostal-Restaurante La Marina*, opposite the harbour at Andenes del Puerto 4, has a good-value menú for 1300 ptas; the dining room has a nautical flavour, or you can eat out the front and watch the boats come in and people go by. *Chi Chi's*, at Carrer del Mar 16, is a lively little place that serves up good Tex-Mex tucker with starters from around 700 ptas and mains mostly 1500 to 2200 ptas.

A good spot for brekky is the café downstairs from *Hostal-Residencia Parque* at Carrer Vicent Cuervo 3; they do a mean plate of bacon and eggs for 450 ptas and a tasty *sandwich* (toasted ham and cheese) for 350 ptas.

If you want better Italian food than what's on offer in the port area, head for *Pizzería da Franco er Romano* on Avinguda Bartomeu Vicent Ramon (below Hostal Sol y Brisa). Pizzas are 700 to 925 ptas, pastas 600 to 900 ptas and other main courses 1000 to 1500 ptas. It also has an excellent menú for 1250 ptas. The whitewashed walls, dark timber trim and gingham tablecloths combine to create a pleasant atmosphere – highly recommended.

Nearby at Carrer Vicent Cuervo 15, *Restaurante Hong Kong* has cheap Chinese food with filling menús starting from 700 ptas.

Most of Ibiza's more up-market restaurants are up in D'Alt Vila. There's a cluster of places just inside the entrance to the old town, spread along Plaça de Vila. *Restaurante El Olivo* is one of the best of these, and main courses like pork fillet stuffed with goat's cheese or crispy duck ravioli are in the 1700 to 2500 ptas range. Also good is the small and stylish *La Plaza*, which has similar prices and specialises in game and seafood dishes.

There are several more restaurants along the adjacent Plaça Desamparats. The popular *El Portalon* is fronted by an open-sided courtyard dining area and has main courses in the 1800 to 3200 ptas range. If you're looking for somewhere intimate and romantic, head for the candle-lit *La Scala* at the far end of the plaza.

If you're doing your own cooking you can buy fresh fruit and vegies from the small open-air Mercat de Verdures on Carrer de ses Verdures, opposite the entrance to D'Alt Vila.

Entertainment
Sa Penya is Ibiza city's nightlife centre. Dozens of bars keep the port area jumping from around sunset until the early hours, and after they wind down you can continue on to one of the island's world-famous discos – if you can afford the outrageous cover charges or score a free pass, that is.

Bars Carrer de Barcelona, a pedestrian-only street that runs parallel with the harbour, is lined with an impressive collection of funky bars. Most have tall tables and stools out on the street and all pump out loud music and cold drinks: *Tango*, *La Biela* and *Pub Tenesse* are just a few of the places worth checking out. There are plenty more further east along Carrer Garijo Cipriano, including *Bar Mambo* at No 10 and *Flash* at No 9.

Don't be surprised if you should receive unsolicited invitations from attractive strangers. The local bar scene is highly competitive and lots of places employ slick and very persuasive touts to 'invite' passers-by to join them for a drink, sometimes with the lure of free passes to the big discos.

Ca'n Pou Bar, opposite the harbour at Carrer de Lluis Tur i Palau 19, is a bit more relaxed and less hyped than most of Sa Penya's other bars. Another good place if you're just after a quiet drink is *Café del Parque*, on the plaza of the same name. It's a laid-back place with comfy cane chairs and tables out the front and soothing sky-blue and timber-panelled walls inside. It also plays good funk and soul music, which can make for a nice change from all that pounding techno-disco stuff.

The gay scene is based towards the eastern end of Sa Penya, particularly along the far end of Carrer de la Virgen. At No 44, *Samsara* has live floor shows most nights at 12.30 pm, and the *Capricho Bar* next door is a popular watering hole.

Discos Ibiza enjoys a reputation for having one of the best club scenes in all of Europe, and during the summer months the island is virtually a continuous party from sunset to sunrise (and beyond). Fuelled by an overdeveloped sense of competitiveness, the island's entrepreneurs have built a truly amazing collection of discos – huge, throbbing temples to which thousands of disciples flock nightly to pay homage to the gods of hedonism.

A 'disco sunrise' is definitely part of the Ibiza experience, and even if you're not a disco buff you should try to check out at least one of these unique entertainment megaplexes while you're here.

With the exception of Pacha (the only club to open year round), the major discos operate nightly between June and September and most open their doors from around midnight till dawn, although things don't usually hot up until 3 am or later. Each of these places has something different to offer, and special theme nights, fancy-dress parties and the like are regular features.

Note, however, that entertainment Ibiza-style doesn't come cheap: most places charge between 2000 and 5000 ptas entry (and then sting you big-time for drinks). If you hang around the right bars in Sa Penya you might be lucky enough to score a flier that entitles you to free or discounted entry. These are handed out by club promoters whose job it is to entice people with 'the look' (ie very hip and/or very attractive) to their discos.

The big names are *Pacha*, on the north side of Ibiza city's port; *Privilege* (the disco formerly known as Ku) and *Amnesia*, both six km out of Ibiza city on the road to Sant Antoni; and *Kiss* and *Space*, both south of Ibiza city in Platja d'en Bossa. Space is the place to head for when everywhere else has closed – it opens at 6 am!

During summer, Ibiza's 'Discobus' service operates nightly from 10 pm until sunrise, doing a continuous circuit between the major discos, bars and hotels in Ibiza city, Platja d'en Bossa, Sant Rafel and Sant Antoni.

Getting There & Away
Ibiza's airport is seven km south-west of the capital. Iberia (☎ 30 25 80) has an office in Ibiza city at Passeig Vara de Rey 15.

Buses to other parts of the island generally depart from a series of stops along Avinguda Isidoro Macabich (the western continuation of Avinguda Bartomeu Rosselló). Tickets can be bought from the bus companies' ticket booths or on board the buses. See Ibiza's Getting Around section for more details.

Trasmediterránea (☎ 31 41 73) has an office in Ibiza city on the corner of Avinguda Bartomeu Vicent Ramon and Carrer Ramon y Cajal. See the Getting There & Away section at the beginning of this chapter for information on inter-island ferries.

Getting Around
Buses between the airport and Avinguda Isidoro Macabich operate hourly between 7

am and 10.30 pm (100 ptas); otherwise, a taxi should cost around 1600 ptas.

Ibiza's commercial centre is quite compact, with most places of interest lying within five to 10 minutes walk of the harbour.

EAST COAST
Cala Llonga
A busy highway speeds you north out of Ibiza city towards Santa Eulària on the east coast. Alternatively, you could take the slower but more scenic coastal road via Cala Llonga – take the turn-off to Jesús a couple of km north of Ibiza city. This route winds through low hills and groves of olive trees, with detours along the way to several beaches including the very pleasant **Sol d'en Serra**.

Cala Llonga is set on an attractive bay with high rocky cliffs sheltering a lovely sandy beach, but the town itself has many high-rise hotels. This resort seems to be especially popular with elderly English types who probably find Ibiza city just a little too racy. Still, the beaches are fine and there's a golf course and horse-riding ranch nearby.

There's also a good camping ground, *Camping Cala Llonga*, 300 metres back from the beach (open during summer only). Sites are shaded by pine trees, and facilities include a pool, a bar-restaurant and a supermarket.

Santa Eulària d'es Riu
Ibiza's third-largest town, Santa Eulària is a bustling and agreeable place with reasonable beaches and a large harbour. A whitewashed 16th century church overlooks the town from a hillside at the top of the old quarter, but the majority of the architecture in the new town is of the 20th century tourist-resort genre.

Orientation & Information The main highway, known as Carrer Sant Jaume as it passes through the town centre, is a hectic traffic artery lined with souvenir shops and restaurants.

The tourist office is just off the highway at Carrer de Mariano Riquer Wallis 4. It opens weekdays from 9.30 am to 1.30 pm and 4.30 to 7 pm, and Saturday from 9.30 am to 1.30 pm. There's a telephone office right next door.

Places to Stay Modern hotels and apartments crowd Santa Eulària's beachfront, but a couple of blocks inland you'll find a cluster of affordable hostales. The excellent *Hostal-Residencia Sa Rota* (☎ 33 00 22), Carrer Sant Vincent 59, has bright rooms with modern bath or shower. Singles/doubles cost from 2300/3800 to 3300/5000 ptas.

Also on Carrer Sant Vicent at No 24, the German-owned *Hostal Central* (☎ 33 00 43) is open all year and has a cosy pizza bar and restaurant downstairs. Rooms with heating, showers and terraces range from 2000/3000 to 3000/4000 ptas. The three storey *Hostal Rey* (☎ 33 0210), Carrer de Sant Josep 17, has similar standards and prices.

Ca's Català (☎ 33 10 06, Carrer del Sol s/n, is a real find. This 12 room hotel has the feel of a private villa, with its colourful flowerpots and sunny rooms overlooking a garden courtyard and swimming pool. There's also a cosy lounge and dining room, a separate TV lounge, a book library and a self-service bar, and the amiable English owners, Kim and Jill, add a personal touch. Singles start at 3500 ptas and doubles range from 6000 to 8500 ptas (plus IVA); add another 850 ptas if you want a cooked buffet breakfast.

Places to Eat Most of the restaurants and cafés along the beachfront are either overly expensive or pretty tacky: at *Mel's English Snack Bar* you can enjoy 'home cooking at its very best', with choices including beans on toast, scrambled eggs and roast dinners. Nice one, Mel.

As with accommodation, if you're after a feed you'd be better off heading inland. Four blocks back there are plenty of decent eateries along Carrer Sant Vicent: the friendly folk at *Restaurante La Bota*, at No 43, offer a good menú for 950 ptas, while the atmospheric *Pizzeria Pepito* at No 24 has pizzas and pastas for around 800 ptas and paellas,

seafood and meat dishes in the 900 to 1500 ptas range.

Getting There & Away The main bus stop is on Avinguda Doctor Ricardo Gotarredona: regular buses connect Santa Eulària with Ibiza city, Sant Antoni and the northern beaches. During summer there are also daily boat services from the harbour to Es Canar, Cala Llonga and other local beaches, as well as to Ibiza city and Formentera.

Santa Eulària to S'Aigua Blanca
To the north of Santa Eulària is the resort town of **Cala Nova**, which is heavily developed and probably best avoided, although there are several camping grounds in the vicinity worth considering. The best of these is the well set-up *Camping Cala Nova* (☎ 33 17 74), 500 metres north of the main town. It has barbecue areas, good shady sites and is just 100 metres from an excellent beach. One km south of Cala Nova and a short stroll from the popular Punta Arabi beach is *Camping Florida* (☎ 33 16 98). Its bungalows sleep four people and are good value at 4000 to 6000 ptas per night, or there are six-bed bungalows with private bathrooms at 7000 to 9000 ptas per night.

Further north and back on the main road is the sleepy little town of **Sant Carles de Peralta**. A good place to stop for a bite or a drink here is the popular *Bar Anita*, opposite the church in the centre of town. There's a nice courtyard at the front, and it serves tasty tapas as well as pizzas, bocadillos and platos combinados.

About a km north of Sant Carles there's a turn-off to the right to **Cala de Boix**, which is the only true black-sand beach in the Balearic Islands – if you've never been to the Canary Islands it will give you an idea of what to expect. This area is undeveloped apart from a beach bar and a couple of restaurants, and the main bay is bounded by rocky points on either side of a relatively uncrowded beach. There's also a good place to stay, the *Hostal Cala Boix* (☎ 33 52 24), which consists of 14 neat rooms above the restaurant *S'Arribada*. All rooms have private bathrooms and some have sea views. B&B ranges from 3300 to 4000 ptas a double (plus IVA). There's another solitary pensión around the next headland at **Pou d'es Lleó**, although the beaches here aren't so good.

Back on the main road the next turning leads to the resort area of **Es Figueral**, and a little further on a handwritten sign marks the turn-off to the lovely beaches of S'Aigua Blanca. There isn't too much in the way of development down this way apart from a handful of private villas and apartments. Being a bit out of the way, these beaches are particularly popular with Ibiza's 'young and restless' crowd, most of whom don't seem to bother wearing swimsuits. At the end of the road you come to a series of narrow sandy beaches of dark sand and crystal-clear water, with a sprinkling of black rocks lurking offshore. There's a good open-sided bar-café beside the beach which has deck chairs for rent.

A couple of hundred metres back from the beachfront is the three storey *Pensión Sa Plana* (☎ 33 50 73), a laid-back 30 room place with a great pool, outdoor courtyard and pool-side bar and barbecue. The restaurant has a menú for 1000 ptas, or you can order à la carte. Each room has its own bathroom and a terrace with fine views. Singles/doubles cost around 4000/4500 ptas.

Cala Sant Vicent

The package-tour resort of Cala Sant Vicent is built around the shores of a protected bay on the north-east coast, a long stretch of sandy beach backed by a string of modern mid-rise hotels. It's not a bad place to stop for a swim if you happen to be passing by, and you could also take one of the boat trips that leave here daily to visit the small island of **Tagomago**.

NORTH COAST & INTERIOR
Cala Sant Vicent to Portinatx

The main road heads due west from Cala Sant Vicent, passing by the small village of **Sant Vicent de sa Cala** and then twisting its way through the mountains to **Sant Joan de Labritja**. Sant Joan is an unremarkable little

place, although it does have one cheap pensión – *Casa de Huéspedes Can Pla Roig* (☎ 33 30 12), with double rooms from 2300 ptas or 3500 ptas with bath.

Less than a km beyond Sant Joan this road intersects with the main north-south highway. From here you have a choice of heading south down to Ibiza city or north to Portinatx.

Portinatx

Portinatx is the north coast's major tourist resort, with an intensive development of hotels spread around its three adjoining beaches – S'Arenal Petit, S'Arenal Gran and Platja Es Port. The beaches themselves are indeed beautiful – a string of rocky coves and sandy beaches backed by pine trees – but unless you're looking for large crowds, beach toys or souvenirs there are better places to spend time.

Cala Xarraca

This beach, just west of Portinatx, is worth a visit. Set in a picturesque, partly protected bay with a rocky shoreline and a dark-sand beach, development is limited to a solitary bar-restaurant overlooked by a couple of private houses.

This northern part of Ibiza contains some of the island's most attractive landscapes, and if you need a break from the beaches the area's coastal hills and inland mountains are popular with bushwalkers and cyclists.

Sant Llorenç de Balafia

Between Portinatx and Ibiza city and just off the main highway, Sant Llorenç is a tiny village consisting of a cluster of houses and farms surrounding a typical whitewashed Ibizan church.

Sant Miquel de Balansat & Port de Sant Miquel

One of the largest inland towns, Sant Miquel is overlooked by a box-like whitewashed church which was built on a hilltop during the 14th century. It's worth a quick look, but there isn't much else in the town of interest to visitors.

Several km north, Port de Sant Miquel is yet another overdeveloped resort town, dominated by the huge *Hotel Club San Miguel*, which has consumed an entire hillside above the admittedly fine beaches.

A turn-off to the right just before you enter town takes you around a headland to the entrance to the **Cova de Can Marca**, a collection of underground caverns spectacularly lit by coloured lights. The caves are open daily for tours.

Beyond the caves, a *very* rough unsealed road continues for four km around the coast to the lovely and unspoiled bay of **Cala Benirrás**, which has two bar-restaurants and a handful of houses. In case you're not driving a hire car, there's also a sealed road which leads to Cala Benirrás: it's off the Sant Joan-Sant Miquel road, midway between the towns.

Around the coast about three km west of Port de Sant Miquel is Ibiza's famed *Hotel Hacienda* (☎ 33 45 00). If you can afford the hefty price tags and want to rub shoulders with the rich and famous, this is *the* place to stay. Set on an isolated and rugged clifftop, the rooms and rooftop terrace enjoy spectacular coastal views and great sunsets. It's a luxurious and surprisingly stylish five star hotel with outstanding facilities including three pools, tennis courts, in-house masseurs, mountain bikes, a disco and one of the island's best restaurants. Room tariffs range seasonally from 22,000 to 35,000 ptas a double; suites range from 25,000 to 40,000 ptas.

Santa Gertrudis de Fruitera

If you blinked at the wrong time you could easily miss Santa Gertrudis, but this tiny village in the centre of the island is definitely worth a visit. Clustered around the central Plaça de l'Església you'll find an unusual collection of art and craft galleries and antique and bric-a-brac shops, plus several good bars. The most famous of the latter is *Bar Costa*, and while you're here it's almost obligatory to try a *bocadillo completo* – a delicious warmed roll smeared with tomato and filled with *jamón serrano* and cheese.

The bar's interior is somewhat bizarre, with dozens of legs of ham hanging from the ceiling of the front bar and the walls of the back rooms crammed with a collection of weird and fascinating paintings. Bar Costa opens every day (except Tuesday) until 1 or 2 am.

Also in town is the excellent *Restaurant La Plaza* (☎ 19 70 75), which specialises in French cuisine and has an intimate dining room and a lovely courtyard out the back. Main courses are mostly in the 1800 to 2500 ptas range.

Sant Rafel

Midway between Ibiza city and Sant Antoni de Portmany, Sant Rafel is home to a couple of Ibiza's biggest and best discos. By day the town is known as a craft centre and has a pretty good collection of ceramics workshops, sculpture galleries, shops and markets.

WEST COAST
Sant Antoni de Portmany

Sant Antoni, widely known as 'San An', is big, tacky and about as Spanish as bangers and mash. The locals joke (somewhat sadly) that even soccer hooligans need holidays, and somehow they all seem to end up in San An at one time or another. It's the perfect destination if you've come in search of booze-ups, brawls and hangovers, but otherwise it's probably best to treat San An as you might a really annoying person: just ignore it and hope it goes away.

So unless your travel agent secretly hates you and sends you here on a package tour, the only reason you might end up in Sant Antoni is because there are direct boats to and from Denia on the mainland, or to sample the notorious nightlife which is...well...wild, to say the least.

Sant Antoni is connected with Ibiza city and the rest of the island by regular bus services. There are also boat services to local beaches like Cala Bassa and Cala Comte, as well as to Portinatx, Formentera and Denia. The tourist office (☎ 33 07 28) is at Carrer Mariano Riquer Wallis 4, and if you need somewhere to stay this is the place to ask about hostales and hotels.

Not far north of Sant Antoni there are several pleasant and undeveloped beaches, such as **Cala Salada**, a wide bay with sandy shores backed by a pine forest. From here, a rough track continues north around the coast towards the beach at **Ses Fontanelles**, but unless you have a 4WD this route isn't really passable. If you're keen to get here there's easier access from the main road.

Cala Bassa to Cala d'Hort

Heading west and south from Sant Antoni you'll come to the rocky and popular bay of Cala Bassa. Not far back from the beach, *Camping Cala Bassa* (☎ 34 45 99) is an okay second-class camping ground that opens during summer.

Further south, **Cala Vedella** is one of the smaller and more low-key resort towns on Ibiza. There's a fine beach in the centre of town, backed by a couple of restaurants. The main accommodation option here is the big and bland apartment-hotel *Apartamentos Puerto Cala Vedella* (☎ 80 80 13). It caters mainly for the package-tour set but will offer short-term rentals if there are vacancies. Nightly tariffs range from 5000 to 9000 ptas for one bedroom apartments and from 6000 to 15,000 ptas for two and three bedroom apartments.

A little further south, Cala d'Hort has a spectacular setting overlooking two rugged rocky islets, Es Vedra and Es Vedranell. The water here is an inviting shade of blue and the beach is a long arc of sand sprinkled with pebbles and rocks, sheltered by low cliffs on either side. As yet the developers still haven't ruined this place, and there's nothing here apart from two good bar-restaurants. One of these, *Restaurante y Habitaciones Del Carmen* (☎ 14 26 61), has rooms upstairs with bath, terraces and sea views for 5500 to 6500 ptas a double. The restaurant downstairs specialises in seafood and paellas.

SOUTH COAST
Ses Salines

Platja de ses Salines and the adjacent Platja d'es Cavallet, at the southernmost tip of the island, are the best and most popular beaches within striking distance of Ibiza city. You can be here in half an hour on the local bus, or considerably quicker if you have your own transport. The area takes its name from the numerous salt pans in the area, which have been exploited since Carthaginian times and remained the mainstay of the Ibizan economy until the tourism boom.

If you're taking the bus from Ibiza city you'll be dropped at the western end of Ses Salines beside a small bar; you can buy groceries, sunscreen, postcards and other essential beach gear at the attached shop. Across the road on the other side of the sand dunes a long crescent-shaped bay stretches away into the distance, with a broad sandy beach broken by patches of rocks. These beaches are popular with Ibiza's party-hard crowd, and there are four or five open-air beach bars spread around the bay. Each has a slightly different vibe and plays a different type of music, and most people just stroll along the shore until they find a spot that suits their mood. The western end is more 'family-oriented', and it seems that swimsuits become less common the further east you go. Stroll on if the *au naturel* look appeals to you: Es Cavallet, the next bay around to the east, is Ibiza's official nudist beach.

Places to Stay There are two accommodation options immediately behind the beach (and opposite the bus stop): *Casa de Huéspedes Escandell* (☎ 39 65 83) is a simple little guesthouse which has six double rooms with shared bathrooms for 3500 ptas, and one downstairs room with its own bathroom for 4000 ptas. Nearby, *Hostal Mar y Sal* (☎ 39 65 84) has its own bar and restaurant and double rooms with bath from 3600 to 4600 ptas (plus IVA).

Places to Eat All of Ses Salines' beach bars offer some type of food. About halfway along the beach, *The Jockey Club* is a funky tropical-style bar fronted by rows of coloured banana lounges (500 ptas to hire for the day). It's a good spot for a drink or a bite, with timber decking shaded by palm-tree branches, good music and meals ranging from grilled sardines (1200 ptas) to a pan-fried fillet of fish with vegies (2000 ptas).

At the eastern end of the beach, *Sa Trincha* is more casual and a bit more affordable, serving up burgers, bocadillos, salads and fruit smoothies. This place has its own DJ booth, and things can get kind of wild and crazy down this end of the beach.

Getting There & Away Autobuses Voramar El Gaucho (☎ 34 03 82) runs 10 buses a day down to Ses Salines from Ibiza city, departing from Avinguda Isidoro Macabich (105 ptas one way).

Formentera

A short boat ride south of Ibiza, Formentera is the smallest and least developed of the four main Balearic Islands. This idyllic island has fine beaches and some excellent short walking and cycling trails to explore. It's a popular day trip from Ibiza and can get pretty crowded in midsummer, but most of the time it is still possible to find yourself a strip of sand out of sight of tourist colonies and out of earshot of other tourists.

Formentera's landscape is rugged, harsh and at times bleak, and, with the exception of the eastern plateau, the island is predominantly flat. The coast is alternately fringed with jagged rocky cliffs and beaches backed by low sand dunes dotted with hardy coastal scrub. A handful of farmers scrape a living out of the soils in the central and eastern sections, but elsewhere the island is a patchwork of pine plantations, sunbleached salt beds, low stone walls and vacant fields.

Orientation

Formentera is less than 20 km across from east to west. Ferries arrive at the port town of La Savina, a functional and largely uninteresting harbour town wedged between two large salt lakes, the Estany d'es Peix and Estany Pudent (the aptly named Smelly Lake). Three km south of La Savina is the island's administrative capital, Sant Francesc Xavier, and another five km south is Cap de Barbaria, the southernmost point. Es Pujols, the main tourist resort, is three km east of La Savina.

The main road runs down the middle of the island, passing by the fine beaches of Platja de Migjorn along the south coast and through the fishing village of Es Caló (13 km east of La Savina) before climbing to Sa Talaia, the island's highest point (192 metres). At the far eastern point of the island is the Far de sa Mola lighthouse.

Maps The tourist office's *Green Tours* brochure includes a rundown and map of 19 excellent walking and cycling trails that take you through some of the island's most scenic areas.

Information

Formentera's tourist office (☎ 32 20 57) is in La Savina, hidden behind the row of rental agencies that line the port. Opening hours vary seasonally: during summer it opens from 10 am to 2 pm and 5 to 7 pm (closed Saturday afternoon and Sunday). Most of the banks are in Sant Francesc Xavier. There is a Telefónica phone centre and a laundrette in Es Pujols.

Things to See & Do

Apart from the walking and cycling trails and the beaches, sightseeing is fairly limited. Points of interest include a series of crumbling **stone watchtowers** along the coastline, a ruined **Roman fortress** on the south coast and another 40 minor **archaeological sites** (most of which are signposted off the main roads).

Beaches Some of the island's best and most popular beaches are the **Platja de Llevant** and the **Platja de ses Illetes** – beautiful strips of white sand which line the east and west sides, respectively, of the narrow promontory which stretches north towards Ibiza.

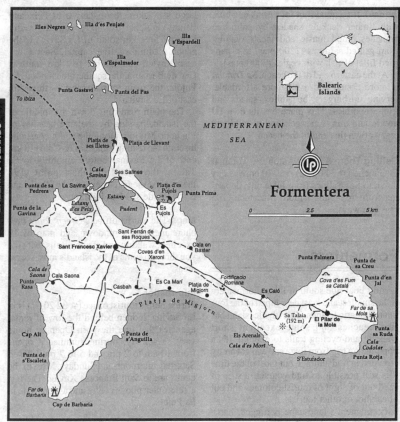

Formentera

MEDITERRANEAN SEA

Balearic Islands

0   2.5   5 km

A two km walking trail leads from the La Savina-Es Pujols road to the far end of the promontory, from where you can wade across a narrow strait to **S'Espalmador**, a tiny islet with beautiful, quiet beaches. The promontory itself is largely undeveloped apart from a series of popular beach cafés and bars.

East of Sant Ferrán, towards Es Caló, a series of bumpy roads and unsealed tracks lead down to the beaches along the south coast, known collectively as the **Platja de Migjorn**. These beaches are quite secluded and particularly popular with nudists,

despite their sometimes rocky and seaweed-strewn shorelines. Most of these beach settlements consist of a handful of houses and apartments, a couple of bar-restaurants and the odd hostal.

San Francesc Xavier Formentera's capital, San Francesc Xavier, is an attractive white-washed village with some good cafés overlooking small, sunny plazas. The town's older buildings include a 14th century chapel and an 18th century fortress, and its interesting Ethnological Museum is well worth a visit.

Cap de Barbaria A narrow sealed road heads south out of the capital and winds through stone-walled farmlands to Cap de Barbaria, the island's southernmost point. It's a pleasant ride or drive down to the lonely white lighthouse at the road's end, although there isn't much to do once you get there apart from clamber around the cliff tops and wish you were a seagull. There are a couple of subterranean caves to explore, and from the lighthouse a 10 minute walking track leads east around the coast to the **Torre d'es Cap de Barbaria**, an 18th century watch-tower.

Cala Saona A third of the way down the road to Cap de Barbaria, you can turn off (west) to the small and lovely beach settlement of Cala Saona. The beach here is one of the island's best, a generous expanse of white sand sprinkled with bright beach umbrellas and backed by pine trees. Development is limited to one very big hotel (see Places to Stay & Eat) and a couple of bar-restaurants with open-air terraces overlooking the clear, pale aqua and blue-black waters.

Coves d'en Xeroni Beside the main road just east of Sant Ferrán are the Coves d'en Xeroni, an unexceptional series of underground caves. Entry costs 400 ptas (200 ptas for children), and the caves open daily from 10 am to 8 pm between May and October.

Es Caló This small (but rapidly expanding) fishing settlement is set around a tiny rocky cove ringed by faded timber boat shelters. The coastline here is jagged and rocky, but immediately west of Es Caló you'll find some good swimming holes and rock pools with small patches of sand hidden amongst the rocks.

From Es Caló, the road suddenly twists and climbs its way up to the island's highest point. Close to the top, *Bar-Restaurant El Mirador* has spectacular views back down across the whole island and as far as Ibiza. Eating here isn't particularly cheap, although for the price of a coffee or a beer you can enjoy the same views.

Eastern End The eastern end of the island is an elevated limestone plateau. It doesn't hold much interest: most of the coastline is only accessible by boat, and the interior is mainly taken up by pine forests and farms. A solitary road runs arrow-straight to the island's eastern tip, passing through the non-descript town of Es Pilar de la Mola. At the end of the road stand the Far de sa Mola lighthouse and a nearby monument to Jules Verne, who used this setting for part of one of his novels.

Places to Stay & Eat
There are no camping grounds on Formentera, and freelance camping is prohibited.

Sad to say, most of the accommodation places on the coast cater mainly to German and English package-tour agencies, and are overpriced and/or booked out in summer. For independent budget travellers, the best bet is to base yourself in one of the small inland towns and bicycle to the beaches.

If you decide to stay longer, there are agencies in the main towns where you can enquire about renting apartments. The tourist office can also help out with information on accommodation.

Es Pujols Once a sleepy fishing village, Es Pujols has been radically transformed by Spain's tourism boom. Rows of sunbleached timber boat shelters still line the beachfront, but nowadays they are overshadowed by modern hotels, apartments and restaurants, and tourism has all but replaced fishing as the town's main source of income. Nevertheless, the scale of development here remains smaller and more low-key than in most of the resorts on Ibiza or Mallorca. And if the town's sandy beaches are too crowded for your liking, there are plenty of others that are more secluded and still within easy striking distance.

Es Pujols' popularity makes it a relatively pricey place to stay, and unless you have an agency booking you may have trouble getting hold of a room during summer.

Right on the beachfront, *Hostal Tahiti* (☎ 32 81 22) at Carrer Fonoll Marí 16 is a

BALEARIC ISLANDS

large, modern three star place ranging from 4700/7800 to 5200/8600 ptas for singles/ doubles with B&B. There are three other hostales along Carrer Miramar (the main street), all with similar setups that include modern rooms with bath and attached bars and restaurants: *Hostal Voramar* (☎ 32 81 19), 100 metres inland, has double rooms ranging from 4200 to 8000 ptas; 50 metres further back, *Hostal Rosales* (☎ 32 81 23) has rooms ranging from 4500/ 7800 to 7700/ 14,000 ptas; while nearby, on the corner of Carrer d'Espalmador, *Hostal-Residencia Sa Volta* (☎ 32 81 25) charges between 3600/ 6600 and 5500/9600 ptas.

There's another cluster of hostales a km or so around the coast west of Es Pujols, including *Hostal Sa Roqueta* (☎ 32 85 06), which has double rooms from 3800 to 5600 ptas.

Es Pujols has an international collection of restaurants, with choices including French, Argentine, German and Mexican. On the beachfront the popular *Caminito* serves up excellent Argentine food and has a menú for 1800 ptas. *The Grapevine*, a tiny and affordable bar-eatery just back from the beach on Carrer de Punta Prima, is a good spot for a burger or a snack.

Sant Francesc Xavier There's only one hostal here: the friendly *Restaurant-Casa Rafal* (☎ 32 22 05) on Carrer Isidoro Macabich has rooms upstairs or out the back costing 2000/3500 ptas, or 3000/5000 ptas with bath.

Sant Ferrán Just 1.6 km south of Es Pujols, this unassuming little town has a couple of decent budget hostales. At Carrer Major 68, the popular *Hostal Pepe* (☎ 32 80 33) has 45 simple and breezy rooms with bath; B&B ranges from 2875/4685 to 3110/4975 ptas. The hostal's legendary bar has been a popular hippy hang-out since the 1960s. On the main road, *Hostal Illes Pitises* (☎ 32 81 89) has modern rooms with bath ranging from 2000/4750 to 3000/6875 ptas.

La Savina Formentera's port town isn't the most thrilling place, but if you decide to opt for convenience there are a couple of choices. Closest to the ferry docks, *Hostal Bahia* (☎ 32 21 42) has singles/doubles for around 3500/5200 ptas. A better bet is the impressive *Hostal La Savina* (☎ 32 22 79), overlooking the Estany d'es Peix from Avinguda Mediterránea 22 (on the main road out of town). Rooms with shower range from 2750/4250 to 3750/4750 ptas; doubles with bath and harbour views are 5100 to 5800 ptas.

Cala Saona The only accommodation at this lovely beach settlement is the *Hotel Cala Saona* (☎ 32 20 30), a modernish if somewhat bland three star hotel with 116 air-con rooms, a pool, tennis courts, restaurant etc. Rooms start at 5325/7600 ptas, soaring to 10,360/14,800 ptas in the high season (plus IVA).

South Coast There are numerous hostales spread along Formentera's south coast (otherwise known as Platja de Migjorn).

Es Ca Marí is a small resort with a cluster of places and reasonable beaches. *Hostal Ca Mari* (☎ 32 81 80) is actually three hostales in one: their rooms and apartments all share a central bar, restaurant, pool and grocery shop. B&B tariffs range from 3800 to 5600 ptas per person per day. Nearby, the mid-range *Hostal Costa Azul* (☎ 32 80 24) also has rooms or apartments at similar prices. A few hundred metres east, *Club Formentera Playa* is an appallingly overblown four star resort. Give it a miss unless you're looking for a mindless, organised-activities type holiday.

There are a couple of other secluded hostales further along this stretch of coast. The exclusive *Hostal Santi* (☎ 32 83 75) has its own bar-restaurant and charges between 7000 and 10,000 ptas a double, while several hundred metres further east the 40 room *Hostal Maysi* (☎ 32 85 47) is better value, charging from 3400/5500 to 4400/6500 ptas for singles/doubles.

Further east again (and due south of Es Caló) is the whitewashed mass-market holiday village of *Club Maryland* – very large, very depressing.

Es Caló Overlooking a small rocky harbour, *Fonda Rafalet* (☎ 32 70 16) has good rooms (some with sea views) ranging from 2500/4800 to 3000/5500 ptas. It also incorporates a bar and a pricey seafood restaurant, and at the time of writing a new accommodation block was being built next door.

Across the (main) road, *Casa de Huéspedes Miramar* (☎ 32 70 60) has eight simple upstairs rooms sharing a communal bathroom. Nightly costs are 2000/3000 ptas for singles/doubles; the front rooms have sea views (and traffic noise), the back rooms have bush views.

Es Pilar de la Mola Formentera's easternmost town has a handful of bars and restaurants. You can sit out the front of *Bar Can Toni* and watch the lighthouse-bound traffic go back and forth while you tuck into the two-course menú (850 ptas, drinks extra). Two km further east, near the lighthouse itself, *Bar Es Puig* specialises in mixed platters of hams, sausages and cheeses, herbal liquors and local wines. But ask '*¿Cuánto cuesta?*' before you order – the menu is 'priceless'.

Entertainment
Es Pujols has the only nightlife to speak of. In summer the town is pretty lively, with a cluster of bars along Carrer Miramar that stay open until 3 or 4 am. Close to the beachfront, Carrer d'Espardell has a couple of popular watering holes including the *Tennis Bar* and the small *Indiana Café*. There are also two good discos, *Magoos* and *Tipic*, to take you through until sunrise.

Getting There & Away
Three companies – Trasmapi-Flebasa Lines (☎ 31 07 11), Umafisa Lines (☎ 31 45 13) and Inserco (☎ 31 11 57) – operate some 20 to 25 ferry services daily between Ibiza city and Formentera. The first ferries depart from Ibiza city at around 7.30 am and the last

return from Formentera at around 9 pm. Services are more frequent during summer.

The jet ferries take about 25 minutes for the trip and cost around 3600 ptas return, while the car ferries take about an hour and cost 1500 to 2400 ptas return. Return fares for vehicles are around 5000 ptas for a small car, 1200 ptas for a scooter and 350 ptas for a bike. Prices vary seasonally and from company to company, so check around.

Pitra (☎ 96-642 31 20) operates twice-weekly ferries from Denia on the mainland to Formentera (via Sant Antoni de Portmany on Ibiza).

Getting Around
The local branch of Greenpeace has stuck a notice in the window of the tourist office in La Savina: 'The world is collapsing, the energy is exhausted. RENT A BIKE.' And unless you're in a tearing hurry (or lazy), pedal power is the best and most leisurely way to get around this little island. There's also a regular bus service connecting all the main towns.

If you need to hire transport you'll find rental agencies all over the island, including a string of places opposite the harbour in La Savina. Avis and Hertz have representatives here: local agencies include Moto Rent Mitjorn (☎ 32 22 55), Autos Isla Blanca (☎ 32 25 59) and Moto Rent La Savina (☎ 32 22 75). Daily rates are around 600 ptas for a bike, 1000 ptas for a mountain bike, 2000 to 4000 ptas for scooters or motorbikes, 5000 to 6000 ptas for small cars, and 7000 to 9000 ptas for a Suzuki 4WD.

Menorca

Menorca is perhaps the least overrun and most low-key of the Balearic Islands. In 1993 the island was declared a Biosphere Reserve by UNESCO, with the aim of preserving its important environmental areas such as the S'Albufera d'es Grau wetlands and its unique collection of archaeological relics and monuments.

BALEARIC ISLANDS

While it has a reputation for being modest, retiring and even staid, in truth it just isn't as brash as the other islands. It's also more family-oriented, so if partying all night is a priority you'd be better off going to Ibiza or Mallorca.

The second-largest and northernmost of the Balearics, Menorca also has a wetter climate and is usually a few degrees cooler than the other islands – although this can be a blessing in summer. It is also known as the 'windy island', and particularly during the colder months is relentlessly buffeted by chilling *tramuntana* winds.

Orientation
The capital, Maó (Mahón in Castilian), is at the eastern end of the island. Maó's busy port is the arrival point for most ferries, and Menorca's airport is seven km south-west. The main road runs along the middle of the island to Ciutadella, Menorca's second town, with secondary roads leading north and south to the major coastal resorts and beaches.

The northern half of the island is an undulating area of green, rolling hills with a rugged, rocky coastline. The southern half is flatter and drier, with a smoother coastline and sandy beaches between high cliffs.

Activities
As befits any island, water sports are the dominant activities here. There are yacht clubs in Maó, Ciutadella, Fornells and Es Castell, and many of the resorts have marinas with boats and sailboards for hire. There are also several scuba-diving centres around the island, as well as a couple of horse-riding ranches.

The only golf course is at Son Parc, on the north coast near Fornells.

Special Events
Each town on Menorca has a festival to celebrate the feast day of its patron saint. The first and biggest festival is the Festa de Sant Joan, held in Ciutadella over the last weekend in June. The season finishes with the Festa de Mare de Déu de Gràcia in Maó on 8 September.

Menorca's festivals are steeped in traditions that date back to the Middle Ages: jousting tournaments and other medieval games are a common feature. The locals pride themselves particularly on their riding skills, and during the fiestas prancing horses are ridden into the crowds, rearing onto their hind legs and spinning in circles.

Accommodation
If you're on a budget it's probably best to base yourself at either Maó or Ciutadella, at least initially. Both have a handful of good, affordable hostales, but elsewhere around the island bargains are few and far between.

The only camping ground is near the resort of Santa Galdana, about 8 km south of Ferreries. It is only open in summer.

Getting Around
Bus Menorca's airport is seven km south-west of Maó. There are no bus services from the airport; a taxi into Maó will cost around 1200 ptas.

There are three bus companies operating services on Menorca. The major operator is TMSA (☎ 36 03 61), which runs six buses a day between Maó and Ciutadella via Alaior, Es Mercadal and Ferreries. It also has connecting services to the major resorts along the south coast, including S'Algar, Punta Prima, Cala en Porter, Platja Sant Tomas and Santa Galdana.

The other two companies are Autocares Fornells (☎ 37 66 21), which covers the north coast between Maó and Fornells, and Autocares Torres (☎ 38 45 11), with services to the coast south of Ciutadella.

Car, Motorcycle & Bicycle Rental If you're planning to hire a car, rates vary from around 3500 to 8000 ptas a day, depending on the season and the type of car. During summer, minimum hire periods apply.

In Maó, places worth trying include Ibercars (☎ 36 42 08), GB International

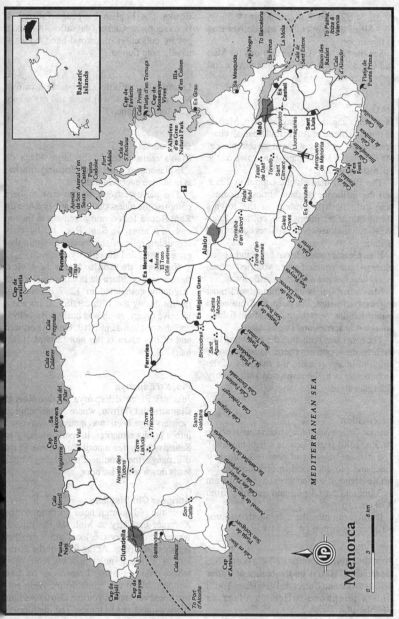

Menorca

BALEARIC ISLANDS

(☎ 36 24 32) and Autos Confort (☎ 36 94 70). All of these operators will deliver cars to the airport.

See the Getting Around sections for Maó and Ciutadella for details of motorcycle and bicycle rentals.

MAÓ

Menorca's capital and largest town, Maó, is an unusual blend of Anglo and Spanish characteristics – in some ways more reminiscent of Gibraltar or Malta than of any town on the Spanish mainland.

The British made it the capital in 1713, and the influence of their almost hundred-year rule is still evident in the town's architecture, traditions and culture. Even today, the majority of its visitors come from Britain.

It's a pleasant and relaxed town and a good place to base yourself when you first arrive. Good beaches are a short bus ride away.

Maó's harbour is its dominant and most impressive feature. The deep, well-protected waters handle everything from small fishing boats to car ferries and huge tankers.

The town was built atop the cliffs that line the harbour's southern shore. Although some older buildings remain, the majority of the architecture is in the restrained 18th century Georgian style.

Information

Tourist Office Menorca's main tourist office (☎ 36 37 90) is at Plaça de s'Esplanada 40. The staff are helpful and generous with their time, and provide good information on the whole island. It's open weekdays from 8 am to 3 pm and 5 to 7 pm, and Saturday from 9.30 am to 1 pm.

During summer there is another tourist office at the airport (☎ 15 71 15).

Post & Communications Maó's post office (postcode 07700) is on the corner of Carrer del Bon Aire and Carrer de l'Església. You'll find a telephone office on Plaça de s'Esplanada.

Books The English Language Library & Bookshop, at Carrer Vassallo 48, has a patchy collection of second-hand books – mostly pulp fiction.

Laundry Servinautic 215, beside a café at Moll de Llevant 4, will wash and dry a 7 kg load for 1700 ptas.

Old Quarter

Maó's main plaza is the large Plaça de s'Esplanada. A **craft and clothing market** is held here every Saturday.

The narrow streets to the east of here comprise the oldest part of Maó. The **Arc de Sant Roc**, a 16th century archway at the top end of Carrer de Sant Roc, is the only remaining relic of the medieval walls that once surrounded the old city.

Església de Santa Maria la Major, further east on Plaça de la Constitució, was originally completed in 1287 but largely rebuilt during the 18th century. It houses a massive organ which was built in Barcelona and shipped across in 1810. On the northern end of this plaza is the **ajuntament** (town hall).

Plaça d'Espanya

Just off Plaça d'Espanya is the **Mercat Claustre del Carme**, where former church cloisters have been imaginatively converted into a produce market. It opens Monday to Saturday from dawn until 2 pm. From Plaça d'Espanya, the winding Costa de ses Voltes leads down to the harbour.

Xoriguer Gin Distillery

From the old quarter, head north up to the Xoriguer distillery at Moll de Ponent 93, where you can try the local gin – another legacy of the Brits. At the front of the distillery is a liquor outlet and souvenir shop where visitors help themselves to free samples. Menorcan gin is distinctively aromatic and very tasty; you can also try various strange liqueurs and tonics. The distillery is

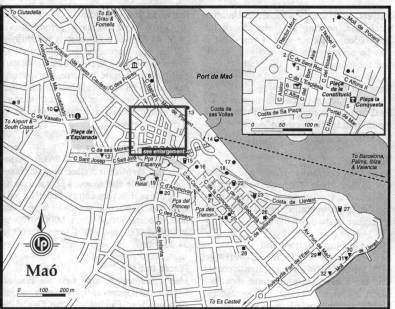

Maó

PLACES TO STAY
20 Hostal Orsi
21 Hostal-Residencia Jume
24 Hostal Roca
25 Hostal-Residencia La Isla
26 Hotel Sheila
28 Hostal Sa Roqueta
29 Hotel Port Mahón

PLACES TO EAT
3 La Dolce Vita
12 El Greco
19 American Bar
30 Ristorante Roma
31 Café Alba
32 Restaurante Gregal

OTHER
1 Acuarium Menorca
2 Arc de Sant Roc
4 Ajuntament
5 Església de Santa Maria la Major
6 Post Office
7 Museu de Mallorca
8 Xoriguer Gin Distillery
9 English Language Library & Bookshop
10 TMSA Bus Depot
11 Main Tourist Office
13 Estació Marítim
14 Main Ferry Docks
15 Nou de Copes
16 Claustre del Carme Market
17 Servinautic 215 (Laundrette)
18 Motos Rayda
22 Texas Bar
23 Nashville Beer & Soundgarden
27 Menor Bar

open weekdays from 8 am to 7 pm and Saturday from 9 am to 1 pm.

Acuarium Menorca
Not far from the distillery at Moll de Ponent 73, the aquarium houses an unexciting collection of uninterested fish. It's open daily from 10 am to 5 pm, but isn't really worth the 250 ptas entry (150 ptas for kids). Instead, go after 5 pm when it turns into a bar and entry is free (although you have to buy at least one drink).

Museu de Mallorca
The supposedly impressive collection of this museum is housed in a former Franciscan

convent off Plaça d'es Monestir. Unfortunately the building has been closed for 'restoration' work for several years, but it may be open by the time you visit; check with the tourist office for the latest.

Beaches

The closest decent beaches to the capital are **Es Grau** to the north and **Punta Prima** to the south. Both are connected to Maó by regular bus services.

Boat Trips

Numerous operators offer boat cruises around the harbour. These can be a pleasant way to kill a few hours, but don't pay extra for the 'glass-bottomed boat trips': there isn't much to see down there.

Places to Stay – bottom end

At Carrer de la Infanta 19, *Hostal Orsi* (☎ 36 47 51) is owned by a young English couple who are a mine of information about the island. It's bright and clean, well located and highly recommended. Singles/doubles/triples range from 1850/3200/4500 to 2200/3800/5400 ptas, doubles with shower from 3600 to 4400 ptas. There are also bikes for rent (see Getting Around for details).

Hostal-Residencia La Isla (☎ 36 64 92), at Carrer de Santa Catalina 4, is a large, family-run hostal which has excellent rooms with modern bathrooms ranging from 1700/3400 to 2000/4000 ptas. The downstairs restaurant has a good menú at 900 ptas.

Maó's other budget options are less praiseworthy. *Hostal-Residencia Jume* (☎ 36 48 78), at Carrer de la Concepció 6, charges between 2185 and 2570 ptas per person for B&B. Rooms have their own bathrooms and are comfortable enough, but the staff are surly and unhelpful.

At Carrer del Carme 37, *Hostal Roca* (☎ 35 15 39) is one of the cheapest options, with shabby rooms above a cluttered bar at 1500/2500 ptas. Further east, *Hostal Sa Roqueta* (☎ 36 43 35) is a long way from the action at Carrer del Carme 122. It has 20 plain but clean rooms from 1700/3000 to 2000/3500 ptas.

Places to Stay – middle

At Carrer Santa Cecilia 41, *Hotel Sheila* (☎ 36 48 55) has been recently refurbished and has very impressive (if slightly stark) rooms with safes, TV, phones and (optional) piped music. Despite the name, it's Spanish-run and has its own bangers-and-mash-free restaurant, plus a bar and guest lounge. Rooms are fairly pricey at 5500/8550 to 7050/12,050 ptas.

Places to Stay – top end

The *Hotel Port Mahón* (☎ 36 26 00), Avinguda Port de Maó, is a sleek four star hotel with 74 marble-clad rooms, a pool and pleasant gardens. It's very comfy, but it's a long walk into the centre if you don't have transport. Rooms range from 6000/9000 to 10,000/18,000 ptas, suites from 20,000 to 34,000 ptas.

Places to Eat

Maó's architecture may have an English flavour, but it seems as though every second restaurant here is an Italian bistro. One of the best of these is *La Dolce Vita* at Carrer de Sant Roc 25, which has great home-made bread, fresh salads, pastas and pizzas (575 to 900 ptas) and an excellent menú at 1000 ptas. Note that it is only open for dinner.

Just off Plaça de s'Esplanada at Carrer de ses Moreres 49, *El Greco* is an elegant little eatery that specialises in a blend of French and Spanish cuisine. Its menú costs 1350 ptas or you can eat à la carte, with mains in the 700 to 1500 ptas range.

The *American Bar* in Plaça Reial is a spacious café fronted by open-air tables. It's a good place to linger over the newspaper or write postcards, and has a limited but tasty menú for 950 ptas.

Maó's harbour is lined with restaurants and bars and most have outdoor terraces where you can soak up the waterfront atmosphere. A walk along here is a good way to work up an appetite while you decide where to eat.

Moll de Llevant, at the eastern end of the harbour, is home to Maó's most up-market restaurants – while you eat you can gaze enviously at the fleet of expensive yachts moored opposite. One of the best eateries here is *Ristorante Roma* at Moll de Llevant 295. A bustling and stylish Italian bistro, it's surprisingly good value with pizzas and pastas from 600 to 900 ptas, other mains from 875 to 1400 ptas and a menú at 1100 ptas. Next door at No 299, *Café Alba* has a menú for 950 ptas, while further along at No 306, the classy *Restaurant Gregal* specialises in seafood and has a light lunch menú at 1200 ptas and main courses ranging from 1500 to 3500 ptas.

Closer to the centre of town, there are plenty more restaurants (not to mention gift and souvenir shops) opposite the ferry docks along Moll de Ponent. At No 28, *Passage to India* serves up tasty Indian tucker with main courses in the 1000 to 1500 ptas range. Nearby at No 15, *Casanova* lured us in with a signboard proclaiming: 'Here you can taste authentic Italian cousin'. Was this was a spelling mistake or the ultimate family restaurant? As it turned out, seared Sicilian wasn't on the menu, but the pastas and salads were excellent and there is a separate vegetarian menu with dishes from 550 to 800 ptas.

Entertainment

Nightlife in Maó is pretty low-key in comparison to Mallorca or Ibiza. Most of the bars and discos are down along the waterfront, but you'll need to wear your walking boots as they are well spread out.

Heading east along the Moll de Llevant, one of the first places you'll come to is the *Texas Bar*, a lively wood-panelled country and/or western joint (Yee-ha!). Tacky but fun. A bit further along, the *Nashville Beer & Soundgarden* is a large tavern featuring mainstream rock bands; it opens Wednesday to Saturday nights until around 4 am.

In case you're starting to wonder what country you're in, the *Menor Bar* a couple of hundred metres further east is much funkier and much more Spanish. With its old sandstone walls and heavy timber ceiling beams, has an appropriately maritime flavour.

Nou de Copes, in a laneway between the top of Costa de ses Voltes and the Claustre del Carme, is a popular little music bar with a cave-like interior carved out of the old walls above the harbour.

Getting There & Away

TMSA (☎ 36 03 61) buses depart from either its depot at Avinguda Josep M Quadrado 7 or from nearby Plaça de s'Esplanada. It has around six buses each day from Maó to Ciutadella (450 ptas) via Alaior (140 ptas), Es Mercadal (220 ptas) and Ferreries (290 ptas). It also has regular services to the south-coast beaches including Punta Prima (200 ptas) and Cala Tomas (340 ptas).

Getting Around

Motos Rayda (☎ 35 47 86), at Moll de Llevant 35-36, hires out mountain bikes (800 ptas per day), scooters and Vespas (1500 to 2500 ptas per day).

Just Bicicletas (☎ 36 47 51), based at Hostal Orsi at Carrer de la Infanta 19, also hires out mountain bikes for 800 ptas a day or 4900 ptas a week.

THE INTERIOR – MAÓ TO CIUTADELLA

Menorca's main road, from Maó to Ciutadella, divides the island into north and south. It passes through the towns of Alaior, Es Mercadal and Ferreries, and along the way smaller roads branch off towards the beaches and resorts of the north and south coasts.

Many of the island's most significant archaeological relics are signposted off the main road (see the boxed aside 'Menorca's Prehistoric Heritage' for details).

The small town of **Alaior** is the home to local cheese and shoe industries. Cheeses from the Quesos Coinga factory are sold all over Menorca, but if you're passing through you can visit the tasting and sales room at the front of the factory; it's open weekdays from 9 am to 1 pm and 5 to 8 pm and Saturday from 9 am to 1 pm. On Saturday morning a small craft market is held at the front of the church of Santa Eulalia.

In the centre of the island is the small and nondescript village of **Es Mercadal** – perhaps most notable as the turn-off for

Menorca's Prehistoric Heritage

Menorca's beaches aren't its only attractions. The interior of the island is liberally sprinkled with reminders of its rich and ancient heritage.

Many of the most significant sites and monuments are open to the public (and free!), although some are on private property and you'll need to ask permission before visiting.

These archaeological relics have been embraced by Menorca's tourism promoters, who often liken the island to an open-air museum. As such the major sites have been made readily accessible to visitors – sometimes to their detriment. While these places provide fascinating insights into the past, most of them aren't as well presented as they could be and as a result they somehow lack the mystique they should hold. The major monuments are definitely worth a look, but at many of the minor sites there isn't a whole lot to see apart from crumbling ruins.

The monuments are linked to three main periods: the Pre-Talayotic Period (or cave era) from 2000 to 1300 BC; the Talayotic Period (or Bronze Age) from 1300 to 800 BC; and the Post-Talayotic Period (or Iron Age) from 800 to around 100 BC. Similarly, there are three types of structures: navetas, talayots and taulas.

Navetas, built from large rocks in the shape of upturned boat hulls, are thought to have been used as either tombs or meeting places – perhaps both.

Talayots, large stone mounds that are found all over the island, were perhaps used as defensive watchtowers for each settlement.

Unique to Menorca, **taulas** are huge stone tablets that have been precisely balanced in the shape of a 'T'. It has been suggested that taulas could have been used as sacrificial altars, but, as with Stonehenge, nobody is really sure how these enormous slabs of stone were moved into position or what they actually signify.

Just off the main road three km west of Maó, the talayotic settlement known as **Talatí de Dalt** is one of the most interesting sites. It's about five minutes walk from the car park to the main feature, a well-preserved and much photographed taula. Unusually it has an attached column, probably a second taula that fell here by accident.

About four km further along on the north side of the road is the **Rafal Rubí**, a pair of well-preserved burial navetas.

The nearby **Torralba d'en Salord** is another talayotic settlement. It also features an impressive taula, but the rest of the settlement is quite deteriorated.

South of Alaior is the large **Torre d'en Gaumes** settlement, which now has its own car park, kiosk and a signposted walking trail that leads you around the site. It includes three talayots on a hilltop and a collection of circular dwellings.

Further south on the coast at **Cales Coves** some 90 caves have been carved into the coastal cliffs – these were apparently used for ritual burials. More recently some of the caves have been homes to hippy colonies, and nearby the large **Cova des Xoroi** has been enterprisingly converted into a disco.

South of Ciutadella, **Son Catlar** is the largest talayotic settlement in the Balearic Islands. Its five talayots and the remains of its dwellings cover around six hectares. East of Ciutadella (near the 40 km road marker), the **Naveta des Tudons** is a stone burial chamber that was restored in 1961.

The tourist office's excellent *Archaeological Guide to Menorca* is a handy guide to the major sites. ∎

Fornells. You also turn here to get to **Monte El Toro**, Menorca's highest point at 357 metres. A steep and twisting road leads up to the summit, which is shared by a 16th century church and Augustine monastery, a cluster of satellite dishes and radio towers, and a statue of Christ (built to honour the islanders who died defending the Republican cause during the Spanish Civil War). There are great views of the whole island; on a clear day you can see as far as Mallorca.

Ferreries is Menorca's highest town. On Saturday morning the excellent Mercat de Ferreries is held here, with stall holders selling fresh produce as well as traditional Menorcan crafts and artworks. On other days there are few reasons to linger. The turn-off to the resort of Santa Galdana is just west of here.

CIUTADELLA

Founded by the Carthaginians, Ciutadella was virtually destroyed following the Turkish invasion of 1558 and much of the city was subsequently rebuilt during the 17 century. It was the capital of Menorca up until the arrival of the British.

Known as 'Vella i Bella', it's an attractive and distinctly Spanish city with a picturesque port and a historic old quarter.

Information

Tourist Office Ciutadella's tourist office (☎ 38 26 39) is opposite the cathedral on Plaça d'es Born. During summer it opens on weekdays from 9.30 am to 1.30 pm and 5 to 7 pm, and on Saturday from 9.30 am to 1 pm.

Post & Communications The post office (postcode 07760) is at the southern end of Plaça d'es Born, and there's a Telefónica office on nearby Plaça dels Pins.

Things to See & Do

Ciutadella has few actual 'sights' or 'attractions', which in a way is part of its appeal. It's a living, breathing town that goes about its business without too many concessions to tourism, and it's a pleasure just to wander around exploring the old quarter and the port.

The main square, the large Plaça d'es Born, is surrounded by palm trees and gracious 19th century buildings including the **ajuntament**, the post office and the **Palau Torresaura**. In the centre of the square is a tall, thin obelisk, built to commemorate those who died trying to defend the city from the Turkish invasion on 9 July 1558.

Costa d'es Moll takes you down to the port from Plaça d'es Born. Heading in the other direction, the cobbled laneways and streets between Placa d'es Born and Plaça d'Alfons III hold plenty of interest, with simple whitewashed buildings alongside ornate churches and elegant palaces. The pedestrian walkway of **Ses Voltes**, the heart of the commercial district, is lined with glamorous shops and boutiques, restaurants and smoky bars.

Architectural landmarks worth looking out for include the 14th century **catedral**, built in Catalan Gothic style on the original site of an Islamic mosque; the baroque 17th century churches **Església dels Socors** and **Església del Roser** (now used as an exhibition gallery); and the impressive palaces of the nobility such as **Palau Martorell** and **Palau Saura**.

Ciutadella has a **market** each Thursday, when the town is flooded with shoppers.

Special Events The Festa de Sant Joan de Ciutadella, held over a weekend in late June, is one of Spain's best-known and most traditional festivals.

Places to Stay – bottom end

Hostal-Residencia Oasis (☎ 38 21 97), at Carrer de Sant Isidre 33, is set around a spacious garden courtyard and has pleasant rooms, most with bathrooms, from 1700/3000 to 2500/4300 ptas.

Cafè Ses Persianes (☎ 38 14 45), a hip little bar on Plaça d'Artrutx, has rooms upstairs at around 3800 ptas a double.

Places to Stay – middle

Hotel Gèminis (☎ 38 58 96), Carrer Josepa Rossinyol 4, is a friendly and stylish two star place. Excellent rooms with bathroom, TV, phone and heating cost from 2500/4500 to 3500/6500 ptas (plus IVA).

Hostal-Residencia Ciutadella (☎ 38 34 62), well located at Carrer Sant Eloi 10, is another good mid-range option. Cosy rooms with dark timber furniture, a phone and private bathroom cost 2500 ptas for singles (available low season only) and from 4000 to 6700 ptas for doubles; tariffs include breakfast.

If both the above places are full, there's always the big and bland *Hotel Alfonso III* (☎ 38 01 50) at Cami de Maó 53 (the main road into town). Rooms range from 2500/4400 to 3000/5800 ptas (plus IVA).

Places to Eat

There's a great collection of bars and restaurants clustered around Ciutadella's small port, many of them set in the old city walls or carved out of the cliffs that line the waterfront. If you join the evening *paseo* and stroll along here you won't have any trouble finding somewhere to eat.

For a good Italian feed, try *Il Palato Fino*

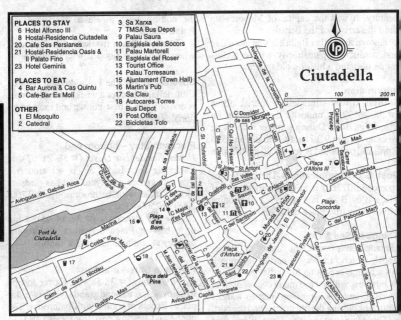

PLACES TO STAY
6 Hotel Alfonso III
8 Hostal-Residencia Ciutadella
20 Cafe Ses Persianes
21 Hostal-Residencia Oasis &
   Il Palato Fino
23 Hotel Geminis

PLACES TO EAT
4 Bar Aurora & Cas Quintu
5 Cafe-Bar Es Molí

OTHER
1 El Mosquito
2 Catedral

3 Sa Xarxa
7 TMSA Bus Depot
9 Palau Saura
10 Església dels Socors
11 Palau Martorell
12 Església del Roser
13 Tourist Office
14 Palau Torresaura
15 Ajuntament (Town Hall)
16 Martin's Pub
17 Sa Clau
18 Autocares Torres
   Bus Depot
19 Post Office
22 Bicicletas Tolo

Ciutadella

0   100   200 m

BALEARIC ISLANDS

– it's out the back of Hostal Oasis' courtyard at Carrer de Sant Isidre 33.

There are a couple of good bar-restaurants on the central Plaça d'Alfons III. *Cas Quintu*'s corner bar has a great tapas selection – try the calamar a la plancha (500 ptas) or the tasty albóndigas (meatballs) (250 ptas) – and the adjoining restaurant offers a menú for 1000 ptas. *Bar Aurora* next door is also worth a visit.

On the opposite corner (topped by a huge white windmill), *Cafè-Bar Es Molí* is a popular tavern set in ancient stone walls, with arched ceilings, old wine barrels and a couple of pool tables.

Entertainment

After dinner, be sure to check out *Sa Clau*, on the waterfront at the bottom of Costa d'es Moll. Set in the old city walls, it's a hip and very stylish little piano bar that features live jazz and blues.

Halfway up Costa d'es Moll, *Martin's Pub*

pumps out throbbing bakalao music most nights until around 4 am.

A little further north at the top of Carrer de sa Muradeta, *El Mosquito* is a funky salsa club with a great vibe. A sign out the front says 'Enjoy El Mosquito', and frankly, it's hard not to.

Sa Xarxa, a music bar over on Carrer de Sant Sebastià, pulls a young crowd of Iggy Pop and Nirvana fans.

Getting There & Away

TMSA (☎ 38 03 03) runs buses between Ciutadella and Maó; its depot is close to the centre at Carrer de Barcelona 8. Autocares Torres (☎ 38 47 20) serves the coast south of Ciutadella; its buses leave from Plaça del Pins.

Getting Around

Bicicletas Tolo (☎ 38 15 76), opposite Hostal Oasis at Carrer de Sant Isidre 28, rent out mountain bikes (700 ptas per day)

Vespas and scooters (1500 to 4200 ptas per day, two-day minimum).

NORTH COAST

Menorca's north coast is rugged and rocky, dotted with numerous small and scenic coves. It's much less developed than the south coast, and with your own transport and a bit of footwork you'll be able to discover some of Menorca's best off-the-beaten-track beaches.

Maó to Fornells

The closest beach to the north of Maó is **Sa Mesquida**, but it isn't very appealing. Further north is **Es Grau**, a fairly plain little village set on an open bay. The beach is okay, and there are a couple of bar-restaurants here (but no accommodation).

Inland from Es Grau and separated from the coast by a barrier of high sand dunes is **S'Albufera d'es Grau**, the largest freshwater lagoon in the Balearic Islands. Home to many species of wetland birds and an important stopover for migrating birds, S'Albufera and the surrounding countryside have been designated the 'nucleus zone' of Menorca's Biosphere Reserve. As such, the area is now a natural park, protected from the ever-growing threat of development. Also included in the park is the island of **Illa d'en Colom**, which is just a couple of hundred metres offshore. There are boat trips across to the island from Es Grau.

Continuing north, it's a great drive from Maó through green and undulating countryside up to **Cap de Favàritx**, a narrow rocky cape at the top of the S'Albufera d'es Grau zone. The last leg of the drive is across a lunar-like landscape of black rock. At the end of the road a lighthouse stands watch while a relentless sea pounds the jagged cliffs.

South of the cape there are some fine sandy bays and beaches which can be reached on foot, including **Cala Presili** and **Platja d'en Tortuga**. If you park just before the gate to the lighthouse and climb up the rocks behind you, you'll see a couple of the beaches that are just waiting for scramblers like yourself to grace their sands.

Fornells

The picturesque and whitewashed town of Fornells is on a large and shallow bay that is popular with windsurfers. A former fishing village, Fornells has been made famous by its waterfront seafood restaurants, most of which serve up the local speciality *caldereta de llagosta*, a lobster stew.

It's a nice place – perhaps too nice, to judge by the steady stream of white-shoe tourists who come here. Another downside of its 'discovery' is that it's an expensive place to eat or sleep in.

Things to See & Do If the sight of those fishing boats bobbing in the bay conjures up romantic imaginings, you could always hire one of Servinautic's (☎ 37 66 36) small motor boats and go exploring. There's also a windsurfing school just south of town.

A couple of km west at **Platjas de Fornells**, the development frenzy has been unleashed on the coastal hills surrounding a small beach. The exclusive villas of the Menorca Country Club resort dominate this ritzy *urbanizació*.

If you want to escape the crowds, continue west to the beach of **Binimella**, from where you can walk around to the unspoilt beaches at **Cala Pregonda**.

Places to Stay There are several hostales in the centre of Fornells. *Hostal La Palma* (☎ 37 66 34), at Plaça S'Algaret 3, offers the best value. Out the back of this bar-restaurant are cheerful rooms with private bathrooms, balconies and views of the surrounding countryside. Singles (not available during summer) cost 3000 ptas, and doubles are 5000 to 5750 ptas.

Right next door, *Hostal-Residencia S'Algaret* (☎ 37 65 52) is relatively overpriced, with B&B ranging from 4770/7000 to 6700/11,300 ptas. Fifty metres along Carrer Major at No 17 is *Hostal Fornells* (☎ 37 66 76), a slick new place with a good pool plus a bar and restaurant. Rooms with all the mod cons range from 3500/5000 to 7000/14,000 ptas.

Places to Eat The restaurants along the fore-shore are all pretty expensive, and if you're here to try caldereta de llagosta you're up for around 5500 ptas.

If you're planning to spend that sort of money head for *Es Cranc*, a couple of hundred metres north of the centre on Carrer de Tramuntana. It has a simple dining room but the food is very good, and it's less touristy than the waterfront places. Steak and seafood dishes are mostly 1400 to 2500 ptas, or you can splash out on caldereta de llagosta (6200 ptas) or paella de llagosta (12,400 ptas for two people).

Near Ciutadella

One thing you realise after exploring the island is that the newly paved and well-signposted roads invariably lead to heavily developed *urbanizacions*. On the other hand, if you find yourself bouncing along a narrow, pot-holed shocker lined with crumbling stone walls, it probably leads somewhere interesting.

A good example is the road from Ciutadella to **Cala Morell**. It's hard to find and bumpy as hell, but it leads to a low-key, tasteful development of whitewashed villas. Steep steps leads down to the small port/beach, which is a blend of sand, rocks, concrete platforms and timber decking and is backed by a couple of bar-restaurants. There's also a rough track leading around the cliffs to the **Cala Morell Necropolis**, a fascinating collection of burial caves which were carved into these coastal cliffs in prehistoric times.

Instead of turning left to Cala Morell, you can also continue straight on to **La Vall**. At the end of the road you come to a set of gates, beyond which is a privately owned nature and wildlife park with a parking area, a small lake and good untouched beaches. The owners charge 600 ptas entry per car; if you want to save money you could try parking further back up the road and walking in. La Vall is open daily from 10 am to 7 pm.

SOUTH COAST

Menorca's southern coastline tends to have the better beaches. Consequently this coast has been the main focus of developers and many of the best beaches are backed by *urbanizacions*, condos and time-share resorts.

After you've travelled around for a while, you start to see a recurring image – a jagged coastline, a small inlet with a sandy beach backed by a growing cluster of modern whitewashed villas. Menorca may not have the long, sweeping beaches of Mallorca, but neither does it have the vast concrete high-rises that have engulfed the larger island. Instead it has opted for smaller-scale developments in the 'Moorish-Mediterranean' style, largely modelled on the resort of Binibeca Vell (south of Maó) that was designed by the architect Antonio Sintes in 1972.

These resorts are perhaps more aesthetically pleasing, but they're still largely the domain of package tourists and time-share touts, and there can be a disconcerting uniformity about them.

South of Ciutadella the coastline is mostly rocky and rugged, with just a couple of smallish beaches at the resorts of **Santandria** and **Cala Blanca**. On the island's south-west corner is the large resort of **Cala en Bosc**, a busy boating and diving centre. Not far east of here are the popular sandy beaches of **Son Xoriguer**, which are connected to Ciutadella by frequent buses.

The stretch of coast between Son Xoriguer and Santa Galdana isn't easily accessible, but as a result it has some of the least spoiled beaches on the south coast. A series of rough tracks and walking trails lead down to the lovely beaches of **Son Saura**, **Cala en Turqueta** and **Es Castellet de Macarelleta** some of these pass through private property and you'll need to ask permission to use them.

South-west of Ferreries is the big resort of Santa Galdana. Two-thirds of the way down this road you'll see *Camping S'Atalai*, a simple and pleasant camping ground shaded by pine trees.

Santa Galdana is just the place to head for if karaoke bars, English pubs, mini-golf courses and huge hotels comprise your idea of a good holiday. If the crowds don't appeal, there are a couple of good beaches on either side of the resort.

Heading west, a walking track leads around the coast to the popular **Macarella**, which has a couple of beach bars, and a little further on is the previously mentioned Es Castellet de Macarelleta. To the east of Santa Galdana is the fine beach of **Cala Mitjana**.

The walking track down to the coast branches off the main road just north of the resort.

Most of the coast south of Maó is more intensively developed. There are regular buses down to the resort of **Punta Prima**, which has one of the nicest beaches. There are a couple of affordable hostales here if you decide to stay: *Hostal Mar Blava* (☎ 15 90 29), one block back from the main beach, has good double rooms from 4000 to 6000 ptas (plus IVA).

Murcia

The autonomous community and province of Murcia, in the south-east of Spain, is framed by the coastal provinces of Alicante (in Valencia) and Almería (Andalucía) and the inland provinces of Albacete (Castilla-La Mancha) and Granada (Andalucía).

The climate is subarid, with little more than 300 mm of annual rain, which is distributed by a system of water wheels, aqueducts and Islamic canals *(acequias)*.

The landscape is diverse, ranging from 250 km of coastline – the Costa Cálida – to extensive mountainous regions with more than 300 peaks, of which at least one, Revolcadores, is more than 2000 metres high. In between are the plateau regions of Jumilla and Yecla, mainly used for wine production, and the fertile orchards of the valley of El Guadalentín, through which the Río Segura and the Río Mula flow. In addition, there are vast areas of dry plains which at present cannot support any agriculture at all.

The highest mountains are to the north-west, in the Moratalla uplands. North of Moratalla is the district of La Puerta, with extensive pine forests crossed by the Benamor and Hondares rivers. In the middle of the province is the Segura valley, its ancient Muslim villages dotted around the rugged countryside of Archena, Ulea and Ojós, sheltered by the red ochre rock of the Sierra de Ricote.

The city of Murcia – the capital of the region and province – has a population of more than 310,000, and sits in the centre of the orchard region, which supplies a large canning industry. On the coast is Cartagena, one of Spain's most important commercial and naval ports, with a population of 175,000. Inland, the former frontier town of Lorca is famous for its spectacular Semana Santa processions.

Also worth a visit is the Parque Natural de Sierra Espuña, a popular destination for climbers and hikers, with 240 sq km of unspoilt highlands.

HIGHLIGHTS

- Semana Santa celebrations in the town of Lorca
- Murcia's Catedral de Santa María
- The variety of architectural styles in Murcia's Casino
- Hiking in the Parque Natural de Sierra Espuña

The telephone code for Murcia province is ☎ 968.

MURCIA

Founded in 825 AD on the site of a Roman colony by Abd ar-Rahman II, caliph of Córdoba, the Islamic town of Mursiya and its surrounding countryside became an independent kingdom in 1224, only to be conquered by Castilla in 1243. Over the years much of Murcia's land was lost to Jaén, Valencia, Albacete, Cuenca, Granada and Almería, until the province was reduced to its present size of 11,300 sq km in 1833.

During the War of the Spanish Succession, the countryside surrounding the city was flooded to defend it against attack by the Austrians. In 1936, during the Spanish Civil War, it was the scene of bitter fighting and many of its churches were burnt down.

Today, despite much industrial growth on the outskirts, it remains an attractive univer-

Murcia

0   20   40 km

CASTILLA - LA MANCHA

VALENCIA

To Albacete

ANDALUCÍA

MEDITERRANEAN SEA

Costa   Cálida

Golfo de Mazarrón

MURCIA

---

sity city, with many of its most important Renaissance monuments intact.

Orientation

The centre of town is immediately north of the Río Segura, using the Puente Viejo (old bridge) as the starting point. The bus station (☎ 29 22 11), is at Calle Sierra de la Pila, a good 20 minute walk west of the centre. The RENFE station is south of the Puente Viejo and a slightly longer walk. Immediately north of the Puente Viejo is Gran Vía Escultor Francisco Salzillo, the main commercial thoroughfare.

All of Murcia's sights are within walking distance, mostly between the river and the university, north-east of the centre. From the cathedral, Calle de la Trapería – the *calle mayor* of medieval and Renaissance Murcia – runs north through the old town and is the heart of the pedestrianised shopping zone.

Information

Tourist Office The municipal tourist office (☎ 21 98 01), on Calle Plano de San Francisco, opens Monday to Friday from 9 am to 2 pm and 5.30 to 7.30 pm, Saturday from 10 am to 1 pm. The regional tourist office (☎ 36

61 00), on Calle San Cristóbal, just north of the casino, keeps the same hours and has information on the whole province.

Money There are plenty of banks with outside ATMs giving cash advances on Visa, MasterCard and American Express, particularly on Gran Vía Escultor Francisco Salzillo and Calle Trapería.

Post & Communications The central post office (postcode 30080) is on Plaza Circular. There is only one phone and fax office, and that's opposite the church in Calle San Lorenzo. It is open Monday to Thursday from 10 am to 2 pm and 6 to 9 pm, Friday from 10 am to 2 pm only.

Medical & Emergency Services In a medical emergency call the Cruz Roja on ☎ 22 22 22. The Hospital General (☎ 25 69 00) is just north of the river at Avenida Intendente Jorge Palacios 1.

The Policía Municipal (☎ 26 66 00) are at Avenida San Juan de la Cruz 12. In an emergency ring ☎ 092.

Catedral de Santa María

On the east side of Plaza Cardenal Belluga, the ornate cathedral – built on the site of a former mosque – is Murcia's most famous monument. Construction work began in Gothic style in 1358, though in the 16th century it was partly rebuilt and from 1748 there were dramatic alterations, including the construction of the baroque façade, designed by Jaime Bort.

Inside, don't miss the 16th century **Capilla de Junterón**, built in Renaissance style by Jerónimo Quijano, who was also responsible for the panelling in the sacristy. For spectacular views of the city, climb the 92-metre Renaissance tower, designed and built by two Italians, Francisco and Jacobo Florentino (not related).

In the 19th century cloister and chapterhouse, the **museo** contains many treasures, including a Roman sarcophagus, a sculpture by Salzillo, an 18th century silver monstrance by Antonio Pérez and a 14th century

altarpiece by Bernabé de Módena. The cathedral and museum are open daily from 10 am to 1 pm and from 5 to 7 pm. Entry to the museum is 200 ptas.

Casino

The casino, at Calle Trapería 22, is a gentlemen's club which opened in 1847. Its decorative façade, completed in 1901, is the work of architect Don Pedro Cerdán Martínez, while the vestibule and Arabic patio were designed by *madrileño* artist Manuel Castraños. The library was designed in 1916 by the English firm Waking Gillow. The building also features an enormous central gallery, a Pompeiian patio, a billiard room, a French ballroom, a ladies' powder room in neobaroque style and a restaurant. It is open daily from 9 am to 11 pm; entry is 100 ptas.

Museums

North of Plaza de Santo Domingo, the **Museo Arqueológico**, in the Casa de Cultura at Gran Vía Alfonso X El Sabio 9, has a fine collection of prehistoric, Roman and Islamic artefacts. Most of the year it is open Monday to Friday from 9 am to 2 pm and 5 to 8 pm, Saturday from 10 am to 1.30 pm. In July, August and September, it is open Monday to Friday from 9 am to 1.30 pm only. Entry is free.

The **Museo de Bellas Artes**, at Calle Obispo Frutos 12, contains works by José de Ribero, Hernández Amores and Martínez Pozo and has a good selection of contemporary art. It is open Monday to Friday from 9 am to 2 pm and 5 to 8 pm, and Saturday from 10 am to 2 pm. In July, August and the first two weeks of September it is open in the morning only. Entry is free.

West of town at Plaza de San Agustín, just before the bus station, is the Ermita de Jesús, a baroque chapel housing the **Museo Salzillo**, devoted to the Murcian sculptor Francisco Salzillo. Born in 1707, he died in 1783, and while his work can be seen in many churches, here you can see the figures carried in the Semana Santa processions which are among the most impressive in Spain. The exhibition also features hi

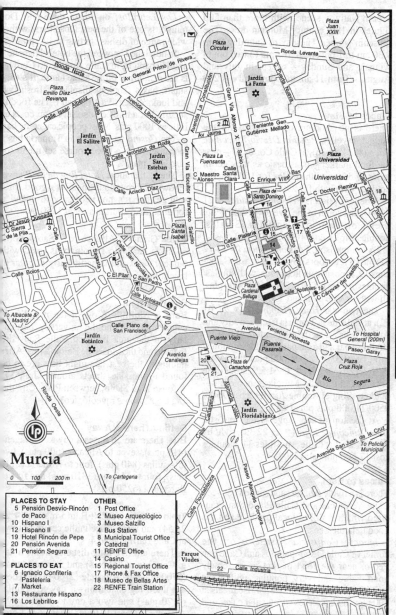

Murcia

0   100   200 m

To Cartegena

PLACES TO STAY	OTHER
5 Pensión Desvío-Rincón de Paco	1 Post Office
10 Hispano I	2 Museo Arqueológico
12 Hispano II	3 Museo Salzillo
19 Hotel Rincón de Pepe	4 Bus Station
20 Pensión Avenida	8 Municipal Tourist Office
21 Pensión Segura	9 Catedral
	11 RENFE Office
PLACES TO EAT	14 Casino
6 Ignacio Confitería Pastelería	15 Regional Tourist Office
7 Market	17 Phone & Fax Office
13 Restaurante Hispano	18 Museo de Bellas Artes
16 Los Lebrillos	22 RENFE Train Station

superb Nativity scene, with more than 500 figures in 18th century Murcian dress. The museum is open Tuesday to Saturday from 9.30 am to 1 pm and 4 to 7 pm (3 to 6 pm in winter), and Sunday – except in July and August – from 11 am to 1 pm. Entry is 200 ptas.

Places to Stay

There is no shortage of pensiones for the budget traveller. *Pensión Desvío-Rincón de Paco* (☎ 21 84 36), at Calle Cortés 27 – near the food market – is as basic as they get in terms of décor, with singles for 1500 ptas or doubles with bath for 2900 ptas.

A better option is *Pensión Avenida* (☎ 21 52 94), just south of the river over the Puente Viejo, on Avenida Canalejas. Singles/doubles/triples cost 1000/3000/5000 ptas.

By comparison, *Pensión Segura* (☎ 21 12 81), just a few doors down at Plaza de Camachos 19, is positively luxurious, with singles/doubles/triples for just 2300/3600/5000 ptas, all with private bath and TV.

The two-star *Hotel Hispano I* (☎ 21 61 52), at Calle de la Trapería 8 (closed July and August), has a wide range of facilities including a bar and a car park. Singles/doubles/triples cost 3500/5500/6000 ptas plus IVA.

Hotel Hispano II (☎ 21 61 52), around the back at Calle Radio Murcia 3, is more upmarket. Singles/doubles/triples cost 7500/9500/11,000 ptas plus IVA.

At the top of the range is the four-star *Hotel Rincón de Pepe* (☎ 21 22 39), right by the cathedral at Calle Apóstoles 34. Doubles cost 17,600 ptas plus IVA.

Places to Eat

There is a lively *market* sandwiched between Calle Verónicas and Calle Plano San Francisco which is full of local produce and has good delicatessens.

Ignacio Confitería Pastelería on the corner of Calle Desamparados and Calle San Pedro, near the food market, is extremely good value and very popular, with great tapas from 175 ptas and two-course meals at 400 ptas. It also serves spectacular cakes and pastries.

Los Lebrillos, on Plaza de Santo Domingo, is one of the best tapas bars, with a wide range of dishes starting at 125 ptas.

Sandwiched between the hotels Hispano I and Hispano II, in Calle Arquitecto Cerdán, is the *restaurant* of the same name. It's very smart, has a fabulous display of fresh fish and looks expensive – but isn't. The food is superb, but a three course set menu costs as little as 1000 ptas. Most people eat at the bar.

The *Casino* on Calle de la Trapería has a restaurant with a three course set menu for just 1100 ptas.

The restaurant at *Hotel Rincón de Pepe* is renowned throughout Spain. It's good for a splurge, but it's not necessary to spend a fortune: main courses start at 1250 ptas.

Cafés Gran Vía Alfonso X El Sabio, north of Plaza de Santo Domingo, is lined with outdoor cafés and is particularly popular at lunchtime.

Entertainment

Bars & Nightlife Most of the nightlife is concentrated around the university, particularly in the area between Calle Saavedra Fajardo and the Museo de Bellas Artes. After midnight, the best late-night bars are to be found in the side streets around Gran Vía Alfonso X El Sabio, between Plaza Circular and the Museo Arqueológico.

Getting There & Away

Bus There are 20 buses a day to Cartagena (415 ptas), seven to Alicante (600 ptas), two to Águilas (840 ptas), four to Almería (2110 ptas), four to Málaga (3810 ptas) and five to Barcelona (5250 ptas).

Train There is a RENFE information (☎ 2. 21 54) and sales office in the centre of town at Calle Barrionuevo 4.

There are five long-distance trains a day to Cartagena (700 ptas) and four to Madrid (5700 ptas) via Albacete (2700 ptas). There are three regional trains a day to Águila (1120 ptas) and two a day to Valencia via Alicante. At least 10 trains a day go to Lorc via Totana, and two of them continue to Granada.

Alicante, Albacete and Valencia provide links to Barcelona.

Car & Motorcycle For Cartagena, take the N-301 southbound. If you're heading north-west, the N-301 also takes you to Albacete and on towards Madrid. For the Parque Natural de Sierra Espuña you need the N-340 to Alhama de Murcia or Totana (the road continues to Lorca, Almería and on to the Costa del Sol). The A-7 runs north-east to Alicante and Valencia.

Getting Around

To get into town from the bus station take the No 3 bus. From the train station take No 9 or No 11.

CARTAGENA

The Iberian settlement of Mastia was captured in around 223 BC by a Carthaginian army led by Hasdrubal and became the town of Carthago Nova. It continued to flourish under the Romans, and under Muslim rule became, for a while, the independent emirate of Cartajana. The Arabs did much to improve its agriculture and it was around this time that Cartagena's reputation for building warships was established.

In 1242 Cartagena was conquered by Fernando III of Castilla. It remains one of Spain's most important commercial and naval ports, and minerals – which have been mined since Carthaginian times – still play a major role in the local economy.

Information

The tourist office (☎ 52 21 31), is right by the port, housed in the Palacio Consistorial, on Plaza del Ayuntamiento. It is open Monday to Friday from 10 am to 1 pm and 5 to 8 pm, Saturday from 10 am to 2 pm.

The post office is on Calle Arco de la Caridad, and the postcode is 30200. There are plenty of free parking spaces at the port. In a medical emergency call the Cruz Roja on ☎ 50 17 27.

Things to See

Right by the quay, at the west end of Paseo de Alfonso XII, is the **Submarino Isaac Peral**, one of the oldest submarines in the world, built in 1888. Nearby are the remains of the **Teatro Romano**, discovered by accident in 1987. The rows of seats were built into the northern side of La Concepción hill, and inscriptions indicate that it was built in 1 BC.

The **Museo Arqueológico Municipal**, north-west of the town centre at Calle Ramón y Cajal 45, is built on the site of the 4th century Roman necropolis of San Antón and contains important Carthaginian, Roman, Visigothic and Muslim antiquities. It is open Tuesday to Friday from 10 am to 1 pm and 4 to 6 pm, Saturday and Sunday from 10 am to 1 pm. Entry is free.

The **Museo Naval**, near Plaza de España at Calle Menéndez Pelayo 8, is open Tuesday to Friday from 10 am to 3 pm and 4 to 6 pm, Saturday from 10 am to 12.30 pm. Entry is free. The **Museo de Arqueología Submarina**, by the lighthouse on the far side of the harbour on Calle Dique de Navidad, has a collection of antiquities recovered from the sea, including exhibits from shipwrecks. It is open Tuesday to Sunday from 10 am to 3 pm. Entry is 400 ptas.

The **Iglesia de Santa María de Gracia**, on Calle San Miguel, was originally built in the 18th century and contains several works by Salzillo. It is open daily from 8 to 10 am and 7 to 9 pm.

Places to Stay & Eat

Pensión Isabelita (☎ 50 77 35), just around the corner from the tourist office on Plaza José María Artés, has perfectly acceptable doubles with/without bath for 3300/2700 ptas.

Hotel Peninsular (☎ 50 00 33), also very central at Calle Cuatro Santos 3, is extremely comfortable and has singles/doubles with private bath and telephone for 3500/5000 ptas plus IVA. Facilities include bar, laundry, fax service and moneychanging facilities.

A 10 minute walk from the port, the two star hotel *Los Habaneros* (☎ 50 52 50), at

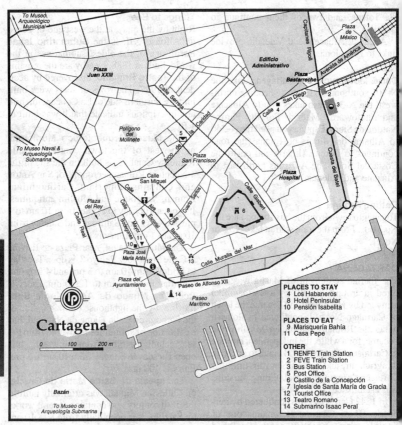

MURCIA

Cartagena

0   100   200 m

Bazán

To Museo de
Arqueología Submarina

PLACES TO STAY
4 Los Habaneros
8 Hotel Peninsular
10 Pensión Isabelita

PLACES TO EAT
9 Marisquería Bahía
11 Casa Pepe

OTHER
1 RENFE Train Station
2 FEVE Train Station
3 Bus Station
5 Post Office
6 Castillo de la Concepción
7 Iglesia de Santa María de Gracia
12 Tourist Office
13 Teatro Romano
14 Submarino Isaac Peral

Calle San Diego 60, is a step up in luxury, with doubles for 6000 ptas plus IVA.

Most of the bars and restaurants are concentrated around Plaza del Ayuntamiento, Plaza José María Artés and the side streets off Calle Mayor. Quality and prices tend to be pretty similar.

Opposite Pensión Isabelita is *Casa Pepe*, where you can get a menú for 850 ptas. Particularly highly rated is the very traditional *Marisquería Bahía*, Calle Escorial 6, which specialises in paellas and fresh fish. A menú there costs 1100 ptas. For more up-market surroundings, try the restaurant at *Los Habaneros*, where a menú costs 1250 ptas.

Getting There & Away

There are 12 buses day to Los Alcázares (350 ptas) on the Mar Menor, two to Águilas and Almería (700 ptas), and two to Lorca (635 ptas).

There are four trains a day to Madrid (5700 ptas) via Albacete (3400 ptas) and Murcia (700 ptas), and one to Valencia via Alicante and Murcia. For Lorca, change at Murcia.

If you're driving, the N-332 will take you

north-east to Los Alcázares and on to Alicante, or west to Mazarrón and on to Águilas.

THE COSTA CÁLIDA

The Costa Cálida (Warm Coast) stretches either side of Cartagena, from the **Mar Menor** (Lesser Sea) to **Águilas**. It is the Mar Menor which attracts the most tourists: a salt-water lagoon of 170 sq km, separated from the sea by a narrow strip of land known as **La Manga**, which is 22 km long.

With an average depth of seven metres, the water in the Mar Menor is so warm that you can swim at virtually any time of year, and with a high salt and iodine content it is said to be very therapeutic – so much so that every year thousands of tourists cover themselves in the healing muds of the Mota de la Calcetera, close to Lo Pagán.

Resorts such as **Los Alcázares** are very popular with the Spanish and are well served by tourist facilities, but the cheaper accommodation gets booked up pretty quickly.

West of Cartagena, on the Golfo de Mazarrón, the coast is much quieter. The main resorts are Puerto de Mazarrón and Águilas, with very little development in between and some beautiful, unspoilt beaches.

LORCA

In Roman times Lorca, then known as Illurco, was a modest stopover on the road between the Pyrenees and Cádiz, but by the Visigothic era it was fundamental to the defence of the kingdom of Murcia owing to its strategic position on the border of the Muslim region Al-Andalus. It finally fell to the Muslims, who called it Lurka, in around 780 AD.

On 23 November 1243, the same day Fernando III took Sevilla, his son – the future Alfonso X El Sabio – reconquered Lorca, though the city continued to be raided by the Muslims until the fall of Granada.

Orientation & Information

Lorca sits on the banks of the Río Guadalentín and is overlooked by a 13th century castle. The tourist office (☎ 46 61 57), at Calle Lope Gisbert 12, is open Monday to Friday from 9.30 am to 2 pm and 5 to 7.30 pm. The post office is at Calle Musso Valiente 1. The postcode is 30800.

There is an underground car park in the centre of town, just 100 metres south-west of the tourist office.

Things to See

The **Centro de Artesanía**, beside the tourist office, sells traditional arts and crafts and some fairly funky stuff too. It is open Monday to Friday from 10 am to 2 pm and 5 to 8 pm.

The 17th century **Casa de los Guevara** is a splendid example of baroque architecture; unfortunately, all you can see of it is the inside of the tourist office as the rest of the building is currently undergoing restoration.

There are more baroque buildings around the **Plaza de España**, otherwise known as Plaza Mayor, in the centre of town. These include the **Pósito y Juzgados**, a 16th century public granary, now the courthouse, and the **Casa Consistorial**, which is now the *ayuntamiento*. Most impressive of all is the **Colegiata de San Patricio**: its façade is baroque but the interior is mostly Renaissance. It is open daily from 11 am to 1 pm and 4.30 to 6.30 pm.

Peculiar to Lorca are two extraordinary museums – one for the Blancos and another for the Azules – featuring the magnificent embroidery used in the Semana Santa processions. The **Museo de Bordados del Paso Blanco**, on Plaza de Santa Domingo, is open Monday to Friday from 11 am to 1 pm and 5 to 7 pm; entry is 200 ptas. The **Museo de Bordados del Paso Azul**, at Calle de Nogalte 7, is open Monday to Friday from 11 am to 1 pm and 5 to 8 pm; entry is free.

The **Museo Arqueológico**, on Plaza de Juan Moreno, is open Monday to Friday from 11 am to 2 pm and 5 to 8 pm, Saturday and Sunday from 11 am to 2 pm. Entry is free.

Special Events

Lorca is renowned throughout Spain for its Semana Santa celebrations, in which two

MURCIA

brotherhoods – the Azules (Blues) and the Blancos (Whites) – have competed every year since 1855 to see who can put on the most lavish display.

Places to Stay & Eat

For some bizarre reason there is only one pensión in the centre of town: the spotless *Hostal del Carmen* (☎ 46 80 06) at Rincón de los Valientes 3. Singles/doubles cost 2500/4000 ptas with bath; basic doubles cost 3000 ptas. To find it, turn into Calle Cuesta San Francisco from the underground car park, then take a left. The hostal is in a tiny square on the right after Calle Andrés Pascual – the fifth turning on the right from the Cruz Roja building.

The other options are quite a hike over the other side of the river, so it's a good excuse to have a splurge. The three star *Hotel Alameda* (☎ 40 66 00), at Calle Musso Valiente 8, has rooms for 4000/7000 ptas plus IVA, and the modern, four star *Jardines de Lorca* (☎ 47 05 99), on Alameda Rafael Méndez, has doubles for 9000 ptas plus IVA.

For the best tapas in town head for *Casa Roberto*, at Calle Musso Valiente 5. *Rincón de los Valientes*, right next to the Hostal del Carmen, serves fine fare, with a menú for 1000 ptas. *Jardines de Lorca* has its own excellent restaurant with a menú for 1500 ptas plus IVA.

Getting There & Away

There are eight buses a day to Murcia (395 ptas), two to Almería (800 ptas) and three to Granada (1515 ptas). The bus station is in the centre, about 150 metres south of the tourist office. There are more than 10 trains a day to Murcia (515 ptas).

By road, the N-340/E-15 runs south-west to Almería or north-east to Murcia via Totana and on (as the A-7/E-15) to Alicante.

PARQUE NATURAL DE SIERRA ESPUÑA

A 40 minute drive south-west of Murcia towards Lorca, just north of the N-340, the Parque Natural de Sierra Espuña is a paradise for hikers and climbing enthusiasts, with 240 sq km of unspoilt highlands. Emerging from the sprawling pine forests are towering limestone formations, of which the most impressive is **La Pared Sur del Valle de Leiva** (the south wall of the Leiva valley). The park is home to the mouflon (Barbary sheep), a species introduced from Africa whose main Spanish habitat is here.

In the north-western part of the park you can see the Pozos de la Nieve (snow wells), built in the 16th century. The snow was compressed into ice and transported to nearby towns and cities in the summer – a practice which lasted until earlier this century.

Access to the park is best via Alhama de Murcia or Totana. For further details pick up a map from the tourist office in Murcia or Lorca.

Andalucía

This large region stretching right across the south of Spain is one of the country's most diverse. In simple geographic terms, it consists of two east-west mountain chains divided by the fertile valley of the Río Guadalquivir. Of the two mountain chains, the Sierra Morena rolls along Andalucía's borders with Extremadura and Castilla-La Mancha, while the Sistema Penibético is a complicated mass of rugged *sierras* broadening out, wedge-shaped, from the southwest to the east; it includes mainland Spain's highest peak, Mulhacén (3478 metres), in the Sierra Nevada south-east of Granada. The Mediterranean coastline is mostly a narrow plain, which includes not only the intensively developed Costa del Sol west of Málaga, but also, east of Almería – you'll be delighted to discover – rugged Cabo de Gata, where there are some very beautiful and relatively untouched beaches. Andalucía's Atlantic coast, known as the Costa de la Luz, also has magnificent beaches and is little developed.

The regional capital, Sevilla, is notorious for its extreme heat in summer, yet winters in the inland towns can be chilly, and snow lies for most of the year on the high peaks of the Sierra Nevada. The Sierra de Grazalema in the south-west, exposed to Atlantic winds, is the wettest and one of the greenest parts of Spain; the deserts of Almería in the east are the driest and one of the brownest. Some of these wild, beautiful back-country regions – many of them now under a degree of protection as *parques naturales* – offer great walking and climbing and opportunities for many other activities. Bear in mind, though, that July and August can be oppressively hot away from the coast. The best seasons for walking in most of Andalucía are from about mid-April to mid-June, September and the first half of October. In the west, Andalucía's only national park, Doñana, protects part of the Guadalquivir delta, with its huge bird population.

HIGHLIGHTS

- Sevilla, the magical capital of the south
- The pretty patios and mesmerising Mezquita of Córdoba
- Granada, the city with Spain's greatest Muslim heritage in the Alhambra and the Albaicín, but a buzzing modern life too
- Green and mountainous Parque Natural Sierra de Grazalema, dotted with white villages
- The mysterious valleys of Las Alpujarras, huddled beneath Spain's highest mountain range, the Sierra Nevada
- A succulent seafood dinner watching the sun go down over the Guadalquivir estuary at Sanlúcar de Barrameda
- Flamingos – at Laguna de Fuente de Piedra, Parque Nacional de Doñana or Cabo de Gata
- Cabo de Gata, where semidesert meets the Mediterranean along a coastline of isolated beaches and dramatic cliffs
- The Costa de la Luz – long, sandy, little-developed Atlantic beaches
- Fiestas: Semana Santa and the Feria de Abril in Sevilla, *carnaval* in Cádiz, the Horse Fair at Jerez de la Frontera, almost any weekend at El Rocío, and many more

Andalucía's famously vibrant people are perhaps even more addicted to fiestas, music, colour, spectacle and fun than other Spaniards. This is the heartland of *flamenco* and bullfighting. Sevilla's Semana Santa processions (see the boxed aside later in this chapter) are the most magnificent in the

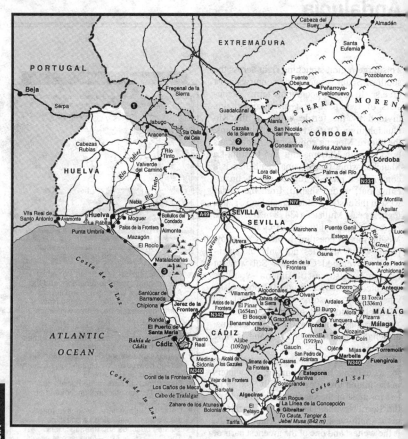

country; Cádiz's *carnaval* and Sevilla's
Feria de Abril (April fair) are two of the
biggest parties you could ever hope to find;
and the annual festive pilgrimage known as
the Romería del Rocío (see the boxed aside)
is probably the largest religious (or quasi-
religious) event in Europe. Yet nearly every
other town and village, too, holds its own
Semana Santa processions and summer
feria. If you're here in mid-July, don't miss
the sight of flotillas of gaily bedecked boats
putting out from every harbour on the coast
for a ceremonial blessing of the waters on the
Día de la Virgen del Carmen.

History

Andalucía's natural blessings have long
favoured the development of prosperous
civilisations. Some time around 1500 or
1000 BC the vanished civilisation of Tartessus (biblical Tarshish) flourished here –
perhaps between Cádiz and Huelva. In
Roman times Andalucía was the most civilised area in the empire outside Italy.

Andalucía was the obvious base for the
Muslim invaders who started arriving from
Africa in the 8th century. Córdoba (until the
11th century), then Sevilla (until the 13th),
and finally Granada (until the 15th) took

NATIONAL PARKS & RESERVES
1. Parque Natural Sierra de Aracena y Picos de Aroche
2. Parque Natural Sierra Norte
3. Parque Nacional de Doñana
4. Parque Natural Los Alcornocales
5. Parque Natural Sierra de Grazalema
6. Parque Natural Sierra de las Nieves
7. Parque Natural Sierra Subbética
8. Parque Natural de Cazorla, Segura y Las Villas
9. Parque Natural Sierra Nevada
10. Parque Natural de Cabo de Gata-Níjar

Andalucía

MEDITERRANEAN SEA

ANDALUCÍA

turns as the leading city of Muslim Spain, which was known as Al-Andalus (from which the modern name Andalucía comes). At its peak, Córdoba ruled most of Spain and Portugal. Andalucía's Islamic heritage – great buildings such as the Alhambra in Granada, the Mezquita in Córdoba, the Alcázar and Giralda in Sevilla, plus countless other castles, towers, and villages – is one of its most fascinating aspects today.

The Christian Reconquista arrived in the 13th century when the north and west of Andalucía, including Córdoba and Sevilla, fell, leaving the Emirate of Granada as the last bastion of Al-Andalus. Granada held out till 1492, when it fell to the Catholic Monarchs, Fernando and Isabel. Columbus' discovery of America the same year brought great wealth to Sevilla, and later Cádiz, the ports through which most of the trade with the new continent was conducted. But Andalucía's Castilian conquerors effectively killed off its deeper source of prosperity by handing out great swathes of territory to their nobles, who set sheep to run on irrigated food-growing lands. Spain's decline in the 17th to 19th centuries bit as hard here as anywhere. Peasants went hungry while the owners of huge estates either let the land go to seed or sold what they produced.

By the late 19th century Andalucía – especially the west – was a hotbed of rural unrest. During the Spanish Civil War it split along class lines: savage atrocities were committed by both sides, most notoriously in Granada, Málaga and Sevilla after they fell to the Nationalists. The hungry years after the war were particularly hungry in Andalucía, and hundreds of thousands of people left to work in the industrial cities of northern Spain.

The overall improvement in the Spanish economy since the 1960s, plus the tourism boom, of which Andalucía has been a prime beneficiary, have made a difference. Andalucía's major cities today are bright, cosmopolitan places, its people increasingly well educated, and rural poverty has been dealt a blow by government subsidies. Yet unemployment still runs at over 30% in six of its eight provinces.

Books & Publications

A nice little guide you can pick up locally is *Excursions in Southern Spain* by David Baird, which details 40 mainly off-the-beaten track trips in Andalucía. It's motorist-oriented but useful for anyone. Walkers might find the *Hiking* booklet, sold for around 600 ptas by most main Andalucían tourist offices, handy. Though its 'maps' are barely sketches, and its route descriptions perfunctory at best, it does list 25 walks in each province and can serve as a useful basic planning tool.

El Giraldillo, a monthly what's-on magazine covering all Andalucía, is useful for tracking down flamenco concerts, fiestas and other events. You can pick it up free at some tourist offices, or access it on the Internet (http:\\www.elgiraldillo.es).

Medical & Emergency Services

Throughout Andalucía, you can call ☎ 061 in a serious medical emergency.

Youth Hostels

Andalucía's youth hostels are mostly good, modern places with a high proportion of twin rooms. The central booking office is Inturjoven (☎ 95-455 82 93; fax 95-455 82 92), Calle del Miño 24, Los Remedios, 41011 Sevilla. You can also book with the hostels themselves. Standard prices for under-26s are 900/1100 ptas in the low/high season (1050/1250 ptas with breakfast), and for 26 and overs 1200/1400 ptas (1350/1550 ptas with breakfast). At the Córdoba, Granada, Málaga, Almería and Sevilla hostels the high season is all year; at Jerez de la Frontera it's April to September; at Sierra Nevada it's December and February to April; at other hostels it's from mid-June to mid-September, long weekends year round, and the Easter school holidays. The prices include sheets but you must add IVA.

Getting There & Away

If you're heading on to Morocco from Andalucía by ferry, you have a choice of at least five departure ports: Almería, Málaga, Gibraltar, Algeciras (the busiest) and Tarifa. Details of services are given in each city entry in this chapter. Anyone coming back from Morocco with a vehicle should expect rigorous customs searches on arrival.

Sevilla Province

The wonderful city of Sevilla overshadows the rest of the province, but country-lovers could head out to the Parque Natural Sierra Norte, while travellers heading east have the option of stopping off at interesting old towns such as Carmona and Osuna.

The telephone code for Sevilla province is ☎ 95.

SEVILLA

Sevilla, capital of the south with 700,000 people, is one of the most exciting cities in Spain. It takes a stony heart not to be captivated by its unique atmosphere – stylish, confident, magnificent, ancient, proud yet also relaxed, convivial, intimate, joyful and fun-loving. One of the first people recorded as falling in love with Sevilla was the Muslim poet-king Al-Mutamid in the 11th century. The place works its old enchantment every bit as well today.

Except along the banks of the Río Guadalquivir – navigable to the Atlantic Ocean 100 km away and source of Sevilla's greatness in times past – this is not a city of great long vistas. The beauty of its dense centre unfolds more subtly as you wend your way around its narrow streets and small plazas. Its two great monuments – the Muslim Alcázar and the Christian *catedral* – reveal most of their splendour only once you're inside them.

A great city in Muslim times and again in the 16th and 17th centuries, Sevilla has known bad times, too, so it knows how to enjoy the good ones when they come. The year 1992, when the eyes of the world turned on Sevilla's world Expo, was one of the best. You might think the atmosphere today was still a carry-over from 1992 if you didn't know that Sevilla has been throwing one of Spain's wildest parties, the Feria de Abril, every year for more than a century, or that just before the feria, during Semana Santa, it stages processions which have few rivals for the title of the most magnificent in the country.

Aside from its historic and artistic sights and other inner-city attractions, the city enjoys some good green parks on the fringes of the centre. It's also one of the homes of flamenco and bullfighting, and has a lively entertainment scene. But above all, Sevilla is an atmosphere. Being out on its streets among its happy, celebratory crowds on a warm night is a not-to-be-forgotten experience. To put it in one Spanish word, the city has *alegría*.

There are a couple of catches, of course. One is that Sevilla is expensive. You might pay 5000 or 6000 ptas for a room that would cost 3000 ptas in other towns. And prices go even higher during the two big festivals (if you can get a room). Another thing to bear in mind is that Sevilla gets obscenely hot in July and August and is not much fun to be in. Locals, sensibly, leave the city then.

History

The Taifa Kings The Romans and Visigoths called Sevilla Híspalis. Under the Romans it was a significant town, especially as a port, but overshadowed by Córdoba. Come the Muslims, who called it Ishbiliya, Sevilla again began by playing second fiddle to Córdoba. But after the collapse of the Córdoba Caliphate in 1031 Sevilla became the most powerful of the small *taifa* states into which Al-Andalus broke up. By 1078 it held sway from the Algarve to Murcia. Its Abbadid dynasty rulers Al-Mutadid (1042-69) and Al-Mutamid (1069-91) were both poets, too, and Al-Mutamid was the first of a long line of rulers to succumb to the city's powers of enchantment, presiding over a languid, hedonistic court in the Alcázar.

Almoravids & Almohads When Toledo fell to the Christians in 1085, the scared Al-Mutamid asked the Muslim fundamentalist Berber rulers of Morocco, the Almoravids, for help against the growing northern threat. The Almoravids came, defeated Alfonso VI, and went back to Morocco – but then returned in 1091 to help themselves to Al-Andalus, too. The harsh Almoravids persecuted Jews and Christians, reunified Al-Andalus and ruled it from Marrakesh as a colony. But their austere grip soon weakened – partly, it seems, because of the charms of Al-Andalus. A new strict Muslim Berber sect, the Almohads, displaced the Almoravids in Morocco, then moved into Al-Andalus, which they had under full control by 1173. Arts and learning revived under the Almohads: Caliph Yacoub Yousouf rather liked Sevilla, making it capital of his whole realm (which included Algeria and Tunisia as well as Morocco and Al-Andalus), and building a great mosque where the cathedral now stands. His successor Yousouf Yacoub al-Mansour added the Giralda tower and thrashed the Christian armies at Alarcos in 1195. The Christians,

ANDALUCÍA

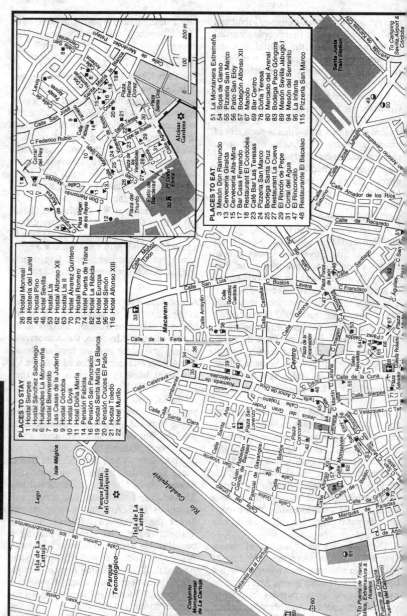

PLACES TO STAY

1 Hostal Sierpes
2 Hostal Sánchez Sabariego
5 Huéspedes La Montoreña
6 Hostal Pino
7 Hostal Bienvenido
8 Las Casas de la Judería
9 Hostal Córdoba
10 Hostal Goya
12 Hotel Doña María
14 Pensión Fabiola
16 Pensión San Pancracio
19 Hostal Santa María La Blanca
20 Pensión Cruces El Patio
21 Hostal Toledo
22 Hotel Murillo
26 Hostal Monreal
28 Hostería del Laurel
45 Hostal Pino
46 Hotel Sevilla
53 Hostal Lis
62 Hostal Alfonso XII
63 Hostal Lis II
70 Hotel Alvarez Quintero
73 Hostal Romero
74 Hotel Puerta de Triana
82 Hotel La Rábida
84 Hotel Europa
96 Hotel Simón
116 Hotel Alfonso XIII

PLACES TO EAT

3 Mesón Don Raimundo
13 Cervecería Giralda
15 Cervecería Alta-Mira
17 Bar Casa Fernando
18 Restaurant El Cordobés
23 Café Bar Las Teresas
24 Pizzería San Marco
25 Bodega Santa Cruz
27 Restaurant La Cueva
29 El Rincón de Pepe
31 Corral del Agua
47 El Rinconcillo
48 Restaurante El Bacalao
51 La Montanera Extremeña
54 Sopa de Ganso
55 Pizzería San Marco
56 Patio San Eloy
57 Bodegón Alfonso XII
67 Manolo
69 Bar Centro
78 Doña Teresa
80 Mercado del Arenal
83 Bodega Paco Góngora
89 Mesón Sevilla Jabugo
94 Mesón del Serranito
95 La Infanta
115 Pizzería San Marco

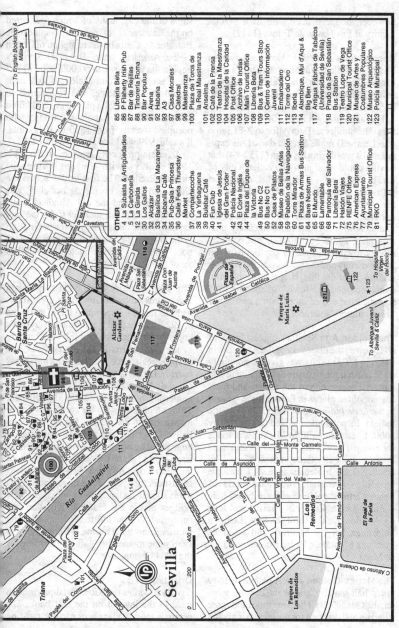

however, bounced back with their pivotal victory at Las Navas de Tolosa (1212).

Reconquista After this, Almohad power in Spain dwindled, enabling Castilla's Fernando III El Santo (the Saint) to capture several major Andalucían cities culminating in Sevilla, after two years siege, in 1248.

Fernando brought in 24,000 Castilian settlers. His intellectual son Alfonso X El Sabio (the Learned) made Sevilla one of his capitals and it was during his reign (1252-84) that Sevilla could most justly be called a city of three cultures – Christians, *mudéjares* (Muslims under Christian rule) and Jews. By the 14th century Sevilla was the most important Castilian city, but the reign of the monarch who loved it more intensely than any other, Pedro I (1350-69), was beset by bloody royal feuds and by conflict between the monarchy and the nobles (see the Alcázar section later in this chapter). A pogrom which emptied the Jewish quarter in 1391 signalled the end of more than a century of 'three cultures' tolerance.

The Golden Age Sevilla's biggest break of all followed the discovery of the Americas in 1492. In 1503 the city was given a monopoly on Spanish trade with the new continent and rapidly became one of the richest and most cosmopolitan places in Europe – the *'puerto y puerta de Indias'* (port and gateway of the Indies). Its population tripled to 150,000 by 1600. Even though little Madrid was made the national capital in 1561, Sevilla remained Spain's major city through most of the 17th century. Lavish Renaissance and baroque buildings sprouted, and many stars of Spain's artistic golden age were based here – artists such as Zurbarán, Murillo and Juan de Valdés Leal (though Sevilla-born Velázquez left for Madrid), and sculptors Martínez Montañés, Pedro Roldán and Juan de Mesa.

The Not-so-Golden Age A plague in 1649 killed half the city, and as the century wore on, the Guadalquivir became more and more silted up and difficult for the increasingly big ships of the day, many of which foundered on the sandbar at its mouth by Sanlúcar de Barrameda. Cádiz began to siphon off much of the American trade. By 1700 Sevilla's population was down to 60,000, and in 1717 the Casa de la Contratación, which controlled this commerce, was transferred to Cádiz. Another Sevilla plague in 1800 killed 13,000. Then the Napoleonic troops who occupied the city from 1810 to 1812 stole, it's said, 999 works of art when they left.

A certain prosperity returned in the mid-19th century with the beginnings of industrialisation. The first bridge across the Guadalquivir, the Puente de Isabel II, was built in 1845, and the old Almohad walls were knocked down in 1869 to let the city expand. While the majority of the population in the city and the countryside remained very poor, romantics were attracted by Sevilla's air of faded grandeur.

The 20th Century Middle-class optimism was expressed by Sevilla's first great international fair, the Exposición Iberoamericana of 1929, but the civil war brought everyone's hopes to nothing. The city fell very quickly to the Nationalists at the start of the war despite resistance in the working class *barrios*. Urban development from the 1950s onwards did little for the look of the city, with numerous historic buildings demolished. Things looked up with the coming to power in Madrid of the PSOE, led by *sevillano* Felipe González, and the city was given a huge boost by being chosen to hold the 1992 Expo world fair, on the 500th anniversary of the discovery of America. As well as millions of visitors that year and a huge boost to its international image, Sevilla got eight new bridges across the Guadalquivir, the new super-fast AVE rail link to Madrid, and many thousand new hotel rooms. It's now trying to keep some momentum going by bidding for the 2004 Olympics.

Orientation

Sevilla straddles the Río Guadalquivir, with most of the interest on the east bank. The centre is mostly a tangle of narrow, twisting

ANDALUCÍA

old streets and small plazas, with the exception of Plaza Nueva and Avenida de la Constitución, which runs south from Plaza Nueva. Just east of Avenida de la Constitución are the cathedral, the Giralda tower and the Alcázar fortress palace, the city's major monuments. The quaint Barrio de Santa Cruz, immediately east of the cathedral and Alcázar, has a good many budget lodgings.

The main transport terminals are on the periphery of the central area: Santa Justa train station 1.5 km north-east of the cathedral at Avenida Kansas City s/n, the Plaza de Armas bus station one km north-west of the cathedral near the Puente de Chapina bridge, and the Prado de San Sebastián bus station 750 metres south-east of the cathedral on Plaza San Sebastián.

Information

Tourist Offices The main tourist office is at Avenida de la Constitución 21 (☎ 422 14 04). Open weekdays from 9 am to 7 pm and Saturday from 10 am to 2 pm, it's often very busy. It has a list of over 30 foreign consulates in the city. There are also two municipal tourist offices – one south of the centre at Paseo de las Delicias 9 (☎ 423 44 65), open Monday to Friday from 8.30 am to 6.30 pm, the other on Calle de Arjona by the Puente de Isabel II (☎ 421 36 30), open weekdays from 9 am to 8.45 pm, and on weekend mornings.

Money There's no shortage of banks and ATMs in the central area. American Express on Plaza Nueva cashes banknotes and travellers' cheques commission-free. Santa Justa station has ATMs, and an exchange office giving poor rates.

Post & Communications The main post office (postcode 41080) is at Avenida de la Constitución 32, opposite the Archivo de Indias. Sevilla has two Internet cafés where you can access the Net over a coffee or a *bocadillo*. Both are on Calle Betis on the west bank of the Guadalquivir: Big Ben at No 54 charges 500 ptas for 30 minutes

access; Café Metro is at No 29. Both also offer e-mail receiving services.

Bookshops Librería Beta at Avenida de la Constitución 9 and 27, and Calle Sierpes 81, has guidebooks and novels in English, and maps. For a wider choice of books in English, there's the English Bookshop out east of the centre at Calle Marqués del Nervión 70.

Laundry Tintorería Roma at Calle Castelar 4 will wash, dry and fold a load of washing for 1000 ptas. It's open weekdays from 9.30 am to 1.30 pm and 4.30 to 8.30 pm, Saturday from 9.30 am to 1.30 pm.

Medical & Emergency Services The main general hospital is the Hospital Virgen del Rocío (☎ 424 81 81) at Avenida Manuel Siurot s/n, one km south of the Parque de María Luisa. For an ambulance call ☎ 442 55 65. The Policía Municipal (☎ 092) are in the Pabellón de Brasil, Paseo de las Delicias 15 (at the south end of the Parque María Luisa), and the Policía Nacional (☎ 091) are on Plaza Concordia.

Dangers & Annoyances Sevilla has a reputation for petty crime against tourists – pickpockets, bag-snatchers and the like – so take care.

Catedral & Giralda

Sevilla's immense cathedral stands on the site of the main Almohad mosque. After Sevilla fell to the Christians in 1248 the mosque was used as a church until 1401, when in view of its decaying state the church authorities decided to knock it down and start again. 'Let us create such a building that future generations will take us for lunatics,' they agreed – or so legend has it. They certainly got themselves a big church. Some 160 metres wide and 140 metres long, it's surpassed in area among the world's cathedrals only by St Peter's (Rome) and St Paul's (London). The building, whose architect is unknown, was completed by 1507 – all Gothic, though the work done after its central

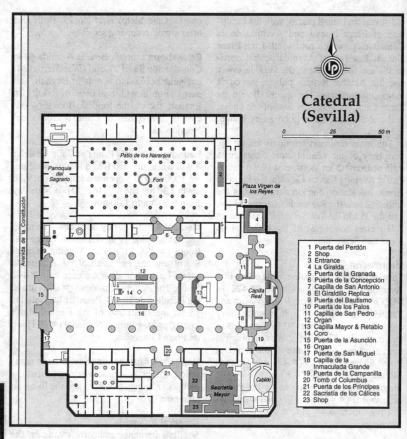

Catedral (Sevilla)

0   25   50 m

1 Puerta del Perdón
2 Shop
3 Entrance
4 La Giralda
5 Puerta de la Granada
6 Puerta de la Concepción
7 Capilla de San Antonio
8 El Giraldillo Replica
9 Puerta del Bautismo
10 Puerta de los Palos
11 Capilla de San Pedro
12 Organ
13 Capilla Mayor & Retablo
14 Coro
15 Puerta de la Asunción
16 Organ
17 Puerta de San Miguel
18 Capilla de la
   Inmaculada Grande
19 Puerta de la Campanilla
20 Tomb of Columbus
21 Puerta de los Príncipes
22 Sacristía de los Cálices
23 Shop

Patio de los Naranjos
Parroquia del Sagrario
Font
Plaza Virgen de los Reyes
Avenida de la Constitución
Capilla Real
Sacristía Mayor
Cabildo

dome collapsed in 1511 was mostly in Renaissance style.

Apart from the Puerta del Perdón on Calle Alemanes (a survival from the pre-1401 building), the bulky exterior of the cathedral gives few hints of the treasures within. More impressive from outside is La Giralda, the tower on its east side.

Over 90 metres high but with foundations only a few metres deep, La Giralda was the minaret of the mosque, and was constructed nearly all in brick in 1184-95. Its proportions, delicate patterned brick decoration and colour – which changes with the light – make

it perhaps Spain's most perfect Islamic building. The topmost parts of La Giralda – from the bell level up – were added in the 16th century, when Spanish Christians were busy 'improving on' surviving Islamic buildings. Opinion divides over whether the addition complements or spoils the rest of La Giralda. It's topped by a bronze weather vane representing Faith and known as El Giraldillo, which is something of a symbol of Sevilla.

Entry The entrance to the cathedral and tower is beside La Giralda, on Plaza Virgen de los Reyes. Both are open Monday to Saturday from 11 am to 6 pm, Sunday from 2 to 5 pm, with last entry one hour before closing time. Entry is 600 ptas (students and pensioners 200 ptas). The Giralda alone is open on Sunday from 10.30 am to 1.30 pm (300 ptas).

Patio de los Naranjos Immediately inside the entrance, this was once the courtyard of the mosque and is still planted with over 60 orange trees. You enter the cathedral proper by the Puerta de la Granada in the patio's south-east corner. Hanging from the roof just outside this entry are a stuffed crocodile – a gift in 1260 to Alfonso X from the Sultan of Egypt, who hoped to marry Alfonso's daughter – and an elephant's tusk, said to have been found in the Roman amphitheatre at Itálica.

La Giralda Turn left inside the cathedral for the climb up to La Giralda's belfry. The ascent is quite easy as there's a series of ramps (not stairs) all the way up. The climb affords great views of the forests of flying buttresses and pinnacles around the outside of the cathedral, as well as of the city beyond.

Cathedral Chapels Back down inside the broad, five-naved cathedral, the sheer size of the place is obscured by the welter of interior structures typical of Spanish cathedrals. These constitute a storehouse of art and artisanry as rich as any church in the country. It's a good idea to start with a wander along the rows of chapels on the north and south sides. As you take in your surrounds, don't forget to look up from time to time to admire the marvellous Gothic vaulting and tracery.

The side chapels hold riches of sculpture, stained glass and painting which have filled books of their own. The westernmost one on the north side has a replica of El Giraldillo. Next to it is the Capilla de San Antonio with Murillo's large 1666 canvas depicting the vision of St Anthony of Padua; thieves cut out the kneeling saint in 1874, but he was later found in New York and put back.

Columbus' Tomb Inside the south door, the Puerta de los Príncipes (so called because it has always been the one favoured by royalty, being the closest to the Alcázar), stands the tomb of Christopher Columbus. The great sailor's remains were brought here from Cuba in 1899. The monument, by Arturo Mélida from about the same time, shows four crowned sepulchre-bearers representing the four kingdoms of Spain at the time of Columbus' voyage: Castilla (carrying Granada on the point of its spear), León, Aragón and Navarra.

Coro Right in the middle of the cathedral is the large *coro* (choir) with 117 carved Gothic-mudéjar stalls. The lower ones have marquetry representations of La Giralda on their seats and show vices and sins on the misericords (the front parts of the movable sections of the seats).

Capilla Mayor East of the coro is the Capilla Mayor, whose Gothic *retablo* is the jewel of the whole cathedral and is said to be the biggest altarpiece in the world. Begun by the Flemish sculptor Pieter Dancart in 1482 and completed by others by 1564, this sea of polychrome and gilded wood holds more than 1000 carved biblical figures. At the centre of the lowest level is the 13th century silver-plated cedar image of the Virgen de la Sede, patroness of the cathedral.

Eastern Chapels East of the Capilla Mayor, in the east wall of the cathedral, are more chapels. The central of these is the Capilla Real (Royal Chapel). The silver and bronze tomb of Fernando III stands in front of the altar (he's mummified inside); the tombs of his son, Alfonso X, and wife, Beatrice of Swabia, are at the sides. The Capilla de San Pedro, immediately north, has a retablo with nine fine Zurbarán paintings of the saint's life.

Sacristía de los Cálices In the south-east corner of the cathedral is a group of rooms which hold some of the building's main art treasures. Westernmost of these is the

ANDALUCÍA

Sacristía de los Cálices, which was built in 1509-37 – architecturally a bridge between the Gothic and Renaissance eras. Goya's painting of the Sevilla martyrs *Santas Justa y Rufina* (1817) hangs above the altar; they died at the hands of the Romans, but that didn't stop Goya putting the Giralda and the cathedral in the background. The other art is from the 16th and 17th centuries and includes Zurbarán's *San Juan Bautista*.

Sacristía Mayor This large, domed room east of the Sacristía de los Cálices is a plater-esque creation of 1528-47: its portal arch has carvings of 16th century foods. Pedro de Campaña's 1547 *Descendimiento*, above the central altar at the south end, and Zurbarán's *Santa Teresa* to its right, are two of the cathedral's masterpieces. Murillo's *San Leandro* and *San Isidoro* face each other across the room. (The pair were leading figures of the Visigothic church in Sevilla; Isidoro is the one who's reading.) This room also holds some of the cathedral's most important treasures, among them a huge 475-kg silver *custodia* (monstrance) made in the 1580s by Juan de Arfe; 17th century images of San Fernando (Fernando III) and La Inmaculada which, like the monstrance, are carried in Sevilla's Corpus Christi pro-cessions; and, in one of the glass cases, the city keys handed over to Fernando III when he took Sevilla.

Cabildo The beautifully domed, oval chap-terhouse was created in 1558-92 for meetings of the cathedral hierarchy, to the design of Hernán Ruiz, architect of the Giralda belfry. At the base of the dome, above the archbishop's throne at the south end, is a Murillo masterpiece, *La Inmacu-lada*. There are also eight Murillo saints around the dome at the same level.

Alcázar

The Alcázar (fortress) is more palace than fort. Built originally for Sevilla's Muslim rulers in the 10th century, it was later taken over by the Christian monarchs of Castilla, some of whom used it as a permanent resi-dence. As recently as 1995 it staged the wedding feast of the Infanta Elena, daughter of King Juan Carlos I, after her marriage in Sevilla's cathedral. The Alcázar has been adapted and/or enlarged in almost every century since its foundation, which makes it complicated to understand but in the end only adds to its fascination. It's an intriguing and beautiful place that shouldn't be missed, not least for its associations with the lives and loves of several famous rulers, above all the extraordinary Pedro I (1350-69), known either as El Cruel or as El Justiciero – the Justice-Dispenser – depending on which side you were on.

History The Alcázar was founded as a fort for the Córdoban governors of Sevilla in 913. As Sevilla prospered in the 11th century, its taifa rulers built themselves a palace called Al-Muwarak, the Blessed, in the western part of the present Alcázar, partly on the site of the present Palacio de Don Pedro. East of this, the 12th century Almohad rulers added another palace around the Patio del Crucero. When Sevilla fell to the Christians in 1248, Fernando III moved into the Alcázar, dying here in 1252. His son Alfonso X replaced the Almohad palace with a Gothic one, now called the Salones de Carlos V. In 1364-66 Pedro I created the Alcázar's crown jewel, the sumptuous mudéjar palace known as the Palacio de Don Pedro, partly on the site of the old taifa rulers' palace. The Catholic Monarchs, Fernando and Isabel, set up court in the Alcázar for several years as they prepared for the conquest of Granada. The whole complex was further adapted and expanded by later rulers, who also created the Alcázar's beautiful gardens.

Entry The entrance is the Puerta del León at the southern corner of Plaza del Triunfo. The Alcázar is open Tuesday to Saturday from 10.30 am to 5 pm (June to September. from 10 am to 1.30 pm and 5 to 7 pm), Sunday and holidays from 10 am to 1 pm. Entry is 600 ptas (free for students with ID).

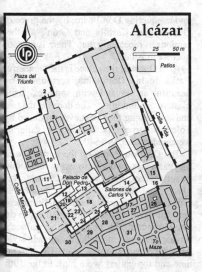

Alcázar

0   25   50 m

Patios

Plaza del Triunfo

Calle Vida

Calle Miranda

Palacio de Don Pedro

Salones de Carlos V

To Maze

1	Patio de Banderas
2	Puerta del León
3	Patio del León
4	Sala de la Justicia
5	Patio del Yeso
6	Apeadero
7	Jardín de la Alcabilla
8	Patio del Crucero
9	Patio de la Montería
10	Salón del Almirante
11	Sala de Audiencias
12	Cuarto del Príncipe
13	Cámara Regia
14	Salón de Tapices
15	Jardín del Chorrón
16	Puerta del Palacio de los Duques de Arcos
17	Entrance to Baños de Doña María de Padilla
18	Patio de las Doncellas
19	Patio de las Muñecas
20	Cuarto del Techo de los Reyes Católicos
21	Jardín del Príncipe
22	Salón del Techo de Felipe II
23	Salón de Embajadores
24	Sala de Infantes
25	Salón del Techo de Carlos V
26	Estanque de Mercurio
27	Jardín de las Danzas
28	Jardín de Troya
29	Jardín de las Galeras
30	Jardín de las Flores
31	Jardín de las Damas

Patio del León This was the garrison yard of the Al-Muwarak palace. Off its south-east corner is the **Sala de la Justicia**, with beautiful mudéjar plasterwork and an *artesonado* ceiling. It was built in the 1340s by Alfonso XI, who disported here with his mistress Leonor de Guzmán. Alfonso's sexual exploits left his heir Pedro I with five half-brothers and a severe case of sibling rivalry. Pedro is said to have had a dozen friends, cousins and half-brothers murdered in his efforts to hang on to his throne. One of the half-brothers, Don Fadrique, met his maker right here in the inaptly named Sala de la Justicia. The room leads on to the pretty **Patio del Yeso**, one of the few surviving parts of the Almohad palace.

Patio de la Montería The rooms on the west side of this courtyard were part of the original Casa de la Contratación founded by the Catholic Monarchs in 1503. The **Salón del Almirante** has 19th and 20th century paintings showing historical events associated with Sevilla. The **Sala de Audiencias** contains the earliest known painting on the subject of the discovery of the Americas (by Alejo Fernández, 16th century), in which

Columbus, Fernando El Católico, Carlos I, Amerigo Vespucci and American Indians can all be seen sheltered beneath the cloak of the Virgen del Buen Aire. Also here is a model of Columbus' ship the *Santa María*.

Patio del Crucero The passage off the Patio de la Montería's east side leads onto this garden, which corresponds to the upper of two levels of the patio of the Almohad palace. Originally this upper level consisted only of raised walkways which met in the middle. On the lower level grew orange trees, the fruit from which could be plucked at hand height by the lucky folk strolling along above. The lower level was built over in the 18th century to support the surrounding buildings after earthquake damage. There's a Pedro I angle to this bit of the Alcázar, too. Ever a man of extremes and notwithstanding the fact that he was married

ANDALUCÍA

to a French princess, Pedro loved to distraction a woman called María de Padilla and gave her the Salones de Carlos V, on the south side of the patio, to live in. María must have liked oranges for the patio is also known as the Patio de María de Padilla.

Palacio de Don Pedro Whatever else Pedro I may have done, posterity owes him a great big thank you for creating this palace.

Unable to trust many of the 'Christians' from closer to home, Pedro maintained a long-standing alliance with the Muslim Emir of Granada, Mohammed V, the man chiefly responsible for the decoration of the Alhambra's Casa Real. So when in 1364 Pedro decided to build himself a new palace in the Alcázar, Mohammed sent along many of his best artisans to help. These were joined by Jews and Muslims from Toledo, and others, mainly Muslim, from Sevilla. Their work not only represented the best of contemporary architecture and design but also drew on the earlier traditions of the Almohads and caliphal Córdoba. What resulted is a uniquely magnificent synthesis of Iberian Muslim art.

Inscriptions on the palace's relatively austere façade, on the Patio de la Montería, encapsulate the unusual nature of the whole enterprise. While one records that the building's creator was 'the very high, noble and conquering Don Pedro, by the grace of God king of Castilla and León', another reminds us repeatedly that 'There is no conqueror but Allah'.

At the heart of the palace is the wonderful **Patio de las Doncellas**, surrounded by beautiful arches and with some exquisite plasterwork and tiling. The doors at the two ends are among the finest ever produced by Toledo's carpenters. The upper galleries were added later, in 1540.

The **Cámara Regia** on the north side of the patio has two rooms with incredibly beautiful ceilings and more wonderful plaster and tilework. The rear room was probably the monarch's bedroom. From here you can move west into the small **Patio de las Muñecas**, the heart of the palace's private quarters, with delicate Granada-style decoration on its lowest level. The mezzanine and top gallery were built in the 19th century for Isabel II, using plasterwork brought from the Alhambra. The **Cuarto del Príncipe** to the north has superb ceilings and was probably the queen's bedroom.

The spectacular **Salón de Embajadores** (Hall of Ambassadors), on the west side of the Patio de las Doncellas, was Pedro I's throne room – as it had been, in earlier form, of the Al-Muwarak palace. Its fabulous wooden dome of multiple star patterns, symbolising the universe, was added in 1427.

✱ ✱

The Red King, the Black Prince & a Big Red Stone

Three centuries before Pedro I set to work on the Salón de Embajadores, the taifa poet-king Al-Mutamid had held soirées here and sung of his beloved, Rumaykka. Pedro put the place to other uses. When his buddy Mohammed V was deposed in Granada by a rival known as the Red King, Pedro invited the Red King to Sevilla and laid on a banquet in the Salón de Embajadores. Armed men suddenly leapt from hiding and seized the Red King and his retinue of 37. All were killed outside the city a few days later.

Legend has it that Pedro's main motive for this deed was to get his hands on a particularly fabulous ruby in the Red King's possession. Later Pedro gave the jewel to England's Edward, the Black Prince, an ally in his struggles with his most troublesome half-brother, Enrique de Trastámara (known to history as Henry the Bastard).

Mohammed V got his kingdom back and the Black Prince helped Pedro keep a lid on Enrique and the nobles who backed him. But when Edward eventually went home (with the ruby), Enrique turned nasty again, and Pedro wound up stabbed to death by his sibling in a tent. The ruby – described by England's Elizabeth I as 'great as a racket ball' – today sits in the Tower of London as part of the English royal crown. ∎

✱ ✱

The dome's shape gives the room the alternative name Sala de la Media Naranja (Hall of the Half Orange). The coloured plasterwork is equally magnificent. The door arches, heavily reminiscent of the Medina Azahara palace near Córdoba, were retained by Pedro from the Al-Muwarak building. On the west side the beautiful **Arco de Pavones** archway – named after its peacock motifs – leads into the **Salón del Techo de Felipe II**, with a Renaissance ceiling created in 1589-91. The **Salón del Techo de Carlos V** to the south has another fine ceiling (1540s) and used to be the palace chapel.

Salones de Carlos V Reached by a staircase from the south-east corner of the Patio de las Doncellas, these are the much remodelled rooms of the Gothic palace built in the 13th century by Alfonso X. It was here that Alfonso's intellectual court gathered and that, a century later, Pedro I installed María de Padilla. The Salón de Tapices or Sala Grande has a collection of huge tapestries showing Carlos I's 1535 conquest of Tunis from the Turkish-backed pirate Barbarossa.

Gardens From the Salones de Carlos V you can make your way out into the Alcázar's large and lovely gardens, the perfect place to ease your body and brain after some intensive sightseeing. The gardens extending in front of the Salones de Carlos V and Palacio de Don Pedro go back to Muslim times but were mostly brought to their present form in the 16th and 17th centuries, while those to the east, beyond a long Almohad wall, are 20th century creations. Immediately in front of the Salones de Carlos V, and extending round to the west side of the Palacio de Don Pedro, is a series of small linked gardens, some with pools and fountains. From one, a passage runs beneath the Salones de Carlos V to the so-called **Baños de Doña María de Padilla**. Here you can see the vaults beneath the Patio del Crucero and a grotto which replaced that patio's pool – in which, we imagine, María de Padilla liked to bathe.

From the new gardens you can return by the **Puerta del Palacio de los Duques de Arcos** to the corner of the Salones de Carlos V, whence a passage leads north to the **Apeadero**, built in 1607-09 as an entrance hall for the palace and now housing a collection of old carriages. From here you leave the Alcázar by the **Patio de las Banderas**, which was the garrison yard of the original 10th century fort.

Archivo de Indias

This building on the west side of Plaza del Triunfo has since 1785 been the main archive on the conquest and colonisation of Spain's American empire. It houses over 40 million documents dating from 1492 through to the end of the empire in the 19th century. Most can only be consulted with special permission, but there are rotating displays of fascinating maps and documents. Entry is free, and it's open Monday to Friday from 10 am to 1 pm.

Barrio de Santa Cruz

This area immediately east of the cathedral and Alcázar was Sevilla's medieval *judería* (Jewish quarter); today it is a tangle of quaint, winding streets and lovely plant-decked plazas. If you're not staying in the area, you should have a wander through it anyway: there are some good places to stop off for food or drink as you go. The judería extended to just east of Calle Santa María La Blanca. The modern barrio's most characteristic plaza is Plaza de Santa Cruz, with a central cross made in 1692 which is one of the finest examples of Sevilla wrought-iron work.

The Centre

The real centre of Sevilla stretches north of the cathedral. It's a densely packed zone of narrow, crooked streets, broken up here and there by plazas around which the life of the city has revolved for aeons.

Plaza de San Francisco & Calle Sierpes

Site of a market in Muslim times, Plaza de San Francisco has been Sevilla's main public and ceremonial square since the 16th

ANDALUCÍA

century. Formerly the scene of Inquisition burnings and executions of criminals, today it's the place where the upper echelons sit on special viewing stands to watch the Semana Santa processions. The *ayuntamiento* (city hall) on the west side was built in the 1530s.

Calle Sierpes, heading north from the plaza, is the main shopping street. Now pedestrianised and without some of its famous old cafés, it has lost some of the animation it must once have had, but is still considered the best place to take the pulse of the city.

Plaza Salvador This was the forum of Roman Híspalis. Now a very popular spot for an open-air drink in the evening, the plaza is dominated by the **Parroquia del Salvador**, a big red baroque church built in 1674-1712 on the site of a mosque. Inside are three huge and profuse baroque retablos, and on the north side the mosque's old patio remains, with orange trees, font, and Roman columns with Visigothic capitals. The church is open Monday to Saturday from 8.30 to 10.30 am and 6.30 to 9 pm, Sunday (except September) from 10.30 am to 2 pm and 7.30 to 9 pm.

Casa de Pilatos One explanation for the name of this finest of Sevilla's noble mansions, on Plaza Pilatos, is that its 16th century creator, Don Fadrique Enríquez de Ribera, was trying to imitate Pontius Pilate's palace in Jerusalem, which he had visited. The building is a handsome mixture of diverse architectural styles: the main courtyard, for instance, has mudéjar plasterwork, 16th century tiling, a Renaissance fountain and Roman sculpture. There's a chapel, gardens, and upper rooms with frescos, tapestries and an art collection to explore. It's open daily from 10 am to 7 pm, though the cost is a bit steep at 500 ptas for each of the two floors.

To the River
A short walk west from the south end of Avenida de la Constitución brings you to the east bank of the Río Guadalquivir, a pleasant place for a stroll.

Torre del Oro This 13th century Muslim watchtower, on the riverbank just north of the Puente de San Telmo, crowned a corner of the Almohad city walls. It was originally covered in golden tiles, hence its name. Inside is the small, crowded Museo Marítimo (maritime museum), open Tuesday to Friday from 10 am to 2 pm, Saturday and Sunday from 11 am to 2 pm (100 ptas).

Hospital de la Caridad A block back from the river at Calle Temprado 3, this still functioning hospital for the elderly is the fruit of the funds and labour of a notorious 17th century libertine, Miguel de Mañara, who changed his ways after experiencing a vision of his own funeral procession. Its church is adorned with a collection of top-class 17th century Sevillan art on the theme of death and redemption through mercy, commissioned by Mañara. Valdés Leal's frightening masterpieces *In Ictu Oculi* (In the Blink of an Eye) and *Finis Gloriae Mundi* flank the west door. Four Murillo paintings along the side walls illustrate the mercy theme. They show Moses drawing water from the rock, the miracle of the loaves and fishes, St John of God (San Juan de Dios) caring for an invalid, and Isabel de Hungría curing the sick.

Mañara is buried at the foot of the high altar, the retablo of which illustrates the ultimate act of mercy – the burial of the dead (in this case Christ). The sculpture is by Pedro Roldán.

The church is open Monday to Saturday from 10 am to 1 pm and 3.30 to 6 pm (closed on holidays).

Plaza de Toros de la Real Maestranza Sevilla's bullring on Paseo de Cristóbal Colón is one of handsomest in the country, and probably the oldest (building began in 1758). Sevilla is one of Spain's bullfighting capitals, and it was in rings such as this and the one at Ronda that bullfighting on foot (instead of horseback) took off in the 18th century. The ring has a museum, open Monday to Saturday from 10 am to 1 pm.

Museo de Bellas Artes Sevilla's fine arts museum, at Plaza del Museo 9 just off Calle Alfonso XII, has an outstanding collection of Spanish art, housed in a beautiful former convent. It's strongest on Sevillan 'golden age' artists such as Murillo, Zurbarán and Valdés Leal, but also holds works by El Greco and Velázquez. It's open Tuesday to Sunday from 9 am to 3 pm and is free for EU citizens (250 ptas for others).

South of the Centre
Antigua Fábrica de Tabacos Sevilla's massive former tobacco factory on Calle San Fernando – workplace of Bizet's operatic heroine Carmen – was erected in the 18th century and served its original purpose until the mid-20th century. The factory had its own jail, stables for its 400 mules, 21 fountains, 24 patios, 10 wells, and even a nursery since most of its workers were women. It's now part of the Universidad de Sevilla and you can wander in daily at any time between 9 am and 9 pm.

Parque de María Luisa A large area south of the Fábrica de Tabacos was transformed for the Exposición Iberoamericana of 1929. It's spattered with all sorts of fancy and funny buildings, many of them harking back to eras of past glory. In its midst the Parque de María Luisa is a fine respite from the hustle of the city, with its maze of paths, flowers, fountains, shaded lawns and 3500 trees of over 100 species. It's open daily from 8 am to 10 pm.

On Plaza de América in the south end of the park is Sevilla's **Museo Arqueológico**. A highlight of its big collection is the hoard of gold jewellery known as the Tesoro del Carambolo, from the mysterious Tartessus culture. There are also good Iberian and Roman sections, the latter including mosaics, a fine *Venus* from Itálica, and busts of the Itálica-born emperors Hadrian (Adriano, sporting a Gorgon-head helmet), and Trajan (Trajano). Facing it is the **Museo de Artes y Costumbres Populares**, in the exhibition's mudéjar pavilion, which appeared as an Arab palace in *Lawrence of Arabia*. Its collection ranges over the clothing, furniture, ceramics and gold and silver ware of Sevilla province from the Reconquista to today. Both museums are open Tuesday to Sunday from 9 am to 2.30 pm and are free.

Plaza de España Facing the north-east side of the park across Avenida de Isabel la Católica, Plaza de España is one of the city's favourite rest and recreation spots, with mini-canals where you can splash around in rowing boats. Around it is the most grandiose of the constructions for 1929, a semicircular brick and tile confection in neo-mudéjar and neo-Renaissance styles.

Isla de La Cartuja
Not quite an island, this tongue of land between two branches of the Guadalquivir, north-west of the centre, was the site of Expo 92. Since the great year it has had a chequered history, and by 1996 large expanses lay unused. However, things look set to take off again and there's already enough going on to make a visit worthwhile. The easiest approach from the city centre is by the Puente de Chapina (also called Puente del Cachorro). Puerta de Triana, the southern end of the site, is just west of this bridge. Bus Nos C 1, C 2 and C 3 (see Getting Around at the end of this section), and No 5 from Puerta de Jerez, all go to Puerta de Triana.

The **Puerta de Triana** area, reopened in 1996, features a Pabellón de la Navegación (shipping pavilion) with exhibits on sea exploration, focusing on Sevilla's role (400 ptas), a replica of Magellan's ship the *Victoria* (250 ptas), and a Torre Mirador (lookout tower; 250 ptas), all open Tuesday to Sunday from 10 am to 1 pm and 5 to 8 pm. Just to the north is the **Conjunto Monumental de La Cartuja**, a 15th century monastery where Columbus used to stay. His body lay here from 1507, the year after his death, to 1542. In 1838 the monastery was bought by a Liverpudlian, William Pickman, who turned it into a ceramics factory and built the five

Semana Santa in Sevilla

Every day from Palm Sunday to Easter Sunday, large, lavishly bedecked images and whole life-size tableaux of Passion scenes are carried from the city's churches through the streets to the Catedral, accompanied by long processions which may take more than an hour to pass, and watched by vast crowds. The origins of these rites go back to the 14th century but they took on their present form in the 17th, when many of the images – some of which are supreme works of art – were created.

The processions are organised by over 50 different *hermandades* or *cofradías* (brotherhoods, some of which include women). Each normally has two *pasos*, as the decorative platforms bearing the images are called. The first carries an image of Christ, crucified or bearing the cross or in a scene from the Passion; the second holds an image of the Virgin. The pasos are carried by teams of bearers called *costaleros*, about 40 per paso, who work in relays. The pasos are heavy – each costalero normally carries about 50 kg – and they move with a swaying motion to the rhythm of their accompanying music and the commands of their *capataz* (leader). Each pair of pasos has between 400 and 2500 costumed followers, known as *nazarenos*. Many of these wear tall pointed capes which cover their heads except for narrow eye slits. The most contrite go barefooted and carry crosses.

Each day from Palm Sunday to Good Friday, seven or eight hermandades leave their churches in the afternoon or early evening and arrive between 5 and 11 pm at Calle Campana at the north end of Calle Sierpes. This is the start of the *carrera oficial* which all then follow – along Calle Sierpes, through Plaza San Francisco and along Avenida de la Constitución to the Catedral, which they enter at the west end and leave at the east, emerging on Plaza Virgen de los Reyes. They get back to their churches some time between 10 pm and 3 am.

The climax of the week is the *madrugada* (early hours) of Good Friday, when some of the most respected and/or popular hermandades file through the city. The first to reach the carrera oficial, about 1.30 am, is the oldest hermandad, El Silencio, which goes in complete silence. Next, about 2 am, comes Jesús del Gran Poder, whose almost wizened Christ, sculpted in 1620 by Juan de Mesa, is one of the masterpieces of Sevillan sculpture. This is followed about 3 am by La Macarena whose Virgen de la Esperanza (or simply La Macarena) is the most passionately adored of all: created about 1700 by an unknown artist, she's the patron of bullfighters and the city's supreme representation of the grieving yet hoping Virgin. Then comes El Calvario with an extraordinary crucifixion sculpture of 1612 by Francisco de Ocampo, followed by Esperanza de Triana from the Triana barrio across the river, and finally about 6 am Los Gitanos, the gypsy hermandad. La Macarena's return about 1.30 pm to her church, the Basílica de la Macarena at Calle Bécquer 1, is attended by enormous crowds.

On the Saturday evening, just four hermandades make their way to the Catedral, and finally, on Easter Sunday morning, one: the Hermandad de la Resurrección.

There are marked differences between the styles of the hermandades. City centre hermandades, such as El Silencio, are traditionally linked with the bourgeosie. They're serious and austere, with

tall, bottle-shaped kilns which stand incongruously beside the monastery buildings. The whole complex was restored for Expo 92. It's open Tuesday to Sunday from 11 am to 9 pm (October to March to 7 pm). Entry is 300 ptas (free for EU citizens on Tuesday).

From here you can wander further north among the exotic exhibition buildings in what's slowly being turned into a technology industries park. Near the riverbank, a big post-Expo theme park-funfair called the Parque de los Descubrimientos closed in 1995, but a replacement, **Isla Mágica**, was due to start up in June 1997. The north end of the Isla de la Cartuja, beyond the Viaducto del Alamillo, will be the site for the 2004 Olympic Games if Sevilla's bid for the games succeeds.

Language Courses

For information on courses at the university, contact the Instituto de Idiomas, Universidad de Sevilla (☎ 455 14 93; fax 456 04 39), Calle Palos de la Frontera s/n, 41004 Sevilla. the main tourist office can give you a list of over 20 private colleges, and the Centro de Información Juvenil near the Torre del Oro on the east bank of the Guadalquivir, open Monday to Friday from 10 am to 2 pm and 5.30 to 8.30 pm, also has information on courses. One school with a solid reputation and beginners' courses starting every two

little or no music, and wear black tunics usually without capes and tied with esparto grass. Hermandades from the working class barrios outside the centre, such as La Macarena, are less sombre, with brass and drum bands accompanying more brightly bedecked pasos. Their nazarenos wear coloured, caped tunics, often of satin, velvet or wool. They also, of course, have to come from further away, and some are on the streets for more than 12 hours.

Programmes giving each hermandad's schedule and route are widely available during Semana Santa, but the best source of information is *ABC* newspaper, which has maps showing their churches, recommended viewing spots *(lugar recomendado)* and all manner of other detail. It's not too hard to work out which procession will be where and when, and pick one up on the way through its own barrio or even as it leaves or re-enters its church, which are always emotional moments.

Crowds along most of the carrera oficial make it hard to get much of a view there, unless you manage to get one of the seats, which go for anything from about 900 ptas on Plaza Virgen de los Reyes to as much as 3000 ptas at the top of Calle Sierpes. But if you arrive early enough in the evening, you can usually get close enough to the west or east end of the cathedral to see plenty without paying.

If you're not in Sevilla for Semana Santa, you can get an inkling of what it's about by visiting some of the churches where the famous images are housed. La Macarena and the Iglesia de Jesús

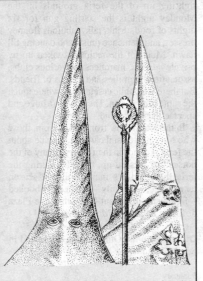

Nazarenos in pointed capes follow the *pasos* through the streets to the cathedral in Sevilla's daily Semana Santa processions.

del Gran Poder, on Plaza de San Lorenzo, are both in the working-class Macarena district, two km north of the Catedral. The *Cristo del Calvario* is in the Iglesia de la Magdalena, Calle de Bailén 5-7. All three churches are open daily from at least 9 to 11 am and 6.30 to 9 pm, and the first two have museums displaying the images' lavish vestments. ■

weeks is CLIC (☎ 437 45 00; fax 437 18 06), Calle Santa Ana 11, 41002 Sevilla (near Alameda de Hércules).

Organised Tours

Open-topped double-decker buses run by Sevirama and Guide Friday operate continuous one-hour city tours daily from 10 am to 8 pm from Paseo de Cristóbal Colón, 100 metres north of the Torre del Oro. There's earphone commentary in a choice of eight languages. Price is 1300 ptas (800 ptas for pensioners and children). The Compañía Hispalense de Tranvías runs tours from the same spot in converted trams, with live commentary.

There are also several daily one-hour river cruises (1000 ptas) from the *embarcadero* (jetty) by the Torre del Oro.

Special Events

Sevilla's lavish Semana Santa processions (see the boxed aside) and its Feria de Abril, the fair which follows a week or two later, are two of Spain's most famous and exciting festivals.

Feria de Abril Sevilla's April Fair, in the second half of the month, is a kind of release after the relative solemnity of Semana Santa. It takes place on a special *recinto* (site), El Real de la Feria, in the Los Remedios area west of the Guadalquivir. The ceremonial lighting up of the feria grounds on the Monday night is the starting gun for six nights of food, drink, talk, fabulous flouncy dresses, and flamenco music and dancing till dawn. Much of the recinto is taken up by private *casetas*, marquees for various clubs, associations, families and groups of friends. But there are public casetas, too, where much the same fun goes on. There's also a huge and spectacular fairground.

In the afternoons, from about 1 pm, those who have horses and carriages parade about the feria grounds in their finery (many of the horses are dressed up, too). It's during the feria that Sevilla's major bullfight season takes place, with daily – and heavily booked – fights starting about 6.30 pm at the Plaza de Toros de la Real Maestranza.

Other Festivals

Other events celebrated in Sevilla include:

5 January
> *Cabalgata de los Reyes Magos* – a very popular parade in which the Reyes Magos (Three Kings) and others throw sweets to the crowds

24-26 July
> *Velá de Santiago* – fiesta of the Triana barrio on the west side of the Guadalquivir

September, even-numbered years
> *Bienal de Flamenco* – one of the country's major flamenco festivals, with events most nights of the month in various locations

Places to Stay

The summer prices given here can come down substantially from October to March, but during Semana Santa and the Feria de Abril they can go up by anything from 20% to 200%, and you should book ahead, too.

Places to Stay – bottom end

Camping *Camping Sevilla* (☎ 451 43 79) is about six km from the centre on the N-IV highway to Córdoba. Prices are 450 ptas per person, 450 ptas per car and 395 ptas per tent.

Youth Hostel The *Albergue Juvenil Sevilla* (☎ 461 31 50) was closed for renovation but may be open by the time you get there. It's at Calle Isaac Peral 2, about 10 minutes by bus No 34 from opposite the main tourist office.

Hostales & Pensiones Barrio de Santa Cruz, close to the cathedral and Alcázar, has lots of places, some of them reasonably good value. The area north of Plaza Nueva, only 10 minutes walk from all the hustle and bustle, is another good bet.

Barrio de Santa Cruz *Hostal Monreal* (☎ 421 41 66), Calle Rodrigo Caro 8, is one of the bigger places with 18 rooms at 2675/4065 ptas for singles/doubles, or 6420 ptas for doubles with bath. *Pensión San Pancracio* (☎ 441 31 04), Plaza de las Cruces 9, has poky singles for 1800 ptas and bigger doubles for 3200 ptas, or 4000 ptas with bath. *Pensión Cruces El Patio* (☎ 422 96 33), Plaza de las Cruces 10, has one dorm room with beds at 1200 ptas, singles at 2500 ptas, and doubles at 4000 and 5000 ptas. Some rooms have shower and toilet. The friendly and well-kept *Hostal Toledo* (☎ 421 53 35), Calle Santa Teresa 15, has 10 clean singles/doubles, all with bath, for 2500/5000 ptas. Except during Semana Santa and the Feria de Abril, they lock the door at 1 am.

Hostal Santa María La Blanca (☎ 442 11 74), Calle Santa María La Blanca 28, has spotless, modern doubles for 3000 ptas, or 4000 ptas with bath. Among several places on Calle Archeros, the 13 room *Hostal Bienvenido* (☎ 441 36 55) at No 14 has singles for 1500 or 1700 ptas, doubles for 3000 ptas. The small *Huéspedes La Montoreña* (☎ 441 24 07), Calle San Clemente 12, has clean, simple singles/doubles at 1500/3000 ptas. Its sign just says 'Huéspedes Camas'.

Not far north of Barrio de Santa Cruz, the 10 room *Hostal Sánchez Sabariego* (☎ 441 44 70) at Corral del Rey 23, with a nice little courtyard, has decent singles/doubles with bath for 2000/4000 ptas.

North of Plaza Nueva *Hostal Pino* (☎ 421 28 10), Calle Tarifa 6, in an old building with a small courtyard, has decent, sizeable rooms for 1600/2600 ptas or 2000/3200 ptas with shower. *Hostal Lis II* (☎ 456 02 28), in a beautiful house at Calle Olavide 5, charges 1700 ptas for singles and 3500 ptas for doubles with toilet. The singles are on the small side. The same family owns the 10 room *Hostal Lis* (☎ 421 30 88), Calle Escarpín 10, where singles/doubles with shower are 2000/3500 ptas. There's a nice tiled lobby. The friendly, 10 room *Hostal Alfonso XII* (☎ 421 15 98), in a nice old building at Calle Monsalves 25, has singles for 2000 ptas and doubles with bath for 4000 ptas.

Places to Stay – middle
Barrio de Santa Cruz *Pensión Fabiola* (☎ 421 83 46) at Calle Fabiola 16, with a plant-filled courtyard, has simple, well-kept rooms for 4000/6500 ptas, or 8000 ptas for doubles with bath. The singles are small. *Hostal Córdoba* (☎ 422 74 98), nearby at Calle Farnesio 12, has singles/doubles for 4500/6000 ptas, and doubles with bath for 7000 ptas. Prices in both places can come down a bit if business is slow. *Hostal Goya* (☎ 421 11 70), Calle Mateos Gago 31, is a bit bigger, with singles/doubles with shower for 4000/5800 ptas.

Hostería del Laurel (☎ 422 02 95), above a characterful old bar at Plaza de los Venerables 5, has 20 clean and simple rooms with bath or shower for 6500/8500 ptas (more in April and May). *Hotel Murillo* (☎ 421 60 95), Calle Lope de Rueda 7, is bigger, with doubles at 7000 ptas.

Not far north of Barrio de Santa Cruz at Corral del Rey 22, *Hostal Sierpes* (☎ 422 49 48) is a good-value larger place with a restaurant, bar, garage space, singles with bath for 4300 ptas, and doubles with shower or bath from 4300 to 6700 ptas. They'll pay your taxi fare from the train or bus station.

West of Avenida de la Constitución This is a good central location. *Hotel Simón* (☎ 422 66 60), Calle García Vinuesa 19, in a fine 18th century Sevillan house, has 29 very pleasant rooms at 5350/7500 ptas for singles/doubles with bath (6420/10,165 ptas

in April and May). Breakfast is available. The 16 room *Hotel Europa* (☎ 421 43 05), Calle Jimios 5, has a nice old-fashioned tiled lobby and decent, quite sizeable rooms with TV for 5000/7000 ptas plus IVA. The bigger *Hotel La Rábida* (☎ 422 09 60), Calle Castelar 24, has an impressive lobby with a fountain, a restaurant, and good rooms with bath at 5600/8825 ptas.

North & West of Plaza Nueva *Hotel Sevilla* (☎ 438 41 61), Calle Daóiz 5, is good value at 6000 ptas plus IVA for doubles with bath. *Hostal Romero* (☎ 421 13 53), Calle Gravina 21, has ordinary rooms with shared bath at 3500/7000 ptas, but a nice courtyard. *Hotel Puerta de Triana* (☎ 421 54 04), Calle Reyes Católicos 5, is a good larger hotel in a modernised old house, with doubles at 10,000 ptas plus IVA.

Places to Stay – top end
Not far north of the cathedral on a quiet street, *Hotel Álvarez Quintero* (☎ 422 12 98), Calle Álvarez Quintero 13, is a modernised old house with 37 all-mod-con rooms. Singles/doubles are 7000/10,000 to 9500/14,000 ptas, plus IVA. Even nearer the cathedral, *Hotel Doña María* (☎ 422 49 90), Calle Don Remondo 19, is in a characterful old building, with 60 varied rooms and suites from 12,000 to 29,000 ptas plus IVA.

In the Barrio de Santa Cruz, *Las Casas de la Judería* (☎ 441 51 50), Callejón de Dos Hermanas 7, are a group of charmingly restored old houses around several patios and fountains, with lots of pretty tiles and plants. The 30 rooms, with air-con and TV, are from 15,500 ptas plus IVA a double.

You can break the bank in style at the *Hotel Alfonso XIII* (☎ 422 28 50), Calle San Fernando 2, a magnificent 1920s fusion of old Sevillan styles in marble, mahogany and tiles. Rooms start at 38,000 ptas plus IVA.

Places to Eat
Sevilla is one of Spain's tapas capitals, with scores and scores of bars serving all sorts of varied and tasty light bites. To catch the atmosphere of the city, you should certainly

do some of your eating in bars. You can go for *media raciones* or *raciones* if tapas won't fill you up fast enough.

Meals Perhaps because tapas are so much the thing, Sevilla is not quite so well endowed with good restaurants, but there are enough to keep you going.

Barrio de Santa Cruz Near the Alcázar, *Restaurant La Cueva*, a touristic but pleasant courtyard restaurant at Calle Rodrigo Caro 18, does a lunch menú of gazpacho, salad, paella and dessert for 1350 ptas (minimum two people). *El Rincón de Pepe* nearby at Calle Gloria 6 has pretty, folksy décor and the same menú, except that you must choose between gazpacho and salad, for 1050 ptas.

The excellent, very popular *Pizzeria San Marco*, in a stylishly refurbished old Muslim bathhouse at Calle Mesón del Moro 6, does pizzas around 725 ptas and pasta dishes around 795 ptas. Calle Santa María La Blanca has several good-value places: at *Cervecería Alta-Mira*, No 6, a media ración of tortilla Alta-Mira (made with potatoes and vegetables) is almost a full meal for 600 ptas; the busy little *Bar Casa Fernando* round the corner has a decent 800-ptas lunch menú; *Restaurant El Cordobés* at No 20 is good for breakfast such as eggs, bacon, bread and coffee for 350 ptas.

For something fancier, *Corral del Agua*, Callejón del Agua 6, has fine, inventive Andalucían food. Its cool, green courtyard is great on a hot day (though often full!). A speciality is solomillo de ternera a la pimienta verde con manzana frita (steak with green pepper and fried apples). A full meal with wine will set you back about 3000 ptas or more. It's closed on Sunday and through January.

West of Avenida de la Constitución *Mesón del Serranito*, Calle Antonio Díaz 9, has a good selection of platos combinados from 750 ptas. Busy *Bodega Paco Góngora* at Calle Padre Marchena 1 does a huge range of good seafood at decent prices – media raciones of fish a la plancha (grilled) are

mostly 600 ptas. It's open daily from 11 am to 4 pm and 7 pm to midnight.

El Centro *Mesón Don Raimundo*, in a former convent at Calle Argote de Molina 20, specialises in seafood and game typical of Sanlúcar de Barrameda and the nearby Guadalquivir marshes. Try the garlicky clam soup with pine nuts, or partridge cooked in sherry. Soups are 500 ptas, main courses around 1600 ptas. It's closed Sunday.

At Plaza de San Francisco 5, *Doña Teresa* is a busy, no-frills spot for breakfast (churros 100 ptas, tostadas from 100 ptas) or platos combinados such as omelette, ham and salad for 600 ptas. Just off Plaza Salvador at Calle Álvarez Quintero 3, *Bar Centro*, popular with American students, does light platos combinados such as pincho de pollo (chicken kebab) with salad and chips for around 500 ptas.

The original *Pizzeria San Marco* (see under Barrio de Santa Cruz earlier in this section) is at Calle de la Cuna 6 in an 18th century mansion. It closes on Sunday.

To the east, the handsomely blue-tiled *Restaurante El Bacalao*, Plaza Ponce de León 15, specialises in what its name suggests, which is a Sevilla favourite. You can take your bacalao a dozen ways for 1700 ptas plus IVA, but it's cheaper as tortillitas (deep fried balls) or croquetas, for 1000 ptas.

Elsewhere *Bodegón Alfonso XII* at Calle Alfonso XII 33 near the Museo de Bellas Artes is good value with deals like scrambled eggs with mushrooms, ham and prawns for 400 ptas, or chicken and chips for 500 ptas. Across the river at Calle Betis 68, there's yet another in the good *Pizzeria San Marco* chain.

The *Mercado del Arenal*, on Calle Pastor y Landero, is the only food market in the central area.

Tapas An evening of tapas-hopping round Sevilla's bars with a couple of friends is one of the most enjoyable experiences the city has to offer. Most of these places are good for popping into at other times of day, too, for a bite and a drink. Sherry or beer are the traditional accompaniments to tapas. In many bars, instead of charging for each item as you go along, they chalk what you spend on the counter in front of you and add it up when you leave.

Though many bars helpfully have a tapas menu – or at least a blackboard – you're bound to find that you don't know what many things are. A few local favourites you'll come across are *caña de lomo*, pork loin (expensive); *chanquetes*, tiny fish, deep-fried; *espinacas con garbanzos*, spinach and chick peas; *papas aliñás*, sliced potatoes and boiled eggs, with tomato, capsicum, onion and a vinegar-and-oil dressing; *pavía*, battered fish or seafood; *pringá*, a small toasted roll with a filling of mixed sausage, black pudding and bacon; and *puntillitas*, baby squid, usually deep-fried.

Barrio de Santa Cruz *Bodega Santa Cruz* on Calle Mateos Gago, a bar popular with visitors and locals, has a big choice of decent-sized tapas at the good price of 150 ptas. A couple of streets away at Calle Santa Teresa 2, *Café Bar Las Teresas* is an atmospheric old-style bar with lots of hanging hams, good tapas from 160 to 200 ptas and media raciones around 600 ptas. The queso viejo (mature cheese) is a speciality.

Cervecería Giralda, Calle Mateos Gago 1, has a wonderful variety of good tapas, some pretty exotic, for 225 to 275 ptas.

West of Avenida de la Constitución *Mesón Sevilla Jabugo I*, Calle Castelar 1, specialises in expensive Jabugo ham though there's lots of other choice. It's a no-frills place, busy most of the day (closed Sunday). *La Infanta*, Calle Arfe 36, with sherry butts for tables, is a haunt of the tweed-jacketed young Sevilla smart set. If you feel well enough dressed, the tapas, from 175 ptas, are exotic and great. *Bodega Paco Góngora* (see under Meals earlier in this section) is good for tapas, too.

El Centro *Mesón Don Raimundo* and *Restaurante El Bacalao* (see under Meals earlier in this section) both do good tapas. There are several inviting bodegas and other good tapas joints around Plaza de la Alfalfa. The *Manolo*, Plaza de la Alfalfa 3, has good fried fish tapas. *Sopa de Ganso* at Calle Pérez Galdós 8 specialises in vegetarian tapas. If grilled meat is more your scene, head for *La Montanera Extremeña* at Calle San Esteban 17.

El Rinconcillo at Calle Gerona 40 is Sevilla's oldest bar, founded in 1670 and still going strong. Its present tiles-and-wood look is 19th century. The tapas are fairly straightforward – espinacas con garbanzos, tortilla de jamón – and good with a 'coronel', a big glass of house wine.

Elsewhere *Patio San Eloy* at Calle San Eloy 9 is a bright, busy place, popular with a young crowd and with a flight of steps at the back to sit on. Tapas of ham, cheese, smoked salmon, pork and more go for 110 to 185 ptas. It's open daily from 11.30 am to 4 pm and 6.30 pm to midnight.

There's another cluster of good places around Plaza del Altozano in Triana, at the west end of the Puente de Isabel II.

Entertainment

Sevilla's nightlife is undoubtedly among the liveliest in Spain. On fine nights throngs of people block the streets outside popular bars and crowd the east bank of the Guadalquivir, which in summer is dotted with temporary bars. Teenagers just bring their own bottles to mass open-air gathering spots such as the Mercado del Arenal. Sevilla also has some great music bars, often with dance space. As everywhere in Spain, the best action is on Friday and Saturday nights.

For more organised events – concerts, dance, theatre, exhibitions and some flamenco performances – check the arts and listings pages of newspapers such as *ABC*, *El Correo* and *El País*, and *El Giraldillo* magazine. Also keep an eye on posters.

Drinking, Music & Dancing Of course you can eat while you drink: for some bars where

ANDALUCÍA

the tapas are an attraction in themselves, see the preceding section.

Until about midnight, Plaza Salvador is a very popular spot for an open-air drink, with a studenty crowd and a couple of little bars selling takeaway drinks.

There are some hugely popular bars just north of the cathedral: *P Flaherty Irish Pub* on Calle Alemanes gets packed with locals and visitors alike – 500 ptas for your pint of Guinness or bitter. *La Subasta* and *Antigüedades* on Calle Argote de Molina are very popular with a slightly older, more conservative crowd.

For a change of gear, head across Avenida de la Constitución to *Casa Morales* at Calle García de Vinuesa 3 – an old-fashioned bodega going since 1850, with wine from the barrel. A little further west, the scene changes again: the crowds – mostly young – from about midnight some nights on Calle de Adriano have to be seen to be believed. Busy music bars on Adriano itself include *A3*, *Habana*, *Bar Populus* and *Arena*. There's also *RKO* on Calle Pastor y Landero. Cheap beer is sold through a hole in the wall at *Bar de Rejillas* on Calle Harinas.

Just to the south, there are some more relaxed bars and bodegas on Calle Dos de Mayo. Check out the art on the walls of the *Maestranza* at No 28.

Calle Pérez Galdós off Plaza Alfalfa has three lively music bars – the discoish *Lamentable* at No 28, *Bare Nostrum* a couple of doors up with some good African sounds, and *Sopa de Ganso* at No 8. This street gets fairly busy by midnight.

Further north, there are a few live music possibilities on Alameda de Hércules (which is also a red-light district). The *Fun Club* music bar at No 86 has live bands on Saturday and often Friday nights – cover is normally about 800 ptas including a drink. The more sedate *Bulebar Café* at No 83 has weekly live music (Wednesday at our last check) from Irish folk to country. *Pub-Sala Princesa* at the north end of the Alameda sometimes has music, too. Across the street, *Habanilla Café* is an aromatic bar with a fairly offbeat crowd.

Calle Betis, on the west bank of the Guadalquivir, is another good spot. *Alambique*, *Mui d'Aqui* and *Big Ben*, side by side two blocks north of the Puente de San Telmo, all play good music and attract an interesting mix of students and travellers. If you're looking for somewhere quieter, try *Café de la Prensa* at Calle Betis 8.

Flamenco Sevilla is one of Spain's flamenco capitals and its Triana barrio on the west bank of the Guadalquivir, which once had a high Gypsy population, was one of the flamenco's birthplaces. Even so, it can be hard to find authentic flamenco being performed unless you're present for the Feria de Abril or the Bienal de Flamenco (see under Special Events earlier in this section), or come across it during some fiesta.

The *Anselma* bar at Calle Pagés del Corro 49 in Triana has an atmosphere redolent of the El Rocío romería and there's flamenco and *sevillana* guitar, singing and dancing most nights. It's open from 8 pm to 1 am except Sunday. Bars which stage fairly regular flamenco performers, of variable quality, include *La Carbonería*, Calle Levies 18; *La Yerbaguena*, Calle González Cuadrado 35 (Wednesday at 9.30 pm at our last check), which has Mexican tapas, too; and *El Mundo*, Calle Siete Revueltas 5 (usually Tuesday at midnight). El Mundo charges an entry fee of 300 ptas which includes one drink.

There are also several tourist-oriented flamenco venues with regular shows, and some of these, though hardly spontaneous, are good. The best is *Los Gallos* on Plaza Santa Cruz, with shows at 9 and 11.30 pm nightly for 3000 ptas.

Other Music, Dance & Theatre The *Teatro de la Maestranza* at Paseo de Cristóbal Colón 22 and *Teatro Lope de Vega* at Avenida de María Luisa s/n stage varied programmes of concerts, dance and drama.

Spectator Sport

Bullfights at the Plaza de Toros de la Real Maestranza on Paseo de Cristóbal Colón are

Top: Beach scene at Port d'Alcúdia, Mallorca
Middle: Plaça de la Vila in the old walled town, D'Alt Vila, Ibiza city
Bottom: On the rocks and *au naturel* in Ses Salines, Ibiza

DAVID WATERMAN

DAVID WATERMAN

Top: Rural scene, Andalucía
Bottom: Rocks of ages at El Torcal, near Antequera, Andalucía

among the best in Spain. The season runs from Easter to October, with fights on Sunday about 6 pm, and almost every day during the Feria de Abril and the week before it. Tickets start at around 2000 ptas. The ring, which holds 13,500 spectators, is one of the country's oldest and most elegant, and its crowds among the most knowledgeable.

Things to Buy

The main shopping area is on and around Calle Sierpes. There's an El Corte Inglés department store on Plaza del Duque de la Victoria. The large Thursday morning flea market on Calle de la Feria in the Barrio de la Macarena is well worth a visit.

Getting There & Away

Air Sevilla airport (☎ 451 06 77) has quite a range of domestic and international flights. Air Europa flies to Barcelona for 13,900 ptas one way. You can get tickets at Halcón Viajes (☎ 421 44 56), Calle Almirante Bonifaz 3. Iberia (☎ 422 89 01), Calle Almirante Lobo 2, has direct daily flights to Barcelona, Madrid, Valencia, London, Paris, Milan, Amsterdam, Brussels and Düsseldorf.

Bus From Prado de San Sebastián bus station (☎ 441 71 11) on Plaza San Sebastián, there are eight or more daily buses to Córdoba (two hours; 1200 ptas), Granada (four hours; 2710 ptas), Málaga (3½ hours; 2245 ptas), Jerez de la Frontera, Sanlúcar de Barrameda and Cádiz (one hour; 1200 to 1330 ptas); and a few to Arcos de la Frontera and Ronda (2½ hours; 1235 ptas), Tarifa, Algeciras (three hours; 2300 ptas), La Línea and the Costa del Sol. This is also the station for frequent buses to Carmona, and a few daily buses to Jaén, Almería, Murcia, Alicante, Valencia and Barcelona.

From Plaza de Armas bus station (☎ 490 80 40), just east of the Puente de Chapina, there are frequent buses to Huelva (1¼ hours; 870 ptas), a few a day to El Rocío and Matalascañas, and 11 to Madrid (six hours; 2680 ptas). Northward, there are frequent buses from here to Zafra (two hours), about 12 daily to Mérida (3¼ hours; 1675 ptas),

around six a day to Badajoz, Cáceres (four hours; 2200 ptas), Plasencia and Salamanca, and a few as far as Galicia. To Lisbon there are three direct buses a week (eight hours; 4350 ptas) and daily buses with a transfer at the border (nine hours to Lisbon for 2540 ptas). For the Algarve you need to change buses at Huelva.

Train There's a central RENFE information and booking office at Calle Zaragoza 31, open Monday to Friday from 9 am to 1.15 pm and 4 to 7 pm. Sevilla's Santa Justa train station (☎ 454 02 02) is about 1.5 km northeast of the centre on Avenida Kansas City. *Consigna* lockers, open from 6 am to midnight, cost 300 to 600 ptas for 24 hours.

There are three types of train to/from Madrid. Up to a dozen super-fast AVE trains each day cover the 471 km in just 2½ hours, costing from 7600 to 9200 ptas in the cheapest class *(turista)*; a couple of Talgos take 3½ hours for 6700 to 7300 ptas in 2nd class; and the evening Tren Hotel takes 3¾ hours for 5100 ptas in a seat. The AVE service is the pride of Spain's rail network: the trains reach speeds of 280 km/hour and if they arrive more than five minutes late, you get your money back. (Don't get excited: this only happens to one train in 250.) Unfortunately for Inter-Railers, Inter-Rail cards are not valid on AVEs; Eurail pass-holders pay 1400 ptas. Inter-Railers must also pay 2300 ptas on the Tren Hotel.

Other daily trains from Sevilla include about 20 to Córdoba (43 minutes by AVE for 2100 to 2500 ptas in turista class; up to 1¾ hours on other trains, from 875 ptas); up to 15 to Jerez de la Frontera and Cádiz (two hours; 1195 to 1400 ptas); three or four each to Granada (4½ hours; 1950 ptas), Málaga (three hours; 1790 ptas), Huelva (1½ hours), Ronda (three hours; 1650 ptas) and Algeciras (five hours; 2340 ptas), with a change at Bobadilla for the last two places; two to Valencia (nine hours; 5300 ptas); four to Barcelona (11 to 14 hours; from 6600 ptas); one to Jaén; and one north to Zafra, Mérida, Cáceres and Plasencia. For Lisbon (16 hours; 6500 ptas in 2nd class), you must change at

Cáceres. There's no train service to the Algarve.

Car Pooling Compartecoche (☎ 490 78 52) at Calle González Cuadrado 49 is an intercity car-pooling service. Its service is free to drivers, while passengers pay an agreed transfer rate. Ring between 10 am and 1.30 pm or 5 and 8 pm for details.

Boat There are no regular passenger services along the Guadalquivir these days, but from around April to October day cruises run to Sanlúcar de Barrameda at the river's mouth and back. Early and late in the season cruises may only go on the weekend. Several companies make the trips, from the *embarcadero* by the Torre del Oro, for around 3500 ptas. It's 4½ hours each way, usually with 4½ hours in Sanlúcar in between.

Getting Around

The Airport Sevilla airport is about seven km from the centre off the N-IV Córdoba road. Airport buses make the 30 minute trip (750 ptas) up to 12 times daily; tourist offices have details.

Bus Bus No C1, going east from in front of Santa Justa train station, follows a clockwise circular route via Avenida de Carlos V (close to Prado de San Sebastián bus station and the city centre), Avenida de María Luisa, Triana and Plaza de Armas bus station. Bus No C2, heading west from Santa Justa, follows the same route in reverse unless it's marked 'Por Cartuja', which means it misses out Plaza de Armas bus station. Bus No 27, from the same stop as No C2, runs to/from Plaza de la Encarnación in the northern part of the centre.

Bus No C3, which does a clockwise circuit, will take you from Calle Menéndez Pelayo (outside Prado de San Sebastián bus station) to Puerta de Jerez (the south end of Avenida de la Constitución), Triana and Plaza de Armas bus station. The anticlockwise C4, going south on Calle de Arjona from Plaza de Armas bus station, goes along

Paseo de Colón to Puerta de Jerez, then to Calle Menéndez Pelayo.

A single bus ride is 120 ptas. You can pick up a route map from tourist offices or from information booths at major stops. Or call ☎ 441 11 52 for city bus information.

AROUND SEVILLA
Itálica

About eight km north-west of central Sevilla, on the edge of the village of Santiponce, Itálica was the first Roman town in Spain – founded for veterans of the Punic Wars in 206 BC – and the birthplace of at least two emperors, Trajan and Hadrian. Abandoned since Visigothic times, its ruins include one of the biggest of all Roman amphitheatres and some excellent mosaics. The site is open Tuesday to Saturday from 9 am to 6.30 pm, Sunday and holidays from 9 am to 3 pm (October to March, Tuesday to Saturday from 9 am to 5.30 pm, Sunday and holidays from 10 am to 4 pm). There are good tapas and platos combinados at the restaurant at the entrance. Frequent buses run to Santiponce from Sevilla's Prado de San Sebastián bus station.

LA CAMPIÑA

This hot, rolling, fertile area south of the Río Guadalquivir, stretching about 100 km east of Sevilla and crossed by the main roads to Córdoba, Granada and Málaga, can be bleak country, with hardly a soul in sight over the long distances separating the few towns. La Campiña is still a land of huge estates, whose efficient modern farming methods do nothing to relieve the plight of Andalucía's centuries-old stratum of landless labourers.

If you're not in a hurry there are a few towns whose surprisingly grand architecture (though evidence of the enormous and long-standing wealth gap) makes them worth a detour.

Carmona

Carmona is just off the N-IV, 38 km east of Sevilla. Frequent buses from Sevilla's Prado de San Sebastián bus station stop just outside the west side of the old town on Calle San

Pedro. The tourist office (☎ 414 22 00) is at Plaza de las Descalzas s/n, two blocks north-east of the Plaza Mayor.

Things to See From Calle San Pedro, the **Puerta de Sevilla**, a Roman gate with Muslim fortifications built over it (open daily from 11 am to 2 pm), leads into the old town. Two blocks east of Plaza Mayor, the 15th century **Iglesia de Santa María** has a mudéjar tower and a pretty patio remaining from an earlier mosque on the site. The east side of the town is overlooked by an Almohad **alcázar** which, in the 13th century, Pedro El Cruel turned into a mudéjar palace in similar style to his parts of the Sevilla Alcázar. It was restored as a *parador* in the 1970s. But Carmona's most remarkable sight lies outside the old town, to the west. This is the **Necrópolis Romana**, Avenida Jorge Bonsor 9, with 900 Roman family tombs hewn from the rock, some of them very elaborate, many-chambered and decorated with frescos. The biggest even have kitchens and dining rooms. From 15 June to 15 September the necropolis is open Tuesday to Saturday from 8.30 am to 2.30 pm; at other times, Tuesday to Friday from 10 am to 2 pm and 4 to 6 pm, Saturday and Sunday from 10 am to 2 pm.

Places to Stay Inexpensive lodgings are in rather short supply. *Pensión Comercio* (☎ 414 00 18), Calle Torre del Oro 30 by the Puerta de Sevilla, has 14 clean rooms at 3000 or 4000 ptas a double, and a restaurant. *Casa Carmelo* (☎ 414 05 72) at Calle San Pedro 15 has doubles from 4000 ptas. The *Parador Alcázar del Rey Don Pedro* (☎ 414 10 10) has rooms from 16,500 ptas plus IVA.

Osuna

Osuna, 91 km from Sevilla just off the A-92, doesn't look much from the highway, but once there you'll find it a pleasant place with some very impressive buildings, several of them created by the ducal family of Osuna, one of Spain's richest since the 17th century. Tourist information is available at the ayuntamiento (☎ 481 00 50) on Plaza Mayor.

Things to See Most impressive are the big buildings on the hill at the top of the town: the old **university**, founded in 1549 (now a school), and the 16th century **Colegiata de Santa María de la Asunción** church, open for guided tours Tuesday to Sunday from 10.30 am to 1.30 pm and 3.30 to 6.30 pm. The Colegiata has a lovely patio, superb mudéjar wood and tile ceilings, and several fine paintings by Ribera. The tour includes the underground Sepulcro Ducal, the family vault of the Osuna family.

Places to Stay *Hostal Las 5 Puertas* (☎ 481 12 43), Calle Carrera 79, has doubles at 3100 to 3400 ptas (more in April and May); *Hostal Caballo Blanco* (☎ 481 01 84), an old coaching inn nearby at Calle Granada 1, is slightly more expensive but better. Both places have restaurants.

Getting There & Away There are half a dozen buses daily to/from Sevilla (Prado de San Sebastián), four to/from Antequera, and also services to/from Málaga. Three trains a day run to/from Sevilla, Antequera, Granada and Málaga.

PARQUE NATURAL SIERRA NORTE

If you're looking to get off the regular tourist trail, this 1648 sq km protected area of the Sierra Morena, stretching right across the north of Sevilla province, could fill the bill. It's a sparsely populated and in places wild region, much of it covered in *dehesas*, woodlands of scattered holm and cork oak rising from scrub or pasture. Many of the villages and small towns bear a clear Islamic imprint, with old forts, part-mudéjar churches and narrow, zigzagging white streets. There are good walks in several areas, including around Cazalla de la Sierra and along the Huéznar valley to its east.

Daily buses to Cazalla de la Sierra and Constantina, the biggest town, leave from Sevilla's Plaza de Armas bus station, and three or four trains a day from Sevilla go to Cazalla-Constantina station, on the C-432 seven km from Cazalla and 12 km from Constantina. The national park's information

ANDALUCÍA

centre (☎ 488 01 10) is near Constantina, at El Robledo, Carretera Constantina-El Pedroso, Paraje La Dehesilla. There's also a tourist office (☎ 488 45 60) at Paseo del Moro 2 in Cazalla de la Sierra.

Places to Stay

Camping Batán de las Monjas (☎ 588 65 98), Carretera Estación de Cazalla Km 7, San Nicolás del Puerto, is open all year. There's a free *zona de acampada* at Isla Margarita, 2.5 km up the Río Huéznar from Cazalla-Constantina station.

The *Albergue Juvenil Constantina* youth hostel (☎ 588 15 89) near the centre of Constantina at Cuesta Blanca s/n has room for 90, all in twin rooms. The half-dozen places in and near Cazalla include *Hostal La Milagrosa* (☎ 488 42 60), Calle Llana 29, with doubles at 3500 ptas, and *Posada El Moro* (☎ 488 43 26), Paseo El Moro s/n, where comfortable doubles with bath are 7000 ptas.

Huelva Province

Andalucía's westernmost province stretches to the Portuguese border, which is crossed by a road bridge over the Río Guadiana near Ayamonte. The province includes most of the Parque Nacional de Doñana, famous for its huge bird population, and around half of the fine beaches of the Costa de la Luz (Coast of Light) which extends down into Cádiz province.

The port city of Huelva was founded by the Phoenicians as a trading settlement, under the name Onuba, about 3000 years ago, but the region first really prospered under the Romans, as the Río Tinto mines – today one of its bigger tourist attractions – were fully exploited. In 1492, it was from the Huelva area that Christopher Columbus set sail, and the sites east of the city associated with his life are visited in a kind of pilgrimage by many people.

The telephone code for Huelva province is ☎ 959.

HUELVA

The capital of the province is distinctly unattractive, and since much of the original town was destroyed by the effects of the Lisbon earthquake in 1755 there is very little to see of any historical value. It does, however, make a convenient base from which to explore the surrounding area.

The commercial harbour is one of Spain's leading ports, but the massive industrial growth of recent years has wrecked the environment. Beggars can be a problem in the city centre and it's not a particularly pleasant place to stay.

Orientation

The main street is Avenida Martín Alonso Pinzón – known as Gran Vía – which leads to Plaza de las Monjas, the central square. Running parallel on the south side is a series of small pedestrianised shopping streets from Calle Concepción through to Calle Berdigón; here you will find plenty of places to eat and drink. Most of the sites are within walking distance.

Information

The tourist office (☎ 25 74 03) is just around the corner from the bus station at Avenida Alemania 12. It is open Monday to Friday from 8.30 am to 7.30 pm and on Saturday from 9 am to 2 pm.

Banco El Monte on Avenida Martín Alonso Pinzón and Banco Nat West on corner of Plaza del Punto and Avenida Italia are two of many banks with 24-hour ATMs. There are four more on the pedestrianised shopping streets. American Express is represented by Ultratur at Calle Puerto 46.

The post office is on the corner of Avenida de Italia and Avenida Tomás Domínguez. The central postcode is 21080.

There is a first-aid centre (Casa de Socorro) at Vía Paisajística (☎ 25 38 00). The Cruz Roja (☎ 26 12 11) is at Paseo Buenos Aires and the hospital (☎ 24 22 22) is at Avenida Federico Mayo.

Things to See

For those interested in the history of the Río

Tinto mines, the **Museo Provincial**, at Calle Alameda Sundheim 13, has an impressive collection of artefacts. In summer it is open Monday to Friday from 8.30 am to 2.30 pm; out of season, from 9.30 am to 2 pm and 4.30 to 7 pm. Entry is free.

Few churches survived the earthquake of 1755, but the **Catedral de la Merced**, north-west of Plaza de las Monjas, off Paseo de Buenos Aires, is worth a look, if only for its image of the Virgen de la Cinta, the patron saint of the city, attributed to Montañés. Nearby, the 15th century **Iglesia de San Pedro**, off Plaza San Pedro, is the city's oldest church, built on the ruins of a mudéjar mosque.

Two km north of the centre, off Avenida de Manuel Siurot, is the **Santuario de Nuestra Señora de la Cinta**, which Columbus visited before embarking on his momentous voyage. The event is portrayed in traditional *azulejo* tiles by the artist Daniel Zuloaga. Bus No 6 will take you there from Plaza de las Monjas.

Special Events
Fiestas Colombinas It was 3 August 1492 when Columbus set off for the Americas. Each year, Huelva celebrates the occasion with seven days of music, dancing, sport, cultural events and bullfighting.

Places to Stay
The nearest camping ground is at Aljaraque, 10 km west. *Camping Las Vegas* (☎ 31 81 41), at Carretera Huelva-Punta Umbría Km 7, charges 500 ptas per adult, 500 ptas a tent and 500 ptas a car.

In town, most of the low-budget accommodation lies in the backstreets between Avenida de Italia and Calle Concepción. *Pensión Virgen del Rocío* (☎ 28 17 16), at Calle Tendaleras 14, has singles for 1800 ptas and doubles with bath for 4500 ptas. There are three pensiones in Calle Rascón, all of which are very basic: *Nuestra Señora de la Cinta* (☎ 24 85 82), at No 29, has rooms for 1100/2000 ptas. Just a couple of doors down, *Calvo* (☎ 24 90 16), at No 31, has rooms for 1100/2400 ptas plus IVA.

Directly opposite, *Las Delicias* (☎ 24 83 92), at No 42, has doubles for 2500 ptas plus IVA.

Hotel Costa de la Luz (☎ 25 64 22), at Calle José María Amo 8, has decent singles/doubles with bath for 3000/5000 ptas plus IVA, but *Hotel Los Condes* (☎ 28 24 00), at Calle Alameda Sundheim 14, is much more up-market, with rooms for 4200/7500 ptas plus IVA.

Hotel Tartessos (☎ 28 27 11), Avenida Martín Alonso Pinzón 13, has rooms for 6000/9500 ptas plus IVA.

The best in town is *Hotel Luz Huelva* (☎ 25 00 11), at Alameda Sundheim 26, which has rooms for 10,980/16,335 ptas plus IVA.

Places to Eat
Burger Alameda on Avenida Martín Alonso Pinzón does a burger, chips and soft drink for 575 ptas.

Mesón La Marmita, at Calle Miguel Redondo 12, is smart but cosy, with a set menu for just 850 ptas plus IVA. *La Cazuela*, at Calle Garci Fernandes 5, specialises in fish, with a set menu for 1500 ptas plus IVA. *La Goleta de Antonio*, at Calle Berdigón 16, also specialises in fish, with main courses costing around 1200 ptas plus IVA. All three are highly recommended.

There are three cafés grouped together at the east end of Avenida Martín Alonso Pinzón: *Odiel Restaurante* is the best, with great ham and eggs for 450 ptas or a set menu for 850 ptas. *La Prensa* and *Heladería El Punto* are also popular haunts.

Entertainment
Taberna El Condado at Calle Sor Ángela de la Cruz 3, is atmospheric, with chillies, garlic and ham hanging from the ceiling; tapas cost from 250 ptas. Most bars in the area start winding down around 11 pm; after midnight people head for Calle Pablo Rada, north of Plaza de las Monjas, where everything is open late.

Getting There & Away
Bus The bus station is a short walk from the city centre at Avenida Portugal 9. There are

ANDALUCÍA

frequent buses to Sevilla (870 ptas) and Madrid (3200 ptas) and there is one a day to Málaga (3160 ptas). Four buses a day leave for Faro in Portugal (720 ptas).

Locally, there are at least three buses a day to Río Tinto (670 ptas) and, on weekdays only, two a day to Aracena (1050 ptas).

Train The train station is on Avenida de Italia, and from it there is a daily train to Madrid (7600 ptas) via Sevilla and Córdoba (2700 ptas), plus three others to Sevilla and one or more via Jabugo to Zafra in Extremadura.

AROUND HUELVA
Columbus Trail
La Rábida, Palos de la Frontera and Moguer – the most important sites associated with Columbus – are within a 40-km return trip from Huelva, but you need your own vehicle to accomplish the whole thing. On the way south out of town you could stop by the **Monumento a Colón** (monument to Columbus), a 34 metre statue by an American sculptor named Whitney, at Punta del Sebo.

From Punta del Sebo it's six km to **La Rábida**. The 14th century Franciscan monastery here has a cross at the entrance, erected in 1892 to commemorate Columbus' stay. It is open Tuesday to Sunday from 10 am to 1 pm and 4 to 6.15 pm.

It was 1485 when Columbus first arrived here from Portugal and was greatly encouraged to pursue his ambitions. After six long years of negotiations with the Catholic Monarchs it was to La Rábida that he returned at an all-time low after his proposals had been rejected. Again he was encouraged, and thanks to Prior Juan Pérez, formerly Queen Isabel's confessor, an agreement was finally signed on 17 April 1492 which gave Columbus all the support he needed to embark on his voyage.

A very popular recent addition at La Rábida, near the monastery, is the Muelle de las Carabelas (Wharf of the Caravels, ☎ 53 05 97), where you can visit accurate replicas of Columbus' three ships, the *Santa María*, the *Pinta* and the *Niña*. It's open Tuesday to Friday from 10 am to 2 pm and 5 to 9 pm, Saturday, Sunday and holidays from 11 am to 8 pm (in winter, Tuesday to Sunday from 10 am to 7 pm). Cost is 420 ptas.

Four km north-east of La Rábida is the former port of **Palos de la Frontera**, now sadly in a state of decay. All that is left of the old pier out into the Río Tinto, rebuilt to celebrate the 400th anniversary of the discovery of America, are the rotting remains of a landing stage. The local economy has changed to the extent that its fishing and maritime industry has been replaced by agricultural activities. Today it is one of the main producers and exporters of wild and cultivated strawberries – a far cry from the 15th century, when its main claim to fame was its expert sailors. The royal decree which ordered the handing over of ships to Columbus was read in the 1473 **Iglesia de San Jorge**, built in Gothic and mudéjar styles. It was here that he and his crew attended mass before setting off on their voyage. They returned to Palos on 15 March 1493.

A further seven km north-east is **Moguer**. The **Convento de Santa Clara**, founded in the 14th century by Don Alonso Jofre Tenorio, the first nobleman of Moguer, features magnificent mudéjar choir stalls, and was visited many times by Columbus while he desperately sought official backing for his first voyage. It was here that he kept vigil for a night upon his safe return, fulfilling a vow that he had made during a terrible storm off the Azores. The convent is open Monday to Friday from 11 am to 1 pm and 4.30 to 6.30 pm. Entry is 250 ptas. From Moguer you can return to Huelva the way you came, or continue north, and then west on the N-431. The distance is much the same either way.

Punta Umbría & Marismas del Odiel
In season there are hourly ferries to the local seaside resort of Punta Umbría from Huelva's harbour, and cruises to the Marismas del Odiel, a nearby marshland nature reserve of 70 sq km renowned for its colonies of herons and spoonbills. For further details contact the Agencia del Medio Ambiente in Huelva on ☎ 24 57 68.

COSTA DE LA LUZ

The C-442, covered by one Damas bus a day Monday to Friday from Huelva, runs south-east behind a fine, 30 km dune-backed beach to Matalascañas. The coast is almost uninhabited apart from the small resort of Mazagón, 18 km from Huelva, which has a few hostales and a camping ground. Eleven km further on, the huge Camping Doñana Playa (☎ 53 62 81), which has room for 6000, is open all year. Matalascañas is covered in the following section.

PARQUE NACIONAL DE DOÑANA & AROUND

The Doñana national park, one of Europe's most important wetlands, covers 507 sq km in the south-east of Huelva province and neighbouring Sevilla province. It's vital not only as one of the last refuges for such endangered species as the pardel lynx and Spanish imperial eagle (both with populations of 30 or 40 here), but also as a crucial major habitat for a great variety of other birds, many of them migratory.

Doñana, made a national park in 1969, fights a continuing battle against agricultural and tourism schemes around its fringes which threaten to reduce its water supplies. The latest is a project by Alfonso de Hohenlohe, the man who brought the jet set to Marbella, to build two luxury hotels, 1200 holiday apartments and a golf course near Sanlúcar de Barrameda.

A good base for visiting the park itself (which requires booking ahead) and some interesting surrounding areas (which don't) is the village of El Rocío at the north-west corner of the park. Another possible base is the beach resort of Matalascañas at the south-west corner of the park.

Bordering the national park are four discrete blocks of land making up the separate, 542 sq km Parque Natural Entorno de Doñana, which includes 265 sq km designated as preparque, or buffer zones for the national park.

Flora, Fauna & Ecosystems

Doñana counts 125 resident and 125 migratory bird species and is a major habitat for greater flamingos, ducks, coots, herons, egrets, stilts, vultures, birds of prey and many more.

Half the national park consists of marismas, marshes formed by branches and tributaries of the Río Guadalquivir. The park contains only about one-tenth of the Guadalquivir marismas, but most of those outside it have been drained and/or channelled for agriculture. The natural marismas are almost dry from July to October. In autumn they start to fill with water, leaving only a few islets of dry land. Hundreds of thousands of ducks, geese, coots and other water birds arrive from northern Europe to spend winter here. As the waters recede in spring, other birds – greater flamingos, spoonbills, storks, herons, avocets, hoopoes, bee-eaters, stilts – arrive for the summer, many of them to nest. In summer great crowds of birds flock around shallow, shrinking ponds known as lucios, and in July, herons, storks and kites move in to take bountiful catches of trapped perch.

Between the park's 30 km Atlantic beach and the marismas is a band up to five km wide of moving sand dunes, which are blown inland at a rate of up to six metres a year. Between the dunes are patches of umbrella pine and undergrowth known as corrales. When dune sand eventually reaches the marismas, it is then carried by rivers back down to the sea, which washes it up on the beach where the wind begins the dune cycle all over again. The beach, moving dunes and corrales together make up 102 sq km of the park.

In other parts of the park, stable sand supports 144 sq km of coto, the habitat of most of the park's abundant mammal population – among them deer, wild boar, feral camels, mongoose, and a few Homo sapiens. Coto vegetation ranges from heather and scrub through dense wooded thickets to stands of umbrella pine and cork oak.

El Rocío

Overlooking the marismas at the north-west corner of the fenced-off national park, El

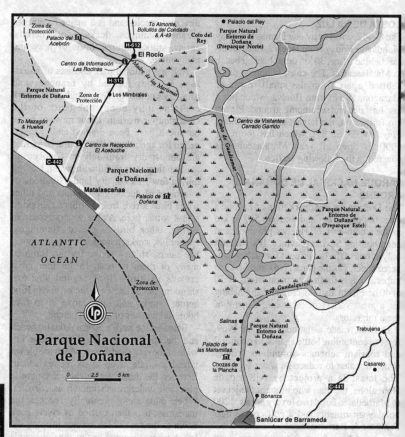

Parque Nacional de Doñana

Rocío has a touch of the Wild West about it. Its sandy streets bear as many hoofprints as tyre marks, and are lined by rows of verandahed buildings which usually stand empty. But this is no ghost town, for the houses are in excellent repair: most of them belong to the 90-odd *hermandades* (brotherhoods) of pilgrim-revellers who converge on El Rocío every Pentecost in one of Europe's most amazing happenings, the Romería del Rocío (see the boxed aside). Indeed, something of a fiesta atmosphere pervades the village during most weekends of the year as hermandades arrive to carry

out lesser rituals and processions. Candelaria (2 February) is the biggest event apart from the Romería.

Information There's a tourist office, open Monday to Friday from 3.30 to 7.30 pm, at Avenida de la Canaliega s/n, just south of the Hotel Puente del Rey. You can get national park information at the Centro de Información Las Rocinas (see under Things to See & Do). An ATM just west of the Ermita accepts Visa, American Express, Plus and Eurocheque cards.

Things to See & Do The heart of the village in every way is the **Ermita del Rocío**, a church built in its present form since 1964, which houses the Virgen del Rocío – a tiny wooden image dressed in long, bejewelled robes.

The marismas in front of El Rocío have year-round water, so this is nearly always a good place to spot birds and wildlife. The bridge on the H-312 one km south of the village is a good viewing spot. Just past the bridge is the **Centro de Información Las Rocinas** (☎ 44 23 40), open daily from 10 am to 8 pm, which has an exhibition on El Rocío and the Romería, and short paths to bird-watching hides by an adjacent patch of wetlands with year-round water. Six km along a road west from Las Rocinas is the **Palacio del Acebrón**, with an exhibition on 'El Hombre y La Marisma' and a 1.5 km walking track through some lovely riverside woodland.

For a longer walk, head across the Puente del Ajolí at the north-east edge of El Rocío and along the track into the woods ahead.

This is the beginning of the **Coto del Rey**, a large woodland zone in the preparque where you can wander freely for hours. It's criss-crossed by numerous tracks which vehicles might manage in dry seasons. Look overhead for birds of prey. Early in the morning or late in the evening you may spot deer or boar.

You can rent horses at several places in El Rocío.

Places to Stay & Eat El Rocío has about half a dozen hostales and hotels. Don't bother even trying for a room at Romería time. *Hostal Vélez* (☎ 44 21 17) at Calle Algaida 2, one block north of the Ermita, has clean, basic singles/doubles with shared bath for 1500/2500 ptas. *Pensión Cristina* (☎ 44 24 13), at Calle Real 32 a short distance east of the Ermita, has reasonable singles/doubles with bath for 3000/4000 ptas, and a decent restaurant where veal/lamb/venison and chips is 700 ptas.

Hotel Toruño (☎ 44 23 23), a little further east at Plaza Acebuchal 22, is a nice new

---

The Romería del Rocío

Like most of Spain's holiest images, Nuestra Señora del Rocío – aka La Blanca Paloma (White Dove) – has legendary origins. Back in the 13th century, the story goes, a hunter from the village of Almonte found her in a tree in the marismas. When he stopped to doze on the way home, the virgin made her own way back to the tree.

Before long a chapel was built on the spot and pilgrims were making for it. In the 17th and 18th centuries hermandades (brotherhoods) began forming in nearby towns to make an annual trip to El Rocío at Pentecost, the seventh weekend after Easter. By 1960 there were 32 hermandades and since then the Romería del Rocío has mushroomed into a vast festive cult that pulls people from all over Spain. There are over 90 hermandades now, some of several thousand men and women, and they still reach El Rocío as they have always done: on foot, on horseback, and in gaily decorated covered wagons pulled by cattle or horses, camping along the way. Those from the east cross the Río Guadalquivir at Sanlúcar de Barrameda in boats, then cross the national park.

Solemn is the last word you'd apply to this quintessentially Andalucían event. Participants dress in fine Andalucían costume and sing, dance, drink, laugh and romance their way to El Rocío. Hundreds of thousands of 'rocieros de fin de semana' converge on the village by other means, pushing the total number up to about a million.

On the Saturday each hermandad in turn pays its respects to the Virgen del Rocío in the Ermita. Things come to an ecstatic climax in the very early hours of Monday, by which time a million people's senses have been stretched by at least 40-odd hours of little sleep and a lot of alcohol. Young members of the hermandad of Almonte, the nearest town to El Rocío, which claims the Virgen for its own, carry her shoulder-high from the church. Violent struggles ensue as others literally battle with the Almonte lads for the honour of carrying La Paloma Blanca. With everyone else trying to get within touching distance, the crush and chaos is immense but somehow good humour survives and the Virgen is carried round to each of the hermandad buildings, finally being returned to the Ermita in the afternoon. ■

ANDALUCÍA

place which has 30 attractively simple rooms with air-con and bath at 5500/7500 ptas. Some have marismas views. *Hotel Puente del Rey* (☎ 44 25 75; fax 44 20 70), at Avenida de la Canaliega s/n by the main road, is a larger, new, three star hotel with rooms at 6400/8000 ptas.

There are several cafés, bars and restaurants around the village.

Centro de Recepción El Acebuche & National Park Tours

Twelve km south on the H-612 from El Rocío, then 1.6 km along an approach road, El Acebuche (☎ 44 87 11) is the main visitor centre for the national park and the starting point for tours into the park. Open daily from 8 am to 8 pm, it has displays on Doñana, an information desk selling books and maps, a café, and footpaths to nearby hides overlooking a lagoon with plenty of birds.

Trips from here into the national park are run by the local guides of the Cooperativa de Guías Marismas del Rocío (☎ 43 04 32), who speak Spanish only. These are the only way to get inside the park without special permission, except for boat trips from Sanlúcar de Barrameda (see that section later in this chapter). You need to book ahead by telephone: for spring, summer and holiday times the trips can get booked up more than a month ahead, but otherwise a week or maybe less is usually adequate. The trips go twice a day (no trips on Monday), last about four hours and cost 2800 ptas per person. They normally start with a long beach drive before taking in moving dunes and corrales, marismas, and woods where you can be pretty certain of seeing a good number of deer and boar. Some ornithologists report being disappointed by the tours' focus on four-footed creatures.

Buses stop on the H-612 outside El Acebuche. From Monday to Saturday, the first morning bus from El Rocío or Matalascañas should get you to El Acebuche for the morning tour. The last buses pass about 7 pm northbound and 6.15 pm southbound (4.30 pm on Sunday).

Matalascañas

This modern resort with a number of tall hotels could hardly be in greater contrast to the wildernesses of the national park, but it *is* set on an excellent beach. From the junction of the H-312 and C-442, Avenida de las Adelfas heads south straight to the beach, passing the tourist office (☎ 43 00 86), which is open Monday to Friday from 10 am to 2 pm and 3.30 to 6 pm, Saturday from 10 am to 2 pm. Matalascañas' bus stop is at the beach end of Avenida de las Adelfas.

Places to Stay & Eat The huge *Camping Rocío Playa* (☎ 43 02 38), open all year with room for 4000, is just above the beach one km west of the end of Avenida de las Adelfas. *Pensión Rocío* (☎ 43 01 41), a minute's walk north of the tourist office at Avenida El Greco 60 (no sign), has rooms with and without bath from 2000 to 3500 ptas a double. *Hostal Los Tamarindos* (☎ 43 01 19), Avenida de las Adelfas 31, and *Hostal El Duque* (☎ 43 00 58), Avenida de las Adelfas 34, have doubles with bath for 3000 to 7000 ptas depending on the season. There are several big tourist hotels.

Restaurante El Pichi, behind the beach near the end of Avenida de las Adelfas, has a three course menú for 950 ptas, platos combinados from 500 ptas, and good-value raciones. You'll find more places nearby and in the Centro Comercial off Avenida de las Adelfas.

Getting There & Away

Bus The Damas line runs three or four buses daily between Sevilla's Plaza de Armas bus station, El Rocío (1½ hours; 615 ptas) and Matalascañas; and one bus Monday to Friday between Huelva and Matalascañas along the coast. The El Rocío-Matalascañas route is also covered by three to five Damas buses daily between Almonte and Matalascañas.

Car & Motorcycle El Rocío is 27 km south along the H-612 from the A-49 Sevilla-

Huelva highway, with Matalascañas on the coast 16 km further south-west. Turn off the A-49 at Bollullos del Condado.

MINAS DE RÍO TINTO

By 1873 these mines were in the hands of the British-run Río Tinto Company, and a rapid programme of railway-building began. At one time there were 135 locomotives and 372 km of tracks to transport mineral ore from the mines to the port at Huelva. In 1954 control of the company returned to the Spanish. Today visitors can take the **miners' train** along 20 km of track through the scarred landscapes of the copper-rich Río Tinto. The train runs on weekend afternoons and costs 700 ptas.

Railway buffs shouldn't miss a visit to the **mining museum** in the centre of Río Tinto village. Displays include a 1907 steam locomotive and the luxurious 'Maharajah' coach, originally designed by the Birmingham Railway Carriage & Wagon Company for a trip by Queen Victoria to India. The trip was cancelled; the coach was sold to the Río Tinto Company and was used instead by King Alfonso XIII of Spain for a royal visit to the mines. The museum, which has mining artefacts from prehistoric to modern times, is open on Tuesday, Thursday and Saturday from 10 am to 2 pm, and on Wednesday from 5 to 8 pm. Entry costs 200 ptas.

Complete tours of the **mines**, including a ride on the train and entry to the museum, cost 1400 ptas. For further details contact the Fundación Río Tinto (☎ 59 00 25) on Plaza del Museo in Río Tinto village.

From a roadside viewing platform two km north of the village, you can see into one of the biggest open-cast mines in the world; the 1200 metre long and 330 metre deep basin of the Corta Atalaya.

To get to Río Tinto village by car, take the N-431 towards Sevilla, and after 14 km turn north onto the N-435, which runs north towards the Sierra de Aracena. The turn-off for Río Tinto is shortly after Zalamea la Real. Alternatively, there are regular buses from Huelva.

ARACENA & AROUND

A local road from Minas de Río Tinto runs north through the mountains to the town of Aracena, 104 km from Huelva. The main reason for visiting is **La Gruta de las Maravillas**. At 1200 metres long this is one of the largest caves of its kind in the world, complete with underground lakes, stalactites and stalagmites. It is open daily from 10.30 am to 1.30 pm and 3 to 6 pm. Entry costs 850 ptas.

Other sights include **Nuestra Señora de los Dolores**, a 13th century Gothic church – originally a mosque – built around the remains of a Muslim castle at the top of the hill, and the **Convento de Santa Catalina**.

The tourist office (☎ 11 03 55), on Plaza de San Pedro, can provide you with a list of places to stay. There is no shortage of budget accommodation.

From Aracena it is 20 km west to **Jabugo**, famed for its *jamón ibérico*, the best cured ham in Spain – though naturally it's pretty expensive. On weekdays there is a daily bus from Huelva (875 ptas).

The 1840 sq km **Parque Natural Sierra de Aracena y Picos de Aroche** stretches from Aracena to the borders of Portugal, Extremadura and Sevilla province. This is the west end of the Sierra Morena, with magnificent forests and wildlife including boar, deer and mountain goat, as well as numerous birds of prey. It's great hiking territory, and there are plenty of places to stay along the way. For further information, you can contact the Aracena tourist office or the park's office (☎ 11 04 75), at Plaza de Santa Lucía 23, Aracena.

Cádiz Province

The province of Cádiz reaches from the mouth of the Río Guadalquivir to the Strait of Gibraltar and inland to the rainy mountains of the Sierra de Grazalema. It's a region of great and varied attractions, from the historic port of Cádiz itself and the nearby triangle of sherry-making towns (Jerez de la

Frontera, Sanlúcar de Barrameda and El Puerto de Santa María), to the long, sandy and little-developed Atlantic beaches along the Costa de la Luz and the beautiful, green Sierra de Grazalema with its remote white hill towns.

The proliferation of 'de la Frontera' place names here stems from the days of the Reconquista. Most of Cádiz province was conquered by Castilla in the 13th century but the territory to its east remained in the hands of the Emirate of Granada until the late 15th century. Hence this region was one of the *fronteras* (frontiers) of Christian-held territory. The region still retains a bit of an untamed feel today, with large tracts of sparsely inhabited sierra, windy coasts and big lowland ranches which breed famous fighting bulls.

The telephone code for Cádiz province is ☎ 956.

CÁDIZ

No one remembers Cádiz when they list the great cities of Andalucía, and yet this port is as famous and historic as almost any of them. It's just that it's out on a limb, almost as intimate with oceans and distant continents as with its own land, and with no Muslim or Reconquista heritage whatsoever.

Once you get past the desolate coastal marshes and grim industrial sprawl of the approach to Cádiz, you emerge into a largely 18th century city of decayed grandeur, crammed on to the head of a long peninsula like some huge, overcrowded Atlantic-going ship. Its 155,000 people, called *gaditanos*, are a mostly unassuming and tolerant lot whose main concern is to make the best of life – whether staying out late to enjoy the after-dark cool in the sweltering summer months, or indulging in Spain's most riotous carnaval in spring.

History

Cádiz may be the oldest city in Europe. It was founded – tradition says in 1100 BC – by the Phoenicians, who called it Gadir and traded Baltic amber as well as Spanish silver and tin here. Later a naval base for the

Romans – who heaped praise on its culinary, sexual and musical delights – Cádiz then faded into obscurity until 1262, when it was taken from the Muslims by Alfonso X.

Cádiz began to boom with the discovery of America. Columbus sailed from here on his second and fourth voyages. It attracted Spain's enemies, too: in 1587 England's Sir Francis Drake 'singed the King of Spain's beard' with a raid on the harbour which delayed the imminent Armada, then in 1596 Anglo-Dutch attackers burnt almost the entire city.

Cádiz's golden age was the 18th century, when it enjoyed 75% of Spanish trade with the Americas. It grew into the richest and most cosmopolitan city in Spain, and gave birth to Spain's first middle class of progressive, liberal inclinations. Most of its fine buildings date from this era.

The Napoleonic Wars brought British warships back, to blockade and bombard the city and shatter the Spanish fleet at the Battle of Trafalgar, nearby, in 1805. After Spain turned against Napoleon in 1808, Cádiz was one of the few cities that never fell to the French, withstanding a two year siege from 1810. During this time a national *cortes* (parliament) convened here, a lopsidedly liberal gathering which adopted Spain's famous 1812 constitution, proclaiming sovereignty of the people and setting the scene for a whole century of struggle between Spanish liberals and conservatives.

The loss of the American colonies in the 19th century plunged Cádiz into decline, from which it has recovered only in the past few decades.

Orientation

Breathing space between the huddled streets of the old city is provided by numerous plazas, of which Plaza San Juan de Dios, towards the east end, is, if any, the main one. From here Calle Nueva and Calle San Francisco lead north-west towards another important square, Plaza de Mina. The train station is in the east of the old city on Plaza Sevilla, with the main bus station, of the Comes line, 800 metres north-west on Plaza

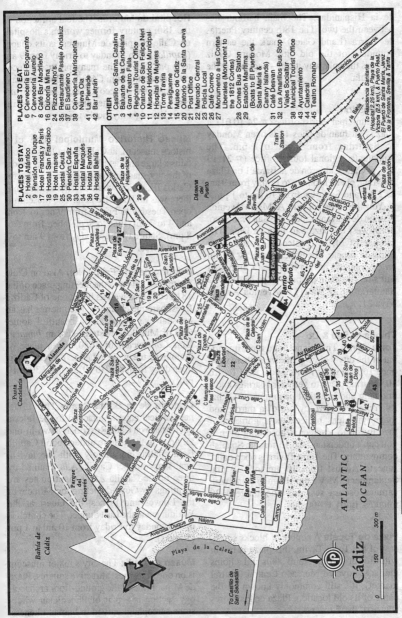

PLACES TO STAY
2 Hotel Atlántico
9 Pensión del Duque
17 Hostal Francia y París
18 Hostal San Francisco
19 Hotel Imares
30 Hostal Ceuta
35 Pensión Cádiz
33 Hostal España
34 Hostal Marqués
36 Hostal Fantoni
40 Hostal Bahía

PLACES TO EAT
6 Cervecería El Bogavante
7 Cervecería Aurelio
8 Café Bar Madrileño
16 Dulcería Mina
24 Pizzería Nino's
35 Restaurante Pasaje Andaluz
37 El Sardinero
39 Cervecería Marisquería
Nueva Ola
41 La Pierrade
42 Bar Letrán

OTHER
1 Castillo de Santa Catalina
3 Baluarte de la Candelaria
4 Gran Teatro Falla
5 Regional Tourist Office
10 Oratorio de San Felipe Neri
11 Museo Histórico Municipal
12 Hospital de Mujeres
13 Torre Tavira
14 Persiguème
15 Museo de Cádiz
20 Oratorio de la Santa Cueva
21 Post Office
22 Mercado Central
23 Policía Local
26 Café Correo
27 Monumento a las Cortes
Liberales (Monument to
the 1812 Cortes)
28 Comes Bus Station
29 Estación Marítima
(Boats to El Puerto de
Santa María &
Cádiz Islands)
31 Café Desván
32 Los Amarillos Bus Stop &
Viajes Socialtur
38 Municipal Tourist Office
43 Ayuntamiento
44 Catedral
45 Teatro Romano

ANDALUCÍA

de la Hispanidad. The main harbour lies between the two. The 18th century Puertas de Tierra (Land Gates) mark the eastern boundary of the old city. Modern Cádiz extends the only way it can – back along the peninsula.

Information

The municipal tourist office (☎ 24 10 01) at Plaza San Juan de Dios 11 is open Monday to Saturday from 9 am to 2 pm. The Andalucía regional tourist office (☎ 21 13 13), at Calle Calderón de la Barca 1 on Plaza de Mina, opens Monday to Friday from 9 am to 2 pm and Saturday from 10 am to 1 pm.

You'll find banks with ATMs on Avenida Ramón de Carranza and Calle San Francisco, north-west of Plaza San Juan de Dios. The main post office (postcode 11080) is on Plaza de Topete. The Policía Local (☎ 092 in an emergency) have a station at Campo del Sur s/n. The main hospital is the Residencia Sanitaria (☎ 27 90 11) at Avenida Ana de Viya 21.

Things to See & Do

Torre Tavira This highest and most important of the city's old watchtowers (there were once 160), at Calle Marqués del Real Tesoro 10, is a fine place to get your bearings and a dramatic and beautiful panorama of Cádiz. Its *cámara oscura*, by use of a mirror and magnifying lens, projects moving images of the city on to a screen – absorbing even if you can't understand the 15-minute Spanish commentary. The Torre Tavira is open daily, June to August from 10 am to 8.30 pm, September to May from 10 am to 6 pm, with cámara oscura sessions about every 30 minutes. Entry is 400 ptas.

Plaza de Topete A couple of blocks southeast of the Torre Tavira, this plaza is bright with flower and cage-bird stalls and adjoins the large covered Mercado Central (central market). It's still commonly known by the name of its old location, Plaza de las Flores (Plaza of the Flowers).

Hospital de Mujeres The real attraction of the 18th century former women's hospital, on Calle Hospital de Mujeres, is its chapel (*capilla*), open Monday to Friday from 9 am to 1 pm. One of the many profusely decorated churches from Cádiz's golden century, this contains El Greco's *Éxtasis de San Francisco*, depicting the grey-cloaked saint experiencing a mystical vision.

Museo Histórico Municipal The city history museum, at Calle Santa Inés 9, contains a large and detailed 18th century model of the city, made in mahogany and marble for Carlos III, which would merit a visit even if there was nothing else here. The museum is open Tuesday to Friday from 9 am to 1 pm and 4 to 7 pm (June to September, from 5 to 8 pm), Saturday and Sunday from 9 am to 1 pm. It's free.

Oratorio de San Felipe Neri Also on Calle Santa Inés, this was the meeting place of the 1812 cortes, as well as being one of Cádiz's finest baroque churches. The interior has an unusual oval shape and a beautiful dome. One of Murillo's masterpieces, an *Inmaculada Concepción* of 1680, has a place of honour in the main retablo. The church is open daily from 8.30 to 10 am and 7.30 to 10 pm.

Oratorio de la Santa Cueva This 1780s neoclassical church, attached to the Iglesia del Rosario on Calle Rosario, is a two-in-one affair, with the austere underground Capilla Baja contrasting sharply with the lavish, oval-shaped upper Capilla Alta. Framed by three of the Capilla Alta's eight arches are paintings by Goya depicting the Miracle of the Loaves and Fishes, the Guest at the Wedding, and the Last Supper. The church is open Monday to Friday from 10 am to 1 pm (50 ptas).

Museo de Cádiz The city's major museum is on one of its most attractive squares, Plaza de Mina. Pride of the ground-floor archaeology section is a pair of Phoenician white-stone sarcophagi carved in human likeness.

There's also some beautiful Phoenician jewellery and Roman glass, and lots of headless Roman statues – plus emperor Trajan, with head, from Baelo Claudia.

A highlight of the 2nd floor fine arts collection is a group of 21 superb canvases of saints, angels and monks by Zurbarán. The museum also has a room of beautiful old puppets used in satirical puppet theatre in Cádiz. It's open Tuesday to Sunday from 9.30 am to 2 pm. Entry is free for EU citizens, 250 ptas for others.

Coastal Walk One block north of Plaza de Mina you emerge on the city's northern seafront, with views across the Bahía de Cádiz to El Puerto de Santa María. From here you could head west along the **Alameda** garden, with the **Baluarte de la Candelaria** bastion at its end, then south beside the sea wall to the **Parque del Genovés**, which was laid out, like the Alameda, in the 19th century. From the park, Avenida Duque de Nájera leads to **Playa de la Caleta** beach (very crowded in summer), on a bay between two forts. The star-shaped **Castillo de Santa Catalina** at the north end, built in 1598 and for a long time Cádiz's main citadel, is open for guided visits every 30 minutes, Monday to Friday from 10 am to 7 pm, Saturday and Sunday from 10 am to 1.30 pm. The Castillo de San Sebastián, far out on the south side of the bay, is in military use and closed to the public. From Playa de la Caleta you can follow the coast eastward to the cathedral.

Catedral & Around The story of Cádiz's yellow-domed cathedral reflects that of the whole city in the 18th and 19th centuries. The decision to build it was taken in 1716 on the strength of the imminent transfer from Sevilla to Cádiz of the Casa de Contratación, which controlled Spanish trade with the Americas. But the cathedral wasn't finished till 1838, by which time not only had neoclassical elements diluted Vicente Acero's original baroque design, but a drying-up of funds had forced cutbacks in both size and quality. It's still a big and impressive construction, with little ornamentation to distract from the marble and stone grandeur of the interior, lit from the 50-metre-high dome. The Cádiz composer Manuel de Falla is buried in the crypt. If you want to see inside the cathedral, set your watch: it's open for tourist visits Monday to Saturday from noon to 1 pm only (100 ptas).

Plaza San Juan de Dios & Around The shabby **Barrio del Pópulo** district between the cathedral and Plaza San Juan de Dios was the kernel of medieval Cádiz, a fortified enclosure wrecked in 1596. Plaza San Juan de Dios is dominated by the neoclassical **ayuntamiento**, built at its south end around 1800.

If by now you're in need of a cool, quiet and leafy resting spot, the bougainvillea-shaded benches in **Plaza Candelaria** fit the bill very nicely.

Playa de la Victoria This wide beach stretches many km back down the ocean side of the peninsula, beginning about one km beyond the Puertas de Tierra. On hot summer weekends the whole city seems to be out here. Bus No 1 'Plaza España-Cortadura' from Plaza de España runs along the peninsula one or two blocks inland from the beach.

Special Events

No other Spanish city celebrates carnaval with the verve of Cádiz, where it turns into a 10 day singing, dancing and drinking fancy-dress party that continues until the weekend after the normal Shrove Tuesday close of carnaval. Everyone – locals and visitors alike – dresses up, and the fun, abetted by huge quantities of alcohol, is wholly infectious. A focus is provided by costumed groups called *murgas* who tour the city on foot or on floats, singing witty satirical ditties, dancing or performing sketches. In addition to the 300 or so officially recognised murgas, whose efforts go before judges in the Gran Teatro Falla, there are also the *ilegales* – any group that fancies taking to the streets and trying to play or sing.

Some of the liveliest scenes are in the working-class Barrio de la Viña, between the

ANDALUCÍA

Mercado Central and Playa de la Caleta, and on Calle Ancha and Calle Columela, where *ilegales* tend to congregate.

Rooms in Cádiz for carnaval time get booked months in advance. Assuming you haven't managed this, you could just go for the night from Sevilla or anywhere else within striking distance. You'll find plenty of other people do this – in fancy dress.

Places to Stay

From October to June (except for Christmas-New Year, carnaval and Semana Santa), many places cut prices by 10% to 20%.

Places to Stay – bottom end

Cheaper places mostly cluster just west of Plaza San Juan de Dios. A good choice is the friendly, family-run *Hostal Fantoni* (28 27 04), in an old house at Calle Flamenco 5. Very clean and recently renovated, and with a roof terrace catching a bit of summer breeze, it has singles/doubles for 1600/3200 ptas, and doubles with bath for 5000 ptas. *Hostal Marqués* (☎ 28 58 54), Calle Marqués de Cádiz 1, has slightly ageing but clean singles/doubles, all with balcony, for 2000/3300 ptas. *Hostal España* (☎ 28 55 00) at No 9 on the same street has nice rooms for 2600/3800 ptas, or doubles with private shower for 4800 ptas.

A bit further north-west, *Pension Cádiz* (☎ 28 58 01) at Calle Feduchy 20 is a popular little place with doubles/triples only, at 3000/4500 ptas with bath. *Hostal Ceuta* (☎ 22 16 54) at Calle Montañés 7 has doubles with bath for around 4000 ptas.

A good choice further into the old city is the clean and friendly *Hostal San Francisco* (☎ 22 18 42) at Calle San Francisco 12. Singles/doubles are 1900/3200 ptas; doubles with shower are 4200 ptas. Rooms at *Hotel Imares* (☎ 21 22 57) across the street at No 9 range from some airless and odorous interior ones to bright and breezy ones overlooking the street. Singles/doubles range from around 2800/4000 to 3300/5300 ptas.

The family-run *Pensión del Duque* at Calle Ancha 13 has decent rooms with bath for 3500/4000 ptas.

Places to Stay – middle & top end

Hostal Bahía (☎ 25 90 61) at Calle Plocia 5 just off Plaza San Juan de Dios has comfortable air-con rooms with TV at 6500 ptas a double. *Hotel Francia y París* (☎ 21 23 18), very well located at Plaza San Francisco 2, is bigger (57 rooms) and more luxurious, with singles/doubles for 7320/9200 ptas plus IVA.

The modern *Hotel Atlántico* parador (☎ 22 69 05) is on the seafront by Parque del Genovés at Avenida Duque de Nájera 9. Doubles are 13,500 ptas plus IVA.

Places to Eat

Naturally, Cádiz is strong on seafood, particularly fried fish *(pescado frito)* and shellfish. Sea urchins *(erizos)* are a local favourite.

Plaza San Juan de Dios offers plenty of choice. If price is crucial, *Bar Letrán* does a reasonable menú for 700 ptas or platos combinados for 500 to 800 ptas; *Restaurante Pasaje Andaluz* has menús from 850 ptas and mains from 400 ptas. *El Sardinero* does similar fare better but for almost twice the price. On the east side of the plaza, *Cervecería Marisquería Nueva Ola* has good seafood and fish raciones or platters from 750 ptas, and platos combinados from 550 to 800 ptas. Or you can go for a sherry (150 ptas) and tapas. *La Pierrade* one block off the plaza at Calle Plocia 2 is a bit more adventurous. The 1250 ptas three course menú might offer mejillones (mussels) al Roquefort, or brocheta de cordero (lamb kebab), and includes wine and bread.

Another good area is around Plaza de Mina. *Café Bar Madrileño* on the plaza itself has a wide choice at reasonable prices: tapas at 150 to 200 ptas, salads around 350 ptas, stuffed peppers or pork brochettes for 700 ptas. *Dulcería Mina* at Calle Antonio López 2 has good pastries and excellent filled baguettes, and is a good spot for breakfast (tea/coffee, juice and tostada for 300 ptas; bacon and eggs 450 ptas). Off another side of the plaza, it's hard to pass by the mouthwatering fresh seafood tapas at *Cervecería Aurelio*, Calle Zorrilla 1. Down at the end of this street, you can enjoy the bay views at

Cervecería El Bogavante while attentive waiters serve up good scrambled eggs with prawns and asparagus for 700 ptas, big salads for 600 ptas, or mains from 800 to 1200 ptas.

Pizzería Nino's on Calle Columela just off Plaza de Topete does fine pizzas from 725 ptas, and pasta, Tex-Mex and burgers from 625 ptas. The nearby *Mercado Central* sells churros which you can take to cafés to enjoy with hot chocolate for breakfast.

Entertainment

There's a great atmosphere in some of the old city's plazas on hot summer nights, with the bars and cafés busy till well after midnight and all ages out enjoying the relative cool. *Café Desván* at Calle Santo Cristo 8 near Plaza Candelaria is a laid-back little bar with a happy hour and sometimes live music. Not far away, *Café Correo* at Calle Cardenal Zapata 6 is a popular spot with good music, but closed Monday and Tuesday. *Persígueme* on the corner of Calle Tinte and Calle Sagasta is another good music bar, with live sounds on Thursday.

From midnight or so in summer the real scene migrates to the Paseo Marítimo along Playa de la Victoria – about three km down the peninsula from the Puertas de Tierra. Here, some 300 metres past the big Hotel Playa Victoria you'll find lively music bars like *La Jarra* and *El Cobertizo Pub*; 350 metres further on is Calle Villa de Paradas, where throngs of people stand in the street with macetas (large plastic mugs) of beer for 250 ptas from bars like *H2O* and *Bar Kemedehe*. A lot of people simply mess around on the beach till deep into the madrugada. A taxi from the old city to this area costs around 600 ptas. Up to about 1.30 am you could use bus No 1 from Plaza de España to get here.

Getting There & Away

Bus Most buses are run by the Comes line (☎ 22 42 71) from Plaza de la Hispanidad. These include at least seven buses daily to Sevilla (one hour; 1200 to 1330 ptas), El Puerto de Santa María, Jerez de la Frontera,

Tarifa and Algeciras (two hours; 1225 ptas), three or more daily to Arcos de la Frontera, Ronda and Málaga, and buses at least daily to Córdoba and Granada.

Los Amarillos runs up to eight buses daily to El Puerto de Santa María and Sanlúcar de Barrameda, and two or three daily to Arcos de la Frontera and El Bosque, from its stop outside Viajes Socialtur (☎ 28 58 52), Avenida Ramón de Carranza 31, which has tickets and information.

Train Up to 30 trains daily run to/from El Puerto de Santa María and Jerez de la Frontera (40 minutes), and up to 15 to/from Sevilla (two hours; 1195 to 1400 ptas). There are three trains daily to/from Córdoba, and two each for Madrid (five hours) and Barcelona (12½ to 16 hours). The station (☎ 25 43 01) on Plaza Sevilla has consigna lockers.

Car & Motorcycle The A-4 *autopista* from Sevilla to Puerto Real on the east side of the Bahía de Cádiz carries a toll of 1395 ptas. The toll-free N-IV is a lot busier and slower. From Puerto Real the N-443 crosses a bridge over the narrowest part of the bay, to join the road in from the south about four km short of the old city.

Boat Trasmediterránea (☎ 22 74 21) at the Estación Marítima operates a passenger and vehicle ferry to the Canary Islands, leaving Cádiz on Saturday and arriving in Santa Cruz de Tenerife and Las Palmas, respectively, 1½ and two days later. The one-way passenger fare is from 26,750 to 53,060 ptas.

EL PUERTO DE SANTA MARÍA

The town of El Puerto de Santa María, 10 km north-east of Cádiz across the Bahía de Cádiz (22 km by road), makes an interesting side trip, best enjoyed by taking the ferry *El Vapor*. Columbus lived here from 1483 to 1486 and received some encouragement from the local Duque de Medinaceli for his travel plans. Here Columbus met the owner of the *Santa María*, Juan de la Cosa, who was his pilot in 1492 and who in 1500 issued the first world map. Later El Puerto became

Sherry

Sherry is fortified wine produced in the towns of Jerez de la Frontera, El Puerto de Santa María and Sanlúcar de Barrameda. A combination of climate, chalky soils that soak up the sun but retain moisture, and a special ageing process called the *solera* system produce this unique wine. Some 95% of sherry is made from the Palomino grape variety.

There are endless varieties of sherry but the main distinction is between *fino* (dry and the colour of straw) and *oloroso* (sweet, dark and with a strong bouquet). Both varieties have several subdivisions. An *amontillado* is an amber, moderately dry fino with a nutty flavour and a higher alcohol content than the paler finos. A *manzanilla* is a camomile-coloured fino from Sanlúcar de Barrameda: its delicate flavour is reckoned to come from sea breezes wafting into the bodegas. An *oloroso* combined with a sweet wine results in a 'cream sherry'. Sherry, especially fino, goes brilliantly with many tapas, but it can also accompany a meal: manzanilla is great with seafood and olorosos are excellent with red meat.

Once sherry grapes have been harvested, they are pressed and the resulting must is left to ferment. Within a few months a frothy veil of yeast called *flor* appears on the surface. The wine is transferred to the *bodegas* (wineries) in barrels *(botas)* of American oak with a capacity of more than 500 litres. The oak adds to the flavour of the wine.

New wine enters the solera process when it is a year old. The barrels, only about five-sixths full, are lined up in rows, called *escalas*, at least three deep: the barrels on the bottom layer, called the solera (from *suelo*, floor), contain the oldest wine. From these, around three times a year, 10% of the wine is drawn off. This is replaced with the same amount of wine from the barrels in the layer above, which is in turn replaced with wine taken from the next layer. The wines are left to age for at least three years, though amontillados are aged for at least five years and olorosos for seven.

Sherry houses are typically beautiful buildings set in attractive gardens. A tour will take you through the bodegas where the wine is stored and aged, inform you about the process and the history of the sherry producers and give you a bit of a tasting. You'll probably be shown the flor, visible through a glass end of a barrel of fino. You may also be given a demonstration of the use of a *venencia*, a cup with a long handle which is used to sample sherry from the barrel. These used to be made from whalebone and silver but have been replaced by plastic and stainless steel. The venencia is expertly manipulated, with the sherry cascading from head level into a glass held at waist level. ■

heavily involved in trade with the Americas and many palaces were built on the proceeds. Recent prosperity has come from sherry, and you can visit two bodegas here.

Orientation & Information

Most of the town is situated on the north bank of the Río Guadalete, just upstream from its mouth. *El Vapor* puts in dead in the centre at the Muelle del Vapor jetty, beside Plaza de las Galeras Reales. The tourist office (☎ 54 24 13), open daily from 10 am to 2 pm and 6 to 8 pm, is a hop, skip and jump away at Calle Guadalete 1. Calle Luna, the main drag with shops and banks, is straight ahead of the jetty. Calle Palacios runs parallel, one block to the left.

Buses come and go from stops outside the Plaza de Toros, off Calle Los Moros about 800 metres north-west of the Muelle del Vapor. Calle Los Moros runs all the way to

the riverfront. The train station is to the east on Plaza de la Estación by the Cádiz-Jerez road, a 10 minute walk from the centre.

Things to See & Do

Most of the sights are between the river and Plaza España, seven blocks from the Muelle del Vapor at the top of Calle Palacios. Stop by the little **Museo Municipal**, Calle Pagador 1 just off Plaza España, which has interesting archaeological and fine arts sections. It's open Monday to Saturday from 10 am to 2 pm (free). The **Iglesia Mayor Prioral**, with a baroque façade, dominates Plaza España. Back towards the river the **Castillo San Marcos** was built by Alfonso X after he took the town in 1260. Right by the river, **Plaza de las Galeras Reales** takes its name from the America-bound ships *(galeras)* which drew their water supplies from its four-spouted fountain. A couple of blocks to the west on Calle Aramburu de Mora is the lovely old fish exchange, the **Antigua Lonja de Pescado**, which is now a restaurant.

The tourist office can help with information about visiting the **18th century palaces** which are dotted around town. A couple in the centre are Palacio Medinaceli on Calle Aramburu de Mora and Palacio de Aranibar near the Castillo San Marcos.

To check out El Puerto's sherry bodegas, you need to call ahead. **Bodegas Osborne** (☎ 85 52 11) is open for visits (300 ptas) Monday to Friday from 10.30 am to 1 pm. In July **Bodegas Terry** (☎ 48 30 00) welcomes visitors (free) Monday to Friday at 9.30 am, 11.30 am and 12.30 pm. Check at the tourist office for times in other months.

Of the town's two beaches, the pine-backed **Playa de la Puntilla**, a half-hour walk south-west of the centre, is the most appealing. Bus No 5 from Plaza de las Galeras Reales goes to **Playa Fuentebravia**, further west.

Special Events
El Puerto's Feria De la Primavera early in May is in large measure dedicated to sherry, with around 180,000 half-bottles being drunk in a week.

Places to Stay
Camping Playa Las Dunas (☎ 87 22 10), Paseo Marítimo La Puntilla, Playa de la Puntilla, has shade and is open year round. Cost is 515 ptas per tent and per adult plus 440 ptas per car.

Las Columnas (☎ 85 20 19), Calle Vicario 8, a rambling old house a few steps south-east of Plaza España, has clean rooms with shared bath at 1200 ptas per person. *Hostal Santamaría* (☎ 85 36 31), Calle Pedro Muñoz Seca 38, two blocks towards the river from Plaza España, has reasonable singles/doubles at 1500/3000 ptas. Moving up the scale a little, *Hostal Manolo* (☎ 85 75 25), Calle Jesús de los Milagros 18, a block inland from Plaza de las Galeras Reales, has a friendly owner and singles/doubles at

2900/3900 ptas, while nearby *Hostal Loreto* (☎ 54 24 10), Calle Ganado 10, charges 2000/4500 ptas for rooms with private bath around a leafy courtyard. Both these places cut prices in the off season.

The top place is *Monasterio San Miguel* (☎ 54 04 40), Calle Virgen de los Milagros 27, with rooms from 10,800/15,100 ptas plus IVA.

Places to Eat
El Puerto is an excellent place to sample seafood. Crowds head for the *Romerijo* and *Romerijo 2* on Calle Ribera del Marisco, near the Muelle del Vapor, where you can buy portions of seafood in paper cones to take away or eat at the tables outside. Huge counters display what's available. Romerijo specialises in boiled fresh seafood while Romerijo 2 fries it up and you buy by the quarter-kilo – prawns 300 ptas, choco (cuttlefish) 500 ptas and so on. Just back from here, *Café Bar Herrera* has good food and prices, with a nice little salad at 250 ptas and pinchitos morenos at 800 ptas. *Restaurante El Resbaladero* in the old fish exchange on Calle Aramburu de Mora offers air-con comfort inside and a medium-to-expensive menu with lots of seafood and fish choices.

For breakfast, or a drink, head to *Milor*, on the corner of Calle Tie Piury and Calle Virgen de los Milagros, two blocks north of the castle. It's a comfy clone of an English pub, open from 8 am weekdays and 10 am on weekends. *Tortillería Bar*, Calle Palacios 2, a little inland from the tourist office, does a huge variety of bocadillos from 175 to 200 ptas including bacalao, chorizo, salmon and Roquefort. *Cafetería las Capuchinas* in the Monasterio San Miguel hotel provides welcome air-con on a hot day. Enjoy a drink or the three course menú at 1250 ptas plus IVA.

Entertainment
El Puerto is a pretty lively place with plenty of bars, and quite a lot more going on in summer. On Saturday night in July/August, there are free concerts in Plaza Colón near

the tourist office. Two flamenco clubs – *Tertulia Flamenca Tomás El Nitri*, at Calle Diego Niño 1, and *Peña Flamenca El Chumni* – have performances from time to time in their 18th century cellars; ask at the tourist office about forthcoming events. There are also *night boat trips* (two hours) on the Bahía de Cádiz from July to September (600 ptas). There's more action, bars, discos etc east of town out at Playa Valdelagrana.

Getting There & Away

Bus A timetable is posted on the window of Bar Sol y Sombra, close to the Plaza de Toros bus stops. There are buses for Cádiz almost half-hourly Monday to Friday from 6.55 am to 9.30 pm (fewer at weekends) and four to nine daily to Jerez de la Frontera and Sanlúcar de Barrameda. More buses for Cádiz and Jerez leave from outside the train station.

Train El Puerto is on the Cádiz-Sevilla line, half an hour from Cádiz, with up to 30 trains daily in each direction, leaving from the station east of Plaza de la Estación.

Boat *El Vapor* sails from the Estación Marítima in Cádiz daily at 10 am, noon, and 2, 6.30 and 8.30 pm, with an extra trip at 4.30 pm on Sunday. Trips back from El Puerto are at 9 and 11 am and 1, 3.30 and 7.30 pm, plus 5.30 pm on Sunday. The crossing takes 45 minutes; 250 ptas one way.

SANLÚCAR DE BARRAMEDA

The northern tip of the sherry triangle and a flourishing summer resort, Sanlúcar is 23 km north-west of El Puerto de Santa María. It has a likeable atmosphere and a fine location on the Guadalquivir estuary looking across to the tip of the Parque Nacional de Doñana.

Columbus set sail from Sanlúcar in 1498 on his third voyage to the Caribbean. So, in 1519, did the Portuguese Ferdinand Magellan, who set off with five ships to find, as Columbus had been trying to do, a westerly route to the spice islands of Indonesia.

Magellan achieved the first-ever voyage round Cape Horn but was killed in the Philippines. By the time his Basque pilot Sebastián Elcano completed the first circumnavigation of the globe by returning to Sanlúcar in 1522, just one ship, the *Santa María de Victoria*, and 18 sailors were left.

Orientation

Sanlúcar stretches about 2.5 km along the south-east side of the estuary. Calzada del Ejército, running 600 metres inland from the seafront Paseo Marítimo, is the main avenue. A block beyond its inland end is Plaza del Cabildo, the central square. The Los Amarillos bus station is on Plaza La Salle, 500 metres south-west of Plaza del Cabildo along Calle San Juan.

The old fishing quarter, Bajo de Guía, site of Sanlúcar's best restaurants and Doñana boat departures, is 750 metres north-east along the riverfront from Calzada del Ejército.

Information

The tourist office (☎ 36 61 10) is towards the inland end of Calzada del Ejército. It's open Monday to Friday from 10 am to 2 pm and 6 to 8 pm, Saturday and Sunday from 10 am to 1 pm. You'll find banks and ATMs on Plaza del Cabildo and Calle San Juan.

The Centro de Interpretación de la Naturaleza (☎ 36 38 13) at the end of Avenida de Bajo de Guía, which runs to Bajo de Guía from near the seaward end of Avenida del Ejército, has displays and information on the Parque Nacional de Doñana and related topics. It's open Monday to Friday from 9 am to 3 pm, weekends and holidays from 9.30 am to 2.30 pm.

Things to See & Do

Walking Tour A tour of the sights doesn't take long as most of them aren't open to visitors. From Plaza del Cabildo, cross Calle Ancha to Plaza San Roque and head uphill on Calle Bretones, where you can look into the **mercado** just before reaching **Las Covachas**, a set of 15th century wine cellars (recently closed for restoration). Here the street turns right and becomes Calle Cuesta de Belén where, Monday to Friday from 10 am to 2 pm, you can look into the **Palacio de Orleans y Borbón**. The creation of this neomudéjar fantasy for the aristocratic Montpensier family in the 19th century was what spurred Sanlúcar's growth as a resort. Today the building is the ayuntamiento.

From the top of Calle Cuesta de Belén, a block to the left along Calle Caballeros is the 15th century **Iglesia de Nuestra Señora de la O**, with a mudéjar façade and ceiling (but under restoration). Adjoining is the **Palacio de los Duques de Medina Sidonia** (not open to visitors) home of the aristocratic family which once owned more of Spain than any other. Some 200 metres further along the street is the 15th century **Castillo de Santiago** (closed for restoration), amid buildings of the Barbadillo sherry company. From the castle you can return directly downhill to the town centre.

Beach Sanlúcar's sandy beach runs along the riverfront and several km beyond to the south-west.

Sherry Bodegas Free tours of Bodegas Barbadillo, the town's biggest sherry firm, at Calle Luis de Eguilaz 11, are given every Thursday at 12.30 pm. Book in advance on ☎ 36 08 94, or through the tourist office. Barbadillo and other sherry houses also do some tours on other weekday mornings; check with the tourist office.

Parque Nacional de Doñana Trips to the national park are made by the boat *Real Fernando* from Bajo de Guía. The four hour trip ventures 10 km up the Guadalquivir with stops for guided walks at some *salinas* (salt lagoons) which attract plentiful bird life, and a restored farmhouse in pine woods. Guides speak Spanish and English. The trips leave Tuesday to Sunday, at 9 am and 4 pm from May to mid-September, 10 am the rest of the year. Tickets (2100 ptas) are sold at the Centro de Interpretación de la Naturaleza (see under Information earlier in this section) and at a kiosk near the boat's pier, which

opens for longer hours. At holiday times you need to book a few days ahead.

Special Events
The Sanlúcar summer gets going with a sherry festival, the Feria de la Manzanilla, in late May or early June, and blossoms in July and August with happenings like the Noches de Bajo de Guía flamenco season (late July), jazz and classical music festivals, one-off concerts by some good visiting bands, and Sanlúcar's unique horse races (see the boxed aside).

Places to Stay
You need to book well ahead for a room at holiday times. At other times, expect about 20% off prices given here. The only bottom-end place seems to be *Hostal La Blanca Paloma* (☎ 36 36 44) at Plaza San Roque 15,

---

Hoofbeats on the Sand
Sanlúcar's *carreras de caballos*, held every year (bar a couple of interruptions for war) since 1845, may be the only sporting event in the world where police crowd control takes the form of gently persuading the spectators to take off their shoes and stand in an estuary. It's an exciting spectacle in which real racehorses, many of them Irish, French, or British-bred thoroughbreds, thunder along the sands near the water's edge between a thick crowd of spectators on the landward side and a thinner one standing in the shallows on the other.

Two three-day meetings are held every August, one around the 9th of the month, the other around the 24th. Exact starting times depend on the tides (!) but the first race normally begins around 6 pm. The finish is about one km south-west of Calzada del Ejército, and most races start at Bajo de Guía. Prize money for the two meetings totals around 15 million ptas.

Serious racegoers will want to get into the area with spectator stands, bookmakers, paddock and winner's enclosure up by the finishing post. The rest of the crowd strings itself back along the course. Here the only bookies, it seems, are children who set up little cardboard-box booths and scrape a line across the track in front, then take money on which horse will cross their 'finish' first! ■

with adequate singles/doubles for 2500/4000 ptas. *Hostal Bohemia* (☎ 36 95 99), Calle Don Claudio 5, off Calle Ancha 300 metres north-east of Plaza del Cabildo, has better rooms with bath at around 5500 ptas a double.

Hotel Los Helechos (☎ 36 76 55) at Calle Madre de Dios 9, off Calle San Juan 200 metres from Plaza del Cabildo, is an excellent mid-range choice with rooms round two pretty courtyards and a cosy bar. Singles/doubles are 5000/7000 ptas plus IVA. The welcoming *Hotel Tartaneros* (☎ 36 20 44), Calle Tartaneros 8 at the inland end of Calzada del Ejército, is a turn-of-the-century industrialist's mansion with comfy if rather bare rooms for 6500/10,000 ptas plus IVA.

Places to Eat
The line of seafood restaurants facing the riverfront at Bajo de Guía are a reason in themselves for visiting Sanlúcar. Spain holds few more idyllic dining experiences than watching the sun go down over the Guadalquivir while tucking into the succulent fresh fare here and washing it down with a glass or two of Sanlúcar's manzanilla sherry. Just wander along and pick a restaurant that suits your pocket. The most popular include *Restaurante Poma, Restaurante Virgen del Carmen, Restaurante Casa Juan* and *Bar Joselito Huerta*. At the Virgen del Carmen most fish mains, plancha (grilled) or frito (fried), are 1000 to 1400 ptas. You shouldn't miss out on the starters: langostinos (king prawns) and the juicy coquines al ajillo (cockles cooked in garlic), both 1000 ptas, are specialities. A half-bottle of manzanilla is 600 ptas.

Elsewhere, there are lots of cafés and bars, many serving manzanilla from the barrel, around Plaza del Cabildo. *Bar El Cura*, Calle Amargura 2, in an alley off Plaza San Roque, does some good-value platos combinados for 500 ptas.

Entertainment
There are some lively music bars and discos on and around Calzada del Ejército and Plaza del Cabildo.

Getting There & Away
Bus Los Amarillos runs up to nine buses daily to/from El Puerto de Santa María and Cádiz, and up to 17 to/from Sevilla. Linesur-Valenciana, whose stop is outside the Bar La Jaula opposite the Hotel Guadalquivir on Calzada del Ejército, runs hourly buses to/from Jerez de la Frontera.

Boat Though you can visit Sanlúcar on excursion boats from Sevilla, you can't take a one-way ride upriver from Sanlúcar to Sevilla.

JEREZ DE LA FRONTERA
The large town of Jerez (population 190,000), 36 km north-east of Cádiz, is world-famous for its wine – sherry – made from grapes grown on the chalky soil around the town. Most people come here to visit its bodegas.

British capital was largely responsible for the development of the wineries from around the 1830s, and Jerez upper-crust society is a mixture of *andaluz* and British due to inter-marriage among families of wine traders over the past 150 years. Since the 1980s most of the wineries, previously owned by about 15 families, have been bought out by multinational companies. Jerez reeks of money with loads of fancy shops, well-heeled residents, wide, spacious streets, old mansions and beautiful churches in its interesting old quarter. It puts on fantastic fiestas with sleek horses, beautiful people, and flamenco. But behind the façade lurk the problems of high unemployment and drug abuse common to many Andalucían towns.

History
The Muslims called the town Scheris or Xeres, from which 'Jerez' and 'sherry' are derived. The drink was already famed in England in Shakespeare's time. Jerez had its share of strife in the late 19th century when anarchism gained ground in Andalucía – one day in 1891 thousands of peasants armed with scythes and sticks marched in and occupied the town for a few hours, succeeding only in bringing down further repression on

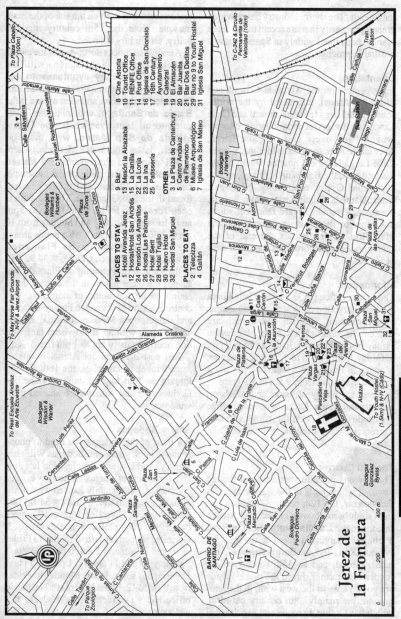

PLACES TO STAY

1   Hotel Avenida Jerez
12 Hostal/Hotel San Andrés
24 Pensión Los Amarillos
26 Hostal Las Palomas
27 Hotel Serit
28 Hotel Trujillo
30 Nuevo Hotel
32 Hostal San Miguel

PLACES TO EAT

2   Telepizza
4   Gaitán
9   Bar
13 Mesón la Alcazaba
15 La Canilla
22 La Lonja
23 La Ina
25 Patisserie

OTHER

3   La Plaza de Canterbury
5   Centro Andaluz
    de Flamenco
6   Museo Arqueológico
7   Iglesia de San Mateo
8   Cine Astoria
10 Tourist Office
11 RENFE Office
14 Post Office
16 Iglesia de San Dionisio
17 16th Century
    Ayuntamiento
18 Catedral
19 El Almacén
20 Bar Juanita
21 Bar Dos Deditos
29 Bus no 9 to Youth Hostel
31 Iglesia San Miguel

ANDALUCÍA

Jerez de la Frontera

their heads. The sherry industry has provided greater prosperity in more recent times. Jerez brandy, consumed widely in Spain, is also a profitable product.

Orientation

Jerez centres on the Alameda Cristina and Plaza del Arenal, connected by the north-south Calle Larga (pedestrianised) and Calle Lancería. Budget accommodation clusters around two streets east of Calle Larga, Avenida de Arcos and Calle Medina. West of Calle Larga is the old quarter, whose north-western part, the Barrio de Santiago, retains a sizeable Gypsy community. North-east from Alameda Cristina runs Calle Sevilla, becoming Avenida Álvaro Domecq, which has some of the up-market hotels and the May Horse Fair grounds. Several of the sherry bodegas are north-east and south-west of the centre.

Information

The tourist office (☎ 33 11 50), Calle Larga 39, has energetic young staff and mountains of information. English and French are spoken. In summer it's open Monday to Friday from 10 am to 1.30 pm and 5 to 9 pm, Saturday from 10 am to 1.30 pm; in winter, Monday to Friday from 9 am to 2 pm and 5 to 7 pm, Saturday from 9 am to 1.30 pm.

There are plenty of banks and ATMs on and around Calle Larga. The post office (postcode 11400) is on the corner of Calle Cerrón and Calle Medina, just east of Calle Larga.

The Old Quarter

The obvious place to start a tour of the old town, of which parts of the walls survive, is the **alcázar**, the 12th century Almohad fortress slightly south-west of Plaza del Arenal. Inside are the **Capilla Santa María la Real**, a chapel converted from a mosque by Alfonso X in 1264, the **Baños Árabes** (Arab baths, closed) and an 18th century palace (under restoration). From the plaza outside are good views to the west with, in the foreground, the mainly 18th century **catedral**, which has Gothic, baroque and neoclassical

features and was built on the site of the main mosque. Note the 15th century mudéjar belfry, set slightly apart.

A couple of blocks north-east of the cathedral is Plaza de la Asunción, with the splendid 16th century **ayuntamiento** and lovely 15th century mudéjar **Iglesia de San Dionisio**. To the north and west of here is the **Barrio de Santiago**, with churches dedicated to all four evangelists: the Gothic **Iglesia de San Mateo**, with mudéjar chapels, is on Plaza del Mercado, where you'll also find the refurbished **Museo Arqueológico**. The pride of the museum's collection is a 7th century BC Greek helmet found in the Río Guadalete. The museum is open Tuesday to Friday from 10 am to 2 pm and 4 to 7 pm, Saturday and Sunday from 10 am to 2.30 pm (250 ptas). Also in this area is the **Centro Andaluz de Flamenco** (Andalucían Flamenco Centre; ☎ 34 92 65), in the Palacio de Pemartín on Plaza de San Juan. Like other places in the district, Jerez claims to be the home of flamenco. The centre is a kind of flamenco library-museum and school, open Monday to Friday from 9 am to 2 pm, with an audio-visual presentation hourly from 10 am to 1 pm (free).

Just east of Plaza del Arenal is one of Jerez's loveliest churches, the 16th century **Iglesia de San Miguel**, built in Isabelline Gothic style and with superb stained-glass windows.

Sherry Bodegas

For most of the bodegas you need to phone ahead to book your visit. Bodegas Williams, Harveys and Domecq are closed in late July and for much of August. The two biggest companies, both handily located west of the alcázar, are González Byass (☎ 34 00 00), Calle Manuel González s/n, and Domecq (☎ 15 15 00), Calle San Ildefonso 3. González is open for visits Monday to Friday at 10 and 11 am and 1 and 6 pm (375 ptas), Saturday 10 and 11 am and 1 pm (475 ptas). Domecq has several tours Monday to Friday from 9 am to 12.30 pm (350 ptas). The tourist office has a complete list of bodegas that welcome visitors.

Other Attractions

One of Jerez's main attractions is the **Real Escuela Andaluz del Arte Ecuestre** (Royal Andalucían School of Equestrian Art; ☎ 31 11 00) on Avenida Duque de Abrantes in the north of town. The school trains horses and riders in dressage, and you can watch them being put through their paces in training sessions on Monday, Tuesday, Wednesday and Friday from 11 am to 1 pm (450 ptas). On Thursday at noon there's an official show where the horses perform to classical music (around 2000 ptas). A couple of km west of the centre is the **Parque Zoológico**, or Zoo Jerez, with lovely gardens and a wild animal recuperation centre (adults 500 ptas, children 300 ptas). It's open Tuesday to Sunday from 10 am to 6 pm, to 8 pm in summer.

Special Events

Jerez's Feria de Caballo (horse fair) in early May is one of Andalucía's biggest festivals, with music and dancing as well as all kinds of horse competitions. Colourful parades of horses pass through the fairgrounds, the aristocratic-looking male riders decked out in flat-topped hats, frilly white shirts, black trousers and leather chaps, their female counterparts in traditional long, frilled, spotted dresses. Flamenco features in the early to mid-September festival of song and dance, the Fiesta de la Bulería. The Fiestas de Otoño from mid-September to mid-October, celebrating the grape harvest, range from cultural events to horse races and dressage competitions, concluding with a massive parade of horses and riders.

Places to Stay

Prices given are for summer unless stated otherwise. Room rates go sky-high during the May horse fair, and you need to book ahead.

Places to Stay – bottom end

The modern *Albergue Juvenil Jerez* youth hostel (☎ 34 28 90) is 1.5 km south of the centre at Avenida Carrero Blanco 30. Bus No 9 from Plaza de las Angustias, or No 1 or 3 from Plaza del Arenal, will take you there.

Other budget choices are more conveniently located around Calle Medina and Avenida de Arcos and on Calle Caballeros, which runs south-east off Plaza del Arenal. The friendly *Hostal/Hotel San Andrés* (☎ 34 09 83), Calle Morenos 12, is a good choice. For 2000 ptas per person you can get a room with private bath and TV, or there are cheaper rooms with shared bath. Free parking is available. Closer to the bus station, *Pensión Los Amarillos*, Calle Medina 30, is run by the same family and charges 1300 ptas per person with shared bath. *Hostal Las Palomas* (☎ 34 37 73), Calle Higueras 17, is another good bet. Spacious, nicely furnished rooms with shared bath go for 1500 ptas per person; there are also doubles with bath for 3000 ptas. *Nuevo Hotel* (☎ 33 16 00), Calle Caballeros 23, in an old mansion, has roomy singles/doubles with bath, TV and winter heating from 2000/3500 ptas. Nearby, *Hostal San Miguel* (☎ 34 85 62), Plaza San Miguel 4, costs 1500/3000 ptas, or 2500/4500 ptas with attached bath.

Places to Stay – middle & top end

Add IVA to the following prices. *Hotel Trujillo* (☎ 34 24 38), Calle Medina 3, has rooms with all mod cons at 3500/5500 ptas in the off season, 4500/7500 ptas from May to October. Nearby, *Hotel Serit* (☎ 34 07 00), Calle Higueras 7, has similar rooms for 4500/6000 ptas. *Hotel Avenida Jerez* (☎ 34 74 11), Avenida Álvaro Domecq 10, has doubles for 14,000 ptas. There are more top-end places on this road.

Places to Eat

These are rather spread out. The restaurants on Pescadería Vieja, a small alley on the west side of Plaza del Arenal which catches a refreshing breeze on a hot day, are moderate to expensive. *La Lonja* has a menú for 1000 ptas, for which you get two courses and a drink. *La Ina* has menús from 850 ptas with bread, drink and dessert. *Bar Juanita*, and *El Almacén* round the corner on Calle Ferros, are local tapas haunts, and good places to sample a fino, too.

There's a *McDonald's* on Calle Larga. At

Calle Larga 8, *La Canilla* is fine for a simple breakfast, under big canvas umbrellas in summer. Cheaper breakfasts can be had in the *Bar* on the corner of Plaza de Plateros, behind Iglesia de San Dionisio.

Mesón la Alcazaba, Calle Medina 19, with a covered patio, is good value with reasonable à-la-carte prices, a menú with plenty of choice at 800 ptas and platos combinados for 500 ptas. The *Patissería*, corner Calles Medina and Higueras, has good cakes, pastries and baguettes. *Telepizza* on Calle Salvatierra, north of the bullring in the heart of the small nightlife area, has cheap deals and does a roaring trade.

For a splash-out meal at *Gaitán*, Calle Gaitán 3, two blocks west of the Alameda Cristina, you can expect to pay around 1000 ptas for starters such as seafood cocktails, a little less for soups, and 1500 to 2000 ptas for main courses.

Entertainment

Check at the tourist office and watch out for posters advertising forthcoming events. The newspaper *Diario de Jerez* has some what's-on information. *Cine Astoria* on Calle Francos is an outdoor cinema and concert area where there's often live music from blues to flamenco; there are sometimes concerts in the bullring, too. *Bar Dos Deditos*, Plaza Vargas 1, behind Pescadería Vieja, has live music some nights, including blues; if there's something on, you can't miss the crowd spilling on to the pavement.

North-east of the centre just before the bullring, *La Plaza de Canterbury*, with loads of bars around a central courtyard, attracts a young crowd. Between the bullring and Plaza Caballo is a small nightlife area centred on Calle Salvatierra, with bars, and a couple of clubs for dancing until late on weekend nights and fiestas.

For flamenco, there are several peñas in the Barrio de Santiago; they're listed on the tourist office map. *El Laga Tío Parrilla*, Plaza del Mercado, has more tourist-oriented flamenco performances on Monday and Saturday nights.

Spectator Sport

Jerez has a motorcycle and car racing track, the Circuito Permanente de Velocidad (☎ 15 11 00), on the C-342 10 km east of town. Motorcycle races are held throughout the year, and in May you may catch a World Championship *grand prix*. There are around three car races annually.

Getting There & Away

Air Jerez airport (☎ 15 00 00), the only one serving Cádiz and the Costa de la Luz, is seven km north-east of town on the N-IV. Aviaco (☎ 15 00 10) has direct flights daily to/from Madrid, and three days a week to/from Barcelona.

Bus The bus station is on Calle Cartuja, the extension of Calle Medina, about a km south-east of the centre. Comes has buses for Cádiz (up to 18 daily), El Puerto de Santa María (six daily; 150 ptas), Vejer de la Frontera and Barbate (one daily), Ronda (four daily; 1255 ptas) and on to Málaga (2370 ptas), and Córdoba (one daily; 1850 ptas). There are plenty of buses to Sevilla (875 ptas) by Linesur-Valenciana and Comes. Linesur-Valenciana also runs to Sanlúcar de Barrameda (205 ptas) hourly from 7 am to 8 pm. Los Amarillos handles buses to *pueblos* inland with plenty to Arcos de la Frontera (280 ptas), and four daily to El Bosque. For bus information you can call ☎ 34 52 07.

Train The train station is a couple of blocks further south-east at the end of Calle Cartuja. Jerez is on the Cádiz-Sevilla line with plenty of trains in both directions. The central RENFE office at Calle Larga 34 is open Monday to Saturday from 9 am to 2 pm and 5 to 8.30 pm.

ARCOS DE LA FRONTERA

Arcos (population 28,000) is 30 km east of Jerez along the N-342 across pretty, rolling agricultural country of wheat and sunflower fields, vineyards and fruit orchards. From a distance, it's a striking sight with its castle and old town atop a ridge, and the Río

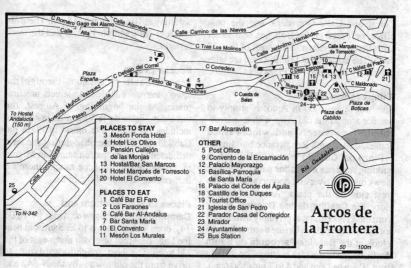

PLACES TO STAY
3 Mesón Fonda Hotel
4 Hotel Los Olivos
8 Pensión Callejón
   de las Monjas
13 Hostal/Bar San Marcos
14 Hotel Marqués de Torresoto
20 Hotel El Convento

PLACES TO EAT
1 Café Bar El Faro
2 Los Faraones
6 Café Bar Al-Andalus
7 Bar Santa María
10 El Convento
11 Mesón Los Murales

17 Bar Alcaraván

OTHER
5 Post Office
9 Convento de la Encarnación
12 Palacio Mayorazgo
15 Basílica-Parroquia
   de Santa María
16 Palacio del Conde del Águila
18 Castillo de los Duques
19 Tourist Office
21 Iglesia de San Pedro
22 Parador Casa del Corregidor
23 Mirador
24 Ayuntamiento
25 Bus Station

**Arcos de
la Frontera**

0   50   100m

Guadalete meandering below – though it's less enchanting from closer up with the modern town spilling out below the ridge. Arcos is said to have a dark, sinister side: there are tales of strange vibes, madness, interbreeding, covens and witchcraft. Whether or not you feel anything mysterious in the atmosphere, Arcos is well worth visiting to explore its old town, which has a street plan little changed since medieval times and some lovely post-Reconquista buildings including Renaissance palaces and two splendid churches.

History
Arcos' strategic location has been prized from way back. It was taken from the Visigoths by the Muslims in 711. In the 11th century it was for a time an independent taifa until absorbed by Sevilla. In 1255 Alfonso X took the town and repopulated it with Castilians and Leonese. Some Muslims stayed but rebelled in 1261 and were evicted by 1264. In 1440 the town passed to the Ponce de León family, known as the Duques de Arcos, who were active in the conquest of the Emirate of Granada. When the last Duque de Arcos died heirless in 1780, his

cousin, the Duquesa de Benavente, took over his lands. She was partly responsible for replacing sheep farming with cereals, olives, vines and horse breeding as the dominant economic activity around Arcos. During the period of liberal rule of 1820-23, the so-called *señorío* system of land ownership by noble families was abolished, but the rural poverty that was part and parcel of the system continued until well into the 20th century.

Orientation & Information
From the bus station, on Calle Corregidores in part of the new town, it's a one km uphill walk to the old town. About halfway up is Plaza España, from where Paseo de los Boliches and Calle Corredera both head east up to the old town's main square, Plaza del Cabildo. The rest of the old town spreads north and east along the ridge and its gentler slopes from here. The tourist office (☎ 70 22 64) on Plaza del Cabildo, open Monday to Saturday from 9 am to 2 pm and 5 to 7 pm, Sunday from 11 am to 1.30 pm, has lively staff who can provide a useful map and other information.

Banks and ATMs, on Calle Debajo del

ANDALUCÍA

Corral and Calle Corredera, and the post office, on Paseo de los Boliches near Hotel Los Olivos, are down to the west of the old town. The postcode is 11630. There are telephones by the church on Plaza del Cabildo.

Things to See & Do
The best thing to do in Arcos is simply to wander around the old town with its narrow cobblestone streets and whitewashed houses, dotted with Renaissance buildings.

Plaza del Cabildo is surrounded by fine buildings and has a **mirador** with panoramic views over the river and countryside. On the west side of the plaza, Arcos' crowning glory, the **Castillo de los Duques**, dating from the 11th century, is privately owned and not open to the public. On the north side, take a look at the **Basílica-Parroquia de Santa María**, begun in the 15th century – open daily from 10 am to 1 pm and 4 to 7 pm (150 ptas). On the east, the **parador**, with striking views from its restaurant and terrace, is a 1960s reconstruction of a 16th century magistrate's house, the **Casa del Corregidor**. The **ayuntamiento** on the south side of the plaza has a mudéjar panelled ceiling and a portrait of Carlos IV attributed to Goya.

Explore the streets east of here, which pass by some lovely buildings such as the 16th century **Convento de la Encarnación** on Calle Marqués de Torresoto, which has a Gothic façade. On Calle Núñez de Prado is the impressive 15th century Gothic **Iglesia de San Pedro**, with a large collection of religious paintings; its bell tower affords great views but has recently been closed. The church is open Monday to Saturday from 10 am to 1 pm and 4 to 7 pm (150 ptas). Nearby, the 17th century **Palacio Mayorazgo** has an exhibition of Semana Santa posters dating back to 1974.

The attractive building with an arch over Calle Deán Espinosa just below Plaza del Cabildo is the 15th century mudéjar **Palacio del Conde del Águila**.

Organised Tours
The tourist office organises hour-long guided tours of the old town Monday to Saturday at 10 am, noon and 5 pm. There are also tours of traditional patios and the town at night.

Special Events
Semana Santa processions through the town's narrow cobblestone streets are dramatic. At the beginning of August, the three-day Fiesta de la Virgen de las Nieves includes late-night live music in Plaza del Cabildo. On 29 September, during the feria dedicated to Arcos' patron saint San Miguel in the last few days of the month, there's a hair-raising running of the bulls.

Places to Stay – bottom end
Camping *Camping Lago de Arcos* (☎ 70 05 14), open year round, is in El Santiscal near the Lago de Arcos reservoir north-east of the old town. The most straightforward route to drive from the old town is by the N-342 and the Carretera El Bosque y Ubrique. Turn left after the bridge across the dam. A local bus runs here from Arcos.

Pensiones & Hostales There are a couple of budget places in the old town. *Hostal San Marcos* (☎ 70 07 21), above the bar and restaurant of the same name at Calle Marqués de Torresoto 6, a short walk east of Plaza del Cabildo, has a handful of good, simple rooms with hand-painted furniture and attached bath. There's a roof terrace with fine views. Singles/doubles cost 2000/4000 ptas, or 1500/3000 ptas in winter. *Pensión Callejón de las Monjas* (☎ 70 23 02), Calle Deán Espinosa 4, is right by the picture-postcard arch over this street, just west of Plaza del Cabildo. Doubles cost 3500 and 4500 ptas. There's a barber's chair in reception and the owner will offer to cut your hair.

Mesón Fonda Hotel on Calle Debajo de Corral near Plaza España costs 1600 ptas per person in rooms with shared bath, but upgrading is planned. The restaurant below has a cheap menú (750 ptas).

Hostal Andalucía (☎ 70 07 14) at Polígono Industrial El Retiro, on the N-342 highway about 300 metres south-west of the bus station, offers the best deal in town i you're not too picky about your surroundings: it's above a car yard and backed by workshops. Large rooms with attached bath and fan cost 1500 ptas a person, which is excellent value for singles.

Places to Stay – middle & top end

Arcos has some charming places to stay in this category. *Hotel El Convento* (☎ 70 23 33), Calle Maldonado 2, in a 17th century convent just east of Plaza del Cabildo, has similar views to the parador's. Fine singles/doubles are 5000/7000 ptas plus IVA from March to October, less in winter. In the same part of town, *Hotel Marqués de Torresoto* (☎ 70 42 56), in a converted mansion at Calle Marqués de Torresoto 4, is 6000/8000 ptas plus IVA. Next door is a pleasant café for snacks and ice creams. Down the hill towards Plaza España, the friendly and attractive *Hotel Los Olivos* (☎ 70 08 11), Paseo de los Boliches 30, has rooms at 5000/9000 ptas plus IVA from March to November, less in winter. *Parador Casa del Corregidor* (☎ 70 05 00) on Plaza del Cabildo, offers typical parador luxury at 10,000/15,000 ptas plus IVA.

Places to Eat

Arcos has places to eat to suit all pockets. In the old town the homely *Bar San Marcos* at Calle Marqués de Torrosoto 6 does platos combinados from 500 to 900 ptas, tapas around 200 ptas and a menú at 880 ptas. Opposite, *El Convento* is a classy restaurant turning out interesting fare – the three course menú is 2300 ptas including a drink. *Mesón Los Murales*, Plaza de Boticas 1, near the Hotel El Convento, has a cheaper menú at 900 ptas. The cave-like *Bar Alcaraván* at Calle Nueva 1, with tables outside under the castle walls, is good for tapas. Simple, economical meals can be had at *Bar Santa María* on Cuesta de Belén and at *Café Bar Al-Andalus* further down the same street, with tables outside.

In the new town, there are a couple of options on Calle Debajo del Corral near Plaza España. *Café Bar El Faro* at No 14 has breakfast at 225 ptas, main dishes from 500

to 700 ptas and a menú at 900 ptas. At No 8, *Los Faraones* does both Spanish and Egyptian Arabic food. There are menús from 1250 to 1550 ptas. The Arabic food is excellent with some tasty vegetarian choices, though the price can quickly add up if you order a few side dishes. There are more eateries down by the river, below the castle.

Entertainment

In July and August, flamenco happens down by the river at Plaza del Cananeo on Thursday night from 10.30 pm.

Getting There & Away

Buses departing from Calle Corregidores from Monday to Friday include 19 a day to Jerez, six to El Bosque, and a few each to Cádiz, Sevilla and Ronda. On some routes there are fewer buses on weekends. For information you can call ☎ 70 20 15.

PARQUE NATURAL SIERRA DE GRAZALEMA

The mountainous Parque Natural Sierra de Grazalema in the north-east of Cádiz province, dotted with attractive white towns and villages, is the wettest part of Spain and one of Andalucía's most beautiful and green areas. This is fine walking country, and there are opportunities for a range of other activities from rock climbing and caving to paragliding and trout fishing. The best times to visit are spring, early summer and autumn. The park extends into the north-west of Málaga province, where it includes the Cueva de la Pileta with ancient rock paintings (see the Around Ronda section later in this chapter).

The rare Spanish fir *(pinsapo)*, a relic of forests more than two million years old, dominates the land above 1000 metres. Other vegetation is typically Mediterranean and includes holm oak, cork oak, gall oak, wild olive and riverside forest. Among the park's fauna are the ibex, chamois, roe deer, mongoose, otter and genet. Birds of prey include Bonelli's eagle, golden eagle, Egyptian vulture and one of Europe's largest colonies of common vultures, which feed on

ANDALUCÍA

carcasses of the area's sheep, pigs, goats and cattle.

Plenty of maps and printed information on the park are available, including suggested walks and drives. Many of the best walking routes are in the north of the park, around and between the towns of El Bosque, Bena-mahoma, Grazalema and Zahara de la Sierra, all of which are good bases and can be linked in circuits of three or four days. Highlight walks include the route through the *pinsapar* (pinsapo forest) between Grazalema and Benamahoma, the ascent of the highest peak in Cádiz province, El Torreón, also called El Pinar (1654 metres), between the same two towns, and the trip into the Garganta Verde gorge south of Zahara.

For some walking routes, including several peaks and entry to the pinsapares, permission is needed. Check at the information offices in El Bosque, Benamahoma, Grazalema or Zahara de la Sierra.

El Bosque

From Arcos de la Frontera, the C-344 heads 33 km east to El Bosque across rolling country which gradually becomes more treed and dotted with farms and livestock. El Bosque is prettily situated below the wooded foothills of the Sierra de Albarracín, the westernmost section of the natural park. The town grew up around the Palacio de Marcenilla, which was owned by the Duques de Arcos. It's better known for sports than for its sights: there's a take-off point for hang-gliders and paragliders in the Sierra de Albarracín, plenty of trout to be fished in the streams near the town, and some good walking.

Orientation & Information Most places you'll need are close to the C-344 (Avenida Diputación) on the west side of town. You can't miss the Punto de Información y Oficina del Parque Natural (☎ 72 70 29), open daily from 9 am to 2 pm and Friday to Sunday from 4 to 6 pm. El Bosque's large public swimming pool (350 ptas), with shade, is on the opposite side of the square fronting the park office.

Places to Stay & Eat The *Albergue Campamento El Bosque* youth hostel (☎ 71 62 12), Molino de Enmedio s/n, is pleasantly situated by a trout stream 800 metres from the C-344 on the west side of town. Turn off by the Hotel Las Truchas. The hostel has bungalows and a shady camping area as well as doubles and triples in the main block. There's a swimming pool, too. Various walks, including alongside the Río El Bosque, start on a track beside the hostel; at the beginning of the track, there's an information board showing the routes. *Camping La Torrecilla* (☎ 71 60 95) is on the far side of town, on Carretera Antigua El Bosque-Ubrique, one km off the C-344. Cost for two adults, one tent and one car is 1425 ptas. Cabins are available from 4000 ptas.

Hostal Enrique Calvillo (☎ 71 61 05), Avenida Diputación 5 near the park information office, has rooms with bath for 2000/3500 ptas. Reception is in the *Casa Calvillo* restaurant a few doors away. *Hotel Las Truchas* (☎ 71 60 61), nearby at Avenida Diputación s/n, has comfy singles/doubles with bath for 4000/6250 ptas and a restaurant terrace overlooking the town and countryside. Try the trout, the local speciality.

Getting There & Away Up to six buses daily run from Arcos de la Frontera, a few from Jerez de la Frontera and Cádiz, and two from Grazalema.

Benamahoma

The small town of Benamahoma, four km from El Bosque towards Grazalema, is another good base for exploring the sierra. It's known for its market gardens, trout farm and cottage industry of rush-backed chairs. There's a park information office (☎ 71 60 63) in an old mill. Nearby on Camino del Nacimiento is *Camping Los Linares* (☎ 71 62 75), which has good facilities including a swimming pool. Benamahoma remembers its past in its Fiestas de Moros y Cristianos (festival of Moors and Christians) on the first Sunday of August.

Grazalema

From Benamahoma the C-344 winds east up to Puerto del Boyar at 1103 metres, where there's a lookout point, before the descent to Grazalema (823 metres). (In bad weather, or simply when the mist comes down, this mountainous road is treacherous.) Grazalema nestles into a hillside, surrounded by beautiful mountain country, with the Sierra del Pinar to the north-west and the Sierra del Endrinal to the south. Towering Pico San Cristóbal (1525 metres), to the north-west, provided the first glimpse of home for Spanish sailors returning with their treasure troves from the Americas.

A haunt of nature-lovers and artists (with a drug rehabilitation centre, too), Grazalema is a neat, pretty, picture-postcard town, especially when dusted with snow. Its steep, narrow cobblestone streets, whitewashed houses and beflowered window boxes reflect its Muslim heritage. Grazalema's population today (2300) is only one-third of what it was in the 19th century, when it prospered on the wool and textile industries and agriculture. Local products still include pure wool blankets and rugs, as well as pork products, cakes and pastries.

Information The centre of town is Plaza de España, where you'll find the tourist office (☎ 13 22 25) with information about the natural park, details of houses to rent, and local crafts and produce for sale. It's open daily from 10 am to 2 pm plus two afternoon hours which vary with the season. There's an ATM outside Unicaja, right by Plaza de España.

Things to See & Do There are a couple of lovely 17th century churches, the **Iglesia de la Aurora** on Plaza de España and the nearby **Iglesia de la Encarnación**, though like other buildings they suffered damage during the 19th century War of Independence and the civil war.

Horizon (☎ 13 23 63), Calle Doctor Mateos Gago 12, caters for a range of activities from horse riding and rock climbing to hot-air balloon trips and paragliding. It's open Tuesday to Friday from 10 am to 2 pm and weekends from 3.30 to 5.30 pm. Horse riding costs 1500 ptas an hour.

Grazalema's public swimming pool, with stunning views, is below Restaurante El Tajo at the east end of town.

Special Events From around 12 to 20 July, Grazalema celebrates Las Fiestas del Carmen, with plenty of late-night music and dance performances. The festivities end on the Monday with a bull-running through the streets.

Places to Stay & Eat *Camping Tajo Rodillo* (☎ 13 20 63) is one km above the town on the C-344 to El Bosque. It's closed in November and February. Cost for two adults, a tent and a car is 1375 ptas. In the town centre, *Casa de las Piedras* (☎ 13 20 14), Calle las Piedras 32, is a charming, long-established hostal with plenty of rooms, all with winter heating. Singles/doubles are 1500/3000 ptas, or 3600/4800 ptas with attached bath. Its restaurant serves a range of hearty medium-priced breakfasts, and *platos del día* such as pisto (mixed vegetables; 450 ptas), gazpacho (400 ptas) and stuffed pork (750 ptas).

The more luxurious *Villa Turística* (☎ 13 21 62) is at El Olivar s/n, above the town to the north. It has manicured lawns with a swimming pool and great views across to the town. Rooms with all mod cons cost from 4000/5750 ptas. There are also apartments with two double rooms from 10,500 ptas.

There are plenty more places to eat and drink on Calle Agua, off Plaza de España. On Calle José Jiménez, there's a good bakery. *Restaurante El Tajo*, with panoramic views at the east end of town, has a classy air. The buffet lunch is 1100 ptas, salads are 450 ptas, and hake or trout, both stuffed with ham, are 950 ptas each.

Getting There & Away There are two buses daily from El Bosque, several from Ubrique, and two from Ronda.

ANDALUCÍA

Zahara de la Sierra

The most northerly town in the natural park and topped by a crag with a ruined castle, Zahara de la Sierra is one of the most dramatic and pretty of all the white towns. It feels quite otherworldly, especially if you've driven the 18 km from Grazalema – another high and potentially treacherous road – through heavy mist. There's a fairly new reservoir below the town, to the north and east. Despite its apparent isolation, Zahara is well set up for those wanting to explore the surrounding country.

History Founded by Muslims in the 8th century, Zahara fell in 1407 to the Castilian prince Fernando de Antequera. Its recapture by Abu al-Hasan of Granada in a daring night raid in 1481 sparked the last phase of the Reconquista, which ended with the fall of Granada in 1492. Zahara itself was back in Christian hands by 1483. In the late 19th century Zahara was a noted hotbed of anarchism.

Information The town centres on Calle San Juan, a cobblestone street with a church at each end. Here you'll find Turismo Rural Bocaleones (☎ 12 31 14), a tourist office-cum-activities cooperative, open daily from 9.30 am to 2 pm. For most walks in the natural park, you need to get permission here. The office can organise horse rides, canoe trips, bicycle and 4WD rental and more. Hostal Marqués de Zahara, next door, has printed information about the town and natural park. It also sells delicious locally made jams!

Things to See & Do The obvious thing to do is to climb up to the 12th century **castillo**, of which one tower survives, reached by a dirt track beside the 18th century baroque **Iglesia de Santa María de la Mesa** on Calle San Juan. There's also a **mirador** on Calle San Juan. Zahara's steep streets invite investigation; there are pretty views across the town and out to the countryside, some framed by tall palm trees or hot-pink bougainvillea.

There are five major routes in the natural park, all good for walking, and some open to four-wheel drive vehicles, bicycles and horses. There are also caving possibilities.

Places to Stay & Eat Camping Cortijo is three km out of town at Arroyomolinos, beside the river near the reservoir. Cost for two adults, a tent and a car is around 1000 ptas. The friendly little Pensión González at Calle San Juan 9 has a few rooms with shared bath at 1000/2000 ptas. There's no name outside. Other hostales include Los Estribos (☎ 13 74 45), Calle Fuerte 3, and Los Tadeos (☎ 13 78 86), Paseo de la Fuente s/n. Hostal Marqués de Zahara (☎ 12 30 61), a converted mansion at Calle San Juan 3, has 10 comfy rooms with winter heating. Singles/doubles are 3300/4850 to 3500/5500 ptas depending on the season. The hostal's restaurant, with a menú at 1450 ptas, is for guests only, but there are other places to eat on this street and a supermarket nearby.

Getting There & Away The Comes line operates two buses Monday to Friday to/from Ronda via Algodonales.

The road from Grazalema climbs to Puerto de los Palomas (Doves' Pass, 1331 metres, but there are more vultures here than doves) before the descent to Zahara (551 metres). From Zahara the CA-351 heads north to join the C-339, which runs north to Algodonales and south-east to Ronda (30 km). The N-342 connects Algodonales with Olvera and Antequera to the east, and Arcos de la Frontera (50 km) to the west.

COSTA DE LA LUZ

The 90 km coast between Cádiz and Tarifa can be windy, and its Atlantic waters are a shade cooler than those of the Mediterranean, but these are small prices to pay for an unspoiled, often wild shore, strung with long, clean white-sand beaches and just a few small towns and villages. Andalucíans are well aware of its attractions and flock down here by the thousand in July and August, bringing a vibrant fiesta atmosphere to the normally quiet coastal settlements.

Top : Sevilla, Andalucía, from La Giralda – formerly a minaret, now the bell tower of the cathedral
Bottom Left: The Puerta de Almodóvar, in Córdoba, Andalucía
Bottom Right: Shop fronts in Sevilla

DAMIEN SIMONIS

BETHUNE CARMICHAEL

DAMIEN SIMONIS

BETHUNE CARMICHAEL

DAMIEN SIMONIS

La Alhambra
Details from the Alhambra, the delightful palace-fortress complex, built by the Nasrid dynasty in the
13th and 14th centuries, that dominates Granada, Andalucía, from a hill top in the north-east of the city

From before Roman times until the advent of 20th century tourism, this coast lived mainly from tuna fishing. Shoals of big tuna, some weighing 300 kg, are still intercepted by walls of net several km long as they head in from the Atlantic towards their Mediterranean spawning grounds in spring, and again as they head out in July and August. Barbate has the main tuna fleet today.

The two finest places to head for are the villages of Los Caños de Meca and Zahara de los Atunes, a few km either side of the town of Barbate. It's advisable to ring ahead for rooms in July and August.

Vejer de la Frontera

This isolated, old-fashioned white town looms mysteriously atop a rocky hill above the busy N-340, 50 km from Cádiz and 10 km inland. It's well worth a wander.

The oldest part of town, still partly walled and with narrow, winding streets clearly signifying its Muslim origins, spreads over the highest part of the hill. Buses stop just below this on La Plazuela, which is more or less the heart of town. There's a tourist office (☎ 45 01 91), open from 10.30 am to 2 pm and 6.30 to 8.30 pm, a couple of blocks further down at Calle San Filmo 6.

Within the walled area, seek out the **Iglesia del Divino Salvador**, whose interior is mudéjar at the altar end and Gothic at the other; and the much-reworked **castillo**, open from 11 am to 2 pm and 5 to 10 pm, with great views from its battlements and a small museum that preserves one of the black cloaks, covering everything but the eyes, that Vejer women wore until just a couple of decades ago.

Places to Stay *Hostal La Janda* (☎ 45 01 42), across town at the meeting of Calle San Ambrosio and Calle Cerro Clarinas, has singles/doubles with bath for 2000/4000 ptas. Down a side street nearby, *Hostal Buena Vista* (☎ 45 09 69), Calle Manuel Machado 20, has good-value doubles with bath for 3000 ptas, and fine views across to the old part of town. The *Hotel Convento de San Francisco* (☎ 45 10 01), in a restored

17th century convent at Plazuela s/n, has singles/doubles at 5985/7615 ptas plus IVA.

Getting There & Away Buses of the Comes line run to/from Cádiz and Barbate around six times a day. More buses for the same places, plus Tarifa and Algeciras (about 10 daily), La Línea, Málaga and Sevilla (all three or more) stop at La Barca de Vejer, on the N-340 at the bottom of the hill.

Barbate

A fishing and canning town of 22,000 people, with a long sandy beach and a big harbour, Barbate becomes a fairly lively resort in summer, but it's mostly a drab place. You might need to use it as a staging post if you're travelling by bus. The Comes bus station (☎ 43 05 94) is over a km back from the beach at the north end of the long main street, Avenida del Generalísimo. The only tourist office (☎ 43 10 06) for the Los Caños de Meca-Barbate-Zahara area is on Calle Ramón y Cajal, just back from the beachfront Paseo Marítimo towards its east end.

Hotel Mediterráneo (☎ 43 02 43), near the market at Calle Albufera 1, has doubles with bath for 4500 ptas but only opens from July to mid-September. The better *Hotel Galia* (☎ 43 04 82), a few blocks from the bus station at Calle Doctor Valencia 5, has doubles from 4500 to 6000 ptas depending on the season. There are plenty of seafood eateries on Paseo Marítimo and elsewhere.

Buses run to/from La Barca de Vejer (see the Vejer de la Frontera section above) up to 10 times daily, Cádiz and Vejer de la Frontera four to eight times, Sevilla once, and Tarifa and Algeciras once every day except Sunday.

Los Caños de Meca

Los Caños, once a hippy hideaway, straggles untidily along a series of sandy coves beneath a pine-clad hill 12 km west of Barbate. It maintains its laid-back, off-the-beaten-track air even at the height of summer.

The coast between Barbate and Los Caños is mostly cliffs, up to 100 metres high. The road between the two places runs inland through the La Breña umbrella pine forest. About halfway along the road, a walking path leads to the Torre del Tajo, a 16th century cliff-top lookout tower. Another tower, the Torre de Meca on the hill behind Los Caños, can also be reached from this road.

The road emerges towards the east end of Los Caños' single street, which mostly seems to be called Avenida Trafalgar. The main beach is straight in front of you. Those who want to strip off and swim do so round the small headland at its east end. At the west end of the village a side road leads out to a lighthouse on a low spit of land with a famous name – Cabo de Trafalgar. Off here, Spanish naval power was terminated in a few hours one day in 1805 by a British fleet under Admiral Nelson. There are further decent beaches either side of Cabo de Trafalgar.

Places to Stay There are three medium-sized camp sites, which are open from April to September and maybe a couple of weeks either side. They get pretty crowded in high summer. Nearest the centre is *Camping Camaleón* (☎ 43 71 54), Avenida Trafalgar s/n, about one km west from the Barbate road corner, with a shady site at about 2200 ptas for two people with a car and tent. *Camping Faro de Trafalgar* (☎ 43 70 17), about another 700 metres west, and *Camping Caños de Meca* (☎ 43 71 20), one km further on in the separate settlement of Zahora, are a little cheaper.

About 10 hostales are strung along Avenida Trafalgar, and there are more at Zahora. Most are pretty similar and have decent rooms with private bath. In August they typically add 1000 ptas to the prices given here.

The quieter end of the village is east from the Barbate road corner. *Hostal Fortuna* (☎ 43 70 75), a couple of hundred metres along, has doubles for 5000 ptas. Further on, the laid-back *Hostal Los Castillejos* is a quaint, turreted little place with lingering hippy vibes. Doubles are 4000 ptas.

West of the Barbate road corner, *Hostal Miramar* (☎ 43 70 24), Avenida Trafalgar

100, boasts a pool and a restaurant and has singles/doubles with bath for 3500/4000 ptas. Past the Camping Camaleón turning, *Hostal El Ancla* (☎ 43 71 00) has doubles or triples with bath, fridge and TV for 5000 ptas.

At Zahora, the single-storey *Hostal Alhambra* (☎ 43 72 16), opposite Camping Caños de Meca, has Alhambra-esque trimmings and nice rooms with little verandahs for 4500 ptas a double, and a restaurant.

Places to Eat *Bar-Restaurante El Caña*, a short distance east from the Barbate road corner, has a fine position atop the small cliff above the beach. Most seafood is around 1000 ptas. There's a *supermarket* across the road.

El Pirata, overlooking the beach a couple of hundred metres west, is a good bet with salads from 300 ptas and seafood media raciones at 500 or 600 ptas. The revueltos de gambas y ortigas (scrambled eggs with shrimps and sea anemones), for 900 ptas, are excellent!

Entertainment Good bars include the cool *Bar Araña* next to Hostal Los Castillejos, *Café-Bar Ketama* across the street from El Pirata, and a couple of places with music on the road out to Cabo de Trafalgar. *La Jaima*, in a kind of nomad's tent with red plush seats, just east of the Barbate road corner, has belly-dancing shows. *Sajorami* restaurant-bar out at Playa Zahora often has live rock, blues or flamenco on summer nights.

Getting There & Away Buses to Los Caños run in summer only. In 1996 the Comes line ran buses from Sevilla, mid-June to early September, daily at 9 am; from Cádiz, July and August, Saturday, Sunday and holidays only, at 10 am. These continue to Barbate. From Barbate there was a daily bus to Los Caños from mid-June to early September at 6.30 pm.

Zahara de los Atunes
Plonked in the middle of nothing except a broad, 12 km long, west-facing sandy beach

Zahara is an elemental sort of place. At the heart of the village stand the crumbling walls of the old Almadraba, once a depot and refuge for the local tuna (atún) fishers, who were an infamously rugged lot. Cervantes, in La Ilustre Fregona, wrote that no-one deserved the name pícaro (rogue or scoundrel) unless they had spent two seasons at Zahara fishing for tuna. The pícaros were evidently good at their job for records state that in 1541 no fewer than 140,000 tuna were brought into Zahara's Almadraba. Today the tuna industry here has dwindled out of sight, but Zahara has revived as an almost fashionable Spanish summer resort. With a little, old-fashioned core of narrow streets, it's altogether a fine spot to let the sun, sea and wind – and, in summer, a spot of lively nightlife – batter your senses.

Unicaja bank on Calle María Luisa has an ATM.

Places to Stay Most places cut prices by about 20% from October to mid-June.

The good Camping Bahía de la Plata (☎ 43 90 40), near the beach at the south end of Zahara, is open all year, charging 2000 ptas for two people with car and tent.

Alternatively, the cheapest place, and the most likely to have a room when everywhere else is full, is Hostal Monte Mar (☎ 43 90 47), Calle Peñón 12, at the northern tip of the village. The rooms are fine, at 4500 ptas a double with bath. The small Hotel Nicolás (☎ 43 92 74), Calle María Luisa 13, has simple but attractive singles/doubles with TV and bath for 4000/5700 ptas, and a restaurant.

The prime beach position is occupied by the Hotel Gran Sol (☎ 43 93 01), Calle Sánchez Rodríguez s/n, with large, comfortable doubles at 9500 ptas plus IVA. Hotel Doña Lola (☎ 43 90 09) at Plaza Thompson 1 is a modern place in attractive old-fashioned style, with good doubles at 9500 ptas.

Places to Eat Most restaurants are on or near Plaza de Tamarón near the Hotel Doña Lola, and most offer pretty similar lists of fish, seafood, salads, meat and sometimes pizzas. Patio la Plazoleta on Plaza de Tamarón is a good one, open to the air; a media ración of pez limón a la plancha (grilled tuna with vegetables and lemon) is 600 ptas, and there are also good pizzas around 800 ptas. Café-Bar Casa Juanita on Calle Sagasta is another pleasant place, a little cheaper – and not a bad spot for your morning coffee and tostada.

Entertainment In July and August a line of marquees and makeshift shacks along the beach south of the Almadraba serve as bars, discos and teterías. They get busy from about midnight. Some have live flamenco or other music.

Getting There & Away The Comes line runs two buses daily (none on Sunday) to/from Cádiz, three daily to/from Barbate (one on Sunday), one daily (none on Sunday) to/from Tarifa and Algeciras, and, at the time of writing, from mid-June to early September one daily to/from Sevilla via Los Caños de Meca.

Bolonia
This tiny village, 10 km down the coast from Zahara and about 20 km from Tarifa, has a fine white-sand beach, a handful of restaurants and small hostales, and the ruins of the Roman town of Baelo Claudia. The ruins include substantial remains of a theatre, a paved forum surrounded by remains of temples and other buildings, and the remains of the workshops which turned out the products that made Baelo Claudia famous in the Roman world: salted fish, and garum, a much-prized vitamin-rich paste made from fish entrails. The site is open for guided visits (250 ptas for foreigners) Tuesday to Sunday at 10 and 11 am, noon and 1 pm, also Tuesday to Saturday at 4 and 5 pm (5 and 6 pm from July to mid-September).

The hostales are all around 5000 ptas for a double with bath in summer. Some fall to 4000 ptas at other times.

The only road to Bolonia heads west off the N-340, 15 km from Tarifa. If you don't have wheels, it's a seven km hilly walk from

❋❋❋❋❋❋❋❋❋❋❋❋

Tunnelling to Africa

Bolonia is the nearest place to the Spanish end of a projected Strait of Gibraltar tunnel which could be shuttling vehicle-carrying trains to Tangier by the second decade of the 21st century. After decades of talk, in 1996 Spain and Morocco finally took a serious step towards doing something about it when they agreed to seek EU funds for the project. The planned 38-km tunnel will begin a couple of km inland, cross the coastline between Bolonia and Punta Paloma, and descend to a depth of 450 metres en route to its southern end just east of Tangier. The railway through it will link up with a new line to be built between Cádiz and Algeciras. The total cost is estimated to be at least 550 billion ptas (US\$4.4 billion). ■

❋❋❋❋❋❋❋❋❋❋❋❋

the main road, as there's no regular bus service. You can also walk the eight km along the coast from Ensenada de Valdevaqueros via Punta Paloma (see the Tarifa section which follows).

TARIFA

Even at peak times, Tarifa is an attractive and laid-back town. Until 10 years or so ago it was relatively unknown but it has since become a mecca for windsurfers. It's strange to see the international surf scene transported to this European setting with a strong Arabic feel, but if you're Australian, Californian or Hawaiian you'll feel right at home: the beaches have clean, white sand and good waves, and inland the country is green and rolling. Then there's the old town to explore, with its pretty, narrow streets, whitewashed houses and flowers cascading from balconies and window boxes. The only negative – unless, of course, you're a windsurfer or own one of the hundreds of windmills on the hill tops inland – is the wind on which Tarifa's new prosperity is based. For much of the year, either the *oriente* (easterly) or *poniente* (westerly) is blowing, ruinous for a relaxed sit on the beach and tiring if you're simply wandering around. August can be blessedly still, hot but not too hot, crowded but not overly so.

History

Tarifa may be as old as Phoenician Cádiz and was definitely a Roman settlement, but it takes its name from Tarif ibn Malik who led a Muslim raid in 710, the year before the main Islamic invasion of the peninsula. The Christians took the town in 1292, but it was not secure until Algeciras was won in 1344. Tarifa was active in the colonisation of the Americas: many of its citizens left for Peru in the 16th and 17th centuries.

Orientation

The main road into Tarifa from the N-340 becomes Calle Batalla del Salado, which ends at east-west Avenida de Andalucía where the Puerta de Jerez leads through the walls into the old town. The main street of the old town is Calle Sancho IV El Bravo, with the Iglesia de San Mateo at its east end. The castle overlooks the port on the south side of the old town. To the south-west protrudes the Punta de Tarifa, a military-occupied promontory that is the southernmost point of continental Europe, with the Strait of Gibraltar to the south and the Atlantic Ocean to the west.

Information

The tourist office (☎ 68 09 93) is near the top end of the main plaza, the palm-lined Paseo de la Alameda, which stretches down the west side of the old town from Avenida de Andalucía almost to the port. The tourist office is open Monday to Friday: in summer from 10 am to 2 pm and 6 to 8 pm, in winter from 8 am to 3 pm. If it's closed, head for the ayuntamiento on Plaza de Santa María for a map and information.

There are banks and ATMs on Calle Sancho IV El Bravo and Calle Batalla del Salado. The post office is at Calle Coronel Moscardó 9, south from the Iglesia San Mateo. The postcode is 11380. The Policía Local (☎ 61 41 86) are in the ayuntamiento. The Cruz Roja (Red Cross; ☎ 64 48 96) is at Calle Alcalde Juan Núñez 5, a short distance west of the bottom of the Alameda.

International newspapers and books in English and German are available at the

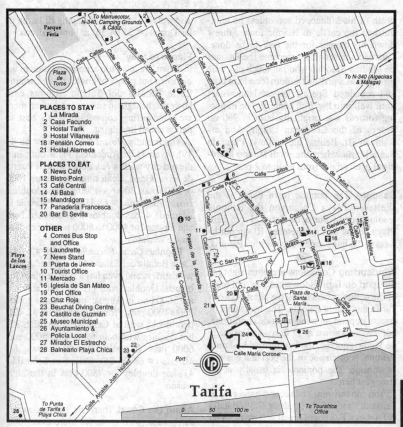

PLACES TO STAY
1 La Mirada
2 Casa Facundo
3 Hostal Tarik
9 Hostal Villanueva
18 Pensión Correo
21 Hostal Alameda

PLACES TO EAT
6 News Café
12 Bistro Point
13 Café Central
14 Ali Baba
15 Mandrágora
17 Panadería Francesca
20 Bar El Sevilla

OTHER
4 Comes Bus Stop and Office
5 Laundrette
7 News Stand
8 Puerta de Jerez
10 Tourist Office
11 Mercado
16 Iglesia de San Mateo
19 Post Office
22 Cruz Roja
23 Beuchat Diving Centre
24 Castillo de Guzmán
25 Museo Municipal
26 Ayuntamiento & Policía Local
27 Mirador El Estrecho
28 Balneario Playa Chica

Tarifa

0   50   100 m

newsstand on Calle Batalla del Salado, opposite Puerta de Jerez. Two doors north up the road is a laundrette which does washing only, at 100 ptas per load.

Things to See & Do

Tarifa is best enjoyed by strolling about the tangled streets of the old town to the castle walls, checking out the castle (if it's open), stopping in at the busy fishing port and sampling the beaches.

Old Town The mudéjar **Puerta de Jerez** was built after the Reconquista. From here

you could look in at the bustling, neo-mudéjar **mercado** on Calle Colón before wending your way to the mainly 15th century **Iglesia de San Mateo**. The streets to the south of the church are little changed since Islamic times. Climb the stairs at the end of Calle Coronel Moscardó and go left on Calle Aljaranda to reach the **Mirador El Estrecho** atop part of the castle walls, with spectacular views across to Africa.

The **Castillo de Guzmán** (recently closed to visitors) extending west from here is named after the Reconquista hero Guzmán El Bueno, who, when threatened with the death of his kidnapped son unless he relinquished the castle to Islamic forces, threw down his dagger for the task to be done. Guzmán's descendants became the Duques de Medina Sidonia, who ran much of Cádiz province as a private fiefdom for a long time and remained Spain's largest landowners until well into the 20th century. The imposing fortress was originally built in 960 on orders of the Córdoban caliph, Abd ar-Rahman III. Behind the castle is Plaza de Santa María, where the small **Museo Municipal** opens daily from noon to 2 pm.

Beaches The popular town beach is the sheltered Playa Chica, on the isthmus leading out to Punta de Tarifa. From here Playa de los Lances stretches 10 km northwest to the huge sand dune at Punta Paloma.

Windsurfing Conditions are often right for the sport on Tarifa's town beaches, but most of the action occurs along the coast between Tarifa and Punta Paloma. The best spots of course depend on wind and tide conditions, but the one known as El Porro on Ensenada de Valdevaqueros, the bay formed by Punta Paloma, is often one of the best and busiest. In summer the poniente is usually at its strongest here.

You can buy new and second-hand gear in Tarifa at the surf shops along Calle Batalla del Salado. For board rental and classes you need to try places up the coast such as Club Mistral at the Hurricane Hotel (see Places to Stay), or Spin Out in front of Camping Torre de la Peña II, near El Porro. At Club Mistral board rental costs 2200 ptas for one hour or 6700 ptas for a day, and a six-hour beginner's course is 17,500 ptas.

Competitions are held year round with two big events in summer – the World Speed Cup from 1 to 7 July and the World Cup (Formula 42) from 30 July to 4 August.

Diving Tarifa has some good diving. For information, head to Beuchat Diving Centre (☎ 908-25 40 78) on Calle Alcalde Juan Núñez, next door to the Cruz Roja. There's also a diving school at Camping El Jardín de las Dunas (☎ 23 64 36) at Punta Paloma.

Places to Stay

In Town There's little accommodation in the old town but plenty of choice on and around Calle Batalla del Salado. Rooms can, however, be tight in summer and when there are windsurfing competitions. It's best to phone ahead in August.

The friendly *Hostal Villanueva* (☎ 68 41 49), Avenida de Andalucía 11, is built into the old city walls a few doors west of Puerta de Jerez. Good, clean single rooms are 1500 or 2000 ptas; 3000 or 4500 ptas for doubles. *Hostal Alameda* (☎ 68 11 81), at Paseo de la Alameda 4, has doubles with attached bath and air-con for 4000 to 6000 ptas depending on the season.

Popular *Casa Facundo* (☎ 68 42 98), Calle Batalla del Salado 47, is geared up for windsurfers and even has a storage place for boards. Doubles with private bath and TV are 5000 ptas in August; other rooms go for 2500/4000 ptas. *Hostal Tarik* (☎ 68 52 40), two blocks west at Calle San Sebastián 32, has doubles with bath for around 5000 and 6000 ptas. If you're after sea views, *La Mirada* (☎ 68 06 26), Calle San Sebastián 41, has doubles for 7500 ptas in the high season.

Along the Coast There are six year-round camp sites, with room for more than 4000 campers, on or near the beach between Tarifa and Punta Paloma, 10 km north-west. All charge about 2000 ptas for two people with a tent and a car.

At least nine hostales and hotels are dotted along the same stretch, some on the beach, some on the inland side of the N-340, but none is cheap. All have rooms with private bath.

Hostal Millón (☎ 68 52 46), five km from the town centre, has a nice little garden leading on to the beach, its own small restaurant, and reasonable doubles at 9000 ptas (7000 ptas from October to June).

The *Hurricane Hotel* (☎ 68 49 19), six km out, is the place to go if money is no object.

Set in beachside semitropical gardens, it has 33 large and comfy rooms, two pools, a health club, and its own windsurfing school. Singles/doubles range seasonally from 8250/11,000 to 12,375/16,500 ptas on the ocean side, and 6000/8000 to 9750/13,000 ptas on the land side. To these prices you must add IVA, but they include an excellent buffet breakfast.

Hostal Oasis (☎ 68 50 65) and *Hotel La Ensenada* (☎ 68 06 37), both about eight km out, are two of the less pricey places, with doubles ranging from 4300 ptas (5900 ptas at the Oasis) to 8500 ptas depending on the season. *Hotel Las Piñas*, 10 km out, is the closest hotel to Punta Paloma, with doubles from 6000 to 7500 ptas.

Places to Eat

Thanks to Tarifa's high number of international visitors, you're guaranteed some variety from the usual Spanish fare. Lots of places to eat have wholemeal bread *(pan moreno)*.

In Town Calle Sancho IV El Bravo has all manner of takeaway options. Try *Panadería Francesca* for filled French sticks, pizza portions and empanadas. Across the road, the popular *Ali Baba* has filling and tasty Arabic food and benches outside where you can eat. Vegetarians can enjoy excellent felafels for 300 ptas; carnivores pay a bit extra for the kebabs and kebes (spicy meatballs). A few doors away, *Café Central* has good churros y chocolate and a range of large breakfasts for around 400 ptas. Main meals from the long menu are around 900 ptas.

There's excellent food nearby at *Mandrágora*, Calle Independencia 3, on the street running behind the Iglesia de San Mateo. Some of the delicious options are peppers stuffed with bacalao (1000 ptas) and chicken breasts stuffed with cheese (900 ptas).

The best-value seafood in town is to be had at *Bar El Sevilla*, the marisquería on Calle Inválidos west of the centre. There's no name outside; some locals call it El Gallego. Mixed fish and seafood fry-ups cost 150 ptas

for a generous tapa, 850 ptas for a ración (enough for two people) – excellent washed down with a beer! Close by, *Bistro Point*, on the corner of Calle San Francisco and Calle Santísima Trinidad, is popular in the evening for its huge range of sweet and savoury crêpes, and main dishes around 1100 ptas.

The *Hostal Villanueva's* restaurant, on Avenida de Andalucía, does a brisk trade with its 850-ptas lunch menú. Other fare is reasonably priced. At the *News Café*, attached to the newsstand on Calle Batalla del Salado, you can enjoy mouthwatering fruit shakes and fill up on breakfast such as brown bread with tomato and ham, with a hot drink, for 400 ptas.

Along the Coast Most hotels and hostales up here have their own restaurants. The one at the *Hurricane Hotel* has a good lunchtime salad bar for 700 ptas, also home-made pasta and local fish and seafood. *Mesón El Toro*, on the inland side of the N-340 four km from Tarifa, is a good steak and fish house with most mains around 1200 to 1500 ptas. It's open from 7 pm to 1 am (closed Monday).

Entertainment

Nightlife is limited to the bars in town and up the beach, although in July and August the open-air disco at Balneario Playa Chica may be worth checking out.

Getting There & Away

Bus The Comes bus stop and office is on Calle Batalla del Salado two blocks north of the Puerta de Jerez. Comes (☎ 68 40 38) runs seven buses daily to Cádiz and La Línea, 10 to Algeciras (four on Sunday), three each to Sevilla and Málaga, and one each to Jerez de la Frontera and (though not on Sunday) Zahara de los Atunes and Barbate.

Car & Motorcycle The N-340 between Tarifa and Algeciras climbs to 340 metres. Stop at the Mirador del Estrecho, about seven km out of Tarifa, to take in magnificent

ANDALUCÍA

views of the Strait of Gibraltar, the Mediterranean, the Atlantic and two continents.

Boat There are two ferries daily (taking one hour) between Tarifa and Tangier, leaving Tarifa at 10.30 am and 8 pm, returning from Tangier at 7 am and 4.30 pm (Moroccan time). The one-way passenger fare is 2960 ptas; a car and driver is 9300 ptas and a motorcycle 2650 ptas. Buy your ticket in the port at the Touráfrica office, or from Marruecotur, next to the petrol station on Calle Batalla del Salado.

PARQUE NATURAL LOS ALCORNOCALES

This large (1700 sq km) natural park stretches 75 km north from the Strait of Gibraltar across a jumble of sierras of medium height. Much of it is covered in Spain's most extensive cork oak woodlands (*alcornocales*).

There are plenty of walks and possibilities for other activities in the park, but you need your own wheels to make the most of it, as it's sparsely populated and public transport runs mostly along its fringes. The park office (☎ 42 02 77) is at Calle José Tizón 5 in the sleepy white town of Alcalá de los Gazules on the park's western fringe. Another information office is beside the N-340 Tarifa-Algeciras road at El Pelayo, about 12 km from Tarifa and close to the modern *Albergue Juvenil Algeciras* (☎ 67 90 60) at Carretera Nacional 340, Km 95.6. There's a bus stop at the front of the hostel, which has a few singles, 18 doubles, 16 four-person rooms and a swimming pool.

The small town of **Jimena de la Frontera**, on the C-3331 on the park's eastern boundary, is a good base for the generally higher and more rugged northern part of the park. Jimena is crowned by a fine Muslim castle, has a couple of hostales, and is served by train and bus from Algeciras and Ronda, and bus from La Línea. The C-3331 heading north-west from here will take you to **La Sauceda**, an abandoned village that's now the site of a camping area and cabins (☎ 95-

215 02 02 for information), close to the park's highest peak, Aljibe (1092 metres).

ALGECIRAS

Algeciras, the major port linking Spain with Africa, is an unattractive, polluted place with little to hold your interest for longer than it takes to organise your crossing to Tangier or Ceuta. During the summer, the port is hectic with large numbers of Moroccan workers making the journey home from northern Europe for their holidays. Algeciras is also an industrial town, a big fishing port and a centre for drug smuggling.

History

Algeciras was an important port under the Romans. In 711 it fell to the Islamic invaders who held on to it until 1344 when it was conquered by Alfonso XI. Later Mohammed V of Granada attacked and razed it to the ground before abandoning it. In 1704 Algeciras was repopulated by many of those who left Gibraltar after the British took it. During the Franco era, industry was developed.

Orientation

Algeciras is on the west side of the Bahía de Algeciras, opposite Gibraltar. Avenida Virgen del Carmen runs from north to south along the seafront, becoming Avenida de la Marina around the entrance to the port. From here Calle Juan de la Cierva (becoming Calle San Bernardo) runs inland beside a rail track to the main bus station (about 350 metres) and the train station (400 metres). The town's central plaza, Plaza Alta, is a couple of blocks inland from Avenida Virgen del Carmen, reached from Calle Pablo Mayayo. Plaza Palma, with a bustling daily market (close on Sunday), is one block west of Avenida de la Marina.

Information

Tourist Offices The English-speaking main tourist office (☎ 57 26 36) is at Calle Juan de la Cierva s/n, a block inland from Avenida de la Marina. It's open Monday to Friday from 9 am to 2 pm. The Spanish-speaking municipal tourist office is in a kiosk outside the

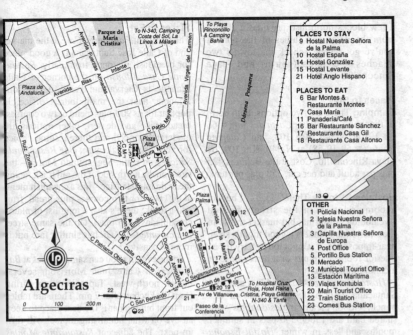

PLACES TO STAY
9 Hostal Nuestra Señora
 de la Palma
10 Hostal España
14 Hostal González
15 Hostal Levante
21 Hotel Anglo Hispano

PLACES TO EAT
6 Bar Montes &
 Restaurante Montes
7 Casa María
11 Panadería/Café
16 Bar Restaurante Sánchez
17 Restaurante Casa Gil
18 Restaurante Casa Alfonso

OTHER
1 Policía Nacional
2 Iglesia Nuestra Señora
 de la Palma
3 Capilla Nuestra Señora
 de Europa
4 Post Office
5 Portillo Bus Station
8 Mercado
12 Municipal Tourist Office
13 Estación Marítima
19 Viajes Kontubia
20 Main Tourist Office
22 Train Station
23 Comes Bus Station

Algeciras

0   100   200 m

main entrance to the port. In July and August it's open Monday to Friday from 10 am to 2 pm and 4 to 8 pm, and sporadically at weekends. In other months it's only open Monday to Friday from 10 am to 2 pm.

Money There are banks and ATMs on Avenida Virgen del Carmen and around Plaza Alta, plus at least one ATM inside the port. Exchange rates are better at the banks than at travel agencies. You'll get a better deal buying dirham if you wait until you reach Morocco.

Post & Communications There's a post office on Calle José Antonio just south of Plaza Alta. There are telephones in the port, on Avenida de la Marina, near the market and at the train station.

Medical & Emergency Services The Policía Nacional (☎ 66 04 00) are at Avenida

de las Fuerzas Armadas 6 next to Parque de María Cristina. For an ambulance dial ☎ 65 15 55. The Hospital Cruz Roja (☎ 60 31 44) is central at Paseo de la Conferencia s/n, on the southern extension of Avenida de la Marina.

Left Luggage The train station has plenty of consigna lockers (400 ptas daily). In the port, storage is available from 7.30 am to 10 pm at 100 ptas a bag: there are no lockers, so bags need to be secured.

Things to See & Do
If you have to spend any time in Algeciras, wander up to the pretty, palm-fringed **Plaza Alta**, which has a lovely tiled fountain. On its west side are the 18th century **Iglesia Nuestra Señora de la Palma** and 17th century **Capilla Nuestra Señora de Europa**, both worth a look. Some of the houses around here are delightfully tumbledown. The leafy **Parque de María Cristina**

ANDALUCÍA

a few blocks north also provides a change from the noise and fumes of the port. If you've got wheels, check the town's two beaches – **Getares** (south) and **Playa Rinconcillo** (north).

Places to Stay

Camping There are two options, both north of the town – *Camping Costa del Sol* (☎ 66 02 19) at N-340, Km 108, and *Camping Bahía* (☎ 69 19 58) at N-340, Km 109, by Playa Rinconcillo. Cost at the Bahía is 425 ptas per adult and per car, 350 ptas per tent.

Hostales & Hotels There's loads of budget accommodation in the streets behind Avenida de la Marina, but market traffic in the small hours renders a good night's sleep near-impossible. If it's not too hot, try for an interior room. Earplugs or a heavy dose of alcohol might help.

Hostal González (☎ 65 28 43), Calle José Santacana 7, is perhaps the pick of this bunch. Good, clean singles/doubles with shared bath are 1500/3500 ptas in summer months and less in winter. *Hostal España* (☎ 66 82 62), Calle José Santacana 4, has large, clean rooms at 1000 ptas per person but it's right by the market. On the west side of Plaza Palma at No 12, *Hostal Nuestra Señora de la Palma* (☎ 63 24 81) has comfortable rooms with bath for 1925/3850 ptas. *Hostal Levante* (☎ 65 15 05), Calle Duque de Almodóvar 21, is a little removed from the thick of things; OK rooms with a shower are 1500/2500 ptas though the corridors are a bit musty.

If you have more to spend, the 19th century *Hotel Anglo Hispano* (☎ 57 25 90), Avenida de Villanueva 7, just west of the main tourist office, is a good choice. Doubles are 5000 ptas plus IVA, less in winter. *Hotel Reina Cristina* (☎ 60 26 22), Paseo de la Conferencia s/n, a brisk five minute walk south of the port, is an old colonial-style hotel set amid tropical gardens. Doubles cost 17,500 ptas, or 13,500 ptas in winter, plus IVA. This hotel, a suitable place to observe sea traffic passing through the Strait of Gibraltar, was the haunt of spies in WWII.

Places to Eat

The excellent *Panadería-Café* at the market end of Calle José Santacana is a good place for breakfast; it's open from early. *Restaurante Casa Alfonso* on the corner of Calle Juan de la Cierva and Paseo de la Conferencia, near the main tourist office, is popular for its 900-ptas menú of two courses, bread, wine and dessert; other options are moderately priced and there's some choice for vegetarians. Likewise, *Bar Restaurante Sánchez* on Calle Segismundo Moret – the street on the north side of the rail track facing the main tourist office – has a cheapish menú at 800 ptas for two courses plus bread, fruit and a drink; there's also a long list of platos combinados (575 ptas). On the same street *Restaurante Casa Gil* has similar fare but is more expensive.

In the evening you can sample tapas at *Bar Montes* on Calle Juan Morrison, several blocks north-west. Tapas keep appearing from the kitchen after 7 pm. There are tables out front but the bar is the best place to keep an eye on what tantalising morsel will turn up next. The adjacent *Restaurante Montes* has an 1100 ptas menú with quite a wide choice, and an extensive à-la-carte seafood list from 1200 ptas. Across the road, the popular *Casa María* on Calle Emilio Castellar, has a menú for 975 ptas.

Entertainment

In summer there are flamenco, rock and other concerts at some of the more pleasant spots in town – the Plaza de Toros, Parque de María Cristina, Plaza de Andalucía and Playa Rinconcillo. The main tourist office gives out a list of events.

Getting There & Away

The daily paper *Europa Sur* has up-to-date transport arrival and departure details.

Bus The main bus station, that of the Comes line (☎ 65 34 56), is under the Hotel Octavio on Calle San Bernardo. To Tarifa (215 ptas) there are 10 buses daily Monday to Saturday but only four on Sunday and holidays. Buses run to La Línea (40 minutes; 225 ptas) every half-hour from 7 am to 9.30 pm. Other daily services include nine buses to Cádiz, four to Sevilla, two to Jimena de la Frontera (one on Saturday, none on Sunday), and two to Madrid. There's one bus (none on Sunday) to Zahara de los Atunes and Barbate.

Portillo (☎ 65 10 55) at Avenida Virgen del Carmen 15 operates 10 buses daily to Málaga (1285 ptas; 2½ hours), seven to the Costa del Sol towns (Marbella 735 ptas) and two to Granada (2420 ptas).

Bacoma (☎ 66 65 89), inside the port, runs up to four services daily to Alicante (5720 ptas), Valencia (6245 ptas) and Barcelona (9340 ptas).

There are also buses to France, Germany, Holland and France. Information and tickets are available at Viajes Kontubia, next to the main tourist office. Buses depart from outside Viajes Kontubia.

Train Three or four trains daily run between Algeciras and Bobadilla via Ronda from the station adjacent to Calle San Bernardo, taking in some dramatic scenery en route. At Bobadilla, you can change for Granada, Málaga, Sevilla and Madrid. For information call ☎ 63 02 02.

Boat Trasmediterránea, Isleña de Navegación and Moroccan companies operate frequent daily roll-on, roll-off car ferries and hydrofoils (also called fast ferries or *rápidos*) to/from Tangier and Ceuta, the Spanish enclave on the Moroccan coast. Buy your ticket in the port or at the agencies on Avenida de la Marina – prices are the same everywhere.

To Tangier, ferries take two hours, hydrofoils one hour. Trasmediterránea (☎ 66 52 00) and the Moroccan companies run a basic service of six ferries daily and three or four hydrofoils. In July and August, there are ferries almost round the clock to cater for the huge demand. In September, there are eight ferries daily. One-way fares are: adults 2960 ptas, children 1480 ptas, cars 9300 ptas and motorcycles 2650 ptas.

To Ceuta, ferries take 90 minutes, hydrofoils 35 minutes. There are five or six ferries

and the same number of fast ferries daily, weather permitting, plus extra in July and August. One-way fares on fast ferries are 3002 ptas for adults and 1502 ptas for children; ferries are cheaper at 1884 ptas for adults, 943 ptas for children. Cars cost 4793 to 8665 ptas and motorcycles 1860 to 2801 ptas, depending on their dimensions.

LA LÍNEA

La Línea de la Concepción (to give it its full name), 20 km east of Algeciras, is the unavoidable stepping stone to Gibraltar. A left turn as you exit the bus station will bring you out on Avenida 20 de Abril, which runs the 300 metres or so from the main square, Plaza de la Constitución, to the Gibraltar border. There's a tourist office (☎ 76 99 50) on the plaza.

Places to Stay

Pensión La Perla (☎ 76 95 13) at Calle Clavel 10, two blocks north of Plaza de la Constitución, has clean, spacious pink-trimmed singles/doubles for 1700/3000 ptas. *Hostal La Esteponera* (☎ 10 66 68), several blocks west at Calle Carteya 10, has doubles from 1600 ptas (2400 ptas from May to September). *Hostal La Campana* (☎ 10 30 59) at Calle Carboneros 3, off the west side of Plaza de la Constitución, has decent rooms with bath and TV for 3500 ptas a double (a bit more in summer).

Getting There & Away

Bus There are four buses daily to/from Málaga (three hours; 1225 ptas), stopping in the Costa del Sol towns; three each to/from Cádiz (2½ hours; 1440 ptas) and Sevilla (four hours; 2500 ptas), two to/from Granada (2360 ptas), one Monday to Saturday to/from Ronda (990 ptas), and buses every 30 minutes to/from Algeciras.

Car & Motorcycle To avoid vehicle queues at the Gibraltar border, many visitors park in La Línea, then walk across. The underground car park on Plaza de la Constitución charges 100 ptas an hour or 810 ptas for 24 hours; parking meters are a little less.

Gibraltar

Looming like some great ship off almost the southernmost tip of Spain, the British colony of Gibraltar is such a compound of curiosities that a visit can hardly fail to stir one's interest.

Gibraltar's territory is about six km long and one km wide and most of it is one huge lump of limestone rising to 426 metres, which is almost sheer along its east side. To the ancient Greeks and Romans, Gibraltar was one of the two Pillars of Hercules, set up by the mythical hero to mark the edge of the known world. The other pillar is the coastal mountain Jebel Musa in Morocco, 25 km south across the storm-prone Strait of Gibraltar.

History

Neanderthals, Phoenicians and Greeks left traces here, but Gibraltar really entered the history books in 711 AD, when Tariq ibn Ziyad, the Muslim governor of Tangier, landed here to launch the Islamic invasion of the Iberian Peninsula. The Rock has carried his name ever since – Jebel Tariq (Tariq's Mountain).

Castilla finally wrested the Rock from the Muslims in 1462. Then in 1704 an Anglo-Dutch fleet captured Gibraltar during the War of the Spanish Succession. Spain ceded the Rock to Britain in 1713, but didn't finally give up military attempts to regain it until the failure of Great Siege of 1779-83. Britain developed it into an important naval base. During the Franco period Gibraltar was an extremely sore point between Britain and Spain, and the border was closed from 1967 to 1985. In the 1990s there has been a big reduction in the British military presence and although Gibraltar's current conservative government says it cannot contemplate losing British sovereignty (most of the population seem to agree), some form of joint sovereignty between Spain and Britain might be the ultimate outcome.

By the mid-1990s Gibraltar had become the base for scores of high-speed launches which smuggled into Spain large quantities of cigarettes from Gibraltar and also drugs from Morocco. A clampdown on their activities led to riots in 1995. Meanwhile efforts to turn the place into an offshore banking centre had led to accusations of illicit money-laundering. These are played down by the Gibraltar authorities, though in 1996 the chief minister Peter Caruana was moved to announce that his government would act against money-laundering and smuggling should it arise.

Population & People

Gibraltar has around 27,000 people, of whom 75% are classed as Gibraltarians, 14% British, and 7% Moroccan. The Gibraltarians are of mixed Genoese, Jewish, Spanish and British ancestry (the Genoese element comes from ship repairers brought by the British in the 18th century). The Moroccans are mostly temporary workers.

Gibraltarians speak both English and Spanish and, at times, a curious mix of the two. Signs are in English.

Orientation

To reach Gibraltar by land you must pass through the Spanish border town of La Línea (see that section earlier in this chapter). Immediately south of the border, the road crosses the runway of Gibraltar airport. The town and harbours of Gibraltar lie along the Rock's less steep west side, facing the Bahía de Algeciras (or Bay of Gibraltar).

Information

Tourist Offices Gibraltar has several helpful tourist offices with good give-away material. One is opposite British customs and immigration at the border; others are at the restaurant The Piazza, Main St (☎ 74982), and the Gibraltar Museum, 18-20 Bomb House Lane (☎ 74805). All are open Monday to Friday from 10 am to 6 pm, the last two also Saturday from 10 am to 2 pm.

Visas & Documents To enter Gibraltar you need a passport or, for EU nationalities that

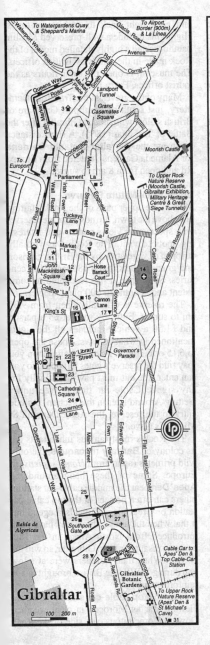

PLACES TO STAY
3 Emile Youth Hostel
5 Continental Hotel
7 Miss Seruya Guest House
15 Cannon Hotel
18 White's Hotel
21 Hotel Bristol
26 Toc H Hostel
29 Queen's Hotel
31 Rock Hotel

PLACES TO EAT
2 Market Restaurant
6 The Clipper
9 Viceroy of India
12 The Piazza
17 Three Roses Bar
22 Maxi Manger
25 Minister's Restaurant
28 Piccadilly Gardens

OTHER
1 Bus No 9
4 Tourafrica International
8 Post Office
10 Bus No 10
11 Police Station
13 Tourist Office
14 St Bernard's Hospital
16 Roman Catholic Cathedral
19 Gibraltar Museum & Tourist Office
20 Bus No 3
23 Anglican Cathedral
24 Gibraltar Bookshop
27 Trafalgar Cemetery
30 Lower Cable-Car Station

possess them, an identity card. EU, USA, Canada, Australia, New Zealand, Israel, South Africa and Singapore passport-holders are among those who do not need visas for Gibraltar. You can contact Gibraltar's Immigration Department (☎ 71543) if you need further information.

Those who need visas for *Spain* should have at least a double-entry Spanish visa so that they can return to Spain from Gibraltar. You might be able to slip back into Spain without showing your passport but you certainly can't count on it.

Money The currencies are the Gibraltar pound (£) and the pound sterling, which are interchangeable. You can use pesetas, but conversion rates aren't in your favour. Exchange rates for buying pesetas are,

ANDALUCÍA

however, a bit better than in Spain. Change any unspent Gibraltar pounds before you leave.

Banks are generally open Monday to Friday from 9 am to 3.30 pm. There are several on Main St. There are also *bureaux de change*, open longer hours.

Post & Communications The main post office, open Monday to Friday from 10 am to 4.30 pm, Saturday from 10 am to 1 pm, is at 104 Main St.

To phone Gibraltar from Spain, the telephone code is ☎ 9567; from other countries dial the international access code, then ☎ 350 (the country code for Gibraltar) and the local number.

In Gibraltar, you can make international as well as local calls from street pay phones. To phone Spain, just dial the area code and number; to phone other countries, dial the international access code ☎ 00, then the country code, area code and number.

Bookshops Gibraltar is a good place to stock up on English-language reading material. Of its three bookshops, Gibraltar Bookshop at 300 Main St is the best.

Medical & Emergency Services St Bernard's Hospital (☎ 79700) on Hospital Hill has 24-hour emergency facilities. Police wear British uniforms and their station (☎ 72500) is at 120 Irish Town. In an emergency call ☎ 199 for police or ambulance.

Electricity Electric current is the same as in Britain, 220V or 240V, with plugs of three flat pins.

The Town
Gibraltar's city centre, with its British pubs and British shoppers, is distinctly unexotic. Most Spanish and Islamic buildings were destroyed in 18th century sieges, though British fortifications, gates and gun emplacements are all over the place.

The **Gibraltar Museum**, 18-20 Bomb House Lane, contains very worthwhile historical, architectural and military displays

and goes right back to prehistoric times. Highlights include a well-preserved Muslim bathhouse and a highly detailed model of the Rock made in the 1860s by British officers. The museum is open the same hours as the tourist offices. Entry is £2.

Many of the graves in the **Trafalgar Cemetery**, just south of Southport Gate, are of British sailors who died at Gibraltar after the Battle of Trafalgar (1805). A short distance south are the **Gibraltar Botanic Gardens** (or Alameda Gardens), entered from Europa Rd and open from 8 am to sunset.

Upper Rock Nature Reserve
Most of the upper parts of the Rock, starting just above the town, are now a nature reserve, with spectacular views and several interesting spots to visit. The Rock was virtually stripped of vegetation by the British garrison and grazing goats in the 18th and 19th centuries. Since then it has recovered to some extent and is home to 600 plant species.

The reserve is officially open from 9.30 am to sunset. Entry by road at £5 a person and £1.50 a vehicle includes all the sights mentioned in what follows. These are open to 6.15 or 6.30 pm. From late afternoon you may find the reserve's gates left open, so you can enter free but must pay individually for any sights. Cable-car tickets (see under Getting Around later in this section) include entry to the reserve, the Apes' Den and St Michael's Cave.

The Rock's most famous inhabitants are its colony of **Barbary macaques**, the only wild primates (apart from *Homo sapiens*) in Europe. Some of these hang around the **Apes' Den** near the middle cable-car station; others can often be seen at the top cable-car station or Great Siege Tunnels. Legend has it that when the apes (which may have been introduced from North Africa in the 18th century) disappear from Gibraltar, so will the British. When their numbers were at a low ebb during WWII, the British brought in ape reinforcements.

From the **top cable-car station**, there are views as far as Morocco in clear weather. Down the precipitous east side of the Rock is the biggest of the old **water catchments** which channelled rain into underground reservoirs. Today this source of water has been replaced by desalination plants. About 20 minutes walk south down St Michael's Rd (or 20 minutes up from the Apes' Den), **St Michael's Cave** is a big natural grotto with fine stalagmites and stalactites. It was once home to Neolithic inhabitants of the Rock. Today, apart from attracting tourists in droves, it's used for concerts, plays and even fashion shows. There's a café outside.

Princess Caroline's Battery, about 30 minutes walk north (downhill) from the top cable-car station, houses a **Military Heritage Centre**. From here a road leads up to the **Great Siege Tunnels**. These impressive artificial galleries were hewn out by hand by the British during the 1779-83 siege to provide new gun emplacements. They constitute a tiny proportion of the more than 70 km of tunnels in the Rock, most of which are off limits to the public.

Worth a stop on Willis' Rd, which leads down to the town from Princess Caroline's Battery, are the **Gibraltar, A City Under Siege** exhibition and the **Tower of Homage**, the last vestige of Gibraltar's Muslim castle built in 1333.

Dolphins

The Bahía de Algeciras has a sizeable year-round population of dolphins. Dolphin Safari (☎ 71914) and the yacht *Fortuna* (☎ 74598) both offer dolphin-spotting boat trips daily from Tuesday to Sunday. The trips last about 2½ hours and cost £15 per adult and £7 or £7.50 per child. You'll be unlucky if you don't get plenty of close-up dolphin contact. Both boats go from Watergardens Quay.

Places to Stay

The recently opened independent *Emile Youth Hostel* (☎ 51106) at Montagu Bastion, Line Wall Rd, is a step up from Gibraltar's previous budget options. It has 44 places in two to eight-person rooms, for £10 including continental breakfast. The ramshackle old *Toc H Hostel* (☎ 73431), tucked into the city

walls at the south end of Line Wall Rd, is the cheapest place with beds at £5 a night and cold showers. *Miss Seruya Guest House* (☎ 73220), 92/1A Irish Town (1st floor), has four tiny and very basic rooms and one shower. Singles/doubles cost from £8/12 to £16/18.

The *Queen's Hotel* (☎ 74000) at 1 Boyd St is more comfortable, with a restaurant, bar, games room, and rooms at £16/24, or £20/36 with private bath or shower. Reduced rates of £14/20 and £16/24 are offered for students and young travellers. The *Cannon Hotel* (☎ 51711) at 9 Cannon Lane also has decent rooms, each sharing a bathroom with one other room, for £25 single or double including English breakfast.

The rooms at the *Hotel Bristol* (☎ 76800), 10 Cathedral Square, are pleasant enough and a decent size, with TV, but expensive at £42/55 interior or £46/60 exterior. The *Continental Hotel* (☎ 76900), 1 Engineer Lane, has cosy rooms at £42/55.

At the luxury end, *White's Hotel* (☎ 70500), centrally placed at 2 Governor's Parade, normally charges £95 or more but at weekends there are doubles for £49.50. The *Rock Hotel* (☎ 73000) at 3 Europa Rd has a bit more history – past guests have included Winston Churchill and Noel Coward. Singles/doubles from £60/80 to £95/100 include breakfast. Both hotels have good restaurants and pools.

If Gibraltar prices don't grab you, there are some economical options in La Línea.

Places to Eat

Most of the many pubs do typical British pub meals. One of the best is *The Clipper* at 78B Irish Town, where a generous serve of fish and chips and a pint of beer will set you back £6. *Three Roses Bar* at 60 Governor's St does an all-day breakfast of two eggs, sausage, bacon, fried bread, beans, tomato and mushrooms for £2.80. At the popular *Piccadilly Gardens* pub on Rosia Rd sit outside and have a three course lunch for £6.

Maxi Manger on Main St is a good fast-food spot with burgers (including veggie

ANDALUCÍA

ones) for £1.60, calamari for £2.25, fish and chips for £3.

The *Market Restaurant* on Market Place is good value with fish, chips and peas for £3, or a big British breakfast for £2.80. There's great Indian food at the *Viceroy of India* at 9/11 Horse Barrack Court, which has a three course lunch for £6.50. À la carte there are vegetarian dishes for £2 to £3, and main courses from £6 to £10. *The Piazza*, 156 Main St, does decent burgers and pizzas for £4.50 to £6, and fish and meat main courses from £5.50 to £8. *Minister's Restaurant*, 310 Main St, is good for fish, meat or pasta from £3.50.

Things to Buy

British expats from the Costa del Sol flock to Gibraltar to stock up on British goods at cheaper prices than in Spain. There are lots of British high street stores, such as Marks & Spencer, Safeway (in the Europort development at the north end of the main harbour), and British Home Stores. There are even a few Indian corner shops on streets such as Irish Town. Shops are normally open Monday to Friday from 9 am to 7.30 pm, and Saturday morning.

Getting There & Away

The border is open 24 hours daily.

Air GB Airways (☎ 79300, in Britain ☎ 0345-222111) flies daily to London for £99 one way. It also has flights to Morocco, though these are cheaper if bought from travel agents in Spain. In Gibraltar a one month return to Marrakesh is £133. Monarch Airlines was due to start Luton-Gibraltar flights in May 1997.

Bus There are no regular buses to Gibraltar itself but the bus station in La Línea is only a five minute walk from the border.

Car & Motorcycle Vehicle queues at the border often make it less time-consuming to park in La Línea, then walk across the border. To take a car into Gibraltar you need an insurance certificate, registration document,

nationality plate and driving licence. Petrol is about 30% cheaper than in Spain.

Ferry There are normally three ferries a week each way between Gibraltar and Tangier, taking two hours for £18/28 one way/return. In Gibraltar, buy tickets at Tourafrica International (☎ 77666), 2A Main St. Ferries from Algeciras are more frequent and cheaper.

Getting Around

The 1.5-km walk from the border to the town centre is quite fun as it crosses the airport runway. A left turn off Corral Rd at the northern end of town will take you through the Landport Tunnel, once the only land entry through Gibraltar's walls, into Grand Casemates Square. Alternatively, bus Nos 3 and 9 go from the border into town about every 15 minutes. No 9 goes to Market Place, from 8 am to 9 pm. No 3 goes south along Line Wall Rd, with a stop at Cathedral Square, then up Europa Rd and on to Europa Point at the south end of the Rock. Bus No 10 runs from the border to Europort (with a stop at Safeway supermarket), then to Reclamation Rd near the centre. On Sunday bus services are limited. All buses are 40p a ride.

All of Gibraltar can be covered on foot, and much of it (including the upper Rock) by car or motorcycle, but there are other options worth considering. The most obvious is the cable car which, weather permitting, leaves its lower station on Red Sands Rd Monday to Saturday every 10 minutes between 9.30 am and 5.15 pm. Fares are £3.45/4.65 one way/return. For the Apes' Den, get off at the middle station.

If you're in a hurry, take a taxi tour of the Rock's main sights for around £25.

Málaga Province

Best known for Spain's most densely packed holiday coast, the Costa del Sol, Málaga province in south central Andalucía also contains some wild and dramatic hill country, a lively capital city and some very attractive country towns such as Ronda and Antequera. Málaga's international airport is many people's point of entry into Spain.

The telephone code for Málaga province is ☎ 95.

MÁLAGA

Málaga, the capital of the Costa del Sol yet mercifully distinct from it, is ignored by many visitors who slip straight off from the airport to the resort towns. But this thriving, cosmopolitan, southern port city of 556,000 people is well worth investigating. Though surrounded by rings of ugly industrial and housing developments, its centre, with the backdrop of a sparkling blue Mediterranean, has wide, leafy boulevards, some charmingly dilapidated streets and a handful of impressive monuments. A lively city with a liberal tradition, Málaga stays open late and inspires a fierce devotion among its citizens. Its Semana Santa processions are among Spain's biggest and its August feria is celebrated exuberantly.

History

Málaga was established in the 8th century BC by Phoenician traders, who are credited with planting the area's first vineyards. The city flourished in the Muslim era, especially as part of the Granada taifa in the 11th century and of the Emirate of Granada from 1296. Its fall to the Christians in 1487 was a big nail in the emirate's coffin.

The expulsion of the Moriscos, who had been active in agriculture, contributed to famine and epidemics in the 17th century, but prosperity arrived in the 19th century with a dynamic middle class led by the Riojan Larios and Heredia families, who founded textile factories, sugar mills, shipyards and steel mills. The popularity of Málaga dessert wine in Victorian England was also profitable until a bug devastated the vineyards around the city. Málaga's first tourism drive helped to compensate: the city had already been popularised by the romantic movement and in the 1920s it became the favourite winter resort of rich *madrileños*.

In the 1930s the civil war ravaged the city and province. With a firm tradition of anarchism and syndicalism, Málaga was a Republican stronghold. Republicans burnt churches and convents, then the city was bombed by Italian planes before falling in February 1937 to the Nationalists. Particularly vicious reprisals followed.

In the 1960s Franco flogged tourism on the Costa del Sol, and Málaga has since flourished; its industry is healthy, too, though youth unemployment is high.

Orientation

The central thoroughfare is the east-west Alameda Principal. At its east end is the long, leafy Paseo del Parque. To the west it continues as Avenida de Andalucía. The main streets heading north off the Alameda are Calle Molina Lario, with the cathedral; Calle Marqués de Larios, ending at the central Plaza de la Constitución, around which is what remains of the old quarter; and Calle Puerta del Mar, which is the centre of the modern shopping district. On the hill above Paseo del Parque are the Alcazaba and Gibralfaro.

Information

Tourist Offices Málaga's helpful multilingual tourist office (☎ 221 34 45) is at Pasaje Chinitas 4, an alley off Plaza de la Constitución. Transport details are posted on the wall. The office is open Monday to Friday from 9 am to 7 pm, Saturday from 10 am to 7 pm and Sunday from 10 am to 2 pm. The office has details of the many foreign consulates in and near Málaga. There's also a small branch at the bus station.

Money There are plenty of banks with ATMs on Calle Puerta del Mar and Calle Marqués de Larios.

Post & Communications The main post office (postcode 29080) is at Avenida de Andalucía 1.

Books El Corte Inglés, opposite the post office, stocks English-language press,

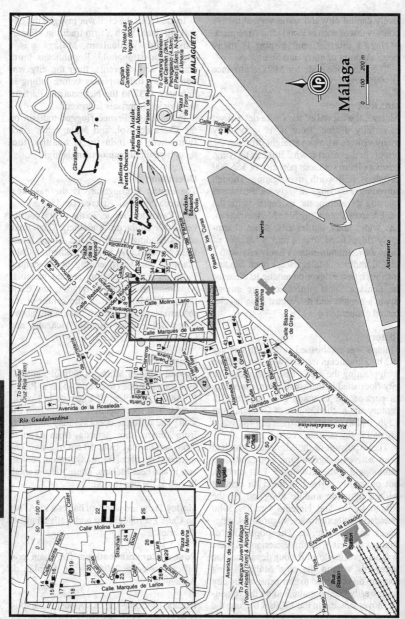

Málaga

English Cemetery

To Hotel Las
Vegas (600m)

To Camping Balneario
del Carmen (3km);
Pedregalejo (4.5km);
El Palo (5.5km), N-340;
LA MALAGUETA

Plaza
de Toros

Calle Reding

Paseo de Reding

Gibralfaro

Jardines de Puerta Obscura

Jardines Alcalde
Pedro Ruiz Alonso

Alcazaba

Calle Alcazabilla

Plaza
Merced

Campos Marín

Calle Granada

Recinto
Eduardo
Ocón

Paseo del Parque

Paseo de los Curas

Calle Beatas

Calle Méndez Núñez

C Caldería

Calle Molina Lario

See Enlargement

Calle Marqués de Larios

Puerto

Estación
Marítima

Calle Blasco de Grey

Carretería

Calle Cisneros

Cuenca Nueva

Henita
del Rey

Puerta
Nueva

Avenida de la Roseleda

To Hospital
Cruz Roja (1km)

Río Guadalmedina

Pintora

Alameda

Calle Trinidad Grund

Alameda Manuel Agustín Heredia

Alameda de Colón

Calle Bazton

Río Guadalmedina

Post
Office

El Corte
Inglés

Calle de Salita

Avenida de Andalucía

To Albergue Juvenil Málaga
(Youth Hostel) (1km) & Airport (10km)

Paseo de los Tilos

Explanada de la Estación

Train
Station

Bus
Station

Calle Molina Lario

Calle Cister

Calle Santa María

Strachan

Bolsa

de Lara

Plaza de
la Marina

Calle Sancha

Calle Marqués de Larios

ANDALUCÍA

0 100 200 m

0   50   100 m

PLACES TO STAY					
9	Hostal Aurora	8	La Cancela	6	Salsa
12	Hostal Cisneros	13	Entrepan Fastfood	7	Parador Málaga
14	Hostal Lampérez	15	Café Central		Gibralfaro
17	Hostal Chinitas	16	Café Chinitas	10	Viajes Alhambra &
18	Hotel Larios	20	Bar Restaurant Mesón		American Express
24	Hostal Córdoba		El Chinitas	11	Museo de Artes y
26	Hotel Don Curro	30	Bar Restaurante		Costumbres
28	Hostal Victoria		Tormes		Populares
29	Hostal Derby	33	Bar Galeria Terra	19	Tourist Office
36	Hotel Carlos V	34	El Jardín	21	Librería de Ocasion
43	Hostal Avenida	35	Café Teatro	22	Catedral
44	Hotel Venecia	37	Un Bar de Cine	23	RENFE Office
45	Hotel Sur	39	Aduana	25	Iberia Office
46	Hostal El Ruedo	40	Rag-Time Café	27	Air Europa &
48	Hostal El Cenachero	41	Marisquerías		Trasmediterránea
		47	El Yamal		Office
		49	Mesón Danés	31	Tetería
PLACES TO EAT				32	Museo Picasso &
4	Sociedad Naturo-	OTHER			Museo Bellas Artes
	Vegetariana de Málaga	1	Policía Local	38	Roman Theatre
5	Café Bar La Nueva	2	Teatro Cervantes	42	Mercado
	Cabaña	3	Casa Natal de Picasso	50	Central-Alameda

guides and novels, and maps. Librería de Ocasión, Calle Salinas 7, also has books in English.

Medical & Emergency Services The Policía Local (☎ 260 00 92, or 092 in an emergency) are at Avenida de la Rosaleda 19 on the east side of the Río Guadalmedina. The Hospital Cruz Roja (☎ 225 04 50, or 222 22 22 in an emergency) is at Avenida Jorge Silvela 64, a km further north.

Dangers & Annoyances Take care of your valuables in the dark corners of the centre, where pickpockets and bag-snatchers operate.

Luggage Lockers at the train and bus stations cost 400 ptas a day.

Alcazaba
The Alcazaba is the Muslim palace-fortress at the lower, west end of the hill that dominates the city centre. It looks splendid in spring when the jacaranda trees at its base are in full purple bloom. With a double wall and a large number of defensive towers, the Alcazaba was begun in 1057 by the fearsome taifa ruler Badis. The entrance has typically Muslim staggered passages to make access

difficult. The first of three parallel palaces inside is a Badis original; the others were restored in the Nasrid style earlier this century. For years the Alcazaba housed a **Museo Arqueológico**, with some excellent Muslim ceramics. This recently closed but was due to reopen, possibly at another site, at the end of 1997.

The Alcazaba is open Tuesday to Friday from 9.30 am to 1.30 pm and 5 to 8 pm (4 to 7 pm in winter), Saturday and Sunday from 10 am to 2 pm (winter 10 am to 1 pm). Entry costs 30 ptas.

Below the Alcazaba, a Roman theatre is being excavated.

Gibralfaro
Above the Alcazaba towers the older Muslim castle, the Gibralfaro, built on the site of an earlier Phoenician fort by Abd ar-Rahman I, the Córdoban emir in the 8th century. What you see today is the result of rebuilding in the 14th and 15th centuries when Málaga was the main port for the Emirate of Granada. The Gibralfaro is open daily from 9 am to 1.50 pm and 4 to 8 pm.

The Alcazaba and Gibralfaro are connected by a rampart, but you can't use it. Walk up to the Gibralfaro by the rough path from the south side of the Alcazaba or take

ANDALUCÍA

bus No 35 from Paseo del Parque (roughly every 45 minutes from 11 am to 7 pm daily).

Catedral

Málaga's cathedral, on Calle Molina Lario, was begun in the 16th century on the site of the former main mosque and took two centuries to complete. Like many of Málaga's old buildings, it is falling down, but restoration has recently begun. It is known locally as La Manquita (the One-Armed) owing to the fact that only the west tower was ever completed. Money allocated for the east tower was contributed to the campaign against the British in the American War of Independence. Recently the Costa del Sol's American Society has handed over money towards the current repairs in belated thanks. The cathedral has an 18th century baroque façade but the inside is both Gothic and Renaissance. Of most interest are the 17th century finely carved wooden choir stalls. The cathedral is open Monday to Saturday from 10 am to 1 pm and 4.30 to 6.30 pm (200 ptas). During Mass, at 8.30 am daily and several times on Sunday, entry is free.

Museo Picasso & Museo de Bellas Artes

The lovely 16th century Palacio de los Condes de Buenavista on Calle San Agustín is due to be converted by the year 2000 into an important new museum devoted to the Málaga-born Pablo Picasso, based on a large donation of Picasso's work by his daughter-in-law Christine Ruiz-Picasso. The city's Museo de Bellas Artes (fine arts museum), which has occupied the building since 1961, is due to move to another (at the time of writing, undecided) site. Its extensive collection concentrates on work by *malagueños*, though others such as Ribera, Zurbarán, Murillo and Alonso Cano are also well represented.

Alameda Principal & Paseo del Parque

The Alameda Principal, now a busy thoroughfare, was constructed in the late 18th century as a boulevard on what were then the sands of the Guadalmedina estuary. Until the Paseo del Parque was built, it was the city's

main gathering and strolling place. It is adorned with old trees from the Indies and lined with 18th and 19th century buildings.

In the 1890s the palm-lined Paseo del Parque, an extension of the Alameda, was built on land reclaimed from the sea. Over time the garden along its south side has been filled with rare and exotic tropical plants, making a pleasant refuge from the bustle of the city. The 18th century **aduana** (customs house) on the paseo's north side originally had the sea lapping at its doors.

Museo de Artes y Costumbres Populares

The Museum of Popular Arts, housed in an old inn on Pasillo Santa Isabel, is a fun place to visit, especially for children. The building is little changed from the 17th century when the stables and storehouses were on the ground floor and the rooms above. The collection focuses on everyday life and includes items connected with farming and fishing. Note the glass cabinets containing painted clay figures *(barros)* of the highwayman, the couple dancing, the rider from Ronda and other characters from malagueño folklore. These barros exercised a strong fascination on 19th and early 20th century travellers influenced by the romantic movement. The museum is open Monday to Friday from 10 am to 1.30 pm and 4 to 7 pm (200 ptas; free for students and children under 14).

Casa Natal de Picasso

Picasso fans might like to stop by the house where he was born, at Plaza de la Merced 15. The recently restored house is operated by the Fundación Picasso, a body which organises cultural events in memory of the painter, but there's not a lot to see: a few Picasso sketches and paintings, articles about him and a video about his life. Current opening times are Monday to Friday from 11 am to 2 pm and 5 to 8 pm.

English Cemetery

The leafy English Cemetery is on Paseo de Reding, just beyond the Plaza de Toros. It was built on land ceded to the British consul in 1830 at his request to found a foreign cemetery. (Prior to this, non-Catholic bodies were buried at night upright in the sand at the foot of the beach. Corpses were exposed to being ravaged by dogs, washed out to sea or back to shore.) Unlike the wall niches customary in Andalucían cemeteries, this one has gravestones and monuments, with some fascinating inscriptions. A variety of people of many nationalities, from poets to consuls to children, are buried here.

The cemetery is open daily from 8 am to 1 pm and Monday to Friday only from 2.30 to 6 pm.

Language Courses

We've had good reports about Spanish courses run by the Universidad de Málaga (☎ 221 40 07; fax 221 25 13). Two-week intensive courses cost around 45,000 ptas and accommodation with a Spanish family (2500 ptas per day) can be arranged. For more information, write to Universidad de Málaga, Cursos de Español para Extranjeros, Apartado 310, 29080 Málaga. There are also some good private language schools in Málaga: the main tourist office can help with information.

Special Events

Semana Santa in Málaga is solemn and spectacular. The *pasos* are large and heavy, some needing up to 150 people to carry them. On the Monday, the procession following the image of Jesús Cautivo (Christ taken prisoner) is joined by as many as 25,000 people, some barefooted, hooded, or with their ankles in chains. As in most cities, events reach their climax on Good Friday. The best place to see the processions is the steps on the east bank of the Río Guadalmedina.

Other festivals include:

16 July
  Procesión de la Virgen del Carmen – held at dusk in Málaga and towns along the coast. Fishing fleets cast out to sea with the lead boat bearing the image of the virgin. On shore, crowds shout her praises and set off flares and fireworks.

12-20 August
  Feria de Málaga – Málaga's August Fair takes place in the city centre and in fairgrounds on the outskirts. The busy programme includes bullfights, flamenco and rock concerts. Events culminate in a lantern-lit sardine bake on the beach.

Places to Stay – bottom end

Camping *Camping Balneario del Carmen* (☎ 229 00 21), Avenida Pintor Joaquín Sorolla 26, El Cano, near the coast three km east of the centre, is open year round. Cost is 475 ptas per person, per tent and per car (less in winter). Bus No 11 (see Getting Around) passes by.

Youth Hostel The *Albergue Juvenil Málaga* (☎ 230 85 00) at Plaza Pío XII, 1.5 km west of the centre and a couple of blocks north of Avenida de Andalucía, is inconvenient for the centre but on the right side of town for the bus and train stations. It has 100 places, all in double rooms. Bus No 18 (see Getting Around) will take you most of the way.

Hostales Most of Málaga's hostales are in the blocks north and south of the Alameda Principal. Budget rooms are on the whole tatty, and the cathedral bells toll on the quarter-hour through the night, a recipe for disturbed sleep. Expect to pay more than the prices quoted during July, August and Semana Santa.

North of the Alameda Hostal *Chinitas* (☎ 221 46 83) at Pasaje Chinitas 2, east off Plaza de la Constitución, is run by a friendly family and has clean, basic singles/doubles for 1700/3400 ptas. Close by, *Hostal Lampérez* (☎ 221 94 84), at Calle Santa María 6, costs 1500/2500 ptas. Rooms vary; the bathroom is a bit grim.

West of Plaza de la Constitución, *Hostal Aurora* (☎ 222 40 04), Calle Muro de Puerta Nueva 1, off Calle Cisneros, has six clean, attractive rooms for 2000/4000 ptas. The owners are welcoming. *Hostal Cisneros* (☎ 221 26 33), Calle Cisneros 7, is spotless and friendly. Rooms are 2500/4500 ptas, or 5500 ptas for doubles with bath.

ANDALUCÍA

Close to the Alameda Principal, the friendly *Hostal Derby* (☎ 222 13 01), Calle San Juan de Dios 1, has spacious rooms with big windows and private bath from 3000/4000 ptas. One block north, Calle Bolsa has yet more possibilities. The homely *Hostal Córdoba* (☎ 221 44 69) at No 9 has rooms with shared bath from 1300/2500 ptas.

South of the Alameda *Hostal Avenida* (☎ 221 77 28), Alameda Principal 5, has clean, basic rooms with shared bath at 1400/2800 ptas plus IVA. *Hostal El Ruedo* (☎ 221 58 20), Calle Trinidad Grund 3, one block south of the Alameda Principal, is an old place with friendly owners and rooms at 1700/3200 ptas. *El Cenachero* (☎ 222 40 88), Calle Barroso 5, is a good bet at 3000/4700 ptas for rooms with bath, or doubles for 3500 ptas with shared bath.

Places to Stay – middle

Add IVA to these prices and expect to pay more in July and August. All have private bathroom and TV.

A few steps west of the cathedral, *Hotel Carlos V* (☎ 221 51 27), Calle Cister 10, has comfortable rooms for 3000/5700 ptas. The popular *Hostal Victoria* (☎ 222 42 24), Calle Sancha de Lara 3, has 16 rooms at 4000/5900 ptas. On the south side of the Alameda, *Hotel Venecia* (☎ 221 36 36), Alameda Principal 9, and *Hotel Sur* (☎ 222 48 03), Calle Trinidad Grund 13, have similar rates.

Places to Stay – top end

Add IVA to all prices. In the centre, *Hotel Larios*, (☎ 222 22 00), Calle Marqués de Larios 2, has doubles for 17,000 ptas (rising to a whopping 35,000 ptas for Semana Santa). The large *Hotel Don Curro* (☎ 222 72 00), Calle Sancha de Lara 9, has singles/doubles at 8000/11,500 ptas. East of the centre, the *Hotel Las Vegas* (☎ 221 77 12), Paseo de Sancha 22, has rooms for 9500/11,800 ptas and the added attraction of a pool and proximity to the beach.

The *Parador Málaga Gibralfaro* (☎ 222 19 02), with an unbeatable location on the Gibralfaro hill, has recently been refurbished and also has a pool. Doubles are 16,500 ptas but there are winter discounts.

Places to Eat

Malagueño cuisine concentrates on fish fried quickly in olive oil. *Fritura malagueño* consists of fried fish, anchovies and squid. Cold soups are popular. As well as *gazpacho* (in the tomato season) and *sopa de ajo* (garlic soup), try *sopa de almendra con uvas* (almond soup with grapes). Málaga's sweet Muscatel wine is added to some chicken dishes and confectionery.

Seafood Sample fish dishes at the marisquerías (seafood eateries) with tables outside on slightly seedy Calle Comisario, an alley off the north side of the Alameda Principal. The seafront eateries at Pedregalejo, 4.5 km east of the centre, do good fish, or you could continue one km east to *Tintero II* on the seafront at El Palo, where plates of seafood are brought out by the waiters and you shout for what you want.

Near Plaza de la Constitución *Café Central*, with tables outside on the busy east side of the plaza, is a noisy local favourite; its coffee will satisfy even hardened caffeine addicts. Prices for food are reasonable, and there's plenty of choice. Round the corner on pedestrian Pasaje Chinitas, mellow *Café Chinitas* is good for coffees, pastries, fresh juices, milk shakes, breakfasts and snacks. Nearby, *Bar Restaurante Mesón El Chinitas* on Calle Monroy is a fancy place with prices to match – most main dishes are around 1500 ptas. It's open daily for lunch and dinner.

Entrepan Fastfood on Calle Dr Manuel Pérez Bryan, off the west side of Calle Marqués de Larios, has good breakfasts from 175 ptas, plus other meals and tapas.

Just north of Plaza de la Constitución, *Café Bar La Nueva Cabaña* on Calle Calderería, open till late on weekdays and to 4 pm on weekends, is good for tea, coffee and pastries. *La Cancela*, nearby at Calle Belgrano 5, has an appetising menu at moderate prices.

Near the Cathedral *El Jardín* on Calle Cister, with a pleasant terrace facing the cathedral, has a fancy interior and an elaborate menu with lots of seafood; the menú is 1100 ptas. It's open daily from 8 am to late. *Bar Galería Terral*, on the corner of Calle Cister and Calle Pedro de Toledo, is a good spot for tapas. The *Tetería* on pedestrian Calle San Agustín, opposite the Museo de Bellas Artes, does all manner of teas, including an 'antidepresivo', plus crêpes, pastries and sorbets. Open daily from 4 pm until late, it's popular with students. *Bar Restaurante Tormes* at Calle San Agustín 13 is open for late breakfast, lunch and dinner (closed Monday); the three course menú is 1100 ptas.

Near the Market The colourful *Mercado Central*, built in the 19th century in a mudéjar-influenced style, has terrific fresh produce inside as well. Nearby, there are loads of cafés on pedestrian Calle Herrerería del Rey. These open early and pack up promptly at 1 pm. There are also some atmospheric *bars* serving local wine from barrels, among them one on the corner of Calles Puerta del Mar and Herredería del Rey. A few blocks west of the market, *El Corte Inglés* has a supermarket.

South of the Alameda Head for this area if you're after something different from the usual fare. *El Yamal*, at Calle Blasco de Grey 3, does good Arabic food; couscous with vegetables costs 900 ptas. *Mesón Danés*, Calle Barroso 5, offers Spanish and Danish food; the menú is 985 ptas. Both places close on Sunday.

Vegetarian Vegetarians should try *Sociedad Naturo-Vegetariana de Málaga*, upstairs at Calle Carretería 82 (1st floor), open for lunch.

Entertainment
Two monthly publications – *Guía del Ocio* (160 ptas) from kiosks, and *¿Qué Hacer? ¿Dónde Ir?* from the tourist office – have entertainment listings. Nightlife clusters around Calle Granada and Calle Beatas in the centre and in La Malagueta, the area near the seafront immediately east of the centre. Pedregalejo, 4.5 km east of the centre, with numerous bars and discos, buzzes until late on weekends and other nights in the summer.

In the centre, *Café Teatro*, Calle Afligidos, is a slightly offbeat place, open from 8.30 pm, which sometimes has live music. Posters there advertise forthcoming live music around town. *Un Bar de Cine*, Calle Alcazabilla 2, near Cine Albéniz also sometimes has live music. *Salsa*, on the corner of Calle Belgrano and Calle Méndez Núñez, has live salsa on Wednesday night from midnight to late. *Rag-Time Café*, Calle Reding 12 in La Malagueta, has blues, jazz or flamenco depending on the night. The *Plaza de Toros* on Paseo de Reding stages big-name rock gigs as well as bullfights.

The *Teatro Cervantes* on Calle Ramos Marín has a regular programme of classical music, opera, dance and theatre.

Getting There & Away
Air Málaga's busy international airport (☎ 224 00 00) is 10 km west of the centre, halfway to Torremolinos. Cheap charter flights transport many of the millions of tourists who pass through each year. Plenty of agencies sell one-way seats on these: flights to London are usually 15,000 ptas or less. Servitour (☎ 204 82 92) and Flightline (☎ 204 83 40) have tickets to Britain: Flightline also has flights to Germany, Holland and Belgium. Iberia (☎ 213 61 47), at Calle Molina Lario 13, has direct scheduled flights to/from London (daily) and several other European cities. Alitalia, British Airways, Royal Air Maroc and Lufthansa are other carriers serving Málaga.

Most domestic flights are operated by Iberia, Aviaco and Binter Mediterráneo (which share the Iberia office), and Air Europa (☎ 260 08 80), Calle Don Juan Díaz 4. Iberia has seven flights daily to Madrid (16,550 ptas one way) and two or three to Barcelona (22,800 ptas). Air Europa flies most days to Madrid (from 9900 ptas) and Barcelona (13,900 ptas), and a few times a

ANDALUCÍA

week to Palma de Mallorca, Salamanca, Santiago de Compostela and elsewhere. Binter Mediterráneo flies daily to Melilla. All airlines have offices at the airport.

Bus The bus station (☎ 235 00 61) is on Paseo de los Tilos, one km west of the centre.

There are frequent buses along the coast in both directions, and several daily to inland towns including Antequera and Ronda. Other services include to Sevilla (10 or more daily; 3½ hours; 2245 ptas), Córdoba (six daily; 2½ hours; 1400 ptas), Granada (up to 16 daily; 2½ hours; 1400 ptas), Murcia (3765 ptas), Alicante (4285 ptas), Valencia (five daily; 11 hours; 5745 ptas), Barcelona (four daily; 18 hours; 8630 ptas), and Madrid (six daily; 8½ hours; 2710 to 3010 ptas). There are also buses to Germany, Switzerland, the UK, Portugal, France and the Netherlands.

Train The train station (☎ 236 02 02) is on Explanada de la Estación round the corner from the bus station. The city centre RENFE office (☎ 221 31 22) at Calle Strachan 2 is open Monday to Friday from 9 am to 1.30 pm and 4.30 to 7.30 pm.

Most days there are eight trains to Madrid: five Talgos, two 2nd class night trains, and one slow day train which goes on to Zaragoza (4300 ptas to Madrid). The fastest Talgo takes four hours (8000 ptas). Bobadilla (where you need to change for Granada and Ronda) and Córdoba are on the Madrid line. The fastest Talgo takes around two hours to Córdoba (2200 ptas), to which there are also three 2nd class trains daily.

To Sevilla (three hours) there are three trains daily, one requiring a change at Bobadilla. From Bobadilla, there are three connections daily to Granada (three hours).

For Valencia and Barcelona there are two 2nd class trains daily, one overnight. A 2nd class seat to Barcelona costs 7300 ptas and the trip takes 14½ hours. There's also a slightly quicker night train to Barcelona via Zaragoza.

Cercanías trains run to the airport and continue to Torremolinos and Fuengirola

(285 ptas), about every half-hour from 6.30 am to 10.30 pm.

Car Rental There are several agencies at the airport, some with cars for under 20,000 ptas a week. Mocar Autorent (☎ 261 45 15), Calle Brújula 3, one km west of the centre, has cars from 6000 ptas a day or 22,500 ptas a week.

Boat Trasmediterránea (☎ 222 43 91), Calle Don Juan Díaz 4, operates ferries daily (except Sunday from mid-September to mid-June) to/from Melilla. The trip takes 7½ hours and costs 3370 ptas for passengers, 8330 ptas for a standard-size car and 3305 ptas for a 250 cc motorbike. You can buy tickets most easily at the Estación Marítima, more or less directly south of the town centre.

Getting Around
The Airport Buses to the airport (115 ptas) run about every half-hour between 6.30 am and 11.30 pm from the south side of the cathedral, stopping at the train and bus stations en route. Trains (20 minutes; 125 ptas) run every half-hour from 6.30 am to 10.30 pm between the airport, Málaga's main station and the Centro-Alameda station on the west side of the Río Guadalmedina just south of Avenida de Andalucía. From the airport they go on to Torremolinos and Fuengirola. The airport station is a five minute walk from the terminal: follow the 'Ferrocarril' signs. A taxi to the airport costs around 1300 ptas.

Bus Useful buses around town (100 ptas) include No 4 from the train station to the centre, No 11 to Pedregalejo and El Palo from Paseo del Parque, and No 18 west along the Alameda Principal and Avenida de Andalucía.

Taxi Fares within the centre, including those to the train and bus stations, are around 400 ptas.

COSTA DEL SOL
The much-maligned Costa del Sol might best

be described as an international strip stuck on the bottom of Spain, home to more than 300,000 expatriates, particularly from Britain, Germany and Scandinavia.

Comprising a string of resorts running south-west from Málaga towards Gibraltar, it is geared for – and incredibly popular with – package-deal tourists and the time-share crowd. With more than 25 camp sites and 40 luxury hotels, as well as hundreds of pensiones and hostales, there is accommodation to suit every budget. The Costa del Sol pulls in the crowds because of its weather, beaches, warm Mediterranean water and cheap package deals, though it still manages to pull in the jet set with its abundance of exclusive facilities.

These resorts were once simple fishing villages, but there is little sign of the villages now. Instead, the Costa del Sol is arguably the finest example in all Europe of how overdevelopment can ruin a spectacular landscape.

Most people still think of it in terms of the most famous resorts: Torremolinos – which has acquired such a bad reputation that it has been dubbed 'Terrible Torre' – Fuengirola and Marbella. In fact, it is a series of townscapes from one end to the other, as *urbanización* after *urbanización* – complete with bars, restaurants, banks and shops – has raped the land which used to punctuate the towns.

Despite all that, when you know where to go, the Costa del Sol can be a fabulous place to live, and the real Spain is still only a few minutes inland by car. But you do need a car to appreciate the beauty of it: otherwise you're unlikely to experience more than the average package tourist.

Markets

Colourful, bustling street markets take place on different days in each town and are well worth a wander. You can often get away with bartering for a bargain, though clothes and leather goods with well-known brand names are almost inevitably fakes. The markets are in Marbella on Monday, Fuengirola on Tuesday, Estepona and Mijas-Costa on

---

❋ ❋ ❋ ❋ ❋ ❋ ❋ ❋ ❋ ❋ ❋ ❋ ❋

Carretera de Cádiz

Life on the Costa del Sol revolves around the Carretera de Cádiz (N-340), without which it is impossible to get from A to B. This road was formerly dubbed 'Death Highway' due to the number of fatalities on it, but much has been done in recent years to improve its safety.

Town bypasses have been built to take motorway traffic off what essentially is the only local road, and both central and side barriers have been put up to prevent dangerous turn-offs. Countless bridges and underpasses have been built to enable motorists supposedly safe access to and from the various *urbanizaciones*, yet still the danger remains.

So pivotal is the N-340 to everyday life that even the most luxurious of hotels use a km mark rather than an address. In practice, this means that many visitors spot their turn-off at the last minute – or miss it altogether – leading to panic-stricken driving manoeuvres. This confusion is compounded by the fact that many of the km marks have been changed, and a lot of the old signs are still on the road.

Undoubtedly the most useful sign for the motorist is 'Cambio de Sentido', which appears every couple of km and lets you know where you can change direction. Meanwhile, beware of other motorists and watch out for cats and dogs and/or inebriated pedestrians trying to cross.

Take special care when it's been raining: after months of hot weather, the roads are particularly lethal when wet. You'd expect people to slow down in these conditions, but they don't...and the way in which they sit on your rear bumper when they want to overtake is quite intimidating. ■

❋ ❋ ❋ ❋ ❋ ❋ ❋ ❋ ❋ ❋ ❋ ❋ ❋

Wednesday, San Pedro de Alcántara and Torremolinos on Thursday, Benalmádena on Friday and Nueva Andalucía on Saturday.

Activities

The Costa del Sol is a sport-lover's paradise, with more than 40 golf clubs from one end to the other, along with tennis and squash courts, riding schools, diving centres, swimming pools and gymnasiums. Many beaches offer facilities for water sports such as windsurfing, sailing, water-skiing and paragliding. For those who like gambling there are two casinos: the Casino de Torrequebrada (☎ 244 25 45) in Benalmádena at

N-340, Km 226, and Casino Nueva Andalucía (☎ 281 40 00), at N-340, Km 173, just west of Marbella.

Special Events

During Semana Santa there are spectacular processions in Benalmádena and Marbella. In May, the celebration of the Cruces de Mayo – for which the streets and squares are decorated with flowers – is best seen in Coín. During the summer months practically every town honours its patron saint: in Marbella the main festivities take place in June, in Estepona between 3 and 10 July, in Torremolinos from 24 to 29 September and in Fuengirola between 6 and 12 October.

Accommodation

Prices given in this section are for the high season of July, August and, in some places, September. They come down sharply at other times in most places.

Torremolinos

It is difficult to imagine why anyone would stop for longer than it takes to drink a beer in this hideous high-rise resort, designed to squeeze as many paying customers as possible into the smallest imaginable space.

Phoenicians, Greeks, Roman and Muslims all once settled here. The main legacy of the Islamic period is the watchtower at the end of Calle San Miguel, referred to in a 1947 decree as Torre de los Molinos (Tower of the Mills), from which the resort takes its name.

In 1930 groups of English people started arriving at the Englishman's Castle, an estate belonging to the first expatriate, George Langworthy, who had converted it into what was then the only place of residence for foreigners on the Costa del Sol.

In the tourist boom of the 1950s and 60s it was Torremolinos that made the coast of Málaga famous, and it was basically all downhill from then on, to the extent that today you'll be surprised if you hear someone speak Spanish.

The tourist office (☎ 237 95 12), in the ayuntamiento on Calle Rafael Quintana, is open Monday to Friday from 9.30 am to 1.30 pm.

The pedestrianised Calle San Miguel, just east of the train station, is pretty much the centre of town, and there is no shortage of places to stay within a few minutes walk. *Hostal Prudencio* (☎ 238 14 52), Calle Carmen 43, is a stone's throw from the beach, with singles/doubles for 2800/5600 ptas. *Hostal Guillot* (☎ 238 01 44), Calle Río Mundo 4, is nowhere near as pleasant, but has cheaper doubles at 3500 ptas. The tourist office can supply you with a list of options; alternatively, just head for the nearest travel agent and for a small fee get them to book you a room.

With more than 250 restaurants in town – let alone bars and nightclubs – competition is fairly intense, and you won't have a problem finding cheap food and entertainment. The nightlife can be fairly outrageous and it's a popular destination with gay travellers and transvestites.

Trains to Torremolinos run every half-hour from Málaga city and airport.

Fuengirola

Almost – but not quite – as ghastly as Torremolinos, Fuengirola is another high-rise resort, 30 minutes away by train. From both the train and bus stations it's just a two minute walk to the tourist office. What is left of the old town lies south of Avenida Condes de San Isidro and Avenida Matías Sáenz de Tejada, and stretches to the seafront. The centre is Plaza de la Constitucíon, and most accommodation is a short walk from here.

The tourist office (☎ 246 74 57) at Avenida Jesús Santos Rein 6 is open Monday to Friday from 9.30 am to 1.30 pm and 4 to 7 pm, Saturday from 10 am to 1.30 pm. The post office is just off Plaza de la Constitucíon.

The English-run *Pensión Coca* (☎ 247 41 89), Calle de la Cruz 3, has decent rooms at 2800/4800 ptas. *Pensión Andalucía* (☎ 246 33 30), Calle Troncón 59, has doubles only at 3300 ptas (4500 ptas in August). Both are just a short walk from the beach.

The old town has plenty of places to eat

and drink – many owned by expatriates – though if you take a stroll down the pedestrianised Paseo Marítimo by the port you'll find wall-to-wall restaurants with competitive prices. For the best value international restaurant in town, head for *El Tomate*, at Calle Troncón 19.

Sports fans may as well head straight for *Linekers* bar, by the yacht club at the eastern end of the port. Run by the brother of British footballer Gary Lineker, it has satellite coverage of all major international events and is open until 3 am.

Fuengirola is served by the same trains from Málaga as Torremolinos. There are four buses a day between Fuengirola and Sevilla (2060 ptas), 11 to Madrid (2850 ptas), three to Barcelona (8605 ptas), four to Granada (1425 ptas) and 35 to Marbella (270 ptas).

Mijas

A pretty little town of Muslim origin nine km north of Fuengirola, with whitewashed houses covered with bougainvillea and jasmine, Mijas would be worth a detour just for its panoramic views if it hadn't already been ruined by busloads of tourists in search of 'the typical Andalucían village'. There is no shortage of bars, restaurants and tacky souvenir shops, though out of season it's still worth a visit. The festival of San Antón is celebrated on 17 January with an open-air party, and in the first fortnight of September homage is paid to La Virgen de la Peña, the patron saint.

There are buses between Mijas and Fuengirola every 30 minutes throughout the day (95 ptas).

Marbella

In the 1950s, when Prince Alfonso von Hohenlohe built the exclusive Marbella Club, the area quickly acquired a reputation as a playground of the international jet set. Sheltered by the beautiful Sierra Blanca, it has always been the most fashionable resort on the Costa del Sol, but by the late 1980s it was going through a period of decline.

Marbella suffered perhaps more than any town from the rapid growth of *urbani-zaciones* along the coast. Now that holidaymakers had bars and restaurants within walking distance of their villas and apartments, they were reluctant to drive into town and risk the journey back on the notorious N-340. That, coupled with the effects of the recession, meant that there wasn't much money around. Meanwhile, the ayuntamiento had allowed the resort to fall into a state of neglect.

Jesús Gil y Gil, a flamboyant and controversial businessman, came to the rescue when he won a landslide victory to become mayor. Almost overnight he increased the number of police on the streets to deal with the drug addicts and prostitutes. Nearby Puerto Banús was whitewashed back to its former glory, avenidas were lined with palm trees, marble pavements were laid, plazas were spruced up and underground car parks were built to deal with the traffic problem.

Today Marbella has regained its reputation as the quality resort of the Costa del Sol. The beaches are clean, with excellent facilities, and the tourists are back.

Information The tourist office (☎ 277 14 42), on Glorieta de la Fontanilla, opens Monday to Friday from 9.30 am to 8 pm and Saturday from 10 am to 2 pm. There is a smaller office (☎ 282 35 50) by the ayuntamiento at Plaza de los Naranjos 1. For information on all Andalucía, contact the Centro Internacional de Turismo de Andalucía (☎ 283 87 85) at N-340, Km 189.6. It is open Monday to Friday from 9 am to 3 pm.

There are two banks with ATMs opposite Plaza de la Alameda on Avenida Ramón y Cajal: Central Hispano and Banco Argentaria. The postcode is 29600.

Things to See Just north of Avenida Ramón y Cajal is the charming **Plaza de los Naranjos**, the heart of the *casco antiguo* (old town), with its 16th century **ayuntamiento** and the church of **Nuestra Señora de la Encarnación**.

The **Museo del Grabado Español Contemporáneo**, on Calle Hospital Bazán, houses works by Picasso, Miró and Dalí; it

ANDALUCÍA

is open Tuesday to Friday from 11 am to 2 pm and 5.30 to 8.15 pm, Monday from 11 am to 2 pm and Sunday from 11.30 am to 2.15 pm. North-east of Plaza de los Naranjos, in Parque del Arroyo de la Represa, is Spain's only **Bonsai Museum**, open daily from 11 am to 1.30 pm and 4 to 7.30 pm.

The lively **Monday market** takes place in the streets between the football stadium and Avenida General López Domínguez, east of the old town.

Places to Stay The excellent modern HI *Albergue Juvenil Marbella* (☎ 277 14 91), above the old town at Calle Trapiche 2, has rooms with just two or three beds. Half have private bath.

There are plenty of pensiones in the old town. The British-run *Hostal del Pilar* (☎ 282 99 36), at Calle Mesoncillo 4, is deservedly popular with backpackers at 2000 ptas a person.

Hostal El Castillo (☎ 277 17 39), by the remains of the Islamic castle and city walls at Plaza San Bernabé 2, has singles/doubles for 2400/4500 ptas with bath.

The newly renovated *Hostal Enriqueta* (☎ 282 75 52), at Calle Los Caballeros 18, has doubles/triples with bath for 5000/7500 plus IVA.

Out of town, the famous *Marbella Club* (☎ 282 22 11), at N-340, Km 178, has doubles for 39,000 ptas plus IVA. Of the five-star hotels, *Hotel Don Carlos* (☎ 283 11 40), at N-340, Km 192, has singles/doubles for 23,500/30,000 ptas plus IVA, *Hotel Los Monteros* (☎ 277 17 00) at N-340, Km 188, has rooms for 29,000/36,000 ptas plus IVA, and *Hotel Puente Romano* (☎ 282 09 00) at N-340, Km 177.5, has rooms for 34,000/42,900 ptas plus IVA.

Places to Eat The restaurants around Plaza de los Naranjos are popular with visitors, but naturally they cost a lot more. For a local adventure try *El Gallo* at Calle Lobatos 44 – egg and chips for 300 ptas and the cheapest gambas pil pil in town at 500 ptas – or eat in the courtyard of *El Patio Andaluz*, a charming, dilapidated old posada (coaching inn) on

Calle San Juan de Dios: sardines, boquerones and chips with wine will set you back just 800 ptas. Also popular with locals is *Casa de los Martínez* at Calle Ramón y Cajal 7, where tapas cost around 150 ptas.

For something more up-market book a patio table at *Pícaros* (☎ 282 86 50) at Calle Aduar 1. The chef is from New York and the décor is beautiful, but main courses start from just 800 ptas and the bar is open till late.

Of all the restaurants down by the beach, *Palms*, on the east side of the Puerto Deportivo, is the most popular, specialising in interesting salads from 850 ptas.

The best Indian restaurant in town is *Gulzar*, opposite Hotel Skol on Calle Camilo José Cela.

Entertainment *Bar Tu Casa*, off the south-west corner of Plaza de los Naranjos at Calle Valdés 2, is a convenient meeting place, open from morning till late with all-day food. The inimitable Carmel – who moonlights as a stand-up comic – is a mine of information. The cosy *Bar Vera Cruz* at Calle Buitrago 7 – run by Canadian Billy – is open from 7.30 pm to 3 am (closed Sunday).

Bodega San Bernabé, south of Plaza de la Alameda on Calle Carlos Mackintosh, is wonderfully traditional, with tapas of ham and cheese only. *Bodega La Venencia*, a stone's throw from the beach on Avenida Miguel Cano, serves great tapas from 125 ptas.

After midnight, most of the youngsters head for the bars at the Puerto Deportivo. The older set tends to head for the streets around Calle Camilo José Cela, where *Frank's Corner*, *The Rock Club* (entry free after 11 pm), *Atrium* and *Havana* are the main hang-outs.

Getting There & Away There are frequent buses between Marbella and Málaga (545 ptas) and throughout the day there are regular buses to Puerto Banús (125 ptas) and Estepona (240 ptas). There are four buses daily to La Línea (670 ptas), four to Sevilla (1805 ptas) and 11 to Madrid (2980 ptas).

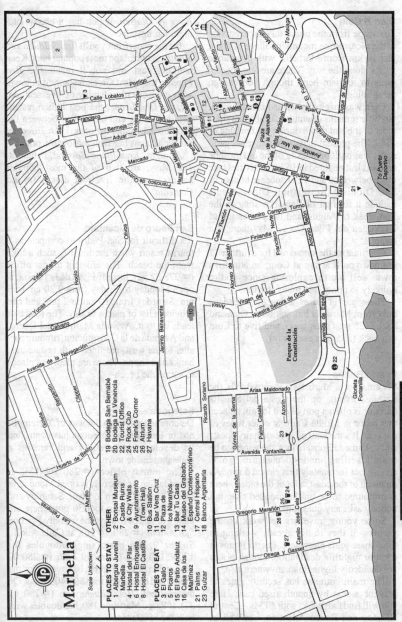

Marbella

Scale Unknown

PLACES TO STAY
1 Albergue Juvenil
4 Marbella
6 Hostal del Pilar
7 Hostal Enriqueta
8 Hostal El Castillo

PLACES TO EAT
3 El Gallo
5 Picaros
15 El Patio Andaluz
16 Casa de los Martínez
21 Palms
23 Gulzar

OTHER
2 Bonsai Museum
9 Ayuntamiento (Town Hall)
10 Bus Station
11 Bar Vera Cruz
12 Plaza de los Naranjos
13 Bar Tu Casa
14 Museo del Grabado Español Contemporáneo
17 Central Hispano
18 Banco Argentaria
19 Bodega San Bernabé
20 Bodega La Venencia
22 Tourist Office
24 Castle Ruins & City Walls
25 Rock Club
26 Atrium
27 Havana

ANDALUCÍA

Ojén & Coín

To escape from the coast, take an excursion to the picturesque mountain village of Ojén, just 10 km from Marbella, with panoramic views along the way. There are few concessions to tourism here, though you can go paragliding.

Ojén was originally a Muslim settlement, but little remains of architectural value since most of it burnt down during the uprising of 1569. The present parish church, mudéjar in style, was built on the site of the old mosque and was last restored in 1670. Festivities take place between 9 and 12 October in honour of San Dionisio Aeropajita. Other events include a festival of flamenco song in the first week of August and the procession of La Virgen del Pilar. On 12 May there is a romería.

Continue on the same road for a further 17 km and you'll arrive at Coín; an attractive town well worth exploring since you're unlikely to bump into many tourists.

There are 11 buses a day on weekdays only from Marbella bus station to Ojén and back (125 ptas each way), and five to Coín and back (335 ptas each way).

Puerto Banús

Six km west of Marbella is Puerto Banús, the flashiest marina on the Costa del Sol. Its harbour is often a port of call for gin palaces that moor in Monte Carlo at other times of the year. It's the land of stick-on hairy chests and gold medallions: in fact, there used to be a stall selling made-to-measure 'gold' chains, but fortunately that closed down. As on much of the coast, a lot of the money here is rumoured to be on the crooked side, but nobody asks any questions.

Some young travellers get work on the yachts – if they're not already working as time-share touts elsewhere. Puerto Banús is a major nightlife destination, though prices are decidedly higher than anywhere else.

The main entrance has security gates to prevent access by unauthorised cars. Here you will find two banks with ATMs – Central Hispano and Banco Atlántico – as well as

Bang & Olufsen, which has a classy late-night bar upstairs.

By the waterfront you'll find *Salduba* and *Sinatra's*, two of the most popular bars. Keep walking east and you'll reach *The Red Pepper*, the oldest Greek restaurant in town, with a spectacular display of live seafood. Next is *Don Leone*, the best Italian restaurant, and at the end of an alley between the two, tucked around the back, is *La Tasca*, an excellent tapas bar with reasonable prices.

At night, *Joy's Piano Bar* and, behind it, *The Navy*, are two of the most popular haunts. For the liveliest disco, try *La Comedia*.

San Pedro de Alcántara

It's difficult for San Pedro to compete as a tourist resort when the town is such a hike from the beach. The efficient tourist office (☎ 278 52 52), just off Plaza de la Iglesia, is open Monday to Friday from 9.30 am to 9 pm, Saturday from 10 am to 2 pm, and can provide a list of places to stay. The road that leads up to it, Avenida Marqués del Duero, and Avenida de la Constitución, running parallel to the west, are lined with restaurants, banks and shops. There are plenty of places to eat on the beach.

Estepona

Determined not to go the way of Torremolinos or Fuengirola, Estepona has controlled its development carefully and remains a pleasant seaside town.

The tourist office (☎ 280 09 13), at Avenida San Lorenzo 1, is open Monday to Friday from 9.30 am to 9 pm, Saturday and Sunday from 10 am to 1.30 pm. There are plenty of places to stay: the friendly *Pensíon San Antoni* (☎ 280 14 76), at Calle Adolfo Suárez 9, has basic singles/doubles for 1700/3100 ptas. *Hostal El Pilar* (☎ 280 00 18), at Plaza Las Flores 10, overlooks the square and has rooms for 1800/4000 ptas. On the seafront, *Hotel Buenavista* (☎ 280 01 37), at Paseo Marítimo 180, has doubles with bath for 5500 ptas.

West of Estepona

Eight km further on is the turning for the old Islamic town of **Casares**, 10 km inland. Dubbed 'the hanging village' for the way in which it clings to the edge of a cliff below the well-preserved remains of a Muslim castle, it is well worth an excursion and the surrounding countryside offers excellent hiking opportunities. Unfortunately, if you're relying on public transport there are only two buses daily (and none on Sunday) from Estepona (240 ptas), leaving at 1.15 and 7pm. The return buses leave Casares at 6.45 am and 4 pm, which doesn't leave a lot of time.

Further west, just off the coastal road, is the village of **Manilva**. The best reason for coming here is the *Roman Oasis* restaurant (☎ 289 23 80), at Baños Romanos, three km off the N-340 (watch out for the yellow arrows). It's only open from 1 June to 30 September, but you couldn't hope to find more spectacular surroundings and it's well worth a splurge. Most of the meat is barbecued; the speciality is leg of lamb (4400 ptas), which two people can't possibly finish. There's a play area for kids and an adults-only area with jacuzzi and sun-beds. The wacky owner, Paul Hickling, has an extraordinary number of parrots and other birds, and the finest collection of vintage port in southern Spain (up to 8000 ptas a glass). Lunch can easily drag on till dinner as nobody wants to leave, but if you have any energy left, you can bathe in the Roman sulphur pools nearby.

RONDA

An hour or so's journey up from the Costa del Sol is Ronda (population 35,000), a world away from the coastal hustle. Set astride the awesome, 100 metre deep El Tajo gorge amid the beautiful Serranía de Ronda mountains, it deservedly attracts its quota of visitors, but many of them return to the coast in the afternoon.

For much of the Muslim period Ronda was capital of its own independent, or nearly independent, statelet. Despite being close to the western frontier of Muslim territory, its almost impregnable position kept it out of Christian hands until 1485.

Orientation

The old Muslim town, known as La Ciudad, stands on the south-east side of El Tajo, with the post-Reconquista town to the north-west. Three bridges cross the gorge, the main one being the Puente Nuevo. Both parts of town come to an abrupt end on the south-west with cliffs plunging away to the valley of the Río Guadalevín far below. Most places to stay and eat, and the bus and train stations, are in the newer part of town.

Information

In summer the main tourist office (☎ 287 12 72) at Plaza de España 1 is open daily from 9.30 am to 2 pm and 4.30 to 7 pm; in winter, Monday to Friday from 10 am to 2 pm. There's also a municipal tourist office (☎ 287 08 18) in the Palacio de Mondragón.

Banks and ATMs are mainly on Calle Virgen de la Paz and Plaza Carmen Abela. The main post office is at Calle Virgen de la Paz 18-20. The postcode is 29400. The Policía Local (☎ 287 13 69) are at Plaza Duquesa de Parcent s/n.

Plaza de España & Puente Nuevo

Chapter 10 of Ernest Hemingway's *For Whom the Bell Tolls* tells how at the start of the Spanish Civil War the 'fascists' of a small town were rounded up in the town hall, then clubbed and flailed as they walked a gauntlet between two lines of townspeople 'in the plaza on the top of the cliff above the river'. At the end of the line the victims, dead or still alive, were thrown over the cliff. The episode was based on events in Ronda, though the actual perpetrators were apparently a gang from Málaga. The Parador de Ronda on Plaza de España was the town hall before it became a hotel.

The majestic Puente Nuevo spanning El Tajo from Plaza de España is two centuries old. An established Ronda tale relates that its architect, Juan Martín de Aldehuela, fell to his death while trying to engrave the completion date on the bridge. The word *año* (year)

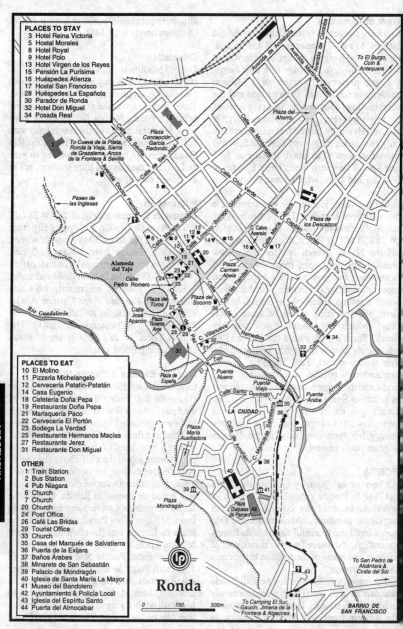

PLACES TO STAY
3 Hotel Reina Victoria
5 Hostal Morales
8 Hotel Royal
9 Hotel Polo
13 Hotel Virgen de los Reyes
15 Pensión La Purísima
16 Huéspedes Atienza
17 Hostal San Francisco
28 Huéspedes La Española
30 Parador de Ronda
32 Hotel Don Miguel
34 Posada Real

PLACES TO EAT
10 El Molino
11 Pizzeria Michelangelo
12 Cervecería Patatín-Patatán
14 Casa Eugenio
18 Cafetería Doña Pepa
19 Restaurante Doña Pepa
21 Marisquería Paco
22 Cervecería El Portón
23 Bodega La Verdad
25 Restaurante Hermanos Macías
27 Restaurante Jerez
31 Restaurante Don Miguel

OTHER
1 Train Station
2 Bus Station
4 Pub Niagara
6 Church
7 Church
20 Church
24 Post Office
26 Café Las Bridas
29 Tourist Office
33 Church
35 Casa del Marqués de Salvatierra
36 Puerta de la Exijara
37 Baños Árabes
38 Minarete de San Sebastián
39 Palacio de Mondragón
40 Iglesia de Santa María La Mayor
41 Museo del Bandolero
42 Ayuntamiento & Policía Local
43 Iglesia del Espíritu Santo
44 Puerta del Almocabar

ANDALUCÍA

To El Burgo,
Coín &
Antequera

To Cueva de la Pileta,
Ronda la Vieja, Sierra
de Grazalema, Arcos
de la Frontera & Sevilla

Paseo de
las Inglesas

Alameda
del Tajo

Río Guadalevín

Plaza del
Ahorro

Plaza
Concepción
García
Redondo

Plaza de
los Descalzos

Plaza
Carmen
Abela

Plaza del
Socorro

Plaza
Teniente
Arce

Plaza
de la Paz

Plaza de
España

Plaza de
Toros

Calle
Pedro Romero

Calle
José
Aparicio

Puente
Nuevo

Puente
Viejo

Puente
Árabe

LA CIUDAD

Calle Santo
Domingo

Plaza
María
Auxiliadora

Plaza
Mondragón

Plaza
Duquesa
de Parcent

Ronda

To San Pedro de
Alcántara &
Costa del Sol

To Camping El Sur,
Gaucín, Jimena de la
Frontera & Algeciras

BARRIO DE
SAN FRANCISCO

0   150   300m

and some other, incomplete hieroglyphics, by the shield on the side of the bridge, may encourage you to disbelieve sources that say the hapless engineer died in 1802, nine years after the bridge was opened.

La Ciudad

Though the old Muslim town has been heavily modified over the centuries, it retains a typical medina character with a warren of narrow streets twisting between white buildings. The following route around it starts from the Puente Nuevo and returns you to the new town by the Puente Viejo.

Head south first for **Plaza María Auxiliadora**, where there are fine views, then continue to the **Palacio de Mondragón**, thought to have been built for Abomelic, ruler of Ronda and son of a sultan of Morocco, in 1314. It was altered soon after the Christian conquest. The ground floor has three courtyards, of which only the Patio Mudéjar preserves an Islamic character with its rich tiling and arches, one of which leads into a small cliff-top garden. Some rooms of the palace house a museum with displays mostly on prehistoric life of the Ronda area. The palace is open daily from 10 am to 7 pm (Saturday and Sunday to 3 pm). Entry is 200 ptas (100 ptas for students).

A minute's walk beyond is Plaza Duquesa de Parcent, where the **Iglesia de Santa María La Mayor** stands on the site of Muslim Ronda's main mosque. The tower betrays clear Islamic origins, and the handsome galleries beside it, built for viewing festivities, also date from Muslim times. Just inside the entrance is an arch covered with Arabic inscriptions which was the mosque's mihrab. The church was begun in Gothic style, but as building went on over the centuries, tastes changed so that it wound up with an 18th century baroque north end. It's open daily from 10 am to 8 pm in summer, 6 pm in winter (entry 150 ptas).

Near Plaza Duquesa de Parcent at Calle Armiñán 65, the **Museo del Bandolero** covers the folklore and popular history of the Ronda area, which was once renowned for its bandits. Just off the same street, the little

Minarete de San Sebastián was built in Granada style, as part of a mosque, in the 14th century. Beside the museum, steps lead down to an impressive stretch of the old **walls** of La Ciudad. Follow them north down to the **Puerta de la Exijara**, originally the gate of Islamic Ronda's Jewish quarter. From here a path leads down the hillside to the beautiful **Baños Árabes** (Muslim baths), built in the 13th and 14th centuries. They were due to reopen, after restoration, in spring 1997. Just to their north is the old **Puente Árabe** over the Río Guadalevín, immediately downstream of which, at the start of the gorge, is the **Puente Viejo**, dating in its current version from 1616.

From the Puente Viejo make your way back up to Plaza de España via a small park along the gorge's edge. Before doing so you could detour to the **Casa del Marqués de Salvatierra** on Calle Marqués de Salvatierra, an 18th century mansion open for guided visits (250 ptas) every half-hour from 11 am to 2 pm and 4 to 7 pm (closed Sunday afternoon and Thursday).

Plaza de Toros & Around

Ronda's elegant bullring on Calle Virgen de la Paz is a mecca for aficionados. Built in

---

Ronda's Fighting Romeros

Ronda can justly claim to be the home of bullfighting. It was here in the 18th and 19th centuries that three generations of the Romero family established most of the basics of modern bullfighting on foot (previously it had been done on horseback as a kind of cavalry training-cum-sport for the nobility). Francisco Romero, born in 1698, invented the use of the cape to attract the bull and its cloth replacement in the kill, the *muleta*; his son Juan introduced the matador's supporting team, the *cuadrilla*; and his grandson Pedro (1754-1839), one of the all-time greats, perfected a strict classical style still known as the Ronda School before becoming director of the first bullfighting college (in Sevilla) at the age of 77. Pedro's skill was such, it's said, that outlaws from the bandit-ridden mountains around Ronda would risk capture to see him in action. ∎

ANDALUCÍA

1785, it's one of the oldest in Spain, with one of the biggest arenas, and has been the scene of some of the most important events in bullfighting history (see the boxed aside 'Ronda's Fighting Romeros'). Open daily from 10 am to 7 pm (225 ptas), it contains a small **Museo Taurino** with posters for the first bullfights held here, one of Pedro Romero's costumes and photos of famous visitors including Ernest Hemingway and Orson Welles.

Behind the Plaza de Toros, walk along from the clifftop **Plaza Teniente Arce** to the shady **Alameda del Tajo** park – recently partly closed for remodelling, as was the cliff-top **Paseo de las Inglesas** along to the Hotel Reina Victoria.

Walks

A path leads down into the valley at the foot of the gorge from Plaza María Auxiliadora. From the bottom a road leads up to the Barrio de San Francisco, at the south end of town, or you could work your way north-east, crossing the river, and find the path up to the Hotel Reina Victoria.

Special Events

Ronda's bullring stages relatively few fights, but around 8 September it holds some of the most unusual anywhere – the Corridas Goyescas, in which the bullfighters wear 19th century-style costumes as portrayed by Goya's Ronda bullfight scenes. These are the excuse for a general fiesta.

Places to Stay – bottom end

Camping El Sur (☎ 287 59 39), in a pleasant setting two km south-west of town on the Algeciras road, has a swimming pool and restaurant and is open all year, charging around 1750 ptas for two adults with a car and tent.

Huéspedes La Española (☎ 287 10 52) is well located at Calle José Aparicio 3, the narrow street between the main tourist office and the bullring, and has basic but clean singles/doubles from 1200/2400 ptas. The bright and friendly *Pensión La Purísima* (☎ 287 10 50) at Calle de Sevilla 10 has nine rooms at 1300/2600 ptas (1500/3000 ptas in summer). *Hostal Morales* (☎ 287 15 38), Calle de Sevilla 51, is also decent value at 1400/2800 ptas. *Huéspedes Atienza* (☎ 287 52 36) at Calle Calvo Asensio 3 is dingy and stuffy, but for 1000/2000 ptas the rooms are clean enough.

The 16 room *Hostal San Francisco* (☎ 287 32 99) at Calle María Cabrera 18 is good value at 1500/3000 ptas with bathroom. It's sometimes full, however.

Places to Stay – middle

The 30 room *Hotel Virgen de los Reyes* (☎ 287 11 40), Calle Lorenzo Borrego Gómez 13, has solid singles/doubles with TV and small bathrooms, for 3000/5000 ptas. *Hotel Royal* (☎ 287 11 41), Calle Virgen de la Paz 42, has similar standards and prices. *Hotel Polo* (☎ 287 24 47), Calle Mariano Soubirón 8, is a bit better. Its 33 air-con rooms are 6000/8500 ptas (4700/6500 ptas from mid-October to mid-March) plus IVA. The least expensive gorge views are at the *Hotel Don Miguel* (☎ 287 77 22), Calle Villanueva 8, where doubles are 9000 ptas (7500 ptas from November to February) plus IVA.

Places to Stay – top end

Posada Real (☎ 287 71 76) at Calle Real 42 is a charming small hotel in a 500 year old mansion. The 10 rooms are all different, with singles at 10,000 ptas and doubles for 12,500 or 15,000 ptas, plus IVA. There's a cosy bar, a restaurant, and a nice little garden with a pool.

Hotel Reina Victoria (☎ 287 12 40), Avenida Doctor Fleming 25, was built by a British company in the 1900s, when Ronda was a trendy outing from Gibraltar by the railway from Algeciras (also British-built, a decade earlier). The air of faded comfort recalls hill station hotels in far-flung parts of the British Empire. There are 90 rooms: singles/doubles are from 8000/13,000 to 9800/15,000 ptas, plus IVA – a bit less in June, July and November to February. The hotel has fine cliff-top gardens.

The stylish, modern *Parador de Ronda* (☎ 287 75 00), Plaza de España s/n, is right on the edge of the gorge with a pool almost on the cliff top. Singles/doubles are from 13,200/16,500 ptas plus IVA – about 20% less from November to February.

Places to Eat

Typical Ronda food is hearty mountain fare, strong on stews (*cocido*, *estofado* or *cazuela*), trout (*trucha*), game such as rabbit (*conejo*), partridge (*perdiz*) and quail (*codorniz*), and, of course, oxtail (*rabo de toro*).

Restaurante Jerez is the best (and most expensive) of a line of tourist-oriented restaurants on Calle José Aparicio, with offerings from soups and salads at 400 to 600 ptas to oxtail (1550 ptas) or partridge (2100 ptas) – all plus IVA. *Restaurante Don Miguel* on Plaza de España has tables overlooking El Tajo and huntin' and shootin' fare such as partridge stew and roast stag leg for 1500 to 2000 ptas. The menú at 2150 ptas plus IVA is nothing out of the ordinary, however.

You'll find generally better value on and around Plaza del Socorro, including three places on Calle Pedro Romero, which leads here from the bullring. Here, neighbours *Cervecería El Portón* and *Bodega La Verdad* at Nos 7 and 5 are both good tapas joints: seafood is the thing at the former; the latter also has wines from the barrel. *Restaurante Hermanos Macías* does a very rondeño 925 ptas menú. There are more good tapas – seafood and jamón – at *Marisquería Paco* on Plaza del Socorro.

The reliable and old-fashioned *Restaurante Doña Pepa* at Plaza Socorro 10 has menús for 1275 and 1700 ptas and a long a-la-carte list. Its sibling *Cafetería Doña Pepa*, a few doors along at Calle Marina 1, is slightly cheaper – and open for breakfast. Vegetarians have options at both these places. *El Molino*, with tables on Plaza del Socorro, is popular for its pizzas and pasta at 500 to 700 ptas and platos combinados from 500 ptas.

The bright *Cervecería Patatín-Patatán* at Calle Lorenzo Borrego Gómez 7 has sherry and very tasty tapas, mostly priced between 75 and 150 ptas and featuring a small slice of steak (*filetito*) – also good fried potatoes

with dips from 300 ptas. The busy *Pizzeria Michelangelo* next door at No 5 serves up economical pizzas and pasta for 500 to 600 ptas.

Casa Eugenio at Calle de Sevilla 7 must have the cheapest platos combinados in town – eg bacon, egg and chips for 350 ptas.

Entertainment

Café Las Bridas at Calle Los Remedios 18 usually has live flamenco or rock on Friday and Saturday around midnight. Entry is free. *Pub Niagara* on Avenida Doctor Fleming plays some good music.

Getting There & Away

Bus The bus station (☎ 287 26 57) is at Plaza Concepción García Redondo 2. Buses leave nine to 12 times daily for Málaga (two to three hours; 875 to 1110 ptas); three to five times a day for Sevilla (2½ hours; 1235 ptas), Arcos de la Frontera, Jerez de la Frontera, Cádiz, San Pedro de Alcántara, Marbella (560 ptas), Fuengirola and Torremolinos; and once daily Monday to Saturday for Gaucín and La Línea (990 ptas). For buses to towns and villages in the nearby sierras, see those destination sections in this chapter.

Train Ronda is on the scenic Bobadilla-Algeciras line, served by three or four trains each way daily. Change at Bobadilla for Sevilla (around three hours from Ronda; 1650 ptas), Málaga (2½ hours; 1080 ptas), Granada (3½ hours; 1490 ptas) and Córdoba (three hours; 1490 ptas). The station (☎ 287 16 73) is on Avenida de Andalucía.

Car & Motorcycle The C-339 winding up from San Pedro de Alcántara is the main approach from the coast. You can also reach Ronda by older and even more scenic roads linking villages on the way, such as the C-344 from Coín, which winds round the Sierra de las Nieves; or the C-3331 from near Algeciras or Gibraltar to Jimena de la Frontera, then the C-341 along a high ridge route between the Guadiaro and Genal valleys.

ANDALUCÍA

Getting Around

Occasional buses run to Plaza de España from Avenida Martínez Astein, across the road from the train station.

AROUND RONDA

Beautiful green hill country, dotted with isolated towns and villages, stretches in all directions from Ronda. To the west and north you can continue over into the remote northeast of Cádiz province (see the Parque Natural Sierra de Grazalema section earlier in this chapter).

Parque Natural Sierra de las Nieves

This 180 sq km natural park south-east of Ronda encompasses some fine walking country in the craggy, deeply fissured Sierra de las Nieves and Sierra de Tolox. These mountains are noted for their stands of the rare Spanish fir (pinsapo), mainly on the damper northern slopes, and a fauna that includes ibex and mouflon (wild sheep).

For information, ask at the main tourist office in Ronda or the tourist offices in the small towns north and east of the park: Calle Enmedio 11, El Burgo (☎ 216 00 02); Calle Seminarista Duarte 34, Yunquera; Calle Coín 2, Alozaina (☎ 248 10 17); and Plaza Alta No 5 Bajo, Tolox (☎ 248 00 44).

A motorable track crosses the park from the C-339, about 15 km south of Ronda, to Tolox, which clings to a steep hillside five km off the C-344. Several walking routes start at Los Quejigales, about seven km in from the C-339, where there's a camping area. A full day's hike from here would take you via the Puerto de los Pilones pass (1783 metres) to Torrecilla (1919 metres), the highest peak in these sierras. Another goes north-east to the Los Sauces camping area, from where it's three or four hours walk via the Barranco del Portillo gorge to El Burgo. There are plenty of shorter walks from Los Quejigales, Tolox, El Burgo and Yunquera.

Places to Stay There's another camping area, La Fuensanta, between El Burgo and Los Sauces; *Camping Pinsapo Azul* (☎ 248 27 54), on the edge of the park near Yunquera, charges around 375 ptas per person, per car and per tent.

Hostal Sierra de las Nieves (☎ 216 01 17), Calle Comandante Benítez 26, El Burgo, and *Hostal Asencio* (☎ 248 27 16), Calle Mesones 1, Yunquera, both have doubles with bathroom for around 4000 ptas. The Asencio also has cheaper rooms with shared bath. *La Posada del Canónigo* (☎ 216 01 85), Calle Mesones 24, El Burgo, is an old mansion converted into a cosy small hotel with doubles at 5500 ptas. There are three cheapish hostales open from about mid-June to mid-October at Tolox.

Getting There & Away The Ferron Coín company runs buses between Ronda and Málaga via El Burgo, Alozaina and Yunquera twice daily, and also has a daily Ronda-Tolox service. The Portillo line runs from Málaga to Tolox.

Cueva de la Pileta

Some of Spain's most fascinating prehistoric rock art lies within this impressive cave some 15 km south-west of Ronda. Visits have a genuine sense of exploration: the entrance is on a rocky hillside and you'll be guided by lamplight by one of the Bullón family, from the only farmhouse in the valley. A member of the family discovered the paintings back in 1905 when searching for bat-dung fertiliser. The paintings show an archer, animals including a pregnant horse, fish and abstract symbols.

Cueva de la Pileta is signposted from the MA-501 about four km south of Benaoján. One-hour tours are given daily at 10 and 11 am, noon, and 1, 4 and 5 pm. They cost 600 to 800 ptas per person, depending on the size of the group.

The nearest you can get by public transport is Benaoján. From Ronda there are four daily trains and buses Monday to Friday at 8.30 am and 1 pm.

EL CHORRO & BOBASTRO

Fifty km north-west of Málaga the Río Guadalhorce carves its way through the awesome Garganta del Chorro (Gorge of El

Bandoleros & Guerrilleros

The complicated sierras of Andalucía, full of ravines, caves, and hidden valleys, are an age-old refuge for those who didn't get on with the authorities of the day. As long ago as the 9th century Bobastro, near El Chorro gorge, was the epicentre of prolonged and widespread opposition to Córdoban rule led by a sort of Islamic Robin Hood, Umar ibn Hafsun. Ibn Hafsun came from a landed family but turned to banditry after killing a neighbour in a quarrel. Quickly gaining followers and popular support – partly, it's said, because he defended the peasants against taxes and forced labour – he at one stage controlled territory from Cartagena to the Strait of Gibraltar.

Later, under Christian rule, the bandits *(bandoleros)* who preyed on the rich became folk heroes of a kind. The most famous was José María Hinojosa or El Tempranillo (the Early One), born in 1800 near Lucena in Córdoba province. By the age of 22 he claimed: 'The king may reign in Spain, but in the sierra I do'. Blond and courteous to women, El Tempranillo reputedly demanded an ounce of gold for each vehicle crossing his domain.

A favourite haunt of El Tempranillo and his like was the Venta de Alfarnate, Andalucía's oldest inn (going since 1690), just outside the village of Alfarnate about 40 km north-east of Málaga on a mountain road to Granada. Frequently taken over by bandits in the 19th century, the Venta is now a kind of museum to them as well as a popular country restaurant. (Foodwise it's famous for its *huevos a la bestia*, a kind of hill country mixed grill of fried eggs and assorted pork products.)

It was the activities of these bandits that led the government to set up the Guardia Civil, Spain's rural police force, in 1844. Many were then forced into the service of the *caciques* (local landowners and political bosses), or even of the Guardia Civil itself. El Tempranillo met his end this way, murdered by an old comrade.

The last of the bandolero breed was Pasos Largos (Big Steps), a murderous, agile and clever poacher who haunted the area between El Burgo and Yunquera, east of Ronda. He was killed in 1934, officially in a shootout with the Guardia Civil, though some say his killer was a traitorous companion.

After the civil war the Andalucían sierras became the refuge of a new kind of outlaw (though with the same enemy, the Guardia Civil): communist *guerrilleros* waging the last resistance to Franco. The Sierra Bermeja, north of Estepona, and the mountains of Axarquía, east of Málaga, were among their hideouts. This little known chapter of Spanish history closed in the 1950s. But on the panoramic peak of one of Axarquía's mountains, El Lucero, remain the ruins of a Guardia Civil post built to keep watch for just such guerrilleros. ■

Chorro), up to 400 metres deep and as little as 10 metres wide. The gorge, about seven km long, is traversed not only by the main railway in and out of Málaga (with the aid of 12 tunnels and six bridges), but also by a footpath which for long sections becomes a concrete catwalk clinging to the gorge walls 100 metres above the river.

The path, the Camino del Rey, is in a perilously decaying state but, until lately at least, this hasn't stopped adventurous souls from making their way along it. Reconstruction work was due to start in 1997. You can reach it by walking from El Chorro train station near its southern end, or from the Restaurant El Mirador on the MA-444 about seven km north-east of the village of Ardales. El Chorro also provides marvellous rock climbing, and there are other good walks in the area.

Not far away is Bobastro, the impregnable hill-top fort of the 9th century Muslim rebel Umar ibn Hafsun (see the boxed aside 'Bandoleros & Guerrilleros'). From El Chorro station, take the road up the far (west) side of the valley, which veers away to the west after about two km. Two km further on, soon after Bar La Ermita, a road to the left leads six km up to a mountain top where you'll find remains of old fortress walls, caves that were once inhabited, and a Mozarabic church cut into the rock. The legend is that Ibn Hafsun converted to Christianity some time before his death in 917 and was buried in this church. When Bobastro was finally conquered by Abd ar-Rahman III in 927, Ibn Hafsun's remains were taken away for posthumous crucifixion outside Córdoba's Mezquita.

Places to Stay & Eat

La Garganta (☎ 249 72 19), by El Chorro

station, has apartments in a converted flour mill for four to seven people at 5500 to 8500 ptas. There's also a restaurant here. Up the hill there are cottages to rent at the British-run *La Almona*. To the south, there are hostales in Ardales, Alora and Carratraca.

Getting There & Away
Córdoba-bound trains that leave Málaga at 1.50 and 8.25 pm stop at El Chorro after 45 minutes. Return trains leave El Chorro at 8.49 am and 3.08 pm. If you're driving from Málaga, head west to Pizarra, then north to Alora on the C-337. Beyond Alora the roads demand care. One heads north to El Chorro, then west passing the Bobastro turn-off to meet the MA-444 a short distance south of the Restaurant El Mirador.

ANTEQUERA
Antequera (population 40,000), 50 km inland from Málaga, is one of Andalucía's most attractive towns. It's set on the edge of a plain 540 metres above sea level, with rugged mountainous country to the south and east, and two outstanding natural sites within 25 km.

Orientation & Information
The old heart of the town is below the north-west side of the hill-top Muslim Alcazaba. The main street, Calle Infante Don Fernando, begins here on Plaza San Sebastián and runs west. The tourist office (☎ 270 25 05) is at Plaza San Sebastián 7.

Things to See
The Muslim castle, the **Alcazaba**, affords great views, and its gardens sport a nice line in topiary. Antequera was a favourite spot of the emirs of Granada before it became the first of their towns to fall to Castilla, in 1410. Two impressive 16th century structures up here are the **Arco de los Gigantes** gate, incorporating inscribed stones from Roman Antequera, and the **Colegiata de Santa María la Mayor** church, in Renaissance

style. The Colegiata is open Tuesday to Sunday from 10 am to 2 pm.

In the town below, the pride of the **Museo Municipal**, in the 18th century Palacio de Nájera on Plaza Coso Viejo, is a 1.5 metre bronze Roman statue of a boy, 'Efebo', found on a local farm in the 1970s. The museum is open Tuesday to Friday from 10 am to 1.30 pm, Saturday 10 am to 1 pm, Sunday 11 am to 1 pm (200 ptas). About the finest of Antequera's 24 churches is the **Iglesia del Carmen**, on Plaza del Carmen a couple of blocks east of the museum – a 16th century mudéjar construction with a lavish 18th century baroque interior. It's open Tuesday to Sunday from 10 am to 2 pm (200 ptas).

Some of Europe's largest megalithic dolmens stand on the fringes of the town. Two, the **Cueva de Menga** and **Cueva de Viera**, are about 1.5 km from the centre on the road leading north-east out to the N-331. In around 2500 or 2000 BC the local folk managed to quarry huge blocks of stone from nearby hills and transport them here to construct these tombs – originally covered in earth – for their chieftains. Menga, the larger, is 25 metres long, four metres high and composed of 31 slabs, the largest weighing 180 tonnes. At midsummer, the sun rising behind the 'head' on the landmark Peña de los Enamorados mountain to north-east shines directly into its mouth. Menga and Viera are open Tuesday to Sunday from 10 am to 2 pm, and Tuesday to Friday for two afternoon hours varying by season. Ask here or at the tourist office whether a third big dolmen further out of town, the **Cueva del Romeral**, is open.

Places to Stay
The no-frills *Camas El Gallo* (☎ 284 21 04) at Calle Nueva 2 just south of Plaza San Sebastián has small doubles from 1500 ptas. Half a km west, *Hostal Reyes* (☎ 284 10 28) at Calle Tercia 4, off Calle Infante Don Fernando, has singles/doubles from 1350/2700 ptas. *Pensión Manzanito* (☎ 284 10 23) at Plaza San Sebastián 5 charges 2600/4500

ptas for singles/doubles. The larger *Hostal Colón* (☎ 284 00 10), Calle Infante Don Fernando 29, has rooms ranging from 3200 to 5000 ptas a double. *Hotel Nuevo Infante* (☎ 270 02 93) at Calle Infante Don Fernando 5 is surprisingly peaceful and has good doubles at 6000 ptas. The *Parador de Antequera* (☎ 284 02 61), Paseo Calle García del Olmo s/n, in a quiet area north of the bullring, has nice gardens and doubles for 11,500 ptas plus IVA.

Places to Eat

Bar Manzanito on Plaza San Sebastián has reasonably priced meals. *Mesón Papabellotas* on Calle Encarnación facing the lovely old Plaza Coso Viejo is more expensive: you could just have a drink and tapas and admire the interesting old photos. *La Espuela* in the 19th century bullring at the west end of Calle Infante Don Fernando has good local cooking and a fairly economical menú.

Getting There & Away

The bus station, about one km from the centre at Campillo Alto s/n, and the train station, about two km out at Calle Divina Pastora 8, are in the north-west of town. There are several buses daily to/from Málaga, about five to/from Sevilla (Prado de San Sebastián) and three each to/from Granada and Córdoba by Alsina Graells.

Three trains a day run to/from Granada, three to/from Sevilla (one with a change at Bobadilla), and two (with a change at Bobadilla) to/from Málaga.

AROUND ANTEQUERA
El Torcal

Millions of years of wind and water action have sculpted this 1336 metre mountain south of Antequera into some of the most weird and wonderful rock formations you'll see anywhere. The 12 sq km of gnarled, serrated, pillared and deeply fissured limestone were originally formed as sea bed 150 million years ago. A visitor centre here is open Tuesday to Sunday from 10.30 am to 2

pm and 4 to 5.30 pm. Camping is not allowed.

A few marked – and sometimes busy – walking trails set off from the visitor centre. You're also free to roam on your own, though this isn't sensible when it's cloudy. El Torcal harbours 664 plant species, and 82 species of bird and 22 mammals (including ibex) have been spotted here – but the real stars are the rocks themselves.

Getting There & Away On SUNDAY, the 9 am Villanueva de la Concepción bus from Antequera bus station will drop you at the Cruce del Torcal junction, from where it's four km uphill to the visitor centre. The return bus passes the Cruce about 6.20 pm. Bus schedules from Monday to Friday allow no more than a quick poke around El Torcal, and on Saturday there's no service.

Drivers from Antequera should head south down Calle Picadero near the west end of Calle Infante Don Fernando, then follow the C-3310 towards Villanueva de la Concepción. Twelve km from the town, a turn uphill to the right leads four km to the car park and visitor centre.

Laguna de Fuente de Piedra

When it's not dried up by drought, this shallow lake, close to the A-92 about 20 km north-west of Antequera, is one of Europe's two main breeding grounds for the spectacular greater flamingo (the other is the Camargue in France). In 1996, after a wet winter, a record 13,000 flamingo chicks hatched here, from 16,000 nesting pairs. The birds arrive in January or February, with the chicks hatching in April and May, and stay till about August. The Centro de Información José Andrés Valverde (☎ 211 10 50) at the lake is open Tuesday to Sunday from 10 am to 3 pm and 4 to 7 pm. *Camping La Laguna* (☎ 273 52 94), on the edge of nearby Fuente de Piedra village, is open all year at 700 ptas for two people with a car and tent. *Hostal La Laguna* (☎ 273 52 92) at Km 135 on the A-92 near Fuente de Piedra has doubles for 5000 ptas.

ANDALUCÍA

Getting There & Away Buses run between Antequera bus station and Fuente de Piedra village seven times a day Monday to Friday, five times on Saturday and three times on Sunday.

Fuente de Piedra train station, about 500 metres from the lake, is on the Málaga-Córdoba line, with two trains each way daily, but schedules don't permit a day trip from either Málaga or Antequera.

EAST OF MÁLAGA

The coast east of Málaga, sometimes described as the Costa del Sol Oriental, is a lot less developed than the coast to the west, but not much more attractive until you approach Nerja, 56 km from Málaga.

Behind the coast, the region known as La Axarquía climbs to the sierras along the border of Granada province. Known for its strong sweet wine made from sun-dried grapes, La Axarquía was otherwise one of Andalucía's forgotten areas until a modicum of tourist and expat interest developed in the last decade or so. Riven by deep valleys lined with terraces and irrigation channels that go back to Muslim times, it's dotted with white hillside villages also of obvious Muslim origin. Signposted driving routes with names like Ruta del Sol y del Vino and Ruta Mudéjar have been devised to link groups of villages along the snaking hilly roads. Information on these, and on accommodation and sights in La Axarquía, is available at the tourist offices in Nerja, Cómpeta and elsewhere.

Nerja

Nerja is older, whiter and more charming than the towns to its west, though it's inundated by tourism, which has pushed it far beyond its old confines since the 1960s. The tourist office (☎ 252 15 31) is in the centre at Puerta del Mar 4, near the Balcón de Europa lookout point, which has good coastal views. The best beach is Playa Burriana, on the east side of town.

Places to Stay & Eat In August you should try to arrive early in the day to ensure a room.

A good, economical choice among the couple of dozen hostales and pensiones is *Hostal Mena* (☎ 252 05 41) at Calle El Barrio 15, a short distance west of the tourist office. It has singles/doubles from 1000/2000 to 1250/2500 ptas (about 50% more in the high season). Nearby and a bit more expensive, with doubles ranging from 2800 to 5000 ptas depending on the season, are *Hostal Atenbeni* (☎ 252 13 41) at Calle Diputación Provincial 12, and *Hostal Alhambra* (☎ 252 21 74) on the corner of Calle Antonio Millón and Calle Chaparil.

Hotel Cala Bella (☎ 252 07 00) and *Hotel Portofino* (☎ 252 01 50) on Puerta del Mar have some rooms with good beach views – 3750 to 5750 ptas a double at the Cala Bella, 7500 ptas at the Portofino (all plus IVA). Top-end places include the *Hotel Balcón de Europa* (☎ 252 08 00), next to the Balcón itself and with its own little beach (doubles from 9750 to 13,700 ptas plus IVA), and the *Parador de Nerja* (☎ 252 00 50), Calle Almuñécar 8, above Playa Burriana (doubles 13,500 to 16,500 ptas plus IVA).

One of the best feeds is out at the open-air *Merendero Ayo* towards the east end of Playa Burriana, where a plate of paella, cooked on the spot in great sizzling pans, is 675 ptas. There are reasonably priced salads and more expensive fish and meat, too.

Getting There & Away Alsina Graells (☎ 252 15 04), on the N-340 near the top of Calle Pintada, has around 15 buses daily to/from Málaga, about seven each to/from the Cueva de Nerja, Almuñécar and Almería, and two to/from Granada.

Lual Rent A Car (☎ 252 30 66), Edificio Casablanca, Avenida Castilla Pérez, has excellent deals.

Around Nerja

The big tourist attraction is the **Cueva de Nerja**, three km east of the town, just off the N-340. This enormous set of caverns remains very impressive despite the crowds traipsing continually through it. Hollowed out by water around 5 million years ago, it was inhabited by Stone Age hunters around

15,000 BC. Unfortunately their rock paintings are off limits to visitors. The cave is open daily from 10.30 am to 2 pm and 3.30 to 6 pm (500 ptas). The *Restaurant Cueva de Nerja* by the entrance has a decent 790 ptas menú.

Further east the coast becomes more rugged and scenic and with your own wheels you can head out to some good **beaches** reached by tracks down from the N-340 around eight to 10 km from Nerja.

Seven km inland from Nerja and linked to it by several buses daily is the very pretty village of **Frigiliana**, scene of the final bloody defeat of the Moriscos of La Axarquía after they joined the 1569 Alpujarras rebellion.

Cómpeta & Around

A good base for exploring La Axarquía is the typically pretty village of Cómpeta, about 17 km inland from La Caleta, which is just east of Torre del Mar. Cómpeta has a tourist office (☎ 255 33 01) at Calle Rampa 3, some of La Axarquía's best wine, and quite a range of places to stay and eat.

Things to See & Do Cómpeta is a good base for varied walks. If you fancy an easier way up 2080-metre **Maroma**, the highest peak here, the English-run Los Pinos Photo Workshops (☎ 211 53 55) takes groups to within a couple of hours walk of the summit by 4WD (about 3000 ptas per person).

The village of **Árchez**, a few km down the valley from Cómpeta, has a very beautiful Almohad minaret next to its church. From Árchez one road winds eight km south-west to **Arenas**, where a steep but driveable track climbs to the ruined Muslim **Castillo de Bentomiz**, crowning a hill top with fine panoramas. In October 1996 Arenas staged its first annual Feria de la Mula, a colourful affair dedicated to that rapidly disappearing Andalucían beast of burden, the mule. Another road from Árchez, west through the villages of Salares, Sedella and Canillas de Aceituno, eventually links up with the C-335 north of Vélez Málaga. The C-335 heads up through the **Boquete de Zafarraya**, a dramatic cleft in the mountains, towards Alhama de Granada. One bus a day, between Torre del Mar and Granada, makes its way over the latter road.

Places to Stay The options in Cómpeta include *Hostal Los Montes* (☎ 251 60 15) on the central Plaza Almijara, which has rooms for 2600 ptas a double; the English-run *Casa La Piedra* (☎ 251 63 29) at Plazoleta 17 with good singles/doubles in an attractive village house at 2000/4000 ptas or 3000/5000 ptas for B&B; and the hill-top *Hostal Alberdini* (☎ 251 62 41) at La Lomilla one km east of the village (turn right at the Venta de Palma bar on the Torrox road), with spectacular views, rooms from 2000/3500 to 2500/4500 ptas and a reasonably priced restaurant.

Getting There & Away Three buses a day (two on Saturday and Sunday) run from Málaga to Cómpeta via Torre del Mar.

Córdoba Province

The big draw here is the city of Córdoba, centre of Muslim power in the peninsula for three centuries, whose Mezquita (mosque) is one of the most magnificent of all Islamic buildings. The city lies on the Río Guadalquivir, which runs from east to west across the middle of the province. To the north rises the Sierra Morena. To the south is a fertile rolling area called La Campiña, rising to the Sierras Subbéticas in the south-east.

The telephone code for Córdoba province is ☎ 957.

CÓRDOBA

Córdoba (population 315,000) is provincial and relaxed, yet also sophisticated and wealthy. It's a fascinating place to explore with its labyrinthine old Jewish and Muslim quarters and numerous reminders of its past splendour – above all the famous Mezquita, one of the outstanding creations of Al-Andalus.

Córdoba's splendid patios, a feature of

ANDALUCÍA

ANDALUCÍA

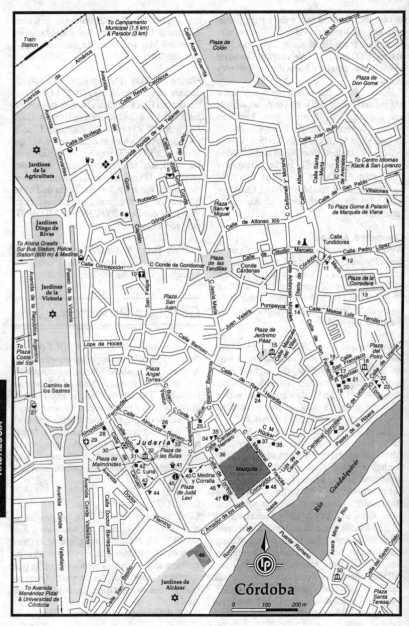

To Campamento
Municipal (1.5 km)
& Parador (3 km)

Train
Station

Plaza de
Colón

Plaza de
Don Gome

Calle Moriscos

C. de los

Avenida
de
América

Avenida
de
Cervantes

Calle Reyes Católicos

Calle Acera Guerra

Calle
del
Gran
Capitán

Avenida Ronda de los Tejares

Calle
del Caño

Calle
José
Cruz
Conde

Calle Juan Rufo

Calle Santa
María

C Conde
de Arenales

To Centro Idiomas
Klack & San Lorenzo

Calle de San Pablo

Villalones

To Plaza Gome & Palacio
de Marqués de Viana

Calle
Tundidores

Calle Pedro López

Plaza de la
Corredera

Plaza
del
Potro

Río Guadalquivir

Córdoba

0   100   200 m

Jardines
de la
Agricultura

Jardines
Diego de
Rivas

To Alsina Graells
Sur Bus Station, Police
Station (600 m) & Medina

Jardines
de la
Victoria

Paseo de la Victoria

Avenida de la República Argentina

To
Plaza
Costa
del Sol

Camino de
los Sastres

Avenida Conde de Vallellano

Calle Conde de Vallellano

To Avenida
Menéndez Pidal
& Universidad de
Córdoba

Calle la Bodega

Robledo

Góngora

Calle Concepción

C Conde de Gondomar

San Felipe

Plaza
San Juan

Lope de Hoces

Plaza
Angel
Torres

Calle Fernández

Almodóvar

Juderia

Plaza de
Maimónides

Plaza de
las Bulas

C Luna

Plaza de
Judá Leví

Fleming

Calle Doctor Barraquer

Calle San Basilio

Jardines de
Alcázar

C Amador de los Ríos

Ronda

Puente Romano

Acera Mira al Río

Calle del Santo Cristo

Plaza
Santa
Teresa

Plaza
San
Miguel

Calle de Alfonso XIII

Calle de Claudio Marcelo

Plaza
de las
Tendillas

Calle
Conde
Cárdenas

Jesús María

Pompeyos

Juan Valera

Calle Barroso

Calle de Rey Heredia

Calle — de — Rey — Heredia

Plaza de
Jerónimo
Páez

Calle Marqués del Villar

Calle de San Fernando

Plaza de la
Corredera

Calle Maese Luis

Tarnillo

Plaza
del
Potro

Calle de Lineros

C del Lucano

Calle Torres

C. de la Ribera

Paseo de la Ribera

Mazquita

Corredor

Luis de la Cerda

C. Cardenal González

C Magistral G Francés

C M Rücker

Calle Cardenal Herrero

Calle Belmonte

C Buen Pastor

C Conde

Cespedes

C Luque

Almanzor

Romero

Lucena

Diario de Córdoba

Calle San Francisco

Calle Barroso

Isasa

C Medina
y Corrella

Calle de Torrijos

1

2   3

4

5

6

7

8

9

10

11

12

13

14

15

16

17

18

19   20

21

22

23

24

25

26

27

28

29

30

31   32

33

34   35

36

37

38

39

40

41

42

43

44

45

46

47

48

49

50

Calle Pedro López

C Conde de Gondomar

Calle de San Pablo

PLACES TO STAY		23	Restaurant	10	San Nicolás de la Villa
14	Pensión San Francisco	26	El Churrasco	12	La Bulería
16	Hostal La Fuente	33	Restaurante El Rincón	13	Mercado
19	Hotel Maestre		de Carmen	15	Museo Arqueológico
20	Hostal Los Arcos	34	Self-Service Los Patios	18	Museo de Bellas Artes
21	Hostal Maestre	35	El Caballo Rojo		& Museo Julio
24	Hostal Rey Heredia	43	Mesón la Muralla		Romero de Torres
25	Hostal Seneca	44	Mesón de la Luna	27	Secorbus Bus Station
37	Hotel El Conquistador	46	Restaurante Bandolero	28	Puerta de Almodóvar
38	Hostal Martínez Rücker			29	Hospital Cruz Roja
39	Hostal Santa Ana	**OTHER**		30	Sinagoga
41	Albergue Juvenil	1	Autocares San	31	Zoco
	Córdoba		Sebastián	32	Museo Taurino
42	Hotel Amistad Córdoba	2	Pub Salsa Ya	36	Puerta del Perdón
48	Hostal El Triunfo	3	El Corte Inglés	40	Filmoteca de Andalucía
		4	RENFE office	45	Municipal Tourist Office
PLACES TO EAT		5	Post Office	47	Regional Tourist
7	Taberna San Miguel	6	Gran Teatro de		Office
11	Taberna Salinas		Córdoba	49	Alcázar de los Reyes
17	Taberna Sociedad de	8	Roman Temple	50	Torre de la Calahorra &
	Plateros	9	Auto Transportes		Museo Vivo de
22	Restaurant		López		Al-Andalus

most old buildings, drip with foliage and blooms. Many people time a visit to coincide with the spring Concurso de Patios, when the patios are open to the public and at their most beautiful, and the skies are big and blue but the heat tolerable. The city's site on a sweep of the Río Guadalquivir is impressive when the mighty river is swollen from winter rains.

Modern Córdoba centred on Plaza de las Tendillas brings one back to the 20th century with its shops and traffic, though it's less polluted and less hectic than some of Andalucía's other cities.

History

The thriving Roman colony of Corduba, founded in 169 BC, became the capital of Hispania Ulterior, one of the two initial Roman provinces on the peninsula. After a political reorganisation in the 1st century BC, Corduba was the capital of Baetica province (covering today's Andalucía and southern Extremadura). In this major cultural centre were born the two Senecas, philosophers of renown, and the poet Lucan, companion to Nero. In 711 Córdoba fell to the Islamic invaders and soon became the capital of Muslim Spain. At first it was subordinate to the Caliphate of Damascus, but in 756 Abd ar-Rahman I set himself up as an independent emir. He was the last surviving member of the Umayyad dynasty of Damascus which had ruled the Islamic world; a rival clan, the Abbasids, had usurped power in Damascus and transferred their capital to Baghdad. Córdoba's heyday came in the 10th century under Abd ar-Rahman III (912-61), who severed ties with Baghdad in 929 by founding an independent caliphate. Córdoba was now the biggest city in western Europe, with an estimated population of 100,000. It had dazzling mosques, patios, gardens and fountains plus public baths, libraries, observatories, aqueducts and a university. Its economy flourished on the agriculture of its irrigated hinterland and the products of its own skilled artisans – leather and metal work, textiles, glazed tiles and more. The court of Abd ar-Rahman III was frequented by Jewish, Arab and Christian scholars and in Córdoba Christians, Muslims and Jews lived in harmony.

The Córdoban emirate and caliphate unified Al-Andalus for long periods despite frequent discontent among the ruled, sometimes even open rebellion. At its peak, the caliphate encompassed most of the Iberian Peninsula south of the Río Duero, the Balearic Islands and some of North Africa. Córdoba became a place of pilgrimage for

ANDALUCÍA

Muslims who could not get to Mecca or Jerusalem, and in the Mezquita was kept a relic, one of Mohammed's arm bones, which became a psychological weapon against the Christians and was partly responsible for the development of the opposing cult of Santiago (St James).

Towards the end of the 10th century, Al-Mansour, a fearsome general, took over the reins of power from the caliphs. Al-Mansour struck terror into Christian Spain, making 57 or so forays (*razzias*) in 20 years. He even destroyed the cathedral at Santiago de Compostela, forcing Christian slaves to bring its doors and bells to Córdoba where the bells were hung upside-down as gigantic oil lamps in the Mezquita. After the death of Al-Mansour's son in 1008 the caliphate descended into anarchy. Berber troops terrorised and looted the city and in 1031 the caliphate finally collapsed into 20 or so taifas. Córdoba became a part of the Sevilla taifa in 1070. Until Almoravid and Almohad rule in the 12th century, intellectual life continued with great scholars such as the Muslim Averroës and the Jew Maimonides among Córdoba's 12th century citizens. Their work was, however, curtailed by their overlords, and both ended up fleeing to North Africa.

Córdoba, no longer great, was taken by Fernando III in 1236 and much of the population fled. Fernando returned the bells to Santiago de Compostela cathedral. Córdoba became an unimportant provincial town, a situation which began to change only with the coming of industry in the late 19th century and, later, tourism. Today it is a bustling modern city with a carefully preserved old quarter.

Orientation

Córdoba centres on the Mezquita, which stands on the banks of the Río Guadalquivir. The judería (medieval Jewish quarter) west and north of the Mezquita, and the old Muslim quarter to the east, make up the old town. The commercial centre of modern Córdoba is Plaza de las Tendillas, a few hundred metres north of the Mezquita.

Information

Tourist Offices The Junta de Andalucía tourist office (☎ 47 12 35) is on the western side of the Mezquita at Calle de Torrijos 10. It's open Monday to Saturday from 9.30 am to 7 pm and Sunday from 10 am to 2 pm, and has plenty of written material available, including a brochure listing Córdoba's tapas bars. English is spoken. The municipal tourist office (☎ 47 20 00 ext 209) is on Plaza de Judá Levi, two blocks west of the Mezquita. Opening hours are Monday to Saturday 9 am to 2 pm and 4.30 to 6.30 pm, Sunday from 9 am to 2 pm. Here the staff are helpful but only speak Spanish.

Money There are plenty of banks and ATMs on and around Avenida del Gran Capitán and Plaza de las Tendillas in the centre of the commercial district.

Post & Communications The main post office (postcode 14080) is on Calle de José Cruz Conde, which heads north off Plaza de las Tendillas.

Books Librería Luque, Calle Conde de Gondomar 13, has a good selection of novels in English.

Medical & Emergency Services For urgent police assistance, call ☎ 092; there's a police station at Campo Madre de Dios s/n, just over a km east of the Mezquita, and another on Avenida de Medina Azahara right by the main bus station. For an ambulance call ☎ 29 55 70; the Hospital Cruz Roja (Red Cross Hospital, ☎ 29 34 11) is central at Paseo de la Victoria s/n.

Opening Hours Opening times for Córdoba's major sights rarely remain static. With the exception of the Mezquita, most places are closed on Monday and they close earlier in the winter than in the summer.

Mezquita

This astonishing building can seem rather bewildering at first. The contrast between the original Islamic structure and later Christian alterations, as well as the sheer darkness imposed by Christianity, demand a stretch of the imagination to picture the building as it was in Muslim times, open to and in harmony with its immediate surroundings. The Mezquita has some truly beautiful architectural features – among them its domed mihrab and the famous rows of columns supporting two-tier arches assembled in mesmerising stripes of red brick and white stone.

From the outside the building looks like a fortress. It is surrounded by immense stone walls punctuated by ornately decorated gates; it is low-slung except for the protruding roof of the cathedral within and the lower domes of the mihrab.

History Abd ar-Rahman I founded the Mezquita in 785 on the site of a church which for 50 years had been partitioned between Muslims and Christians. Abd ar-Rahman I purchased the Christian half from the Christian community. Abd ar-Rahman II in the 9th century and Al-Hakim II in the 960s extended the Mezquita southwards to cater for Córdoba's expanding population. Al-Hakim II also added the mihrab, with its beautiful domed skylights to solve the lighting problem created by the Mezquita's increased size. Under Al-Mansour, extensions were made to the east and the mihrab lost its central position.

What you see today is its final Islamic form with one marked alteration – a 16th century cathedral right in the middle (hence the often-used description 'Mezquita-Catedral'). For this the extensions made under Abd ar-Rahman II and Al-Mansour were partly dismantled.

Entry The main entrance is by the Puerta del Perdón, a 14th century mudéjar gateway on Calle Cardenal Herrero, with the ticket office immediately to its left. The Mezquita is open Monday to Saturday from 10 am to 7 pm, Sunday from 2 to 7 pm; from October to March, closing time is 5.30 pm. Entry is 750 ptas. You can enter free for daily mass from 9 to 10 am.

Beside the Puerta del Perdón is a 16th century tower which replaced the original minaret. Inside is the Mezquita's pretty courtyard, the **Patio de los Naranjos** (Courtyard of the Orange Trees), from which a small door leads into the Mezquita itself.

Inside the Mezquita You come first to Abd ar-Rahman I's section, completed by his son Hisham, comprising the first 12 aisles, a forest of pillars and arches. Beyond this are the main Christian structures, aligned east-west roughly in the centre of the Mezquita, and surrounded on all sides by more Islamic aisles, pillars and arches. At the south end of the building, approached by rows of particularly elegant columns, capitals and arches, is the **mihrab**, acclaimed as the most beautiful of all Islamic prayer rooms. The mihrab's inner sanctum or niche is roped off and you're unlikely to be able to see its lovely shell-shaped dome. The horseshoe arch at its entrance, however, is superbly decorated with Byzantine mosaics and stucco work. There are more brilliant Byzantine mosaics on the dome of the area before the niche, where the Caliphs and their retinues would have prayed. Gold inscriptions from the Koran provide further decoration.

Wandering around, it's possible to lose yourself in the aisles with views of only the incredible columns and arches, unspoiled by the sombre Christian alterations. In Muslim times the Mezquita would have been well lit, and doors open along its sides.

Columns, Capitals & Arches Abd ar-Rahman I's section of the Mezquita incorporated columns and capitals – of various coloured marbles, granite and alabaster – from the site's previous Visigothic church, from Roman buildings in Córdoba and further afield, and even from ancient Carthage. The columns were of differing heights so tall ones had to be sunk into the floor. They support two tiers of arches, giving an effect reminiscent of Roman aqueducts and/or date palms. The use of bicoloured materials for the arches was inspired. Subsequent alterations required more columns, most of which were made by Córdoban craftsmen. The final Islamic building had 1300 columns, of which 850 remain.

Christian Alterations After Fernando III took Córdoba in 1236, the Mezquita was turned into a cathedral. Early modifications such as the 1370s mudéjar **Capilla de Villaviciosa** (now closed), were carried out with restraint. But in the reign of Carlos I the centre of the Mezquita was ripped out to allow construction of the **Capilla Mayor** and **coro**, which in a different setting would be more pleasing. The Capilla Mayor has a rich jasper and marble retablo; the coro's fine mahogany stalls were carved in the 18th century by Pedro Duque Cornejo. There are further chapels, one next to the mihrab, and others lining the east wall of the whole Mezquita building.

Alcázar de los Reyes

The Alcázar, south-west of the Mezquita, was built as a residence and fortress in 1328 by Alfonso XI on the site of previous Visigothic and Islamic buildings. Isabel and Fernando received Columbus here before he set off on his voyage of discovery, and from 1490 to 1821 the Inquisition operated out of here. A square mudéjar building with three of its four watchtowers still standing, the Alcázar has been much altered and is currently undergoing renovations which mean you can't explore the towers and ramparts, but you can stroll around its extensive, pretty gardens which reach to the banks of the Guadalquivir. It also houses a museum, with some Roman mosaics of most interest.

Opening hours are Tuesday to Saturday from 10 am to 2 pm and 6 to 8 pm (October to April from 4 to 7 pm), Sunday from 9.30 am to 3 pm. The cost until renovations are completed is 300 ptas (students 150 ptas). On Friday entry is free.

Judería

The judería extends northwards from west of the Mezquita, almost to the beginning of Avenida del Gran Capitán. A pleasure to get lost in (like the Islamic quarter east of the Mezquita), it's a maze of narrow streets and small plazas, of whitewashed buildings with flowers dripping from window boxes, and wrought-iron doorways giving glimpses of plant-filled patios.

One approach to the quarter is through **Puerta de Almodóvar**, the ancient gate in the city walls that still stand at the bottom of Paseo de la Victoria. From here Calle Judíos cuts south through the heart of the quarter to Plaza de Maimónides. On Calle Judíos a few steps north of this plaza is the small 14th century **sinagoga**, one of Spain's very few surviving medieval synagogues. It retains its original women's gallery and mudéjar stucco work on the upper part of its walls. Opening hours are Tuesday to Saturday from 10 am to 2 pm and 3.30 to 5.30 pm, Sunday from 10 am to 1.30 pm (50 ptas). Opposite is the **Zoco** or Souk, a craft centre built around a patio, with fairly up-market silver and leather goods for sale, and artisans at work.

Next door to the Zoco, at Plaza de las Bulas 5, is the **Museo Taurino** (bullfighting museum), which celebrates Córdoba's great *toreros*: there are rooms dedicated to El Cordobés and Manolete, even with the skin, tail and ear of the bull that finished off Manolete in 1947. The museum is open Tuesday to Saturday from 10 am to 2 pm and 6 to 8 pm (October to April, from 4 to 7 pm), Sunday from 9.30 am to 3 pm. Cost is 425 ptas (free on Tuesday).

Other Museums

Museo Arqueológico Córdoba's most impressive museum is in a Renaissance mansion on Plaza de Jerónimo Páez, off Calle Marqués del Villar. A reclining stone lion takes pride of place in the Iberian section, and the Roman period is well represented with large, intricate mosaics, elegant ceramics and tinted glass bowls. The rooms upstairs are devoted to Islamic Córdoba, including bronze animals from the caliphs' palace at Medina Azahara. The museum is open Tuesday to Saturday from 10 am to 2 pm and 6 to 8 pm, Sunday from 10 am to 1.30

pm. Entry is 250 ptas (free with an EU passport).

Museo Vivo de Al-Andalus The 'Living Museum of Al-Andalus' in the 14th century Torre de la Calahorra at the south end of the much restored Puente Romano (Roman bridge) is the city's attempt to recreate the world of Al-Andalus and catch the tourist dollar. Although some aspects are rather kitsch, it contains excellent models of the Mezquita and Granada's Alhambra. Some of the commentary in the sound-and-light display is interesting. It's open daily, May to September from 10 am to 2 pm and 4.30 to 8.30 pm; other months from 10 am to 6 pm daily. Cost is 400 ptas.

Museo de Bellas Artes On the attractive Plaza del Potro, 500 metres or so east of the Mezquita, this was closed for a supposedly short period for restoration when we visited. It houses a collection of works by Córdoban artists and others including Zurbarán, Ribera and Goya. Cost was 250 ptas (free for EU residents).

Museo Julio Romero de Torres Across the courtyard from the Museo de Bellas Artes, this has a wonderful collection of Romero de Torres' dark, sensual portraits of Córdoban women. It's open Tuesday to Saturday from 10 am to 2 pm and 6 to 8 pm (October to April, from 4 to 7 pm), Sunday from 9.30 am to 3 pm. Entry is 425 ptas; free on Tuesday.

Plaza de la Corredera
This lively square, 500 metres or so northeast of the Mezquita, has been undergoing repairs, hopefully keeping intact the square's colourful character, which is due in part to its decayed elegance. On the south side of the plaza is Córdoba's food market; the plaza itself is given over to a flea market and buskers most days and is busiest on Saturday.

Other Attractions
As you're roaming around old Córdoba, you'll notice several beautiful churches. Most of these were built soon after the Reconquista and are Gothic in style, though their façades are plain and you'll also notice other architectural influences, especially mudéjar. **San Nicolás de la Villa** on Calle Conde de Gondomar, with a huge octagonal tower, and **San Lorenzo** on Calle María Auxiliadora, with a beautiful rose window, are two of the best.

A collapsed **Roman temple** has been exposed and partly restored on Calle Claudio de Marcelo.

Language Courses
For information on courses at the university contact the Secretaria de Cursos para Extranjeros (☎ 21 81 33) at the Universidad de Córdoba, Avenida Menéndez Pidal, 14071 Córdoba. The privately run Centro de Idiomas Klack (☎ 49 13 03), Calle Manchado 9, runs courses that last from two to 16 weeks for 32,000 to 197,000 ptas.

Organised Tours
Córdoba Vision (☎ 29 95 77), Calle Escritor Conde Zamora s/n, operates tours in and around the city. Three-hour city tours including the Mezquita and judería are 2650 ptas. Book at major hotels and agents around town.

Special Events
Semana Santa is celebrated with typical Andalucían fervour and is Córdoba's biggest festival. Other special events include:

First two weeks of May
  Concurso de Patios (Festival of the Patios) – many of Córdoba's fantastic private patios, and more humble ones, are open to the public to show off their spring floral displays. At the same time there's a busy cultural programme including flamenco song and dance performances.
Late May and early June
  Feria de la Nuestra Señora de la Salud – party time for Córdoba
Two weeks starting in late June
  Festival Internacional de Guitarra (International Guitar Festival) – a daily programme of varied live music from classical and flamenco to rock and blues

Córdoba's Patios

Córdoba's patios have two roots – Roman and Muslim. For the Romans, the patios provided a meeting place; during Islamic times, patios were used for rest and recreation. Today these trends continue – patios provide a haven of peace and quiet, shade during the searing heat of the summer, and a place to entertain.

As you wander around the streets and alleys of Córdoba in May, you'll notice 'Patio' signs; this means that you're invited to view what is for the rest of the year closed to the world by heavy wooden doors or partially hidden by wrought-iron gates. At this time of year the patios are at their prettiest as new blooms proliferate, though not all displays are on a grand scale.

Around 40 patios are entered into the annual competition for the title of best patio. The tourist office can provide a detailed map of patios available for viewing. If you don't have a lot of spare time, the patios in the vicinity of Calle San Basilio, 500 metres or so west of the Mezquita, are some of the best.

The patios are generally open in the morning from 10 am to lunchtime and again in the evening from 9 pm for a few hours. Entry is usually free but sometimes a container is placed at the exit for donations.

The Renaissance **Palacio de Marqués de Viana** just over a km north-east of the Mezquita at Plaza de Don Gome 2, has 14 patios, some of which are outstanding. It's open all year: summer hours are Monday to Saturday (closed Wednesday) from 10 am to 1 pm and 4 to 6 pm, Sunday from 10 am to 2 pm. To view the patios costs 200 ptas; to enter the palace costs 400 ptas. ∎

Places to Stay

Many of Córdoba's places to stay are built around charming patios, but single rooms for a decent price are in short supply. Prices here are for spring (when it's best to ring ahead); you may get reductions in the off season.

Places to Stay – bottom end

Camping Córdoba's *Campamento Municipal* (☎ 28 21 65) is at Avenida del Brillante 50 on the road to Villaviciosa, 1.5 km north of the train station. Open year round, it costs 500 ptas per adult, 350 ptas per tent and 500 ptas per car.

Youth Hostels Córdoba's ultramodern youth hostel, *Albergue Juvenil Córdoba* (☎ 29 01 66), is perfectly positioned on Plaza de Judá Levi, has excellent facilities and no curfew.

Hostales *Hostal Martínez Rücker* (☎ 47 25 62), Calle Martínez Rücker 14, with singles/doubles from 1500/3500 ptas, is particularly friendly and only a stone's throw east of the Mezquita. A short walk east at Calle Cardenal González 25, *Hostal Santa Ana* (☎ 48 58 37) has one single at 1500 ptas and doubles at 3000 ptas, or 4500 ptas with bath; rooms upstairs are more appealing. Heading north-west a little, the friendly *Hostal Rey Heredia* (☎ 47 41 82), Calle Rey Heredia 26, has rooms around a plant-filled patio for 1500/3000 ptas.

Further away from the tourist masses, there are some good hostales to the east. *Pensión San Francisco* (☎ 47 27 16), Calle de San Fernando 24, is good value with one small single at 1500 ptas and doubles from 3500 ptas. *Hostal La Fuente* (☎ 48 78 27), Calle de San Fernando 51, has compact singles at 1800 ptas and doubles from 4500 ptas; it's newly refurbished (the shower pressure is excellent!), has a courtyard for sitting outside and its café serves a decent breakfast. Close by at Calle Romero Barroso 14, *Hostal Los Arcos* (☎ 48 56 43) has modern rooms around a pretty courtyard from 2000/3500 ptas, 4000 ptas with attached bath. Next door at No 16, *Hostal Maestre* (☎ 47 53 95) has plenty of clean, spacious rooms with private bath at 2200/4000 ptas.

Places to Stay – middle

Hostal El Triunfo (☎ 47 55 00), Calle Corregidor Luis de la Cerda 79, on the south side of the Mezquita, has singles/doubles/triples with air-con and TV for 3500/5800/6900 ptas plus IVA. There's a restaurant, too. A block north of the Mezquita, *Hostal Seneca* (☎ 47 32 34), at Calle Conde y Luque 7, is charming with friendly management, a *típico* patio and a breakfast room; rooms with shared bath cost 2300/4250 ptas, with attached bath 5250 ptas. You're advised to

ANDALUCÍA

phone ahead. *Hotel Maestre* (☎ 47 24 10), at Calle Romero Barroso 4-6, has bright rooms with attached bath for 3500/6000 ptas, 2900/4900 ptas in winter; parking, free at off-peak times, is available.

Places to Stay – top end

Add IVA to prices quoted. *Hotel El Conquistador* (☎ 48 11 02), Calle Magistral González Francés 15-17 right by the east side of the Mezquita, has sumptuous doubles for 15,500 ptas. *Hotel Amistad Córdoba* (☎ 42 03 35), Plaza de Maimónides 3, has similar prices but does weekend and summer deals with rooms down to 9000 ptas. It's in two converted 18th century mansions and is entered by a door in the ancient city wall.

Córdoba's modern *parador* (☎ 28 04 09), Avenida de la Arruzafa s/n, is three km north of the centre on the site of Abd ar-Rahman I's country palace, where it's claimed Europe's first palm trees were planted. Doubles are 15,000 ptas.

Places to Eat

A couple of dishes are common to most Córdoban restaurants. *Salmorejo* is a type of gazpacho with chopped hard-boiled eggs floating on top. *Rabo de toro* is bulls' tail stew. Some of the top places to eat feature recipes from Al-Andalus such as garlic soup with raisins, honeyed lamb, fried eggplant, and meats stuffed with dates and pine nuts. The local tipple is wine from nearby Montilla and Moriles, made by a similar process to sherry.

There are lots of places to eat right by the Mezquita, some expensive, some mediocre and some awful. There are better-value places to eat a short walk west into the Judería. A longer walk east or north will produce even better options for the budget-conscious and/or inquisitive.

Around the Mezquita *Self-Service Los Patios*, right by the Mezquita at Calle Cardenal Herrero 14, has functional main courses and desserts with nothing over 600 ptas. A typical main dish is fried merluza (hake) and

salad (595 ptas). The lovely covered patio offers respite from the heat.

On the same street at No 28, *El Caballo Rojo* specialises in food from the time of the caliphs. The menú is a hefty 2950 ptas plus IVA and mains are around 2000 ptas, but here you're guaranteed something different from the usual fare. For a first class meal try *Restaurante Bandolero*, Calle de Torrijos 6, near the tourist office. It has platos combinados from 700 to 900 ptas; à la carte, expect to pay around 4000 ptas per person. Delicious items on the menu include red peppers stuffed with seafood (1500 ptas) and seafood soup (975 ptas).

Judería *El Churrasco*, Calle Almanzor Romero 16, is said to be Córdoba's best restaurant. The menu is fancy, the food rich, portions generous and service attentive, with prices to match. The menú is 3000 ptas and most mains are around 2000 ptas, though salmon and rabo de toro are less. A few doors away *Restaurante El Rincón de Carmen* has a café that does good snacks and breakfast. Comfy cane chairs and relaxed background music provide welcome relief to the footsore.

Mesón de la Luna and *Mesón la Muralla*, in the city walls on Calle de la Luna, share a courtyard and both have menús from 1200 to 1900 ptas which feature local specialities.

East & North of the Mezquita The two *restaurants* side by side on pedestrian Calle Torres, facing Plaza del Potro, both have menús from 1000 ptas. This is a fine place to sit on a balmy evening at sunset.

Taberna Sociedad de Plateros, in the same vicinity at Calle San Francisco 6 but off the main tourist beat, is a popular tavern with a good range of tapas and raciones – nothing over 600 ptas. The homely *Taberna Salinas* at Calle Tundidores 3, just short of Plaza de la Corredera, offers good, cheap local fare – bacalao with bitter oranges makes an interesting change. Decent vegetarian options, each for 600 ptas, include chickpeas with

ANDALUCÍA

spinach, wild mushrooms in a sauce, and pisto (fried vegetables). The restaurant is closed on Sunday.

Taberna San Miguel on Plaza San Miguel, north of Plaza de las Tendillas, is another popular watering hole with good tapas. It's closed on Sunday and from 4 to 8 pm other days.

Self-Catering There's a good *food market* on the south side of Plaza de la Corredera, open from Monday to Saturday (when it's busiest). Both the old and new parts of town have good bakeries with pastries, cakes and bocadillos.

Entertainment

For information about what's on around the town, grab a copy of *Salir* from the tourist office. Or consult *Diario Córdoba*, Córdoba's daily newspaper.

Most nightlife action is around Plaza de las Tendillas. In particular, try Plaza San Miguel and Calle del Caño. Locals recommend *Pub Salsa Ya*, in an alley behind El Corte Inglés, which is on Avenida Ronda de los Tejares. The pubs and bars around Plaza Costa del Sol, a km west of Plaza de las Tendillas, are also popular.

The *Gran Teatro de Córdoba*, Avenida del Gran Capitán 3, has an ongoing programme of events including film festivals, theatre, dance, and varied concerts. The *Filmoteca de Andalucía*, on the west side of the Mezquita at Calle Medina y Corrella 5, has regular foreign films and, from time to time, film festivals.

Various flamenco performances are widely advertised. *La Bulería*, at Calle Pedro López 3, behind Plaza de la Corredera, is slightly off the tourist trail. The show gets going every night at 10.30. You pay 1500 ptas for your first drink. *El Tablao*, Calle Cardenal Herrero 12, does a tourist-oriented performance (2500 ptas) during the spring and summer, again from 10.30 pm. Córdoba's municipal orchestra performs in the gardens of the Alcázar on Sunday morning!

Things to Buy

There are plenty of trinkets and high-quality goods to be had in the tourist shops around the Mezquita. Córdoba is known for its leather goods and silver jewellery, particularly filigree. The Zoco on Calle Judíos has good but pricey products. For jewellery, it may pay to look in the central commercial district rather than the Mezquita area. Córdoba's attractive traditional pottery, in distinctive green, blue and black on a white background, is inexpensive and widely available in town.

Getting There & Away

Bus The main bus station is a km or so west of Plaza de las Tendillas. A new central bus station on the west side of the train station is scheduled to open in 1998. Meanwhile, there's a plethora of others. Buses to cities around Andalucía leave from the Alsina Graells Sur station (☎ 23 64 74) at Avenida Medina Azahara 29-31, a km west of Plaza de las Tendillas. There are a few consigna lockers here (300 ptas for 24 hours). Daily services include five to Málaga (1510 ptas), seven to Granada (1735 ptas), at least nine to Sevilla (1200 ptas) and one to Almería (2995 ptas). Buses to Barcelona and other cities on the Mediterranean coast, operated by Bacoma (☎ 45 65 14), leave from the same station. There's a night bus to Barcelona (8025 ptas) via Albacete and Valencia, and another to Benidorm (4775 ptas) stopping in Alicante.

At least six buses daily to Madrid (1290 ptas) are run by Secorbus (☎ 46 80 40), Camino de los Sastres 1, on the corner of Avenida de la República Argentina, 600 metres north-west of the Mezquita.

Auto Transportes López (☎ 47 45 92) on Paseo de la Victoria, near the corner of Calle Concepción, runs services to Extremadura.

Train The train station is north-west of Córdoba's commercial centre at Avenida de América 13. There are plenty of trains daily to/from Sevilla. Options range from AVEs (45 minutes; from 2100 ptas) to stopping trains (1¾ hours; 875 ptas). To Madrid,

AVEs take 1¾ to two hours (from 5500 ptas) and there are plenty of other trains; the cheapest is an afternoon Intercity which takes 4½ hours and costs 3100 ptas. Several trains daily run to Málaga (1300 to 2400 ptas). For Granada, you need to change at Bobadilla, but connections are usually good (3¾ to 5½ hours; from 1700 ptas). There's a RENFE office (☎ 47 58 84) at Avenida Ronda de los Tejares 10.

Getting Around

Córdoba is quite compact. Thanks to the one-way system, it's almost as quick to walk from the train or main bus station to the centre as to take a bus. A taxi is around 450 ptas. Bus No 3 runs into the centre from Avenida de América, outside the train station, if you're desperate. You can pick it up on Ronda de Isasa, just south of the Mezquita, for the return trip. The same bus will get you most of the way to the main bus station.

AROUND CÓRDOBA
Medina Azahara

About 10 km north-west of Córdoba in the foothills of the Sierra Morena lie the ruins of Medina Azahara, the sumptuous palace begun by Abd ar-Rahman III for his wife Azahara in 936. It took 25 years to build but lasted only till 1010, when it was ransacked by rampaging Berber troops as the caliphate disintegrated. The palace was also the court of the caliphs, their needs having outgrown the Alcázar and its environs. From what remains, it's difficult to imagine the scale and grandeur of the palace in its heyday. Excavations began in 1911 but less than 10% of the site has been completed.

The city-palace was constructed in a series of terraces. The highest parts were occupied by the palace; then came the central part with gardens and orchards; the lower sections comprised a mosque, houses, baths, an inn, a market and more.

Apart from the 1944 reconstruction of the Salón de Abd ar-Rahman III there's not much to see other than low-lying ruins, trees and bushes. This hall is beautiful with its horseshoe arches repeating the red-and-white striped patterns of Córdoba's Mezquita. Its chambers are richly decorated.

The site is open Tuesday to Saturday from 10 am to 2 pm and 6 to 8.30 pm (October to April, from 4 to 6.30 pm), Sunday from 10 am to 2 pm. Entry is free for EU citizens, 250 ptas for others.

Getting There & Away If you're driving from Córdoba, take Avenida de Medina Azahara, which leads to Carretera Palma del Río, the C-431. Follow this for six km to the turn-off for Medina Azahara. Otherwise, the easiest way is a tour or a taxi. Córdoba Vision (☎ 29 95 77) runs tours to Medina Azahara three times daily for 2150 ptas (see under Organised Tours in the Córdoba section). A taxi is around 4000 ptas for the return trip including a half-hour wait. Buses (100 ptas) depart Córdoba roughly hourly from Autocares San Sebastián, Calle La Bodega, off Avenida de Cervantes, but leave you with a three-km walk uphill from the Cruce de Medina Azahara turn-off on the C-431.

SOUTH OF CÓRDOBA
Towards Málaga

Just east of the N-331 and on the Córdoba-Málaga railway, **Montilla** is the production centre for Córdoba's sherry-like wines. You can visit a couple of bodegas, but you need to call first. The main one is Alvear (☎ 65 01 00).

Nature-lovers with their own transport could detour to the **Laguna de Zoñar**, four km south-west of Aguilar, which has a high winter and spring population of water birds. Conservation efforts here have saved the western European population of the white-headed duck (pato malvasía), a polygamous creature which can hardly walk on land because of its underdeveloped feet designed for diving. Since 1977 its numbers here have jumped from 50 to over 700. The Centro de Información El Lagar (☎ 66 11 52), two km from Aguilar on the C-329, is open daily from 10 am to 3 pm and 4 to 7 pm.

ANDALUCÍA

Priego de Córdoba

Priego de Córdoba, 100 km south-east of Córdoba, combines a higgledy-piggledy medieval quarter, the Barrio de la Villa, with a dramatic setting on a cliff known as the Adarve and some marvellous baroque churches from the 18th century, when the town blossomed on the profits of its silk industry.

The helpful tourist office (☎ 70 06 25) at Calle del Río 33, just off the handsome central Plaza de la Constitución, can help with access to some of the churches. At the end of Calle del Río is the spectacular 16th to 18th century **Fuente del Rey**, a fountain with 139 spouts. In the Barrio de la Villa, you'll find an imposing Muslim **castillo** (closed to visitors) and the **Iglesia de la Asunción**, whose *sagrario* (sacristy) is one of Spain's great baroque creations. Outstanding among seven or eight other fine churches are the **Iglesia de San Pedro**, just west of the castle, and the **Iglesia de La Aurora** on Calle Argentina.

The basic *Hostal Andalucía* (☎ 54 01 74), in the centre at Calle del Río 13, has doubles for 2200 ptas. The welcoming *Hostal Rafi* (☎ 54 07 49), also central at Calle Isabel La Católica 4, has good rooms at 4300 ptas a double, and a restaurant.

The Carrera line (☎ 23 14 01) runs several buses daily to Priego de Córdoba from its station at Avenida República Argentina 30 in Córdoba.

Parque Natural Sierra Subbética

This 316 sq km natural park west of Priego de Córdoba has some rugged limestone hills, wooded river valleys and good walking possibilities.

Granada Province

As well as the world-famous city of Granada, the province includes the highest mountains of the Sierra Nevada, which stretch east into Almería. South of the Sierra Nevada are the beautiful and rather mysterious valleys known as Las Alpujarras.

The telephone code for Granada province is ☎ 958.

GRANADA

At first, modern Granada with its traffic-choked main streets and high-rise apartment blocks seems a disappointing world away from its Muslim past. However, the delights of the Alhambra, which dominates the skyline from its hill-top perch, and the fascinating warren of streets that make up the Albaicín, the old Islamic quarter, are highlights of a visit to Spain.

The city has more to offer. Its setting, with the backdrop of the often snow-clad Sierra Nevada, is magnificent; its greenness is a delight in often parched Andalucía and the climate pleasant especially in spring and autumn. Granada also has some impressive and historic post-Reconquista buildings, a vibrant, youthful population thanks to its university, a buzzing cultural life, some excellent bars and a hopping nightlife.

Granada is a wealthy city of 270,000 people with an international feel mostly due to its high numbers of tourists. It seems to absorb tourism well except for peak periods inside the Alhambra and the Capilla Real. In tandem with its wealth subsists a whole underclass: you'll see quite a few beggars.

History

An Iberian tribe, the Túrdulos, established their settlement, Elibyrge, here in the 5th century BC. The Romans arrived late in the 3rd century BC, settling in the vicinity of the Alcazaba and Albaicín. The Visigoths built walls round the city and laid the foundations of the Alcazaba. Muslim forces, with the help of the city's Jews, took the city in 711. It was ruled from Córdoba until 1031, and later from Sevilla by the Almoravids and then the Almohads. The Islamic city was called Karnattah, from which 'Granada' is derived (*granada* also happens to be the Spanish for pomegranate, which has been adopted as part of the city's coat of arms).

After the fall of Córdoba (1236) and

Sevilla (1248), Muslims sought refuge in Granada, where the founder of the famous Nasrid dynasty, Mohammed ibn Yousouf ibn Nasr (also called Mohammed al-Ahmar), had recently established an independent emirate. Stretching from the Strait of Gibraltar to east of Almería, this became the final remnant of Al-Andalus, ruled by the Nasrids from the lavish Alhambra palace for 250 years. Such was the state of play at the time the emirate was established, the Nasrids actually helped Fernando III take Sevilla and paid tribute to Castilla from this time until 1476. However, throughout their rule, they played off Castilla and Aragón against each other, at times also seeking assistance from the Marinid rulers of Morocco.

Granada became one of the richest and most populous cities in 13th century Europe, flourishing on the talents of its swelled population of traders and artisans. The two centuries of artistic and scientific splendour peaked under Yousouf I and Mohammed V in the 14th century.

But by the end of the 15th century the Nasrid dynasty was in decline. Its economy had stagnated, the rulers had retreated into a pleasure-loving existence inside the Alhambra, and violent rivalry had developed over the succession. One faction supported the emir, Abu al-Hasan, and his harem favourite Zoraya. The other faction backed Boabdil, Abu al-Hasan's son by his wife Aixa. In 1482 Boabdil rebelled, setting off a confused civil war. The Christian armies which launched an invasion of the Granada emirate the same year took full advantage. The scene had been set for war by the unification of Castilla and Aragón through the marriage of Isabel and Fernando, and Abu al-Hasan's refusal to pay tribute to Castilla from 1476.

Capturing Boabdil in 1483, the Catholic Monarchs extracted from him a promise to surrender much of the emirate if they would help him regain Granada itself. Following Abu al-Hasan's death in 1485, Boabdil won control of the city as the Christians pushed across the rest of the emirate, besieging towns and devastating the countryside. In 1491 they finally laid siege to Granada. After

eight months siege, Boabdil agreed to surrender the city in return for the Alpujarras valleys and 30,000 gold coins, plus political and religious freedom for his subjects. To forestall trouble from hawk factions in the city, he allowed Castilian troops into the Alhambra on the night of 1-2 January 1492. Next day Isabel and Fernando entered the city ceremonially in Muslim dress. They set up court in the Alhambra for several years.

Under them, Granada became a dynamic Castilian city but religious persecution, despite promises to the contrary, soured the scene. Jews were expelled from Spain soon after the city's conquest, and persecution of Muslims increased at the end of the century, leading to revolts across the former emirate. In 1502, Muslims were given the ultimatum to convert or leave Spain. Most were baptised and remained, to be known as Moriscos (converted Muslims). But following another revolt in the 1560s, centred on the Alpujarras, the Moriscos of the Granada area were deported to other parts of Spain. By the beginning of the 17th century, having lost much of its talented populace, Granada had fallen into a decline which was only arrested by the interest drummed up by the romantic movement in the 1830s. This set the stage for the restoration of Granada's Islamic heritage and the arrival of tourism. Many historic buildings were, however, torn down to make way for wide thoroughfares.

Early 20th century Granada frowned on liberalism, leading to the horrors unleashed after the Nationalists took over the city at the start of the civil war in 1936. An estimated 4000 *granadinos* with left or liberal connections were killed, among them Federico García Lorca, Granada's famous poet/dramatist/artist/musician. Granada today still has a reputation for conservatism.

Orientation

The two main streets, Gran Vía de Colón and Calle Reyes Católicos, meet at Plaza Isabel La Católica. North-east of here, Calle Reyes Católicos passes through Plaza Nueva to Plaza Santa Ana, from where Carrera del Darro leads up to the old Islamic district, the

PLACES TO STAY
7 Hotel Washington Irving
8 Posada Doña Lupe
10 Hotel Alhambra Palace
17 La Luz es Como El Agua
22 Hostal Terminus
28 Hotel Dauro
29 Youth Hostel

PLACES TO EAT
2 El Ladrillo
4 Mirador de Morayma
14 Casa Cristóbal

OTHER
1 Monasterio de la Cartuja
3 Colegiata de Nuestra Salvador
5 Mirador San Nicolás

6 Casa del Castril
  (Museo Arqueológico)
9 Centro Cultural Manuel de Falla
11 El Pie de la Vela
12 Baños Arabes
13 El Corral del Príncipe
15 Iglesia San Miguel
16 Convento Santa Isabel
18 Bus Stop for Viznar
19 Bar El Eshavira
20 Autedia Bus Station
21 Bacoma Bus Station
23 Train Station
24 Hospital de San Juan de Dios
25 Convento de San Jerónimo
26 Universidad (Facultad de Derecho)
27 Policía Nacional
30 Alsina Graells Bus Station

Granada

0   200   400 m

To Viznar

Paseo de la Cartuja

Real de Cartuja

Carretera   de   Murcia

Calle Cruz
de Arqueros

Ancha de Capuchinos

Avenida de Madrid

Jardines
del
Triunfo

Gran Vía de Colón

To Camping Sierra Nevada
& N-323 (Jaén & Madrid)

Avenida del Doctor Olóriz

Avenida de Madrid

Avenida de Andaluces

Avenida   de   la

Constitución

Parque
Fuente
Nueva

Calle Rector

Calle Doctor Severo Ochoa

Calle San Juan de Dios

24

25

23

21   22

Martín Ocete

To N-342 (Airport,
Fuente Vaqueros &
Málaga)

Avenida de la Fuente Nueva

Calle Melchor Almag

Camino   de   Ronda

Placeta
Fatima

2

Calle de Elvira

Plaza del
Triunfo

ANDALUCÍA

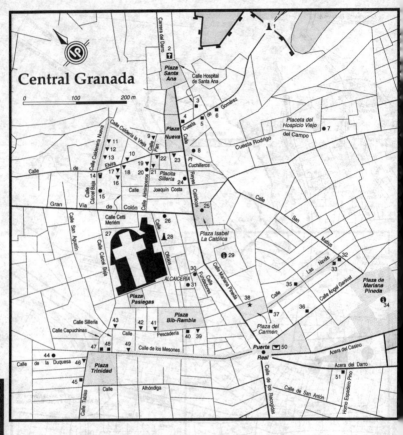

Central Granada

0   100   200 m

Albaicín. To the south, Calle Reyes Católicos extends to Puerta Real, Granada's main plaza. From here, Acera del Darro heads south-east to cross the Río Genil.

The Alhambra, atop the hill to the north-east of the centre, overlooks Carrera del Darro and the Albaicín. Cuesta de Gomérez leads up to the Alhambra from Plaza Nueva.

Most major sights are within walking distance of the centre though there are buses if you get fed up with walking uphill. The Alsina Graells bus station (south-west) and train station (west) are out of the centre with plenty of buses heading to and fro.

Information
Tourist Offices The municipal tourist office (☎ 22 66 88) is at Plaza de Mariana Pineda east of Puerta Real. The helpful English-speaking staff have plenty of information to give away about Granada and Granada province. Opening hours are Monday to Friday from 10.30 am to 1.30 pm and 4.30 to 6.30 pm, Saturday from 10 am to 1 pm. The Junta de Andalucía has a more central tourist office (☎ 22 59 90) in the Corral del Carbón on Calle Mariana Pineda. Staff here are more pressed, and charge for maps and other printed material. Bus and train information

PLACES TO STAY		16	Café/Bar Nueva	14	Bar Avellano
3	Hostal Vienna		Riviera	15	Granada 10
4	Hostal Britz	17	La Nueva Bodega	20	La Taberna del
5	Hostal Austria	18	Mesón Andaluz		Irlandés
6	Hostal Gomérez	19	Café/Bar Almireceros	24	RENFE office
32	Hostal Roma	21	Antigua Castañeda	25	Iberia & Aviaco Office
33	Hotel Dauro II	22	Bodegas Castañeda	26	Librería Atlantida
35	Hotel Navás	23	Café	27	Catedral and Capilla
36	Hostal Fabiola	39	Café Bib-Rambla		Real
37	Hostal Residencia	41	Pizzeria Gallio	28	La Madraza (Casa
	Lisboa	42	Cunini		del Cabildo
40	Hotel Los Tilos	43	El Cepillo		Antiguo)
45	Hostal Zurita	46	Bar/Cervecería	29	Corral del Carbón,
47	Huéspedes		Reca		Tourist Office
	Capuchinas	49	Mesón El Patio		(Junta de
48	Pensión Romero				Andalucía) &
51	Hotel Montecarlo	OTHER			Artespaña
		1	Puerta de las	30	La Sabanilla
PLACES TO EAT			Granadas	31	Alcaicería
9	Restaurante León	2	Iglesia de Santa Ana	34	Municipal Tourist
10	Boabdil	7	Universidad - Centro		Office
11	El Panadero Loco		de Lenguas	38	Policía Local
12	Medina Zahara		Modernas	44	Pub Liberta
13	Naturii Albaicín	8	Café Aljibe	50	Post Office

s posted outside. Opening hours are
Monday to Friday from 9 am to 7 pm, Saturday from 10 am to 2 pm.

Money There are several banks with ATMs
on Gran Vía de Colón and Calle Reyes
Católicos.

Post & Communications The main post
office (postcode 18080) is at Puerta Real s/n.
There are numerous public phones around
the centre.

Books *Tales of the Alhambra* by Washington
Irving makes a great read whilst on site in
Granada. Librería Urbano, Calle Tablas 6,
south-west off Plaza de la Trinidad, Librería
Continental, Puerta Real, and Librería
Atlántida, Gran Vía de Colón 9, stock books
in English.

Medical & Emergency Services The
Policía Local (☎ 20 94 61) are at Plaza del
Carmen 5, just north of Puerta Real. The
Policía Nacional station (☎ 27 83 00) is at
Calle de la Duquesa 15, north-west off Plaza
de la Trinidad. For urgent medical help, the
Cruz Roja (☎ 22 22 22) is at Calle Escoriaza

8, near Paseo de la Bomba and the Río Genil.
The Hospital de San Juan de Dios (☎ 20 43
00) is in a fairly central position at Calle San
Juan de Dios 15.

La Alhambra & El Generalife

Nothing can prepare you for the delights of
the Alhambra. Perched on top of La Sabika,
the hill which overlooks Granada, this
monument is the stuff of fairy tales. It may
initially disappoint with its simple, unadorned red fortress towers and walls,
though its Sierra Nevada backdrop and the
cypresses and elms in which it nestles are
undeniably magnificent. Inside the marvel-
lously decorated Casa Real (Royal Palace)
and the Generalife (the Alhambra's gardens),
you're in for a treat. Water has been used as
an art form in both places, and even around
the exterior of the Alhambra the sound of
running water and the greenness contribute
to a sense of calm, a world away from the
bustle of the city and the general dryness of
much of Spain.

This tranquillity can be completely shat-
tered by the hordes of visitors who traipse
through the complex (4600 on an average

ANDALUCÍA

day), so try to visit first thing in the morning, late in the afternoon or – a magical experience – at night. (Note that for night visits, only the major rooms of the Casa Real are open.)

The Alhambra has two main parts, the Alcazaba (fortress) and the Casa Real. Also within it are the Palacio de Carlos V, the Iglesia de Santa María de la Alhambra, two hotels, a few restaurants, souvenir shops and refreshment stalls. The Generalife is a short walk to the north-east.

History The Alhambra, from the Arabic *al-qala hamra* (red castle), began life as a fortress as early as the 9th century. The Nasrids of the 13th and 14th centuries turned it into a fortress-palace complex adjoined by a small city (medina), of which nothing remains. The founder of the Nasrid dynasty, Mohammed ibn Yousouf ibn Nasr, set up home on the hill top, restoring and expanding the Alcazaba. His 14th-century successors, Yousouf I and Mohammed V, built the Casa Real; Mohammed V was also responsible for much of the decoration of the palace. In 1492 the Catholic Monarchs moved in after their conquest of Granada. They appointed a Morisco to restore the decoration of the Casa Real, and in time the palace mosque was replaced with a church and a convent, the Convento de San Francisco, was built. Carlos I, the grandson of the Catholic Monarchs, had a wing of the Casa Real destroyed to make space for a huge Renaissance palace, which was called the Palacio de Carlos V using his title as Holy Roman Emperor. In the 18th century the Alhambra was abandoned to thieves and beggars, and during the Napoleonic occupation it was used as a barracks and narrowly escaped being blown up. In 1870 it was declared a national monument after the huge interest taken in it by romantic writers such as Washington Irving, who wrote his wonderful *Tales of the Alhambra* in his study in some of the palace rooms during an extended stay. Since then it has been salvaged and heavily restored.

Getting There The Tren Alhambra, a little tourist road train, makes its way up to the Alhambra from Plaza Nueva daily from 9 am to 7 pm (to 9 pm in summer). Trains leave every 30 minutes and tickets (return only) cost 250 ptas. Bus No 2 from Plaza Nueva (every 40 minutes) heads up to the Alhambra, too. Coming by car from outside Granada, you can reach the Alhambra without heading into the city centre by following the signs from the Carretera de Circunvalación which partly rings the city.

Walking up Cuesta de Gomérez from Plaza Nueva you soon reach the **Puerta de las Granadas** (Gate of the Pomegranates) a solid gateway with three pomegranates built by Carlos I. Above the gate are the Bosque Alhambra woods. Here a path to the left rises steeply to the austere **Puerta de la Justicia** (Gate of Justice), constructed by Yousouf I in 1348, which is the main entrance to the Alhambra. From the gate, a passage leads to the Plaza de los Aljibes, with the main ticket office.

Opening hours from April to September are Monday to Saturday 9 am to 8 pm, Sunday 9 am to 6 pm; the Casa Real is also open Tuesday, Thursday and Saturday from 10 pm to midnight. Hours from October to March are 9 am to 6 pm daily, with the Casa Real also open on Saturday from 8 to 10 pm. Tickets cost 675 ptas, 250 ptas for the Generalife only, free for disabled people and children under eight. Entry is free for all on Sunday. Tickets have tear-away sections for each part of the Alhambra; each section must be used on the same day. Tickets are stamped with a half-hour time slot in which you must enter the Casa Real, though you can spend as long as you like in there.

In the ticket office there is a branch of the tourist office and, to one side, guides sit at a table awaiting business: for a tour in English they charge 8000 to 10,000 ptas for one to 10 people. If you want a tour, they're cheaper arranged elsewhere (see Organised Tours).

Alcazaba What remains are the ramparts and several towers, the most important and tallest being the **Torre de la Vela** (watch

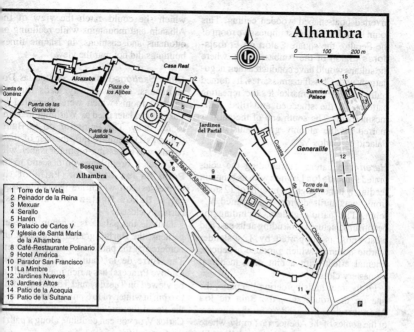

Alhambra

0   100   200 m

1 Torre de la Vela
2 Peinador de la Reina
3 Mexuar
4 Serallo
5 Harén
6 Palacio de Carlos V
7 Iglesia de Santa María
   de la Alhambra
8 Café-Restaurante Polinario
9 Hotel América
10 Parador San Francisco
11 La Mimbre
12 Jardines Nuevos
13 Jardines Altos
14 Patio de la Acequia
15 Patio de la Sultana

ower). Here a narrow, winding staircase
ads to the top terrace, which has splendid
iews of the city and surrounds. It was here
nat the cross and banners of the Reconquista
ere raised in January 1492. The tower's bell
. rung on festive occasions only, but in the
ast it tolled to control the irrigation system
f the Vega.

asa Real This is what all the fuss is about.
he Royal Palace (also called the Palacio
azaríes), with its intricately carved stucco
alls, fine knotted wooden ceilings, elabo-
ite honeycomb vaulting and beautifully
roportioned rooms and courtyards, stands
. marked contrast to the austere walls and
wers of the fortress. Arabic inscriptions
cur in the stucco work.

exuar These rooms, through which you
ter the palace, date from the 14th century
d were used for bureaucratic and judicial
rposes. The general public would not have

been allowed beyond them. The first room,
the council chamber, has been much altered
and contains both Muslim and Christian
motifs. At its far end is a small, lavishly
decorated room (originally a prayer room)
that looks out upon the Río Darro below.
From here you pass into the **Patio del
Mexuar** or Patio del Cuarto Dorado, with a
small fountain, and the mudéjar **Cuarto
Dorado** (Golden Room) on the left. Opposite the Cuarto Dorado is the entrance to the
Serallo, through a beautiful façade of glazed
tiles, stucco work and carved wood.

Serallo This was the official residence of the
emir or sultan. Its rooms surround the **Patio
de los Arrayanes** (Patio of the Myrtles),
named for the hedges that flank the rectangular pool and fountains. Finely carved
arches sit atop marble pillars to form porticoes at the north and south ends of the patio.
Through the north portico is the **Sala de la
Barca** (Salon of the Boat) with a beautiful

inverted boat-shaped wooden ceiling. This room leads into the most impressive room of the Serallo, the square **Salón de Embajadores** (Salon of the Ambassadors), where the sultans would have conducted their negotiations with Christian emissaries. Its domed cedar ceiling is remarkable, the repeating patterns of the stuccoed and tiled walls mesmerising. The south end of the patio is marred by the gloomy grey walls of the Palacio de Carlos V.

Harén The harem, surrounding the celebrated **Patio de los Leones** with its fountain feeding water through the mouths of 12 stone lions, was built during Mohammed V's reign. The patio's gallery, including the beautiful structures protruding at its east and west ends, is supported by 124 slender marble columns which produce a delicate oriental effect with a hint of a medieval monastery cloister.

Of the four halls bordering the patio, the one on the south side, the **Sala de los Abencerrajes**, is legendary for the murders of the nobles of the Abencerraj family, whose head, the story goes, dared to dally with Zoraya, the harem favourite of Abu al-Hasan. (Historians also say the Abencerrajes favoured Boabdil in the palace power struggle.) The room's highlight is its tall, domed ceiling, with stalactite vaulting producing a star-like effect and windows giving the room a wonderful light.

At the east end of the patio is the **Sala de los Reyes** (Hall of the Kings) with paintings of royalty, medieval scenes and motifs on its leather-lined ceiling. Its name comes from the painting on the central part of the ceiling, which is thought to depict 10 Nasrid emirs.

On the north side of the patio is the **Sala de las Dos Hermanas** (Hall of the Two Sisters), as beautiful and richly decorated as the Sala de los Abencerrajes, and named for the two slabs of white marble either side of its fountain. It was the room of the sultan's favourite paramour. At its far end is the enchanting **Sala de los Ajimeces**. This was the favoured lady's dressing room and bedroom, with low-slung windows through which she could catch the view of the Albaicín and mountains while reclining on ottomans and cushions. In Islamic times buildings did not mar the view.

Other Sections From the Sala de las Dos Hermanas, a passageway leads through deserted rooms which were decorated by Carlos I and later used by Washington Irving as his study. The **Peinador de la Reina** (Queen's Dressing-room), the last of these rooms, was a dressing-room for Isabel, wife of Carlos I. From here you descend to the **Patio de los Cipreses** (Patio of the Cypresses), off which are the richly decorated **Baños Reales** (Royal Baths) currently closed.

Outside the palace is a group of recent gardens, the **Partal**, graded in terraces and bordered by the palace towers and ramparts. The Torre de la Cautiva (Tower of the Captive Princess) has a rich interior and can be viewed on Tuesday and Thursday from 2 to 6 pm in winter, or to 8 pm in summer. From the Partal there is an exit to the Palacio de Carlos V, or you can continue along a path to the Generalife.

Generalife The name means 'garden of the architect'. These palace gardens planted on the hillside facing the Casa Real are a beautiful and soothing composition of walkways, terraces, patios and fountains, flowers of every imaginable hue in season, trimmed hedges and tall, long-established trees, especially cypresses. The Muslim rulers' summer palace is in the farthest corner. Within the palace, the **Patio de la Acequia** (Court of the Long Pond) has a long pool framed by flower beds and fountains whose shapes sensuously echo the arched porticoes at each end. The northern portico leads into the **Patio de la Sultana**, almost as lovely and recently under restoration, where the Nasrid ruler Abu al-Hasan supposedly caught his lover, Zoraya, with the head of the Abencerraj clan, leading to the murders in the Sala de los Abencerrajes of the Casa Real. Above here are the modern **Jardines Altos** (upper gardens), and a stairway with cascading waterfalls. Back towards the entry/exit are the **Jardines Nuevos** (new gardens). A pleasant alternative route back to town is along Cuesta de los Chinos, which runs down a gully between the Generalife and the Alhambra proper to the Río Darro.

Palacio de Carlos V This huge Renaissance palace, also called the Casa Real Nueva, is the dominating building of the Christian era in the Alhambra. Begun in 1527 by Pedro Machuca, a Toledo architect and painter who studied under Michelangelo in Italy, it was never completed. The building is square, but contains a surprising two-tiered circular courtyard surrounded by 32 columns. Were the palace in a different setting its merits would be more readily appreciated, but here it seems intrusive.

The palace houses two museums. On the ground floor, the **Museo Nacional de Arte Hispano-Árabe** contains artefacts from the Alhambra and the province of Granada, including pre-Muslim finds. Its highlight is the beautiful, tall Alhambra Vase, decorated with gazelles. It's open Tuesday to Saturday from 9 am to 2 pm. Entry is 250 ptas but free with an EU passport.

The **Museo de Bellas Artes** on the upper floor has an impressive collection of paintings and sculptures. Most notable are the statue of Virgin and Child by Diego de Siloé, various pieces by Alonso Cano, and an enamelled screen formerly the property of El Gran Capitán (Gonzalo Fernández de Córdoba), the military right-hand man of Isabel and Fernando. Opening hours are Tuesday to Saturday from 10 am to 2.30 pm. Entry is free.

Other Christian Buildings The **Iglesia de Santa María** was built between 1581 and 1617 on the site of the former palace mosque. Entry is free. The **Convento de San Francisco**, now a parador, was erected upon an Islamic palace. Isabel and Fernando were laid to rest in a sepulchre in what is now the parador's patio before being transferred to the Capilla Real. Today, its outdoor terrace bar makes a fine setting for refreshments.

Capilla Real
The Royal Chapel, on Calle Oficios adjoining the cathedral, is Granada's outstanding Christian building. Built in elaborate late Gothic style, it was commissioned by the Catholic Monarchs to be their mausoleum, but was not completed until 1521 – hence their temporary interment in the Convento de San Francisco.

The illustrious monarchs lie in simple lead coffins in the crypt beneath their marble monuments in the chancel, which is enclosed by a stunning gilded wrought-iron screen created in 1520 by Bartolomé de Jaén. The coffins, from left to right, are those of Felipe El Hermoso (the Handsome, husband of the monarchs' daughter Juana la Loca), Fernando, Isabel, Juana la Loca (the Mad) and Miguel, the eldest grandchild of Isabel and Fernando. The carved effigies reclining above the crypt were the idea of Carlos I as a more fitting tribute to his parents and grandparents than the simple coffins. The slightly lower of the two monuments, representing Isabel and Fernando, is the work of a Tuscan, Domenico Fancelli. The other monument, to Felipe and Juana, is higher apparently due to Felipe being the son of the Holy Roman Emperor, Maximilian. This is the work of Bartolomé Ordóñez (1520) from Burgos. The chancel's densely decorated plateresque retablo is the work of Felipe de Vigarni (1522). Note the kneeling figures of Isabel and Fernando, attributed to Diego de Siloé, and the paintings below depicting the defeat of the Muslims and subsequent conversions to Christianity. Cardinal Cisneros is there, too.

In the sacristy is a museum with an impressive collection including Isabel's sceptre and silver crown and Fernando's sword. Isabel's personal art collection, mainly Flemish, occupies one room; there is also Botticelli's *Prayer in the Garden of Olives*, and two fine statues of the kneeling monarchs by Vigarni.

The Capilla Real's opening hours are Monday to Saturday from 10.30 am to 1 pm and 3.30 to 6.30 pm, Sunday from 11 am to 1 pm. Entry is 200 ptas; free on Sunday.

ANDALUCÍA

Catedral

Adjoining the Capilla Real, the chunky Gothic/Renaissance cathedral with its cavernous interior was begun in 1521, and directed by Diego de Siloé from 1528 to 1563. Work was not completed until the 18th century. The main façade on Plaza de las Pasiegas, with its four heavy buttresses and arched doorway, was designed by Alonso Cano. The lavish Puerta del Perdón on the north façade has statues carved by Diego de Siloé. Much of the interior is also the work of de Siloé, including the gilded and painted sanctuary. Here, too, are the Catholic Monarchs at prayer carved by Pedro de Mena – look to each side of the tabernacle, above the lovely carved and painted pulpits – and Alonso Cano's busts of Adam and Eve.

The cathedral is open from Monday to Saturday from 10.30 am to 1 pm and 3.30 to 6.30 pm. On Sunday, it's closed in the morning. Entry (from Gran Vía de Colón) costs 200 ptas. You should be able to slip in for free during early-morning Masses.

Islamic Buildings near the Capilla Real

La Madraza Opposite the Capilla Real remains part of the old Muslim university, La Madraza, also called the Casa del Cabildo Antiguo as it was later used as a town hall. Now with a painted baroque façade, the much-altered building retains an octagonal domed prayer-room with stucco lacework and pretty tiles. Upstairs is another room with typical Islamic decorations. The building is now part of the modern university, but you can take a look at most times during the day.

Corral del Carbón This place's name (charcoal yard) disguises its original function as a 14th century *caravanserai* or inn for merchants, commonplace in the oriental world but not in Spain. The building has had a chequered history, having been used as an inn for coal dealers (hence its modern name), and later a theatre, before its restoration. It now houses a tourist office and government-run crafts shop. To find it, cross Calle de los Reyes Católicos from Capilla Real and look for the sign that points down an alley. You can't miss the lovely Islamic façade with its elaborate horseshoe arch.

Alcaicería The Alcaicería was the Muslim silk exchange, but what you see now is a restoration after a 19th century fire, filled with tourist shops. Take a look here before the shops open, when it still manages to convey some charm in the early-morning light and quiet. The buildings, separated by narrow alleys, are just south-west of the Capilla Real.

Albaicín

A wander around the hilly streets and narrow, aged alleys of the Albaicín, Granada's old Muslim quarter, is a must. The Albaicín covers much of the hill that faces the Alhambra across the valley of the Río Darro. Its name derives from 1227 when Muslims from Baeza populated the district after their city was conquered by the Christians. It became a densely populated residential area of Islamic Granada and after the Reconquista it survived as the Muslim quarter. Muslim ramparts, cisterns, gates, fountains and houses remain, and many of the Albaicín's churches and *cármenes* (large walled villas with gardens) stand on or incorporate the remains of Islamic buildings.

Carrera del Darro One way to approach the Albaicín is up Carrera del Darro from Plaza Nueva. At the north-east end of Plaza Nueva is the **Iglesia de Santa Ana**, which incorporates a former mosque's minaret in its bell tower, as do several churches in the Albaicín. Stop by at Carrera del Darro 31 to see the remains of the 11th century **Baños Árabes** (Muslim baths), open Monday to Saturday from 10 am to 2 pm. Entry (free) is through a pretty patio complete with plants, birds in cages and a pond.

At Carrera del Darro 43 is the Renaissance Casa del Castril, home to the **Museo Arqueológico**, which has some interesting finds from Granada province. On the upper floor, the Islamic room has some lovely azulejos, carved wood and fine ceramics. As you emerge from this room you are greeted with a splendid vista of the Alhambra. The museum is open Tuesday to Sunday from 10 am to 2 pm. Entry is 250 ptas (free with an EU passport).

Paseo de los Tristes & Cuesta del Chapiz
Shortly after the museum, Carrera del Darro becomes Paseo de los Tristes (also called Paseo del Padre Manjón), with a number of cafés and restaurants with outdoor tables. This is a great spot to take in the view of the Alhambra's fortifications directly above.

Upper Albaicín From the top end of Paseo de los Tristes, Cuesta del Chapiz heads north, uphill, then curves west into Plaza del Salvador, where the **Colegiata de Nuestra Salvador**, a 16th century church, still contains the Islamic courtyard of the mosque it replaced. It's open daily from 10 am to 1 pm and 4 to 7 pm (100 ptas). From here Calle Panaderos leads to **Plaza Larga**, with an Islamic gateway at the top end of the Albaicín's surviving Muslim ramparts, and lively bars offering cheap menús. From Calle Panaderos, Calle Horno Moral and Calle Charca lead to the **Mirador San Nicolás**, which has fantastic views of the Alhambra and the Sierra Nevada – you can't miss the rail at sunset!

Descent from Mirador San Nicolás Descending from the mirador along Camino Nuevo San Nicolás, which becomes Calle Santa Isabel la Real, you pass the **Convento Santa Isabel**, a former Islamic palace. Its church, open daily from 10 am to 6 pm, has a mudéjar ceiling. Nearby is **Plaza de San Miguel Bajo**, where the Iglesia San Miguel occupies the site of a former mosque. To wend your way back to the centre, follow Plaza Cauchiles San Miguel and then Calle San José. Calle San José ends near the top end of picturesque **Calle Calderería Nueva** with its teterías, a stone's throw from Plaza Nueva. Alternatively, enjoy getting lost – but not too late at night.

Sacromonte
Camino del Sacromonte leads from Cuesta del Chapiz up Sacromonte hill to the **Iglesia de San Cecilio**, passing by caves dug into the hillside; these caves have been occupied by Gypsies since the 18th century.

Plaza Bib-Rambla, Plaza de la Trinidad & Around
Just south-west of the Alcaicería is the large and pleasant **Plaza Bib-Rambla**, where there are restaurants, flower stalls, toy shops and a central fountain with statues of giants at its base. This was the scene of Inquisition lashings and burnings, jousting and bullfights. Today buskers, mime artists and street sellers provide more gentle entertainment.

A block to the south-west is Calle de los Mesones, a pedestrianised street with modern shops. At its north end is the leafy **Plaza de la Trinidad**, from which Calle de la Duquesa leads past the university founded by Carlos I (now the Law Faculty, with the main modern campus out of the centre to the north) to the **Convento de San Jerónimo** on Calle del Gran Capitán. Dating from the early 16th century, this features more work by the talented and ubiquitous Diego de Siloé, including the larger of the convent's two cloisters and much of the attached church. Either side of the church's altar are statues of El Gran Capitán and his wife María; El Gran Capitán is reputedly buried beneath the altar. The convent is open daily from 10 am to 1.30 pm, plus 3 to 6.30 pm in winter and 4 to 7.30 pm in summer (200 ptas).

Monasterio de La Cartuja
More impressive is the ornate La Cartuja Monastery, a 20 minute walk north of the Convento de San Jerónimo (or take bus No 8 from Gran Vía de Colon). The monastery, with an imposing sand-coloured stone exterior, was built between the 16th and 18th centuries. Its baroque interior oozes wealth, especially the astonishingly lavish sagrario, decorated in brown and white marble and stucco, and the *sanctum sanctorum* (holy

sanctuary), a riot of colour and patterns with its twisted marble columns, loads of statues, paintings, gilt and beautiful frescoed cupola. In contrast, four dark chapels off the cloister display religious paintings, some in a state of disrepair, of bizarre scenes of martyrdom and the Inquisition. The monastery is open Monday to Saturday from 10 am to 1 pm and 3.30 to 7 pm, Sunday from 10 am to noon and 3.30 to 7 pm; it closes at 6 pm in winter (200 ptas).

Huerta de San Vicente

This house where Federico García Lorca spent summers and wrote some of his well-known works, a 15 minute walk from the centre, was once surrounded by orchards. Today the new Parque Federico García Lorca separates it from whizzing traffic in an attempt to recreate the tranquil rural environment that inspired Lorca. The house contains some original furnishings including Lorca's desk and piano, some of his drawings and other memorabilia, plus exhibitions connected with his life and work. There are guided tours in Spanish on the half-hour. To find it, head down Calle de las Recogidas from Puerta Real and cross Camino de Ronda. A block further on is Calle del Arabial, and the park is just along it to the right. The house is open Tuesday to Sunday from 10 am to 1 pm and 4 to 7 pm (winter), 6 to 9 pm (summer), and entry is free (see under Around Granada later in this section for more Lorca sites).

Language Courses

With the city's attractions and its youthful population, Granada makes a good place to study Spanish. The university offers a variety of intensive programmes with a four-week course priced at 53,000 ptas. For more information contact Universidad de Granada, Centro de Lenguas Modernas, Cursos Para Extranjeros, Placeta del Hospicio Viejo s/n (Realejo), 18071 Granada (☎ 22 07 90; fax 22 08 44). Colegio Nueva Universidad, Calle Natalio Rivas 1, 18001 Granada (☎ 27 54 24; fax 27 50 15), is another possibility.

Organised Tours

Grana Vision (☎ 13 58 04) does guided tours of the Alhambra and Generalife (3300 ptas). Granada Histórica tours, which include the cathedral, Capilla Real, La Cartuja, the Albaicín and Sacromonte (also 3300 ptas) flamenco shows (3500 ptas) and excursions further afield. Phone direct or book through any travel agent.

Special Events

Semana Santa and the Corpus Christi feria nine weeks later are the big two. Benches are set up in Plaza del Carmen for viewing the Semana Santa processions. At Corpus Christi, fairgrounds, drinking and dancing sevillanas are the go. Other festivals include

2 January
> *Día de la Toma* (Day of the Conquest) – celebrates the completion of the Reconquista with the taking of Granada by the Catholic Monarchs.

3 May
> *Día de la Cruz* (Day of the Cross) – squares patios and balconies are adorned with crosses (the *Cruces de Mayo*) made of flowers. Horse riders, polka-dot dresses and sevillana dancing add to the colour.

Late June/early July
> *Festival Internacional de Música y Danza* – international music and dance festival with open air performances (some free) in the Generalife and Palacio de Carlos V. For information, contact Centro Manuel de Falla, Paseo de los Mártires s/n.

November
> *Festival Internacional de Jazz* – for information contact Calle del Gran Capitán 24.

Places to Stay

There should be no problem finding a room in Granada except during Semana Santa. Prices are no higher than elsewhere in Spain and there are some good budget options. The most expensive places are in and around the Alhambra. Expect to pay more than the prices quoted during Semana Santa and July or August.

Places to Stay – bottom end

Camping There are several camp sites within about five km of Granada, all accessible by bus. All charge around 500 ptas per adult, 300 to 350 ptas per tent, and 400 to 600 ptas per vehicle. Closest and biggest, though closed from November to February, is *Camping Sierra Nevada* (☎ 15 00 62) at Avenida de Madrid 107, three km north-west of the centre. There are big, clean bathrooms, a pool and a laundry. Take bus No 3 from the centre. Other options include:

Camping Granada (☎ 34 05 48), Cerro de la Cruz s/n, Peligros, four km north of Granada (take exit 123 from the N-323) – open all year
Camping María Eugenia (☎ 20 06 06), Carretera N-342, Km 286, en route to Santa Fe
Los Álamos (☎ 20 84 79), Carretera N-342, Km 290, en route to Santa Fe

Youth Hostels The *Albergue Juvenil Granada* (☎ 27 26 38), Camino de Ronda 171, is right by the Alsina Graells bus station. The large, modern, white building with pool has recently been renovated.

Hostales & Pensiones Cheap hostales are mainly located near Plaza Nueva, around Plaza de la Trinidad and near Plaza del Carmen. One exception, handy for the Alhambra, is *Posada Doña Lupe* (☎ 22 14 73), Avenida del Generalife s/n, with more than 40 rooms. Management is friendly, English is spoken and there is a small, clean pool on a large roof-terrace. Clean singles/doubles/triples with bathroom cost 1000/1950/2950 ptas, or 700 ptas per bed if you bring your own bedding. Better doubles with a balcony are 4950 ptas. All prices include a light breakfast. Bus No 2 from Plaza Nueva stops outside.

Near Plaza Nueva There's plenty of choice on Cuesta de Gomérez, the busy street running from Plaza Nueva up to the Alhambra. The friendly *Hostal Britz* (☎ 22 36 52) at No 1, facing Plaza Nueva, has clean, adequate singles/doubles for 2000/3200 ptas, and doubles with bath for 4500 ptas. *Hostal Gomérez* (☎ 22 44 37) at No 10 has a lively, helpful owner who speaks English, French and Italian. The nine well-kept rooms cost 1300/2200 ptas. Close by, *Hostal Vienna* (☎ 22 18 59), Calle Hospital de Santa Ana 2,

first left off Cuesta de Gomérez, is a popular choice. Rooms vary; some have private bathrooms. Tolerable singles, reasonable doubles and good triples cost 1500/3000/4000 ptas. Management is obliging and English and German are spoken. The same people run *Hostal Austria* (☎ 22 70 75), Cuesta de Gomérez 4. All rooms have attached bathrooms. Singles cost 2000 and 2500 ptas, doubles 2500 and 3500 ptas.

Near Puerta Real & Plaza del Carmen *Hostal Fabiola* (☎ 22 35 72), Calle Ángel Ganivet 5, 3rd floor, is a friendly, family-run place. The 19 good rooms, some with balcony and all with private bathroom, cost 1800/3500/5000 ptas for singles/doubles/triples. Two blocks north at Plaza del Carmen 27, the friendly *Hostal-Residencia Lisboa* (☎ 22 14 13) has singles/doubles for 3000/4700 ptas with bath, 2000/3300 ptas without. *Hostal Roma* (☎ 22 62 77), Calle de Las Navás 1, has good, clean singles for 2000 and 2500 ptas, doubles for 3000 and 4000 ptas.

Near Plaza de la Trinidad Some of the many hostales in this area are full up with university students in term-time but have rooms free in the summer. The following places should have rooms available year-round. The good, family-run *Pensión Romero* (☎ 26 60 79) at Calle Sillería 1, on the corner of Calle Los Mesones, opposite Plaza de la Trinidad, has rooms for 1300/2500 ptas, some with balconies. *Hostal Zurita* (☎ 27 50 20), Plaza de la Trinidad 7, has good-value rooms for 1875/3750 ptas, and doubles for 4500 ptas with bathroom. There's off-street parking, too. *Huéspedes Capuchinas* (☎ 26 53 94), Calle Capuchinas 2 (2nd floor), has clean rooms for 1500/2500 ptas.

Elsewhere *Hostal Terminus* (☎ 20 03 11), Avenida de Andaluces 10, a stone's throw from the train station, has basic rooms with shared bathroom for 1500/2500 ptas. *Hostal La Luz es Como el Agua* (☎ 20 13 68), in a beautiful building at Calle Cruz de Arqueros

ANDALUCÍA

3, two blocks north-east of Plaza del Triunfo on the edge of the Albaicín, has just three double rooms, but they're clean and good value at 3600 ptas. It has a restaurant with good food and a terrace. The Belgian owner is multilingual.

Places to Stay – middle

Many of the middle-range hotels are on or near the busy Acera del Darro. Others are in the vicinity of the Alhambra. Add IVA to all prices given here. *Hotel Montecarlo* (☎ 25 79 00), Acera del Darro 44, has good singles/doubles with all mod cons for 4000/6000 ptas. *Hotel Los Tilos* (☎ 26 67 12), Plaza Bib-Rambla 4, costs 3500/6000 ptas, with doubles at 4500 ptas in winter. Up the scale a bit, Hotel Navás (☎ 22 59 59), Calle de Las Navás 24, charges 6800/10,250 ptas. *Hotel Dauro* (☎ 22 21 55), Acera del Darro 19, and *Hotel Dauro II* (☎ 22 15 81), Calle de Las Navás 5, are both at 7600/11000 ptas. *Hotel América* (☎ 22 74 71, Calle Real da Alhambra 53, is within the Alhambra grounds. Cost is 6,500/11,000 ptas. It has only 13 rooms: reserve well in advance. *Hotel Washington Irving* (☎ 22 75 50), Paseo del Generalife 2, near the Bosque Alhambra, has been around since last century. Rooms are 8000/10,500 ptas.

Places to Stay – top end

Parador San Francisco (☎ 22 14 40), Calle Real de Alhambra s/n, is the top place to stay in Granada. The converted monastery can't be beat for its location within the Alhambra and its historical connections. Rooms cost 18,000/26,000 ptas plus IVA. Book well ahead. The distinctive neo-Islamic *Hotel Alhambra Palace* (☎ 22 14 68), Peña Partida 2, close to the Bosque Alhambra, has wonderful views over the city. Rooms are 14,200/17,600 ptas plus IVA.

Places to Eat

Granadino cuisine uses the seafood and tropical fruits from the nearby coast and the meats and sausages of the interior. A hint of the Muslim past is evident in seasonings and desserts. *Rabo de toro* (bull's tail stew) and *habas con jamón* (broad beans with ham) are *platos típicos*. A *tortilla Sacromonte* is an omelette combining calf's brains, jamón, prawns or oysters, and greens. Bar flies will be pleasantly surprised to find that tapas are often free at night.

Prices are higher in choice locations such as in and around the Alhambra, Plaza Bib-Rambla, Plaza Nueva and some of the tea shops *(teteriás)* on Calle Calderería Nueva.

Near Plaza Nueva Two blocks west of Plaza Nueva *La Nueva Bodega*, Calle Cetti Meriém 3, and *Café/Bar Nueva Riviera* next door have similar fare and prices, and seem to be run by the same outfit. Menús start at 850 ptas; vegetarians can be accommodated. Roquefort salad (550 ptas), excellent spinach soup (600 ptas), bacalao, and trout with mushrooms enliven the menu. Across the road on the corner of Calle de Elvira, *Mesón Andaluz* is slightly more expensive with mains from 900 to 1300 ptas and menús from 950 ptas, all plus IVA. Round the corner on Calle de Elvira, *Boabdil* has reasonable food with menús from 725 ptas. A line of blackboards out the front display the options.

Back towards Plaza Nueva, *Restaurante León*, Calle Pan 3, is popular with menús from 850 to 1100 ptas plus IVA. Classier food in a more típico setting can be had at *Bodegas Castañeda* (an institution among locals and tourists alike) and *Antigua Castañeda*, almost side by side on Calle de Elvira and Calle Almireceros. Both places have barrels of Alpujarras wine and offer delicious, beautifully presented food. Try the montaditos (250 ptas), slices of bread with toppings such as smoked salmon or smoked trout with a touch of caviar. More elaborate meals cost around 1200 ptas. Down the scale but good value, especially for breakfast, is *Café-Bar Almireceros* on Calle Almireceros opposite the Antigua Castañeda.

Alhambra Even the kiosks inside the Alhambra complex charge hefty prices *Café-Restaurante Polinario*, opposite the Iglesia de Santa María, has expensive bocadillos etc and a buffet lunch at 1300 pta

ANDALUCÍA

plus IVA. *Parador San Francisco* has a pricey restaurant and a more affordable terrace bar out the back with a lovely view, which is open from 11 am to 11 pm daily. Teas and coffees cost 200 ptas and snacks are available.

La Mimbre on the corner of Avenida del Generalife and Cuesta de los Chinos has outdoor tables in a leafy garden under the Alhambra walls. It specialises in granadino fare, with main dishes at 900 ptas and a menú at 1300 ptas.

Albaicín On the south-east edge of the Albaicín, atmospheric Calle Calderería Nueva has several restaurants, teterías, health-food shops and takeaway food places (see also Vegetarian & Arabic Food). *El Panadero Loco* at No 14 is a good wholemeal bakery that also sells takeaway pizzas. It's open Monday to Saturday from 10 am to 2 pm and 5 to 8 pm, and Sunday evening only.

Near the top of the Albaicín, Plaza Larga and nearby Calle Panaderos have lively café-bars with cheap menús around 550 ptas. A couple of blocks north, *El Ladrillo* on Placeta Fátima spills out into the street in fine weather. It's a fun, popular seafood place open for lunch and dinner. Big platters of seafood go for 1200 ptas. For a splash-out, try the highly regarded *Mirador de Morayma*, Calle Pianista Carrillo 2, off Cuesta San Agustín on the west side of Cuesta del Chapiz. It occupies a lovely carmen (walled villa).

On the south-west edge of the Albaicín, Plaza San Miguel Bajo has a couple of lively bars with meals and tapas, popular with students. Down from here, close to Plaza del Triunfo, *La Luz es Como el Agua* at Cruz de Arqueros 3 is a hostal with a recommended restaurant.

Plaza Bib-Rambla & Around *Café Bib-Rambla*, with tables on the plaza, is a great place for breakfast. Coffee and toast with butter and excellent marmalade cost 400 ptas outside, and only 210 ptas at the bar inside. *Pizzeria Gallio*, Plaza Bib-Rambla 10, does tasty Italian food. Try pizza Florentina, with

spinach and béchamel sauce (745 ptas plus IVA). Drinks aren't cheap, with coffee at 200 ptas and a beer at 330 ptas. A little to the west on Calle Pescadería is *Cunini*, an expensive seafood restaurant with tables outside – prices are lower inside at the bar. A few doors away is *El Cepillo*, a popular cheaper seafood restaurant; it gets packed at lunchtime. Menús are 750 ptas and it's closed on Sunday.

Plaza de la Trinidad & Around *Bar-Cervecería Reca* on the plaza is full to overflowing at peak times. A beer and two plates of tapas – each with a couple of bites of seafood, a dumpling, fried eggplant and spicy salsa – will set you back 270 ptas. *Mesón El Patio*, Calle de Los Mesones 50, is a medium-priced restaurant with the usual Spanish-granadino mix of food and a pleasant patio. Tasty cured olives and warm bread precede your meal.

Campo del Príncipe South of the Alhambra is Campo del Príncipe, another area that buzzes at night. Of its several restaurants, *Casa Cristóbal* has menús from 850 ptas and does wonderful sangría.

Vegetarian & Arabic Food *Naturii Albaicín* at Calle Calderería Nueva 10 is a cosy, intimate place that has an interesting veggie menu with an Arabic twist. No alcohol is served. Hunks of delicious wholemeal bread accompany the meal. Mains are around 700 ptas, menús 850 to 1050 ptas, and fresh juices are available. *Restaurante Vegetariano Raíces*, about a 15 minute walk from the centre at Calle Pablo Picasso 30, is a further option for vegetarians. Take Acero de Darro, cross the Río Genil, and the sixth street on your right is Pablo Picasso. Alternatively, take bus No 11 from the centre. It's open Tuesday to Sunday from 1.30 to 4 pm and 8.30 to 11 pm.

On the Calle de Elvira side of Plaza Nueva, there's a *café* with genuine pitta bread, tasty felafel and hummus (each 250 ptas), and fresh juices, to take away or eat at the few tables inside. *Medina Zahara*, Calle

Calderería Nueva 12, has similar food though not quite as good; it's open to 1 am.

Markets & Shops For fresh fruit and veggies, the *produce market* spills down Calle San Agustín beside the cathedral. There are usually a few fruit and vegetable stalls on Calle Pescadería. Basic groceries can be bought at the stores at the Gran Vía end of Calle Calderería Nueva.

Entertainment

Available at kiosks at the beginning of each month, *Guía del Ocio* lists entertainment. *Ideal*, Granada's daily newspaper, has entertainment listings near the back.

Bars, Live Music & Discos Granada is reputed to have a sedate nightlife, but you can as easily dance the night away here as in most places in Spain. Keep your eye out for posters advertising live music shows and non-touristy flamenco.

Around Plaza Nueva The streets just west of Plaza Nueva are lively on weekend nights. *Bodega Castañeda* and *Antigua Castañeda* (see Places to Eat), with free tapas, make good stops to start the evening. Nearby, there are popular bars with good music on Placita Sillería and Calle Joaquín Costa, while *La Taberna del Irlandés* on Calle Almireceros offers Tetley's Bitter, Guinness and Fosters as well as Spanish tipples. Also close by, *Bar Avellano* on the corner of Calle de Elvira and Calle Cárcel Baja has great music – African, blues and pop classics. Beers cost 250 ptas. It's best after midnight on the weekend. *Granada 10*, the disco on Calle Cárcel Baja, has varied dance music. It opens about midnight and gets going about 2 am. Don't look too scruffy. Cover is 800 ptas, beers a hefty 700 ptas.

Cafe Aljibe above Plaza Cuchilleros on the east side of Plaza Nueva is great for late live music, though only open sporadically. *La Sabinilla*, on Calle Fundadores near the Alcaicería, is Granada's oldest bar and, though showing its age, is still worth a visit.

Elsewhere Don't miss *Bar El Eshavira*, a basement jazz, blues, flamenco and salsa club down a dark alley at Placeta de la Cuna, towards the north end of Calle de Elvira. It was closed Tuesday and Saturday when we were last in town, but open other nights from 11.30 pm.

Al Pie de la Vela, on Carrera del Darro near Calle Concepción, is another popular bar often with live music. There are more places to check out further up on Paseo de los Tristes.

Pub Liberta, Calle de la Duquesa 8 near Plaza de la Trinidad, celebrates the blues. A talented young four-piece band were entertaining when we visited. Entry is free and the music starts about 9 pm.

From about 11 pm on the weekend, you can't miss the crowds heading for Calle Pedro Antonio de Alarcón, a km or so southwest of the centre, where a string of disco-bars offer cheap deals on drinks with tapas thrown in.

Some of the Sacromonte caves turn into discos during university terms.

Flamenco As elsewhere in Spain, it's difficult to see flamenco that's not geared to tourists – but some shows are more authentic than others and do at least attract Spaniards as well as foreigners. These include the almost-nightly ones at *El Corral del Príncipe* on Campo del Príncipe (1000 ptas) and the Friday and Saturday midnight shows at *Tarantos*, Camino del Sacromonte 9 (2500 ptas). Tarantos' 10 pm shows attract more foreigners. *Jardines Neptuno* on Calle del Arabial has a tourist-oriented flamenco performance at 10.15 pm daily (3300 ptas).

For some of these shows you can prebook tickets at the venues or through hotels and travel agents. Some travellers go to the Sacromonte caves to see flamenco but it is extremely touristy and a bit of a rip-off.

Other Entertainment The notice board in the foyer of La Madraza, on Calle Oficios opposite the Capilla Real, has large posters listing forthcoming cultural events. The *municipal band* often performs at noon or

Sunday at Plaza de las Pasiegas, between the cathedral and Plaza Bib-Rambla. *Centro Cultural Manuel de Falla*, Paseo de los Mártires s/n, near the Alhambra, is the venue for orchestral concerts which take place at around 8 pm, usually once a week.

Things to Buy

A distinctive local craft is marquetry *(taracea)*, which is used on boxes, tables, chess sets and more – the best has shell, silver or mother-of-pearl inlays. Other granadino crafts include embossed leather, guitars, wrought iron, brass and copperware, basket-weaving, textiles and, of course, pottery. Places to look include the Alcaicería, the Albaicín and Cuesta de Gomérez. Watch marquetry experts at work in the shop opposite the Iglesia de Santa María in the Alhambra, and in two shops on Cuesta de Gomérez. There's also a guitar-maker on Cuesta de Gomérez. The government-run Artespaña in the Corral del Carbón has a good range of granadino handicrafts. It's open Monday to Friday from 10 am to 1.30 pm and 4.30 to 8 pm, Saturday from 10 am to 1.30 pm.

Getting There & Away

Air Aviaco, which shares the Iberia office (☎ 22 75 92) at Plaza Isabel la Católica 2, has flights daily to/from Madrid and Barcelona, and three times a week to/from Valencia. The airport (☎ 24 52 00) is 17 km west of the centre on the N-342.

Bus A new bus station has been built on Avenida de Madrid, four km north-west of the centre, but no date has been set for its opening. Meanwhile long-distance buses leave from several bus stations. The main bus station is at Camino de Ronda 97, 1.5 km south-west of the centre. From here Alsina Graells (☎ 25 13 58) runs to Las Alpujarras (see that section later in this chapter for details), Córdoba (seven daily; 3½ hours; 1735 ptas), Sevilla (eight daily; four hours; 2710 ptas), Málaga (12 daily; 2½ hours; 1400 ptas), Jaén, Úbeda, Almuñécar and

Nerja. Nine buses daily to Madrid (six hours; 1875 ptas) also go from here.

Bacoma (☎ 28 42 51) at Avenida de Andaluces 12, beside the train station, has services to Alicante, Valencia, Barcelona and Madrid (four daily).

Buses to Guadix (1½ hours) and Almería (3½ hours) are run by Autedia (☎ 27 87 25) from Calle Rector Martín Ocete 10, off Avenida de la Constitución three blocks towards the centre from the train station.

Train The central RENFE office (☎ 22 31 19) is at Calle Reyes Católicos 63 and is open Monday to Friday from 9 am to 1.30 pm and 4.30 to 7 pm. The station is 1.5 km west of the centre on Avenida de Andaluces, off Avenida de la Constitución. Consigna lockers cost 400 ptas for 24 hours.

Three trains daily run to/from Antequera (1¾ hours) and Sevilla (four to 4½ hours; from 1950 ptas), and Almería (2¾ hours; 1215 ptas) via Guadix (565 ptas). One of the Sevilla services requires a change at Bobadilla. For Málaga and Córdoba (both four hours; 1580 to 1820 ptas) there are two to three trains daily, all involving a change at Bobadilla. For Linares-Baeza there are at least four trains daily.

To Madrid there's a day train taking six hours for 4000 ptas in a 2nd class seat and a night train taking 9½ hours (3300 ptas). There's one train daily to Valencia and Barcelona (13 to 14 hours; 6800 ptas).

Getting Around

The Airport Four airport buses daily (two on Sunday) leave from outside the Banesto bank on Plaza Isabel la Católica. Call ☎ 27 86 77 for information. A taxi will set you back 2200 ptas.

Bus City buses cost 100 ptas. The tourist offices have a handy map showing all routes. To get from the Camino de Ronda bus station to the centre, take bus N 11 from across the road, which has a circular route. Get off at the cathedral stop – you can't see the cathedral itself from the bus. To reach the centre from the train station, walk straight ahead to

Avenida de la Constitución and pick up bus No 3 or 11.

Taxi Taxis line up on Plaza Nueva. Most fares within the city are around 400 to 500 ptas.

AROUND GRANADA

Granada is surrounded by a fertile plain known as La Vega, planted with poplar groves and crops ranging from potatoes and maize to melons and tobacco. The Vega has always been vital to the city and was an inspiration to Federico García Lorca, who was born and, as fate had it, killed here.

Fuente Vaqueros

The house where Lorca was born in 1898, in this village 17 km west of Granada, is now the **Casa Museo Federico García Lorca**. The place really makes his spirit come alive, with numerous charming photos, posters and costumes for plays that he wrote and directed, and paintings illustrating some of his poems. A short video at the end of the visit captures him in action with the touring Teatro Barraca.

The museum is open for guided tours in Spanish (200 ptas) from Tuesday to Sunday hourly from 10 am to 1 pm and 4 to 6 pm. To get there take an Ureña bus from outside Granada train station. On weekdays these depart hourly from 9 am to 9 pm (except 10 am); on weekends the service is two-hourly. There's a timetable at the roundabout in the village centre.

Viznar

To follow the Lorca trail to the bitter end you have to make your way out to this village eight km north-east of the city. When the civil war broke out and the Nationalists took over the city in 1936, Lorca was arrested and taken with hundreds of others to Viznar to be shot. Outside the village, on the road to Alfacar, is the rather unkempt and sometimes locked **Parque Lorca**, with a granite block marking the spot where he is believed to have been killed. His body has never been found. The *Albergue Juvenil Viznar* (☎ 54 33 07) at

Camino de la Fuente Grande s/n is a good modern youth hostel accommodating 111 people, with its own swimming pool. Buses to Viznar leave from the Puerta de Elvira on Plaza del Triunfo, Monday to Friday at 7.30 am, 2.15 and 8 pm, returning from Viznar at 7 and 8 am and 4 pm. On Saturday there's one bus, at 1.30 pm from Granada and 8.30 am from Viznar.

ALHAMA DE GRANADA

The main road west from Granada is the N-342/A-92, which will take you to Sevilla or Málaga. An alternative route to the Málaga area is the C-340 heading south-west via this picturesque ancient spa town 53 km from Granada. Alhama stands at the top of a ravine carved through rolling countryside by the Río Alhama. There's a tourist office (☎ 36 02 71) on Plaza de los Presos uphill from the central Plaza de la Constitución.

The Town The centre is of obvious Muslim origin, with narrow zigzagging streets. Just off Plaza de la Constitución and close to the edge of the gorge is the pretty **Iglesia del Carmen**, dating from the 16th century and with some fine stone carving. The main **Iglesia de la Encarnación** on Plaza de los Presos, also from the 16th century, was a gift from the Catholic Monarchs, whose conquest of Alhama in 1482 was a key early step in their war against Granada. It has a mudéjar pulpit and ceiling, but is only open Tuesday to Friday from noon to 1 pm. There's a **Roman bridge** about one km below the town near the modern bridge used by the C-340 towards Granada.

Balneario Beside the C-340 bridge is the turning to the *balneario* (spa), one km or so down a road through a minor gorge. The warm springs here have been channelled into baths since Roman times, and during the spa's season (10 June to 10 October) you can go inside the Hotel Balneario Alhama de Granada to look at the old Muslim bathhouse (daily from 11.30 am to 1.30 pm; 100 ptas). In the woodland park in front of the hotel is a public open-air pool with lovely hot waters.

A 500 ptas ticket from the hotel admits you to this and a second public pool, the Baño Nuevo, one km along a riverside path. Both pools are open daily, in season, from 11 am to 2 pm and 4 to 7 pm.

Places to Stay *Hostal San José* (☎ 35 01 56) at Plaza de la Constitución 27, has reasonable rooms at 2600 ptas a double, or 3500 ptas with bathroom. At the balneario, *Hotel Baño Nuevo* (☎ 35 00 11) has doubles for 4350 ptas plus IVA, while *Hotel Balneario Alhama de Granada* (same ☎) charges 7800 ptas plus IVA. Both are open from 10 June to 10 October.

Getting There & Away One Alsina Graells bus a day passes through Alhama each way between Granada and Torre del Mar, on the coast 33 km east of Málaga, From Torre del Mar there are frequent buses to Málaga and Nerja.

GUADIX

The N-342/A-92 to Murcia starts off through wild, forested, mountainous country north-east of Granada before entering an arid, almost lunar landscape. The dusty and rather shabby town of Guadix (population 20,000), 55 km from Granada, is famous for its cave dwellings – not prehistoric remnants but modern-day homes of the ordinary townsfolk, nearly half of whom inhabit the town's cave quarter, known as Ermita Nueva or Barrio de Santiago. Cave dwelling is fairly widespread across eastern Granada province, but Guadix has the biggest concentration of underground homes. There's a tourist office (☎ 66 26 65) at Carretera de Granada s/n.

Things to See

Your average late 20th century cave has a whitewashed wall across the front and a chimney – often with TV aerial attached – sticking out the top. Some have many rooms and all mod cons, and are even second homes for city dwellers. The habit of living in them apparently goes back to Muslims expelled from the old town after the Reconquista.

There's a **Cueva Museo** in Ermita Nueva, recreating typical cave life and open Tuesday to Sunday from 10 am to 2 pm and 4 to 5 pm.

Guadix has an interesting sandstone **catedral** designed in Renaissance style by Diego de Siloé the 16th century. It's open for tourist visits daily except Sunday from 11 am to 1 pm and 4 to 7 pm. Also have a look at the remains of the Muslim fort, the **Alcazaba**, with views over the Ermita Nueva. It's open daily except Sunday (and Saturday afternoon) from 9.30 am to 1.30 pm and 3.30 to 6.30 pm.

Places to Stay

Cuevas Pedro Antonio de Alarcón (☎ 66 49 86), a recently opened cave hotel in Barrio de San Torcuato, about one km from the centre, has comfortable modern two-room grottoes, sleeping four, for 7800 ptas. It has a good restaurant, too! Doubles with bath are 3500 ptas at *Hostal Río Verde* (☎ 66 45 81) at Carretera Murcia 1 (near the edge of town), and 4840 ptas at the nearby *Pensión Mulhacén* (☎ 66 07 50), Avenida Buenos Aires 41.

Getting There & Away

Guadix is about 1½ hours from both Granada and Almería by several Autedia buses daily or by three daily trains.

SIERRA NEVADA

The Sierra Nevada, which includes mainland Spain's highest peak, Mulhacén (3478 metres), forms an almost year-round snowy backdrop to Granada. The range has 14 peaks over 3000 metres. A good starting point for walks and drives is the Alpujarras valleys on the south side of the range (see the Las Alpujarras section later in this chapter). The Sierra Nevada ski resort, also known as Solynieve (☎ 24 91 00 or 24 91 19 for information), is on the north flank of the mountains at Pradollano, 33 km south-east of Granada. This is Spain's most southerly ski resort and one of its biggest and liveliest. It was considerably expanded for the world alpine skiing championships held here in 1996.

ANDALUCÍA

The resort has 39 downhill runs (five black, 18 red, 14 blue and two green) totalling 61 km, and 19 lifts. Two cable cars run up from Pradollano (2100 metres) to Borreguiles (2645 metres), where lifts take you to the higher slopes, some of which start almost at the top of 3396-metre Pico del Veleta, the second-highest peak in the Sierra Nevada. The longest run, Águila, drops 1150 metres in its 5.9 km course from Veleta to Pradollano. The season normally lasts from December to April. A ski pass costs from 2725 to 3150 ptas for one day, or 13,950 to 16,000 ptas for six days: the highest prices are from about 24 December to 6 January, from 10 to 25 February and for Semana Santa. Skis and boots can be rented at the stations of the Al-Andalus cable car for 2200/7600 ptas for one/six days; snowboards are 3000/11,000 ptas.

Places to Stay

The *Albergue Juvenil Sierra Nevada* youth hostel (☎ 48 03 05; fax 48 13 77) at Pradollano has 110 places, all in double rooms. At the time of writing it only opens for the ski season. The only other economical accommodation appears to be the *Albergue Universitario* (☎ 48 01 22) above the parador at the top of Pradollano. Reservations are highly advisable at both these places.

Otherwise the best deals are skiing-and-accommodation packages, which you're advised to book at least two weeks ahead through the resort's central booking service (☎ 24 91 11). Unfortunately for those with limited time, most packages are for six days. The cheapest, at the Hotel Telecabina (☎ 24 91 20) or Hostal El Ciervo (☎ 48 04 09), cost from about 24,000 to 38,500 ptas per person with breakfast and lift passes included, or 32,000 to 50,000 ptas with three hours of ski school daily as well. An independently booked double room in one of these hotels costs 7000 to 10,000 ptas. Several Granada hotels also offer ski packages.

Outside the ski season only a few hotels stay open.

Getting There & Away

Viajes Bonal (☎ 27 31 00, 27 24 97) runs a bus to the ski resort from next to the Palacio de Congresos on Paseo del Violón in Granada daily at 9 am. It returns from Pradollano at 5 pm. A taxi from Granada costs about 5000 ptas.

The paved road from Granada continues 13 km past Pradollano right up to the top of Pico del Veleta. A dirt road branching off at about 3250 metres, below the peak, continues over to Capileira in Las Alpujarras, but recently has only been open to those who have obtained permits from local ayuntamientos (see the Mulhacén & Pico del Veleta section under Las Alpujarras for more on this road).

LAS ALPUJARRAS

On the south side of the Sierra Nevada lies one of the oddest crannies of Andalucía, the 70 km long valley – or, rather, jumble of valleys – known as Las Alpujarras (or La Alpujarra). Arid hillsides split by deep ravines alternate with dozens of steep white villages surrounded, oasis-like, by gardens, orchards and woodlands of chestnut, oak, poplar or pine. For centuries one of Spain's most isolated corners, the Alpujarras has experienced a burst of tourism in the last decade or two. But it remains a world unto itself, with a sense of remoteness, timelessness and mystery which is born in part of a bizarre history that saw a flourishing Muslim community replaced en masse by Christian settlers in the 16th century. Reminders of the Muslim past are ubiquitous in the form of the Alpujarras' Berber-style villages and the terracing and irrigation of the land, while the four centuries of Christian habitation have seen some unique folklore and customs evolve.

There are innumerable good walks linking valley villages or heading up into the Sierra Nevada, where Mulhacén (3478 metres) is mainland Spain's highest peak. The best time to be in the high mountains – mid-July to early October – unfortunately doesn't coincide very well with the most pleasant months down in the valley, which are April to June

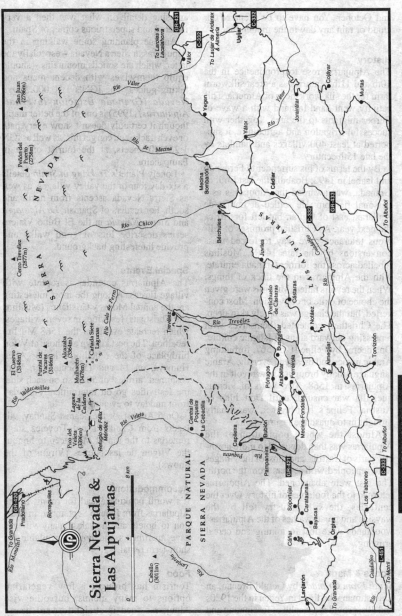

and October. You have to be prepared for cloud or rain any day in the mountains.

History

The Alpujarras rose to prominence in the 10th and 11th centuries as a great silkworm farm for the silk workshops of Almería. This activity went hand in hand with a wave of Berber migrants to the area. Together with successful irrigation and agriculture, it supported at least 400 villages and hamlets by the late 15th century.

By the terms of his surrender to Fernando and Isabel in 1492, Boabdil, the last Emir of Granada, was awarded the Alpujarras as a personal fiefdom. He settled at Laujar de Andarax, east of Ugíjar, but left for Africa the next year. As Christian promises of religious tolerance gave way to forced mass conversions by the late 1490s, Muslims rebelled across the former Granada emirate, with the Alpujarras in the thick of things. When the revolts failed, Muslims were given the choice of exile or conversion. Most converted, but the change was barely skin-deep. The Christians contented themselves with repressing outward signs of Islamic culture. One decree by Felipe II in 1567, forbidding Arabic names and dress and even the Arabic language, finally brought a new revolt in the Alpujarras in 1568. Two years of vicious guerrilla war ensued, until Don Juan of Austria, Felipe's half-brother, was finally brought in to quash the insurrection.

Almost the whole population of the Alpujarras was then deported to more northerly parts of Castilla, and most of the villages were repeopled with settlers from the north. The rest were abandoned. The Alpujarras returned to the footnotes of history. Over the centuries, the silk industry fell by the wayside and great swathes of the Alpujarras' woodlands were lost to mining and cereal growing.

Books & Maps

South From Granada by Gerald Brenan, an Englishman who lived in Yegen in the 1920s and 30s, provides a wealth of fascinating and amusing detail on what was then a very isolated and superstitious corner of Spain.

Anyone planning some walking in the Alpujarras or Sierra Nevada – especially the latter, which are serious mountains – should equip themselves with decent maps and hiking guides. The IGN's 1:50,000 *Sierra Nevada (Granada Estación Invernal-Alpujarras)* (1995) is one of the better maps, though it certainly doesn't show every path or even track. You can get this, as well as IGN 1:25,000 sheets, at the tourist office in Pampaneira.

Lonely Planet's *Trekking in Spain* details a six-day tour of the valley villages, as well as Sierra Nevada ascents from north and south. For readers of Spanish, *La Alpujarra* and *Sierra Nevada* in the El Búho Viajero series describe lots of good walks and provide interesting background.

Special Events

The Alpujarras calendar is replete with village fiestas. Among the most interesting are the annual Moros y Cristianos (Muslims and Christians) festivities in several villages, which recreate events of the 1568 Muslim rebellion. The best known are those at Válor, birthplace of the rebellion's leader Aben Humeya, on 14 and 15 September. With costumed 'armies' of 50 or so on each side, the festivities go on intermittently all day from midday to evening.

On 5 August, or the nearest Sunday, villagers from Capileira and Trevélez stage romerías to the top of Mulhacén to honour the Virgen de las Nieves (Virgin of the Snows).

Accommodation

It's worth booking ahead for rooms in the Alpujarras from June to September. In addition to hotels and hostales, many villages have apartments and houses available for short-term rental.

Food

Tourism has brought a few vegetarian options to many menus, but otherwise Alpujarras food is straightforward hearty country fare, with lots of good meat and local trout. Restaurants tend to be pretty reasonably priced. Trevélez is famous for the quality of its *jamón serrano*, but many other villages produce good hams, too. The *plato alpujarreño*, which you'll find on almost every menu, consists of fried potatoes, fried eggs, sausage, ham and maybe a black pudding, usually for around 600 ptas.

Getting There & Away

Buses to the Alpujarras are run by Alsina Graells (☎ 78 50 02 in Órgiva). From Granada, three buses a day run to Órgiva, Pampaneira (two hours), Bubión, Capileira, then back down to Bubión and Pampaneira and on to Pitres (2¾ hours), with two continuing to Trevélez (3¼ hours) and Bérchules (3¾ hours). There is also a twice-daily Granada-Ugíjar service via Órgiva and Yegen; a Málaga-Órgiva service daily except Sunday; a daily Almería-Ugíjar service; and an Almería-Bérchules bus via Ugíjar and Yegen on Saturday and Sunday.

Órgiva

The main town of the western Alpujarras (population 6000, sometimes spelt Órjiva) is at its most interesting on Thursday morning, when both locals and the Alpujarras' sizeable international community – which has a strong alternative/new age component – converge to buy and sell everything from vegetables and wholefoods to hippie art and jewellery at a colourful market by the Río Chico on the west side of town.

There are banks, some with ATMs, on and near the main street, Calle Dr Fleming, and a post office (postcode 18400) towards the top of the town at Calle Mulhacén 5. The Policía Local (☎ 78 52 12) are at Calle Dr Fleming 1.

Places to Stay & Eat Camping Órgiva (☎ 78 43 07) has a pool and restaurant but only a small, almost shadeless area for camping. Two adults with a car and tent pay 1600 ptas. It's two km south of the centre on the road down to the Río Guadalfeo, and open all year.

> ### Alpujarras Houses
>
> Travellers who have been to Morocco may notice a marked resemblance between villages in the Alpujarras and those in the Atlas mountains, from where the Alpujarran style was introduced in Muslim times by Berber settlers.
>
> Most houses are of two storeys, with the lower one used for storage and animals. The characteristic *terraos* or flat roofs, with their protruding chimney pots, consist of a layer of *launa* (a type of clay) packed on to flat stones which are laid on beams of chestnut, ash or pine. Nowadays there's often a sheet of plastic between the stones and the launa for extra waterproofing. Whitewash is a fairly modern introduction too: some poorer Alpujarras villages remain stone-coloured as they all used to be. ■

Hostal Mirasol (☎ 78 51 08) at Avenida González Robles 3 overlooking the Thursday market site, has adequate singles/doubles with bath for 1500/3000 ptas plus IVA. The adjacent *Hotel Mirasol* (same ☎ and address) has newer, more comfortable rooms with TV for 3000/5000 ptas plus IVA.

Pensión Alma Alpujarreña (☎ 78 40 85), Avenida González Robles 49, just below the traffic lights at the foot of Calle Dr Fleming, has singles/doubles for 1700/3500 ptas, or doubles with bath for 4000 ptas, and a three course menú for 900 ptas plus IVA.

La Zahona bakery on Calle Dr Fleming does good cakes and pastries, which go well with a drink at the pavement tables of the adjacent *Café Heladería Galindo*.

Pampaneira, Bubión & Capileira

This trio of villages 14 to 20 km north-east of Órgiva, on the flank of the highest part of the Sierra Nevada, are three of the prettiest, most dramatically sited – and most visited by tourists – in Las Alpujarras. Their houses seem to clamber over each other in an effort not to slide down into the deep, steep Barranco de Poqueira ravine, while streets decked with flowery balconies climb haphazardly between them. Given the somewhat Himalayan character of this landscape, it's not

ANDALUCÍA

entirely surprising that there's a small Tibetan Buddhist monastery, Osel Ling (Place of the Clear Light), high above the valley opposite Pampaneira.

Pampaneira (altitude 1050 metres) and Bubión (1300 metres) have about 350 inhabitants each; Capileira (1440 metres) has 600. Capileira is the best base for walks in the surrounding valleys and mountains.

Information Parque Natural Sierra Nevada Centro de Información (☎ 76 31 27), on Pampaneira's square, Plaza de la Libertad, appears to be the only tourist office in the Alpujarras. It has a wealth of information on the Alpujarras and the 1400 sq km Parque Natural Sierra Nevada, which covers the entire mountain range. It's open daily from at least 10.30 am to 2 pm and 4.30 to 7 pm, and English is spoken. There's also a small information kiosk by the main road in Capileira.

La General, at the end of Calle Doctor Castilla in Capileira, is the only bank in any of these villages. It has an ATM. All three villages have small supermarkets.

Things to See All three villages – like many others in Las Alpujarras – have 16th century mudéjar-style churches (open only at Mass times, which are posted on the doors). They also have plentiful craft shops, some selling fashions from Bali and pottery from all over Andalucía as well as the more homespun Alpujarras cotton rugs, colourful and affordable descendants of a textile tradition that goes back to Muslim times. All three villages have small weaving workshops which you can poke you head into.

Activities Organisations such as Nevadensis, which runs the tourist office at Pampaneira, Rustic Blue (☎ 76 33 81) and Global Spirit (☎ 76 30 54) in Bubión offer activities such as guided hikes or treks, mountain bike trips, horse riding and climbing.

Walks From Capileira you can drop down to three bridges over the Río Poqueira in the gorge below the village. From the top one a

trail climbs the far bank to La Cebadilla hamlet and a power station (1½ hours from Capileira). From the middle and lower bridges paths descend the far side of the valley: branches lead back across and up to Bubión and Pampaneira, or you could carry on down to lower villages such as Soportújar or Carataunas, or even Órgiva (four to five hours), and get a bus back. You can walk from Capileira to Trevélez in about five hours by taking the broad track heading to the right off the Mulhacén road at the third switchback above Capileira (four km from the village and a couple of hundred metres after the 8 Km marker).

From Bubión a marked six-km section of the GR-7 long-distance footpath leads southeast across to Pitres in the next valley. It's signposted just down the main road from the Restaurant Teide (see also the Mulhacén & Pico del Veleta section later in this chapter).

Places to Stay & Eat – Pampaneira Two good hostales face each other across Calle José Antonio at the entrance to the village. *Hostal Pampaneira* (☎ 76 30 02) has doubles (only) with bathroom for 3000 ptas, and its own restaurant, which is the cheapest in the village (trout or pork chops at 500 or 550 ptas). *Hostal Ruta del Mulhacén* (☎ 76 30 10) has singles/doubles with bath for 2500/3500 ptas. Of the three restaurants just along the street on Plaza de la Libertad, *Restaurante Casa Diego*, with a pleasant upstairs terrace, is a good choice. Main dishes are from 650 to 1100 ptas: trout with ham, and local ham and eggs, are among the cheaper dishes.

Places to Stay & Eat – Bubión *Hostal Las Terrazas* (☎ 76 30 34), at Plaza del Sol 7 below the main road, has pleasant though smallish singles/doubles with bath for 2350/3300 ptas plus IVA. The *Villa Turística de Bubión* (☎ 76 31 11), just off the main road at the top of the village, is the only top-end place in the Alpujarras. Rooms, at 14,000 ptas plus IVA, have their own kitchens and fireplaces. Rustic Blue (see under Activities earlier in this section) offers houses to rent here and elsewhere in the Alpujarras.

Restaurante Teide by the main road is good, with a three course menú for 1100 ptas including a drink. À la carte there are several mains under 800 ptas, including trout with ham. Add IVA to prices. Up the road are a few convivial bars such as the pub-like *Café Bar ¿A Dónde Vamos?*, and *Taberna Ca' Boabdil/Balcón de Bubión* which plays good music.

Places to Stay & Eat – Capileira *Mesón Hostal Poqueira* (☎ 76 30 48), just off the main road at Calle Doctor Castilla 6, has good singles/doubles with bath for 1800/3000 ptas, and a popular restaurant. *Hostal Atalaya* (☎ 76 30 25), 100 metres down the main road at Calle Perchel 3, has the same prices but is smaller and less appealing. Or there's the slightly dearer *Hostal Paco López* (☎ 76 30 76), just up the main road at Carretera de la Sierra 5. *Casa Rosendo* (☎ 76 30 70) a little further up the road has apartments for three to six people at 8000 to 10,000 ptas plus IVA. *Cervecería Capi* on Calle Doctor Castilla does generous raciones of things like albóndigas (meatballs) or carne en salsa for around 600 ptas. *Casa Ibero* below the church (follow the signs from there) offers a change from normal Alpujarras fare with a menu that ranges from hot pitta bread with cheese and ham (450 ptas) or couscous several ways (675 to 1050 ptas) to lamb with ginger sauce (1100 ptas).

Mulhacén & Pico del Veleta
Rising above the top of the Poqueira valley, Mulhacén is named after Moulay (Emir) Abu al-Hasan, father of Boabdil. A 40 km road over the Sierra Nevada from Capileira to the Sierra Nevada ski resort on the north side of the range passes within one km of its summit. This is said to be the highest road in Europe. Blocked by snow for much of the year, in an average year it's passable from about mid-July to early October. It's manageable, with a bit of care, in an ordinary car, but to drive right over it you need a permit from a local

ayuntamiento – which in Las Alpujarras means Pampaneira, Bubión or Capileira. The permits are not given out regardless, so if you want one, think of a good reason why you have to go this way!

Without a permit, at the time of writing, you can drive 20 km up from Capileira to a checkpoint at about 2800 metres, from where it's around 2½ hours walk to the top of Mulhacén. A good base for those entirely dependent on their feet is the *Refugio Félix Méndez* (☎ 34 33 49), a 60-place mountain refuge at around 3000 metres, a short distance off the road three km west of Mulhacén (about seven hours from Capileira). The refuge is normally open from April or May to October and serves meals; dinner, bunk and breakfast comes to around 2500 ptas. It's worth ringing ahead to check that it won't be full.

Another walker's approach to Mulhacén and the other high Sierra Nevada peaks is from Trevélez, via the Trevélez valley and the Cañada de Siete Lagunas, a lake-dotted basin below the east side of Mulhacén. The important thing on this route is to steer clear of the boggy bottom of the valley of the Río Culo de Perro (Dog's Arse River). It's possible to reach the peak in one hard day, but better is to camp in the Cañada, five or six hours up from Trevélez.

Pitres & Around
Pitres is almost as pretty as the villages in the Poqueira gorge but less touristy. It has a bank (no ATM) on the main square. *Camping El Balcón de Pitres* (☎ 76 61 11), by the GR-421 on the west side of the village, charges around 1600 ptas for two adults with a car and tent. It has a decent restaurant and a swimming pool. *Refugio Los Albergues* (☎ 34 31 76), two minutes walk (signposted) down a path from the GR-421 on the east side of the village, is a small, privately run hikers' hostel, with bunks at 800 ptas, one double room for 2500 ptas, and an equipped kitchen. It's open all year except 10 January to 15 February. The friendly German owner is full of information on the locality and the many good walks in it. *Fonda Sierra Nevada* on

Pitres' plaza has singles/doubles at 1200/2400 ptas. There's a handful of cafés and restaurants around the plaza.

Trevélez

Trevélez (population 800; altitude 1476 metres), set in a valley almost as impressive as the Poqueira gorge, claims to be the highest village in Spain (Taüll in Cataluña, at 1495 metres, might have something to say about that), and produces some of the country's best jamón serrano. Hams are trucked in from around Spain for curing in Trevélez's cold, dry mountain air.

First impressions of Trevélez are disappointing as you're confronted by a welter of jamón and souvenir shops along the main road, but a wander into the upper parts reveals a lively village of typical Alpujarran quaintness. There's a bank, La General, on Plaza Iglesia, but no ATM.

Places to Stay & Eat *Restaurante González* (☎ 85 85 33) on Plaza de Don Francisco Abellán, by the main road at the foot of the village, has doubles with shared bathroom for 2500 ptas and a good restaurant with trout and potatoes for 600 ptas. There are three or four other places with rooms just along the road.

Hostal Fernando (☎ 85 85 65), Pista del Barrio Medio s/n, by the road up towards the top of the village, has decent doubles with bath for 3000 ptas, or two-person apartments with terraces for 4000 ptas. Past here, the road reaches Plaza Barrio Medio, where there are signs to the *Hotel La Fragua* (☎ 85 85 73), Calle San Antonio 4, with the most comfortable rooms in town at 5500 ptas with bath. Its restaurant, *Mesón La Fragua*, a short walk away, offers relatively exotic fare such as partridge in walnut sauce (1400 ptas) as well as the usual trout, ham, pork etc. Between the hotel and the restaurant, *Café Bar Castellón* on Calle Cárcel has singles/doubles for 1200/2400 ptas.

Mesón Haraicel just above Plaza de Don Francisco Abellán has a few outside tables and good food which includes trout and meat main courses from 750 ptas. Jamón de

Trevélez crops up on every menu. If you want some to take away, the shops up in the village tend to be cheaper than those on the main road. You should be able to get one kg for 1000 ptas or less, or a whole ham for around 7000 ptas (double for the special ibérico and pata negra varieties).

East of Trevélez

Seven km south of Trevélez, the GR-421 crosses the low Portichuelo de Cástaras pass and turns east into a barer landscape which gets even barer still as you head on towards Almería province. There are, however, oases of greenery around the villages, and these central and eastern parts of the Alpujarras, though less obviously picturesque than the west, are still impressive areas which would reward those with time to explore them.

Bérchules, 17 km from Trevélez, is an attractive village set in a green valley which stretches a long way back into the hills. *Casa Resu* (☎ 76 90 92) in the centre at Calle Iglesia 18 has basic singles/doubles for 1000/2000 ptas. At **Mecina Bombarón**, six km east, *Los Molinos* (☎ 85 10 76) has attractive apartments for six to eight people in converted flour mills near the Río de Mecina just north-east of the village.

Five km beyond is **Yegen**, where Gerald Brenan's house, just off the main plaza, has a plaque. Yegen could be a good walking or touring base even if you're not a Brenanophile. *Café-Bar La Fuente* on the plaza has singles/doubles for 1300/2600 ptas; *El Parador de El Tinao* (☎ 85 12 12) on the road has doubles with bath for 3500 ptas, also four and six-person apartments for 4800 to 7200 ptas; *El Rincón de Yegen* (☎ 85 12 70) by the road on the east edge of the village has more expensive apartments.

At **Válor**, a peaceful place between two ravines five km east of Yegen, *Hostal Las Perdices* (☎ 85 18 21) on Calle Torrecilla has good rooms with bath for 3000 ptas a double. Parts of the landscape below Yegen and Válor have a particularly bleak and moon-like quality.

Ugíjar (population 3000), seven km south-east of Válor, is the main market town hereabouts, with two hostales. From here the Alpujarras, and the C-322, continue east into Almería province.

THE COAST

Granada's 80 km coastline is rugged and cliff-lined, with the coastal N-340 highway winding up and down between scattered towns and villages. The tourism industry calls this the Costa Tropical because of the crops such as sugar cane, custard apples, avocadoes and mangoes that are grown where the coastal plain broadens out a bit. The N-323 from Granada arrives near the coast just west of Motril after threading through an impressive gorge carved by the Río Guadalfeo. East of uninspiring Motril, the mountains often come right down to the shore, the settlements are mostly drab and the beaches shingly.

West of Motril the terrain is a bit less abrupt and there are a couple of beach towns worth a halt if the mood takes you.

Salobreña

Salobreña's huddle of white houses rises on a crag between the N-340 and the sea, just two km west of the N-323 junction. Up at the top is an impressive Muslim castle, open for visits, and below is a long dark-sand beach. There's a tourist office (☎ 82 83 45) on Plaza de Goya, and half a dozen hostales, some of them pretty cheap. *Camping El Peñón* (☎ 61 02 07) by the beach is nicer than the camping ground at Almuñécar, but closes from November to March.

Almuñécar

Fifteen km further west, Almuñécar appears from the road as an uninviting agglomeration of apartment blocks, but it has a more attractive older heart beneath the 16th century Castillo San Miguel. Popular mainly with Spanish tourists, Almuñécar is a bright and not-too-expensive resort, though the town beaches are pebbly. The area is also a bit of a scuba-diving centre and there are three or four outfits locally which will take divers out or teach beginners.

Orientation & Information The bus station is at Avenida Juan Carlos I 1, just south of the N-340 and north of the old centre. The tourist office (☎ 63 11 25) is in the Palacete La Najarra on Avenida de Europa, just back from the east end of Playa de San Cristóbal.

Things to See On Playa de San Cristóbal is an aviary with 120 types of tropical bird, named the **Parque Ornitológico Loro Sexi**. *Loro* means parrot and Sexi was the Phoenician name for Almuñécar. Antiquity-lovers should visit the **Museo Arqueológico**, in a set of Roman galleries called the Cueva de Siete Palacios, with local Phoenician, Roman and Islamic finds plus a rare, 3500 year old Egyptian amphora, and seek out the **Phoenician necropolis** and **Roman aqueduct**.

Places to Stay The cheaper places are a few blocks south of the bus station in the streets around Plaza Rosa. Among them are the basic but clean *Hostal Victoria* (☎ 63 00 22), Plaza Victoria 6, which has doubles with bath at 2700 ptas (3200 ptas in the high season); the better *Hostal Victoria II* (☎ 63 17 34), Plaza Victoria 22, with doubles from 2700 to 4200 ptas; and the good *Hostal Plaza Damasco* (☎ 63 01 65), Calle Cerrajeros 8, charging 3500 to 5000 ptas plus IVA. A few more up-market places are on Avenida de Europa, near the tourist office, and Playa de San Cristóbal.

Getting There & Away Several buses a day run along the coast to Nerja, Málaga and Almería, and inland to Granada, from Avenida Juan Carlos.

Jaén Province

The province of Jaén, in the north-east of Andalucía, is one of the world's largest olive-growing regions. It is divided by the Río Guadalquivir, which rises in the mountainous Parque Natural de Cazorla, Segura y

Las Villas in the east of the province, flowing initially northward, then west.

South of the river lies the provincial capital Jaén. Less than 60 km away are the beautiful towns of Úbeda and Baeza, and it is well worth a detour to visit them. Both retain traces of Roman, Islamic and Gothic periods, but are most characterised by their Renaissance architecture.

The telephone code for Jaén province is ☎ 953.

JAÉN

Originally a Carthaginian town, Jaén was captured by the Romans, who exploited its silver mines and named it Auringis. In Muslim times it became the capital of the statelet of Jayyan, taken in 1246 by Fernando III's Christian armies, and in the late 15th century it was a base for the final Christian campaign against the Granada emirate.

Orientation

Avenida de Madrid and Paseo de la Constitución are the two main streets, with Plaza de la Constitución marking the centre of town. Most of the sights are within a few minutes walk of the pedestrianised old town, which is immediately north-west of the cathedral. Between Calle de la Maestra, which begins at Plaza de Santa María, next to the cathedral, and Plaza de la Constitución you will find most of the low-budget accommodation.

Information

The tourist office (☎ 22 27 37) is a few minutes walk from the bus station, at Calle Arquitecto del Berges 1, just off Paseo de la Estación. It is open Monday to Friday from 9 am to 8 pm and Saturday from 9 am to 2 pm.

There is no shortage of banks along Paseo de la Estación and around the Plaza de la Constitución; many of them have ATMs. The central post office is on Plaza de los Jardinillos (postcode 23080). In a medical emergency call ☎ 061 or the Cruz Roja on ☎ 25 15 40. The general hospital is just west of the Museo Provincial at Avenida del Ejército Español 14.

Things to See

Built on the site of a former mosque, work on the enormous Renaissance **catedral** first started in 1492 and continued until its completion in 1802. It is open daily from 8.30 am to 1 pm and 4.30 to 7 pm. The cathedral museum is open on Saturday and Sunday from 11 am to 1 pm.

The 11th century **baños árabes** – the largest baths to survive in Spain – were discovered earlier this century and restored in the 1980s. They were found beneath the **Palacio de Villardompado**, built in the 16th century and now a museum of arts and crafts. Both the baths and the museum are open Tuesday to Friday from 10 am to 2 pm and 5 to 8 pm, Saturday and Sunday from 10.30 am to 2 pm. Entry is 100 ptas (free with an EU passport).

The **Museo Provincial**, at Paseo de la Estación 29, is renowned for its fine collection of Iberian sculptures dating from the 5th century BC. It is open Tuesday to Saturday from 9 am to 2 pm and Sunday from 10 am to 2 pm. Entry is 100 ptas (free with an EU passport).

The **Iglesia de la Magdalena**, on Calle Santo Domingo, is Jaén's oldest church and was built over an earlier mosque. Gothic in style, with a 15th century façade, it is open daily from 6 to 8 pm.

Castillo de Santa Catalina, on the hill to the west of town, offers spectacular panoramic views of the city and the olive groves beyond. There is no bus, but you can walk there in just over an hour from the centre of town, using a path up the hill which begins where Calle de Buenavista meets the Carretera de Circunvalación, or take a taxi for 800 ptas. The castle ruins are open Thursday to Tuesday from 10.30 am to 1.30 pm.

Places to Stay

Most hotels are well signposted from the road.

For budget travellers, *Hostal Carlos V* (☎ 22 20 91), at Avenida de Madrid 4, is the nearest pensión to the bus station, with basic singles/doubles for 2300/3200 ptas.

Hostal Martín (☎ 22 06 33), just off the

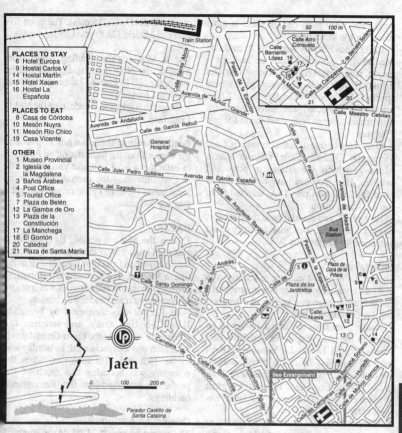

PLACES TO STAY
6 Hotel Europa
9 Hostal Carlos V
14 Hostal Martín
15 Hotel Xauen
16 Hostal La
 Española

PLACES TO EAT
8 Casa de Córdoba
10 Mesón Nuyra
11 Mesón Río Chico
19 Casa Vicente

OTHER
1 Museo Provincial
2 Iglesia de
 la Magdalena
3 Baños Árabes
4 Post Office
5 Tourist Office
7 Plaza de Belén
12 La Gamba de Oro
13 Plaza de la
 Constitución
17 La Manchega
18 El Gorrión
20 Catedral
21 Plaza de Santa María

Train Station

Paseo de la Estación

Calle Santa Alicia

Avenida de Muñoz Grande

Avenida de Andalucía

Calle de García Rebull

General
Hospital

Calle Juan Pedro Gutiérez

Avenida del Ejército Español

Calle del Sagrado

Calle de Fermín Palma

Avenida de Madrid

Calle del Arquitecto Bergés

Paseo de Castilla

Bus
Station

Plaza de
Coca de la
Piñera

Calle de San Andrés

Calle Santo Domingo

Calle de la Estación

Plaza de los
Jardinillos

Calle Gracia

Calle Nueva

Carretera de Circunvalación

Calle de Buenvista

Calle Aguilas

Calle Almendros

See Enlargement

Jaén

0   100   200 m

Parador Castillo de
Santa Catalina

C de Bernabé Soriano

Calle Arro
Consuelo

Calle
Bernardo
López

Calle de la Maestra

Calle las Campanas

Calle Maestro Cebrian

0   50   100 m

Calle las Campanas

Calle de Bernabé Soriano

Calle de Muñoz Garnica

C de Bernabé Soriano

ANDALUCÍA

south-east side of Plaza de la Constitución at Calle Cuatro Torres 5, is shabby but adequate, with basic rooms for 2000/3000 ptas.

Hostal La Española (☎ 23 02 54), just north-west of the cathedral at Calle Bernardo López 9, has the most character, with rooms for 1600/3200 ptas.

A step up in quality is *Hotel Europa* (☎ 22 27 00), just off the junction of Avenida de Madrid and Avenida de Granada at Plaza de Belén, where decent rooms with bath cost 4550/6500 ptas plus IVA.

Better still is *Hotel Xauen* (☎ 26 40 11), just off the south-west side of Plaza de la

Constitución at Plaza Deán Mazas 3. Rooms cost 5200/7000 ptas plus IVA.

But if one place calls for a real splurge it's the *Parador Castillo de Santa Catalina* (☎ 23 00 00). Doubles cost 16,000 ptas plus IVA.

Places to Eat

There is no shortage of bars and restaurants serving traditional food at reasonable prices.

Casa de Córdoba, directly opposite Hotel Europa, is hugely popular and always busy, with a restaurant at the back of the bar. Its speciality is solomillo a la pimienta (pepper steak) for 1000 ptas, though there is a set menu for the same price.

Calle Nueva, a tiny street off Avenida de Madrid, just north of Plaza de la Constitución, is jam-packed with places to eat and drink. If you're looking for somewhere special, *Mesón Nuyra* and *Méson Río Chico* are highly respected; the latter also has a downstairs taverna with a set menu for just 700 ptas.

One of the best restaurants in town is *Casa Vicente* (☎ 23 22 22), Calle Francisco Martín Mora 1, which specialises in pork and venison. Here you can have a three course meal for 2500 ptas plus IVA, selected from the à-la-carte menu.

Best of all, you could dine at the *parador*, though a set meal with wine is likely to set you back 4000 ptas plus IVA.

Entertainment
One of Jaén's most endearing traditions is that most bars give free tapas with drinks. In Calle Nueva there is a spectacular seafood bar, *La Gamba de Oro*.

Aside from that, the best bars are to be found in the old town, in the pedestrianised streets around Hostal La Española. Don't miss *El Gorrión*, the oldest house in Jaén, dating back to 1808, and *La Manchega*, both in Calle Arco Consuelo. They have a great atmosphere and good tapas; the latter has staple fare for 500 ptas.

There is very little in the way of entertainment other than eating and drinking, so it's not exactly a destination for serious nightclubbing. Anyone desperate for a disco could try the university zone, between Avenida de Muñoz Grande and the train station.

Getting There & Away
Bus The bus station is on Plaza de Coca de la Piñera, off Paseo de la Estación. There are 10 buses a day to Baeza (445 ptas) and Úbeda (535 ptas), three a day to Cazorla (930 ptas) and 13 a day to Granada (870 ptas).

Train The train station is at the northern end of Paseo de la Estación. There is one train a day to Cádiz (3125 ptas) via Córdoba (1080 ptas) and Sevilla (2085 ptas). There are five a day to Madrid (2830 ptas).

Car & Motorcycle Heading south from Madrid, the N-IV goes straight to Bailén, where the N-323 leads to Jaén and continues south to Granada.

To get to Baeza and Úbeda, take the N-321 from Jaén.

Getting Around There is a bus stop around the corner from the train station on Paseo de la Estación: a No 1 will take you to Plaza de la Constitución – the central point for all local buses – for 150 ptas, or you can get a taxi for 400 ptas.

BAEZA
During the Muslim period, Bayyasa, as it was then known, was the capital of a region which extended from the Guadalquivir to the Sierra Morena. The second most important town in the region after Jaén, it was a centre of commerce renowned for its bazars.

In 1227 it was conquered by Fernando III's Christian army, and became the Christians' capital of the upper Guadalquivir until Jaén was also reclaimed. Its heyday was in the 16th and 17th centuries, when the economy was booming and much of the profit was ploughed into fine Renaissance buildings.

Orientation & Information
The tourist office (☎ 74 04 44) is south of Paseo de la Constitución – the centre of town – on Plaza del Pópulo. It is open Monday to Friday from 9 am to 2.30 pm and Saturday from 10 am to 12.30pm.

The main commercial streets are Calle de San Pablo and Calle de San Francisco, which meet at Plaza de España. All the sights are within walking distance from here.

The local feria takes place from 10 to 15 August.

Things to See
Plaza de Leones, named after the fountain in its centre, is surrounded by Renaissance architecture such as the 16th century **antigua**

carnicería (old butcher's shop), the **Casa del Pópulo**, the **Puerta de Jaén** and the **Arco de Villalar**.

Nearby, the **ayuntamiento**, on Paseo Cardenal Benavides, is a national monument. It was once both courthouse and prison, and is considered one of the most valuable examples of Andalucían plateresque. It is open Monday to Friday from 9 am to 2 pm.

On the south side of Plaza Santa María is the **Santa Iglesia Catedral**, originally constructed on the site of a mosque. Its main façade was built in the 16th century. The oldest part is the Puerta de la Luna, built in 13th century Gothic-mudéjar style. The cathedral is open daily from 10.30 am to 1 pm and 5 to 7 pm.

Close by, the **Palacio de Jabalquinto**, built in flamboyant Gothic style, is open Monday to Friday from 11 am to 1 pm and 5 to 7 pm.

Places to Stay & Eat

Pensión El Patio (☎ 74 02 00), at Calle Conde Romanones 13, has singles/doubles with shower for 1500/3000 ptas. *Hostal Comercio* (☎ 74 01 00), at Calle San Pablo 21, has rooms for 1400/2800 ptas, and a good-value restaurant. The most up-market place in town is *Hotel Baeza* (☎ 74 81 30), at Calle Concepción 3, with doubles for 9000 ptas plus IVA.

For places to eat, head for the bars around Paseo de la Constitución.

Getting There & Away

The bus station (☎ 74 04 68) is a short walk north of the town centre on Avenida Alcalde Puche Pardo. At least seven buses a day run between Baeza and Úbeda. The nearest train station is Linares-Baeza, 13 km away. There are connecting buses for most trains from Monday to Saturday.

ÚBEDA

Known by the Romans as Bétula and by the Muslims as Ubbadat-al-Arab, the town was reclaimed by the Christians in 1234. It flourished in the 16th century as a producer of textiles, and as a result of its prosperity the architect Andrés de Vandelvira was appointed to design the Renaissance buildings which remain its chief attraction today.

Information

The tourist office (☎ 75 08 97) is housed in the ayuntamiento on Plaza de los Caídos, and the bus station (☎ 75 21 57) is west of town on Calle San José. Most low-budget accommodation is around Avenida Ramón y Cajal, near the bus station. All the sights are within walking distance. The Fiestas de San Miguel take place from 27 September to 4 October.

Things to See

At the centre of town is Plaza de Vázquez Molina, featuring the **Sacra Capilla del Salvador** – the most spectacular church in Úbeda – the **Palacio del Marqués de Mancera**, built by the Viceroy of Peru, and the church of **Santa María de los Reales Alcázares**. Other sights include the Cárcel del Obispo – the Bishop's prison – and the *antiguo pósito* (old communal granary).

Places to Stay & Eat

Hostal Castillo (☎ 75 04 30), at Calle Ramón y Cajal 20, has basic singles/doubles for 1600/2800 ptas, and its own restaurant. *Hostal Victoria* (☎ 75 29 52), halfway between the Iglesia de San Isidoro and the bullring, at Calle Alaminos 5, has rooms with bath for 2500/4000 ptas.

In the old town itself, the luxurious *Palacio de la Rambla* (☎ 75 01 96), at Plaza del Marqués 1, has doubles for 13,000 ptas, but you do need to book in advance. *Parador Condestable Dávalos* (☎ 75 03 45), on Plaza de Vázquez de Molina, has doubles for 16,500 ptas plus IVA, and a superb restaurant with a fixed menu for 3000 ptas plus IVA. Otherwise, most of the low-budget restaurants can be found along Avenida Ramón y Cajal.

PARQUE NATURAL DE CAZORLA, SEGURA Y LAS VILLAS

This is Spain's largest protected area (2140 sq km) and one of its most beautiful, composed of a jumble of sierras – the highest peaks are over 2000 metres – covered in forest and riven by deep gorges and river valleys. The Río Guadalquivir rises towards the south of the park and flows north through the 24 km long Embalse del Tranco reservoir before turning west. The park's wildlife is unusually visible: you might actually *see* ibex, boar, mouflon (wild sheep) and deer if you get out and walk a bit.

The town of Cazorla is a good access point, though to get around the park you need your own wheels – or at least a good pair of feet – as there are virtually no buses. Aside from the natural attractions, the spectacular hill-top villages of Hornos and Segura de la Sierra towards the north of the park are well worth heading for. The best weather is usually from late April to early June and September to early October.

Information

Quercus (☎ 72 01 15), on Plaza de la Constitución, where the buses arrive in Cazorla, can sell you 4WD tours. The Oficina del Parque Natural (☎ 72 01 25), at Calle Martínez Falero 11, Cazorla, can provide you with a map and a list of facilities, or you could go straight to the Torre del Vinagre visitor centre (☎ 72 01 02), inside the park at Carretera del Tranco, Km 18 (about five km south of the Embalse del Tranco).

Places to Stay

There is no shortage of accommodation in Cazorla itself. *Hostal Betis* (☎ 72 05 40), at Plaza Corredera 19, and *Hostal Guadalquivir* (☎ 72 02 68), at Calle Nueva 6, are among the cheapest, with basic doubles for 2500/2800 ptas. There are quite a few mid-range hotels, too: *Andalucía* (☎ 72 12 68), at Calle Martínez Falero 42, has doubles for 4700 plus IVA. Most of the bars are around Plaza Santa María.

There are also a number of lodgings and camping grounds within the park itself, including the *Parador El Adelantado* (☎ 72 10 75), on the road east from Cazorla, with doubles for 12,500 plus IVA, and a variety of cheaper places.

Getting There & Away

There are three buses a day to Cazorla's Plaza de la Constitución from Úbeda, at least one a day from Jaén and one a day from Granada. To get there from Úbeda by car or motorcycle, take the N-322 east to Torreperogil, then turn south-east to Peal de Becerro and Cazorla.

Almería Province

Andalucía's easternmost province is its sunniest, with over 3000 hours of sunshine a year. It's also the most parched part of Spain, with large expanses of rocky desert, particularly east of Almería city.

Isolated and for a long time forgotten and impoverished, the province has used its main natural resource – sunshine – to stage a bit of a comeback in recent decades, partly through tourism and partly through intensive cultivation of vegetables, fruit and flowers in plastic greenhouses, an oppressive sight which you can't fail to notice as you travel through. The 'capital' of *plasticultura* is the ugly, sprawling town of El Ejido, west of Almería, which claims to have more banks per person than anywhere in Spain.

The telephone code for Almería province is ☎ 950.

ALMERÍA

As the chief port of the Córdoba caliphate and, later, capital of an independent taifa, the Islamic city of Al-Mariyat grew wealthy on a textile industry which wove silk from the silkworms of the Alpujarras. At its peak it may have numbered almost as many people as the 155,000 who call Almería home today. The Alcazaba, the large fort dominating the city, is the chief reminder of this distant heyday. Devastated by an earthquake in 1522, Almería only began to recover in the 19th century. Today it's a mostly modern city and the hub of a mining and vegetable, fruit and flower-growing region – a likeable and lively enough place to linger for a night or so.

Orientation

The city centre lies between the Alcazaba in the west and the Rambla de Belén, a dry river bed being transformed into a strip of park, in the east. Paseo de Almería, cutting northwest from Rambla de Belén to the intersection called Puerta de Purchena, is the main artery.

Information

The helpful tourist office (☎ 27 43 55) at Parque de Nicolás Salmerón s/n is open Monday to Friday from 9 am to 7 pm, Saturday from 9 am to 1 pm.

There are numerous banks on Paseo de Almería. The post office (postcode 04080) is at Plaza de Juan Cassinello 1. The Policía Municipal (☎ 21 00 19, or in an emergency 092) are at Calle Santos Zárate 11. The main hospital is the Hospital Torrecárdenas (☎ 21 21 00) at Pasaje Torrecárdenas s/n in the north of the city.

Alcazaba

Though earthquakes and other ravages of time have spared little of its apparently once Alhambra-like internal splendour, the hilltop Alcazaba is still a large and impressive monument. Founded in the first half of the 10th century by the great Córdoba caliph Abd ar-Rahman III, its hefty walls and towers dominate the city and command great views when you get up atop them. The entrance, off Calle Almanzor, is open daily: from mid-June to September, 10 am to 2 pm and 5 to 8.30 pm; otherwise 9 am to 1.30 pm and 3.30 to 6.30 pm. Entry costs 250 ptas (free to EU passport holders).

The Alcazaba consists of three compounds (recintos). The lowest, the Primer Recinto, is today mainly gardens. Originally it served as a military camp and a refuge for the population in times of siege. From its top corner, the Muralla de Jairán (or Cortina de la Hoya) crosses the valley north of the Alcazaba. This wall was part of extra city defences built in the 11th century by Jairan, the first ruler of the Almería taifa.

The Segundo Recinto was the heart of the Alcazaba. By the wall at its east end is the Ermita de San Juan chapel, converted from a mosque by the Catholic Monarchs, who took Almería in 1489. On the north side of the recinto is the Muslim rulers' palace, the Palacio de Almotacín. The Ventana de la Odalisca (Concubine's Window) here gets its name from a slave girl who, the legend goes, jumped to her death after her Christian prisoner lover had been thrown from the window when caught attempting to escape.

The Tercer Recinto, at the north-west end of the Alcazaba, is a fortress added by the Catholic Monarchs. It's in much better shape than the rest of the Alcazaba: no doubt its sturdy stone walls and round towers proved more earthquake-resistant.

Catedral

Almería's weighty cathedral is at the heart of the old part of the city, a tangle of narrow streets south of the Alcazaba. Begun in 1524 to replace Al-Mariyat's main mosque, which had been converted into a cathedral, then wrecked by the 1522 earthquake, its fortress-like appearance – with six towers – was dictated by raids from Barbary pirates from North Africa. The north façade on Plaza de la Catedral is an elaborate mid-16th century creation by Juan de Orea.

The spacious interior, entered by the Puerta de Perdones on Calle Velázquez, has a Gothic ribbed ceiling and makes use of jasper and local marble in some of its trimmings. The chapel behind the main altar contains the tomb of Bishop Villalán, founder of the cathedral, whose broken-nosed image is another work of de Orea, as is the Sacristía Mayor with its fine carved stone roof, windows and arches.

The cathedral is open for tourist visits Monday to Friday from 10 am to 2 pm and 3.30 to 6 pm, Saturday from 10 am to 3 pm. The fee of 300 ptas includes a guide leaflet.

Museums

Almería's city museum is closed pending the construction of a new building on Plaza de la Estación. In the meantime its prehistoric collection, with finds from Los Millares (see

ANDALUCÍA

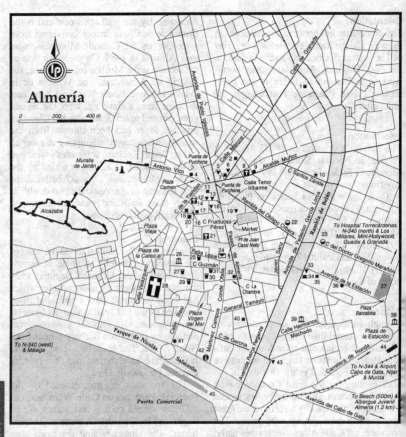

Almería

0   200   400 m

Muralla de Jairán

Alcazaba

Plaza Vieja

Puerta de Purchena

Antonio Vico

Plaza Carmen

Puerta de Purchena

C de la Tiendas

C Fructuoso Pérez

Plaza Vieja

Plaza de la Catedral

Padre Luque

C Guzmán

Calle Velázquez

Plaza Virgen del Mar

Calle Real

Parque de Nicolás

Salmerón

To N-340 (west) & Málaga

Puerto Comercial

Calle Marcos

Calle de Granada

Alcalde Muñoz

Calle Tenor Iribarme

C Santos Zárate

Rambla del Obispo Orbera

Market

Pl de Juan Cassi Nello

Avenida de Pablo Iglesias

Avenida de Federico García Lorca

Rambla de Belén

To Hospital Torrecárdenas, N-340 (north) & Los Millares, Mini-Hollywood, Guadix & Granada

C del Doctor Gregorio Marañón

Avenida de la Estación

Plaza Barcelona

Plaza de la Estación

Conde Ofalia

Paseo de Almería

Javier Sanz

Avenida Reina Regente

C La Chambre

General Tamayo

Martínez Campos

C de Gerona

Calle Hermanos Machado

To N-344 & Airport, Cabo de Gata, Níjar & Murcia

To Beach (500m) & Albergue Juvenil Almería (1.2 km)

Carretera de Ronda

Avenida del Cabo de Gata

North of Almería later in this chapter), is in the Biblioteca Pública on Calle Hermanos Machado, open Monday to Friday from 10 am to 2 pm and 4 to 6 pm, Saturday from 10 am to 1 pm; and the Iberian and Roman sections are in the Archivo Histórico Provincial at Calle Infanta 12, open Monday to Friday from 9 am to 2.30 pm.

Beach

Almería has a long grey-sand beach fronting the mainly pedestrianised Paseo Marítimo, east of the centre.

Places to Stay

The modern *Albergue Juvenil Almería* youth hostel (☎ 26 97 88) at Calle Isla de Fuerteventura s/n has room for 170 people, nearly all in double rooms. It's 1.5 km east of the centre, off Calle Úbeda. You can get close to it on the line 4 '500 Viviendas' bus. Currently this travels westbound from the east end of Rambla Obispo Orbera, but the work on Rambla de Belén may cause rerouting. Ask the driver for the Albergue Juvenil or the Estadio de la Juventud stadium, which is next door to the hostel.

Most hostales and hotels here raise their

PLACES TO STAY		13	Marisquería El Alcázar	24	Post Office
1	Hostal Maribel	18	Bodega Las Botas	25	Georgia Pub Jazz
2	Hostal Sevilla	19	Restaurant Sol de		Club
4	Hotel Residencia La		Almería	26	Archivo Histórico
	Perla	33	Cafetería Santa Rita		Provincial
7	Hostal Andalucía		La Rambla	27	Vertice Pub
11	Hostal Universal	34	Portocarrero Café	28	Catedral
15	Hotel Residencia	43	Cafetería	29	Vhada
	Torreluz		Restaurante	30	Velvet Trajano
17	Hotel Torreluz		Central	31	El Cafetín
20	Hotel Complejo			32	Iberia & Aviaco
	Torreluz	**OTHER**		36	Bernardo Travel
35	Hostal-Residencia	3	Christ Statue		Agency
	Americano	8	Templo de San	37	Bus Station
40	Hotel Residencia		Sebastián	38	Museo de Almería
	Costasol	9	RENFE Office		(Future Site)
		10	Policía Municipal	39	Biblioteca Pública
PLACES TO EAT		14	Templo de Santiago	41	Trasmediterránea
5	Restauran Alfareros	16	Plaza Flores		Office
6	Boutique del Pan San	21	Iglesia de San Pedro	42	Tourist Office
	Andrés	22	Bus to Youth Hostel	44	Train Station
12	Cervecería Baviera	23	Bus to Airport	45	Estación Marítima

prices by 10% to 20% from June or July to September.

Hostal-Residencia Americano (☎ 25 80 11) at Avenida de la Estación 6 is a good choice if you want to be near the bus or train station. Plain but clean singles/doubles, well kept and a decent size, are 1800/3500 ptas with washbasin, 2200/3800 ptas with shower or 2500/4500 ptas with bath.

Hostal Universal (☎ 23 55 57), in the centre at Puerta de Purchena 3, has about 20 simple but sizeable and clean rooms for 1500/3000 ptas all year, with shared bathroom. The building was once a minor mansion, as the broad staircase and spacious, plant-draped lobby indicate.

Hostal Andalucía (☎ 23 77 33), nearby at Calle de Granada 9, was also probably once rather grand. Today it offers bare, adequate rooms for 1300/2400 ptas, or 2000/3000 ptas with bath. *Hostal Sevilla* (☎ 23 00 09), Calle de Granada 23, has better rooms with TV and bath for 2850/4500 ptas.

Hostal Maribel (☎ 23 51 73), Avenida de Federico García Lorca 153, 600 metres north-east of Puerta de Purchena, has clean if small rooms for 1800/3750 ptas (2000/3950 ptas with bath).

In the middle and top price brackets you get private bath, TV, air-con in summer and heating in winter. *Hotel Residencia La Perla* (☎ 23 88 77) at Plaza Carmen 7, just off Puerta de Purchena, has singles/doubles for 4350/6675 ptas plus IVA, and a cafeteria. *Hotel Residencia Costasol* (☎ 23 40 11) at Paseo de Almería 58 has good rooms for 7325/9160 ptas plus IVA (year round), and its own restaurant.

Plaza Flores has a group of three sizeable places (all ☎ 23 47 99) to suit almost any pocket: the *Hotel Complejo Torreluz* at No 6, the *Hotel Residencia Torreluz* at No 1, and the *Hotel Torreluz* at No 5. Doubles are, respectively, 6995, 8860 and 15,840 ptas plus IVA, year round.

Places to Eat

The cafés lining the Puerta de Purchena end of Paseo de Almería are better for a spot of breakfast, a coffee or maybe tapas than for a full meal. Another good nearby spot for a coffee and croissant or pastry is *Boutique del Pan San Andrés*, Calle de Granada 19.

For more substantial eating, the friendly *Restaurán Alfareros* at Calle Marcos 6, near Puerta de Purchena, has a good, three course lunch and dinner menú, including wine and a decent choice of fish and meat main courses, for 900 ptas. It's open daily from 1 to 4 pm and 8 to 10 pm. There's also a

ANDALUCÍA

handful of good places on Calle Tenor Iribarme, just off Paseo de Almería. *Marisquería El Alcázar* is good for fish and seafood, with a big choice available as tapas, media raciones and raciones. Most raciones are 800 to 1000 ptas at a table, or about 20% less at the bar. On the same street, *Cervecería Baviera* has a decent, three course menú for 1000 ptas, while round the corner at Calle Fructuoso Pérez 3 is *Bodega Las Botas*, an atmospheric sherry bar that also does varied tapas and raciones and a menú for 2000 ptas.

Restaurant Sol de Almería by the covered market offers several daily menús for around 900 ptas, including a drink. Some are only two courses, but they're quite substantial. It's open lunchtime, and evenings from 7.30 to 10 pm. The *market* itself is a good source of fresh food of all kinds.

A few glossy but not over-expensive places line up on Avenida de Federico García Lorca beside Rambla de Belén. The bright *Cafetería Restaurante Central* does platos combinados from 700 ptas and raciones and main dishes from 700 to 1300 ptas (half-raciones available, too). The *Portocarrero Café* and *Cafetería Santa Rita La Rambla* are nice for a lighter bite.

Entertainment

There are a dozen or two music bars and discos on streets like Calle Padre Luque, Calle San Pedro, Calle Guzmán, Calle Eduardo Pérez and Calle Real, between the post office and the cathedral. Some open from early evening. The area gets liveliest on Friday and Saturday nights from about 11 pm – so lively, in fact, that in 1996 the city council, in a rare fit of Spanish sensitivity to noise, banned motorcycles and mopeds from the zone at those times and forbade bars from setting up tables outside.

Getting There & Away

Air Almería receives charter flights from several European countries and has daily scheduled services to Barcelona and Madrid by Aviaco, which shares the Iberia offices at Calle Lachambre 2 (☎ 23 86 84) and the airport (☎ 21 37 90). You can pick up one-way international fares from agencies such as Bernardo (☎ 25 01 80) at Avenida de la Estación 16, or Viajes Como at the airport. The airport (☎ 22 19 54) is nine km east of the city off the N-344. There are also daily flights to Melilla by Binter Mediterráneo.

Bus The bus station (☎ 21 00 29) is 400 metres east of Rambla de Belén on Plaza Barcelona, and from it there are at least three buses daily to Guadix (1½ hours), Granada (3½ hours), Sevilla, Málaga, Murcia (3½ to five hours), Alicante (5½ hours) and Madrid (eight hours). Other daily services go to Ugíjar, Úbeda, Jaén, Córdoba, Benidorm, Valencia (eight hours) and Barcelona (13 hours); see destination sections for buses within Almería province.

Train The train station is 200 metres south of Rambla de Belén on Plaza de la Estación. You can buy tickets at the town centre RENFE office, Calle Alcalde Muñoz 7, as well as at the station (☎ 25 11 35). Direct trains run to/from Granada (2¾ hours; 1215 ptas) three times daily; Córdoba (8¼ hours; 2700 ptas) and Sevilla (10 hours; 3300 ptas) daily except Saturday (overnight); Madrid twice daily (6¾ or 10 hours; from 3500 ptas); and Barcelona (14½ hours) via Valencia on Wednesday, Friday and Sunday. All trains go through Guadix (1½ to two hours) and most through Linares-Baeza (4¼ hours).

Car & Motorcycle The N-344 is a faster and better road than the N-340 if you're heading east.

Boat From the Estación Marítima, Trasmediterránea sails to the Spanish North African enclave of Melilla at least once daily from Tuesday to Sunday between early September and mid-June. The crossing takes a scheduled 6½ hours. The cheapest passenger accommodation, a *butaca* (seat), is 3370 ptas one way; cabins are from 5525 to 9380 ptas per person; a car or van up to 4.5 metres long and 1.80 metres high is 13,330 ptas. You can buy tickets at the Estación Marítima or the Trasmediterránea office (☎ 23 61 55) at Parque Nicolás Salmerón 19.

Getting Around

The line 14 'El Alquián' bus runs between the city and the airport every 30 to 45 minutes from 7 am to 9.30 pm. At the time of writing it departs the city westbound from the west end of Calle del Doctor Gregorio Marañón, but check that it hasn't been rerouted because of work on Rambla de Belén.

You can call a taxi 24 hours a day on ☎ 22 61 61.

NORTH OF ALMERÍA
Los Millares & Beyond

Prehistory fans might want to head out to this site, about 20 km north of Almería on the N-324, which veers north-west off the N-340 at Benahadux. Occupied from about 2700 to 1800 BC, Los Millares was probably the site of Spain's first metalworking culture. Its people's ability to smelt and shape copper was a crucial step between the Stone and Bronze ages. The site, still being excavated, contains remains of strong defensive walls, dwelling huts, a foundry, and over 100 tombs. At the last check, it was open Tuesday to Sunday from 9.30 am to 1 pm, and Tuesday, Thursday and Saturday in summer from 6.30 to 9 pm.

Buses from Almería to the small spa town of Alhama de Almería should be able to drop you at the site entrance. Alhama is on the C-332, which heads west through the Almerían Alpujarras into the Granada Alpujarras. Laujar de Andarax (population 2000) is the main town of the Almerían Alpujarras and has a few places to stay.

Mini-Hollywood & Texas Hollywood

North of Benahadux, the Almería desert takes on a particularly moon-like appearance, with deep canyons and rocky wastes that look straight out of the Arizona badlands. Back in the 1960s, makers of Western movies spotted the resemblance, too, and shot dozens of films here. Locals played Indians, outlaws and US cavalry while Clint Eastwood, Charles Bronson, Raquel Welch and co did the talking bits. The big-time movie industry has since moved on, leaving behind a couple of complete Wild West town sets.

Mini-Hollywood (☎ 36 52 36), the best-known, is 24 km from Almería at Km 138 on the N-340. More than 100 films have been shot here, among them *A Fistful of Dollars* and *The Good, the Bad and the Ugly*. At 5 pm daily, and at high noon from June to September and on Saturday, Sunday and holidays year round, a mock bank hold-up, shoot-out, saloon brawl and other stunts are staged. It's open daily from 10 am to 7.30 pm and entry is 950 ptas (children 525 ptas).

A few km further along the N-340 towards Tabernas, then a few minutes up a track to the north, Texas Hollywood (☎ 16 54 58) has not only a Western town set but a Mexican pueblo, Indian tepees, buffalo and camels! It claims a hand in *The Magnificent Seven* and many other Westerns.

Buses from Almería bus station to Tabernas (there are up to six a day) should be willing to drop you at the turn-offs for these places.

NÍJAR

Some of Andalucía's most attractive and unusual glazed pottery, and colourful striped cotton rugs known as *jarapas*, are made in this small town four km north of the N-344, 31 km east of Almería. It's well worth a little detour if you're driving this way. Shops selling the products, many of which are quite affordable, line the main street, Avenida García Lorca. There are three hostales.

CABO DE GATA

The stark desert landscape of eastern Almería meets the Mediterranean most dramatically where the Sierra del Cabo de Gata, of volcanic origin, plunges towards azure and turquoise waters around this isolated headland east of Almería city. Some of Spain's most beautiful and emptiest beaches are strung between cliffs and capes of awesome grandeur, and the whole area has a

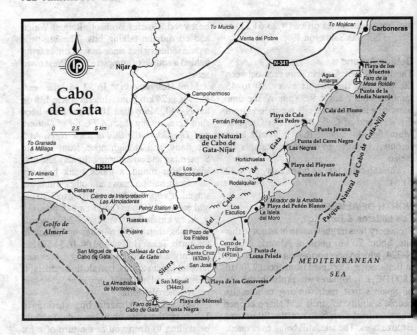

Cabo de Gata

0 2.5 5 km

To Granada & Málaga

To Almería

N-344

To Murcia

Venta del Pobre

To Mojácar

Carboneras

N-341

Níjar

Campohermoso

Fernán Pérez

Parque Natural de Cabo de Gata-Níjar

Los Albericoques

Rodalquilar

Hortichuelas

Retamar

Centro de Interpretación Las Almoladeras

Petrol Station

Golfo de Almería

Ruescas

Pujaire

El Pozo de los Frailes

Los Escullos

San Miguel de Cabo de Gata

Salinas de Cabo de Gata

Cerro de Santa Cruz (432m)

Cerro de los Frailes (491m)

San José

Punta de Loma Pelada

La Almadraba de Monteleva

San Miguel (344m)

Playa de los Genoveses

Faro de Cabo de Gata

Playa de Mónsul

Punta Negra

Agua Amarga

Faro de la Mesa Roldán

Playa de los Muertos

Punta de la Media Naranja

Cala del Plomo

Playa de Cala San Pedro

Punta Javana

Punta del Cerro Negro

Las Negras

Playa del Playazo

Punta de la Polacra

Mirador de la Amatista

Playa del Peñón Blanco

La Isleta del Moro

MEDITERRANEAN SEA

Parque Natural de Cabo de Gata-Níjar

wild, elemental feel that's virtually unique on the Spanish Mediterranean. With just 100 mm of rain in an average year, it's the driest place in Europe. Though Cabo de Gata is certainly not undiscovered, it's far enough from the beaten track to seem positively deserted compared with most Andalucían beach areas. There are no towns, just a scattering of villages which – with a couple of exceptions in July and August – remain very low-key.

It's possible to walk along, or not far from, the coast all the way round from Retamar in the north-west to Agua Amarga in the north-east, but in summer bear in mind that there's very little shade. The west side of the promontory is straight and flat, with a sandy beach stretching most of its length; the south and east are more rugged and indented, and generally more exciting. There's good snorkelling in many places.

It's worth calling ahead for accommodation anywhere on Cabo de Gata during Semana Santa and from June to September. Room rates given in what follows are for the peak months, July and August: most places charge 20% to 40% less at the quietest times of year. Camping is only officially allowed in the four organised camp sites.

The only bank is Caja Rural de Almería in Pujaire. There's an ATM in San Miguel de Cabo de Gata.

Getting There & Away

Bus All the following buses leave from Almería bus station. There are none from Mojácar or Carboneras.

Las Negras & Rodalquilar – daily except Sunday by Autocares Marín Amat (☎ 22 81 78)

San José – two daily Monday to Friday, and one or Saturday, by Autocares Bernardo (☎ 26 42 92) from about June to September, an extra bus each way on Saturday, and one on Sunday

San Miguel de Cabo de Gata – four or more daily by Autocares Becerra (☎ 22 44 03)

Car & Motorcycle The only petrol station on Cabo de Gata is halfway along the Ruescas-San José road.

Centro de Interpretación Las Almoladeras

About 2.5 km before Ruescas on the road from Almería, this is the main information centre for the **Parque Natural de Cabo de Gata-Níjar**, which covers the 60 km or so of coast around Cabo de Gata, plus a thick strip of hinterland and a two km wide marine fringe. The centre (☎ 16 04 35) is well worth a stop if you're on your own wheels – but buses may not be willing to drop you any nearer than Ruescas. It's open daily from at least 9.30 am to 2 pm and 5 to 7 pm, and has displays on the area's fauna, flora and human activities, as well as tourist information.

San Miguel de Cabo de Gata

Often called just Cabo de Gata, this is the main village on the west side of the promontory. Fronted by a long straight beach, it's an odd mixture of bijou holiday homes and a down-at-heel old nucleus, with a small fishing fleet, at the south end. South of the village stretch the **Salinas de Cabo de Gata** salt-extraction lagoons. In spring many greater flamingos and other water birds call in here while migrating to breeding grounds further north (France's Camargue, in the case of the flamingos). A few flamingos and many other birds stay at Cabo de Gata to breed, then others arrive in summer as their breeding grounds elsewhere dry up: by the end of August there can be 1000 flamingos here. Autumn brings the biggest numbers of migratory birds as they call here on their return south. The best place to watch the birds is the hide in a wood-fenced area just off the road three km south of the village. You should see flamingos and a good variety of other bird life any time of year except winter, when the salinas are drained after the autumn salt harvest.

Places to Stay & Eat *Camping Cabo de Gata* (☎ 16 04 42) is near the beach, two km down a side road just south of Ruescas (altogether 6.5 km from San Miguel de Cabo de Gata). It's open all year, charging 450 ptas per adult, per car and per tent, and has a restaurant, swimming pool and bicycles to rent.

Restaurante Mediterráneo (☎ 37 11 37) towards the south end of the village seafront has a handful of singles/doubles with shared bathroom for 2500/4000 ptas. It serves decent food with seafood and meat main dishes for 700 to 1000 ptas. *Hostal Las Dunas* (☎ 37 00 72) at Calle Barrionuevo 5, about 250 metres back from the beach at the north end of the village, is a clean, modern place where singles/doubles with bath are 4500/6500 ptas plus IVA.

Faro de Cabo de Gata & Around

The salt collected from the salinas is piled up in great heaps at **La Almadraba de Monteleva**, a drab village at their south end. Beyond here the road winds four km up round the cliffs to the **Faro de Cabo de Gata**, the lighthouse at the promontory's tip. A turning by Bar José y María (with tapas and seafood), just before the lighthouse, leads up to **Punta Negra**, 3.5 km east, with an old Arab watchtower atop some very high cliffs, and awesome views especially to the east. Here the road ends but a walking track continues on to Playa de Mónsul (about 1½ hours away), Playa de los Genoveses and San José.

San José & Around

San José, spreading round a bay towards the south end of the east side of Cabo de Gata, is the largest settlement on the promontory. Though it becomes a mildly chic little resort in summer, it's still a small and rambling place with sandy streets and no high-rise development. Out of season it's almost empty.

Orientation & Information The road in from the north becomes San José's main street, Calle Correo, with the beach a couple of blocks down to the left (east). On Calle Correo you'll find a natural park and tourist information office (☎ 38 02 99), open daily from 10.15 am to 2 pm (closed winter Wednesdays), a Spar supermarket and, further on up the hill, the post office (postcode 04118). The tourist office can help you organise bicycle rental, horse riding, boat trips, windsurfing or diving.

Beaches San José has a sandy central beach, with a harbour at its east end, but two of the finest beaches on Cabo de Gata lie along a dirt road to the south-west, well away from human settlement. **Playa de los Genoveses**, a broad strip of fine yellow sand about one km long, with shallow waters, and rocky headlands at each end, is 4.5 km from San José. **Playa de Mónsul**, 2.5 km further on, is a shorter length of fine grey sand, backed by huge lumps of volcanic rock. Two km beyond Playa de Mónsul, the road is blocked to vehicles – but not to walkers – for the climb up to Punta Negra.

Places to Stay *Camping Tau* (☎ 38 01 66), open from April to September, has a shady site about 300 metres from the beach, with room for 185 people at around 450 ptas per person, per tent and per car. Follow the 'Albergue' sign pointing left down Camino de Cala Higuera as you enter San José from the north, and go about 800 metres.

The *Albergue Juvenil de San José* (☎ 38 03 53; fax 38 02 13) at Calle Montemar s/n is a friendly, non-HI and non-REAJ youth hostel run by the local municipality. It holds 88 people in bunk rooms of up to eight, at 1000 to 1300 ptas depending on the season. It opens from late June to the end of September and also for Christmas-New Year, Semana Santa, weekends between Semana Santa and late June, and long weekends year round. To find it head towards Camping Tau but turn right after you cross a river bed, then first left up the hill.

On Calle Correo in the village centre, *Café Bar Fonda Costa Rica* (☎ 38 01 03) has eight decent doubles with bath for 5000 ptas. *Hostal Bahía* (☎ 38 03 07), on Calle Correo just north of the centre, has attractive, sparkling clean singles/doubles with bathroom

and TV, in a bright, modern building, for 5000/7500 ptas.

For a bit of a hideaway, try Cala Higuera, a pebbly beach about 1.25 km by dirt road beyond Camping Tau. The accommodation here, run by the friendly Alberto Palfí, has no name (or telephone) but you can ask for *Alberto Cala Higuera*. There are seven rustic rooms for two or three people, some with kitchen, costing from 3000 to 6000 ptas, and a terrace bar with food. To find it, continue past Camping Tau to a T-junction with a wooden fence in front of you, then go right and follow the 'Bar' signs.

There are half a dozen more expensive hostales and hotels. If you fancy staying a while, consider renting an apartment. Two people can pay as little as 2000 ptas a day in the low season for a 10 day stay, though more like 6000 ptas in high summer.

Places to Eat *Bar-Restaurante El Emigrante* across Calle Correo from the Hostal Bahía is a clean, attractive, modern place with good service and good food. Fish and meat mains are around 900 to 1000 ptas, tortillas are 300 to 400 ptas, and a big mixed salad is 350 ptas.

Restaurante Carolina y Vanessa on Calle Correo in the centre does platos combinados for 700 to 800 ptas, also paella and fish. At the far end of the beach, near the harbour, there's a line of brighter, more expensive places mostly with fish and meat mains in the 1100 to 1200 ptas region.

San José to Las Negras
The rugged coast north-east of San José makes room for only two small settlements, the odd old fort and a few beaches before the village of Las Negras, 17 km away as the crow flies. The road spends most of its time ducking inland and, though you can walk off-road most of the way, you're also off coast much of the time.

Six km north-east of San José as the crow flies (10 km by road), the hamlet of **Los Escullos** has a short, mainly sandy beach and a restored old fort, the Castillo de San Felipe. The large and moderately shaded

Camping Los Escullos (☎ 38 98 11), 900 metres back from the beach, is open all year and has a pool and supermarket. There are two reasonable mid-range hotels: *Hotel Los Escullos* (☎ 38 97 33) by the beach, with about 20 rooms at 7000 or 8000 ptas, and *Casa Emilio* (☎ 38 97 32), with eight singles/doubles for 4000/6000 ptas. All three places have restaurants.

La Isleta del Moro, two km further north-east, is a tiny pueblo with a couple of fishing boats, and Playa del Peñón Blanco stretching to the east. Women still wash clothes at public sinks in the square. *Hostal Isleta del Moro* (☎ 38 97 13) has rooms with bath for 3000/5000 ptas all year, and a restaurant with fresh seafood. *Casa Café de la Loma* on a small hill above the village, run by a friendly young German, has a few rooms at 2000 ptas per person (2500 ptas with bath) – again all year – and a café in summer, and holds t'ai-chi workshops and similar activities.

From here the road climbs to the **Mirador de la Amatista** lookout point before heading inland past the former gold-mining village of Rodalquilar. The turning to **Playa del Playazo** is 300 metres after a turn marked 'La Polacra' just past Rodalquilar. It's two km along a level track to this good sand beach between two headlands, one topped by the Castillo de San Ramón fort. From here walkers can stick close to the coast as far as **Las Negras**, which is on a pebbly beach, with a few bars and cafés and several holiday apartments and houses to let. *Camping Náutico La Caleta* (☎ 52 52 37), open all year, is one km round to the south in a separate pebbly cove with little shade.

Las Negras to Agua Amarga

There's no road along this cliff-lined and most secluded stretch of the Cabo de Gata coast, but walkers can take an up-and-down path of about 11 km, which gives access to several beaches. The **Playa de Cala San Pedro** nudist beach, with its ruined fort, is about four km from Las Negras. **Cala del Plomo** is about 3.5 km further on. You may be able to find a fishing boat to take you to

these beaches: ask in the La Palma bar on the beach at Las Negras.

Drivers must head inland through Horti-chuelas. A dirt road heads north-east across country from the bus shelter at the south end of the village of Fernán Pérez. Keep to the main track at all turnings and after 9.5 km you'll come out on the N-341, which links the N-344 to Carboneras. Turn right on the N-341, then right again at the Agua Amarga turning after 1.25 km.

Agua Amarga

Agua Amarga (sometimes spelt Aguamarga) is a pleasant fishing-cum-tourist settlement, popular with Italians, that stretches along a straight sandy beach. It has a supermarket and a post office, and you can change money at Karidemo (☎ 13 80 22), on Calle Mare Nostrum, on Monday, Wednesday and Friday from 10.30 am to 12.45 pm and 5.30 to 8.30 pm.

Three km up the road to the east, there's a turning to the cliff-top Faro de la Mesa Roldán lighthouse (1.25 km), which has an old lookout tower for a neighbour. The views up here are marvellous. From the car park by the turning you can walk down to the Playa de los Muertos nudist beach. The road continues north to Carboneras, a minor resort with a big cement works, and Mojácar, 30 km from Agua Amarga.

Places to Stay & Eat *Hostal Restaurante La Palmera* (☎ 13 82 08) at the east end of the beach has 10 pleasant rooms with bath for 10,000 ptas (a bit less if you can do without a sea view). On Calle La Lomilla, a little bit up from the west end of the beach, *Restaurante-Hostal René y Michèle 'El Family'* (☎ & fax 13 80 14) has just two nice rooms with bath for 7000 ptas, a pool, and an excellent four course menú for 1700 ptas. The rooms are often booked well ahead for summer. The restaurant opens nightly at 7 pm and on Saturday and Sunday at 1 pm. There are also houses and apartments for rent in Agua Amarga.

Restaurante Ajoblanco on Calle Ferro-carril Minero has most main dishes at 950

ANDALUCÍA

ptas or more but also does takeaways and dishes of the day from 600 ptas. *Chiringuito Las Tarahis* at the west end of the beach does tortillas from 500 ptas and fish and meat dishes from 1200 ptas.

MOJÁCAR

Mojácar, up the coast north-east from Cabo de Gata and 85 km from Almería, is two towns: the old Mojácar Pueblo, a jumble of white, cube-shaped houses perched on a hill top two km inland, and the new Mojácar Playa, a coastal resort strip, seven km long but only a couple of blocks wide. Though even the Pueblo is dominated by tourism now, it remains very picturesque, and Mojácar Playa has been developed in a less intense way than other Spanish package-tourism honey-pots. It has few high-rise buildings, a good, long, clean beach, and quite a lively summer scene. The whole place is pretty quiet in winter. The Pueblo goes back at least to Muslim times. From the 13th century onwards, it found itself on the Granada emirate's eastern frontier with the Christians, finally falling to the Catholic Monarchs in 1488. Tucked away in an isolated corner of one of Spain's most backward regions, it was decaying and half-abandoned by the 1960s, before the mayor started luring artists and others with give-away property offers. Mojácar became chic and trendy, then a holiday resort. Today its two parts have a combined permanent population of around 6000.

Orientation & Information

Pueblo and Playa are joined by a road which heads uphill from a junction known as El Cruce, by the Parque Comercial shopping centre towards the north end of Mojácar Playa.

The tourist office (☎ 47 51 62) is on Calle Glorieta, just north-east of Mojácar Pueblo's main square Plaza Nueva, in the same building as the post office. It's open Monday to Friday from 9.30 am to 2 pm and 4.30 to 7 pm, Saturday from 10 am to 1 pm. Banesto next door has an ATM, as does Banco Andalucía in the Centro Comercial at El

Cruce. There's another post office in the Centro Comercial, too. The postcode for all Mojácar is 04638.

Things to See & Do

Seeing the Pueblo is mainly a matter of wandering the quaint, winding streets with their flower-decked balconies and nosing into the craft shops, art galleries and boutiques. **El Castillo** at the very top of the village is not a castle, and is private property to boot, but there are good views from the walkway around it. The fortress-style **Iglesia de Santa María** just north of Plaza del Ayuntamiento dates from 1560 and may have once been a mosque. The **Puerta de la Ciudad** gate on Calle La Guardia is one of the few vestiges of Muslim Mojácar.

The most touching spot is the **Fuente Público** (public fountain) on Calle La Fuente in the lower part of the Pueblo's seaward side. Though remodelled in modern times, it maintains the Muslim tradition of turning water into art. Flowing from 12 spouts into marble troughs, the water tinkles along a courtyard decked with hanging plants. An inscription records the moving speech, made according to legend on this spot in 1488 by Alavez, the last Islamic governor of Mojácar, to Garcilaso, the envoy of the conquering Catholic Monarchs. It translates, in part, as follows:

I am just as much a Spaniard as you. Though my people have lived in Spain for more than 700 years, you say to us: 'You are foreigners, go back to the sea'. In Africa an inhospitable coast awaits us, which will surely tell us, as you do – and certainly with more reason – 'You are foreigners: cross the sea by which you came and go back to your own land'. Treat us like brothers, not enemies, and let us continue working the land of our ancestors.

Special Events

The Moros y Cristianos festival in mid-June re-enacts the Christian conquest of Mojácar, along with dances, processions and other typical fiesta goings-on.

Places to Stay

Prices given here are for the summer high

PLACES TO STAY
1 Hotel Mamabel's
16 Pensión La Luna
20 Pensión El Torreón
22 Pensión Casa Justa
23 Hostal La Esquinica

PLACES TO EAT
5 Café-Bar Indalo
9 Restaurante El
   Viento del Desierto
11 Hamburguesería
12 Bar

OTHER
2 'Mojácar Bus' Stop
3 Tourist Office &
   Post Office
4 El Castillo
6 La Muralla
7 Budú Pub
8 Market
10 Plaza Frontón
13 Bar La Escalera
14 Iglesia de Santa María
15 Car Park
17 Plaza del Ayuntamiento
18 Ayuntamiento
19 Puerta de la Ciudad
21 Disco Bar Sahara
24 Fuente Público
25 Centro de Artesanía

Mojácar Pueblo

season, which typically means July and August but also includes June and September in some places. Outside these times you can expect about 15% to 30% off.

Mojácar Pueblo *Pensión Casa Justa* (☎ 47 83 72), Calle Morote 7, is good value with rooms at 1500/3000 ptas all year, or 4000 ptas for doubles with bath. *Hostal La Esquinica* (☎ 47 50 09), nearby at Calle Cano 1, charges 1750/3500 ptas and has its own café. *Pensión La Luna* (☎ 47 80 32), Calle Estación Nueva 15, is more comfortable and has 10 individually decorated doubles with bath for 5000 ptas, and good meals.

Hotel Mamabel's (☎ 47 24 48) at Calle Embajadores 3 has just four excellent rooms – big, characterfully decorated, with sea views and bath – for 6500 ptas. There's an excellent restaurant, too. *Pensión El Torreón* (☎ 47 52 59), Calle Jazmín s/n, is another beautiful house with great views, and rooms

at 5500 ptas (5000 ptas with shared bath). Apparently Walt Disney was born here!

Mojácar Playa The shady *Camping El Cantal* (☎ 47 82 04), one km south of El Cruce at the El Cantal bus stop, is open all year with room for 800 people at around 500 ptas per adult, per car and per tent. *Hotel Bahía* (☎ 47 80 10), just to its south, has doubles with bath for 5000 ptas. You may find it closed in winter.

Hotel El Puntazo (☎ 47 82 65), two km south of El Cruce, is a decent medium-sized hotel with doubles from 6410 to 9715 ptas, all with bath and TV. The best have air-con and balconies. There are also four-person apartments for 9050 ptas, and a pool and restaurant.

Hotel Playa Río Abajo (☎ 47 89 28) at the north end of Mojácar Playa has 19 nice rooms in chalets in a pleasant garden fronting the beach for 6500 ptas, or 8500 ptas with TV and a beach view. It has its own pool, restaurant and bar. From La Rumina bus stop, head towards the beach and you'll find it.

Places to Eat

Mojácar Pueblo *Restaurante El Viento del Desierto* on Plaza Frontón by the church is good value with main courses such as chicken kebabs, beef Bourguignon or rabbit in mustard for 550 to 700 ptas. There's a cheap *hamburguesería* next door, doing things like eggs, chips and bacon for 450 ptas. The unnamed *bar* down the street at Calle Iglesia 4 does platos combinados and seafood raciones from only 450 ptas.

Café-Bar Indalo up in the shopping precinct north-west of Plaza Nueva serves reasonable meat and seafood for 650 to 900 ptas, and raciones and tortillas from 400 ptas. The restaurant at *Hotel Mamabel's* serves up some of the best food in Mojácar, with main courses from 1200 ptas.

Mojácar Playa *Restaurante Chino La Gran Muralla*, two km south of El Cruce near the Pueblo Indalo bus stop, has fair-value Chinese set meals from 625 to 1750 ptas. *Antonella*, half a km further south near the Lance Nuevo bus stop, pulls in the customers with its pizzas and pasta at 600 to 1200 ptas. Out of season it usually opens evenings only. *Mesón Casa Egea* towards the south end of Mojácar Playa, at the Las Ventánicas bus stop, is popular for its fish and meat main courses in the 500 to 800 ptas range.

Entertainment

Lively bars in Mojácar Pueblo include *Bar La Escalera* on Calle Horno, *Budú Pub* on Calle Estación Nueva, *La Muralla* round the corner on Calle Aire Alto, and *Disco Bar Sahara* on Calle Cuesta de la Fuente. To work off some energy after midnight, head down the hill to one of Mojácar's open-air discos: *Master Disco* just below the petrol station halfway north of Camping El Cantal, *Tito's* towards the south end of the beach near Las Ventánicas bus stop (sometimes with live jazz or blues), or *Tuareg*, amid oasis-like gardens on the Carboneras road 3.5 km beyond the south end of Mojácar Playa. Bear in mind that these may not open at quiet times.

Getting There & Away

Long-distance buses stop outside the Centro Comercial at El Cruce; some also go up to the Centro de Artesanía at the foot of Mojácar Pueblo. There are at least three buses daily to/from Almería (1¾ hours) and Murcia (2½ hours), and two to/from Granada (4½ hours) and Madrid (nine hours). All these except the Granada buses are run by the Andreo line (☎ 39 04 10). Buses to Alicante, Valencia and Barcelona go from Vera, 16 km north. You can check the latest schedules for all buses at the tourist office.

Getting Around

The 'Mojácar Bus' service runs from near the tourist office in Mojácar Pueblo down to El Cruce, then to the south end of Mojácar Playa (Hotel Indalo stop), then to the north end of Mojácar Playa (La Rumina stop), then back to El Cruce and the Pueblo. It goes about every half-hour from 9 am to 9 pm in summer, and about every hour from 9 am to 6 pm in winter.

For a taxi call ☎ 47 81 84.

Extremadura

Extremadura, a large, sparsely populated tableland bordering Portugal, is one of Spain's least-known gems. It's not totally unvisited by tourists but is far enough off the beaten track to give you a genuine sense of exploration – something that *extremeños* themselves have a flair for: many epic 16th century conquistadors of the Americas, including Francisco Pizarro and Hernán Cortés, sprang from this land.

Though much of the Extremadura countryside is flat, bleak and unforgiving, wooded sierras rise up along its northern, eastern and southern fringes. Across the north, the Sierra de Gredos and its western extensions separate Extremadura from Castilla y León. In the south and south-east, the lower Sierra Morena straddles the border with Andalucía. In the central east, the Sierra de Guadalupe takes over from Castilla-La Mancha's Montes de Toledo. The north in particular is a sequence of beautiful ranges and green valleys, dotted with old-fashioned, often isolated villages that make for great exploring, with some fine walking possibilities too.

Extremadura's most interesting towns form a convenient triangle in the centre of the region. Cáceres and Trujillo are full of reminders both of the conquistadors and of the Reconquista. Mérida was the main city of the entire Iberian Peninsula in Roman times and today has Spain's finest collection of Roman ruins.

Two of Spain's major rivers, the Tajo and the Guadiana, cross Extremadura from east to west. Both have been dammed more than once to form large reservoirs. The river basins are mostly broad and covered with thin grass, heath and scrub, but here and there the rivers flow through a craggier landscape. Those with an interest in wildlife shouldn't miss the Parque Natural Monfragüe, which straddles the Río Tajo between Plasencia and Trujillo and has some of the most spectacular bird life in the country.

The name Extremadura is often – and under-

HIGHLIGHTS

- Charming Trujillo, cradle of conquistadors
- Spectacular birds of prey at Parque Natural Monfragüe
- Exploring the lush valleys, anicient villages and high ranges of the north
- Cáceres' perfectly preserved medieval centre
- Spain's finest Roman remains at Mérida
- The biggest meal you may ever eat, at *Restaurante La Troya* in Trujillo or Cáceres
- For those who can afford it, a night in one of Spain's most exotic *paradores* – a 14th century mansion in Cáceres, a 15th century castle in Jarandilla de la Vera or a 16th century convent at Trujillo

standably – thought to derive from *extrema et dura* (Latin for 'outermost and hard'). Extreme is certainly the right word for the climate, which is very hot in summer and bitingly chilly in winter. The best times to come are the second half of April, May, September and the first half of October. Extremadura is best avoided in July and August.

Those in the know reckon the name more probably means 'beyond the Río Duero'. In the 10th and 11th centuries the name was given to territory in what's now southern Castilla y León that was held by the Christian kingdoms of León and Castilla. In the 13th century – when most of Extremadura finally fell to Alfonso IX of León – the name was transferred to the newly acquired lands.

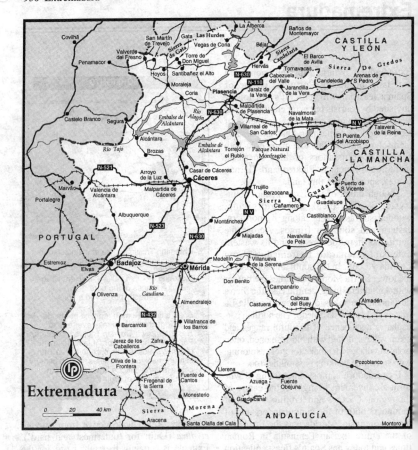

Extremadura

0   20   40 km

Huge parcels of land, granted to the knightly orders and nobility who had led the Reconquista, were turned over to livestock, especially sheep, leaving scant chance of gain for the rest of the population. Thus it was that so many extremeños were willing to try their luck in the Americas in the 16th century (see the boxed aside 'Extremadura & America' later in this chapter). The riches some of these folk came back with turned Extremadura briefly into a prosperous place and something of a cultural centre. But Spain's expulsion of the Moriscos (converted Muslims) in the 17th century

contributed to a new decline. Extremadura was hit hard again by the Peninsular War of the early 19th century.

In the 1970s a new wave of emigration took many hard-up extremeños to jobs in Cataluña, the País Vasco and abroad. There's still little industry: sheep and pig farming, and olive, cork and fruit-growing are among the most important economic activities.

Food & Drinks

Extremadura is often said to have two types of food: the fine fare that originated in its wealthy monasteries and convents, and a

EXTREMADURA

more rough and ready peasant cuisine. The Convento de San Benito at Alcántara concocted recipes so good that even the French borrowed them when Napoleon came this way in the 19th century. *Perdiz* (partridge) *al estilo/modo de Alcántara* is a dish you'll find on most good extremeño menus.

From the peasant tradition comes *caldereta*, a hearty casserole of lamb *(cordero)* or kid *(cabrito)*, usually with chilli, onion and garlic, and often liver or wine. You can expect simple roast lamb *(cordero asado)* to be pretty good too. But you might think twice about ordering *chanfaina*, an offal stew. *Ancas de rana*, frogs' legs, usually come deep-fried *(rebozadas)*.

Extremadura is pig country too and the *cerdos ibéricos* that feed on the acorns from its plentiful oak trees end up as some of the choicest *jamón* (cured ham) in Spain. Jamón from the villages of Montánchez and Piornal is among the best. There's a whole range of sausages and other pork products too. It's perhaps better not to know what goes into one speciality, a kind of black pudding known as *patatera*, but we're going to tell you anyway: boiled potatoes, paprika, salt, garlic and ibérico pig fat.

Among a variety of local cheeses is the Camembert-like *torta del Casar* from Casar de Cáceres, 12 km north of Cáceres.

Basic Extremadura country wine is known as *pitarra*. More unusual and potent is the range of fruit liqueurs (15% to 20% alc/vol) and *aguardientes* (eaux de vie, 40%-plus alc/vol) from the Valle del Jerte and elsewhere. Flavours include cherry *(cereza)*, raspberry *(frambuesa)*, blackberry *(zarzamora)* and even acorn *(bellota)*. A bottle of one of these in a shop can cost anywhere from 800 to 2000 ptas. Aguardiente de cerezas is the same as Kirsch.

Northern Extremadura

In contrast to the even, bare landscapes of central Extremadura, the far north presents a crinkled, folded and much greener aspect.

Here you're in the western reaches of the Cordillera Central, a complicated jigsaw of uplands and valleys forming an arc around Plasencia from the Sierra de Gredos in the east to the Sierra de Gata in the west. It's a rather remote and often very beautiful region that's well worth taking time over as you move between Extremadura and Castilla y León – perfect for those who like exploring remote valleys, old-fashioned villages, narrow roads and mountain paths. In the north-east, three lush, wooded valleys – La Vera, the Valle del Jerte and the Valle del Ambroz – stretch down towards Plasencia. Watered by rushing mountain streams, called *gargantas*, and dotted with almost medieval villages of narrow streets and overhanging houses, these valleys attract just enough visitors to provide a good network of places to stay. There are some excellent walking routes along them and over the ranges in between. A useful tool for exploring this area is the Editorial Alpina guide booklet *Sistema Central: Valle del Jerte, Valle del Ambroz, La Vera*, which includes a 1:50,000 map of the area showing many walking routes. Try to get it before you come: if not, the tourist office in Cabezuela del Valle may have copies.

In the northernmost tip of Extremadura, the isolated and mysterious Las Hurdes region has a harsher sort of beauty, while the Sierra de Gata in the north-west is equally isolated but prettier and more fertile.

Throughout this region your own wheels are a big help, but if you do use the buses, you can at least walk over into the next valley without worrying about how to get back to your car!

The telephone code for the northern region is ☎ 927.

LA VERA

La Vera is the north side of the valley of the Río Tiétar, at the foot of the western Sierra de Gredos and the Sierra de Tormantos. Its many crops include raspberries, tobacco, asparagus and paprika. The C-501 from Plasencia to Arenas de San Pedro in Castilla y León runs right along the valley.

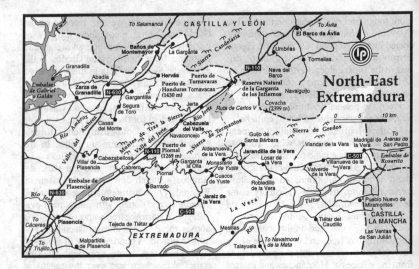

Information

There are tourist offices at Plaza Mayor 1, Jaraiz de la Vera (☎ 46 00 24), and at Plaza España (also called Plaza de la Constitución) 1, beside the church in Jarandilla de la Vera (☎ 56 04 60). They have a very basic leaflet suggesting some good walks along the valley and into the hills. Most sizeable villages have banks and post offices.

Things to See & Do

A good area to head for is the middle of the valley. **Cuacos de Yuste**, 45 km from Plasencia, has its share of the medieval streets that are typical of La Vera villages, with half-timbered houses leaning at odd angles, and overhanging upper storeys supported by timber or stone pillars. Look for the Casa de Juan de Austria on Plaza de Juan de Austria, where Carlos I's illegitimate son Don Juan of Austria – later a charismatic general and admiral – stayed while visiting his father at the Monasterio de Yuste.

Two km north-west of Cuacos, up a side road, is the **Monasterio de Yuste**, to which the gouty Carlos I, having handed over the world's biggest empire to his legitimate sons,

retired in 1557 to spend his dying years. The serenity of the setting makes it easy to understand his choice. After his death Carlos lay in the crypt here for 18 years before being removed to El Escorial, outside Madrid. The monastery is occupied by a closed order of Hieronymite monks, but the church and the simple royal chambers – with the ailing monarch's bed placed to give him a direct view of the altar – are open Monday to Saturday from 9.30 am to 12.30 pm and 3.30 to 6 pm, and Sunday and holidays from 9.30 to 11.30 am, 1 to 1.30 pm and 3.30 to 6 pm. Entry is by guided tour in Spanish for 100 ptas.

The road to the monastery continues seven km to **Garganta la Olla**, another picturesque village, from where you can either head down to Jaraiz de la Vera or, more exciting, up over the 1269 metre **Puerto de Piornal** pass to Piornal and the Valle del Jerte.

Jarandilla de la Vera, 10 km north-east of Cuacos de Yuste, is a bigger village, with a 15th century fortress-church on the main square (below the main road), and a *parador* occupying the 15th century Castillo de los Condes de Oropesa, where Carlos I stayed for a few months while Yuste was being readied for him. A Roman bridge over the Garganta Jaranda below the village makes a focus for short rambles. Of the longer hikes, the Ruta de Carlos V (see Valle del Jerte below) is one of the most enticing. To start from the Jarandilla end, head north-west out of the village along the C-501 for a few minutes. Opposite the 'Camping Jaranda 300m' sign is a curve of disused road on the right, with a track leading off it and running up between a hedge and a red-brick building. At the end of the hedge the track bends left, then right. At this second bend look for a faint arrow on the wall pointing you up a path to the left beside a wire fence. This is the Ruta de Carlos V.

Other La Vera villages with some particu-larly fine traditional architecture are **Jaraiz de la Vera**, **Valverde de la Vera** and **Villanueva de la Vera**.

Places to Stay & Eat

There are camping grounds – often with good riverside positions – at Aldeanueva de la Vera, Cuacos de Yuste, Jarandilla de la Vera, Losar de la Vera, Madrigal de la Vera and Villanueva de la Vera. Most are only open from March/April to September/ October, but *Camping Godoy* (☎ 57 04 11) at Losar and *Camping Alardos* (☎ 56 50 66) at Madrigal stay open all year. There's a free *zona de acampada*, with no facilities, in a pine wood at Garganta la Olla.

On the main road in Cuacos de Yuste,

Woolly Wanderers

If you travel the byways of Extremadura, Castilla y León or Castilla-La Mancha you may occasionally find your road crossing or running beside a broad grassy track, which might have signs announcing that it's a *cañada real* or a *vía pecuaria*. What you've stumbled upon is one of Spain's age-old livestock migration routes. The Visigoths, 14 or 15 centuries ago, are reckoned to have been the first to take their flocks and herds south from Castilla y León to winter on the plains of Extremadura – a practice which not only avoided the icy northern winters but allowed pastures to regenerate.

This twice-yearly *trashumancia* (migration of animals) – northward in early summer, southward in late autumn – grew to epic proportions in the late Middle Ages when sheep farming became the mainstay of the Spanish economy. Huge clouds of dust raised by the migrating flocks were a characteristic sight in a countryside that was now often emptied of other agriculture and human habitation by the dominance of this single beast over an entire country. The powerful sheep owners' guild known as the Mesta – with the support of a monarchy which took its cut from the wool trade – was able to establish a vast network of drove roads which is said eventually to have totalled 124,000 km. At an average 33 metres wide, these covered an area of 4210 sq km – almost 1% of Spain!

The biggest drove roads – veritable sheep freeways up to 75 metres wide – were the *cañadas reales* (royal drove roads). The Cañada Real de la Plata – roughly following the Roman Via Lata from north-west to south-west Spain – passes just west of Salamanca, enters Extremadura by the Valle del Ambroz, crosses the Parque Natural Monfragüe and is then used by stretches of the C-524 to Trujillo. If you cross the Sierra de Gredos in Castilla y León by the Puerto del Pico pass, on the N-502 between Ávila and Arenas de San Pedro, you're on the Cañada Real Leonesa Occidental (and again on a Roman road), The Cañada Real Galiana stretches right down Castilla-La Mancha from Cardoso de la Sierra in the Sierra de Guadarrama, north of Madrid, to Almadén, west of Ciudad Real.

Come the late 20th century and a decline in the importance of sheep farming and in the attractions of the shepherd's life, allied to the easy availability of truck and train transport for those beasts that still migrate, the trashumancia has dwindled to a trickle. Many of the cañadas have been made unusable by new roads, spreading towns and cities, reservoirs, rubbish tips and farms. The nearest most Spaniards come to a migrating sheep today is when Proyecto 2001, a campaign dedicated to keeping the drove roads open, takes a flock of 2000 or so through the centre of Madrid each October. Proyecto 2001, which has EU financial backing, has staged full-scale trashumancias each year since 1993, moving thousands of sheep back and forth between Extremadura and northern León and between northern and southern Castilla-La Mancha. Its motivation is to revitalise the trashumancia, arrest the loss of public land, and maintain the drove roads for their environmental value. It argues that the twice-yearly migrations help to keep woodlands clean, eliminate excess scrub and avert exhaustion of pastures. ■

Pensión Sol de Vettonia (☎ 17 22 41) has good singles/doubles for 1900/2700 ptas; *Hostal Moregón* (☎ 17 21 81) two doors along gives you private bathroom and TV for 3500/6000 ptas. Both have restaurants.

In Jarandilla de la Vera, *Hostal Jaranda* (☎ 56 02 06), on the main road at Avenida Soledad Vega Ortiz 101, has big, bright rooms with bath for 2675/5350 ptas, and an excellent-value three course menú with wine for 850 ptas. *Hostal Marbella* (☎ 56 02 18) a few doors along is a bit cheaper. *Hostal La Posada de Pizarro* (☎ 56 05 10) at Calle Cuesta de los Carros 1, in the lower part of the village, has doubles with shower for 6500 ptas. The *Parador de Jarandilla* (☎ 56 01 17) is suitably splendid, with singles/doubles from 10,800/13,500 to 12,000/15,000 ptas plus IVA.

Getting There & Away

Mirat (☎ 42 36 43) runs a bus Sunday to Friday between Cáceres, Plasencia and Madrigal de la Vera, stopping at the villages on the C-501 in La Vera. It also has two buses Monday to Friday between Plasencia and Navalmoral de la Mata via Jaraiz de la Vera, Cuacos de Yuste, Jarandilla de la Vera and Losar de la Vera (one continues to Madrid). Daily services between Madrid and La Vera are run by Doaldi (☎ 17 03 59), from Madrid's Estación Sur de Autobuses, and La Sepulvedana from Paseo de Florida 11.

VALLE DEL JERTE

This valley, separated by the Sierra de Tormantos from La Vera, grows half Spain's cherries and turns into a sea of white when the trees blossom in April. The N-110 Plasencia-Ávila road runs right up it, crossing into Castilla y León at the 1275 metre Puerto de Tornavacas at the head of the valley. There's a tourist office (☎ 47 21 22) in the Sede Mancomunidad de Municipios del Valle del Jerte building at Cabezuela del Valle, open Monday to Friday from 10 am to 1 pm.

Things to See & Do

The village of **Piornal**, at a height of 1200 metres on the south-east flank of the valley, is a good base for walks along the Sierra de Tormantos by the PR-19 path, or down to Navaconcejo in the valley by the PR-15. The lower part of the village, below the main road, is the more old-fashioned. Temperatures in Piornal are lower than down in the valley and the village can be pleasant in August but cold in September.

In the valley bottom, **Cabezuela del Valle** has a particularly medieval main street, Calle El Hondón. A 35 km road crosses from just north of here over the 1430 metre Puerto de Honduras to Hervás in the Valle del Ambroz. For hikers, the PR-10 trail to Gargantilla climbs roughly parallel – a one day walk. From **Jerte** there are walks in the beautiful **Reserva Natural de la Garganta de los Infiernos**, focused on a mountain river tumbling down the north-west side of the Sierra de Tormantos.

Tornavacas, another village with a huddled, medieval centre, near the head of the valley, is the starting point of the **Ruta de Carlos V**. This 28 km trail (No PR-1) is marked by red and white arrows and follows the scenic route by which Carlos I (who was also Charles V of the Holy Roman Empire – hence the path's name) was carried over the mountains to Jarandilla de la Vera on his way to Yuste. It is possible to walk it in one long day – just as Carlos' bearers did back then. To find the start of the route, from Tornavacas' Plaza de la Iglesia head down Calle Real de Medio past the *ayuntamiento* (town hall), and keep going down past the post office. The first turn is to the left, just past the Ermita de los Humilladeros, a little chapel with black railings. Cross a small bridge and turn right. The route crosses the Sierra de Tormantos by the 1479 metre Collado (or Puerto) de las Yeguas.

Places to Stay & Eat

Camping Río Jerte (☎ 17 30 06), 1.5 km south-west of Navaconcejo, is open from March to October; *Camping Valle del Jerte* (☎ 47 05 27) by the Río Jerte two km south-west of Jerte village, near the entrance to the Reserva Natural de la Garganta de los Infiernos, is open from mid-March to September. There's a *zona de acampada* at Piornal, towards the top of the village.

Also in Piornal, *Casa Verde* (☎ 908-92 19 72), Calle Libertad 38, is a friendly hostel-style place charging 2000 ptas a person in decent doubles with private bath. To find it, follow Calle Cuesta up from the plaza where the bus stops. It's advisable to ring ahead as it's often full, especially in spring. *Pensión Los Piornos* (☎ 47 60 55) on Plaza de las Eras, near the bus stop, charges 2000/2500 ptas for plain singles/doubles.

In Cabezuela del Valle, *Hotel Aljama* (☎ 47 22 91), Calle Federico Bajo s/n, almost touching the church across the street, has nice modern rooms for 2500/4500 ptas plus IVA. There are numerous places to eat and drink on nearby Calle El Hondón.

Hotel Los Arenales (☎ 47 02 50), two km south-west of Jerte on the N-110, has good singles/doubles with bath for 4000/6000 ptas plus IVA, and a restaurant.

Hostal Puerto de Tornavacas (☎ 47 01 01), a couple of km up the N-110 from Tornavacas, is a country inn-style place with singles for 2500 ptas and doubles with bath for 4600 ptas, and a restaurant specialising in extremeño food.

Good local trout is available in almost every eatery in the Valle del Jerte.

Getting There & Away

From Plasencia, the León Álvarez company runs one daily bus to Piornal, and four a day Monday to Friday (one on Saturday and Sunday) up the Valle del Jerte to Tornavacas, with one a day continuing to Madrid.

VALLE DEL AMBROZ

This broader valley west of the Valle del Jerte is followed by the N-630 running north from Plasencia to Béjar and Salamanca in Castilla y León.

Hervás

The valley's main focus of interest is this pleasant small town with the best surviving 15th century **barrio judío** (Jewish quarter) in Extremadura, where many Jews took refuge in hope of avoiding the Inquisition. El Lagar crafts shop on Rincón de Don Benito has displays on old Jewish life. You can climb up to the **Iglesia de Santa María**, on the site of a ruined Knights Templar castle at the highest point of the town, to get your bearings. The **Museo Pérez Comendador-Leroux** in an 18th century mansion on the main street, Calle de Asensio Neila, houses works of the interesting Hervás-born sculptor Enrique Pérez Comendador (1900-81) and his wife, the French painter Magdalena Leroux. It's open Tuesday to Sunday for varying hours and is free.

Granadilla

About 22 km west of Hervás by paved roads across the valley, Granadilla is a picturesque old fortified village that was abandoned after the creation in the 1960s of the Embalse de Gabriel y Galán reservoir, which almost surrounds it. Since then it has been restored as an educational centre and you can visit, free, from 10 am to 1 pm and 5 to 7 pm daily (closed Saturday morning, Sunday afternoon and from 15 December to 30 January).

Places to Stay & Eat

Camping El Pinajarro (☎ 48 16 73), 1.5 km from Hervás on the more southerly of the two approach roads from the N-630, is open from mid-March to late September, charging around 450 ptas per adult, per car and per tent. *Hostal Sinagoga* (☎ 48 11 91), outside the town centre at Avenida de la Provincia 2, is an adequate but dull modern place charging 2500/5000 ptas for singles/doubles with bath and TV. You may find the odd house with an 'Habitaciones' or 'Camas' sign in the *barrio judío*. There are several reasonable cafés and restaurants in the town centre.

Getting There & Away

Los Tres Pilares (☎ 41 14 23) runs two buses Monday to Friday between Plasencia and Hervás. Enatcar has a few services daily between Cáceres, Plasencia and Salamanca via the Valle del Ambroz, stopping at the Empalme de Hervás junction on the N-630, two km from the town.

LAS HURDES

Las Hurdes was long synonymous with grinding poverty and chilling tales of witchcraft, evil spirits and even cannibalism. As far back as the 16th century the Carmelite monastery in the Valle de Las Batuecas, across the border in Castilla y León, was founded to counteract the demons, and in the 1930s Luis Buñuel made Las Hurdes the subject of his film about rural poverty, *Las Hurdes – Terre Sans Pain*. Time hasn't stood still here – or not quite – and today Las Hurdes has shaken off the worst of its poverty, but the atmosphere in some of its more remote and inbred villages remains distinctly spooky.

The rocky terrain yields only small terraces of cultivable land along the river banks, but has an austere, dark beauty where the hills haven't been stripped for timber or by fire. The huddles of traditional, small stone houses look almost as much like slate-roofed sheep pens as human dwellings. Here and there are clusters of beehives which produce high-quality honey.

Things to See & Do

Experiencing Las Hurdes is a matter of sensing the atmosphere of its villages and enjoying the harsh beauty of its countryside. The heart of Las Hurdes is the valley of the Río Hurdano, north-west from Vegas de Coria on the C-512 Coria-Salamanca road.

From Nuñomoral, 7.5 km up the valley, a road heads west up a side valley to such isolated and traditional villages as **Fragosa** – turn to the left (south) at Martinlandrán – **Cottolengo** and, at the end of the road nine km from Nuñomoral, **El Gasco**. Various tracks head off into the hills from this valley – there's a good walk from El Gasco to the beautiful 70 metre waterfall, **El Chorro de la Miacera**.

Back in the main valley, five km northwest of Nuñomoral, is **Asegur**, which has many stone houses that look as though they grew out of the hillside. Four km further north is **Casares de las Hurdes**, which is almost cosmopolitan. Between Asegur and Casares, another side road heads west to

Casabrubia and **La Huetre** (2.3 km), from where you could head off for more walks into the hills.

Beyond Casares de las Hurdes, the road winds seven km up through Carabusino and Robledo to the border of Salamanca province (Castilla y León). You could continue to Ciudad Rodrigo (25 km), but a right turn just 20 metres before the border marker will take you winding nine km down through forest to the picturesque, isolated village of **Riomalo de Arriba**. From Riomalo de Arriba the road continues 16 km down through Ladrillar and Cabezo to **Las Mestas**, a relatively lively place in the evenings. From Las Mestas you can turn north to the Valle de las Batuecas and La Alberca (see the Sierra de la Peña Francia section in the Castilla y León chapter), or continue 3.5 km down to rejoin the C-512, 3.5 km west of Riomalo de Abajo.

Places to Stay & Eat

The nearest camping grounds are on the C-512 at Riomalo de Abajo and Pinofranqueado. *Camping Del Pino* (☎ 67 41 41) at Pinofranqueado is open all year. Also on the C-512 there are hostales in Pinofranqueado, Caminomorisco, Vegas de Coria and Riomalo de Abajo. *Pensión El Abuelo* (☎ 43 51 14) in Caminomorisco has singles/doubles for 1800/2400 ptas, or 2000/3000 ptas with private shower, and its restaurant has a menú for 1000 ptas. *Hostal Riomalo* (☎ 43 30 20) in Riomalo de Abajo has singles/doubles with shower or bath for 3000/3500 ptas.

Pensión Hurdano (☎ 43 30 12) in the middle of Nuñomoral has decent singles/doubles for 1300/2000 ptas – some doubles have private bath. It also has a reasonably priced comedor serving good portions, with virtually everything at about 600 ptas. *Pensión Marisol* (☎ 10 60 58) in La Huetre has basic doubles for just 1200 ptas. *Hostal Montesol* (☎ 43 30 25) at Calle Lindón 7, Casares de las Hurdes, has better doubles (only) for 3000 or 3500 ptas plus IVA. Its restaurant menú costs 1000 ptas.

Nearly all the places to stay have restaurants or comedores.

Las Hurdes

Getting There & Away

Autocares Cleo (☎ 10 45 08) runs a daily bus Monday to Friday from Plasencia to Vegas de Coria, Nuñomoral, La Huetre, Casares de las Hurdes and back, and another (also Monday to Friday) to Martinlandrán, Fragosa, Cottolengo, El Gasco and back.

Hitching to and around Las Hurdes can be painfully slow.

SIERRA DE GATA

The Muslims built several castles here, and after the Reconquista, which came in 1212, the area was controlled by the Knights Templar and knights of the Orden de Alcántara. The traditional architecture features a lot of granite stonework with external staircases, and several villages have impressive 16th century churches. Olives and other fruit are grown in the lower parts of the area's wooded valleys.

The two main roads through the region – the C-526 north from Coria to Ciudad Rodrigo and the C-513 west from the Valle del Ambroz to Penamacor in Portugal – cross near the biggest and one of the most attractive villages, **Hoyos**, which has some impressive *casas señoriales* (mansions) as well as a ruined 16th century convent and a church. To the east, **Santibáñez el Alto** has a substantial castle dating back to the 9th century, with fine views; **Torre de Don Miguel** has more casas señoriales and an elm tree in its plaza which some say is 500 years old; **Gata** has some of the best traditional architecture and another ruined convent.

In the west, locals speak a unique dialect thought to be derived from Asturian and Leonese settlers in the Reconquista. **San Martín de Trevejo**, where the dialect is called *mañegu*, is a pretty place of traditional buildings amid a landscape of oak and chestnut woods. **Valverde del Fresno**, where the dialect is called *varverdeiru*, is larger but also picturesque, with a ruined castle and a handsome *plaza mayor*.

EXTREMADURA

Places to Stay

At Santibáñez el Alto, *Camping Borbollón* (no ☎) is open from March to September, at 400 ptas per adult, per car and per tent. In Hoyos, *Pensión El Redoble* (☎ 51 40 18), Plaza de la Paz 12, has singles/doubles for 1500/2500 ptas. *Pensión Avenida* (☎ 10 20 79), at Avenida Almenara 12 in Gata, is a little more comfortable at 2500/3000 ptas plus IVA. In Valverde del Fresno you can choose between *Pensión Sajeras* (☎ 51 02 49), Calle Francisco Pizarro 43, with basic rooms at 900/1700 ptas, and *Hotel La Palmera* (☎ 51 03 23), Calle Santos Robledo, where rooms with bath are 3000/5000 ptas.

Getting There & Away

There are one or two buses daily into the region from Coria and Cáceres.

CORIA

South of the Sierra de Gata, Coria (population 11,000) is a good stop on the way to/from Plasencia or Cáceres. Still surrounded by its **Roman walls**, reckoned to be the most perfectly preserved in Europe, Coria was the seat of a bishopric as long ago as Roman times and of a large seminary till the 1970s. There's a tourist office (☎ 50 13 51) on Avenida de Extremadura.

The impressive **catedral** on Plaza Catedral, open from 9 am to 1 pm and 5 to 7 pm except Sunday afternoons, was built between the 14th and 17th centuries. Primarily a Gothic construction, it has plateresque decoration on the façades, a tall tower and a very wide nave. Its Capilla de la Reliquias houses the 'Mantel de la Última Cena' (Tablecloth of the Last Supper), a tattered, yellowish cloth four metres long said to have been brought here by the mother of the Roman emperor Constantine. In a field south of the cathedral stands a fine old stone bridge, abandoned in the 17th century by the Río Alagón, which now takes a more southerly course.

Places to Stay & Eat

Pensión Piro (☎ 50 00 27) at Plaza del Rollo 6 has singles/doubles for 1600/2000 ptas and a good restaurant where lunch or dinner will set you back around 1100 ptas. *Hotel Los Kekes* (☎ 50 09 00) on Avenida Sierra de Gata has rooms with bath from 3375/4700 ptas plus IVA.

Getting There & Away

The bus station (☎ 50 01 10) is on Calle Guijo. There are daily buses to/from Plasencia, Gata, Cáceres and Salamanca.

PLASENCIA

This bustling old town of 36,000, rising above a bend of the Río Jerte, is the natural hub for the valleys and mountains of northern Extremadura. Founded in 1186 by Alfonso VIII of Castilla, Plasencia only lost out to Cáceres as northern Extremadura's most important town in the 19th century. It retains an attractive old quarter of narrow streets with some stately buildings.

Orientation & Information

The heart of town is the lively, arcaded Plaza Mayor, meeting place of no fewer than 10 streets and the scene of a Tuesday market since the 12th century. The bus station is at Calle Tornavacas 2, about one km to the north-east, and the train station is on Avenida Ambroz, across the river to the south.

The tourist office (☎ 42 21 59) is at Calle del Rey 17, on one of the streets leading north-east off Plaza Mayor. The post office (postcode 10600) is at Avenida Alfonso VIII s/n, and the Policía Nacional (☎ 41 00 46) are at Rúa Zapatería 14.

Things To See

The outstanding building is the **catedral** on Plaza de la Catedral, a quick wiggle south from Plaza Mayor. It's actually two cathedrals: the Romanesque Catedral Vieja round the side, and the 16th century Catedral Nueva, a mainly Gothic building with a handsome plateresque façade. The Catedral Nueva was never finished, so seems disproportionately tall for its length. The carvings on its early 16th century choir stalls alternate between the sacred and the obscene: their carver, Rodrigo Alemán, is said to have been an unwillingly converted Jew who took the chance to mock the Christian church. The cathedral museum gives access to a lovely Cistercian cloister.

Nearby on Plazuela Marqués de la Puebla, in part of the old Hospital Provincial, is the **Museo Etnográfico** (closed Monday; free) with an interesting display of local crafts and costumes. The impressive 16th century **Palacio del Marqués de Mirabel** on Plaza de San Vicente Ferrer houses the Duque de Arión's one room Museo Cinegético, a museum of hunting trophies and weapons.

Among the numerous old churches and mansions in town, some of those most worth a look are the **Casa del Deán** facing the Catedral Vieja; the 13th century **Palacio Monroy** on Calle Santa Isabel; the **Iglesia de San Nicolás**, one of the oldest churches in Extremadura, on Plaza de San Vicente Ferrer; and the **Iglesia de San Martín** on Plazuela de San Martín.

Places to Stay & Eat

Add IVA to all room prices. *Hostal La Muralla* (☎ 41 38 74), at Calle Berrozana 6 two blocks north-west of Plaza Mayor, has singles/doubles from 1500/2800 to 1800/3200 ptas, or 2900/3000 to 3700/3800 ptas with shower, and a good, economical restaurant. *Hotel Rincón Extremeño* (☎ 41 11 50), just off Plaza Mayor at Calle Vidrieras 6, has helpful management and rooms with shower or bath from 2800/4200 to 3300/4700 ptas. The *Hotel Alfonso VIII* (☎ 41 02 50), at Avenida Alfonso VIII 32, is the top place in town, with rooms at 6500/10,000 ptas.

There are several restaurants on and around Plaza Mayor and lots of bars – many serving free tapas with drinks – just to its east on Calle Talavera and nearby streets such as Calle Patalón.

Getting There & Away

Plasencia is fairly well served by buses, with at least four daily to Salamanca, one or two to Madrid, 12 or more to Cáceres (fewer at weekends), five to Mérida and Sevilla, and other services as far afield as Badajoz, Bilbao, La Coruña and Barcelona. But direct buses to Trujillo, via the Parque Natural Monfragüe, only go on Tuesday, Thursday and Friday. For buses to other places in northern Extremadura, see the sections for individual destinations.

Trains run three times daily to Madrid (three hours), three or four times to Cáceres (1¼ hours), two or three times to Mérida, once to Badajoz and once (except Sunday) to Sevilla (seven hours). You can call ☎ 41 00 49 for information.

PARQUE NATURAL MONFRAGÜE

This natural park in the Tajo valley is famous for its bird life, notably some of Spain's most spectacular colonies of birds of prey. Among its 178 feathery species is the largest known concentration (said to be over 200 pairs) of Europe's biggest bird of prey, the rare black vulture, and important populations of two other rare large birds, the Spanish imperial eagle (about 10 pairs) and the black stork (about 30 pairs). March to October are the best months to come as the vultures, storks and others winter in Africa – but remember that July and August are very hot in Extremadura. The park is also an important habitat for the pardel lynx. Its vegetation ranges from classic Mediterranean woodland and scrub to riverbank woodland and *dehesas* (see the boxed aside). There are also stands of eucalypts, introduced in the Franco era but no longer planted here because of their desiccating effect on the land.

Orientation & Information

At the hamlet of Villarreal de San Carlos on the C-524 Plasencia-Trujillo road there's an information centre (☎ 45 51 04), open daily from 9 am to 2.30 pm and 4 to 6 pm (June to September, from 5 to 7 pm). Much of the park is an out-of-bounds *reserva integral*, but from Villarreal several marked walking trails of up to six hours (return) take you to some good lookout points, some of which you can drive to as well. Villarreal is near the confluence of the Tajo and Tiétar rivers, both of which are dammed not far upstream.

Things to See & Do

One of the best spots to head for is the hill-top **Castillo de Monfragüe**, a ruined 9th century Muslim fort about 1½ hours walk south from Villarreal (or a few minutes drive). Just below the castillo, the modern Ermita (or Santuario) de Monfragüe chapel houses a 12th century image of the Virgin brought from Palestine. But above all, this is a great spot for watching birds in flight from the Peña Falcón crag on the opposite (west) bank of the Río Tajo. Peña Falcón's residents at the last count included 80 pairs of huge griffon vultures, three pairs of black storks, and one pair each of Egyptian vultures, peregrine falcons, golden eagles and eagle owls – the latter another giant of the bird world with a 1.5 metre wingspan. You can get a closer look at Peña Falcón from Salto del Gitano, by the road below the Castillo de Monfragüe on the east side of the Tajo.

Another walk (2½ hours return) goes west from Villarreal de San Carlos to **Cerro Gimio**, where you can see black vultures nesting. This bird is distinguishable from the griffon vulture by being all black. A further good bird-viewing spot is the **Mirador de la Tajadilla**, about a three hour walk east of Villarreal (you can also drive there), which is noted for griffon vultures and Egyptian vultures in flight (the griffon is the bigger).

Places to Stay & Eat

There are a couple of bars at Villarreal de San Carlos where you can get a bite to eat, but the nearest accommodation is *Camping Monfragüe* (☎ 45 92 20), open all year, 14 km north on the C-524. The cost is 425 ptas plus IVA per adult, per tent and per car. The nearest rooms are in the village of Torrejón el Rubio, 16 km south, which has three places on the C-524: *Pensión Avenida* (☎ 45 50 50), *Pensión Monfragüe* (☎ 45 50 26) and the *Hotel Carvajal* (☎ 45 52 54). The Avenida and the Monfragüe both have doubles with shared bath for 3000 ptas (the Monfragüe also has singles for 1550 ptas); the Carvajal has singles/doubles with shower for 3000/5000 ptas plus IVA, and a modestly priced restaurant.

Getting There & Away

Your own wheels are a big advantage. The only bus service is by the Izquierdo company, which runs buses on Tuesday, Thursday and Friday from Trujillo to Plasencia and back, with stops at Torrejón el Rubio and Villarreal de San Carlos (465 ptas from Trujillo). Schedules at the time of writing would give you a worthwhile 6½ hours at Monfragüe before returning.

Monfragüe train station (called Palazuelo-Empalme on some maps) is 16 km north of Villarreal de San Carlos and 1.5 km west of the C-524 and Camping Monfragüe. It's served by three trains a day in each direction on the Cáceres-Madrid line.

Hitching along the C-524 might not be too difficult in spring and summer.

Getting Around

Centro de Educación Ambiental de la Dehesa (☎ 45 50 96) at Calle Gabriel y Galán 17, Torrejón el Rubio, advertises bicycles to rent. There may also be bikes available at Camping Monfragüe.

✿ ✿ ✿ ✿ ✿ ✿ ✿ ✿ ✿ ✿ ✿ ✿

Dehesas

The Spanish word *dehesa* means, simply, pastureland, but in parts of Extremadura, where the pastures are often dotted with evergreen oaks, it takes on a dimension that sends environmentalists into raptures of delight. *Dehesas de encina* (holm oak) *y alcornoque* (cork oak) are a textbook case of sustainable exploitation. The bark of the cork oak can be stripped every 10 years or so for cork *(corcho)* – you'll see the scars on some trees, a bright terracotta colour if they're new. The holm oak can be pruned about every four years and the offcuts used for charcoal. Meanwhile livestock can graze the pastures and in autumn pigs are turned out to gobble up the fallen acorns *(bellotas)* – a diet considered to produce the best ham of all.

Such at least is the theory. In practice a growing number of Extremadura's dehesas are used to a lot less than their full potential. Some belong to absentee landlords who use them only for shooting; others are left untended simply because people are finding easier ways of earning a crust. ∎

✿ ✿ ✿ ✿ ✿ ✿ ✿ ✿ ✿ ✿ ✿ ✿

Central Extremadura

CÁCERES

At the heart of Cáceres, Extremadura's second most populous city with 72,000 inhabitants, stands an old town so little changed since the 15th and 16th centuries that it's often used as a film set and has now been added to UNESCO's list of World Heritage cities. Apart from this 'Ciudad Monumental', there isn't much to see in Cáceres, but it's a pleasant and lively place, with a sizeable student population thanks to the presence here of several faculties of the Universidad Extremeña.

There was once a Roman town, Norba Caesarina, here, but it wasn't until the Muslim period that Cáceres achieved much significance. A key goal for anyone hoping to control Extremadura, the city was taken by the Christian kingdom of León three times between 1142 and 1184 but was recaptured by the Muslims on each occasion. The fourth Christian conquest, by Alfonso IX of León in 1227, proved to be permanent. Noble Leonese families started settling here in the late 13th century, and during the 15th and 16th centuries they turned its walled nucleus into one of the most impressive concentrations of medieval stonemasonry in Europe.

Orientation

The heart of Cáceres is the 150 metre long Plaza Mayor, with the Ciudad Monumental rising on its east side. Around Plaza Mayor and the Ciudad Monumental extends a tangle of humbler old streets which gives way, about 450 metres to the south-west, to the straight Avenida de España lining the Parque Calvo Sotelo and Paseo de Cánovas – the modern half of central Cáceres. From the Cruz de los Caídos monument at the south end of Paseo de Cánovas, Avenida de Alemania runs one km south-west to the train station. The bus station is 200 metres east of the train station, just off Avenida de la Hispanidad.

Information

The tourist office (☎ 24 63 47) is on the east side of Plaza Mayor. It's open weekdays from 9 am to 2 pm and 5 to 7 pm, weekends from 9.30 am to 2 pm.

You'll find banks and ATMs along Calle Pintores, off the south end of Plaza Mayor. The main post office (postcode 10080) is at Paseo Primo de Rivera 2 facing Parque Calvo Sotelo. The telephone code is ☎ 927.

The Policía Nacional (☎ 091) are at Avenida Virgen de la Montaña 3, off the east side of Parque Calvo Sotelo. The Hospital Provincial (☎ 24 23 00) is on the west side of Parque Calvo Sotelo.

Ciudad Monumental

The Ciudad Monumental is worth two visits – one by day to look around and visit such buildings as you can, and one by night to soak up the atmosphere of accumulated ages. Especially outside university terms, it can seem very quiet, but as a kind of medieval Nobs' Hill it probably never bustled like the streets outside its walls. Many of its mansions – all carved with the heraldic shields of their founding families – are still in private (though often absentee) hands; others are occupied by the bureaucrats of the provincial government, the local bishop and sections of the university.

The Ciudad Monumental is still almost surrounded by **walls** and **towers** rebuilt by the Almohads about 1184.

Plaza de Santa María Entering the Ciudad Monumental from Plaza Mayor through an 18th century arch, the **Arco de la Estrella**, you'll see ahead the **Iglesia de Santa María**, Cáceres' 15th century Gothic cathedral. From February to September, Santa María's tower will be topped by the ungainly nests of the white storks which come from Africa to make their homes on every worthwhile vertical protuberance in the old city. The clacking beaks of the chicks demanding food are sometimes the loudest sound you'll hear. On one corner of the church is a statue of San Pedro de Alcántara, a 16th century extremeño ascetic who dedicated himself to reforming the Franciscan order. Inside the church, stick 100 ptas in the slot to the right of the sacristy/museum door to light up the fine carved-cedar retablo of 1549-51.

The church stands on one of the Ciudad Monumental's handsomest plazas, Plaza de Santa María, which is also fronted by such other fine buildings – all in 16th century Renaissance style – as the **Palacio Episcopal** (Bishop's Palace), the **Palacio de Mayoralgo**, and the **Palacio de Ovando**, built by Cáceres' leading clan of the 16th and 17th centuries. Just off the north-east corner of the plaza is the **Palacio Carvajal**, another old mansion now used to lodge visiting dignitaries and as the offices of the local tourism department. Free guided visits are available every half-hour, Monday to Friday from 10 am to 2 pm, Saturday from 10 am to 1.30 pm and 5 to 7.30 pm, Sunday and holidays from 10 am to 1.30 pm.

Not far away in the north-western corner of the walled city, the **Palacio Toledo-Moctezuma** was once the home of a daughter of the Aztec emperor Moctezuma, brought to Cáceres as the bride of the conquistador Juan Cano de Saavedra. Today it's the Archivo Histórico Provincial and sometimes stages exhibitions: otherwise, only the unexciting patio is open.

Plaza de San Jorge Back on Plaza de Santa María, you can head south-east past the fine Renaissance-style **Palacio de la Diputación** (provincial government headquarters) to Plaza de San Jorge, above which rises the **Iglesia de San Francisco Javier**, an 18th century Jesuit church. Its coat of white paint was added a few years ago for the filming of *1492, The Conquest of Paradise* which starred Gerard Depardieu as Christopher Columbus.

The **Casa-Museo Árabe Yussuf Al-Borch**, nearby at Cuesta del Marqués 4, is a private house decked out by its owner with all sorts of oriental and Islamic trappings to capture the feel of Muslim times. Its opening hours are erratic. The **Arco del Cristo** at the bottom of this street is a Roman gate.

Plaza de San Mateo & Plaza Veletas From Plaza de San Jorge, Cuesta de la Compañía climbs to Plaza de San Mateo, where the **Iglesia de San Mateo**, traditionally the church of the landowning nobility, has a plateresque portal and a rococo retablo – though it's usually only open for services. Just to the east on Plaza Veleta is the **Torre de las Cigüeñas** (Tower of the Storks), the only one of Cáceres' many towers which did not have its battlements lopped off in the late 15th century, on Isabel la Católica's orders, to put a stop to rivalry between the city's fractious nobility. The building is now the local military headquarters.

Across the square at Plaza Veletas 1 is the excellent **Museo de Cáceres**. The museum is housed in a 16th century mansion built over an elegant 12th century cistern *(aljibe)* – the only surviving bit of Cáceres' Muslim castle – which is its prize exhibit. It also has an interesting archaeological section, upstairs rooms devoted to *artes y costumbres populares* (textile crafts, ceramics, wood-carving, copperware, exotic old costumes), and, in a separate building at the back, a good little fine arts section which includes works by El Greco, Picasso and Miró. The museum is open Tuesday to Saturday from 9 am to 2.30 pm, and Sunday from 10.15 am to 2.30 pm. Entry is 200 ptas.

Other Buildings Also worth a glance as you wander the Ciudad Monumental are the **Palacio de los Golfines de Arriba** on Calle Olmos, which was Franco's headquarters for a few weeks early in the civil war; the **Casa Mudéjar**, one of few buildings in Cáceres to show Muslim influence, on Cuesta de Aldana; and, on Plaza Caldereros, the **Casa de la Generala**, now the university law faculty, and the **Palacio de los Rivera**, the university's rectorate.

Special Events
Every year from 1992 to 1996, Cáceres staged the Spanish edition of the WOMAD (World of Music & Dance) festival, with international bands ranging from reggae and Celtic to African and Indian playing in the

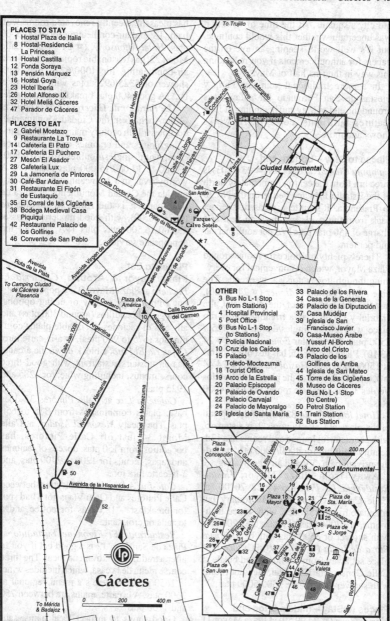

PLACES TO STAY
1 Hostal Plaza de Italia
8 Hostal-Residencia
 La Princesa
11 Hostal Castilla
12 Fonda Soraya
13 Pensión Márquez
16 Hostal Goya
23 Hotel Iberia
26 Hotel Alfonso IX
32 Hotel Meliá Cáceres
47 Parador de Cáceres

PLACES TO EAT
2 Gabriel Mostazo
9 Restaurante La Troya
14 Cafetería El Pato
17 Cafetería El Puchero
27 Mesón El Asador
28 Cafetería Lux
29 La Jamonería de Pintores
30 Café-Bar Adarve
31 Restaurante El Figón
 de Eustaquio
35 El Corral de las Cigüeñas
38 Bodega Medieval Casa
 Piquiqui
42 Restaurante Palacio de
 los Golfines
46 Convento de San Pablo

OTHER
3 Bus No L-1 Stop
 (from Stations)
4 Hospital Provincial
5 Post Office
6 Bus No L-1 Stop
 (to Stations)
7 Policía Nacional
10 Cruz de los Caídos
15 Palacio
 Toledo-Moctezuma
18 Tourist Office
19 Arco de la Estrella
20 Palacio Episcopal
21 Palacio de Ovando
22 Palacio Carvajal
24 Palacio de Mayoralgo
25 Iglesia de Santa María
33 Palacio de los Rivera
34 Casa de la Generala
36 Palacio de la Diputación
37 Casa Mudéjar
39 Iglesia de San
 Francisco Javier
40 Casa-Museo Árabe
 Yussuf Al-Borch
41 Arco del Cristo
43 Palacio de los
 Golfines de Arriba
44 Iglesia de San Mateo
45 Torre de las Cigüeñas
48 Museo de Cáceres
49 Bus No L-1 Stop
 (to Centre)
50 Petrol Station
51 Train Station
52 Bus Station

Cáceres

0   200   400 m

EXTREMADURA

old city's squares. At the time of writing it was uncertain whether this would continue, but it's well worth keeping an eye on the papers for announcements if you're heading this way in the first half of May.

In a more traditional vein, the Feria y Fiestas de San Fernando for a few days around the end of May and beginning of June features bullfights, concerts, fireworks shows and more.

Places to Stay – bottom end

Camping Ciudad de Cáceres (☎ 23 04 03) is three km from the centre, immediately north of the Estadio Príncipe Felipe on the N-630 to Plasencia. It's quite a pleasant site, set back from the road, and open all year at a charge of 450 ptas plus IVA per adult, per car and per tent.

There's plenty of choice for rooms around Plaza Mayor, which is convenient for everything though it gets noisy at weekends. The nine room *Pensión Márquez* (☎ 24 49 60), just off the low end of the plaza at Calle Gabriel y Galán 2, is a friendly family-run place with clean singles/doubles at 1250/2500 ptas. The similar *Fonda Soraya* (☎ 24 43 10), Plaza Mayor 25, has just three rooms at 1500/3000 ptas. *Hostal Castilla* (☎ 24 44 04), one block west of the plaza at Calle Ríos Verdes 3, has adequate rooms for 2000/4000 ptas.

Hotel Iberia (☎ 24 82 00), off the top end of the plaza at Calle Pintores 2, is a step up, with characterful lounge and rooms in a 17th century building for 4000/5000 ptas including private bath, TV and air-con/heating.

Away from Plaza Mayor, *Hostal-Residencia La Princesa* (☎ 22 70 00) at Calle Camino Llano has 34 ordinary but adequate rooms. Singles, with shared bathrooms, are 2000 ptas; doubles are 3200 ptas with shower or 3500 ptas with bath. *Hostal Plaza de Italia* (☎ 24 77 60) is a nice new place set away from the hustle and bustle at Calle Constancia 12. Clean, pleasant rooms with shower and TV are 3500/5000 ptas.

Places to Stay – middle & top end

Hostal Goya (☎ 24 99 50) at Plaza Mayor 11

has pleasant, recently renovated rooms with bath, TV and air-con/heating for 5000/6500 ptas. *Hotel Alfonso IX* (☎ 24 64 00), Calle Moret 22, has reasonable rooms with TV and air-con/heating for 4000/6275 ptas with shower or 5325/6925 ptas with bath, plus IVA. A good 400 ptas breakfast is available.

The *Parador de Cáceres* (☎ 21 17 59), at Calle Ancha 6 in the Ciudad Monumental, occupies a 14th century mansion full of intriguing nooks and crannies and has all mod cons, with singles/doubles from 10,800/13,500 to 12,000/15,000 ptas plus IVA. A worthy rival, in a 16th century mansion just outside the Ciudad Monumental at Plaza de San Juan 11, is the *Hotel Meliá Cáceres* (☎ 21 58 00), with good modern rooms at 13,500/16,500 ptas plus IVA, and all the appropriate services.

Places to Eat

Plaza Mayor & Around *Cafetería El Puchero* at Plaza Mayor 9 is a popular hangout with a huge variety of eating options, from good bocadillos (around 300 ptas) and all sorts of raciones to sizeable platos combinados (675 to 900 ptas), or à-la-carte fare. *Cafetería El Pato*, a block down the arcade, has an upstairs restaurant with good three course menús, including wine, for 1285 and 1925 ptas.

Cafetería Lux at Calle Pintores 32 does basic platos combinados from 375 to 650 ptas. The meaty *Mesón El Asador*, at Calle Moret 34 just off Calle Pintores, has bocadillos from 150 ptas, dozens of raciones and tapas, menús for 1200 to 2400 ptas, and à-la-carte fare too.

Café-Bar Adarve on a short street between Calle Pintores and Gran Vía is not a bad spot for breakfast – 185 ptas for coffee and a tostada or croissant.

Restaurante El Figón de Eustaquio at Plaza de San Juan 12 is a good bet if you're after a traditional extremeño meal. The three course menú de la casa, which includes wine, is 1650 ptas, or there's a menú regional at 2600 ptas. À la carte, mains are between 750 and 1700 ptas.

Good shops to inspect local hams, sausages, cheeses and fruit liquor are *La Jamonería de Pintores* on Calle Pintores, and *Gabriel Mostazo* at the corner of Calle San Pedro and Calle San Antón.

Ciudad Monumental The Ciudad Monumental has a couple of good, atmospheric restaurants – the expensive *Bodega Medieval Casa Piquiqui* at Calle Orellana 1, with suckling pig, kid, game and other extremeño specialities, and the even more expensive *Restaurante Palacio de los Golfines* on Adarve del Padre Rosalio. If you've 4000 or 5000 ptas to spend, the restaurant at the *Parador de Cáceres*, Calle Ancha 6, is also reportedly pretty good – especially its caldereta de cordero.

For a more economical bite, drop into *El Corral de las Cigüeñas* on Cuesta de Aldana. Or visit the *Convento de San Pablo* on Plaza de San Mateo, where the nuns bake and sell tasty snacks such as bizcochitas (small sponge cakes; 250 ptas a serve) or pastas con almendra (almond pastries; 475 ptas). The renowned yemas de San Pablo (candied egg yolks; 650 ptas) aren't to everyone's taste, though. A *torno* – a revolving dumb waiter – enables the nuns, who are members of a closed order, to sell the goodies without seeing or being seen by the customers. Hours are Monday to Friday from 9 am to 1 pm and 5 to 8 pm, Saturday from 9 am to 1 pm.

Elsewhere If you're in the mood for a *really* big feed, Cáceres has a *Restaurante La Troya*, the sister establishment of the one in Trujillo (see that section), at Calle Juan XXIII 1. From the Cruz de los Caídos, head west on Calle Gil Cordero: Juan XXIII is the third street on the left.

Entertainment
The bottom (north) end of Plaza Mayor, and nearby streets such as Calle Gabriel y Galán and Calle General Ezponda, are full of very lively bars, many with music. Particularly at weekends during university terms, you can party here for most of the night. The other nightlife zone – which includes a couple of discos – is around Plaza Albatros, 300 metres west up the hill from the north end of Parque Calvo Sotelo.

Getting There & Away
Bus Daily services include at least nine buses to Plasencia; eight or more to Salamanca (three to four hours; 2000 ptas); about 10 to Trujillo (400 ptas); up to three (except Saturday) to Guadalupe (960 ptas); at least seven to Madrid (3½ to 4¼ hours; 2385 ptas) and Mérida (1¼ hours; 500 to 650 ptas); 11 to Badajoz (fewer at weekends; 750 to 825 ptas); six or more to Zafra and Sevilla (four hours; 2200 ptas); and at least one to Córdoba, Valladolid, León, Santiago de Compostela and even Barcelona. You can call ☎ 23 25 50 or ☎ 23 42 54 for bus information. The bus station has a left-luggage *consigna*.

Train There are five trains a day to Madrid (3½ to five hours; from 2200 ptas), three or more to Plasencia (1¼ hours), Mérida (one hour) and Badajoz (two hours), one to Sevilla (5½ hours; 2075 ptas) and one to Barcelona. The single daily train to Lisbon (six hours; from 4400 ptas) leaves in the middle of the night. You can call ☎ 23 37 61 for train information.

Getting Around
Bus No L-1 from the stop beside the petrol station by the big roundabout outside the train station – also close to the bus station – will take you into town. The nearest stop to the centre is the third, on Paseo Primo de Rivera. Returning to the stations, you can catch this bus by the Kiosco Colón on Avenida de España.

ALCÁNTARA
This historic and pleasant small town is 62 km north-west of Cáceres on a possible route to Portugal, the C-523. There's a tourist office (☎ 39 08 63) on the way in from Cáceres at Avenida de Mérida 21. The telephone code here is ☎ 927.

Alcántara is Arabic for 'the bridge'. The finest **Roman bridge** in Spain – 204 metres long, 61 metres high, and built without mortar – spans the Río Tajo west of the town, not far below a huge modern dam holding back the 80 km long Embalse de Alcántara. There's a memorial to the bridge's 2nd century AD architect, Caius Julius Lacer, in a small Roman temple on the river bank.

The town itself has old walls, remains of a castle, and numerous fine old buildings. From 1218 it was the headquarters of the Orden de Alcántara, an order of Reconquista knights which ruled much of western Extremadura as a kind of private kingdom. The order built the 16th century **Convento de San Benito**, famous for its recipes, with Renaissance exterior, Gothic cloister, plateresque church interior and beautiful three tier gallery. The 13th century **Iglesia de Santa María de Almócovar**, a mix of Romanesque and Herrerian styles, contains tombs of masters of the Orden de Alcántara and paintings by the noted 16th century extremeño artist Luis Morales, known as El Divino Morales.

The *Hostal Kantara Al Saif* (☎ 39 09 78) at Avenida de Mérida s/n has doubles with bath from 4000 to 6000 ptas, depending on the season (plus IVA).

There are daily buses (none on Sunday) from Cáceres.

TRUJILLO

Trujillo is one of the most perfect little towns in Spain. With just 9000 people, it can't be much bigger now than it was in 1529 when its most famous son, Francisco Pizarro, set off with his four half-brothers and a few other local buddies for an expedition that culminated a few years later in the bloody conquest of the Inca empire.

Trujillo is blessed with a broad and fine Plaza Mayor, from which rises its remarkably preserved old town, packed with aged buildings exuding history. If you arrive from the Plasencia direction you might imagine that you've driven through a time warp into the 16th century.

Information

The tourist office (☎ 32 26 77), on Plaza Mayor, is open Tuesday to Sunday from 9

am to 2 pm and 5 to 7 pm. The post office is at Calle Encarnación 28, south of the centre. The postcode is 10200 and the telephone code ☎ 927.

The Policía Local (☎ 908-70 65 17) are in an alley off the south-west side of Plaza Mayor.

Things to See

Plaza Mayor An equestrian **statue of Pizarro**, done by an American, Charles Rumsey, in the 1920s, dominates Plaza Mayor. There's a tale that Rumsey originally did the piece as a statue of Hernán Cortés, to present to Mexico, but Mexico (which takes a poor view of Cortés) didn't want it, so it was given to Trujillo as Pizarro instead!

On the plaza's south side, the corner of the **Palacio de la Conquista** (currently closed to visitors) sports the carved images of Pizarro and his lover Inés Yupanqui (sister of the Inca emperor Atahualpa) and, to the right, their daughter Francisca Pizarro Yupanqui with her husband (and uncle) Hernando Pizarro. The mansion was built in the 1560s for Hernando and Francisca after Hernando – the only Pizarro brother not to die a bloody death in Peru – had done 20 years in jail in Spain for the killing of Diego de Almagro. Above the corner balcony another carving shows the Pizarro family shield – two bears and a pine tree – surrounded by the walls of Cuzco, plus Pizarro's ships at Tumbes, and Atahualpa with his hands in two chests of gold surrounded by seven Inca chiefs.

Overseeing the Plaza Mayor from the north-east corner is the **Iglesia de San Martín**, a mainly 16th century construction with a number of noble tombs inside, but normally only open for services. Its towers, like most others in Trujillo and in old Cáceres, support the precarious nests of storks. Across the street from the east end of the church is the 16th century **Palacio de los Duques de San Carlos**, now a convent but open for visits daily from 9.30 am to 1 pm and 4.30 to 6.30 pm (100 ptas). It has a classical-style patio and a very grand staircase.

Through an alley from the south-west

Trujillo

0   100   200 m

PLACES TO STAY
7 Hostal La Cadena
16 Hostal Nuria
20 Camas Boni
21 Casa Roque
22 Parador de Trujillo

PLACES TO EAT
6 Café-Bar El Escudo
8 Restaurante La Troya
9 Hostal Pizarro
17 Bar Pillete
18 Bar La Victoria

OTHER
1 Castillo

2 Museo de la Coria
3 Casa-Museo de Pizarro
4 Iglesia de Santa María la
   Mayor
5 Iglesia de Santiago
10 Iglesia de San Martín
11 Pizarro Statue
12 Tourist Office
13 Palacio Juan Pizarro de
   Orellana
14 Policía Local
15 Palacio de la Conquista
19 Palacio de los Duques de
   San Carlos
23 Post Office
24 Bus Station

corner of the Plaza Mayor is the **Palacio Juan Pizarro de Orellana**, which was converted from a miniature fortress into a Renaissance mansion by a cousin of the Pizarros who took part in the conquest of Peru and lived to reap the benefits back home. It's now a school, the Colegio del Sagrado Corazón de Jesús, and you can visit its patio, decorated with Pizarro and Orellana coats of arms, daily from 9.30 am to 2 pm and 4 to 6.30 pm.

Upper Town The 900 metres of **walls** which circle the upper town date from Muslim times. It was here that after the Reconquista the newly settled noble families erected their mansions and churches. The defensive towers which topped their buildings were, like those of Cáceres, later demolished on orders of Isabel la Católica.

The **Iglesia de Santiago** on Plaza Santiago is one of Trujillo's oldest churches. It was founded in the 13th century by the Knights of Santiago, and their conch-shell emblem is a recurring motif. The church is open from 10.30 am to 2 pm and 4.30 to 6.30 pm (50 ptas).

The **Iglesia de Santa María la Mayor** on

EXTREMADURA

Extremadura & America

Many people from Extremadura jumped at the chance of a new start in life that was opened up by Columbus' discovery of the Americas in 1492. A further westward impetus was provided by the fall of Granada the same year, which ended the Reconquista of Muslim Spain to which many of Extremadura's knightly families had looked for a chance of booty and new land.

In 1501 Fray Nicolás de Ovando, a member of a leading Cáceres family, was named governor of the Indies by the Catholic Monarchs. He set up his capital, Santo Domingo, in what's now the Dominican Republic on the Caribbean island of Hispaniola. With him went 2500 followers, many of them from Extremadura, including Francisco Pizarro, an illegitimate son of a minor noble family from Trujillo. In 1504, Hernán Cortés, from a similar family in Medellín, on the Río Guadiana east of Mérida, arrived in Santo Domingo too.

Both young men prospered in the new world. Cortés took part in the conquest of Cuba in 1511 and settled there to raise livestock and trade the gold that was mined by the Indians whose labour he had been granted. Pizarro, in 1513, accompanied Vasco Núñez de Balboa to Darién, where they discovered the Pacific Ocean. Balboa, from Jerez de los Caballeros in south-west Extremadura, had run into debt in the Caribbean and escaped his creditors by hiding in a barrel on a ship to the mainland. Settling in Panama and, like Cortés, being granted Indian labour, Pizarro grew cattle, raised maize, raised cattle, and eventually rose to be mayor of the town of Panama. (In between times he was given the job of arresting the unfortunate Balboa for treason. Balboa was executed in 1519.)

In 1518 the governor of Cuba asked Cortés to lead an expedition to what's now Mexico, which was rumoured to be full of gold and silver. Cortés set off the following year with 550 men and 11 horses. By 1521, with a combination of incredible courage, cunning, fortitude, luck and ruthlessness, Cortés and his small band had conquered Tenochtitlán (Mexico City), the mountain capital of the Aztec empire. The rest of the empire – a large slice of modern Mexico – was brought to heel by 1524. Though initially named governor of what he had conquered, Cortés soon found royal officials arriving to usurp his authority. He returned to Spain in 1528 to see King Carlos I, with rich gifts and a retinue of Indian chiefs. The king confirmed him as captain general of Nueva España but not as governor, though he did make him a *marqués* and give him a massive grant of Indian labour. Cortés returned to Mexico in 1530 but, increasingly discontented, returned again to Spain in 1540, this time to a cool reception from the representatives of the king. He never returned to Mexico, dying in a village near Sevilla in 1547. There's a monument to him in Medellín.

While Cortés was conquering the Aztecs, Pizarro was becoming obsessed by tales of another empire of silver and gold south of Panama. In 1524 he formed a partnership with two other colonists,

Plaza de Santa María is an interesting hotch-potch of 13th to 16th century styles, with a Romanesque tower. Inside are the tombs of leading Trujillo families of the Middle Ages, plus that of Diego García de Paredes (1466-1530), known as 'El Sansón extremeño' (the Samson of Extremadura), a Trujillo warrior of legendary strength who fought for the Reyes Católicos (Catholic Monarchs) against Granada and later in Italy and against the Turks. According to Cervantes he could stop a mill wheel with one finger. The church also has a fine retablo with Flemish-style paintings done in about 1485 by Fernando Gallego from Salamanca. The church is open from 10.30 am to 4 pm and 4.30 to 7 pm (50 ptas).

A little higher, the 15th century **Casa-Museo de Pizarro** was the ancestral home of the great conquistador family. The family was a noble one, originally from Asturias (where, one imagines, they got the idea of putting a bear on their escutcheon) and was rewarded for its part in the reconquest of Trujillo by being allowed to build within the city walls. Recently restored in the style of the 15th and 16th centuries, the house contains informative displays (in Spanish) on the Inca empire and the Pizarros. Whether Francisco Pizarro ever lived here is doubtful. Though the eldest of his father Gonzalo's nine children – by four women – Francisco was (like five of the others) illegitimate and not accepted as an heir. However, it was here, on his visit to Trujillo in 1529, that Francisco was brought in triumph by his siblings. The house is open Tuesday to Sunday from 11 am to 2 pm and 4.30 to 8 pm (250 ptas).

✤ ✤

Diego de Almagro and the priest Hernando de Luque, to search for this. Their first expeditions, in 1524 and 1526, failed, though on the second one they did reach the Inca town of Tumbes, on the coast of what's now Peru. Unable to gain the support of the Spanish governor in Panama for a bigger expedition, Pizarro followed Cortés' trail back to Spain in 1529 to see the king, bringing llamas and other gifts. He won royal backing for his project and – no doubt learning much from the experience of Cortés, whom he met in Toledo – got himself named, in advance, governor of what was to be called Nueva Castilla.

Before sailing back to Panama, Pizarro visited Trujillo, where he received a hero's welcome and picked up his four half-brothers – Hernando, Juan and Gonzalo Pizarro from his father's side and Martín de Alcántara from his mother's – and other relatives and friends to join the expedition. This finally set off from Panama in 1531, with 180 men and 37 horses. With a perhaps even more incredible combination of the same factors by which Cortés had succeeded in Mexico, Pizarro and his men crossed the Andes and in 1532 managed to capture the Inca emperor Atahualpa in the city of Cajamarca despite his having an army of 30,000 on hand. The Inca empire, with its capital in Cuzco, extended north to Colombia and south to Chile and Argentina. Atahualpa offered to buy his freedom from Pizarro by filling with gold the room where he was held captive. The conquistadors took the gold but the following year executed Atahualpa and named his brother, Manco, as a puppet emperor.

When Manco rebelled in 1536, Juan Pizarro was killed in the battle for Cuzco. In 1538 a civil war broke out between the Pizarros and Diego de Almagro, ending with the execution of Almagro by Hernando Pizarro. Francisco Pizarro and Martín de Alcántara were assassinated by Almagro's son in Lima in 1541 (Pizarro is buried in Lima cathedral). Inca resistance was finally quelled by about 1545, but in 1548 Gonzalo Pizarro rebelled against the new Spanish viceroy and was executed.

Other members of the Pizarro expedition survived to make their mark elsewhere. In about 1540 Hernando de Soto, from either Jerez de los Caballeros or nearby Barcarrota (both places claim him), became the first European to discover the Mississippi. Shortly afterwards Francisco de Orellana, from Trujillo, did the same for the Amazon, floating down it by raft for eight months from the Andes to the Atlantic.

Altogether 600 or 700 people from Trujillo made their way to the Americas in the 16th century. So it's not really surprising that there are at least seven Trujillos in North, Central and South America today. There's an even higher number of Guadalupes, for conquistadors and colonists from all over Spain took with them to the new world the name of the Virgin of Guadalupe in eastern Extremadura, whose shrine was one of the most venerated and most visited of all in medieval Spain. The cult of the Virgen de Guadalupe remains widespread in Latin America today. ■

✤ ✤

Against the walls north-west of the Pizarro house, the **Museo de la Coria** has further displays on the conquest of the Americas, in a restored former convent. It's run by a private foundation and is only open on Saturday, Sunday and holidays from 11.30 am to 2 pm (free).

At the top of the hill and affording great views, Trujillo's **castillo** is an impressive though empty castle, of 10th century Muslim origin, strengthened later by the Christians. It's open daily till dusk (free).

Places to Stay

Camas Boni (☎ 32 16 04), about 100 metres east of Plaza Mayor at Calle Domingo de Ramos 7, is good value with singles/doubles from 1500/3000 ptas and doubles with bath for 4000 ptas. Rooms are on the small side but well kept. *Casa Roque* (☎ 32 23 13), further along the street at No 30, is a second choice, with singles at 1500 ptas, and doubles with bath at 3500 ptas. On Plaza Mayor at No 27, *Hostal Nuria* (☎ 32 09 07) has nice singles/doubles with bath for 3000/5000 ptas. The friendly eight room *Hostal La Cadena* (☎ 32 14 63) at No 8 is also good, at 4000/5000 ptas.

The *Parador de Trujillo* (☎ 32 13 50), on Plaza de Santa Clara, is in a beautiful former convent dating from the 16th century. Doubles start at 13,500 ptas plus IVA.

Places to Eat

If you're a meat-eater, the 1900-ptas menú at *Restaurante La Troya*, Plaza Mayor 10, will save you from eating much else for the next couple of days. What the bare three course

EXTREMADURA

list of offerings doesn't tell you is that portions are gigantic and that they also give you a large potato omelette and a salad for starters, and an extra main course later on! Caldereta, of course, is a main course speciality. If you're not *that* hungry there are great tapas here too. Elsewhere on Plaza Mayor the *Hostal La Cadena* and *Hostal Pizarro* do normal-size meals, *Cafetería Nuria* has platos combinados for 750 to 900 ptas, *Bar La Victoria* does raciones at 500 or 600 ptas, and *Bar Pillete* is the classiest café and has the best position.

Café-Bar El Escudo up the hill on Plaza Santiago has moderately priced raciones and platos combinados too.

The *Parador de Trujillo* has an excellent restaurant, but you're looking at around 4000 ptas for a full meal.

Getting There & Away

The bus station (☎ 32 12 02) is 500 metres south of Plaza Mayor, on Carretera de Mérida. At least 12 buses daily run to Madrid (2½ to four hours; 2000 ptas), seven or more to Cáceres (45 minutes; 400 ptas) and eight or more to Mérida (1¼ hours) and Badajoz. There's daily service to Salamanca, Zafra, Huelva and Barcelona. Buses run on Tuesday, Thursday and Friday to Torrejón el Rubio, Villarreal de San Carlos (for the Parque Natural Monfragüe) and Plasencia. Other days you need to change buses at Cáceres to reach Plasencia.

GUADALUPE

There's one main reason for visiting Guadalupe, and that's to see the Monasterio de Nuestra Señora, built by King Alfonso XI following the defeat of a Moroccan invasion at the Battle of El Salado in 1340. The monastery was established on the site where a 14th century shepherd is said to have found an effigy of the Virgin carved by St Luke, and later became one of Spain's most important pilgrimage sites and an important centre for the study of medicine and surgery.

In the 15th and 16th centuries, the Virgin of Guadalupe was so revered that she was made patron of all the territories conquered by Spain in America. Christopher Columbus named the Caribbean island in her honour, and on 29 July 1496 his Indian servants were baptised in the fountain in front of the monastery. The entries are registered in the first Book of Baptisms.

Today Guadalupe remains one of Spain's most important religious centres, and the local economy relies heavily upon tourism to the extent that there is little else to do in town but eat, drink and visit tacky souvenir shops. Lovers of remote country, however, could head off into the wild, craggy sierras of this corner of Extremadura, which are split by deep valleys and are home to woodlands of chestnut and oak as well as olive groves and vineyards. Several minor roads wind through the hills, and there are hiking possibilities.

Information

The tourist office (☎ 15 41 28) is on Plaza de Santa María, otherwise known as Plaza Mayor. The post office is next to the medical centre in Calle Gregorio López. Centro Hispano bank, also in Calle Gregorio López, has an outside ATM. The postcode is 10140 and the phone code is ☎ 927.

Things to See

The **monasterio**, on Plaza de Santa María, is open daily from 9.30 am to 1 pm and 3.30 to 6.30 pm. Visitors gather in the waiting room until there are enough people for the one hour guided tour (300 ptas).

The architectural style of the monastery buildings varies dramatically, as they were constructed at various times between the 14th and 18th centuries. The tour starts with the mudéjar cloister, in the centre of which is a small Gothic temple, and continues with the **Museo de Bordados**, containing embroidered vestments and altar cloths. In the **sacristía** there are eight paintings by Francisco de Zurbarán, while the image of the Virgin is kept in the rococo **camarín**.

Special Events

There are fiestas and processions during Semana Santa and on 8 September, 30 September and 12 October. At such times it is essential to book accommodation well in advance.

Places to Stay

There is a pretty camp site in a valley two km before the village with good facilities including bar, restaurant and swimming pool. This is *Camping Las Villuercas* (☎ 36 71 39), at Carretera de Villanueva, charging 375 ptas per person and 375 ptas per car.

There is no shortage of places to stay in Guadalupe, all a short walk from the monastery. *Pensión Tena* (☎ 36 71 04), at Calle Ventilla 1, has singles/doubles with bath for 2000/3000 ptas. *Mesón Típico Isabel* (☎ 36 71 26), on Plaza de Santa María, has rooms above the bar. Singles/doubles with private shower cost 3000/4000 ptas.

Hostal Lujuan (☎ 36 71 70), at Calle Gregorio López 19, has rooms with bath for 3000/4000 ptas plus IVA. *Hostal Cerezo II* (☎ 36 73 79), at Plaza de Santa María 33, has rooms with bath for 2750/4750 ptas plus IVA. *Hostal Cerezo I* (☎ 36 73 79), at Calle Gregorio López 20, has singles with shower for 2600 ptas and doubles with bath for 4000 ptas plus IVA.

Parador Zurbarán (☎ 36 70 75), a converted 15th century hospital at Calle Marqués de la Romana 10, opposite the monastery, has doubles from 9500 ptas plus IVA. Much better is *Hospedería del Real Monasterio* (☎ 36 70 00), at Plaza Juan Carlos 1, with rooms for 4700/6900 ptas plus IVA, but you'll need to book in advance.

Places to Eat

Most places to stay have cafés or restaurants offering set menus for around 1100 ptas plus IVA. The *Hospedería del Real Monasterio* has a set menu for 2000 ptas plus IVA, and a bar with a spectacular courtyard which you should go out of your way to visit.

The *parador* has a rather sedate restaurant with a set menu for 2200 ptas plus IVA, but you're likely to have a much better time at the nearby *Mesón El Cordero*, at Calle Convento 2. It's probably the best restaurant in town and specialises in cordero asado en

horno de leña (roast lamb from a wood-fired oven) for 1550 ptas. Alternatively, there's a 2120 ptas set menu.

Most bars start closing around 10 pm and by 11 pm the place is dead, though it may be different in the peak season.

Getting There & Away

All buses leave from the medical centre next to the ayuntamiento on Avenida de Blas Pérez. From Monday to Friday there are two buses a day to Cáceres (960 ptas) via Trujillo. From Monday to Saturday there are two a day to Madrid (2100 ptas) via Talavera de la Reina. There are two buses daily to Miajadas: change there for Mérida and Badajoz.

Southern Extremadura

MÉRIDA

The city of Mérida stands on the site of the Roman Augusta Emerita, originally founded in 25 BC as a settlement for veterans of Rome's campaigns in Cantabria. It became the capital of the Roman province of Lusitania, and with more than 40,000 inhabitants it was the largest Roman city on the Iberian Peninsula. The population was diverse: funeral inscriptions and the different religious rites reveal that Romans and Iberians lived side by side with people from the Middle East and Africa.

Before long, Emerita had become the political and cultural hub of Hispania, even minting its own coins until the practice was banned by Caligula. Its decline began in 713 AD, when it was conquered by the Muslims, and continued after the Reconquista by Alfonso IX in 1230 as the inhabitants moved away, leaving it abandoned until the era of the Catholic Monarchs.

Today, Mérida has more Roman ruins than anywhere else in Spain, around which a lively, modern city with a population of 41,000 has sprung up. Since 1983 it has been the seat of the Junta de Extremadura, the Extremadura regional government.

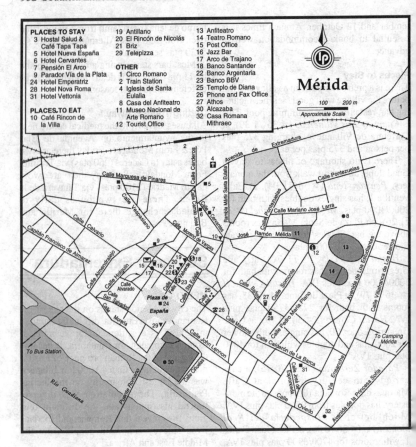

PLACES TO STAY		19 Antillano	13 Anfiteatro
3	Hostal Salud &	20 El Rincón de Nicolás	14 Teatro Romano
	Café Tapa Tapa	21 Briz	15 Post Office
5	Hotel Nueva España	29 Telepizza	16 Jazz Bar
6	Hotel Cervantes		17 Arco de Trajano
7	Pensión El Arco	OTHER	18 Banco Santander
9	Parador Vía de la Plata	1 Circo Romano	22 Banco Argentaria
24	Hotel Emperatriz	2 Train Station	23 Banco BBV
28	Hotel Nova Roma	3 Iglesia de Santa	25 Templo de Diana
31	Hotel Vettonia	Eulalia	26 Phone and Fax Office
		8 Casa del Anfiteatro	27 Athos
PLACES TO EAT		11 Museo Nacional de	30 Alcazaba
10	Café Rincon de	Arte Romano	32 Casa Romana
	la Villa	12 Tourist Office	Mithraeo

Mérida

0   100   200 m

Approximate Scale

Orientation

From the train station, on Calle Carderos, it's just a 10 minute walk to Plaza de España, the centre of town. Much of the accommodation lies between the two. From the bus station, on the other side of the Río Guadiana, it's a 20 minute walk, but you have a spectacular view of the Puente Romano from the new suspension bridge.

The most important Roman ruins are concentrated on the east side of town, but all are within walking distance. The pedestrianised Calle Santa Eulalia, which starts from Plaza de España, is the heart of the shopping zone.

Information

Tourist Office The helpful tourist office (☎ 31 53 53), on Calle Pedro María Plano, is right by the gates to the Roman theatre and amphitheatre. It is open Monday to Friday from 9 am to 1.45 pm and 5 to 6.45 pm (4 to 5.45 pm in winter), Saturday and Sunday from 9 am to 1.45 pm.

Money Most of the banks are around Plaza de España and the pedestrianised shopping zone. Banco BBV, Banco Santander and Banco Argentaria on Calle Felix Valverde Lillo are among many with 24-hour ATMs.

Post & Communications The central post office is on Plaza de la Constitución, and the postcode is 06800. There is a phone and fax office at Calle Maestros (☎ 30 34 84). The phone code is ☎ 924.

Medical Services For an ambulance call ☎ 37 08 28 or ☎ 31 11 08. The Hospital General (☎ 38 10 00) is on Calle Enrique Sánchez de León, south-west of the bus station.

Things to See
Roman Ruins For 600 ptas you can buy a ticket which gives you entry to the Teatro Romano, the Anfiteatro, the Casa del Anfiteatro, the Casa Romana del Mithraeo and the Alcazaba, all open daily from 9 am to 1.45 pm and 5 to 7.15 pm (4 to 6.15 pm in winter).

The **Teatro Romano**, which has recently been restored, was built around 15 BC to seat 6000 spectators, while the adjoining **Anfiteatro**, constructed in 8 BC for gladiatorial contests, had a capacity of 15,000. Nearby, the 3rd century **Casa del Anfiteatro** has remains of paintings and exceptionally good mosaics. The 2nd century **Casa Romana del Mithraeo**, a former stately home discovered by chance in 1964 while a piece of land was being levelled, has mosaics in almost every room and top-quality Pompeiian frescos. The **Alcazaba** – originally a Roman and Visigothic building – was converted into a Muslim castle in 855 AD and was later used as a monastery.

Other Roman monuments are dotted around the city and can be seen at any time; of these the **Puente Romano** is one of the most important. With 64 granite arches and a length of 792 metres, it is one of the longest bridges ever built by the Romans. In Calle Trajano, the **Arco de Trajano**, 15 metres high, was originally a monumental gate to the provincial forum. Nearby, in Calle Romero Leal, is the **Templo de Diana**, relatively well preserved since most of it was incorporated into a mansion in the 16th century. North-east of the amphitheatre, on Avenida de la Princesa Sofía, are the overgrown remains of the **Circo Romano**, the

only surviving hippodrome of its kind in Spain.

Museo Nacional de Arte Romano This museum, designed by architect Rafael Moneo, was opened in 1986 and houses a superb collection of statues, mosaics, frescos, coins and other Roman artefacts. Opening times are Tuesday to Saturday from 10 am to 2 pm and 5 to 7 pm (4 to 6 pm in winter), Sunday from 10 am to 2 pm only. Entry is 400 ptas.

Iglesia de Santa Eulalia Originally built in the 4th century in honour of the city's patron saint, the church was completely rebuilt in Romanesque style in the 13th century. It's open Monday to Saturday from 10 am to 1.45 pm and 5 to 6.45 pm (4 to 5.45 pm in winter).

Special Events
In July and August there is a festival at the Roman theatre featuring ancient and more recent drama classics.

Places to Stay
The nearest camp site is *Camping Mérida* (☎ 30 34 53), two km out of town at Carretera de Madrid, Km 337. It is open all year round and costs 425 ptas per person, per tent and per car.

Pensión El Arco (☎ 31 83 21), at Calle Cervantes 16, is the only pensión in the centre of town. It's great value for money and deservedly popular with backpackers: spotless singles/doubles/triples cost 1600/ 3000/ 4200 ptas with shared bathroom.

Hostal Salud (☎ 31 22 59), less than a five minute walk from the train station at Calle Vespasiano 41, has decent singles/doubles with private bath for 2500/4500 ptas. *Hotel Nueva España* (☎ 31 33 56), at Avenida de Extremadura 6, has simple rooms with private bath for 2500/4500 ptas. *Hotel Vettonia* (☎ 31 14 62), at Calle Calderón de la Barca 26, has distinctly average rooms with private bath for 2800/4400, plus IVA.

Moving up-market, *Hotel Cervantes* (☎ 31 49 61) at Calle Camilo José Cela 8 has comfortable rooms for 5000/8000 ptas plus

IVA. The international-style *Hotel Nova Roma* (☎ 31 12 61), at Calle Suárez Somonte 42, has singles/doubles for 8000/10,450 ptas plus IVA, but *Hotel Emperatriz* (☎ 31 31 11), a former palace at Plaza de España 19, is far preferable, with singles/doubles costing 6000/10,950 ptas plus IVA.

Parador Vía de la Plata (☎ 31 38 00) – originally a Roman forum, it has subsequently been a mosque, a convent and an asylum – at Plaza de la Constitución 3, has singles/doubles for 9200/16,500 plus IVA.

Places to Eat

For anyone craving junk food, *Telepizza*, on the corner of Plaza de España, has pizzas from 700 ptas.

There are three great bar-restaurants next door to each other on Calle Felix Valverde Lillo. *Briz*, at No 5, does a great montado de lomo (loin of pork sandwich) for 350 ptas and has a restaurant out the back with set menus for 1350 ptas. Next door is the upmarket *El Rincón de Nicolás*, with set menus for 2000 ptas. The lively *Antillano*, at No 15, is very popular with locals and has set menus for just 1200 ptas.

Parador Vía de la Plata has a menú for 3500 ptas plus IVA featuring local specialities such as marinated partridge, but best of all is the excellent *Los Eméritos*, at the Hotel Emperatriz, where you can dine in the stylish surroundings of the covered courtyard. Surprisingly, its fixed-price menu costs just 1500 ptas and offers a wide range, from regional specialities to bacon, eggs and chips.

Cafés *Tapa Tapa*, adjoining Hostal Salud, has a good range of tapas at 300 ptas, and raciones such as estofado de carne en salsa for 600 ptas. *Rincón de la Villa* is a good place to meet, conveniently situated at the top of Rambla Mártir Santa Eulalia, the main shopping street. There are three telephones outside which take credit cards.

Entertainment

During the day, Plaza de España has a variety of bars and is a popular place to sit and watch the world go by.

Most of the nightlife is concentrated on – believe it or not – Calle John Lennon. (Interestingly, the right-wing element of the Extremadura regional government is fighting to change the name to Calle Margaret Thatcher.) The street is full of late-night bars catering for every kind of taste. There is also a large disco called *Mai Kel's*, which out of season is open from 11 pm until 5 am on Friday and Saturday nights only.

Three blocks away, at Calle Baños 3, is *Athos*, the only gay bar in the whole of Extremadura – or so they claim – featuring a late-night bar, hard-core videos and a somewhat raunchy dance floor.

Best of all, just around the corner from the Arco de Trajano, on Calle Trajano, there's a classy late-night jazz bar, called – rather unimaginatively – *Jazz Bar*.

Getting There & Away

Bus There are at least eight buses a day to Badajoz (610 ptas), Sevilla (1675 ptas) and Madrid (3625 ptas) and at least seven to Cáceres (650 ptas). To get to Guadalupe, take one of five daily buses to Trujillo (830 ptas) and change at Miajadas.

Train There are three long-distance trains a day to Barcelona (7000 ptas) via Cáceres (1100 ptas), Madrid (2900 ptas), Zaragoza (5300 ptas) and Lleida (6200 ptas), and three a day to Badajoz (1100 ptas). There are two long-distance trains a day to Ciudad Real for connections with Sevilla, Córdoba, Granada, Cádiz and Valencia.

There is one regional train a day to Sevilla (1560 ptas), two a day to Madrid (2725 ptas), two a day to Zafra (480 ptas) and at least three a day to Badajoz (735 ptas).

Car & Motorcycle Heading north from Sevilla, the N-630 goes directly to Mérida via Zafra and continues to Cáceres. Southwest from Madrid, the N-V via Trujillo is the fastest route.

Getting Around

To get a bus into town from the train station, walk 50 metres up Calle Carderos and turn left into Avenida de Extremadura. The bus stop is right next to the Hornito de Santa Eulalia, a small shrine in front of the Iglesia de Santa Eulalia. Bus No L2 will take you to Plaza de España.

To get into town from the bus station, take a No 6 from the bus stop opposite. Alternatively, you could take a taxi from the rank outside for 400 ptas.

BADAJOZ

Just seven km from the Portuguese border, Badajoz – the provincial capital of the southern half of Extremadura – stands on the banks of the Río Guadiana. A modern, sprawling, industrial city with 150,000 inhabitants, it retains few monuments of interest.

Formerly the capital of a small Muslim kingdom, it was conquered by Alfonso IX of León in 1229 and subsequently became the scene of much military conflict. It was first occupied by the Portuguese in 1385, and again in 1396, 1542 and 1660. In 1701 it was besieged by the Allies during the War of the Spanish Succession, and in 1812 the French were driven out by the British.

Orientation

Plaza de España is the centre of the old town; west of it are the pedestrianised shopping streets, with plenty of places to eat and drink. The main commercial centre is around Calle Juan Carlos I.

Most low-budget accommodation is just a short walk away, but two of the international hotels are on the other side of the river. The bus station (☎ 25 86 61), on Calle José Rebollo López, is a 20 minute walk, at the southern edge of town beyond the ring road. The train station (☎ 27 11 70), on Avenida de Carolina Coronado, is even further out, on the other side of the river, north-west of town.

Information

Tourist Office The exceptionally helpful tourist office (☎ 22 49 81), on Pasaje de San Juan, just off Plaza de España, opens Monday to Friday from 8 am to 3 pm and occasionally on Saturday from 9 am to 1 pm. For regional information, the Junta de Extremadura (☎ 22 27 63) is at Plaza de la Libertad 3, just south-west of Paseo de San Francisco. It is open Monday to Friday from 9 am to 2 pm and 5 to 7 pm, Saturday and Sunday from 9 am to 2 pm.

Money Banco Central Hispano and Banco El Monte, both on Plaza de España, have 24-hour ATMs. There are plenty of others nearby on Plaza de Minayo and the adjoining Paseo de San Francisco.

Post & Communications The central post office (postcode 06080) is on Calle Correos, at the southern corner of Paseo de San Francisco. The phone code is ☎ 924.

Medical Services The Cruz Roja (☎ 22 22 22) is south-west of the centre at Calle Tomás Romero de Castilla 2. The Hospital Provincial de San Sebastián (☎ 22 47 43) is centrally located at Plaza de Minayo 2.

Things to See

The 13th century **Catedral de San Juan** is on Plaza de España, built in fortress style on the site of an earlier mosque. It is open Tuesday to Saturday from 11 am to 1 pm. There is a museum in the chapterhouse with paintings by various artists including Luis de Morales, open on Friday and Saturday only from 11 am to 1 pm. Entry is free.

The remains of the **Alcazaba Musulmana** and the Renaissance palace within lie in a public park to the north-east of Plaza de España. The **Museo Arqueológico** is housed in a former mosque within the enclosure. It is open Tuesday to Sunday from 10 am to 3 pm; entry is free.

The **Museo Provincial de Bellas Artes**, at Calle Meléndez Valdés 32, has more than 900 paintings and sculptures including works by Picasso, Dalí, Morales and Zurbarán. It is open Monday to Friday from 9 am to 2 pm and on Saturday from 10 am to 1 pm. Entry is free.

The **Puente de Palmas**, an impressive granite bridge built over the Río Guadiana in 1596, is 582 metres long, with 32 arches, and leads into the city via the late 16th century town gate, the **Puerta de Palmas**.

Special Events

The Romería de Bótoa takes place on the first Sunday in May and the Romería de San Isidro is celebrated on the Sunday closest to 15 May. The week-long Feria de San Juan starts on 24 June.

Places to Stay

Hostal de las Heras (☎ 22 40 14), at Calle Pedro de Valdivia 6, has basic singles/doubles for 1300/2300 ptas, or 2300/3500 ptas with bath. *Hostal Santarem* (☎ 22 44 55), at Calle de Montesinos 24, has equally basic singles/doubles for 1600/2500 ptas and a restaurant with a 600 ptas set menu.

Hotel Cervantes (☎ 22 37 10), an attractive old building at Calle Trinidad 2, has decent singles/doubles with bath for 3200/5200 ptas plus IVA. *Hotel Condedu* (☎ 22 46 41), at Calle Muñoz Torrero 29, has very comfortable rooms with bath for 4300/6300 ptas plus IVA.

North-west of town, over the Puente de la Universidad, there are two up-market hotels, both of which look pretty awful from the outside but are actually very good. *Hotel Lisboa* (☎ 27 29 00), at Avenida de Adolfo Díaz Ambrona 13, has rooms for 5600/7000 ptas plus IVA. *Hotel Río* (☎ 27 26 00) is opposite on the same street, with rooms for 9750/13,750 ptas plus IVA.

Best of all is *Gran Hotel Zurbarán* (☎ 22 37 41), closer to the centre opposite Parque de Castelar, which costs 10,750/17,500 ptas plus IVA.

Places to Eat

There is an all-day supermarket, *Simago*, next to the post office on Paseo San Francisco. A couple of doors down is *Pizza Flash*, a fast-food restaurant with pizzas from 700 ptas and a wide variety of other dishes.

Mesón El Tronco, at Calle Muñoz Torrero 16, specialises in regional food, and does a roaring trade with eight set menus at just 850 ptas.

Los Monjes Zurbarán, in the Gran Hotel Zurbarán opposite Parque de Castelar, is very up-market, with a 5000 ptas set menu.

Meat-lovers shouldn't miss out on *Los Gabrieles*, in the centre of the old town at Calle Vicente Barrantes 21 (closed Sunday evening). It looks like an ordinary bar, but the restaurant at the back is an exceptional treat, specialising in asado de cochinillo (suckling pig) for 1700 ptas and asado de cordero (roast lamb) for 1100 ptas. There is also a set menu for 1600 ptas.

On the other side of the river, *Hotel Río* has its own facilities, and the nearby *La Toja*, at Calle Sánchez de la Rocha 2, is one of the best restaurants in Badajoz and well worth a splurge. Its specialities are merluza a la gallega (1900 ptas), rape al estilo Pontevedra (2000 ptas), chuletón de ternera a la gallega (1500 ptas) and paletilla de cordero al horno (2000 ptas), though there is a set menu for 1500 ptas.

Cafés *Café La Ria*, at Plaza de España 7, has decent Western fare, with hamburgers from 275 ptas and bacon, eggs and chips for 650 ptas.

Café San Juan, directly opposite the tourist office, is large and airy, with cast-iron pillars and a superb collection of old radios. Bacon, eggs and coffee costs 500 ptas.

Entertainment

Mesón La Revancha, on Calle Felipe Checa, is a small but popular hang-out, heaving from afternoon till late. Also open in the afternoons is *Alquibla*, a cool, moody jazz and blues bar on Calle Virgen Soledad, usually open until 3 or 4 am.

There are plenty more late-night bars in the streets to the east of Plaza de España. *Bocoy*, at Calle de Afligidos 22, *Anas* and *Blue Berlin*, both on Calle de San Blas, the more up-market *Mesón San Andrés La*

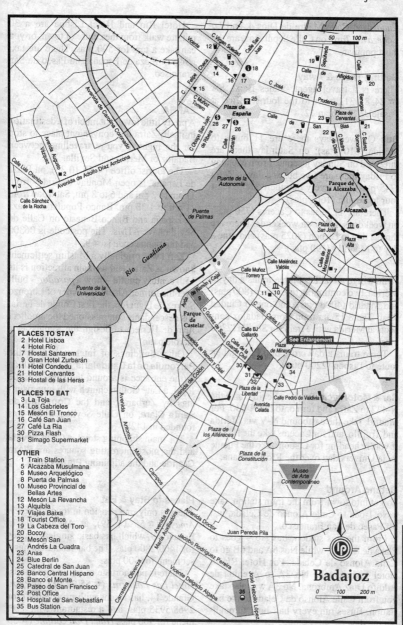

Badajoz

0   50   100 m

0   100   200 m

PLACES TO STAY
2   Hotel Lisboa
4   Hotel Río
7   Hostal Santarem
9   Gran Hotel Zurbarán
11 Hotel Condedu
21 Hotel Cervantes
33 Hostal de las Heras

PLACES TO EAT
3   La Toja
14 Los Gabrieles
15 Mesón El Tronco
16 Café San Juan
27 Café La Ria
30 Pizza Flash
31 Simago Supermarket

OTHER
1   Train Station
5   Alcazaba Musulmana
6   Museo Arquelógico
8   Puerta de Palmas
10 Museo Provincial de
    Bellas Artes
13 Mesón La Revancha
17 Alquibla
18 Viajes Baixa
18 Tourist Office
19 La Cabeza del Toro
20 Bocoy
22 Mesón San
    Andrés La Cuadra
23 Anas
24 Blue Berlin
25 Catedral de San Juan
26 Banco Central Hispano
28 Banco el Monte
29 Paseo de San Francisco
32 Post Office
34 Hospital de San Sebastián
35 Bus Station

EXTREMADURA

Cuadra, at Calle Madre de Dios 4, and *La Cabeza del Toro*, on Calle Sepúlveda, are the most popular.

Getting There & Away

There is a travel agent, Viajes Baixa SA (☎ 24 83 31), next to the tourist office at Pasaje de San Juan 12.

Bus On weekdays there are 11 buses to Mérida (610 ptas); on Saturday there are three and on Sunday just one. From Monday to Friday there are five buses a day to Zafra (745 ptas), and every day there are at least four to Sevilla (1665 ptas).

There are 11 buses to Cáceres (750 ptas) on weekdays, fewer on weekends. There are three a day to Lisbon (2025 ptas) and nine a day to Madrid (3190 ptas).

Train There are at least three trains a day to Mérida, two continuing to Cáceres (800 ptas) and Madrid (4000 ptas), and one to Ciudad Real. The 8.15 am train from Badajoz connects at Mérida with a train for Sevilla (2300 ptas).

Three trains a day cross into Portugal en route to Lisbon (2200 ptas).

Car & Motorcycle To get to Sevilla, take the N-432 to Zafra and turn onto the N-630. For Madrid, take the eastbound N-V via Mérida and Trujillo, and for Cáceres take the N-523. If you're heading for Lisbon, take the Puente de la Universidad over the Río Guadiana.

Getting Around

To get into town from the train station, take a No 1 bus to Calle Alonso de Celada, just off Paseo de San Francisco.

From the bus station, bus No 4 goes to Plaza de España, while Nos 6A and 6B go to Calle Alonso de Celada. For Hotel Río or Hotel Lisboa, take No 3A to Avenida de Adolfo Díaz Ambrona. No 3A will also take you from Calle Alonso de Celada to the bus station. Buses run every half-hour throughout the day.

Hotel Río and Hotel Lisboa are a 30 minute walk from the centre of town, or you can take a taxi for 500 ptas. There are taxi ranks in Plaza de España and Paseo de San Francisco.

ZAFRA

A pretty little town, not much of a destination in itself, Zafra is a convenient place to stop for the night if you're travelling between Badajoz or Mérida and Sevilla.

The tourist office (☎ 55 10 36), on Plaza de España, is open Monday to Friday from 11 am to 2 pm and 6 to 8 pm, Saturday from 11 am to 1.30 pm. Banco Popular on Plaza de España and Banco Banesto on Calle de Sevilla have ATMs. The postcode is 06300 and the phone code is ☎ 924.

Zafra was originally a Muslim settlement known as Zafar, and its main attraction is its 15th century **castle** – now a *parador* – built over the former Alcázar by order of Lorenzo Suárez de Figueroa, the first Conde de Feria. His descendants commissioned the architect Juan de Herrera to design the Renaissance marble patio.

Other buildings of interest include the **Parroquia de la Candelaria**, at Calle Tetuán 4 (the entrance is around the side on Calle José), a Late Gothic church with nine paintings by Zurbarán; and the **Convento de Santa Clara**, on Calle Sevilla, which was founded in 1428.

The main shopping street is **Calle Sevilla** and the most interesting squares are **Plaza Grande** and the adjoining **Plaza Chica**.

Places to Stay & Eat

There is only one pensión in town, *Pensión Amaya* (☎ 55 14 39), at Avenida de la Estación 9, which has basic singles/doubles for 1400/2800 ptas. The bar-restaurant has a set menu for 900 ptas.

There is no shortage of mid-range hotels. *Hotel Las Palmeras* (☎ 55 22 08), at Plaza Grande 14, has rooms with private bath for 2968/5935 ptas, and a restaurant with a set menu for 900 ptas. *Hotel Don Quijote* (☎ 55

47 71), at Calle Huelva 3, has rooms for 5500/8500 ptas plus IVA, and its restaurant has a set menu for 900 ptas.

Hotel Restaurante El Ancla (☎ 55 43 82), at Plaza de España 8, has rooms for 5000/9000 ptas plus IVA, and a restaurant with a set menu for 1500 ptas.

Parador Hernán Cortés (☎ 55 45 40), at Plaza Corazón de María 7, has doubles for 15,000 ptas plus IVA, and its restaurant has a set menu for 3500 ptas plus IVA.

Getting There & Away
The bus station (☎ 55 39 07) is on Carretera Badajoz-Granada, just north-east of the centre, and the train station (☎ 55 02 15) is a good 20 minute walk south-east of the centre at the end of Avenida de la Estación.

Glossary

Unless otherwise indicated, these terms are in Castilian Spanish.

abierto – open
aficionado – enthusiast
agroturismo – another word for *turismo rural*
ajuntament – Catalan for city or town hall
albergue juvenil – youth hostel; not to be confused with *hostal*
alcázar – Muslim-era fortress
altar mayor – high altar
alud – avalanche
apartado de correos – post office box
apnea – snorkelling
armadura – wooden *mudéjar* ceiling, especially one like an inverted ship's hull
artesonado – *mudéjar* wooden ceiling with interlaced beams leaving a pattern of spaces for decoration
auto de fe – elaborate execution ceremony staged by the Inquisition
autonomía – autonomous community or region: Spain's 50 *provincias* are grouped into 17 of these
autopista – tollway
autovía – toll-free dual-carriage highway
AVE – Tren de Alta Velocidad Español; high-speed train
ayuntamiento – city or town hall
azulejo – glazed tile

bakalao – ear-splitting Spanish techno music (not to be confused with *bacalao*, salted cod)
barrio – district, quarter (of a town or city)
biblioteca – library
bici todo terreno – mountain bike
bodega – literally, a cellar (especially a wine cellar); also means a winery, or a traditional wine bar likely to serve wine from the barrel
bota – sherry cask or animal-skin wine vessel
botijo – jug, usually an earthenware one
BTT – abbreviation for *bici todo terreno*
buceo – scuba diving

cajero automático – automatic teller machine (ATM)
calle – street
callejón – lane
cambio – in general, change; also currency exchange
caña – a small beer in a glass
capilla – chapel
capilla mayor – chapel containing the high altar of a church
carmen – walled villa with gardens, in Granada
carnaval – carnival; a period of fancy-dress parades and merrymaking in many places, usually ending on the Tuesday 47 days before Easter Sunday
carretera – highway
carta – menu
casa de labranza – a *casa rural* in Cantabria
casa de pagès – a *casa rural* in Cataluña
casa rural – a village or country house or farmstead with rooms to let
casco – literally, helmet; often used to refer to the old part of a city (more correctly, *casco antiguo*)
castellers – Catalan human-castle builders
castillo – castle
castro – Celtic or Celtiberian fortified village
catedral – cathedral
caza – hunting
cercanías – local trains serving big cities' suburbs and nearby towns
cerrado – closed
cervecería – beer bar
churrigueresque – ornate style of baroque architecture named after the brothers Alberto and José Churriguera
cofradía – same as *hermandad*
colegiata – collegiate church
coll, collado – Catalan for a mountain pass
comarca – district (sometimes translated as county), the next administrative division down from *provincia*
comedor – dining room
comisaría – National Police station

960

consigna – left-luggage office or lockers

converso – Jew who converted to Christianity in medieval Spain

copas – drinks (literally, glasses); *ir de copas* is to go out for a few drinks

cordillera – mountain chain

coro – choir (part of a church, usually in the middle)

Correos – post office

corrida de toros – bullfight

costa – coast

cruceiro – standing crucifix found at many crossroads in Galicia

cuenta – bill (check)

cuesta – lane (usually on a hill)

dolmen – prehistoric megalithic tomb

duro – literally, hard; also a common name for a 5 ptas coin

embalse – reservoir

embarcadero – pier or landing stage

encierro – running of bulls Pamplona-style (also happens in many other places around Spain)

entrada – entrance

ermita – hermitage or chapel

església – Catalan for *iglesia*

estació – Catalan for *estación*

estación de autobuses – bus station

estación de esquí – ski station or resort

estación de ferrocarril – train station

extremeño – Extremaduran; a native of Extremadura

faro – lighthouse

feria – fair; can refer to trade fairs as well as to city, town or village fairs which are basically several days of merrymaking; can also mean a bullfight or festival stretching over days or weeks

ferrocarril – railway

fiesta – festival, public holiday or party

fin de semana – weekend

flamenco – means flamingo as well as flamenco

gallego – Galician; a native of Galicia

gatos – literally, cats; also a colloquial name for *madrileños*

gitano – Gypsy

glorieta – big roundabout

hermandad – brotherhood, in particular one that takes part in religious processions

hórreo – Galician or Asturian grain store

hostal – commercial establishment providing accommodation in the one to three star category; not to be confused with *albergue juvenil*

humedal – wetland

iglesia – church

infanta – princess

infante – prince

IVA – *impuesto sobre el valor añadido*, or value-added tax

judería – Jewish *barrio* in medieval Spain

librería – bookshop

lidia – the art of bullfighting

lista de correos – poste restante

litera – couchette or sleeping carriage

llegada – arrival

locutorio – private telephone centre

macarra – Madrid's rough but (usually) likeable lads

madrileño – a person from Madrid

madrugada – the 'early hours', from around 3 am to dawn – a pretty lively time in some Spanish cities!

manchego – La Manchan; a person from La Mancha

marcha – action, life, 'the scene'

medina – Arabic word for town or city

menú del día – fixed-price meal available at lunchtime, sometimes in the evening too

mercado – market

meseta – the high tableland of central Spain

mihrab – prayer niche in a mosque indicating the direction of Mecca

mirador – lookout point

modernisme – literally, modernism; the architectural and artistic style, influenced by Art Nouveau and sometimes known as Catalan modernism, whose leading practitioner was Antoni Gaudí

modernista – an exponent of *modernisme*

morería – former Islamic quarter in a town

Morisco – a Muslim converted (often only superficially) to Christianity in medieval Spain

moro – 'Moor' or Muslim (usually in a medieval context)

movida – similar to *marcha*; a *zona de movida* is an area of a town where lively bars and maybe discos are clustered

Mozarab – Christian living under Muslim rule in medieval Spain; those who left for Christian territory often took their Islamic-influenced Mozarabic style of architecture and decoration with them

mudéjar – a Muslim living under Christian rule in medieval Spain; also refers to their decorative style of architecture

muelle – wharf or pier

museo – museum

museu – Catalan for *museo*

muwallad – descendant of Christians who had converted to Islam, in medieval Spain

nezakalturismoa – Basque for *turismo rural*

oficina de turismo – tourist office

Pantocrator – Christ the All-Ruler or Christ in Majesty, a central emblem of Romanesque art

parador – one of a chain of luxurious state-owned hotels, many of them in historic buildings

paso – literally, a step; also means an image carried in a religious procession and/or the platform it's carried on

peña – a club, usually of flamenco *aficionados* or Real Madrid or Barcelona football fans; sometimes a dining club

pinchos – Basque for *tapas*

piscina – swimming pool

plateresque – Italian-influenced style of Renaissance architecture noted for its intricately decorated façades; its principal exponent was Alonso de Covarrubias

platja – Catalan for *playa*

plato combinado – literally 'combined plate', a largeish serve of meat/seafood/omelette with trimmings

playa – beach

plaza de toros – bullring

porrón – jug with a long, thin spout through which you (try to) pour wine into your mouth

port – port or mountain pass (Catalan)

presa – dam

provincia – province; Spain is divided into 50 of them

pueblo – village

puente – bridge; also means the extra day or two off that many people take when a holiday falls close to a weekend

puerta – gate or door

puerto – port or mountain pass

ración – meal-sized serve of *tapas*

rastro – flea market, car-boot (trunk) sale

REAJ – Red Española de Albergues Juveniles, the Spanish HI youth hostel network

Reconquista – the Christian reconquest of the Iberian Peninsula from the Muslims (8th to 15th centuries)

refugi – Catalan for *refugio*

refugio – shelter or refuge, especially a mountain refuge with basic accommodation for hikers

reja – grille, especially a wrought-iron one dividing a chapel from the rest of a church

RENFE – Red Nacional de los Ferrocarriles Españoles, the national rail network

retablo – altarpiece

ría – estuary in Galicia or Asturias

río – river

riu – Catalan for river

rodalies – Catalan for *cercanías*

romería – festive pilgrimage or procession

ronda – ring road

sacristía – sacristy, the part of a church in which vestments, sacred objects and other valuables are kept

salida – exit or departure

Semana Santa – Holy Week, the week leading up to Easter Sunday

sida – AIDS

sidrería – cider bar

sierra – mountain range

s/n – sin numero (without number), sometimes seen in addresses

supermercado – supermarket

taifa – small Muslim kingdom in medieval Spain

tapas – bar snacks traditionally served on a saucer or lid *(tapa)*

tarjeta de crédito – credit card

tarjeta de residencia – residence card

tarjeta telefónica – phonecard

techumbre – roof, or specifically a common type of *armadura*

terraza – terrace; often means a café's or bar's outdoor tables

tertulia – informal discussion group or other regular social gathering

tetería – teahouse, usually in Middle Eastern style with low seats round low tables

tienda – shop or tent

trascoro – screen behind the *coro*

turismo – means both tourism and saloon car; *el turismo* can also mean the tourist office

turismo rural – rural tourism: usually refers to accommodation in *casas rurales* and associated activities such as walking and horse riding

urbanització – Catalan for *urbanización*

urbanización – suburban housing development

vall – valley (Catalan)

valle – valley

v.o. – *versión original*, a foreign-language film subtitled in Spanish

zona de acampada – country camp site with no facilities, no supervision and no charge

Index

MAPS

TEXT

Map references are in **bold** type.

LONELY PLANET PHRASEBOOKS

Building bridges,
Breaking barriers,
Beyond babble-on

Listen for the gems

Speak your own words

Ask your own questions

Master of your own image

- handy pocket-sized books
- easy to understand Pronunciation chapter
- clear and comprehensive Grammar chapter
- romanisation alongside script to allow ease of pronunciation
- script throughout so users can point to phrases
- extensive vocabulary sections, words and phrases for every situations
- full of cultural information and tips for the traveller

'...vital for a real DIY spirit and attitude in language learning' – Backpacker

'the phrasebooks have good cultural backgrounders and offer solid advice for challenging situations in remote locations' – San Francisco Examiner

'...they are unbeatable for their coverage of the world's more obscure languages' – The Geographical Magazine

---

Arabic (Egyptian)
Arabic (Moroccan)
Australia
  Australian English, Aboriginal and Tor-
  res Strait languages
Baltic States
  Estonian, Latvian, Lithuanian
Bengali
Burmese
Brazilian
Cantonese
Central Europe
  Czech, French, German, Hungarian,
  Italian and Slovak
Eastern Europe
  Bulgarian, Czech, Hungarian, Polish,
  Romanian and Slovak
Egyptian Arabic
Ethiopian (Amharic)
Fijian
French
German
Greek

Hindi/Urdu
Indonesian
Italian
Japanese
Korean
Lao
Latin American Spanish
Malay
Mandarin
Mediterranean Europe
  Albanian, Croatian, Greek, Italian,
  Macedonian, Maltese, Serbian,
  Slovene
Mongolian
Moroccan Arabic
Nepali
Papua New Guinea
Pilipino (Tagalog)
Quechua
Russian
Scandinavian Europe
  Danish, Finnish, Icelandic, Norwegian
  and Swedish

South-East Asia
  Burmese, Indonesian, Khmer, Lao,
  Malay, Tagalog (Pilipino), Thai and
  Vietnamese
Spanish
Sri Lanka
Swahili
Thai
Thai Hill Tribes
Tibetan
Turkish
Ukrainian
USA
  US English, Vernacular Talk,
  Native American languages and
  Hawaiian
Vietnamese
Western Europe
  Basque, Catalan, Dutch, French, Ger-
  man, Irish, Italian, Portuguese, Scot-
  tish Gaelic, Spanish (Castilian) and
  Welsh

LONELY PLANET TRAVEL ATLASES

Lonely Planet has long been famous for the number and quality of its guidebook maps. Now we've gone one step further and in conjunction with Steinhart Katzir Publishers produced a handy companion series: Lonely Planet travel atlases – maps of a country produced in book form.

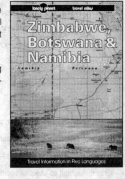

Unlike other maps, which look good but lead travellers astray, our travel atlases have been researched on the road by Lonely Planet's experienced team of writers. All details are carefully checked to ensure the atlas corresponds with the equivalent Lonely Planet guidebook.

The handy atlas format means no holes, wrinkles, torn sections or constant folding and unfolding. These atlases can survive long periods on the road, unlike cumbersome fold-out maps. The comprehensive index ensures easy reference.

- full-colour throughout
- maps researched and checked by Lonely Planet authors
- place names correspond with Lonely Planet guidebooks
  – no confusing spelling differences
- legend and travelling information in English, French, German, Japanese and Spanish
- size: 230 x 160 mm

Available now:
Chile & Easter Island • Egypt • India & Bangladesh • Israel & the Palestinian Territories •Jordan, Syria & Lebanon • Kenya • Laos • Portugal • South Africa, Lesotho & Swaziland • Thailand • Turkey • Vietnam • Zimbabwe, Botswana & Namibia

---

LONELY PLANET TV SERIES & VIDEOS

Lonely Planet travel guides have been brought to life on television screens around the world. Like our guides, the programmes are based on the joy of independent travel, and look honestly at some of the most exciting, picturesque and frustrating places in the world. Each show is presented by one of three travellers from Australia, England or the USA and combines an innovative mixture of video, Super-8 film, atmospheric soundscapes and original music.

Videos of each episode – containing additional footage not shown on television – are available from good book and video shops, but the availability of individual videos varies with regional screening schedules.

Video destinations include: Alaska • American Rockies • Australia – The South-East • Baja California & the Copper Canyon • Brazil • Central Asia • Chile & Easter Island • Corsica, Sicily & Sardinia – The Mediterranean Islands • East Africa (Tanzania & Zanzibar) • Ecuador & the Galapagos Islands • Greenland & Iceland • Indonesia • Israel & the Sinai Desert • Jamaica • Japan • La Ruta Maya • Morocco • New York • North India • Pacific Islands (Fiji, Solomon Islands & Vanuatu) • South India • South West China • Turkey • Vietnam • West Africa • Zimbabwe, Botswana & Namibia

The Lonely Planet TV series is produced by:
Pilot Productions
The Old Studio
18 Middle Row
London W10 5AT UK

For video availability and ordering information contact your nearest Lonely Planet office.

Music from the TV series is available on CD & cassette.

PLANET TALK

Lonely Planet's FREE quarterly newsletter

We love hearing from you and think you'd like to hear from us.

When...is the right time to see reindeer in Finland?
Where...can you hear the best palm-wine music in Ghana?
How...do you get from Asunción to Areguá by steam train?
What...is the best way to see India?

For the answer to these and many other questions read PLANET TALK.

Every issue is packed with up-to-date travel news and advice including:

* a letter from Lonely Planet co-founders Tony and Maureen Wheeler
* go behind the scenes on the road with a Lonely Planet author
* feature article on an important and topical travel issue
* a selection of recent letters from travellers
* details on forthcoming Lonely Planet promotions
* complete list of Lonely Planet products

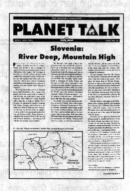

To join our mailing list contact any Lonely Planet office.

Also available: Lonely Planet T-shirts. 100% heavyweight cotton.

LONELY PLANET ONLINE

Get the latest travel information before you leave or while you're on the road

Whether you've just begun planning your next trip, or you're chasing down specific info on currency regulations or visa requirements, check out Lonely Planet Online for up-to-the-minute travel information.

As well as travel profiles of your favourite destinations (including maps and photos), you'll find current reports from our researchers and other travellers, updates on health and visas, travel advisories, and discussion of the ecological and political issues you need to be aware of as you travel.

There's also an online travellers' forum where you can share your experience of life on the road, meet travel companions and ask other travellers for their recommendations and advice. We also have plenty of links to other online sites useful to independent travellers.

And of course we have a complete and up-to-date list of all Lonely Planet travel products including guides, phrasebooks, atlases, Journeys and videos and a simple online ordering facility if you can't find the book you want elsewhere.

www.lonelyplanet.com
or
AOL keyword: lp

LONELY PLANET PRODUCTS

Lonely Planet is known worldwide for publishing practical, reliable and no-nonsense travel information in our guides and on our web site. The Lonely Planet list covers just about every accessible part of the world. Currently there are eight series: *travel guides, shoestring guides, walking guides, city guides, phrasebooks, audio packs, travel atlases* and *Journeys* – a unique collection of travel writing.

EUROPE

Amsterdam • Austria • Baltic States phrasebook • Britain • Central Europe on a shoestring • Central Europe phrasebook • Czech & Slovak Republics • Denmark • Dublin • Eastern Europe on a shoestring • Eastern Europe phrasebook • Estonia, Latvia & Lithuania • Finland • France • French phrasebook • German phrasebook • Greece • Greek phrasebook • Hungary • Iceland, Greenland & the Faroe Islands • Ireland • Italian phrasebook • Italy • Mediterranean Europe on a shoestring • Mediterranean Europe phrasebook • Paris • Poland • Portugal • Portugal travel atlas • Prague • Russia, Ukraine & Belarus • Russian phrasebook • Scandinavian & Baltic Europe on a shoestring • Scandinavian Europe phrasebook • Slovenia • Spain • Spanish phrasebook • St Petersburg • Switzerland • Trekking in Greece • Trekking in Spain • Ukrainian phrasebook • Vienna • Walking in Britain • Walking in Switzerland • Western Europe on a shoestring • Western Europe phrasebook

Travel Literature: The Olive Grove: Travels in Greece

NORTH AMERICA

Alaska • Backpacking in Alaska • Baja California • California & Nevada • Canada • Florida • Hawaii • Honolulu • Los Angeles • Mexico • Miami • New England • New Orleans • New York City • New York, New Jersey & Pennsylvania • Pacific Northwest USA • Rocky Mountain States • San Francisco • Southwest USA • USA phrasebook • Washington, DC & the Capital Region

CENTRAL AMERICA & THE CARIBBEAN

Bermuda • Central America on a shoestring • Costa Rica • Cuba • Eastern Caribbean • Guatemala, Belize & Yucatán: La Ruta Maya • Jamaica

SOUTH AMERICA

Argentina, Uruguay & Paraguay • Bolivia • Brazil • Brazilian phrasebook • Buenos Aires • Chile & Easter Island • Chile & Easter Island travel atlas • Colombia • Ecuador & the Galápagos Islands • Latin American Spanish phrasebook • Peru • Quechua phrasebook • Rio de Janeiro • South America on a shoestring • Trekking in the Patagonian Andes • Venezuela

Travel Literature: Full Circle: A South American Journey

ANTARCTICA

Antarctica

ISLANDS OF THE INDIAN OCEAN

Madagascar & Comoros • Maldives• Mauritius, Réunion & Seychelles

AFRICA

Africa - the South • Africa on a shoestring • Arabic (Moroccan) phrasebook • Cape Town • Central Africa • East Africa • Egypt • Egypt travel atlas• Ethiopian (Amharic) phrasebook • Kenya • Kenya travel atlas • Malawi, Mozambique & Zambia • Morocco • North Africa • South Africa, Lesotho & Swaziland • South Africa, Lesotho & Swaziland travel atlas • Swahili phrasebook • Trekking in East Africa • West Africa • Zimbabwe, Botswana & Namibia • Zimbabwe, Botswana & Namibia travel atlas

Travel Literature: The Rainbird: A Central African Journey • Songs to an African Sunset: A Zimbabwean Story

MAIL ORDER

Lonely Planet products are distributed worldwide. They are also available by mail order from Lonely Planet, so if you have difficulty finding a title please write to us. North American and South American residents should write to Embarcadero West, 155 Filbert St, Suite 251, Oakland CA 94607, USA; European and African residents should write to 10 Barley Mow Passage, Chiswick, London W4 4PH; and residents of other countries to PO Box 617, Hawthorn, Victoria 3122, Australia.

NORTH-EAST ASIA

Beijing • Cantonese phrasebook • China • Hong Kong • Hong Kong, Macau & Guangzhou • Japan • Japanese phrasebook • Japanese audio pack • Korea • Korean phrasebook • Mandarin phrasebook • Mongolia • Mongolian phrasebook • North-East Asia on a shoestring • Seoul • Taiwan • Tibet • Tibet phrasebook • Tokyo

Travel Literature: Lost Japan

MIDDLE EAST & CENTRAL ASIA

Arab Gulf States • Arabic (Egyptian) phrasebook • Central Asia • Iran • Israel & the Palestinian Territories • Israel & the Palestinian Territories travel atlas • Istanbul • Jerusalem • Jordan & Syria • Jordan, Syria & Lebanon travel atlas • Middle East • Turkey • Turkish phrasebook • Turkey travel atlas • Yemen

Travel Literature: The Gates of Damascus • Kingdom of the Film Stars: Journey into Jordan

ALSO AVAILABLE:

Travel with Children • Traveller's Tales

INDIAN SUBCONTINENT

Bangladesh • Bengali phrasebook • Delhi • Hindi/Urdu phrasebook • India • India & Bangladesh travel atlas • Indian Himalaya • Karakoram Highway • Nepal • Nepali phrasebook • Pakistan • Rajasthan • Sri Lanka • Sri Lanka phrasebook • Trekking in the Indian Himalaya • Trekking in the Karakoram & Hindukush • Trekking in the Nepal Himalaya

Travel Literature: In Rajasthan • Shopping for Buddhas

SOUTH-EAST ASIA

Bali & Lombok • Bangkok • Burmese phrasebook • Cambodia • Ho Chi Minh City • Indonesia • Indonesian phrasebook • Indonesian audio pack • Jakarta • Java • Laos • Lao phrasebook • Laos travel atlas • Malay phrasebook • Malaysia, Singapore & Brunei • Myanmar (Burma) • Philippines • Pilipino phrasebook • Singapore • South-East Asia on a shoestring • South-East Asia phrasebook • Thailand • Thailand travel atlas • Thai phrasebook • Thai audio pack • Thai Hill Tribes phrasebook • Vietnam • Vietnamese phrasebook • Vietnam travel atlas

AUSTRALIA & THE PACIFIC

Australia • Australian phrasebook • Bushwalking in Australia • Bushwalking in Papua New Guinea • Fiji • Fijian phrasebook • Islands of Australia's Great Barrier Reef • Melbourne • Micronesia • New Caledonia • New South Wales & the ACT • New Zealand • Northern Territory • Outback Australia • Papua New Guinea • Papua New Guinea phrasebook • Queensland • Rarotonga & the Cook Islands • Samoa • Solomon Islands • South Australia • Sydney • Tahiti & French Polynesia • Tasmania • Tonga • Tramping in New Zealand • Vanuatu • Victoria • Western Australia

Travel Literature: Islands in the Clouds • Sean & David's Long Drive

THE LONELY PLANET STORY

Lonely Planet published its first book in 1973 in response to the numerous 'How did you do it?' questions Maureen and Tony Wheeler were asked after driving, bussing, hitching, sailing and railing their way from England to Australia.

Written at a kitchen table and hand collated, trimmed and stapled, *Across Asia on the Cheap* became an instant local bestseller, inspiring thoughts of another book.

Eighteen months in South-East Asia resulted in their second guide, *South-East Asia on a shoestring*, which they put together in a backstreet Chinese hotel in Singapore in 1975. The 'yellow bible', as it quickly became known to backpackers around the world, soon became *the* guide to the region. It has sold well over half a million copies and is now in its 9th edition, still retaining its familiar yellow cover.

Today there are over 240 titles, including travel guides, walking guides, language kits & phrasebooks, travel atlases and travel literature. The company is the largest independent travel publisher in the world. Although Lonely Planet initially specialised in guides to Asia, today there are few corners of the globe that have not been covered.

The emphasis continues to be on travel for independent travellers. Tony and Maureen still travel for several months of each year and play an active part in the writing, updating and quality control of Lonely Planet's guides.

They have been joined by over 70 authors and 170 staff at our offices in Melbourne (Australia), Oakland (USA), London (UK) and Paris (France). Travellers themselves also make a valuable contribution to the guides through the feedback we receive in thousands of letters each year and on our web site.

The people at Lonely Planet strongly believe that travellers can make a positive contribution to the countries they visit, both through their appreciation of the countries' culture, wildlife and natural features, and through the money they spend. In addition, the company makes a direct contribution to the countries and regions it covers. Since 1986 a percentage of the income from each book has been donated to ventures such as famine relief in Africa; aid projects in India; agricultural projects in Central America; Greenpeace's efforts to halt French nuclear testing in the Pacific; and Amnesty International.

'I hope we send people out with the right attitude about travel. You realise when you travel that there are so many different perspectives about the world, so we hope these books will make people more interested in what they see. Guidebooks can't really guide people. All you can do is point them in the right direction.'

– Tony Wheeler

LONELY PLANET PUBLICATIONS

Australia
PO Box 617, Hawthorn 3122, Victoria
tel: (03) 9819 1877 fax: (03) 9819 6459
e-mail: talk2us@lonelyplanet.com.au

USA
Embarcadero West, 155 Filbert St, Suite 251,
Oakland, CA 94607
tel: (510) 893 8555 TOLL FREE: 800 275-8555
fax: (510) 893 8563
e-mail: info@lonelyplanet.com

UK
10 Barley Mow Passage, Chiswick,
London W4 4PH
tel: (0181) 742 3161 fax: (0181) 742 2772
e-mail: lonelyplanetuk@compuserve.com

France:
71 bis rue du Cardinal Lemoine, 75005 Paris
tel: 1 44 32 06 20 fax: 1 46 34 72 55
e-mail: 100560.415@compuserve.com

**World Wide Web: http://www.lonelyplanet.com
or *AOL keyword: lp***